PENSION AND EMPLOYEE BENEFIT STATUTES AND REGULATIONS

SELECTED SECTIONS

2017 EDITION

SEAN M. ANDERSON
Teaching Assistant Professor
University of Illinois College of Law

DAVID A. PRATT
Professor of Law
Albany Law School

ANDREW W. STUMPFF
Lecturer, University of Michigan Law School
Adjunct Professor, University of Alabama Law School

FOUNDATION
PRESS

© 2002–2004 FOUNDATION PRESS
© 2005–2013 THOMSON REUTERS / FOUNDATION PRESS
© 2015 LEG, Inc. d/b/a West Academic
© 2017 LEG, Inc. d/b/a West Academic
    444 Cedar Street, Suite 700
    St. Paul, MN 55101
    1-877-888-1330

Printed in the United States of America

ISBN: 978-1-68328-461-1

ACKNOWLEDGMENTS

We would like to acknowledge, with gratitude, the contributions of the following: Professor Bruce Wolk, who prepared earlier editions; Theresa Colbert for outstanding legal assistance; Ariele Doolittle, Esq., research assistant par excellence; and Tessa Boury and her associates at Foundation Press, who have provided essential help and support at every stage.

Table of Contents

INTERNAL REVENUE CODE OF 1986

EMPLOYEE RETIREMENT INCOME SECURITY ACT OF 1974

AGE DISCRIMINATION IN EMPLOYMENT ACT OF 1967

AMERICANS WITH DISABILITIES ACT OF 1990

ERISA REORGANIZATION PLAN

TREASURY REGULATIONS

AGE DISCRIMINATION REGULATIONS

ERISA REGULATIONS

PENSION AND EMPLOYEE BENEFIT STATUTES AND REGULATIONS

SELECTED SECTIONS

2017 EDITION

INTERNAL REVENUE CODE OF 1986

§ 25B. Elective deferrals and IRA contributions by certain individuals.

(a) Allowance of credit—In the case of an eligible individual, there shall be allowed as a credit against the tax imposed by this subtitle for the taxable year an amount equal to the applicable percentage of so much of the qualified retirement savings contributions of the eligible individual for the taxable year as do not exceed $2,000.

(b) Applicable percentage—For purposes of this section—

(1) Joint returns—In the case of a joint return, the applicable percentage is—

(A) if the adjusted gross income of the taxpayer is not over $30,000, 50 percent,

(B) if the adjusted gross income of the taxpayer is over $30,000 but not over $32,500, 20 percent,

(C) if the adjusted gross income of the taxpayer is over $32,500 but not over $50,000, 10 percent, and

(D) if the adjusted gross income of the taxpayer is over $50,000, zero percent.

(2) Other returns—In the case of—

(A) a head of household, the applicable percentage shall be determined under paragraph (1) except that such paragraph shall be applied by substituting for each dollar amount therein (as adjusted under paragraph (3)) a dollar amount equal to 75 percent of such dollar amount, and

(B) any taxpayer not described in paragraph (1) or subparagraph (A), the applicable percentage shall be determined under paragraph (1) except that such paragraph shall be applied by substituting for each dollar amount therein (as adjusted under paragraph (3)) a dollar amount equal to 50 percent of such dollar amount.

(3) Inflation adjustment—In the case of any taxable year beginning in a calendar year after 2006, each of the dollar amounts in paragraph (1) shall be increased by an amount equal to—

(A) such dollar amount, multiplied by

(B) the cost-of-living adjustment determined under section 1(f)(3) for the calendar year in which the taxable year begins, determined by substituting "calendar year 2005" for "calendar year 1992" in subparagraph (B) thereof.

Any increase determined under the preceding sentence shall be rounded to the nearest multiple of $500.

(c) Eligible individual—For purposes of this section—

(1) In general—The term "eligible individual" means any individual if such individual has attained the age of 18 as of the close of the taxable year.

(2) Dependents and full-time students not eligible—The term "eligible individual" shall not include—

(A) any individual with respect to whom a deduction under section 151 is allowed to another taxpayer for a taxable year beginning in the calendar year in which such individual's taxable year begins, and

(B) any individual who is a student (as defined in section 152(f)(2)).

(d) Qualified retirement savings contributions—For purposes of this section—

(1) In general—The term "qualified retirement savings contributions" means, with respect to any taxable year, the sum of—

(A) the amount of the qualified retirement contributions (as defined in section 219(e)) made by the eligible individual,

(B) the amount of—

(i) any elective deferrals (as defined in section 402(g)(3)) of such individual, and

(ii) any elective deferral of compensation by such individual under an eligible deferred compensation plan (as defined in section 457(b)) of an eligible employer described in section 457(e)(1)(A), and

(C) the amount of voluntary employee contributions by such individual to any qualified retirement plan (as defined in section 4974(c)).

(2) Reduction for certain distributions—

(A) In general—The qualified retirement savings contributions determined under paragraph (1) shall be reduced (but not below zero) by the aggregate distributions received by the individual during the testing period from any entity of a type to which contributions under paragraph (1) may be made. The preceding sentence shall not apply to the portion of any distribution which is not includible in gross income by reason of a trustee-to-trustee transfer or a rollover distribution.

(B) Testing period—For purposes of subparagraph (A), the testing period, with respect to a taxable year, is the period which includes—

(i) such taxable year,

(ii) the 2 preceding taxable years, and

(iii) the period after such taxable year and before the due date (including extensions) for filing the return of tax for such taxable year.

(C) Excepted distributions—There shall not be taken into account under subparagraph (A)—

(i) any distribution referred to in section 72(p), 401(k)(8), 401(m)(6), 402(g)(2), 404(k), or 408(d)(4), and

(ii) any distribution to which section 408A(d)(3) applies.

(D) Treatment of distributions received by spouse of individual—For purposes of determining distributions received by an individual under subparagraph (A) for any taxable year, any distribution received by the spouse of such individual shall be treated as received by such individual if such individual and spouse file a joint return for such taxable year and for the taxable year during which the spouse receives the distribution.

(e) Adjusted gross income—For purposes of this section, adjusted gross income shall be determined without regard to sections 911, 931, and 933.

(f) Investment in the contract—Notwithstanding any other provision of law, a qualified retirement savings contribution shall not fail to be included in determining the investment in the contract for purposes of section 72 by reason of the credit under this section.

§ 45E. Small employer pension plan startup costs.

(a) General rule—For purposes of section 38, in the case of an eligible employer, the small employer pension plan startup cost credit determined under this section for any taxable year is an amount equal to 50 percent of the qualified startup costs paid or incurred by the taxpayer during the taxable year.

(b) Dollar limitation—The amount of the credit determined under this section for any taxable year shall not exceed—

    (1) $500 for the first credit year and each of the 2 taxable years immediately following the first credit year, and

    (2) zero for any other taxable year.

(c) Eligible employer—For purposes of this section—

    (1) In general—The term "eligible employer" has the meaning given such term by section 408(p)(2)(C)(i).

    (2) Requirement for new qualified employer plans—Such term shall not include an employer if, during the 3-taxable year period immediately preceding the 1st taxable year for which the credit under this section is otherwise allowable for a qualified employer plan of the employer, the employer or any member of any controlled group including the employer (or any predecessor of either) established or maintained a qualified employer plan with respect to which contributions were made, or benefits were accrued, for substantially the same employees as are in the qualified employer plan.

(d) Other definitions—For purposes of this section—

    (1) Qualified startup costs—

        (A) In general—The term "qualified startup costs" means any ordinary and necessary expenses of an eligible employer which are paid or incurred in connection with—

            (i) the establishment or administration of an eligible employer plan, or

            (ii) the retirement-related education of employees with respect to such plan.

        (B) Plan must have at least 1 participant—Such term shall not include any expense in connection with a plan that does not have at least 1 employee eligible to participate who is not a highly compensated employee.

    (2) Eligible employer plan—The term "eligible employer plan" means a qualified employer plan within the meaning of section 4972(d).

    (3) First credit year—The term "first credit year" means—

        (A) the taxable year which includes the date that the eligible employer plan to which such costs relate becomes effective, or

        (B) at the election of the eligible employer, the taxable year preceding the taxable year referred to in subparagraph (A).

(e) Special rules—For purposes of this section—

(1) Aggregation rules—All persons treated as a single employer under subsection (a) or (b) of section 52, or subsection (m) or (o) of section 414, shall be treated as one person. All eligible employer plans shall be treated as 1 eligible employer plan.

(2) Disallowance of deduction—No deduction shall be allowed for that portion of the qualified startup costs paid or incurred for the taxable year which is equal to the credit determined under subsection (a).

(3) Election not to claim credit—This section shall not apply to a taxpayer for any taxable year if such taxpayer elects to have this section not apply for such taxable year.

§ 72. Annuities; certain proceeds of endowment and life insurance contracts.

(a) General rule for annuities—(a) General rules for annuities.

(1) Income inclusion. Except as otherwise provided in this chapter, gross income includes any amount received as an annuity (whether for a period certain or during one or more lives) under an annuity, endowment, or life insurance contract.

(2) Partial annuitization. If any amount is received as an annuity for a period of 10 years or more or during one or more lives under any portion of an annuity, endowment, or life insurance contract—

(**A**) such portion shall be treated as a separate contract for purposes of this section,

(**B**) for purposes of applying subsections (b), (c), and (e), the investment in the contract shall be allocated pro rata between each portion of the contract from which amounts are received as an annuity and the portion of the contract from which amounts are not received as an annuity, and

(**C**) a separate annuity starting date under subsection (c)(4) shall be determined with respect to each portion of the contract from which amounts are received as an annuity.

(b) Exclusion ratio—

(1) In general—Gross income does not include that part of any amount received as an annuity under an annuity, endowment, or life insurance contract which bears the same ratio to such amount as the investment in the contract (as of the annuity starting date) bears to the expected return under the contract (as of such date).

(2) Exclusion limited to investment—The portion of any amount received as an annuity which is excluded from gross income under paragraph (1) shall not exceed the unrecovered investment in the contract immediately before the receipt of such amount.

(3) Deduction where annuity payments cease before entire investment recovered—

(**A**) **In general**—If—

(**i**) after the annuity starting date, payments as an annuity under the contract cease by reason of the death of an annuitant, and

(**ii**) as of the date of such cessation, there is unrecovered investment in the contract,

the amount of such unrecovered investment (in excess of any amount specified in subsection (e)(5) which was not included in gross income) shall be allowed as a deduction to the annuitant for his last taxable year.

(B) Payments to other persons—In the case of any contract which provides for payments meeting the requirements of subparagraphs (B) and (C) of subsection (c)(2), the deduction under subparagraph (A) shall be allowed to the person entitled to such payments for the taxable year in which such payments are received.

(C) Net operating loss deductions provided—For purposes of section 172, a deduction allowed under this paragraph shall be treated as if it were attributable to a trade or business of the taxpayer.

(4) Unrecovered investment—For purposes of this subsection, the unrecovered investment in the contract as of any date is—

(A) the investment in the contract (determined without regard to subsection (c)(2)) as of the annuity starting date, reduced by

(B) the aggregate amount received under the contract on or after such annuity starting date and before the date as of which the determination is being made, to the extent such amount was excludable from gross income under this subtitle.

(c) Definitions—

(1) Investment in the contract—For purposes of subsection (b), the investment in the contract as of the annuity starting date is—

(A) the aggregate amount of premiums or other consideration paid for the contract, minus

(B) the aggregate amount received under the contract before such date, to the extent that such amount was excludable from gross income under this subtitle or prior income tax laws.

(2) Adjustment in investment where there is refund feature—If—

(A) the expected return under the contract depends in whole or in part on the life expectancy of one or more individuals;

(B) the contract provides for payments to be made to a beneficiary (or to the estate of an annuitant) on or after the death of the annuitant or annuitants; and

(C) such payments are in the nature of a refund of the consideration paid,

then the value (computed without discount for interest) of such payments on the annuity starting date shall be subtracted from the amount determined under paragraph (1). Such value shall be computed in accordance with actuarial tables prescribed by the Secretary. For purposes of this paragraph and of subsection (e)(2)(A), the term "refund of the consideration paid" includes amounts payable after the death of an annuitant by reason of a provision in the contract for a life annuity with minimum period of payments certain, but (if part of the consideration was contributed by an employer) does not include that part of any payment to a beneficiary (or to the estate of the annuitant) which is not attributable to the consideration paid by the employee for the contract as determined under paragraph (1)(A).

(3) Expected return—For purposes of subsection (b), the expected return under the contract shall be determined as follows:

(A) Life expectancy—If the expected return under the contract, for the period on and after the annuity starting date, depends in whole or in part on the life expectancy of one or more individuals, the expected return shall be computed with reference to actuarial tables prescribed by the Secretary.

(B) Installment payments—If subparagraph (A) does not apply, the expected return is the aggregate of the amounts receivable under the contract as an annuity.

(4) Annuity starting date—For purposes of this section, the annuity starting date in the case of any contract is the first day of the first period for which an amount is received as an annuity under the contract.

(d) Special rules for qualified employer retirement plans—

(1) Simplified method of taxing annuity payments—

(A) In general—In the case of any amount received as an annuity under a qualified employer retirement plan—

(i) subsection (b) shall not apply, and

(ii) the investment in the contract shall be recovered as provided in this paragraph.

(B) Method of recovering investment in contract—

(i) In general—Gross income shall not include so much of any monthly annuity payment under a qualified employer retirement plan as does not exceed the amount obtained by dividing—

(I) the investment in the contract (as of the annuity starting date), by

(II) the number of anticipated payments determined under the table contained in clause (iii) (or, in the case of a contract to which subsection (c)(3)(B) applies, the number of monthly annuity payments under such contract).

(ii) Certain rules made applicable—Rules similar to the rules of paragraphs (2) and (3) of subsection (b) shall apply for purposes of this paragraph.

(iii) Number of anticipated payments—If the annuity is payable over the life of a single individual, the number of anticipated payments shall be determined as follows:

If the age of the annuitant on the annuity starting date is:	The number of anticipated payments is:
Not more than 55	360
More than 55 but not more than 60	310
More than 60 but not more than 65	260
More than 65 but not more than 70	210
More than 70	160

(iv) Number of anticipated payments where more than one life—If the annuity is payable over the lives of more than 1 individual, the number of anticipated payments shall be determined as follows:

If the combined ages of annuitants are: *The number is:*

If the combined ages of annuitants are:	The number is:
Not more than 110	410
More than 110 but not more than 120	360
More than 120 but not more than 130	310
More than 130 but not more than 140	260
More than 140	210

(C) Adjustment for refund feature not applicable—For purposes of this paragraph, investment in the contract shall be determined under subsection (c)(1) without regard to subsection (c)(2).

(D) Special rule where lump sum paid in connection with commencement of annuity payments—If, in connection with the commencement of annuity payments under any qualified employer retirement plan, the taxpayer receives a lump-sum payment—

    (i) such payment shall be taxable under subsection (e) as if received before the annuity starting date, and

    (ii) the investment in the contract for purposes of this paragraph shall be determined as if such payment had been so received.

(E) Exception—This paragraph shall not apply in any case where the primary annuitant has attained age 75 on the annuity starting date unless there are fewer than 5 years of guaranteed payments under the annuity.

(F) Adjustment where annuity payments not on monthly basis—In any case where the annuity payments are not made on a monthly basis, appropriate adjustments in the application of this paragraph shall be made to take into account the period on the basis of which such payments are made.

(G) Qualified employer retirement plan—For purposes of this paragraph, the term "qualified employer retirement plan" means any plan or contract described in paragraph (1), (2), or (3) of section 4974(c).

(2) Treatment of employee contributions under defined contribution plans—For purposes of this section, employee contributions (and any income allocable thereto) under a defined contribution plan may be treated as a separate contract.

(e) Amounts not received as annuities—

(1) Application of subsection—

    (A) In general—This subsection shall apply to any amount which—

        (i) is received under an annuity, endowment, or life insurance contract, and

        (ii) is not received as an annuity, if no provision of this subtitle (other than this subsection) applies with respect to such amount.

    (B) Dividends—For purposes of this section, any amount received which is in the nature of a dividend or similar distribution shall be treated as an amount not received as an annuity.

(2) General rule—Any amount to which this subsection applies—

(A) if received on or after the annuity starting date, shall be included in gross income, or 72(e)(2)(B) if received before the annuity starting date—

  (i) shall be included in gross income to the extent allocable to income on the contract, and

  (ii) shall not be included in gross income to the extent allocable to the investment in the contract.

(3) Allocation of amounts to income and investment—For purposes of paragraph (2)(B)—

  (A) Allocation to income—Any amount to which this subsection applies shall be treated as allocable to income on the contract to the extent that such amount does not exceed the excess (if any) of—

    (i) the cash value of the contract (determined without regard to any surrender charge) immediately before the amount is received, over

    (ii) the investment in the contract at such time.

  (B) Allocation to investment—Any amount to which this subsection applies shall be treated as allocable to investment in the contract to the extent that such amount is not allocated to income under subparagraph (A).

* * *

(5) Retention of existing rules in certain cases—

  (A) In general—In any case to which this paragraph applies—

    (i) paragraphs (2)(B) and (4)(A) shall not apply, and

    (ii) if paragraph (2)(A) does not apply, the amount shall be included in gross income, but only to the extent it exceeds the investment in the contract.

* * *

  (D) Contracts under qualified plans—Except as provided in paragraph (8), this paragraph shall apply to any amount received—

    (i) from a trust described in section 401(a) which is exempt from tax under section 501(a),

    (ii) from a contract—

      (I) purchased by a trust described in clause (i),

      (II) purchased as part of a plan described in section 403(a),

      (III) described in section 403(b), or

      (IV) provided for employees of a life insurance company under a plan described in section 818(a)(3), or

    (iii) from an individual retirement account or an individual retirement annuity.

Any dividend described in section 404(k) which is received by a participant or beneficiary shall, for purposes of this subparagraph, be treated as paid under a separate contract to which clause (ii)(I) applies.

* * *

(6) Investment in the contract—For purposes of this subsection, the investment in the contract as of any date is—

(A) the aggregate amount of premiums or other consideration paid for the contract before such date, minus

(B) the aggregate amount received under the contract before such date, to the extent that such amount was excludable from gross income under this subtitle or prior income tax laws.

(7) [Repealed]

(8) Extension of paragraph (2)(b) to qualified plans—

(A) In general—Notwithstanding any other provision of this subsection, in the case of any amount received before the annuity starting date from a trust or contract described in paragraph (5)(D), paragraph (2)(B) shall apply to such amounts.

(B) Allocation of amount received—For purposes of paragraph (2)(B), the amount allocated to the investment in the contract shall be the portion of the amount described in subparagraph (A) which bears the same ratio to such amount as the investment in the contract bears to the account balance. The determination under the preceding sentence shall be made as of the time of the distribution or at such other time as the Secretary may prescribe.

(C) Treatment of forfeitable rights—If an employee does not have a nonforfeitable right to any amount under any trust or contract to which subparagraph (A) applies, such amount shall not be treated as part of the account balance.

(D) Investment in the contract before 1987—In the case of a plan which on May 5, 1986, permitted withdrawal of any employee contributions before separation from service, subparagraph (A) shall apply only to the extent that amounts received before the annuity starting date (when increased by amounts previously received under the contract after December 31, 1986) exceed the investment in the contract as of December 31, 1986.

* * *

(f) Special rules for computing employees' contributions—In computing, for purposes of subsection (c)(1)(A), the aggregate amount of premiums or other consideration paid for the contract, and for purposes of subsection (e)(6), the aggregate premiums or other consideration paid, amounts contributed by the employer shall be included, but only to the extent that—

(1) such amounts were includible in the gross income of the employee under this subtitle or prior income tax laws; or

(2) if such amounts had been paid directly to the employee at the time they were contributed, they would not have been includible in the gross income of the employee under the law applicable at the time of such contribution.

* * *

(m) Special rules applicable to employee annuities and distributions under employee plans—

(1) [Repealed]

(2) Computation of consideration paid by the employee—In computing—

(A) the aggregate amount of premiums or other consideration paid for the contract for purposes of subsection (c)(1)(A) (relating to the investment in the contract), and

(B) the aggregate premiums or other consideration paid for purposes of subsection (e)(6) (relating to certain amounts not received as an annuity),

any amount allowed as a deduction with respect to the contract under section 404 which was paid while the employee was an employee within the meaning of section 401(c)(1) shall be treated as consideration contributed by the employer, and there shall not be taken into account any portion of the premiums or other consideration for the contract paid while the employee was an owner-employee which is properly allocable (as determined under regulations prescribed by the Secretary) to the cost of life, accident, health, or other insurance.

(3) Life insurance contracts—

(A) This paragraph shall apply to any life insurance contract—

(i) purchased as a part of a plan described in section 403(a), or

(ii) purchased by a trust described in section 401(a) which is exempt from tax under section 501(a) if the proceeds of such contract are payable directly or indirectly to a participant in such trust or to a beneficiary of such participant.

(B) Any contribution to a plan described in subparagraph (A)(i) or a trust described in subparagraph (A)(ii) which is allowed as a deduction under section 404, and any income of a trust described in subparagraph (A)(ii), which is determined in accordance with regulations prescribed by the Secretary to have been applied to purchase the life insurance protection under a contract described in subparagraph (A), is includible in the gross income of the participant for the taxable year when so applied.

(C) In the case of the death of an individual insured under a contract described in subparagraph (A), an amount equal to the cash surrender value of the contract immediately before the death of the insured shall be treated as a payment under such plan or a distribution by such trust, and the excess of the amount payable by reason of the death of the insured over such cash surrender value shall not be includible in gross income under this section and shall be treated as provided in section 101.

* * *

(10) Determination of investment in the contract in the case of qualified domestic relations orders—Under regulations prescribed by the Secretary, in the case of a distribution or payment made to an alternate payee who is the spouse or former spouse of the participant pursuant to a qualified domestic relations order (as defined in section 414(p)), the investment in the contract as of the date prescribed in such regulations shall be allocated on a pro rata basis between the present value of such distribution or payment and the present value of all other benefits payable with respect to the participant to which such order relates.

* * *

(p) Loans treated as distributions—For purposes of this section—

(1) Treatment as distributions—

(A) Loans—If during any taxable year a participant or beneficiary receives (directly or indirectly) any amount as a loan from a qualified employer plan, such amount shall be treated as having been received by such individual as a distribution under such plan.

(B) Assignments or pledges—If during any taxable year a participant or beneficiary assigns (or agrees to assign) or pledges (or agrees to pledge) any portion of his interest in a qualified employer plan, such portion shall be treated as having been received by such individual as a loan from such plan.

(2) Exception for certain loans—

(A) General rule—Paragraph (1) shall not apply to any loan to the extent that such loan (when added to the outstanding balance of all other loans from such plan whether made on, before, or after August 13, 1982), does not exceed the lesser of—

(i) $50,000, reduced by the excess (if any) of—

(I) the highest outstanding balance of loans from the plan during the 1-year period ending on the day before the date on which such loan was made, over

(II) the outstanding balance of loans from the plan on the date on which such loan was made, or

(ii) the greater of (I) one-half of the present value of the nonforfeitable accrued benefit of the employee under the plan, or (II) $10,000.

For purposes of clause (ii), the present value of the nonforfeitable accrued benefit shall be determined without regard to any accumulated deductible employee contributions (as defined in subsection (o)(5)(B)).

(B) Requirement that loan be repayable within 5 years—

(i) In general—Subparagraph (A) shall not apply to any loan unless such loan, by its terms, is required to be repaid within 5 years.

(ii) Exception for home loans—Clause (i) shall not apply to any loan used to acquire any dwelling unit which within a reasonable time is to be used (determined at the time the loan is made) as the principal residence of the participant.

(C) Requirement of level amortization—Except as provided in regulations, this paragraph shall not apply to any loan unless substantially level amortization of such loan (with payments not less frequently than quarterly) is required over the term of the loan.

(D) Related employers and related plans—For purposes of this paragraph—

(i) the rules of subsections (b), (c), and (m) of section 414 shall apply, and

(ii) all plans of an employer (determined after the application of such subsections) shall be treated as 1 plan.

(3) Denial of interest deductions in certain cases—

(A) In general—No deduction otherwise allowable under this chapter shall be allowed under this chapter for any interest paid or accrued on any loan to which paragraph (1) does not apply by reason of paragraph (2) during the period described in subparagraph (B).

(B) Period to which subparagraph (a) applies—For purposes of subparagraph (A), the period described in this subparagraph is the period—

(i) on or after the 1st day on which the individual to whom the loan is made is a key employee (as defined in section 416(i)), or

(ii) such loan is secured by amounts attributable to elective deferrals described in subparagraph (A) or (C) of section 402(g)(3).

(4) Qualified employer plan, etc—For purposes of this subsection—

(A) Qualified employer plan—

(i) In general—The term "qualified employer plan" means—

(I) a plan described in section 401(a) which includes a trust exempt from tax under section 501(a),

(II) an annuity plan described in section 403(a), and

(III) a plan under which amounts are contributed by an individual's employer for an annuity contract described in section 403(b).

(ii) Special rule—The term "qualified employer plan" shall include any plan which was (or was determined to be) a qualified employer plan or a government plan.

(B) Government plan—The term "government plan" means any plan, whether or not qualified, established and maintained for its employees by the United States, by a State or political subdivision thereof, or by an agency or instrumentality of any of the foregoing.

* * *

(t) 10-percent additional tax on early distributions from qualified retirement plans—

(1) Imposition of additional tax—If any taxpayer receives any amount from a qualified retirement plan (as defined in section 4974(c)), the taxpayer's tax under this chapter for the taxable year in which such amount is received shall be increased by an amount equal to 10 percent of the portion of such amount which is includible in gross income.

(2) Subsection not to apply to certain distributions—Except as provided in paragraphs (3) and (4), paragraph (1) shall not apply to any of the following distributions:

(A) In general—Distributions which are—

(i) made on or after the date on which the employee attains age 59½,

(ii) made to a beneficiary (or to the estate of the employee) on or after the death of the employee,

(iii) attributable to the employee's being disabled within the meaning of subsection (m)(7),

(iv) part of a series of substantially equal periodic payments (not less frequently than annually) made for the life (or life expectancy) of the employee or the joint lives (or joint life expectancies) of such employee and his designated beneficiary,

(v) made to an employee after separation from service after attainment of age 55,

(vi) dividends paid with respect to stock of a corporation which are described in section 404(k),

(vii) made on account of a levy under section 6331 on the qualified retirement plan, or

(viii) payments under a phased retirement annuity under section 8366a(a)(5) or 8412 a(a)(5) of title 5, United States Code, or a composite retirement annuity under section 8366a(a)(1) or 8412a(a)(1) of such title.

(B) Medical expenses—Distributions made to the employee (other than distributions described in subparagraph (A), (C) or (D)) to the extent such distributions do not exceed the amount allowable as a deduction under section 213 to the employee for amounts paid during the taxable year for medical care (determined without regard to whether the employee itemizes deductions for such taxable year).

(C) Payments to alternate payees pursuant to qualified domestic relations orders—Any distribution to an alternate payee pursuant to a qualified domestic relations order (within the meaning of section 414(p)(1)).

(D) Distributions to unemployed individuals for health insurance premiums—

(i) In general—Distributions from an individual retirement plan to an individual after separation from employment—

(I) if such individual has received unemployment compensation for 12 consecutive weeks under any Federal or State unemployment compensation law by reason of such separation,

(II) if such distributions are made during any taxable year during which such unemployment compensation is paid or the succeeding taxable year, and

(III) to the extent such distributions do not exceed the amount paid during the taxable year for insurance described in section 213(d)(1)(D) with respect to the individual and the individual's spouse and dependents (as defined in section 152, determined without regard to subsections (b)(1), (b)(2), and (d)(1)(B) thereof).

(ii) Distributions after reemployment—Clause (i) shall not apply to any distribution made after the individual has been employed for at least 60 days after the separation from employment to which clause (i) applies.

(iii) Self-employed individuals—To the extent provided in regulations, a self-employed individual shall be treated as meeting the requirements of clause (i)(I) if, under Federal or State law, the individual would have received unemployment compensation but for the fact the individual was self-employed.

(E) Distributions from individual retirement plans for higher education expenses—Distributions to an individual from an individual retirement plan to the extent such distributions do not exceed the qualified higher education expenses (as defined in paragraph (7)) of the taxpayer for the taxable year. Distributions shall not be taken into account under the preceding sentence if such distributions are described in subparagraph (A), (C), or (D) or to the extent paragraph (1) does not apply to such distributions by reason of subparagraph (B).

(F) Distributions from certain plans for first home purchases—Distributions to an individual from an individual retirement plan which are qualified first-time homebuyer distributions (as defined in paragraph (8)). Distributions shall not be taken into account under the preceding sentence if such distributions are described in subparagraph (A), (C), (D), or (E) or to the extent paragraph (1) does not apply to such distributions by reason of subparagraph (B).

(G) Distributions from retirement plans to individuals called to active duty—

(i) In general—Any qualified reservist distribution.

(ii) Amount distributed may be repaid—Any individual who receives a qualified reservist distribution may, at any time during the 2-year period beginning on the day after the end of the active duty period, make one or more contributions to an individual retirement plan of such individual in an aggregate amount not to exceed the amount of such distribution. The dollar limitations otherwise applicable to contributions to individual retirement plans shall not apply to any contribution made pursuant to the preceding sentence. No deduction shall be allowed for any contribution pursuant to this clause.

(iii) Qualified reservist distribution—For purposes of this subparagraph, the term "qualified reservist distribution" means any distribution to an individual if—

(I) such distribution is from an individual retirement plan, or from amounts attributable to employer contributions made pursuant to elective deferrals described in subparagraph (A) or (C) of section 402(g)(3) or section 501(c)(18)(D)(iii),

(II) such individual was (by reason of being a member of a reserve component (as defined in section 101 of title 37, United States Code)) ordered or called to active duty for a period in excess of 179 days or for an indefinite period, and

(III) such distribution is made during the period beginning on the date of such order or call and ending at the close of the active duty period.

(iv) Application of subparagraph—This subparagraph applies to individuals ordered or called to active duty after September 11, 2001. In no event shall the 2-year period referred to in clause (ii) end on or before the date which is 2 years after the date of the enactment of this subparagraph.

(3) Limitations—

(A) Certain exceptions not to apply to individual retirement plans—Subparagraphs (A)(v) and (C) of paragraph (2) shall not apply to distributions from an individual retirement plan.

(B) Periodic payments under qualified plans must begin after separation—Paragraph (2)(A)(iv) shall not apply to any amount paid from a trust described in section 401(a) which is exempt from tax under section 501(a) or from a contract described in section 72(e)(5)(D)(ii) unless the series of payments begins after the employee separates from service.

(4) Change in substantially equal payments—

(A) In general—If—

(i) paragraph (1) does not apply to a distribution by reason of paragraph (2)(A)(iv), and

(ii) the series of payments under such paragraph are subsequently modified (other than by reason of death or disability or a distribution to which paragraph (10) applies)—

(I) before the close of the 5-year period beginning with the date of the first payment and after the employee attains age 59½, or

(II) before the employee attains age 59½, the taxpayer's tax for the 1st taxable year in which such modification occurs shall be increased by an amount, determined under regulations, equal to the tax which (but for paragraph (2)(A)(iv)) would have been imposed, plus interest for the deferral period.

(B) Deferral period—For purposes of this paragraph, the term "deferral period" means the period beginning with the taxable year in which (without regard to paragraph (2)(A)(iv)) the distribution would have been includible in gross income and ending with the taxable year in which the modification described in subparagraph (A) occurs.

(5) Employee—For purposes of this subsection, the term "employee" includes any participant, and in the case of an individual retirement plan, the individual for whose benefit such plan was established.

(6) Special rules for simple retirement accounts—In the case of any amount received from a simple retirement account (within the meaning of section 408(p)) during the 2-year period beginning on the date such individual first participated in any qualified salary reduction arrangement maintained by the individual's employer under section 408(p)(2), paragraph (1) shall be applied by substituting "25 percent" for "10 percent".

(7) Qualified higher education expenses—For purposes of paragraph (2)(E)—

(A) In general—The term "qualified higher education expenses" means qualified higher education expenses (as defined in section 529(e)(3)) for education furnished to—

(i) the taxpayer,

(ii) the taxpayer's spouse, or

(iii) any child (as defined in section 152(f)(1)) or grandchild of the taxpayer or the taxpayer's spouse,

at an eligible educational institution (as defined in section 529(e)(5)).

(B) Coordination with other benefits—The amount of qualified higher education expenses for any taxable year shall be reduced as provided in section 25A(g)(2).

(8) Qualified first-time homebuyer distributions—For purposes of paragraph (2)(F)—

(A) In general—The term "qualified first-time homebuyer distribution" means any payment or distribution received by an individual to the extent such payment or distribution is used by the individual before the close of the 120th day after the day on which such payment or distribution is received to pay qualified acquisition costs with respect to a principal residence of a first-time homebuyer who is such individual, the spouse of such individual, or any child, grandchild, or ancestor of such individual or the individual's spouse.

(B) Lifetime dollar limitation—The aggregate amount of payments or distributions received by an individual which may be treated as qualified first-time homebuyer distributions for any taxable year shall not exceed the excess (if any) of—

(i) $10,000, over

(ii) the aggregate amounts treated as qualified first-time homebuyer distributions with respect to such individual for all prior taxable years.

(C) Qualified acquisition costs—For purposes of this paragraph, the term "qualified acquisition costs" means the costs of acquiring, constructing, or reconstructing a residence. Such term includes any usual or reasonable settlement, financing, or other closing costs.

(D) First-time homebuyer; other definitions—For purposes of this paragraph—

(i) **First-time homebuyer**—The term "first-time homebuyer" means any individual if—

(I) such individual (and if married, such individual's spouse) had no present ownership interest in a principal residence during the 2-year period ending on the date of acquisition of the principal residence to which this paragraph applies, and

(II) subsection (h) or (k) of section 1034 (as in effect on the day before the date of the enactment of this paragraph) did not suspend the running of any period of time specified in section 1034 (as so in effect) with respect to such individual on the day before the date the distribution is applied pursuant to subparagraph (A).

(ii) **Principal residence**—The term "principal residence" has the same meaning as when used in section 121.

(iii) **Date of acquisition**—The term "date of acquisition" means the date—

(I) on which a binding contract to acquire the principal residence to which subparagraph (A) applies is entered into, or

(II) on which construction or reconstruction of such a principal residence is commenced.

(E) Special rule where delay in acquisition—If any distribution from any individual retirement plan fails to meet the requirements of subparagraph (A) solely by reason of a delay or cancellation of the purchase or construction of the residence, the amount of the distribution may be contributed to an individual retirement plan as provided in section 408(d)(3)(A)(i) (determined by substituting "120th day" for "60th day" in such section), except that—

(i) section 408(d)(3)(B) shall not be applied to such contribution, and

(ii) such amount shall not be taken into account in determining whether section 408(d)(3)(B) applies to any other amount.

(9) Special rule for rollovers to section 457 plans—For purposes of this subsection, a distribution from an eligible deferred compensation plan (as defined in section 457(b)) of an eligible employer described in section 457(e)(1)(A) shall be treated as a distribution from a qualified retirement plan described in 4974(c)(1) to the extent that such distribution is attributable to an amount transferred to an eligible deferred compensation plan from a qualified retirement plan (as defined in section 4974(c)).

(10) Distributions to qualified public safety employees in governmental plans—

(A) In general—In the case of a distribution to a qualified public safety employee from a governmental plan (within the meaning of section 414(d)), paragraph (2)(A)(v) shall be applied by substituting "age 50" for "age 55".

(B) Qualified public safety employee—For purposes of this paragraph, the term "qualified public safety employee" means—

(i) any employee of a State or political subdivision of a State who provides police protection, firefighting services, or emergency medical services for any area within the jurisdiction of such State or political subdivision; or

(ii) any Federal law enforcement officer described in section 8331(20) or 8401(17) of title 5, United States Code, any Federal customs and border protection officer described in section 8331(31) or 8401(36) of such title, any Federal firefighter described in section 8331(21) or 8401(14) of such title, any air traffic controller described in 8331(30) or 8401(35) of such title, any nuclear materials courier described in section 8331(27) or 8401(33) of such title, any member of the United States Capitol Police, any member of the Supreme Court Police, any diplomatic security special agent of the Department of State, any nuclear materials courier described in section 8331(27) or 8401(33) of such title, any member of the United States Capitol Police, any member of the Supreme Court Police, or any diplomatic security special agent of the Department of State.

* * *

§ 79. Group-term life insurance purchased for employees.

(a) General rule. There shall be included in the gross income of an employee for the taxable year an amount equal to the cost of group-term life insurance on his life provided for part or all of such year under a policy (or policies) carried directly or indirectly by his employer (or employers); but only to the extent that such cost exceeds the sum of—

(1) the cost of $50,000 of such insurance, and

(2) the amount (if any) paid by the employee toward the purchase of such insurance.

(b) Exceptions. Subsection (a) shall not apply to—

(1) the cost of group-term life insurance on the life of an individual which is provided under a policy carried directly or indirectly by an employer after such individual has terminated his employment with such employer and is disabled (within the meaning of section 72(m)(7)),

(2) the cost of any portion of the group-term life insurance on the life of an employee provided during part or all of the taxable year of the employee under which—

(A) the employer is directly or indirectly the beneficiary, or

(B) a person described in section 170(c) is the sole beneficiary,

for the entire period during such taxable year for which the employee receives such insurance, and

(3) the cost of any group-term life insurance which is provided under a contract to which section 72(m)(3) applies.

(c) Determination of cost of insurance. For purposes of this section and section 6052, the cost of group-term insurance on the life of an employee provided during any period shall be determined on the basis of uniform premiums (computed on the basis of 5-year age brackets) prescribed by regulations by the Secretary.

(d) Nondiscrimination requirements.

(1) In general. In the case of a discriminatory group-term life insurance plan

(A) subsection (a)(1) shall not apply with respect to any key employee, and

(B) the cost of group-term life insurance on the life of any key employee shall be the greater of—

(i) such cost determined without regard to subsection (c), or

(ii) such cost determined with regard to subsection (c).

(2) Discriminatory group-term life insurance plan. For purposes of this subsection, the term "discriminatory group-term life insurance plan" means any plan of an employer for providing group-term life insurance unless—

(A) the plan does not discriminate in favor of key employees as to eligibility to participate, and

(B) the type and amount of benefits available under the plan do not discriminate in favor of participants who are key employees.

(3) Nondiscriminatory eligibility classification

(A) In general. A plan does not meet requirements of subparagraph (A) of paragraph (2) unless—

(i) such plan benefits 70 percent or more of all employees of the employer,

(ii) at least 85 percent of all employees who are participants under the plan are not key employees,

(iii) such plan benefits such employees as qualify under a classification set up by the employer and found by the Secretary not to be discriminatory in favor of key employees, or

(iv) in the case of a plan which is part of a cafeteria plan, the requirements of section 125 are met.

(B) Exclusion of certain employees. For purposes of subparagraph (A), there may be excluded from consideration—

(i) employees who have not completed 3 years of service;

(ii) part-time or seasonal employees;

(iii) employees not included in the plan who are included in a unit of employees covered by an agreement between employee representatives and one or more employers which the Secretary finds to be a collective bargaining agreement, if the benefits provided under the plan were the subject of good faith bargaining between such employee representatives and such employer or employers; and

(iv) employees who are nonresident aliens and who receive no earned income (within the meaning of section 911(d)(2) from the employer which constitutes income from sources within the United States (within the meaning of section 861(a)(3).

(4) Nondiscriminatory benefits. A plan does not meet the requirements of paragraph (2)(B) unless all benefits available to participants who are key employees are available to all other participants.

(5) Special rule. A plan shall not fail to meet the requirements of paragraph (2)(B) merely because the amount of life insurance on behalf of the employees under the plan bears a uniform relationship to the total compensation or the basic or regular rate of compensation of such employees.

(6) Key employee defined. For purposes of this subsection, the term "key employee" has the meaning given to such term by paragraph (1) of section 416(i). Such term also includes any former employee if such employee when he retired or separated from service was a key employee.

(7) Exemption for church plans.

(A) In general. This subsection shall not apply to a church plan maintained for church employees.

(B) Definitions. For purposes of subparagraph (A), the terms "church plan" and "church employee" have the meaning given such terms by paragraphs (1) and (3)(B) of section 414(e), respectively, except that—

(i) section 414(e) shall be applied by substituting "section 501(c)(3)" for "section 501" each place it appears, and

(ii) the term "church employee" shall not include an employee of—

(I) an organization described in section 170(b)(1)(A)(ii) above the secondary school level (other than a school for religious training),

(II) an organization described in section 170(b)(1)(A)(iii), and

(III) an organization described in section 501(c)(3), the basis of the exemption for which is substantially similar to the basis for exemption of an organization described in subclause (II).

(8) Treatment of former employees. To the extent provided in regulations, this subsection shall be applied separately with respect to former employees.

(e) Employee includes former employee. For purposes of this section, the term "employee" includes a former employee.

(f) Exception for life insurance purchased in connection with qualified transfer of excess pension assets. Subsection (b)(3) and section 72(m)(3) shall not apply in the case of any cost paid (whether directly or indirectly) with assets held in an applicable life insurance account (as defined in section 420(e)(4) under a defined benefit plan.

§ 83. Property transferred in connection with performance of services.

(a) General rule—If, in connection with the performance of services, property is transferred to any person other than the person for whom such services are performed, the excess of—

(1) the fair market value of such property (determined without regard to any restriction other than a restriction which by its terms will never lapse) at the first time the rights of the person having the beneficial interest in such property are transferable or are not subject to a substantial risk of forfeiture, whichever occurs earlier, over

(2) the amount (if any) paid for such property,

shall be included in the gross income of the person who performed such services in the first taxable year in which the rights of the person having the beneficial interest in such property are transferable or are not subject to a substantial risk of forfeiture, whichever is applicable. The preceding sentence shall not apply if such person sells or otherwise disposes of such property in an arm's length transaction before his rights in such property become transferable or not subject to a substantial risk of forfeiture.

(b) Election to include in gross income in year of transfer—

(1) In general—Any person who performs services in connection with which property is transferred to any person may elect to include in his gross income, for the taxable year in which such property is transferred, the excess of—

(A) the fair market value of such property at the time of transfer (determined without regard to any restriction other than a restriction which by its terms will never lapse), over

(B) the amount (if any) paid for such property. If such election is made, subsection (a) shall not apply with respect to the transfer of such property, and if such property is subsequently forfeited, no deduction shall be allowed in respect of such forfeiture.

(2) Election—An election under paragraph (1) with respect to any transfer of property shall be made in such manner as the Secretary prescribes and shall be made not later than 30 days after the date of such transfer. Such election may not be revoked except with the consent of the Secretary.

(c) Special rules—For purposes of this section—

(1) Substantial risk of forfeiture—The rights of a person in property are subject to a substantial risk of forfeiture if such person's rights to full enjoyment of such property are conditioned upon the future performance of substantial services by any individual.

(2) Transferability of property—The rights of a person in property are transferable only if the rights in such property of any transferee are not subject to a substantial risk of forfeiture.

(3) Sales which may give rise to suit under section 16(b) of the securities exchange act of 1934—So long as the sale of property at a profit could subject a person to suit under section 16(b) of the Securities Exchange Act of 1934, such person's rights in such property are—

(A) subject to a substantial risk of forfeiture, and

(B) not transferable.

(4) For purposes of determining an individual's basis in property transferred in connection with the performance of services, rules similar to the rules of section 72(w) shall apply.

(d) Certain restrictions which will never lapse—

(1) Valuation—In the case of property subject to a restriction which by its terms will never lapse, and which allows the transferee to sell such property only at a price determined under a formula, the price so determined shall be deemed to be the fair market value of the property unless established to the contrary by the Secretary, and the burden of proof shall be on the Secretary with respect to such value.

(2) Cancellation—If, in the case of property subject to a restriction which by its terms will never lapse, the restriction is cancelled, then, unless the taxpayer establishes—

(A) that such cancellation was not compensatory, and

(B) that the person, if any, who would be allowed a deduction if the cancellation were treated as compensatory, will treat the transaction as not compensatory, as evidenced in such manner as the Secretary shall prescribe by regulations,

the excess of the fair market value of the property (computed without regard to the restrictions) at the time of cancellation over the sum of—

(C) the fair market value of such property (computed by taking the restriction into account) immediately before the cancellation, and

(D) the amount, if any, paid for the cancellation,

shall be treated as compensation for the taxable year in which such cancellation occurs.

(e) Applicability of section—This section shall not apply to—

(1) a transaction to which section 421 applies,

(2) a transfer to or from a trust described in section 401(a) or a transfer under an annuity plan which meets the requirements of section 404(a)(2),

(3) the transfer of an option without a readily ascertainable fair market value,

(4) the transfer of property pursuant to the exercise of an option with a readily ascertainable fair market value at the date of grant, or

(5) group-term life insurance to which section 79 applies.

(f) Holding period—In determining the period for which the taxpayer has held property to which subsection (a) applies, there shall be included only the period beginning at the first time his rights in such property are transferable or are not subject to a substantial risk of forfeiture, whichever occurs earlier.

(g) Certain exchanges—If property to which subsection (a) applies is exchanged for property subject to restrictions and conditions substantially similar to those to which the property given in such exchange was subject, and if section 354, 355, 356, or 1036 (or so much of section 1031 as relates to section 1036) applied to such exchange, or if such exchange was pursuant to the exercise of a conversion privilege—

(1) such exchange shall be disregarded for purposes of subsection (a), and

(2) the property received shall be treated as property to which subsection (a) applies.

(h) Deduction by employer—In the case of a transfer of property to which this section applies or a cancellation of a restriction described in subsection (d), there shall be allowed as a deduction under section 162, to the person for whom were performed the services in connection with which such property was transferred, an amount equal to the amount included under subsection (a), (b), or (d)(2) in the gross income of the person who performed such services. Such deduction shall be allowed for the taxable year of such person in which or with which ends the taxable year in which such amount is included in the gross income of the person who performed such services.

§ 86. Social security and tier 1 railroad retirement benefits.

(a) In general—

(1) In general—Except as provided in paragraph (2), gross income for the taxable year of any taxpayer described in subsection (b) (notwithstanding section 207 of the Social Security Act) includes social security benefits in an amount equal to the lesser of—

(A) one-half of the social security benefits received during the taxable year, or

(B) one-half of the excess described in subsection (b)(1).

(2) Additional amount—In the case of a taxpayer with respect to whom the amount determined under subsection (b)(1)(A) exceeds the adjusted base amount, the amount included in gross income under this section shall be equal to the lesser of—

(A) the sum of—

(i) 85 percent of such excess, plus

(ii) the lesser of the amount determined under paragraph (1) or an amount equal to one-half of the difference between the adjusted base amount and the base amount of the taxpayer, or

(B) 85 percent of the social security benefits received during the taxable year.

(b) Taxpayers to whom subsection (a) applies—

(1) In general—A taxpayer is described in this subsection if—

(A) the sum of—

(i) the modified adjusted gross income of the taxpayer for the taxable year, plus

(ii) one-half of the social security benefits received during the taxable year, exceeds

(B) the base amount.

(2) Modified adjusted gross income—For purposes of this subsection, the term "modified adjusted gross income" means adjusted gross income—

(A) determined without regard to this section and sections 135, 137, 199, 221, 222, 911, 931, and 933, and

(B) increased by the amount of interest received or accrued by the taxpayer during the taxable year which is exempt from tax.

(c) Base amount and adjusted base amount—For purposes of this section—

(1) Base amount—The term "base amount" means—

(A) except as otherwise provided in this paragraph, $25,000,

(B) $32,000 in the case of a joint return, and

(C) zero in the case of a taxpayer who—

(i) is married as of the close of the taxable year (within the meaning of section 7703) but does not file a joint return for such year, and

(ii) does not live apart from his spouse at all times during the taxable year.

(2) Adjusted base amount—The term "adjusted base amount" means—

(A) except as otherwise provided in this paragraph, $34,000,

(B) $44,000 in the case of a joint return, and

(C) zero in the case of a taxpayer described in paragraph (1)(C).

(d) Social security benefit—

(1) In general—For purposes of this section, the term "social security benefit" means any amount received by the taxpayer by reason of entitlement to—

(A) a monthly benefit under title II of the Social Security Act, or

(B) a tier 1 railroad retirement benefit.

* * *

§ 101. Certain death benefits.

(a) Proceeds of life insurance contracts payable by reason of death.

(1) General rule. Except as otherwise provided in paragraph (2), subsection (d), subsection (f), and subsection (j), gross income does not include amounts received (whether in a single sum or otherwise) under a life insurance contract, if such amounts are paid by reason of the death of the insured.

(2) Transfer for valuable consideration. In the case of a transfer for a valuable consideration, by assignment or otherwise, of a life insurance contract or any interest therein, the amount excluded from gross income by paragraph (1) shall not exceed an amount equal to the sum of the actual value of such consideration and the premiums and other amounts subsequently paid by the transferee. The preceding sentence shall not apply in the case of such a transfer—

(A) if such contract or interest therein has a basis for determining gain or loss in the hands of a transferee determined in whole or in part by reference to such basis of such contract or interest therein in the hands of the transferor, or

(B) if such transfer is to the insured, to a partner of the insured, to a partnership in which the insured is a partner, or to a corporation in which the insured is a shareholder or officer.

The term "other amounts" in the first sentence of this paragraph includes interest paid or accrued by the transferee on indebtedness with respect to such contract or any interest therein if such interest paid or accrued is not allowable as a deduction by reason of section 264(a)(4).

(c) Interest. If any amount excluded from gross income by subsection (a) is held under an agreement to pay interest thereon, the interest payments shall be included in gross income.

(d) Payment of life insurance proceeds at a date later than death.

(1) General rule. The amounts held by an insurer with respect to any beneficiary shall be prorated (in accordance with such regulations as may be prescribed by the Secretary) over the period or periods with respect to which such payments are to be made. There shall be excluded from the gross income of such beneficiary in the taxable year received any amount determined by such proration. Gross income includes, to the extent not excluded by the preceding sentence, amounts received under agreements to which this subsection applies.

(2) Amount held by an insurer. An amount held by an insurer with respect to any beneficiary shall mean an amount to which subsection (a) applies which is—

(A) held by any insurer under an agreement provided for in the life insurance contract, whether as an option or otherwise, to pay such amount on a date or dates later than the death of the insured, and

(B) equal to the value of such agreement to such beneficiary

(i) as of the date of death of the insured (as if any option exercised under the life insurance contract were exercised at such time), and

(ii) as discounted on the basis of the interest rate used by the insurer in calculating payments under the agreement and mortality tables prescribed by the Secretary.

(3) Application of subsection. This subsection shall not apply to any amount to which subsection (c) is applicable.

* * *

(g) Treatment of certain accelerated death benefits.

(1) In general. For purposes of this section, the following amounts shall be treated as an amount paid by reason of the death of an insured:

(A) Any amount received under a life insurance contract on the life of an insured who is a terminally ill individual.

(B) Any amount received under a life insurance contract on the life of an insured who is a chronically ill individual.

(2) Treatment of viatical settlements.

(A) In general. If any portion of the death benefit under a life insurance contract on the life of an insured described in paragraph (1) is sold or assigned to a viatical settlement provider, the amount paid for the sale or assignment of such portion shall be treated as an amount paid under the life insurance contract by reason of the death of such insured.

* * *

(3) Special rules for chronically ill insureds. In the case of an insured who is a chronically ill individual—

(A) In general. Paragraphs (1) and (2) shall not apply to any payment received for any period unless—

(i) such payment is for costs incurred by the payee (not compensated for by insurance or otherwise) for qualified long-term care services provided for the insured for such period, and

(ii) the terms of the contract giving rise to such payment satisfy—

(I) the requirements of section 7702B(b)(1)(B), and

(II) the requirements (if any) applicable under subparagraph (B).

For purposes of the preceding sentence, the rule of section 7702B(b)(2)(B) shall apply.

(B) Other requirements. The requirements applicable under this subparagraph are—

(i) those requirements of section 7702B(g) and section 4980C which the Secretary specifies as applying to such a purchase, assignment, or other arrangement,

(ii) standards adopted by the National Association of Insurance Commissioners which specifically apply to chronically ill individuals (and, if such standards are adopted, the analogous requirements specified under clause (i) shall cease to apply), and

(iii) standards adopted by the State in which the policyholder resides (and if such standards are adopted, the analogous requirements specified under clause (i) and (subject to section 4980C(f)) standards under clause (ii), shall cease to apply).

(C) Per diem payments. A payment shall not fail to be described in subparagraph (A) by reason of being made on a per diem or other periodic basis without regard to the expenses incurred during the period to which the payment relates.

(D) Limitation on exclusion for periodic payments. For limitation on amount of periodic payments which are treated as described in paragraph (1), see section 7702B(d).

(4) Definitions. For purposes of this subsection—

(A) Terminally ill individual. The term "terminally ill individual" means an individual who has been certified by a physician as having an illness or physical condition which can reasonably be expected to result in death in 24 months or less after the date of the certification.

(B) Chronically ill individual. The term "chronically ill individual" has the meaning given such term by section 7702B(c)(2); except that such term shall not include a terminally ill individual.

(C) Qualified long-term care services. The term "qualified long-term care services" has the meaning given such term by section 7702B(c).

(D) Physician. The term "physician" has the meaning given to such term by section 1861(r)(1) of the Social Security Act.

(5) Exception for business-related policies. This subsection shall not apply in the case of any amount paid to any taxpayer other than the insured if such taxpayer has an insurable interest with respect to the life of the insured by reason of the insured being a director, officer, or employee of the taxpayer or by reason of the insured being financially interested in any trade or business carried on by the taxpayer.

* * *

(j) Treatment of certain employer-owned life insurance contracts.

(1) General rule. In the case of an employer-owned life insurance contract, the amount excluded from gross income of an applicable policyholder by reason of paragraph (1) of subsection (a) shall not exceed an amount equal to the sum of the premiums and other amounts paid by the policyholder for the contract.

(2) Exceptions. In the case of an employer-owned life insurance contract with respect to which the notice and consent requirements of paragraph (4) are met, paragraph (1) shall not apply to any of the following:

(A) Exceptions based on insured's status. Any amount received by reason of the death of an insured who, with respect to an applicable policyholder—

(i) was an employee at any time during the 12-month period before the insured's death, or

(ii) is, at the time the contract is issued—

(I) a director,

(II) a highly compensated employee within the meaning of section 414(q) (without regard to paragraph (1)(B)(ii) thereof), or

(III) a highly compensated individual within the meaning of section 105(h)(5), except that "35 percent" shall be substituted for "25 percent" in subparagraph (C) thereof.

(B) Exception for amounts paid to insured's heirs. Any amount received by reason of the death of an insured to the extent—

(i) the amount is paid to a member of the family (within the meaning of section 267(c)(4)) of the insured, any individual who is the designated beneficiary of the insured under the contract (other than the applicable policyholder), a trust established for the benefit of any such member of the family or designated beneficiary, or the estate of the insured, or

(ii) the amount is used to purchase an equity (or capital or profits) interest in the applicable policyholder from any person described in clause (i).

(3) Employer-owned life insurance contract.

(A) In general. For purposes of this subsection, the term "employer-owned life insurance contract" means a life insurance contract which—

(i) is owned by a person engaged in a trade or business and under which such person (or a related person described in subparagraph (B)(ii)) is directly or indirectly a beneficiary under the contract, and

(ii) covers the life of an insured who is an employee with respect to the trade or business of the applicable policyholder on the date the contract is issued.

For purposes of the preceding sentence, if coverage for each insured under a master contract is treated as a separate contract for purposes of sections 817(h), 7702, and 7702A, coverage for each such insured shall be treated as a separate contract.

(B) Applicable policyholder. For purposes of this subsection—

(i) In general. The term "applicable policyholder" means, with respect to any employer-owned life insurance contract, the person described in subparagraph (A)(i) which owns the contract.

(ii) Related persons. The term "applicable policyholder" includes any person which—

(I) bears a relationship to the person described in clause (i) which is specified in section 267(b) or 707(b)(1), or

(II) is engaged in trades or businesses with such person which are under common control (within the meaning of subsection (a) or (b) of section 52).

(4) Notice and consent requirements. The notice and consent requirements of this paragraph are met if, before the issuance of the contract, the employee—

(A) is notified in writing that the applicable policyholder intends to insure the employee's life and the maximum face amount for which the employee could be insured at the time the contract was issued,

(B) provides written consent to being insured under the contract and that such coverage may continue after the insured terminates employment, and

(C) is informed in writing that an applicable policyholder will be a beneficiary of any proceeds payable upon the death of the employee.

(5) Definitions. For purposes of this subsection—

(A) Employee. The term "employee" includes an officer, director, and highly compensated employee (within the meaning of section 414(q)).

(B) Insured. The term "insured" means, with respect to an employer-owned life insurance contract, an individual covered by the contract who is a United States citizen or resident. In the case of a contract covering the joint lives of 2 individuals, references to an insured include both of the individuals.

§ 104. Compensation for injuries or sickness.

(a) In general. Except in the case of amounts attributable to (and not in excess of) deductions allowed under section 213 (relating to medical, etc., expenses) for any prior taxable year, gross income does not include—

(1) amounts received under workmen's compensation acts as compensation for personal injuries or sickness;

(2) the amount of any damages (other than punitive damages) received (whether by suit or agreement and whether as lump sums or as periodic payments) on account of personal physical injuries or physical sickness;

(3) amounts received through accident or health insurance (or through an arrangement having the effect of accident or health insurance) for personal injuries or sickness (other than amounts received by an employee, to the extent such amounts (A) are attributable to contributions by the employer which were not includible in the gross income of the employee, or (B) are paid by the employer);

(4) amounts received as a pension, annuity, or similar allowance for personal injuries or sickness resulting from active service in the armed forces of any country or in the Coast and Geodetic Survey or the Public Health Service, or as a disability annuity payable under the provisions of section 808 of the Foreign Service Act of 1980;

(5) amounts received by an individual as disability income attributable to injuries incurred as a direct result of a terroristic or military action (as defined in section 692(c)(2)); and

(6) amounts received pursuant to—

> **(A)** section 1201 of the Omnibus Crime Control and Safe Streets Act of 1968 (42 U.S.C. 3796); or

> **(B)** a program established under the laws of any State which provides monetary compensation for surviving dependents of a public safety officer who has died as the direct and proximate result of a personal injury sustained in the line of duty,

except that subparagraph (B) shall not apply to any amounts that would have been payable if death of the public safety officer had occurred other than as the direct and proximate result of a personal injury sustained in the line of duty.

For purposes of paragraph (3), in the case of an individual who is, or has been, an employee within the meaning of section 401(c)(1) (relating to self-employed individuals), contributions made on behalf of such individual while he was such an employee to a trust described in section 401(a) which is exempt from tax under section 501(a), or under a plan described in section 403(a), shall, to the extent allowed as deductions under section 404, be treated as contributions by the employer which were not includible in the gross income of the employee. For purposes of paragraph (2), emotional distress shall not be treated as a physical injury or physical sickness. The preceding sentence shall not apply to an amount of damages not in excess of the amount paid for medical care (described in subparagraph (A) or (B) of section 213(d)(1)) attributable to emotional distress.

* * *

(d) Cross references.

> **(1)** For exclusion from employee's gross income of employer contributions to accident and health plans, see section 106.

> **(2)** For exclusion of part of disability retirement pay from the application of subsection (a)(4) of this section, see section 1403 of title 10, United States Code (relating to career compensation laws).

§ 105. Amounts received under accident and health plans.

(a) Amounts attributable to employer contributions. Except as otherwise provided in this section, amounts received by an employee through accident or health insurance for personal injuries or sickness shall be included in gross income to the extent such amounts (1) are attributable to contributions by the employer which were not includible in the gross income of the employee, or (2) are paid by the employer.

(b) Amounts expended for medical care. Except in the case of amounts attributable to (and not in excess of) deductions allowed under section 213 (relating to medical, etc., expenses) for any prior taxable year, gross income does not include amounts referred to in subsection (a) if such amounts are paid, directly or indirectly, to the taxpayer to reimburse the taxpayer for expenses incurred by him for the medical care (as defined in section 213(d)) of the taxpayer, his spouse, his dependents (as defined in section 152), determined without regard to subsections (b)(1), (b)(2), and (d)(1)(B) thereof), and any child (as defined in section 152(f)(1)) of the taxpayer who as of the end of the taxable year has not attained age 27. Any child to whom section 152(e) applies shall be treated as a dependent of both parents for purposes of this subsection.

(c) Payments unrelated to absence from work. Gross income does not include amounts referred to in subsection (a) to the extent such amounts—

(1) constitute payment for the permanent loss or loss of use of a member or function of the body, or the permanent disfigurement, of the taxpayer, his spouse, or a dependent (as defined in section 152, determined without regard to subsections (b)(1), (b)(2), and (d)(1)(B) thereof), and

(2) are computed with reference to the nature of the injury without regard to the period the employee is absent from work.

(e) Accident and health plans. For purposes of this section and section 104—

(1) amounts received under an accident or health plan for employees, and

(2) amounts received from a sickness and disability fund for employees maintained under the law of a State or the District of Columbia,

shall be treated as amounts received through accident or health insurance.

(f) Rules for application of section 213. For purposes of section 213(a) (relating to medical, dental, etc., expenses) amounts excluded from gross income under subsection (c) shall not be considered as compensation (by insurance or otherwise) for expenses paid for medical care.

(g) Self-employed individual not considered an employee. For purposes of this section, the term "employee" does not include an individual who is an employee within the meaning of section 401(c)(1) (relating to self-employed individuals).

(h) Amount paid to highly compensated individuals under a discriminatory self-insured medical expense reimbursement plan.

(1) In general. In the case of amounts paid to a highly compensated individual under a self-insured medical reimbursement plan which does not satisfy the requirements of paragraph (2) for a plan year, subsection (b) shall not apply to such amounts to the extent they constitute an excess reimbursement of such highly compensated individual.

(2) Prohibition of discrimination. A self-insured medical reimbursement plan satisfies the requirements of this paragraph only if—

(A) the plan does not discriminate in favor of highly compensated individuals as to eligibility to participate; and

(B) the benefits provided under the plan do not discriminate in favor of participants who are highly compensated individuals.

(3) Nondiscriminatory eligibility classifications.

(A) In general. A self-insured medical reimbursement plan does not satisfy the requirements of subparagraph (A) of paragraph (2) unless such plan benefits—

(i) 70 percent or more of all employees, or 80 percent or more of all the employees who are eligible to benefit under the plan if 70 percent or more of all employees are eligible to benefit under the plan; or

(ii) such employees as qualify under a classification set up by the employer and found by the Secretary not to be discriminatory in favor of highly compensated individuals.

(B) Exclusion of certain employees. For purposes of subparagraph (A), there may be excluded from consideration—

 (i) employees who have not completed 3 years of service;

 (ii) employees who have not attained age 25;

 (iii) part-time or seasonal employees;

 (iv) employees not included in the plan who are included in a unit of employees covered by an agreement between employee representatives and one or more employers which the Secretary finds to be a collective bargaining agreement, if accident and health benefits were the subject of good faith bargaining between such employee representatives and such employer or employers; and

 (v) employees who are nonresident aliens and who receive no earned income (within the meaning of section 911(d)(2)) from the employer which constitutes income from sources within the United States (within the meaning of section 861(a)(3)).

(4) Nondiscriminatory benefits. A self-insured medical reimbursement plan does not meet the requirements of subparagraph (B) of paragraph (2) unless all benefits provided for participants who are highly compensated individuals are provided for all other participants.

(5) Highly compensated individual defined. For purposes of this subsection, the term "highly compensated individual" means an individual who is—

 (A) one of the 5 highest paid officers,

 (B) a shareholder who owns (with the application of section 318) more than 10 percent in value of the stock of the employer, or

 (C) among the highest paid 25 percent of all employees (other than employees described in paragraph (3)(B) who are not participants).

(6) Self-insured medical reimbursement plan. The term "self-insured medical reimbursement plan" means a plan of an employer to reimburse employees for expenses referred to in subsection (b) for which reimbursement is not provided under a policy of accident and health insurance.

(7) Excess reimbursement of highly compensated individual. For purposes of this section, the excess reimbursement of a highly compensated individual which is attributable to a self-insured medical reimbursement plan is—

 (A) in the case of a benefit available to highly compensated individuals but not to all other participants (or which otherwise fails to satisfy the requirements of paragraph (2)(B)), the amount reimbursed under the plan to the employee with respect to such benefit, and

 (B) in the case of benefits (other than benefits described in subparagraph (A) paid to a highly compensated individual by a plan which fails to satisfy the requirements of paragraph (2), the total amount reimbursed to the highly compensated individual for the plan year multiplied by a fraction—

  (i) the numerator of which is the total amount reimbursed to all participants who are highly compensated individuals under the plan for the plan year, and

(ii) the denominator of which is the total amount reimbursed to all employees under the plan for such plan year.

In determining the fraction under subparagraph (B), there shall not be taken into account any reimbursement which is attributable to a benefit described in subparagraph (A).

(8) Certain controlled groups, etc. All employees who are treated as employed by a single employer under subsection (b), (c), or (m) of section 414 shall be treated as employed by a single employer for purposes of this section.

(9) Regulations. The Secretary shall prescribe such regulations as may be necessary to carry out the provisions of this section.

(10) Time of inclusion. Any amount paid for a plan year that is included in income by reason of this subsection shall be treated as received or accrued in the taxable year of the participant in which the plan year ends.

* * *

§ 106. Contributions by employer to accident and health plans.

[handwritten: emp. provided health care escapes federal & state income & employment taxes]

(a) General rule. Except as otherwise provided in this section, gross income of an employee does not include employer-provided coverage under an accident or health plan.

(b) Contributions to Archer MSAs.

(1) In general. In the case of an employee who is an eligible individual, amounts contributed by such employee's employer to any Archer MSA of such employee shall be treated as employer-provided coverage for medical expenses under an accident or health plan to the extent such amounts do not exceed the limitation under section 220(b)(1) (determined without regard to this subsection) which is applicable to such employee for such taxable year.

(2) No constructive receipt. No amount shall be included in the gross income of any employee solely because the employee may choose between the contributions referred to in paragraph (1) and employer contributions to another health plan of the employer.

(3) Special rule for deduction of employer contributions. Any employer contribution to an Archer MSA, if otherwise allowable as a deduction under this chapter, shall be allowed only for the taxable year in which paid.

(4) Employer MSA contributions required to be shown on return. Every individual required to file a return under section 6012 for the taxable year shall include on such return the aggregate amount contributed by employers to the Archer MSAs of such individual or such individual's spouse for such taxable year.

(5) MSA contributions not part of COBRA coverage. Paragraph (1) shall not apply for purposes of section 4980B.

(6) Definitions. For purposes of this subsection, the terms "eligible individual" and "Archer MSA" have the respective meanings given to such terms by section 220.

(7) Cross reference. For penalty on failure by employer to make comparable contributions to the Archer MSAs of comparable employees, see section 4980E.

(c) Inclusion of long-term care benefits provided through flexible spending arrangements.

(1) In general. Gross income of an employee shall include employer-provided coverage for qualified long-term care services (as defined in section 7702B(c)) to the extent that such coverage is provided through a flexible spending or similar arrangement.

(2) Flexible spending arrangement. For purposes of this subsection, a flexible spending arrangement is a benefit program which provides employees with coverage under which—

    (A) specified incurred expenses may be reimbursed (subject to reimbursement maximums and other reasonable conditions), and

    (B) the maximum amount of reimbursement which is reasonably available to a participant for such coverage is less than 500 percent of the value of such coverage.

In the case of an insured plan, the maximum amount reasonably available shall be determined on the basis of the underlying coverage.

(d) Contributions to health savings accounts.

(1) In general. In the case of an employee who is an eligible individual (as defined in section 223(c)(1)), amounts contributed by such employee's employer to any health savings account (as defined in section 223(d)) of such employee shall be treated as employer-provided coverage for medical expenses under an accident or health plan to the extent such amounts do not exceed the limitation under section 223(b) (determined without regard to this subsection) which is applicable to such employee for such taxable year.

(2) Special rules. Rules similar to the rules of paragraphs (2), (3), (4), and (5) of subsection (b) shall apply for purposes of this subsection.

(3) Cross reference. For penalty on failure by employer to make comparable contributions to the health savings accounts of comparable employees, see section 4980G.

(e) FSA and HRA terminations to fund HSAs.

(1) In general. A plan shall not fail to be treated as a health flexible spending arrangement or health reimbursement arrangement under this section or section 105 merely because such plan provides for a qualified HSA distribution.

(2) Qualified HSA distribution. The term "qualified HSA distribution" means a distribution from a health flexible spending arrangement or health reimbursement arrangement to the extent that such distribution—

    (A) does not exceed the lesser of the balance in such arrangement on September 21, 2006, or as of the date of such distribution, and

    (B) is contributed by the employer directly to the health savings account of the employee before January 1, 2012.

Such term shall not include more than 1 distribution with respect to any arrangement.

* * *

(f) Reimbursements for medicine restricted to prescribed drugs and insulin. For purposes of this section and section 105, reimbursement for expenses incurred for a medicine or a drug shall be treated as a reimbursement for medical expenses only if such medicine or drug is a prescribed drug (determined without regard to whether such drug is available without a prescription) or is insulin.

§ 119. Meals or lodging furnished for the convenience of the employer.

(a) Meals and lodging furnished to employee, his spouse, and his dependents, pursuant to employment. There shall be excluded from gross income of an employee the value of any meals or lodging furnished to him, his spouse, or any of his dependents by or on behalf of his employer for the convenience of the employer, but only if—

    (1) in the case of meals, the meals are furnished on the business premises of the employer, or

    (2) in the case of lodging, the employee is required to accept such lodging on the business premises of his employer as a condition of his employment.

(b) Special rules. For purposes of subsection (a)—

    (1) Provisions of employment contract or state statute not to be determinative. In determining whether meals or lodging are furnished for the convenience of the employer, the provisions of an employment contract or of a State statute fixing terms of employment shall not be determinative of whether the meals or lodging are intended as compensation.

    (2) Certain factors not taken into account with respect to meals. In determining whether meals are furnished for the convenience of the employer, the fact that a charge is made for such meals, and the fact that the employee may accept or decline such meals, shall not be taken into account.

    (3) Certain fixed charges for meals.

        (A) In general. If—

            (i) an employee is required to pay on a periodic basis a fixed charge for his meals, and

            (ii) such meals are furnished by the employer for the convenience of the employer,

        there shall be excluded from the employee's gross income an amount equal to such fixed charge.

        (B) Application of subparagraph (A). Subparagraph (A) shall apply—

            (i) whether the employee pays the fixed charge out of his stated compensation or out of his own funds, and

            (ii) only if the employee is required to make the payment whether he accepts or declines the meals.

    (4) Meals furnished to employees on business premises where meals of most employees are otherwise excludable. All meals furnished on the business premises of an employer to such employer's employees shall be treated as furnished for the convenience of the employer if, without regard to this paragraph, more than half of the employees to whom such meals are furnished on such premises are furnished such meals for the convenience of the employer.

* * *

(d) Lodging furnished by certain educational institutions to employees.

(1) In general. In the case of an employee of an educational institution, gross income shall not include the value of qualified campus lodging furnished to such employee during the taxable year.

(2) Exception in cases of inadequate rent. Paragraph (1) shall not apply to the extent of the excess of—

(A) the lesser of—

(i) 5 percent of the appraised value of the qualified campus lodging, or

(ii) the average of the rentals paid by individuals (other than employees or students of the educational institution) during such calendar year for lodging provided by the educational institution which is comparable to the qualified campus lodging provided to the employee, over

(B) the rent paid by the employee for the qualified campus lodging during such calendar year.

The appraised value under subparagraph (A)(i) shall be determined as of the close of the calendar year in which the taxable year begins, or, in the case of a rental period not greater than 1 year, at any time during the calendar year in which such period begins.

(3) Qualified campus lodging. For purposes of this subsection, the term "qualified campus lodging" means lodging to which subsection (a) does not apply and which is—

(A) located on, or in the proximity of, a campus of the educational institution, and

(B) furnished to the employee, his spouse, and any of his dependents by or on behalf of such institution for use as a residence.

(4) Educational institution, etc. For purposes of this subsection—

(A) **In general.** The term "educational institution" means—

(i) an institution described in section 170(b)(1)(A)(ii) (or an entity organized under State law and composed of public institutions so described), or

(ii) an academic health center.

(B) **Academic health center.** For purposes of subparagraph (A), the term "academic health center" means an entity—

(i) which is described in section 170(b)(1)(A)(iii),

(ii) which receives (during the calendar year in which the taxable year of the taxpayer begins) payments under subsection (d)(5)(B) or (h) of section 1886 of the Social Security Act (relating to graduate medical education), and

(iii) which has as one of its principal purposes or functions the providing and teaching of basic and clinical medical science and research with the entity's own faculty.

§ 125. Cafeteria plans.

(a) **In general**—Except as provided in subsection (b), no amount shall be included in the gross income of a participant in a cafeteria plan solely because, under the plan, the participant may choose among the benefits of the plan.

(b) **Exception for highly compensated participants and key employees—**

(1) Highly compensated participants—In the case of a highly compensated participant, subsection (a) shall not apply to any benefit attributable to a plan year for which the plan discriminates in favor of—

(A) highly compensated individuals as to eligibility to participate, or

(B) highly compensated participants as to contributions and benefits.

(2) Key employees—In the case of a key employee (within the meaning of section 416(i)(1)), subsection (a) shall not apply to any benefit attributable to a plan for which the qualified benefits provided to key employees exceed 25 percent of the aggregate of such benefits provided for all employees under the plan. For purposes of the preceding sentence, qualified benefits shall be determined without regard to the second sentence of subsection (f).

(3) Year of inclusion—For purposes of determining the taxable year of inclusion, any benefit described in paragraph (1) or (2) shall be treated as received or accrued in the taxable year of the participant or key employee in which the plan year ends.

(c) Discrimination as to benefits or contributions—For purposes of subparagraph (B) of subsection (b)(1), a cafeteria plan does not discriminate where qualified benefits and total benefits (or employer contributions allocable to statutory nontaxable benefits and employer contributions for total benefits) do not discriminate in favor of highly compensated participants.

(d) Cafeteria plan defined—For purposes of this section—

(1) In general—The term "cafeteria plan" means a written plan under which—

(A) all participants are employees, and

(B) the participants may choose among 2 or more benefits consisting of cash and qualified benefits.

(2) Deferred compensation plans excluded—

(A) In general—The term "cafeteria plan" does not include any plan which provides for deferred compensation.

(B) Exception for cash and deferred arrangements—Subparagraph (A) shall not apply to a profit-sharing or stock bonus plan or rural cooperative plan (within the meaning of section 401(k)(7)) which includes a qualified cash or deferred arrangement (as defined in section 401(k)(2)) to the extent of amounts which a covered employee may elect to have the employer pay as contributions to a trust under such plan on behalf of the employee.

(C) Exception for certain plans maintained by educational institutions—Subparagraph (A) shall not apply to a plan maintained by an educational organization described in section 170(b)(1)(A)(ii) to the extent of amounts which a covered employee may elect to have the employer pay as contributions for post-retirement group life insurance if—

(i) all contributions for such insurance must be made before retirement, and

(ii) such life insurance does not have a cash surrender value at any time.

For purposes of section 79, any life insurance described in the preceding sentence shall be treated as group-term life insurance.

(D) Exception for health savings accounts—Subparagraph (A) shall not apply to a plan to the extent of amounts which a covered employee may elect to have the employer pay as contributions to a health savings account established on behalf of the employee.

(e) Highly compensated participant and individual defined—For purposes of this section—

(1) Highly compensated participant—The term "highly compensated participant" means a participant who is—

(A) an officer,

(B) a shareholder owning more than 5 percent of the voting power or value of all classes of stock of the employer,

(C) highly compensated, or

(D) a spouse or dependent (within the meaning of section 152, determined without regard to subsections (b)(1), (b)(2), and (d)(1)(B) thereof) of an individual described in subparagraph (A), (B), or (C).

(2) Highly compensated individual—The term "highly compensated individual" means an individual who is described in subparagraphs (A), (B), (C), or (D) of paragraph (1).

(f) Qualified benefits defined—For purposes of this section—

(1) In general. The term "qualified benefit" means any benefit which, with the application of subsection (a), is not includible in the gross income of the employee by reason of an express provision of this chapter (other than section 106(b), 117, 127, or 132. Such term includes any group term life insurance which is includible in gross income only because it exceeds the dollar limitation of section 79 and such term includes any other benefit permitted under regulations.

(2) Long-term care insurance not qualified. The term "qualified benefit" shall not include any product which is advertised, marketed, or offered as long-term care insurance.

(3) Certain exchange-participating qualified health plans not qualified.

(A) In general. The term "qualified benefit" shall not include any qualified health plan (as defined in section 1301(a) of the Patient Protection and Affordable Care Act offered through an Exchange established under section 1311 of such Act.

(B) Exception for exchange-eligible employers. Subparagraph (A) shall not apply with respect to any employee if such employee's employer is a qualified employer (as defined in section 1312(f)(2) of the Patient Protection and Affordable Care Act offering the employee the opportunity to enroll through such an Exchange in a qualified health plan in a group market.

* * *

(i) Limitation on health flexible spending arrangements [This subsection applies to taxable years beginning after December 31, 2012, as provided by § 10902(b) of P.L. 111-148, as amended.].

(1) In general. For purposes of this section, if a benefit is provided under a cafeteria plan through employer contributions to a health flexible spending arrangement, such benefit shall not be treated as a qualified benefit unless the cafeteria plan provides that an employee may not elect for any taxable year to have salary reduction contributions in excess of $2,500 made to such arrangement.

(2) Adjustment for inflation. In the case of any taxable year beginning after December 31, 2013, the dollar amount in paragraph (1) shall be increased by an amount equal to—

(A) such amount, multiplied by

(B) the cost-of-living adjustment determined under section 1(f)(3) for the calendar year in which such taxable year begins by substituting "calendar year 2012" for "calendar year 1992" in subparagraph (B) thereof.

If any increase determined under this paragraph is not a multiple of $50, such increase shall be rounded to the next lowest multiple of $50.

(j) Simple cafeteria plans for small businesses.

(1) In general. An eligible employer maintaining a simple cafeteria plan with respect to which the requirements of this subsection are met for any year shall be treated as meeting any applicable nondiscrimination requirement during such year.

* * *

§ 127. Educational assistance programs.

(a) Exclusion from gross income.

(1) In general. Gross income of an employee does not include amounts paid or expenses incurred by the employer for educational assistance to the employee if the assistance is furnished pursuant to a program which is described in subsection (b).

(2) $5,250 maximum exclusion. If, but for this paragraph, this section would exclude from gross income more than $5,250 of educational assistance furnished to an individual during a calendar year, this section shall apply only to the first $5,250 of such assistance so furnished.

(b) Educational assistance program.

(1) In general. For purposes of this section, an educational assistance program is a separate written plan of an employer for the exclusive benefit of his employees to provide such employees with educational assistance. The program must meet the requirements of paragraphs (2) through (6) of this subsection.

(2) Eligibility. The program shall benefit employees who qualify under a classification set up by the employer and found by the Secretary not to be discriminatory in favor of employees who are highly compensated employees (within the meaning of section 414(q)) or their dependents. For purposes of this paragraph, there shall be excluded from consideration employees not included in the program who are included in a unit of employees covered by an agreement which the Secretary of Labor finds to be a collective bargaining agreement between employee representatives and one or more employers, if there is evidence that educational assistance benefits were the subject of good faith bargaining between such employee representatives and such employer or employers.

(3) Principal shareholders or owners. Not more than 5 percent of the amounts paid or incurred by the employer for educational assistance during the year may be provided for the class of individuals who are shareholders or owners (or their spouses or dependents), each of whom (on any day of the year) owns more than 5 percent of the stock or of the capital or profits interest in the employer.

(4) Other benefits as an alternative. A program must not provide eligible employees with a choice between educational assistance and other remuneration includible in gross income. For purposes of this section, the business practices of the employer (as well as the written program) will be taken into account.

(5) No funding required. A program referred to in paragraph (1) is not required to be funded.

(6) Notification of employees. Reasonable notification of the availability and terms of the program must be provided to eligible employees.

(c) Definitions; special rules. For purposes of this section—

(1) Educational assistance. The term "educational assistance" means—

(A) the payment, by an employer, of expenses incurred by or on behalf of an employee for education of the employee (including, but not limited to, tuition, fees, and similar payments, books, supplies, and equipment), and

(B) the provision, by an employer, of courses of instruction for such employee (including books, supplies, and equipment),

but does not include payment for, or the provision of, tools or supplies which may be retained by the employee after completion of a course of instruction, or meals, lodging, or transportation. The term "educational assistance" also does not include any payment for, or the provision of any benefits with respect to, any course or other education involving sports, games, or hobbies.

(2) Employee. The term "employee" includes, for any year, an individual who is an employee within the meaning of section 401(c)(1) (relating to self-employed individuals).

(3) Employer. An individual who owns the entire interest in an unincorporated trade or business shall be treated as his own employer. A partnership shall be treated as the employer of each partner who is an employee within the meaning of paragraph (2).

* * *

§ 132. Certain fringe benefits.

(a) Exclusion from gross income. Gross income shall not include any fringe benefit which qualifies as a—

(1) no-additional-cost service,

(2) qualified employee discount,

(3) working condition fringe,

(4) de minimis fringe,

(5) qualified transportation fringe,

(6) qualified moving expense reimbursement,

(7) qualified retirement planning services, or

(8) qualified military base realignment and closure fringe.

(b) No-additional-cost service defined. For purposes of this section, the term "no-additional-cost service" means any service provided by an employer to an employee for use by such employee if—

(1) such service is offered for sale to customers in the ordinary course of the line of business of the employer in which the employee is performing services, and

(2) the employer incurs no substantial additional cost (including forgone revenue) in providing such service to the employee (determined without regard to any amount paid by the employee for such service).

(c) Qualified employee discount defined. For purposes of this section—

(1) Qualified employee discount. The term "qualified employee discount" means any employee discount with respect to qualified property or services to the extent such discount does not exceed—

(A) in the case of property, the gross profit percentage of the price at which the property is being offered by the employer to customers, or

(B) in the case of services, 20 percent of the price at which the services are being offered by the employer to customers.

* * *

(3) Employee discount defined. The term "employee discount" means the amount by which—

(A) the price at which the property or services are provided by the employer to an employee for use by such employee, is less than

(B) the price at which such property or services are being offered by the employer to customers.

(4) Qualified property or services. The term "qualified property or services" means any property (other than real property and other than personal property of a kind held for investment) or services which are offered for sale to customers in the ordinary course of the line of business of the employer in which the employee is performing services.

(d) Working condition fringe defined. For purposes of this section, the term "working condition fringe" means any property or services provided to an employee of the employer to the extent that, if the employee paid for such property or services, such payment would be allowable as a deduction under section 162 or 167.

(e) De minimis fringe defined. For purposes of this section—

(1) In general. The term "de minimis fringe" means any property or service the value of which is (after taking into account the frequency with which similar fringes are provided by the employer to the employer's employees) so small as to make accounting for it unreasonable or administratively impracticable.

(2) Treatment of certain eating facilities. The operation by an employer of any eating facility for employees shall be treated as a de minimis fringe if—

(A) such facility is located on or near the business premises of the employer, and

(B) revenue derived from such facility normally equals or exceeds the direct operating costs of such facility.

The preceding sentence shall apply with respect to any highly compensated employee only if access to the facility is available on substantially the same terms to each member of a group of employees which is defined under a reasonable classification set up by the employer which does not discriminate in favor of highly compensated employees. For purposes of subparagraph (B), an employee entitled under section 119 to exclude the value of a meal provided at such facility shall be treated as having paid an amount for such meal equal to the direct operating costs of the facility attributable to such meal.

(f) Qualified transportation fringe.

(1) In general. For purposes of this section, the term "qualified transportation fringe" means any of the following provided by an employer to an employee:

(A) Transportation in a commuter highway vehicle if such transportation is in connection with travel between the employee's residence and place of employment.

(B) Any transit pass.

(C) Qualified parking.

(D) Any qualified bicycle commuting reimbursement.

(2) Limitation on exclusion. The amount of the fringe benefits which are provided by an employer to any employee and which may be excluded from gross income under subsection (a)(5) shall not exceed—

(A) $175 per month in the case of the aggregate of the benefits described in subparagraphs (A) and (B) of paragraph (1),

(B) $175 per month in the case of qualified parking, and

(C) the applicable annual limitation in the case of any qualified bicycle commuting reimbursement.

(3) Cash reimbursements. For purposes of this subsection, the term "qualified transportation fringe" includes a cash reimbursement by an employer to an employee for a benefit described in paragraph (1). The preceding sentence shall apply to a cash reimbursement for any transit pass only if a voucher or similar item which may be exchanged only for a transit pass is not readily available for direct distribution by the employer to the employee.

(4) No constructive receipt. No amount shall be included in the gross income of an employee solely because the employee may choose between any qualified transportation fringe (other than a qualified bicycle commuting reimbursement) and compensation which would otherwise be includible in gross income of such employee.

(5) Definitions. For purposes of this subsection—

(A) Qualified parking. The term "qualified parking" means parking provided to an employee on or near the business premises of the employer or on or near a location from which the employee commutes to work by transportation described in subparagraph (A), in a commuter highway vehicle, or by carpool. Such term shall not include any parking on or near property used by the employee for residential purposes.

* * *

(6) Inflation adjustment.

(A) In general. In the case of any taxable year beginning in a calendar year after 1999, the dollar amounts contained in subparagraphs (A) and (B) of paragraph (2) shall be increased by an amount equal to—

(i) such dollar amount, multiplied by

(ii) the cost-of-living adjustment determined under section 1(f)(3) for the calendar year in which the taxable year begins, by substituting "calendar year 1998" for "calendar year 1992".

In the case of any taxable year beginning in a calendar year after 2002, clause (ii) shall be applied by substituting 'calendar year 2001' for 'calendar year 1998' for purposes of adjusting the dollar amount contained in paragraph (2)(A).

(B) Rounding. If any increase determined under subparagraph (A) is not a multiple of $5, such increase shall be rounded to the next lowest multiple of $5.

(7) Coordination with other provisions. For purposes of this section, the terms "working condition fringe" and "de minimis fringe" shall not include any qualified transportation fringe (determined without regard to paragraph (2)).

(g) Qualified moving expense reimbursement. For purposes of this section, the term "qualified moving expense reimbursement" means any amount received (directly or indirectly) by an individual from an employer as a payment for (or a reimbursement of) expenses which would be deductible as moving expenses under section 217 if directly paid or incurred by the individual. Such term shall not include any payment for (or reimbursement of) an expense actually deducted by the individual in a prior taxable year.

(h) Certain individuals treated as employees for purposes of subsections (a)(1) and (2). For purposes of paragraphs (1) and (2) of subsection (a)—

(1) Retired and disabled employees and surviving spouse of employee treated as employee. With respect to a line of business of an employer, the term "employee" includes—

(A) any individual who was formerly employed by such employer in such line of business and who separated from service with such employer in such line of business by reason of retirement or disability, and

(B) any widow or widower of any individual who died while employed by such employer in such line of business or while an employee within the meaning of subparagraph (A).

(2) Spouse and dependent children.

(A) In general. Any use by the spouse or a dependent child of the employee shall be treated as use by the employee.

(B) Dependent child. For purposes of subparagraph (A), the term "dependent child" means any child (as defined in section 152(f)(1)) of the employee—

(i) who is a dependent of the employee, or

(ii) both of whose parents are deceased and who has not attained age 25.

For purposes of the preceding sentence, any child to whom section 152(e) applies shall be treated as the dependent of both parents.

(3) Special rule for parents in the case of air transportation. Any use of air transportation by a parent of an employee (determined without regard to paragraph (1)(B)) shall be treated as use by the employee.

(i) Reciprocal agreements. For purposes of paragraph (1) of subsection (a), any service provided by an employer to an employee of another employer shall be treated as provided by the employer of such employee if—

    (1) such service is provided pursuant to a written agreement between such employers, and

    (2) neither of such employers incurs any substantial additional costs (including foregone revenue) in providing such service or pursuant to such agreement.

(j) Special rules.

    (1) Exclusions under subsection (a)(1) and (2) apply to highly compensated employees only if no discrimination. Paragraphs (1) and (2) of subsection (a) shall apply with respect to any fringe benefit described therein provided with respect to any highly compensated employee only if such fringe benefit is available on substantially the same terms to each member of a group of employees which is defined under a reasonable classification set up by the employer which does not discriminate in favor of highly compensated employees.

* * *

    (4) On-premises gyms and other athletic facilities.

        (A) In general. Gross income shall not include the value of any on-premises athletic facility provided by an employer to his employees.

        (B) On-premises athletic facility. For purposes of this paragraph, the term "on-premises athletic facility" means any gym or other athletic facility—

            (i) which is located on the premises of the employer,

            (ii) which is operated by the employer, and

            (iii) substantially all the use of which is by employees of the employer, their spouses, and their dependent children (within the meaning of subsection (h)).

* * *

(l) Section not to apply to fringe benefits expressly provided for elsewhere. This section (other than subsections (e) and (g)) shall not apply to any fringe benefits of a type the tax treatment of which is expressly provided for in any other section of this chapter.

(m) Qualified retirement planning services.

    (1) In general. For purposes of this section, the term "qualified retirement planning services" means any retirement planning advice or information provided to an employee and his spouse by an employer maintaining a qualified employer plan.

    (2) Nondiscrimination rule. Subsection (a)(7) shall apply in the case of highly compensated employees only if such services are available on substantially the same terms to each member of the group of employees normally provided education and information regarding the employer's qualified employer plan.

    (3) Qualified employer plan. For purposes of this subsection, the term "qualified employer plan" means a plan, contract, pension, or account described in section 219(g)(5).

* * *

§ 162. Trade or business expenses.

* * *

(m) Certain excessive employee remuneration. (1) In general. In the case of any publicly held corporation, no deduction shall be allowed under this chapter for applicable employee remuneration with respect to any covered employee to the extent that the amount of such remuneration for the taxable year with respect to such employee exceeds $1,000,000.

(2) Publicly held corporation. For purposes of this subsection, the term "publicly held corporation" means any corporation issuing any class of common equity securities required to be registered under section 12 of the Securities Exchange Act of 1934.

(3) Covered employee. For purposes of this subsection, the term "covered employee" means any employee of the taxpayer if—

(A) as of the close of the taxable year, such employee is the chief executive officer of the taxpayer or is an individual acting in such a capacity, or

(B) the total compensation of such employee for the taxable year is required to be reported to shareholders under the Securities Exchange Act of 1934 by reason of such employee being among the 4 highest compensated officers for the taxable year (other than the chief executive officer).

(4) Applicable employee remuneration. For purposes of this subsection—

(A) In general. Except as otherwise provided in this paragraph, the term "applicable employee remuneration" means, with respect to any covered employee for any taxable year, the aggregate amount allowable as a deduction under this chapter for such taxable year (determined without regard to this subsection) for remuneration for services performed by such employee (whether or not during the taxable year).

(B) Exception for remuneration payable on commission basis. The term "applicable employee remuneration" shall not include any remuneration payable on a commission basis solely on account of income generated directly by the individual performance of the individual to whom such remuneration is payable.

(C) Other performance-based compensation. The term "applicable employee remuneration" shall not include any remuneration payable solely on account of the attainment of one or more performance goals, but only if—

(i) the performance goals are determined by a compensation committee of the board of directors of the taxpayer which is comprised solely of 2 or more outside directors,

(ii) the material terms under which the remuneration is to be paid, including the performance goals, are disclosed to shareholders and approved by a majority of the vote in a separate shareholder vote before the payment of such remuneration, and

(iii) before any payment of such remuneration, the compensation committee referred to in clause (i) certifies that the performance goals and any other material terms were in fact satisfied.

(D) Exception for existing binding contracts. The term "applicable employee remuneration" shall not include any remuneration payable under a written binding contract which was in effect on February 17, 1993, and which was not modified thereafter in any material respect before such remuneration is paid.

(E) Remuneration. For purposes of this paragraph, the term "remuneration" includes any remuneration (including benefits) in any medium other than cash, but shall not include—

> **(i)** any payment referred to in so much of section 3121(a)(5) as precedes subparagraph (E) thereof, and

> **(ii)** any benefit provided to or on behalf of an employee if at the time such benefit is provided it is reasonable to believe that the employee will be able to exclude such benefit from gross income under this chapter.

For purposes of clause (i), section 3121(a)(5) shall be applied without regard to section 3121(v)(1).

(F) Coordination with disallowed golden parachute payments. The dollar limitation contained in paragraph (1) shall be reduced (but not below zero) by the amount (if any) which would have been included in the applicable employee remuneration of the covered employee for the taxable year but for being disallowed under section 280G.

(G) Coordination with excise tax on specified stock compensation. The dollar limitation contained in paragraph (1) with respect to any covered employee shall be reduced (but not below zero) by the amount of any payment (with respect to such employee) of the tax imposed by section 4985 directly or indirectly by the expatriated corporation (as defined in such section) or by any member of the expanded affiliated group (as defined in such section) which includes such corporation.

(5) Special rule for application to employers participating in the troubled assets relief program.

> **(A) In general.** In the case of an applicable employer, no deduction shall be allowed under this chapter—

> > **(i)** in the case of executive remuneration for any applicable taxable year which is attributable to services performed by a covered executive during such applicable taxable year, to the extent that the amount of such remuneration exceeds $500,000, or

> > **(ii)** in the case of deferred deduction executive remuneration for any taxable year for services performed during any applicable taxable year by a covered executive, to the extent that the amount of such remuneration exceeds $500,000 reduced (but not below zero) by the sum of—

> > > **(I)** the executive remuneration for such applicable taxable year, plus

> > > **(II)** the portion of the deferred deduction executive remuneration for such services which was taken into account under this clause in a preceding taxable year.

* * *

§ 213. Medical, dental, etc., expenses.

(a) Allowance of deduction. There shall be allowed as a deduction the expenses paid during the taxable year, not compensated for by insurance or otherwise, for medical care of the taxpayer, his spouse, or a dependent (as defined in section 152, determined without regard to subsections (b)(1), (b)(2), and (d)(1)(B) thereof), to the extent that such expenses exceed 10 percent of adjusted gross income.

Note that subsection (f) provides a special rule for 2013 through 2016 for taxpayers aged 65 or older.

(b) Limitation with respect to medicine and drugs. An amount paid during the taxable year for medicine or a drug shall be taken into account under subsection (a) only if such medicine or drug is a prescribed drug or is insulin.

* * *

(d) Definitions. For purposes of this section—

(1) The term "medical care" means amounts paid—

(A) for the diagnosis, cure, mitigation, treatment, or prevention of disease, or for the purpose of affecting any structure or function of the body,

(B) for transportation primarily for and essential to medical care referred to in subparagraph (A),

(C) for qualified long-term care services (as defined in section 7702B(c)), or

(D) for insurance (including amounts paid as premiums under part B of title XVIII of the Social Security Act, relating to supplementary medical insurance for the aged) covering medical care referred to in subparagraphs (A) and (B) or for any qualified long-term care insurance contract (as defined in section 7702B(b)).

In the case of a qualified long-term care insurance contract (as defined in section 7702B(b)), only eligible long-term care premiums (as defined in paragraph (10)) shall be taken into account under subparagraph (D).

(2) Amounts paid for certain lodging away from home treated as paid for medical care. Amounts paid for lodging (not lavish or extravagant under the circumstances) while away from home primarily for and essential to medical care referred to in paragraph (1)(A) shall be treated as amounts paid for medical care if—

(A) the medical care referred to in paragraph (1)(A) is provided by a physician in a licensed hospital (or in a medical care facility which is related to, or the equivalent of, a licensed hospital), and

(B) there is no significant element of personal pleasure, recreation, or vacation in the travel away from home.

The amount taken into account under the preceding sentence shall not exceed $50 for each night for each individual.

(3) Prescribed drug. The term "prescribed drug" means a drug or biological which requires a prescription of a physician for its use by an individual.

(4) Physician. The term "physician" has the meaning given to such term by section 1861(r) of the Social Security Act.

(5) Special rule in the case of child of divorced parents, etc. Any child to whom section 152(e) applies shall be treated as a dependent of both parents for purposes of this section.

* * *

(9) Cosmetic surgery.

   (A) In general. The term "medical care" does not include cosmetic surgery or other similar procedures, unless the surgery or procedure is necessary to ameliorate a deformity arising from, or directly related to, a congenital abnormality, a personal injury resulting from an accident or trauma, or disfiguring disease.

   (B) Cosmetic surgery defined. For purposes of this paragraph, the term "cosmetic surgery" means any procedure which is directed at improving the patient's appearance and does not meaningfully promote the proper function of the body or prevent or treat illness or disease.

(10) Eligible long-term care premiums.

   (A) In general. For purposes of this section, the term "eligible long-term care premiums" means the amount paid during a taxable year for any qualified long-term care insurance contract (as defined in section 7702B(b)) covering an individual, to the extent such amount does not exceed the limitation determined under the following table:

In the case of an individual with an attained age before the close of the taxable year of:	The limitation is:
40 or less	$ 200
More than 40 but not more than 50	375
More than 50 but not more than 60	750
More than 60 but not more than 70	2,000
More than 70	2,500

   (B) Indexing.

      (i) In general. In the case of any taxable year beginning in a calendar year after 1997, each dollar amount contained in subparagraph (A) shall be increased by the medical care cost adjustment of such amount for such calendar year. If any increase determined under the preceding sentence is not a multiple of $10, such increase shall be rounded to the nearest multiple of $10.

      (ii) Medical care cost adjustment. For purposes of clause (i), the medical care cost adjustment for any calendar year is the percentage (if any) by which—

         (I) the medical care component of the Consumer Price Index (as defined in section 1(f)(5)) for August of the preceding calendar year, exceeds

         (II) such component for August of 1996.

The Secretary shall, in consultation with the Secretary of Health and Human Services, prescribe an adjustment which the Secretary determines is more appropriate for purposes of this paragraph than the adjustment described in the preceding sentence, and the adjustment so prescribed shall apply in lieu of the adjustment described in the preceding sentence.

(11) Certain payments to relatives treated as not paid for medical care. An amount paid for a qualified long-term care service (as defined in section 7702B(c)) provided to an individual shall be treated as not paid for medical care if such service is provided—

(A) by the spouse of the individual or by a relative (directly or through a partnership, corporation, or other entity) unless the service is provided by a licensed professional with respect to such service, or

(B) by a corporation or partnership which is related (within the meaning of section 267(b) or 707(b)) to the individual.

For purposes of this paragraph, the term 'relative' means an individual bearing a relationship to the individual which is described in any of subparagraphs (A) through (G) of section 152(d)(2). This paragraph shall not apply for purposes of section 105(b) with respect to reimbursements through insurance.

(e) Exclusion of amounts allowed for care of certain dependents. Any expense allowed as a credit under section 21 shall not be treated as an expense paid for medical care.

(f) Special rule for 2013, 2014, 2015, and 2016. In the case of any taxable year beginning after December 31, 2012, and ending before January 1, 2017, subsection (a) shall be applied with respect to a taxpayer by substituting "7.5 percent" for "10 percent" if such taxpayer or such taxpayer's spouse has attained age 65 before the close of such taxable year.

§ 219. Retirement savings.

(a) Allowance of deduction—In the case of an individual, there shall be allowed as a deduction an amount equal to the qualified retirement contributions of the individual for the taxable year.

(b) Maximum amount of deduction—

(1) In general—The amount allowable as a deduction under subsection (a) to any individual for any taxable year shall not exceed the lesser of—

(A) the deductible amount, or

(B) an amount equal to the compensation includible in the individual's gross income for such taxable year.

(2) Special rule for employer contributions under simplified employee pensions—This section shall not apply with respect to an employer contribution to a simplified employee pension.

* * *

(4) Special rule for simple retirement accounts—This section shall not apply with respect to any amount contributed to a simple retirement account established under section 408(p).

(5) Deductible amount—For purposes of paragraph (1)(A)—

(A) In general—The deductible amount is $5,000.

(B) Catch-up contributions for individuals 50 or older—

(i) In general—In the case of an individual who has attained the age of 50 before the close of the taxable year, the deductible amount for such taxable year shall be increased by the applicable amount.

(ii) Applicable amount—For purposes of clause (i), the applicable amount is $1,000.

(C) Cost-of-living adjustment—

(i) In general—In the case of any taxable year beginning in a calendar year after 2008, the $5,000 amount under subparagraph (A) shall be increased by an amount equal to—

(I) such dollar amount, multiplied by

(II) the cost-of-living adjustment determined under section 1(f)(3) for the calendar year in which the taxable year begins, determined by substituting "calendar year 2007" for "calendar year 1992" in subparagraph (B) thereof.

(ii) Rounding rules—If any amount after adjustment under clause (i) is not a multiple of $500, such amount shall be rounded to the next lower multiple of $500.

(c) Kay Bailey Hutchison Spousal IRA—

(1) In general—In the case of an individual to whom this paragraph applies for the taxable year, the limitation of paragraph (1) of subsection (b) shall be equal to the lesser of—

(A) the dollar amount in effect under subsection (b)(1)(A) for the taxable year, or

(B) the sum of—

(i) the compensation includible in such individual's gross income for the taxable year, plus

(ii) the compensation includible in the gross income of such individual's spouse for the taxable year reduced by—

(I) the amount allowed as a deduction under subsection (a) to such spouse for such taxable year,

(II) the amount of any designated nondeductible contribution (as defined in section 408(o)) on behalf of such spouse for such taxable year, and

(III) the amount of any contribution on behalf of such spouse to a Roth IRA under section 408A for such taxable year.

(2) Individuals to whom paragraph (1) applies—Paragraph (1) shall apply to any individual if—

(A) such individual files a joint return for the taxable year, and

(B) the amount of compensation (if any) includible in such individual's gross income for the taxable year is less than the compensation includible in the gross income of such individual's spouse for the taxable year.

(d) Other limitations and restrictions—

(1) Beneficiary must be under age 70½—No deduction shall be allowed under this section with respect to any qualified retirement contribution for the benefit of an individual if such individual has attained age 70½ before the close of such individual's taxable year for which the contribution was made.

(2) Recontributed amounts—No deduction shall be allowed under this section with respect to a rollover contribution described in section 402(c), 403(a)(4), 403(b)(8), 408(d)(3), or 457(e)(16).

(3) Amounts contributed under endowment contract—In the case of an endowment contract described in section 408(b), no deduction shall be allowed under this section for that portion of the amounts paid under the contract for the taxable year which is properly allocable, under regulations prescribed by the Secretary, to the cost of life insurance.

(4) Denial of deduction for amount contributed to inherited annuities or accounts—No deduction shall be allowed under this section with respect to any amount paid to an inherited individual retirement account or individual retirement annuity (within the meaning of section 408(d)(3)(C)(ii)).

(e) Qualified retirement contribution—For purposes of this section, the term "qualified retirement contribution" means—

(1) any amount paid in cash for the taxable year by or on behalf of an individual to an individual retirement plan for such individual's benefit, and

(2) any amount contributed on behalf of any individual to a plan described in section 501(c)(18).

(f) Other definitions and special rules—

(1) Compensation—For purposes of this section, the term "compensation" includes earned income (as defined in section 401(c)(2)). The term "compensation" does not include any amount received as a pension or annuity and does not include any amount received as deferred compensation. The term "compensation" shall include any amount includible in the individual's gross income under section 71 with respect to a divorce or separation instrument described in subparagraph (A) of section 71(b)(2). For purposes of this paragraph, section 401(c)(2) shall be applied as if the term trade or business for purposes of section 1402 included service described in subsection (c)(6). The term compensation includes any differential wage payment (as defined in section 3401(h)(2))

(2) Married individuals—The maximum deduction under subsection (b) shall be computed separately for each individual, and this section shall be applied without regard to any community property laws.

(3) Time when contributions deemed made—For purposes of this section, a taxpayer shall be deemed to have made a contribution to an individual retirement plan on the last day of the preceding taxable year if the contribution is made on account of such taxable year and is made not later than the time prescribed by law for filing the return for such taxable year (not including extensions thereof).

(4) [Stricken]

(5) Employer payments—For purposes of this title, any amount paid by an employer to an individual retirement plan shall be treated as payment of compensation to the employee (other than a self-employed individual who is an employee within the meaning of section 401(c)(1)) includible in his gross income in the taxable year for which the amount was contributed, whether or not a deduction for such payment is allowable under this section to the employee.

(6) Excess contributions treated as contribution made during subsequent year for which there is an unused limitation—

(A) **In general**—If for the taxable year the maximum amount allowable as a deduction under this section for contributions to an individual retirement plan exceeds the amount contributed, then the taxpayer shall be treated as having made an additional contribution for the taxable year in an amount equal to the lesser of—

(i) the amount of such excess, or

(ii) the amount of the excess contributions for such taxable year (determined under section 4973(b)(2) without regard to subparagraph (C) thereof).

(B) **Amount contributed**—For purposes of this paragraph, the amount contributed—

(i) shall be determined without regard to this paragraph, and

(ii) shall not include any rollover contribution.

(C) **Special rule where excess deduction was allowed for closed year**—Proper reduction shall be made in the amount allowable as a deduction by reason of this paragraph for any amount allowed as a deduction under this section for a prior taxable year for which the period for assessing deficiency has expired if the amount so allowed exceeds the amount which should have been allowed for such prior taxable year.

(7) Special rule for compensation earned by members of the armed forces for service in a combat zone—For purposes of subsections (b)(1)(B) and (c), the amount of compensation includible in an individual's gross income shall be determined without regard to section 112.

(8) Election not to deduct contributions—For election not to deduct contributions to individual retirement plans, see section 408(o)(2)(B)(ii).

(g) Limitation on deduction for active participants in certain pension plans—

(1) In general—If (for any part of any plan year ending with or within a taxable year) an individual or the individual's spouse is an active participant, each of the dollar limitations contained in subsections (b)(1)(A) and (c)(1)(A) for such taxable year shall be reduced (but not below zero) by the amount determined under paragraph (2).

(2) Amount of reduction—

(A) **In general**—The amount determined under this paragraph with respect to any dollar limitation shall be the amount which bears the same ratio to such limitation as—

(i) the excess of—

(I) the taxpayer's adjusted gross income for such taxable year, over

(II) the applicable dollar amount, bears to

(ii) $10,000 ($20,000 in the case of a joint return).

(B) **No reduction below $200 until complete phase-out**—No dollar limitation shall be reduced below $200 under paragraph (1) unless (without regard to this subparagraph) such limitation is reduced to zero.

(C) **Rounding**—Any amount determined under this paragraph which is not a multiple of $10 shall be rounded to the next lowest $10.

(3) Adjusted gross income; applicable dollar amount—For purposes of this subsection—

(A) Adjusted gross income—Adjusted gross income of any taxpayer shall be determined—

(i) after application of sections 86 and 469, and

(ii) without regard to sections 135, 137, 221, 222, and 911 or the deduction allowable under this section.

(B) Applicable dollar amount—The term "applicable dollar amount" means the following:

(i) In the case of a taxpayer filing a joint return, $80,000.

(ii) In the case of any other taxpayer (other than a married individual filing a separate return), $50,000.

(iii) In the case of a married individual filing a separate return, zero.

(4) Special rule for married individuals filing separately and living apart—A husband and wife who—

(A) file separate returns for any taxable year, and

(B) live apart at all times during such taxable year, shall not be treated as married individuals for purposes of this subsection.

(5) Active participant—For purposes of this subsection, the term "active participant" means, with respect to any plan year, an individual—

(A) who is an active participant in—

(i) a plan described in section 401(a) which includes a trust exempt from tax under section 501(a),

(ii) an annuity plan described in section 403(a),

(iii) a plan established for its employees by the United States, by a State or political subdivision thereof, or by an agency or instrumentality of any of the foregoing,

(iv) an annuity contract described in section 403(b),

(v) a simplified employee pension (within the meaning of section 408(k)), or

(vi) any simple retirement account (within the meaning of section 408(p)), or

(B) who makes deductible contributions to a trust described in section 501(c)(18).

The determination of whether an individual is an active participant shall be made without regard to whether or not such individual's rights under a plan, trust, or contract are nonforfeitable. An eligible deferred compensation plan (within the meaning of section 457(b)) shall not be treated as a plan described in subparagraph (A)(iii).

* * *

(7) Special rule for spouses who are not active participants—If this subsection applies to an individual for any taxable year solely because their spouse is an active participant, then, in applying this subsection to the individual (but not their spouse)—

(A) the applicable dollar amount under paragraph (3)(B)(i) shall be $150,000; and

(B) the amount applicable under paragraph (2)(A)(ii) shall be $10,000.

(8) Inflation adjustment—In the case of any taxable year beginning in a calendar year after 2006, each of the dollar amounts in paragraphs (3)(B)(i), (3)(B)(ii), and (7)(A) shall each be increased by an amount equal to—

(A) such dollar amount, multiplied by

(B) the cost-of-living adjustment determined under section 1(f)(3) for the calendar year in which the taxable year begins, determined by substituting "calendar year 2005" for "calendar year 1992" in subparagraph (B) thereof.

Any increase determined under the preceding sentence shall be rounded to the nearest multiple of $1,000.

* * *

§ 223. Health savings accounts.

(a) Deduction allowed—In the case of an individual who is an eligible individual for any month during the taxable year, there shall be allowed as a deduction for the taxable year an amount equal to the aggregate amount paid in cash during such taxable year by or on behalf of such individual to a health savings account of such individual.

(b) Limitations—

(1) In general—The amount allowable as a deduction under subsection (a) to an individual for the taxable year shall not exceed the sum of the monthly limitations for months during such taxable year that the individual is an eligible individual.

(2) Monthly limitation—The monthly limitation for any month is 1/12 of—

(A) in the case of an eligible individual who has self-only coverage under a high deductible health plan as of the first day of such month, $2,250.

(B) in the case of an eligible individual who has family coverage under a high deductible health plan as of the first day of such month, $4,500.

(3) Additional contributions for individuals 55 or older—

(A) In general—In the case of an individual who has attained age 55 before the close of the taxable year, the applicable limitation under subparagraphs (A) and (B) of paragraph (2) shall be increased by the additional contribution amount.

(B) Additional contribution amount—For purposes of this section, the additional contribution amount is the amount determined in accordance with the following table:

For taxable years beginning in: *The additional contribution amount is:*

* * *

2009 and thereafter..............................*$1,000*

(4) Coordination with other contributions—The limitation which would (but for this paragraph) apply under this subsection to an individual for any taxable year shall be reduced (but not below zero) by the sum of—

(A) the aggregate amount paid for such taxable year to Archer MSAs of such individual,

(B) the aggregate amount contributed to health savings accounts of such individual which is excludable from the taxpayer's gross income for such taxable year under section 106(d) (and such amount shall not be allowed as a deduction under subsection (a)), and

(C) the aggregate amount contributed to health savings accounts of such individual for such taxable year under section 408(d)(9) (and such amount shall not be allowed as a deduction under subsection (a)).

Subparagraph (A) shall not apply with respect to any individual to whom paragraph (5) applies.

(5) Special rule for married individuals—In the case of individuals who are married to each other, if either spouse has family coverage—

(A) both spouses shall be treated as having only such family coverage (and if such spouses each have family coverage under different plans, as having the family coverage with the lowest annual deductible), and

(B) the limitation under paragraph (1) (after the application of subparagraph (A) and without regard to any additional contribution amount under paragraph (3))—

(i) shall be reduced by the aggregate amount paid to Archer MSAs of such spouses for the taxable year, and

(ii) after such reduction, shall be divided equally between them unless they agree on a different division.

(6) Denial of deduction to dependents—No deduction shall be allowed under this section to any individual with respect to whom a deduction under section 151 is allowable to another taxpayer for a taxable year beginning in the calendar year in which such individual's taxable year begins.

(7) Medicare eligible individuals—The limitation under this subsection for any month with respect to an individual shall be zero for the first month such individual is entitled to benefits under title XVIII of the Social Security Act and for each month thereafter.

(c) Definitions and special rules—For purposes of this section—

(1) Eligible individual—

(A) In general—The term "eligible individual" means, with respect to any month, any individual if—

(i) such individual is covered under a high deductible health plan as of the 1st day of such month, and

(ii) such individual is not, while covered under a high deductible health plan, covered under any health plan—

(I) which is not a high deductible health plan, and

(II) which provides coverage for any benefit which is covered under the high deductible health plan.

(B) Certain coverage disregarded—Subparagraph (A)(ii) shall be applied without regard to—

(i) coverage for any benefit provided by permitted insurance,

(ii) coverage (whether through insurance or otherwise) for accidents, disability, dental care, vision care, or long-term care, and

(iii) for taxable years beginning after December 31, 2006, coverage under a health flexible spending arrangement during any period immediately following the end of a plan year of such arrangement during which unused benefits or contributions remaining at the end of such plan year may be paid or reimbursed to plan participants for qualified benefit expenses incurred during such period if—

(I) the balance in such arrangement at the end of such plan year is zero, or

(II) the individual is making a qualified HSA distribution (as defined in section 106(e)) in an amount equal to the remaining balance in such arrangement as of the end of such plan year, in accordance with rules prescribed by the Secretary.

(C) Special rule for individuals eligible for certain veterans benefits—An individual shall not fail to be treated as an eligible individual for any period merely because the individual receives hospital care or medical services under any law administered by the Secretary of Veterans Affairs for a service-connected disability (within the meaning of section 101(16) of title 38, United States Code).

(2) High deductible health plan—

(A) In general—The term "high deductible health plan" means a health plan—

(i) which has an annual deductible which is not less than—

(I) $1,000 for self-only coverage, and

(II) twice the dollar amount in subclause (I) for family coverage, and

(ii) the sum of the annual deductible and the other annual out-of-pocket expenses required to be paid under the plan (other than for premiums) for covered benefits does not exceed—

(I) $5,000 for self-only coverage, and

(II) twice the dollar amount in subclause (I) for family coverage.

(B) Exclusion of certain plans—Such term does not include a health plan if substantially all of its coverage is coverage described in paragraph (1)(B).

(C) Safe harbor for absence of preventive care deductible—A plan shall not fail to be treated as a high deductible health plan by reason of failing to have a deductible for preventive care (within the meaning of section 1871 of the Social Security Act, except as otherwise provided by the Secretary).

(D) Special rules for network plans—In the case of a plan using a network of providers—

(i) Annual out-of-pocket limitation—Such plan shall not fail to be treated as a high deductible health plan by reason of having an out-of-pocket limitation for services provided outside of such network which exceeds the applicable limitation under subparagraph (A)(ii).

(ii) Annual deductible—Such plan's annual deductible for services provided outside of such network shall not be taken into account for purposes of subsection (b)(2).

(3) Permitted insurance—The term "permitted insurance" means—

(A) insurance if substantially all of the coverage provided under such insurance relates to—

(i) liabilities incurred under workers' compensation laws,

(ii) tort liabilities,

(iii) liabilities relating to ownership or use of property, or

(iv) such other similar liabilities as the Secretary may specify by regulations,

(B) insurance for a specified disease or illness, and

(C) insurance paying a fixed amount per day (or other period) of hospitalization.

(4) Family coverage—The term "family coverage" means any coverage other than self-only coverage.

(5) Archer MSA—The term "Archer MSA" has the meaning given such term in section 220(d).

(d) Health savings account—For purposes of this section—

(1) In general—The term "health savings account" means a trust created or organized in the United States as a health savings account exclusively for the purpose of paying the qualified medical expenses of the account beneficiary, but only if the written governing instrument creating the trust meets the following requirements:

(A) Except in the case of a rollover contribution described in subsection (f)(5) or section 220(f)(5), no contribution will be accepted—

(i) unless it is in cash, or

(ii) to the extent such contribution, when added to previous contributions to the trust for the calendar year, exceeds the sum of—

(I) the dollar amount in effect under subsection (b)(2)(B), and

(II) the dollar amount in effect under subsection (b)(3)(B).

(B) The trustee is a bank (as defined in section 408(n)), an insurance company (as defined in section 816), or another person who demonstrates to the satisfaction of the Secretary that the manner in which such person will administer the trust will be consistent with the requirements of this section.

(C) No part of the trust assets will be invested in life insurance contracts.

(D) The assets of the trust will not be commingled with other property except in a common trust fund or common investment fund.

(E) The interest of an individual in the balance in his account is nonforfeitable.

(2) Qualified medical expenses—

(A) In general—The term "qualified medical expenses" means, with respect to an account beneficiary, amounts paid by such beneficiary for medical care (as defined in section 213(d) for such individual, the spouse of such individual, and any dependent (as defined in section 152) of such individual, but only to the extent such amounts are not compensated for by insurance or otherwise. Such term shall include an amount paid for medicine or a drug only if such medicine or drug is a prescribed drug (determined without regard to whether such drug is available without a prescription) or is insulin.

(B) Health insurance may not be purchased from account—Subparagraph (A) shall not apply to any payment for insurance.

(C) Exceptions—Subparagraph (B) shall not apply to any expense for coverage under—

(i) a health plan during any period of continuation coverage required under any Federal law,

(ii) a qualified long-term care insurance contract (as defined in section 7702B(b)),

(iii) a health plan during a period in which the individual is receiving unemployment compensation under any Federal or State law, or

(iv) in the case of an account beneficiary who has attained the age specified in section 1811 of the Social Security Act, any health insurance other than a medicare supplemental policy (as defined in section 1882 of the Social Security Act).

(3) Account beneficiary—The term "account beneficiary" means the individual on whose behalf the health savings account was established.

(4) Certain rules to apply—Rules similar to the following rules shall apply for purposes of this section:

(A) Section 219(d)(2) (relating to no deduction for rollovers).

(B) Section 219(f)(3) (relating to time when contributions deemed made).

(C) Except as provided in section 106(d), section 219(f)(5) (relating to employer payments).

(D) Section 408(g) (relating to community property laws).

(E) Section 408(h) (relating to custodial accounts).

(e) Tax treatment of accounts—

(1) In general—A health savings account is exempt from taxation under this subtitle unless such account has ceased to be a health savings account. Notwithstanding the preceding sentence, any such account is subject to the taxes imposed by section 511 (relating to imposition of tax on unrelated business income of charitable, etc. organizations).

(2) Account terminations—Rules similar to the rules of paragraphs (2) and (4) of section 408(e) shall apply to health savings accounts, and any amount treated as distributed under such rules shall be treated as not used to pay qualified medical expenses.

(f) Tax treatment of distributions—

(1) Amounts used for qualified medical expenses—Any amount paid or distributed out of a health savings account which is used exclusively to pay qualified medical expenses of any account beneficiary shall not be includible in gross income.

(2) Inclusion of amounts not used for qualified medical expenses—Any amount paid or distributed out of a health savings account which is not used exclusively to pay the qualified medical expenses of the account beneficiary shall be included in the gross income of such beneficiary.

(3) Excess contributions returned before due date of return—

(A) In general—If any excess contribution is contributed for a taxable year to any health savings account of an individual, paragraph (2) shall not apply to distributions from the health savings accounts of such individual (to the extent such distributions do not exceed the aggregate excess contributions to all such accounts of such individual for such year) if—

(i) such distribution is received by the individual on or before the last day prescribed by law (including extensions of time) for filing such individual's return for such taxable year, and

(ii) such distribution is accompanied by the amount of net income attributable to such excess contribution.

Any net income described in clause (ii) shall be included in the gross income of the individual for the taxable year in which it is received.

(B) Excess contribution—For purposes of subparagraph (A), the term "excess contribution" means any contribution (other than a rollover contribution described in paragraph (5) or section 220(f)(5)) which is neither excludable from gross income under section 106(d) nor deductible under this section.

(4) Additional tax on distributions not used for qualified medical expenses—

(A) In general—The tax imposed by this chapter on the account beneficiary for any taxable year in which there is a payment or distribution from a health savings account of such beneficiary which is includible in gross income under paragraph (2) shall be increased by 20 percent of the amount which is so includible.

(B) Exception for disability or death—Subparagraph (A) shall not apply if the payment or distribution is made after the account beneficiary becomes disabled within the meaning of section 72(m)(7) or dies.

(C) Exception for distributions after medicare eligibility—Subparagraph (A) shall not apply to any payment or distribution after the date on which the account beneficiary attains the age specified in section 1811 of the Social Security Act.

(5) Rollover contribution—An amount is described in this paragraph as a rollover contribution if it meets the requirements of subparagraphs (A) and (B).

(A) In general—Paragraph (2) shall not apply to any amount paid or distributed from a health savings account to the account beneficiary to the extent the amount received is paid into a health savings account for the benefit of such beneficiary not later than the 60th day after the day on which the beneficiary receives the payment or distribution.

(B) Limitation—This paragraph shall not apply to any amount described in subparagraph (A) received by an individual from a health savings account if, at any time during the 1-year period ending on the day of such receipt, such individual received any other amount described in subparagraph (A) from a health savings account which was not includible in the individual's gross income because of the application of this paragraph.

(6) Coordination with medical expense deduction—For purposes of determining the amount of the deduction under section 213, any payment or distribution out of a health savings account for qualified medical expenses shall not be treated as an expense paid for medical care.

(7) **Transfer of account incident to divorce**—The transfer of an individual's interest in a health savings account to an individual's spouse or former spouse under a divorce or separation instrument described in subparagraph (A) of section 71(b)(2) shall not be considered a taxable transfer made by such individual notwithstanding any other provision of this subtitle, and such interest shall, after such transfer, be treated as a health savings account with respect to which such spouse is the account beneficiary.

(8) **Treatment after death of account beneficiary**—

(A) **Treatment if designated beneficiary is spouse**—If the account beneficiary's surviving spouse acquires such beneficiary's interest in a health savings account by reason of being the designated beneficiary of such account at the death of the account beneficiary, such health savings account shall be treated as if the spouse were the account beneficiary.

(B) **Other cases**—

(i) **In general**—If, by reason of the death of the account beneficiary, any person acquires the account beneficiary's interest in a health savings account in a case to which subparagraph (A) does not apply—

(I) such account shall cease to be a health savings account as of the date of death, and

(II) an amount equal to the fair market value of the assets in such account on such date shall be includible if such person is not the estate of such beneficiary, in such person's gross income for the taxable year which includes such date, or if such person is the estate of such beneficiary, in such beneficiary's gross income for the last taxable year of such beneficiary.

(ii) **Special rules**—

(I) **Reduction of inclusion for predeath expenses**—The amount includible in gross income under clause (i) by any person (other than the estate) shall be reduced by the amount of qualified medical expenses which were incurred by the decedent before the date of the decedent's death and paid by such person within 1 year after such date.

(II) **Deduction for estate taxes**—An appropriate deduction shall be allowed under section 691(c) to any person (other than the decedent or the decedent's spouse) with respect to amounts included in gross income under clause (i) by such person.

(g) **Cost-of-living adjustment**—

(1) **In general**—Each dollar amount in subsections (b)(2) and (c)(2)(A) shall be increased by an amount equal to—

(A) such dollar amount, multiplied by

(B) the cost-of-living adjustment determined under section 1(f)(3) for the calendar year in which such taxable year begins determined by substituting for "calendar year 1992" in subparagraph (B) thereof—

(i) except as provided in clause (ii), "calendar year 1997", and

(ii) in the case of each dollar amount in subsection (c)(2)(A), "calendar year 2003".

In the case of adjustments made for any taxable year beginning after 2007, section 1(f)(4) shall be applied for purposes of this paragraph by substituting "March 31" for "August 31", and the Secretary shall publish the adjusted amounts under subsections (b)(2) and (c)(2)(A) for taxable years beginning in any calendar year no later than June 1 of the preceding calendar year.

(2) Rounding—If any increase under paragraph (1) is not a multiple of $50, such increase shall be rounded to the nearest multiple of $50.

* * *

§ 280G. Golden parachute payments.

(a) General rule. No deduction shall be allowed under this chapter for any excess parachute payment.

(b) Excess parachute payment. For purposes of this section—

(1) In general. The term "excess parachute payment" means an amount equal to the excess of any parachute payment over the portion of the base amount allocated to such payment.

(2) Parachute payment defined.

(A) In general. The term "parachute payment" means any payment in the nature of compensation to (or for the benefit of) a disqualified individual if—

(i) such payment is contingent on a change—

(I) in the ownership or effective control of the corporation, or

(II) in the ownership of a substantial portion of the assets of the corporation, and

(ii) the aggregate present value of the payments in the nature of compensation to (or for the benefit of) such individual which are contingent on such change equals or exceeds an amount equal to 3 times the base amount.

For purposes of clause (ii), payments not treated as parachute payments under paragraph (4)(A), (5), or (6) shall not be taken into account.

(B) Agreements. The term "parachute payment" shall also include any payment in the nature of compensation to (or for the benefit of) a disqualified individual if such payment is made pursuant to an agreement which violates any generally enforced securities laws or regulations. In any proceeding involving the issue of whether any payment made to a disqualified individual is a parachute payment on account of a violation of any generally enforced securities laws or regulations, the burden of proof with respect to establishing the occurrence of a violation of such a law or regulation shall be upon the Secretary.

(C) Treatment of certain agreements entered into within 1 year before change of ownership. For purposes of subparagraph (A)(i), any payment pursuant to—

(i) an agreement entered into within 1 year before the change described in subparagraph (A)(i), or

(ii) an amendment made within such 1-year period of a previous agreement,

shall be presumed to be contingent on such change unless the contrary is established by clear and convincing evidence.

(3) Base amount.

(A) In general. The term "base amount" means the individual's annualized includible compensation for the base period.

(B) Allocation. The portion of the base amount allocated to any parachute payment shall be an amount which bears the same ratio to the base amount as—

(i) the present value of such payment, bears to

(ii) the aggregate present value of all such payments.

(4) Treatment of amounts which taxpayer establishes as reasonable compensation. In the case of any payment described in paragraph (2)(A)—

(A) the amount treated as a parachute payment shall not include the portion of such payment which the taxpayer establishes by clear and convincing evidence is reasonable compensation for personal services to be rendered on or after the date of the change described in paragraph (2)(A)(i), and

(B) the amount treated as an excess parachute payment shall be reduced by the portion of such payment which the taxpayer establishes by clear and convincing evidence is reasonable compensation for personal services actually rendered before the date of the change described in paragraph (2)(A)(i).

For purposes of subparagraph (B), reasonable compensation for services actually rendered before the date of the change described in paragraph (2)(A)(i) shall be first offset against the base amount.

(5) Exemption for small business corporations, etc.

(A) In general. Notwithstanding paragraph (2), the term "parachute payment" does not include—

(i) any payment to a disqualified individual with respect to a corporation which (immediately before the change described in paragraph (2)(A)(i)) was a small business corporation (as defined in section 1361(b) but without regard to paragraph (1)(C) thereof), and

(ii) any payment to a disqualified individual with respect to a corporation (other than a corporation described in clause (i)) if—

(I) immediately before the change described in paragraph (2)(A)(i), no stock in such corporation was readily tradeable on an established securities market or otherwise, and

(II) the shareholder approval requirements of subparagraph (B) are met with respect to such payment.

The Secretary may, by regulations, prescribe that the requirements of subclause (I) of clause (ii) are not met where a substantial portion of the assets of any entity consists (directly or indirectly) of stock in such corporation and interests in such other entity are readily tradeable on an established securities market, or otherwise. Stock described in section 1504(a)(4) shall not be taken into account under clause (ii)(I) if the payment does not adversely affect the shareholder's redemption and liquidation rights.

(B) Shareholder approval requirements. The shareholder approval requirements of this subparagraph are met with respect to any payment if—

(i) such payment was approved by a vote of the persons who owned, immediately before the change described in paragraph (2)(A)(i), more than 75 percent of the voting power of all outstanding stock of the corporation, and

(ii) there was adequate disclosure to shareholders of all material facts concerning all payments which (but for this paragraph) would be parachute payments with respect to a disqualified individual.

The regulations prescribed under subsection (e) shall include regulations providing for the application of this subparagraph in the case of shareholders which are not individuals (including the treatment of nonvoting interests in an entity which is a shareholder) and where an entity holds a de minimis amount of stock in the corporation.

(6) Exemption for payments under qualified plans. Notwithstanding paragraph (2), the term "parachute payment" shall not include any payment to or from—

(A) a plan described in section 401(a) which includes a trust exempt from tax under section 501(a),

(B) an annuity plan described in section 403(a),

(C) a simplified employee pension (as defined in section 408(k), or

(D) a simple retirement account described in section 408(p).

(c) Disqualified individuals. For purposes of this section, the term "disqualified individual" means any individual who is—

(1) an employee, independent contractor, or other person specified in regulations by the Secretary who performs personal services for any corporation, and

(2) is an officer, shareholder, or highly-compensated individual.

For purposes of this section, a personal service corporation (or similar entity) shall be treated as an individual. For purposes of paragraph (2), the term "highly-compensated individual" only includes an individual who is (or would be if the individual were an employee) a member of the group consisting of the highest paid 1 percent of the employees of the corporation or, if less, the highest paid 250 employees of the corporation.

(d) Other definitions and special rules. For purposes of this section—

(1) Annualized includible compensation for base period. The term "annualized includible compensation for the base period" means the average annual compensation which—

(A) was payable by the corporation with respect to which the change in ownership or control described in paragraph (2)(A) of subsection (b) occurs, and

(B) was includible in the gross income of the disqualified individual for taxable years in the base period.

(2) Base period. The term "base period" means the period consisting of the most recent 5 taxable years ending before the date on which the change in ownership or control described in paragraph (2)(A) of subsection (b) occurs (or such portion of such period during which the disqualified individual performed personal services for the corporation).

(3) Property transfers. Any transfer of property—

(A) shall be treated as a payment, and

(B) shall be taken into account as its fair market value.

(4) Present value. Present value shall be determined by using a discount rate equal to 120 percent of the applicable Federal rate (determined under section 1274(d)), compounded semiannually.

(5) Treatment of affiliated groups. Except as otherwise provided in regulations, all members of the same affiliated group (as defined in section 1504), determined without regard to section 1504(b), shall be treated as 1 corporation for purposes of this section. Any person who is an officer of any member of such group shall be treated as an officer of such 1 corporation.

(e) Special rule for application to employers participating in the Troubled Assets Relief Program.

(1) In general. In the case of the severance from employment of a covered executive of an applicable employer during the period during which the authorities under section 101(a) of the Emergency Economic Stabilization Act of 2008 are in effect (determined under section 120 of such Act), this section shall be applied to payments to such executive with the following modifications:

(A) Any reference to a disqualified individual (other than in subsection (c)) shall be treated as a reference to a covered executive.

(B) Any reference to a change described in subsection (b)(2)(A)(i) shall be treated as a reference to an applicable severance from employment of a covered executive, and any reference to a payment contingent on such a change shall be treated as a reference to any payment made during an applicable taxable year of the employer on account of such applicable severance from employment.

(C) Any reference to a corporation shall be treated as a reference to an applicable employer.

(D) The provisions of subsections (b)(2)(C), (b)(4), (b)(5), and (d)(5) shall not apply.

(2) Definitions and special rules. For purposes of this subsection:

(A) Definitions. Any term used in this subsection which is also used in section 162(m)(5) shall have the meaning given such term by such section.

(B) Applicable severance from employment. The term "applicable severance from employment" means any severance from employment of a covered executive—

(i) by reason of an involuntary termination of the executive by the employer, or

(ii) in connection with any bankruptcy, liquidation, or receivership of the employer.

(C) Coordination and other rules.

(i) In general. If a payment which is treated as a parachute payment by reason of this subsection is also a parachute payment determined without regard to this subsection, this subsection shall not apply to such payment.

(ii) Regulatory authority. The Secretary may prescribe such guidance, rules, or regulations as are necessary—

(I) to carry out the purposes of this subsection and the Emergency Economic Stabilization Act of 2008, including the extent to which this subsection applies in the case of any acquisition, merger, or reorganization of an applicable employer,

(II) to apply this section and section 4999 in cases where one or more payments with respect to any individual are treated as parachute payments by reason of this subsection, and other payments with respect to such individual are treated as parachute payments under this section without regard to this subsection, and

(III) to prevent the avoidance of the application of this section through the mischaracterization of a severance from employment as other than an applicable severance from employment.

(f) Regulations. The Secretary shall prescribe such regulations as may be necessary or appropriate to carry out the purposes of this section (including regulations for the application of this section in the case of related corporations and in the case of personal service corporations).

§ 401. Qualified pension, profit-sharing, and stock bonus plans.

(a) Requirements for qualification—A trust created or organized in the United States and forming part of a stock bonus, pension, or profit-sharing plan of an employer for the exclusive benefit of his employees or their beneficiaries shall constitute a qualified trust under this section—

(1) if contributions are made to the trust by such employer, or employees, or both, or by another employer who is entitled to deduct his contributions under section 404(a)(3)(B) (relating to deduction for contributions to profit-sharing and stock bonus plans), or by a charitable remainder trust pursuant to a qualified gratuitous transfer (as defined in section 664(g)(1)), for the purpose of distributing to such employees or their beneficiaries the corpus and income of the fund accumulated by the trust in accordance with such plan;

(2) if under the trust instrument it is impossible, at any time prior to the satisfaction of all liabilities with respect to employees and their beneficiaries under the trust, for any part of the corpus or income to be (within the taxable year or thereafter) used for, or diverted to, purposes other than for the exclusive benefit of his employees or their beneficiaries (but this paragraph shall not be construed, in the case of a multiemployer plan, to prohibit the return of a contribution within 6 months after the plan administrator determines that the contribution was made by a mistake of fact or law (other than a mistake relating to whether the plan is described in section 401(a) or the trust which is part of such plan is exempt from taxation under section 501(a), or the return of any withdrawal liability payment determined to be an overpayment within 6 months of such determination));

(3) if the plan of which such trust is a part satisfies the requirements of section 410 (relating to minimum participation standards); and

(4) if the contributions or benefits provided under the plan do not discriminate in favor of highly compensated employees (within the meaning of section 414(q)). For purposes of this paragraph, there shall be excluded from consideration employees described in section 410(b)(3)(A) and (C).

(5) Special rules relating to nondiscrimination requirements—

(A) Salaried or clerical employees—A classification shall not be considered discriminatory within the meaning of paragraph (4) or section 410(b)(2)(A)(i) merely because it is limited to salaried or clerical employees.

(B) Contributions and benefits may bear uniform relationship to compensation—A plan shall not be considered discriminatory within the meaning of paragraph (4) merely because the contributions or benefits of, or on behalf of, the employees under the plan bear a uniform relationship to the compensation (within the meaning of section 414(s)) of such employees.

(C) Certain disparity permitted—A plan shall not be considered discriminatory within the meaning of paragraph (4) merely because the contributions or benefits of, or on behalf of, the employees under the plan favor highly compensated employees (as defined in section 414(q)) in the manner permitted under subsection (l).

(D) Integrated defined benefit plan—

(i) In general—A defined benefit plan shall not be considered discriminatory within the meaning of paragraph (4) merely because the plan provides that the employer-derived accrued retirement benefit for any participant under the plan may not exceed the excess (if any) of—

(I) the participant's final pay with the employer, over

(II) the employer-derived retirement benefit created under Federal law attributable to service by the participant with the employer.

For purposes of this clause, the employer-derived retirement benefit created under Federal law shall be treated as accruing ratably over 35 years.

(ii) Final pay—For purposes of this subparagraph, the participant's final pay is the compensation (as defined in section 414(q)(4)) paid to the participant by the employer for any year—

(I) which ends during the 5-year period ending with the year in which the participant separated from service for the employer, and

(II) for which the participant's total compensation from the employer was highest.

(E) 2 or more plans treated as single plan—For purposes of determining whether 2 or more plans of an employer satisfy the requirements of paragraph (4) when considered as a single plan—

(i) Contributions—If the amount of contributions on behalf of the employees allowed as a deduction under section 404 for the taxable year with respect to such plans, taken together, bears a uniform relationship to the compensation (within the meaning of section 414(s)) of such employees, the plans shall not be considered discriminatory merely because the rights of employees to, or derived from, the employer contributions under the separate plans do not become nonforfeitable at the same rate.

(ii) Benefits—If the employees' rights to benefits under the separate plans do not become nonforfeitable at the same rate, but the levels of benefits provided by the separate plans satisfy the requirements of regulations prescribed by the Secretary to take account of the differences in such rates, the plans shall not be considered discriminatory merely because of the difference in such rates.

(F) Social security retirement age—For purposes of testing for discrimination under paragraph (4)—

(i) the social security retirement age (as defined in section 415(b)(8)) shall be treated as a uniform retirement age, and

(ii) subsidized early retirement benefits and joint and survivor annuities shall not be treated as being unavailable to employees on the same terms merely because such benefits or annuities are based in whole or in part on an employee's social security retirement age (as so defined).

(G) Governmental plans—Paragraphs (3) and (4) shall not apply to a governmental plan (within the meaning of section 414(d)).

(6) A plan shall be considered as meeting the requirements of paragraph (3) during the whole of any taxable year of the plan if on one day in each quarter it satisfied such requirements.

(7) A trust shall not constitute a qualified trust under this section unless the plan of which such trust is a part satisfies the requirements of section 411 (relating to minimum vesting standards).

(8) A trust forming part of a defined benefit plan shall not constitute a qualified trust under this section unless the plan provides that forfeitures must not be applied to increase the benefits any employee would otherwise receive under the plan.

(9) Required distributions—

(A) In general—A trust shall not constitute a qualified trust under this subsection unless the plan provides that the entire interest of each employee—

(i) will be distributed to such employee not later than the required beginning date, or

(ii) will be distributed, beginning not later than the required beginning date, in accordance with regulations, over the life of such employee or over the lives of such employee and a designated beneficiary (or over a period not extending beyond the life expectancy of such employee or the life expectancy of such employee and a designated beneficiary).

(B) Required distribution where employee dies before entire interest is distributed—

(i) Where distributions have begun under subparagraph (A)(ii)—A trust shall not constitute a qualified trust under this section unless the plan provides that if—

(I) the distribution of the employee's interest has begun in accordance with subparagraph (A)(ii), and

(II) the employee dies before his entire interest has been distributed to him, the remaining portion of such interest will be distributed at least as rapidly as under the method of distributions being used under subparagraph (A)(ii) as of the date of his death.

(ii) 5-year rule for other cases—A trust shall not constitute a qualified trust under this section unless the plan provides that, if an employee dies before the distribution of the employee's interest has begun in accordance with subparagraph (A)(ii), the entire interest of the employee will be distributed within 5 years after the death of such employee.

(iii) Exception to 5-year rule for certain amounts payable over life of beneficiary—If—

(I) any portion of the employee's interest is payable to (or for the benefit of) a designated beneficiary,

(II) such portion will be distributed (in accordance with regulations) over the life of such designated beneficiary (or over a period not extending beyond the life expectancy of such beneficiary), and

(III) such distributions begin not later than 1 year after the date of the employee's death or such later date as the Secretary may by regulations prescribe,

for purposes of clause (ii), the portion referred to in subclause (I) shall be treated as distributed on the date on which such distributions begin.

(iv) Special rule for surviving spouse of employee—If the designated beneficiary referred to in clause (iii)(I) is the surviving spouse of the employee—

(I) the date on which the distributions are required to begin under clause (iii)(III) shall not be earlier than the date on which the employee would have attained age 70½, and

(II) if the surviving spouse dies before the distributions to such spouse begin, this subparagraph shall be applied as if the surviving spouse were the employee.

(C) Required beginning date—For purposes of this paragraph—

(i) In general—The term "required beginning date" means April 1 of the calendar year following the later of—

(I) the calendar year in which the employee attains age 70½, or

(II) the calendar year in which the employee retires.

(ii) Exception—Subclause (II) of clause (i) shall not apply—

(I) except as provided in section 409(d), in the case of an employee who is a 5-percent owner (as defined in section 416) with respect to the plan year ending in the calendar year in which the employee attains age 70½, or

(II) for purposes of section 408(a)(6) or (b)(3).

(iii) Actuarial adjustment—In the case of an employee to whom clause (i)(II) applies who retires in a calendar year after the calendar year in which the employee attains age 70½, the employee's accrued benefit shall be actuarially increased to take into account the period after age 70½ in which the employee was not receiving any benefits under the plan.

(iv) Exception for governmental and church plans—Clauses (ii) and (iii) shall not apply in the case of a governmental plan or church plan. For purposes of this clause, the term "church plan" means a plan maintained by a church for church employees, and the term "church" means any church (as defined in section 3121(w)(3)(A)) or qualified church-controlled organization (as defined in section 3121(w)(3)(B)).

(D) Life expectancy—For purposes of this paragraph, the life expectancy of an employee and the employee's spouse (other than in the case of a life annuity) may be redetermined but not more frequently than annually.

(E) Designated beneficiary—For purposes of this paragraph, the term "designated beneficiary" means any individual designated as a beneficiary by the employee.

(F) Treatment of payments to children—Under regulations prescribed by the Secretary, for purposes of this paragraph, any amount paid to a child shall be treated as if it had been paid to the surviving spouse if such amount will become payable to the surviving spouse upon such child reaching majority (or other designated event permitted under regulations).

(G) Treatment of incidental death benefit distributions—For purposes of this title, any distribution required under the incidental death benefit requirements of this subsection shall be treated as a distribution required under this paragraph.

(10) Other requirements—

(A) Plans benefiting owner-employees—In the case of any plan which provides contributions or benefits for employees some or all of whom are owner-employees (as defined in subsection (c)(3)), a trust forming part of such plan shall constitute a qualified trust under this section only if the requirements of subsection (d) are also met.

(B) Top-heavy plans—

(i) In general—In the case of any top-heavy plan, a trust forming part of such plan shall constitute a qualified trust under this section only if the requirements of section 416 are met.

(ii) Plans which may become top-heavy—Except to the extent provided in regulations, a trust forming part of a plan (whether or not a top-heavy plan) shall constitute a qualified trust under this section only if such plan contains provisions—

(I) which will take effect if such plan becomes a top-heavy plan, and

(II) which meet the requirements of section 416.

(iii) Exemption for governmental plans—This subparagraph shall not apply to any governmental plan.

(11) Requirement of joint and survivor annuity and preretirement survivor annuity—

(A) In general—In the case of any plan to which this paragraph applies, except as provided in section 417, a trust forming part of such plan shall not constitute a qualified trust under this section unless—

(i) in the case of a vested participant who does not die before the annuity starting date, the accrued benefit payable to such participant is provided in the form of a qualified joint and survivor annuity, and

(ii) in the case of a vested participant who dies before the annuity starting date and who has a surviving spouse, a qualified preretirement survivor annuity is provided to the surviving spouse of such participant.

(B) Plans to which paragraph applies—This paragraph shall apply to—

(i) any defined benefit plan,

(ii) any defined contribution plan which is subject to the funding standards of section 412, and

(iii) any participant under any other defined contribution plan unless—

(I) such plan provides that the participant's nonforfeitable accrued benefit (reduced by any security interest held by the plan by reason of a loan outstanding to such participant) is payable in full, on the death of the participant, to the participant's surviving spouse (or, if there is no surviving spouse or the surviving spouse consents in the manner required under section 417(a)(2), to a designated beneficiary),

(II) such participant does not elect a payment of benefits in the form of a life annuity, and

(III) with respect to such participant, such plan is not a direct or indirect transferee (in a transfer after December 31, 1984) of a plan which is described in clause (i) or (ii) or to which this clause applied with respect to the participant.

Clause (iii)(III) shall apply only with respect to the transferred assets (and income therefrom) if the plan separately accounts for such assets and any income therefrom.

(C) Exception for certain ESOP benefits—

(i) In general—In the case of—

(I) a tax credit employee stock ownership plan (as defined in section 409(a)), or

(II) an employee stock ownership plan (as defined in section 4975(e)(7)),

subparagraph (A) shall not apply to that portion of the employee's accrued benefit to which the requirements of section 409(h) apply.

(ii) Nonforfeitable benefit must be paid in full, etc—In the case of any participant, clause (i) shall apply only if the requirements of subclauses (I), (II), and (III) of subparagraph (B)(iii) are met with respect to such participant.

(D) Special rule where participant and spouse married less than 1 year—A plan shall not be treated as failing to meet the requirements of subparagraphs (B)(iii) or (C) merely because the plan provides that benefits will not be payable to the surviving spouse of the participant unless the participant and such spouse had been married throughout the 1-year period ending on the earlier of the participant's annuity starting date or the date of the participant's death.

(E) Exception for plans described in section 404(c)—This paragraph shall not apply to a plan which the Secretary has determined is a plan described in section 404(c) (or a continuation thereof) in which participation is substantially limited to individuals who, before January 1, 1976, ceased employment covered by the plan.

(F) Cross reference—For—

(i) provisions under which participants may elect to waive the requirements of this paragraph, and

(ii) other definitions and special rules for purposes of this paragraph,

see section 417.

(12) A trust shall not constitute a qualified trust under this section unless the plan of which such trust is a part provides that in the case of any merger or consolidation with, or transfer of assets or liabilities to, any other plan after September 2, 1974, each participant in the plan would (if the plan then terminated) receive a benefit immediately after the merger, consolidation, or transfer which is equal to or greater than the benefit he would have been entitled to receive immediately before the merger, consolidation, or transfer (if the plan had then terminated). The preceding sentence does not apply to any multiemployer plan with respect to any transaction to the extent that participants either before or after the transaction are covered under a multiemployer plan to which title IV of the Employee Retirement Income Security Act of 1974 applies.

(13) Assignment and alienation—

(A) In general—A trust shall not constitute a qualified trust under this section unless the plan of which such trust is a part provides that benefits provided under the plan may not be assigned or alienated. For purposes of the preceding sentence, there shall not be taken into account any voluntary and revocable assignment of not to exceed 10 percent of any benefit payment made by any participant who is receiving benefits under the plan unless the assignment or alienation is made for purposes of defraying plan administration costs. For purposes of this paragraph a loan made to a participant or beneficiary shall not be treated as an assignment or alienation if such loan is secured by the participant's accrued nonforfeitable benefit and is exempt from the tax imposed by section 4975 (relating to tax on prohibited transactions) by reason of section 4975(d)(1). This paragraph shall take effect on January 1, 1976 and shall not apply to assignments which were irrevocable on September 2, 1974.

(B) Special rules for domestic relations orders—Subparagraph (A) shall apply to the creation, assignment, or recognition of a right to any benefit payable with respect to a participant pursuant to a domestic relations order, except that subparagraph (A) shall not apply if the order is determined to be a qualified domestic relations order.

(C) Special rule for certain judgments and settlements—Subparagraph (A) shall not apply to any offset of a participant's benefits provided under a plan against an amount that the participant is ordered or required to pay to the plan if—

(i) the order or requirement to pay arises—

(I) under a judgment of conviction for a crime involving such plan,

(II) under a civil judgment (including a consent order or decree) entered by a court in an action brought in connection with a violation (or alleged violation) of part 4 of subtitle B of title I of the Employee Retirement Income Security Act of 1974, or

(III) pursuant to a settlement agreement between the Secretary of Labor and the participant, or a settlement agreement between the Pension Benefit Guaranty Corporation and the participant, in connection with a violation (or alleged violation) of part 4 of such subtitle by a fiduciary or any other person,

(ii) the judgment, order, decree, or settlement agreement expressly provides for the offset of all or part of the amount ordered or required to be paid to the plan against the participant's benefits provided under the plan, and

(iii) in a case in which the survivor annuity requirements of section 401(a)(11) apply with respect to distributions from the plan to the participant, if the participant has a spouse at the time at which the offset is to be made—

(I) either such spouse has consented in writing to such offset and such consent is witnessed by a notary public or representative of the plan (or it is established to the satisfaction of a plan representative that such consent may not be obtained by reason of circumstances described in section 417(a)(2)(B)), or an election to waive the right of the spouse to either a qualified joint and survivor annuity or a qualified preretirement survivor annuity is in effect in accordance with the requirements of section 417(a),

(II) such spouse is ordered or required in such judgment, order, decree, or settlement to pay an amount to the plan in connection with a violation of part 4 of such subtitle, or

(III) in such judgment, order, decree, or settlement, such spouse retains the right to receive the survivor annuity under a qualified joint and survivor annuity provided pursuant to section 401(a)(11)(A)(i) and under a qualified preretirement survivor annuity provided pursuant to section 401(a)(11)(A)(ii), determined in accordance with subparagraph (D).

A plan shall not be treated as failing to meet the requirements of this subsection, subsection (k), section 403(b), or section 409(d) solely by reason of an offset described in this subparagraph.

(D) Survivor annuity—

(i) **In general**—The survivor annuity described in subparagraph (C)(iii)(III) shall be determined as if—

(I) the participant terminated employment on the date of the offset,

(II) there was no offset,

(III) the plan permitted commencement of benefits only on or after normal retirement age,

(IV) the plan provided only the minimum-required qualified joint and survivor annuity, and

(V) the amount of the qualified preretirement survivor annuity under the plan is equal to the amount of the survivor annuity payable under the minimum-required qualified joint and survivor annuity.

    (ii) Definition—For purposes of this subparagraph, the term "minimum-required qualified joint and survivor annuity" means the qualified joint and survivor annuity which is the actuarial equivalent of the participant's accrued benefit (within the meaning of section 411(a)(7)) and under which the survivor annuity is 50 percent of the amount of the annuity which is payable during the joint lives of the participant and the spouse.

    (14) A trust shall not constitute a qualified trust under this section unless the plan of which such trust is a part provides that, unless the participant otherwise elects, the payment of benefits under the plan to the participant will begin not later than the 60th day after the latest of the close of the plan year in which—

    (A) the date on which the participant attains the earlier of age 65 or the normal retirement age specified under the plan,

    (B) occurs the 10th anniversary of the year in which the participant commenced participation in the plan, or

    (C) the participant terminates his service with the employer.

In the case of a plan which provides for the payment of an early retirement benefit, a trust forming a part of such plan shall not constitute a qualified trust under this section unless a participant who satisfied the service requirements for such early retirement benefit, but separated from the service (with any nonforfeitable right to an accrued benefit) before satisfying the age requirement for such early retirement benefit, is entitled upon satisfaction of such age requirement to receive a benefit not less than the benefit to which he would be entitled at the normal retirement age, actuarially reduced under regulations prescribed by the Secretary.

    (15) A trust shall not constitute a qualified trust under this section unless under the plan of which such trust is a part—

    (A) in the case of a participant or beneficiary who is receiving benefits under such plan, or

    (B) in the case of a participant who is separated from the service and who has nonforfeitable rights to benefits,

such benefits are not decreased by reason of any increase in the benefit levels payable under title II of the Social Security Act or any increase in the wage base under such title II, if such increase takes place after September 2, 1974, or (if later) the earlier of the date of first receipt of such benefits or the date of such separation, as the case may be.

    (16) A trust shall not constitute a qualified trust under this section if the plan of which such trust is a part provides for benefits or contributions which exceed the limitations of section 415.

    (17) Compensation limit—

    (A) In general—A trust shall not constitute a qualified trust under this section unless, under the plan of which such trust is a part, the annual compensation of each employee taken into account under the plan for any year does not exceed $200,000.

    (B) Cost-of-living adjustment—The Secretary shall adjust annually the $200,000 amount in subparagraph (A) for increases in the cost-of-living at the same time and in the same manner as adjustments under section 415(d); except that the base period shall be the calendar quarter beginning July 1, 2001, and any increase which is not a multiple of $5,000 shall be rounded to the next lowest multiple of $5,000.

(18) **[Repealed]**

(19) A trust shall not constitute a qualified trust under this section if under the plan of which such trust is a part any part of a participant's accrued benefit derived from employer contributions (whether or not otherwise nonforfeitable), is forfeitable solely because of withdrawal by such participant of any amount attributable to the benefit derived from contributions made by such participant. The preceding sentence shall not apply to the accrued benefit of any participant unless, at the time of such withdrawal, such participant has a nonforfeitable right to at least 50 percent of such accrued benefit (as determined under section 411). The first sentence of this paragraph shall not apply to the extent that an accrued benefit is permitted to be forfeited in accordance with section 411(a)(3)(D)(iii) (relating to proportional forfeitures of benefits accrued before September 2, 1974, in the event of withdrawal of certain mandatory contributions).

(20) A trust forming part of a pension plan shall not be treated as failing to constitute a qualified trust under this section merely because the pension plan of which such trust is a part makes 1 or more distributions within 1 taxable year to a distributee on account of a termination of the plan of which the trust is a part, or in the case of a profit-sharing or stock bonus plan, a complete discontinuance of contributions under such plan. This paragraph shall not apply to a defined benefit plan unless the employer maintaining such plan files a notice with the Pension Benefit Guaranty Corporation (at the time and in the manner prescribed by the Pension Benefit Guaranty Corporation) notifying the Corporation of such payment or distribution and the Corporation has approved such payment or distribution or, within 90 days after the date on which such notice was filed, has failed to disapprove such payment or distribution. For purposes of this paragraph, rules similar to the rules of section 402(a)(6)(B) (as in effect before its repeal by section 521 of the Unemployment Compensation Amendments of 1992) shall apply.

(21) **[Repealed]**

(22) If a defined contribution plan (other than a profit-sharing plan)—

(A) is established by an employer whose stock is not readily tradable on an established market, and

(B) after acquiring securities of the employer, more than 10 percent of the total assets of the plan are securities of the employer,

any trust forming part of such plan shall not constitute a qualified trust under this section unless the plan meets the requirements of subsection (e) of section 409. The requirements of subsection (e) of section 409 shall not apply to any employees of an employer who are participants in any defined contribution plan established and maintained by such employer if the stock of such employer is not readily tradable on an established market and the trade or business of such employer consists of publishing on a regular basis a newspaper for general circulation. For purposes of the preceding sentence, subsections (b), (c), (m), and (o) of section 414 shall not apply except for determining whether stock of the employer is not readily tradable on an established market.

(23) A stock bonus plan shall not be treated as meeting the requirements of this section unless such plan meets the requirements of subsections (h) and (o) of section 409, except that in applying section 409(h) for purposes of this paragraph, the term "employer securities" shall include any securities of the employer held by the plan.

(24) Any group trust which otherwise meets the requirements of this section shall not be treated as not meeting such requirements on account of the participation or inclusion in such trust of the moneys of any plan or governmental unit described in section 818(a)(6).

(25) Requirement that actuarial assumptions be specified—A defined benefit plan shall not be treated as providing definitely determinable benefits unless, whenever the amount of any benefit is to be determined on the basis of actuarial assumptions, such assumptions are specified in the plan in a way which precludes employer discretion.

(26) Additional participation requirements—

(A) In general—In the case of a trust which is a part of a defined benefit plan, such trust shall not constitute a qualified trust under this subsection unless on each day of the plan year such trust benefits at least the lesser of—

(i) 50 employees of the employer, or

(ii) the greater of—   → HCE & NHCE

(I) 40 percent of all employees of the employer, or

(II) 2 employees (or if there is only 1 employee, such employee).

(B) Treatment of excludable employees—

(i) In general—A plan may exclude from consideration under this paragraph employees described in paragraphs (3) and (4)(A) of section 410(b).

(ii) Separate application for certain excludable employees—If employees described in section 410(b)(4)(B) are covered under a plan which meets the requirements of subparagraph (A) separately with respect to such employees, such employees may be excluded from consideration in determining whether any plan of the employer meets such requirements if—

(I) the benefits for such employees are provided under the same plan as benefits for other employees,

(II) the benefits provided to such employees are not greater than comparable benefits provided to other employees under the plan, and

(III) no highly compensated employee (within the meaning of section 414(q)) is included in the group of such employees for more than 1 year.

(C) Special rule for collective bargaining units—Except to the extent provided in regulations, a plan covering only employees described in section 410(b)(3)(A) may exclude from consideration any employees who are not included in the unit or units in which the covered employees are included.

(D) Paragraph not to apply to multiemployer plans—Except to the extent provided in regulations, this paragraph shall not apply to employees in a multiemployer plan (within the meaning of section 414(f)) who are covered by collective bargaining agreements.

(E) Special rule for certain dispositions or acquisitions—Rules similar to the rules of section 410(b)(6)(C) shall apply for purposes of this paragraph.

(F) Separate lines of business—At the election of the employer and with the consent of the Secretary, this paragraph may be applied separately with respect to each separate line of business of the employer. For purposes of this paragraph, the term "separate line of business" has the meaning given such term by section 414(r) (without regard to paragraph (2)(A) or (7) thereof).

(G) Exception for governmental plans—This paragraph shall not apply to a governmental plan (within the meaning of section 414(d)).

(H) Regulations—The Secretary may by regulation provide that any separate benefit structure, any separate trust, or any other separate arrangement is to be treated as a separate plan for purposes of applying this paragraph.

(27) Determinations as to profit-sharing plans—

(A) Contributions need not be based on profits—The determination of whether the plan under which any contributions are made is a profit-sharing plan shall be made without regard to current or accumulated profits of the employer and without regard to whether the employer is a tax-exempt organization.

(B) Plan must designate type—In the case of a plan which is intended to be a money purchase pension plan or a profit-sharing plan, a trust forming part of such plan shall not constitute a qualified trust under this subsection unless the plan designates such intent at such time and in such manner as the Secretary may prescribe.

(28) Additional requirements relating to employee stock ownership plans—

(A) In general—In the case of a trust which is part of an employee stock ownership plan (within the meaning of section 4975(e)(7)) or a plan which meets the requirements of section 409(a), such trust shall not constitute a qualified trust under this section unless such plan meets the requirements of subparagraphs (B) and (C).

(B) Diversification of investments—

(i) In general—A plan meets the requirements of this subparagraph if each qualified participant in the plan may elect within 90 days after the close of each plan year in the qualified election period to direct the plan as to the investment of at least 25 percent of the participant's account in the plan (to the extent such portion exceeds the amount to which a prior election under this subparagraph applies). In the case of the election year in which the participant can make his last election, the preceding sentence shall be applied by substituting "50 percent" for "25 percent".

(ii) Method of meeting requirements—A plan shall be treated as meeting the requirements of clause (i) if—

(I) the portion of the participant's account covered by the election under clause (i) is distributed within 90 days after the period during which the election may be made, or

(II) the plan offers at least 3 investment options (not inconsistent with regulations prescribed by the Secretary) to each participant making an election under clause (i) and within 90 days after the period during which the election may be made, the plan invests the portion of the participant's account covered by the election in accordance with such election.

(iii) Qualified participant—For purposes of this subparagraph, the term "qualified participant" means any employee who has completed at least 10 years of participation under the plan and has attained age 55.

(iv) Qualified election period—For purposes of this subparagraph, the term "qualified election period" means the 6-plan-year period beginning with the later of—

(I) the 1st plan year in which the individual first became a qualified participant, or

(II) the 1st plan year beginning after December 31, 1986.

(v) Exception—This subparagraph shall not apply to an applicable defined contribution plan (as defined in paragraph (35)(E)).

For purposes of the preceding sentence, an employer may elect to treat an individual first becoming a qualified participant in the 1st plan year beginning in 1987 as having become a participant in the 1st plan year beginning in 1988.

(C) Use of independent appraiser—A plan meets the requirements of this subparagraph if all valuations of employer securities which are not readily tradable on an established securities market with respect to activities carried on by the plan are by an independent appraiser. For purposes of the preceding sentence, the term "independent appraiser" means any appraiser meeting requirements similar to the requirements of the regulations prescribed under section 170(a)(1).

(29) Benefit limitations—In the case of a defined benefit plan (other than a multiemployer plan or a CSEC plan) to which the requirements of section 412 apply, the trust of which the plan is a part shall not constitute a qualified trust under this subsection unless the plan meets the requirements of section 436.

(30) Limitations on elective deferrals—In the case of a trust which is part of a plan under which elective deferrals (within the meaning of section 402(g)(3)) may be made with respect to any individual during a calendar year, such trust shall not constitute a qualified trust under this subsection unless the plan provides that the amount of such deferrals under such plan and all other plans, contracts, or arrangements of an employer maintaining such plan may not exceed the amount of the limitation in effect under section 402(g)(1)(A) for taxable years beginning in such calendar year.

(31) Direct transfer of eligible rollover distributions—

(A) In general—A trust shall not constitute a qualified trust under this section unless the plan of which such trust is a part provides that if the distributee of any eligible rollover distribution—

(i) elects to have such distribution paid directly to an eligible retirement plan, and

(ii) specifies the eligible retirement plan to which such distribution is to be paid (in such form and at such time as the plan administrator may prescribe),

such distribution shall be made in the form of a direct trustee-to-trustee transfer to the eligible retirement plan so specified.

(B) Certain mandatory distributions—

(i) In general—In case of a trust which is part of an eligible plan, such trust shall not constitute a qualified trust under this section unless the plan of which such trust is a part provides that if—

(I) a distribution described in clause (ii) in excess of $1,000 is made, and

(II) the distributee does not make an election under subparagraph (A) and does not elect to receive the distribution directly,

the plan administrator shall make such transfer to an individual retirement plan of a designated trustee or issuer and shall notify the distributee in writing (either separately or as part of the notice under section 402(f)) that the distribution may be transferred to another individual retirement plan.

(ii) Eligible plan—For purposes of clause (i), the term "eligible plan" means a plan which provides that any nonforfeitable accrued benefit for which the present value (as determined under section 411(a)(11)) does not exceed $5,000 shall be immediately distributed to the participant.

(C) Limitation—Subparagraphs (A) and (B) shall apply only to the extent that the eligible rollover distribution would be includible in gross income if not transferred as provided in subparagraph (A) (determined without regard to sections 402(c), 403(a)(4), 403(b)(8), and 457(e)(16)). The preceding sentence shall not apply to such distribution if the plan to which such distribution is transferred—

(i) is a qualified trust which is part of a plan which is a defined contribution plan and agrees to separately account for amounts so transferred, including separately accounting for the portion of such distribution which is includible in gross income and the portion of such distribution which is not so includible, or

(ii) is an eligible retirement plan described in clause (i) or (ii) of section 402(c)(8)(B).

(D) Eligible rollover distribution—For purposes of this paragraph, the term "eligible rollover distribution" has the meaning given such term by section 402(f)(2)(A).

(E) Eligible retirement plan—For purposes of this paragraph, the term "eligible retirement plan" has the meaning given such term by section 402(c)(8)(B), except that a qualified trust shall be considered an eligible retirement plan only if it is a defined contribution plan, the terms of which permit the acceptance of rollover distributions.

(32) Treatment of failure to make certain payments if plan has liquidity shortfall—

(A) In general—A trust forming part of a pension plan to which section 430(j)(4) or 433(f)(5) applies shall not be treated as failing to constitute a qualified trust under this section merely because such plan ceases to make any payment described in subparagraph (B) during any period that such plan has a liquidity shortfall (as defined in section 430(j)(4) or 433(f)(5)).

(B) Payments described—A payment is described in this subparagraph if such payment is—

(i) any payment, in excess of the monthly amount paid under a single life annuity (plus any social security supplements described in the last sentence of section 411(a)(9)), to a participant or beneficiary whose annuity starting date (as defined in section 417(f)(2)) occurs during the period referred to in subparagraph (A),

(ii) any payment for the purchase of an irrevocable commitment from an insurer to pay benefits, and

(iii) any other payment specified by the Secretary by regulations.

(C) Period of shortfall—For purposes of this paragraph, a plan has a liquidity shortfall during the period that there is an underpayment of an installment under section 430(j)(3) or 433(f) by reason of section 430(j)(4)(A) or 433(f)(5), respectively.

(33) Prohibition on benefit increases while sponsor is in bankruptcy—

(A) In general—A trust which is part of a plan to which this paragraph applies shall not constitute a qualified trust under this section if an amendment to such plan is adopted while the employer is a debtor in a case under title 11, United States Code, or similar Federal or State law, if such amendment increases liabilities of the plan by reason of—

(i) any increase in benefits,

(ii) any change in the accrual of benefits, or

(iii) any change in the rate at which benefits become nonforfeitable under the plan,

with respect to employees of the debtor, and such amendment is effective prior to the effective date of such employer's plan of reorganization.

(B) Exceptions—This paragraph shall not apply to any plan amendment if—

(i) the plan, were such amendment to take effect, would have a funding target attainment percentage (as defined in section 430(d)(2)) of 100 percent or more,

(ii) the Secretary determines that such amendment is reasonable and provides for only de minimis increases in the liabilities of the plan with respect to employees of the debtor,

(iii) such amendment only repeals an amendment described in section 412(d)(2), or

(iv) such amendment is required as a condition of qualification under this part.

(C) Plans to which this paragraph applies—This paragraph shall apply only to plans (other than multiemployer plans or CSEC plans) covered under section 4021 of the Employee Retirement Income Security Act of 1974.

(D) Employer—For purposes of this paragraph, the term "employer" means the employer referred to in section 412(b)(1), without regard to section 412(b)(2).

(34) Benefits of missing participants on plan termination—In the case of a plan covered by title IV of the Employee Retirement Income Security Act of 1974, a trust forming part of such plan shall not be treated as failing to constitute a qualified trust under this section merely because the pension plan of which such trust is a part, upon its termination, transfers benefits of missing participants to the Pension Benefit Guaranty Corporation in accordance with section 4050 of such Act.

(35) Diversification requirements for certain defined contribution plans—

(A) In general—A trust which is part of an applicable defined contribution plan shall not be treated as a qualified trust unless the plan meets the diversification requirements of subparagraphs (B), (C), and (D).

(B) Employee contributions and elective deferrals invested in employer securities—In the case of the portion of an applicable individual's account attributable to employee contributions and elective deferrals which is invested in employer securities, a plan meets the requirements of this subparagraph if the applicable individual may elect to direct the plan to divest any such securities and to reinvest an equivalent amount in other investment options meeting the requirements of subparagraph (D).

(C) Employer contributions invested in employer securities—In the case of the portion of the account attributable to employer contributions other than elective deferrals which is invested in employer securities, a plan meets the requirements of this subparagraph if each applicable individual who—

(i) is a participant who has completed at least 3 years of service, or

(ii) is a beneficiary of a participant described in clause (i) or of a deceased participant,

may elect to direct the plan to divest any such securities and to reinvest an equivalent amount in other investment options meeting the requirements of subparagraph (D).

(D) Investment options—

(i) In general—The requirements of this subparagraph are met if the plan offers not less than 3 investment options, other than employer securities, to which an applicable individual may direct the proceeds from the divestment of employer securities pursuant to this paragraph, each of which is diversified and has materially different risk and return characteristics.

(ii) Treatment of certain restrictions and conditions—

(I) Time for making investment choices—A plan shall not be treated as failing to meet the requirements of this subparagraph merely because the plan limits the time for divestment and reinvestment to periodic, reasonable opportunities occurring no less frequently than quarterly.

(II) Certain restrictions and conditions not allowed—Except as provided in regulations, a plan shall not meet the requirements of this subparagraph if the plan imposes restrictions or conditions with respect to the investment of employer securities which are not imposed on the investment of other assets of the plan. This subclause shall not apply to any restrictions or conditions imposed by reason of the application of securities laws.

(E) Applicable defined contribution plan—For purposes of this paragraph—

(i) In general—The term "applicable defined contribution plan" means any defined contribution plan which holds any publicly traded employer securities.

(ii) Exception for certain ESOPs—Such term does not include an employee stock ownership plan if—

(I) there are no contributions to such plan (or earnings thereunder) which are held within such plan and are subject to subsection (k) or (m), and

(II) such plan is a separate plan for purposes of section 414(l) with respect to any other defined benefit plan or defined contribution plan maintained by the same employer or employers.

(iii) Exception for one participant plans—Such term does not include a one-participant retirement plan.

(iv) One-participant retirement plan—For purposes of clause (iii), the term "one-participant retirement plan" means a retirement plan that on the first day of the plan year—

(I) covered only one individual (or the individual and the individual's spouse) and the individual (or the individual and the individual's spouse) owned 100 percent of the plan sponsor (whether or not incorporated), or

(II) covered only one or more partners (or partners and their spouses) in the plan sponsor.

(F) Certain plans treated as holding publicly traded employer securities—

(i) In general—Except as provided in regulations or in clause (ii), a plan holding employer securities which are not publicly traded employer securities shall be treated as holding publicly traded employer securities if any employer corporation, or any member of a controlled group of corporations which includes such employer corporation, has issued a class of stock which is a publicly traded employer security.

(ii) Exception for certain controlled groups with publicly traded securities—Clause (i) shall not apply to a plan if—

(I) no employer corporation, or parent corporation of an employer corporation, has issued any publicly traded employer security, and

(II) no employer corporation, or parent corporation of an employer corporation, has issued any special class of stock which grants particular rights to, or bears particular risks for, the holder or issuer with respect to any corporation described in clause (i) which has issued any publicly traded employer security.

(iii) Definitions—For purposes of this subparagraph, the term—

(I) "controlled group of corporations" has the meaning given such term by section 1563(a), except that "50 percent" shall be substituted for "80 percent" each place it appears,

(II) "employer corporation" means a corporation which is an employer maintaining the plan, and

(III) "parent corporation" has the meaning given such term by section 424(e).

(G) Other definitions—For purposes of this paragraph—

(i) Applicable individual—The term "applicable individual" means—

(I) any participant in the plan, and

(II) any beneficiary who has an account under the plan with respect to which the beneficiary is entitled to exercise the rights of a participant.

(ii) Elective deferral—The term "elective deferral" means an employer contribution described in section 402(g)(3)(A).

(iii) Employer security—The term "employer security" has the meaning given such term by section 407(d)(1) of the Employee Retirement Income Security Act of 1974.

(iv) Employee stock ownership plan—The term "employee stock ownership plan" has the meaning given such term by section 4975(e)(7).

(v) Publicly traded employer securities—The term "publicly traded employer securities" means employer securities which are readily tradable on an established securities market.

(vi) Year of service—The term "year of service" has the meaning given such term by section 411(a)(5).

(H) Transition rule for securities attributable to employer contributions—

(i) Rules phased in over 3 years—

(I) In general—In the case of the portion of an account to which subparagraph (C) applies and which consists of employer securities acquired in a plan year beginning before January 1, 2007, subparagraph (C) shall only apply to the applicable percentage of such securities. This subparagraph shall be applied separately with respect to each class of securities.

(II) Exception for certain participants aged 55 or over—Subclause (I) shall not apply to an applicable individual who is a participant who has attained age 55 and completed at least 3 years of service before the first plan year beginning after December 31, 2005.

(ii) Applicable percentage—For purposes of clause (i), the applicable percentage shall be determined as follows:

Plan year to which subparagraph (C) applies—	The applicable percentage is—
1st	33
2d	66
3d and following	100.

(36) Distributions during working retirement—A trust forming part of a pension plan shall not be treated as failing to constitute a qualified trust under this section solely because the plan provides that a distribution may be made from such trust to an employee who has attained age 62 and who is not separated from employment at the time of such distribution.

(37) Death benefits under USERRA-qualified active military service—A trust shall not constitute a qualified trust unless the plan provides that, in the case of a participant who dies while performing qualified military service (as defined in section 414(u)), the survivors of the participant are entitled to any additional benefits (other than benefit accruals relating to the period of qualified military service) provided under the plan had the participant resumed and then terminated employment on account of death.

Paragraphs (11), (12), (13), (14), (15), (19), and (20) shall apply only in the case of a plan to which section 411 (relating to minimum vesting standards) applies without regard to subsection (e)(2) of such section.

(b) Certain retroactive changes in plan—A stock bonus, pension, profit-sharing, or annuity plan shall be considered as satisfying the requirements of subsection (a) for the period beginning with the date on which it was put into effect, or for the period beginning with the earlier of the date on which there was adopted or put into effect any amendment which caused the plan to fail to satisfy such requirements, and ending with the time prescribed by law for filing the return of the employer for his taxable year in which such plan or amendment was adopted (including extensions thereof) or such later time as the Secretary may designate, if all provisions of the plan which are necessary to satisfy such requirements are in effect by the end of such period and have been made effective for all purposes for the whole of such period.

(c) Definitions and rules relating to self-employed individuals and owner-employees—
For purposes of this section—

(1) Self-employed individual treated as employee—

(A) In general—The term "employee" includes, for any taxable year, an individual who is a self-employed individual for such taxable year.

(B) Self-employed individual—The term "self-employed individual" means, with respect to any taxable year, an individual who has earned income (as defined in paragraph (2)) for such taxable year. To the extent provided in regulations prescribed by the Secretary, such term also includes, for any taxable year—

(i) an individual who would be a self-employed individual within the meaning of the preceding sentence but for the fact that the trade or business carried on by such individual did not have net profits for the taxable year, and

(ii) an individual who has been a self-employed individual within the meaning of the preceding sentence for any prior taxable year.

(2) Earned income—

(A) In general—The term "earned income" means the net earnings from self-employment (as defined in section 1402(a)), but such net earnings shall be determined—

(i) only with respect to a trade or business in which personal services of the taxpayer are a material income-producing factor,

(ii) without regard to paragraphs (4) and (5) of section 1402(c),

(iii) in the case of any individual who is treated as an employee under sections 3121(d)(3)(A), (C), or (D), without regard to paragraph (2) of section 1402(c),

(iv) without regard to items which are not included in gross income for purposes of this chapter, and the deductions properly allocable to or chargeable against such items,

(v) with regard to the deductions allowed by section 404 to the taxpayer, and

(vi) with regard to the deduction allowed to the taxpayer by section 164(f).

For purposes of this subparagraph, section 1402, as in effect for a taxable year ending on December 31, 1962, shall be treated as having been in effect for all taxable years ending before such date. For purposes of this part only (other than sections 419 and 419A), this subparagraph shall be applied as if the term "trade or business" for purposes of section 1402 included service described in section 1402(c)(6).

(C)[B] Income from disposition of certain property—For purposes of this section, the term "earned income" includes gains (other than any gain which is treated under any provision of this chapter as gain from the sale or exchange of a capital asset) and net earnings derived from the sale or other disposition of, the transfer of any interest in, or the licensing of the use of property (other than good will) by an individual whose personal efforts created such property.

(3) Owner-employee—The term "owner-employee" means an employee who—

(A) owns the entire interest in an unincorporated trade or business, or

(B) in the case of a partnership, is a partner who owns more than 10 percent of either the capital interest or the profits interest in such partnership.

To the extent provided in regulations prescribed by the Secretary, such term also means an individual who has been an owner-employee within the meaning of the preceding sentence.

(4) Employer—An individual who owns the entire interest in an unincorporated trade or business shall be treated as his own employer. A partnership shall be treated as the employer of each partner who is an employee within the meaning of paragraph (1).

(5) Contributions on behalf of owner-employees—The term "contribution on behalf of an owner-employee" includes, except as the context otherwise requires, a contribution under a plan—

(A) by the employer for an owner-employee, and

(B) by an owner-employee as an employee.

(6) Special rule for certain fishermen—For purposes of this subsection, the term "self-employed individual" includes an individual described in section 3121(b)(20) (relating to certain fishermen).

(d) Contribution limit on owner-employees—A trust forming part of a pension or profit-sharing plan which provides contributions or benefits for employees some or all of whom are owner-employees shall constitute a qualified trust under this section only if, in addition to meeting the requirements of subsection (a), the plan provides that contributions on behalf of any owner-employee may be made only with respect to the earned income of such owner-employee which is derived from the trade or business with respect to which such plan is established.

(e) [Repealed]

(f) Certain custodial accounts and contracts—For purposes of this title, a custodial account, an annuity contract, or a contract (other than a life, health or accident, property, casualty, or liability insurance contract) issued by an insurance company qualified to do business in a State shall be treated as a qualified trust under this section if—

(1) the custodial account or contract would, except for the fact that it is not a trust, constitute a qualified trust under this section, and

(2) in the case of a custodial account the assets thereof are held by a bank (as defined in section 408(n)) or another person who demonstrates, to the satisfaction of the Secretary, that the manner in which he will hold the assets will be consistent with the requirements of this section.

For purposes of this title, in the case of a custodial account or contract treated as a qualified trust under this section by reason of this subsection, the person holding the assets of such account or holding such contract shall be treated as the trustee thereof.

(g) Annuity defined—For purposes of this section and sections 402, 403, and 404, the term "annuity" includes a face-amount certificate, as defined in section 2(a)(15) of the Investment Company Act of 1940 (15 U. S. C., sec. 80a-2); but does not include any contract or certificate issued after December 31, 1962, which is transferable, if any person other than the trustee of a trust described in section 401(a) which is exempt from tax under section 501(a) is the owner of such contract or certificate.

(h) Medical, etc., benefits for retired employees and their spouses and dependents— Under regulations prescribed by the Secretary, and subject to the provisions of section 420, a pension or annuity plan may provide for the payment of benefits for sickness, accident, hospitalization, and medical expenses of retired employees, their spouses and their dependents, but only if—

> **(1)** such benefits are subordinate to the retirement benefits provided by the plan,

> **(2)** a separate account is established and maintained for such benefits,

> **(3)** the employer's contributions to such separate account are reasonable and ascertainable,

> **(4)** it is impossible, at any time prior to the satisfaction of all liabilities under the plan to provide such benefits, for any part of the corpus or income of such separate account to be (within the taxable year or thereafter) used for, or diverted to, any purpose other than the providing of such benefits,

> **(5)** notwithstanding the provisions of subsection (a)(2), upon the satisfaction of all liabilities under the plan to provide such benefits, any amount remaining in such separate account must, under the terms of the plan, be returned to the employer, and

> **(6)** in the case of an employee who is a key employee, a separate account is established and maintained for such benefits payable to such employee (and his spouse and dependents) and such benefits (to the extent attributable to plan years beginning after March 31, 1984, for which the employee is a key employee) are only payable to such employee (and his spouse and dependents) from such separate account.

For purposes of paragraph (6), the term "key employee" means any employee, who at any time during the plan year or any preceding plan year during which contributions were made on behalf of such employee, is or was a key employee as defined in section 416(i). In no event shall the requirements of paragraph (1) be treated as met if the aggregate actual contributions for medical benefits, when added to actual contributions for life insurance protection under the plan, exceed 25 percent of the total actual contributions to the plan (other than contributions to fund past service credits) after the date on which the account is established. For purposes of this subsection, the term "dependent" shall include any individual who is a child (as defined in section 152(f)(1)) of a retired employee who as of the end of the calendar year has not attained age 27.

(i) Certain union-negotiated pension plans—In the case of a trust forming part of a pension plan which has been determined by the Secretary to constitute a qualified trust under subsection (a) and to be exempt from taxation under section 501(a) for a period beginning after contributions were first made to or for such trust, if it is shown to the satisfaction of the Secretary that—

> **(1)** such trust was created pursuant to a collective bargaining agreement between employee representatives and one or more employers,

> **(2)** any disbursements of contributions, made to or for such trust before the time as of which the Secretary determined that the trust constituted a qualified trust, substantially complied with the terms of the trust, and the plan of which the trust is a part, as subsequently qualified, and

(3) before the time as of which the Secretary determined that the trust constitutes a qualified trust, the contributions to or for such trust were not used in a manner which would jeopardize the interests of its beneficiaries,

then such trust shall be considered as having constituted a qualified trust under subsection (a) and as having been exempt from taxation under section 501(a) for the period beginning on the date on which contributions were first made to or for such trust and ending on the date such trust first constituted (without regard to this subsection) a qualified trust under subsection (a).

(j) [Repealed]

(k) Cash or deferred arrangements—

(1) General rule—A profit-sharing or stock bonus plan, a pre-ERISA money purchase plan, or a rural cooperative plan shall not be considered as not satisfying the requirements of subsection (a) merely because the plan includes a qualified cash or deferred arrangement.

(2) Qualified cash or deferred arrangement—A qualified cash or deferred arrangement is any arrangement which is part of a profit-sharing or stock bonus plan, a pre-ERISA money purchase plan, or a rural cooperative plan which meets the requirements of subsection (a)—

(A) under which a covered employee may elect to have the employer make payments as contributions to a trust under the plan on behalf of the employee, or to the employee directly in cash;

(B) under which amounts held by the trust which are attributable to employer contributions made pursuant to the employee's election—

(i) may not be distributable to participants or other beneficiaries earlier than—

(I) severance from employment, death, or disability,

(II) an event described in paragraph (10),

(III) in the case of a profit-sharing or stock bonus plan, the attainment of age 59½, or

(IV) in the case of contributions to a profit-sharing or stock bonus plan to which section 402(e)(3) applies, upon hardship of the employee, or

(V) in the case of a qualified reservist distribution (as defined in section 72(t)(2)(G)(iii)), the date on which a period referred to in subclause (III) of such section begins, and

(ii) will not be distributable merely by reason of the completion of a stated period of participation or the lapse of a fixed number of years;

(C) which provides that an employee's right to his accrued benefit derived from employer contributions made to the trust pursuant to his election is nonforfeitable, and

(D) which does not require, as a condition of participation in the arrangement, that an employee complete a period of service with the employer (or employers) maintaining the plan extending beyond the period permitted under section 410(a)(1) (determined without regard to subparagraph (B)(i) thereof).

(3) Application of participation and discrimination standards—

(A) A cash or deferred arrangement shall not be treated as a qualified cash or deferred arrangement unless—

    (i) those employees eligible to benefit under the arrangement satisfy the provisions of section 410(b)(1), and

    (ii) the actual deferral percentage for eligible highly compensated employees (as defined in paragraph (5)) for the plan year bears a relationship to the actual deferral percentage for all other eligible employees for the preceding plan year which meets either of the following tests:

        (I) The actual deferral percentage for the group of eligible highly compensated employees is not more than the actual deferral percentage of all other eligible employees multiplied by 1.25.

        (II) The excess of the actual deferral percentage for the group of eligible highly compensated employees over that of all other eligible employees is not more than 2 percentage points, and the actual deferral percentage for the group of eligible highly compensated employees is not more than the actual deferral percentage of all other eligible employees multiplied by 2.

If 2 or more plans which include cash or deferred arrangements are considered as 1 plan for purposes of section 401(a)(4) or 410(b), the cash or deferred arrangements included in such plans shall be treated as 1 arrangement for purposes of this subparagraph.

If any highly compensated employee is a participant under 2 or more cash or deferred arrangements of the employer, for purposes of determining the deferral percentage with respect to such employee, all such cash or deferred arrangements shall be treated as 1 cash or deferred arrangement. An arrangement may apply clause (ii) by using the plan year rather than the preceding plan year if the employer so elects, except that if such an election is made, it may not be changed except as provided by the Secretary.

(B) For purposes of subparagraph (A), the actual deferral percentage for a specified group of employees for a plan year shall be the average of the ratios (calculated separately for each employee in such group) of—

    (i) the amount of employer contributions actually paid over to the trust on behalf of each such employee for such plan year, to

    (ii) the employee's compensation for such plan year.

(C) A cash or deferred arrangement shall be treated as meeting the requirements of subsection (a)(4) with respect to contributions if the requirements of subparagraph (A)(ii) are met.

(D) For purposes of subparagraph (B), the employer contributions on behalf of any employee—

    (i) shall include any employer contributions made pursuant to the employee's election under paragraph (2), and

    (ii) under such rules as the Secretary may prescribe, may, at the election of employer, include—

        (I) matching contributions (as defined in section 401(m)(4)(A)) which meet the requirements of paragraph (2)(B) and (C), and

(II) qualified nonelective contributions (within the meaning of section 401(m)(4)(C)).

(E) For purposes of this paragraph, in the case of the first plan year of any plan (other than a successor plan), the amount taken into account as the actual deferral percentage of nonhighly compensated employees for the preceding plan year shall be—

(i) 3 percent, or

(ii) if the employer makes an election under this subclause, the actual deferral percentage of nonhighly compensated employees determined for such first plan year.

(F) Special rule for early participation—If an employer elects to apply section 410(b)(4)(B) in determining whether a cash or deferred arrangement meets the requirements of subparagraph (A)(i), the employer may, in determining whether the arrangement meets the requirements of subparagraph (A)(ii), exclude from consideration all eligible employees (other than highly compensated employees) who have not met the minimum age and service requirements of section 410(a)(1)(A).

(G) Governmental plan—A governmental plan (within the meaning of section 414(d)) shall be treated as meeting the requirements of this paragraph.

(4) Other requirements—

(A) Benefits (other than matching contributions) must not be contingent on election to defer—A cash or deferred arrangement of any employer shall not be treated as a qualified cash or deferred arrangement if any other benefit is conditioned (directly or indirectly) on the employee electing to have the employer make or not make contributions under the arrangement in lieu of receiving cash. The preceding sentence shall not apply to any matching contribution (as defined in section 401(m)) made by reason of such an election.

(B) Eligibility of state and local governments and tax-exempt organizations—

(i) Tax-exempts eligible—Except as provided in clause (ii), any organization exempt from tax under this subtitle may include a qualified cash or deferred arrangement as part of a plan maintained by it.

(ii) Governments ineligible—A cash or deferred arrangement shall not be treated as a qualified cash or deferred arrangement if it is part of a plan maintained by a State or local government or political subdivision thereof, or any agency or instrumentality thereof. This clause shall not apply to a rural cooperative plan or to a plan of an employer described in clause (iii).

(iii) Treatment of Indian tribal governments—An employer which is an Indian tribal government (as defined in section 7701(a)(40)), a subdivision of an Indian tribal government (determined in accordance with section 7871(d)), an agency or instrumentality of an Indian tribal government or subdivision thereof, or a corporation chartered under Federal, State, or tribal law which is owned in whole or in part by any of the foregoing may include a qualified cash or deferred arrangement as part of a plan maintained by the employer.

(C) Coordination with other plans—Except as provided in section 401(m), any employer contribution made pursuant to an employee's election under a qualified cash or deferred arrangement shall not be taken into account for purposes of determining whether any other plan meets the requirements of section 401(a) or 410(b). This subparagraph shall not apply for purposes of determining whether a plan meets the average benefit requirement of section 410(b)(2)(A)(ii).

(5) Highly compensated employee—For purposes of this subsection, the term "highly compensated employee" has the meaning given such term by section 414(q).

(6) Pre-ERISA money purchase plan—For purposes of this subsection, the term "pre-ERISA money purchase plan" means a pension plan—

(A) which is a defined contribution plan (as defined in section 414(i)),

(B) which was in existence on June 27, 1974, and which, on such date, included a salary reduction arrangement, and

(C) under which neither the employee contributions nor the employer contributions may exceed the levels provided for by the contribution formula in effect under the plan on such date.

(7) Rural cooperative plan—For purposes of this subsection—

(A) In general—The term "rural cooperative plan" means any pension plan—

(i) which is a defined contribution plan (as defined in section 414(i)), and

(ii) which is established and maintained by a rural cooperative.

(B) Rural cooperative defined—For purposes of subparagraph (A), the term "rural cooperative" means—

(i) any organization which—

(I) is engaged primarily in providing electric service on a mutual or cooperative basis, or

(II) is engaged primarily in providing electric service to the public in its area of service and which is exempt from tax under this subtitle or which is a State or local government (or an agency or instrumentality thereof), other than a municipality (or an agency or instrumentality thereof),

(ii) any organization described in paragraph (4) or (6) of section 501(c) and at least 80 percent of the members of which are organizations described in clause (i),

(iii) a cooperative telephone company described in section 501(c)(12),

(iv) any organization which—

(I) is a mutual irrigation or ditch company described in section 501(c)(12) (without regard to the 85 percent requirement thereof), or

(II) is a district organized under the laws of a State as a municipal corporation for the purpose of irrigation, water conservation, or drainage, and

(v) an organization which is a national association of organizations described in clause (i), (ii), (iii), or (iv).

(C) Special rule for certain distributions—A rural cooperative plan which includes a qualified cash or deferred arrangement shall not be treated as violating the requirements of section 401(a) or of paragraph (2) merely by reason of a hardship distribution or a distribution to a participant after attainment of age 59½. For purposes of this section, the term "hardship distribution" means a distribution described in paragraph (2)(B)(i)(IV) (without regard to the limitation of its application to profit-sharing or stock bonus plans).

(8) Arrangement not disqualified if excess contributions distributed—

(A) **In general**—A cash or deferred arrangement shall not be treated as failing to meet the requirements of clause (ii) of paragraph (3)(A) for any plan year if, before the close of the following plan year—

(i) the amount of excess contributions for such plan year (and any income allocable to such contributions through the end of such year) is distributed, or

(ii) to the extent provided in regulations, the employee elects to treat the amount of the excess contributions as an amount distributed to the employee and then contributed by the employee to the plan.

Any distribution of excess contributions (and income) may be made without regard to any other provision of law.

(B) **Excess contributions**—For purposes of subparagraph (A), the term "excess contributions" means, with respect to any plan year, the excess of—

(i) the aggregate amount of employer contributions actually paid over to the trust on behalf of highly compensated employees for such plan year, over

(ii) the maximum amount of such contributions permitted under the limitations of clause (ii) of paragraph (3)(A) (determined by reducing contributions made on behalf of highly compensated employees in order of the actual deferral percentages beginning with the highest of such percentages).

(C) **Method of distributing excess contributions**—Any distribution of the excess contributions for any plan year shall be made to highly compensated employees on the basis of the amount of contributions by, or on behalf of, each of such employees.

(D) **Additional tax under section 72(t) not to apply**—No tax shall be imposed under section 72(t) on any amount required to be distributed under this paragraph.

(E) **Treatment of matching contributions forfeited by reason of excess deferral or contribution or permissible withdrawal**—For purposes of paragraph (2)(C), a matching contribution (within the meaning of subsection (m)) shall not be treated as forfeitable merely because such contribution is forfeitable if the contribution to which the matching contribution relates is treated as an excess contribution under subparagraph (B), an excess deferral under section 402(g)(2)(A), a permissible withdrawal under section 414(w), or an excess aggregate contribution under section 401(m)(6)(B).

(F) **Cross reference**—For excise tax on certain excess contributions, see section 4979.

(9) Compensation—For purposes of this subsection, the term "compensation" has the meaning given such term by section 414(s).

(10) Distributions upon termination of plan—

(A) **In general**—An event described in this subparagraph is the termination of the plan without establishment or maintenance of another defined contribution plan (other than an employee stock ownership plan as defined in section 4975(e)(7)).

(B) Distributions must be lump sum distributions—

(i) In general—A termination shall not be treated as described in subparagraph (A) with respect to any employee unless the employee receives a lump sum distribution by reason of the termination.

(ii) Lump-sum distribution—For purposes of this subparagraph, the term "lump-sum distribution" has the meaning given such term by section 402(e)(4)(D) (without regard to subclauses (I), (II), (III), and (IV) of clause (i) thereof). Such term includes a distribution of an annuity contract from—

(I) a trust which forms a part of a plan described in section 401(a) and which is exempt from tax under section 501(a), or

(II) an annuity plan described in section 403(a).

(11) Adoption of simple plan to meet nondiscrimination tests—

(A) In general—A cash or deferred arrangement maintained by an eligible employer shall be treated as meeting the requirements of paragraph (3)(A)(ii) if such arrangement meets—

(i) the contribution requirements of subparagraph (B),

(ii) the exclusive plan requirements of subparagraph (C), and

(iii) the vesting requirements of section 408(p)(3).

(B) Contribution requirements—

(i) In general—The requirements of this subparagraph are met if, under the arrangement—

(I) an employee may elect to have the employer make elective contributions for the year on behalf of the employee to a trust under the plan in an amount which is expressed as a percentage of compensation of the employee but which in no event exceeds the amount in effect under section 408(p)(2)(A)(ii),

(II) the employer is required to make a matching contribution to the trust for the year in an amount equal to so much of the amount the employee elects under subclause (I) as does not exceed 3 percent of compensation for the year, and

(III) no other contributions may be made other than contributions described in subclause (I) or (II).

(ii) Employer may elect 2-percent nonelective contribution—An employer shall be treated as meeting the requirements of clause (i)(II) for any year if, in lieu of the contributions described in such clause, the employer elects (pursuant to the terms of the arrangement) to make nonelective contributions of 2 percent of compensation for each employee who is eligible to participate in the arrangement and who has at least $5,000 of compensation from the employer for the year. If an employer makes an election under this subparagraph for any year, the employer shall notify employees of such election within a reasonable period of time before the 60th day before the beginning of such year.

(iii) Administrative requirements—

(I) In general—Rules similar to the rules of subparagraphs (B) and (C) of section 408(p)(5) shall apply for purposes of this subparagraph.

(II) Notice of election period—The requirements of this subparagraph shall not be treated as met with respect to any year unless the employer notifies each employee eligible to participate, within a reasonable period of time before the 60th day before the beginning of such year (and, for the first year the employee is so eligible, the 60th day before the first day such employee is so eligible), of the rules similar to the rules of section 408(p)(5)(C) which apply by reason of subclause (I).

(C) Exclusive plan requirement—The requirements of this subparagraph are met for any year to which this paragraph applies if no contributions were made, or benefits were accrued, for services during such year under any qualified plan of the employer on behalf of any employee eligible to participate in the cash or deferred arrangement, other than contributions described in subparagraph (B).

(D) Definitions and special rule—

(i) Definitions—For purposes of this paragraph, any term used in this paragraph which is also used in section 408(p) shall have the meaning given such term by such section.

(ii) Coordination with top-heavy rules—A plan meeting the requirements of this paragraph for any year shall not be treated as a top-heavy plan under section 416 for such year if such plan allows only contributions required under this paragraph.

(12) Alternative methods of meeting nondiscrimination requirements—

(A) In general—A cash or deferred arrangement shall be treated as meeting the requirements of paragraph (3)(A)(ii) if such arrangement—

(i) meets the contribution requirements of subparagraph (B) or (C), and

(ii) meets the notice requirements of subparagraph (D).

(B) Matching contributions—

(i) In general—The requirements of this subparagraph are met if, under the arrangement, the employer makes matching contributions on behalf of each employee who is not a highly compensated employee in an amount equal to—

(I) 100 percent of the elective contributions of the employee to the extent such elective contributions do not exceed 3 percent of the employee's compensation, and

(II) 50 percent of the elective contributions of the employee to the extent that such elective contributions exceed 3 percent but do not exceed 5 percent of the employee's compensation.

(ii) Rate for highly compensated employees—The requirements of this subparagraph are not met if, under the arrangement, the rate of matching contribution with respect to any elective contribution of a highly compensated employee at any rate of elective contribution is greater than that with respect to an employee who is not a highly compensated employee.

(iii) Alternative plan designs—If the rate of any matching contribution with respect to any rate of elective contribution is not equal to the percentage required under clause (i), an arrangement shall not be treated as failing to meet the requirements of clause (i) if—

(I) the rate of an employer's matching contribution does not increase as an employee's rate of elective contributions increase, and

(II) the aggregate amount of matching contributions at such rate of elective contribution is at least equal to the aggregate amount of matching contributions which would be made if matching contributions were made on the basis of the percentages described in clause (i).

(C) Nonelective contributions—The requirements of this subparagraph are met if, under the arrangement, the employer is required, without regard to whether the employee makes an elective contribution or employee contribution, to make a contribution to a defined contribution plan on behalf of each employee who is not a highly compensated employee and who is eligible to participate in the arrangement in an amount equal to at least 3 percent of the employee's compensation.

(D) Notice requirement—An arrangement meets the requirements of this paragraph if, under the arrangement, each employee eligible to participate is, within a reasonable period before any year, given written notice of the employee's rights and obligations under the arrangement which—

(i) is sufficiently accurate and comprehensive to appraise the employee of such rights and obligations, and

(ii) is written in a manner calculated to be understood by the average employee eligible to participate.

(E) Other requirements—

(i) Withdrawal and vesting restrictions—An arrangement shall not be treated as meeting the requirements of subparagraph (B) or (C) of this paragraph unless the requirements of subparagraphs (B) and (C) of paragraph (2) are met with respect to all employer contributions (including matching contributions) taken into account in determining whether the requirements of subparagraphs (B) and (C) of this paragraph are met.

(ii) Social security and similar contributions not taken into account—An arrangement shall not be treated as meeting the requirements of subparagraph (B) or (C) unless such requirements are met without regard to subsection (l), and, for purposes of subsection (l), employer contributions under subparagraph (B) or (C) shall not be taken into account.

(F) Other plans—An arrangement shall be treated as meeting the requirements under subparagraph (A)(i) if any other plan maintained by the employer meets such requirements with respect to employees eligible under the arrangement.

(13) Alternative method for automatic contribution arrangements to meet nondiscrimination requirements—

(A) In general—A qualified automatic contribution arrangement shall be treated as meeting the requirements of paragraph (3)(A)(ii).

(B) Qualified automatic contribution arrangement—For purposes of this paragraph, the term "qualified automatic contribution arrangement" means any cash or deferred arrangement which meets the requirements of subparagraphs (C) through (E).

(C) Automatic deferral—

(i) In general—The requirements of this subparagraph are met if, under the arrangement, each employee eligible to participate in the arrangement is treated as having elected to have the employer make elective contributions in an amount equal to a qualified percentage of compensation.

(ii) Election out—The election treated as having been made under clause (i) shall cease to apply with respect to any employee if such employee makes an affirmative election—

(I) to not have such contributions made, or

(II) to make elective contributions at a level specified in such affirmative election.

(iii) Qualified percentage—For purposes of this subparagraph, the term "qualified percentage" means, with respect to any employee, any percentage determined under the arrangement if such percentage is applied uniformly, does not exceed 10 percent, and is at least—

(I) 3 percent during the period ending on the last day of the first plan year which begins after the date on which the first elective contribution described in clause (i) is made with respect to such employee,

(II) 4 percent during the first plan year following the plan year described in subclause (I),

(III) 5 percent during the second plan year following the plan year described in subclause (I), and

(IV) 6 percent during any subsequent plan year.

(iv) Automatic deferral for current employees not required—Clause (i) may be applied without taking into account any employee who—

(I) was eligible to participate in the arrangement (or a predecessor arrangement) immediately before the date on which such arrangement becomes a qualified automatic contribution arrangement (determined after application of this clause), and

(II) had an election in effect on such date either to participate in the arrangement or to not participate in the arrangement.

(D) Matching or nonelective contributions—

(i) In general—The requirements of this subparagraph are met if, under the arrangement, the employer—

(I) makes matching contributions on behalf of each employee who is not a highly compensated employee in an amount equal to the sum of 100 percent of the elective contributions of the employee to the extent that such contributions do not exceed 1 percent of compensation plus 50 percent of so much of such contributions as exceed 1 percent but do not exceed 6 percent of compensation, or

(II) is required, without regard to whether the employee makes an elective contribution or employee contribution, to make a contribution to a defined contribution plan on behalf of each employee who is not a highly compensated employee and who is eligible to participate in the arrangement in an amount equal to at least 3 percent of the employee's compensation.

(ii) **Application of rules for matching contributions**—The rules of clauses (ii) and (iii) of paragraph (12)(B) shall apply for purposes of clause (i)(I).

(iii) **Withdrawal and vesting restrictions**—An arrangement shall not be treated as meeting the requirements of clause (i) unless, with respect to employer contributions (including matching contributions) taken into account in determining whether the requirements of clause (i) are met—

(I) any employee who has completed at least 2 years of service (within the meaning of section 411(a)) has a nonforfeitable right to 100 percent of the employee's accrued benefit derived from such employer contributions, and

(II) the requirements of subparagraph (B) of paragraph (2) are met with respect to all such employer contributions.

(iv) **Application of certain other rules**—The rules of subparagraphs (E)(ii) and (F) of paragraph (12) shall apply for purposes of subclauses (I) and (II) of clause (i).

(E) Notice requirements—

(i) **In general**—The requirements of this subparagraph are met if, within a reasonable period before each plan year, each employee eligible to participate in the arrangement for such year receives written notice of the employee's rights and obligations under the arrangement which—

(I) is sufficiently accurate and comprehensive to apprise the employee of such rights and obligations, and

(II) is written in a manner calculated to be understood by the average employee to whom the arrangement applies.

(ii) **Timing and content requirements**—A notice shall not be treated as meeting the requirements of clause (i) with respect to an employee unless—

(I) the notice explains the employee's right under the arrangement to elect not to have elective contributions made on the employee's behalf (or to elect to have such contributions made at a different percentage),

(II) in the case of an arrangement under which the employee may elect among 2 or more investment options, the notice explains how contributions made under the arrangement will be invested in the absence of any investment election by the employee, and

(III) the employee has a reasonable period of time after receipt of the notice described in subclauses (I) and (II) and before the first elective contribution is made to make either such election.

(l) Permitted disparity in plan contributions or benefits—

(1) In general—The requirements of this subsection are met with respect to a plan if—

(A) in the case of a defined contribution plan, the requirements of paragraph (2) are met, and

(B) in the case of a defined benefit plan, the requirements of paragraph (3) are met.

(2) Defined contribution plan—

(A) In general—A defined contribution plan meets the requirements of this paragraph if the excess contribution percentage does not exceed the base contribution percentage by more than the lesser of—

(i) the base contribution percentage, or

(ii) the greater of—

(I) 5.7 percentage points, or

(II) the percentage equal to the portion of the rate of tax under section 3111(a) (in effect as of the beginning of the year) which is attributable to old-age insurance.

(B) Contribution percentages—For purposes of this paragraph—

(i) Excess contribution percentage—The term "excess contribution percentage" means the percentage of compensation which is contributed by the employer under the plan with respect to that portion of each participant's compensation in excess of the integration level.

(ii) Base contribution percentage—The term "base contribution percentage" means the percentage of compensation contributed by the employer under the plan with respect to that portion of each participant's compensation not in excess of the integration level.

(3) Defined benefit plan—A defined benefit plan meets the requirements of this paragraph if—

(A) Excess plans—

(i) In general—In the case of a plan other than an offset plan—

(I) the excess benefit percentage does not exceed the base benefit percentage by more than the maximum excess allowance,

(II) any optional form of benefit, preretirement benefit, actuarial factor, or other benefit or feature provided with respect to compensation in excess of the integration level is provided with respect to compensation not in excess of such level, and

(III) benefits are based on average annual compensation.

(ii) Benefit percentages—For purposes of this subparagraph, the excess and base benefit percentages shall be computed in the same manner as the excess and base contribution percentages under paragraph (2)(B), except that such determination shall be made on the basis of benefits attributable to employer contributions rather than contributions.

(B) Offset plans—In the case of an offset plan, the plan provides that—

(i) a participant's accrued benefit attributable to employer contributions (within the meaning of section 411(c)(1)) may not be reduced (by reason of the offset) by more than the maximum offset allowance, and

(ii) benefits are based on average annual compensation.

(4) Definitions relating to paragraph (3)—For purposes of paragraph (3)—

(A) Maximum excess allowance—The maximum excess allowance is equal to—

(i) in the case of benefits attributable to any year of service with the employer taken into account under the plan, 3/4 of a percentage point, and

(ii) in the case of total benefits, 3/4 of a percentage point, multiplied by the participant's years of service (not in excess of 35) with the employer taken into account under the plan.

In no event shall the maximum excess allowance exceed the base benefit percentage.

(B) Maximum offset allowance—The maximum offset allowance is equal to—

(i) in the case of benefits attributable to any year of service with the employer taken into account under the plan, 3/4 percent of the participant's final average compensation, and

(ii) in the case of total benefits, 3/4 percent of the participant's final average compensation, multiplied by the participant's years of service (not in excess of 35) with the employer taken into account under the plan.

In no event shall the maximum offset allowance exceed 50 percent of the benefit which would have accrued without regard to the offset reduction.

(C) Reductions—

(i) **In general**—The Secretary shall prescribe regulations requiring the reduction of the 3/4 percentage factor under subparagraph (A) or (B)—

(I) in the case of a plan other than an offset plan which has an integration level in excess of covered compensation, or

(II) with respect to any participant in an offset plan who has final average compensation in excess of covered compensation.

(ii) **Basis of reductions**—Any reductions under clause (i) shall be based on the percentages of compensation replaced by the employer-derived portions of primary insurance amounts under the Social Security Act for participants with compensation in excess of covered compensation.

(D) Offset plan—The term "offset plan" means any plan with respect to which the benefit attributable to employer contributions for each participant is reduced by an amount specified in the plan.

(5) Other definitions and special rules—For purposes of this subsection—

(A) Integration level—

(i) **In general**—The term "integration level" means the amount of compensation specified under the plan (by dollar amount or formula) at or below which the rate at which contributions or benefits are provided (expressed as a percentage) is less than such rate above such amount.

(ii) Limitation—The integration level for any year may not exceed the contribution and benefit base in effect under section 230 of the Social Security Act for such year.

(iii) Level to apply to all participants—A plan's integration level shall apply with respect to all participants in the plan.

(iv) Multiple integration levels—Under rules prescribed by the Secretary, a defined benefit plan may specify multiple integration levels.

(B) Compensation—The term "compensation" has the meaning given such term by section 414(s).

(C) Average annual compensation—The term "average annual compensation" means the participant's highest average annual compensation for—

(i) any period of at least 3 consecutive years, or

(ii) if shorter, the participant's full period of service.

(D) Final average compensation—

(i) In general—The term "final average compensation" means the participant's average annual compensation for—

(I) the 3-consecutive year period ending with the current year, or

(II) if shorter, the participant's full period of service.

(ii) Limitation—A participant's final average compensation shall be determined by not taking into account in any year compensation in excess of the contribution and benefit base in effect under section 230 of the Social Security Act for such year.

(E) Covered compensation—

(i) In general—The term "covered compensation" means, with respect to an employee, the average of the contribution and benefit bases in effect under section 230 of the Social Security Act for each year in the 35-year period ending with the year in which the employee attains the social security retirement age.

(ii) Computation for any year—For purposes of clause (i), the determination for any year preceding the year in which the employee attains the social security retirement age shall be made by assuming that there is no increase in the bases described in clause (i) after the determination year and before the employee attains the social security retirement age.

(iii) Social security retirement age—For purposes of this subparagraph, the term "social security retirement age" has the meaning given such term by section 415(b)(8).

(F) Regulations—The Secretary shall prescribe such regulations as are necessary or appropriate to carry out the purposes of this subsection, including—

(i) in the case of a defined benefit plan which provides for unreduced benefits commencing before the social security retirement age (as defined in section 415(b)(8)), rules providing for the reduction of the maximum excess allowance and the maximum offset allowance, and

(ii) in the case of an employee covered by 2 or more plans of the employer which fail to meet the requirements of subsection (a)(4) (without regard to this subsection), rules preventing the multiple use of the disparity permitted under this subsection with respect to any employee.

For purposes of clause (i), unreduced benefits shall not include benefits for disability (within the meaning of section 223(d) of the Social Security Act).

(6) Special rule for plan maintained by railroads—In determining whether a plan which includes employees of a railroad employer who are entitled to benefits under the Railroad Retirement Act of 1974 meets the requirements of this subsection, rules similar to the rules set forth in this subsection shall apply. Such rules shall take into account the employer-derived portion of the employees' tier 2 railroad retirement benefits and any supplemental annuity under the Railroad Retirement Act of 1974.

(m) Nondiscrimination test for matching contributions and employee contributions—

(1) In general—A defined contribution plan shall be treated as meeting the requirements of subsection (a)(4) with respect to the amount of any matching contribution or employee contribution for any plan year only if the contribution percentage requirement of paragraph (2) of this subsection is met for such plan year.

(2) Requirements—

(A) Contribution percentage requirement—A plan meets the contribution percentage requirement of this paragraph for any plan year only if the contribution percentage for eligible highly compensated employees for such plan year does not exceed the greater of—

(i) 125 percent of such percentage for all other eligible employees for the preceding plan year, or

(ii) the lesser of 200 percent of such percentage for all other eligible employees for the preceding plan year, or such percentage for all other eligible employees for the preceding plan year plus 2 percentage points.

This subparagraph may be applied by using the plan year rather than the preceding plan year if the employer so elects, except that if such an election is made, it may not be changed except as provided the Secretary.

(B) Multiple plans treated as a single plan—If two or more plans of an employer to which matching contributions, employee contributions, or elective deferrals are made are treated as one plan for purposes of section 410(b), such plans shall be treated as one plan for purposes of this subsection. If a highly compensated employee participates in two or more plans of an employer to which contributions to which this subsection applies are made, all such contributions shall be aggregated for purposes of this subsection.

(3) Contribution percentage—For purposes of paragraph (2), the contribution percentage for a specified group of employees for a plan year shall be the average for the ratios (calculated separately for each employee in such group) of—

(A) the sum of the matching contributions and employee contributions paid under the plan on behalf of each such employee for such plan year, to

(B) the employee's compensation (within the meaning of section 414(s)) for such plan year.

Under regulations, an employer may elect to take into account (in computing the contribution percentage) elective deferrals and qualified nonelective contributions under the plan or any other plan of the employer. If matching contributions are taken into account for purposes of subsection (k)(3)(A)(ii) for any plan year, such contributions shall not be taken into account under subparagraph (A) for such year. Rules similar to the rules of subsection (k)(3)(E) shall apply for purposes of this subsection.

(4) Definitions—For purposes of this subsection—

(A) Matching contribution—The term "matching contribution" means—

(i) any employer contribution made to a defined contribution plan on behalf of an employee on account of an employee contribution made by such employee, and

(ii) any employer contribution made to a defined contribution plan on behalf of an employee on account of an employee's elective deferral.

(B) Elective deferral—The term "elective deferral" means any employer contribution described in section 402(g)(3).

(C) Qualified nonelective contributions—The term "qualified nonelective contribution" means any employer contribution (other than a matching contribution) with respect to which—

(i) the employee may not elect to have the contribution paid to the employee in cash instead of being contributed to the plan, and

(ii) the requirements of subparagraphs (B) and (C) of subsection (k)(2) are met.

(5) Employees taken into consideration—

(A) In general—Any employee who is eligible to make an employee contribution (or, if the employer takes elective contributions into account, elective contributions) or to receive a matching contribution under the plan being tested under paragraph (1) shall be considered an eligible employee for purposes of this subsection.

(B) Certain nonparticipants—If an employee contribution is required as a condition of participation in the plan, any employee who would be a participant in the plan if such employee made such a contribution shall be treated as an eligible employee on behalf of whom no employer contributions are made.

(C) Special rule for early participation—If an employer elects to apply section 410(b)(4)(B) in determining whether a plan meets the requirements of section 410(b), the employer may, in determining whether the plan meets the requirements of paragraph (2), exclude from consideration all eligible employees (other than highly compensated employees) who have not met the minimum age and service requirements of section 410(a)(1)(A).

(6) Plan not disqualified if excess aggregate contributions distributed before end of following plan year—

(A) In general—A plan shall not be treated as failing to meet the requirements of paragraph (1) for any plan year if, before the close of the following plan year, the amount of the excess aggregate contributions for such plan year (and any income allocable to such contributions through the end of such year) is distributed (or, if forfeitable, is forfeited). Such contributions (and such income) may be distributed without regard to any other provision of law.

(B) Excess aggregate contributions—For purposes of subparagraph (A), the term "excess aggregate contributions" means, with respect to any plan year, the excess of—

(i) the aggregate amount of the matching contributions and employee contributions (and any qualified nonelective contribution or elective contribution taken into account in computing the contribution percentage) actually made on behalf of highly compensated employees for such plan year, over

(ii) the maximum amount of such contributions permitted under the limitations of paragraph (2)(A) (determined by reducing contributions made on behalf of highly compensated employees in order of their contribution percentages beginning with the highest of such percentages).

(C) Method of distributing excess aggregate contributions—Any distribution of the excess aggregate contributions for any plan year shall be made to highly compensated employees on the basis of the amount of contributions on behalf of, or by, each such employee. Forfeitures of excess aggregate contributions may not be allocated to participants whose contributions are reduced under this paragraph.

(D) Coordination with subsection (k) and 402(g)—The determination of the amount of excess aggregate contributions with respect to a plan shall be made after—

(i) first determining the excess deferrals (within the meaning of section 402(g)), and

(ii) then determining the excess contributions under subsection (k).

(7) Treatment of distributions—

(A) Additional tax of section 72(t) not applicable—No tax shall be imposed under section 72(t) on any amount required to be distributed under paragraph (6).

(B) Exclusion of employee contributions—Any distribution attributable to employee contributions shall not be included in gross income except to the extent attributable to income on such contributions.

(8) Highly compensated employee—For purposes of this subsection, the term "highly compensated employee" has the meaning given to such term by section 414(q).

(9) Regulations—The Secretary shall prescribe such regulations as may be necessary to carry out the purposes of this subsection and subsection (k), including regulations permitting appropriate aggregation of plans and contributions.

(10) Alternative method of satisfying tests—A defined contribution plan shall be treated as meeting the requirements of paragraph (2) with respect to matching contributions if the plan—

(A) meets the contribution requirements of subparagraph (B) of subsection (k)(11),

(B) meets the exclusive plan requirements of subsection (k)(11)(C), and

(C) meets the vesting requirements of section 408(p)(3).

(11) Additional alternative method of satisfying tests—

(A) In general—A defined contribution plan shall be treated as meeting the requirements of paragraph (2) with respect to matching contributions if the plan—

    (i) meets the contribution requirements of subparagraph (B) or (C) of subsection (k)(12),

    (ii) meets the notice requirements of subsection (k)(12)(D), and

    (iii) meets the requirements of subparagraph (B).

(B) Limitation on matching contributions—The requirements of this subparagraph are met if—

    (i) matching contributions on behalf of any employee may not be made with respect to an employee's contributions or elective deferrals in excess of 6 percent of the employee's compensation,

    (ii) the rate of an employer's matching contribution does not increase as the rate of an employee's contributions or elective deferrals increase, and

    (iii) the matching contribution with respect to any highly compensated employee at any rate of an employee contribution or rate of elective deferral is not greater than that with respect to an employee who is not a highly compensated employee.

(12) Alternative method for automatic contribution arrangements—A defined contribution plan shall be treated as meeting the requirements of paragraph (2) with respect to matching contributions if the plan—

    (A) is a qualified automatic contribution arrangement (as defined in subsection (k)(13)), and

    (B) meets the requirements of paragraph (11)(B).

(13) Cross reference—For excise tax on certain excess contributions, see section 4979.

(n) Coordination with qualified domestic relations orders—The Secretary shall prescribe such rules or regulations as may be necessary to coordinate the requirements of subsection (a)(13)(B) and section 414(p) (and the regulations issued by the Secretary of Labor thereunder) with the other provisions of this chapter.

(o) Cross reference—For exemption from tax of a trust qualified under this section, see section 501(a).

§ 402. Taxability of beneficiary of employees' trust.

(a) Taxability of beneficiary of exempt trust—Except as otherwise provided in this section, any amount actually distributed to any distributee by any employees' trust described in section 401(a) which is exempt from tax under section 501(a) shall be taxable to the distributee, in the taxable year of the distributee in which distributed, under section 72 (relating to annuities).

(b) Taxability of beneficiary of nonexempt trust—

(1) Contributions—Contributions to an employees' trust made by an employer during a taxable year of the employer which ends with or within a taxable year of the trust for which the trust is not exempt from tax under section 501(a) shall be included in the gross income of the employee in accordance with section 83 (relating to property transferred in connection with performance of services), except that the value of the employee's interest in the trust shall be substituted for the fair market value of the property for purposes of applying such section.

(2) Distributions—The amount actually distributed or made available to any distributee by any trust described in paragraph (1) shall be taxable to the distributee, in the taxable year in which so distributed or made available, under section 72 (relating to annuities), except that distributions of income of such trust before the annuity starting date (as defined in section 72(c)(4)) shall be included in the gross income of the employee without regard to section 72(e)(5) (relating to amounts not received as annuities).

(3) Grantor trusts—A beneficiary of any trust described in paragraph (1) shall not be considered the owner of any portion of such trust under subpart E of part I of subchapter J (relating to grantors and others treated as substantial owners).

(4) Failure to meet requirements of section 410(b)—

(A) Highly compensated employees—If 1 of the reasons a trust is not exempt from tax under section 501(a) is the failure of the plan of which it is a part to meet the requirements of section 401(a)(26) or 410(b), then a highly compensated employee shall, in lieu of the amount determined under paragraph (1) or (2) include in gross income for the taxable year with or within which the taxable year of the trust ends an amount equal to the vested accrued benefit of such employee (other than the employee's investment in the contract) as of the close of such taxable year of the trust.

(B) Failure to meet coverage tests—If a trust is not exempt from tax under section 501(a) for any taxable year solely because such trust is part of a plan which fails to meet the requirements of section 401(a)(26) or 410(b), paragraphs (1) and (2) shall not apply by reason of such failure to any employee who was not a highly compensated employee during—

(i) such taxable year, or

(ii) any preceding period for which service was creditable to such employee under the plan.

(C) Highly compensated employee—For purposes of this paragraph, the term 'highly compensated employee' has the meaning given such term by section 414(q).

(c) Rules applicable to rollovers from exempt trusts—

(1) Exclusion from income—If—

(A) any portion of the balance to the credit of an employee in a qualified trust is paid to the employee in an eligible rollover distribution,

(B) the distributee transfers any portion of the property received in such distribution to an eligible retirement plan, and

(C) in the case of a distribution of property other than money, the amount so transferred consists of the property distributed,

then such distribution (to the extent so transferred) shall not be includible in gross income for the taxable year in which paid.

(2) Maximum amount which may be rolled over—In the case of any eligible rollover distribution, the maximum amount transferred to which paragraph (1) applies shall not exceed the portion of such distribution which is includible in gross income (determined without regard to paragraph (1)). The preceding sentence shall not apply to such distribution to the extent—

> **(A)** such portion is transferred in a direct trustee-to-trustee transfer to a qualified trust or to an annuity contract described in section 403(b) and such trust or contract provides for separate accounting for amounts so transferred (and earnings thereon), including separately accounting for the portion of such distribution which is includible in gross income and the portion of such distribution which is not so includible, or

> **(B)** such portion is transferred to an eligible retirement plan described in clause (i) or (ii) of paragraph (8)(B).

In the case of a transfer described in subparagraph (A) or (B), the amount transferred shall be treated as consisting first of the portion of such distribution that is includible in gross income (determined without regard to paragraph (1)).

> **(3) Transfer must be made within 60 days of receipt—**

> > **(A) In general**—Except as provided in subparagraph (B), paragraph (1) shall not apply to any transfer of a distribution made after the 60th day following the day on which the distributee received the property distributed.

> > **(B) Hardship exception**—The Secretary may waive the 60-day requirement under subparagraph (A) where the failure to waive such requirement would be against equity or good conscience, including casualty, disaster, or other events beyond the reasonable control of the individual subject to such requirement.

> **(4) Eligible rollover distribution**—For purposes of this subsection, the term "eligible rollover distribution" means any distribution to an employee of all or any portion of the balance to the credit of the employee in a qualified trust; except that such term shall not include—

> > **(A)** any distribution which is one of a series of substantially equal periodic payments (not less frequently than annually) made—

> > > **(i)** for the life (or life expectancy) of the employee or the joint lives (or joint life expectancies) of the employee and the employee's designated beneficiary, or

> > > **(ii)** for a specified period of 10 years or more,

> > **(B)** any distribution to the extent such distribution is required under section 401(a)(9), and

> > **(C)** any distribution which is made upon hardship of the employee.

If all or any portion of a distribution during 2009 is treated as an eligible rollover distribution but would not be so treated if the minimum distribution requirements under section 401(a)(9) had applied during 2009, such distribution shall not be treated as an eligible rollover distribution for purposes of section 401(a)(31) or 3405(c) or subsection (f) of this section.

> **(5) Transfer treated as rollover contribution under section 408**—For purposes of this title, a transfer to an eligible retirement plan described in clause (i) or (ii) of paragraph (8)(B) resulting in any portion of a distribution being excluded from gross income under paragraph (1) shall be treated as a rollover contribution described in section 408(d)(3).

> **(6) Sales of distributed property**—For purposes of this subsection—

(A) Transfer of proceeds from sale of distributed property treated as transfer of distributed property—The transfer of an amount equal to any portion of the proceeds from the sale of property received in the distribution shall be treated as the transfer of property received in the distribution.

(B) Proceeds attributable to increase in value—The excess of fair market value of property on sale over its fair market value on distribution shall be treated as property received in the distribution.

(C) Designation where amount of distribution exceeds rollover contribution—In any case where part or all of the distribution consists of property other than money—

 (i) the portion of the money or other property which is to be treated as attributable to amounts not included in gross income, and

 (ii) the portion of the money or other property which is to be treated as included in the rollover contribution,

shall be determined on a ratable basis unless the taxpayer designates otherwise. Any designation under this subparagraph for a taxable year shall be made not later than the time prescribed by law for filing the return for such taxable year (including extensions thereof). Any such designation, once made, shall be irrevocable.

(D) Nonrecognition of gain or loss—No gain or loss shall be recognized on any sale described in subparagraph (A) to the extent that an amount equal to the proceeds is transferred pursuant to paragraph (1).

(7) Special rule for frozen deposits—

 (A) In general—The 60-day period described in paragraph (3) shall not—

  (i) include any period during which the amount transferred to the employee is a frozen deposit, or

  (ii) end earlier than 10 days after such amount ceases to be a frozen deposit.

 (B) Frozen deposits—For purposes of this subparagraph, the term "frozen deposit" means any deposit which may not be withdrawn because of—

  (i) the bankruptcy or insolvency of any financial institution, or

  (ii) any requirement imposed by the State in which such institution is located by reason of the bankruptcy or insolvency (or threat thereof) of 1 or more financial institutions in such State.

A deposit shall not be treated as a frozen deposit unless on at least 1 day during the 60-day period described in paragraph (3) (without regard to this paragraph) such deposit is described in the preceding sentence.

(8) Definitions—For purposes of this subsection—

 (A) Qualified trust—The term "qualified trust" means an employees' trust described in section 401(a) which is exempt from tax under section 501(a).

 (B) Eligible retirement plan—The term "eligible retirement plan" means—

  (i) an individual retirement account described in section 408(a),

  (ii) an individual retirement annuity described in section 408(b) (other than an endowment contract),

(iii) a qualified trust,

(iv) an annuity plan described in section 403(a),

(v) an eligible deferred compensation plan described in section 457(b) which is maintained by an eligible employer described in section 457(e)(1)(A), and

(vi) an annuity contract described in section 403(b).

If any portion of an eligible rollover distribution is attributable to payments or distributions from a designated Roth account (as defined in section 402A), an eligible retirement plan with respect to such portion shall include only another designated Roth account and a Roth IRA.

(9) Rollover where spouse receives distribution after death of employee—If any distribution attributable to an employee is paid to the spouse of the employee after the employee's death, the preceding provisions of this subsection shall apply to such distribution in the same manner as if the spouse were the employee.

(10) Separate accounting—Unless a plan described in clause (v) of paragraph (8)(B) agrees to separately account for amounts rolled into such plan from eligible retirement plans not described in such clause, the plan described in such clause may not accept transfers or rollovers from such retirement plans.

(11) Distributions to inherited individual retirement plan of nonspouse beneficiary—

(A) In general—If, with respect to any portion of a distribution from an eligible retirement plan described in paragraph (8)(B)(iii) of a deceased employee, a direct trustee-to-trustee transfer is made to an individual retirement plan described in clause (i) or (ii) of paragraph (8)(B) established for the purposes of receiving the distribution on behalf of an individual who is a designated beneficiary (as defined by section 401(a)(9)(E)) of the employee and who is not the surviving spouse of the employee—

(i) the transfer shall be treated as an eligible rollover distribution,

(ii) the individual retirement plan shall be treated as an inherited individual retirement account or individual retirement annuity (within the meaning of section 408(d)(3)(C)) for purposes of this title, and

(iii) section 401(a)(9)(B) (other than clause (iv) thereof) shall apply to such plan.

(B) Certain trusts treated as beneficiaries—For purposes of this paragraph, to the extent provided in rules prescribed by the Secretary, a trust maintained for the benefit of one or more designated beneficiaries shall be treated in the same manner as a designated beneficiary.

(d) Taxability of beneficiary of certain foreign situs trusts—For purposes of subsections (a), (b), and (c), a stock bonus, pension, or profit-sharing trust which would qualify for exemption from tax under section 501(a) except for the fact that it is a trust created or organized outside the United States shall be treated as if it were a trust exempt from tax under section 501(a).

(e) Other rules applicable to exempt trusts—

(1) Alternate payees—

(A) Alternate payee treated as distributee—For purposes of subsection (a) and section 72, an alternate payee who is the spouse or former spouse of the participant shall be treated as the distributee of any distribution or payment made to the alternate payee under a qualified domestic relations order (as defined in section 414(p)).

(B) Rollovers—If any amount is paid or distributed to an alternate payee who is the spouse or former spouse of the participant by reason of any qualified domestic relations order (within the meaning of section 414(p)), subsection (c) shall apply to such distribution in the same manner as if such alternate payee were the employee.

(2) Distributions by united states to nonresident aliens—The amount includible under subsection (a) in the gross income of a nonresident alien with respect to a distribution made by the United States in respect of services performed by an employee of the United States shall not exceed an amount which bears the same ratio to the amount includible in gross income without regard to this paragraph as—

(A) the aggregate basic pay paid by the United States to such employee for such services, reduced by the amount of such basic pay which was not includible in gross income by reason of being from sources without the United States, bears to

(B) the aggregate basic pay paid by the United States to such employee for such services.

In the case of distributions under the civil service retirement laws, the term "basic pay" shall have the meaning provided in section 8331(3) of title 5, United States Code.

(3) Cash or deferred arrangements—For purposes of this title, contributions made by an employer on behalf of an employee to a trust which is a part of a qualified cash or deferred arrangement (as defined in section 401(k)(2)) or which is part of a salary reduction agreement under section 403(b) shall not be treated as distributed or made available to the employee nor as contributions made to the trust by the employee merely because the arrangement includes provisions under which the employee has an election whether the contribution will be made to the trust or received by the employee in cash.

(4) Net unrealized appreciation—

(A) Amounts attributable to employee contributions—For purposes of subsection (a) and section 72, in the case of a distribution other than a lump sum distribution, the amount actually distributed to any distributee from a trust described in subsection (a) shall not include any net unrealized appreciation in securities of the employer corporation attributable to amounts contributed by the employee (other than deductible employee contributions within the meaning of section 72(o)(5)). This subparagraph shall not apply to a distribution to which subsection (c) applies.

(B) Amounts attributable to employer contributions—For purposes of subsection (a) and section 72, in the case of any lump sum distribution which includes securities of the employer corporation, there shall be excluded from gross income the net unrealized appreciation attributable to that part of the distribution which consists of securities of the employer corporation. In accordance with rules prescribed by the Secretary, a taxpayer may elect, on the return of tax on which a lump sum distribution is required to be included, not to have this subparagraph apply to such distribution.

(C) Determination of amounts and adjustments—For purposes of subparagraphs (A) and (B), net unrealized appreciation and the resulting adjustments to basis shall be determined in accordance with regulations prescribed by the Secretary.

(D) Lump-sum distribution—For purposes of this paragraph—

(i) In general—The term "lump sum distribution" means the distribution or payment within one taxable year of the recipient of the balance to the credit of an employee which becomes payable to the recipient—

(I) on account of the employee's death,

(II) after the employee attains age 59½,

(III) on account of the employee's separation from service, or

(IV) after the employee has become disabled (within the meaning of section 72(m)(7)),

from a trust which forms a part of a plan described in section 401(a) and which is exempt from tax under section 501 or from a plan described in section 403(a). Subclause (III) of this clause shall be applied only with respect to an individual who is an employee without regard to section 401(c)(1), and subclause (IV) shall be applied only with respect to an employee within the meaning of section 401(c)(1). For purposes of this clause, a distribution to two or more trusts shall be treated as a distribution to one recipient. For purposes of this paragraph, the balance to the credit of the employee does not include the accumulated deductible employee contributions under the plan (within the meaning of section 72(o)(5)).

(ii) Aggregation of certain trusts and plans—For purposes of determining the balance to the credit of an employee under clause (i)—

(I) all trusts which are part of a plan shall be treated as a single trust, all pension plans maintained by the employer shall be treated as a single plan, all profit-sharing plans maintained by the employer shall be treated as a single plan, and all stock bonus plans maintained by the employer shall be treated as a single plan, and

(II) trusts which are not qualified trusts under section 401(a) and annuity contracts which do not satisfy the requirements of section 404(a)(2) shall not be taken into account.

(iii) Community property laws—The provisions of this paragraph shall be applied without regard to community property laws.

(iv) Amounts subject to penalty—This paragraph shall not apply to amounts described in subparagraph (A) of section 72(m)(5) to the extent that section 72(m)(5) applies to such amounts.

(v) Balance to credit of employee not to include amounts payable under qualified domestic relations order—For purposes of this paragraph, the balance to the credit of an employee shall not include any amount payable to an alternate payee under a qualified domestic relations order (within the meaning of section 414(p)).

(vi) Transfers to cost-of-living arrangement not treated as distribution—For purposes of this paragraph, the balance to the credit of an employee under a defined contribution plan shall not include any amount transferred from such defined contribution plan to a qualified cost-of-living arrangement (within the meaning of section 415(k)(2)) under a defined benefit plan.

(vii) Lump-sum distributions of alternate payees—If any distribution or payment of the balance to the credit of an employee would be treated as a lump-sum distribution, then, for purposes of this paragraph, the payment under a qualified domestic relations order (within the meaning of section 414(p)) of the balance to the credit of an alternate payee who is the spouse or former spouse of the employee shall be treated as a lump-sum distribution. For purposes of this clause, the balance to the credit of the alternate payee shall not include any amount payable to the employee.

(E) Definitions relating to securities—For purposes of this paragraph—

(i) Securities—The term "securities" means only shares of stock and bonds or debentures issued by a corporation with interest coupons or in registered form.

(ii) Securities of the employer—The term "securities of the employer corporation" includes securities of a parent or subsidiary corporation (as defined in subsections (e) and (f) of section 424) of the employer corporation.

(5) [Repealed]

(6) Direct trustee-to-trustee transfers—Any amount transferred in a direct trustee-to-trustee transfer in accordance with section 401(a)(31) shall not be includible in gross income for the taxable year of such transfer.

(f) Written explanation to recipients of distributions eligible for rollover treatment—

(1) In general—The plan administrator of any plan shall, within a reasonable period of time before making an eligible rollover distribution, provide a written explanation to the recipient—

(A) of the provisions under which the recipient may have the distribution directly transferred to an eligible retirement plan and that the automatic distribution by direct transfer applies to certain distributions in accordance with section 401(a)(31)(B),

(B) of the provision which requires the withholding of tax on the distribution if it is not directly transferred to an eligible retirement plan,

(C) of the provisions under which the distribution will not be subject to tax if transferred to an eligible retirement plan within 60 days after the date on which the recipient received the distribution,

(D) if applicable, of the provisions of subsections (d) and (e) of this section, and

(E) of the provisions under which distributions from the eligible retirement plan receiving the distribution may be subject to restrictions and tax consequences which are different from those applicable to distributions from the plan making such distribution.

(2) Definitions—For purposes of this subsection—

(A) Eligible rollover distribution—The term "eligible rollover distribution" has the same meaning as when used in subsection (c) of this section, paragraph (4) of section 403(a), subparagraph (A) of section 403(b)(8), or subparagraph (A) of section 457(e)(16). Such term shall include any distribution to a designated beneficiary which would be treated as an eligible rollover distribution by reason of subsection (c)(11), or section 403(a)(4)(B), 403(b)(8)(B), or 457(e)(16)(B), if the requirements of subsection (c)(11) were satisfied.

(B) Eligible retirement plan—The term "eligible retirement plan" has the meaning given such term by subsection (c)(8)(B).

(g) Limitation on exclusion for elective deferrals—

(1) In general—

(A) Limitation—Notwithstanding subsections (e)(3) and (h)(1)(B), the elective deferrals of any individual for any taxable year shall be included in such individual's gross income to the extent the amount of such deferrals for the taxable year exceeds the applicable dollar amount. The preceding sentence shall not apply the portion of such excess as does not exceed the designated Roth contributions of the individual for the taxable year.

(B) Applicable dollar amount—For purposes of subparagraph (A), the applicable dollar amount is $15,000.

(C) Catch-up contributions—In addition to subparagraph (A), in the case of an eligible participant (as defined in section 414(v)), gross income shall not include elective deferrals in excess of the applicable dollar amount under subparagraph (B) to the extent that the amount of such elective deferrals does not exceed the applicable dollar amount under section 414(v)(2)(B)(i) for the taxable year (without regard to the treatment of the elective deferrals by an applicable employer plan under section 414(v)).

(2) Distribution of excess deferrals—

(A) In general—If any amount (hereinafter in this paragraph referred to as "excess deferrals") is included in the gross income of an individual under paragraph (1) (or would be included but for the last sentence thereof) for any taxable year—

(i) not later than the 1st March 1 following the close of the taxable year, the individual may allocate the amount of such excess deferrals among the plans under which the deferrals were made and may notify each such plan of the portion allocated to it, and

(ii) not later than the 1st April 15 following the close of the taxable year, each such plan may distribute to the individual the amount allocated to it under clause (i) (and any income allocable to such amount through the end of such taxable year).

The distribution described in clause (ii) may be made notwithstanding any other provision of law.

(B) Treatment of distribution under section 401(k)—Except to the extent provided under rules prescribed by the Secretary, notwithstanding the distribution of any portion of an excess deferral from a plan under subparagraph (A)(ii), such portion shall, for purposes of applying section 401(k)(3)(A)(ii), be treated as an employer contribution.

(C) Taxation of distribution—In the case of a distribution to which subparagraph (A) applies—

(i) except as provided in clause (ii), such distribution shall not be included in gross income, and

(ii) any income on the excess deferral shall, for purposes of this chapter, be treated as earned and received in the taxable year in which such income is distributed.

No tax shall be imposed under section 72(t) on any distribution described in the preceding sentence.

(D) Partial distributions—If a plan distributes only a portion of any excess deferral and income allocable thereto, such portion shall be treated as having been distributed ratably from the excess deferral and the income.

(3) Elective deferrals—For purposes of this subsection, the term "elective deferrals" means, with respect to any taxable year, the sum of—

(A) any employer contribution under a qualified cash or deferred arrangement (as defined in section 401(k)) to the extent not includible in gross income for the taxable year under subsection (e)(3) (determined without regard to this subsection),

(B) any employer contribution to the extent not includible in gross income for the taxable year under subsection (h)(1)(B) (determined without regard to this subsection),

(C) any employer contribution to purchase an annuity contract under section 403(b) under a salary reduction agreement (within the meaning of section 3121(a)(5)(D)), and

(D) any elective employer contribution under section 408(p)(2)(A)(i).

An employer contribution shall not be treated as an elective deferral described in subparagraph (C) if under the salary reduction agreement such contribution is made pursuant to a one-time irrevocable election made by the employee at the time of initial eligibility to participate in the agreement or is made pursuant to a similar arrangement involving a one-time irrevocable election specified in regulations.

(4) Cost-of-living adjustment—In the case of taxable years beginning after December 31, 2006, the Secretary shall adjust the $15,000 amount under paragraph (1)(B) at the same time and in the same manner as under section 415(d), except that the base period shall be the calendar quarter beginning July 1, 2005, and any increase under this paragraph which is not a multiple of $500 shall be rounded to the next lowest multiple of $500.

(5) Disregard of community property laws—This subsection shall be applied without regard to community property laws.

(6) Coordination with section 72—For purposes of applying section 72, any amount includible in gross income for any taxable year under this subsection but which is not distributed from the plan during such taxable year shall not be treated as an investment in the contract.

(7) Special rule for certain organizations—

(A) In general—In the case of a qualified employee of a qualified organization, with respect to employer contributions described in paragraph (3)(C) made by such organization, the limitation of paragraph (1) for any taxable year shall be increased by whichever of the following is the least:

(i) $3,000,

(ii) $15,000 reduced by the sum of—

(I) the amounts not included in gross income for prior taxable years by reason of this paragraph, plus

      (II) the aggregate amount of designated Roth contributions (as defined in section 402A(c)) permitted for prior taxable years by reason of this paragraph, or

      (iii) the excess of $5,000 multiplied by the number of years of service of the employee with the qualified organization over the employer contributions described in paragraph (3) made by the organization on behalf of such employee for prior taxable years (determined in the manner prescribed by the Secretary).

    (B) Qualified organization—For purposes of this paragraph, the term "qualified organization" means any educational organization, hospital, home health service agency, health and welfare service agency, church, or convention or association of churches. Such term includes any organization described in section 414(e)(3)(B)(ii). Terms used in this subparagraph shall have the same meaning as when used in section 415(c)(4) (as in effect before the enactment of the Economic Growth and Tax Relief Reconciliation Act of 2001).

    (C) Qualified employee—For purposes of this paragraph, the term "qualified employee" means any employee who has completed 15 years of service with the qualified organization.

    (D) Years of service—For purposes of this paragraph, the term "years of service" has the meaning given such term by section 403(b).

  (8) Matching contributions on behalf of self-employed individuals not treated as elective employer contributions—Except as provided in section 401(k)(3)(D)(ii), any matching contribution described in section 401(m)(4)(A) which is made on behalf of a self-employed individual (as defined in section 401(c)) shall not be treated as an elective employer contribution under a qualified cash or deferred arrangement (as defined in section 401(k)) for purposes of this title.

(h) Special rules for simplified employee pensions—For purposes of this chapter—

  (1) In general—Except as provided in paragraph (2), contributions made by an employer on behalf of an employee to an individual retirement plan pursuant to a simplified employee pension (as defined in section 408(k))—

    (A) shall not be treated as distributed or made available to the employee or as contributions made by the employee, and

    (B) if such contributions are made pursuant to an arrangement under section 408(k)(6) under which an employee may elect to have the employer make contributions to the simplified employer pension on behalf of the employee, shall not be treated as distributed or made available or as contributions made by the employee merely because the simplified employee pension includes provisions for such election.

  (2) Limitations on employer contributions—Contributions made by an employer to a simplified employee pension with respect to an employee for any year shall be treated as distributed or made available to such employee and as contributions made by the employee to the extent such contributions exceed the lesser of—

    (A) 25 percent of the compensation (within the meaning of section 414(s)) from such employer includible in the employee's gross income for the year (determined without regard to the employer contributions to the simplified employee pension), or

(B) the limitation in effect under section 415(c)(1)(A), reduced in the case of any highly compensated employee (within the meaning of section 414(q)) by the amount taken into account with respect to such employee under section 408(k)(3)(D).

(3) Distributions—Any amount paid or distributed out of an individual retirement plan pursuant to a simplified employee pension shall be included in gross income by the payee or distributee, as the case may be, in accordance with the provisions of section 408(d).

(i) Treatment of self-employed individuals—For purposes of this section, except as otherwise provided in subparagraph (A) of subsection (d)(4), the term "employee" includes a self-employed individual (as defined in section 401(c)(1)(B)) and the employer of such individual shall be the person treated as his employer under section 401(c)(4).

(j) Effect of disposition of stock by plan on net unrealized appreciation—

(1) In general—For purposes of subsection (e)(4), in the case of any transaction to which this subsection applies, the determination of net unrealized appreciation shall be made without regard to such transaction.

(2) Transaction to which subsection applies—This subsection shall apply to any transaction in which—

(A) the plan trustee exchanges the plan's securities of the employer corporation for other such securities, or

(B) the plan trustee disposes of securities of the employer corporation and uses the proceeds of such disposition to acquire securities of the employer corporation within 90 days (or such longer period as the Secretary may prescribe), except that this subparagraph shall not apply to any employee with respect to whom a distribution of money was made during the period after such disposition and before such acquisition.

(k) Treatment of simple retirement accounts—Rules similar to the rules of paragraphs (1) and (3) of subsection (h) shall apply to contributions and distributions with respect to a simple retirement account under section 408(p).

(l) Distributions from governmental plans for health and long-term care insurance—

(1) In general—In the case of an employee who is an eligible retired public safety officer who makes the election described in paragraph (6) with respect to any taxable year of such employee, gross income of such employee for such taxable year does not include any distribution from an eligible retirement plan maintained by the employer described in paragraph (4)(B) to the extent that the aggregate amount of such distributions does not exceed the amount paid by such employee for qualified health insurance premiums for such taxable year.

(2) Limitation—The amount which may be excluded from gross income for the taxable year by reason of paragraph (1) shall not exceed $3,000.

(3) Distributions must otherwise be includible—

(A) In general—An amount shall be treated as a distribution for purposes of paragraph (1) only to the extent that such amount would be includible in gross income without regard to paragraph (1).

(B) Application of section 72—Notwithstanding section 72, in determining the extent to which an amount is treated as a distribution for purposes of subparagraph (A), the aggregate amounts distributed from an eligible retirement plan in a taxable year (up to the amount excluded under paragraph (1)) shall be treated as includible in gross income (without regard to subparagraph (A)) to the extent that such amount does not exceed the aggregate amount which would have been so includible if all amounts to the credit of the eligible public safety officer in all eligible retirement plans maintained by the employer described in paragraph (4)(B) were distributed during such taxable year and all such plans were treated as 1 contract for purposes of determining under section 72 the aggregate amount which would have been so includible. Proper adjustments shall be made in applying section 72 to other distributions in such taxable year and subsequent taxable years.

(4) Definitions—For purposes of this subsection—

(A) Eligible retirement plan—For purposes of paragraph (1), the term "eligible retirement plan" means a governmental plan (within the meaning of section 414(d)) which is described in clause (iii), (iv), (v), or (vi) of subsection (c)(8)(B).

(B) Eligible retired public safety officer—The term "eligible retired public safety officer" means an individual who, by reason of disability or attainment of normal retirement age, is separated from service as a public safety officer with the employer who maintains the eligible retirement plan from which distributions subject to paragraph (1) are made.

(C) Public safety officer— The term "public safety officer" shall have the same meaning given such term by section 1204(9)(A) of the Omnibus Crime Control and Safe Streets Act of 1968 (42 U.S.C. 3796b(9)(A)), as in effect immediately before the enactment of the National Defense Authorization Act for Fiscal Year 2013 [enacted Jan. 2, 2013].

(D) Qualified health insurance premiums—The term "qualified health insurance premiums" means premiums for coverage for the eligible retired public safety officer, his spouse, and dependents (as defined in section 152), by an accident or health plan or qualified long-term care insurance contract (as defined in section 7702B(b)).

(5) Special rules—For purposes of this subsection—

(A) Direct payment to insurer required—Paragraph (1) shall only apply to a distribution if payment of the premiums is made directly to the provider of the accident or health plan or qualified long-term care insurance contract by deduction from a distribution from the eligible retirement plan.

(B) Related plans treated as 1—All eligible retirement plans of an employer shall be treated as a single plan.

(6) Election described—

(A) In general—For purposes of paragraph (1), an election is described in this paragraph if the election is made by an employee after separation from service with respect to amounts not distributed from an eligible retirement plan to have amounts from such plan distributed in order to pay for qualified health insurance premiums.

(B) Special rule—A plan shall not be treated as violating the requirements of section 401, or as engaging in a prohibited transaction for purposes of section 503(b), merely because it provides for an election with respect to amounts that are otherwise distributable under the plan or merely because of a distribution made pursuant to an election described in subparagraph (A).

(7) Coordination with medical expense deduction—The amounts excluded from gross income under paragraph (1) shall not be taken into account under section 213.

(8) Coordination with deduction for health insurance costs of self-employed individuals—The amounts excluded from gross income under paragraph (1) shall not be taken into account under section 162(l).

§ 402A. Optional treatment of elective deferrals as Roth contributions.

(a) General rule—If an applicable retirement plan includes a qualified Roth contribution program—

(1) any designated Roth contribution made by an employee pursuant to the program shall be treated as an elective deferral for purposes of this chapter, except that such contribution shall not be excludable from gross income, and

(2) such plan (and any arrangement which is part of such plan) shall not be treated as failing to meet any requirement of this chapter solely by reason of including such program.

(b) Qualified Roth contribution program—For purposes of this section—

(1) In general—The term "qualified Roth contribution program" means a program under which an employee may elect to make designated Roth contributions in lieu of all or a portion of elective deferrals the employee is otherwise eligible to make under the applicable retirement plan.

(2) Separate accounting required—A program shall not be treated as a qualified Roth contribution program unless the applicable retirement plan—

(A) establishes separate accounts ("designated Roth account") for the designated Roth contributions of each employee and any earnings properly allocable to the contributions, and

(B) maintains separate recordkeeping with respect to each account.

(c) Definitions and rules relating to designated Roth contributions—For purposes of this section—

(1) Designated Roth contribution—The term "designated Roth contribution" means any elective deferral which—

(A) is excludable from gross income of an employee without regard to this section, and

(B) the employee designates (at such time and in such manner as the Secretary may prescribe) as not being so excludable.

(2) Designation limits—The amount of elective deferrals which an employee may designate under paragraph (1) shall not exceed the excess (if any) of—

(A) the maximum amount of elective deferrals excludable from gross income of the employee for the taxable year (without regard to this section), over

(B) the aggregate amount of elective deferrals of the employee for the taxable year which the employee does not designate under paragraph (1).

(3) Rollover contributions—

(A) In general—A rollover contribution of any payment or distribution from a designated Roth account which is otherwise allowable under this chapter may be made only if the contribution is to—

> **(i)** another designated Roth account of the individual from whose account the payment or distribution was made, or

> **(ii)** a Roth IRA of such individual.

(B) Coordination with limit—Any rollover contribution to a designated Roth account under subparagraph (A) shall not be taken into account for purposes of paragraph (1).

(4) Taxable rollovers to designated Roth accounts.

(A) In general. Notwithstanding sections 402(c), 403(b)(8), and 457(e)(16), in the case of any distribution to which this paragraph applies—

> **(i)** there shall be included in gross income any amount which would be includible were it not part of a qualified rollover contribution,

> **(ii)** section 72(t) shall not apply, and

> **(iii)** unless the taxpayer elects not to have this clause apply, any amount required to be included in gross income for any taxable year beginning in 2010 by reason of this paragraph shall be so included ratably over the 2-taxable-year period beginning with the first taxable year beginning in 2011.

Any election under clause (iii) for any distributions during a taxable year may not be changed after the due date for such taxable year.

(B) Distributions to which paragraph applies. In the case of an applicable retirement plan which includes a qualified Roth contribution program, this paragraph shall apply to a distribution from such plan other than from a designated Roth account which is contributed in a qualified rollover contribution (within the meaning of section 408A(e)) to the designated Roth account maintained under such plan for the benefit of the individual to whom the distribution is made.

(C) Coordination with limit. Any distribution to which this paragraph applies shall not be taken into account for purposes of paragraph (1).

(D) Other rules. The rules of subparagraphs (D), (E), and (F) of section 408A(d)(3) (as in effect for taxable years beginning after 2009) shall apply for purposes of this paragraph.

(E) Special rule for certain transfers. In the case of an applicable retirement plan which includes a qualified Roth contribution program—

> **(i)** the plan may allow an individual to elect to have the plan transfer any amount not otherwise distributable under the plan to a designated Roth account maintained for the benefit of the individual,

> **(ii)** such transfer shall be treated as a distribution to which this paragraph applies which was contributed in a qualified rollover contribution (within the meaning of section 408A(e)) to such account, and

(iii) the plan shall not be treated as violating the provisions of section 401(k)(2)(B)(i), 403(b)(7)(A)(ii), 403(b)(11), or 457(d)(1)(A), or of section 8433 of title 5, United States Code, solely by reason of such transfer.

(d) Distribution rules—For purposes of this title—

(1) Exclusion—Any qualified distribution from a designated Roth account shall not be includible in gross income.

(2) Qualified distribution—For purposes of this subsection—

(A) In general—The term "qualified distribution" has the meaning given such term by section 408A(d)(2)(A) (without regard to clause (iv) thereof).

(B) Distributions within nonexclusion period—A payment or distribution from a designated Roth account shall not be treated as a qualified distribution if such payment or distribution is made within the 5-taxable-year period beginning with the earlier of—

(i) the first taxable year for which the individual made a designated Roth contribution to any designated Roth account established for such individual under the same applicable retirement plan, or

(ii) if a rollover contribution was made to such designated Roth account from a designated Roth account previously established for such individual under another applicable retirement plan, the first taxable year for which the individual made a designated Roth contribution to such previously established account.

(C) Distributions of excess deferrals and contributions and earnings thereon—The term "qualified distribution" shall not include any distribution of any excess deferral under section 402(g)(2) or any excess contribution under section 401(k)(8), and any income on the excess deferral or contribution.

(3) Treatment of distributions of certain excess deferrals—Notwithstanding section 72, if any excess deferral under section 402(g)(2) attributable to a designated Roth contribution is not distributed on or before the 1st April 15 following the close of the taxable year in which such excess deferral is made, the amount of such excess deferral shall—

(A) not be treated as investment in the contract, and

(B) be included in gross income for the taxable year in which such excess is distributed.

(4) Aggregation rules—Section 72 shall be applied separately with respect to distributions and payments from a designated Roth account and other distributions and payments from the plan.

(e) Other definitions—For purposes of this section—

(1) Applicable retirement plan—The term "applicable retirement plan" means—

(A) an employees' trust described in section 401(a) which is exempt from tax under section 501(a),

(B) a plan under which amounts are contributed by an individual's employer for an annuity contract described in section 403(b), and

(C) an eligible deferred compensation plan (as defined in section 457(b) of an eligible employer described in section 457(e)(1)(A).

(2) Elective deferral—The term "elective deferral" means—

(A) any elective deferral described in subparagraph (A) or (C) of section 402(g)(3), and

(B) any elective deferral of compensation by an individual under an eligible deferred compensation plan (as defined in section 457(b)) of an eligible employer described in section 457(e)(1)(A).

§ 403. Taxation of employee annuities.

(a) Taxability of beneficiary under a qualified annuity plan—

(1) Distributee taxable under section 72—If an annuity contract is purchased by an employer for an employee under a plan which meets the requirements of section 404(a)(2) (whether or not the employer deducts the amounts paid for the contract under such section), the amount actually distributed to any distributee under the contract shall be taxable to the distributee (in the year in which so distributed) under section 72 (relating to annuities).

(2) Special rule for health and long-term care insurance—To the extent provided in section 402(l), paragraph (1) shall not apply to the amount distributed under the contract which is otherwise includible in gross income under this subsection.

(3) Self-employed individuals—For purposes of this subsection, the term "employee" includes an individual who is an employee within the meaning of section 401(c)(1), and the employer of such individual is the person treated as his employer under section 401(c)(4).

(4) Rollover amounts—

(A) General rule—If—

(i) any portion of the balance to the credit of an employee in an employee annuity described in paragraph (1) is paid to him in an eligible rollover distribution (within the meaning of section 402(c)(4)),

(ii) the employee transfers any portion of the property he receives in such distribution to an eligible retirement plan, and

(iii) in the case of a distribution of property other than money, the amount so transferred consists of the property distributed,

then such distribution (to the extent so transferred) shall not be includible in gross income for the taxable year in which paid.

(B) Certain rules made applicable— The rules of paragraphs (2) through (7) and (11) and (9) of section 402(c) and section 402(f) shall apply for purposes of subparagraph (A).

(5) Direct trustee-to-trustee transfer—Any amount transferred in a direct trustee-to-trustee transfer in accordance with section 401(a)(31) shall not be includible in gross income for the taxable year of such transfer.

(b) Taxability of beneficiary under annuity purchased by section 501(c)(3) organization or public school—

(1) General rule—If—

(A) an annuity contract is purchased—

(i) for an employee by an employer described in section 501(c)(3) which is exempt from tax under section 501(a),

(ii) for an employee (other than an employee described in clause (i)), who performs services for an educational organization described in section 170(b)(1)(A)(ii), by an employer which is a State, a political subdivision of a State, or an agency or instrumentality of any one or more of the foregoing, or

(iii) for the minister described in section 414(e)(5)(A) by the minister or by an employer,

(B) such annuity contract is not subject to subsection (a),

(C) the employee's rights under the contract are nonforfeitable, except for failure to pay future premiums,

(D) except in the case of a contract purchased by a church, such contract is purchased under a plan which meets the nondiscrimination requirements of paragraph 12, and

(E) in the case of a contract purchased under a salary reduction agreement, the contract meets the requirements of section 401(a)(30),

then contributions and other additions by such employer for such annuity contract shall be excluded from the gross income of the employee for the taxable year to the extent that the aggregate of such contributions and additions (when expressed as an annual addition (within the meaning of section 415(c)(2))) does not exceed the applicable limit under section 415. The amount actually distributed to any distributee under such contract shall be taxable to the distributee (in the year in which so distributed) under section 72 (relating to annuities). For purposes of applying the rules of this subsection to contributions and other additions by an employer for a taxable year, amounts transferred to a contract described in this paragraph by reason of a rollover contribution described in paragraph (8) of this subsection or section 408(d)(3)(A)(ii) shall not be considered contributed by such employer.

(2) Special rule for health and long-term care insurance—To the extent provided in section 402(l), paragraph (1) shall not apply to the amount distributed under the contract which is otherwise includible in gross income under this subsection.

(3) Includible compensation—For purposes of this subsection, the term "includible compensation" means, in the case of any employee, the amount of compensation which is received from the employer described in paragraph (1)(A), and which is includible in gross income (computed without regard to section 911) for the most recent period (ending not later than the close of the taxable year) which under paragraph (4) may be counted as one year of service, and which precedes the taxable year by no more than five years. Such term does not include any amount contributed by the employer for any annuity contract to which this subsection applies. Such term includes—

(A) any elective deferral (as defined in section 402(g)(3)), and

(B) any amount which is contributed or deferred by the employer at the election of the employee and which is not includible in the gross income of the employee by reason of section 125, 132(f)(4), or 457.

(4) Years of service—In determining the number of years of service for purposes of this subsection, there shall be included—

(A) one year for each full year during which the individual was a full-time employee of the organization purchasing the annuity for him, and

(B) a fraction of a year (determined in accordance with regulations prescribed by the Secretary) for each full year during which such individual was a part-time employee of such organization and for each part of a year during which such individual was a full-time or part-time employee of such organization.

In no case shall the number of years of service be less than one.

(5) Application to more than one annuity contract—If for any taxable year of the employee this subsection applies to 2 or more annuity contracts purchased by the employer, such contracts shall be treated as one contract.

(6) [Repealed]

(7) Custodial accounts for regulated investment company stock—

(A) Amounts paid treated as contributions—For purposes of this title, amounts paid by an employer described in paragraph (1)(A) to a custodial account which satisfies the requirements of section 401(f)(2) shall be treated as amounts contributed by him for an annuity contract for his employee if—

(i) the amounts are to be invested in regulated investment company stock to be held in that custodial account, and

(ii) under the custodial account no such amounts may be paid or made available to any distributee (unless such amount is a distribution to which section 72(t)(2)(G) applies) before the employee dies, attains age 59½, has a severance from employment, becomes disabled (within the meaning of section 72(m)(7)), or in the case of contributions made pursuant to a salary reduction agreement (within the meaning of section 3121(a)(5)(D)), encounters financial hardship.

(B) Account treated as plan—For purposes of this title, a custodial account which satisfies the requirements of section 401(f)(2) shall be treated as an organization described in section 401(a) solely for purposes of subchapter F and subtitle F with respect to amounts received by it (and income from investment thereof).

(C) Regulated investment company—For purposes of this paragraph, the term "regulated investment company" means a domestic corporation which is a regulated investment company within the meaning of section 851(a).

(8) Rollover amounts—

(A) General rule—If—

(i) any portion of the balance to the credit of an employee in an annuity contract described in paragraph (1) is paid to him in an eligible rollover distribution (within the meaning of section 402(c)(4)),

(ii) the employee transfers any portion of the property he receives in such distribution to an eligible retirement plan described in section 402(c)(8)(B), and

(iii) in the case of a distribution of property other than money, the property so transferred consists of the property distributed,

then such distribution (to the extent so transferred) shall not be includible in gross income for the taxable year in which paid.

(B) Certain rules made applicable—The rules of paragraphs (2) through (7), (9), and (11) of section 402(c) and section 402(f) shall apply for purposes of subparagraph (A), except that section 402(f) shall be applied to the payor in lieu of the plan administrator.

(9) Retirement income accounts provided by churches, etc—

(A) Amounts paid treated as contributions—For purposes of this title—

(i) a retirement income account shall be treated as an annuity contract described in this subsection, and

(ii) amounts paid by an employer described in paragraph (1)(A) to a retirement income account shall be treated as amounts contributed by the employer for an annuity contract for the employee on whose behalf such account is maintained.

(B) Retirement income account—For purposes of this paragraph, the term "retirement income account" means a defined contribution program established or maintained by a church, or a convention or association of churches, including an organization described in section 414(e)(3)(A), to provide benefits under section 403(b) for an employee described in paragraph (1) or his beneficiaries.

(10) Distribution requirements—Under regulations prescribed by the Secretary, this subsection shall not apply to any annuity contract (or to any custodial account described in paragraph (7) or retirement income account described in paragraph (9)) unless requirements similar to the requirements of sections 401(a)(9) and 401(a)(31) are met (and requirements similar to the incidental death benefit requirements of section 401(a) are met) with respect to such annuity contract (or custodial account or retirement income account). Any amount transferred in a direct trustee-to-trustee transfer in accordance with section 401(a)(31) shall not be includible in gross income for the taxable year of the transfer.

(11) Requirement that distributions not begin before age 59½, severance from employment, death, or disability—This subsection shall not apply to any annuity contract unless under such contract distributions attributable to contributions made pursuant to a salary reduction agreement (within the meaning of section 402(g)(3)(C)) may be paid only—

(A) when the employee attains age 59½, has a severance from employment, dies, or becomes disabled (within the meaning of section 72(m)(7)), or

(B) in the case of hardship, or

(C) for distributions to which section 72(t)(2)(G) applies.

Such contract may not provide for the distribution of any income attributable to such contributions in the case of hardship.

(12) Nondiscrimination requirements—

(A) In general—For purposes of paragraph (1)(D), a plan meets the nondiscrimination requirements of this paragraph if—

(i) with respect to contributions not made pursuant to a salary reduction agreement, such plan meets the requirements of paragraphs (4), (5), (17), and (26) of section 401(a), section 401(m), and section 410(b) in the same manner as if such plan were described in section 401(a), and

(ii) all employees of the organization may elect to have the employer make contributions of more than $200 pursuant to a salary reduction agreement if any employee of the organization may elect to have the organization make contributions for such contracts pursuant to such agreement.

For purposes of clause (i), a contribution shall be treated as not made pursuant to a salary reduction agreement if under the agreement it is made pursuant to a 1-time irrevocable election made by the employee at the time of initial eligibility to participate in the agreement or is made pursuant to a similar arrangement involving a one-time irrevocable election specified in regulations. For purposes of clause (ii), there may be excluded any employee who is a participant in an eligible deferred compensation plan (within the meaning of section 457) or a qualified cash or deferred arrangement of the organization or another annuity contract described in this subsection. Any nonresident alien described in section 410(b)(3)(C) may also be excluded. Subject to the conditions applicable under section 410(b)(4), there may be excluded for purposes of this subparagraph employees who are students performing services described in section 3121(b)(10) and employees who normally work less than 20 hours per week.

(B) Church—For purposes of paragraph (1)(D), the term "church" has the meaning given to such term by section 3121(w)(3)(A). Such term shall include any qualified church-controlled organization (as defined in section 3121(w)(3)(B)).

(C) State and local governmental plans—For purposes of paragraph (1)(D), the requirements of subparagraph (A)(i) (other than those relating to section 401(a)(17)) shall not apply to a governmental plan (within the meaning of section 414(d)) maintained by a State or local government or political subdivision thereof (or agency or instrumentality thereof).

(13) Trustee-to-trustee transfers to purchase permissive service credit—No amount shall be includible in gross income by reason of a direct trustee-to-trustee transfer to a defined benefit governmental plan (as defined in section 414(d)) if such transfer is—

(A) for the purchase of permissive service credit (as defined in section 415(n)(3)(A)) under such plan, or

(B) a repayment to which section 415 does not apply by reason of subsection (k)(3) thereof.

(14) Death benefits under USERRA-qualified active military service—This subsection shall not apply to an annuity contract unless such contract meets the requirements of section 401(a)(37).

(c) Taxability of beneficiary under nonqualified annuities or under annuities purchased by exempt organizations—Premiums paid by an employer for an annuity contract which is not subject to subsection (a) shall be included in the gross income of the employee in accordance with section 83 (relating to property transferred in connection with performance of services), except that the value of such contract shall be substituted for the fair market value of the property for purposes of applying such section. The preceding sentence shall not apply to that portion of the premiums paid which is excluded from gross income under subsection (b). In the case of any portion of any contract which is attributable to premiums to which this subsection applies, the amount actually paid or made available under such contract to any beneficiary which is attributable to such premiums shall be taxable to the beneficiary (in the year in which so paid or made available) under section 72 (relating to annuities).

§ 404. Deduction for contributions of an employer to an employees' trust or annuity plan and compensation under a deferred-payment plan.

(a) **General rule**—If contributions are paid by an employer to or under a stock bonus, pension, profit-sharing, or annuity plan, or if compensation is paid or accrued on account of any employee under a plan deferring the receipt of such compensation, such contributions or compensation shall not be deductible under this chapter; but if they would otherwise be deductible, they shall be deductible under this section, subject, however, to the following limitations as to the amounts deductible in any year:

(1) **Pension trusts**—

(A) **In general**—In the taxable year when paid, if the contributions are paid into a pension trust (other than a trust to which paragraph (3) applies), and if such taxable year ends within or with a taxable year of the trust for which the trust is exempt under section 501(a), in the case of a defined benefit plan other than a multiemployer plan, in an amount determined under subsection (o), and in the case of any other plan in an amount determined as follows:

(i) the amount necessary to satisfy the minimum funding standard provided by section 412(a) for plan years ending within or with such taxable year (or for any prior plan year), if such amount is greater than the amount determined under clause (ii) or (iii) (whichever is applicable with respect to the plan),

(ii) the amount necessary to provide with respect to all of the employees under the trust the remaining unfunded cost of their past and current service credits distributed as a level amount, or a level percentage of compensation, over the remaining future service of each such employee, as determined under regulations prescribed by the Secretary, but if such remaining unfunded cost with respect to any 3 individuals is more than 50 percent of such remaining unfunded cost, the amount of such unfunded cost attributable to such individuals shall be distributed over a period of at least 5 taxable years,

(iii) an amount equal to the normal cost of the plan, as determined under regulations prescribed by the Secretary, plus, if past service or other supplementary pension or annuity credits are provided by the plan, an amount necessary to amortize the unfunded costs attributable to such credits in equal annual payments (until fully amortized) over 10 years, as determined under regulations prescribed by the Secretary.

In determining the amount deductible in such year under the foregoing limitations the funding method and the actuarial assumptions used shall be those used for such year under section 431, and the maximum amount deductible for such year shall be an amount equal to the full funding limitation for such year determined under section 431.

(B) **Special rule in case of certain amendments**—In the case of a multiemployer plan which the Secretary of Labor finds to be collectively bargained which makes an election under this subparagraph (in such manner and at such time as may be provided under regulations prescribed by the Secretary), if the full funding limitation determined under section 431(c)(6) for such year is zero, if as a result of any plan amendment applying to such plan year, the amount determined under section 431(c)(6)(A)(ii) exceeds the amount determined under section 431(c)(6)(A)(i), and if the funding method and the actuarial assumptions used are those used for such year under section 431, the maximum amount deductible in such year under the limitations of this paragraph shall be an amount equal to the lesser of—

(i) the full funding limitation for such year determined by applying section 431(c)(6) but increasing the amount referred to in subparagraph (A) thereof by the decrease in the present value of all unamortized liabilities resulting from such amendment, or

(ii) the normal cost under the plan reduced by the amount necessary to amortize in equal annual installments over 10 years (until fully amortized) the decrease described in clause (i).

In the case of any election under this subparagraph, the amount deductible under the limitations of this paragraph with respect to any of the plan years following the plan year for which such election was made shall be determined as provided under such regulations as may be prescribed by the Secretary to carry out the purposes of this subparagraph.

(C) Certain collectively-bargained plans—In the case of a plan which the Secretary of Labor finds to be collectively bargained, established or maintained by an employer doing business in not less than 40 States and engaged in the trade or business of furnishing or selling services described in section 168(i)(10)(C), with respect to which the rates have been established or approved by a State or political subdivision thereof, by any agency or instrumentality of the United States, or by a public service or public utility commission or other similar body of any State or political subdivision thereof, and in the case of any employer which is a member of a controlled group with such employer, subparagraph (B) shall be applied by substituting for the words "plan amendment" the words "plan amendment or increase in benefits payable under title II of the Social Security Act". For purposes of this subparagraph, the term "controlled group" has the meaning provided by section 1563(a), determined without regard to section 1563(a)(4) and (e)(3)(C).

(D) Amount determined on basis of unfunded current liability—In the case of a defined benefit plan which is a multiemployer plan, except as provided in regulations, the maximum amount deductible under the limitations of this paragraph shall not be less than the excess (if any) of—

(i) 140 percent of the current liability of the plan determined under section 431(c)(6)(D), over

(ii) the value of the plan's assets determined under section 431(c)(2).

(E) Carryover—Any amount paid in a taxable year in excess of the amount deductible in such year under the foregoing limitations shall be deductible in the succeeding taxable years in order of time to the extent of the difference between the amount paid and deductible in each such succeeding year and the maximum amount deductible for such year under the foregoing limitations.

(2) Employees' annuities—In the taxable year when paid, in an amount determined in accordance with paragraph (1), if the contributions are paid toward the purchase of retirement annuities, or retirement annuities and medical benefits as described in section 401(h), and such purchase is a part of a plan which meets the requirements of section 401(a)(3), (4), (5),(6), (7), (8), (9), (11), (12), (13), (14), (15), (16), (17), (19), (20), (22), (26), (27), (31), and (37) and, if applicable, the requirements of section 401(a)(10) and of section 401(d), and if refunds of premiums, if any, are applied within the current taxable year or next succeeding taxable year towards the purchase of such retirement annuities, or such retirement annuities and medical benefits.

(3) Stock bonus and profit-sharing trusts—

(A) Limits on deductible contributions—

(i) In general—In the taxable year when paid, if the contributions are paid into a stock bonus or profit-sharing trust, and if such taxable year ends within or with a taxable year of the trust with respect to which the trust is exempt under section 501(a), in an amount not in excess of the greater of—

(I) 25 percent of the compensation otherwise paid or accrued during the taxable year to the beneficiaries under the stock bonus or profit-sharing plan, or

(II) the amount such employer is required to contribute to such trust under section 401(k)(11) for such year.

(ii) Carryover of excess contributions—Any amount paid into the trust in any taxable year in excess of the limitation of clause (i) (or the corresponding provision of prior law) shall be deductible in the succeeding taxable years in order of time, but the amount so deductible under this clause in any 1 such succeeding taxable year together with the amount allowable under clause (i) shall not exceed the amount described in subclause (I) or (II) of clause (i), whichever is greater, with respect to such taxable year.

(iii) Certain retirement plans excluded—For purposes of this subparagraph, the term "stock bonus or profit-sharing trust" shall not include any trust designed to provide benefits upon retirement and covering a period of years, if under the plan the amounts to be contributed by the employer can be determined actuarially as provided in paragraph (1).

(iv) 2 or more trusts treated as 1 trust—If the contributions are made to 2 or more stock bonus or profit-sharing trusts, such trusts shall be considered a single trust for purposes of applying the limitations in this subparagraph.

(v) Defined contribution plans subject to the funding standards—Except as provided by the Secretary, a defined contribution plan which is subject to the funding standards of section 412 shall be treated in the same manner as a stock bonus or profit-sharing plan for purposes of this subparagraph.

(B) Profit-sharing plan of affiliated group—In the case of a profit-sharing plan, or a stock bonus plan in which contributions are determined with reference to profits, of a group of corporations which is an affiliated group within the meaning of section 1504, if any member of such affiliated group is prevented from making a contribution which it would otherwise have made under the plan, by reason of having no current or accumulated earnings or profits or because such earnings or profits are less than the contributions which it would otherwise have made, then so much of the contribution which such member was so prevented from making may be made, for the benefit of the employees of such member, by the other members of the group, to the extent of current or accumulated earnings or profits, except that such contribution by each such other member shall be limited, where the group does not file a consolidated return, to that proportion of its total current and accumulated earnings or profits remaining after adjustment for its contribution deductible without regard to this subparagraph which the total prevented contribution bears to the total current and accumulated earnings or profits of all the members of the group remaining after adjustment for all contributions deductible without regard to this subparagraph. Contributions made under the preceding sentence shall be deductible under subparagraph (A) of this paragraph by the employer making such contribution, and, for the purpose of determining amounts which may be carried forward and deducted under the second sentence of subparagraph (A) of this paragraph in succeeding taxable years, shall be deemed to have been made by the employer on behalf of whose employees such contributions were made.

(4) Trusts created or organized outside the united states—If a stock bonus, pension, or profit-sharing trust would qualify for exemption under section 501 (a) except for the fact that it is a trust created or organized outside the United States, contributions to such a trust by an employer which is a resident, or corporation, or other entity of the United States, shall be deductible under the preceding paragraphs.

(5) Other plans—If the plan is not one included in paragraph (1), (2), or (3), in the taxable year in which an amount attributable to the contribution is includible in the gross income of employees participating in the plan, but, in the case of a plan in which more than one employee participates only if separate accounts are maintained for each employee. For purposes of this section, any vacation pay which is treated as deferred compensation shall be deductible for the taxable year of the employer in which paid to the employee.

(6) Time when contributions deemed made—For purposes of paragraphs (1), (2), and (3), a taxpayer shall be deemed to have made a payment on the last day of the preceding taxable year if the payment is on account of such taxable year and is made not later than the time prescribed by law for filing the return for such taxable year (including extensions thereof).

(7) Limitation on deductions where combination of defined contribution plan and defined benefit plan—

(A) In general—If amounts are deductible under the foregoing paragraphs of this subsection (other than paragraph (5)) in connection with 1 or more defined contribution plans and 1 or more defined benefit plans or in connection with trusts or plans described in 2 or more of such paragraphs, the total amount deductible in a taxable year under such plans shall not exceed the greater of—

(i) 25 percent of the compensation otherwise paid or accrued during the taxable year to the beneficiaries under such plans, or

(ii) the amount of contributions made to or under the defined benefit plans to the extent such contributions do not exceed the amount of employer contributions necessary to satisfy the minimum funding standard provided by section 412 with respect to any such defined benefit plans for the plan year which ends with or within such taxable year (or for any prior plan year).

A defined contribution plan which is a pension plan shall not be treated as failing to provide definitely determinable benefits merely by limited employer contributions to amounts deductible under this section. In the case of a defined benefit plan which is a single employer plan, the amount necessary to satisfy the minimum funding standard provided by section 412 shall not be less than the excess (if any) of the plan's funding target (as defined in section 430(d)(1)) over the value of the plan's assets (as determined under section 430(g)(3)).

(B) Carryover of contributions in excess of the deductible limit—Any amount paid under the plans in any taxable year in excess of the limitation of subparagraph (A) shall be deductible in the succeeding taxable years in order of time, but the amount so deductible under this subparagraph in any 1 such succeeding taxable year together with the amount allowable under subparagraph (A) shall not exceed 25 percent of the compensation otherwise paid or accrued during such taxable year to the beneficiaries under the plans.

(C) Paragraph not to apply in certain cases—

(i) Beneficiary test—This paragraph shall not have the effect of reducing the amount otherwise deductible under paragraphs (1), (2), and (3), if no employee is a beneficiary under more than 1 trust or under a trust and an annuity plan.

(ii) Elective deferrals—If, in connection with 1 or more defined contribution plans and 1 or more defined benefit plans, no amounts (other than elective deferrals (as defined in section 402(g)(3))) are contributed to any of the defined contribution plans for the taxable year, then subparagraph (A) shall not apply with respect to any of such defined contribution plans and defined benefit plans.

(iii) Limitation—In the case of employer contributions to 1 or more defined contribution plans—

(I) if such contributions do not exceed 6 percent of the compensation otherwise paid or accrued during the taxable year to the beneficiaries under such plans, this paragraph shall not apply to such contributions or to employer contributions to the defined benefit plans to which this paragraph would otherwise apply by reason of contributions to the defined contribution plans, and

(II) if such contributions exceed 6 percent of such compensation, this paragraph shall be applied by only taking into account such contributions to the extent of such excess.

For purposes of this clause, amounts carried over from preceding taxable years under subparagraph (B) shall be treated as employer contributions to 1 or more defined contributions plans to the extent attributable to employer contributions to such plans in such preceding taxable years.

(iv) Guaranteed plans—In applying this paragraph, any single-employer plan covered under section 4021 of the Employee Retirement Income Security Act of 1974 shall not be taken into account.

(v) Multiemployer plans—In applying this paragraph, any multiemployer plan shall not be taken into account.

(D) Insurance contract plans—For purposes of this paragraph, a plan described in section 412(e)(3) shall be treated as a defined benefit plan.

(8) Self-employed individuals—In the case of a plan included in paragraph (1), (2), or (3) which provides contributions or benefits for employees some or all of whom are employees within the meaning of section 401(c)(1), for purposes of this section—

(A) the term "employee" includes an individual who is an employee within the meaning of section 401(c)(1), and the employer of such individual is the person treated as his employer under section 401(c)(4);

(B) the term "earned income" has the meaning assigned to it by section 401(c)(2);

(C) the contributions to such plan on behalf of an individual who is an employee within the meaning of section 401(c)(1) shall be considered to satisfy the conditions of section 162 or 212 to the extent that such contributions do not exceed the earned income of such individual (determined without regard to the deductions allowed by this section) derived from the trade or business with respect to which such plan is established, and to the extent that such contributions are not allocable (determined in accordance with regulations prescribed by the Secretary) to the purchase of life, accident, health, or other insurance; and

(D) any reference to compensation shall, in the case of an individual who is an employee within the meaning of section 401(c)(1), be considered to be a reference to the earned income of such individual derived from the trade or business with respect to which the plan is established.

(9) Certain contributions to employee stock ownership plans—

(A) Principal payments—Notwithstanding the provisions of paragraphs (3) and (7), if contributions are paid into a trust which forms a part of an employee stock ownership plan (as described in section 4975(e)(7)), and such contributions are, on or before the time prescribed in paragraph (6), applied by the plan to the repayment of the principal of a loan incurred for the purpose of acquiring qualifying employer securities (as described in section 4975(e)(8)), such contributions shall be deductible under this paragraph for the taxable year determined under paragraph (6). The amount deductible under this paragraph shall not, however, exceed 25 percent of the compensation otherwise paid or accrued during the taxable year to the employees under such employee stock ownership plan. Any amount paid into such trust in any taxable year in excess of the amount deductible under this paragraph shall be deductible in the succeeding taxable years in order of time to the extent of the difference between the amount paid and deductible in each such succeeding year and the maximum amount deductible for such year under the preceding sentence.

(B) Interest payment—Notwithstanding the provisions of paragraphs (3) and (7), if contributions are made to an employee stock ownership plan (described in subparagraph (A)) and such contributions are applied by the plan to the repayment of interest on a loan incurred for the purpose of acquiring qualifying employer securities (as described in subparagraph (A)), such contributions shall be deductible for the taxable year with respect to which such contributions are made as determined under paragraph (6).

(C) S corporations—This paragraph shall not apply to an S corporation.

(D) Qualified gratuitous transfers—A qualified gratuitous transfer (as defined in section 664(g)(1)) shall have no effect on the amount or amounts otherwise deductible under paragraph (3) or (7) or under this paragraph.

(10) Contributions by certain ministers to retirement income accounts—In the case of contributions made by a minister described in section 414(e)(5) to a retirement income account described in section 403(b)(9) and not by a person other than such minister, such contributions—

(A) shall be treated as made to a trust which is exempt from tax under section 501(a) and which is part of a plan which is described in section 401(a), and

(B) shall be deductible under this subsection to the extent such contributions do not exceed the limit on elective deferrals under section 402(g) or the limit on annual additions under section 415.

For purposes of this paragraph, all plans in which the minister is a participant shall be treated as one plan.

(11) Determinations relating to deferred compensation—For purposes of determining under this section—

    (A) whether compensation of an employee is deferred compensation; and

    (B) when deferred compensation is paid,

no amount shall be treated as received by the employee, or paid, until it is actually received by the employee.

(12) Definition of compensation—For purposes of paragraphs (3), (7), (8), and (9) and subsection (h)(1)(C), the term "compensation" shall include amounts treated as "participant's compensation" under subparagraph (C) or (D) of section 415(c)(3).

(b) Method of contributions, etc., having the effect of a plan; certain deferred benefits—

    (1) Method of contributions, etc., having the effect of a plan—If—

        (A) there is no plan, but

        (B) there is a method or arrangement of employer contributions or compensation which has the effect of a stock bonus, pension, profit-sharing, or annuity plan, or other plan deferring the receipt of compensation (including a plan described in paragraph (2)),

subsection (a) shall apply as if there were such a plan.

    (2) Plans providing certain deferred benefits—

        (A) In general—For purposes of this section, any plan providing for deferred benefits (other than compensation) for employees, their spouses, or their dependents shall be treated as a plan deferring the receipt of compensation. In the case of such a plan, for purposes of this section, the determination of when an amount is includible in gross income shall be made without regard to any provisions of this chapter excluding such benefits from gross income.

        (B) Exception—Subparagraph (A) shall not apply to any benefit provided through a welfare benefit fund (as defined in section 419(e)).

(c) Certain negotiated plans—If contributions are paid by an employer—

    (1) under a plan under which such contributions are held in trust for the purpose of paying (either from principal or income or both) for the benefit of employees and their families and dependents at least medical or hospital care, or pensions on retirement or death of employees; and

    (2) such plan was established prior to January 1, 1954, as a result of an agreement between employee representatives and the Government of the United States during a period of Government operation, under seizure powers, of a major part of the productive facilities of the industry in which such employer is engaged,

such contributions shall not be deductible under this section nor be made nondeductible by this section, but the deductibility thereof shall be governed solely by section 162 (relating to trade or business expenses). For purposes of this chapter and subtitle B, in the case of any individual who before July 1, 1974, was a participant in a plan described in the preceding sentence—

    (A) such individual, if he is or was an employee within the meaning of section 401(c)(1), shall be treated (with respect to service covered by the plan) as being an employee other than an employee within the meaning of section 401(c)(1) and as being an employee of a participating employer under the plan,

(B) earnings derived from service covered by the plan shall be treated as not being earned income within the meaning of section 401(c)(2), and

(C) such individual shall be treated as an employee of a participating employer under the plan with respect to service before July 1, 1975, covered by the plan.

Section 277 (relating to deductions incurred by certain membership organizations in transactions with members) does not apply to any trust described in this subsection. The first and third sentences of this subsection shall have no application with respect to amounts contributed to a trust on or after any date on which such trust is qualified for exemption from tax under section 501(a).

(d) Deductibility of payments of deferred compensation, etc., to independent contractors—If a plan would be described in so much of subsection (a) as precedes paragraph (1) thereof (as modified by subsection (b)) but for the fact that there is no employer-employee relationship, the contributions or compensation—

(1) shall not be deductible by the payor thereof under this chapter, but

(2) shall (if they would be deductible under this chapter but for paragraph (1)) be deductible under this subsection for the taxable year in which an amount attributable to the contribution or compensation is includible in the gross income of the persons participating in the plan.

(e) Contributions allocable to life insurance protection for self-employed individuals— In the case of a self-employed individual described in section 401(c)(1), contributions which are allocable (determined under regulations prescribed by the Secretary) to the purchase of life, accident, health, or other insurance shall not be taken into account under paragraph (1), (2), or (3) of subsection (a).

(f) [Repealed]

(g) Certain employer liability payments considered as contributions—

(1) In general—For purposes of this section, any amount paid by an employer under section 4041(b), 4062, 4063, or 4064, or part 1 of subtitle E of title IV of the Employee Retirement Income Security Act of 1974 shall be treated as a contribution to which this section applies by such employer to or under a stock bonus, pension, profit-sharing, or annuity plan.

(2) Controlled group deductions—In the case of a payment described in paragraph (1) made by an entity which is liable because it is a member of a commonly controlled group of corporations, trades, or businesses, within the meaning of subsection (b) or (c) of section 414, the fact that the entity did not directly employ participants of the plan with respect to which the liability payment was made shall not affect the deductibility of a payment which otherwise satisfies the conditions of section 162 (relating to trade or business expenses) or section 212 (relating to expenses for the production of income).

(3) Timing of deduction of contributions—

(A) In general—Except as otherwise provided in this paragraph, any payment described in paragraph (1) shall (subject to the last sentence of subsection (a)(1)(A)) be deductible under this section when paid.

(B) Contributions under standard terminations—Subparagraph (A) shall not apply (and subsection (a)(1)(A) shall apply) to any payments described in paragraph (1) which are paid to terminate a plan under section 4041(b) of the Employee Retirement Income Security Act of 1974 to the extent such payments result in the assets of the plan being in excess of the total amount of benefits under such plan which are guaranteed by the Pension Benefit Guaranty Corporation under section 4022 of such Act.

(C) **Contributions to certain trusts**—Subparagraph (A) shall not apply to any payment described in paragraph (1) which is made under section 4062(c) of such Act and such payment shall be deductible at such time as may be prescribed in regulations which are based on principles similar to the principles of subsection (a)(1)(A).

(4) References to employee retirement income security act of 1974—For purposes of this subsection, any reference to a section of the Employee Retirement Income Security Act of 1974 shall be treated as a reference to such section as in effect on the date of the enactment of the Retirement Protection Act of 1994.

(h) Special rules for simplified employee pensions—

(1) In general—Employer contributions to a simplified employee pension shall be treated as if they are made to a plan subject to the requirements of this section. Employer contributions to a simplified employee pension are subject to the following limitations:

(A) Contributions made for a year are deductible—

(i) in the case of a simplified employee pension maintained on a calendar year basis, for the taxable year with or within which the calendar year ends, or

(ii) in the case of a simplified employee pension which is maintained on the basis of the taxable year of the employer, for such taxable year.

(B) Contributions shall be treated for purposes of this subsection as if they were made for a taxable year if such contributions are made on account of such taxable year and are made not later than the time prescribed by law for filing the return for such taxable year (including extensions thereof).

(C) The amount deductible in a taxable year for a simplified employee pension shall not exceed 25 percent of the compensation paid to the employees during the calendar year ending with or within the taxable year (or during the taxable year in the case of a taxable year described in subparagraph (A)(ii)). The excess of the amount contributed over the amount deductible for a taxable year shall be deductible in the succeeding taxable years in order of time, subject to the 25 percent limit of the preceding sentence.

(2) Effect on certain trusts—For any taxable year for which the employer has a deduction under paragraph (1), the otherwise applicable limitations in subsection (a)(3)(A) shall be reduced by the amount of the allowable deductions under paragraph (1) with respect to participants in the trust subject to subsection (a)(3)(A).

(3) Coordination with subsection (a)(7)—For purposes of subsection (a)(7), a simplified employee pension shall be treated as if it were a separate stock bonus or profit-sharing trust.

(i) [Repealed]

(j) Special rules relating to application with section 415—

(1) No deduction in excess of section 415 limitation—In computing the amount of any deduction allowable under paragraphs (1), (2), (3), (4), (7), or (9) of subsection (a) for any year—

(A) in the case of a defined benefit plan, there shall not be taken into account any benefits for any year in excess of any limitation on such benefits under section 415 for such year, or

(B) in the case of a defined contribution plan, the amount of any contributions otherwise taken into account shall be reduced by any annual additions in excess of the limitation under section 415 for such year.

(2) No advance funding of cost-of-living adjustments—For purposes of clause (i), (ii) or (iii) of subsection (a)(1)(A), and in computing the full funding limitation, there shall not be taken into account any adjustments under section 415(d)(1) for any year before the year for which such adjustment first takes effect.

(k) Deduction for dividends paid on certain employer securities—

(1) General rule—In the case of a C corporation, there shall be allowed as a deduction for a taxable year the amount of any applicable dividend paid in cash by such corporation with respect to applicable employer securities. Such deduction shall be in addition to the deductions allowed under subsection (a).

(2) Applicable dividend—For purposes of this subsection—

(A) In general—The term "applicable dividend" means any dividend which, in accordance with the plan provisions—

(i) is paid in cash to the participants in the plan or their beneficiaries,

(ii) is paid to the plan and is distributed in cash to participants in the plan or their beneficiaries not later than 90 days after the close of the plan year in which paid,

(iii) is, at the election of such participants or their beneficiaries—

(I) payable as provided in clause (i) or (ii), or

(II) paid to the plan and reinvested in qualifying employer securities, or

(iv) is used to make payments on a loan described in subsection (a)(9) the proceeds of which were used to acquire the employer securities (whether or not allocated to participants) with respect to which the dividend is paid.

(B) Limitation on certain dividends—A dividend described in subparagraph (A)(iv) which is paid with respect to any employer security which is allocated to a participant shall not be treated as an applicable dividend unless the plan provides that employer securities with a fair market value of not less than the amount of such dividend are allocated to such participant for the year which (but for subparagraph (A)) such dividend would have been allocated to such participant.

(3) Applicable employer securities—For purposes of this subsection, the term "applicable employer securities" means, with respect to any dividend, employer securities which are held on the record date for such dividend by an employee stock ownership plan which is maintained by—

(A) the corporation paying such dividend, or

(B) any other corporation which is a member of a controlled group of corporations (within the meaning of section 409(l)(4)) which includes such corporation.

(4) Time for deduction—

(A) In general—The deduction under paragraph (1) shall be allowable in the taxable year of the corporation in which the dividend is paid or distributed to a participant or his beneficiary.

(B) Reinvestment dividends—For purposes of subparagraph (A), an applicable dividend reinvested pursuant to clause (iii)(II) of paragraph (2)(A) shall be treated as paid in the taxable year of the corporation in which such dividend is reinvested in qualifying employer securities or in which the election under clause (iii) of paragraph (2)(A) is made, whichever is later.

(C) Repayment of loans—In the case of an applicable dividend described in clause (iv) of paragraph (2)(A), the deduction under paragraph (1) shall be allowable in the taxable year of the corporation in which such dividend is used to repay the loan described in such clause.

(5) Other rules—For purposes of this subsection—

(A) Disallowance of deduction—The Secretary may disallow the deduction under paragraph (1) for any dividend if the Secretary determines that such dividend constitutes, in substance, an avoidance or evasion of taxation.

(B) Plan qualification—A plan shall not be treated as violating the requirements of section 401, 409, or 4975(e)(7), or as engaging in a prohibited transaction for purposes of section 4975(d)(3), merely by reason of any payment or distribution described in paragraph (2)(A).

(6) Definitions—For purposes of this subsection—

(A) Employer securities—The term "employer securities" has the meaning given such term by section 409(l).

(B) Employee stock ownership plan—The term "employee stock ownership plan" has the meaning given such term by section 4975(e)(7). Such term includes a tax credit employee stock ownership plan (as defined in section 409).

(7) Full vesting—In accordance with section 411, an applicable dividend described in clause (iii)(II) of paragraph (2)(A) shall be subject to the requirements of section 411(a)(1).

(l) Limitation on amount of annual compensation taken into account—For purposes of applying the limitations of this section, the amount of annual compensation of each employee taken into account under the plan for any year shall not exceed $200,000. The Secretary shall adjust the $200,000 amount at the same time, and by the same amount, as the adjustment under section 401(a)(17)(B). For purposes of clause (i), (ii), or (iii) of subsection (a)(1)(A), and in computing the full funding limitation, any adjustment under the preceding sentence shall not be taken into account for any year before the year for which such adjustment first takes effect.

(m) Special rules for simple retirement accounts—

(1) In general—Employer contributions to a simple retirement account shall be treated as if they are made to a plan subject to the requirements of this section.

(2) Timing—

(A) Deduction—Contributions described in paragraph (1) shall be deductible in the taxable year of the employer with or within which the calendar year for which the contributions were made ends.

(B) Contributions after end of year—For purposes of this subsection, contributions shall be treated as made for a taxable year if they are made on account of the taxable year and are made not later than the time prescribed by law for filing the return for the taxable year (including extensions thereof).

(n) Elective deferrals not taken into account for purposes of deduction limits—Elective deferrals (as defined in section 402(g)(3)) shall not be subject to any limitation contained in paragraph (3), (7), or (9) of subsection (a) or paragraph (1)(C) of subsection (h), and such elective deferrals shall not be taken into account in applying any such limitation to any other contributions.

(o) Deduction limit for single-employer plans—For purposes of subsection (a)(1)(A)—

(1) In general—In the case of a defined benefit plan to which subsection (a)(1)(A) applies (other than a multiemployer plan), the amount determined under this subsection for any taxable year shall be equal to the greater of—

(A) the sum of the amounts determined under paragraph (2) with respect to each plan year ending with or within the taxable year, or

(B) the sum of the minimum required contributions under section 430 for such plan years.

(2) Determination of amount—

(A) In general—The amount determined under this paragraph for any plan year shall be equal to the excess (if any) of—

(i) the sum of—

(I) the funding target for the plan year,

(II) the target normal cost for the plan year, and

(III) the cushion amount for the plan year, over

(ii) the value (determined under section 430(g)(3)) of the assets of the plan which are held by the plan as of the valuation date for the plan year.

(B) Special rule for certain employers—If section 430(i) does not apply to a plan for a plan year, the amount determined under subparagraph (A)(i) for the plan year shall in no event be less than the sum of—

(i) the funding target for the plan year (determined as if section 430(i) applied to the plan), plus

(ii) the target normal cost for the plan year (as so determined).

(3) Cushion amount—For purposes of paragraph (2)(A)(i)(III)—

(A) In general—The cushion amount for any plan year is the sum of—

(i) 50 percent of the funding target for the plan year, and

(ii) the amount by which the funding target for the plan year would increase if the plan were to take into account—

(I) increases in compensation which are expected to occur in succeeding plan years, or

(II) if the plan does not base benefits for service to date on compensation, increases in benefits which are expected to occur in succeeding plan years (determined on the basis of the average annual increase in benefits over the 6 immediately preceding plan years).

(B) Limitations—

(i) In general—In making the computation under subparagraph (A)(ii), the plan's actuary shall assume that the limitations under subsection (l) and section 415(b) shall apply.

(ii) Expected increases—In the case of a plan year during which a plan is covered under section 4021 of the Employee Retirement Income Security Act of 1974, the plan's actuary may, notwithstanding subsection (l), take into account increases in the limitations which are expected to occur in succeeding plan years.

(4) Special rules for plans with 100 or fewer participants—

(A) In general—For purposes of determining the amount under paragraph (3) for any plan year, in the case of a plan which has 100 or fewer participants for the plan year, the liability of the plan attributable to benefit increases for highly compensated employees (as defined in section 414(q)) resulting from a plan amendment which is made or becomes effective, whichever is later, within the last 2 years shall not be taken into account in determining the target liability.

(B) Rule for determining number of participants—For purposes of determining the number of plan participants, all defined benefit plans maintained by the same employer (or any member of such employer's controlled group (within the meaning of section 412(d)(3))) shall be treated as one plan, but only participants of such member or employer shall be taken into account.

(5) Special rule for terminating plans—In the case of a plan which, subject to section 4041 of the Employee Retirement Income Security Act of 1974, terminates during the plan year, the amount determined under paragraph (2) shall in no event be less than the amount required to make the plan sufficient for benefit liabilities (within the meaning of section 4041(d) of such Act).

(6) Actuarial assumptions— Any computation under this subsection for any plan year shall use the same actuarial assumptions which are used for the plan year under section 430 (determined by not taking into account any adjustment under clause (iv) of subsection (h)(2)(C) thereof).

(7) Definitions—Any term used in this subsection which is also used in section 430 shall have the same meaning given such term by section 430.

(8) CSEC Plans—Solely for purposes of this subsection, a CSEC plan shall be treated as though section 430 applied to such plan and the minimum required contribution for any plan year shall be the amount described in section 412(a)(2)(D).

§ 408. Individual retirement accounts.

(a) Individual retirement account—For purposes of this section, the term "individual retirement account" means a trust created or organized in the United States for the exclusive benefit of an individual or his beneficiaries, but only if the written governing instrument creating the trust meets the following requirements:

(1) Except in the case of a rollover contribution described in subsection (d)(3), in section 402(c), 403(a)(4), 403(b)(8), or 457(e)(16), no contribution will be accepted unless it is in cash, and contributions will not be accepted for the taxable year on behalf of any individual in excess of the amount in effect for such taxable year under section 219(b)(1)(A).

(2) The trustee is a bank (as defined in subsection (n)) or such other person who demonstrates to the satisfaction of the Secretary that the manner in which such other person will administer the trust will be consistent with the requirements of this section.

(3) No part of the trust funds will be invested in life insurance contracts.

(4) The interest of an individual in the balance of his account is nonforfeitable.

(5) The assets of the trust will not be commingled with other property except in a common trust fund or common investment fund.

(6) Under regulations prescribed by the Secretary, rules similar to the rules of section 401(a)(9) and the incidental death benefit requirements of section 401(a) shall apply to the distribution of the entire interest of an individual for whose benefit the trust is maintained.

(b) Individual retirement annuity—For purposes of this section, the term "individual retirement annuity" means an annuity contract, or an endowment contract (as determined under regulations prescribed by the Secretary), issued by an insurance company which meets the following requirements:

(1) The contract is not transferable by the owner.

(2) Under the contract—

(A) the premiums are not fixed,

(B) the annual premium on behalf of any individual will not exceed the dollar amount in effect under section 219(b)(1)(A), and

(C) any refund of premiums will be applied before the close of the calendar year following the year of the refund toward the payment of future premiums or the purchase of additional benefits.

(3) Under regulations prescribed by the Secretary, rules similar to the rules of section 401(a)(9) and the incidental death benefit requirements of section 401(a) shall apply to the distribution of the entire interest of the owner.

(4) The entire interest of the owner is nonforfeitable.

Such term does not include such an annuity contract for any taxable year of the owner in which it is disqualified on the application of subsection (e) or for any subsequent taxable year. For purposes of this subsection, no contract shall be treated as an endowment contract if it matures later than the taxable year in which the individual in whose name such contract is purchased attains age 70½; if it is not for the exclusive benefit of the individual in whose name it is purchased or his beneficiaries; or if the aggregate annual premiums under all such contracts purchased in the name of such individual for any taxable year exceed the dollar amount in effect under section 219(b)(1)(A).

(c) Accounts established by employers and certain associations of employees—A trust created or organized in the United States by an employer for the exclusive benefit of his employees or their beneficiaries, or by an association of employees (which may include employees within the meaning of section 401(c)(1)) for the exclusive benefit of its members or their beneficiaries, shall be treated as an individual retirement account (described in subsection (a)), but only if the written governing instrument creating the trust meets the following requirements:

(1) The trust satisfies the requirements of paragraphs (1) through (6) of subsection (a).

(2) There is a separate accounting for the interest of each employee or member (or spouse of an employee or member).

The assets of the trust may be held in a common fund for the account of all individuals who have an interest in the trust.

(d) Tax treatment of distributions—

(1) In general—Except as otherwise provided in this subsection, any amount paid or distributed out of an individual retirement plan shall be included in gross income by the payee or distributee, as the case may be, in the manner provided under section 72.

(2) Special rules for applying section 72—For purposes of applying section 72 to any amount described in paragraph (1)—

(A) all individual retirement plans shall be treated as 1 contract,

(B) all distributions during any taxable year shall be treated as 1 distribution, and

(C) the value of the contract, income on the contract, and investment in the contract shall be computed as of the close of the calendar year in which the taxable year begins.

For purposes of subparagraph (C), the value of the contract shall be increased by the amount of any distributions during the calendar year.

(3) Rollover contribution—An amount is described in this paragraph as a rollover contribution if it meets the requirements of subparagraphs (A) and (B).

(A) In general—Paragraph (1) does not apply to any amount paid or distributed out of an individual retirement account or individual retirement annuity to the individual for whose benefit the account or annuity is maintained if—

(i) the entire amount received (including money and any other property) is paid into an individual retirement account or individual retirement annuity (other than an endowment contract) for the benefit of such individual not later than the 60th day after the day on which he receives the payment or distribution; or

(ii) the entire amount received (including money and any other property) is paid into an eligible retirement plan for the benefit of such individual not later than the 60th day after the date on which the payment or distribution is received, except that the maximum amount which may be paid into such plan may not exceed the portion of the amount received which is includible in gross income (determined without regard to this paragraph).

For purposes of clause (ii), the term "eligible retirement plan" means an eligible retirement plan described in clause (iii), (iv), (v), or (vi) of section 402(c)(8)(B).

(B) Limitation—This paragraph does not apply to any amount described in subparagraph (A)(i) received by an individual from an individual retirement account or individual retirement annuity if at any time during the 1-year period ending on the day of such receipt such individual received any other amount described in that subparagraph from an individual retirement account or an individual retirement annuity which was not includible in his gross income because of the application of this paragraph.

(C) Denial of rollover treatment for inherited accounts, etc—

(i) In general—In the case of an inherited individual retirement account or individual retirement annuity—

(I) this paragraph shall not apply to any amount received by an individual from such an account or annuity (and no amount transferred from such account or annuity to another individual retirement account or annuity shall be excluded from gross income by reason of such transfer), and

(II) such inherited account or annuity shall not be treated as an individual retirement account or annuity for purposes of determining whether any other amount is a rollover contribution.

(ii) Inherited individual retirement account or annuity—An individual retirement account or individual retirement annuity shall be treated as inherited if—

(I) the individual for whose benefit the account or annuity is maintained acquired such account by reason of the death of another individual, and

(II) such individual was not the surviving spouse of such other individual.

(D) Partial rollovers permitted—

(i) In general—If any amount paid or distributed out of an individual retirement account or individual retirement annuity would meet the requirements of subparagraph (A) but for the fact that the entire amount was not paid into an eligible plan as required by clause (i) or (ii) of subparagraph (A), such amount shall be treated as meeting the requirements of subparagraph (A) to the extent it is paid into an eligible plan referred to in such clause not later than the 60th day referred to in such clause.

(ii) Eligible plan—For purposes of clause (i), the term "eligible plan" means any account, annuity, contract, or plan referred to in subparagraph (A).

(E) Denial of rollover treatment for required distributions—This paragraph shall not apply to any amount to the extent such amount is required to be distributed under subsection (a)(6) or (b)(3).

(F) Frozen deposits—For purposes of this paragraph, rules similar to the rules of section 402(c)(7) (relating to frozen deposits) shall apply.

(G) Simple retirement accounts—In the case of any payment or distribution out of a simple retirement account (as defined in subsection (p)) to which section 72(t)(6) applies, this paragraph shall not apply unless such payment or distribution is paid into another simple retirement account.

(H) Application of section 72—

(i) In general—If—

(I) a distribution is made from an individual retirement plan, and

(II) a rollover contribution is made to an eligible retirement plan described in section 402(c)(8)(B)(iii), (iv), (v), or (vi) with respect to all or part of such distribution, then, notwithstanding paragraph (2), the rules of clause (ii) shall apply for purposes of applying section 72.

(ii) Applicable rules—In the case of a distribution described in clause (i)—

(I) section 72 shall be applied separately to such distribution,

(II) notwithstanding the pro rata allocation of income on, and investment in, the contract to distributions under section 72, the portion of such distribution rolled over to an eligible retirement plan described in clause (i) shall be treated as from income on the contract (to the extent of the aggregate income on the contract from all individual retirement plans of the distributee), and

(III) appropriate adjustments shall be made in applying section 72 to other distributions in such taxable year and subsequent taxable years.

(I) Waiver of 60-day requirement—The Secretary may waive the 60-day requirement under subparagraphs (A) and (D) where the failure to waive such requirement would be against equity or good conscience, including casualty, disaster, or other events beyond the reasonable control of the individual subject to such requirement.

(4) Contributions returned before due date of return—Paragraph (1) does not apply to the distribution of any contribution paid during a taxable year to an individual retirement account or for an individual retirement annuity if—

(A) such distribution is received on or before the day prescribed by law (including extensions of time) for filing such individual's return for such taxable year,

(B) no deduction is allowed under section 219 with respect to such contribution, and

(C) such distribution is accompanied by the amount of net income attributable to such contribution.

In the case of such a distribution, for purposes of section 61, any net income described in subparagraph (C) shall be deemed to have been earned and receivable in the taxable year in which such contribution is made.

(5) Distributions of excess contributions after due date for taxable year and certain excess rollover contributions—

(A) In general—In the case of any individual, if the aggregate contributions (other than rollover contributions) paid for any taxable year to an individual retirement account or for an individual retirement annuity do not exceed the dollar amount in effect under section 219(b)(1)(A), paragraph (1) shall not apply to the distribution of any such contribution to the extent that such contribution exceeds the amount allowable as a deduction under section 219 for the taxable year for which the contribution was paid—

(i) if such distribution is received after the date described in paragraph (4),

(ii) but only to the extent that no deduction has been allowed under section 219 with respect to such excess contribution.

If employer contributions on behalf of the individual are paid for the taxable year to a simplified employee pension, the dollar limitation of the preceding sentence shall be increased by the lesser of the amount of such contributions or the dollar limitation in effect under section 415(c)(1)(A) for such taxable year.

(B) Excess rollover contributions attributable to erroneous information—If—

    (i) the taxpayer reasonably relies on information supplied pursuant to subtitle F for determining the amount of a rollover contribution, but

    (ii) the information was erroneous,

subparagraph (A) shall be applied by increasing the dollar limit set forth therein by that portion of the excess contribution which was attributable to such information.

For purposes of this paragraph, the amount allowable as a deduction under section 219 shall be computed without regard to section 219(g).

(6) Transfer of account incident to divorce—The transfer of an individual's interest in an individual retirement account or an individual retirement annuity to his spouse or former spouse under a divorce or separation instrument described in subparagraph (A) of section 71(b)(2) is not to be considered a taxable transfer made by such individual notwithstanding any other provision of this subtitle, and such interest at the time of the transfer is to be treated as an individual retirement account of such spouse, and not of such individual. Thereafter such account or annuity for purposes of this subtitle is to be treated as maintained for the benefit of such spouse.

(7) Special rules for simplified employee pensions or simple retirement accounts—

    (A) Transfer or rollover of contributions prohibited until deferral test met—Notwithstanding any other provision of this subsection or section 72(t), paragraph (1) and section 72(t)(1) shall apply to the transfer or distribution from a simplified employee pension of any contribution under a salary reduction arrangement described in subsection (k)(6) (or any income allocable thereto) before a determination as to whether the requirements of subsection (k)(6)(A)(iii) are met with respect to such contribution.

    (B) Certain exclusions treated as deductions—For purposes of paragraphs (4) and (5) and section 4973, any amount excludable or excluded from gross income under section 402(h) or 402(k) shall be treated as an amount allowable or allowed as a deduction under section 219.

(8) Distributions for charitable purposes—

    (A) In general—So much of the aggregate amount of qualified charitable distributions with respect to a taxpayer made during any taxable year which does not exceed $100,000 shall not be includible in gross income of such taxpayer for such taxable year.

    (B) Qualified charitable distribution—For purposes of this paragraph, the term 'qualified charitable distribution' means any distribution from an individual retirement plan (other than a plan described in subsection (k) or (p))—

        (i) which is made directly by the trustee to an organization described in section 170(b)(1)(A) (other than any organization described in section 509(a)(3) or any fund or account described in section 4966(d)(2)), and

        (ii) which is made on or after the date that the individual for whose benefit the plan is maintained has attained age 70 1/2.

A distribution shall be treated as a qualified charitable distribution only to the extent that the distribution would be includible in gross income without regard to subparagraph (A).

(C) Contributions must be otherwise deductible—For purposes of this paragraph, a distribution to an organization described in subparagraph (B)(i) shall be treated as a qualified charitable distribution only if a deduction for the entire distribution would be allowable under section 170 (determined without regard to subsection (b) thereof and this paragraph).

(D) Application of section 72—Notwithstanding section 72, in determining the extent to which a distribution is a qualified charitable distribution, the entire amount of the distribution shall be treated as includible in gross income without regard to subparagraph (A) to the extent that such amount does not exceed the aggregate amount which would have been so includible if all amounts in all individual retirement plans of the individual were distributed during such taxable year and all such plans were treated as 1 contract for purposes of determining under section 72 the aggregate amount which would have been so includible. Proper adjustments shall be made in applying section 72 to other distributions in such taxable year and subsequent taxable years.

(E) Denial of deduction—Qualified charitable distributions which are not includible in gross income pursuant to subparagraph (A) shall not be taken into account in determining the deduction under section 170.

(F) Termination— This paragraph shall not apply to distributions made in taxable years beginning after December 31, 2013.

(9) Distribution for health savings account funding—

(A) In general—In the case of an individual who is an eligible individual (as defined in section 223(c)) and who elects the application of this paragraph for a taxable year, gross income of the individual for the taxable year does not include a qualified HSA funding distribution to the extent such distribution is otherwise includible in gross income.

(B) Qualified HSA funding distribution—For purposes of this paragraph, the term "qualified HSA funding distribution" means a distribution from an individual retirement plan (other than a plan described in subsection (k) or (p)) of the employee to the extent that such distribution is contributed to the health savings account of the individual in a direct trustee-to-trustee transfer.

(C) Limitations—

(i) Maximum dollar limitation—The amount excluded from gross income by subparagraph (A) shall not exceed the excess of—

(I) the annual limitation under section 223(b) computed on the basis of the type of coverage under the high deductible health plan covering the individual at the time of the qualified HSA funding distribution, over

(II) in the case of a distribution described in clause (ii)(II), the amount of the earlier qualified HSA funding distribution.

(ii) One-time transfer—

(I) In general—Except as provided in subclause (II), an individual may make an election under subparagraph (A) only for one qualified HSA funding distribution during the lifetime of the individual. Such an election, once made, shall be irrevocable.

(II) Conversion from self-only to family coverage—If a qualified HSA funding distribution is made during a month in a taxable year during which an individual has self-only coverage under a high deductible health plan as of the first day of the month, the individual may elect to make an additional qualified HSA funding distribution during a subsequent month in such taxable year during which the individual has family coverage under a high deductible health plan as of the first day of the subsequent month.

(D) Failure to maintain high deductible health plan coverage—

(i) In general—If, at any time during the testing period, the individual is not an eligible individual, then the aggregate amount of all contributions to the health savings account of the individual made under subparagraph (A)—

(I) shall be includible in the gross income of the individual for the taxable year in which occurs the first month in the testing period for which such individual is not an eligible individual, and

(II) the tax imposed by this chapter for any taxable year on the individual shall be increased by 10 percent of the amount which is so includible.

(ii) Exception for disability or death—Subclauses (I) and (II) of clause (i) shall not apply if the individual ceased to be an eligible individual by reason of the death of the individual or the individual becoming disabled (within the meaning of section 72(m)(7)).

(iii) Testing period—The term "testing period" means the period beginning with the month in which the qualified HSA funding distribution is contributed to a health savings account and ending on the last day of the 12th month following such month.

(E) Application of section 72—Notwithstanding section 72, in determining the extent to which an amount is treated as otherwise includible in gross income for purposes of subparagraph (A), the aggregate amount distributed from an individual retirement plan shall be treated as includible in gross income to the extent that such amount does not exceed the aggregate amount which would have been so includible if all amounts from all individual retirement plans were distributed. Proper adjustments shall be made in applying section 72 to other distributions in such taxable year and subsequent taxable years.

(e) Tax treatment of accounts and annuities—

(1) Exemption from tax—Any individual retirement account is exempt from taxation under this subtitle unless such account has ceased to be an individual retirement account by reason of paragraph (2) or (3). Notwithstanding the preceding sentence, any such account is subject to the taxes imposed by section 511 (relating to imposition of tax on unrelated business income of charitable, etc. organizations).

(2) Loss of exemption of account where employee engages in prohibited transaction—

(A) In general—If, during any taxable year of the individual for whose benefit any individual retirement account is established, that individual or his beneficiary engages in any transaction prohibited by section 4975 with respect to such account, such account ceases to be an individual retirement account as of the first day of such taxable year. For purposes of this paragraph—

(i) the individual for whose benefit any account was established is treated as the creator of such account, and

(ii) the separate account for any individual within an individual retirement account maintained by an employer or association of employees is treated as a separate individual retirement account.

(B) Account treated as distributing all its assets—In any case in which any account ceases to be an individual retirement account by reason of subparagraph (A) as of the first day of any taxable year, paragraph (1) of subsection (d) applies as if there were a distribution on such first day in an amount equal to the fair market value (on such first day) of all assets in the account (on such first day).

(3) Effect of borrowing on annuity contract—If during any taxable year the owner of an individual retirement annuity borrows any money under or by use of such contract, the contract ceases to be an individual retirement annuity as of the first day of such taxable year. Such owner shall include in gross income for such year an amount equal to the fair market value of such contract as of such first day.

(4) Effect of pledging account as security—If, during any taxable year of the individual for whose benefit an individual retirement account is established, that individual uses the account or any portion thereof as security for a loan, the portion so used is treated as distributed to that individual.

(5) Purchase of endowment contract by individual retirement account—If the assets of an individual retirement account or any part of such assets are used to purchase an endowment contract for the benefit of the individual for whose benefit the account is established—

(A) to the extent that the amount of the assets involved in the purchase are not attributable to the purchase of life insurance, the purchase is treated as a rollover contribution described in subsection (d)(3), and

(B) to the extent that the amount of the assets involved in the purchase are attributable to the purchase of life, health, accident, or other insurance such amounts are treated as distributed to that individual (but the provisions of subsection (f) do not apply).

(6) Commingling individual retirement account amounts in certain common trust funds and common investment funds—Any common trust fund or common investment fund of individual retirement account assets which is exempt from taxation under this subtitle does not cease to be exempt on account of the participation or inclusion of assets of a trust exempt from taxation under section 501(a) which is described in section 401(a).

(f) [Repealed]

(g) Community property laws—This section shall be applied without regard to any community property laws.

(h) Custodial accounts—For purposes of this section, a custodial account shall be treated as a trust if the assets of such account are held by a bank (as defined in subsection (n)) or another person who demonstrates, to the satisfaction of the Secretary, that the manner in which he will administer the account will be consistent with the requirements of this section, and if the custodial account would, except for the fact that it is not a trust, constitute an individual retirement account described in subsection (a). For purposes of this title, in the case of a custodial account treated as a trust by reason of the preceding sentence, the custodian of such account shall be treated as the trustee thereof.

(i) Reports—The trustee of an individual retirement account and the issuer of an endowment contract described in subsection (b) or an individual retirement annuity shall make such reports regarding such account, contract, or annuity to the Secretary and to the individuals for whom the account, contract, or annuity is, or is to be, maintained with respect to contributions (and the years to which they relate), distributions aggregating $10 or more in any calendar year, and such other matters as the Secretary may require. The reports required by this subsection—

(1) shall be filed at such time and in such manner as the Secretary prescribes, and

(2) shall be furnished to individuals—

(A) not later than January 31 of the calendar year following the calendar year to which such reports relate, and

(B) in such manner as the Secretary prescribes.

In the case of a simple retirement account under subsection (p), only one report under this subsection shall be required to be submitted each calendar year to the Secretary (at the time provided under paragraph (2)) but, in addition to the report under this subsection, there shall be furnished, within 31 days after each calendar year, to the individual on whose behalf the account is maintained a statement with respect to the account balance as of the close of, and the account activity during, such calendar year.

(j) Increase in maximum limitations for simplified employee pensions—In the case of any simplified employee pension, subsections (a)(1) and (b)(2) of this section shall be applied by increasing the amounts contained therein by the amount of the limitation in effect under section 415(c)(1)(A).

(k) Simplified employee pension defined—

(1) **In general**—For purposes of this title, the term "simplified employee pension" means an individual retirement account or individual retirement annuity—

(A) with respect to which the requirements of paragraphs (2), (3), (4), and (5) of this subsection are met, and

(B) if such account or annuity is part of a top-heavy plan (as defined in section 416), with respect to which the requirements of section 416(c)(2) are met.

(2) **Participation requirements**—This paragraph is satisfied with respect to a simplified employee pension for a year only if for such year the employer contributes to the simplified employee pension of each employee who—

(A) has attained age 21,

(B) has performed service for the employer during at least 3 of the immediately preceding 5 years, and

(C) received at least $450 in compensation (within the meaning of section 414(q)(4)) from the employer for the year.

For purposes of this paragraph, there shall be excluded from consideration employees described in subparagraph (A) or (C) of section 410(b)(3). For purposes of any arrangement described in subsection (k)(6), any employee who is eligible to have employer contributions made on the employee's behalf under such arrangement shall be treated as if such a contribution was made.

(3) **Contributions may not discriminate in favor of the highly compensated, etc**—

(A) In general—The requirements of this paragraph are met with respect to a simplified employee pension for a year if for such year the contributions made by the employer to simplified employee pensions for his employees do not discriminate in favor of any highly compensated employee (within the meaning of section 414(q)).

(B) Special rules—For purposes of subparagraph (A), there shall be excluded from consideration employees described in subparagraph (A) or (C) of section 410(b)(3).

(C) Contributions must bear uniform relationship to total compensation—For purposes of subparagraph (A), and except as provided in subparagraph (D), employer contributions, to simplified employee pensions (other than contributions under an arrangement described in paragraph (6)) shall be considered discriminatory unless contributions thereto bear a uniform relationship to the compensation (not in excess of the first $200,000) of each employee maintaining a simplified employee pension.

(D) Permitted disparity—For purposes of subparagraph (C), the rules of section 401(l)(2) shall apply to contributions to simplified employee pensions (other than contributions under an arrangement described in paragraph (6)).

(4) Withdrawals must be permitted—A simplified employee pension meets the requirements of this paragraph only if—

(A) employer contributions thereto are not conditioned on the retention in such pension of any portion of the amount contributed, and

(B) there is no prohibition imposed by the employer on withdrawals from the simplified employee pension.

(5) Contributions must be made under written allocation formula—The requirements of this paragraph are met with respect to a simplified employee pension only if employer contributions to such pension are determined under a definite written allocation formula which specifies—

(A) the requirements which an employee must satisfy to share in an allocation, and

(B) the manner in which the amount allocated is computed.

(6) Employee may elect salary reduction arrangement—

(A) Arrangements which qualify—

(i) In general—A simplified employee pension shall not fail to meet the requirements of this subsection for a year merely because, under the terms of the pension, an employee may elect to have the employer make payments—

(I) as elective employer contributions to the simplified employee pension on behalf of the employee, or

(II) to the employee directly in cash.

(ii) 50 percent of eligible employees must elect—Clause (i) shall not apply to a simplified employee pension unless an election described in clause (i)(I) is made or is in effect with respect to not less than 50 percent of the employees of the employer eligible to participate.

(iii) Requirements relating to deferral percentage—Clause (i) shall not apply to a simplified employee pension for any year unless the deferral percentage for such year of each highly compensated employee eligible to participate is not more than the product of—

> **(I)** the average of the deferral percentages for such year of all employees (other than highly compensated employees) eligible to participate, multiplied by

> **(II)** 1.25.

(iv) Limitations on elective deferrals—Clause (i) shall not apply to a simplified employee pension unless the requirements of section 401(a)(30) are met.

(B) Exception where more than 25 employees—This paragraph shall not apply with respect to any year in the case of a simplified employee pension maintained by an employer with more than 25 employees who were eligible to participate (or would have been required to be eligible to participate if a pension was maintained) at any time during the preceding year.

(C) Distributions of excess contributions—

(i) In general—Rules similar to the rules of section 401(k)(8) shall apply to any excess contribution under this paragraph. Any excess contribution under a simplified employee pension shall be treated as an excess contribution for purposes of section 4979.

(ii) Excess contribution—For purposes of clause (i), the term "excess contributions" means, with respect to a highly compensated employee, the excess of elective employer contributions under this paragraph over the maximum amount of such contributions allowable under subparagraph (A)(iii).

(D) Deferral percentage—For purposes of this paragraph, the deferral percentage for an employee for a year shall be the ratio of—

(i) the amount of elective employer contributions actually paid over to the simplified employee pension on behalf of the employee for the year, to

(ii) the employee's compensation (not in excess of the first $200,000) for the year.

(E) Exception for state and local and tax-exempt pensions—This paragraph shall not apply to a simplified employee pension maintained by—

(i) a State or local government or political subdivision thereof, or any agency or instrumentality thereof, or

(ii) an organization exempt from tax under this title.

(F) Exception where pension does not meet requirements necessary to insure distribution of excess contributions—This paragraph shall not apply with respect to any year for which the simplified employee pension does not meet such requirements as the Secretary may prescribe as are necessary to insure that excess contributions are distributed in accordance with subparagraph (C), including—

(i) reporting requirements, and

(ii) requirements which, notwithstanding paragraph (4), provide that contributions (and any income allocable thereto) may not be withdrawn from a simplified employee pension until a determination has been made that the requirements of subparagraph (A)(iii) have been met with respect to such contributions.

(G) Highly compensated employee—For purposes of this paragraph, the term "highly compensated employee" has the meaning given such term by section 414(q).

(H) Termination—This paragraph shall not apply to years beginning after December 31, 1996. The preceding sentence shall not apply to a simplified employee pension of an employer if the terms of simplified employee pensions of such employer, as in effect on December 31, 1996, provide that an employee may make the election described in subparagraph (A).

(7) Definitions—For purposes of this subsection and subsection (l)—

(A) Employee, employer, or owner-employee—The terms "employee", "employer", and "owner-employee" shall have the respective meanings given such terms by section 401(c).

(B) Compensation—Except as provided in paragraph (2)(C), the term "compensation" has the meaning given such term by section 414(s).

(C) Year—The term "year" means—

(i) the calendar year, or

(ii) if the employer elects, subject to such terms and conditions as the Secretary may prescribe, to maintain the simplified employee pension on the basis of the employer's taxable year.

(8) Cost-of-living adjustment—The Secretary shall adjust the $450 amount in paragraph (2)(C) at the same time and in the same manner as under section 415(d) and shall adjust the $200,000 amount in paragraphs (3)(C) and (6)(D)(ii) at the same time, and by the same amount, as any adjustment under section 401(a)(17)(B); except that any increase in the $450 amount which is not a multiple of $50 shall be rounded to the next lowest multiple of $50.

(9) Cross reference—For excise tax on certain excess contributions, see section 4979.

(l) Simplified employer reports—

(1) In general—An employer who makes a contribution on behalf of an employee to a simplified employee pension shall provide such simplified reports with respect to such contributions as the Secretary may require by regulations. The reports required by this subsection shall be filed at such time and in such manner, and information with respect to such contributions shall be furnished to the employee at such time and in such manner, as may be required by regulations.

(2) Simple retirement accounts—

(A) No employer reports—Except as provided in this paragraph, no report shall be required under this section by an employer maintaining a qualified salary reduction arrangement under subsection (p).

(B) Summary description—The trustee of any simple retirement account established pursuant to a qualified salary reduction arrangement under subsection (p) and the issuer of an annuity established under such an arrangement shall provide to the employer maintaining the arrangement, each year a description containing the following information:

(i) The name and address of the employer and the trustee or issuer.

(ii) The requirements for eligibility for participation.

(iii) The benefits provided with respect to the arrangement.

(iv) The time and method of making elections with respect to the arrangement.

(v) The procedures for, and effects of, withdrawals (including rollovers) from the arrangement.

(C) Employee notification—The employer shall notify each employee immediately before the period for which an election described in subsection (p)(5)(C) may be made of the employee's opportunity to make such election. Such notice shall include a copy of the description described in subparagraph (B).

(m) Investment in collectibles treated as distributions—

(1) In general—The acquisition by an individual retirement account or by an individually-directed account under a plan described in section 401(a) of any collectible shall be treated (for purposes of this section and section 402) as a distribution from such account in an amount equal to the cost to such account of such collectible.

(2) Collectible defined—For purposes of this subsection, the term "collectible" means—

(A) any work of art,

(B) any rug or antique,

(C) any metal or gem,

(D) any stamp or coin,

(E) any alcoholic beverage, or

(F) any other tangible personal property specified by the Secretary for purposes of this subsection.

(3) Exception for certain coins and bullion—For purposes of this subsection, the term "collectible" shall not include—

(A) any coin which is

(i) a gold coin described in paragraph (7), (8), (9), or (10) of section 5112(a) of title 31, United States Code,

(ii) a silver coin described in section 5112(e) of title 31, United States Code,

(iii) a platinum coin described in section 5112(k) of title 31, United States Code, or

(iv) a coin issued under the laws of any State, or

(B) any gold, silver, platinum, or palladium bullion of a fineness equal to or exceeding the minimum fineness that a contract market (as described in section 7 of the Commodity Exchange Act, 7 U.S.C. 7) requires for metals which may be delivered in satisfaction of a regulated futures contract, if such bullion is in the physical possession of a trustee described under subsection (a) of this section.

(n) Bank—For purposes of subsection (a)(2), the term "bank" means—

(1) any bank (as defined in section 581),

(2) an insured credit union (within the meaning of paragraph (6) or (7) of section 101 of the Federal Credit Union Act), and

(3) a corporation which, under the laws of the State of its incorporation, is subject to supervision and examination by the Commissioner of Banking or other officer of such State in charge of the administration of the banking laws of such State.

(o) Definitions and rules relating to nondeductible contributions to individual retirement plans—

(1) In general—Subject to the provisions of this subsection, designated nondeductible contributions may be made on behalf of an individual to an individual retirement plan.

(2) Limits on amounts which may be contributed—

(A) In general—The amount of the designated nondeductible contributions made on behalf of any individual for any taxable year shall not exceed the nondeductible limit for such taxable year.

(B) Nondeductible limit—For purposes of this paragraph—

(i) In general—The term "nondeductible limit" means the excess of—

(I) the amount allowable as a deduction under section 219 (determined without regard to section 219(g)), over

(II) the amount allowable as a deduction under section 219 (determined with regard to section 219(g)).

(ii) Taxpayer may elect to treat deductible contributions as nondeductible—If a taxpayer elects not to deduct an amount which (without regard to this clause) is allowable as a deduction under section 219 for any taxable year, the nondeductible limit for such taxable year shall be increased by such amount.

(C) Designated nondeductible contributions—

(i) In general—For purposes of this paragraph, the term "designated nondeductible contribution" means any contribution to an individual retirement plan for the taxable year which is designated (in such manner as the Secretary may prescribe) as a contribution for which a deduction is not allowable under section 219.

(ii) Designation—Any designation under clause (i) shall be made on the return of tax imposed by chapter 1 for the taxable year.

(3) Time when contributions made—In determining for which taxable year a designated nondeductible contribution is made, the rule of section 219(f)(3) shall apply.

(4) Individual required to report amount of designated nondeductible contributions—

(A) In general—Any individual who—

(i) makes a designated nondeductible contribution to any individual retirement plan for any taxable year, or

(ii) receives any amount from any individual retirement plan for any taxable year, shall include on his return of the tax imposed by chapter 1 for such taxable year and any succeeding taxable year (or on such other form as the Secretary may prescribe for any such taxable year) information described in subparagraph (B).

(B) Information required to be supplied—The following information is described in this subparagraph:

(i) The amount of designated nondeductible contributions for the taxable year.

(ii) The amount of distributions from individual retirement plans for the taxable year.

(iii) The excess (if any) of—

(I) the aggregate amount of designated nondeductible contributions for all preceding taxable years, over

(II) the aggregate amount of distributions from individual retirement plans which was excludable from gross income for such taxable years.

(iv) The aggregate balance of all individual retirement plans of the individual as of the close of the calendar year in which the taxable year begins.

(v) Such other information as the Secretary may prescribe.

(C) Penalty for reporting contributions not made—For penalty where individual reports designated nondeductible contributions not made, see section 6693(b).

(p) Simple retirement accounts—

(1) In general—For purposes of this title, the term "simple retirement account" means an individual retirement plan (as defined in section 7701(a)(37))—

(A) with respect to which the requirements of paragraphs (3), (4), and (5) are met; and

(B) except in the case of a rollover contribution described in subsection (d)(3)(G) or a rollover contribution otherwise described in subsection (d)(3) or in section 402(c), 403(a)(4), 403(b)(8), or 457(e)(16), which is made after the 2-year period described in section 72(t)(6), with respect to which the only contributions allowed are contributions under a qualified salary reduction arrangement.

(2) Qualified salary reduction arrangement—

(A) In general—For purposes of this subsection, the term "qualified salary reduction arrangement" means a written arrangement of an eligible employer under which—

(i) an employee eligible to participate in the arrangement may elect to have the employer make payments—

(I) as elective employer contributions to a simple retirement account on behalf of the employee, or

(II) to the employee directly in cash,

(ii) the amount which an employee may elect under clause (i) for any year is required to be expressed as a percentage of compensation and may not exceed a total of the applicable dollar amount for any year,

(iii) the employer is required to make a matching contribution to the simple retirement account for any year in an amount equal to so much of the amount the employee elects under clause (i)(I) as does not exceed the applicable percentage of compensation for the year, and

(iv) no contributions may be made other than contributions described in clause (i) or (iii).

(B) Employer may elect 2-percent nonelective contribution—

(i) In general—An employer shall be treated as meeting the requirements of subparagraph (A)(iii) for any year if, in lieu of the contributions described in such clause, the employer elects to make nonelective contributions of 2 percent of compensation for each employee who is eligible to participate in the arrangement and who has at least $5,000 of compensation from the employer for the year. If an employer makes an election under this subparagraph for any year, the employer shall notify employees of such election within a reasonable period of time before the 60-day period for such year under paragraph (5)(C).

(ii) Compensation limitation—The compensation taken into account under clause (i) for any year shall not exceed the limitation in effect for such year under section 401(a)(17).

(C) Definitions—For purposes of this subsection—

(i) Eligible employer—

(I) In general—The term "eligible employer" means, with respect to any year, an employer which had no more than 100 employees who received at least $5,000 of compensation from the employer for the preceding year.

(II) 2-year grace period—An eligible employer who establishes and maintains a plan under this subsection for 1 or more years and who fails to be an eligible employer for any subsequent year shall be treated as an eligible employer for the 2 years following the last year the employer was an eligible employer. If such failure is due to any acquisition, disposition, or similar transaction involving an eligible employer, the preceding sentence shall not apply.

(ii) Applicable percentage—

(I) In general—The term "applicable percentage" means 3 percent.

(II) Election of lower percentage—An employer may elect to apply a lower percentage (not less than 1 percent) for any year for all employees eligible to participate in the plan for such year if the employer notifies the employees of such lower percentage within a reasonable period of time before the 60-day election period for such year under paragraph (5)(C). An employer may not elect a lower percentage under this subclause for any year if that election would result in the applicable percentage being lower than 3 percent in more than 2 of the years in the 5-year period ending with such year.

(III) Special rule for years arrangement not in effect—If any year in the 5-year period described in subclause (II) is a year prior to the first year for which any qualified salary reduction arrangement is in effect with respect to the employer (or any predecessor), the employer shall be treated as if the level of the employer matching contribution was at 3 percent of compensation for such prior year.

(D) Arrangement may be only plan of employer—

(i) In general—An arrangement shall not be treated as a qualified salary reduction arrangement for any year if the employer (or any predecessor employer) maintained a qualified plan with respect to which contributions were made, or benefits were accrued, for service in any year in the period beginning with the year such arrangement became effective and ending with the year for which the determination is being made. If only individuals other than employees described in subparagraph (A) of section 410(b)(3) are eligible to participate in such arrangement, then the preceding sentence shall be applied without regard to any qualified plan in which only employees so described are eligible to participate.

(ii) Qualified plan—For purposes of this subparagraph, the term "qualified plan" means a plan, contract, pension, or trust described in subparagraph (A) or (B) of section 219(g)(5).

(E) Applicable dollar amount; cost-of-living adjustment—

(i) In general—For purposes of subparagraph (A)(ii), the applicable dollar amount is $10,000.

(ii) Cost-of-living adjustment—In the case of a year beginning after December 31, 2005, the Secretary shall adjust the $10,000 amount under clause (i) at the same time and in the same manner as under section 415(d), except that the base period taken into account shall be the calendar quarter beginning July 1, 2004, and any increase under this subparagraph which is not a multiple of $500 shall be rounded to the next lower multiple of $500.

(3) Vesting requirements—The requirements of this paragraph are met with respect to a simple retirement account if the employee's rights to any contribution to the simple retirement account are nonforfeitable. For purposes of this paragraph, rules similar to the rules of subsection (k)(4) shall apply.

(4) Participation requirements—

(A) In general—The requirements of this paragraph are met with respect to any simple retirement account for a year only if, under the qualified salary reduction arrangement, all employees of the employer who—

(i) received at least $5,000 in compensation from the employer during any 2 preceding years, and

(ii) are reasonably expected to receive at least $5,000 in compensation during the year,

are eligible to make the election under paragraph (2)(A)(i) or receive the nonelective contribution described in paragraph (2)(B).

(B) Excludable employees—An employer may elect to exclude from the requirement under subparagraph (A) employees described in section 410(b)(3).

(5) Administrative requirements—The requirements of this paragraph are met with respect to any simple retirement account if, under the qualified salary reduction arrangement—

(A) an employer must—

(i) make the elective employer contributions under paragraph (2)(A)(i) not later than the close of the 30-day period following the last day of the month with respect to which the contributions are to be made, and

(ii) make the matching contributions under paragraph (2)(A)(iii) or the nonelective contributions under paragraph (2)(B) not later than the date described in section 404(m)(2)(B),

(B) an employee may elect to terminate participation in such arrangement at any time during the year, except that if an employee so terminates, the arrangement may provide that the employee may not elect to resume participation until the beginning of the next year, and

(C) each employee eligible to participate may elect, during the 60-day period before the beginning of any year (and the 60-day period before the first day such employee is eligible to participate), to participate in the arrangement, or to modify the amounts subject to such arrangement, for such year.

(6) Definitions—For purposes of this subsection—

(A) Compensation—

(i) In general—The term "compensation" means amounts described in paragraphs (3) and (8) of section 6051(a). For purposes of the preceding sentence, amounts described in section 6051(a)(3) shall be determined without regard to section 3401(a)(3).

(ii) Self-employed—In the case of an employee described in subparagraph (B), the term "compensation" means net earnings from self-employment determined under section 1402(a) without regard to any contribution under this subsection. The preceding sentence shall be applied as if the term "trade or business" for purposes of section 1402 included service described in section 1402(c)(6).

(B) Employee—The term "employee" includes an employee as defined in section 401(c)(1).

(C) Year—The term "year" means the calendar year.

(7) Use of designated financial institution—A plan shall not be treated as failing to satisfy the requirements of this subsection or any other provision of this title merely because the employer makes all contributions to the individual retirement accounts or annuities of a designated trustee or issuer. The preceding sentence shall not apply unless each plan participant is notified in writing (either separately or as part of the notice under subsection (l)(2)(C)) that the participant's balance may be transferred without cost or penalty to another individual account or annuity in accordance with subsection (d)(3)(G).

(8) Coordination with maximum limitation under subsection (a)—In the case of any simple retirement account, subsections (a)(1) and (b)(2) shall be applied by substituting "the sum of the dollar amount in effect under paragraph (2)(A)(ii) of this subsection and the employer contribution required under subparagraph (A)(iii) or (B)(i) of paragraph (2) of this subsection, whichever is applicable" for "the dollar amount in effect under section 219(b)(1)(A)".

(9) Matching contributions on behalf of self-employed individuals not treated as elective employer contributions—Any matching contribution described in paragraph

(2)(A)(iii) which is made on behalf of a self-employed individual (as defined in section 401(c)) shall not be treated as an elective employer contribution to a simple retirement account for purposes of this title.

(10) Special rules for acquisitions, dispositions, and similar transactions—

(A) In general—An employer which fails to meet any applicable requirement by reason of an acquisition, disposition, or similar transaction shall not be treated as failing to meet such requirement during the transition period if—

(i) the employer satisfies requirements similar to the requirements of section 410(b)(6)(C)(i)(II); and

(ii) the qualified salary reduction arrangement maintained by the employer would satisfy the requirements of this subsection after the transaction if the employer which maintained the arrangement before the transaction had remained a separate employer.

(B) Applicable requirement—For purposes of this paragraph, the term "applicable requirement" means—

(i) the requirement under paragraph (2)(A)(i) that an employer be an eligible employer;

(ii) the requirement under paragraph (2)(D) that an arrangement be the only plan of an employer; and

(iii) the participation requirements under paragraph (4).

(C) Transition period—For purposes of this paragraph, the term "transition period" means the period beginning on the date of any transaction described in subparagraph (A) and ending on the last day of the second calendar year following the calendar year in which such transaction occurs.

(q) Deemed IRAs under qualified employer plans—

(1) General rule—If—

(A) a qualified employer plan elects to allow employees to make voluntary employee contributions to a separate account or annuity established under the plan, and

(B) under the terms of the qualified employer plan, such account or annuity meets the applicable requirements of this section or section 408A for an individual retirement account or annuity,

then such account or annuity shall be treated for purposes of this title in the same manner as an individual retirement plan and not as a qualified employer plan (and contributions to such account or annuity as contributions to an individual retirement plan and not to the qualified employer plan). For purposes of subparagraph (B), the requirements of subsection (a)(5) shall not apply.

(2) Special rules for qualified employer plans—For purposes of this title, a qualified employer plan shall not fail to meet any requirement of this title solely by reason of establishing and maintaining a program described in paragraph (1).

(3) Definitions—For purposes of this subsection—

(A) Qualified employer plan—The term "qualified employer plan" has the meaning given such term by section 72(p)(4)(A)(i); except that such term shall also include an eligible deferred compensation plan (as defined in section 457(b)) of an eligible employer described in section 457(e)(1)(A).

(B) Voluntary employee contribution—The term "voluntary employee contribution" means any contribution (other than a mandatory contribution within the meaning of section 411(c)(2)(C))—

(i) which is made by an individual as an employee under a qualified employer plan which allows employees to elect to make contributions described in paragraph (1), and

(ii) with respect to which the individual has designated the contribution as a contribution to which this subsection applies.

* * *

§ 408A. Roth IRAs.

(a) General rule—Except as provided in this section, a Roth IRA shall be treated for purposes of this title in the same manner as an individual retirement plan.

(b) Roth IRA—For purposes of this title, the term "Roth IRA" means an individual retirement plan (as defined in section 7701(a)(37)) which is designated (in such manner as the Secretary may prescribe) at the time of establishment of the plan as a Roth IRA. Such designation shall be made in such manner as the Secretary may prescribe.

(c) Treatment of contributions—

(1) No deduction allowed—No deduction shall be allowed under section 219 for a contribution to a Roth IRA.

(2) Contribution limit—The aggregate amount of contributions for any taxable year to all Roth IRAs maintained for the benefit of an individual shall not exceed the excess (if any) of—

(A) the maximum amount allowable as a deduction under section 219 with respect to such individual for such taxable year (computed without regard to subsection (d)(1) or (g) of such section), over

(B) the aggregate amount of contributions for such taxable year to all other individual retirement plans (other than Roth IRAs) maintained for the benefit of the individual.

(3) Limits based on modified adjusted gross income—

(A) Dollar limit—The amount determined under paragraph (2) for any taxable year shall not exceed an amount equal to the amount determined under paragraph (2)(A) for such taxable year, reduced (but not below zero) by the amount which bears the same ratio to such amount as—

(i) the excess of—

(I) the taxpayer's adjusted gross income for such taxable year, over

(II) the applicable dollar amount, bears to

(ii) $15,000 ($10,000 in the case of a joint return or a married individual filing a separate return).

The rules of subparagraphs (B) and (C) of section 219(g)(2) shall apply to any reduction under this subparagraph.

(B) Definitions—For purposes of this paragraph—

(i) adjusted gross income shall be determined in the same manner as under section 219(g)(3), except that any amount included in gross income under subsection (d)(3) shall not be taken into account, and

(ii) the applicable dollar amount is—

(I) in the case of a taxpayer filing a joint return, $150,000,

(II) in the case of any other taxpayer (other than a married individual filing a separate return), $95,000, and

(III) in the case of a married individual filing a separate return, zero.

(C) Marital status—Section 219(g)(4) shall apply for purposes of this paragraph.

(D) Inflation adjustment—In the case of any taxable year beginning in a calendar year after 2006, the dollar amounts in subclauses (I) and (II) of subparagraph (D)(ii) shall each be increased by an amount equal to—

(i) such dollar amount, multiplied by

(ii) the cost-of-living adjustment determined under section 1(f)(3) for the calendar year in which the taxable year begins, determined by substituting "calendar year 2005" for "calendar year 1992" in subparagraph (B) thereof.

Any increase determined under the preceding sentence shall be rounded to the nearest multiple of $1,000.

(4) Contributions permitted after age 70½—Contributions to a Roth IRA may be made even after the individual for whom the account is maintained has attained age 70½.

(5) Mandatory distribution rules not to apply before death—Notwithstanding subsections (a)(6) and (b)(3) of section 408 (relating to required distributions), the following provisions shall not apply to any Roth IRA:

(A) Section 401(a)(9)(A).

(B) The incidental death benefit requirements of section 401(a).

(6) Rollover contributions—

(A) In general—No rollover contribution may be made to a Roth IRA unless it is a qualified rollover contribution.

(B) Coordination with limit—A qualified rollover contribution shall not be taken into account for purposes of paragraph (2).

(7) Time when contributions made—For purposes of this section, the rule of section 219(f)(3) shall apply.

(d) Distribution rules—For purposes of this title—

(1) Exclusion—Any qualified distribution from a Roth IRA shall not be includible in gross income.

(2) Qualified distribution—For purposes of this subsection—

(A) In general—The term "qualified distribution" means any payment or distribution—

(i) made on or after the date on which the individual attains age 59½,

(ii) made to a beneficiary (or to the estate of the individual) on or after the death of the individual,

(iii) attributable to the individual's being disabled (within the meaning of section 72(m)(7)), or

(iv) which is a qualified special purpose distribution.

(B) Distributions within nonexclusion period—A payment or distribution from a Roth IRA shall not be treated as a qualified distribution under subparagraph (A) if such payment or distribution is made within the 5-taxable year period beginning with the 1st taxable year for which the individual made a contribution to a Roth IRA (or such individual's spouse made a contribution to a Roth IRA) established for such individual.

(C) Distributions of excess contributions and earnings—The term "qualified distribution" shall not include any distribution of any contribution described in section 408(d)(4) and any net income allocable to the contribution.

(3) Rollovers from an eligible retirement plan other than a Roth IRA—

(A) In general—Notwithstanding sections 402(c), 403(b)(8), 408(d)(3), and 457(e)(16), in the case of any distribution to which this paragraph applies—

(i) there shall be included in gross income any amount which would be includible were it not part of a qualified rollover contribution,

(ii) section 72(t) shall not apply, and

(iii) unless the taxpayer elects not to have this clause apply, any amount required to be included in gross income for any taxable year beginning in 2010 by reason of this paragraph shall be so included ratably over the 2-taxable-year period beginning with the first taxable year beginning in 2011.

Any election under clause (iii) for any distributions during a taxable year may not be changed after the due date for such taxable year.

(B) Distributions to which paragraph applies—This paragraph shall apply to a distribution from an eligible retirement plan (as defined by section 402(c)(8)(B)) maintained for the benefit of an individual which is contributed to a Roth IRA maintained for the benefit of such individual in a qualified rollover contribution. This paragraph shall not apply to a distribution which is a qualified rollover contribution from a Roth IRA or a qualified rollover contribution from a designated Roth account which is a rollover contribution described in section 402A(c)(3)(A).

(C) Conversions—The conversion of an individual retirement plan (other than a Roth IRA) to a Roth IRA shall be treated for purposes of this paragraph as a distribution to which this paragraph applies.

(D) Additional reporting requirements—Trustees of Roth IRAs, trustees of individual retirement plans, persons subject to section 6047(d)(1), or all of the foregoing persons, whichever is appropriate, shall include such additional information in reports required under section 408(i) or 6047 as the Secretary may require to ensure that amounts required to be included in gross income under subparagraph (A) are so included.

(E) Special rules for contributions to which 2-year averaging applies—In the case of a qualified rollover contribution to a Roth IRA of a distribution to which subparagraph (A)(iii) applied, the following rules shall apply:

(i) Acceleration of inclusion—

(I) In general—The amount otherwise required to be included in gross income for any taxable year beginning in 2010 or the first taxable year in the 2-year period under subparagraph (A)(iii) shall be increased by the aggregate distributions from Roth IRAs for such taxable year which are allocable under paragraph (4) to the portion of such qualified rollover contribution required to be included in gross income under subparagraph (A)(i).

(II) Limitation on aggregate amount included—The amount required to be included in gross income for any taxable year under subparagraph (A)(iii) shall not exceed the aggregate amount required to be included in gross income under subparagraph (A)(iii) for all taxable years in the 2-year period (without regard to subclause (I)) reduced by amounts included for all preceding taxable years.

(ii) Death of distributee—

(I) In general—If the individual required to include amounts in gross income under such subparagraph dies before all of such amounts are included, all remaining amounts shall be included in gross income for the taxable year which includes the date of death.

(II) Special rule for surviving spouse—If the spouse of the individual described in subclause (I) acquires the individual's entire interest in any Roth IRA to which such qualified rollover contribution is properly allocable, the spouse may elect to treat the remaining amounts described in subclause (I) as includible in the spouse's gross income in the taxable years of the spouse ending with or within the taxable years of such individual in which such amounts would otherwise have been includible. Any such election may not be made or changed after the due date for the spouse's taxable year which includes the date of death.

(F) Special rule for applying section 72—

(i) In general—If—

(I) any portion of a distribution from a Roth IRA is properly allocable to a qualified rollover contribution described in this paragraph; and

(II) such distribution is made within the 5-taxable year period beginning with the taxable year in which such contribution was made,

then section 72(t) shall be applied as if such portion were includible in gross income.

(ii) Limitation—Clause (i) shall apply only to the extent of the amount of the qualified rollover contribution includible in gross income under subparagraph (A)(i).

(4) Aggregation and ordering rules—

(A) Aggregation rules—Section 408(d)(2) shall be applied separately with respect to Roth IRAs and other individual retirement plans.

(B) Ordering rules—For purposes of applying this section and section 72 to any distribution from a Roth IRA, such distribution shall be treated as made—

(i) from contributions to the extent that the amount of such distribution, when added to all previous distributions from the Roth IRA, does not exceed the aggregate contributions to the Roth IRA; and

(ii) from such contributions in the following order:

(I) Contributions other than qualified rollover contributions to which paragraph (3) applies.

(II) Qualified rollover contributions to which paragraph (3) applies on a first-in, first-out basis.

Any distribution allocated to a qualified rollover contribution under clause (ii)(II) shall be allocated first to the portion of such contribution required to be included in gross income.

(5) Qualified special purpose distribution—For purposes of this section, the term "qualified special purpose distribution" means any distribution to which subparagraph (F) of section 72(t)(2) applies.

(6) Taxpayer may make adjustments before due date—

(A) In general—Except as provided by the Secretary, if, on or before the due date for any taxable year, a taxpayer transfers in a trustee-to-trustee transfer any contribution to an individual retirement plan made during such taxable year from such plan to any other individual retirement plan, then, for purposes of this chapter, such contribution shall be treated as having been made to the transferee plan (and not the transferor plan).

(B) Special rules—

(i) Transfer of earnings—Subparagraph (A) shall not apply to the transfer of any contribution unless such transfer is accompanied by any net income allocable to such contribution.

(ii) No deduction—Subparagraph (A) shall apply to the transfer of any contribution only to the extent no deduction was allowed with respect to the contribution to the transferor plan.

(7) Due date—For purposes of this subsection, the due date for any taxable year is the date prescribed by law (including extensions of time) for filing the taxpayer's return for such taxable year.

(e) Qualified rollover contribution—For purposes of this section—

(1) In general—The term "qualified rollover contribution" means a rollover contribution—

(A) to a Roth IRA from another such account,

(B) from an eligible retirement plan, but only if—

(i) in the case of an individual retirement plan, such rollover contribution meets the requirements of section 408(d)(3), and

(ii) in the case of any eligible retirement plan (as defined in section 402(c)(8)(B) other than clauses (i) and (ii) thereof), such rollover contribution meets the requirements of section 402(c), 403(b)(8), or 457(e)(16), as applicable.

For purposes of section 408(d)(3)(B), there shall be disregarded any qualified rollover contribution from an individual retirement plan (other than a Roth IRA) to a Roth IRA.

(2) Military death gratuity—

(A) In general—The term 'qualified rollover contribution' includes a contribution to a Roth IRA maintained for the benefit of an individual made before the end of the 1-year period beginning on the date on which such individual receives an amount under section 1477 of title 10, United States Code, or section 1967 of title 38 of such Code, with respect to a person, to the extent that such contribution does not exceed—

(i) the sum of the amounts received during such period by such individual under such sections with respect to such person, reduced by

(ii) the amounts so received which were contributed to a Coverdell education savings account under section 530(d)(9).

(B) Annual limit on number of rollovers not to apply—Section 408(d)(3)(B) shall not apply with respect to amounts treated as a rollover by the subparagraph (A).

(C) Application of section 72—For purposes of applying section 72 in the case of a distribution which is not a qualified distribution, the amount treated as a rollover by reason of subparagraph (A) shall be treated as investment in the contract.

(f) Individual retirement plan—For purposes of this section—

(1) a simplified employee pension or a simple retirement account may not be designated as a Roth IRA; and

(2) contributions to any such pension or account shall not be taken into account for purposes of subsection (c)(2)(B).

§ 409. Qualifications for tax credit employee stock ownership plans.

* * *

(e) Voting rights—

(1) In general—A plan meets the requirements of this subsection if it meets the requirements of paragraph (2) or (3), whichever is applicable.

(2) Requirements where employer has a registration-type class of securities—If the employer has a registration-type class of securities, the plan meets the requirements of this paragraph only if each participant or beneficiary in the plan is entitled to direct the plan as to the manner in which securities of the employer which are entitled to vote and are allocated to the account of such participant or beneficiary are to be voted.

(3) Requirement for other employers—If the employer does not have a registration-type class of securities, the plan meets the requirements of this paragraph only if each participant or beneficiary in the plan is entitled to direct the plan as to the manner in which voting rights under securities of the employer which are allocated to the account of such participant or beneficiary are to be exercised with respect to any corporate matter which involves the voting of such shares with respect to the approval or disapproval of any corporate merger or consolidation, recapitalization, reclassification, liquidation, dissolution, sale of substantially all assets of a trade or business, or such similar transaction as the Secretary may prescribe in regulations.

(4) Registration-type class of securities defined—For purposes of this subsection, the term "registration-type class of securities" means—

(A) a class of securities required to be registered under section 12 of the Securities Exchange Act of 1934, and

(B) a class of securities which would be required to be so registered except for the exemption from registration provided in subsection (g)(2)(H) of such section 12.

(5) 1 vote per participant—A plan meets the requirements of paragraph (3) with respect to an issue if—

(A) the plan permits each participant 1 vote with respect to such issue, and

(B) the trustee votes the shares held by the plan in the proportion determined after application of subparagraph (A).

* * *

(h) Right to demand employer securities; put option—

(1) In general—A plan meets the requirements of this subsection if a participant who is entitled to a distribution from the plan—

(A) has a right to demand that his benefits be distributed in the form of employer securities, and

(B) if the employer securities are not readily tradable on an established market, has a right to require that the employer repurchase employer securities under a fair valuation formula.

(2) Plan may distribute cash in certain cases—

(A) In general—A plan which otherwise meets the requirements of this subsection or of section 4975(e)(7) shall not be considered to have failed to meet the requirements of section 401(a) merely because under the plan the benefits may be distributed in cash or in the form of employer securities.

(B) Exception for certain plans restricted from distributing securities—

(i) In general—A plan to which this subparagraph applies shall not be treated as failing to meet the requirements of this subsection or section 401(a) merely because it does not permit a participant to exercise the right described in paragraph (1)(A) if such plan provides that the participant entitled to a distribution has a right to receive the distribution in cash, except that such plan may distribute employer securities subject to a requirement that such securities may be resold to the employer under terms which meet the requirements of paragraph (1)(B).

(ii) Applicable plans—This subparagraph shall apply to a plan which otherwise meets the requirements of this subsection or section 4975(e)(7) and which is established and maintained by—

(I) an employer whose charter or bylaws restrict the ownership of substantially all outstanding employer securities to employees or to a trust described in section 401(a), or

(II) an S corporation.

(3) Special rule for banks—In the case of a plan established and maintained by a bank (as defined in section 581) which is prohibited by law from redeeming or purchasing its own securities, the requirements of paragraph (1)(B) shall not apply if the plan provides that participants entitled to a distribution from the plan shall have a right to receive a distribution in cash.

(4) Put option period—An employer shall be deemed to satisfy the requirements of paragraph (1)(B) if it provides a put option for a period of at least 60 days following the date of distribution of stock of the employer and, if the put option is not exercised within such 60-day period, for an additional period of at least 60 days in the following plan year (as provided in regulations promulgated by the Secretary).

(5) Payment requirement for total distribution—If an employer is required to repurchase employer securities which are distributed to the employee as part of a total distribution, the requirements of paragraph (1)(B) shall be treated as met if—

(A) the amount to be paid for the employer securities is paid in substantially equal periodic payments (not less frequently than annually) over a period beginning not later than 30 days after the exercise of the put option described in paragraph (4) and not exceeding 5 years, and

(B) there is adequate security provided and reasonable interest paid on the unpaid amounts referred to in subparagraph (A).

For purposes of this paragraph, the term "total distribution" means the distribution within 1 taxable year to the recipient of the balance to the credit of the recipient's account.

(6) Payment requirement for installment distributions—If an employer is required to repurchase employer securities as part of an installment distribution, the requirements of paragraph (1)(B) shall be treated as met if the amount to be paid for the employer securities is paid not later than 30 days after the exercise of the put option described in paragraph (4).

(7) Exception where employee elected diversification—Paragraph (1)(A) shall not apply with respect to the portion of the participant's account which the employee elected to have reinvested under section 401(a)(28)(B) or subparagraph (B) or (C) of section 401(a)(35).

* * *

(l) Employer securities defined—For purposes of this section—

(1) In general—The term "employer securities" means common stock issued by the employer (or by a corporation which is a member of the same controlled group) which is readily tradable on an established securities market.

(2) Special rule where there is no readily tradable common stock—If there is no common stock which meets the requirements of paragraph (1), the term "employer securities" means common stock issued by the employer (or by a corporation which is a member of the same controlled group) having a combination of voting power and dividend rights equal to or in excess of—

(A) that class of common stock of the employer (or of any other such corporation) having the greatest voting power, and

(B) that class of common stock of the employer (or of any other such corporation) having the greatest dividend rights.

(3) Preferred stock may be issued in certain cases—Noncallable preferred stock shall be treated as employer securities if such stock is convertible at any time into stock which meets the requirements of paragraph (1) or (2) (whichever is applicable) and if such conversion is at a conversion price which (as of the date of the acquisition by the tax credit employee stock ownership plan) is reasonable. For purposes of the preceding sentence, under regulations prescribed by the Secretary, preferred stock shall be treated as noncallable if after the call there will be a reasonable opportunity for a conversion which meets the requirements of the preceding sentence.

(4) Application to controlled group of corporations—

(A) In general—For purposes of this subsection, the term "controlled group of corporations" has the meaning given to such term by section 1563(a) (determined without regard to subsections (a)(4) and (e)(3)(C) of section 1563).

(B) Where common parent owns at least 50 percent of first tier subsidiary—For purposes of subparagraph (A), if the common parent owns directly stock possessing at least 50 percent of the voting power of all classes of stock and at least 50 percent of each class of nonvoting stock in a first tier subsidiary, such subsidiary (and all other corporations below it in the chain which would meet the 80 percent test of section 1563(a) if the first tier subsidiary were the common parent) shall be treated as includible corporations.

(C) Where common parent owns 100 percent of first tier subsidiary—For purposes of subparagraph (A), if the common parent owns directly stock possessing all of the voting power of all classes of stock and all of the nonvoting stock, in a first tier subsidiary, and if the first tier subsidiary owns directly stock possessing at least 50 percent of the voting power of all classes of stock, and at least 50 percent of each class of nonvoting stock, in a second tier subsidiary of the common parent, such second tier subsidiary (and all other corporations below it in the chain which would meet the 80 percent test of section 1563(a) if the second tier subsidiary were the common parent) shall be treated as includible corporations.

(5) Nonvoting common stock may be acquired in certain cases—Nonvoting common stock of an employer described in the second sentence of section 401(a)(22) shall be treated as employer securities if an employer has a class of nonvoting common stock outstanding and the specific shares that the plan acquires have been issued and outstanding for at least 24 months.

* * *

(o) Distribution and payment requirements—A plan meets the requirements of this subsection if—

(1) Distribution requirement—

(A) In general—The plan provides that, if the participant and, if applicable pursuant to section 401(a)(11) and 417, with the consent of the participant's spouse elects the distribution of the participant's account balance in the plan will commence not later than 1 year after the close of the plan year—

(i) in which the participant separates from service by reason of the attainment of normal retirement age under the plan, disability, or death, or

(ii) which is the 5th plan year following the plan year in which the participant otherwise separates from service, except that this clause shall not apply if the participant is reemployed by the employer before distribution is required to begin under this clause.

(B) Exception for certain financed securities—For purposes of this subsection, the account balance of a participant shall not include any employer securities acquired with the proceeds of the loan described in section 404(a)(9) until the close of the plan year in which such loan is repaid in full.

(C) Limited distribution period—The plan provides that, unless the participant elects otherwise, the distribution of the participant's account balance will be in substantially equal periodic payments (not less frequently than annually) over a period not longer than the greater of—

(i) 5 years, or

(ii) in the case of a participant with an account balance in excess of $800,000, 5 years plus 1 additional year (but not more than 5 additional years) for each $160,000 or fraction thereof by which such balance exceeds $800,000.

(2) Cost-of-living adjustment—The Secretary shall adjust the dollar amounts under paragraph (1)(C) at the same time and in the same manner as under section 415(d).

* * *

§ 409A. Inclusion in gross income of deferred compensation under nonqualified deferred compensation plans

(a) Rules relating to constructive receipt—

(1) Plan failures—

(A) Gross income inclusion—

(i) In general—If at any time during a taxable year a nonqualified deferred compensation plan—

(I) fails to meet the requirements of paragraphs (2), (3), and (4), or

(II) is not operated in accordance with such requirements,

all compensation deferred under the plan for the taxable year and all preceding taxable years shall be includible in gross income for the taxable year to the extent not subject to a substantial risk of forfeiture and not previously included in gross income.

(ii) Application only to affected participants—Clause (i) shall only apply with respect to all compensation deferred under the plan for participants with respect to whom the failure relates.

(B) Interest and additional tax payable with respect to previously deferred compensation—

(i) **In general**—If compensation is required to be included in gross income under subparagraph (A) for a taxable year, the tax imposed by this chapter for the taxable year shall be increased by the sum of—

(I) the amount of interest determined under clause (ii), and

(II) an amount equal to 20 percent of the compensation which is required to be included in gross income.

(ii) **Interest**—For purposes of clause (i), the interest determined under this clause for any taxable year is the amount of interest at the underpayment rate plus 1 percentage point on the underpayments that would have occurred had the deferred compensation been includible in gross income for the taxable year in which first deferred or, if later, the first taxable year in which such deferred compensation is not subject to a substantial risk of forfeiture.

(2) Distributions—

(A) In general—The requirements of this paragraph are met if the plan provides that compensation deferred under the plan may not be distributed earlier than—

(i) separation from service as determined by the Secretary (except as provided in subparagraph (B)(i)),

(ii) the date the participant becomes disabled (within the meaning of subparagraph (C)),

(iii) death,

(iv) a specified time (or pursuant to a fixed schedule) specified under the plan at the date of the deferral of such compensation,

(v) to the extent provided by the Secretary, a change in the ownership or effective control of the corporation, or in the ownership of a substantial portion of the assets of the corporation, or

(vi) the occurrence of an unforeseeable emergency.

(B) Special rules—

(i) **Specified employees**—In the case of any specified employee, the requirement of subparagraph (A)(i) is met only if distributions may not be made before the date which is 6 months after the date of separation from service (or, if earlier, the date of death of the employee). For purposes of the preceding sentence, a specified employee is a key employee (as defined in section 416(i) without regard to paragraph (5) thereof) of a corporation any stock in which is publicly traded on an established securities market or otherwise.

(ii) **Unforeseeable emergency**—For purposes of subparagraph (A)(vi)—

(I) **In general**—The term 'unforeseeable emergency' means a severe financial hardship to the participant resulting from an illness or accident of the participant, the participant's spouse, or a dependent (as defined in section 152(a)) of the participant, loss of the participant's property due to casualty, or other similar extraordinary and unforeseeable circumstances arising as a result of events beyond the control of the participant.

(II) Limitation on distributions—The requirement of subparagraph (A)(vi) is met only if, as determined under regulations of the Secretary, the amounts distributed with respect to an emergency do not exceed the amounts necessary to satisfy such emergency plus amounts necessary to pay taxes reasonably anticipated as a result of the distribution, after taking into account the extent to which such hardship is or may be relieved through reimbursement or compensation by insurance or otherwise or by liquidation of the participant's assets (to the extent the liquidation of such assets would not itself cause severe financial hardship).

(C) Disabled—For purposes of subparagraph (A)(ii), a participant shall be considered disabled if the participant—

(i) is unable to engage in any substantial gainful activity by reason of any medically determinable physical or mental impairment which can be expected to result in death or can be expected to last for a continuous period of not less than 12 months, or

(ii) is, by reason of any medically determinable physical or mental impairment which can be expected to result in death or can be expected to last for a continuous period of not less than 12 months, receiving income replacement benefits for a period of not less than 3 months under an accident and health plan covering employees of the participant's employer.

(3) Acceleration of benefits—The requirements of this paragraph are met if the plan does not permit the acceleration of the time or schedule of any payment under the plan, except as provided in regulations by the Secretary.

(4) Elections—

(A) In general—The requirements of this paragraph are met if the requirements of subparagraphs (B) and (C) are met.

(B) Initial deferral decision—

(i) In general—The requirements of this subparagraph are met if the plan provides that compensation for services performed during a taxable year may be deferred at the participant's election only if the election to defer such compensation is made not later than the close of the preceding taxable year or at such other time as provided in regulations.

(ii) First year of eligibility—In the case of the first year in which a participant becomes eligible to participate in the plan, such election may be made with respect to services to be performed subsequent to the election within 30 days after the date the participant becomes eligible to participate in such plan.

(iii) Performance-based compensation—In the case of any performance-based compensation based on services performed over a period of at least 12 months, such election may be made no later than 6 months before the end of the period.

(C) Changes in time and form of distribution—The requirements of this subparagraph are met if, in the case of a plan which permits under a subsequent election a delay in a payment or a change in the form of payment—

(i) the plan requires that such election may not take effect until at least 12 months after the date on which the election is made,

(ii) in the case of an election related to a payment not described in clause (ii), (iii), or (vi) of paragraph (2)(A), the plan requires that the payment with respect to which such election is made be deferred for a period of not less than 5 years from the date such payment would otherwise have been made, and

(iii) the plan requires that any election related to a payment described in paragraph (2)(A)(iv) may not be made less than 12 months prior to the date of the first scheduled payment under such paragraph.

(b) Rules relating to funding—

(1) Offshore property in a trust—In the case of assets set aside (directly or indirectly) in a trust (or other arrangement determined by the Secretary) for purposes of paying deferred compensation under a nonqualified deferred compensation plan, for purposes of section 83 such assets shall be treated as property transferred in connection with the performance of services whether or not such assets are available to satisfy claims of general creditors—

(A) at the time set aside if such assets (or such trust or other arrangement) are located outside of the United States, or

(B) at the time transferred if such assets (or such trust or other arrangement) are subsequently transferred outside of the United States.

This paragraph shall not apply to assets located in a foreign jurisdiction if substantially all of the services to which the nonqualified deferred compensation relates are performed in such jurisdiction.

(2) Employer's financial health—In the case of compensation deferred under a nonqualified deferred compensation plan, there is a transfer of property within the meaning of section 83 with respect to such compensation as of the earlier of—

(A) the date on which the plan first provides that assets will become restricted to the provision of benefits under the plan in connection with a change in the employer's financial health, or

(B) the date on which assets are so restricted,

whether or not such assets are available to satisfy claims of general creditors.

(3) Treatment of employer's defined benefit plan during restricted period—

(A) In general—If—

(i) during any restricted period with respect to a single-employer defined benefit plan, assets are set aside or reserved (directly or indirectly) in a trust (or other arrangement as determined by the Secretary) or transferred to such a trust or other arrangement for purposes of paying deferred compensation of an applicable covered employee under a nonqualified deferred compensation plan of the plan sponsor or member of a controlled group which includes the plan sponsor, or

(ii) a nonqualified deferred compensation plan of the plan sponsor or member of a controlled group which includes the plan sponsor provides that assets will become restricted to the provision of benefits under the plan to an applicable covered employee in connection with such restricted period (or other similar financial measure determined by the Secretary) with respect to the defined benefit plan, or assets are so restricted,

such assets shall, for purposes of section 83, be treated as property transferred in connection with the performance of services whether or not such assets are available to satisfy claims of general creditors. Clause (i) shall not apply with respect to any assets which are so set aside before the restricted period with respect to the defined benefit plan.

(B) Restricted period—For purposes of this section, the term "restricted period" means, with respect to any plan described in subparagraph (A)—

(i) any period during which the plan is in at-risk status (as defined in section 430(i));

(ii) any period the plan sponsor is a debtor in a case under title 11, United States Code, or similar Federal or State law, and

(iii) the 12-month period beginning on the date which is 6 months before the termination date of the plan if, as of the termination date, the plan is not sufficient for benefit liabilities (within the meaning of section 4041 of the Employee Retirement Income Security Act of 1974).

(C) Special rule for payment of taxes on deferred compensation included in income—If an employer provides directly or indirectly for the payment of any Federal, State, or local income taxes with respect to any compensation required to be included in gross income by reason of this paragraph—

(i) interest shall be imposed under subsection (a)(1)(B)(i)(I) on the amount of such payment in the same manner as if such payment was part of the deferred compensation to which it relates,

(ii) such payment shall be taken into account in determining the amount of the additional tax under subsection (a)(1)(B)(i)(II) in the same manner as if such payment was part of the deferred compensation to which it relates, and

(iii) no deduction shall be allowed under this title with respect to such payment.

(D) Other definitions—For purposes of this section—

(i) Applicable covered employee—The term "applicable covered employee" means any—

(I) covered employee of a plan sponsor,

(II) covered employee of a member of a controlled group which includes the plan sponsor, and

(III) former employee who was a covered employee at the time of termination of employment with the plan sponsor or a member of a controlled group which includes the plan sponsor.

(ii) Covered employee—The term "covered employee" means an individual described in section 162(m)(3) or an individual subject to the requirements of section 16(a) of the Securities Exchange Act of 1934.

(4) Income inclusion for offshore trusts and employer's financial health—For each taxable year that assets treated as transferred under this subsection remain set aside in a trust or other arrangement subject to paragraph (1), (2), or (3), any increase in value in, or earnings with respect to, such assets shall be treated as an additional transfer of property under this subsection (to the extent not previously included in income).

(5) Interest on tax liability payable with respect to transferred property—

(A) In general—If amounts are required to be included in gross income by reason of paragraph (1), (2), or (3) for a taxable year, the tax imposed by this chapter for such taxable year shall be increased by the sum of—

(i) the amount of interest determined under subparagraph (B), and

(ii) an amount equal to 20 percent of the amounts required to be included in gross income.

(B) Interest—For purposes of subparagraph (A), the interest determined under this subparagraph for any taxable year is the amount of interest at the underpayment rate plus 1 percentage point on the underpayments that would have occurred had the amounts so required to be included in gross income by paragraph (1), (2), or (3) been includible in gross income for the taxable year in which first deferred or, if later, the first taxable year in which such amounts are not subject to a substantial risk of forfeiture.

(c) No inference on earlier income inclusion or requirement of later inclusion—Nothing in this section shall be construed to prevent the inclusion of amounts in gross income under any other provision of this chapter or any other rule of law earlier than the time provided in this section. Any amount included in gross income under this section shall not be required to be included in gross income under any other provision of this chapter or any other rule of law later than the time provided in this section.

(d) Other definitions and special rules—For purposes of this section—

(1) Nonqualified deferred compensation plan—The term 'nonqualified deferred compensation plan' means any plan that provides for the deferral of compensation, other than—

(A) a qualified employer plan, and

(B) any bona fide vacation leave, sick leave, compensatory time, disability pay, or death benefit plan.

(2) Qualified employer plan—The term 'qualified employer plan' means—

(A) any plan, contract, pension, account, or trust described in subparagraph (A) or (B) of section 219(g)(5) (without regard to subparagraph (A)(iii)),

(B) any eligible deferred compensation plan (within the meaning of section 457(b)), and

(C) any plan described in section 415(m).

(3) Plan includes arrangements, etc—The term 'plan' includes any agreement or arrangement, including an agreement or arrangement that includes one person.

(4) Substantial risk of forfeiture—The rights of a person to compensation are subject to a substantial risk of forfeiture if such person's rights to such compensation are conditioned upon the future performance of substantial services by any individual.

(5) Treatment of earnings—References to deferred compensation shall be treated as including references to income (whether actual or notional) attributable to such compensation or such income.

(6) Aggregation rules—Except as provided by the Secretary, rules similar to the rules of subsections (b) and (c) of section 414 shall apply.

(e) Regulations—The Secretary shall prescribe such regulations as may be necessary or appropriate to carry out the purposes of this section, including regulations—

(1) providing for the determination of amounts of deferral in the case of a nonqualified deferred compensation plan which is a defined benefit plan,

(2) relating to changes in the ownership and control of a corporation or assets of a corporation for purposes of subsection (a)(2)(A)(v),

(3) exempting arrangements from the application of subsection (b) if such arrangements will not result in an improper deferral of United States tax and will not result in assets being effectively beyond the reach of creditors,

(4) defining financial health for purposes of subsection (b)(2), and

(5) disregarding a substantial risk of forfeiture in cases where necessary to carry out the purposes of this section.

§ 410. Minimum participation standards

(a) Participation—

(1) Minimum age and service conditions—

(A) General rule—A trust shall not constitute a qualified trust under section 401(a) if the plan of which it is a part requires, as a condition of participation in the plan, that an employee complete a period of service with the employer or employers maintaining the plan extending beyond the later of the following dates—

(i) the date on which the employee attains the age of 21; or

(ii) the date on which he completes 1 year of service (1,000 hours)

(B) Special rules for certain plans—

(i) In the case of any plan which provides that after not more than 2 years of service each participant has a right to 100 percent of his accrued benefit under the plan which is nonforfeitable (within the meaning of section 411) at the time such benefit accrues, clause (ii) of subparagraph (A) shall be applied by substituting "2 years of service" for "1 year of service".

(ii) In the case of any plan maintained exclusively for employees of an educational institution (as defined in section 170(b)(1)(A)(ii)) by an employer which is exempt from tax under section 501(a) which provides that each participant having at least 1 year of service has a right to 100 percent of his accrued benefit under the plan which is nonforfeitable (within the meaning of section 411) at the time such benefit accrues, clause (i) of subparagraph (A) shall be applied by substituting "26" for "21". This clause shall not apply to any plan to which clause (i) applies.

(2) Maximum age conditions—A trust shall not constitute a qualified trust under section 401(a) if the plan of which it is a part excludes from participation (on the basis of age) employees who have attained a specified age.

(3) Definition of year of service—

(A) General rule—For purposes of this subsection, the term "year of service" means a 12-month period during which the employee has not less than 1,000 hours of service. For purposes of this paragraph, computation of any 12-month period shall be made with reference to the date on which the employee's employment commenced, except that, under regulations prescribed by the Secretary of Labor, such computation may be made by reference to the first day of a plan year in the case of an employee who does not complete 1,000 hours of service during the 12-month period beginning on the date his employment commenced.

(B) Seasonal industries—In the case of any seasonal industry where the customary period of employment is less than 1,000 hours during a calendar year, the term "year of service" shall be such period as may be determined under regulations prescribed by the Secretary of Labor.

(C) Hours of service—For purposes of this subsection, the term "hour of service" means a time of service determined under regulations prescribed by the Secretary of Labor.

(D) Maritime industries—For purposes of this subsection, in the case of any maritime industry, 125 days of service shall be treated as 1,000 hours of service. The Secretary of Labor may prescribe regulations to carry out this subparagraph.

(4) Time of participation—A plan shall be treated as not meeting the requirements of paragraph (1) unless it provides that any employee who has satisfied the minimum age and service requirements specified in such paragraph, and who is otherwise entitled to participate in the plan, commences participation in the plan no later than the earlier of—

(A) the first day of the first plan year beginning after the date on which such employee satisfied such requirements, or

(B) the date 6 months after the date on which he satisfied such requirements,

unless such employee was separated from the service before the date referred to in subparagraph (A) or (B), whichever is applicable.

(5) Breaks in service—

(A) General rule—Except as otherwise provided in subparagraphs (B), (C), and (D), all years of service with the employer or employers maintaining the plan shall be taken into account in computing the period of service for purposes of paragraph (1).

(B) Employees under 2-year 100 percent vesting—In the case of any employee who has any 1-year break in service (as defined in section 411(a)(6)(A)) under a plan to which the service requirements of clause (i) of paragraph (1)(B) apply, if such employee has not satisfied such requirements, service before such break shall not be required to be taken into account.

(C) 1-year break in service—In computing an employee's period of service for purposes of paragraph (1) in the case of any participant who has any 1-year break in service (as defined in section 411(a)(6)(A)), service before such break shall not be required to be taken into account under the plan until he has completed a year of service (as defined in paragraph (3)) after his return.

(D) Nonvested participants—

(i) In general—For purposes of paragraph (1), in the case of a nonvested participant, years of service with the employer or employers maintaining the plan before any period of consecutive 1-year breaks in service shall not be required to be taken into account in computing the period of service if the number of consecutive 1-year breaks in service within such period equals or exceeds the greater of—

(I) 5, or

(II) the aggregate number of years of service before such period.

(ii) Years of service not taken into account—If any years of service are not required to be taken into account by reason of a period of breaks in service to which clause (i) applies, such years of service shall not be taken into account in applying clause (i) to a subsequent period of breaks in service.

(iii) Nonvested participant defined—For purposes of clause (i), the term "nonvested participant" means a participant who does not have any nonforfeitable right under the plan to an accrued benefit derived from employer contributions.

(E) Special rule for maternity or paternity absences—

(i) General rule—In the case of each individual who is absent from work for any period—

(I) by reason of the pregnancy of the individual,

(II) by reason of the birth of a child of the individual,

(III) by reason of the placement of a child with the individual in connection with the adoption of such child by such individual, or

(IV) for purposes of caring for such child for a period beginning immediately following such birth or placement,

the plan shall treat as hours of service, solely for purposes of determining under this paragraph whether a 1-year break in service (as defined in section 411(a)(6)(A)) has occurred, the hours described in clause (ii).

(ii) Hours treated as hours of service—The hours described in this clause are—

(I) the hours of service which otherwise would normally have been credited to such individual but for such absence, or

(II) in any case in which the plan is unable to determine the hours described in subclause (I), 8 hours of service per day of such absence,

except that the total number of hours treated as hours of service under this clause by reason of any such pregnancy or placement shall not exceed 501 hours.

(iii) Year to which hours are credited—The hours described in clause (ii) shall be treated as hours of service as provided in this subparagraph—

(I) only in the year in which the absence from work begins, if a participant would be prevented from incurring a 1-year break in service in such year solely because the period of absence is treated as hours of service as provided in clause (i); or

(II) in any other case, in the immediately following year.

(iv) **Year defined**—For purposes of this subparagraph, the term "year" means the period used in computations pursuant to paragraph (3).

(v) **Information required to be filed**—A plan shall not fail to satisfy the requirements of this subparagraph solely because it provides that no credit will be given pursuant to this subparagraph unless the individual furnishes to the plan administrator such timely information as the plan may reasonably require to establish—

(I) that the absence from work is for reasons referred to in clause (i), and

(II) the number of days for which there was such an absence.

(b) Minimum coverage requirements—

(1) In general—A trust shall not constitute a qualified trust under section 401(a) unless such trust is designated by the employer as part of a plan which meets 1 of the following requirements:

(A) The plan benefits at least 70 percent of employees who are not highly compensated employees.

(B) The plan benefits—

(i) a percentage of employees who are not highly compensated employees which is at least 70 percent of

(ii) the percentage of highly compensated employees benefiting under the plan.

(C) The plan meets the requirements of paragraph (2).

(2) Average benefit percentage test—

(A) **In general**—A plan shall be treated as meeting the requirements of this paragraph if—

(i) the plan benefits such employees as qualify under a classification set up by the employer and found by the Secretary not to be discriminatory in favor of highly compensated employees, and

(ii) the average benefit percentage for employees who are not highly compensated employees is at least 70 percent of the average benefit percentage for highly compensated employees.

(B) **Average benefit percentage**—For purposes of this paragraph, the term "average benefit percentage" means, with respect to any group, the average of the benefit percentages calculated separately with respect to each employee in such group (whether or not a participant in any plan).

(C) **Benefit percentage**—For purposes of this paragraph—

(i) **In general**—The term "benefit percentage" means the employer-provided contribution or benefit of an employee under all qualified plans maintained by the employer, expressed as a percentage of such employee's compensation (within the meaning of section 414(s)).

(ii) Period for computing percentage—At the election of an employer, the benefit percentage for any plan year shall be computed on the basis of contributions or benefits for—

(I) such plan year, or

(II) any consecutive plan year period (not greater than 3 years) which cnds with such plan year and which is specified in such election.

An election under this clause, once made, may be revoked or modified only with the consent of the Secretary.

(D) Employees taken into account—For purposes of determining who is an employee for purposes of determining the average benefit percentage under subparagraph (B)—

(i) except as provided in clause (ii), paragraph (4)(A) shall not apply, or

(ii) if the employer elects, paragraph (4)(A) shall be applied by using the lowest age and service requirements of all qualified plans maintained by the employer.

(E) Qualified plan—For purposes of this paragraph, the term "qualified plan" means any plan which (without regard to this subsection) meets the requirements of section 401(a).

(3) Exclusion of certain employees—For purposes of this subsection, there shall be excluded from consideration—

(A) employees who are included in a unit of employees covered by an agreement which the Secretary of Labor finds to be a collective bargaining agreement between employee representatives and one or more employers, if there is evidence that retirement benefits were the subject of good faith bargaining between such employee representatives and such employer or employers,

(B) in the case of a trust established or maintained pursuant to an agreement which the Secretary of Labor finds to be a collective bargaining agreement between air pilots represented in accordance with title II of the Railway Labor Act and one or more employers, all employees not covered by such agreement, and

(C) employees who are nonresident aliens and who receive no earned income (within the meaning of section 911(d)(2)) from the employer which constitutes income from sources within the United States (within the meaning of section 861(a)(3)).

Subparagraph (A) shall not apply with respect to coverage of employees under a plan pursuant to an agreement under such subparagraph. For purposes of subparagraph (B), management pilots who are not represented in accordance with title II of the Railway Labor Act shall be treated as covered by a collective bargaining agreement described in such subparagraph if the management pilots manage the flight operations of air pilots who are so represented and the management pilots are, pursuant to the terms of the agreement, included in the group of employees benefitting under the trust described in such subparagraph. Subparagraph (B) shall not apply in the case of a plan which provides contributions or benefits for employees whose principal duties are not customarily performed aboard an aircraft in flight (other than management pilots described in the preceding sentence).

(4) Exclusion of employees not meeting age and service requirements—

   (A) In general—If a plan—

      (i) prescribes minimum age and service requirements as a condition of participation, and

      (ii) excludes all employees not meeting such requirements from participation,

then such employees shall be excluded from consideration for purposes of this subsection.

   (B) Requirements may be met separately with respect to excluded group—If employees not meeting the minimum age or service requirements of subsection (a)(1) (without regard to subparagraph (B) thereof) are covered under a plan of the employer which meets the requirements of paragraph (1) separately with respect to such employees, such employees may be excluded from consideration in determining whether any plan of the employer meets the requirements of paragraph (1).

   (C) Requirements not treated as being met before entry date—An employee shall not be treated as meeting the age and service requirements described in this paragraph until the first date on which, under the plan, any employee with the same age and service would be eligible to commence participation in the plan.

(5) Line of business exception—

   (A) In general—If, under section 414(r), an employer is treated as operating separate lines of business for a year, the employer may apply the requirements of this subsection for such year separately with respect to employees in each separate line of business.

   (B) Plan must be nondiscriminatory—Subparagraph (A) shall not apply with respect to any plan maintained by an employer unless such plan benefits such employees as qualify under a classification set up by the employer and found by the Secretary not to be discriminatory in favor of highly compensated employees.

(6) Definitions and special rules—For purposes of this subsection—

   (A) Highly compensated employee—The term "highly compensated employee" has the meaning given such term by section 414(q).

   (B) Aggregation rules—An employer may elect to designate—

      (i) 2 or more trusts,

      (ii) 1 or more trusts and 1 or more annuity plans, or

      (iii) 2 or more annuity plans,

as part of 1 plan intended to qualify under section 401(a) to determine whether the requirements of this subsection are met with respect to such trusts or annuity plans. If an employer elects to treat any trusts or annuity plans as 1 plan under this subparagraph, such trusts or annuity plans shall be treated as 1 plan for purposes of section 401(a)(4).

   (C) Special rules for certain dispositions or acquisitions—

      (i) In general—If a person becomes, or ceases to be, a member of a group described in subsection (b), (c), (m), or (o) of section 414, then the requirements of this subsection shall be treated as having been met during the transition period with respect to any plan covering employees of such person or any other member of such group if—

 (I) such requirements were met immediately before each such change, and

 (II) the coverage under such plan is not significantly changed during the transition period (other than by reason of the change in members of a group) or such plan meets such other requirements as the Secretary may prescribe by regulation.

 (ii) Transition period—For purposes of clause (i), the term "transition period" means the period—

 (I) beginning on the date of the change in members of a group, and

 (II) ending on the last day of the 1st plan year beginning after the date of such change.

(D) Special rule for certain employee stock ownership plans—A trust which is part of a tax credit employee stock ownership plan which is the only plan of an employer intended to qualify under section 401(a) shall not be treated as not a qualified trust under section 401(a) solely because it fails to meet the requirements of this subsection if—

 (i) such plan benefits 50 percent or more of all the employees who are eligible under a nondiscriminatory classification under the plan, and

 (ii) the sum of the amounts allocated to each participant's account for the year does not exceed 2 percent of the compensation of that participant for the year.

(E) Eligibility to contribute—In the case of contributions which are subject to section 401(k) or 401(m), employees who are eligible to contribute (or elect to have contributions made on their behalf) shall be treated as benefiting under the plan (other than for purposes of paragraph (2)(A)(ii)).

(F) Employers with only highly compensated employees—A plan maintained by an employer which has no employees other than highly compensated employees for any year shall be treated as meeting the requirements of this subsection for such year.

(G) Regulations—The Secretary shall prescribe such regulations as may be necessary or appropriate to carry out the purposes of this subsection.

(c) Application of participation standards to certain plans—

(1) The provisions of this section (other than paragraph (2) of this subsection) shall not apply to—

(A) a governmental plan (within the meaning of section 414(d)),

(B) a church plan (within the meaning of section 414(e)) with respect to which the election provided by subsection (d) of this section has not been made,

(C) a plan which has not at any time after September 2, 1974, provided for employer contributions, and

(D) a plan established and maintained by a society, order, or association described in section 501(c)(8) or (9) if no part of the contributions to or under such plan are made by employers of participants in such plan.

(2) A plan described in paragraph (1) shall be treated as meeting the requirements of this section for purposes of section 401(a), except that in the case of a plan described in subparagraph (B), (C), or (D) of paragraph (1), this paragraph shall apply only if such plan meets the requirements of section 401(a)(3) (as in effect on September 1, 1974).

(d) Election by church to have participation, vesting, funding, etc., provisions apply—

(1) In general—If the church or convention or association of churches which maintains any church plan makes an election under this subsection (in such form and manner as the Secretary may by regulations prescribe), then the provisions of this title relating to participation, vesting, funding, etc. (as in effect from time to time) shall apply to such church plan as if such provisions did not contain an exclusion for church plans.

(2) Election irrevocable—An election under this subsection with respect to any church plan shall be binding with respect to such plan, and, once made, shall be irrevocable.

§ 411. Minimum vesting standards.

(a) General rule—A trust shall not constitute a qualified trust under section 401(a) unless the plan of which such trust is a part provides that an employee's right to his normal retirement benefit is nonforfeitable upon the attainment of normal retirement age (as defined in paragraph (8)) and in addition satisfies the requirements of paragraphs (1), (2), and (11) of this subsection and the requirements of subsection (b)(3), and also satisfies, in the case of a defined benefit plan, the requirements of subsection (b)(1) and, in the case of a defined contribution plan, the requirements of subsection (b)(2).

(1) Employee contributions—A plan satisfies the requirements of this paragraph if an employee's rights in his accrued benefit derived from his own contributions are nonforfeitable.

(2) Employer contributions—

(A) Defined benefit plans—

(i) In general—In the case of a defined benefit plan, a plan satisfies the requirements of this paragraph if it satisfies the requirements of clause (ii) or (iii).

(ii) 5-year vesting—A plan satisfies the requirements of this clause if an employee who has completed at least 5 years of service has a nonforfeitable right to 100 percent of the employee's accrued benefit derived from employer contributions.

(iii) 3 to 7 year vesting—A plan satisfies the requirements of this clause if an employee has a nonforfeitable right to a percentage of the employee's accrued benefit derived from employer contributions determined under the following table:

Years of service:	The nonforfeitable percentage is:
3	20
4	40
5	60
6	80
7 or more	100.

(B) Defined contribution plans—

(i) In general—In the case of a defined contribution plan, a plan satisfies the requirements of this paragraph if it satisfies the requirements of clause (ii) or (iii).

      (ii) 3-year vesting—A plan satisfies the requirements of this clause if an employee who has completed at least 3 years of service has a nonforfeitable right to 100 percent of the employee's accrued benefit derived from employer contributions.

      (iii) 2 to 6 year vesting—A plan satisfies the requirements of this clause if an employee has a nonforfeitable right to a percentage of the employee's accrued benefit derived from employer contributions determined under the following table:

Years of service:	The nonforfeitable percentage is:
2	20
3	40
4	60
5	80
6 or more	100.

  (3) Certain permitted forfeitures, suspensions, etc—For purposes of this subsection—

    (A) Forfeiture on account of death—A right to an accrued benefit derived from employer contributions shall not be treated as forfeitable solely because the plan provides that it is not payable if the participant dies (except in the case of a survivor annuity which is payable as provided in section 401(a)(11)).

    (B) Suspension of benefits upon reemployment of retiree—A right to an accrued benefit derived from employer contributions shall not be treated as forfeitable solely because the plan provides that the payment of benefits is suspended for such period as the employee is employed, subsequent to the commencement of payment of such benefits—

      (i) in the case of a plan other than a multiemployer plan, by the employer who maintains the plan under which such benefits were being paid; and

      (ii) in the case of a multiemployer plan, in the same industry, the same trade or craft, and the same geographic area covered by the plan as when such benefits commenced.

The Secretary of Labor shall prescribe such regulations as may be necessary to carry out the purposes of this subparagraph, including regulations with respect to the meaning of the term "employed".

    (C) Effect of retroactive plan amendments—A right to an accrued benefit derived from employer contributions shall not be treated as forfeitable solely because plan amendments may be given retroactive application as provided in section 412(d)(2).

    (D) Withdrawal of mandatory contributions—

      (i) A right to an accrued benefit derived from employer contributions shall not be treated as forfeitable solely because the plan provides that, in the case of a participant who does not have a nonforfeitable right to at least 50 percent of his accrued benefit derived from employer contributions, such accrued benefit may be forfeited on account of the withdrawal by the participant of any amount attributable to the benefit derived from mandatory contributions (as defined in subsection (c)(2)(C)) made by such participant.

(ii) Clause (i) shall not apply to a plan unless the plan provides that any accrued benefit forfeited under a plan provision described in such clause shall be restored upon repayment by the participant of the full amount of the withdrawal described in such clause plus, in the case of a defined benefit plan, interest. Such interest shall be computed on such amount at the rate determined for purposes of subsection (c)(2)(C) on the date of such repayment (computed annually from the date of such withdrawal). The plan provision required under this clause may provide that such repayment must be made (I) in the case of a withdrawal on a account of separation from service, before the earlier of 5 years after the first date on which the participant is subsequently re-employed by the employer, or the close of the first period of 5 consecutive 1-year breaks in service commencing after the withdrawal; or (II) in the case of any other withdrawal, 5 years after the date of the withdrawal.

(iii) In the case of accrued benefits derived from employer contributions which accrued before September 2, 1974, a right to such accrued benefit derived from employer contributions shall not be treated as forfeitable solely because the plan provides that an amount of such accrued benefit may be forfeited on account of the withdrawal by the participant of an amount attributable to the benefit derived from mandatory contributions (as defined in subsection (c)(2)(C)) made by such participant before September 2, 1974 if such amount forfeited is proportional to such amount withdrawn. This clause shall not apply to any plan to which any mandatory contribution is made after September 2, 1974. The Secretary shall prescribe such regulations as may be necessary to carry out the purposes of this clause.

(iv) For purposes of this subparagraph, in the case of any class-year plan, a withdrawal of employee contributions shall be treated as a withdrawal of such contributions on a plan year by plan year basis in succeeding order of time.

(v) For nonforfeitability where the employee has a nonforfeitable right to at least 50 percent of his accrued benefit, see section 401(a)(19).

(E) Cessation of contributions under a multiemployer plan—A right to an accrued benefit derived from employer contributions under a multiemployer plan shall not be treated as forfeitable solely because the plan provides that benefits accrued as a result of service with the participant's employer before the employer had an obligation to contribute under the plan may not be payable if the employer ceases contributions to the multiemployer plan.

(F) Reduction and suspension of benefits by a multiemployer plan—A participant's right to an accrued benefit derived from employer contributions under a multiemployer plan shall not be treated as forfeitable solely because—

(i) the plan is amended to reduce benefits under section 418D or under section 4281 of the Employee Retirement Income Security Act of 1974, or

(ii) benefit payments under the plan may be suspended under section 418E or under section 4281 of the Employee Retirement Income Security Act of 1974.

(G) Treatment of matching contributions forfeited by reason of excess deferral or contribution or permissible withdrawal—A matching contribution (within the meaning of section 401(m)) shall not be treated as forfeitable merely because such contribution is forfeitable if the contribution to which the matching contribution relates is treated as an excess contribution under section 401(k)(8)(B), an excess deferral under section 402(g)(2)(A), a permissible withdrawal under section 414(w), or an excess aggregate contribution under section 401(m)(6)(B).

(4) Service included in determination of nonforfeitable percentage or erroneous automatic contribution—In computing the period of service under the plan for purposes of determining the nonforfeitable percentage under paragraph (2), all of an employee's years of service with the employer or employers maintaining the plan shall be taken into account, except that the following may be disregarded:

(A) years of service before age 18,

(B) years of service during a period for which the employee declined to contribute to a plan requiring employee contributions;

(C) years of service with an employer during any period for which the employer did not maintain the plan or a predecessor plan (as defined under regulations prescribed by the Secretary);

(D) service not required to be taken into account under paragraph (6);

(E) years of service before January 1, 1971, unless the employee has had at least 3 years of service after December 31, 1970;

(F) years of service before the first plan year to which this section applies, if such service would have been disregarded under the rules of the plan with regard to breaks in service as in effect on the applicable date; and

(G) in the case of a multiemployer plan, years of service—

    (i) with an employer after—

        (I) a complete withdrawal of that employer from the plan (within the meaning of section 4203 of the Employee Retirement Income Security Act of 1974), or

        (II) to the extent permitted in regulations prescribed by the Secretary, a partial withdrawal described in section 4205(b)(2)(A)(i) of such Act in conjunction with the decertification of the collective bargaining representative, and

    (ii) with any employer under the plan after the termination date of the plan under section 4048 of such Act.

(5) Year of service—

(A) General rule—For purposes of this subsection, except as provided in subparagraph (C), the term "year of service" means a calendar year, plan year, or other 12-consecutive month period designated by the plan (and not prohibited under regulations prescribed by the Secretary of Labor) during which the participant has completed 1,000 hours of service.

(B) Hours of service—For purposes of this subsection, the term "hours of service" has the meaning provided by section 410(a)(3)(C).

(C) Seasonal industries—In the case of any seasonal industry where the customary period of employment is less than 1,000 hours during a calendar year, the term "year of service" shall be such period as may be determined under regulations prescribed by the Secretary of Labor.

(D) Maritime industries—For purposes of this subsection, in the case of any maritime industry, 125 days of service shall be treated as 1,000 hours of service. The Secretary of Labor may prescribe regulations to carry out the purposes of this subparagraph.

(6) Breaks in service—

(A) Definition of 1-year break in service—For purposes of this paragraph, the term "1-year break in service" means a calendar year, plan year, or other 12-consecutive-month period designated by the plan (and not prohibited under regulations prescribed by the Secretary of Labor) during which the participant has not completed more than 500 hours of service.

(B) 1 year of service after 1-year break in service—For purposes of paragraph (4), in the case of any employee who has any 1-year break in service, years of service before such break shall not be required to be taken into account until he has completed a year of service after his return.

(C) 5 consecutive 1-year breaks in service under defined contribution plan—For purposes of paragraph (4), in the case of any participant in a defined contribution plan, or an insured defined benefit plan which satisfies the requirements of subsection (b)(1)(F), who has 5 consecutive 1-year breaks in service, years of service after such 5-year period shall not be required to be taken into account for purposes of determining the nonforfeitable percentage of his accrued benefit derived from employer contributions which accrued before such 5-year period.

(D) Nonvested participants—

(i) In general—For purposes of paragraph (4), in the case of a nonvested participant, years of service with the employer or employers maintaining the plan before any period of consecutive 1-year breaks in service shall not be required to be taken into account if the number of consecutive 1-year breaks in service within such period equals or exceeds the greater of—

(I) 5, or

(II) the aggregate number of years of service before such period.

(ii) Years of service not taken into account—If any years of service are not required to be taken into account by reason of a period of breaks in service to which clause (i) applies, such years of service shall not be taken into account in applying clause (i) to a subsequent period of breaks in service.

(iii) Nonvested participant defined—For purposes of clause (i), the term "nonvested participant" means a participant who does not have any nonforfeitable right under the plan to an accrued benefit derived from employer contributions.

(E) Special rule for maternity or paternity absences—

(i) General rule—In the case of each individual who is absent from work for any period—

(I) by reason of the pregnancy of the individual,

(II) by reason of the birth of a child of the individual,

(III) by reason of the placement of a child with the individual in connection with the adoption of such child by such individual, or

(IV) for purposes of caring for such child for a period beginning immediately following such birth or placement,

the plan shall treat as hours of service, solely for purposes of determining under this paragraph whether a 1-year break in service has occurred, the hours described in clause (ii).

(ii) Hours treated as hours of service—The hours described in this clause are—

(I) the hours of service which otherwise would normally have been credited to such individual but for such absence, or

(II) in any case in which the plan is unable to determine the hours described in subclause (I), 8 hours of service per day of absence,

except that the total number of hours treated as hours of service under this clause by reason of any such pregnancy or placement shall not exceed 501 hours.

(iii) Year to which hours are credited—The hours described in clause (ii) shall be treated as hours of service as provided in this subparagraph—

(I) only in the year in which the absence from work begins, if a participant would be prevented from incurring a 1-year break in service in such year solely because the period of absence is treated as hours of service as provided in clause (i); or

(II) in any other case, in the immediately following year.

(iv) Year defined—For purposes of this subparagraph, the term "year" means the period used in computations pursuant to paragraph (5).

(v) Information required to be filed—A plan shall not fail to satisfy the requirements of this subparagraph solely because it provides that no credit will be given pursuant to this subparagraph unless the individual furnishes to the plan administrator such timely information as the plan may reasonably require to establish—

(I) that the absence from work is for reasons referred to in clause (i), and

(II) the number of days for which there was such an absence.

(7) Accrued benefit—

(A) In general—For purposes of this section, the term "accrued benefit" means—

(i) in the case of a defined benefit plan, the employee's accrued benefit determined under the plan and, except as provided in subsection (c)(3), expressed in the form of an annual benefit commencing at normal retirement age, or

(ii) in the case of a plan which is not a defined benefit plan, the balance of the employee's account.

(B) Effect of certain distributions—Notwithstanding paragraph (4), for purposes of determining the employee's accrued benefit under the plan, the plan may disregard service performed by the employee with respect to which he has received—

(i) a distribution of the present value of his entire nonforfeitable benefit if such distribution was in an amount (not more than the dollar limit under section 411 (a)(11)(A)) permitted under regulations prescribed by the Secretary, or

(ii) a distribution of the present value of his nonforfeitable benefit attributable to such service which he elected to receive.

Clause (i) of this subparagraph shall apply only if such distribution was made on termination of the employee's participation in the plan. Clause (ii) of this subparagraph shall apply only if such distribution was made on termination of the employee's participation in the plan or under such other circumstances as may be provided under regulations prescribed by the Secretary.

(C) Repayment of subparagraph (b) distributions—For purposes of determining the employee's accrued benefit under a plan, the plan may not disregard service as provided in subparagraph (B) unless the plan provides an opportunity for the participant to repay the full amount of the distribution described in such subparagraph (B) with, in the case of a defined benefit plan, interest at the rate determined for purposes of subsection (c)(2)(C) and provides that upon such repayment the employee's accrued benefit shall be recomputed by taking into account service so disregarded. This subparagraph shall apply only in the case of a participant who—

(i) received such a distribution in any plan year to which this section applies, which distribution was less than the present value of his accrued benefit,

(ii) resumes employment covered under the plan, and

(iii) repays the full amount of such distribution with, in the case of a defined benefit plan, interest at the rate determined for purposes of subsection (c)(2)(C).

The plan provision required under this subparagraph may provide that such repayment must be made (I) in the case of a withdrawal on account of separation from service, before the earlier of 5 years after the first date on which the participant is subsequently re-employed by the employer, or the close of the first period of 5 consecutive 1-year breaks in service commencing after the withdrawal; or (II) in the case of any other withdrawal, 5 years after the date of the withdrawal.

(D) Accrued benefit attributable to employee contributions—The accrued benefit of an employee shall not be less than the amount determined under subsection (c)(2)(B) with respect to the employee's accumulated contributions.

(8) Normal retirement age—For purposes of this section, the term "normal retirement age" means the earlier of—

(A) the time a plan participant attains normal retirement age under the plan, or

(B) the later of—

(i) the time a plan participant attains age 65, or

(ii) the 5th anniversary of the time a plan participant commenced participation in the plan.

(9) Normal retirement benefit—For purposes of this section, the term "normal retirement benefit" means the greater of the early retirement benefit under the plan, or the benefit under the plan commencing at normal retirement age. The normal retirement benefit shall be determined without regard to—

(A) medical benefits, and

(B) disability benefits not in excess of the qualified disability benefit.

For purposes of this paragraph, a qualified disability benefit is a disability benefit provided by a plan which does not exceed the benefit which would be provided for the participant if he separated from the service at normal retirement age. For purposes of this paragraph, the early retirement benefit under a plan shall be determined without regard to any benefits commencing before benefits payable under title II of the Social Security Act become payable which—

(i) do not exceed such social security benefits, and

(ii) terminate when such social security benefits commence.

(10) Changes in vesting schedule—

(A) General rule—A plan amendment changing any vesting schedule under the plan shall be treated as not satisfying the requirements of paragraph (2) if the nonforfeitable percentage of the accrued benefit derived from employer contributions (determined as of the later of the date such amendment is adopted, or the date such amendment becomes effective) of any employee who is a participant in the plan is less than such nonforfeitable percentage computed under the plan without regard to such amendment.

(B) Election of former schedule—A plan amendment changing any vesting schedule under the plan shall be treated as not satisfying the requirements of paragraph (2) unless each participant having not less than 3 years of service is permitted to elect, within a reasonable period after the adoption of such amendment, to have his nonforfeitable percentage computed under the plan without regard to such amendment.

(11) Restrictions on certain mandatory distributions—

(A) In general—If the present value of any nonforfeitable accrued benefit exceeds $5,000 a plan meets the requirements of this paragraph only if such plan provides that such benefit may not be immediately distributed without the consent of the participant.

(B) Determination of present value—For purposes of subparagraph (A), the present value shall be calculated in accordance with section 417(e)(3).

(C) Dividend distributions of ESOPs arrangement—This paragraph shall not apply to any distribution of dividends to which section 404(k) applies.

(D) Special rule for rollover contributions—A plan shall not fail to meet the requirements of this paragraph if, under the terms of the plan, the present value of the nonforfeitable accrued benefit is determined without regard to that portion of such benefit which is attributable to rollover contributions (and earnings allocable thereto). For purposes of this subparagraph, the term "rollover contributions" means any rollover contribution under sections 402(c), 403(a)(4), 403(b)(8), 408(d)(3)(A)(ii), and 457(e)(16).

(12) [Repealed]

(13) Special rules for plans computing accrued benefits by reference to hypothetical account balance or equivalent amounts—

(A) In general—An applicable defined benefit plan shall not be treated as failing to meet—

(i) subject to subparagraph (B), the requirements of subsection (a)(2), or

(ii) the requirements of subsection (a)(11) or (c) or the requirements of section 417(e) with respect to accrued benefits derived from employer contributions,

solely because the present value of the accrued benefit (or any portion thereof) of any participant is, under the terms of the plan, equal to the amount expressed as the balance in the hypothetical account described in paragraph (3) or as an accumulated percentage of the participant's final average compensation.

(B) 3-year vesting—In the case of an applicable defined benefit plan, such plan shall be treated as meeting the requirements of subsection (a)(2) only if an employee who has completed at least 3 years of service has a nonforfeitable right to 100 percent of the employee's accrued benefit derived from employer contributions.

(C) Applicable defined benefit plan and related rules—For purposes of this subsection—

(i) In general—The term "applicable defined benefit plan" means a defined benefit plan under which the accrued benefit (or any portion thereof) is calculated as the balance of a hypothetical account maintained for the participant or as an accumulated percentage of the participant's final average compensation.

(ii) Regulations to include similar plans—The Secretary shall issue regulations which include in the definition of an applicable defined benefit plan any defined benefit plan (or any portion of such a plan) which has an effect similar to an applicable defined benefit plan.

(b) Accrued benefit requirements—

(1) Defined benefit plans—

(A) 3-percent method—A defined benefit plan satisfies the requirements of this paragraph if the accrued benefit to which each participant is entitled upon his separation from the service is not less than—

(i) 3 percent of the normal retirement benefit to which he would be entitled if he commenced participation at the earliest possible entry age under the plan and served continuously until the earlier of age 65 or the normal retirement age specified under the plan, multiplied by

(ii) the number of years (not in excess of 33⅓) of his participation in the plan.

In the case of a plan providing retirement benefits based on compensation during any period, the normal retirement benefit to which a participant would be entitled shall be determined as if he continued to earn annually the average rate of compensation which he earned during consecutive years of service, not in excess of 10, for which his compensation was the highest. For purposes of this subparagraph, social security benefits and all other relevant factors used to compute benefits shall be treated as remaining constant as of the current year for all years after such current year.

(B) 133⅓ percent rule—A defined benefit plan satisfies the requirements of this paragraph for a particular plan year if under the plan the accrued benefit payable at the normal retirement age is equal to the normal retirement benefit and the annual rate at which any individual who is or could be a participant can accrue the retirement benefits payable at normal retirement age under the plan for any later plan year is not more than 133⅓ percent of the annual rate at which he can accrue benefits for any plan year beginning on or after such particular plan year and before such later plan year. For purposes of this subparagraph—

(i) any amendment to the plan which is in effect for the current year shall be treated as in effect for all other plan years;

(ii) any change in an accrual rate which does not apply to any individual who is or could be a participant in the current year shall be disregarded;

(iii) the fact that benefits under the plan may be payable to certain employees before normal retirement age shall be disregarded; and

(iv) social security benefits and all other relevant factors used to compute benefits shall be treated as remaining constant as of the current year for all years after the current year.

(C) **Fractional rule**—A defined benefit plan satisfies the requirements of this paragraph if the accrued benefit to which any participant is entitled upon his separation from the service is not less than a fraction of the annual benefit commencing at normal retirement age to which he would be entitled under the plan as in effect on the date of his separation if he continued to earn annually until normal retirement age the same rate of compensation upon which his normal retirement benefit would be computed under the plan, determined as if he had attained normal retirement age on the date on which any such determination is made (but taking into account no more than the 10 years of service immediately preceding his separation from service). Such fraction shall be a fraction, not exceeding 1, the numerator of which is the total number of his years of participation in the plan (as of the date of his separation from the service) and the denominator of which is the total number of years he would have participated in the plan if he separated from the service at the normal retirement age. For purposes of this subparagraph, social security benefits and all other relevant factors used to compute benefits shall be treated as remaining constant as of the current year for all years after such current year.

(D) **Accrual for service before effective date**—Subparagraphs (A), (B), and (C) shall not apply with respect to years of participation before the first plan year to which this section applies, but a defined benefit plan satisfies the requirements of this subparagraph with respect to such years of participation only if the accrued benefit of any participant with respect to such years of participation is not less than the greater of—

(i) his accrued benefit determined under the plan, as in effect from time to time prior to September 2, 1974, or

(ii) an accrued benefit which is not less than one-half of the accrued benefit to which such participant would have been entitled if subparagraph (A), (B), or (C) applied with respect to such years of participation.

(E) **First two years of service**—Notwithstanding subparagraphs (A), (B), and (C) of this paragraph, a plan shall not be treated as not satisfying the requirements of this paragraph solely because the accrual of benefits under the plan does not become effective until the employee has two continuous years of service. For purposes of this subparagraph, the term "years of service" has the meaning provided by section 410(a)(3)(A).

(F) Certain insured defined benefit plans—Notwithstanding subparagraphs (A), (B), and (C), a defined benefit plan satisfies the requirements of this paragraph if such plan—

(i) is funded exclusively by the purchase of insurance contracts, and

(ii) satisfies the requirements of subparagraphs (B) and (C) of section 412(e)(3) (relating to certain insurance contract plans),

but only if an employee's accrued benefit as of any applicable date is not less than the cash surrender value his insurance contracts would have on such applicable date if the requirements of subparagraphs (D), (E), and (F) of section 412(e)(3) were satisfied.

(G) Accrued benefit may not decrease on account of increasing age or service—Notwithstanding the preceding subparagraphs, a defined benefit plan shall be treated as not satisfying the requirements of this paragraph if the participant's accrued benefit is reduced on account of any increase in his age or service. The preceding sentence shall not apply to benefits under the plan commencing before entitlement to benefits payable under title II of the Social Security Act which benefits under the plan—

(i) do not exceed such social security benefits, and

(ii) terminate when such social security benefits commence.

(H) Continued accrual beyond normal retirement age—

(i) In general—Notwithstanding the preceding subparagraphs, a defined benefit plan shall be treated as not satisfying the requirements of this paragraph if, under the plan, an employee's benefit accrual is ceased, or the rate of an employee's benefit accrual is reduced, because of the attainment of any age.

(ii) Certain limitations permitted—A plan shall not be treated as failing to meet the requirements of this subparagraph solely because the plan imposes (without regard to age) a limitation on the amount of benefits that the plan provides or a limitation on the number of years of service or years of participation which are taken into account for purposes of determining benefit accrual under the plan.

(iii) Adjustments under plan for delayed retirement taken into account—In the case of any employee who, as of the end of any plan year under a defined benefit plan, has attained normal retirement age under such plan—

(I) if distribution of benefits under such plan with respect to such employee has commenced as of the end of such plan year, then any requirement of this subparagraph for continued accrual of benefits under such plan with respect to such employee during such plan year shall be treated as satisfied to the extent of the actuarial equivalent of in-service distribution of benefits, and

(II) if distribution of benefits under such plan with respect to such employee has not commenced as of the end of such year in accordance with section 401(a)(14)(C), and the payment of benefits under such plan with respect to such employee is not suspended during such plan year pursuant to subsection (a)(3)(B), then any requirement of this subparagraph for continued accrual of benefits under such plan with respect to such employee during such plan year shall be treated as satisfied to the extent of any adjustment in the benefit payable under the plan during such plan year attributable to the delay in the distribution of benefits after the attainment of normal retirement age.

The preceding provisions of this clause shall apply in accordance with regulations of the Secretary. Such regulations may provide for the application of the preceding provisions of this clause, in the case of any such employee, with respect to any period of time within a plan year.

(iv) Disregard of subsidized portion of early retirement benefit—A plan shall not be treated as failing to meet the requirements of clause (i) solely because the subsidized portion of any early retirement benefit is disregarded in determining benefit accruals.

(v) Coordination with other requirements—The Secretary shall provide by regulation for the coordination of the requirements of this subparagraph with the requirements of subsection (a), sections 404, 410, and 415, and the provisions of this subchapter precluding discrimination in favor of highly compensated employees.

(2) Defined contribution plans—

(A) In general—A defined contribution plan satisfies the requirements of this paragraph if, under the plan, allocations to the employee's account are not ceased, and the rate at which amounts are allocated to the employee's account is not reduced, because of the attainment of any age.

(B) Application to target benefit plans—The Secretary shall provide by regulation for the application of the requirements of this paragraph to target benefit plans.

(C) Coordination with other requirements—The Secretary may provide by regulation for the coordination of the requirements of this paragraph with the requirements of subsection (a), sections 404, 410, and 415, and the provisions of this subchapter precluding discrimination in favor of highly compensated employees.

(3) Separate accounting required in certain cases—A plan satisfies the requirements of this paragraph if—

(A) in the case of a defined benefit plan, the plan requires separate accounting for the portion of each employee's accrued benefit derived from any voluntary employee contributions permitted under the plan; and

(B) in the case of any plan which is not a defined benefit plan, the plan requires separate accounting for each employee's accrued benefit.

(4) Year of participation—

(A) Definition—For purposes of determining an employee's accrued benefit, the term "year of participation" means a period of service (beginning at the earliest date on which the employee is a participant in the plan and which is included in a period of service required to be taken into account under section 410(a)(5) determined without regard to section 410(a)(5)(E)) as determined under regulations prescribed by the Secretary of Labor which provide for the calculation of such period on any reasonable and consistent basis.

(B) Less than full time service—For purposes of this paragraph, except as provided in subparagraph (C), in the case of any employee whose customary employment is less than full time, the calculation of such employee's service on any basis which provides less than a ratable portion of the accrued benefit to which he would be entitled under the plan if his customary employment were full time shall not be treated as made on a reasonable and consistent basis.

(C) Less than 1,000 hours of service during year—For purposes of this paragraph, in the case of any employee whose service is less than 1,000 hours during any calendar year, plan year or other 12-consecutive month period designated by the plan (and not prohibited under regulations prescribed by the Secretary of Labor) the calculation of his period of service shall not be treated as not made on a reasonable and consistent basis solely because such service is not taken into account.

(D) Seasonal industries—In the case of any seasonal industry where the customary period of employment is less than 1,000 hours during a calendar year, the term "year of participation" shall be such period as determined under regulations prescribed by the Secretary of Labor.

(E) Maritime industries—For purposes of this subsection, in the case of any maritime industry, 125 days of service shall be treated as a year of participation. The Secretary of Labor may prescribe regulations to carry out the purposes of this subparagraph.

(5) Special rules relating to age—

(A) Comparison to similarly situated younger individual—

(i) In general—A plan shall not be treated as failing to meet the requirements of paragraph (1)(H)(i) if a participant's accrued benefit, as determined as of any date under the terms of the plan, would be equal to or greater than that of any similarly situated, younger individual who is or could be a participant.

(ii) Similarly situated—For purposes of this subparagraph, a participant is similarly situated to any other individual if such participant is identical to such other individual in every respect (including period of service, compensation, position, date of hire, work history, and any other respect) except for age.

(iii) Disregard of subsidized early retirement benefits—In determining the accrued benefit as of any date for purposes of this subparagraph, the subsidized portion of any early retirement benefit or retirement-type subsidy shall be disregarded.

(iv) Accrued benefit—For purposes of this subparagraph, the accrued benefit may, under the terms of the plan, be expressed as an annuity payable at normal retirement age, the balance of a hypothetical account, or the current value of the accumulated percentage of the employee's final average compensation.

(B) Applicable defined benefit plans—

(i) Interest credits—

(I) In general—An applicable defined benefit plan shall be treated as failing to meet the requirements of paragraph (1)(H) unless the terms of the plan provide that any interest credit (or an equivalent amount) for any plan year shall be at a rate which is not greater than a market rate of return. A plan shall not be treated as failing to meet the requirements of this subclause merely because the plan provides for a reasonable minimum guaranteed rate of return or for a rate of return that is equal to the greater of a fixed or variable rate of return.

(II) Preservation of capital—An applicable defined benefit plan shall be treated as failing to meet the requirements of paragraph (1)(H) unless the plan provides that an interest credit (or equivalent amount) of less than zero shall in no event result in the account balance or similar amount being less than the aggregate amount of contributions credited to the account.

(III) Market rate of return—The Secretary may provide by regulation for rules governing the calculation of a market rate of return for purposes of subclause (I) and for permissible methods of crediting interest to the account (including fixed or variable interest rates) resulting in effective rates of return meeting the requirements of subclause (I).

(ii) Special rule for plan conversions—If, after June 29, 2005, an applicable plan amendment is adopted, the plan shall be treated as failing to meet **the** requirements of paragraph (1)(H) unless the requirements of clause (iii) are met with respect to each individual who was a participant in the plan immediately before the adoption of the amendment.

(iii) Rate of benefit accrual—Subject to clause (iv), **the** requirements of this clause are met with respect to any participant if the accrued benefit of the participant under the terms of the plan as in effect after the amendment is not less than the sum of—

(I) the participant's accrued benefit for years of service before the effective date of the amendment, determined under the terms of the plan as in effect before the amendment, plus

(II) the participant's accrued benefit for years of service after the effective date of the amendment, determined under the terms of the plan as in effect after the amendment.

(iv) Special rules for early retirement subsidies—For purposes of clause (iii)(I), the plan shall credit the accumulation account or similar amount with the amount of any early retirement benefit or retirement-type subsidy for the plan year in which the participant retires if, as of such time, the participant has met the age, years of service, and other requirements under the plan for entitlement to such benefit or subsidy.

(v) Applicable plan amendment—For purposes of this subparagraph—

(I) In general—The term "applicable plan amendment" means an amendment to a defined benefit plan which has the effect of converting the plan to an applicable defined benefit plan.

(II) Special rule for coordinated benefits—If the benefits of 2 or more defined benefit plans established or maintained by an employer are coordinated in such a manner as to have the effect of the adoption of an amendment described in subclause (I), the sponsor of the defined benefit plan or plans providing for such coordination shall be treated as having adopted such a plan amendment as of the date such coordination begins.

(III) Multiple amendments—The Secretary shall issue regulations to prevent the avoidance of the purposes of this subparagraph through the use of 2 or more plan amendments rather than a single amendment.

(IV) Applicable defined benefit plan—For purposes of this subparagraph, the term "applicable defined benefit plan" has the meaning given such term by section 411(a)(13).

(vi) Termination requirements—An applicable defined benefit plan shall not be treated as meeting the requirements of clause (i) unless the plan provides that, upon the termination of the plan—

(I) if the interest credit rate (or an equivalent amount) under the plan is a variable rate, the rate of interest used to determine accrued benefits under the plan shall be equal to the average of the rates of interest used under the plan during the 5-year period ending on the termination date, and

(II) the interest rate and mortality table used to determine the amount of any benefit under the plan payable in the form of an annuity payable at normal retirement age shall be the rate and table specified under the plan for such purpose as of the termination date, except that if such interest rate is a variable rate, the interest rate shall be determined under the rules of subclause (I).

(C) Certain offsets permitted—A plan shall not be treated as failing to meet the requirements of paragraph (1)(H)(i) solely because the plan provides offsets against benefits under the plan to the extent such offsets are otherwise allowable in applying the requirements of section 401(a).

(D) Permitted disparities in plan contributions or benefits—A plan shall not be treated as failing to meet the requirements of paragraph (1)(H) solely because the plan provides a disparity in contributions or benefits with respect to which the requirements of section 401(l) are met.

(E) Indexing permitted—

(i) In general—A plan shall not be treated as failing to meet the requirements of paragraph (1)(H) solely because the plan provides for indexing of accrued benefits under the plan.

(ii) Protection against loss—Except in the case of any benefit provided in the form of a variable annuity, clause (i) shall not apply with respect to any indexing which results in an accrued benefit less than the accrued benefit determined without regard to such indexing.

(iii) Indexing—For purposes of this subparagraph, the term "indexing" means, in connection with an accrued benefit, the periodic adjustment of the accrued benefit by means of the application of a recognized investment index or methodology.

(F) Early retirement benefit or retirement-type subsidy—For purposes of this paragraph, the terms "early retirement benefit" and "retirement-type subsidy" have the meaning given such terms in subsection (d)(6)(B)(i).

(G) Benefit accrued to date—For purposes of this paragraph, any reference to the accrued benefit shall be a reference to such benefit accrued to date.

(c) Allocation of accrued benefits between employer and employee contributions—

(1) Accrued benefit derived from employer contributions—For purposes of this section, an employee's accrued benefit derived from employer contributions as of any applicable date is the excess, if any, of the accrued benefit for such employee as of such applicable date over the accrued benefit derived from contributions made by such employee as of such date.

(2) Accrued benefit derived from employee contributions—

    (A) Plans other than defined benefit plans—In the case of a plan other than a defined benefit plan, the accrued benefit derived from contributions made by an employee as of any applicable date is—

        (i) except as provided in clause (ii), the balance of the employee's separate account consisting only of his contributions and the income, expenses, gains, and losses attributable thereto, or

        (ii) if a separate account is not maintained with respect to an employee's contributions under such a plan, the amount which bears the same ratio to his total accrued benefit as the total amount of the employee's contributions (less withdrawals) bears to the sum of such contributions and the contributions made on his behalf by the employer (less withdrawals).

    (B) Defined benefit plans—In the case of a defined benefit plan, the accrued benefit derived from contributions made by an employee as of any applicable date is the amount equal to the employee's accumulated contributions expressed as an annual benefit commencing at normal retirement age, using an interest rate which would be used under the plan under section 417(e)(3) (as of the determination date).

    (C) Definition of accumulated contributions—For purposes of this subsection, the term "accumulated contributions" means the total of—

        (i) all mandatory contributions made by the employee,

        (ii) interest (if any) under the plan to the end of the last plan year to which subsection (a)(2) does not apply (by reason of the applicable effective date), and

        (iii) interest on the sum of the amounts determined under clauses (i) and (ii) compounded annually—

            (I) at the rate of 120 percent of the Federal mid-term rate (as in effect under section 1274 for the 1st month of a plan year) for the period beginning with the 1st plan year to which subsection (a)(2) applies (by reason of the applicable effective date) and ending with the date on which the determination is being made, and

            (II) at the interest rate which would be used under the plan under section 417(e)(3) (as of the determination date) for the period beginning with the determination date and ending on the date on which the employee attains normal retirement age.

For purposes of this subparagraph, the term "mandatory contributions" means amounts contributed to the plan by the employee which are required as a condition of employment, as a condition of participation in such plan, or as a condition of obtaining benefits under the plan attributable to employer contributions.

    (D) Adjustments—The Secretary is authorized to adjust by regulation the conversion factor described in subparagraph (B) from time to time as he may deem necessary.

(3) Actuarial adjustment—For purposes of this section, in the case of any defined benefit plan, if an employee's accrued benefit is to be determined as an amount other than an annual benefit commencing at normal retirement age, or if the accrued benefit derived from contributions made by an employee is to be determined with respect to a benefit other than an annual benefit in the form of a single life annuity (without ancillary benefits) commencing at normal retirement age, the employee's accrued benefit, or the accrued benefits derived from contributions made by an employee, as the case may be, shall be the actuarial equivalent of such benefit or amount determined under paragraph (1) or (2).

(d) Special rules—

(1) Coordination with section 401(a)(4)—A plan which satisfies the requirements of this section shall be treated as satisfying any vesting requirements resulting from the application of section 401(a)(4) unless—

(A) there has been a pattern of abuse under the plan (such as a dismissal of employees before their accrued benefits become nonforfeitable) tending to discriminate in favor of employees who are highly compensated employees (within the meaning of section 414(q)), or

(B) there have been, or there is reason to believe there will be, an accrual of benefits or forfeitures tending to discriminate in favor of employees who are highly compensated employees (within the meaning of section 414(q)).

(2) Prohibited discrimination—Subsection (a) shall not apply to benefits which may not be provided for designated employees in the event of early termination of the plan under provisions of the plan adopted pursuant to regulations prescribed by the Secretary to preclude the discrimination prohibited by section 401(a)(4).

(3) Termination or partial termination; discontinuance of contributions—Notwithstanding the provisions of subsection (a), a trust shall not constitute a qualified trust under section 401(a) unless the plan of which such trust is a part provides that—

(A) upon its termination or partial termination, or

(B) in the case of a plan to which section 412 does not apply, upon complete discontinuance of contributions under the plan,

the rights of all affected employees to benefits accrued to the date of such termination, partial termination, or discontinuance, to the extent funded as of such date, or the amounts credited to the employees' accounts, are nonforfeitable. This paragraph shall not apply to benefits or contributions which, under provisions of the plan adopted pursuant to regulations prescribed by the Secretary to preclude the discrimination prohibited by section 401(a)(4), may not be used for designated employees in the event of early termination of the plan. For purposes of this paragraph, in the case of the complete discontinuance of contributions under a profit-sharing or stock bonus plan, such plan shall be treated as having terminated on the day on which the plan administrator notifies the Secretary (in accordance with regulations) of the discontinuance.

(4) [Repealed]

(5) Treatment of voluntary employee contributions—In the case of a defined benefit plan which permits voluntary employee contributions, the portion of an employee's accrued benefit derived from such contributions shall be treated as an accrued benefit derived from employee contributions under a plan other than a defined benefit plan.

(6) Accrued benefit not to be decreased by amendment—

(A) In general—A plan shall be treated as not satisfying the requirements of this section if the accrued benefit of a participant is decreased by an amendment of the plan, other than an amendment described in section 412(d)(2), or section 4281 of the Employee Retirement Income Security Act of 1974.

(B) Treatment of certain plan amendments—For purposes of subparagraph (A), a plan amendment which has the effect of—

(i) eliminating or reducing an early retirement benefit or a retirement-type subsidy (as defined in regulations), or

(ii) eliminating an optional form of benefit,

with respect to benefits attributable to service before the amendment shall be treated as reducing accrued benefits. In the case of a retirement-type subsidy, the preceding sentence shall apply only with respect to a participant who satisfies (either before or after the amendment) the preamendment conditions for the subsidy. The Secretary shall by regulations provide that this subparagraph shall not apply to any plan amendment which reduces or eliminates benefits or subsidies which create significant burdens or complexities for the plan and plan participants, unless such amendment adversely affects the rights of any participant in a more than de minimis manner. The Secretary may by regulations provide that this subparagraph shall not apply to a plan amendment described in clause (ii) (other than a plan amendment having an effect described in clause (i)).

(C) Special rule for ESOPs—For purposes of this paragraph, any—

(i) tax credit employee stock ownership plan (as defined in section 409(a)), or

(ii) employee stock ownership plan (as defined in section 4975(e)(7)),

shall not be treated as failing to meet the requirements of this paragraph merely because it modifies distribution options in a nondiscriminatory manner.

(D) Plan transfers—

(i) In general—A defined contribution plan (in this subparagraph referred to as the "transferee plan") shall not be treated as failing to meet the requirements of this subsection merely because the transferee plan does not provide some or all of the forms of distribution previously available under another defined contribution plan (in this subparagraph referred to as the "transferor plan") to the extent that—

(I) the forms of distribution previously available under the transferor plan applied to the account of a participant or beneficiary under the transferor plan that was transferred from the transferor plan to the transferee plan pursuant to a direct transfer rather than pursuant to a distribution from the transferor plan,

(II) the terms of both the transferor plan and the transferee plan authorize the transfer described in subclause (I),

(III) the transfer described in subclause (I) was made pursuant to a voluntary election by the participant or beneficiary whose account was transferred to the transferee plan,

(IV) the election described in subclause (III) was made after the participant or beneficiary received a notice describing the consequences of making the election, and

(V) the transferee plan allows the participant or beneficiary described in subclause (III) to receive any distribution to which the participant or beneficiary is entitled under the transferee plan in the form of a single sum distribution.

(ii) Special rule for mergers, etc—Clause (i) shall apply to plan mergers and other transactions having the effect of a direct transfer, including consolidations of benefits attributable to different employers within a multiple employer plan.

(E) Elimination of form of distribution—Except to the extent provided in regulations, a defined contribution plan shall not be treated as failing to meet the requirements of this section merely because of the elimination of a form of distribution previously available thereunder. This subparagraph shall not apply to the elimination of a form of distribution with respect to any participant unless—

(i) a single sum payment is available to such participant at the same time or times as the form of distribution being eliminated, and

(ii) such single sum payment is based on the same or greater portion of the participant's account as the form of distribution being eliminated.

(e) Application of vesting standards to certain plans—

(1) The provisions of this section (other than paragraph (2)) shall not apply to—

(A) A governmental plan (within the meaning of section 414(d)),

(B) a church plan (within the meaning of section 414(e)) with respect to which the election provided by section 410(d) has not been made,

(C) a plan which has not, at any time after September 2, 1974, provided for employer contributions, and

(D) a plan established and maintained by a society, order, or association described in section 501(c)(8) or (9), if no part of the contributions to or under such plan are made by employers of participants in such plan.

(2) A plan described in paragraph (1) shall be treated as meeting the requirements of this section, for purposes of section 401(a), if such plan meets the vesting requirements resulting from the application of sections 401(a)(4) and 401(a)(7) as in effect on September 1, 1974.

§ 412. Minimum funding standards.

(a) Requirement to meet minimum funding standard—

(1) In general—A plan to which this section applies shall satisfy the minimum funding standard applicable to the plan for any plan year.

(2) Minimum funding standard—For purposes of paragraph (1), a plan shall be treated as satisfying the minimum funding standard for a plan year if—

(A) in the case of a defined benefit plan which is not a multiemployer plan or a CSEC plan, the employer makes contributions to or under the plan for the plan year which, in the aggregate, are not less than the minimum required contribution determined under section 430 for the plan for the plan year,

(B) in the case of a money purchase plan which is not a multiemployer plan, the employer makes contributions to or under the plan for the plan year which are required under the terms of the plan,

(C) in the case of a multiemployer plan, the employers make contributions to or under the plan for any plan year which, in the aggregate, are sufficient to ensure that the plan does not have an accumulated funding deficiency under section 431 as of the end of the plan year, and

(D) in the case of a CSEC plan, the employers make contributions to or under the plan for any plan year which, in the aggregate, are sufficient to ensure that the plan does not have an accumulated funding deficiency under section 433 as of the end of the plan year.

(b) Liability for contributions—

(1) In general—Except as provided in paragraph (2), the amount of any contribution required by this section (including any required installments under paragraphs (3) and (4) of section 430(j) or under section 433(f)) shall be paid by the employer responsible for making contributions to or under the plan.

(2) Joint and several liability where employer member of controlled group— If the employer referred to in paragraph (1) is a member of a controlled group, each member of such group shall be jointly and severally liable for payment of such contributions.

(3) Multiemployer plans in critical status—Paragraph (1) shall not apply in the case of a multiemployer plan for any plan year in which the plan is in critical status pursuant to section 432. This paragraph shall only apply if the plan sponsor adopts a rehabilitation plan in accordance with section 432(e) and complies with such rehabilitation plan (and any modifications of the plan).

(c) Variance from minimum funding standards—

(1) Waiver in case of business hardship—

(A) In general—If—

(i) an employer is (or in the case of a multiemployer plan or a CSEC plan, 10 percent or more of the number of employers contributing to or under the plan are) unable to satisfy the minimum funding standard for a plan year without temporary substantial business hardship (substantial business hardship in the case of a multiemployer plan), and

(ii) application of the standard would be adverse to the interests of plan participants in the aggregate,

the Secretary may, subject to subparagraph (C), waive the requirements of subsection (a) for such year with respect to all or any portion of the minimum funding standard. The Secretary shall not waive the minimum funding standard with respect to a plan for more than 3 of any 15 (5 of any 15 in the case of a multiemployer plan) consecutive plan years

(B) Effects of waiver—If a waiver is granted under subparagraph (A) for any plan year—

(i) in the case of a defined benefit plan which is not a multiemployer plan or a CSEC plan, the minimum required contribution under section 430 for the plan year shall be reduced by the amount of the waived funding deficiency and such amount shall be amortized as required under section 430(e),

(ii) in the case of a multiemployer plan, the funding standard account shall be credited under section 431(b)(3)(C) with the amount of the waived funding deficiency and such amount shall be amortized as required under section 431(b)(2)(C), and

(iii) in the case of a CSEC plan, the funding standard account shall be credited under section 433(b)(3)(C) with the amount of the waived funding deficiency and such amount shall be amortized as required under section 433(b)(2)(C).

(C) Waiver of amortized portion not allowed—The Secretary may not waive under subparagraph (A) any portion of the minimum funding standard under subsection (a) for a plan year which is attributable to any waived funding deficiency for any preceding plan year.

(2) Determination of business hardship—For purposes of this subsection, the factors taken into account in determining temporary substantial business hardship (substantial business hardship in the case of a multiemployer plan) shall include (but shall not be limited to) whether or not—

(A) the employer is operating at an economic loss,

(B) there is substantial unemployment or underemployment in the trade or business and in the industry concerned,

(C) the sales and profits of the industry concerned are depressed or declining, and

(D) it is reasonable to expect that the plan will be continued only if the waiver is granted.

(3) Waived funding deficiency—For purposes of this section and part III of this subchapter, the term "waived funding deficiency" means the portion of the minimum funding standard under subsection (a) (determined without regard to the waiver) for a plan year waived by the Secretary and not satisfied by employer contributions.

(4) Security for waivers for single-employer plans, consultations—

(A) Security may be required—

(i) In general—Except as provided in subparagraph (C), the Secretary may require an employer maintaining a defined benefit plan which is a single-employer plan (within the meaning of section 4001(a)(15) of the Employee Retirement Income Security Act of 1974) to provide security to such plan as a condition for granting or modifying a waiver under paragraph (1) or for granting an extension under section 433(d).

(ii) Special rules—Any security provided under clause (i) may be perfected and enforced only by the Pension Benefit Guaranty Corporation, or at the direction of the Corporation, by a contributing sponsor (within the meaning of section 4001(a)(13) of the Employee Retirement Income Security Act of 1974), or a member of such sponsor's controlled group (within the meaning of section 4001(a)(14) of such Act).

(B) Consultation with the pension benefit guaranty corporation—Except as provided in subparagraph (C), the Secretary shall, before granting or modifying a waiver under this subsection or an extension under section 433(d) with respect to a plan described in subparagraph (A)(i)—

    (i) provide the Pension Benefit Guaranty Corporation with—

        (I) notice of the completed application for any waiver, modification or extension, and

        (II) an opportunity to comment on such application within 30 days after receipt of such notice, and

    (ii) consider—

        (I) any comments of the Corporation under clause (i)(II), and

        (II) any views of any employee organization (within the meaning of section 3(4) of the Employee Retirement Income Security Act of 1974) representing participants in the plan which are submitted in writing to the Secretary in connection with such application.

Information provided to the Corporation under this subparagraph shall be considered tax return information and subject to the safeguarding and reporting requirements of section 6103(p).

    (C) Exception for certain waivers or extensions—

    (i) In general—The preceding provisions of this paragraph shall not apply to any plan with respect to which the sum of—

        (I) the aggregate unpaid minimum required contributions (within the meaning of section 4971(c)(4)) for the plan year and all preceding plan years,

        (II) the present value of all waiver amortization installments determined for the plan year and succeeding plan years under section 430(e)(2) or 433(b)(2)(C), whichever is applicable, and

        (III) the total amounts not paid by reason of an extension in effect under section 433(d),

is less than $1,000,000.

    (ii) Treatment of waivers or extensions for which applications are pending—The amount described in clause (i)(I) shall include any increase in such amount which would result if all applications for waivers or extensions with respect to the minimum funding standard under this subsection which are pending with respect to such plan were denied.

(5) Special rules for single-employer plans—

    (A) Application must be submitted before date 2 1/2 months after close of year—In the case of a defined benefit plan which is not a multiemployer plan, no waiver may be granted under this subsection with respect to any plan for any plan year unless an application therefor is submitted to the Secretary not later than the 15th day of the 3rd month beginning after the close of such plan year.

    (B) Special rule if employer is member of controlled group—In the case of a defined benefit plan which is not a multiemployer plan, if an employer is a member of a controlled group, the temporary substantial business hardship requirements of paragraph (1) shall be treated as met only if such requirements are met—

(**i**) with respect to such employer, and

(**ii**) with respect to the controlled group of which such employer is a member (determined by treating all members of such group as a single employer).

The Secretary may provide that an analysis of a trade or business or industry of a member need not be conducted if the Secretary determines such analysis is not necessary because the taking into account of such member would not significantly affect the determination under this paragraph.

(6) Advance notice—

(**A**) **In general**—The Secretary shall, before granting a waiver under this subsection, require each applicant to provide evidence satisfactory to the Secretary that the applicant has provided notice of the filing of the application for such waiver to each affected party (as defined in section 4001(a)(21) of the Employee Retirement Income Security Act of 1974). Such notice shall include a description of the extent to which the plan is funded for benefits which are guaranteed under title IV of the Employee Retirement Income Security Act of 1974 and for benefit liabilities.

(**B**) **Consideration of relevant information**—The Secretary shall consider any relevant information provided by a person to whom notice was given under subparagraph (A).

(7) Restriction on plan amendments—

(**A**) **In general**—No amendment of a plan which increases the liabilities of the plan by reason of any increase in benefits, any change in the accrual of benefits, or any change in the rate at which benefits become nonforfeitable under the plan shall be adopted if a waiver under this subsection or an extension of time under section 431(d) or 433(d) is in effect with respect to the plan, or if a plan amendment described in subsection (d)(2) which reduces the accrued benefit of any participant has been made at any time in the preceding 12 months (24 months in the case of a multiemployer plan). If a plan is amended in violation of the preceding sentence, any such waiver, or extension of time, shall not apply to any plan year ending on or after the date on which such amendment is adopted.

(**B**) **Exception**—Subparagraph (A) shall not apply to any plan amendment which—

(**i**) the Secretary determines to be reasonable and which provides for only de minimis increases in the liabilities of the plan,

(**ii**) only repeals an amendment described in subsection (d)(2), or

(**iii**) is required as a condition of qualification under part I of subchapter D, of chapter 1.

(d) Miscellaneous rules—

(1) Change in method or year—If the funding method or a plan year for a plan is changed, the change shall take effect only if approved by the Secretary.

(2) Certain retroactive plan amendments—For purposes of this section, any amendment applying to a plan year which—

(A) is adopted after the close of such plan year but no later than 2 1/2 months after the close of the plan year (or, in the case of a multiemployer plan, no later than 2 years after the close of such plan year),

(B) does not reduce the accrued benefit of any participant determined as of the beginning of the first plan year to which the amendment applies, and

(C) does not reduce the accrued benefit of any participant determined as of the time of adoption except to the extent required by the circumstances,

shall, at the election of the plan administrator, be deemed to have been made on the first day of such plan year. No amendment described in this paragraph which reduces the accrued benefits of any participant shall take effect unless the plan administrator files a notice with the Secretary notifying him of such amendment and the Secretary has approved such amendment, or within 90 days after the date on which such notice was filed, failed to disapprove such amendment. No amendment described in this subsection shall be approved by the Secretary unless the Secretary determines that such amendment is necessary because of a temporary substantial business hardship (as determined under subsection (c)(2)) or a substantial business hardship (as so determined) in the case of a multiemployer plan or a CSEC plan and that a waiver under subsection (c) (or, in the case of a multiemployer plan, any extension of the amortization period under section 431(d) or section 433(d)) is unavailable or inadequate.

(3) Controlled group—For purposes of this section, the term "controlled group" means any group treated as a single employer under subsection (b), (c), (m), or (o) of section 414.

(e) Plans to which section applies—

(1) In general—Except as provided in paragraphs (2) and (4), this section applies to a plan if, for any plan year beginning on or after the effective date of this section for such plan under the Employee Retirement Income Security Act of 1974—

(A) such plan included a trust which qualified (or was determined by the Secretary to have qualified) under section 401(a), or

(B) such plan satisfied (or was determined by the Secretary to have satisfied) the requirements of section 403(a).

(2) Exceptions—This section shall not apply to—

(A) any profit-sharing or stock bonus plan,

(B) any insurance contract plan described in paragraph (3),

(C) any governmental plan (within the meaning of section 414(d)),

(D) any church plan (within the meaning of section 414(e)) with respect to which the election provided by section 410(d) has not been made,

(E) any plan which has not, at any time after September 2, 1974, provided for employer contributions, or

(F) any plan established and maintained by a society, order, or association described in section 501(c)(8) or (9), if no part of the contributions to or under such plan are made by employers of participants in such plan.

No plan described in subparagraph (C), (D), or (F) shall be treated as a qualified plan for purposes of section 401(a) unless such plan meets the requirements of section 401(a)(7) as in effect on September 1, 1974.

(3) Certain insurance contract plans—A plan is described in this paragraph if—

(A) the plan is funded exclusively by the purchase of individual insurance contracts,

(B) such contracts provide for level annual premium payments to be paid extending not later than the retirement age for each individual participating in the plan, and commencing with the date the individual became a participant in the plan (or, in the case of an increase in benefits, commencing at the time such increase becomes effective),

(C) benefits provided by the plan are equal to the benefits provided under each contract at normal retirement age under the plan and are guaranteed by an insurance carrier (licensed under the laws of a State to do business with the plan) to the extent premiums have been paid,

(D) premiums payable for the plan year, and all prior plan years, under such contracts have been paid before lapse or there is reinstatement of the policy,

(E) no rights under such contracts have been subject to a security interest at any time during the plan year, and

(F) no policy loans are outstanding at any time during the plan year.

A plan funded exclusively by the purchase of group insurance contracts which is determined under regulations prescribed by the Secretary to have the same characteristics as contracts described in the preceding sentence shall be treated as a plan described in this paragraph.

(4) Certain terminated multiemployer plans—This section applies with respect to a terminated multiemployer plan to which section 4021 of the Employee Retirement Income Security Act of 1974 applies until the last day of the plan year in which the plan terminates (within the meaning of section 4041A(a)(2) of such Act).

§ 413. Collectively bargained plans, etc.

(a) Application of subsection (b)—Subsection (b) applies to—

(1) a plan maintained pursuant to an agreement which the Secretary of Labor finds to be a collective-bargaining agreement between employee representatives and one or more employers, and

(2) each trust which is a part of such plan.

(b) General rule—If this subsection applies to a plan, notwithstanding any other provision of this title—

(1) Participation—Section 410 shall be applied as if all employees of each of the employers who are parties to the collective-bargaining agreement and who are subject to the same benefit computation formula under the plan were employed by a single employer.

(2) Discrimination, etc—Sections 401(a)(4) and 411(d)(3) shall be applied as if all participants who are subject to the same benefit computation formula and who are employed by employers who are parties to the collective bargaining agreement were employed by a single employer.

(3) Exclusive benefit—For purposes of section 401(a), in determining whether the plan of an employer is for the exclusive benefit of his employees and their beneficiaries, all plan participants shall be considered to be his employees.

(4) Vesting—Section 411 (other than subsection (d)(3)) shall be applied as if all employers who have been parties to the collective-bargaining agreement constituted a single employer, except that the application of any rules with respect to breaks in service shall be made under regulations prescribed by the Secretary of Labor.

(5) Funding—The minimum funding standard provided by section 412 shall be determined as if all participants in the plan were employed by a single employer.

(6) Liability for funding tax—For a plan year the liability under section 4971 of each employer who is a party to the collective bargaining agreement shall be determined in a reasonable manner not inconsistent with regulations prescribed by the Secretary—

(A) first on the basis of their respective delinquencies in meeting required employer contributions under the plan, and

(B) then on the basis of their respective liabilities for contributions under the plan.

For purposes of this subsection and the last sentence of section 4971(a), an employer's withdrawal liability under part 1 of subtitle E of title IV of the Employee Retirement Income Security Act of 1974 shall not be treated as a liability for contributions under the plan.

(7) Deduction limitations—Each applicable limitation provided by section 404(a) shall be determined as if all participants in the plan were employed by a single employer. The amounts contributed to or under the plan by each employer who is a party to the agreement, for the portion of his taxable year which is included within such a plan year, shall be considered not to exceed such a limitation if the anticipated employer contributions for such plan year (determined in a manner consistent with the manner in which actual employer contributions for such plan year are determined) do not exceed such limitation. If such anticipated contributions exceed such a limitation, the portion of each such employer's contributions which is not deductible under section 404 shall be determined in accordance with regulations prescribed by the Secretary.

(8) Employees of labor unions—For purposes of this subsection, employees of employee representatives shall be treated as employees of an employer described in subsection (a)(1) if such representatives meet the requirements of sections 401(a)(4) and 410 with respect to such employees.

(9) Plans covering a professional employee—Notwithstanding subsection (a), in the case of a plan (and trust forming part thereof) which covers any professional employee, paragraph (1) shall be applied by substituting "section 410(a) " for "section 410 ", and paragraph (2) shall not apply.

(c) Plans maintained by more than one employer—In the case of a plan maintained by more than one employer—

(1) Participation—Section 410(a) shall be applied as if all employees of each of the employers who maintain the plan were employed by a single employer.

(2) Exclusive benefit—For purposes of section 401(a), in determining whether the plan of an employer is for the exclusive benefit of his employees and their beneficiaries all plan participants shall be considered to be his employees.

(3) Vesting—Section 411 shall be applied as if all employers who maintain the plan constituted a single employer, except that the application of any rules with respect to breaks in service shall be made under regulations prescribed by the Secretary of Labor.

(4) Funding—

    (A) In general—In the case of a plan established after December 31, 1988, each employer shall be treated as maintaining a separate plan for purposes of section 412 unless such plan uses a method for determining required contributions which provides that any employer contributes not less than the amount which would be required if such employer maintained a separate plan.

    (B) Other plans—In the case of a plan not described in subparagraph (A), the requirements of section 412 shall be determined as if all participants in the plan were employed by a single employer unless the plan administrator elects not later than the close of the first plan year of the plan beginning after the date of enactment of the Technical and Miscellaneous Revenue Act of 1988 to have the provisions of subparagraph (A) apply. An election under the preceding sentence shall take effect for the plan year in which made and, once made, may be revoked only with the consent of the Secretary.

(5) Liability for funding tax—For a plan year the liability under section 4971 of each employer who maintains the plan shall be determined in a reasonable manner not inconsistent with regulations prescribed by the Secretary—

    (A) first on the basis of their respective delinquencies in meeting required employer contributions under the plan, and

    (B) then on the basis of their respective liabilities for contributions under the plan.

(6) Deduction limitations—

    (A) In general—In the case of a plan established after December 31, 1988, each applicable limitation provided by section 404(a) shall be determined as if each employer were maintaining a separate plan.

    (B) Other plans—

        (i) In general—In the case of a plan not described in subparagraph (A), each applicable limitation provided by section 404(a) shall be determined as if all participants in the plan were employed by a single employer, except that if an election is made under paragraph (4)(B), subparagraph (A) shall apply to such plan.

        (ii) Special rule—If this subparagraph applies, the amounts contributed to or under the plan by each employer who maintains the plan (for the portion of the taxable year included within a plan year) shall be considered not to exceed any such limitation if the anticipated employer contributions for such plan year (determined in a reasonable manner not inconsistent with regulations prescribed by the Secretary) do not exceed such limitation. If such anticipated contributions exceed such a limitation, the portion of each such employer's contributions which is not deductible under section 404 shall be determined in accordance with regulations prescribed by the Secretary.

(7) Allocations—

    (A) In general—Except as provided in subparagraph (B), allocations of amounts under paragraphs (4), (5), and (6) among the employers maintaining the plan shall not be inconsistent with regulations prescribed for this purpose by the Secretary.

(B) Assets and liabilities of plan—For purposes of applying paragraphs (4)(A) and (6)(A), the assets and liabilities of each plan shall be treated as the assets and liabilities which would be allocated to a plan maintained by the employer if the employer withdrew from the multiple employer plan.

(d) CSEC plans—Notwithstanding any other provision of this section, in the case of a CSEC plan—

(1) Funding—The requirements of section 412 shall be determined as if all participants in the plan were employed by a single employer.

(2) Application of provisions—Paragraphs (1), (2), (3), and (5) of subsection (c) shall apply.

(3) Deduction limitations—Each applicable limitation provided by section 404(a) [26 USCS section 404(a)] shall be determined as if all participants in the plan were employed by a single employer. The amounts contributed to or under the plan by each employer who maintains the plan (for the portion of the taxable year included within a plan year) shall be considered not to exceed such applicable limitation if the anticipated employer contributions for such plan year of all employers (determined in a reasonable manner not inconsistent with regulations prescribed by the Secretary) do not exceed such limitation. If such anticipated contributions exceed such limitation, the portion of each such employer's contributions which is not deductible under section 404 shall be determined in accordance with regulations prescribed by the Secretary.

(4) Allocations—Allocations of amounts under paragraph (3) and subsection (c)(5) among the employers maintaining the plan shall not be inconsistent with the regulations prescribed for this purpose by the Secretary.

§ 414. Definitions and special rules.

(a) Service for predecessor employer—For purposes of this part—

(1) in any case in which the employer maintains a plan of a predecessor employer, service for such predecessor shall be treated as service for the employer, and

(2) in any case in which the employer maintains a plan which is not the plan maintained by a predecessor employer, service for such predecessor shall, to the extent provided in regulations prescribed by the Secretary, be treated as service for the employer.

(b) Employees of controlled group of corporations—For purposes of sections 401, 408(k), 408(p), 410, 411, 415, and 416, all employees of all corporations which are members of a controlled group of corporations (within the meaning of section 1563(a), determined without regard to section 1563(a)(4) and (e)(3)(C)) shall be treated as employed by a single employer. With respect to a plan adopted by more than one such corporation, the applicable limitations provided by section 404(a) shall be determined as if all such employers were a single employer, and allocated to each employer in accordance with regulations prescribed by the Secretary.

(c) Employees of partnerships, proprietorships, etc., which are under common control—

(1) In general—Except as provided in paragraph (2), for purposes of sections 401, 408(k), 408(p), 410, 411, 415, and 416, under regulations prescribed by the Secretary, all employees of trades or businesses (whether or not incorporated) which are under common control shall be treated as employed by a single employer. The regulations prescribed under this subsection shall be based on principles similar to the principles which apply in the case of subsection (b).

(2) Special rules relating to church plans—

(A) General rule—Except as provided in subparagraphs (B) and (C), for purposes of this subsection and subsection (m), an organization that is otherwise eligible to participate in a church plan shall not be aggregated with another such organization and treated as a single employer with such other organization for a plan year beginning in a taxable year unless—

(i) one such organization provides (directly or indirectly) at least 80 percent of the operating funds for the other organization during the preceding taxable year of the recipient organization, and

(ii) there is a degree of common management or supervision between the organizations such that the organization providing the operating funds is directly involved in the day-to-day operations of the other organization.

(B) Nonqualified church-controlled organizations— Notwithstanding subparagraph (A), for purposes of this subsection and subsection (m), an organization that is a nonqualified church-controlled organization shall be aggregated with 1 or more other nonqualified church-controlled organizations, or with an organization that is not exempt from tax under section 501, and treated as a single employer with such other organization, if at least 80 percent of the directors or trustees of such other organization are either representatives of, or directly or indirectly controlled by, such nonqualified church-controlled organization. For purposes of this subparagraph, the term 'nonqualified church-controlled organization' means a churchcontrolled tax-exempt organization described in section 501(c)(3) that is not a qualified church-controlled organization (as defined in section 3121(w)(3)(B)).

(C) Permissive aggregation among church-related organizations—The church or convention or association of churches with which an organization described in subparagraph (A) is associated (within the meaning of subsection (e)(3)(D)), or an organization designated by such church or convention or association of churches, may elect to treat such organizations as a single employer for a plan year. Such election, once made, shall apply to all succeeding plan years unless revoked with notice provided to the Secretary in such manner as the Secretary shall prescribe.

(D) Permissive disaggregation of church-related organizations—For purposes of subparagraph (A), in the case of a church plan, an employer may elect to treat churches (as defined in section 403(b)(12)(B)) separately from entities that are not churches (as so defined), without regard to whether such entities maintain separate church plans. Such election, once made, shall apply to all succeeding plan years unless revoked with notice provided to the Secretary in such manner as the Secretary shall prescribe.

(d) Governmental plan—For purposes of this part, the term "governmental plan" means a plan established and maintained for its employees by the Government of the United States, by the government of any State or political subdivision thereof, or by any agency or instrumentality of any of the foregoing. The term "governmental plan" also includes any plan to which the Railroad Retirement Act of 1935 or 1937 applies and which is financed by contributions required under that Act and any plan of an international organization which is exempt from taxation by reason of the International Organizations Immunities Act (59 Stat. 669). The term "governmental plan" includes a plan which is established and maintained by an Indian tribal government (as defined in section 7701(a)(40)), a subdivision of an Indian tribal government (determined in accordance with section 7871(d)), or an agency or instrumentality of either, and all of the participants of which are employees of such entity substantially all of whose services as such an employee are in the performance of essential governmental functions but not in the performance of commercial activities (whether or not an essential government function).

(e) Church plan—

(1) In general—For purposes of this part, the term "church plan" means a plan established and maintained (to the extent required in paragraph (2)(B)) for its employees (or their beneficiaries) by a church or by a convention or association of churches which is exempt from tax under section 501.

(2) Certain plans excluded—The term "church plan" does not include a plan—

(A) which is established and maintained primarily for the benefit of employees (or their beneficiaries) of such church or convention or association of churches who are employed in connection with one or more unrelated trades or businesses (within the meaning of section 513); or

(B) if less than substantially all of the individuals included in the plan are individuals described in paragraph (1) or (3)(B) (or their beneficiaries).

* * *

(f) Multiemployer plan—

(1) Definition—For purposes of this part, the term "multiemployer plan" means a plan—

(A) to which more than one employer is required to contribute,

(B) which is maintained pursuant to one or more collective bargaining agreements between one or more employee organizations and more than one employer, and

(C) which satisfies such other requirements as the Secretary of Labor may prescribe by regulation.

(2) Cases of common control—For purposes of this subsection, all trades or businesses (whether or not incorporated) which are under common control within the meaning of subsection (c) are considered a single employer.

* * *

(h) Tax treatment of certain contributions—

(1) In general—Effective with respect to taxable years beginning after December 31, 1973, for purposes of this title, any amount contributed—

(A) to an employees' trust described in section 401(a), or

(B) under a plan described in section 403(a),

shall not be treated as having been made by the employer if it is designated as an employee contribution.

(2) Designation by units of government—For purposes of paragraph (1), in the case of any plan established by the government of any State or political subdivision thereof, or by any agency or instrumentality of any of the foregoing, or a governmental plan described in the last sentence of section 414(d) (relating to plans of Indian tribal governments), where the contributions of employing units are designated as employee contributions but where any employing unit picks up the contributions, the contributions so picked up shall be treated as employer contributions.

(i) Defined contribution plan—For purposes of this part, the term "defined contribution plan" means a plan which provides for an individual account for each participant and for benefits based solely on the amount contributed to the participant's account, and any income, expenses, gains and losses, and any forfeitures of accounts of other participants which may be allocated to such participant's account.

(j) Defined benefit plan—For purposes of this part, the term "defined benefit plan" means any plan which is not a defined contribution plan.

(k) Certain plans—A defined benefit plan which provides a benefit derived from employer contributions which is based partly on the balance of the separate account of a participant shall—

> **(1)** for purposes of section 410 (relating to minimum participation standards), be treated as a defined contribution plan,

> **(2)** for purposes of sections 72(d) (relating to treatment of employee contributions as separate contract), 411(a)(7)(A) (relating to minimum vesting standards), 415 (relating to limitations on benefits and contributions under qualified plans), and 401(m) (relating to nondiscrimination tests for matching requirements and employee contributions), be treated as consisting of a defined contribution plan to the extent benefits are based on the separate account of a participant and as a defined benefit plan with respect to the remaining portion of benefits under the plan, and

> **(3)** for purposes of section 4975 (relating to tax on prohibited transactions), be treated as a defined benefit plan.

(l) Merger and consolidations of plans or transfers of plan assets—

> **(1) In general**—A trust which forms a part of a plan shall not constitute a qualified trust under section 401 and a plan shall be treated as not described in section 403(a) unless in the case of any merger or consolidation of the plan with, or in the case of any transfer of assets or liabilities of such plan to, any other trust plan after September 2, 1974, each participant in the plan would (if the plan then terminated) receive a benefit immediately after the merger, consolidation, or transfer which is equal to or greater than the benefit he would have been entitled to receive immediately before the merger, consolidation, or transfer (if the plan had then terminated). The preceding sentence does not apply to any multiemployer plan with respect to any transaction to the extent that participants either before or after the transaction are covered under a multiemployer plan to which Title IV of the Employee Retirement Income Security Act of 1974 applies.

> **(2) Allocation of assets in plan spin-offs, etc—**

>> **(A) In general**—In the case of a plan spin-off of a defined benefit plan, a trust which forms part of—

>>> **(i)** the original plan, or

>>> **(ii)** any plan spun off from such plan, shall not constitute a qualified trust under this section unless the applicable percentage of excess assets are allocated to each of such plans.

(B) Applicable percentage—For purposes of subparagraph (A), the term "applicable percentage" means, with respect to each of the plans described in clauses (i) and (ii) of subparagraph (A), the percentage determined by dividing—

(i) the excess (if any) of—

(I) the sum of the funding target and target normal cost determined under section 430, over

(II) the amount of the assets required to be allocated to the plan after the spin-off (without regard to this paragraph), by

(ii) the sum of the excess amounts determined separately under clause (i) for all such plans.

(C) Excess assets—For purposes of subparagraph (A), the term "excess assets" means an amount equal to the excess (if any) of—

(i) the fair market value of the assets of the original plan immediately before the spin-off, over

(ii) the amount of assets required to be allocated after the spin-off to all plans (determined without regard to this paragraph).

(D) Certain spun-off plans not taken into account—

(i) In general—A plan involved in a spin-off which is described in clause (ii), (iii), or (iv) shall not be taken into account for purposes of this paragraph, except that the amount determined under subparagraph (C)(ii) shall be increased by the amount of assets allocated to such plan.

(ii) Plans transferred out of controlled groups—A plan is described in this clause if, after such spin-off, such plan is maintained by an employer who is not a member of the same controlled group as the employer maintaining the original plan.

(iii) Plans transferred out of multiple employer plans—A plan as described in this clause if, after the spin-off, any employer maintaining such plan (and any member of the same controlled group as such employer) does not maintain any other plan remaining after the spin-off which is also maintained by another employer (or member of the same controlled group as such other employer) which maintained the plan in existence before the spin-off.

(iv) Terminated plans—A plan is described in this clause if, pursuant to the transaction involving the spin-off, the plan is terminated.

(v) Controlled group—For purposes of this subparagraph, the term "controlled group" means any group treated as a single employer under subsection (b), (c), (m), or (o).

(E) Paragraph not to apply to multiemployer plans—This paragraph does not apply to any multiemployer plan with respect to any spin-off to the extent that participants either before or after the spin-off are covered under a multiemployer plan to which title IV of the Employee Retirement Income Security Act of 1974 applies.

* * *

(m) Employees of an affiliated service group—

(1) In general—For purposes of the employee benefit requirements listed in paragraph (4), except to the extent otherwise provided in regulations, all employees of the members of an affiliated service group shall be treated as employed by a single employer.

(2) Affiliated service group—For purposes of this subsection, the term "affiliated service group" means a group consisting of a service organization (hereinafter in this paragraph referred to as the "first organization") and one or more of the following:

(A) any service organization which—

(i) is a shareholder or partner in the first organization, and

(ii) regularly performs services for the first organization or is regularly associated with the first organization in performing services for third persons, and

(B) any other organization if—

(i) a significant portion of the business of such organization is the performance of services (for the first organization, for organizations described in subparagraph (A), or for both) of a type historically performed in such service field by employees, and

(ii) 10 percent or more of the interests in such organization is held by persons who are highly compensated employees (within the meaning of section 414(q)) of the first organization or an organization described in subparagraph (A).

(3) Service organizations—For purposes of this subsection, the term "service organization" means an organization the principal business of which is the performance of services.

(4) Employee benefit requirements—For purposes of this subsection, the employee benefit requirements listed in this paragraph are—

(A) paragraphs (3), (4), (7), (16), (17), and (26) of section 401(a), and

(B) sections 408(k), 408(p), 410, 411, 415, and 416.

(5) Certain organizations performing management functions—For purposes of this subsection, the term "affiliated service group" also includes a group consisting of—

(A) an organization the principal business of which is performing, on a regular and continuing basis, management functions for 1 organization (or for 1 organization and other organizations related to such 1 organization), and

(B) the organization (and related organizations) for which such functions are so performed by the organization described in subparagraph (A).

For purposes of this paragraph, the term "related organizations" has the same meaning as the term "related persons" when used in section 144(a)(3).

(6) Other definitions—For purposes of this subsection—

(A) Organization defined—The term "organization" means a corporation, partnership, or other organization.

(B) Ownership—In determining ownership, the principles of section 318(a) shall apply.

(n) Employee leasing—

(1) In general—For purposes of the requirements listed in paragraph (3), with respect to any person (hereinafter in this subsection referred to as the "recipient") for whom a leased employee performs services—

(A) the leased employee shall be treated as an employee of the recipient, but

(B) contributions or benefits provided by the leasing organization which are attributable to services performed for the recipient shall be treated as provided by the recipient.

(2) Leased employee—For purposes of paragraph (1), the term "leased employee" means any person who is not an employee of the recipient and who provides services to the recipient if—

(A) such services are provided pursuant to an agreement between the recipient and any other person (in this subsection referred to as the "leasing organization"),

(B) such person has performed such services for the recipient (or for the recipient and related persons) on a substantially full-time basis for a period of at least 1 year, and

(C) such services are performed under primary direction or control by the recipient.

(3) Requirements—For purposes of this subsection, the requirements listed in this paragraph are—

(A) paragraphs (3), (4), (7), (16), (17), and (26) of section 401(a),

(B) sections 408(k), 408(p), 410, 411, 415, and 416, and

(C) sections 79, 106, 117(d), 125, 127, 129, 132, 137, 274(j), 505, and 4980B.

(4) Time when first considered as employee—

(A) In general—In the case of any leased employee, paragraph (1) shall apply only for purposes of determining whether the requirements listed in paragraph (3) are met for periods after the close of the period referred to in paragraph (2)(B).

(B) Years of service—In the case of a person who is an employee of the recipient (whether by reason of this subsection or otherwise), for purposes of the requirements listed in paragraph (3), years of service for the recipient shall be determined by taking into account any period for which such employee would have been a leased employee but for the requirements of paragraph (2)(B).

(5) Safe harbor—

(A) In general—In the case of requirements described in subparagraphs (A) and (B) of paragraph (3), this subsection shall not apply to any leased employee with respect to services performed for a recipient if—

(i) such employee is covered by a plan which is maintained by the leasing organization and meets the requirements of subparagraph (B), and

(ii) leased employee (determined without regard to this paragraph) do not constitute more than 20 percent of the recipient's nonhighly compensated work force.

(B) Plan requirements—A plan meets the requirements of this subparagraph if—

(i) such plan is a money purchase pension plan with a nonintegrated employer contribution rate for each participant of at least 10 percent of compensation,

(ii) such plan provides for full and immediate vesting, and

(iii) each employee of the leasing organization (other than employees who perform substantially all of their services for the leasing organization) immediately participates in such plan.

Clause (iii) shall not apply to any individual whose compensation from the leasing organization in each plan year during the 4-year period ending with the plan year is less than $1,000.

* * *

(o) Regulations—The Secretary shall prescribe such regulations (which may provide rules in addition to the rules contained in subsections (m) and (n)) as may be necessary to prevent the avoidance of any employee benefit requirement listed in subsection (m)(4) or (n)(3) or any requirement under section 457 through the use of—

(1) separate organizations,

(2) employee leasing, or

(3) other arrangements.

The regulations prescribed under subsection (n) shall include provisions to minimize the record-keeping requirements of subsection (n) in the case of an employer which has no top-heavy plans (within the meaning of section 416(g)) and which uses the services of persons (other than employees) for an insignificant percentage of the employer's total workload.

(p) Qualified domestic relations order defined—For purposes of this subsection and section 401(a)(13)—

(1) In general—

(A) Qualified domestic relations order—The term "qualified domestic relations order" means a domestic relations order—

(i) which creates or recognizes the existence of an alternate payee's right to, or assigns to an alternate payee the right to, receive all or a portion of the benefits payable with respect to a participant under a plan, and

(ii) with respect to which the requirements of paragraphs (2) and (3) are met.

(B) Domestic relations order—The term "domestic relations order" means any judgment, decree, or order (including approval of a property settlement agreement) which—

(i) relates to the provision of child support, alimony payments, or marital property rights to a spouse, former spouse, child, or other dependent of a participant, and

(ii) is made pursuant to a State domestic relations law (including a community property law).

(2) Order must clearly specify certain facts—A domestic relations order meets the requirements of this paragraph only if such order clearly specifies—

(A) the name and the last known mailing address (if any) of the participant and the name and mailing address of each alternate payee covered by the order,

(B) the amount or percentage of the participant's benefits to be paid by the plan to each such alternate payee, or the manner in which such amount or percentage is to be determined,

(C) the number of payments or period to which such order applies, and

(D) each plan to which such order applies.

(3) Order may not alter amount, form, etc., of benefits—A domestic relations order meets the requirements of this paragraph only if such order—

(A) does not require a plan to provide any type or form of benefit, or any option, not otherwise provided under the plan,

(B) does not require the plan to provide increased benefits (determined on the basis of actuarial value), and

(C) does not require the payment of benefits to an alternate payee which are required to be paid to another alternate payee under another order previously determined to be a qualified domestic relations order.

(4) Exception for certain payments made after earliest retirement age—

(A) In general—A domestic relations order shall not be treated as failing to meet the requirements of subparagraph (A) of paragraph (3) solely because such order requires that payment of benefits be made to an alternate payee—

(i) in the case of any payment before a participant has separated from service, on or after the date on which the participant attains (or would have attained) the earliest retirement age,

(ii) as if the participant had retired on the date on which such payment is to begin under such order (but taking into account only the present value of the benefits actually accrued and not taking into account the present value of any employer subsidy for early retirement), and

(iii) in any form in which such benefits may be paid under the plan to the participant (other than in the form of a joint and survivor annuity with respect to the alternate payee and his or her subsequent spouse).

For purposes of clause (ii), the interest rate assumption used in determining the present value shall be the interest rate specified in the plan or, if no rate is specified, 5 percent.

(B) Earliest retirement age—Purposes of this paragraph, the term "earliest retirement age" means the earlier of—

(i) the date on which the participant is entitled to a distribution under the plan, or

(ii) the later of—

(I) the date the participant attains age 50, or

(II) the earliest date on which the participant could begin receiving benefits under the plan if the participant separated from service.

(5) Treatment of former spouse as surviving spouse for purposes of determining survivor benefits—To the extent provided in any qualified domestic relations order—

(A) the former spouse of a participant shall be treated as a surviving spouse of such participant for purposes of sections 401(a)(11) and 417 (and any spouse of the participant shall not be treated as a spouse of the participant for such purposes), and

(B) if married for at least 1 year, the surviving former spouse shall be treated as meeting the requirements of section 417(d).

(6) Plan procedures with respect to orders—

(A) Notice and determination by administrator—In the case of any domestic relations order received by a plan—

(i) the plan administrator shall promptly notify the participant and each alternate payee of the receipt of such order and the plan's procedures for determining the qualified status of domestic relations orders, and

(ii) within a reasonable period after receipt of such order, the plan administrator shall determine whether such order is a qualified domestic relations order and notify the participant and each alternate payee of such determination.

(B) Plan to establish reasonable procedures—Each plan shall establish reasonable procedures to determine the qualified status of domestic relations orders and to administer distributions under such qualified orders.

(7) Procedures for period during which determination is being made—

(A) In general—During any period in which the issue of whether a domestic relations order is a qualified domestic relations order is being determined (by the plan administrator, by a court of competent jurisdiction, or otherwise), the plan administrator shall separately account for the amounts (hereinafter in this paragraph referred to as the "segregated amounts") which would have been payable to the alternate payee during such period if the order had been determined to be a qualified domestic relations order.

(B) Payment to alternate payee if order determined to be qualified domestic relations order—If within the 18-month period described in subparagraph (E) the order (or modification thereof) is determined to be a qualified domestic relations order, the plan administrator shall pay the segregated amounts (including any interest thereon) to the person or persons entitled thereto.

(C) Payment to plan participant in certain cases—If within the 18-month period described in subparagraph (E)—

(i) it is determined that the order is not a qualified domestic relations order, or

(ii) the issue as to whether such order is a qualified domestic relations order is not resolved,

then the plan administrator shall pay the segregated amounts (including any interest thereon) to the person or persons who would have been entitled to such amounts if there had been no order.

(D) Subsequent determination or order to be applied prospectively only—Any determination that an order is a qualified domestic relations order which is made after the close of the 18-month period described in subparagraph (E) shall be applied prospectively only.

(E) Determination of 18-month period—For purposes of this paragraph, the 18-month period described in this subparagraph is the 18-month period beginning with the date on which the first payment would be required to be made under the domestic relations order.

(8) Alternate payee defined—The term "alternate payee" means any spouse, former spouse, child or other dependent of a participant who is recognized by a domestic relations order as having a right to receive all, or a portion of, the benefits payable under a plan with respect to such participant.

(9) Subsection not to apply to plans to which section 401(a)(13) does not apply—This subsection shall not apply to any plan to which section 401(a)(13) does not apply. For purposes of this title, except as provided in regulations, any distribution from an annuity contract under section 403(b) pursuant to a qualified domestic relations order shall be treated in the same manner as a distribution from a plan to which section 401(a)(13) applies.

(10) Waiver of certain distribution requirements—With respect to the requirements of subsections (a) and (k) of section 401, section 403(b), section 409(d), and section 457(d), plan shall not be treated as failing to meet such requirements solely by reason of payments to an alternative payee pursuant to a qualified domestic relations order.

(11) Application of rules to certain other plans—For purposes of this title, a distribution or payment from a governmental plan (as defined in subsection (d)) or a church plan (as described in subsection (e)) or an eligible deferred compensation plan (within the meaning of section 457(b)) shall be treated as made pursuant to a qualified domestic relations order if it is made pursuant to a domestic relations order which meets the requirement of clause (i) of paragraph (1)(A).

(12) Tax treatment of payments from a section 457 plan—If a distribution or payment from an eligible deferred compensation plan described in section 457(b) is made pursuant to a qualified domestic relations order, rules similar to the rules of section 402(e)(1)(A) shall apply to such distribution or payment.

(13) Consultation with the Secretary—In prescribing regulations under this subsection and section 401(a)(13), the Secretary of Labor shall consult with the Secretary.

(q) Highly compensated employee—

    (1) In general—The term "highly compensated employee" means any employee who—

        (A) was a 5-percent owner at any time during the year or the preceding year, or

        (B) for the preceding year—

            (i) had compensation from the employer in excess of $80,000, and

            (ii) if the employer elects the application of this clause for such preceding year, was in the top-paid group of employees for such preceding year.

The Secretary shall adjust the $80,000 amount under subparagraph (B) at the same time and in the same manner as under section 415(d), except that the base period shall be the calendar quarter ending September 30, 1996.

    (2) 5-percent owner—An employee shall be treated as a 5-percent owner for any year if at any time during such year such employee was a 5-percent owner (as defined in section 416(i)(1)) of the employer.

    (3) Top-paid group—An employee is in the top-paid group of employees for any year if such employee is in the group consisting of the top 20 percent of the employees when ranked on the basis of compensation paid during such year.

(4) Compensation—For purposes of this subsection, the term "compensation" has the meaning given such term by section 415(c)(3).

(5) Excluded employees—For purposes of subsection (r) and for purposes of determining the number of employees in the top-paid group, the following employees shall be excluded—

(A) employees who have not completed 6 months of service,

(B) employees who normally work less than 17½ hours per week,

(C) employees who normally work during not more than 6 months during any year,

(D) employees who have not attained age 21, and

(E) except to the extent provided in regulations, employees who are included in a unit of employees covered by an agreement which the Secretary of Labor finds to be a collective bargaining agreement between employee representatives and the employer.

Except as provided by the Secretary, the employer may elect to apply subparagraph (A), (B), (C), or (D) by substituting a shorter period of service, smaller number of hours or months, or lower age for the period of service, number of hours or months, or age (as the case may be) than that specified in such subparagraph.

(6) Former employees—A former employee shall be treated as a highly compensated employee if—

(A) such employee was a highly compensated employee when such employee separated from service, or

(B) such employee was a highly compensated employee at any time after attaining age 55.

(7) Coordination with other provisions—Subsections (b), (c), (m), (n), and (o) shall be applied before the application of this subsection.

(8) Special rule for nonresident aliens—For purposes of this subsection and subsection (r), employees who are nonresident aliens and who receive no earned income (within the meaning of section 911(d)(2)) from the employer which constitutes income from sources within the United States (within the meaning of section 861(a)(3)) shall not be treated as employees.

* * *

(r) Special rules for separate line of business—

(1) In general—For purposes of sections 129(d)(8) and 410(b), an employer shall be treated as operating separate lines of business during any year if the employer for bona fide business reasons operates separate lines of business.

(2) Line of business must have 50 employees, etc—A line of business shall not be treated as separate under paragraph (1) unless—

(A) such line of business has at least 50 employees who are not excluded under subsection (q)(5),

(B) the employer notifies the Secretary that such line of business is being treated as separate for purposes of paragraph (1), and

(C) such line of business meets guidelines prescribed by the Secretary or the employer receives a determination from the Secretary that such line of business may be treated as separate for purposes of paragraph (1).

(3) Safe harbor rule—

(A) In general—The requirements of subparagraph (C) of paragraph (2) shall not apply to any line of business if the highly compensated employee percentage with respect to such line of business is—

(i) not less than one-half, and

(ii) not more than twice,

the percentage which highly compensated employees are of all employees of the employer. An employer shall be treated as meeting the requirements of clause (i) if at least 10 percent of all highly compensated employees of the employer perform services solely for such line of business.

(B) Determination may be based on preceding year—The requirements of subparagraph (A) shall be treated as met with respect to any line of business if such requirements were met with respect to such line of business for the preceding year and if—

(i) no more than a de minimis number of employees were shifted to or from the line of business after the close of the preceding year, or

(ii) the employees shifted to or from the line of business after the close of the preceding year contained a substantially proportional number of highly compensated employees.

(4) Highly compensated employee percentage defined—For purposes of this subsection, the term "highly compensated employee percentage" means the percentage which highly compensated employees performing services for the line of business are of all employees performing services for the line of business.

(5) Allocation of benefits to line of business—For purposes of this subsection, benefits which are attributable to services provided to a line of business shall be treated as provided by such line of business.

(6) Headquarters personnel, etc—The Secretary shall prescribe rules providing for—

(A) the allocation of headquarters personnel among the lines of business of the employer, and

(B) the treatment of other employees providing services for more than 1 line of business of the employer or not in lines of business meeting the requirements of paragraph (2).

(7) Separate operating units—For purposes of this subsection, the term "separate line of business" includes an operating unit in a separate geographic area separately operated for a bona fide business reason.

(8) Affiliated service groups—This subsection shall not apply in the case of any affiliated service group (within the meaning of section 414(m)).

(s) Compensation—For purposes of any applicable provision—

(1) In general—Except as provided in this subsection, the term "compensation" has the meaning given such term by section 415(c)(3).

(2) Employer may elect not to treat certain deferrals as compensation—An employer may elect not to include as compensation any amount which is contributed by the employer pursuant to a salary reduction agreement and which is not includible in the gross income of an employee under section 125, 132(f)(4), 402(e)(3), 402(h) or 403(b).

(3) Alternative determination of compensation—The Secretary shall by regulation provide for alternative methods of determining compensation which may be used by an employer, except that such regulations shall provide that an employer may not use an alternative method if the use of such method discriminates in favor of highly compensated employees (within the meaning of subsection (q)).

(4) Applicable provision—For purposes of this subsection, the term "applicable provision" means any provision which specifically refers to this subsection.

(t) Application of controlled group rules to certain employee benefits—

(1) In general—All employees who are treated as employed by a single employer under subsection (b), (c), or (m) shall be treated as employed by a single employer for purposes of an applicable section. The provisions of subsection (o) shall apply with respect to the requirements of an applicable section.

(2) Applicable section—For purposes of this subsection, the term "applicable section" means section 79, 106, 117(d), 120, 125, 127, 129, 132, 137, 274(j), 505, or 4980B.

(u) Special rules relating to veterans' reemployment rights under USERRA and to differential wage payments to members on active duty—

(1) Treatment of certain contributions made pursuant to veterans' reemployment rights—If any contribution is made by an employer or an employee under an individual account plan with respect to an employee, or by an employee to a defined benefit plan that provides for employee contributions, and such contribution is required by reason of such employee's rights under chapter 43 of title 38, United States Code, resulting from qualified military service, then—

(A) such contribution shall not be subject to any otherwise applicable limitation contained in section 402(g), 402(h), 403(b), 404(a), 404(h), 408, 415, or 457, and shall not be taken into account in applying such limitations to other contributions or benefits under such plan or any other plan, with respect to the year in which the contribution is made,

(B) such contribution shall be subject to the limitations referred to in subparagraph (A) with respect to the year to which the contribution relates (in accordance with rules prescribed by the Secretary), and

(C) such plan shall not be treated as failing to meet the requirements of section 401(a)(4), 401(a)(26), 401(k)(3), 401(k)(11), 401(k)(12), 401(m), 403(b)(12), 408(k)(3), 408(k)(6), 408(p), 410(b), or 416 by reason of the making of (or the right to make) such contribution.

For purposes of the preceding sentence, any elective deferral or employee contribution made under paragraph (2) shall be treated as required by reason of the employee's rights under such chapter 43.

(2) Reemployment rights under USERRA with respect to elective deferrals—

(A) In general—For purposes of this subchapter and section 457, if an employee is entitled to the benefits of chapter 43 of title 38, United States Code, with respect to any plan which provides for elective deferrals, the employer sponsoring the plan shall be treated as meeting the requirements of such chapter 43 with respect to such elective deferrals only if such employer—

> **(i)** permits such employee to make additional elective deferrals under such plan (in the amount determined under subparagraph (B) or such lesser amount as is elected by the employee) during the period which begins on the date of the reemployment of such employee with such employer and has the same length as the lesser of—

> > **(I)** the product of 3 and the period of qualified military service which resulted in such rights, and

> > **(II)** 5 years, and

> **(ii)** makes a matching contribution with respect to any additional elective deferral made pursuant to clause (i) which would have been required had such deferral actually been made during the period of such qualified military service.

(B) Amount of makeup required—The amount determined under this subparagraph with respect to any plan is the maximum amount of the elective deferrals that the individual would have been permitted to make under the plan in accordance with the limitations referred to in paragraph (1)(A) during the period of qualified military service if the individual had continued to be employed by the employer during such period and received compensation as determined under paragraph (7). Proper adjustment shall be made to the amount determined under the preceding sentence for any elective deferrals actually made during the period of such qualified military service.

(C) Elective deferral—For purposes of this paragraph, the term "elective deferral" has the meaning given such term by section 402(g)(3); except that such term shall include any deferral of compensation under an eligible deferred compensation plan (as defined in section 457(b)).

(D) After-tax employee contributions—References in subparagraphs (A) and (B) to elective deferrals shall be treated as including references to employee contributions.

(3) Certain retroactive adjustments not required—For purposes of this subchapter and subchapter E, no provision of chapter 43 of title 38, United States Code, shall be construed as requiring—

(A) any crediting of earnings to an employee with respect to any contribution before such contribution is actually made, or

(B) any allocation of any forfeiture with respect to the period of qualified military service.

(4) Loan repayment suspensions permitted—If any plan suspends the obligation to repay any loan made to an employee from such plan for any part of any period during which such employee is performing service in the uniformed services (as defined in chapter 43 of title 38, United States Code), whether or not qualified military service, such suspension shall not be taken into account for purposes of section 72(p), 401(a), or 4975(d)(1).

(5) Qualified military service—For purposes of this subsection, the term "qualified military service" means any service in the uniformed services (as defined in chapter 43 of title 38, United States Code) by any individual if such individual is entitled to reemployment rights under such chapter with respect to such service.

(6) Individual account plan—For purposes of this subsection, the term "individual account plan" means any defined contribution plan (including any tax-sheltered annuity plan under section 403(b), any simplified employee pension under section 408(k), any qualified salary reduction arrangement under section 408(p), and any eligible deferred compensation plan (as defined in section 457(b)).

(7) Compensation—For purposes of sections 403(b)(3), 415(c)(3), and 457(e)(5), an employee who is in qualified military service shall be treated as receiving compensation from the employer during such period of qualified military service equal to—

(A) the compensation the employee would have received during such period if the employee were not in qualified military service, determined based on the rate of pay the employee would have received from the employer but for absence during the period of qualified military service, or

(B) if the compensation the employee would have received during such period was not reasonably certain, the employee's average compensation from the employer during the 12-month period immediately preceding the qualified military service (or, if shorter, the period of employment immediately preceding the qualified military service).

(8) USERRA requirements for qualified retirement plans—For purposes of this subchapter and section 457, an employer sponsoring a retirement plan shall be treated as meeting the requirements of chapter 43 of title 38, United States Code, only if each of the following requirements is met:

(A) An individual reemployed under such chapter is treated with respect to such plan as not having incurred a break in service with the employer maintaining the plan by reason of such individual's period of qualified military service.

(B) Each period of qualified military service served by an individual is, upon reemployment under such chapter, deemed with respect to such plan to constitute service with the employer maintaining the plan for the purpose of determining the nonforfeitability of the individual's accrued benefits under such plan and for the purpose of determining the accrual of benefits under such plan.

(C) An individual reemployed under such chapter is entitled to accrued benefits that are contingent on the making of, or derived from, employee contributions or elective deferrals only to the extent the individual makes payment to the plan with respect to such contributions or deferrals. No such payment may exceed the amount the individual would have been permitted or required to contribute had the individual remained continuously employed by the employer throughout the period of qualified military service. Any payment to such plan shall be made during the period beginning with the date of reemployment and whose duration is 3 times the period of the qualified military service (but not greater than 5 years).

(9) Treatment in the case of death or disability resulting from active military service—

(A) In general—For benefit accrual purposes, an employer sponsoring a retirement plan may treat an individual who dies or becomes disabled (as defined under the terms of the plan) while performing qualified military service with respect to the employer maintaining the plan as if the individual has resumed employment in accordance with the individual's reemployment rights under chapter 43 of title 38, United States Code, on the day preceding death or disability (as the case may be) and terminated employment on the actual date of death or disability. In the case of any such treatment, and subject to subparagraphs (B) and (C), any full or partial compliance by such plan with respect to the benefit accrual requirements of paragraph (8) with respect to such individual shall be treated for purposes of paragraph (1) as if such compliance were required under such chapter 43.

(B) Nondiscrimination requirement—Subparagraph (A) shall apply only if all individuals performing qualified military service with respect to the employer maintaining the plan (as determined under subsections (b), (c), (m), and (o)) who die or became disabled as a result of performing qualified military service prior to reemployment by the employer are credited with service and benefits on reasonably equivalent terms.

(C) Determination of benefits—The amount of employee contributions and the amount of elective deferrals of an individual treated as reemployed under subparagraph (A) for purposes of applying paragraph (8)(C) shall be determined on the basis of the individual's average actual employee contributions or elective deferrals for the lesser of—

(i) the 12-month period of service with the employer immediately prior to qualified military service, or

(ii) if service with the employer is less than such 12-month period, the actual length of continuous service with the employer.

(10) Plans not subject to title 38—This subsection shall not apply to any retirement plan to which chapter 43 of title 38, United States Code, does not apply.

(11) References—For purposes of this section, any reference to chapter 43 of title 38, United States Code, shall be treated as a reference to such chapter as in effect on December 12, 1994 (without regard to any subsequent amendment).

(12) Treatment of differential wage payments—

(A) In general—Except as provided in this paragraph, for purposes of applying this title to a retirement plan to which this subsection applies—

(i) an individual receiving a differential wage payment shall be treated as an employee of the employer making the payment,

(ii) the differential wage payment shall be treated as compensation, and

(iii) the plan shall not be treated as failing to meet the requirements of any provision described in paragraph (1)(C) by reason of any contribution or benefit which is based on the differential wage payment.

(B) Special rule for distributions—

(i) In general—Notwithstanding subparagraph (A)(i), for purposes of section 401(k)(2)(B)(i)(I), 403(b)(7)(A)(ii), 403(b)(11)(A), or 457(d)(1)(A)(ii), an individual shall be treated as having been severed from employment during any period the individual is performing service in the uniformed services described in section 3401(h)(2)(A).

(ii) Limitation—If an individual elects to receive a distribution by reason of clause (i), the plan shall provide that the individual may not make an elective deferral or employee contribution during the 6-month period beginning on the date of the distribution.

(C) Nondiscrimination requirement—Subparagraph (A)(iii) shall apply only if all employees of an employer (as determined under subsections (b), (c), (m), and (o)) performing service in the uniformed services described in section 3401(h)(2)(A) are entitled to receive differential wage payments on reasonably equivalent terms and, if eligible to participate in a retirement plan maintained by the employer, to make contributions based on the payments on reasonably equivalent terms. For purposes of applying this subparagraph, the provisions of paragraphs (3), (4), and (5) of section 410(b) shall apply.

(D) Differential wage payment—For purposes of this paragraph, the term "differential wage payment" has the meaning given such term by section 3401(h)(2).

(v) Catch-up contributions for individuals age 50 or over—

(1) In general—An applicable employer plan shall not be treated as failing to meet any requirement of this title solely because the plan permits an eligible participant to make additional elective deferrals in any plan year.

(2) Limitation on amount of additional deferrals—

(A) In general—A plan shall not permit additional elective deferrals under paragraph (1) for any year in an amount greater than the lesser of—

(i) the applicable dollar amount, or

(ii) the excess (if any) of—

(I) the participant's compensation (as defined in section 415(c)(3)) for the year, over

(II) any other elective deferrals of the participant for such year which are made without regard to this subsection.

(B) Applicable dollar amount—For purposes of this paragraph—

(i) In the case of an applicable employer plan other than a plan described in section 401(k)(11) or 408(p), the applicable dollar amount is $5,000.

(ii) In the case of an applicable employer plan described in section 401(k)(11) or 408(p), the applicable dollar amount is $2,500.

(C) Cost-of-living adjustment—In the case of a year beginning after December 31, 2006, the Secretary shall adjust annually the $5,000 amount in subparagraph (B)(i) and the $2,500 amount in subparagraph (B)(ii) for increases in the cost-of-living at the same time and in the same manner as adjustments under section 415(d); except that the base period taken into account shall be the calendar quarter beginning July 1, 2005, and any increase under this subparagraph which is not a multiple of $500 shall be rounded to the next lower multiple of $500.

(D) Aggregation of plans—For purposes of this paragraph, plans described in clauses (i), (ii), and (iv) of paragraph (6)(A) that are maintained by the same employer (as determined under subsection (b), (c), (m) or (o)) shall be treated as a single plan, and plans described in clause (iii) of paragraph (6)(A) that are maintained by the same employer shall be treated as a single plan.

(3) Treatment of contributions—In the case of any contribution to a plan under paragraph (1)—

    (A) such contribution shall not, with respect to the year in which the contribution is made—

        (i) be subject to any otherwise applicable limitation contained in section 401(a)(30), 402(h), 403(b), 408, 415(c), and 457(b)(2) (determined without regard to section 457(b)(3)), or

        (ii) be taken into account in applying such limitations to other contributions or benefits under such plan or any other such plan, and

    (B) except as provided in paragraph (4), such plan shall not be treated as failing to meet the requirements of section 401(a)(4), 401(k)(3), 401(k)(11), 403(b)(12), 408(k), 410(b), or 416 by reason of the making of (or the right to make) such contribution.

(4) Application of nondiscrimination rules—

    (A) In general—An applicable employer plan shall be treated as failing to meet the non-discrimination requirements under section 401(a)(4) with respect to benefits, rights, and features unless the plan allows all eligible participants to make the same election with respect to the additional elective deferrals under this subsection.

    (B) Aggregation—For purposes of subparagraph (A), all plans maintained by employers who are treated as a single employer under subsection (b), (c), (m), or (o) of section 414 shall be treated as 1 plan, except that a plan described in clause (i) of section 410(b)(6)(C) shall not be treated as a plan of the employer until the expiration of the transition period with respect to such plan (as determined under clause (ii) of such section).

(5) Eligible participant—For purposes of this subsection, the term "eligible participant" means a participant in a plan—

    (A) who would attain age 50 by the end of the taxable year,

    (B) with respect to whom no other elective deferrals may (without regard to this subsection) be made to the plan for the plan (or other applicable) year by reason of the application of any limitation or other restriction described in paragraph (3) or comparable limitation or restriction contained in the terms of the plan.

(6) Other definitions and rules—For purposes of this subsection—

    (A) Applicable employer plan—The term "applicable employer plan" means—

        (i) an employees' trust described in section 401(a) which is exempt from tax under section 501(a),

        (ii) a plan under which amounts are contributed by an individual's employer for an annuity contract described in section 403(b),

        (iii) an eligible deferred compensation plan under section 457 of an eligible employer described in section 457(e)(1)(A), and

        (iv) an arrangement meeting the requirements of section 408(k) or (p).

    (B) Elective deferral—The term "elective deferral" has the meaning given such term by subsection (u)(2)(C).

(C) Exception for section 457 plans—This subsection shall not apply to a participant for any year for which a higher limitation applies to the participant under section 457(b)(3).

(w) Special rules for certain withdrawals from eligible automatic contribution arrangements—

(1) In general—If an eligible automatic contribution arrangement allows an employee to elect to make permissible withdrawals—

(A) the amount of any such withdrawal shall be includible in the gross income of the employee for the taxable year of the employee in which the distribution is made,

(B) no tax shall be imposed under section 72(t) with respect to the distribution, and

(C) the arrangement shall not be treated as violating any restriction on distributions under this title solely by reason of allowing the withdrawal.

In the case of any distribution to an employee by reason of an election under this paragraph, employer matching contributions shall be forfeited or subject to such other treatment as the Secretary may prescribe.

(2) Permissible withdrawal—For purposes of this subsection—

(A) In general—The term "permissible withdrawal" means any withdrawal from an eligible automatic contribution arrangement meeting the requirements of this paragraph which—

(i) is made pursuant to an election by an employee, and

(ii) consists of elective contributions described in paragraph (3)(B) (and earnings attributable thereto).

(B) Time for making election—Subparagraph (A) shall not apply to an election by an employee unless the election is made no later than the date which is 90 days after the date of the first elective contribution with respect to the employee under the arrangement.

(C) Amount of distribution—Subparagraph (A) shall not apply to any election by an employee unless the amount of any distribution by reason of the election is equal to the amount of elective contributions made with respect to the first payroll period to which the eligible automatic contribution arrangement applies to the employee and any succeeding payroll period beginning before the effective date of the election (and earnings attributable thereto).

(3) Eligible automatic contribution arrangement—For purposes of this subsection, the term "eligible automatic contribution arrangement" means an arrangement under an applicable employer plan—

(A) under which a participant may elect to have the employer make payments as contributions under the plan on behalf of the participant, or to the participant directly in cash,

(B) under which the participant is treated as having elected to have the employer make such contributions in an amount equal to a uniform percentage of compensation provided under the plan until the participant specifically elects not to have such contributions made (or specifically elects to have such contributions made at a different percentage), and

(**C**) which meets the requirements of paragraph (4).

(4) Notice requirements—

(**A**) **In general**—The administrator of a plan containing an arrangement described in paragraph (3) shall, within a reasonable period before each plan year, give to each employee to whom an arrangement described in paragraph (3) applies for such plan year notice of the employee's rights and obligations under the arrangement which—

(**i**) is sufficiently accurate and comprehensive to apprise the employee of such rights and obligations, and

(**ii**) is written in a manner calculated to be understood by the average employee to whom the arrangement applies.

(**B**) **Time and form of notice**—A notice shall not be treated as meeting the requirements of subparagraph (A) with respect to an employee unless—

(**i**) the notice includes an explanation of the employee's right under the arrangement to elect not to have elective contributions made on the employee's behalf (or to elect to have such contributions made at a different percentage),

(**ii**) the employee has a reasonable period of time after receipt of the notice described in clause (i) and before the first elective contribution is made to make such election, and

(**iii**) the notice explains how contributions made under the arrangement will be invested in the absence of any investment election by the employee.

(**5**) **Applicable employer plan**—For purposes of this subsection, the term "applicable employer plan" means—

(**A**) an employees' trust described in section 401(a) which is exempt from tax under section 501(a),

(**B**) a plan under which amounts are contributed by an individual's employer for an annuity contract described in section 403(b),

(**C**) an eligible deferred compensation plan described in section 457(b) which is maintained by an eligible employer described in section 457(e)(1)(A),

(**D**) a simplified employee pension the terms of which provide for a salary reduction arrangement described in section 408(k)(6), and

(**E**) a simple retirement account (as defined in section 408(p)).

(**6**) **Special rule**—A withdrawal described in paragraph (1) (subject to the limitation of paragraph (2)(C)) shall not be taken into account for purposes of section 401(k)(3).

(x) Special rules for eligible combined defined benefit plans and qualified cash or deferred arrangements—

(**1**) **General rule**—Except as provided in this subsection, the requirements of this title shall be applied to any defined benefit plan or applicable defined contribution plan which are part of an eligible combined plan in the same manner as if each such plan were not a part of the eligible combined plan. In the case of a termination of the defined benefit plan and the applicable defined contribution plan forming part of an eligible combined plan, the plan administrator shall terminate each such plan separately.

(2) Eligible combined plan—For purposes of this subsection—

(A) In general—The term "eligible combined plan" means a plan—

(i) which is maintained by an employer which, at the time the plan is established, is a small employer,

(ii) which consists of a defined benefit plan and an applicable defined contribution plan,

(iii) the assets of which are held in a single trust forming part of the plan and are clearly identified and allocated to the defined benefit plan and the applicable defined contribution plan to the extent necessary for the separate application of this title under paragraph (1), and

(iv) with respect to which the benefit, contribution, vesting, and nondiscrimination requirements of subparagraphs (B), (C), (D), (E), and (F) are met.

For purposes of this subparagraph, the term small employer has the meaning given such term by section 4980D(d)(2), except that such section shall be applied by substituting 500 for 50 each place it appears.

(B) Benefit requirements—

(i) In general—The benefit requirements of this subparagraph are met with respect to the defined benefit plan forming part of the eligible combined plan if the accrued benefit of each participant derived from employer contributions, when expressed as an annual retirement benefit, is not less than the applicable percentage of the participant's final average pay. For purposes of this clause, final average pay shall be determined using the period of consecutive years (not exceeding 5) during which the participant had the greatest aggregate compensation from the employer.

(ii) Applicable percentage—For purposes of clause (i), the applicable percentage is the lesser of—

(I) 1 percent multiplied by the number of years of service with the employer, or

(II) 20 percent.

(iii) Special rule for applicable defined benefit plans—If the defined benefit plan under clause (i) is an applicable defined benefit plan as defined in section 411(a)(13)(B) which meets the interest credit requirements of section 411(b)(5)(B)(i), the plan shall be treated as meeting the requirements of clause (i) with respect to any plan year if each participant receives a pay credit for the year which is not less than the percentage of compensation determined in accordance with the following table:

If the participant's age as of the beginning of the year is—	The percentage is—
30 or less	2
Over 30 but less than 40	4
40 or over but less than 50	6
50 or over	8.

(iv) Years of service—For purposes of this subparagraph, years of service shall be determined under the rules of paragraphs (4), (5), and (6) of section 411(a), except that the plan may not disregard any year of service because of a participant making, or failing to make, any elective deferral with respect to the qualified cash or deferred arrangement to which subparagraph (C) applies.

(C) Contribution requirements—

    (i) In general—The contribution requirements of this subparagraph with respect to any applicable defined contribution plan forming part of an eligible combined plan are met if—

        (I) the qualified cash or deferred arrangement included in such plan constitutes an automatic contribution arrangement, and

        (II) the employer is required to make matching contributions on behalf of each employee eligible to participate in the arrangement in an amount equal to 50 percent of the elective contributions of the employee to the extent such elective contributions do not exceed 4 percent of compensation.

Rules similar to the rules of clauses (ii) and (iii) of section 401(k)(12)(B) shall apply for purposes of this clause.

    (ii) Nonelective contributions—An applicable defined contribution plan shall not be treated as failing to meet the requirements of clause (i) because the employer makes nonelective contributions under the plan but such contributions shall not be taken into account in determining whether the requirements of clause (i)(II) are met.

(D) Vesting requirements—The vesting requirements of this subparagraph are met if—

    (i) in the case of a defined benefit plan forming part of an eligible combined plan an employee who has completed at least 3 years of service has a nonforfeitable right to 100 percent of the employee's accrued benefit under the plan derived from employer contributions, and

    (ii) in the case of an applicable defined contribution plan forming part of eligible combined plan—

        (I) an employee has a nonforfeitable right to any matching contribution made under the qualified cash or deferred arrangement included in such plan by an employer with respect to any elective contribution, including matching contributions in excess of the contributions required under subparagraph (C)(i)(II), and

        (II) an employee who has completed at least 3 years of service has a nonforfeitable right to 100 percent of the employee's accrued benefit derived under the arrangement from nonelective contributions of the employer.

For purposes of this subparagraph, the rules of section 411 shall apply to the extent not inconsistent with this subparagraph.

(E) Uniform provision of contributions and benefits—In the case of a defined benefit plan or applicable defined contribution plan forming part of an eligible combined plan, the requirements of this subparagraph are met if all contributions and benefits under each such plan, and all rights and features under each such plan, must be provided uniformly to all participants.

(F) Requirements must be met without taking into account social security and similar contributions and benefits or other plans—

(i) **In general**—The requirements of this subparagraph are met if the requirements of clauses (ii) and (iii) are met.

(ii) **Social security and similar contributions**—The requirements of this clause are met if—

(I) the requirements of subparagraphs (B) and (C) are met without regard to section 401(l), and

(II) the requirements of sections 401(a)(4) and 410(b) are met with respect to both the applicable defined contribution plan and defined benefit plan forming part of an eligible combined plan without regard to section 401(l).

(iii) **Other plans and arrangements**—The requirements of this clause are met if the applicable defined contribution plan and defined benefit plan forming part of an eligible combined plan meet the requirements of sections 401(a)(4) and 410(b) without being combined with any other plan.

(3) Nondiscrimination requirements for qualified cash or deferred arrangement—

(A) In general—A qualified cash or deferred arrangement which is included in an applicable defined contribution plan forming part of an eligible combined plan shall be treated as meeting the requirements of section 401(k)(3)(A)(ii) if the requirements of paragraph (2)(C) are met with respect to such arrangement.

(B) Matching contributions—In applying section 401(m)(11) to any matching contribution with respect to a contribution to which paragraph (2)(C) applies, the contribution requirement of paragraph (2)(C) and the notice requirements of paragraph (5)(B) shall be substituted for the requirements otherwise applicable under clauses (i) and (ii) of section 401(m)(11)(A).

(4) Satisfaction of top-heavy rules—A defined benefit plan and applicable defined contribution plan forming part of an eligible combined plan for any plan year shall be treated as meeting the requirements of section 416 for the plan year.

(5) Automatic contribution arrangement—For purposes of this subsection—

(A) In general—A qualified cash or deferred arrangement shall be treated as an automatic contribution arrangement if the arrangement—

(i) provides that each employee eligible to participate in the arrangement is treated as having elected to have the employer make elective contributions in an amount equal to 4 percent of the employee's compensation unless the employee specifically elects not to have such contributions made or to have such contributions made at a different rate, and

(ii) meets the notice requirements under subparagraph (B).

(B) Notice requirements—

(i) **In general**—The requirements of this subparagraph are met if the requirements of clauses (ii) and (iii) are met.

(ii) **Reasonable period to make election**—The requirements of this clause are met if each employee to whom subparagraph (A)(i) applies—

(I) receives a notice explaining the employee's right under the arrangement to elect not to have elective contributions made on the employee's behalf or to have the contributions made at a different rate, and

(II) has a reasonable period of time after receipt of such notice and before the first elective contribution is made to make such election.

(iii) Annual notice of rights and obligations—The requirements of this clause are met if each employee eligible to participate in the arrangement is, within a reasonable period before any year, given notice of the employee's rights and obligations under the arrangement.

The requirements of clauses (i) and (ii) of section 401(k)(12)(D) shall be met with respect to the notices described in clauses (ii) and (iii) of this subparagraph.

(6) Coordination with other requirements—

(A) Treatment of separate plans—Section 414(k) shall not apply to an eligible combined plan.

(B) Reporting—An eligible combined plan shall be treated as a single plan for purposes of sections 6058 and 6059.

(7) Applicable defined contribution plan—For purposes of this subsection—

(A) In general—The term "applicable defined contribution plan" means a defined contribution plan which includes a qualified cash or deferred arrangement.

(B) Qualified cash or deferred arrangement—The term "qualified cash or deferred arrangement" has the meaning given such term by section 401(k)(2).

(y) Cooperative and small employer charity pension plans.

(1) In general—For purposes of this title, except as provided in this subsection, a CSEC plan is a defined benefit plan (other than a multiemployer plan)—

(A) to which section 104 of the Pension Protection Act of 2006 applies, without regard to—

(i) section 104(a)(2) of such Act;

(ii) the amendments to such section 104 by section 202(b) of the Preservation of Access to Care for Medicare Beneficiaries and Pension Relief Act of 2010; and

(iii) paragraph (3)(B);

(B) that, as of June 25, 2010, was maintained by more than one employer and all of the employers were organizations described in section 501(c)(3); or

(C) that, as of June 25, 2010, was maintained by an employer—

(i) described in section 501(c)(3) of such Code,

(ii) chartered under part B of subtitle II of title 36, United States Code,

(iii) with employees in at least 40 States, and

(iv) whose primary exempt purpose is to provide services with respect to children.

(2) Aggregation—All employers that are treated as a single employer under subsection (b) or (c) shall be treated as a single employer for purposes of determining if a plan was maintained by more than one employer under subparagraph (B) and (C) of paragraph (1).

(3) Election—

(A) In general—If a plan falls within the definition of a CSEC plan under this subsection (without regard to this paragraph), such plan shall be a CSEC plan unless the plan sponsor elects not later than the close of the first plan year of the plan beginning after December 31, 2013, not to be treated as a CSEC plan. An election under the preceding sentence shall take effect for such plan year and, once made, may be revoked only with the consent of the Secretary.

(B) Special rule—If a plan described in subparagraph (A) is treated as a CSEC plan, section 104 of the Pension Protection Act of 2006, as amended by the Preservation of Access to Care for Medicare Beneficiaries and Pension Relief Act of 2010, shall cease to apply to such plan as of the first date as of which such plan is treated as a CSEC plan.

(z) Certain plan transfers and mergers.

(1) In general.—Under rules prescribed by the Secretary, except as provided in paragraph (2), no amount shall be includible in gross income by reason of—

(A) a transfer of all or a portion of the accrued benefit of a participant or beneficiary, whether or not vested, from a church plan that is a plan described in section 401(a) or an annuity contract described in section 403(b) to an annuity contract described in section 403(b), if such plan and annuity contract are both maintained by the same church or convention or association of churches,

(B) a transfer of all or a portion of the accrued benefit of a participant or beneficiary, whether or not vested, from an annuity contract described in section 403(b) to a church plan that is a plan described in section 401(a), if such plan and annuity contract are both maintained by the same church or convention or association of churches, or **(C)** a merger of a church plan that is a plan described in section 401(a), or an annuity contract described in section 403(b), with an annuity contract described in section 403(b), if such plan and annuity contract are both maintained by the same church or convention or association of churches.

(2) Limitation. Paragraph (1) shall not apply to a transfer or merger unless the participant's or beneficiary's total accrued benefit immediately after the transfer or merger is equal to or greater than the participant's or beneficiary's total accrued benefit immediately before the transfer or merger, and such total accrued benefit is nonforfeitable after the transfer or merger.

(3) Qualification. A plan or annuity contract shall not fail to be considered to be described in section 401(a) or 403(b) merely because such plan or annuity contract engages in a transfer or merger described in this subsection.

(4) Definitions. For purposes of this subsection—

(A) Church or convention or association of churches. The term "church or convention or association of churches" includes an organization described in subparagraph (A) or (B)(ii) of subsection (e)(3).

(B) Annuity contract. The term "annuity contract" includes a custodial account described in section 403(b)(7) and a retirement income account described in section 403(b)(9).

(C) Accrued benefit. The term "accrued benefit" means—

(i) in the case of a defined benefit plan, the employee's accrued benefit determined under the plan, and

(ii) in the case of a plan other than a defined benefit plan, the balance of the employee's account under the plan.

§ 415. Limitations on benefits and contribution under qualified plans.

(a) General rule—

(1) Trusts—A trust which is a part of a pension, profit-sharing, or stock bonus plan shall not constitute a qualified trust under section 401(a) if—

(A) in the case of a defined benefit plan, the plan provides for the payment of benefits with respect to a participant which exceed the limitation of subsection (b), or

(B) in the case of a defined contribution plan, contributions and other additions under the plan with respect to any participant for any taxable year exceed the limitation of subsection (c).

(2) Section applies to certain annuities and accounts—In the case of—

(A) an employee annuity plan described in section 403(a),

(B) an annuity contract described in section 403(b), or

(C) a simplified employee pension described in section 408(k),

such a contract, plan, or pension shall not be considered to be described in section 403(a), 403(b), or 408(k), as the case may be, unless it satisfies the requirements of subparagraph (A) or subparagraph (B) of paragraph (1), whichever is appropriate, and has not been disqualified under subsection (g). In the case of an annuity contract described in section 403(b), the preceding sentence shall apply only to the portion of the annuity contract which exceeds the limitation of subsection (b) or the limitation of subsection (c), whichever is appropriate.

(b) Limitation for defined benefit plans—

(1) In general—Benefits with respect to a participant exceed the limitation of this subsection if, when expressed as an annual benefit (within the meaning of paragraph (2)), such annual benefit is greater than the lesser of—

(A) $160,000, or

(B) 100 percent of the participant's average compensation for his high 3 years.

(2) Annual benefit—

(A) In general—For purposes of paragraph (1), the term "annual benefit" means a benefit payable annually in the form of a straight life annuity (with no ancillary benefits) under a plan to which employees do not contribute and under which no rollover contributions (as defined in sections 402(c), 403(a)(4), 403(b)(8), 408(d)(3), and 457(e)(16)) are made.

(B) Adjustment for certain other forms of benefit—If the benefit under the plan is payable in any form other than the form described in subparagraph (A), or if the employees contribute to the plan or make rollover contributions (as defined in sections 402(c), 403(a)(4), 403(b)(8), 408(d)(3), and 457(e)(16)), the determinations as to whether the limitation described in paragraph (1) has been satisfied shall be made, in accordance with regulations prescribed by the Secretary, by adjusting such benefit so that it is equivalent to the benefit described in subparagraph (A). For purposes of this subparagraph, any ancillary benefit which is not directly related to retirement income benefits shall not be taken into account; and that portion of any joint and survivor annuity which constitutes a qualified joint and survivor annuity (as defined in section 417) shall not be taken into account.

(C) Adjustment to $160,000 limit where benefit begins before age 62—If the retirement income benefit under the plan begins before age 62, the determination as to whether the $160,000 limitation set forth in paragraph (1)(A) has been satisfied shall be made, in accordance with regulations prescribed by the Secretary, by reducing the limitation of paragraph (1)(A) so that such limitation (as so reduced) equals an annual benefit (beginning when such retirement income benefit begins) which is equivalent to a $160,000 annual benefit beginning at age 62.

(D) Adjustment to $160,000 limit where benefit begins after age 65—If the retirement income benefit under the plan begins after age 65, the determination as to whether the $160,000 limitation set forth in paragraph (1)(A) has been satisfied shall be made, in accordance with regulations prescribed by the Secretary, by increasing the limitation of paragraph (1)(A) so that such limitation (as so increased) equals an annual benefit (beginning when such retirement income benefit begins) which is equivalent to a $160,000 annual benefit beginning at age 65.

(E) Limitation on certain assumptions—

(i) For purposes of adjusting any limitation under subparagraph (C) and, except as provided in clause (ii), for purposes of adjusting any benefit under subparagraph (B), the interest rate assumption shall not be less than the greater of 5 percent or the rate specified in the plan.

(ii) For purposes of adjusting any benefit under subparagraph (B) for any form of benefit subject to section 417(e)(3), the interest rate assumption shall not be less than the greatest of—

(I) 5.5 percent,

(II) the rate that provides a benefit of not more than 105 percent of the benefit that would be provided if the applicable interest rate (as defined in section 417(e)(3)) were the interest rate assumption, or

(III) the rate specified under the plan.

(iii) For purposes of adjusting any limitation under subparagraph (D), the interest rate assumption shall not be greater than the lesser of 5 percent or the rate specified in the plan.

(iv) For purposes of this subsection, no adjustments under subsection (d)(1) shall be taken into account before the year for which such adjustment first takes effect.

(v) For purposes of adjusting any benefit or limitation under subparagraph (B), (C), or (D), the mortality table used shall be the applicable mortality table (within the meaning of section 417(e)(3)(B)).

(vi) In the case of a plan maintained by an eligible employer (as defined in section 408(p)(2)(C)(i)), clause (ii) shall be applied without regard to subclause (II) thereof.

(F) [Repealed]

(G) Special limitation for qualified police or firefighters—In the case of a qualified participant, subparagraph (C) of this paragraph shall not apply.

(H) Qualified participant defined—For purposes of subparagraph (G), the term "qualified participant" means a participant—

(i) in a defined benefit plan which is maintained by a State, Indian tribal government (as defined in section 7701(a)(40)), or any political subdivision thereof,

(ii) with respect to whom the period of service taken into account in determining the amount of the benefit under such defined benefit plan includes at least 15 years of service of the participant—

(I) as a full-time employee of any police department or fire department which is organized and operated by the State, Indian tribal government (as so defined), or any political subdivision maintaining such defined benefit plan to provide police protection, firefighting services, or emergency medical services for any area within the jurisdiction of such State, Indian tribal government (as so defined), or any political subdivision, or

(II) as a member of the Armed Forces of the United States.

(I) Exemption for survivor and disability benefits provided under governmental plans—Subparagraph (C) of this paragraph and paragraph (5) shall not apply to—

(i) income received from a governmental plan (as defined in section 414(d)) as a pension, annuity, or similar allowance as the result of the recipient becoming disabled by reason of personal injuries or sickness, or

(ii) amounts received from a governmental plan by the beneficiaries, survivors, or the estate of an employee as the result of the death of the employee.

(3) Average compensation for high 3 years—For purposes of paragraph (1), a participant's high 3 years shall be the period of consecutive calendar years (not more than 3) during which the participant had the greatest aggregate compensation from the employer. In the case of an employee within the meaning of section 401(c)(1), the preceding sentence shall be applied by substituting for "compensation from the employer" the following: "the participant's earned income (within the meaning of section 401(c)(2) but determined without regard to any exclusion under section 911)".

(4) Total annual benefits not in excess of $10,000—Notwithstanding the preceding provisions of this subsection, the benefits payable with respect to a participant under any defined benefit plan shall be deemed not to exceed the limitation of this subsection if—

(A) the retirement benefits payable with respect to such participant under such plan and under all other defined benefit plans of the employer do not exceed $10,000 for the plan year, or for any prior plan year, and

(B) the employer has not at any time maintained a defined contribution plan in which the participant participated.

(5) Reduction for participation or service of less than 10 years—

(A) Dollar limitation—In the case of an employee who has less than 10 years of participation in a defined benefit plan, the limitation referred to in paragraph (1)(A) shall be the limitation determined under such paragraph (without regard to this paragraph) multiplied by a fraction—

    (i) the numerator of which is the number of years (or part thereof) of participation in the defined benefit plan of the employer, and

    (ii) the denominator of which is 10.

(B) Compensation and benefits limitations—The provisions of subparagraph (A) shall apply to the limitations under paragraphs (1)(B) and (4), except that such subparagraph shall be applied with respect to years of service with an employer rather than years of participation in a plan.

(C) Limitation on reduction—In no event shall subparagraph (A) or (B) reduce the limitations referred to in paragraphs (1) and (4) to an amount less than 1/10 of such limitation (determined without regard to this paragraph).

(D) Application to changes in benefit structure—To the extent provided in regulations, subparagraph (A) shall be applied separately with respect to each change in the benefit structure of a plan.

(6) Computation of benefits and contributions—The computation of—

(A) benefits under a defined contribution plan, for purposes of section 401(a)(4),

(B) contributions made on behalf of a participant in a defined benefit plan, for purposes of section 401(a)(4), and

(C) contributions and benefits provided for a participant in a plan described in section 414(k), for purposes of this section

shall not be made on a basis inconsistent with regulations prescribed by the Secretary.

(7) Benefits under certain collectively bargained plans—For a year, the limitation referred to in paragraph (1)(B) shall not apply to benefits with respect to a participant under a defined benefit plan (other than a multiemployer plan)—

(A) which is maintained for such year pursuant to a collective bargaining agreement between employee representatives and one or more employers,

(B) which, at all times during such year, has at least 100 participants,

(C) under which benefits are determined solely by reference to length of service, the particular years during which service was rendered, age at retirement, and date of retirement,

(D) which provides that an employee who has at least 4 years of service has a nonforfeitable right to 100 percent of his accrued benefit derived from employer contributions, and

(E) which requires, as a condition of participation in the plan, that an employee complete a period of not more than 60 consecutive days of service with the employer or employers maintaining the plan.

This paragraph shall not apply to a participant whose compensation for any 3 years during the 10-year period immediately preceding the year in which he separates from service exceeded the average compensation for such 3 years of all participants in such plan. This paragraph shall not apply to a participant for any period for which he is a participant under another plan to which this section applies which is maintained by an employer maintaining this plan. For any year for which the paragraph applies to benefits with respect to a participant, paragraph (1)(A) and subsection (d)(1)(A) shall be applied with respect to such participant by substituting one-half the amount otherwise applicable for such year under paragraph (1)(A) for "$160,000".

(8) Social security retirement age defined—For purposes of this subsection, the term "social security retirement age" means the age used as the retirement age under section 216(l) of the Social Security Act, except that such section shall be applied—

(A) without regard to the age increase factor, and

(B) as if the early retirement age under section 216(l)(2) of such Act were 62.

(9) Special rule for commercial airline pilots—

(A) In general—Except as provided in subparagraph (B), in the case of any participant who is a commercial airline pilot, if, as of the time of the participant's retirement, regulations prescribed by the Federal Aviation Administration require an individual to separate from service as a commercial airline pilot after attaining any age occurring on or after age 60 and before age 62, paragraph (2)(C) shall be applied by substituting such age for age 62.

(B) Individuals who separate from service before age 60—If a participant described in subparagraph (A) separates from service before age 60, the rules of paragraph (2)(C) shall apply.

* * *

(11) Special limitation rule for governmental and multiemployer plans—In the case of a governmental plan (as defined in section 414(d)) or a multiemployer plan (as defined in section 414(f)), subparagraph (B) of paragraph (1) shall not apply. Subparagraph (B) of paragraph (1) shall not apply to a plan maintained by an organization described in section 3121(w)(3)(A) except with respect to highly compensated benefits. For purposes of this paragraph, the term "highly compensated benefits" means any benefits accrued for an employee in any year on or after the first year in which such employee is a highly compensated employee (as defined in section 414(q)) of the organization described in section 3121(w)(3)(A). For purposes of applying paragraph (1)(B) to highly compensated benefits, all benefits of the employee otherwise taken into account (without regard to this paragraph) shall be taken into account.

(c) Limitation for defined contribution plans—

(1) In general—Contributions and other additions with respect to a participant exceed the limitation of this subsection if, when expressed as an annual addition (within the meaning of paragraph (2)) to the participant's account, such annual addition is greater than the lesser of—

(A) $40,000, or

(B) 100 percent of the participant's compensation.

(2) Annual addition—For purposes of paragraph (1), the term "annual addition" means the sum for any year of—

(A) employer contributions,

(B) the employee contributions, and

(C) forfeitures.

For the purposes of this paragraph, employee contributions under subparagraph (B) are determined without regard to any rollover contributions (as defined in sections 402(c), 403(a)(4), 403(b)(8), 408(d)(3), and 457(e)(16)) without regard to employee contributions to a simplified employee pension which are excludable from gross income under section 408(k)(6). Subparagraph (B) of paragraph (1) shall not apply to any contribution for medical benefits (within the meaning of section 419A(f)(2)) after separation from service which is treated as an annual addition.

(3) Participant's compensation—For purposes of paragraph (1)—

(A) In general—The term "participant's compensation" means the compensation of the participant from the employer for the year.

(B) Special rule for self-employed individuals—In the case of an employee within the meaning of section 401(c)(1), subparagraph (A) shall be applied by substituting "the participant's earned income (within the meaning of section 401(c)(2) but determined without regard to any exclusion under section 911)" for "compensation of the participant from the employer".

(C) Special rules for permanent and total disability—In the case of a participant in any defined contribution plan—

(i) who is permanently and totally disabled (as defined in section 22(e)(3)),

(ii) who is not a highly compensated employee (within the meaning of section 414(q)), and

(iii) with respect to whom the employer elects, at such time and in such manner as the Secretary may prescribe, to have this subparagraph apply,

the term "participant's compensation" means the compensation the participant would have received for the year if the participant was paid at the rate of compensation paid immediately before becoming permanently and totally disabled. This subparagraph shall apply only if contributions made with respect to amounts treated as compensation under this subparagraph are nonforfeitable when made. If a defined contribution plan provides for the continuation of contributions on behalf of all participants described in clause (i) for a fixed or determinable period, this subparagraph shall be applied without regard to clauses (ii) and (iii).

(D) Certain deferrals included—The term "participant's compensation" shall include—

(i) any elective deferral (as defined in section 402(g)(3)), and

(ii) any amount which is contributed or deferred by the employer at the election of the employee and which is not includible in the gross income of the employee by reason of section 125, 132(f)(4), or 457.

(E) Annuity contracts—In the case of an annuity contract described in section 403(b), the term "participant's compensation" means the participant's includible compensation determined under section 403(b)(3).

* * *

(d) Cost-of-living adjustments—

(1) In general—The Secretary shall adjust annually—

(A) the $160,000 amount in subsection (b)(1)(A),

(B) in the case of a participant who separated from service, the amount taken into account under subsection (b)(1)(B), and

(C) the $40,000 amount in subsection (c)(1)(A),

for increases in the cost-of-living in accordance with regulations prescribed by the Secretary.

(2) Method—The regulations prescribed under paragraph (1) shall provide for—

(A) an adjustment with respect to any calendar year based on the increase in the applicable index for the calendar quarter ending September 30 of the preceding calendar year over such index for the base period, and

(B) adjustment procedures which are similar to the procedures used to adjust benefit amounts under section 215(i)(2)(A) of the Social Security Act.

(3) Base period—For purpose of paragraph (2)—

(A) $160,000 amount—The base period taken into account for purposes of paragraph (1)(A) is the calendar quarter beginning July 1, 2001.

(B) Separations after December 31, 1994—The base period taken into account for purposes of paragraph (1)(B) with respect to individuals separating from service with the employer after December 31, 1994, is the calendar quarter beginning July 1 of the calendar year preceding the calendar year in which such separation occurs.

(C) Separations before January 1, 1995—The base period taken into account for purposes of paragraph (1)(B) with respect to individuals separating from service with the employer before January 1, 1995, is the calendar quarter beginning October 1 of the calendar year preceding the calendar year in which such separation occurs.

(D) $40,000 amount—The base period taken into account for purposes of paragraph (1)(C) is the calendar quarter beginning July 1, 2001.

(4) Rounding—

(A) $160,000 amount—Any increase under subparagraph (A) of paragraph (1) which is not a multiple of $5,000 shall be rounded to the next lowest multiple of $5,000. This subparagraph shall also apply for purposes of any provision of this title that provides for adjustments in accordance with the method contained in this subsection, except to the extent provided in such provision.

(B) $40,000 amount—Any increase under subparagraph (C) of paragraph (1) which is not a multiple of $1,000 shall be rounded to the next lowest multiple of $1,000.

(e) [Repealed]

(f) Combining of plans—

(1) In general—For purposes of applying the limitations of subsections (b) and (c)—

(A) all defined benefit plans (whether or not terminated) of an employer are to be treated as one defined benefit plan, and

(B) all defined contribution plans (whether or not terminated) of an employer are to be treated as one defined contribution plan.

(2) Exception for multiemployer plans—Notwithstanding paragraph (1) and subsection (g), a multiemployer plan (as defined in section 414(f)) shall not be combined or aggregated—

(A) with any other plan which is not a multiemployer plan for purposes of applying subsection (b)(1)(B) to such other plan, or

(B) with any other multiemployer plan for purposes of applying the limitations established in this section.

(g) Aggregation of plans—Except as provided in subsection (f)(3), the Secretary, in applying the provisions of this section to benefits or contributions under more than one plan maintained by the same employer, and to any trusts, contracts, accounts, or bonds referred to in subsection (a)(2), with respect to which the participant has the control required under section 414(b) or (c), as modified by subsection (h), shall, under regulations prescribed by the Secretary, disqualify one or more trusts, plans, contracts, accounts, or bonds, or any combination thereof until such benefits or contributions do not exceed the limitations contained in this section. In addition to taking into account such other factors as may be necessary to carry out the purposes of subsection (f), the regulations prescribed under this paragraph shall provide that no plan which has been terminated shall be disqualified until all other trusts, plans, contracts, accounts, or bonds have been disqualified.

(h) 50 percent control—For purposes of applying subsections (b) and (c) of section 414 to this section, the phrase "more than 50 percent" shall be substituted for the phrase "at least 80 percent" each place it appears in section 1563(a)(1).

* * *

(k) Special rules—

(1) Defined benefit plan and defined contribution plan—For purposes of this title, the term "defined contribution plan" or "defined benefit plan" means a defined contribution plan (within the meaning of section 414(i)) or a defined plan (within the meaning of section 414(j)), whichever applies, which is—

(A) a plan described in section 401(a) which includes a trust which is exempt from tax under section 501(a),

(B) an annuity plan described in section 403(a),

(C) an annuity contract described in section 403(b), or

(D) a simplified employee pension.

* * *

(4) Special rules for sections 403(b) and 408—For purposes of this section, any annuity contract described in section 403(b) for the benefit of a participant shall be treated as a defined contribution plan maintained by each employer with respect to which the participant has the control required under subsection (b) or (c) of section 414 (as modified by subsection (h)). For purposes of this section, any contribution by an employer to a simplified employee pension plan for an individual for a taxable year shall be treated as an employer contribution to a defined contribution plan for such individual for such year.

(l) Treatment of certain medical benefits—

(1) In general—For purposes of this section, contributions allocated to any individual medical account which is part of a pension or annuity plan shall be treated as an annual addition to a defined contribution plan for purposes of subsection (c). Subparagraph (B) of subsection (c)(1) shall not apply to any amount treated as an annual addition under the preceding sentence.

(2) Individual medical benefit account—For purposes of paragraph (1), the term "individual medical benefit account" means any separate account—

(A) which is established for a participant under a pension or annuity plan, and

(B) from which benefits described in section 401(h) are payable solely to such participant, his spouse, or his dependents.

(m) Treatment of qualified governmental excess benefit arrangements—

(1) Governmental plan not affected—In determining whether a governmental plan (as defined in section 414(d)) meets the requirements of this section, benefits provided under a qualified governmental excess benefit arrangement shall not be taken into account. Income accruing to a governmental plan (or to a trust that is maintained solely for the purpose of providing benefits under a qualified governmental excess benefit arrangement) in respect of a qualified governmental excess benefit arrangement shall constitute income derived from the exercise of an essential governmental function upon which such governmental plan (or trust) shall be exempt from tax under section 115.

(2) Taxation of participant—For purposes of this chapter—

(A) the taxable year or years for which amounts in respect of a qualified governmental excess benefit arrangement are includible in gross income by a participant, and

(B) the treatment of such amounts when so includible by the participant,

shall be determined as if such qualified governmental excess benefit arrangement were treated as a plan for the deferral of compensation which is maintained by a corporation not exempt from tax under this chapter and which does not meet the requirements for qualification under section 401.

(3) Qualified governmental excess benefit arrangement—For purposes of this subsection, the term "qualified governmental excess benefit arrangement" means a portion of a governmental plan if—

(A) such portion is maintained solely for the purpose of providing to participants in the plan that part of the participant's annual benefit otherwise payable under the terms of the plan that exceeds the limitations on benefits imposed by this section,

(B) under such portion no election is provided at any time to the participant (directly or indirectly) to defer compensation, and

(C) benefits described in subparagraph (A) are not paid from a trust forming a part of such governmental plan unless such trust is maintained solely for the purpose of providing such benefits.

(n) Special rules relating to purchase of permissive service credit—

(1) In general—If a participant makes 1 or more contributions to a defined benefit governmental plan (within the meaning of section 414(d)) to purchase permissive service credit under such plan, then the requirements of this section shall be treated as met only if—

(A) the requirements of subsection (b) are met, determined by treating the accrued benefit derived from all such contributions as an annual benefit for purposes of subsection (b), or

(B) the requirements of subsection (c) are met, determined by treating all such contributions as annual additions for purposes of subsection (c).

(2) Application of limit—For purposes of—

(A) applying paragraph (1)(A), the plan shall not fail to meet the reduced limit under subsection (b)(2)(C) solely by reason of this subsection, and

(B) applying paragraph (1)(B), the plan shall not fail to meet the percentage limitation under subsection (c)(1)(B) solely by reason of this subsection.

(3) Permissive service credit—For purposes of this subsection—

(A) In general—The term "permissive service credit" means service credit—

(i) recognized by the governmental plan for purposes of calculating a participant's benefit under the plan,

(ii) which such participant has not received under such governmental plan, and

(iii) which such participant may receive only by making a voluntary additional contribution, in an amount determined under such governmental plan, which does not exceed the amount necessary to fund the benefit attributable to such service credit.

Such term may include service credit for periods for which there is no performance of service, and, notwithstanding clause (ii), may include service credited in order to provide an increased benefit for service credit which a participant is receiving under the plan.

(B) Limitation on nonqualified service credit—A plan shall fail to meet the requirements of this section if—

(i) more than 5 years of nonqualified service credit are taken into account for purposes of this subsection, or

(ii) any nonqualified service credit is taken into account under this subsection before the employee has at least 5 years of participation under the plan.

(C) Nonqualified service credit—For purposes of subparagraph (B), the term 'nonqualified service credit' means permissive service credit other than that allowed with respect to—

(i) service (including parental, medical, sabbatical, and similar leave) as an employee of the Government of the United States, any State or political subdivision thereof, or any agency or instrumentality of any of the foregoing (other than military service or service for credit which was obtained as a result of a repayment described in subsection (k)(3)),

(ii) service (including parental, medical, sabbatical, and similar leave) as an employee (other than as an employee described in clause (i)) of an educational organization described in section 170(b)(1)(A)(ii) which is a public, private, or sectarian school which provides elementary or secondary education (through grade 12), or a comparable level of education, as determined under the applicable law of the jurisdiction in which the service was performed,

(iii) service as an employee of an association of employees who are described in clause (i), or

(iv) military service (other than qualified military service under section 414(u)) recognized by such governmental plan.

In the case of service described in clauses (i), (ii), or (iii), such service will be nonqualified service if recognition of such service would cause a participant to receive a retirement benefit for the same service under more than one plan.

(D) Special rules for trustee-to-trustee transfers—In the case of a trustee-to-trustee transfer to which section 403(b)(13)(A) or 457(e)(17)(A) applies (without regard to whether the transfer is made between plans maintained by the same employer)—

(i) the limitations of subparagraph (B) shall not apply in determining whether the transfer is for the purchase of permissive service credit, and

(ii) the distribution rules applicable under this title to the defined benefit governmental plan to which any amounts are so transferred shall apply to such amounts and any benefits attributable to such amounts.

§ 416. Special rules for top heavy plans.

(a) General rule—A trust shall not constitute a qualified trust under section 401(a) for any plan year if the plan of which it is a part is a top-heavy plan for such plan year unless such plan meets—

(1) the vesting requirements of subsection (b), and

(2) the minimum benefit requirements of subsection (c).

(b) Vesting requirements—

(1) In general—A plan satisfies the requirements of this subsection if it satisfies the requirements of either of the following subparagraphs:

(A) 3-year vesting—A plan satisfies the requirements of this subparagraph if an employee who has completed at least 3 years of service with the employer or employers maintaining the plan has a nonforfeitable right to 100 percent of his accrued benefit derived from employer contributions.

(B) 6-year graded vesting—A plan satisfies the requirements of this subparagraph if an employee has a nonforfeitable right to a percentage of his accrued benefit derived from employer contributions determined under the following table:

Years of service:	*The nonforfeitable percentage is:*
2	20
3	40
4	60
5	80
6 or more	100

(2) Certain rules made applicable—Except to the extent inconsistent with the provisions of this subsection, the rules of section 411 shall apply for purposes of this subsection.

(c) Plan must provide minimum benefits—

(1) Defined benefit plans—

(A) In general—A defined benefit plan meets the requirements of this subsection if the accrued benefit derived from employer contributions of each participant who is a non-key employee, when expressed as an annual retirement benefit, is not less than the applicable percentage of the participant's average compensation for years in the testing period.

(B) Applicable percentage—For purposes of subparagraph (A), the term "applicable percentage" means the lesser of—

(i) 2 percent multiplied by the number of years of service with the employer, or

(ii) 20 percent.

(C) Years of service—For purposes of this paragraph—

(i) In general—Except as provided in clause (ii) or (iii), years of service shall be determined under the rules of paragraphs (4), (5), and (6) of section 411(a).

(ii) Exception for years during which plan was not top-heavy—A year of service with the employer shall not be taken into account under this paragraph if—

(I) the plan was not a top-heavy plan for any plan year ending during such year of service, or

(II) such year of service was completed in a plan year beginning before January 1, 1984.

(iii) Exception for plan under which no key employee (or former key employee) benefits for plan year—For purposes of determining an employee's years of service with the employer, any service with the employer shall be disregarded to the extent that such service occurs during a plan year when the plan benefits (within the meaning of section 410(b)) no key employee or former key employee.

(D) Average compensation for high 5 years—For purposes of this paragraph—

(i) In general—A participant's testing period shall be the period of consecutive years (not exceeding 5) during which the participant had the greatest aggregate compensation from the employer.

(ii) Year must be included in year of service—The years taken into account under clause (i) shall be properly adjusted for years not included in a year of service.

(iii) Certain years not taken into account—Except to the extent provided in the plan, a year shall not be taken into account under clause (i) if—

(I) such year ends in a plan year beginning before January 1, 1984, or

(II) such year begins after the close of the last year in which the plan was a top-heavy plan.

(E) Annual retirement benefit—For purposes of this paragraph, the term "annual retirement benefit" means a benefit payable annually in the form of a single life annuity (with no ancillary benefits) beginning at the normal retirement age under the plan.

(2) Defined contribution plans—

(A) In general—A defined contribution plan meets the requirements of the subsection if the employer contribution for the year for each participant who is a non-key employee is not less than 3 percent of such participant's compensation (within the meaning of section 415). Employer matching contributions (as defined in section 401(m)(4)(A)) shall be taken into account for purposes of this subparagraph (and any reduction under this sentence shall not be taken into account in determining whether section 401(k)(4)(A) applies).

(B) Special rule where maximum contribution less than 3 percent—

(i) In general—The percentage referred to in subparagraph (A) for any year shall not exceed the percentage at which contributions are made (or required to be made) under the plan for the year for the key employee for whom such percentage is the highest for the year.

(ii) Treatment of aggregation groups—

(I) For purposes of this subparagraph, all defined contribution plans required to be included in an aggregation group under subsection (g)(2)(A)(i) shall be treated as one plan.

(II) This subparagraph shall not apply to any plan required to be included in an aggregation group if such plan enables a defined benefit plan required to be included in such group to meet the requirements of section 401(a)(4) or 410.

(d) [Repealed]

(e) Plan must meet requirements without taking into account social security and similar contributions and benefits—A top-heavy plan shall not be treated as meeting the requirement of subsection (b) or (c) unless such plan meets such requirement without taking into account contributions or benefits under chapter 2 (relating to tax on self-employment income), chapter 21 (relating to Federal Insurance Contributions Act), title II of the Social Security Act, or any other Federal or State law.

(f) Coordination where employer has 2 or more plans—The Secretary shall prescribe such regulations as may be necessary or appropriate to carry out the purposes of this section where the employer has 2 or more plans including (but not limited to) regulations to prevent inappropriate omissions or required duplication of minimum benefits or contributions.

(g) Top-heavy plan defined—For purposes of this section—

(1) In general—

(A) Plans not required to be aggregated—Except as provided in subparagraph (B), the term "top-heavy plan" means, with respect to any plan year—

(i) any defined benefit plan if, as of the determination date, the present value of the cumulative accrued benefits under the plan for key employees exceeds 60 percent of the present value of the cumulative accrued benefits under the plan for all employees, and

(ii) any defined contribution plan if, as of the determination date, the aggregate of the accounts of key employees under the plan exceeds 60 percent of the aggregate of the accounts of all employees under such plan.

(B) Aggregated plans—Each plan of an employer required to be included in an aggregation group shall be treated as a top-heavy plan if such group is a top-heavy group.

(2) Aggregation—For purposes of this subsection—

(A) Aggregation group—

(i) Required aggregation—The term "aggregation group" means—

(I) each plan of the employer in which a key employee is a participant, and

(II) each other plan of the employer which enables any plan described in subclause (I) to meet the requirements of section 401(a)(4) or 410.

(ii) Permissive aggregation—The employer may treat any plan not required to be included in an aggregation group under clause (i) as being part of such group if such group would continue to meet the requirements of sections 401(a)(4) and 410 with such plan being taken into account.

(B) Top-heavy group—The term "top-heavy group" means any aggregation group if—

(i) the sum (as of the determination date) of—

(I) the present value of the cumulative accrued benefits for key employees under all defined benefit plans included in such group, and

(II) the aggregate of the accounts of key employees under all defined contribution plans included in such group,

(ii) exceeds 60 percent of a similar sum determined for all employees.

(3) Distributions during last year before determination date taken into account—

(A) In general—For purposes of determining—

(i) the present value of the cumulative accrued benefit for any employee, or

(ii) the amount of the account of any employee,

such present value or amount shall be increased by the aggregate distributions made with respect to such employee under the plan during the 1-year period ending on the determination date. The preceding sentence shall also apply to distributions under a terminated plan which if it had not been terminated would have been required to be included in an aggregation group.

(B) 5-year period in case of in-service distribution—In the case of any distribution made for a reason other than severance from employment, death, or disability, subparagraph (A) shall be applied by substituting "5-year period" for "1-year period".

(4) Other special rules—For purposes of this subsection—

(A) Rollover contributions to plan not taken into account—Except to the extent provided in regulations, any rollover contribution (or similar transfer) initiated by the employee and made after December 31, 1983, to a plan shall not be taken into account with respect to the transferee plan for purposes of determining whether such plan is a top-heavy plan (or whether any aggregation group which includes such plan is a top-heavy group).

(B) Benefits not taken into account if employee ceases to be key employee—If any individual is a non-key employee with respect to any plan for any plan year, but such individual was a key employee with respect to such plan for any prior plan year, any accrued benefit for such employee (and the account of such employee) shall not be taken into account.

(C) Determination date—The term "determination date" means, with respect to any plan year—

> **(i)** the last day of the preceding plan year, or

> **(ii)** in the case of the first plan year of any plan, the last day of such plan year.

(D) Years—To the extent provided in regulations, this section shall be applied on the basis of any year specified in such regulations in lieu of plan years.

(E) Benefits not taken into account if employee not employed for last year before determination date—If any individual has not performed services for the employer maintaining the plan at any time during the 1-year period ending on the determination date, any accrued benefit for such individual (and the account of such individual) shall not be taken into account.

(F) Accrued benefits treated as accruing ratably—The accrued benefit of any employee (other than a key employee) shall be determined—

> **(i)** under the method which is used for accrual purposes for all plans of the employer, or

> **(ii)** if there is no method described in clause (i), as if such benefit accrued not more rapidly than the slowest accrual rate permitted under section 411(b)(1)(C).

(G) Simple retirement accounts—The term "top-heavy plan" shall not include a simple retirement account under section 408(p).

(H) Cash or deferred arrangements using alternative methods of meeting nondiscrimination requirements—The term "top-heavy plan" shall not include a plan which consists solely of—

> **(i)** a cash or deferred arrangement which meets the requirements of section 401(k)(12) or 401(k)(13), and

> **(ii)** matching contributions with respect to which the requirements of section 401(m)(11) or 401(m)(12) are met.

If, but for this subparagraph, a plan would be treated as a top-heavy plan because it is a member of an aggregation group which is a top-heavy group, contributions under the plan may be taken into account in determining whether any other plan in the group meets the requirements of subsection (c)(2).

(h) [Repealed]

(i) Definitions—For purposes of this section—

(1) Key employee—

(A) In general—The term "key employee" means an employee who, at any time during the plan year, is—

(i) an officer of the employer having an annual compensation greater than $130,000,

(ii) a 5-percent owner of the employer, or

(iii) a 1-percent owner of the employer having an annual compensation from the employer of more than $150,000.

For purposes of clause (i), no more than 50 employees (or, if lesser, the greater of 3 or 10 percent of the employees) shall be treated as officers. In the case of plan years beginning after December 31, 2002, the $130,000 amount in clause (i) shall be adjusted at the same time and in the same manner as under section 415(d), except that the base period shall be the calendar quarter beginning July 1, 2001, and any increase under this sentence which is not a multiple of $5,000 shall be rounded to the next lower multiple of $5,000. Such term shall not include any officer or employee of an entity referred to in section 414(d) (relating to governmental plans). For purposes of determining the number of officers taken into account under clause (i), employees described in section 414(q)(5) shall be excluded.

(B) Percentage owners—

(i) 5-percent owner—For purposes of this paragraph, the term "5-percent owner" means—

(I) if the employer is a corporation, any person who owns (or is considered as owning within the meaning of section 318) more than 5 percent of the outstanding stock of the corporation or stock possessing more than 5 percent of the total combined voting power of all stock of the corporation, or

(II) if the employer is not a corporation, any person who owns more than 5 percent of the capital or profits interest in the employer.

(ii) 1-percent owner—For purposes of this paragraph, the term "1-percent owner" means any person who would be described in clause (i) if "1 percent" were substituted for "5 percent" each place it appears in clause (i).

(iii) Constructive ownership rules—For purposes of this subparagraph—

(I) subparagraph (C) of section 318(a)(2) shall be applied by substituting "5 percent" for "50 percent", and

(II) in the case of any employer which is not a corporation, ownership in such employer shall be determined in accordance with regulations prescribed by the Secretary which shall be based on principles similar to the principles of section 318 (as modified by subclause (I)).

(C) Aggregation rules do not apply for purposes of determining ownership in the employer—The rules of subsections (b), (c), and (m) of section 414 shall not apply for purposes of determining ownership in the employer.

(D) Compensation—For purposes of this paragraph, the term "compensation" has the meaning given such term by section 414(q)(4).

(2) Non-key employee—The term "non-key employee" means any employee who is not a key employee.

(3) Self-employed individuals—In the case of a self-employed individual described in section 401(c)(1)—

(A) such individual shall be treated as an employee, and

(B) such individual's earned income (within the meaning of section 401(c)(2)) shall be treated as compensation.

(4) Treatment of employees covered by collective bargaining agreements—The requirements of subsections (b), (c), and (d) shall not apply with respect to any employee included in a unit of employees covered by an agreement which the Secretary of Labor finds to be a collective bargaining agreement between employee representatives and 1 or more employers if there is evidence that retirement benefits were the subject of good faith bargaining between such employee representatives and such employer or employers.

(5) Treatment of beneficiaries—The terms "employee" and "key employee" include their beneficiaries.

(6) Treatment of simplified employee pensions—

(A) Treatment as defined contribution plans—A simplified employee pension shall be treated as a defined contribution plan.

(B) Election to have determinations based on employer contributions—In the case of a simplified employee pension, at the election of the employer, paragraphs (1)(A)(ii) and (2)(B) of subsection (g) shall be applied by taking into account aggregate employer contributions in lieu of the aggregate of the accounts of employees.

§ 417. Definitions and special rules for purposes of minimum survivor annuity requirements.

(a) Election to waive qualified joint and survivor annuity or qualified preretirement survivor annuity—

(1) In general—A plan meets the requirements of section 401(a)(11) only if—

(A) under the plan, each participant—

(i) may elect at any time during the applicable election period to waive the qualified joint and survivor annuity form of benefit or the qualified preretirement survivor annuity form of benefit (or both),

(ii) if the participant elects a waiver under clause (i), may elect the qualified optional survivor annuity at any time during the applicable election period, and

(iii) may revoke any such election at any time during the applicable election period, and

(B) the plan meets the requirements of paragraphs (2), (3), and (4) of this subsection.

(2) Spouse must consent to election—Each plan shall provide that an election under paragraph (1)(A)(i) shall not take effect unless—

(A)(i) the spouse of the participant consents in writing to such election, (ii) such election designates a beneficiary (or a form of benefits) which may not be changed without spousal consent (or the consent of the spouse expressly permits designations by the participant without any requirement of further consent by the spouse), and (iii) the spouse's consent acknowledges the effect of such election and is witnessed by a plan representative or a notary public, or

(B) it is established to the satisfaction of a plan representative that the consent required under subparagraph (A) may not be obtained because there is no spouse, because the spouse cannot be located, or because of such other circumstances as the Secretary may by regulations prescribe.

Any consent by a spouse (or establishment that the consent of a spouse may not be obtained) under the preceding sentence shall be effective only with respect to such spouse.

(3) Plan to provide written explanations—

(A) Explanation of joint and survivor annuity—Each plan shall provide to each participant, within a reasonable period of time before the annuity starting date (and consistent with such regulations as the Secretary may prescribe), a written explanation of—

(i) the terms and conditions of the qualified joint and survivor annuity and of the qualified optional survivor annuity,

(ii) the participant's right to make, and the effect of, an election under paragraph (1) to waive the joint and survivor annuity form of benefit,

(iii) the rights of the participant's spouse under paragraph (2), and

(iv) the right to make, and the effect of, a revocation of an election under paragraph (1).

(B) Explanation of qualified preretirement survivor annuity—

(i) In general—Each plan shall provide to each participant, within the applicable period with respect to such participant (and consistent with such regulations as the Secretary may prescribe), a written explanation with respect to the qualified preretirement survivor annuity comparable to that required under subparagraph (A).

(ii) Applicable period—For purposes of clause (i), the term "applicable period" means, with respect to a participant, whichever of the following periods ends last:

(I) The period beginning with the first day of the plan year in which the participant attains age 32 and ending with the close of the plan year preceding the plan year in which the participant attains age 35.

(II) A reasonable period after the individual becomes a participant.

(III) A reasonable period ending after paragraph (5) ceases to apply to the participant.

(IV) A reasonable period ending after section 401(a)(11) applies to the participant.

In the case of a participant who separates from service before attaining age 35, the applicable period shall be a reasonable period after separation.

(4) Requirement of spousal consent for using plan assets as security for loans— Each plan shall provide that, if section 401(a)(11) applies to a participant when part or all of the participant's accrued benefit is to be used as security for a loan, no portion of the participant's accrued benefit may be used as security for such loan unless—

(A) the spouse of the participant (if any) consents in writing to such use during the 90-day period ending on the date on which the loan is to be so secured, and

(B) requirements comparable to the requirements of paragraph (2) are met with respect to such consent.

(5) Special rules where plan fully subsidizes costs—

(A) In general—The requirements of this subsection shall not apply with respect to the qualified joint and survivor annuity form of benefit or the qualified preretirement survivor annuity form of benefit, as the case may be, if such benefit may not be waived (or another beneficiary selected) and if the plan fully subsidizes the costs of such benefit.

(B) Definition—For purposes of subparagraph (A), a plan fully subsidizes the costs of a benefit if under the plan the failure to waive such benefit by a participant would not result in a decrease in any plan benefits with respect to such participant and would not result in increased contributions from such participant.

(6) Applicable election period defined—For purposes of this subsection, the term "applicable election period" means—

(A) in the case of an election to waive the qualified joint and survivor annuity form of benefit, the 180-day period ending on the annuity starting date, or

(B) in the case of an election to waive the qualified preretirement survivor annuity, the period which begins on the first day of the plan year in which the participant attains age 35 and ends on the date of the participant's death.

In the case of a participant who is separated from service, the applicable election period under subparagraph (B) with respect to benefits accrued before the date of such separation from service shall not begin later than such date.

(7) Special rules relating to time for written explanation—Notwithstanding any other provision of this subsection—

(A) Explanation may be provided after annuity starting date—

(i) In general—A plan may provide the written explanation described in paragraph (3)(A) after the annuity starting date. In any case to which this subparagraph applies, the applicable election period under paragraph (6) shall not end before the 30th day after the date on which such explanation is provided.

(ii) Regulatory authority—The Secretary may by regulations limit the application of clause (i), except that such regulations may not limit the period of time by which the annuity starting date precedes the provision of the written explanation other than by providing that the annuity starting date may not be earlier than termination of employment.

(B) Waiver of 30-day period—A plan may permit a participant to elect (with any applicable spousal consent) to waive any requirement that the written explanation be provided at least 30 days before the annuity starting date (or to waive the 30-day requirement under subparagraph (A)) if the distribution commences more than 7 days after such explanation is provided.

(b) Definition of qualified joint and survivor annuity—For purposes of this section and section 401(a)(11), the term "qualified joint and survivor annuity" means an annuity—

(1) for the life of the participant with a survivor annuity for the life of the spouse which is not less than 50 percent of (and is not greater than 100 percent of) the amount of the annuity which is payable during the joint lives of the participant and the spouse, and

(2) which is the actuarial equivalent of a single annuity for the life of the participant.

Such term also includes any annuity in a form having the effect of an annuity described in the preceding sentence.

(c) Definition of qualified preretirement survivor annuity—For purposes of this section and section 401(a)(11) —

(1) In general—Except as provided in paragraph (2), the term "qualified preretirement survivor annuity" means a survivor annuity for the life of the surviving spouse of the participant if—

(A) the payments to the surviving spouse under such annuity are not less than the amounts which would be payable as a survivor annuity under the qualified joint and survivor annuity under the plan (or the actuarial equivalent thereof) if—

(i) in the case of a participant who dies after the date on which the participant attained the earliest retirement age, such participant had retired with an immediate qualified joint and survivor annuity on the day before the participant's date of death, or

(ii) in the case of a participant who dies on or before the date on which the participant would have attained the earliest retirement age, such participant had—

(I) separated from service on the date of death,

(II) survived to the earliest retirement age,

(III) retired with an immediate qualified joint and survivor annuity at the earliest retirement age, and

(IV) died on the day after the day on which such participant would have attained the earliest retirement age, and

(B) under the plan, the earliest period for which the surviving spouse may receive a payment under such annuity is not later than the month in which the participant would have attained the earliest retirement age under the plan.

In the case of an individual who separated from service before the date of such individual's death, subparagraph (A)(ii)(I) shall not apply.

(2) Special rule for defined contribution plans—In the case of any defined contribution plan or participant described in clause (ii) or (iii) of section 401(a)(11)(B), the term "qualified preretirement survivor annuity" means an annuity for the life of the surviving spouse the actuarial equivalent of which is not less than 50 percent of the portion of the account balance of the participant (as of the date of death) to which the participant had a nonforfeitable right (within the meaning of section 411(a)).

(3) Security interests taken into account—For purposes of paragraphs (1) and (2), any security interest held by the plan by reason of a loan outstanding to the participant shall be taken into account in determining the amount of the qualified preretirement survivor annuity.

(d) Survivor annuities need not be provided if participant and spouse married less than 1 year—

(1) In general—Except as provided in paragraph (2), a plan shall not be treated as failing to meet the requirements of section 401(a)(11) merely because the plan provides that a qualified joint and survivor annuity (or a qualified preretirement survivor annuity) will not be provided unless the participant and spouse had been married throughout the 1-year period ending on the earlier of—

   (A) the participant's annuity starting date, or

   (B) the date of the participant's death.

(2) Treatment of certain marriages within 1 year of annuity starting date for purposes of qualified joint and survivor annuities—For purposes of paragraph (1), if—

   (A) a participant marries within 1 year before the annuity starting date, and

   (B) the participant and the participant's spouse in such marriage have been married for at least a 1-year period ending on or before the date of the participant's death,

such participant and such spouse shall be treated as having been married throughout the 1-year period ending on the participant's annuity starting date.

(e) Restrictions on cash-outs—

(1) Plan may require distribution if present value not in excess of dollar limit—A plan may provide that the present value of a qualified joint and survivor annuity or a qualified preretirement survivor annuity will be immediately distributed if such value does not exceed the amount that can be distributed without the participant's consent under section 411(a)(11). No distribution may be made under the preceding sentence after the annuity starting date unless the participant and the spouse of the participant (or where the participant has died, the surviving spouse) consents in writing to such distribution.

(2) Plan may distribute benefit in excess of dollar limit only with consent—If—

   (A) the present value of the qualified joint and survivor annuity or the qualified preretirement survivor annuity exceeds the amount that can be distributed without the participant's consent under section 411(a)(11), and

   (B) the participant and the spouse of the participant (or where the participant has died, the surviving spouse) consent in writing to the distribution, the plan may immediately distribute the present value of such annuity.

(3) Determination of present value—

(A) In general—For purposes of paragraphs (1) and (2), the present value shall not be less than the present value calculated by using the applicable mortality table and the applicable interest rate.

(B) Applicable mortality table—For purposes of subparagraph (A), the term "applicable mortality table" means a mortality table, modified as appropriate by the Secretary, based on the mortality table specified for the plan year under subparagraph (A) of section 430(h)(3) (without regard to subparagraph (C) or (D) of such section).

(C) Applicable interest rate—For purposes of subparagraph (A), the term "applicable interest rate" means the adjusted first, second, and third segment rates applied under rules similar to the rules of section 430(h)(2)(C) (determined by not taking into account any adjustment under clause (iv) thereof) for the month before the date of the distribution or such other time as the Secretary may by regulations prescribe.

(D) Applicable segment rates—For purposes of subparagraph (C), the adjusted first, second, and third segment rates are the first, second, and third segment rates which would be determined under section 430(h)(2)(C) (determined by not taking into account any adjustment under clause (iv) thereof) if section 430(h)(2)(D) were applied by substituting the average yields for the month described in subparagraph (C) for the average yields for the 24-month period described in such section.

(f) Other definitions and special rules—For purposes of this section and section 401(a)(11) —

(1) Vested participant—The term "vested participant" means any participant who has a nonforfeitable right (within the meaning of section 411(a)) to any portion of such participant's accrued benefit.

(2) Annuity starting date—

(A) In general—The term "annuity starting date" means—

(i) the first day of the first period for which an amount is payable as an annuity, or

(ii) in the case of a benefit not payable in the form of an annuity, the first day on which all events have occurred which entitle the participant to such benefit.

(B) Special rule for disability benefits—For purposes of subparagraph (A), the first day of the first period for which a benefit is to be received by reason of disability shall be treated as the annuity starting date only if such benefit is not an auxiliary benefit.

(3) Earliest retirement age—The term "earliest retirement age" means the earliest date on which, under the plan, the participant could elect to receive retirement benefits.

(4) Plan may take into account increased costs—A plan may take into account in any equitable manner (as determined by the Secretary) any increased costs resulting from providing a qualified joint or survivor annuity or a qualified preretirement survivor annuity.

(5) Distributions by reason of security interests—If the use of any participant's accrued benefit (or any portion thereof) as security for a loan meets the requirements of subsection (a)(4), nothing in this section or section 411(a)(11) shall prevent any distribution required by reason of a failure to comply with the terms of such loan.

(6) Requirements for certain spousal consents—No consent of a spouse shall be effective for purposes of subsection (e)(1) or (e)(2) (as the case may be) unless requirements comparable to the requirements for spousal consent to an election under subsection (a)(1)(A) are met.

(7) Consultation with the Secretary of Labor—In prescribing regulations under this section and section 401(a)(11), the Secretary shall consult with the Secretary of Labor.

(g) Definition of qualified optional survivor annuity—

(1) In general—For purposes of this section, the term "qualified optional survivor annuity" means an annuity—

(A) for the life of the participant with a survivor annuity for the life of the spouse which is equal to the applicable percentage of the amount of the annuity which is payable during the joint lives of the participant and the spouse, and

(B) which is the actuarial equivalent of a single annuity for the life of the participant.

Such term also includes any annuity in a form having the effect of an annuity described in the preceding sentence.

(2) Applicable percentage—

(A) In general—For purposes of paragraph (1), if the survivor annuity percentage—

(i) is less than 75 percent, the applicable percentage is 75 percent, and

(ii) is greater than or equal to 75 percent, the applicable percentage is 50 percent.

(B) Survivor annuity percentage—For purposes of subparagraph (A), the term "survivor annuity percentage" means the percentage which the survivor annuity under the plan's qualified joint and survivor annuity bears to the annuity payable during the joint lives of the participant and the spouse.

§ 419. Treatment of funded welfare benefit plans.

(a) General rule—Contributions paid or accrued by an employer to a welfare benefit fund—

(1) shall not be deductible under this chapter, but

(2) if they would otherwise be deductible, shall (subject to the limitation of subsection (b)) be deductible under this section for the taxable year in which paid.

(b) Limitation—The amount of the deduction allowable under subsection (a)(2) for any taxable year shall not exceed the welfare benefit fund's qualified cost for the taxable year.

(c) Qualified cost—For purposes of this section—

(1) In general—Except as otherwise provided in this subsection, the term "qualified cost" means, with respect to any taxable year, the sum of—

(A) the qualified direct cost for such taxable year, and

(B) subject to the limitation of section 419A(b), any addition to a qualified asset account for the taxable year.

(2) Reduction for funds after-tax income—In the case of any welfare benefit fund, the qualified cost for any taxable year shall be reduced by such fund's after-tax income for such taxable year.

(3) Qualified direct cost—

(A) In general—The term "qualified direct cost" means, with respect to any taxable year, the aggregate amount (including administrative expenses) which would have been allowable as a deduction to the employer with respect to the benefits provided during the taxable year, if—

(i) such benefits were provided directly by the employer, and

(ii) the employer used the cash receipts and disbursements method of accounting.

(B) Time when benefits provided—For purposes of subparagraph (A), a benefit shall be treated as provided when such benefit would be includible in the gross income of the employee if provided directly by the employer (or would be so includible but for any provision of this chapter excluding such benefit from gross income).

* * *

(d) Carryover of excess contributions—If—

(1) the amount of the contributions paid (or deemed paid under this subsection) by the employer during any taxable year to a welfare benefit fund, exceeds

(2) the limitation of subsection (b),

such excess shall be treated as an amount paid by the employer to such fund during the succeeding taxable year.

(e) Welfare benefit fund—For purposes of this section—

(1) In general—The term "welfare benefit fund" means any fund—

(A) which is part of a plan of an employer, and

(B) through which the employer provides welfare benefits to employees or their beneficiaries.

(2) Welfare benefit—The term "welfare benefit" means any benefit other than a benefit with respect to which—

(A) section 83(h) applies,

(B) section 404 applies (determined without regard to section 404(b)(2)), or

(C) section 404A applies.

* * *

§ 419A. Qualified asset account; limitation on additions to account.

(a) General rule—For purposes of this subpart and section 512, the term "qualified asset account" means any account consisting of assets set aside to provide for the payment of—

(1) disability benefits,

(2) medical benefits,

(3) SUB or severance pay benefits, or

(4) life insurance benefits.

(b) Limitation on additions to account—No addition to any qualified asset account may be taken into account under section 419(c)(1)(B) to the extent such addition results in the amount in such account exceeding the account limit.

(c) Account limit—For purposes of this section—

(1) In general—Except as otherwise provided in this subsection, the account limit for any qualified asset account for any taxable year is the amount reasonably and actuarially necessary to fund—

(A) claims incurred but unpaid (as of the close of such taxable year) for benefits referred to in subsection (a), and

(B) administrative costs with respect to such claims.

(2) Additional reserve for post-retirement medical and life insurance benefits—The account limit for any taxable year may include a reserve funded over the working lives of the covered employees and actuarially determined on a level basis (using assumptions that are reasonable in the aggregate) as necessary for—

(A) post-retirement medical benefits to be provided to covered employees (determined on the basis of current medical costs), or

(B) post-retirement life insurance benefits to be provided to covered employees.

* * *

(f) Definitions and other special rules—For purposes of this section—

* * *

(5) Special rule for collective bargained and employee pay-all plans—No account limits shall apply in the case of any qualified asset account under a separate welfare benefit fund—

(A) under a collective bargaining agreement, or

(B) an employee pay-all plan under section 501(c)(9) if—

(i) such plan has at least 50 employees (determined without regard to subsection (h)(1)), and

(ii) no employee is entitled to a refund with respect to amounts in the fund, other than a refund based on the experience of the entire fund.

(6) Exception for 10-or-more employer plans—

(A) In general—This subpart shall not apply in the case of any welfare benefit fund which is part of a 10-or-more employer plan. The preceding sentence shall not apply to any plan which maintains experience-rating arrangements with respect to individual employers.

(B) 10 or more employer plan—For purposes of subparagraph (A), the term "10 or more employer plan" means a plan—

    (i) to which more than 1 employer contributes, and

    (ii) to which no employer normally contributes more than 10 percent of the total contributions contributed under the plan by all employers.

* * *

§ 420. Transfers of excess pension assets to retiree health accounts.

(a) General rule—If there is a qualified transfer of any excess pension assets of a defined benefit plan to a health benefits account, or an applicable life insurance account, which is part of such plan—

    (1) a trust which is part of such plan shall not be treated as failing to meet the requirements of subsection (a) or (h) of section 401 solely by reason of such transfer (or any other action authorized under this section),

    (2) no amount shall be includible in the gross income of the employer maintaining the plan solely by reason of such transfer,

    (3) such transfer shall not be treated—

        (A) as an employer reversion for purposes of section 4980, or

        (B) as a prohibited transaction for purposes of section 4975, and

    (4) the limitations of subsection (d) shall apply to such employer.

(b) Qualified transfer— For purposes of this section—

    (1) In general. The term "qualified transfer" means a transfer

        (A) of excess pension assets of a defined benefit plan to a health benefits account, or an applicable life insurance account, which is part of such plan,

        (B) which does not contravene any other provision of law, and

        (C) with respect to which the following requirements are met in connection with the plan—

            (i) the use requirements of subsection (c)(1),

            (ii) the vesting requirements of subsection (c)(2), and

            (iii) the minimum cost requirements of subsection (c)(3).

    (2) Only 1 transfer per year. No more than 1 transfer with respect to any plan during a taxable year may be treated as a qualified transfer for purposes of this section. If there is a transfer from a defined benefit plan to both a health benefits account and an applicable life insurance account during any taxable year, such transfers shall be treated as 1 transfer for purposes of this paragraph.

    (3) Limitation on amount transferred. The amount of excess pension assets which may be transferred to an account in a qualified transfer shall not exceed the amount which is reasonably estimated to be the amount the employer maintaining the plan will pay (whether directly or through reimbursement) out of such account during the taxable year of the transfer for qualified current retiree liabilities.

(4) Expiration. No transfer made after December 31, 2025, shall be treated as a qualified transfer.

(5) [Redesignated]

(c) Requirements of plans transferring assets—

(1) Use of transferred assets—

(A) In general— Any assets transferred to a health benefits account, or an applicable life insurance account, in a qualified transfer (and any income allocable thereto) shall be used only to pay qualified current retiree liabilities (other than liabilities of key employees not taken into account under subsection (e)(1)(D)) for the taxable year of the transfer (whether directly or through reimbursement). In the case of a qualified future transfer or collectively bargained transfer to which subsection (f) applies, any assets so transferred may also be used to pay liabilities described in subsection (f)(2)(C).

(B) Amounts not used to pay for health benefits or life insurance.

(i) In general. Any assets transferred to a health benefits account, or an applicable life insurance account, in a qualified transfer (and any income allocable thereto) which are not used as provided in subparagraph (A) shall be transferred out of the account to the transferor plan.

(ii) Tax treatment of amounts. Any amount transferred out of an account under clause (i)—

(I) shall not be includible in the gross income of the employer for such taxable year, but

(II) shall be treated as an employer reversion for purposes of section 4980 (without regard to subsection (d) thereof).

(C) Ordering rule. For purposes of this section, any amount paid out of a health benefits account, or an applicable life insurance account, shall be treated as paid first out of the assets and income described in subparagraph (A).

(2) Requirements relating to pension benefits accruing before transfer. The requirements of this paragraph are met if the plan provides that the accrued pension benefits of any participant or beneficiary under the plan become nonforfeitable in the same manner which would be required if the plan had terminated immediately before the qualified transfer (or in the case of a participant who separated during the 1-year period ending on the date of the transfer, immediately before such separation).

(3) Minimum cost requirements—

(A) In general—The requirements of this paragraph are met if each group health plan or arrangement under which applicable health benefits are provided, and each group-term life insurance plan under which applicable life insurance benefits are provided, provides that the applicable employer cost for each taxable year during the cost maintenance period shall not be less than the higher of the applicable employer costs for each of the 2 taxable years immediately preceding the taxable year of the qualified transfer or, in the case of a transfer which involves a plan maintained by an employer described in subsection (f)(2)(E)(i)(III), if the plan meets the requirements of subsection (f)(2)(D)(i)(II).

(B) Applicable employer cost. For purposes of this paragraph, the term "applicable employer cost" means, with respect to any taxable year, the amount determined by dividing—

(i) the qualified current retiree liabilities of the employer for such taxable year determined—

(I) separately with respect to applicable health benefits and applicable life insurance benefits,

(II) without regard to any reduction under subsection (e)(1)(B), and

(III) in the case of a taxable year in which there was no qualified transfer, in the same manner as if there had been such a transfer at the end of the taxable year, by

(ii) the number of individuals to whom coverage was provided during such taxable year for the benefits with respect to which the determination under clause (i) is made.

* * *

(D) Cost maintenance period— For purposes of this paragraph, the term 'cost maintenance period' means the period of 5 taxable years beginning with the taxable year in which the qualified transfer occurs. If a taxable year is in two or more overlapping cost maintenance periods, this paragraph shall be applied by taking into account the highest applicable employer cost required to be provided under subparagraph (A) for such taxable year.

(E) Regulations—

(i) **In general.** The Secretary shall prescribe such regulations as may be necessary to prevent an employer who significantly reduces retiree health coverage or retiree life insurance coverage, as the case may be, during the cost maintenance period from being treated as satisfying the minimum cost requirement of this subsection.

(ii) **Insignificant cost reductions for retiree health coverage permitted.**

(I) **In general.** An eligible employer shall not be treated as failing to meet the requirements of this paragraph for any taxable year if, in lieu of any reduction of retiree health coverage permitted under the regulations prescribed under clause (i), the employer reduces applicable employer cost by an amount not in excess of the reduction in costs which would have occurred if the employer had made the maximum permissible reduction in retiree health coverage under such regulations. In applying such regulations to any subsequent taxable year, any reduction in applicable employer cost under this clause shall be treated as if it were an equivalent reduction in retiree health coverage.

(II) **Eligible employer.** For purposes of subclause (I), an employer shall be treated as an eligible employer for any taxable year if, for the preceding taxable year, the qualified current retiree liabilities of the employer with respect to applicable health benefits were at least 5 percent of the gross receipts of the employer. For purposes of this subclause, the rules of paragraphs (2), (3)(B), and (3)(C) of section 448(c) shall apply in determining the amount of an employer's gross receipts.

(d) Limitations on employer— For purposes of this title—

(1) Deduction limitations. No deduction shall be allowed—

(A) for the transfer of any amount to a health benefits account, or an applicable life insurance account, in a qualified transfer (or any retransfer to the plan under subsection (c)(1)(B)),

(B) for qualified current retiree liabilities paid out of the assets (and income) described in subsection (c)(1), or

(C) for any amounts to which subparagraph (B) does not apply and which are paid for qualified current retiree liabilities for the taxable year to the extent such amounts are not greater than the excess (if any) of—

(i) the amount determined under subparagraph (A) (and income allocable thereto), over

(ii) the amount determined under subparagraph (B).

(2) No contributions allowed. An employer may not contribute[,] any amount to a health benefits account or welfare benefit fund (as defined in section 419(e)(1)) with respect to qualified current retiree liabilities for which transferred assets are required to be used under subsection (c)(1).

(e) Definition and special rules— For purposes of this section—

(1) Qualified current retiree liabilities. For purposes of this section—

(A) In general. The term "qualified current retiree liabilities" means, with respect to any taxable year, the aggregate amounts (including administrative expenses) which would have been allowable as a deduction to the employer for such taxable year with respect to applicable health benefits and applicable life insurance benefits provided during such taxable year if—

(i) such benefits were provided directly by the employer, and

(ii) the employer used the cash receipts and disbursements method of accounting.

For purposes of the preceding sentence, the rule of section 419(c)(3)(B) shall apply.

(B) Reductions for amounts previously set aside. The amount determined under subparagraph (A) shall be reduced by the amount (determined separately for applicable health benefits and applicable life insurance benefits) which bears the same ratio to such amount as—

(i) the value (as of the close of the plan year preceding the year of the qualified transfer) of the assets in all health benefits accounts or applicable life insurance accounts or welfare benefit funds (as defined in section 419(e)(1)) set aside to pay for the qualified current retiree liability, bears to

(ii) the present value of the qualified current retiree liabilities for all plan years (determined without regard to this subparagraph)

(C) Applicable health benefits. The term 'applicable health benefits' means health benefits or coverage which are provided to—

(i) retired employees who, immediately before the qualified transfer, are entitled to receive such benefits by reason of retirement and who are entitled to pension benefits under the plan, and

(ii) their spouses and dependents.

(D) Applicable life insurance benefits. The term "applicable life insurance benefits" means group-term life insurance coverage provided to retired employees who, immediately before the qualified transfer, are entitled to receive such coverage by reason of retirement and who are entitled to pension benefits under the plan, but only to the extent that such coverage is provided under a policy for retired employees and the cost of such coverage is excludable from the retired employee's gross income under section 79.

(E) Key employees excluded. If an employee is a key employee (within the meaning of section 416(i)(1)) with respect to any plan year ending in a taxable year, such employee shall not be taken into account in computing qualified current retiree liabilities for such taxable year or in calculating applicable employer cost under subsection (c)(3)(B).

(2) Excess pension assets. The term "excess pension assets" means the excess (if any) of—

(A) the lesser of—

(i) the fair market value of the plan's assets (reduced by the prefunding balance and funding standard carryover balance determined under section 430(f), or

(ii) the value of plan assets as determined under section 430(g)(3) after reduction under section 430(f), over

(B) 125 percent of the sum of the funding target and the target normal cost determined under section 430 for such plan year.

(3) Health benefits account. The term "health benefits account" means an account established and maintained under section 401(h).

(4) Applicable life insurance account. The term "applicable life insurance account" means a separate account established and maintained for amounts transferred under this section for qualified current retiree liabilities based on premiums for applicable life insurance benefits.

(5) Coordination with sections 430 and 433. In the case of a qualified transfer, any assets so transferred shall not, for purposes of this section and sections 430 and 433, be treated as assets in the plan.

(6) Application to multiemployer plans. In the case of a multiemployer plan, this section shall be applied to any such plan—

(A) by treating any reference in this section to an employer as a reference to all employers maintaining the plan (or, if appropriate, the plan sponsor), and

(B) in accordance with such modifications of this section (and the provisions of this title relating to this section) as the Secretary determines appropriate to reflect the fact the plan is not maintained by a single employer.

(f) Qualified transfers to cover future retiree costs and collectively bargained retiree benefits.

(1) In general. An employer maintaining a defined benefit plan (other than a multiemployer plan) may, in lieu of a qualified transfer, elect for any taxable year to have the plan make—

(A) a qualified future transfer, or

(B) a collectively bargained transfer.

Except as provided in this subsection, a qualified future transfer and a collectively bargained transfer shall be treated for purposes of this title and the Employee Retirement Income Security Act of 1974 as if it were a qualified transfer.

(2) Qualified future and collectively bargained transfers. For purposes of this subsection—

(A) In general. The terms "qualified future transfer" and "collectively bargained transfer" mean a transfer which meets all of the requirements for a qualified transfer, except that—

(i) the determination of excess pension assets shall be made under subparagraph (B),

(ii) the limitation on the amount transferred shall be determined under subparagraph (C),

(iii) the minimum cost requirements of subsection (c)(3) shall be modified as provided under subparagraph (D), and

(iv) in the case of a collectively bargained transfer, the requirements of subparagraph (E) shall be met with respect to the transfer.

(B) Excess pension assets.

(i) In general. In determining excess pension assets for purposes of this subsection, subsection (e)(2) shall be applied by substituting "120 percent" for "125 percent".

(ii) Requirement to maintain funded status. If, as of any valuation date of any plan year in the transfer period, the amount determined under subsection (e)(2)(B) (after application of clause (i)) exceeds the amount determined under subsection (e)(2)(A), either—

(I) the employer maintaining the plan shall make contributions to the plan in an amount not less than the amount required to reduce such excess to zero as of such date, or

(II) there is transferred from the health benefits account or applicable life insurance account, as the case may be, to the plan an amount not less than the amount required to reduce such excess to zero as of such date.

(C) Limitation on amount transferred. Notwithstanding subsection (b)(3), the amount of the excess pension assets which may be transferred—

(i) in the case of a qualified future transfer shall be equal to the sum of—

(I) if the transfer period includes the taxable year of the transfer, the amount determined under subsection (b)(3) for such taxable year, plus

(II) in the case of all other taxable years in the transfer period, the sum of the qualified current retiree liabilities which the plan reasonably estimates, in accordance with guidance issued by the Secretary, will be incurred for each of such years, and

(ii) in the case of a collectively bargained transfer, shall not exceed the amount which is reasonably estimated, in accordance with the provisions of the collective bargaining agreement and generally accepted accounting principles, to be the amount the employer maintaining the plan will pay (whether directly or through reimbursement) out of such account during the collectively bargained cost maintenance period for collectively bargained retiree liabilities.

(D) Minimum cost requirements.

(i) In general. The requirements of subsection (c)(3) shall be treated as met if—

(I) in the case of a qualified future transfer, each group health plan or arrangement under which applicable health benefits are provided, and each group-term life insurance plan or arrangement under which applicable life insurance benefits are provided, provides applicable health benefits or applicable life insurance benefits, as the case may be, during the period beginning with the first year of the transfer period and ending with the last day of the 4th year following the transfer period such that the annual average amount of the applicable employer cost during such period is not less than the applicable employer cost determined under subsection (c)(3)(A) with respect to the transfer, and

(II) in the case of a collectively bargained transfer, each collectively bargained plan under which collectively bargained health benefits or collectively bargained life insurance benefits are provided provides that the collectively bargained employer cost for each taxable year during the collectively bargained cost maintenance period shall not be less than the amount specified by the collective bargaining agreement.

(ii) Election to maintain benefits for future transfers. An employer may elect, in lieu of the requirements of clause (i)(I), to meet the requirements of subsection (c)(3) with respect to applicable health benefits or applicable life insurance benefits by meeting the requirements of such subsection (as in effect before the amendments made by section 535 of the Tax Relief Extension Act of 1999 [enacted Dec. 17, 1999]) for each of the years described in the period under clause (i)(I). Such election may be made separately with respect to applicable health benefits and applicable life insurance benefits. In the case of an election with respect to applicable life insurance benefits, the first sentence of this clause shall be applied as if subsection (c)(3) as in effect before the amendments made by such Act applied to such benefits.

(iii) Collectively bargained employer cost. For purposes of this subparagraph, the term "collectively bargained employer cost" means the average cost per covered individual of providing collectively bargained health benefits, collectively bargained life insurance benefits, or both, as the case may be, as determined in accordance with the applicable collective bargaining agreement. Such agreement may provide for an appropriate reduction in the collectively bargained employer cost to take into account any portion of the collectively bargained health benefits, collectively bargained life insurance benefits, or both, as the case may be, that is provided or financed by a government program or other source.

(E) Special rules for collectively bargained transfers.

(i) In general. A collectively bargained transfer shall only include a transfer which—

(I) is made in accordance with a collective bargaining agreement,

(II) before the transfer, the employer designates, in a written notice delivered to each employee organization that is a party to the collective bargaining agreement, as a collectively bargained transfer in accordance with this section, and

(III) involves a defined benefit plan maintained by an employer which, in its taxable year ending in 2005, provided health benefits or coverage to retirees and their spouses and dependents under all of the health benefit plans maintained by the employer, but only if the aggregate cost (including administrative expenses) of such benefits or coverage which would have been allowable as a deduction to the employer (if such benefits or coverage had been provided directly by the employer and the employer used the cash receipts and disbursements method of accounting) is at least 5 percent of the gross receipts of the employer (determined in accordance with the last sentence of subsection (c)(3)(E)(ii)(II)) for such taxable year, or a plan maintained by a successor to such employer.

(ii) Use of assets. Any assets transferred to a health benefits account, or an applicable life insurance account, in a collectively bargained transfer (and any income allocable thereto) shall be used only to pay collectively bargained retiree liabilities (other than liabilities of key employees not taken into account under paragraph (6)(B)(iii)) for the taxable year of the transfer or for any subsequent taxable year during the collectively bargained cost maintenance period (whether directly or through reimbursement).

(3) Coordination with other transfers. In applying subsection (b)(3) to any subsequent transfer during a taxable year in a transfer period or collectively bargained cost maintenance period, qualified current retiree liabilities shall be reduced by any such liabilities taken into account with respect to the qualified future transfer or collectively bargained transfer to which such period relates.

(4) Special deduction rules for collectively bargained transfers. In the case of a collectively bargained transfer—

(A) the limitation under subsection (d)(1)(C) shall not apply, and

(B) notwithstanding subsection (d)(2), an employer may contribute an amount to a health benefits account or welfare benefit fund (as defined in section 419(e)(1) []) with respect to collectively bargained retiree liabilities for which transferred assets are required to be used under subsection (c)(1)(B), and the deductibility of any such contribution shall be governed by the limits applicable to the deductibility of contributions to a welfare benefit fund under a collective bargaining agreement (as determined under section 419A(f)(5)(A)) without regard to whether such contributions are made to a health benefits account or welfare benefit fund and without regard to the provisions of section 404 or the other provisions of this section.

The Secretary shall provide rules to ensure that the application of this paragraph does not result in a deduction being allowed more than once for the same contribution or for 2 or more contributions or expenditures relating to the same collectively bargained retiree liabilities.

(5) Transfer period. For purposes of this subsection, the term "transfer period" means, with respect to any transfer, a period of consecutive taxable years (not less than 2) specified in the election under paragraph (1) which begins and ends during the 10-taxable-year period beginning with the taxable year of the transfer.

(6) Terms relating to collectively bargained transfers. For purposes of this subsection—

(A) Collectively bargained cost maintenance period. The term "collectively bargained cost maintenance period" means, with respect to each covered retiree and his covered spouse and dependents, the shorter of—

(i) the remaining lifetime of such covered retiree and, in the case of a transfer to a health benefits account, his covered spouse and dependents, or

(ii) the period of coverage provided by the collectively bargained plan (determined as of the date of the collectively bargained transfer) with respect to such covered retiree and, in the case of a transfer to a health benefits account, his covered spouse and dependents.

(B) Collectively bargained retiree liabilities.

(i) In general. The term "collectively bargained retiree liabilities" means the present value, as of the beginning of a taxable year and determined in accordance with the applicable collective bargaining agreement, of all collectively bargained health benefits, and collectively bargained life insurance benefits, (including administrative expenses) for such taxable year and all subsequent taxable years during the collectively bargained cost maintenance period.

(ii) Reduction for amounts previously set aside. The amount determined under clause (i) shall be reduced by the value (as of the close of the plan year preceding the year of the collectively bargained transfer) of the assets in all health benefits accounts, applicable life insurance accounts, or welfare benefit funds (as defined in section 419(e)(1)) set aside to pay for the collectively bargained retiree liabilities. The preceding sentence shall be applied separately for collectively bargained health benefits and collectively bargained life insurance benefits.

(iii) Key employees excluded. If an employee is a key employee (within the meaning of section 416(i)(1)) with respect to any plan year ending in a taxable year, such employee shall not be taken into account in computing collectively bargained retiree liabilities for such taxable year or in calculating collectively bargained employer cost under subsection (c)(3)(C).

(C) Collectively bargained health benefits. The term "collectively bargained health benefits" means health benefits or coverage—

(i) which are provided to retired employees who, immediately before the collectively bargained transfer, are entitled to receive such benefits by reason of retirement and who are entitled to pension benefits under the plan, and their spouses and dependents, and

(ii) if specified by the provisions of the collective bargaining agreement governing the collectively bargained transfer, which will be provided at retirement to employees who are not retired employees at the time of the transfer and who are entitled to receive such benefits and who are entitled to pension benefits under the plan, and their spouses and dependents.

(D) Collectively bargained life insurance benefits. The term "collectively bargained life insurance benefits" means, with respect to any collectively bargained transfer—

(i) applicable life insurance benefits which are provided to retired employees who, immediately before the transfer, are entitled to receive such benefits by reason of retirement, and

(ii) if specified by the provisions of the collective bargaining agreement governing the transfer, applicable life insurance benefits which will be provided at retirement to employees who are not retired employees at the time of the transfer.

(E) Collectively [bargained] plan. The term "collectively bargained plan" means a group health plan or arrangement for retired employees and their spouses and dependents, or a group-term life insurance plan or arrangement for retired employees, that is maintained pursuant to 1 or more collective bargaining agreements.

(g) Segment rates determined without pension stabilization. For purposes of this section, section 430 shall be applied without regard to subsection (h)(2)(C)(iv) thereof.

§ 421. General rules.

(a) Effect of qualifying transfer—If a share of stock is transferred to an individual in a transfer in respect of which the requirements of section 422(a) or 423(a) are met—

(1) no income shall result at the time of the transfer of such share to the individual upon his exercise of the option with respect to such share;

(2) no deduction under section 162 (relating to trade or business expenses) shall be allowable at any time to the employer corporation, a parent or subsidiary corporation of such corporation, or a corporation issuing or assuming a stock option in a transaction to which section 424(a) applies, with respect to the share so transferred; and

(3) no amount other than the price paid under the option shall be considered as received by any of such corporations for the share so transferred.

(b) Effect of disqualifying disposition—If the transfer of a share of stock to an individual pursuant to his exercise of an option would otherwise meet the requirements of section 422(a) or 423(a) except that there is a failure to meet any of the holding period requirements of section 422(a)(1) or 423(a)(1), then any increase in the income of such individual or deduction from the income of his employer corporation for the taxable year in which such exercise occurred attributable to such disposition, shall be treated as an increase in income or a deduction from income in the taxable year of such individual or of such employer corporation in which such disposition occurred. No amount shall be required to be deducted and withheld under chapter 24 with respect to any increase in income attributable to a disposition described in the preceding sentence.

* * *

§ 422. Incentive stock options.

(a) In general. Section 421(a) shall apply with respect to the transfer of a share of stock to an individual pursuant to his exercise of an incentive stock option if—

(1) no disposition of such share is made by him within 2 years from the date of the granting of the option nor within 1 year after the transfer of such share to him, and

(2) at all times during the period beginning on the date of the granting of the option and ending on the day 3 months before the date of such exercise, such individual was an employee of either the corporation granting such option, a parent or subsidiary corporation of such corporation, or a corporation or a parent or subsidiary corporation of such corporation issuing or assuming a stock option in a transaction to which section 424(a) applies.

(b) Incentive stock option. For purposes of this part, the term 'incentive stock option' means an option granted to an individual for any reason connected with his employment by a corporation, if granted by the employer corporation or its parent or subsidiary corporation, to purchase stock of any of such corporations, but only if—

(1) the option is granted pursuant to a plan which includes the aggregate number of shares which may be issued under options and the employees (or class of employees) eligible to receive options, and which is approved by the stockholders of the granting corporation within 12 months before or after the date such plan is adopted;

(2) such option is granted within 10 years from the date such plan is adopted, or the date such plan is approved by the stockholders, whichever is earlier;

(3) such option by its terms is not exercisable after the expiration of 10 years from the date such option is granted;

(4) the option price is not less than the fair market value of the stock at the time such option is granted;

(5) such option by its terms is not transferable by such individual otherwise than by will or the laws of descent and distribution, and is exercisable, during his lifetime, only by him; and

(6) such individual, at the time the option is granted, does not own stock possessing more than 10 percent of the total combined voting power of all classes of stock of the employer corporation or of its parent or subsidiary corporation.

Such term shall not include any option if (as of the time the option is granted) the terms of such option provide that it will not be treated as an incentive stock option.

(c) Special rules.

(1) Good faith efforts to value stock. If a share of stock is transferred pursuant to the exercise by an individual of an option which would fail to qualify as an incentive stock option under subsection (b) because there was a failure in an attempt, made in good faith, to meet the requirement of subsection (b)(4), the requirement of subsection (b)(4) shall be considered to have been met. To the extent provided in regulations by the Secretary, a similar rule shall apply for purposes of subsection (d).

(2) Certain disqualifying dispositions where amount realized is less than value at exercise. If—

(A) an individual who has acquired a share of stock by the exercise of an incentive stock option makes a disposition of such share within either of the periods described in subsection (a)(1), and

(B) such disposition is a sale or exchange with respect to which a loss (if sustained) would be recognized to such individual,

then the amount which is includible in the gross income of such individual, and the amount which is deductible from the income of his employer corporation, as compensation attributable to the exercise of such option shall not exceed the excess (if any) of the amount realized on such sale or exchange over the adjusted basis of such share.

(3) Certain transfers by insolvent individuals. If an insolvent individual holds a share of stock acquired pursuant to his exercise of an incentive stock option, and if such share is transferred to a trustee, receiver, or other similar fiduciary in any proceeding under title 11 or any other similar insolvency proceeding, neither such transfer, nor any other transfer of such share for the benefit of his creditors in such proceeding, shall constitute a disposition of such share for purposes of subsection (a)(1).

(4) Permissible provisions. An option which meets the requirements of subsection (b) shall be treated as an incentive stock option even if—

(A) the employee may pay for the stock with stock of the corporation granting the option,

(B) the employee has a right to receive property at the time of exercise of the option, or

(C) the option is subject to any condition not inconsistent with the provisions of subsection (b).

Subparagraph (B) shall apply to a transfer of property (other than cash) only if section 83 applies to the property so transferred.

(5) 10-percent shareholder rule. Subsection (b)(6) shall not apply if at the time such option is granted the option price is at least 110 percent of the fair market value of the stock subject to the option and such option by its terms is not exercisable after the expiration of 5 years from the date such option is granted.

(6) Special rule when disabled. For purposes of subsection (a)(2), in the case of an employee who is disabled (within the meaning of section 22(e)(3)), the 3-month period of subsection (a)(2) shall be 1 year.

(7) Fair market value. For purposes of this section, the fair market value of stock shall be determined without regard to any restriction other than a restriction which, by its terms, will never lapse.

(d) $100,000 per year limitation.

(1) In general. To the extent that the aggregate fair market value of stock with respect to which incentive stock options (determined without regard to this subsection) are exercisable for the 1st time by any individual during any calendar year (under all plans of the individual's employer corporation and its parent and subsidiary corporations) exceeds $100,000, such options shall be treated as options which are not incentive stock options.

(2) Ordering rule. Paragraph (1) shall be applied by taking options into account in the order in which they were granted.

(3) Determination of fair market value. For purposes of paragraph (1), the fair market value of any stock shall be determined as of the time the option with respect to such stock is granted.

§ 423. Employee stock purchase plans.

(a) General rule—Section 421(a) shall apply with respect to the transfer of a share of stock to an individual pursuant to his exercise of an option granted under an employee stock purchase plan (as defined in subsection (b)) if—

(1) no disposition of such share is made by him within 2 years after the date of the granting of the option nor within 1 year after the transfer of such share to him; and

(2) at all times during the period beginning with the date of the granting of the option and ending on the day 3 months before the date of such exercise, he is an employee of the corporation granting such option, a parent or subsidiary corporation of such corporation, or a corporation or a parent or subsidiary corporation of such corporation issuing or assuming a stock option in a transaction to which section 424(a) applies.

(b) Employee stock purchase plan—For purposes of this part, the term "employee stock purchase plan" means a plan which meets the following requirements:

(1) the plan provides that options are to be granted only to employees of the employer corporation or of its parent or subsidiary corporation to purchase stock in any such corporation;

(2) such plan is approved by the stockholders of the granting corporation within 12 months before or after the date such plan is adopted;

(3) under the terms of the plan, no employee can be granted an option if such employee, immediately after the option is granted, owns stock possessing 5 percent or more of the total combined voting power or value of all classes of stock of the employer corporation or of its parent or subsidiary corporation. For purposes of this paragraph, the rules of section 424(d) shall apply in determining the stock ownership of an individual, and stock which the employee may purchase under outstanding options shall be treated as stock owned by the employee;

(4) under the terms of the plan, options are to be granted to all employees of any corporation whose employees are granted any of such options by reason of their employment by such corporation, except that there may be excluded—

(A) employees who have been employed less than 2 years,

(B) employees whose customary employment is 20 hours or less per week,

(C) employees whose customary employment is for not more than 5 months in any calendar year, and

(D) highly compensated employees (within the meaning of section 414(q));

(5) under the terms of the plan, all employees granted such options shall have the same rights and privileges, except that the amount of stock which may be purchased by any employee under such option may bear a uniform relationship to the total compensation, or the basic or regular rate of compensation, of employees, and the plan may provide that no employee may purchase more than a maximum amount of stock fixed under the plan;

(6) under the terms of the plan, the option price is not less than the lesser of—

(A) an amount equal to 85 percent of the fair market value of the stock at the time such option is granted, or

(B) an amount which under the terms of the option may not be less than 85 percent of the fair market value of the stock at the time such option is exercised;

(7) under the terms of the plan, such option cannot be exercised after the expiration of—

(A) 5 years from the date such option is granted if, under the terms of such plan, the option price is to be not less than 85 percent of the fair market value of such stock at the time of the exercise of the option, or

(B) 27 months from the date such option is granted, if the option price is not determinable in the manner described in subparagraph (A);

(8) under the terms of the plan, no employee may be granted an option which permits his rights to purchase stock under all such plans of his employer corporation and its parent and subsidiary corporations to accrue at a rate which exceeds $25,000 of fair market value of such stock (determined at the time such option is granted) for each calendar year in which such option is outstanding at any time. For purposes of this paragraph—

(A) the right to purchase stock under an option accrues when the option (or any portion thereof) first becomes exercisable during the calendar year;

(B) the right to purchase stock under an option accrues at the rate provided in the option, but in no case may such rate exceed $25,000 of fair market value of such stock (determined at the time such option is granted) for any one calendar year; and

(C) a right to purchase stock which has accrued under one option granted pursuant to the plan may not be carried over to any other option; and

(9) under the terms of the plan, such option is not transferable by such individual otherwise than by will or the laws of descent and distribution, and is exercisable, during his lifetime, only by him.

For purposes of paragraphs (3) to (9), inclusive, where additional terms are contained in an offering made under a plan, such additional terms shall, with respect to options exercised under such offering, be treated as a part of the terms of such plan.

(c) Special rule where option price is between 85 percent and 100 percent of value of stock—If the option price of a share of stock acquired by an individual pursuant to a transfer to which subsection (a) applies was less than 100 percent of the fair market value of such share at the time such option was granted, then, in the event of any disposition of such share by him which meets the holding period requirements of subsection (a), or in the event of his death (whenever occurring) while owning such share, there shall be included as compensation (and not as gain upon the sale or exchange of a capital asset) in his gross income, for the taxable year in which falls the date of such disposition or for the taxable year closing with his death, whichever applies, an amount equal to the lesser of—

(1) the excess of the fair market value of the share at the time of such disposition or death over the amount paid for the share under the option, or

(2) the excess of the fair market value of the share at the time the option was granted over the option price.

If the option price is not fixed or determinable at the time the option is granted, then for purposes of this subsection, the option price shall be determined as if the option were exercised at such time. In the case of the disposition of such share by the individual, the basis of the share in his hands at the time of such disposition shall be increased by an amount equal to the amount so includible in his gross income. No amount shall be required to be deducted and withheld under chapter 24 with respect to any amount treated as compensation under this subsection.

§ 430. Minimum funding standards for single-employer defined benefit pension plans.

(a) Minimum required contribution—For purposes of this section and section 412(a)(2)(A), except as provided in subsection (f), the term "minimum required contribution" means, with respect to any plan year of a defined benefit plan which is not a multiemployer plan—

(1) in any case in which the value of plan assets of the plan (as reduced under subsection (f)(4)(B)) is less than the funding target of the plan for the plan year, the sum of—

(A) the target normal cost of the plan for the plan year,

(B) the shortfall amortization charge (if any) for the plan for the plan year determined under subsection (c), and

(C) the waiver amortization charge (if any) for the plan for the plan year as determined under subsection (e);

(2) in any case in which the value of plan assets of the plan (as reduced under subsection (f)(4)(B)) equals or exceeds the funding target of the plan for the plan year, the target normal cost of the plan for the plan year reduced (but not below zero) by such excess.

(b) Target normal cost—For purposes of this section.

(1) In general—Except as provided in subsection (i)(2) with respect to plans in at-risk status, the term "target normal cost" means, for any plan year, the excess of—

(A) the sum of—

(i) the present value of all benefits which are expected to accrue or to be earned under the plan during the plan year, plus

(ii) the amount of plan-related expenses expected to be paid from plan assets during the plan year, over

(B) the amount of mandatory employee contributions expected to be made during the plan year.

(2) Special rule for increase in compensation—For purposes of this subsection, if any benefit attributable to services performed in a preceding plan year is increased by reason of any increase in compensation during the current plan year, the increase in such benefit shall be treated as having accrued during the current plan year.

(c) Shortfall amortization charge—

(1) In general—For purposes of this section, the shortfall amortization charge for a plan for any plan year is the aggregate total (not less than zero) of the shortfall amortization installments for such plan year with respect to any shortfall amortization base which has not been fully amortized under this subsection.

(2) Shortfall amortization installment—For purposes of paragraph (1)—

(A) Determination—The shortfall amortization installments are the amounts necessary to amortize the shortfall amortization base of the plan for any plan year in level annual installments over the 7-plan-year period beginning with such plan year.

(B) Shortfall installment—The shortfall amortization installment for any plan year in the 7-plan-year period under subparagraph (A) with respect to any shortfall amortization base is the annual installment determined under subparagraph (A) for that year for that base.

(C) Segment rates—In determining any shortfall amortization installment under this paragraph, the plan sponsor shall use the segment rates determined under subparagraph (C) of subsection (h)(2), applied under rules similar to the rules of subparagraph (B) of subsection (h)(2).

(D) Special election for eligible plan years.

(i) In general. If a plan sponsor elects to apply this subparagraph with respect to the shortfall amortization base of a plan for any eligible plan year (in this subparagraph and paragraph (7) referred to as an "election year"), then, notwithstanding subparagraphs (A) and (B)—

(I) the shortfall amortization installments with respect to such base shall be determined under clause (ii) or (iii), whichever is specified in the election, and

(II) the shortfall amortization installment for any plan year in the 9-plan-year period described in clause (ii) or the 15-plan-year period described in clause (iii), respectively, with respect to such shortfall amortization base is the annual installment determined under the applicable clause for that year for that base.

(ii) 2 plus 7 amortization schedule. The shortfall amortization installments determined under this clause are—

(I) in the case of the first 2 plan years in the 9-plan-year period beginning with the election year, interest on the shortfall amortization base of the plan for the election year (determined using the effective interest rate for the plan for the election year), and

(II) in the case of the last 7 plan years in such 9-plan-year period, the amounts necessary to amortize the remaining balance of the shortfall amortization base of the plan for the election year in level annual installments over such last 7 plan years (using the segment rates under subparagraph (C) for the election year).

(iii) 15-year amortization. The shortfall amortization installments determined under this subparagraph are the amounts necessary to amortize the shortfall amortization base of the plan for the election year in level annual installments over the 15-plan-year period beginning with the election year (using the segment rates under subparagraph (C) for the election year).

(iv) Election.

(I) In general. The plan sponsor of a plan may elect to have this subparagraph apply to not more than 2 eligible plan years with respect to the plan, except that in the case of a plan described in section 106 of the Pension Protection Act of 2006, the plan sponsor may only elect to have this subparagraph apply to a plan year beginning in 2011.

(II) Amortization schedule. Such election shall specify whether the amortization schedule under clause (ii) or (iii) shall apply to an election year, except that if a plan sponsor elects to have this subparagraph apply to 2 eligible plan years, the plan sponsor must elect the same schedule for both years.

(III) Other rules. Such election shall be made at such time, and in such form and manner, as shall be prescribed by the Secretary, and may be revoked only with the consent of the Secretary. The Secretary shall, before granting a revocation request, provide the Pension Benefit Guaranty Corporation an opportunity to comment on the conditions applicable to the treatment of any portion of the election year shortfall amortization base that remains unamortized as of the revocation date.

(v) Eligible plan year. For purposes of this subparagraph, the term "eligible plan year" means any plan year beginning in 2008, 2009, 2010, or 2011, except that a plan year shall only be treated as an eligible plan year if the due date under subsection (j)(1) for the payment of the minimum required contribution for such plan year occurs on or after the date of the enactment of this subparagraph.

(vi) Reporting. A plan sponsor of a plan who makes an election under clause (i) shall—

(I) give notice of the election to participants and beneficiaries of the plan, and

(II) inform the Pension Benefit Guaranty Corporation of such election in such form and manner as the Director of the Pension Benefit Guaranty Corporation may prescribe.

(vii) Increases in required installments in certain cases. For increases in required contributions in cases of excess compensation or extraordinary dividends or stock redemptions, see paragraph (7).

(3) Shortfall amortization base—For purposes of this section, the shortfall amortization base of a plan for a plan year is—

(A) the funding shortfall of such plan for such plan year, minus

(B) the present value (determined using the segment rates determined under subparagraph (C) of subsection (h)(2), applied under rules similar to the rules of subparagraph (B) of subsection (h)(2)) of the aggregate total of the shortfall amortization installments and waiver amortization installments which have been determined for such plan year and any succeeding plan year with respect to the shortfall amortization bases and waiver amortization bases of the plan for any plan year preceding such plan year.

(4) Funding shortfall—For purposes of this section, the funding shortfall of a plan for any plan year is the excess (if any) of—

(A) the funding target of the plan for the plan year, over

(B) the value of plan assets of the plan (as reduced under subsection (f)(4)(B)) for the plan year which are held by the plan on the valuation date.

(5) Exemption from new shortfall amortization base—In any case in which the value of plan assets of the plan (as reduced under subsection (f)(4)(A)) is equal to or greater than the funding target of the plan for the plan year, the shortfall amortization base of the plan for such plan year shall be zero.

(6) Early deemed amortization upon attainment of funding target—In any case in which the funding shortfall of a plan for a plan year is zero, for purposes of determining the shortfall amortization charge for such plan year and succeeding plan years, the shortfall amortization bases for all preceding plan years (and all shortfall amortization installments determined with respect to such bases) shall be reduced to zero.

(7) Increases in alternate required installments in cases of excess compensation or extraordinary dividends or stock redemptions.

(A) In general. If there is an installment acceleration amount with respect to a plan for any plan year in the restriction period with respect to an election year under paragraph (2)(D), then the shortfall amortization installment otherwise determined and payable under such paragraph for such plan year shall, subject to the limitation under subparagraph (B), be increased by such amount.

(B) Total installments limited to shortfall base. Subject to rules prescribed by the Secretary, if a shortfall amortization installment with respect to any shortfall amortization base for an election year is required to be increased for any plan year under subparagraph (A)—

(i) such increase shall not result in the amount of such installment exceeding the present value of such installment and all succeeding installments with respect to such base (determined without regard to such increase but after application of clause (ii)), and

(ii) subsequent shortfall amortization installments with respect to such base shall, in reverse order of the otherwise required installments, be reduced to the extent necessary to limit the present value of such subsequent shortfall amortization installments (after application of this paragraph) to the present value of the remaining unamortized shortfall amortization base.

(C) Installment acceleration amount. For purposes of this paragraph—

(i) In general. The term "installment acceleration amount" means, with respect to any plan year in a restriction period with respect to an election year, the sum of—

(I) the aggregate amount of excess employee compensation determined under subparagraph (D) with respect to all employees for the plan year, plus

(II) the aggregate amount of extraordinary dividends and redemptions determined under subparagraph (E) for the plan year.

(ii) Annual limitation. The installment acceleration amount for any plan year shall not exceed the excess (if any) of—

(I) the sum of the shortfall amortization installments for the plan year and all preceding plan years in the amortization period elected under paragraph (2)(D) with respect to the shortfall amortization base with respect to an election year, determined without regard to paragraph (2)(D) and this paragraph, over

(II) the sum of the shortfall amortization installments for such plan year and all such preceding plan years, determined after application of paragraph (2)(D) (and in the case of any preceding plan year, after application of this paragraph).

(iii) Carryover of excess installment acceleration amounts.

(I) In general. If the installment acceleration amount for any plan year (determined without regard to clause (ii)) exceeds the limitation under clause (ii), then, subject to subclause (II), such excess shall be treated as an installment acceleration amount with respect to the succeeding plan year.

(II) Cap to apply. If any amount treated as an installment acceleration amount under subclause (I) or this subclause with respect any succeeding plan year, when added to other installment acceleration amounts (determined without regard to clause (ii)) with respect to the plan year, exceeds the limitation under clause (ii), the portion of such amount representing such excess shall be treated as an installment acceleration amount with respect to the next succeeding plan year.

(III) Limitation on years to which amounts carried for. No amount shall be carried under subclause (I) or (II) to a plan year which begins after the first plan year following the last plan year in the restriction period (or after the second plan year following such last plan year in the case of an election year with respect to which 15-year amortization was elected under paragraph (2)(D)).

(IV) Ordering rules. For purposes of applying subclause (II), installment acceleration amounts for the plan year (determined without regard to any carryover under this clause) shall be applied first against the limitation under clause (ii) and then carryovers to such plan year shall be applied against such limitation on a first-in, first-out basis.

(D) Excess employee compensation. For purposes of this paragraph—

(i) In general. The term "excess employee compensation" means, with respect to any employee for any plan year, the excess (if any) of—

(I) the aggregate amount includible in income under this chapter for remuneration during the calendar year in which such plan year begins for services performed by the employee for the plan sponsor (whether or not performed during such calendar year), over

(II) $1,000,000.

(ii) Amounts set aside for nonqualified deferred compensation. If during any calendar year assets are set aside or reserved (directly or indirectly) in a trust (or other arrangement as determined by the Secretary), or transferred to such a trust or other arrangement, by a plan sponsor for purposes of paying deferred compensation of an employee under a nonqualified deferred compensation plan (as defined in section 409A) of the plan sponsor, then, for purposes of clause (i), the amount of such assets shall be treated as remuneration of the employee includible in income for the calendar year unless such amount is otherwise includible in income for such year. An amount to which the preceding sentence applies shall not be taken into account under this paragraph for any subsequent calendar year.

(iii) Only remuneration for certain post-2009 services counted. Remuneration shall be taken into account under clause (i) only to the extent attributable to services performed by the employee for the plan sponsor after February 28, 2010.

(iv) Exception for certain equity payments.

(I) In general. There shall not be taken into account under clause (i)(I) any amount includible in income with respect to the granting after February 28, 2010, of service recipient stock (within the meaning of section 409A) that, upon such grant, is subject to a substantial risk of forfeiture (as defined under section 83(c)(1)) for at least 5 years from the date of such grant.

(II) Secretarial authority. The Secretary may by regulation provide for the application of this clause in the case of a person other than a corporation.

(v) Other exceptions. The following amounts includible in income shall not be taken into account under clause (i)(I):

(I) Commissions. Any remuneration payable on a commission basis solely on account of income directly generated by the individual performance of the individual to whom such remuneration is payable.

(II) Certain payments under existing contracts. Any remuneration consisting of nonqualified deferred compensation, restricted stock, stock options, or stock appreciation rights payable or granted under a written binding contract that was in effect on March 1, 2010, and which was not modified in any material respect before such remuneration is paid.

(vi) Self-employed individual treated as employee. The term "employee" includes, with respect to a calendar year, a self-employed individual who is treated as an employee under section 401(c) for the taxable year ending during such calendar year, and the term "compensation" shall include earned income of such individual with respect to such self-employment.

(vii) Indexing of amount. In the case of any calendar year beginning after 2010, the dollar amount under clause (i)(II) shall be increased by an amount equal to—

(I) such dollar amount, multiplied by

(II) the cost-of-living adjustment determined under section 1(f)(3) for the calendar year, determined by substituting "calendar year 2009" for "calendar year 1992" in subparagraph (B) thereof. If the amount of any increase under clause (i) is not a multiple of $1,000, such increase shall be rounded to the next lowest multiple of $1,000.

(E) Extraordinary dividends and redemptions.

(i) In general. The amount determined under this subparagraph for any plan year is the excess (if any) of the sum of the dividends declared during the plan year by the plan sponsor plus the aggregate amount paid for the redemption of stock of the plan sponsor redeemed during the plan year over the greater of—

(I) the adjusted net income (within the meaning of section 4043 of the Employee Retirement Income Security Act of 1974) of the plan sponsor for the preceding plan year, determined without regard to any reduction by reason of interest, taxes, depreciation, or amortization, or

(II) in the case of a plan sponsor that determined and declared dividends in the same manner for at least 5 consecutive years immediately preceding such plan year, the aggregate amount of dividends determined and declared for such plan year using such manner.

(ii) Only certain post-2009 dividends and redemptions counted. For purposes of clause (i), there shall only be taken into account dividends declared, and redemptions occurring, after February 28, 2010.

(iii) Exception for intra-group dividends. Dividends paid by one member of a controlled group (as defined in section 412(d)(3)) to another member of such group shall not be taken into account under clause (i).

(iv) Exception for certain redemptions. Redemptions that are made pursuant to a plan maintained with respect to employees, or that are made on account of the death, disability, or termination of employment of an employee or shareholder, shall not be taken into account under clause (i).

(v) Exception for certain preferred stock.

(I) In general. Dividends and redemptions with respect to applicable preferred stock shall not be taken into account under clause (i) to the extent that dividends accrue with respect to such stock at a specified rate in all events and without regard to the plan sponsor's income, and interest accrues on any unpaid dividends with respect to such stock.

(II) Applicable preferred stock. For purposes of subclause (I), the term "applicable preferred stock" means preferred stock which was issued before March 1, 2010 (or which was issued after such date and is held by an employee benefit plan subject to the provisions of title I of Employee Retirement Income Security Act of 1974).

(F) Other definitions and rules. For purposes of this paragraph—

(i) Plan sponsor. The term "plan sponsor" includes any member of the plan sponsor's controlled group (as defined in section 412(d)(3)).

(ii) Restriction period. The term "restriction period" means, with respect to any election year—

(I) except as provided in subclause (II), the 3-year period beginning with the election year (or, if later, the first plan year beginning after December 31, 2009), and

(II) if the plan sponsor elects 15-year amortization for the shortfall amortization base for the election year, the 5-year period beginning with the election year (or, if later, the first plan year beginning after December 31, 2009).

(iii) Elections for multiple plans. If a plan sponsor makes elections under paragraph (2)(D) with respect to 2 or more plans, the Secretary shall provide rules for the application of this paragraph to such plans, including rules for the ratable allocation of any installment acceleration amount among such plans on the basis of each plan's relative reduction in the plan's shortfall amortization installment for the first plan year in the amortization period described in subparagraph (A) (determined without regard to this paragraph).

(iv) Mergers and acquisitions. The Secretary shall prescribe rules for the application of paragraph (2)(D) and this paragraph in any case where there is a merger or acquisition involving a plan sponsor making the election under paragraph (2)(D).

(d) Rules relating to funding target—For purposes of this section—

(1) Funding target—Except as provided in subsection (i)(1) with respect to plans in at-risk status, the funding target of a plan for a plan year is the present value of all benefits accrued or earned under the plan as of the beginning of the plan year.

(2) Funding target attainment percentage—The "funding target attainment percentage" of a plan for a plan year is the ratio (expressed as a percentage) which—

(A) the value of plan assets for the plan year (as reduced under subsection (f)(4)(B)), bears to

(B) the funding target of the plan for the plan year (determined without regard to subsection (i)(1)).

(e) Waiver amortization charge—

(1) Determination of waiver amortization charge—The waiver amortization charge (if any) for a plan for any plan year is the aggregate total of the waiver amortization installments for such plan year with respect to the waiver amortization bases for each of the 5 preceding plan years.

(2) Waiver amortization installment—For purposes of paragraph (1)—

(A) Determination—The waiver amortization installments are the amounts necessary to amortize the waiver amortization base of the plan for any plan year in level annual installments over a period of 5 plan years beginning with the succeeding plan year.

(B) Waiver installment—The waiver amortization installment for any plan year in the 5-year period under subparagraph (A) with respect to any waiver amortization base is the annual installment determined under subparagraph (A) for that year for that base.

(3) Interest rate—In determining any waiver amortization installment under this subsection, the plan sponsor shall use the segment rates determined under subparagraph (C) of subsection (h)(2), applied under rules similar to the rules of subparagraph (B) of subsection (h)(2).

(4) Waiver amortization base—The waiver amortization base of a plan for a plan year is the amount of the waived funding deficiency (if any) for such plan year under section 412(c).

(5) Early deemed amortization upon attainment of funding target—In any case in which the funding shortfall of a plan for a plan year is zero, for purposes of determining the waiver amortization charge for such plan year and succeeding plan years, the waiver amortization bases for all preceding plan years (and all waiver amortization installments determined with respect to such bases) shall be reduced to zero.

(f) Reduction of minimum required contribution by prefunding balance and funding standard carryover balance—

(1) Election to maintain balances—

(A) Prefunding balance—The plan sponsor of a defined benefit plan which is not a multiemployer plan may elect to maintain a prefunding balance.

(B) Funding standard carryover balance—

(i) **In general**—In the case of a defined benefit plan (other than a multiemployer plan) described in clause (ii), the plan sponsor may elect to maintain a funding standard carryover balance, until such balance is reduced to zero.

(ii) **Plans maintaining funding standard account in 2007**—A plan is described in this clause if the plan—

(I) was in effect for a plan year beginning in 2007, and

(II) had a positive balance in the funding standard account under section 412(b) as in effect for such plan year and determined as of the end of such plan year.

(2) Application of balances—A prefunding balance and a funding standard carryover balance maintained pursuant to this paragraph—

(A) shall be available for crediting against the minimum required contribution, pursuant to an election under paragraph (3),

(B) shall be applied as a reduction in the amount treated as the value of plan assets for purposes of this section, to the extent provided in paragraph (4), and

(C) may be reduced at any time, pursuant to an election under paragraph (5).

(3) Election to apply balances against minimum required contribution—

(A) **In general**—Except as provided in subparagraphs (B) and (C), in the case of any plan year in which the plan sponsor elects to credit against the minimum required contribution for the current plan year all or a portion of the prefunding balance or the funding standard carryover balance for the current plan year (not in excess of such minimum required contribution), the minimum required contribution for the plan year shall be reduced as of the first day of the plan year by the amount so credited by the plan sponsor. For purposes of the preceding sentence, the minimum required contribution shall be determined after taking into account any waiver under section 412(c).

(B) **Coordination with funding standard carryover balance**—To the extent that any plan has a funding standard carryover balance greater than zero, no amount of the prefunding balance of such plan may be credited under this paragraph in reducing the minimum required contribution.

(C) **Limitation for underfunded plans**—The preceding provisions of this paragraph shall not apply for any plan year if the ratio (expressed as a percentage) which—

(i) the value of plan assets for the preceding plan year (as reduced under paragraph (4)(C)), bears to

(ii) the funding target of the plan for the preceding plan year (determined without regard to subsection (i)(1)),

is less than 80 percent. In the case of plan years beginning in 2008, the ratio under this subparagraph may be determined using such methods of estimation as the Secretary may prescribe.

(D) **Special rule for certain years of plans maintained by charities.**

(i) In general—For purposes of applying subparagraph (C) for plan years beginning after August 31, 2009, and before September 1, 2011, the ratio determined under such subparagraph for the preceding plan year of a plan shall be the greater of—

(I) such ratio, as determined without regard to this subsection, or

(II) the ratio for such plan for the plan year beginning after August 31, 2007 and before September 1, 2008, as determined under rules prescribed by the Secretary.

(ii) Special rule—In the case of a plan for which the valuation date is not the first day of the plan year—

(I) clause (i) shall apply to plan years beginning after December 31, 2007, and before January 1, 2010, and

(II) clause (i)(II) shall apply based on the last plan year beginning before September 1, 2007, as determined under rules prescribed by the Secretary.

(iii) Limitation to charities—This subparagraph shall not apply to any plan unless such plan is maintained exclusively by one or more organizations described in section 501(c)(3).

(4) Effect of balances on amounts treated as value of plan assets—In the case of any plan maintaining a prefunding balance or a funding standard carryover balance pursuant to this subsection, the amount treated as the value of plan assets shall be deemed to be such amount, reduced as provided in the following subparagraphs:

(A) Applicability of shortfall amortization base—For purposes of subsection (c)(5), the value of plan assets is deemed to be such amount, reduced by the amount of the prefunding balance, but only if an election under paragraph (3) applying any portion of the prefunding balance in reducing the minimum required contribution is in effect for the plan year.

(B) Determination of excess assets, funding shortfall, and funding target attainment percentage—

(i) In general—For purposes of subsections (a), (c)(4)(B), and (d)(2)(A), the value of plan assets is deemed to be such amount, reduced by the amount of the prefunding balance and the funding standard carryover balance.

(ii) Special rule for certain binding agreements with PBGC—For purposes of subsection (c)(4)(B), the value of plan assets shall not be deemed to be reduced for a plan year by the amount of the specified balance if, with respect to such balance, there is in effect for a plan year a binding written agreement with the Pension Benefit Guaranty Corporation which provides that such balance is not available to reduce the minimum required contribution for the plan year. For purposes of the preceding sentence, the term "specified balance" means the prefunding balance or the funding standard carryover balance, as the case may be.

(C) Availability of balances in plan year for crediting against minimum required contribution—For purposes of paragraph (3)(C)(i) of this subsection, the value of plan assets is deemed to be such amount, reduced by the amount of the prefunding balance.

(5) Election to reduce balance prior to determinations of value of plan assets and crediting against minimum required contribution—

(A) In general—The plan sponsor may elect to reduce by any amount the balance of the prefunding balance and the funding standard carryover balance for any plan year (but not below zero). Such reduction shall be effective prior to any determination of the value of plan assets for such plan year under this section and application of the balance in reducing the minimum required contribution for such plan for such plan year pursuant to an election under paragraph (2).

(B) Coordination between prefunding balance and funding standard carryover balance—To the extent that any plan has a funding standard carryover balance greater than zero, no election may be made under subparagraph (A) with respect to the prefunding balance.

(6) Prefunding balance—

(A) In general—A prefunding balance maintained by a plan shall consist of a beginning balance of zero, increased and decreased to the extent provided in subparagraphs (B) and (C), and adjusted further as provided in paragraph (8).

(B) Increases—

(i) In general—As of the first day of each plan year beginning after 2008, the prefunding balance of a plan shall be increased by the amount elected by the plan sponsor for the plan year. Such amount shall not exceed the excess (if any) of—

(I) the aggregate total of employer contributions to the plan for the preceding plan year, over—

(II) the minimum required contribution for such preceding plan year.

(ii) Adjustments for interest—Any excess contributions under clause (i) shall be properly adjusted for interest accruing for the periods between the first day of the current plan year and the dates on which the excess contributions were made, determined by using the effective interest rate for the preceding plan year and by treating contributions as being first used to satisfy the minimum required contribution.

(iii) Certain contributions necessary to avoid benefit limitations disregarded—The excess described in clause (i) with respect to any preceding plan year shall be reduced (but not below zero) by the amount of contributions an employer would be required to make under subsection (b), (c), or (e) of section 436 to avoid a benefit limitation which would otherwise be imposed under such paragraph for the preceding plan year. Any contribution which may be taken into account in satisfying the requirements of more than 1 of such paragraphs shall be taken into account only once for purposes of this clause.

(C) Decreases—The prefunding balance of a plan shall be decreased (but not below zero) by—

(i) as of the first day of each plan year after 2008, the amount of such balance credited under paragraph (2) (if any) in reducing the minimum required contribution of the plan for the preceding plan year, and

(ii) as of the time specified in paragraph (5)(A), any reduction in such balance elected under paragraph (5).

(7) Funding standard carryover balance—

(A) In general—A funding standard carryover balance maintained by a plan shall consist of a beginning balance determined under subparagraph (B), decreased to the extent provided in subparagraph (C), and adjusted further as provided in paragraph (8).

(B) Beginning balance—The beginning balance of the funding standard carryover balance shall be the positive balance described in paragraph (1)(B)(ii)(II).

(C) Decreases—The funding standard carryover balance of a plan shall be decreased (but not below zero) by—

(i) as of the first day of each plan year after 2008, the amount of such balance credited under paragraph (2) (if any) in reducing the minimum required contribution of the plan for the preceding plan year, and

(ii) as of the time specified in paragraph (5)(A), any reduction in such balance elected under paragraph (5).

(8) Adjustments for investment experience—In determining the prefunding balance or the funding standard carryover balance of a plan as of the first day of the plan year, the plan sponsor shall, in accordance with regulations prescribed by the Secretary, adjust such balance to reflect the rate of return on plan assets for the preceding plan year. Notwithstanding subsection (g)(3), such rate of return shall be determined on the basis of fair market value and shall properly take into account, in accordance with such regulations, all contributions, distributions, and other plan payments made during such period.

(9) Elections—Elections under this subsection shall be made at such times, and in such form and manner, as shall be prescribed in regulations of the Secretary.

(g) Valuation of plan assets and liabilities—

(1) Timing of determinations—Except as otherwise provided under this subsection, all determinations under this section for a plan year shall be made as of the valuation date of the plan for such plan year.

(2) Valuation date—For purposes of this section—

(A) In general—Except as provided in subparagraph (B), the valuation date of a plan for any plan year shall be the first day of the plan year.

(B) Exception for small plans—If, on each day during the preceding plan year, a plan had 100 or fewer participants, the plan may designate any day during the plan year as its valuation date for such plan year and succeeding plan years. For purposes of this subparagraph, all defined benefit plans (other than multiemployer plans) maintained by the same employer (or any member of such employer's controlled group) shall be treated as 1 plan, but only participants with respect to such employer or member shall be taken into account.

(C) Application of certain rules in determination of plan size—For purposes of this paragraph—

(i) **Plans not in existence in preceding year**—In the case of the first plan year of any plan, subparagraph (B) shall apply to such plan by taking into account the number of participants that the plan is reasonably expected to have on days during such first plan year.

(ii) **Predecessors**—Any reference in subparagraph (B) to an employer shall include a reference to any predecessor of such employer.

(3) Determination of value of plan assets—For purposes of this section—

(A) In general—Except as provided in subparagraph (B), the value of plan assets shall be the fair market value of the assets.

(B) Averaging allowed—A plan may determine the value of plan assets on the basis of the averaging of fair market values, but only if such method—

(i) is permitted under regulations prescribed by the Secretary,

(ii) does not provide for averaging of such values over more than the period beginning on the last day of the 25th month preceding the month in which the valuation date occurs and ending on the valuation date (or a similar period in the case of a valuation date which is not the 1st day of a month), and

(iii) does not result in a determination of the value of plan assets which, at any time, is lower than 90 percent or greater than 110 percent of the fair market value of such assets at such time.

Any such averaging shall be adjusted for contributions, distributions, and expected earnings (as determined by the plan's actuary on the basis of an assumed earnings rate specified by the actuary but not in excess of the third segment rate applicable under subsection (h)(2)(C)(iii)), as specified by the Secretary.

(4) Accounting for contribution receipts—For purposes of determining the value of assets under paragraph (3)—

(A) Prior year contributions—If—

(i) an employer makes any contribution to the plan after the valuation date for the plan year in which the contribution is made, and

(ii) the contribution is for a preceding plan year,

the contribution shall be taken into account as an asset of the plan as of the valuation date, except that in the case of any plan year beginning after 2008, only the present value (determined as of the valuation date) of such contribution may be taken into account. For purposes of the preceding sentence, present value shall be determined using the effective interest rate for the preceding plan year to which the contribution is properly allocable.

(B) Special rule for current year contributions made before valuation date—If any contributions for any plan year are made to or under the plan during the plan year but before the valuation date for the plan year, the assets of the plan as of the valuation date shall not include—

(i) such contributions, and

(ii) interest on such contributions for the period between the date of the contributions and the valuation date, determined by using the effective interest rate for the plan year.

(h) Actuarial assumptions and methods—

(1) In general—Subject to this subsection, the determination of any present value or other computation under this section shall be made on the basis of actuarial assumptions and methods—

    (A) each of which is reasonable (taking into account the experience of the plan and reasonable expectations), and

    (B) which, in combination, offer the actuary's best estimate of anticipated experience under the plan.

(2) Interest rates—

    (A) Effective interest rate—For purposes of this section, the term "effective interest rate" means, with respect to any plan for any plan year, the single rate of interest which, if used to determine the present value of the plan's accrued or earned benefits referred to in subsection (d)(1), would result in an amount equal to the funding target of the plan for such plan year.

    (B) Interest rates for determining funding target—For purposes of determining the funding target and target normal cost of a plan for any plan year, the interest rate used in determining the present value of the benefits of the plan shall be—

        (i) in the case of benefits reasonably determined to be payable during the 5-year period beginning on the valuation date for the plan year, the first segment rate with respect to the applicable month,

        (ii) in the case of benefits reasonably determined to be payable during the 15-year period beginning at the end of the period described in clause (i), the second segment rate with respect to the applicable month, and

        (iii) in the case of benefits reasonably determined to be payable after the period described in clause (ii), the third segment rate with respect to the applicable month.

    (C) Segment rates—For purposes of this paragraph—

        (i) First segment rate—The term "first segment rate" means, with respect to any month, the single rate of interest which shall be determined by the Secretary for such month on the basis of the corporate bond yield curve for such month, taking into account only that portion of such yield curve which is based on bonds maturing during the 5-year period commencing with such month.

        (ii) Second segment rate—The term "second segment rate" means, with respect to any month, the single rate of interest which shall be determined by the Secretary for such month on the basis of the corporate bond yield curve for such month, taking into account only that portion of such yield curve which is based on bonds maturing during the 15-year period beginning at the end of the period described in clause (i).

        (iii) Third segment rate—The term "third segment rate" means, with respect to any month, the single rate of interest which shall be determined by the Secretary for such month on the basis of the corporate bond yield curve for such month, taking into account only that portion of such yield curve which is based on bonds maturing during periods beginning after the period described in clause (ii).

        (iv) Segment rate stabilization—

(I) In general—If a segment rate described in clause (i), (ii), or (iii) with respect to any applicable month (determined without regard to this clause) is less than the applicable minimum percentage, or more than the applicable maximum percentage, of the average of the segment rates described in such clause for years in the 25-year period ending with September 30 of the calendar year preceding the calendar year in which the plan year begins, then the segment rate described in such clause with respect to the applicable month shall be equal to the applicable minimum percentage or the applicable maximum percentage of such average, whichever is closest. The Secretary shall determine such average on an annual basis and may prescribe equivalent rates for years in any such 25-year period for which the rates described in any such clause are not available.

(II) Applicable minimum percentage; applicable maximum percentage—For purposes of subclause (I), the applicable minimum percentage and the applicable maximum percentage for a plan year beginning in a calendar year shall be determined in accordance with the following table:

If the calendar year is:	The applicable minimum percentage is:	The applicable maximum percentage is:
2012, 2013, 2014, 2015, 2016, 2017, 2018, 2019, or 2020	90%	110%
2021	85%	115%
2022	80%	120%
2023	75%	125%
After 2023	70%	130%

(D) Corporate bond yield curve—For purposes of this paragraph—

(i) In general—The term "corporate bond yield curve" means, with respect to any month, a yield curve which is prescribed by the Secretary for such month and which reflects the average, for the 24-month period ending with the month preceding such month, of monthly yields on investment grade corporate bonds with varying maturities and that are in the top 3 quality levels available.

(ii) Election to use yield curve—Solely for purposes of determining the minimum required contribution under this section, the plan sponsor may, in lieu of the segment rates determined under subparagraph (C), elect to use interest rates under the corporate bond yield curve. For purposes of the preceding sentence such curve shall be determined without regard to the 24-month averaging described in clause (i). Such election, once made, may be revoked only with the consent of the Secretary.

(E) Applicable month—For purposes of this paragraph, the term "applicable month" means, with respect to any plan for any plan year, the month which includes the valuation date of such plan for such plan year or, at the election of the plan sponsor, any of the 4 months which precede such month. Any election made under this subparagraph shall apply to the plan year for which the election is made and all succeeding plan years, unless the election is revoked with the consent of the Secretary.

(F) Publication requirements—The Secretary shall publish for each month the corporate bond yield curve (and the corporate bond yield curve reflecting the modification described in section 417(e)(3)(D)(i) for such month) and each of the rates determined under subparagraph (C) and the averages determined under subparagraph (C)(iv) for such month. The Secretary shall also publish a description of the methodology used to determine such yield curve and such rates which is sufficiently detailed to enable plans to make reasonable projections regarding the yield curve and such rates for future months based on the plan's projection of future interest rates.

* * *

(3) Mortality tables—

(A) In general—Except as provided in subparagraph (C) or (D), the Secretary shall by regulation prescribe mortality tables to be used in determining any present value or making any computation under this section. Such tables shall be based on the actual experience of pension plans and projected trends in such experience. In prescribing such tables, the Secretary shall take into account results of available independent studies of mortality of individuals covered by pension plans.

(B) Periodic revision—The Secretary shall (at least every 10 years) make revisions in any table in effect under subparagraph (A) to reflect the actual experience of pension plans and projected trends in such experience.

(C) Substitute mortality table—

(i) In general—Upon request by the plan sponsor and approval by the Secretary, a mortality table which meets the requirements of clause (iii) shall be used in determining any present value or making any computation under this section during the period of consecutive plan years (not to exceed 10) specified in the request.

(ii) Early termination of period—Notwithstanding clause (i), a mortality table described in clause (i) shall cease to be in effect as of the earliest of—

(I) the date on which there is a significant change in the participants in the plan by reason of a plan spinoff or merger or otherwise, or

(II) the date on which the plan actuary determines that such table does not meet the requirements of clause (iii).

(iii) Requirements—A mortality table meets the requirements of this clause if—

(I) there is a sufficient number of plan participants, and the pension plans have been maintained for a sufficient period of time, to have credible information necessary for purposes of subclause (II), and

(II) such table reflects the actual experience of the pension plans maintained by the sponsor and projected trends in general mortality experience.

(iv) All plans in controlled group must use separate table—Except as provided by the Secretary, a plan sponsor may not use a mortality table under this subparagraph for any plan maintained by the plan sponsor unless—

(I) a separate mortality table is established and used under this subparagraph for each other plan maintained by the plan sponsor and if the plan sponsor is a member of a controlled group, each member of the controlled group, and

(II) the requirements of clause (iii) are met separately with respect to the table so established for each such plan, determined by only taking into account the participants of such plan, the time such plan has been in existence, and the actual experience of such plan.

(v) Deadline for submission and disposition of application—

(I) Submission—The plan sponsor shall submit a mortality table to the Secretary for approval under this subparagraph at least 7 months before the 1st day of the period described in clause (i).

(II) Disposition—Any mortality table submitted to the Secretary for approval under this subparagraph shall be treated as in effect as of the 1st day of the period described in clause (i) unless the Secretary, during the 180-day period beginning on the date of such submission, disapproves of such table and provides the reasons that such table fails to meet the requirements of clause (iii). The 180-day period shall be extended upon mutual agreement of the Secretary and the plan sponsor.

(D) Separate mortality tables for the disabled—Notwithstanding subparagraph (A)—

(i) In general—The Secretary shall establish mortality tables which may be used (in lieu of the tables under subparagraph (A)) under this subsection for individuals who are entitled to benefits under the plan on account of disability. The Secretary shall establish separate tables for individuals whose disabilities occur in plan years beginning before January 1, 1995, and for individuals whose disabilities occur in plan years beginning on or after such date.

(ii) Special rule for disabilities occurring after 1994—In the case of disabilities occurring in plan years beginning after December 31, 1994, the tables under clause (i) shall apply only with respect to individuals described in such subclause who are disabled within the meaning of title II of the Social Security Act and the regulations thereunder.

(iii) Periodic revision—The Secretary shall (at least every 10 years) make revisions in any table in effect under clause (i) to reflect the actual experience of pension plans and projected trends in such experience.

(4) Probability of benefit payments in the form of lump sums or other optional forms—For purposes of determining any present value or making any computation under this section, there shall be taken into account—

(A) the probability that future benefit payments under the plan will be made in the form of optional forms of benefits provided under the plan (including lump sum distributions, determined on the basis of the plan's experience and other related assumptions), and

(B) any difference in the present value of such future benefit payments resulting from the use of actuarial assumptions, in determining benefit payments in any such optional form of benefits, which are different from those specified in this subsection.

(5) Approval of large changes in actuarial assumptions—

(A) In general—No actuarial assumption used to determine the funding target for a plan to which this paragraph applies may be changed without the approval of the Secretary.

(B) Plans to which paragraph applies—This paragraph shall apply to a plan only if—

(i) the plan is a defined benefit plan (other than a multiemployer plan) to which title IV of the Employee Retirement Income Security Act of 1974 applies,

(ii) the aggregate unfunded vested benefits as of the close of the preceding plan year (as determined under section 4006(a)(3)(E)(iii) of the Employee Retirement Income Security Act of 1974) of such plan and all other plans maintained by the contributing sponsors (as defined in section 4001(a)(13) of such Act) and members of such sponsors' controlled groups (as defined in section 4001(a)(14) of such Act) which are covered by title IV (disregarding plans with no unfunded vested benefits) exceed $50,000,000, and

(iii) the change in assumptions (determined after taking into account any changes in interest rate and mortality table) results in a decrease in the funding shortfall of the plan for the current plan year that exceeds $50,000,000, or that exceeds $5,000,000 and that is 5 percent or more of the funding target of the plan before such change.

(i) Special rules for at-risk plans—

(1) Funding target for plans in at-risk status—

(A) In general—In the case of a plan which is in at-risk status for a plan year, the funding target of the plan for the plan year shall be equal to the sum of—

(i) the present value of all benefits accrued or earned under the plan as of the beginning of the plan year, as determined by using the additional actuarial assumptions described in subparagraph (B), and

(ii) in the case of a plan which also has been in at-risk status for at least 2 of the 4 preceding plan years, a loading factor determined under subparagraph (C).

(B) Additional actuarial assumptions—The actuarial assumptions described in this subparagraph are as follows:

(i) All employees who are not otherwise assumed to retire as of the valuation date but who will be eligible to elect benefits during the plan year and the 10 succeeding plan years shall be assumed to retire at the earliest retirement date under the plan but not before the end of the plan year for which the at-risk funding target and at-risk target normal cost are being determined.

(ii) All employees shall be assumed to elect the retirement benefit available under the plan at the assumed retirement age (determined after application of clause (i)) which would result in the highest present value of benefits.

(C) Loading factor—The loading factor applied with respect to a plan under this paragraph for any plan year is the sum of—

(i) $700, times the number of participants in the plan, plus

(ii) 4 percent of the funding target (determined without regard to this paragraph) of the plan for the plan year.

(2) Target normal cost of at-risk plans—In the case of a plan which is in at-risk status for a plan year, the target normal cost of the plan for such plan year shall be equal to the sum of—

(A) the excess of—

(i) the sum of—

(I) the present value of all benefits which are expected to accrue or to be earned under the plan during the plan year, determined using the additional actuarial assumptions described in paragraph (1)(B), plus

(II) the amount of plan-related expenses expected to be paid from plan assets during the plan year, over

(ii) the amount of mandatory employee contributions expected to be made during the plan year, plus

(B) in the case of a plan which also has been in at-risk status for at least 2 of the 4 preceding plan years, a loading factor equal to 4 percent of the amount determined under subsection (b)(1)(A)(i) with respect to the plan for the plan year.

(3) Minimum amount—In no event shall—

(A) the at-risk funding target be less than the funding target, as determined without regard to this subsection, or

(B) the at-risk target normal cost be less than the target normal cost, as determined without regard to this subsection.

(4) Determination of at-risk status—For purposes of this subsection—

(A) In general—A plan is in at-risk status for a plan year if—

(i) the funding target attainment percentage for the preceding plan year (determined under this section without regard to this subsection) is less than 80 percent, and

(ii) the funding target attainment percentage for the preceding plan year (determined under this section by using the additional actuarial assumptions described in paragraph (1)(B) in computing the funding target) is less than 70 percent.

(B) Transition rule—In the case of plan years beginning in 2008, 2009, and 2010, subparagraph (A)(i) shall be applied by substituting the following percentages for "80 percent":

(i) 65 percent in the case of 2008.

(ii) 70 percent in the case of 2009.

(iii) 75 percent in the case of 2010.

In the case of plan years beginning in 2008, the funding target attainment percentage for the preceding plan year under subparagraph (A) may be determined using such methods of estimation as the Secretary may provide.

* * *

(5) Transition between applicable funding targets and between applicable target normal costs—

(A) In general—In any case in which a plan which is in at-risk status for a plan year has been in such status for a consecutive period of fewer than 5 plan years, the applicable amount of the funding target and of the target normal cost shall be, in lieu of the amount determined without regard to this paragraph, the sum of—

(i) the amount determined under this section without regard to this subsection, plus

(ii) the transition percentage for such plan year of the excess of the amount determined under this subsection (without regard to this paragraph) over the amount determined under this section without regard to this subsection.

(B) Transition percentage—For purposes of subparagraph (A), the transition percentage shall be determined in accordance with the following table:

If the consecutive number of years (including the plan year) the plan is in at-risk status is—	The transition percentage is—
1	20
2	40
3	60
4	80.

(C) Years before effective date—For purposes of this paragraph, plan years beginning before 2008 shall not be taken into account.

(6) Small plan exception—If, on each day during the preceding plan year, a plan had 500 or fewer participants, the plan shall not be treated as in at-risk status for the plan year. For purposes of this paragraph, all defined benefit plans (other than multiemployer plans) maintained by the same employer (or any member of such employer's controlled group) shall be treated as 1 plan, but only participants with respect to such employer or member shall be taken into account and the rules of subsection (g)(2)(C) shall apply.

(j) Payment of minimum required contributions—

(1) In general—For purposes of this section, the due date for any payment of any minimum required contribution for any plan year shall be 8 1/2 months after the close of the plan year.

(2) Interest—Any payment required under paragraph (1) for a plan year that is made on a date other than the valuation date for such plan year shall be adjusted for interest accruing for the period between the valuation date and the payment date, at the effective rate of interest for the plan for such plan year.

(3) Accelerated quarterly contribution schedule for underfunded plans—

(A) Failure to timely make required installment—In any case in which the plan has a funding shortfall for the preceding plan year, the employer maintaining the plan shall make the required installments under this paragraph and if the employer fails to pay the full amount of a required installment for the plan year, then the amount of interest charged under paragraph (2) on the underpayment for the period of underpayment shall be determined by using a rate of interest equal to the rate otherwise used under paragraph (2) plus 5 percentage points. In the case of plan years beginning in 2008, the funding shortfall for the preceding plan year may be determined using such methods of estimation as the Secretary may provide.

(B) Amount of underpayment, period of underpayment—For purposes of subparagraph (A)—

(i) Amount—The amount of the underpayment shall be the excess of—

(I) the required installment, over

(II) the amount (if any) of the installment contributed to or under the plan on or before the due date for the installment.

(ii) Period of underpayment—The period for which any interest is charged under this paragraph with respect to any portion of the underpayment shall run from the due date for the installment to the date on which such portion is contributed to or under the plan.

(iii) Order of crediting contributions—For purposes of clause (i)(II), contributions shall be credited against unpaid required installments in the order in which such installments are required to be paid.

(C) Number of required installments; due dates—For purposes of this paragraph—

(i) Payable in 4 installments—There shall be 4 required installments for each plan year.

(ii) Time for payment of installments—The due dates for required installments are set forth in the following table:

In the case of the following required installment:	*The due date is:*
1st	April 15
2nd	July 15
3rd	October 15
4th	January 15 of the following year

(D) Amount of required installment—For purposes of this paragraph—

(i) In general—The amount of any required installment shall be 25 percent of the required annual payment.

(ii) Required annual payment—For purposes of clause (i), the term "required annual payment" means the lesser of—

(I) 90 percent of the minimum required contribution (determined without regard to this subsection) to the plan for the plan year under this section, or

(II) 100 percent of the minimum required contribution (determined without regard to this subsection or to any waiver under section 412(c)) to the plan for the preceding plan year.

Subclause (II) shall not apply if the preceding plan year referred to in such clause was not a year of 12 months.

(E) Fiscal years, short years, and years with alternate valuation date—

(i) Fiscal years—In applying this paragraph to a plan year beginning on any date other than January 1, there shall be substituted for the months specified in this paragraph, the months which correspond thereto.

(ii) Short plan year—This subparagraph shall be applied to plan years of less than 12 months in accordance with regulations prescribed by the Secretary.

(iii) Plan with alternate valuation date—The Secretary shall prescribe regulations for the application of this paragraph in the case of a plan which has a valuation date other than the first day of the plan year.

(F) Quarterly contributions not to include certain increased contributions— Subparagraph (D) shall be applied without regard to any increase under subsection (c)(7).

(4) Liquidity requirement in connection with quarterly contributions—

(A) In general—A plan to which this paragraph applies shall be treated as failing to pay the full amount of any required installment under paragraph (3) to the extent that the value of the liquid assets paid in such installment is less than the liquidity shortfall (whether or not such liquidity shortfall exceeds the amount of such installment required to be paid but for this paragraph).

(B) Plans to which paragraph applies—This paragraph shall apply to a plan (other than a plan described in subsection (g)(2)(B)) which—

(i) is required to pay installments under paragraph (3) for a plan year, and

(ii) has a liquidity shortfall for any quarter during such plan year.

(C) Period of underpayment—For purposes of paragraph (3)(A), any portion of an installment that is treated as not paid under subparagraph (A) shall continue to be treated as unpaid until the close of the quarter in which the due date for such installment occurs.

(D) Limitation on increase—If the amount of any required installment is increased by reason of subparagraph (A), in no event shall such increase exceed the amount which, when added to prior installments for the plan year, is necessary to increase the funding target attainment percentage of the plan for the plan year (taking into account the expected increase in funding target due to benefits accruing or earned during the plan year) to 100 percent.

(E) Definitions—For purposes of this paragraph—

(i) Liquidity shortfall—The term "liquidity shortfall" means, with respect to any required installment, an amount equal to the excess (as of the last day of the quarter for which such installment is made) of—

(I) the base amount with respect to such quarter, over

(II) the value (as of such last day) of the plan's liquid assets.

(ii) Base amount—

(I) In general—The term "base amount" means, with respect to any quarter, an amount equal to 3 times the sum of the adjusted disbursements from the plan for the 12 months ending on the last day of such quarter.

(II) Special rule—If the amount determined under subclause (I) exceeds an amount equal to 2 times the sum of the adjusted disbursements from the plan for the 36 months ending on the last day of the quarter and an enrolled actuary certifies to the satisfaction of the Secretary that such excess is the result of nonrecurring circumstances, the base amount with respect to such quarter shall be determined without regard to amounts related to those nonrecurring circumstances.

(iii) Disbursements from the plan—The term "disbursements from the plan" means all disbursements from the trust, including purchases of annuities, payments of single sums and other benefits, and administrative expenses.

(iv) Adjusted disbursements—The term "adjusted disbursements" means disbursements from the plan reduced by the product of—

(I) the plan's funding target attainment percentage for the plan year, and

(II) the sum of the purchases of annuities, payments of single sums, and such other disbursements as the Secretary shall provide in regulations.

(v) Liquid assets—The term "liquid assets" means cash, marketable securities, and such other assets as specified by the Secretary in regulations.

(vi) Quarter—The term "quarter" means, with respect to any required installment, the 3-month period preceding the month in which the due date for such installment occurs.

(F) Regulations—The Secretary may prescribe such regulations as are necessary to carry out this paragraph.

(k) Imposition of lien where failure to make required contributions—

(1) In general—In the case of a plan to which this subsection applies (as provided under paragraph (2)), if—

(A) any person fails to make a contribution payment required by section 412 and this section before the due date for such payment, and

(B) the unpaid balance of such payment (including interest), when added to the aggregate unpaid balance of all preceding such payments for which payment was not made before the due date (including interest), exceeds $1,000,000,

then there shall be a lien in favor of the plan in the amount determined under paragraph (3) upon all property and rights to property, whether real or personal, belonging to such person and any other person who is a member of the same controlled group of which such person is a member.

(2) Plans to which subsection applies—This subsection shall apply to a defined benefit plan (other than a multiemployer plan) covered under section 4021 of the Employee Retirement Income Security Act of 1974 for any plan year for which the funding target attainment percentage (as defined in subsection (d)(2)) of such plan is less than 100 percent.

(3) Amount of lien—For purposes of paragraph (1), the amount of the lien shall be equal to the aggregate unpaid balance of contribution payments required under this section and section 412 for which payment has not been made before the due date.

(4) Notice of failure; lien—

(A) Notice of failure—A person committing a failure described in paragraph (1) shall notify the Pension Benefit Guaranty Corporation of such failure within 10 days of the due date for the required contribution payment.

(B) Period of lien—The lien imposed by paragraph (1) shall arise on the due date for the required contribution payment and shall continue until the last day of the first plan year in which the plan ceases to be described in paragraph (1)(B). Such lien shall continue to run without regard to whether such plan continues to be described in paragraph (2) during the period referred to in the preceding sentence.

(C) Certain rules to apply—Any amount with respect to which a lien is imposed under paragraph (1) shall be treated as taxes due and owing the United States and rules similar to the rules of subsections (c), (d), and (e) of section 4068 of the Employee Retirement Income Security Act of 1974 shall apply with respect to a lien imposed by subsection (a) and the amount with respect to such lien.

(5) Enforcement—Any lien created under paragraph (1) may be perfected and enforced only by the Pension Benefit Guaranty Corporation, or at the direction of the Pension Benefit Guaranty Corporation, by the contributing sponsor (or any member of the controlled group of the contributing sponsor).

(6) Definitions—For purposes of this subsection—

(A) Contribution payment—The term "contribution payment" means, in connection with a plan, a contribution payment required to be made to the plan, including any required installment under paragraphs (3) and (4) of subsection (j).

(B) Due date; required installment—The terms "due date" and "required installment" have the meanings given such terms by subsection (j).

(C) Controlled group—The term "controlled group" means any group treated as a single employer under subsections (b), (c), (m), and (o) of section 414.

(l) Qualified transfers to health benefit accounts—In the case of a qualified transfer (as defined in section 420), any assets so transferred shall not, for purposes of this section, be treated as assets in the plan.

§ 431. Minimum funding standards for multiemployer plans.

(a) In general—For purposes of section 412, the accumulated funding deficiency of a multiemployer plan for any plan year is the amount, determined as of the end of the plan year, equal to the excess (if any) of the total charges to the funding standard account of the plan for all plan years (beginning with the first plan year for which this part applies to the plan) over the total credits to such account for such years.

(b) Funding standard account—

(1) Account required—Each multiemployer plan to which this part applies shall establish and maintain a funding standard account. Such account shall be credited and charged solely as provided in this section.

(2) Charges to account—For a plan year, the funding standard account shall be charged with the sum of—

(A) the normal cost of the plan for the plan year,

(B) the amounts necessary to amortize in equal annual installments (until fully amortized)—

(i) in the case of a plan which comes into existence on or after January 1, 2008, the unfunded past service liability under the plan on the first day of the first plan year to which this section applies, over a period of 15 plan years,

(ii) separately, with respect to each plan year, the net increase (if any) in unfunded past service liability under the plan arising from plan amendments adopted in such year, over a period of 15 plan years,

(iii) separately, with respect to each plan year, the net experience loss (if any) under the plan, over a period of 15 plan years, and

(iv) separately, with respect to each plan year, the net loss (if any) resulting from changes in actuarial assumptions used under the plan, over a period of 15 plan years,

(C) the amount necessary to amortize each waived funding deficiency (within the meaning of section 412(c)(3)) for each prior plan year in equal annual installments (until fully amortized) over a period of 15 plan years,

(D) the amount necessary to amortize in equal annual installments (until fully amortized) over a period of 5 plan years any amount credited to the funding standard account under section 412(b)(3)(D) (as in effect on the day before the date of the enactment of the Pension Protection Act of 2006), and

(E) the amount necessary to amortize in equal annual installments (until fully amortized) over a period of 20 years the contributions which would be required to be made under the plan but for the provisions of section 412(c)(7)(A)(i)(I) (as in effect on the day before the date of the enactment of the Pension Protection Act of 2006).

(3) Credits to account—For a plan year, the funding standard account shall be credited with the sum of—

(A) the amount considered contributed by the employer to or under the plan for the plan year,

(B) the amount necessary to amortize in equal annual installments (until fully amortized)—

(i) separately, with respect to each plan year, the net decrease (if any) in unfunded past service liability under the plan arising from plan amendments adopted in such year, over a period of 15 plan years,

(ii) separately, with respect to each plan year, the net experience gain (if any) under the plan, over a period of 15 plan years, and

(iii) separately, with respect to each plan year, the net gain (if any) resulting from changes in actuarial assumptions used under the plan, over a period of 15 plan years,

(C) the amount of the waived funding deficiency (within the meaning of section 412(c)(3)) for the plan year, and

(D) in the case of a plan year for which the accumulated funding deficiency is determined under the funding standard account if such plan year follows a plan year for which such deficiency was determined under the alternative minimum funding standard under section 412(g) (as in effect on the day before the date of the enactment of the Pension Protection Act of 2006), the excess (if any) of any debit balance in the funding standard account (determined without regard to this subparagraph) over any debit balance in the alternative minimum funding standard account.

(4) Special rule for amounts first amortized in plan years before 2008—In the case of any amount amortized under section 412(b) (as in effect on the day before the date of the enactment of the Pension Protection Act of 2006) over any period beginning with a plan year beginning before 2008 in lieu of the amortization described in paragraphs (2)(B) and (3)(B), such amount shall continue to be amortized under such section as so in effect.

(5) Combining and offsetting amounts to be amortized—Under regulations prescribed by the Secretary, amounts required to be amortized under paragraph (2) or paragraph (3), as the case may be—

(A) may be combined into one amount under such paragraph to be amortized over a period determined on the basis of the remaining amortization period for all items entering into such combined amount, and

(B) may be offset against amounts required to be amortized under the other such paragraph, with the resulting amount to be amortized over a period determined on the basis of the remaining amortization periods for all items entering into whichever of the two amounts being offset is the greater.

(6) Interest—The funding standard account (and items therein) shall be charged or credited (as determined under regulations prescribed by the Secretary of the Treasury) with interest at the appropriate rate consistent with the rate or rates of interest used under the plan to determine costs.

(7) Special rules relating to charges and credits to funding standard account—For purposes of this part—

(A) Withdrawal liability—Any amount received by a multiemployer plan in payment of all or part of an employer's withdrawal liability under part 1 of subtitle E of title IV of the Employee Retirement Income Security Act of 1974 shall be considered an amount contributed by the employer to or under the plan. The Secretary may prescribe by regulation additional charges and credits to a multiemployer plan's funding standard account to the extent necessary to prevent withdrawal liability payments from being unduly reflected as advance funding for plan liabilities.

(B) Adjustments when a multiemployer plan leaves reorganization—If a multiemployer plan is not in reorganization in the plan year but was in reorganization in the immediately preceding plan year, any balance in the funding standard account at the close of such immediately preceding plan year—

(i) shall be eliminated by an offsetting credit or charge (as the case may be), but

(ii) shall be taken into account in subsequent plan years by being amortized in equal annual installments (until fully amortized) over 30 plan years.

The preceding sentence shall not apply to the extent of any accumulated funding deficiency under section 4243(a) of such Act as of the end of the last plan year that the plan was in reorganization.

(C) Plan payments to supplemental program or withdrawal liability payment fund—Any amount paid by a plan during a plan year to the Pension Benefit Guaranty Corporation pursuant to section 4222 of such Act or to a fund exempt under section 501(c)(22) pursuant to section 4223 of such Act shall reduce the amount of contributions considered received by the plan for the plan year.

(D) Interim withdrawal liability payments—Any amount paid by an employer pending a final determination of the employer's withdrawal liability under part 1 of subtitle E of title IV of such Act and subsequently refunded to the employer by the plan shall be charged to the funding standard account in accordance with regulations prescribed by the Secretary.

(E) Election for deferral of charge for portion of net experience loss—If an election is in effect under section 412(b)(7)(F) (as in effect on the day before the date of the enactment of the Pension Protection Act of 2006) for any plan year, the funding standard account shall be charged in the plan year to which the portion of the net experience loss deferred by such election was deferred with the amount so deferred (and paragraph (2)(B)(iii) shall not apply to the amount so charged).

(F) Financial assistance—Any amount of any financial assistance from the Pension Benefit Guaranty Corporation to any plan, and any repayment of such amount, shall be taken into account under this section and section 412 in such manner as is determined by the Secretary.

(G) Short-term benefits—To the extent that any plan amendment increases the unfunded past service liability under the plan by reason of an increase in benefits which are not payable as a life annuity but are payable under the terms of the plan for a period that does not exceed 14 years from the effective date of the amendment, paragraph (2)(B)(ii) shall be applied separately with respect to such increase in unfunded past service liability by substituting the number of years of the period during which such benefits are payable for "15".

(8) Special relief rules—Notwithstanding any other provision of this subsection—

(A) Amortization of net investment losses—

(i) In general—A multiemployer plan with respect to which the solvency test under subparagraph (C) is met may treat the portion of any experience loss or gain attributable to net investment losses incurred in either or both of the first two plan years ending after August 31, 2008, as an item separate from other experience losses, to be amortized in equal annual installments (until fully amortized) over the period—

(I) beginning with the plan year in which such portion is first recognized in the actuarial value of assets, and

(II) ending with the last plan year in the 30-plan year period beginning with the plan year in which such net investment loss was incurred.

(ii) Coordination with extensions—If this subparagraph applies for any plan year—

(I) no extension of the amortization period under clause (i) shall be allowed under subsection (d), and

(II) if an extension was granted under subsection (d) for any plan year before the election to have this subparagraph apply to the plan year, such extension shall not result in such amortization period exceeding 30 years.

(iii) Net investment losses. For purposes of this subparagraph—

(I) In general—Net investment losses shall be determined in the manner prescribed by the Secretary on the basis of the difference between actual and expected returns (including any difference attributable to any criminally fraudulent investment arrangement).

(II) Criminally fraudulent investment arrangements—The determination as to whether an arrangement is a criminally fraudulent investment arrangement shall be made under rules substantially similar to the rules prescribed by the Secretary for purposes of section 165.

(B) Expanded smoothing period—

(i) In general—A multiemployer plan with respect to which the solvency test under subparagraph (C) is met may change its asset valuation method in a manner which—

(I) spreads the difference between expected and actual returns for either or both of the first 2 plan years ending after August 31, 2008, over a period of not more than 10 years,

(II) provides that for either or both of the first 2 plan years beginning after August 31, 2008, the value of plan assets at any time shall not be less than 80 percent or greater than 130 percent of the fair market value of such assets at such time, or

(III) makes both changes described in subclauses (I) and (II) to such method.

(ii) Asset valuation methods—If this subparagraph applies for any plan year—

(I) the Secretary shall not treat the asset valuation method of the plan as unreasonable solely because of the changes in such method described in clause (i), and

(II) such changes shall be deemed approved by the Secretary under section 302(d)(1) of the Employee Retirement Income Security Act of 1974 and section 412(d)(1).

(iii) Amortization of reduction in unfunded accrued liability—If this subparagraph and subparagraph (A) both apply for any plan year, the plan shall treat any reduction in unfunded accrued liability resulting from the application of this subparagraph as a separate experience amortization base, to be amortized in equal annual installments (until fully amortized) over a period of 30 plan years rather than the period such liability would otherwise be amortized over.

(C) Solvency test—The solvency test under this paragraph is met only if the plan actuary certifies that the plan is projected to have sufficient assets to timely pay expected benefits and anticipated expenditures over the amortization period, taking into account the changes in the funding standard account under this paragraph.

(D) Restriction on benefit increases—If subparagraph (A) or (B) apply to a multiemployer plan for any plan year, then, in addition to any other applicable restrictions on benefit increases, a plan amendment increasing benefits may not go into effect during either of the 2 plan years immediately following such plan year unless—

    (i) the plan actuary certifies that—

        (I) any such increase is paid for out of additional contributions not allocated to the plan immediately before the application of this paragraph to the plan, and

        (II) the plan's funded percentage and projected credit balances for such 2 plan years are reasonably expected to be at least as high as such percentage and balances would have been if the benefit increase had not been adopted, or

    (ii) the amendment is required as a condition of qualification under part I of subchapter D or to comply with other applicable law.

(E) Reporting—A plan sponsor of a plan to which this paragraph applies shall—

    (i) give notice of such application to participants and beneficiaries of the plan, and

    (ii) inform the Pension Benefit Guaranty Corporation of such application in such form and manner as the Director of the Pension Benefit Guaranty Corporation may prescribe.

(c) Additional rules—

(1) Determinations to be made under funding method—For purposes of this part, normal costs, accrued liability, past service liabilities, and experience gains and losses shall be determined under the funding method used to determine costs under the plan.

(2) Valuation of assets—

    (A) In general—For purposes of this part, the value of the plan's assets shall be determined on the basis of any reasonable actuarial method of valuation which takes into account fair market value and which is permitted under regulations prescribed by the Secretary.

    (B) Election with respect to bonds—The value of a bond or other evidence of indebtedness which is not in default as to principal or interest may, at the election of the plan administrator, be determined on an amortized basis running from initial cost at purchase to par value at maturity or earliest call date. Any election under this subparagraph shall be made at such time and in such manner as the Secretary shall by regulations provide, shall apply to all such evidences of indebtedness, and may be revoked only with the consent of the Secretary.

(3) Actuarial assumptions must be reasonable—For purposes of this section, all costs, liabilities, rates of interest, and other factors under the plan shall be determined on the basis of actuarial assumptions and methods—

    (A) each of which is reasonable (taking into account the experience of the plan and reasonable expectations), and

(B) which, in combination, offer the actuary's best estimate of anticipated experience under the plan.

(4) Treatment of certain changes as experience gain or loss—For purposes of this section, if—

(A) a change in benefits under the Social Security Act or in other retirement benefits created under Federal or State law, or

(B) a change in the definition of the term "wages" under section 3121, or a change in the amount of such wages taken into account under regulations prescribed for purposes of section 401(a)(5),

results in an increase or decrease in accrued liability under a plan, such increase or decrease shall be treated as an experience loss or gain.

(5) Full funding—If, as of the close of a plan year, a plan would (without regard to this paragraph) have an accumulated funding deficiency in excess of the full funding limitation—

(A) the funding standard account shall be credited with the amount of such excess, and

(B) all amounts described in subparagraphs (B), (C), and (D) of subsection (b)(2) and subparagraph (B) of subsection (b)(3) which are required to be amortized shall be considered fully amortized for purposes of such subparagraphs.

(6) Full-funding limitation—

(A) In general—For purposes of paragraph (5), the term "full-funding limitation" means the excess (if any) of—

(i) the accrued liability (including normal cost) under the plan (determined under the entry age normal funding method if such accrued liability cannot be directly calculated under the funding method used for the plan), over

(ii) the lesser of—

(I) the fair market value of the plan's assets, or

(II) the value of such assets determined under paragraph (2).

(B) Minimum amount—

(i) In general—In no event shall the full-funding limitation determined under subparagraph (A) be less than the excess (if any) of—

(I) 90 percent of the current liability of the plan (including the expected increase in current liability due to benefits accruing during the plan year), over

(II) the value of the plan's assets determined under paragraph (2).

(ii) Assets—For purposes of clause (i), assets shall not be reduced by any credit balance in the funding standard account.

(C) Full funding limitation—For purposes of this paragraph, unless otherwise provided by the plan, the accrued liability under a multiemployer plan shall not include benefits which are not nonforfeitable under the plan after the termination of the plan (taking into consideration section 411(d)(3)).

(D) Current liability—For purposes of this paragraph—

(i) In general—The term "current liability" means all liabilities to employees and their beneficiaries under the plan.

(ii) Treatment of unpredictable contingent event benefits—For purposes of clause (i), any benefit contingent on an event other than—

(I) age, service, compensation, death, or disability, or

(II) an event which is reasonably and reliably predictable (as determined by the Secretary),

shall not be taken into account until the event on which the benefit is contingent occurs.

(iii) Interest rate used—The rate of interest used to determine current liability under this paragraph shall be the rate of interest determined under subparagraph (E).

(iv) Mortality tables—

(I) Commissioners' standard table—In the case of plan years beginning before the first plan year to which the first tables prescribed under subclause (II) apply, the mortality table used in determining current liability under this paragraph shall be the table prescribed by the Secretary which is based on the prevailing commissioners' standard table (described in section 807(d)(5)(A)) used to determine reserves for group annuity contracts issued on January 1, 1993.

(II) Secretarial authority—The Secretary may by regulation prescribe for plan years beginning after December 31, 1999, mortality tables to be used in determining current liability under this subsection. Such tables shall be based upon the actual experience of pension plans and projected trends in such experience. In prescribing such tables, the Secretary shall take into account results of available independent studies of mortality of individuals covered by pension plans.

(v) Separate mortality tables for the disabled—Notwithstanding clause (iv)—

(I) In general—The Secretary shall establish mortality tables which may be used (in lieu of the tables under clause (iv)) to determine current liability under this subsection for individuals who are entitled to benefits under the plan on account of disability. The Secretary shall establish separate tables for individuals whose disabilities occur in plan years beginning before January 1, 1995, and for individuals whose disabilities occur in plan years beginning on or after such date.

(II) Special rule for disabilities occurring after 1994—In the case of disabilities occurring in plan years beginning after December 31, 1994, the tables under subclause (I) shall apply only with respect to individuals described in such subclause who are disabled within the meaning of title II of the Social Security Act and the regulations thereunder.

(vi) Periodic review—The Secretary shall periodically (at least every 5 years) review any tables in effect under this subparagraph and shall, to the extent such

Secretary determines necessary, by regulation update the tables to reflect the actual experience of pension plans and projected trends in such experience.

(E) Required change of interest rate—For purposes of determining a plan's current liability for purposes of this paragraph—

    (i) In general—If any rate of interest used under the plan under subsection (b)(6) to determine cost is not within the permissible range, the plan shall establish a new rate of interest within the permissible range.

    (ii) Permissible range—For purposes of this subparagraph—

        (I) In general—Except as provided in subclause (II), the term "permissible range" means a rate of interest which is not more than 5 percent above, and not more than 10 percent below, the weighted average of the rates of interest on 30-year Treasury securities during the 4-year period ending on the last day before the beginning of the plan year.

        (II) Secretarial authority—If the Secretary finds that the lowest rate of interest permissible under subclause (I) is unreasonably high, the Secretary may prescribe a lower rate of interest, except that such rate may not be less than 80 percent of the average rate determined under such subclause.

    (iii) Assumptions—Notwithstanding paragraph (3)(A), the interest rate used under the plan shall be—

        (I) determined without taking into account the experience of the plan and reasonable expectations, but

        (II) consistent with the assumptions which reflect the purchase rates which would be used by insurance companies to satisfy the liabilities under the plan.

(7) Annual valuation—

(A) In general—For purposes of this section, a determination of experience gains and losses and a valuation of the plan's liability shall be made not less frequently than once every year, except that such determination shall be made more frequently to the extent required in particular cases under regulations prescribed by the Secretary.

(B) Valuation date—

    (i) Current year—Except as provided in clause (ii), the valuation referred to in subparagraph (A) shall be made as of a date within the plan year to which the valuation refers or within one month prior to the beginning of such year.

    (ii) Use of prior year valuation—The valuation referred to in subparagraph (A) may be made as of a date within the plan year prior to the year to which the valuation refers if, as of such date, the value of the assets of the plan are not less than 100 percent of the plan's current liability (as defined in paragraph (6)(D) without regard to clause (iv) thereof).

    (iii) Adjustments—Information under clause (ii) shall, in accordance with regulations, be actuarially adjusted to reflect significant differences in participants.

    (iv) Limitation—A change in funding method to use a prior year valuation, as provided in clause (ii), may not be made unless as of the valuation date within the prior plan year, the value of the assets of the plan are not less than 125 percent of the plan's current liability (as defined in paragraph (6)(D) without regard to clause (iv) thereof).

(8) Time when certain contributions deemed made—For purposes of this section, any contributions for a plan year made by an employer after the last day of such plan year, but not later than two and one-half months after such day, shall be deemed to have been made on such last day. For purposes of this subparagraph, such two and one-half month period may be extended for not more than six months under regulations prescribed by the Secretary.

(d) Extension of amortization periods for multiemployer plans—

(1) Automatic extension upon application by certain plans—

(A) In general—If the plan sponsor of a multiemployer plan—

(i) submits to the Secretary an application for an extension of the period of years required to amortize any unfunded liability described in any clause of subsection (b)(2)(B) or described in subsection (b)(4), and

(ii) includes with the application a certification by the plan's actuary described in subparagraph (B),

the Secretary shall extend the amortization period for the period of time (not in excess of 5 years) specified in the application. Such extension shall be in addition to any extension under paragraph (2).

(B) Criteria—A certification with respect to a multiemployer plan is described in this subparagraph if the plan's actuary certifies that, based on reasonable assumptions—

(i) absent the extension under subparagraph (A), the plan would have an accumulated funding deficiency in the current plan year or any of the 9 succeeding plan years,

(ii) the plan sponsor has adopted a plan to improve the plan's funding status,

(iii) the plan is projected to have sufficient assets to timely pay expected benefits and anticipated expenditures over the amortization period as extended, and

(iv) the notice required under paragraph (3)(A) has been provided.

(C) [Repealed]

(2) Alternative extension—

(A) In general—If the plan sponsor of a multiemployer plan submits to the Secretary an application for an extension of the period of years required to amortize any unfunded liability described in any clause of subsection (b)(2)(B) or described in subsection (b)(4), the Secretary may extend the amortization period for a period of time (not in excess of 10 years reduced by the number of years of any extension under paragraph (1) with respect to such unfunded liability) if the Secretary makes the determination described in subparagraph (B). Such extension shall be in addition to any extension under paragraph (1).

(B) Determination—The Secretary may grant an extension under subparagraph (A) if the Secretary determines that—

(i) such extension would carry out the purposes of this Act and would provide adequate protection for participants under the plan and their beneficiaries, and

(ii) the failure to permit such extension would—

(I) result in a substantial risk to the voluntary continuation of the plan, or a substantial curtailment of pension benefit levels or employee compensation, and

(II) be adverse to the interests of plan participants in the aggregate.

(C) Action by secretary—The Secretary shall act upon any application for an extension under this paragraph within 180 days of the submission of such application. If the Secretary rejects the application for an extension under this paragraph, the Secretary shall provide notice to the plan detailing the specific reasons for the rejection, including references to the criteria set forth above.

(3) Advance notice—

(A) In general—The Secretary shall, before granting an extension under this subsection, require each applicant to provide evidence satisfactory to such Secretary that the applicant has provided notice of the filing of the application for such extension to each affected party (as defined in section 4001(a)(21) of the Employee Retirement Income Security Act of 1974) with respect to the affected plan. Such notice shall include a description of the extent to which the plan is funded for benefits which are guaranteed under title IV of such Act and for benefit liabilities.

(B) Consideration of relevant information—The Secretary shall consider any relevant information provided by a person to whom notice was given under paragraph (1)

§ 432. Additional funding rules for multiemployer plans in endangered status or critical status.

(a) General rule—For purposes of this part, in the case of a multiemployer plan in effect on July 16, 2006—

(1) if the plan is in endangered status—

(A) the plan sponsor shall adopt and implement a funding improvement plan in accordance with the requirements of subsection (c), and

(B) the requirements of subsection (d) shall apply during the funding plan adoption period and the funding improvement period,

(2) if the plan is in critical status—

(A) the plan sponsor shall adopt and implement a rehabilitation plan in accordance with the requirements of subsection (e), and

(B) the requirements of subsection (f) shall apply during the rehabilitation plan adoption period and the rehabilitation period, and

(3) If the plan is in critical and declining status—

(A) the requirements of paragraph (2) shall apply to the plan; and

(B) the plan sponsor may, by plan amendment, suspend benefits in accordance with the requirements of subsection (e)(9).

(b) Determination of endangered and critical status—For purposes of this section—

(1) Endangered status—A multiemployer plan is in endangered status for a plan year if, as determined by the plan actuary under paragraph (3), the plan is not in critical status for the plan year and is not described in paragraph (5), and, as of the beginning of the plan year, either—

    (A) the plan's funded percentage for such plan year is less than 80 percent, or

    (B) the plan has an accumulated funding deficiency for such plan year, or is projected to have such an accumulated funding deficiency for any of the 6 succeeding plan years, taking into account any extension of amortization periods under section 431(d).

For purposes of this section, a plan shall be treated as in seriously endangered status for a plan year if the plan is described in both subparagraphs (A) and (B).

(2) Critical status—A multiemployer plan is in critical status for a plan year if, as determined by the plan actuary under paragraph (3), the plan is described in 1 or more of the following subparagraphs as of the beginning of the plan year:

    (A) A plan is described in this subparagraph if—

        (i) the funded percentage of the plan is less than 65 percent, and

        (ii) the sum of—

            (I) the fair market value of plan assets, plus

            (II) the present value of the reasonably anticipated employer contributions for the current plan year and each of the 6 succeeding plan years, assuming that the terms of all collective bargaining agreements pursuant to which the plan is maintained for the current plan year continue in effect for succeeding plan years,

is less than the present value of all nonforfeitable benefits projected to be payable under the plan during the current plan year and each of the 6 succeeding plan years (plus administrative expenses for such plan years).

    (B) A plan is described in this subparagraph if—

        (i) the plan has an accumulated funding deficiency for the current plan year, not taking into account any extension of amortization periods under section 431(d), or

        (ii) the plan is projected to have an accumulated funding deficiency for any of the 3 succeeding plan years (4 succeeding plan years if the funded percentage of the plan is 65 percent or less), not taking into account any extension of amortization periods under section 431(d).

    (C) A plan is described in this subparagraph if—

        (i)(I) the plan's normal cost for the current plan year, plus interest (determined at the rate used for determining costs under the plan) for the current plan year on the amount of unfunded benefit liabilities under the plan as of the last date of the preceding plan year, exceeds

            (II) the present value of the reasonably anticipated employer and employee contributions for the current plan year,

(ii) the present value, as of the beginning of the current plan year, of nonforfeitable benefits of inactive participants is greater than the present value of nonforfeitable benefits of active participants, and

(iii) the plan has an accumulated funding deficiency for the current plan year, or is projected to have such a deficiency for any of the 4 succeeding plan years, not taking into account any extension of amortization periods under section 431(d).

(D) A plan is described in this subparagraph if the sum of—

(i) the fair market value of plan assets, plus

(ii) the present value of the reasonably anticipated employer contributions for the current plan year and each of the 4 succeeding plan years, assuming that the terms of all collective bargaining agreements pursuant to which the plan is maintained for the current plan year continue in effect for succeeding plan years,

is less than the present value of all benefits projected to be payable under the plan during the current plan year and each of the 4 succeeding plan years (plus administrative expenses for such plan years).

* * *

(6) Critical and Declining Status—For purposes of this section, a plan in critical status shall be treated as in critical and declining status if the plan is described in one or more of subparagraphs (A), (B), (C), and (D) or paragraph (2) and the plan is projected to become insolvent within the meaning of section 418E during the current plan year or any of the 14 succeeding plan years (19 succeeding plan years if the plan has a ratio of inactive participants to active participants that exceeds 2 to 1 or if the funded percentage of the plan is less than 80 percent).

* * *

(e) Rehabilitation plan must be adopted for multiemployer plans in critical status—

* * *

(9) Benefit suspensions for multiemployer plans in critical and declining status—

(A) In general—Notwithstanding section 411(d)(6) and subject to paragraphs (B) through (I), the plan sponsor of a plan in critical and declining status may, by plan amendment, suspend benefits which the sponsor deems appropriate.

(B) Suspension of benefits—

(i) Suspension of benefits defined—For purposes of this subsection, the term 'suspension of benefits' means the temporary or permanent reduction of any current or future payment obligation of the plan to any participant or beneficiary under the plan, whether or not in pay status at the time of the suspension of benefits.

(ii) Length of suspensions—Any suspension of benefits made under subparagraph (A) shall remain in effect until the earlier of when the plan sponsor provides benefit improvements in accordance with subparagraph (E) or the suspension of benefits expires by its own terms.

(iii) No liability—The plan shall not be liable for any benefit payments not made as a result of a suspension of benefits under this paragraph.

* * *

(C) Conditions for suspensions—The plan sponsor of a plan in critical and declining status for a plan year may suspend benefits only if the following conditions are met:

(i) Taking into account the proposed suspensions of benefits (and, if applicable, a proposed partition of the plan under section 4233 of the Employee Retirement Income Security Act of 1974), the plan actuary certifies that the plan is projected to avoid insolvency within the meaning of section 418E, assuming the suspensions of benefits continue until the suspensions of benefits expire by their own terms or if no such expiration date is set, indefinitely.

(ii) The plan sponsor determines, in a written record to be maintained throughout the period of the benefit suspension, that the plan is still projected to become insolvent unless benefits are suspended under this paragraph, although all reasonable measures to avoid insolvency have been taken (and continue to be taken during the period of the benefit suspension). In its determination, the plan sponsor may take into account factors including the following:

(I) Current and past contribution levels.

(II) Levels of benefit accruals (including any prior reductions in the rate of benefit accruals).

(III) Prior reductions (if any) of adjustable benefits.

(IV) Prior suspensions (if any) of benefits under this subsection.

(V) The impact on plan solvency of the subsidies and ancillary benefits available to active participants.

(VI) Compensation levels of active participants relative to employees in the participants' industry generally.

(VII) Competitive and other economic factors facing contributing employers.

(VIII) The impact of benefit and contribution levels on retaining active participants and bargaining groups under the plan.

(IX) The impact of past and anticipated contribution increases under the plan on employer attrition and retention levels.

(X) Measures undertaken by the plan sponsor to retain or attract contributing employers.

(D) Limitations on suspensions—Any suspensions of benefits made by a plan sponsor pursuant to this paragraph shall be subject to the following limitations:

(i) The monthly benefit of any participant or beneficiary may not be reduced below 110 percent of the monthly benefit which is guaranteed by the Pension Benefit Guaranty Corporation under section 4022A of the Employee Retirement Income Security Act of 1974 on the date of the suspension.

(ii)(I) In the case of a participant or beneficiary who has attained 75 years of age as of the effective date of the suspension, not more than the applicable percentage of the maximum suspendable benefits of such participant or beneficiary may be suspended under this paragraph.

(II) For purposes of subclause (I), the maximum suspendable benefits of a participant or beneficiary is the portion of the benefits of such participant or beneficiary that would be suspended pursuant to this paragraph without regard to this clause;

(III) For purposes of subclause (I), the applicable percentage is a percentage equal to the quotient obtained by dividing--

(aa) the number of months during the period beginning with the month after the month in which occurs the effective date of the suspension and ending with the month during which the participant or beneficiary attains the age of 80, by

(bb) 60 months.

(iii) No benefits based on disability (as defined under the plan) may be suspended under this paragraph.

(iv) Any suspensions of benefits, in the aggregate (and, if applicable, considered in combination with a partition of the plan under section 4233 of the Employee Retirement Income Security Act of 1974), shall be reasonably estimated to achieve, but not materially exceed, the level that is necessary to avoid insolvency.

(v) In any case in which a suspension of benefits with respect to a plan is made in combination with a partition of the plan under section 4233 of the Employee Retirement Income Security Act of 1974, the suspension of benefits may not take effect prior to the effective date of such partition.

(vi) Any suspensions of benefits shall be equitably distributed across the participant and beneficiary population, taking into account factors, with respect to participants and beneficiaries and their benefits, that may include one or more of the following:

(I) Age and life expectancy.

(II) Length of time in pay status.

(III) Amount of benefit.

(IV) Type of benefit: survivor, normal retirement, early retirement.

(V) Extent to which participant or beneficiary is receiving a subsidized benefit.

(VI) Extent to which participant or beneficiary has received post-retirement benefit increases.

(VII) History of benefit increases and reductions.

(VIII) Years to retirement for active employees.

(IX) Any discrepancies between active and retiree benefits.

(X) Extent to which active participants are reasonably likely to withdraw support for the plan, accelerating employer withdrawals from the plan and increasing the risk of additional benefit reductions for participants in and out of pay status.

(XI) Extent to which benefits are attributed to service with an employer that failed to pay its full withdrawal liability.

* * *

(F) Notice requirements—

(i) In general—No suspension of benefits may be made pursuant to this paragraph unless notice of such proposed suspension has been given by the plan sponsor concurrently with an application for approval of such suspension submitted under subparagraph (G) to the Secretary of the Treasury to—

(I) such plan participants and beneficiaries who may be contacted by reasonable efforts,

(II) each employer who has an obligation to contribute (within the meaning of section 4212(a) of the Employee Retirement Income Security Act of 1974) under the plan, and

(III) each employee organization which, for purposes of collective bargaining, represents plan participants employed by such an employer.

(ii) Content of notice—The notice under clause (i) shall contain--

(I) sufficient information to enable participants and beneficiaries to understand the effect of any suspensions of benefits, including an individualized estimate (on an annual or monthly basis) of such effect on each participant or beneficiary,

(II) a description of the factors considered by the plan sponsor in designing the benefit suspensions,

(III) a statement that the application for approval of any suspension of benefits shall be available on the website of the Department of the Treasury and that comments on such application will be accepted,

(IV) information as to the rights and remedies of plan participants and beneficiaries,

(V) if applicable, a statement describing the appointment of a retiree representative, the date of appointment of such representative, identifying information about the retiree representative (including whether the representative is a plan trustee), and how to contact such representative, and

(VI) information on how to contact the Department of the Treasury for further information and assistance where appropriate.

(iii) Form and manner—Any notice under clause (i)—

(I) shall be provided in a form and manner prescribed in guidance by the Secretary of the Treasury, in consultation with the Pension Benefit Guaranty Corporation and the Secretary of Labor, notwithstanding any other provision of law,

(II) shall be written in a manner so as to be understood by the average plan participant, and

(III) may be provided in written, electronic, or other appropriate form to the extent such form is reasonably accessible to persons to whom the notice is required to be provided.

(iv) Other notice requirement—Any notice provided under clause (i) shall fulfill the requirement for notice of a significant reduction in benefits described in section 4980F.

(v) Model notice—The Secretary of the Treasury, in consultation with the Pension Benefit Guaranty Corporation and the Secretary of Labor, shall in the guidance prescribed under clause (iii)(I) establish a model notice that a plan sponsor may use to meet the requirements of this subparagraph.

(G) Approval process by the Secretary of the Treasury in consultation with the Pension Benefit Guaranty Corporation and the Secretary of Labor—

(i) In general—The plan sponsor of a plan in critical and declining status for a plan year that seeks to suspend benefits must submit an application to the Secretary of the Treasury for approval of the suspensions of benefits. If the plan sponsor submits an application for approval of the suspensions, the Secretary of the Treasury shall approve, in consultation with the Pension Benefit Guaranty Corporation and the Secretary of Labor, the application upon finding that the plan is eligible for the suspensions and has satisfied the criteria of subparagraphs (C), (D), (E), and (F).

(ii) Solicitation of comments—Not later than 30 days after receipt of the application under clause (i), the Secretary of the Treasury, in consultation with the Pension Benefit Guaranty Corporation and the Secretary of Labor, shall publish a notice in the Federal Register soliciting comments from contributing employers, employee organizations, and participants and beneficiaries of the plan for which an application was made and other interested parties. The application for approval of the suspension of benefits shall be published on the website of the Department of the Treasury.

(iii) Required action; deemed approval—The Secretary of the Treasury, in consultation with the Pension Benefit Guaranty Corporation and the Secretary of Labor, shall approve or deny any application for suspensions of benefits under this paragraph within 225 days after the submission of such application. An application for suspension of benefits shall be deemed approved unless, within such 225 days, the Secretary of the Treasury notifies the plan sponsor that it has failed to satisfy one or more of the criteria described in this paragraph. If the Secretary of the Treasury, in consultation with the Pension Benefit Guaranty Corporation and the Secretary of Labor, rejects a plan sponsor's application, the Secretary of the Treasury shall provide notice to the plan sponsor detailing the specific reasons for the rejection, including reference to the specific requirement not satisfied. Approval or denial by the Secretary of the Treasury, in consultation with the Pension Benefit Guaranty Corporation and the Secretary of Labor, of an application shall be treated as final agency action for purposes of section 704 of title 5, United States Code.

(iv) Agency review—In evaluating whether the plan sponsor has met the criteria specified in clause (ii) of subparagraph (C), the Secretary of the Treasury, in consultation with the Pension Benefit Guaranty Corporation and the Secretary of Labor, shall review the plan sponsor's consideration of factors under such clause.

(v) Standard for accepting plan sponsor determinations—In evaluating the plan sponsor's application, the Secretary of the Treasury shall accept the plan sponsor's determinations unless it concludes, in consultation with the Pension Benefit Guaranty Corporation and the Secretary of Labor, that the plan sponsor's determinations were clearly erroneous.

(H) Participant ratification process—

(i) In general—No suspension of benefits may take effect pursuant to this paragraph prior to a vote of the participants of the plan with respect to the suspension.

(ii) Administration of vote—Not later than 30 days after approval of the suspension by the Secretary of the Treasury, in consultation with the Pension Benefit Guaranty Corporation and the Secretary of Labor, under subparagraph (G), the Secretary of the Treasury, in consultation with the Pension Benefit Guaranty Corporation and the Secretary of Labor, shall administer a vote of participants and beneficiaries of the plan. Except as provided in clause (v), the suspension shall go into effect following the vote unless a majority of all participants and beneficiaries of the plan vote to reject the suspension. The plan sponsor may submit a new suspension application to the Secretary of the Treasury for approval in any case in which a suspension is prohibited from taking effect pursuant to a vote under this subparagraph.

(iii) Ballots—The plan sponsor shall provide a ballot for the vote (subject to approval by the Secretary of the Treasury, in consultation with the Pension Benefit Guaranty Corporation and the Secretary of Labor) that includes the following:

(I) A statement from the plan sponsor in support of the suspension.

(II) A statement in opposition to the suspension compiled from comments received pursuant to subparagraph (G)(ii).

(III) A statement that the suspension has been approved by the Secretary of the Treasury, in consultation with the Pension Benefit Guaranty Corporation and the Secretary of Labor.

(IV) A statement that the plan sponsor has determined that the plan will become insolvent unless the suspension takes effect.

(V) A statement that insolvency of the plan could result in benefits lower than benefits paid under the suspension.

(VI) A statement that insolvency of the Pension Benefit Guaranty Corporation would result in benefits lower than benefits paid in the case of plan insolvency.

(iv) Communication by plan sponsor—It is the sense of Congress that, depending on the size and resources of the plan and geographic distribution of the plan's participants, the plan sponsor should take such steps as may be necessary to inform participants about proposed benefit suspensions through in-person meetings, telephone or internet-based communications, mailed information, or by other means.

(v) Systemically important plans—

(I) In general—Not later than 14 days after a vote under this subparagraph rejecting a suspension, the Secretary of the Treasury, in consultation with the Pension Benefit Guaranty Corporation and the Secretary of Labor, shall determine whether the plan is a systemically important plan. If the Secretary of the Treasury, in consultation with the Pension Benefit Guaranty Corporation and the Secretary of Labor, determines that the plan is a systemically important plan, not later than the end of the 90-day period beginning on the date the results of the vote are certified, the Secretary of the Treasury shall, notwithstanding such adverse vote--

(aa) permit the implementation of the suspension proposed by the plan sponsor; or

(bb) permit the implementation of a modification by the Secretary of the Treasury, in consultation with the Pension Benefit Guaranty Corporation and the Secretary of Labor, of such suspension (so long as the plan is projected to avoid insolvency within the meaning of section 4245 of the Employee Retirement Income Security Act of 1974 under such modification).

(II) Recommendations—Not later than 30 days after a determination by the Secretary of the Treasury, in consultation with the Pension Benefit Guaranty Corporation and the Secretary of Labor, that the plan is systemically important, the Participant and Plan Sponsor Advocate selected under section 4004 of the Employee Retirement Income Security Act of 1974 may submit recommendations to the Secretary of the Treasury with respect to the suspension or any revisions to the suspension.

(III) Systemically important plan defined—

(aa) In general—For purposes of this subparagraph, a systemically important plan is a plan with respect to which the Pension Benefit Guaranty Corporation projects the present value of projected financial assistance payments exceeds $1,000,000,000 if suspensions are not implemented.

(bb) Indexing—For calendar years beginning after 2015, there shall be substituted for the dollar amount specified in item (aa) an amount equal to the product of such dollar amount and a fraction, the numerator of which is the contribution and benefit base (determined under section 230 of the Social Security Act [42 USCS § 430]) for the preceding calendar year and the denominator of which is such contribution and benefit base for calendar year 2014. If the amount otherwise determined under this item is not a multiple of $1,000,000, such amount shall be rounded to the next lowest multiple of $1,000,000.

(vi) Final authorization to suspend—In any case in which a suspension goes into effect following a vote pursuant to clause (ii) (or following a determination under clause (v) that the plan is a systemically important plan), the Secretary of the Treasury, in consultation with the Pension Benefit Guaranty Corporation and the Secretary of Labor, shall issue a final authorization to suspend with respect to the suspension not later than 7 days after such vote (or, in the case of a suspension that goes into effect under clause (v), at a time sufficient to allow the implementation of the suspension prior to the end of the 90-day period described in clause (v)(I)).

(I) Judicial review—

(i) Denial of application—An action by the plan sponsor challenging the denial of an application for suspension of benefits by the Secretary of the Treasury, in consultation with the Pension Benefit Guaranty Corporation and the Secretary of Labor, may only be brought following such denial.

(ii) Approval of suspension of benefits—

(I) Timing of action—An action challenging a suspension of benefits under this paragraph may only be brought following a final authorization to suspend by the Secretary of the Treasury, in consultation with the Pension Benefit Guaranty Corporation and the Secretary of Labor, under subparagraph (H)(vi).

(II) Standards of review—

(aa) In general—A court shall review an action challenging a suspension of benefits under this paragraph in accordance with section 706 of title 5, United States Code.

(bb) Temporary injunction—A court reviewing an action challenging a suspension of benefits under this paragraph may not grant a temporary injunction with respect to such suspension unless the court finds a clear and convincing likelihood that the plaintiff will prevail on the merits of the case.

(iii) Restricted cause of action—A participant or beneficiary affected by a benefit suspension under this paragraph shall not have a cause of action under this title.

(iv) Limitation on action to suspend benefits—No action challenging a suspension of benefits following the final authorization to suspend or the denial of an application for suspension of benefits pursuant to this paragraph may be brought after one year after the earliest date on which the plaintiff acquired or should have acquired actual knowledge of the existence of such cause of action.

(J) Special rule for emergence from critical status—A plan certified to be in critical and declining status pursuant to projections made under subsection (b)(3) for which a suspension of benefits has been made by the plan sponsor pursuant to this paragraph shall not emerge from critical status under paragraph (4)(B), until such time as--

(i) the plan is no longer certified to be in critical or endangered status under paragraphs (1) and (2) of subsection (b), and

(ii) the plan is projected to avoid insolvency under section 418E.

* * *

§ 433. Minimum funding standards.

(a) General rule—For purposes of section 412, the term "accumulated funding deficiency" for a CSEC plan means the excess of the total charges to the funding standard account for all plan years (beginning with the first plan year to which section 412 applies) over the total credits to such account for such years or, if less, the excess of the total charges to the alternative minimum funding standard account for such plan years over the total credits to such account for such years.

(b) Funding standard account—

(1) Account required—Each plan to which this section applies shall establish and maintain a funding standard account. Such account shall be credited and charged solely as provided in this section.

(2) Charges to account—For a plan year, the funding standard account shall be charged with the sum of—

(A) the normal cost of the plan for the plan year,

(B) the amounts necessary to amortize in equal annual installments (until fully amortized)—

(i) in the case of a plan in existence on January 1, 1974, the unfunded past service liability under the plan on the first day of the first plan year to which section 412 applies, over a period of 40 plan years,

(ii) in the case of a plan which comes into existence after January 1, 1974, but before the first day of the first plan year beginning after December 31, 2013, the unfunded past service liability under the plan on the first day of the first plan year to which section 412 applies, over a period of 30 plan years,

(iii) separately, with respect to each plan year, the net increase (if any) in unfunded past service liability under the plan arising from plan amendments adopted in such year, over a period of 15 plan years,

(iv) separately, with respect to each plan year, the net experience loss (if any) under the plan, over a period of 5 plan years, and

(v) separately, with respect to each plan year, the net loss (if any) resulting from changes in actuarial assumptions used under the plan, over a period of 10 plan years,

(C) the amount necessary to amortize each waived funding deficiency (within the meaning of section 412(c)(3)) for each prior plan year in equal annual installments (until fully amortized) over a period of 5 plan years,

(D) the amount necessary to amortize in equal annual installments (until fully amortized) over a period of 5 plan years any amount credited to the funding standard account under paragraph (3)(D), and

(E) the amount necessary to amortize in equal annual installments (until fully amortized) over a period of 20 years the contributions which would be required to be made under the plan but for the provisions of section 412(c)(7)(A)(i)(I) (as in effect on the day before the enactment of the Pension Protection Act of 2006 [enacted Aug. 17, 2006]).

(3) Credits to account—For a plan year, the funding standard account shall be credited with the sum of—

(A) the amount considered contributed by the employer to or under the plan for the plan year,

(B) the amount necessary to amortize in equal annual installments (until fully amortized)—

(i) separately, with respect to each plan year, the net decrease (if any) in unfunded past service liability under the plan arising from plan amendments adopted in such year, over a period of 15 plan years,

(ii) separately, with respect to each plan year, the net experience gain (if any) under the plan, over a period of 5 plan years, and

(iii) separately, with respect to each plan year, the net gain (if any) resulting from changes in actuarial assumptions used under the plan, over a period of 10 plan years,

(C) the amount of the waived funding deficiency (within the meaning of section 412(c)(3)) for the plan year, and

(D) in the case of a plan year for which the accumulated funding deficiency is determined under the funding standard account if such plan year follows a plan year for which such deficiency was determined under the alternative minimum funding standard, the excess (if any) of any debit balance in the funding standard account (determined without regard to this subparagraph) over any debit balance in the alternative minimum funding standard account.

(4) Combining and offsetting amounts to be amortized—Under regulations prescribed by the Secretary, amounts required to be amortized under paragraph (2) or paragraph (3), as the case may be—

(A) may be combined into one amount under such paragraph to be amortized over a period determined on the basis of the remaining amortization period for all items entering into such combined amount, and

(B) may be offset against amounts required to be amortized under the other such paragraph, with the resulting amount to be amortized over a period determined on the basis of the remaining amortization periods for all items entering into whichever of the two amounts being offset is the greater.

(5) Interest—

(A) In general—Except as provided in subparagraph (B), the funding standard account (and items therein) shall be charged or credited (as determined under regulations prescribed by the Secretary) with interest at the appropriate rate consistent with the rate or rates of interest used under the plan to determine costs.

(B) Exception—The interest rate used for purposes of computing the amortization charge described in subsection (b)(2)(C) or for purposes of any arrangement under subsection (d) for any plan year shall be the greater of—

(i) 150 percent of the Federal mid-term rate (as in effect under section 1274 for the 1st month of such plan year), or

(ii) the rate of interest determined under subparagraph (A).

(6) Amortization schedules in effect—Amortization schedules for amounts described in paragraphs (2) and (3) that are in effect as of the last day of the last plan year beginning before January 1, 2014, by reason of section 104 of the Pension Protection Act of 2006 [26 USCS § 401 note] shall remain in effect pursuant to their terms and this section, except that such amounts shall not be amortized again under this section.

(c) Special rules—

(1) Determinations to be made under funding method—For purposes of this section, normal costs, accrued liability, past service liabilities, and experience gains and losses shall be determined under the funding method used to determine costs under the plan.

(2) Valuation of assets—

(A) In general—For purposes of this section, the value of the plan's assets shall be determined on the basis of any reasonable actuarial method of valuation which takes into account fair market value and which is permitted under regulations prescribed by the Secretary.

(B) Dedicated bond portfolio—The Secretary may by regulations provide that the value of any dedicated bond portfolio of a plan shall be determined by using the interest rate under section 412(b)(5) (as in effect on the day before the enactment of the Pension Protection Act of 2006 [enacted Aug. 17, 2006]).

(3) Actuarial assumptions must be reasonable—For purposes of this section, all costs, liabilities, rates of interest, and other factors under the plan shall be determined on the basis of actuarial assumptions and methods—

(A) each of which is reasonable (taking into account the experience of the plan and reasonable expectations), and

(B) which, in combination, offer the actuary's best estimate of anticipated experience under the plan.

(4) Treatment of certain changes as experience gain or loss—For purposes of this section, if—

(A) a change in benefits under the Social Security Act or in other retirement benefits created under Federal or State law, or

(B) a change in the definition of the term "wages" under section 3121 or a change in the amount of such wages taken into account under regulations prescribed for purposes of section 401(a)(5),

results in an increase or decrease in accrued liability under a plan, such increase or decrease shall be treated as an experience loss or gain.

(5) Funding method and plan year—

(A) Funding methods available—All funding methods available to CSEC plans under section 412 (as in effect on the day before the enactment of the Pension Protection Act of 2006 [enacted Aug. 17, 2006]) shall continue to be available under this section.

(B) Changes—If the funding method for a plan is changed, the new funding method shall become the funding method used to determine costs and liabilities under the plan only if the change is approved by the Secretary. If the plan year for a plan is changed, the new plan year shall become the plan year for the plan only if the change is approved by the Secretary.

(C) Approval required for certain changes in assumptions by certain single-employer plans subject to additional funding requirement—

(i) In general—No actuarial assumption (other than the assumptions described in subsection (h)(3)) used to determine the current liability for a plan to which this subparagraph applies may be changed without the approval of the Secretary.

(ii) Plans to which subparagraph applies—This subparagraph shall apply to a plan only if—

(I) the plan is a CSEC plan,

(II) the aggregate unfunded vested benefits as of the close of the preceding plan year (as determined under section 4006(a)(3)(E)(iii) of the Employee Retirement Income Security Act of 1974) [29 U.S.C.A. § 1306(a)(3)(E)(iii)] of such plan and all other plans maintained by the contributing sponsors (as defined in section 4001(a)(13) of such Act [29 U.S.C.A. § 1301(a)(13)]) and members of such sponsors' controlled groups (as defined in section 4001(a)(14) of such Act [29 U.S.C.A. § 1301(a)(14)]) which are covered by title IV [29 U.S.C.A. §§ 1301 et seq.] (disregarding plans with no unfunded vested benefits) exceed $50,000,000, and

(III) the change in assumptions (determined after taking into account any changes in interest rate and mortality table) results in a decrease in the funding shortfall of the plan for the current plan year that exceeds $50,000,000, or that exceeds $5,000,000 and that is 5 percent or more of the current liability of the plan before such change.

(6) Full funding—If, as of the close of a plan year, a plan would (without regard to this paragraph) have an accumulated funding deficiency (determined without regard to the alternative minimum funding standard account permitted under subsection (e)) in excess of the full funding limitation—

(A) the funding standard account shall be credited with the amount of such excess, and

(B) all amounts described in paragraphs (2)(B), (C), and (D) and (3)(B) of subsection (b) which are required to be amortized shall be considered fully amortized for purposes of such paragraphs.

(7) Full-funding limitation—For purposes of paragraph (6), the term "full-funding limitation" means the excess (if any) of—

(A) the accrued liability (including normal cost) under the plan (determined under the entry age normal funding method if such accrued liability cannot be directly calculated under the funding method used for the plan), over

(B) the lesser of—

(i) the fair market value of the plan's assets, or

(ii) the value of such assets determined under paragraph (2).

(C) Minimum amount—

(i) In general—In no event shall the full-funding limitation determined under subparagraph (A) be less than the excess (if any) of—

(I) 90 percent of the current liability (determined without regard to paragraph (4) of subsection (h)) of the plan (including the expected increase in such current liability due to benefits accruing during the plan year), over

(II) the value of the plan's assets determined under paragraph (2).

(ii) Assets—For purposes of clause (i), assets shall not be reduced by any credit balance in the funding standard account.

(8) Annual valuation—

(A) In general—For purposes of this section, a determination of experience gains and losses and a valuation of the plan's liability shall be made not less frequently than once every year, except that such determination shall be made more frequently to the extent required in particular cases under regulations prescribed by the Secretary.

(B) Valuation date—

(i) Current year—Except as provided in clause (ii), the valuation referred to in subparagraph (A) shall be made as of a date within the plan year to which the valuation refers or within one month prior to the beginning of such year.

(ii) Use of prior year valuation—The valuation referred to in subparagraph (A) may be made as of a date within the plan year prior to the year to which the valuation refers if, as of such date, the value of the assets of the plan are not less than 100 percent of the plan's current liability.

(iii) Adjustments—Information under clause (ii) shall, in accordance with regulations, be actuarially adjusted to reflect significant differences in participants.

(iv) Limitation—A change in funding method to use a prior year valuation, as provided in clause (ii), may not be made unless as of the valuation date within the prior plan year, the value of the assets of the plan are not less than 125 percent of the plan's current liability.

(9) Time when certain contributions deemed made—For purposes of this section, any contributions for a plan year made by an employer during the period—

(A) beginning on the day after the last day of such plan year, and

(B) ending on the day which is 8 1/2 months after the close of the plan year,

shall be deemed to have been made on such last day.

(10) Anticipation of benefit increases effective in the future—In determining projected benefits, the funding method of a collectively bargained CSEC plan described in section 413(a) shall anticipate benefit increases scheduled to take effect during the term of the collective bargaining agreement applicable to the plan.

(d) Extension of amortization periods—The period of years required to amortize any unfunded liability (described in any clause of subsection (b)(2)(B)) of any plan may be extended by the Secretary for a period of time (not in excess of 10 years) if the Secretary determines that such extension would carry out the purposes of the Employee Retirement Income Security Act of 1974 and provide adequate protection for participants under the plan and their beneficiaries, and if the Secretary determines that the failure to permit such extension would result in—

(1) a substantial risk to the voluntary continuation of the plan, or

(2) a substantial curtailment of pension benefit levels or employee compensation.

(e) Alternative minimum funding standard—

(1) In general—A CSEC plan which uses a funding method that requires contributions in all years not less than those required under the entry age normal funding method may maintain an alternative minimum funding standard account for any plan year. Such account shall be credited and charged solely as provided in this subsection.

(2) Charges and credits to account—For a plan year the alternative minimum funding standard account shall be—

(A) charged with the sum of—

    (i) the lesser of normal cost under the funding method used under the plan or normal cost determined under the unit credit method,

    (ii) the excess, if any, of the present value of accrued benefits under the plan over the fair market value of the assets, and

    (iii) an amount equal to the excess (if any) of credits to the alternative minimum standard account for all prior plan years over charges to such account for all such years, and

(B) credited with the amount considered contributed by the employer to or under the plan for the plan year.

(3) Interest—The alternative minimum funding standard account (and items therein) shall be charged or credited with interest in the manner provided under subsection (b)(5) with respect to the funding standard account.

(f) Quarterly contributions required—

(1) In general—If a CSEC plan which has a funded current liability percentage for the preceding plan year of less than 100 percent fails to pay the full amount of a required installment for the plan year, then the rate of interest charged to the funding standard account under subsection (b)(5) with respect to the amount of the underpayment for the period of the underpayment shall be equal to the greater of—

(A) 175 percent of the Federal mid-term rate (as in effect under section 1274 for the 1st month of such plan year), or

(B) the rate of interest used under the plan in determining costs.

(2) Amount of underpayment, period of underpayment—For purposes of paragraph (1)—

(A) Amount—The amount of the underpayment shall be the excess of—

    (i) the required installment, over

    (ii) the amount (if any) of the installment contributed to or under the plan on or before the due date for the installment.

(B) Period of underpayment—The period for which interest is charged under this subsection with regard to any portion of the underpayment shall run from the due date for the installment to the date on which such portion is contributed to or under the plan (determined without regard to subsection (c)(9)).

(C) Order of crediting contributions—For purposes of subparagraph (A)(ii), contributions shall be credited against unpaid required installments in the order in which such installments are required to be paid.

(3) Number of required installments; due dates—For purposes of this subsection—

(A) Payable in 4 installments—There shall be 4 required installments for each plan year.

(B) Time for payment of installments—

In the case of the following required installments—	The due date is—
1st	April 15
2nd	July 15
3rd	October 15
4th	January 15 of the following year.

(4) Amount of required installment—For purposes of this subsection—

(A) In general—The amount of any required installment shall be 25 percent of the required annual payment.

(B) Required annual payment—For purposes of subparagraph (A), the term "required annual payment" means the lesser of—

(i) 90 percent of the amount required to be contributed to or under the plan by the employer for the plan year under section 412 (without regard to any waiver under subsection (c) thereof), or

(ii) 100 percent of the amount so required for the preceding plan year.

Clause (ii) shall not apply if the preceding plan year was not a year of 12 months.

(5) Liquidity requirement—

(A) In general—A plan to which this paragraph applies shall be treated as failing to pay the full amount of any required installment to the extent that the value of the liquid assets paid in such installment is less than the liquidity shortfall (whether or not such liquidity shortfall exceeds the amount of such installment required to be paid but for this paragraph).

(B) Plans to which paragraph applies—This paragraph shall apply to a CSEC plan other than a plan described in section 412(l)(6)(A) (as in effect on the day before the enactment of the Pension Protection Act of 2006 [enacted Aug. 17, 2006]) which—

(i) is required to pay installments under this subsection for a plan year, and

(ii) has a liquidity shortfall for any quarter during such plan year.

(C) Period of underpayment—For purposes of paragraph (1), any portion of an installment that is treated as not paid under subparagraph (A) shall continue to be treated as unpaid until the close of the quarter in which the due date for such installment occurs.

(D) Limitation on increase—If the amount of any required installment is increased by reason of subparagraph (A), in no event shall such increase exceed the amount which, when added to prior installments for the plan year, is necessary to increase the funded current liability percentage (taking into account the expected increase in current liability due to benefits accruing during the plan year) to 100 percent.

(E) Definitions—For purposes of this paragraph—

(i) Liquidity shortfall—The term "liquidity shortfall" means, with respect to any required installment, an amount equal to the excess (as of the last day of the quarter for which such installment is made) of the base amount with respect to such quarter over the value (as of such last day) of the plan's liquid assets.

(ii) Base amount—

(I) In general—The term "base amount" means, with respect to any quarter, an amount equal to 3 times the sum of the adjusted disbursements from the plan for the 12 months ending on the last day of such quarter.

(II) Special rule—If the amount determined under subclause (I) exceeds an amount equal to 2 times the sum of the adjusted disbursements from the plan for the 36 months ending on the last day of the quarter and an enrolled actuary certifies to the satisfaction of the Secretary that such excess is the result of nonrecurring circumstances, the base amount with respect to such quarter shall be determined without regard to amounts related to those nonrecurring circumstances.

(iii) Disbursements from the plan—The term "disbursements from the plan" means all disbursements from the trust, including purchases of annuities, payments of single sums and other benefits, and administrative expenses.

(iv) Adjusted disbursements—The term "adjusted disbursements" means disbursements from the plan reduced by the product of—

(I) the plan's funded current liability percentage for the plan year, and

(II) the sum of the purchases of annuities, payments of single sums, and such other disbursements as the Secretary shall provide in regulations.

(v) Liquid assets—The term "liquid assets" means cash, marketable securities and such other assets as specified by the Secretary in regulations.

(vi) Quarter—The term "quarter" means, with respect to any required installment, the 3-month period preceding the month in which the due date for such installment occurs.

(F) Regulations—The Secretary may prescribe such regulations as are necessary to carry out this paragraph.

(6) Fiscal years and short years—

(A) Fiscal years—In applying this subsection to a plan year beginning on any date other than January 1, there shall be substituted for the months specified in this subsection, the months which correspond thereto.

(B) Short plan year—This subsection shall be applied to plan years of less than 12 months in accordance with regulations prescribed by the Secretary.

(g) Imposition of lien where failure to make required contributions—

(1) In general—In the case of a plan to which this section applies, if—

(A) any person fails to make a required installment under subsection (f) or any other payment required under this section before the due date for such installment or other payment, and

(B) the unpaid balance of such installment or other payment (including interest), when added to the aggregate unpaid balance of all preceding such installments or other payments for which payment was not made before the due date (including interest), exceeds $1,000,000, then there shall be a lien in favor of the plan in the amount determined under paragraph (3) upon all property and rights to property, whether real or personal, belonging to such person and any other person who is a member of the same controlled group of which such person is a member.

(2) Plans to which subsection applies—This subsection shall apply to a CSEC plan for any plan year for which the funded current liability percentage of such plan is less than 100 percent. This subsection shall not apply to any plan to which section 4021 of the Employee Retirement Income Security Act of 1974 [29 U.S.C.A. § 1321] does not apply (as such section is in effect on the date of the enactment of the Retirement Protection Act of 1994 [enacted Dec. 8, 1994]).

(3) Amount of lien—For purposes of paragraph (1), the amount of the lien shall be equal to the aggregate unpaid balance of required installments and other payments required under this section (including interest)—

    (A) for plan years beginning after 1987, and

    (B) for which payment has not been made before the due date.

(4) Notice of failure; lien—

    (A) Notice of failure—A person committing a failure described in paragraph (1) shall notify the Pension Benefit Guaranty Corporation of such failure within 10 days of the due date for the required installment or other payment.

    (B) Period of lien—The lien imposed by paragraph (1) shall arise on the due date for the required installment or other payment and shall continue until the last day of the first plan year in which the plan ceases to be described in paragraph (1)(B). Such lien shall continue to run without regard to whether such plan continues to be described in paragraph (2) during the period referred to in the preceding sentence.

    (C) Certain rules to apply—Any amount with respect to which a lien is imposed under paragraph (1) shall be treated as taxes due and owing the United States and rules similar to the rules of subsections (c), (d), and (e) of section 4068 of the Employee Retirement Income Security Act of 1974 [29 U.S.C.A. § 1368] shall apply with respect to a lien imposed by subsection (a) and the amount with respect to such lien.

(5) Enforcement—Any lien created under paragraph (1) may be perfected and enforced only by the Pension Benefit Guaranty Corporation, or at the direction of the Pension Benefit Guaranty Corporation, by any contributing employer (or any member of the controlled group of the contributing employer).

(6) Definitions—For purposes of this subsection—

    (A) Due date; required installment—The terms "due date" and "required installment" have the meanings given such terms by subsection (f), except that in the case of a payment other than a required installment, the due date shall be the date such payment is required to be made under this section.

    (B) Controlled group—The term "controlled group" means any group treated as a single employer under subsections (b), (c), (m), and (o) of section 414.

(h) Current liability—For purposes of this section—

(1) In general—The term "current liability" means all liabilities to employees and their beneficiaries under the plan.

(2) Treatment of unpredictable contingent event benefits—

(A) In general—For purposes of paragraph (1), any unpredictable contingent event benefit shall not be taken into account until the event on which the benefit is contingent occurs.

(B) Unpredictable contingent event benefit—The term "unpredictable contingent event benefit" means any benefit contingent on an event other than—

(i) age, service, compensation, death, or disability, or

(ii) an event which is reasonably and reliably predictable (as determined by the Secretary).

(3) Interest rate and mortality assumptions used—

(A) Interest rate—The rate of interest used to determine current liability under this section shall be the third segment rate determined under section 430(h)(2)(C).

(B) Mortality tables—

(i) Secretarial authority—The Secretary may by regulation prescribe mortality tables to be used in determining current liability under this subsection. Such tables shall be based upon the actual experience of pension plans and projected trends in such experience. In prescribing such tables, the Secretary shall take into account results of available independent studies of mortality of individuals covered by pension plans.

(ii) Periodic review—The Secretary shall periodically (at least every 5 years) review any tables in effect under this subsection and shall, to the extent the Secretary determines necessary, by regulation update the tables to reflect the actual experience of pension plans and projected trends in such experience.

(C) Separate mortality tables for the disabled—Notwithstanding subparagraph (B)—

(i) In general—In the case of plan years beginning after December 31, 1995, the Secretary shall establish mortality tables which may be used (in lieu of the tables under subparagraph (B)) to determine current liability under this subsection for individuals who are entitled to benefits under the plan on account of disability. The Secretary shall establish separate tables for individuals whose disabilities occur in plan years beginning before January 1, 1995, and for individuals whose disabilities occur in plan years beginning on or after such date.

(ii) Special rule for disabilities occurring after 1994—In the case of disabilities occurring in plan years beginning after December 31, 1994, the tables under clause (i) shall apply only with respect to individuals described in such subclause who are disabled within the meaning of title II of the Social Security Act [42 U.S.C.A. §§ 401 et seq.] and the regulations thereunder.

(4) Certain service disregarded—

(A) In general—In the case of a participant to whom this paragraph applies, only the applicable percentage of the years of service before such individual became a participant shall be taken into account in computing the current liability of the plan.

(B) Applicable percentage—For purposes of this subparagraph, the applicable percentage shall be determined as follows:

If the years of participation are:	The applicable percentage is:
1	20
2	40
3	60
4	80
5 or more	100

(C) Participants to whom paragraph applies—This subparagraph shall apply to any participant who, at the time of becoming a participant—

(i) has not accrued any other benefit under any defined benefit plan (whether or not terminated) maintained by the employer or a member of the same controlled group of which the employer is a member,

(ii) who first becomes a participant under the plan in a plan year beginning after December 31, 1987, and

(iii) has years of service greater than the minimum years of service necessary for eligibility to participate in the plan.

(D) Election—An employer may elect not to have this subparagraph apply. Such an election, once made, may be revoked only with the consent of the Secretary.

(i) Funded current liability percentage—For purposes of this section, the term "funded current liability percentage" means, with respect to any plan year, the percentage which—

(1) the value of the plan's assets determined under subsection (c)(2), is of

(2) the current liability under the plan.

(j) Funding restoration status—Notwithstanding any other provisions of this section—

(1) Normal cost payment—

(A) In general—In the case of a CSEC plan that is in funding restoration status for a plan year, for purposes of section 412, the term "accumulated funding deficiency" means, for such plan year, the greater of—

(i) the amount described in subsection (a), or

(ii) the excess of the normal cost of the plan for the plan year over the amount actually contributed to or under the plan for the plan year.

(B) Normal cost—In the case of a CSEC plan that uses a spread gain funding method, for purposes of this subsection, the term "normal cost" means normal cost as determined under the entry age normal funding method.

(2) Plan amendments—In the case of a CSEC plan that is in funding restoration status for a plan year, no amendment to such plan may take effect during such plan year if such amendment has the effect of increasing liabilities of the plan by means of increases in benefits, establishment of new benefits, changing the rate of benefit accrual, or changing the rate at which benefits become nonforfeitable. This paragraph shall not apply to any plan amendment that is required to comply with any applicable law. This paragraph shall cease to apply with respect to any plan year, effective as of the first day of the plan year (or if later, the effective date of the amendment) upon payment by the plan sponsor of a contribution to the plan (in addition to any contribution required under this section without regard to this paragraph) in an amount equal to the increase in the funding liability of the plan attributable to the plan amendment.

(3) **Funding restoration plan**—The sponsor of a CSEC plan shall establish a written funding restoration plan within 180 days of the receipt by the plan sponsor of a certification from the plan actuary that the plan is in funding restoration status for a plan year. Such funding restoration plan shall consist of actions that are calculated, based on reasonably anticipated experience and reasonable actuarial assumptions, to increase the plan's funded percentage to 100 percent over a period that is not longer than the greater of 7 years or the shortest amount of time practicable. Such funding restoration plan shall take into account contributions required under this section (without regard to this paragraph). If a plan remains in funding restoration status for 2 or more years, such funding restoration plan shall be updated each year after the 1st such year within 180 days of receipt by the plan sponsor of a certification from the plan actuary that the plan remains in funding restoration status for the plan year.

(4) **Annual certification by plan actuary**—Not later than the 90th day of each plan year of a CSEC plan, the plan actuary shall certify to the plan sponsor whether or not the plan is in funding restoration status for the plan year, based on the plan's funded percentage as of the beginning of the plan year. For this purpose, the actuary may conclusively rely on an estimate of—

(A) the plan's funding liability, based on the funding liability of the plan for the preceding plan year and on reasonable actuarial estimates, assumptions, and methods, and

(B) the amount of any contributions reasonably anticipated to be made for the preceding plan year. Contributions described in subparagraph (B) shall be taken into account in determining the plan's funded percentage as of the beginning of the plan year.

(5) **Definitions**—For purposes of this subsection—

(A) **Funding restoration status**—A CSEC plan shall be treated as in funding restoration status for a plan year if the plan's funded percentage as of the beginning of such plan year is less than 80 percent.

(B) **Funded percentage**—The term "funded percentage" means the ratio (expressed as a percentage) which—

(i) the value of plan assets (as determined under subsection (c)(2)), bears to

(ii) the plan's funding liability.

(C) **Funding liability**—The term "funding liability" for a plan year means the present value of all benefits accrued or earned under the plan as of the beginning of the plan year, based on the assumptions used by the plan pursuant to this section, including the interest rate described in subsection (b)(5)(A) (without regard to subsection (b)(5)(B)).

(D) **Spread gain funding method**—The term "spread gain funding method" has the meaning given such term under rules and forms issued by the Secretary.

(E) Plan sponsor—The term "plan sponsor" means, with respect to a CSEC plan, the association, committee, joint board of trustees, or other similar group of representatives of the parties who establish or maintain the plan.

§ 436. Funding-based limits on benefits and benefit accruals under single-employer plans.

(a) General rule—For purposes of section 401(a)(29), a defined benefit plan which is a single-employer plan (other than a CSEC plan) shall be treated as meeting the requirements of this section if the plan meets the requirements of subsections (b), (c), (d), and (e).

(b) Funding-based limitation on shutdown benefits and other unpredictable contingent event benefits under single-employer plans—

(1) In general—If a participant of a defined benefit plan which is a single-employer plan is entitled to an unpredictable contingent event benefit payable with respect to any event occurring during any plan year, the plan shall provide that such benefit may not be provided if the adjusted funding target attainment percentage for such plan year—

(A) is less than 60 percent, or

(B) would be less than 60 percent taking into account such occurrence.

(2) Exemption—Paragraph (1) shall cease to apply with respect to any plan year, effective as of the first day of the plan year, upon payment by the plan sponsor of a contribution (in addition to any minimum required contribution under section 430) equal to—

(A) in the case of paragraph (1)(A), the amount of the increase in the funding target of the plan (under section 430) for the plan year attributable to the occurrence referred to in paragraph (1), and

(B) in the case of paragraph (1)(B), the amount sufficient to result in an adjusted funding target attainment percentage of 60 percent.

(3) Unpredictable contingent event—For purposes of this subsection, the term "unpredictable contingent event benefit" means any benefit payable solely by reason of—

(A) a plant shutdown (or similar event, as determined by the Secretary), or

(B) an event other than the attainment of any age, performance of any service, receipt or derivation of any compensation, or occurrence of death or disability.

(c) Limitations on plan amendments increasing liability for benefits—

(1) In general—No amendment to a defined benefit plan which is a single-employer plan which has the effect of increasing liabilities of the plan by reason of increases in benefits, establishment of new benefits, changing the rate of benefit accrual, or changing the rate at which benefits become nonforfeitable may take effect during any plan year if the adjusted funding target attainment percentage for such plan year is—

(A) less than 80 percent, or

(B) would be less than 80 percent taking into account such amendment.

(2) Exemption—Paragraph (1) shall cease to apply with respect to any plan year, effective as of the first day of the plan year (or if later, the effective date of the amendment), upon payment by the plan sponsor of a contribution (in addition to any minimum required contribution under section 430) equal to—

(A) in the case of paragraph (1)(A), the amount of the increase in the funding target of the plan (under section 430) for the plan year attributable to the amendment, and

(B) in the case of paragraph (1)(B), the amount sufficient to result in an adjusted funding target attainment percentage of 80 percent.

(3) Exception for certain benefit increases—Paragraph (1) shall not apply to any amendment which provides for an increase in benefits under a formula which is not based on a participant's compensation, but only if the rate of such increase is not in excess of the contemporaneous rate of increase in average wages of participants covered by the amendment.

(d) Limitations on accelerated benefit distributions—

(1) Funding percentage less than 60 percent—A defined benefit plan which is a single-employer plan shall provide that, in any case in which the plan's adjusted funding target attainment percentage for a plan year is less than 60 percent, the plan may not pay any prohibited payment after the valuation date for the plan year.

(2) Bankruptcy—A defined benefit plan which is a single-employer plan shall provide that, during any period in which the plan sponsor is a debtor in a case under title 11, United States Code, or similar Federal or State law, the plan may not pay any prohibited payment. The preceding sentence shall not apply on or after the date on which the enrolled actuary of the plan certifies that the adjusted funding target attainment percentage of such plan (determined by not taking into account any adjustment of segment rates under section 430(h)(2)(C)(iv)) is not less than 100 percent.

(3) Limited payment if percentage at least 60 percent but less than 80 percent—

(A) In general—A defined benefit plan which is a single-employer plan shall provide that, in any case in which the plan's adjusted funding target attainment percentage for a plan year is 60 percent or greater but less than 80 percent, the plan may not pay any prohibited payment after the valuation date for the plan year to the extent the amount of the payment exceeds the lesser of—

(i) 50 percent of the amount of the payment which could be made without regard to this section, or

(ii) the present value (determined under guidance prescribed by the Pension Benefit Guaranty Corporation, using the interest and mortality assumptions under section 417(e)) of the maximum guarantee with respect to the participant under section 4022 of the Employee Retirement Income Security Act of 1974.

(B) One-time application—

(i) In general—The plan shall also provide that only 1 prohibited payment meeting the requirements of subparagraph (A) may be made with respect to any participant during any period of consecutive plan years to which the limitations under either paragraph (1) or (2) or this paragraph applies.

(ii) Treatment of beneficiaries—For purposes of this subparagraph, a participant and any beneficiary on his behalf (including an alternate payee, as defined in section 414(p)(8)) shall be treated as 1 participant. If the accrued benefit of a participant is allocated to such an alternate payee and 1 or more other persons, the amount under subparagraph (A) shall be allocated among such persons in the same manner as the accrued benefit is allocated unless the qualified domestic relations order (as defined in section 414(p)(1)(A)) provides otherwise.

(4) Exception—This subsection shall not apply to any plan for any plan year if the terms of such plan (as in effect for the period beginning on September 1, 2005, and ending with such plan year) provide for no benefit accruals with respect to any participant during such period.

(5) Prohibited payment—For purpose of this subsection, the term "prohibited payment" means—

    (A) any payment, in excess of the monthly amount paid under a single life annuity (plus any social security supplements described in the last sentence of section 411(a)(9)), to a participant or beneficiary whose annuity starting date (as defined in section 417(f)(2)) occurs during any period a limitation under paragraph (1) or (2) is in effect,

    (B) any payment for the purchase of an irrevocable commitment from an insurer to pay benefits, and

    (C) any other payment specified by the Secretary by regulations.

Such term shall not include the payment of a benefit which under section 411(a)(11) may be immediately distributed without the consent of the participant.

(e) Limitation on benefit accruals for plans with severe funding shortfalls—

(1) In general—A defined benefit plan which is a single-employer plan shall provide that, in any case in which the plan's adjusted funding target attainment percentage for a plan year is less than 60 percent, benefit accruals under the plan shall cease as of the valuation date for the plan year.

(2) Exemption—Paragraph (1) shall cease to apply with respect to any plan year, effective as of the first day of the plan year, upon payment by the plan sponsor of a contribution (in addition to any minimum required contribution under section 430) equal to the amount sufficient to result in an adjusted funding target attainment percentage of 60 percent.

(f) Rules relating to contributions required to avoid benefit limitations—

(1) Security may be provided—

    (A) In general—For purposes of this section, the adjusted funding target attainment percentage shall be determined by treating as an asset of the plan any security provided by a plan sponsor in a form meeting the requirements of subparagraph (B).

    (B) Form of security—The security required under subparagraph (A) shall consist of—

        (i) a bond issued by a corporate surety company that is an acceptable surety for purposes of section 412 of the Employee Retirement Income Security Act of 1974,

        (ii) cash, or United States obligations which mature in 3 years or less, held in escrow by a bank or similar financial institution, or

        (iii) such other form of security as is satisfactory to the Secretary and the parties involved.

    (C) Enforcement—Any security provided under subparagraph (A) may be perfected and enforced at any time after the earlier of—

(i) the date on which the plan terminates,

(ii) if there is a failure to make a payment of the minimum required contribution for any plan year beginning after the security is provided, the due date for the payment under section 430(j), or

(iii) if the adjusted funding target attainment percentage is less than 60 percent for a consecutive period of 7 years, the valuation date for the last year in the period.

(D) Release of security—The security shall be released (and any amounts thereunder shall be refunded together with any interest accrued thereon) at such time as the Secretary may prescribe in regulations, including regulations for partial releases of the security by reason of increases in the adjusted funding target attainment percentage.

(2) Prefunding balance or funding standard carryover balance may not be used— No prefunding balance or funding standard carryover balance under section 430(f) may be used under subsection (b), (c), or (e) to satisfy any payment an employer may make under any such subsection to avoid or terminate the application of any limitation under such subsection.

(3) Deemed reduction of funding balances—

(A) In general—Subject to subparagraph (C), in any case in which a benefit limitation under subsection (b), (c), (d), or (e) would (but for this subparagraph and determined without regard to subsection (b)(2), (c)(2), or (e)(2)) apply to such plan for the plan year, the plan sponsor of such plan shall be treated for purposes of this title as having made an election under section 430(f) to reduce the prefunding balance or funding standard carryover balance by such amount as is necessary for such benefit limitation to not apply to the plan for such plan year.

(B) Exception for insufficient funding balances—Subparagraph (A) shall not apply with respect to a benefit limitation for any plan year if the application of subparagraph (A) would not result in the benefit limitation not applying for such plan year.

(C) Restrictions of certain rules to collectively bargained plans—With respect to any benefit limitation under subsection (b), (c), or (e), subparagraph (A) shall only apply in the case of a plan maintained pursuant to 1 or more collective bargaining agreements between employee representatives and 1 or more employers.

(g) New plans—Subsections (b), (c), and (e) shall not apply to a plan for the first 5 plan years of the plan. For purposes of this subsection, the reference in this subsection to a plan shall include a reference to any predecessor plan.

(h) Presumed underfunding for purposes of benefit limitations—

(1) Presumption of continued underfunding—In any case in which a benefit limitation under subsection (b), (c), (d), or (e) has been applied to a plan with respect to the plan year preceding the current plan year, the adjusted funding target attainment percentage of the plan for the current plan year shall be presumed to be equal to the adjusted funding target attainment percentage of the plan for the preceding plan year until the enrolled actuary of the plan certifies the actual adjusted funding target attainment percentage of the plan for the current plan year.

(2) Presumption of underfunding after 10th month—In any case in which no certification of the adjusted funding target attainment percentage for the current plan year is made with respect to the plan before the first day of the 10th month of such year, for purposes of subsections (b), (c), (d), and (e), such first day shall be deemed, for purposes of such subsection, to be the valuation date of the plan for the current plan year and the plan's adjusted funding target attainment percentage shall be conclusively presumed to be less than 60 percent as of such first day.

(3) Presumption of underfunding after 4th month for nearly underfunded plans—In any case in which—

> **(A)** a benefit limitation under subsection (b), (c), (d), or (e) did not apply to a plan with respect to the plan year preceding the current plan year, but the adjusted funding target attainment percentage of the plan for such preceding plan year was not more than 10 percentage points greater than the percentage which would have caused such subsection to apply to the plan with respect to such preceding plan year, and

> **(B)** as of the first day of the 4th month of the current plan year, the enrolled actuary of the plan has not certified the actual adjusted funding target attainment percentage of the plan for the current plan year,

until the enrolled actuary so certifies, such first day shall be deemed, for purposes of such subsection, to be the valuation date of the plan for the current plan year and the adjusted funding target attainment percentage of the plan as of such first day shall, for purposes of such subsection, be presumed to be equal to 10 percentage points less than the adjusted funding target attainment percentage of the plan for such preceding plan year.

(i) Treatment of plan as of close of prohibited or cessation period—For purposes of applying this title—

(1) Operation of plan after period—Unless the plan provides otherwise, payments and accruals will resume effective as of the day following the close of the period for which any limitation of payment or accrual of benefits under subsection (d) or (e) applies.

(2) Treatment of affected benefits—Nothing in this subsection shall be construed as affecting the plan's treatment of benefits which would have been paid or accrued but for this section.

(j) Terms relating to funding target attainment percentage—For purposes of this section—

(1) In general—The term "funding target attainment percentage" has the same meaning given such term by section 430(d)(2).

(2) Adjusted funding target attainment percentage—The term "adjusted funding target attainment percentage" means the funding target attainment percentage which is determined under paragraph (1) by increasing each of the amounts under subparagraphs (A) and (B) of section 430(d)(2) by the aggregate amount of purchases of annuities for employees other than highly compensated employees (as defined in section 414(q)) which were made by the plan during the preceding 2 plan years.

(3) Application to plans which are fully funded without regard to reductions for funding balances—In the case of a plan for any plan year, if the funding target attainment percentage is 100 percent or more (determined without regard to the reduction in the value of assets under section 430(f)(4)), the funding target attainment percentage for purposes of paragraphs (1) and (2) shall be determined without regard to such reduction.

* * *

§ 457. Deferred compensation plans of State and local governments and tax-exempt organizations.

(a) Year of inclusion in gross income—

(1) In general—Any amount of compensation deferred under an eligible deferred compensation plan, and any income attributable to the amounts so deferred, shall be includible in gross income only for the taxable year in which such compensation or other income—

(A) is paid to the participant or other beneficiary, in the case of a plan of an eligible employer described in subsection (e)(1)(A), and

(B) is paid or otherwise made available to the participant or other beneficiary, in the case of a plan of an eligible employer described in subsection (e)(1)(B).

(2) Special rule for rollover amounts—To the extent provided in section 72(t)(9), section 72(t) shall apply to any amount includible in gross income under this subsection.

(3) Special rule for health and long-term care insurance—In the case of a plan of an eligible employer described in subsection (e)(1)(A), to the extent provided in section 402(l), paragraph (1) shall not apply to amounts otherwise includible in gross income under this subsection.

(b) Eligible deferred compensation plan defined—For purposes of this section, the term "eligible deferred compensation plan" means a plan established and maintained by an eligible employer—

(1) in which only individuals who perform service for the employer may be participants,

(2) which provides that (except as provided in paragraph (3)) the maximum amount which may be deferred under the plan for the taxable year (other than rollover amounts) shall not exceed the lesser of—

(A) the applicable dollar amount, or

(B) 100 percent of the participant's includible compensation,

(3) which may provide that, for 1 or more of the participant's last 3 taxable years ending before he attains normal retirement age under the plan, the ceiling set forth in paragraph (2) shall be the lesser of—

(A) twice the dollar amount in effect under subsection (b)(2)(A), or

(B) the sum of—

(i) the plan ceiling established for purposes of paragraph (2) for the taxable year (determined without regard to this paragraph), plus

(ii) so much of the plan ceiling established for purposes of paragraph (2) for taxable years before the taxable year as has not previously been used under paragraph (2) or this paragraph,

(4) which provides that compensation will be deferred for any calendar month only if an agreement providing for such deferral has been entered into before the beginning of such month,

(5) which meets the distribution requirements of subsection (d), and

(6) except as provided in subsection (g), which provides that—

(A) all amounts of compensation deferred under the plan,

(B) all property and rights purchased with such amounts, and

(C) all income attributable to such amounts, property, or rights,

shall remain (until made available to the participant or other beneficiary) solely the property and rights of the employer (without being restricted to the provision of benefits under the plan), subject only to the claims of the employer's general creditors.

A plan which is established and maintained by an employer which is described in subsection (e)(1)(A) and which is administered in a manner which is inconsistent with the requirements of any of the preceding paragraphs shall be treated as not meeting the requirements of such paragraph as of the 1st plan year beginning more than 180 days after the date of notification by the Secretary of the inconsistency unless the employer corrects the inconsistency before the 1st day of such plan year.

(c) Limitation—The maximum amount of the compensation of any one individual which may be deferred under subsection (a) during any taxable year shall not exceed the amount in effect under subsection (b)(2)(A) (as modified by any adjustment provided under subsection (b)(3)).

(d) Distribution requirements—

(1) In general—For purposes of subsection (b)(5), a plan meets the distribution requirements of this subsection if—

(A) under the plan amounts will not be made available to participants or beneficiaries earlier than—

(i) the calendar year in which the participant attains age 70½,

(ii) when the participant has a severance from employment with the employer, or

(iii) when the participant is faced with an unforeseeable emergency (determined in the manner prescribed by the Secretary in regulations),

(B) the plan meets the minimum distribution requirements of paragraph (2), and

(C) in the case of a plan maintained by an employer described in subsection (e)(1)(A), the plan meets requirements similar to the requirements of section 401(a)(31).

Any amount transferred in a direct trustee-to-trustee transfer in accordance with section 401(a)(31) shall not be includible in gross income for the taxable year of transfer.

(2) Minimum distribution requirements—A plan meets the minimum distribution requirements of this paragraph if such plan meets the requirements of section 401(a)(9).

(3) Special rule for government plan—An eligible deferred compensation plan of an employer described in subsection (e)(1)(A) shall not be treated as failing to meet the requirements of this subsection solely by reason of making a distribution described in subsection (e)(9)(A).

(e) Other definitions and special rules—For purposes of this section—

(1) Eligible employer—The term "eligible employer" means—

(A) a State, political subdivision of a State, and any agency or instrumentality of a State or political subdivision of a State, and

(B) any other organization (other than a governmental unit) exempt from tax under this subtitle.

(2) Performance of service—The performance of service includes performance of service as an independent contractor and the person (or governmental unit) for whom such services are performed shall be treated as the employer.

(3) Participant—The term "participant" means an individual who is eligible to defer compensation under the plan.

(4) Beneficiary—The term "beneficiary" means a beneficiary of the participant, his estate, or any other person whose interest in the plan is derived from the participant.

(5) Includible compensation—The term "includible compensation" has the meaning given to the term "participant's compensation" by section 415(c)(3).

(6) Compensation taken into account at present value—Compensation shall be taken into account at its present value.

(7) Community property laws—The amount of includible compensation shall be determined without regard to any community property laws.

(8) Income attributable—Gains from the disposition of property shall be treated as income attributable to such property.

(9) Benefits of tax exempt organization plans not treated as made available by reason of certain elections, etc—In the case of an eligible deferred compensation plan of an employer described in subsection (e)(1)(B)—

(A) Total amount payable is dollar limit or less—The total amount payable to a participant under the plan shall not be treated as made available merely because the participant may elect to receive such amount (or the plan may distribute such amount without the participant's consent) if—

(i) the portion of such amount which is not attributable to rollover contributions (as defined in section 411(a)(11)(D)) does not exceed the dollar limit under section 411(a)(11)(A), and

(ii) such amount may be distributed only if—

(I) no amount has been deferred under the plan with respect to such participant during the 2-year period ending on the date of the distribution, and

(II) there has been no prior distribution under the plan to such participant to which this subparagraph applied.

A plan shall not be treated as failing to meet the distribution requirements of subsection (d) by reason of a distribution to which this subparagraph applies.

(B) Election to defer commencement of distributions—The total amount payable to a participant under the plan shall not be treated as made available merely because the participant may elect to defer commencement of distributions under the plan if—

(i) such election is made after amounts may be available under the plan in accordance with subsection (d)(1)(A) and before commencement of such distributions, and

(ii) the participant may make only 1 such election.

(10) Transfers between plans—A participant shall not be required to include in gross income any portion of the entire amount payable to such participant solely by reason of the transfer of such portion from 1 eligible deferred compensation plan to another eligible deferred compensation plan.

(11) Certain plans excluded—

(A) In general—The following plans shall be treated as not providing for the deferral of compensation:

(i) Any bona fide vacation leave, sick leave, compensatory time, severance pay, disability pay, or death benefit plan.

(ii) Any plan paying solely length of service awards to bona fide volunteers (or their beneficiaries) on account of qualified services performed by such volunteers.

* * *

(12) Exception for nonelective deferred compensation of nonemployees—

(A) In general—This section shall not apply to nonelective deferred compensation attributable to services not performed as an employee.

(B) Nonelective deferred compensation—For purposes of subparagraph (A), deferred compensation shall be treated as nonelective only if all individuals (other than those who have not satisfied any applicable initial service requirement) with the same relationship to the payor are covered under the same plan with no individual variations or options under the plan.

* * *

(14) Treatment of qualified governmental excess benefit arrangements—Subsections (b)(2) and (c)(1) shall not apply to any qualified governmental excess benefit arrangement (as defined in section 415(m)(3)), and benefits provided under such an arrangement shall not be taken into account in determining whether any other plan is an eligible deferred compensation plan.

(15) Applicable dollar amount—

(A) In general—The applicable dollar amount is $15,000.

(B) Cost-of-living adjustments—In the case of taxable years beginning after December 31, 2006, the Secretary shall adjust the $15,000 amount under subparagraph (A) at the same time and in the same manner as under section 415(d), except that the base period shall be the calendar quarter beginning July 1, 2005, and any increase under this paragraph which is not a multiple of $500 shall be rounded to the next lowest multiple of $500.

(16) Rollover amounts—

(A) General rule—In the case of an eligible deferred compensation plan established and maintained by an employer described in subsection (e)(1)(A), if—

(i) any portion of the balance to the credit of an employee in such plan is paid to such employee in an eligible rollover distribution (within the meaning of section 402(c)(4)),

(ii) the employee transfers any portion of the property such employee receives in such distribution to an eligible retirement plan described in section 402(c)(8)(B), and

(iii) in the case of a distribution of property other than money, the amount so transferred consists of the property distributed,

then such distribution (to the extent so transferred) shall not be includible in gross income for the taxable year in which paid.

(B) Certain rules made applicable—The rules of paragraphs (2) through (7), (9), and (11) of section 402(c) and section 402(f) shall apply for purposes of subparagraph (A).

(C) Reporting—Rollovers under this paragraph shall be reported to the Secretary in the same manner as rollovers from qualified retirement plans (as defined in section 4974(c)).

(17) Trustee-to-trustee transfers to purchase permissive service credit—No amount shall be includible in gross income by reason of a direct trustee-to-trustee transfer to a defined benefit governmental plan (as defined in section 414(d)) if such transfer is—

(A) for the purchase of permissive service credit (as defined in section 415(n)(3)(A)) under such plan, or

(B) a repayment to which section 415 does not apply by reason of subsection (k)(3) thereof.

(18) Coordination with catch-up contributions for individuals age 50 or older—In the case of an individual who is an eligible participant (as defined by section 414(v)) and who is a participant in an eligible deferred compensation plan of an employer described in paragraph (1)(A), subsections (b)(3) and (c) shall be applied by substituting for the amount otherwise determined under the applicable subsection the greater of—

(A) the sum of—

(i) the plan ceiling established for purposes of subsection (b)(2) (without regard to subsection (b)(3)), plus

(ii) the applicable dollar amount for the taxable year determined under section 414(v)(2)(B)(i), or

(B) the amount determined under the applicable subsection (without regard to this paragraph).

(f) Tax treatment of participants where plan or arrangement of employer is not eligible—

(1) In general—In the case of a plan of an eligible employer providing for a deferral of compensation, if such plan is not an eligible deferred compensation plan, then—

(A) the compensation shall be included in the gross income of the participant or beneficiary for the 1st taxable year in which there is no substantial risk of forfeiture of the rights to such compensation, and

(B) the tax treatment of any amount made available under the plan to a participant or beneficiary shall be determined under section 72 (relating to annuities, etc.).

(2) Exceptions—Paragraph (1) shall not apply to—

(A) a plan described in section 401(a) which includes a trust exempt from tax under section 501(a),

(B) an annuity plan or contract described in section 403,

(C) that portion of any plan which consists of a transfer of property described in section 83,

(D) that portion of any plan which consists of a trust to which section 402(b) applies,

(E) a qualified governmental excess benefit arrangement described in section 415(m), and

(F) that portion of any applicable employment retention plan described in paragraph (4) with respect to any participant.

(3) Definitions—For purposes of this subsection—

(A) Plan includes arrangements, etc—The term "plan" includes any agreement or arrangement.

(B) Substantial risk of forfeiture—The rights of a person to compensation are subject to a substantial risk of forfeiture if such person's rights to such compensation are conditioned upon the future performance of substantial services by any individual.

(4) Employment retention plans—For purposes of paragraph (2)(F)—

(A) In general—The portion of an applicable employment retention plan described in this paragraph with respect to any participant is that portion of the plan which provides benefits payable to the participant not in excess of twice the applicable dollar limit determined under subsection (e)(15).

(B) Other rules—

(i) Limitation—Paragraph (2)(F) shall only apply to the portion of the plan described in subparagraph (A) for years preceding the year in which such portion is paid or otherwise made available to the participant.

(ii) Treatment—A plan shall not be treated for purposes of this title as providing for the deferral of compensation for any year with respect to the portion of the plan described in subparagraph (A).

(C) Applicable employment retention plan—The term "applicable employment retention plan" means an employment retention plan maintained by—

(i) a local educational agency (as defined in section 9101 of the Elementary and Secondary Education Act of 1965 (20 U.S.C. 7801), or

(ii) an education association which principally represents employees of 1 or more agencies described in clause (i) and which is described in section 501(c) (5) or (6) and exempt from taxation under section 501(a).

(D) Employment retention plan—The term "employment retention plan" means a plan to pay, upon termination of employment, compensation to an employee of a local educational agency or education association described in subparagraph (C) for purposes of—

(i) retaining the services of the employee, or

(ii) rewarding such employee for the employee's service with 1 or more such agencies or associations.

(g) Governmental plans must maintain set-asides for exclusive benefit of participants—

(1) In general—A plan maintained by an eligible employer described in subsection (e)(1)(A) shall not be treated as an eligible deferred compensation plan unless all assets and income of the plan described in subsection (b)(6) are held in trust for the exclusive benefit of participants and their beneficiaries.

(2) Taxability of trusts and participants—For purposes of this title—

(A) a trust described in paragraph (1) shall be treated as an organization exempt from taxation under section 501(a), and

(B) notwithstanding any other provision of this title, amounts in the trust shall be includible in the gross income of participants and beneficiaries only to the extent, and at the time, provided in this section.

(3) Custodial accounts and contracts—For purposes of this subsection, custodial accounts and contracts described in section 401(f) shall be treated as trusts under rules similar to the rules under section 401(f).

(4) Death benefits under USERRA-qualified active military service—A plan described in paragraph (1) shall not be treated as an eligible deferred compensation plan unless such plan meets the requirements of section 401(a)(37).

§ 501. Exemption from tax on corporations, certain trusts, etc.

(a) Exemption from taxation—An organization described in subsection (c) or (d) or section 401(a) shall be exempt from taxation under this subtitle unless such exemption is denied under section 502 or 503.

(b) Tax on unrelated business income and certain other activities—An organization exempt from taxation under subsection (a) shall be subject to tax to the extent provided in parts II, III, and VI of this subchapter, but (notwithstanding parts II, III, and VI of this subchapter) shall be considered an organization exempt from income taxes for the purpose of any law which refers to organizations exempt from income taxes.

(c) List of exempt organizations—The following organizations are referred to in subsection (a):

* * *

(9) Voluntary employees' beneficiary associations providing for the payment of life, sick, accident, or other benefits to the members of such association or their dependents or designated beneficiaries, if no part of the net earnings of such association inures (other than through such payments) to the benefit of any private shareholder or individual. For purposes of providing for the payment of sick and accident benefits to members of such an association and their dependents, the term "dependent" shall include any individual who is a child (as defined in section 152(f)(1)) of a member who as of the end of the calendar year has not attained age 27.

* * *

§ 1563. Definitions and special rules.

(a) Controlled group of corporations—For purposes of this part, the term "controlled group of corporations" means any group of—

(1) Parent-subsidiary controlled group—One or more chains of corporations connected through stock ownership with a common parent corporation if—

(A) stock possessing at least 80 percent of the total combined voting power of all classes of stock entitled to vote or at least 80 percent of the total value of shares of all classes of stock of each of the corporations, except the common parent corporation, is owned (within the meaning of subsection (d)(1)) by one or more of the other corporations; and

(B) the common parent corporation owns (within the meaning of subsection (d)(1)) stock possessing at least 80 percent of the total combined voting power of all classes of stock entitled to vote or at least 80 percent of the total value of shares of all classes of stock of at least one of the other corporations, excluding, in computing such voting power or value, stock owned directly by such other corporations.

(2) Brother-sister controlled group—Two or more corporations if 5 or fewer persons who are individuals, estates, or trusts own (within the meaning of subsection (d)(2)) stock possessing more than 50 percent of the total combined voting power of all classes of stock entitled to vote or more than 50 percent of the total value of shares of all classes of stock of each corporation, taking into account the stock ownership of each such person only to the extent such stock ownership is identical with respect to each such corporation.

(3) Combined group—Three or more corporations each of which is a member of a group of corporations described in paragraph (1) or (2), and one of which—

(A) is a common parent corporation included in a group of corporations described in paragraph (1), and also

(B) is included in a group of corporations described in paragraph (2).

(4) Certain insurance companies—Two or more insurance companies subject to taxation under section 801 which are members of a controlled group of corporations described in paragraph (1), (2), or (3). Such insurance companies shall be treated as a controlled group of corporations separate from any other corporations which are members of the controlled group of corporations described in paragraph (1), (2), or (3).

(b) Component member—

(1) General rule—For purposes of this part, a corporation is a component member of a controlled group of corporations on a December 31 of any taxable year (and with respect to the taxable year which includes such December 31) if such corporation—

(A) is a member of such controlled group of corporations on the December 31 included in such year and is not treated as an excluded member under paragraph (2), or

(B) is not a member of such controlled group of corporations on the December 31 included in such year but is treated as an additional member under paragraph (3).

(2) Excluded members—A corporation which is a member of a controlled group of corporations on December 31 of any taxable year shall be treated as an excluded member of such group for the taxable year including such December 31 if such corporation—

(A) is a member of such group for less than one-half the number of days in such taxable year which precede such December 31,

(B) is exempt from taxation under section 501(a) (except a corporation which is subject to tax on its unrelated business taxable income under section 511) for such taxable year,

(C) is a foreign corporation subject to tax under section 881 for such taxable year,

(D) is an insurance company subject to taxation under section 801 (other than an insurance company which is a member of a controlled group described in subsection (a)(4)), or

(E) is a franchised corporation, as defined in subsection (f)(4).

(3) Additional members—A corporation which—

(A) was a member of a controlled group of corporations at any time during a calendar year,

(B) is not a member of such group on December 31 of such calendar year, and

(C) is not described, with respect to such group, in subparagraph (B), (C), (D), or (E) of paragraph (2),

shall be treated as an additional member of such group on December 31 for its taxable year including such December 31 if it was a member of such group for one-half (or more) of the number of days in such taxable year which precede such December 31.

(4) Overlapping groups—If a corporation is a component member of more than one controlled group of corporations with respect to any taxable year, such corporation shall be treated as a component member of only one controlled group. The determination as to the group of which such corporation is a component member shall be made under regulations prescribed by the Secretary which are consistent with the purposes of this part.

(c) Certain stock excluded—

(1) General rule—For purposes of this part, the term "stock" does not include—

(A) nonvoting stock which is limited and preferred as to dividends,

(B) treasury stock, and

(C) stock which is treated as "excluded stock" under paragraph (2).

(2) Stock treated as "excluded stock"—

(A) Parent-subsidiary controlled group—For purposes of subsection (a)(1), if a corporation (referred to in this paragraph as "parent corporation") owns (within the meaning of subsections (d)(1) and (e)(4)), 50 percent or more of the total combined voting power of all classes of stock entitled to vote or 50 percent or more of the total value of shares of all classes of stock in another corporation (referred to in this paragraph as "subsidiary corporation"), the following stock of the subsidiary corporation shall be treated as excluded stock—

(i) stock in the subsidiary corporation held by a trust which is part of a plan of deferred compensation for the benefit of the employees of the parent corporation or the subsidiary corporation,

(ii) stock in the subsidiary corporation owned by an individual (within the meaning of subsection (d)(2)) who is a principal stockholder or officer of the parent corporation. For purposes of this clause, the term "principal stockholder" of a corporation means an individual who owns (within the meaning of subsection (d)(2)) 5 percent or more of the total combined voting power of all classes of stock entitled to vote or 5 percent or more of the total value of shares of all classes of stock in such corporation,

(iii) stock in the subsidiary corporation owned (within the meaning of subsection (d)(2)) by an employee of the subsidiary corporation if such stock is subject to conditions which run in favor of such parent (or subsidiary) corporation and which substantially restrict or limit the employee's right (or if the employee constructively owns such stock, the direct owner's right) to dispose of such stock, or

(iv) stock in the subsidiary corporation owned (within the meaning of subsection (d)(2)) by an organization (other than the parent corporation) to which section 501 (relating to certain educational and charitable organizations which are exempt from tax) applies and which is controlled directly or indirectly by the parent corporation or subsidiary corporation, by an individual, estate, or trust that is a principal stockholder (within the meaning of clause (ii)) of the parent corporation, by an officer of the parent corporation, or by any combination thereof.

(B) Brother-sister controlled group—For purposes of subsection (a)(2), if 5 or fewer persons who are individuals, estates, or trusts (referred to in this subparagraph as "common owners") own (within the meaning of subsection (d)(2)), 50 percent or more of the total combined voting power of all classes of stock entitled to vote or 50 percent or more of the total value of shares of all classes of stock in a corporation, the following stock of such corporation shall be treated as excluded stock—

(i) stock in such corporation held by an employees' trust described in section 401(a) which is exempt from tax under section 501(a), if such trust is for the benefit of the employees of such corporation,

(ii) stock in such corporation owned (within the meaning of subsection (d)(2)) by an employee of the corporation if such stock is subject to conditions which run in favor of any of such common owners (or such corporation) and which substantially restrict or limit the employee's right (or if the employee constructively owns such stock, the direct owner's right) to dispose of such stock. If a condition which limits or restricts the employee's right (or the direct owner's right) to dispose of such stock also applies to the stock held by any of the common owners pursuant to a bona fide reciprocal stock purchase arrangement, such condition shall not be treated as one which restricts or limits the employee's right to dispose of such stock, or

(iii) stock in such corporation owned (within the meaning of subsection (d)(2)) by an organization to which section 501 (relating to certain educational and charitable organizations which are exempt from tax) applies and which is controlled directly or indirectly by such corporation, by an individual, estate, or trust that is a principal stockholder (within the meaning of subparagraph (A)(ii)) of such corporation, by an officer of such corporation, or by any combination thereof.

(d) Rules for determining stock ownership—

(1) Parent-subsidiary controlled group—For purposes of determining whether a corporation is a member of a parent-subsidiary controlled group of corporations (within the meaning of subsection (a)(1)), stock owned by a corporation means—

(A) stock owned directly by such corporation, and

(B) stock owned with the application of paragraphs (1), (2), and (3) of subsection (e).

(2) Brother-sister controlled group—For purposes of determining whether a corporation is a member of a brother-sister controlled group of corporations (within the meaning of subsection (a)(2)), stock owned by a person who is an individual, estate, or trust means—

(A) stock owned directly by such person, and

(B) stock owned with the application of subsection (e).

(e) Constructive ownership—

(1) Options—If any person has an option to acquire stock, such stock shall be considered as owned by such person. For purposes of this paragraph, an option to acquire such an option, and each one of a series of such options, shall be considered as an option to acquire such stock.

(2) Attribution from partnerships—Stock owned, directly or indirectly, by or for a partnership shall be considered as owned by any partner having an interest of 5 percent or more in either the capital or profits of the partnership in proportion to his interest in capital or profits, whichever such proportion is the greater.

(3) Attribution from estates or trusts—

(A) Stock owned, directly or indirectly, by or for an estate or trust shall be considered as owned by any beneficiary who has an actuarial interest of 5 percent or more in such stock, to the extent of such actuarial interest. For purposes of this subparagraph, the actuarial interest of each beneficiary shall be determined by assuming the maximum exercise of discretion by the fiduciary in favor of such beneficiary and the maximum use of such stock to satisfy his rights as a beneficiary.

(B) Stock owned, directly or indirectly, by or for any portion of a trust of which a person is considered the owner under subpart E of part I of subchapter J (relating to grantors and others treated as substantial owners) shall be considered as owned by such person.

(C) This paragraph shall not apply to stock owned by any employees' trust described in section 401(a) which is exempt from tax under section 501(a).

(4) Attribution from corporations—Stock owned, directly or indirectly, by or for a corporation shall be considered as owned by any person who owns (within the meaning of subsection (d)) 5 percent or more in value of its stock in that proportion which the value of the stock which such person so owns bears to the value of all the stock in such corporation.

(5) Spouse—An individual shall be considered as owning stock in a corporation owned, directly or indirectly, by or for his spouse (other than a spouse who is legally separated from the individual under a decree of divorce whether interlocutory or final, or a decree of separate maintenance), except in the case of a corporation with respect to which each of the following conditions is satisfied for its taxable year—

(A) The individual does not, at any time during such taxable year, own directly any stock in such corporation;

(B) The individual is not a director or employee and does not participate in the management of such corporation at any time during such taxable year;

(C) Not more than 50 percent of such corporation's gross income for such taxable year was derived from royalties, rents, dividends, interest, and annuities; and

(D) Such stock in such corporation is not, at any time during such taxable year, subject to conditions which substantially restrict or limit the spouse's right to dispose of such stock and which run in favor of the individual or his children who have not attained the age of 21 years.

(6) Children, grandchildren, parents, and grandparents—

(A) Minor children—An individual shall be considered as owning stock owned, directly or indirectly, by or for his children who have not attained the age of 21 years, and, if the individual has not attained the age of 21 years, the stock owned, directly or indirectly, by or for his parents.

(B) Adult children and grandchildren—An individual who owns (within the meaning of subsection (d)(2), but without regard to this subparagraph) more than 50 percent of the total combined voting power of all classes of stock entitled to vote or more than 50 percent of the total value of shares of all classes of stock in a corporation shall be considered as owning the stock in such corporation owned, directly or indirectly, by or for his parents, grandparents, grandchildren, and children who have attained the age of 21 years.

(C) Adopted child—For purposes of this section, a legally adopted child of an individual shall be treated as a child of such individual by blood.

(f) Other definitions and rules—

(1) Employee defined—For purposes of this section the term "employee" has the same meaning such term is given by paragraphs (1) and (2) of section 3121(d).

(2) Operating rules—

(A) In general—Except as provided in subparagraph (B), stock constructively owned by a person by reason of the application of paragraph (1), (2), (3), (4), (5), or (6) of subsection (e) shall, for purposes of applying such paragraphs, be treated as actually owned by such person.

(B) Members of family—Stock constructively owned by an individual by reason of the application of paragraph (5) or (6) of subsection (e) shall not be treated as owned by him for purposes of again applying such paragraphs in order to make another the constructive owner of such stock.

(3) Special rules—For purposes of this section—

(A) If stock may be considered as owned by a person under subsection (e)(1) and under any other paragraph of subsection (e), it shall be considered as owned by him under subsection (e)(1).

(B) If stock is owned (within the meaning of subsection (d)) by two or more persons, such stock shall be considered as owned by the person whose ownership of such stock results in the corporation being a component member of a controlled group. If by reason of the preceding sentence, a corporation would (but for this sentence) become a component member of two controlled groups, it shall be treated as a component member of one controlled group. The determination as to the group of which such corporation is a component member shall be made under regulations prescribed by the Secretary which are consistent with the purposes of this part.

(C) If stock is owned by a person within the meaning of subsection (d) and such ownership results in the corporation being a component member of a controlled group, such stock shall not be treated as excluded stock under subsection (c)(2), if by reason of treating such stock as excluded stock the result is that such corporation is not a component member of a controlled group of corporations.

* * *

(5) Brother-sister controlled group definition for provisions other than this part—

(A) In general—Except as specifically provided in an applicable provision, subsection (a)(2) shall be applied to an applicable provision as if it read as follows:

"**(2)** Brother-sister controlled group. Two or more corporations if 5 or fewer persons who are individuals, estates, or trusts own (within the meaning of subsection (d)(2) stock possessing—

"**(A)** at least 80 percent of the total combined voting power of all classes of stock entitled to vote, or at least 80 percent of the total value of shares of all classes of stock, of each corporation, and

"**(B)** more than 50 percent of the total combined voting power of all classes of stock entitled to vote or more than 50 percent of the total value of shares of all classes of stock of each corporation, taking into account the stock ownership of each such person only to the extent such stock ownership is identical with respect to each such corporation."

(B) Applicable provision—For purposes of this paragraph, an applicable provision is any provision of law (other than this part) which incorporates the definition of controlled group of corporations under subsection (a).

§ 3121. Definitions.

(a) Wages—For purposes of this chapter, the term "wages" means all remuneration for employment, including the cash value of all remuneration (including benefits) paid in any medium other than cash; except that such term shall not include—

* * *

(5) any payment made to, or on behalf of, an employee or his beneficiary—

(A) from or to a trust described in section 401(a) which is exempt from tax under section 501(a) at the time of such payment unless such payment is made to an employee of the trust as remuneration for services rendered as such employee and not as a beneficiary of the trust,

(B) under or to an annuity plan which, at the time of such payment, is a plan described in section 403(a),

(C) under a simplified employee pension (as defined in section 408(k)(1)), other than any contributions described in section 408(k)(6),

(D) under or to an annuity contract described in section 403(b), other than a payment for the purchase of such contract which is made by reason of a salary reduction agreement (whether evidenced by a written instrument or otherwise),

(E) under or to an exempt governmental deferred compensation plan (as defined in subsection (v)(3)),

(F) to supplement pension benefits under a plan or trust described in any of the foregoing provisions of this paragraph to take into account some portion or all of the increase in the cost of living (as determined by the Secretary of Labor) since retirement but only if such supplemental payments are under a plan which is treated as a welfare plan under section 3(2)(B)(ii) of the Employee Retirement Income Security Act of 1974,

(G) under a cafeteria plan (within the meaning of section 125) if such payment would not be treated as wages without regard to such plan and it is reasonable to believe that (if section 125 applied for purposes of this section) section 125 would not treat any wages as constructively received,

(H) under an arrangement to which section 408(p) applies, other than any elective contributions under paragraph (2)(A)(i) thereof, or

(I) under a plan described in section 457(e)(11)(A)(ii) and maintained by an eligible employer (as defined in section 457(e)(1));

* * *

(v) Treatment of certain deferred compensation and salary reduction arrangements—

(1) Certain employer contributions treated as wages—Nothing in any paragraph of subsection (a) (other than paragraph (1)) shall exclude from the term "wages"—

(A) any employer contribution under a qualified cash or deferred arrangement (as defined in section 401(k)) to the extent not included in gross income by reason of section 402(e)(3) or consisting of designated Roth contributions (as defined in section 402A(c)), or

(B) any amount treated as an employer contribution under section 414(h)(2) where the pickup referred to in such section is pursuant to a salary reduction agreement (whether evidenced by a written instrument or otherwise).

(2) Treatment of certain nonqualified deferred compensation plans—

(A) In general—Any amount deferred under a nonqualified deferred compensation plan shall be taken into account for purposes of this chapter as of the later of—

(i) when the services are performed, or

(ii) when there is no substantial risk of forfeiture of the rights to such amount.

The preceding sentence shall not apply to any excess parachute payment (as defined in section 280G(b)) or to any specified stock compensation (as defined in section 4985) on which tax is imposed by section 4985.

(B) Taxed only once—Any amount taken into account as wages by reason of subparagraph (A) (and the income attributable thereto) shall not thereafter be treated as wages for purposes of this chapter.

(C) Nonqualified deferred compensation plan—For purposes of this paragraph, the term "nonqualified deferred compensation plan" means any plan or other arrangement for deferral of compensation other than a plan described in subsection (a)(5).

(3) Exempt governmental deferred compensation plan—For purposes of subsection (a)(5), the term "exempt governmental deferred compensation plan" means any plan providing for deferral of compensation established and maintained for its employees by the United States, by a State or political subdivision thereof, or by an agency or instrumentality of any of the foregoing. Such term shall not include—

(A) any plan to which section 83, 402(b), 403(c), 457(a), or 457(f)(1) applies,

(B) any annuity contract described in section 403(b), and

(C) the Thrift Savings Fund (within the meaning of subchapter III of chapter 84 of title 5, United States Code).

* * *

§ 3405. Special rules for pensions, annuities, and certain other deferred income.

(a) Periodic payments—

(1) Withholding as if payment were wages—The payor of any periodic payment (as defined in subsection (e)(2)) shall withhold from such payment the amount which would be required to be withheld from such payment if such payment were a payment of wages by an employer to an employee for the appropriate payroll period.

(2) Election of no withholding—An individual may elect to have paragraph (1) not apply with respect to periodic payments made to such individual. Such an election shall remain in effect until revoked by such individual.

(3) When election takes effect—Any election under this subsection (and any revocation of such an election) shall take effect as provided by subsection (f)(3) of section 3402 for withholding exemption certificates.

(4) Amount withheld where no withholding exemption certificate in effect—In the case of any payment with respect to which a withholding exemption certificate is not in effect, the amount withheld under paragraph (1) shall be determined by treating the payee as a married individual claiming 3 withholding exemptions.

(b) Nonperiodic distribution—

(1) Withholding—The payor of any nonperiodic distribution (as defined in subsection (e)(3)) shall withhold from such distribution an amount equal to 10 percent of such distribution.

(2) Election of no withholding—

(A) In general—An individual may elect not to have paragraph (1) apply with respect to any nonperiodic distribution.

(B) Scope of election—An election under subparagraph (A)—

(i) except as provided in clause (ii), shall be on a distribution-by-distribution basis, or

(ii) to the extent provided in regulations, may apply to subsequent nonperiodic distributions made by the payor to the payee under the same arrangement.

(c) Eligible rollover distributions—

(1) In general—In the case of any designated distribution which is an eligible rollover distribution—

(A) subsections (a) and (b) shall not apply, and

(B) the payor of such distribution shall withhold from such distribution an amount equal to 20 percent of such distribution.

(2) Exception—Paragraph (1)(B) shall not apply to any distribution if the distributee elects under section 401(a)(31)(A) to have such distribution paid directly to an eligible retirement plan.

(3) Eligible rollover distribution—For purposes of this subsection, the term "eligible rollover distribution" has the meaning given such term by section 402(f)(2)(A).

* * *

(e) Definitions and special rules—For purposes of this section—

(1) Designated distribution—

(A) In general—Except as provided in subparagraph (B), the term "designated distribution" means any distribution or payment from or under—

(i) an employer deferred compensation plan,

(ii) an individual retirement plan (as defined in section 7701(a)(37)), or

(iii) a commercial annuity.

(B) Exceptions—The term "designated distribution" shall not include—

(i) any amount which is wages without regard to this section,

(ii) the portion of a distribution or payment which it is reasonable to believe is not includible in gross income,

(iii) any amount which is subject to withholding under subchapter A of chapter 3 (relating to withholding of tax on nonresident aliens and foreign corporations) by the person paying such amount or which would be so subject but for a tax treaty, or

(iv) any distribution described in section 404(k)(2).

For purposes of clause (ii), any distribution or payment from or under an individual retirement plan (other than a Roth IRA) shall be treated as includible in gross income.

* * *

(8) Maximum amount withheld—The maximum amount to be withheld under this section on any designated distribution shall not exceed the sum of the amount of money and the fair market value of other property (other than securities of the employer corporation) received in the distribution. No amount shall be required to be withheld under this section in the case of any designated distribution which consists only of securities of the employer corporation and cash (not in excess of $200) in lieu of financial shares. For purposes of this paragraph, the term "securities of the employer corporation" has the meaning given such term by section 402(e)(4)(E).

* * *

§ 4971. Taxes on failure to meet minimum funding standards.

(a) Initial tax—If at any time during any taxable year an employer maintains a plan to which section 412 applies, there is hereby imposed for the taxable year a tax equal to—

(1) in the case of a single-employer plan, 10 percent of the aggregate unpaid minimum required contributions for all plan years remaining unpaid as of the end of any plan year ending with or within the taxable year,

(2) in the case of a multiemployer plan, 5 percent of the accumulated funding deficiency determined under section 431 as of the end of any plan year ending with or within the taxable year, and

(3) in the case of a CSEC plan, 10 percent of the CSEC accumulated funding deficiency as of the end of the plan year ending with or within the taxable year.

(b) Additional tax—If—

(1) a tax is imposed under subsection (a)(1) on any unpaid minimum required contribution and such amount remains unpaid as of the close of the taxable period,

(2) a tax is imposed under subsection (a)(2) on any accumulated funding deficiency and the accumulated funding deficiency is not corrected within the taxable period, or

(3) a tax is imposed under subsection (a)(3) on any CSEC accumulated funding deficiency and the CSEC accumulated funding deficiency is not corrected within the taxable period,

there is hereby imposed a tax equal to 100 percent of the unpaid minimum required contribution, accumulated funding deficiency, or CSEC accumulated funding deficiency, whichever is applicable, to the extent not so paid or corrected.

(c) Definitions—For purposes of this section—

(1) Accumulated funding deficiency—The term "accumulated funding deficiency" has the meaning given to such term by section 431.

(2) Correct—The term "correct" means, with respect to an accumulated funding deficiency or CSEC accumulated funding deficiency, the contribution, to or under the plan, of the amount necessary to reduce such accumulated funding deficiency or CSEC accumulated funding deficiency as of the end of a plan year in which such deficiency arose to zero.

(3) Taxable period—The term "taxable period" means, with respect to an accumulated funding deficiency, CSEC accumulated funding deficiency, or unpaid minimum required contribution, whichever is applicable, the period beginning with the end of the plan year in which there is an accumulated funding deficiency, CSEC accumulated funding deficiency, or unpaid minimum required contribution, whichever is applicable and ending on the earlier of—

(A) the date of mailing of a notice of deficiency with respect to the tax imposed by subsection (a), or

(B) the date on which the tax imposed by subsection (a) is assessed.

(4) Unpaid minimum required contribution—

(A) In general—The term "unpaid minimum required contribution" means, with respect to any plan year, any minimum required contribution under section 430 for the plan year which is not paid on or before the due date (as determined under section 430(j)(1)) for the plan year.

(B) Ordering rule—Any payment to or under a plan for any plan year shall be allocated first to unpaid minimum required contributions for all preceding plan years on a first-in, first-out basis and then to the minimum required contribution under section 430 for the plan year.

(5) CSEC accumulated funding deficiency—The term "CSEC accumulated funding deficiency" means the accumulated funding deficiency determined under section 433.

* * *

(e) Liability for tax—

(1) In general—Except as provided in paragraph (2), the tax imposed by subsection (a), (b), or (f) shall be paid by the employer responsible for contributing to or under the plan the amount described in section 412(a)(2).

(2) Joint and several liability where employer member of controlled group—

(A) In general—If an employer referred to in paragraph (1) is a member of a controlled group, each member of such group shall be jointly and severally liable for the tax imposed by subsection (a), (b), (f), or (g).

(B) Controlled group—For purposes of subparagraph (A), the term "controlled group" means any group treated as a single employer under subsection (b), (c), (m), or (o) of section 414.

(f) Failure to pay liquidity shortfall—

(1) In general—In the case of a plan to which section 430(j)(4) or 433(f) applies, there is hereby imposed a tax of 10 percent of the excess (if any) of—

(A) the amount of the liquidity shortfall for any quarter, over

(B) the amount of such shortfall which is paid by the required installment under section 430(j) or 433(f), whichever is applicable, for such quarter (but only if such installment is paid on or before the due date for such installment).

(2) Additional tax—If the plan has a liquidity shortfall as of the close of any quarter and as of the close of each of the following 4 quarters, there is hereby imposed a tax equal to 100 percent of the amount on which tax was imposed by paragraph (1) for such first quarter.

(3) Definitions and special rule—

(A) Liquidity shortfall; quarter—For purposes of this subsection, the terms "liquidity shortfall" and "quarter" have the respective meanings given such terms by section 430(j) or 433(f), whichever is applicable.

(B) Special rule—If the tax imposed by paragraph (2) is paid with respect to any liquidity shortfall for any quarter, no further tax shall be imposed by this subsection on such shortfall for such quarter.

(4) Waiver by Secretary—If the taxpayer establishes to the satisfaction of the Secretary that—

(A) the liquidity shortfall described in paragraph (1) was due to reasonable cause and not willful neglect, and

(B) reasonable steps have been taken to remedy such liquidity shortfall,

the Secretary may waive all or part of the tax imposed by this subsection.

* * *

§ 4972. Tax on nondeductible contributions to qualified employer plans.

(a) Tax imposed—In the case of any qualified employer plan, there is hereby imposed a tax equal to 10 percent of the nondeductible contributions under the plan (determined as of the close of the taxable year of the employer).

(b) Employer liable for tax—The tax imposed by this section shall be paid by the employer making the contributions.

(c) Nondeductible contributions—For purposes of this section—

(1) In general—The term "nondeductible contributions" means, with respect to any qualified employer plan, the sum of—

(A) the excess (if any) of—

(i) the amount contributed for the taxable year by the employer to or under such plan, over

(ii) the amount allowable as a deduction under section 404 for such contributions (determined without regard to subsection (e) thereof), and

(B) the amount determined under this subsection for the preceding taxable year reduced by the sum of—

(i) the portion of the amount so determined returned to the employer during the taxable year, and

(ii) the portion of the amount so determined deductible under section 404 for the taxable year (determined without regard to subsection (e) thereof).

* * *

(4) Special rule for self-employed individuals—For purposes of paragraph (1), if—

(A) the amount which is required to be contributed to a plan under section 412 on behalf of an individual who is an employee (within the meaning of section 401(c)(1)), exceeds

(B) the earned income (within the meaning of section 404(a)(8)) of such individual derived from the trade or business with respect to which such plan is established,

such excess shall be treated as an amount allowable as a deduction under section 404.

* * *

(6) Exceptions—In determining the amount of nondeductible contributions for any taxable year, there shall not be taken into account—

(A) so much of the contributions to 1 or more defined contribution plans which are not deductible when contributed solely because of section 404(a)(7) as does not exceed the amount of contributions described in section 401(m)(4)(A), or

(B) so much of the contributions to a simple retirement account (within the meaning of section 408(p)) or a simple plan (within the meaning of section 401(k)(11)) which are not deductible when contributed solely because such contributions are not made in connection with a trade or business of the employer.

For purposes of subparagraph (A), the deductible limits under section 404(a)(7) shall first be applied to amounts contributed to a defined benefit plan and then to amounts described in subparagraph (A). Subparagraph (B) shall not apply to contributions made on behalf of the employer or a member of the employer's family (as defined in section 447(e)(1)).

(7) Defined benefit plan exception—In determining the amount of nondeductible contributions for any taxable year, an employer may elect for such year not to take into account any contributions to a defined benefit plan except, in the case of a multiemployer plan, to the extent that such contributions exceed the full-funding limitation (as defined in section 431(c)(6)). For purposes of this paragraph, the deductible limits under section 404(a)(7) shall first be applied to amounts contributed to defined contribution plans and then to amounts described in this paragraph. If an employer makes an election under this paragraph for a taxable year, paragraph (6) shall not apply to such employer for such taxable year.

(d) Definitions—For purposes of this section—

(1) Qualified employer plan—

(A) In general—The term "qualified employer plan" means—

(i) any plan meeting the requirements of section 401(a) which includes a trust exempt from tax under section 501(a),

(ii) an annuity plan described in section 403(a),

(iii) any simplified employee pension (within the meaning of section 408(k)), and

(iv) any simple retirement account (within the meaning of section 408(p)).

(B) Exemption for governmental and tax exempt plans—The term "qualified employer plan" does not include a plan described in subparagraph (A) or (B) of section 4980(c)(1).

(2) Employer—In the case of a plan which provides contributions or benefits for employees some or all of whom are self-employed individuals within the meaning of section 401(c)(1), the term "employer" means the person treated as the employer under section 401(c)(4).

§ 4973. Tax on excess contributions to certain tax-favored accounts and annuities.

(a) Tax imposed—In the case of—

(1) an individual retirement account (within the meaning of section 408(a)),

(2) an Archer MSA (within the meaning of section 220(d)),

(3) an individual retirement annuity (within the meaning of section 408(b)), a custodial account treated as an annuity contract under section 403(b)(7)(A) (relating to custodial accounts for regulated investment company stock), or

(4) a Coverdell education savings account (as defined in section 530),

(5) a health savings account (within the meaning of section 223(d)), or

346

(6) an ABLE account (within the meaning of section 529A),

there is imposed for each taxable year a tax in an amount equal to 6 percent of the amount of the excess contributions to such individual's accounts or annuities (determined as of the close of the taxable year). The amount of such tax for any taxable year shall not exceed 6 percent of the value of the account or annuity (determined as of the close of the taxable year). In the case of an endowment contract described in section 408(b), the tax imposed by this section does not apply to any amount allocable to life, health, accident, or other insurance under such contract. The tax imposed by this subsection shall be paid by such individual.

(b) Excess contributions—For purposes of this section, in the case of individual retirement accounts, or individual retirement annuities the term "excess contributions" means the sum of—

(1) the excess (if any) of—

(A) the amount contributed for the taxable year to the accounts or for the annuities or bonds (other than a contribution to a Roth IRA or a rollover contribution described in section 402(c), 403(a)(4), 403(b)(8), 408(d)(3), or 457(e)(16)), over

(B) the amount allowable as a deduction under section 219 for such contributions, and

(2) the amount determined under this subsection for the preceding taxable year, reduced by the sum of—

(A) the distributions out of the account for the taxable year which were included in the gross income of the payee under section 408(d)(1),

(B) the distributions out of the account for the taxable year to which section 408(d)(5) applies, and

(C) the excess (if any) of the maximum amount allowable as a deduction under section 219 for the taxable year over the amount contributed (determined without regard to section 219(f)(6)) to the accounts or for the annuities (including the amount contributed to a Roth IRA) or bonds for the taxable year.

For purposes of this subsection, any contribution which is distributed from the individual retirement account or the individual retirement annuity in a distribution to which section 408(d)(4) applies shall be treated as an amount not contributed. For purposes of paragraphs (1)(B) and (2)(C), the amount allowable as a deduction under section 219 shall be computed without regard to section 219(g).

* * *

(f) Excess contributions to Roth IRAs—For purposes of this section, in the case of contributions to a Roth IRA (within the meaning of section 408A(b)), the term "excess contributions" means the sum of—

(1) the excess (if any) of—

(A) the amount contributed for the taxable year to Roth IRAs (other than a qualified rollover contribution described in section 408A(e)), over

(B) the amount allowable as a contribution under sections 408A (c)(2) and (c)(3), and

(2) the amount determined under this subsection for the preceding taxable year, reduced by the sum of—

(A) the distributions out of the accounts for the taxable year, and

(B) the excess (if any) of the maximum amount allowable as a contribution under sections 408A (c)(2) and (c)(3) for the taxable year over the amount contributed by the individual to all individual retirement plans for the taxable year.

For purposes of this subsection, any contribution which is distributed from a Roth IRA in a distribution described in section 408(d)(4) shall be treated as an amount not contributed.

* * *

§ 4974. Excise tax on certain accumulations in qualified retirement plans.

(a) General rule—If the amount distributed during the taxable year of the payee under any qualified retirement plan or any eligible deferred compensation plan (as defined in section 457(b)) is less than the minimum required distribution for such taxable year, there is hereby imposed a tax equal to 50 percent of the amount by which such minimum required distribution exceeds the actual amount distributed during the taxable year. The tax imposed by this section shall be paid by the payee.

(b) Minimum required distribution—For purposes of this section, the term "minimum required distribution" means the minimum amount required to be distributed during a taxable year under section 401(a)(9), 403(b)(10), 408(a)(6), 408(b)(3), or 457(d)(2), as the case may be, as determined under regulations prescribed by the Secretary.

(c) Qualified retirement plan—For purposes of this section, the term "qualified retirement plan" means—

(1) a plan described in section 401(a) which includes a trust exempt from tax under section 501(a),

(2) an annuity plan described in section 403(a),

(3) an annuity contract described in section 403(b),

(4) an individual retirement account described in section 408(a), or

(5) an individual retirement annuity described in section 408(b).

Such term includes any plan, contract, account, or annuity which, at any time, has been determined by the Secretary to be such a plan, contract, account, or annuity.

(d) Waiver of tax in certain cases—If the taxpayer establishes to the satisfaction of the Secretary that—

(1) the shortfall described in subsection (a) in the amount distributed during any taxable year was due to reasonable error, and

(2) reasonable steps are being taken to remedy the shortfall, the Secretary may waive the tax imposed by subsection (a) for the taxable year.

§ 4975. Tax on prohibited transactions.

(a) Initial taxes on disqualified person—There is hereby imposed a tax on each prohibited transaction. The rate of tax shall be equal to 15 percent of the amount involved with respect to the prohibited transaction for each year (or part thereof) in the taxable period. The tax imposed by this subsection shall be paid by any disqualified person who participates in the prohibited transaction (other than a fiduciary acting only as such).

(b) Additional taxes on disqualified person—In any case in which an initial tax is imposed by subsection (a) on a prohibited transaction and the transaction is not corrected within the taxable period, there is hereby imposed a tax equal to 100 percent of the amount involved. The tax imposed by this subsection shall be paid by any disqualified person who participated in the prohibited transaction (other than a fiduciary acting only as such).

(c) Prohibited transaction—

(1) General rule—For purposes of this section, the term "prohibited transaction" means any direct or indirect—

(A) sale or exchange, or leasing, of any property between a plan and a disqualified person;

(B) lending of money or other extension of credit between a plan and a disqualified person;

(C) furnishing of goods, services, or facilities between a plan and a disqualified person;

(D) transfer to, or use by or for the benefit of, a disqualified person of the income or assets of a plan;

(E) act by a disqualified person who is a fiduciary whereby he deals with the income or assets of a plan in his own interest or for his own account; or

(F) receipt of any consideration for his own personal account by any disqualified person who is a fiduciary from any party dealing with the plan in connection with a transaction involving the income or assets of the plan.

(2) Special exemption—The Secretary shall establish an exemption procedure for purposes of this subsection. Pursuant to such procedure, he may grant a conditional or unconditional exemption of any disqualified person or transaction or class of disqualified persons or transactions, from all or part of the restrictions imposed by paragraph (1) of this subsection. Action under this subparagraph may be taken only after consultation and coordination with the Secretary of Labor. The Secretary may not grant an exemption under this paragraph unless he finds that such exemption is—

(A) administratively feasible,

(B) in the interests of the plan and of its participants and beneficiaries, and

(C) protective of the rights of participants and beneficiaries of the plan.

Before granting an exemption under this paragraph, the Secretary shall require adequate notice to be given to interested persons and shall publish notice in the Federal Register of the pendency of such exemption and shall afford interested persons an opportunity to present views. No exemption may be granted under this paragraph with respect to a transaction described in subparagraph (E) or (F) of paragraph (1) unless the Secretary affords an opportunity for a hearing and makes a determination on the record with respect to the findings required under subparagraphs (A), (B), and (C) of this paragraph, except that in lieu of such hearing the Secretary may accept any record made by the Secretary of Labor with respect to an application for exemption under section 408(a) of title I of the Employee Retirement Income Security Act of 1974.

* * *

(d) Exemptions—Except as provided in subsection (f)(6), the prohibitions provided in subsection (c) shall not apply to—

(1) any loan made by the plan to a disqualified person who is a participant or beneficiary of the plan if such loan—

> **(A)** is available to all such participants or beneficiaries on a reasonably equivalent basis,

> **(B)** is not made available to highly compensated employees (within the meaning of section 414(q) of the Internal Revenue Code of 1986) in an amount greater than the amount made available to other employees,

> **(C)** is made in accordance with specific provisions regarding such loans set forth in the plan,

> **(D)** bears a reasonable rate of interest, and

> **(E)** is adequately secured;

(2) any contract, or reasonable arrangement, made with a disqualified person for office space, or legal, accounting, or other services necessary for the establishment or operation of the plan, if no more than reasonable compensation is paid therefor; 4975(d);

(3) any loan to a leveraged employee stock ownership plan (as defined in subsection (e)(7)), if—

> **(A)** such loan is primarily for the benefit of participants and beneficiaries of the plan, and

> **(B)** such loan is at a reasonable rate of interest, and any collateral which is given to a disqualified person by the plan consists only of qualifying employer securities (as defined in subsection (e)(8));

* * *

(17) Any transaction in connection with the provision of investment advice described in subsection (e)(3)(B) to a participant or beneficiary in a plan that permits such participant or beneficiary to direct the investment of plan assets in an individual account, if—

> **(A)** the transaction is—

>> **(i)** the provision of the investment advice to the participant or beneficiary of the plan with respect to a security or other property available as an investment under the plan,

>> **(ii)** the acquisition, holding, or sale of a security or other property available as an investment under the plan pursuant to the investment advice, or

>> **(iii)** the direct or indirect receipt of fees or other compensation by the fiduciary adviser or an affiliate thereof (or any employee, agent, or registered representative of the fiduciary adviser or affiliate) in connection with the provision of the advice or in connection with an acquisition, holding, or sale of a security or other property available as an investment under the plan pursuant to the investment advice; and

> **(B)** the requirements of subsection (f)(8) are met.

* * *

(e) Definitions—

350

(1) **Plan**—For purposes of this section, the term "plan" means—

(A) a trust described in section 401(a) which forms a part of a plan, or a plan described in section 403(a), which trust or plan is exempt from tax under section 501(a),

(B) an individual retirement account described in section 408(a),

(C) an individual retirement annuity described in section 408(b),

(D) an Archer MSA described in section 220(d),

(E) a health savings account described in section 223(d),

(F) a Coverdell education savings account described in section 530, or

(G) a trust, plan, account, or annuity which, at any time, has been determined by the Secretary to be described in any preceding subparagraph of this paragraph.

(2) **Disqualified person**—For purposes of this section, the term "disqualified person" means a person who is—

(A) a fiduciary;

(B) a person providing services to the plan;

(C) an employer any of whose employees are covered by the plan;

(D) an employee organization any of whose members are covered by the plan;

(E) an owner, direct or indirect, of 50 percent or more of—

(i) the combined voting power of all classes of stock entitled to vote or the total value of shares of all classes of stock of a corporation,

(ii) the capital interest or the profits interest of a partnership, or

(iii) the beneficial interest of a trust or unincorporated enterprise, which is an employer or an employee organization described in subparagraph (C) or (D);

(F) a member of the family (as defined in paragraph (6)) of any individual described in subparagraph (A), (B), (C), or (E);

(G) a corporation, partnership, or trust or estate of which (or in which) 50 percent or more of—

(i) the combined voting power of all classes of stock entitled to vote or the total value of shares of all classes of stock of such corporation,

(ii) the capital interest or profits interest of such partnership, or

(iii) the beneficial interest of such trust or estate, is owned directly or indirectly, or held by persons described in subparagraph (A), (B), (C), (D), or (E);

(H) an officer, director (or an individual having powers or responsibilities similar to those of officers or directors), a 10 percent or more shareholder, or a highly compensated employee (earning 10 percent or more of the yearly wages of an employer) of a person described in subparagraph (C), (D), (E), or (G); or

(I) a 10 percent or more (in capital or profits) partner or joint venturer of a person described in subparagraph (C), (D), (E), or (G).

The Secretary, after consultation and coordination with the Secretary of Labor or his delegate, may by regulation prescribe a percentage lower than 50 percent for subparagraphs (E) and (G) and lower than 10 percent for subparagraphs (H) and (I).

(3) Fiduciary—For purposes of this section, the term "fiduciary" means any person who—

(A) exercises any discretionary authority or discretionary control respecting management of such plan or exercises any authority or control respecting management or disposition of its assets,

(B) renders investment advice for a fee or other compensation, direct or indirect, with respect to any moneys or other property of such plan, or has any authority or responsibility to do so, or

(C) has any discretionary authority or discretionary responsibility in the administration of such plan.

Such term includes any person designated under section 405(c)(1)(B) of the Employee Retirement Income Security Act of 1974.

(4) Stockholdings—For purposes of paragraphs (2)(E)(i), and (G)(i) there shall be taken into account indirect stockholdings which would be taken into account under section 267(c), except that, for purposes of this paragraph, section 267(c)(4) shall be treated as providing that the members of the family of an individual are the members within the meaning of paragraph (6).

(5) Partnerships; trusts—For purposes of paragraphs (2)(E)(ii) and (iii), (G)(ii) and (iii), and (I) the ownership of profits or beneficial interests shall be determined in accordance with the rules for constructive ownership of stock provided in section 267(c) (other than paragraph (3) thereof), except that section 267(c)(4) shall be treated as providing that the members of the family of an individual are the members within the meaning of paragraph (6).

(6) Member of family—For purposes of paragraph (2)(F), the family of any individual shall include his spouse, ancestor, lineal descendant, and any spouse of a lineal descendant.

(7) Employee stock ownership plan—The term "employee stock ownership plan" means a defined contribution plan—

(A) which is a stock bonus plan which is qualified, or a stock bonus and a money purchase plan both of which are qualified under section 401(a) and which are designed to invest primarily in qualifying employer securities; and

(B) which is otherwise defined in regulations prescribed by the Secretary.

A plan shall not be treated as an employee stock ownership plan unless it meets the requirements of section 409(h), section 409(o), and, if applicable, section 409(n), section 409(p), and section 664(g) and, if the employer has a registration-type class of securities (as defined in section 409(e)(4)), it meets the requirements of section 409(e).

(8) Qualifying employer security—The term "qualifying employer security" means an employer security within the meaning of section 409(l). If any moneys or other property of a plan are invested in shares of an investment company registered under the Investment Company Act of 1940, the investment shall not cause that investment company or that investment company's investment adviser or principal underwriter to be treated as a fiduciary or a disqualified person for purposes of this section, except when an investment company or its investment adviser or principal underwriter acts in connection with a plan covering employees of the investment company, its investment adviser, or its principal underwriter.

* * *

(f) Other definitions and special rules—For purposes of this section—

(1) Joint and several liability—If more than one person is liable under subsection (a) or (b) with respect to any one prohibited transaction, all such persons shall be jointly and severally liable under such subsection with respect to such transaction.

(2) Taxable period—The term "taxable period" means, with respect to any prohibited transaction, the period beginning with the date on which the prohibited transaction occurs and ending on the earliest of—

    (A) the date of mailing a notice of deficiency with respect to the tax imposed by subsection (a) under section 6212,

    (B) the date on which the tax imposed by subsection (a) is assessed, or

    (C) the date on which correction of the prohibited transaction is completed.

(3) Sale or exchange; encumbered property—A transfer of real or personal property by a disqualified person to a plan shall be treated as a sale or exchange if the property is subject to a mortgage or similar lien which the plan assumes or if it is subject to a mortgage or similar lien which a disqualified person placed on the property within the 10-year period ending on the date of the transfer.

(4) Amount involved—The term "amount involved" means, with respect to a prohibited transaction, the greater of the amount of money and the fair market value of the other property given or the amount of money and the fair market value of the other property received; except that, in the case of services described in paragraphs (2) and (10) of subsection (d) the amount involved shall be only the excess compensation. For purposes of the preceding sentence, the fair market value—

    (A) in the case of the tax imposed by subsection (a), shall be determined as of the date on which the prohibited transaction occurs; and

    (B) in the case of the tax imposed by subsection (b), shall be the highest fair market value during the taxable period.

(5) Correction—The terms "correction" and "correct" mean, with respect to a prohibited transaction, undoing the transaction to the extent possible, but in any case placing the plan in a financial position not worse than that in which it would be if the disqualified person were acting under the highest fiduciary standards.

(6) Exemptions not to apply to certain transactions—

    (A) In general—In the case of a trust described in section 401(a) which is part of a plan providing contributions or benefits for employees some or all of whom are owner-employees (as defined in section 401(c)(3)), the exemptions provided by subsection (d) (other than paragraphs (9) and (12)) shall not apply to a transaction in which the plan directly or indirectly—

        (i) lends any part of the corpus or income of the plan to,

        (ii) pays any compensation for personal services rendered to the plan to, or

        (iii) acquires for the plan any property from, or sells any property to, any such owner-employee, a member of the family (as defined in section 267(c)(4)) of any such owner-employee, or any corporation in which any such owner-employee owns, directly or indirectly, 50 percent or more of the total combined voting power of all classes of stock entitled to vote or 50 percent or more of the total value of shares of all classes of stock of the corporation.

(B) Special rules for shareholder-employees, etc—

(i) In general—For purposes of subparagraph (A), the following shall be treated as owner-employees:

(I) A shareholder-employee.

(II) A participant or beneficiary of an individual retirement plan (as defined in section 7701(a)(37)).

(III) An employer or association of employees which establishes such an individual retirement plan under section 408(c).

(ii) Exception for certain transactions involving shareholder-employees—Subparagraph (A)(iii) shall not apply to a transaction which consists of a sale of employer securities to an employee stock ownership plan (as defined in subsection (e)(7)) by a shareholder-employee, a member of the family (as defined in section 267(c)(4)) of such shareholder-employee, or a corporation in which such a shareholder-employee owns stock representing a 50 percent or greater interest described in subparagraph (A).

(iii) Loan exception—For purposes of subparagraph (A)(i), the term "owner-employee" shall only include a person described in subclause (II) or (III) of clause (i).

(C) Shareholder-employee—For purposes of subparagraph (B), the term "shareholder-employee" means an employee or officer of an S corporation who owns (or is considered as owning within the meaning of section 318(a)(1)) more than 5 percent of the outstanding stock of the corporation on any day during the taxable year of such corporation.

(7) S corporation repayment of loans for qualifying employer securities—A plan shall not be treated as violating the requirements of section 401 or 409 or subsection (e)(7), or as engaging in a prohibited transaction for purposes of subsection (d)(3), merely by reason of any distribution (as described in section 1368(a)) with respect to S corporation stock that constitutes qualifying employer securities, which in accordance with the plan provisions is used to make payments on a loan described in subsection (d)(3) the proceeds of which were used to acquire such qualifying employer securities (whether or not allocated to participants). The preceding sentence shall not apply in the case of a distribution which is paid with respect to any employer security which is allocated to a participant unless the plan provides that employer securities with a fair market value of not less than the amount of such distribution are allocated to such participant for the year which (but for the preceding sentence) such distribution would have been allocated to such participant.

(8) Provision of investment advice to participant and beneficiaries—

(A) In general—The prohibitions provided in subsection (c) shall not apply to transactions described in subsection (d)(17) if the investment advice provided by a fiduciary adviser is provided under an eligible investment advice arrangement.

(B) Eligible investment advice arrangement—For purposes of this paragraph, the term "eligible investment advice arrangement" means an arrangement—

(i) which either—

(I) provides that any fees (including any commission or other compensation) received by the fiduciary adviser for investment advice or with respect to the sale, holding, or acquisition of any security or other property for purposes of investment of plan assets do not vary depending on the basis of any investment option selected, or

(II) uses a computer model under an investment advice program meeting the requirements of subparagraph (C) in connection with the provision of investment advice by a fiduciary adviser to a participant or beneficiary, and

(ii) with respect to which the requirements of subparagraphs (D), (E), (F), (G), (H), and (I) are met.

(C) Investment advice program using computer model—

(i) In general—An investment advice program meets the requirements of this subparagraph if the requirements of clauses (ii), (iii), and (iv) are met.

(ii) Computer model—The requirements of this clause are met if the investment advice provided under the investment advice program is provided pursuant to a computer model that—

(I) applies generally accepted investment theories that take into account the historic returns of different asset classes over defined periods of time,

(II) utilizes relevant information about the participant, which may include age, life expectancy, retirement age, risk tolerance, other assets or sources of income, and preferences as to certain types of investments,

(III) utilizes prescribed objective criteria to provide asset allocation portfolios comprised of investment options available under the plan,

(IV) operates in a manner that is not biased in favor of investments offered by the fiduciary adviser or a person with a material affiliation or contractual relationship with the fiduciary adviser, and

(V) takes into account all investment options under the plan in specifying how a participant's account balance should be invested and is not inappropriately weighted with respect to any investment option.

(iii) Certification—

(I) In general—The requirements of this clause are met with respect to any investment advice program if an eligible investment expert certifies, prior to the utilization of the computer model and in accordance with rules prescribed by the Secretary of Labor, that the computer model meets the requirements of clause (ii).

(II) Renewal of certifications—If, as determined under regulations prescribed by the Secretary of Labor, there are material modifications to a computer model, the requirements of this clause are met only if a certification described in subclause (I) is obtained with respect to the computer model as so modified.

(III) Eligible investment expert—The term "eligible investment expert" means any person which meets such requirements as the Secretary of Labor may provide and which does not bear any material affiliation or contractual relationship with any investment adviser or a related person thereof (or any employee, agent, or registered representative of the investment adviser or related person).

(iv) Exclusivity of recommendation—The requirements of this clause are met with respect to any investment advice program if—

(I) the only investment advice provided under the program is the advice generated by the computer model described in clause (ii), and

(II) any transaction described in subsection (d)(17)(A)(ii) occurs solely at the direction of the participant or beneficiary.

Nothing in the preceding sentence shall preclude the participant or beneficiary from requesting investment advice other than that described in clause (i), but only if such request has not been solicited by any person connected with carrying out the arrangement.

(D) Express authorization by separate fiduciary—The requirements of this subparagraph are met with respect to an arrangement if the arrangement is expressly authorized by a plan fiduciary other than the person offering the investment advice program, any person providing investment options under the plan, or any affiliate of either.

(E) Audits—

(i) In general—The requirements of this subparagraph are met if an independent auditor, who has appropriate technical training or experience and proficiency and so represents in writing—

(I) conducts an annual audit of the arrangement for compliance with the requirements of this paragraph, and

(II) following completion of the annual audit, issues a written report to the fiduciary who authorized use of the arrangement which presents its specific findings regarding compliance of the arrangement with the requirements of this paragraph.

(ii) Special rule for individual retirement and similar plans—In the case of a plan described in subparagraphs (B) through (F) (and so much of subparagraph (G) as relates to such subparagraphs) of subsection (e)(1), in lieu of the requirements of clause (i), audits of the arrangement shall be conducted at such times and in such manner as the Secretary of Labor may prescribe.

(iii) Independent auditor—For purposes of this subparagraph, an auditor is considered independent if it is not related to the person offering the arrangement to the plan and is not related to any person providing investment options under the plan.

(F) Disclosure—The requirements of this subparagraph are met if—

(i) the fiduciary adviser provides to a participant or a beneficiary before the initial provision of the investment advice with regard to any security or other property offered as an investment option, a written notification (which may consist of notification by means of electronic communication)—

(I) of the role of any party that has a material affiliation or contractual relationship with the fiduciary adviser in the development of the investment advice program and in the selection of investment options available under the plan,

(II) of the past performance and historical rates of return of the investment options available under the plan,

(III) of all fees or other compensation relating to the advice that the fiduciary adviser or any affiliate thereof is to receive (including compensation provided by any third party) in connection with the provision of the advice or in connection with the sale, acquisition, or holding of the security or other property,

(IV) of any material affiliation or contractual relationship of the fiduciary adviser or affiliates thereof in the security or other property,

(V) the manner, and under what circumstances, any participant or beneficiary information provided under the arrangement will be used or disclosed,

(VI) of the types of services provided by the fiduciary adviser in connection with the provision of investment advice by the fiduciary adviser,

(VII) that the adviser is acting as a fiduciary of the plan in connection with the provision of the advice, and

(VIII) that a recipient of the advice may separately arrange for the provision of advice by another adviser, that could have no material affiliation with and receive no fees or other compensation in connection with the security or other property, and

(ii) at all times during the provision of advisory services to the participant or beneficiary, the fiduciary adviser—

(I) maintains the information described in clause (i) in accurate form and in the manner described in subparagraph (H),

(II) provides, without charge, accurate information to the recipient of the advice no less frequently than annually,

(III) provides, without charge, accurate information to the recipient of the advice upon request of the recipient, and

(IV) provides, without charge, accurate information to the recipient of the advice concerning any material change to the information required to be provided to the recipient of the advice at a time reasonably contemporaneous to the change in information.

(G) Other conditions—The requirements of this subparagraph are met if—

(i) the fiduciary adviser provides appropriate disclosure, in connection with the sale, acquisition, or holding of the security or other property, in accordance with all applicable securities laws,

(ii) the sale, acquisition, or holding occurs solely at the direction of the recipient of the advice,

(iii) the compensation received by the fiduciary adviser and affiliates thereof in connection with the sale, acquisition, or holding of the security or other property is reasonable, and

(iv) the terms of the sale, acquisition, or holding of the security or other property are at least as favorable to the plan as an arm's length transaction would be.

(H) Standards for presentation of information—

(i) In general—The requirements of this subparagraph are met if the notification required to be provided to participants and beneficiaries under subparagraph (F)(i) is written in a clear and conspicuous manner and in a manner calculated to be understood by the average plan participant and is sufficiently accurate and comprehensive to reasonably apprise such participants and beneficiaries of the information required to be provided in the notification.

(ii) Model form for disclosure of fees and other compensation—The Secretary of Labor shall issue a model form for the disclosure of fees and other compensation required in subparagraph (F)(i)(III) which meets the requirements of clause (i).

(I) Maintenance for 6 years of evidence of compliance—The requirements of this subparagraph are met if a fiduciary adviser who has provided advice referred to in subparagraph (A) maintains, for a period of not less than 6 years after the provision of the advice, any records necessary for determining whether the requirements of the preceding provisions of this paragraph and of subsection (d)(17) have been met. A transaction prohibited under subsection (c) shall not be considered to have occurred solely because the records are lost or destroyed prior to the end of the 6-year period due to circumstances beyond the control of the fiduciary adviser.

(J) Definitions—For purposes of this paragraph and subsection (d)(17)—

(i) Fiduciary adviser—The term "fiduciary adviser" means, with respect to a plan, a person who is a fiduciary of the plan by reason of the provision of investment advice referred to in subsection (e)(3)(B) by the person to a participant or beneficiary of the plan and who is—

(I) registered as an investment adviser under the Investment Advisers Act of 1940 (15 U.S.C. 80b-1 et seq.) or under the laws of the State in which the fiduciary maintains its principal office and place of business,

(II) a bank or similar financial institution referred to in subsection (d)(4) or a savings association (as defined in section 3(b)(1) of the Federal Deposit Insurance Act (12 U.S.C. 1813(b)(1)), but only if the advice is provided through a trust department of the bank or similar financial institution or savings association which is subject to periodic examination and review by Federal or State banking authorities,

(III) an insurance company qualified to do business under the laws of a State,

(IV) a person registered as a broker or dealer under the Securities Exchange Act of 1934 (15 U.S.C. 78a et seq.),

(V) an affiliate of a person described in any of subclauses (I) through (IV), or

     (VI) an employee, agent, or registered representative of a person described in subclauses (I) through (V) who satisfies the requirements of applicable insurance, banking, and securities laws relating to the provision of the advice.

For purposes of this title, a person who develops the computer model described in subparagraph (C)(ii) or markets the investment advice program or computer model shall be treated as a person who is a fiduciary of the plan by reason of the provision of investment advice referred to in subsection (e)(3)(B) to a participant or beneficiary and shall be treated as a fiduciary adviser for purposes of this paragraph and subsection (d)(17), except that the Secretary of Labor may prescribe rules under which only 1 fiduciary adviser may elect to be treated as a fiduciary with respect to the plan.

     (ii) Affiliate—The term "affiliate" of another entity means an affiliated person of the entity (as defined in section 2(a)(3) of the Investment Company Act of 1940 (15 U.S.C. 80a-2(a)(3))).

     (iii) Registered representative—The term "registered representative" of another entity means a person described in section 3(a)(18) of the Securities Exchange Act of 1934 (15 U.S.C. 78c(a)(18)) (substituting the entity for the broker or dealer referred to in such section) or a person described in section 202(a)(17) of the Investment Advisers Act of 1940 (15 U.S.C. 80b-2(a)(17)) (substituting the entity for the investment adviser referred to in such section).

* * *

(g) Application of section—This section shall not apply—

     (1) in the case of a plan to which a guaranteed benefit policy (as defined in section 401(b)(2)(B) of the Employee Retirement Income Security Act of 1974) is issued, to any assets of the insurance company, insurance service, or insurance organization merely because of its issuance of such policy;

     (2) to a governmental plan (within the meaning of section 414(d)); or

     (3) to a church plan (within the meaning of section 414(e)) with respect to which the election provided by section 410(d) has not been made.

In the case of a plan which invests in any security issued by an investment company registered under the Investment Company Act of 1940, the assets of such plan shall be deemed to include such security but shall not, by reason of such investment, be deemed to include any assets of such company.

(h) Notification of Secretary of Labor—Before sending a notice of deficiency with respect to the tax imposed by subsection (a) or (b), the Secretary shall notify the Secretary of Labor and provide him a reasonable opportunity to obtain a correction of the prohibited transaction or to comment on the imposition of such tax.

* * *

§ 4976. Taxes with respect to funded welfare benefit plans.

     (a) General rule—If—

     (1) an employer maintains a welfare benefit fund, and

     (2) there is a disqualified benefit provided during any taxable year,

359

there is hereby imposed on such employer a tax equal to 100 percent of such disqualified benefit.

(b) Disqualified benefit—For purposes of subsection (a)

    (1) In general—The term "disqualified benefit" means—

        (A) any post-retirement medical benefit or life insurance benefit provided with respect to a key employee if a separate account is required to be established for such employee under section 419A(d) and such payment is not from such account,

        (B) any post-retirement medical benefit or life insurance benefit provided with respect to an individual in whose favor discrimination is prohibited unless the plan meets the requirements of section 505(b) with respect to such benefit (whether or not such requirements apply to such plan), and

        (C) any portion of a welfare benefit fund reverting to the benefit of the employer.

    (2) Exception for collective bargaining plans—Paragraph (1)(B) shall not apply to any plan maintained pursuant to an agreement between employee representatives and 1 or more employers if the Secretary finds that such agreement is a collective bargaining agreement and that the benefits referred to in paragraph (1)(B) were the subject of good faith bargaining between such employee representatives and such employer or employers.

    (3) Exception for nondeductible contributions—Paragraph (1)(C) shall not apply to any amount attributable to a contribution to the fund which is not allowable as a deduction under section 419 for the taxable year or any prior taxable year (and such contribution shall not be included in any carryover under section 419(d)).

    (4) Exception for certain amounts charged against existing reserve—Subparagraphs (A) and (B) of paragraph (1) shall not apply to post-retirement benefits charged against an existing reserve for post-retirement medical or life insurance benefits (as defined in section 512(a)(3)(E)) or charged against the income on such reserve.

(c) Definitions—For purposes of this section, the terms used in this section shall have the same respective meanings as when used in subpart D of part I of subchapter D of chapter 1.

§ 4979. Tax on certain excess contributions.

(a) General rule—In the case of any plan, there is hereby imposed a tax for the taxable year equal to 10 percent of the sum of—

    (1) any excess contributions under such plan for the plan year ending in such taxable year, and

    (2) any excess aggregate contributions under the plan for the plan year ending in such taxable year.

(b) Liability for tax—The tax imposed by subsection (a) shall be paid by the employer.

(c) Excess contributions—For purposes of this section, the term "excess contributions" has the meaning given such term by sections 401(k)(8)(B), 408(k)(6)(C), and 501(c)(18).

(d) Excess aggregate contribution—For purposes of this section, the term "excess aggregate contribution" has the meaning given to such term by section 401(m)(6)(B). For purposes of determining excess aggregate contributions under an annuity contract described in section 403(b), such contract shall be treated as a plan described in subsection (e)(1).

(e) Plan—For purposes of this section, the term "plan" means—

(1) a plan described in section 401(a) which includes a trust exempt from tax under section 501(a),

(2) any annuity plan described in section 403(a),

(3) any annuity contract described in section 403(b),

(4) a simplified employee pension of an employer which satisfies the requirements of section 408(k), and

(5) a plan described in section 501(c)(18).

Such term includes any plan which, at any time, has been determined by the Secretary to be such a plan.

(f) No tax where excess distributed within specified period after close of year—

(1) In general—No tax shall be imposed under this section on any excess contribution or excess aggregate contribution, as the case may be, to the extent such contribution (together with any income allocable thereto through the end of the plan year for which the contribution was made) is distributed (or, if forfeitable, is forfeited) before the close of the first 2½ months (6 months in the case of an excess contribution or excess aggregate contribution to an eligible automatic contribution arrangement (as defined in section 414(w)(3))) of the following plan year.

(2) Year of inclusion—Any amount distributed as provided in paragraph (1) shall be treated as earned and received by the recipient in the recipient's taxable year in which such distributions were made.

§ 4980. Tax on reversion of qualified plan assets to employer.

(a) Imposition of tax—There is hereby imposed a tax of 20 percent of the amount of any employer reversion from a qualified plan.

(b) Liability for tax—The tax imposed by subsection (a) shall be paid by the employer maintaining the plan.

(c) Definitions and special rules—For purposes of this section—

(1) Qualified plan—The term "qualified plan" means any plan meeting the requirements of section 401(a) or 403(a), other than—

(A) a plan maintained by an employer if such employer has, at all times, been exempt from tax under subtitle A, or

(B) a governmental plan (within the meaning of section 414(d)).

Such term shall include any plan which, at any time, has been determined by the Secretary to be a qualified plan.

(2) Employer reversion—

(A) In general—The term "employer reversion" means the amount of cash and the fair market value of other property received (directly or indirectly) by an employer from the qualified plan.

(B) Exceptions—The term "employer reversion" shall not include—

(i) except as provided in regulations, any amount distributed to or on behalf of any employee (or his beneficiaries) if such amount could have been so distributed before termination of such plan without violating any provision of section 401,

(ii) any distribution to the employer which is allowable under section 401(a)(2) —

(I) in the case of a multiemployer plan, by reason of mistakes of law or fact or the return of any withdrawal liability payment,

(II) in the case of a plan other than a multiemployer plan, by reason of mistake of fact, or

(III) in the case of a plan, by reason of the failure of the plan to initially qualify or the failure of contributions to be deductible, or

(iii) any transfer described in section 420(f)(2)(B)(ii)(II).

* * *

(d) Increase in tax for failure to establish replacement plan or increase benefits—

(1) In general—Subsection (a) shall be applied by substituting "50 percent" for "20 percent" with respect to any employer reversion from a qualified plan unless—

(A) the employer establishes or maintains a qualified replacement plan, or

(B) the plan provides benefit increases meeting the requirements of paragraph (3).

(2) Qualified replacement plan—For purposes of this subsection, the term "qualified replacement plan" means a qualified plan established or maintained by the employer in connection with a qualified plan termination (hereinafter referred to as the "replacement plan") with respect to which the following requirements are met:

(A) Participation requirement—At least 95 percent of the active participants in the terminated plan who remain as employees of the employer after the termination are active participants in the replacement plan.

(B) Asset transfer requirement—

(i) 25 percent cushion—A direct transfer from the terminated plan to the replacement plan is made before any employer reversion, and the transfer is in an amount equal to the excess (if any) of—

(I) 25 percent of the maximum amount which the employer could receive as an employer reversion without regard to this subsection, over

(II) the amount determined under clause (ii).

(ii) Reduction for increase in benefits—The amount determined under this clause is an amount equal to the present value of the aggregate increases in the accrued benefits under the terminated plan of any participants or beneficiaries pursuant to a plan amendment which—

(I) is adopted during the 60-day period ending on the date of termination of the qualified plan, and

(II) takes effect immediately on the termination date.

(iii) Treatment of amount transferred—In the case of the transfer of any amount under clause (i)—

(I) such amount shall not be includible in the gross income of the employer,

(II) no deduction shall be allowable with respect to such transfer, and

(III) such transfer shall not be treated as an employer reversion for purposes of this section.

(C) Allocation requirements—

(i) In general—In the case of any defined contribution plan, the portion of the amount transferred to the replacement plan under subparagraph (B)(i) is—

(I) allocated under the plan to the accounts of participants in the plan year in which the transfer occurs, or

(II) credited to a suspense account and allocated from such account to accounts of participants no less rapidly than ratably over the 7-plan-year period beginning with the year of the transfer.

* * *

(3) Pro rata benefit increases—

(A) In general—The requirements of this paragraph are met if a plan amendment to the terminated plan is adopted in connection with the termination of the plan which provides pro rata increases in the accrued benefits of all qualified participants which—

(i) have an aggregate present value not less than 20 percent of the maximum amount which the employer could receive as an employer reversion without regard to this subsection, and

(ii) take effect immediately on the termination date.

* * *

(6) Subsection not to apply to employer in bankruptcy—This subsection shall not apply to an employer who, as of the termination date of the qualified plan, is in bankruptcy liquidation under chapter 7 of title 11 of the United States Code or in similar proceedings under State law.

§ 4980F. Failure of applicable plans reducing benefit accruals to satisfy notice requirements.

(a) Imposition of tax—There is hereby imposed a tax on the failure of any applicable pension plan to meet the requirements of subsection (e) with respect to any applicable individual.

(b) Amount of tax—

(1) In general—The amount of the tax imposed by subsection (a) on any failure with respect to any applicable individual shall be $100 for each day in the noncompliance period with respect to such failure.

(2) Noncompliance period—For purposes of this section, the term "noncompliance period" means, with respect to any failure, the period beginning on the date the failure first occurs and ending on the date the notice to which the failure relates is provided or the failure is otherwise corrected.

(c) Limitations on amount of tax—

(1) Tax not to apply where failure not discovered and reasonable diligence exercised—No tax shall be imposed by subsection (a) on any failure during any period for which it is established to the satisfaction of the Secretary that any person subject to liability for the tax under subsection (d) did not know that the failure existed and exercised reasonable diligence to meet the requirements of subsection (e).

(2) Tax not to apply to failures corrected within 30 days—No tax shall be imposed by subsection (a) on any failure if—

(A) any person subject to liability for the tax under subsection (d) exercised reasonable diligence to meet the requirements of subsection (e), and

(B) such person provides the notice described in subsection (e) during the 30-day period beginning on the first date such person knew, or exercising reasonable diligence would have known, that such failure existed.

(3) Overall limitation for unintentional failures—

(A) In general—If the person subject to liability for tax under subsection (d) exercised reasonable diligence to meet the requirements of subsection (e), the tax imposed by subsection (a) for failures during the taxable year of the employer (or, in the case of a multiemployer plan, the taxable year of the trust forming part of the plan) shall not exceed $500,000. For purposes of the preceding sentence, all multiemployer plans of which the same trust forms a part shall be treated as 1 plan.

(B) Taxable years in the case of certain controlled groups—For purposes of this paragraph, if all persons who are treated as a single employer for purposes of this section do not have the same taxable year, the taxable years taken into account shall be determined under principles similar to the principles of section 1561.

(4) Waiver by secretary—In the case of a failure which is due to reasonable cause and not to willful neglect, the Secretary may waive part or all of the tax imposed by subsection (a) to the extent that the payment of such tax would be excessive or otherwise inequitable relative to the failure involved.

(d) Liability for tax—The following shall be liable for the tax imposed by subsection (a):

(1) In the case of a plan other than a multiemployer plan, the employer.

(2) In the case of a multiemployer plan, the plan.

(e) Notice requirements for plans significantly reducing benefit accruals—

(1) In general—If an applicable pension plan is amended to provide for a significant reduction in the rate of future benefit accrual, the plan administrator shall provide the notice described in paragraph (2) to each applicable individual (and to each employee organization representing applicable individuals) and to each employer who has an obligation to contribute to the plan.

(2) Notice—The notice required by paragraph (1) shall be written in a manner calculated to be understood by the average plan participant and shall provide sufficient information (as determined in accordance with regulations prescribed by the Secretary) to allow applicable individuals to understand the effect of the plan amendment. The Secretary may provide a simplified form of notice for, or exempt from any notice requirement, a plan—

    (A) which has fewer than 100 participants who have accrued a benefit under the plan, or

    (B) which offers participants the option to choose between the new benefit formula and the old benefit formula.

(3) Timing of notice—Except as provided in regulations, the notice required by paragraph (1) shall be provided within a reasonable time before the effective date of the plan amendment.

(4) Designees—Any notice under paragraph (1) may be provided to a person designated, in writing, by the person to which it would otherwise be provided.

(5) Notice before adoption of amendment—A plan shall not be treated as failing to meet the requirements of paragraph (1) merely because notice is provided before the adoption of the plan amendment if no material modification of the amendment occurs before the amendment is adopted.

(f) Definitions and special rules—For purposes of this section—

(1) Applicable individual—The term "applicable individual" means, with respect to any plan amendment—

    (A) each participant in the plan, and

    (B) any beneficiary who is an alternate payee (within the meaning of section 414(p)(8)) under an applicable qualified domestic relations order (within the meaning of section 414(p)(1)(A)),

whose rate of future benefit accrual under the plan may reasonably be expected to be significantly reduced by such plan amendment.

(2) Applicable pension plan—The term "applicable pension plan" means—

    (A) any defined benefit plan described in section 401(a) which includes a trust exempt from tax under section 501(a), or

    (B) an individual account plan which is subject to the funding standards of section 412.

Such term shall not include a governmental plan (within the meaning of section 414(d)) or a church plan (within the meaning of section 414(e)) with respect to which the election provided by section 410(d) has not been made.

(3) Early retirement—A plan amendment which eliminates or reduces any early retirement benefit or retirement-type subsidy (within the meaning of section 411(d)(6)(B)(i)) shall be treated as having the effect of reducing the rate of future benefit accrual.

(g) New technologies—The Secretary may by regulations allow any notice under subsection (e) to be provided by using new technologies.

§ 7476. Declaratory judgments relating to qualification of certain retirement plans.

(a) Creation of remedy—In a case of actual controversy involving—

(1) a determination by the Secretary with respect to the initial qualification or continuing qualification of a retirement plan under subchapter D of chapter 1, or

(2) a failure by the Secretary to make a determination with respect to

    (A) such initial qualification, or

    (B) such continuing qualification if the controversy arises from a plan amendment or plan termination,

upon the filing of an appropriate pleading, the Tax Court may make a declaration with respect to such initial qualification or continuing qualification. Any such declaration shall have the force and effect of a decision of the Tax Court and shall be reviewable as such. For purposes of this section, a determination with respect to a continuing qualification includes any revocation of or other change in a qualification.

(b) Limitations—

    (1) Petitioner—A pleading may be filed under this section only by a petitioner who is the employer, the plan administrator, an employee who has qualified under regulations prescribed by the Secretary as an interested party for purposes of pursuing administrative remedies within the Internal Revenue Service, or the Pension Benefit Guaranty Corporation.

    (2) Notice—For purposes of this section, the filing of a pleading by any petitioner may be held by the Tax Court to be premature, unless the petitioner establishes to the satisfaction of the court that he has complied with the requirements prescribed by regulations of the Secretary with respect to notice to other interested parties of the filing of the request for a determination referred to in subsection (a).

    (3) Exhaustion of administrative remedies—The Tax Court shall not issue a declaratory judgment or decree under this section in any proceeding unless it determines that the petitioner has exhausted administrative remedies available to him within the Internal Revenue Service. A petitioner shall not be deemed to have exhausted his administrative remedies with respect to a failure by the Secretary to make a determination with respect to initial qualification or continuing qualification of a retirement plan before the expiration of 270 days after the request for such determination was made.

    (4) Plan put into effect—No proceeding may be maintained under this section unless the plan (and, in the case of a controversy involving the continuing qualification of the plan because of an amendment to the plan, the amendment) with respect to which a decision of the Tax Court is sought has been put into effect before the filing of the pleading. A plan or amendment shall not be treated as not being in effect merely because under the plan the funds contributed to the plan may be refunded if the plan (or the plan as so amended) is found to be not qualified.

    (5) Time for bringing action—If the Secretary sends by certified or registered mail notice of his determination with respect to the qualification of the plan to the persons referred to in paragraph (1) (or, in the case of employees referred to in paragraph (1), to any individual designated under regulations prescribed by the Secretary as a representative of such employee), no proceeding may be initiated under this section by any person unless the pleading is filed before the ninety-first day after the day after such notice is mailed to such person (or to his designated representative, in the case of an employee).

(c) Retirement plan—For purposes of this section, the term "retirement plan" means—

(1) a pension, profit-sharing, or stock bonus plan described in section 401(a) or a trust which is part of such a plan, or

(2) an annuity plan described in section 403(a).

* * *

§ 7872. Treatment of loans with below-market interest rates.

(a) Treatment of gift loans and demand loans.

(1) In general—For purposes of this title, in the case of any below-market loan to which this section applies and which is a gift loan or a demand loan, the forgone interest shall be treated as—

    (A) transferred from the lender to the borrower, and

    (B) retransferred by the borrower to the lender as interest.

(2) Time when transfers made—Except as otherwise provided in regulations prescribed by the Secretary, any forgone interest attributable to periods during any calendar year shall be treated as transferred (and retransferred) under paragraph (1) on the last day of such calendar year.

(b) Treatment of other below-market loans—

(1) In general—For purposes of this title, in the case of any below-market loan to which this section applies and to which subsection (a)(1) does not apply, the lender shall be treated as having transferred on the date the loan was made (or, if later, on the first day on which this section applies to such loan), and the borrower shall be treated as having received on such date, cash in an amount equal to the excess of—

    (A) the amount loaned, over

    (B) the present value of all payments which are required to be made under the terms of the loan.

(2) Obligation treated as having original issue discount—For purposes of this title—

    (A) In general—Any below-market loan to which paragraph (1) applies shall be treated as having original issue discount in an amount equal to the excess described in paragraph (1).

    (B) Amount in addition to other original issue discount—Any original issue discount which a loan is treated as having by reason of subparagraph (A) shall be in addition to any other original issue discount on such loan (determined without regard to subparagraph (A)).

(c) Below-market loans to which section applies—

(1) In general—Except as otherwise provided in this subsection, and subsection (g), this section shall apply to—

    (A) Gifts—Any below-market loan which is a gift loan.

    (B) Compensation-related loans—Any below-market loan directly or indirectly between—

        (i) an employer and an employee, or

(ii) an independent contractor and a person for whom such independent contractor provides services.

(C) Corporation-shareholder loans—Any below-market loan directly or indirectly between a corporation and any shareholder of such corporation.

* * *

(3) $10,000 de minimis exception for compensation-related and corporate-shareholder loans—

(A) In general—In the case of any loan described in subparagraph (B) or (C) of paragraph (1), this section shall not apply to any day on which the aggregate outstanding amount of loans between the borrower and lender does not exceed $10,000.

(B) Exception not to apply where 1 of principal purposes is tax avoidance—Subparagraph (A) shall not apply to any loan the interest arrangements of which have as 1 of their principal purposes the avoidance of any Federal tax.

* * *

(e) Definitions of below-market loan and forgone interest—For purposes of this section—

(1) Below-market loan—The term "below-market loan" means any loan if—

(A) in the case of a demand loan, interest is payable on the loan at a rate less than the applicable Federal rate, or

(B) in the case of a term loan, the amount loaned exceeds the present value of all payments due under the loan.

(2) Forgone interest—The term "forgone interest" means, with respect to any period during which the loan is outstanding, the excess of—

(A) the amount of interest which would have been payable on the loan for the period if interest accrued on the loan at the applicable Federal rate and were payable annually on the day referred to in subsection (a)(2), over

(B) any interest payable on the loan properly allocable to such period.

(f) Other definitions and special rules—For purposes of this section—

(1) Present value—The present value of any payment shall be determined in the manner provided by regulations prescribed by the Secretary—

(A) as of the date of the loan, and

(B) by using a discount rate equal to the applicable Federal rate.

(2) Applicable Federal rate—

(A) Term loans—In the case of any term loan, the applicable Federal rate shall be the applicable Federal rate in effect under section 1274(d) (as of the day on which the loan was made), compounded semiannually.

(B) Demand loans—In the case of a demand loan, the applicable Federal rate shall be the Federal short-term rate in effect under section 1274(d) for the period for which the amount of forgone interest is being determined, compounded semiannually.

* * *

(11) Time for determining rate applicable to employee relocation loans—

(A) In general—In the case of any term loan made by an employer to an employee the proceeds of which are used by the employee to purchase a principal residence (within the meaning of section 121), the determination of the applicable Federal rate shall be made as of the date the written contract to purchase such residence was entered into.

(B) Paragraph only to apply to cases to which section 217 applies—Subparagraph (A) shall only apply to the purchase of a principal residence in connection with the commencement of work by an employee or a change in the principal place of work of an employee to which section 217 applies.

* * *

EMPLOYEE RETIREMENT INCOME SECURITY ACT OF 1974

29 U.S.C. § 1001 et seq.

Title I (Subchapter I)—Protection of Employee Benefit Rights

Subtitle A—General Provisions

§ 2. Congressional findings and declaration of policy (§ 1001)

(a) Benefit plans as affecting interstate commerce and the Federal taxing power—

The Congress finds that the growth in size, scope, and numbers of employee benefit plans in recent years has been rapid and substantial; that the operational scope and economic impact of such plans is increasingly interstate; that the continued well-being and security of millions of employees and their dependents are directly affected by these plans; that they are affected with a national public interest; that they have become an important factor affecting the stability of employment and the successful development of industrial relations; that they have become an important factor in commerce because of the interstate character of their activities, and of the activities of their participants, and the employers, employee organizations, and other entities by which they are established or maintained; that a large volume of the activities of such plans are carried on by means of the mails and instrumentalities of interstate commerce; that owing to the lack of employee information and adequate safeguards concerning their operation, it is desirable in the interests of employees and their beneficiaries, and to provide for the general welfare and the free flow of commerce, that disclosure be made and safeguards be provided with respect to the establishment, operation, and administration of such plans; that they substantially affect the revenues of the United States because they are afforded preferential Federal tax treatment; that despite the enormous growth in such plans many employees with long years of employment are losing anticipated retirement benefits owing to the lack of vesting provisions in such plans; that owing to the inadequacy of current minimum standards, the soundness and stability of plans with respect to adequate funds to pay promised benefits may be endangered; that owing to the termination of plans before requisite funds have been accumulated, employees and their beneficiaries have been deprived of anticipated benefits; and that it is therefore desirable in the interests of employees and their beneficiaries, for the protection of the revenue of the United States, and to provide for the free flow of commerce, that minimum standards be provided assuring the equitable character of such plans and their financial soundness.

(b) Protection of interstate commerce and beneficiaries by requiring disclosure and reporting, setting standards of conduct, etc., for fiduciaries—

It is hereby declared to be the policy of this chapter to protect interstate commerce and the interests of participants in employee benefit plans and their beneficiaries, by requiring the disclosure and reporting to participants and beneficiaries of financial and other information with respect thereto, by establishing standards of conduct, responsibility, and obligation for fiduciaries of employee benefit plans, and by providing for appropriate remedies, sanctions, and ready access to the Federal courts.

(c) Protection of interstate commerce, the Federal taxing power, and beneficiaries by vesting of accrued benefits, setting minimum standards of funding, requiring termination insurance—

It is hereby further declared to be the policy of this chapter to protect interstate commerce, the Federal taxing power, and the interests of participants in private pension plans and their beneficiaries by improving the equitable character and the soundness of such plans by requiring them to vest the accrued benefits of employees with significant periods of service, to meet minimum standards of funding, and by requiring plan termination insurance.

§ 3. Definitions (§ 1002)

For purposes of this subchapter:

(1) The terms "employee welfare benefit plan" and "welfare plan" mean any plan, fund, or program which was heretofore or is hereafter established or maintained by an employer or by an employee organization, or by both, to the extent that such plan, fund, or program was established or is maintained for the purpose of providing for its participants or their beneficiaries, through the purchase of insurance or otherwise, (A) medical, surgical, or hospital care or benefits, or benefits in the event of sickness, accident, disability, death or unemployment, or vacation benefits, apprenticeship or other training programs, or day care centers, scholarship funds, or prepaid legal services, or (B) any benefit described in section 186(c) of this title (other than pensions on retirement or death, and insurance to provide such pensions).

(2)(A) Except as provided in subparagraph (B), the terms "employee pension benefit plan" and "pension plan" mean any plan, fund, or program which was heretofore or is hereafter established or maintained by an employer or by an employee organization, or by both, to the extent that by its express terms or as a result of surrounding circumstances such plan, fund, or program—

    (i) provides retirement income to employees, or

    (ii) results in a deferral of income by employees for periods extending to the termination of covered employment or beyond,

regardless of the method of calculating the contributions made to the plan, the method of calculating the benefits under the plan or the method of distributing benefits from the plan. A distribution from a plan, fund, or program shall not be treated as made in a form other than retirement income or as a distribution prior to termination of covered employment solely because such distribution is made to an employee who has attained age 62 and who is not separated from employment at the time of such distribution.

    (B) The Secretary may by regulation prescribe rules consistent with the standards and purposes of this chapter providing one or more exempt categories under which—

    (i) severance pay arrangements, and

    (ii) supplemental retirement income payments, under which the pension benefits of retirees or their beneficiaries are supplemented to take into account some portion or all of the increases in the cost of living (as determined by the Secretary of Labor) since retirement,

shall, for purposes of this subchapter, be treated as welfare plans rather than pension plans. In the case of any arrangement or payment a principal effect of which is the evasion of the standards or purposes of this chapter applicable to pension plans, such arrangement or payment shall be treated as a pension plan. An applicable voluntary early retirement incentive plan (as defined in section 457(e)(11)(D)(ii) of the Title 26) making payments or supplements described in section 457(e)(11)(D)(i) of Title 26, and an applicable employment retention plan (as defined in section 457(f)(4)(C) of Title 26) making payments of benefits described in section 457(f)(4)(A) of Title 26e, shall, for purposes of this subchapter, be treated as a welfare plan (and not a pension plan) with respect to such payments and supplements.

(3) The term "employee benefit plan" or "plan" means an employee welfare benefit plan or an employee pension benefit plan or a plan which is both an employee welfare benefit plan and an employee pension benefit plan.

(4) The term "employee organization" means any labor union or any organization of any kind, or any agency or employee representation committee, association, group, or plan, in which employees participate and which exists for the purpose, in whole or in part, of dealing with employers concerning an employee benefit plan, or other matters incidental to employment relationships; or any employees' beneficiary association organized for the purpose in whole or in part, of establishing such a plan.

(5) The term "employer" means any person acting directly as an employer, or indirectly in the interest of an employer, in relation to an employee benefit plan; and includes a group or association of employers acting for an employer in such capacity.

(6) The term "employee" means any individual employed by an employer.

(7) The term "participant" means any employee or former employee of an employer, or any member or former member of an employee organization, who is or may become eligible to receive a benefit of any type from an employee benefit plan which covers employees of such employer or members of such organization, or whose beneficiaries may be eligible to receive any such benefit.

(8) The term "beneficiary" means a person designated by a participant, or by the terms of an employee benefit plan, who is or may become entitled to a benefit thereunder.

(9) The term "person" means an individual, partnership, joint venture, corporation, mutual company, joint-stock company, trust, estate, unincorporated organization, association, or employee organization.

(10) The term "State" includes any State of the United States, the District of Columbia, Puerto Rico, the Virgin Islands, American Samoa, Guam, Wake Island, and the Canal Zone. The term "United States" when used in the geographic sense means the States and the Outer Continental Shelf lands defined in the Outer Continental Shelf Lands Act (43 U.S.C. 1331-1343).

(11) The term "commerce" means trade, traffic, commerce, transportation, or communication between any State and any place outside thereof.

(12) The term "industry or activity affecting commerce" means any activity, business, or industry in commerce or in which a labor dispute would hinder or obstruct commerce or the free flow of commerce, and includes any activity or industry "affecting commerce" within the meaning of the Labor Management Relations Act, 1947 [29 U.S.C.A. § 11 et seq.], or the Railway Labor Act [45 U.S.C.A. § 151 et seq.].

(13) The term "Secretary" means the Secretary of Labor.

(14) The term "party in interest" means, as to an employee benefit plan—

    (A) any fiduciary (including, but not limited to, any administrator, officer, trustee, or custodian), counsel, or employee of such employee benefit plan;

(B) a person providing services to such plan;

(C) an employer any of whose employees are covered by such plan;

(D) an employee organization any of whose members are covered by such plan;

(E) an owner, direct or indirect, of 50 percent or more of—

    (i) the combined voting power of all classes of stock entitled to vote or the total value of shares of all classes of stock of a corporation.

    (ii) the capital interest or the profits interest of a partnership, or

    (iii) the beneficial interest of a trust or unincorporated enterprise,

which is an employer or an employee organization described in subparagraph (C) or (D);

(F) a relative (as defined in paragraph (15)) of any individual described in subparagraph (A), (B), (C), or (E);

(G) a corporation, partnership, or trust or estate of which (or in which) 50 percent or more of—

    (i) the combined voting power of all classes of stock entitled to vote or the total value of shares of all classes of stock of such corporation,

    (ii) the capital interest or profits interest of such partnership, or

    (iii) the beneficial interest of such trust or estate,

is owned directly or indirectly, or held by persons described in subparagraph (A), (B), (C), (D), or (E);

(H) an employee, officer, director (or an individual having powers or responsibilities similar to those of officers or directors), or a 10 percent or more shareholder directly or indirectly, of a person described in subparagraph (B), (C), (D), (E), or (G), or of the employee benefit plan; or

(I) a 10 percent or more (directly or indirectly in capital or profits) partner or joint venturer of a person described in subparagraph (B), (C), (D), (E), or (G).

The Secretary, after consultation and coordination with the Secretary of the Treasury, may by regulation prescribe a percentage lower than 50 percent for subparagraph (E) and (G) and lower than 10 percent for subparagraph (H) or (I). The Secretary may prescribe regulations for determining the ownership (direct or indirect) of profits and beneficial interests, and the manner in which indirect stockholdings are taken into account. Any person who is a party in interest with respect to a plan to which a trust described in section 501(c)(22) of Title 26 is permitted to make payments under section 1403 of this title shall be treated as a party in interest with respect to such trust.

(15) The term "relative" means a spouse, ancestor, lineal descendant, or spouse of a lineal descendant.

(16)(A) The term "administrator" means—

    (i) the person specifically so designated by the terms of the instrument under which the plan is operated;

    (ii) if an administrator is not so designated, the plan sponsor; or

(iii) in the case of a plan for which an administrator is not designated and a plan sponsor cannot be identified, such other person as the Secretary may by regulation prescribe.

(B) The term "plan sponsor" means (i) the employer in the case of an employee benefit plan established or maintained by a single employer, (ii) the employee organization in the case of a plan established or maintained by an employee organization, or (iii) in the case of a plan established or maintained by two or more employers or jointly by one or more employers and one or more employee organizations, the association, committee, joint board of trustees, or other similar group of representatives of the parties who establish or maintain the plan.

(17) The term "separate account" means an account established or maintained by an insurance company under which income, gains, and losses, whether or not realized, from assets allocated to such account, are, in accordance with the applicable contract, credited to or charged against such account without regard to other income, gains, or losses of the insurance company.

(18) The term "adequate consideration" when used in part 4 of subtitle B of this subchapter means (A) in the case of a security for which there is a generally recognized market, either (i) the price of the security prevailing on a national securities exchange which is registered under section 78f of Title 15, or (ii) if the security is not traded on such a national securities exchange, a price not less favorable to the plan than the offering price for the security as established by the current bid and asked prices quoted by persons independent of the issuer and of any party in interest; and (B) in the case of an asset other than a security for which there is a generally recognized market, the fair market value of the asset as determined in good faith by the trustee or named fiduciary pursuant to the terms of the plan and in accordance with regulations promulgated by the Secretary.

(19) The term "nonforfeitable" when used with respect to a pension benefit or right means a claim obtained by a participant or his beneficiary to that part of an immediate or deferred benefit under a pension plan which arises from the participant's service, which is unconditional, and which is legally enforceable against the plan. For purposes of this paragraph, a right to an accrued benefit derived from employer contributions shall not be treated as forfeitable merely because the plan contains a provision described in section 1053(a)(3) of this title.

(20) The term "security" has the same meaning as such term has under section 77b(1) of Title 15.

(21)(A) Except as otherwise provided in subparagraph (B), a person is a fiduciary with respect to a plan to the extent (i) he exercises any discretionary authority or discretionary control respecting management of such plan or exercises any authority or control respecting management or disposition of its assets, (ii) he renders investment advice for a fee or other compensation, direct or indirect, with respect to any moneys or other property of such plan, or has any authority or responsibility to do so, or (iii) he has any discretionary authority or discretionary responsibility in the administration of such plan. Such term includes any person designated under section 1105(c)(1)(B) of this title.

(B) If any money or other property of an employee benefit plan is invested in securities issued by an investment company registered under the Investment Company Act of 1940 [15 U.S.C.A. § 80a-1 et seq.], such investment shall not by itself cause such investment company or such investment company's investment adviser or principal underwriter to be deemed to be a fiduciary or a party in interest as those terms are defined in this subchapter, except insofar as such investment company or its investment adviser or principal underwriter acts in connection with an employee benefit plan covering employees of the investment company, the investment adviser, or its principal underwriter. Nothing contained in this subparagraph shall limit the duties imposed on such investment company, investment adviser, or principal underwriter by any other law.

(22) The term "normal retirement benefit" means the greater of the early retirement benefit under the plan, or the benefit under the plan commencing at normal retirement age. The normal retirement benefit shall be determined without regard to—

(A) medical benefits, and

(B) disability benefits not in excess of the qualified disability benefit.

For purposes of this paragraph, a qualified disability benefit is a disability benefit provided by a plan which does not exceed the benefit which would be provided for the participant if he separated from the service at normal retirement age. For purposes of this paragraph, the early retirement benefit under a plan shall be determined without regard to any benefit under the plan which the Secretary of the Treasury finds to be a benefit described in section 1054(b)(1)(G) of this title.

(23) The term "accrued benefit" means—

(A) in the case of a defined benefit plan, the individual's accrued benefit determined under the plan and, except as provided in section 1054(c)(3) of this title, expressed in the form of an annual benefit commencing at normal retirement age, or

(B) in the case of a plan which is an individual account plan, the balance of the individual's account.

The accrued benefit of an employee shall not be less than the amount determined under section 1054(c)(2)(B) of this title with respect to the employee's accumulated contribution.

(24) The term "normal retirement age" means the earlier of—

(A) the time a plan participant attains normal retirement age under the plan, or

(B) the later of—

(i) the time a plan participant attains age 65, or

(ii) the 5th anniversary of the time a plan participant commenced participation in the plan.

(25) The term "vested liabilities" means the present value of the immediate or deferred benefits available at normal retirement age for participants and their beneficiaries which are nonforfeitable.

(26) The term "current value" means fair market value where available and otherwise the fair value as determined in good faith by a trustee or a named fiduciary (as defined in section 1102(a)(2) of this title) pursuant to the terms of the plan and in accordance with regulations of the Secretary, assuming an orderly liquidation at the time of such determination.

(27) The term "present value", with respect to a liability, means the value adjusted to reflect anticipated events. Such adjustments shall conform to such regulations as the Secretary of the Treasury may prescribe.

(28) The term "normal service cost" or "normal cost" means the annual cost of future pension benefits and administrative expenses assigned, under an actuarial cost method, to years subsequent to a particular valuation date of a pension plan. The Secretary of the Treasury may prescribe regulations to carry out this paragraph.

(29) The term "accrued liability" means the excess of the present value, as of a particular valuation date of a pension plan, of the projected future benefit costs and administrative expenses for all plan participants and beneficiaries over the present value of future contributions for the normal cost of all applicable plan participants and beneficiaries. The Secretary of the Treasury may prescribe regulations to carry out this paragraph.

(30) The term "unfunded accrued liability" means the excess of the accrued liability, under an actuarial cost method which so provides, over the present value of the assets of a pension plan. The Secretary of the Treasury may prescribe regulations to carry out this paragraph.

(31) The term "advance funding actuarial cost method" or "actuarial cost method" means a recognized actuarial technique utilized for establishing the amount and incidence of the annual actuarial cost of pension plan benefits and expenses. Acceptable actuarial cost methods shall include the accrued benefit cost method (unit credit method), the entry age normal cost method, the individual level premium cost method, the aggregate cost method, the attained age normal cost method, and the frozen initial liability cost method. The terminal funding cost method and the current funding (pay-as-you-go) cost method are not acceptable actuarial cost methods. The Secretary of the Treasury shall issue regulations to further define acceptable actuarial cost methods.

(32) The term "governmental plan" means a plan established or maintained for its employees by the Government of the United States, by the government of any State or political subdivision thereof, or by any agency or instrumentality of any of the foregoing. The term "governmental plan" also includes any plan to which the Railroad Retirement Act of 1935, or 1937 [45 U.S.C.A. § 231 et seq.] applies, and which is financed by contributions required under that Act and any plan of an international organization which is exempt from taxation under the provisions of the International Organizations Immunities Act [22 U.S.C.A. § 288 et seq.]. The term "governmental plan" includes a plan which is established and maintained by an Indian tribal government (as defined in section 7701(a)(40) of Title 26), a subdivision of an Indian tribal government (determined in accordance with section 7871(d) of Title 26), or an agency or instrumentality of either, and all of the participants of which are employees of such entity substantially all of whose services as such an employee are in the performance of essential governmental functions but not in the performance of commercial activities (whether or not an essential government function).

(33)(A) The term "church plan" means a plan established and maintained (to the extent required in clause (ii) of subparagraph (B)) for its employees (or their beneficiaries) by a church or by a convention or association of churches which is exempt from tax under section 501 of Title 26.

* * *

(C) For purposes of this paragraph—

(i) A plan established and maintained for its employees (or their beneficiaries) by a church or by a convention or association of churches includes a plan maintained by an organization, whether a civil law corporation or otherwise, the principal purpose or function of which is the administration or funding of a plan or program for the provision of retirement benefits or welfare benefits, or both, for the employees of a church or a convention or association of churches, if such organization is controlled by or associated with a church or a convention or association of churches.

(ii) The term employee of a church or a convention or association of churches includes--

(I) a duly ordained, commissioned, or licensed minister of a church in the exercise of his ministry, regardless of the source of his compensation;

(II) an employee of an organization, whether a civil law corporation or otherwise, which is exempt from tax under section 501 of Title 26 and which is controlled by or associated with a church or a convention or association of churches; and

(III) an individual described in clause (v).

(iii) A church or a convention or association of churches which is exempt from tax under section 501 of Title 26 shall be deemed the employer of any individual included as an employee under clause (ii).

(iv) An organization, whether a civil law corporation or otherwise, is associated with a church or a convention or association of churches if it shares common religious bonds and convictions with that church or convention or association of churches.

* * *

DCP→ pension plan

(34) The term "individual account plan" or "defined contribution plan" means a pension plan which provides for an individual account for each participant and for benefits based solely upon the amount contributed to the participant's account, and any income, expenses, gains and losses, and any forfeitures of accounts of other participants which may be allocated to such participant's account.

DBP→ pension plan

(35) The term "defined benefit plan" means a pension plan other than an individual account plan; except that a pension plan which is not an individual account plan and which provides a benefit derived from employer contributions which is based partly on the balance of the separate account of a participant—

(A) for the purposes of section 1052 of this title, shall be treated as an individual account plan, and

(B) for the purposes of paragraph (23) of this section and section 1054 of this title, shall be treated as an individual account plan to the extent benefits are based upon the separate account of a participant and as a defined benefit plan with respect to the remaining portion of benefits under the plan.

(36) The term "excess benefit plan" means a plan maintained by an employer solely for the purpose of providing benefits for certain employees in excess of the limitations on contributions and benefits imposed by section 415 of Title 26 on plans to which that section applies without regard to whether the plan is funded. To the extent that a separable part of a plan (as determined by the Secretary of Labor) maintained by an employer is maintained for such purpose, that part shall be treated as a separate plan which is an excess benefit plan.

(37)(A) The term "multiemployer plan" means a plan—

(i) to which more than one employer is required to contribute,

(ii) which is maintained pursuant to one or more collective bargaining agreements between one or more employee organizations and more than one employer, and

(iii) which satisfies such other requirements as the Secretary may prescribe by regulation.

(B) For purposes of this paragraph, all trades or businesses (whether or not incorporated) which are under common control within the meaning of section 1301(b)(1) of this title are considered a single employer.

* * *

(38) The term "investment manager" means any fiduciary (other than a trustee or named fiduciary, as defined in section 1102(a)(2) of this title)—

(A) who has the power to manage, acquire, or dispose of any asset of a plan;

(B) who (i) is registered as an investment adviser under the Investment Advisers Act of 1940 [15 U.S.C.A. § 80b-1 et seq.]; (ii) is not registered as an investment adviser under such Act by reason of paragraph (1) of section203A(a) of such Act [15 U.S.C.A. § 80b-3a(a)], is registered as an investment adviser under the laws of the State (referred to in such paragraph (1)) in which it maintains its principal office and place of business, and, at the time the fiduciary last filed the registration form most recently filed by the fiduciary with such State in order to maintain the fiduciary's registration under the laws of such State, also filed a copy of such form with the Secretary; (iii) is a bank, as defined in that Act; or (iv) is an insurance company qualified to perform services described in subparagraph (A) under the laws of more than one State; and

(C) has acknowledged in writing that he is a fiduciary with respect to the plan.

(39) The terms "plan year" and "fiscal year of the plan" mean, with respect to a plan, the calendar, policy, or fiscal year on which the records of the plan are kept.

(40)(A) The term "multiple employer welfare arrangement" means an employee welfare benefit plan, or any other arrangement (other than an employee welfare benefit plan), which is established or maintained for the purpose of offering or providing any benefit described in paragraph (1) to the employees of two or more employers (including one or more self-employed individuals), or to their beneficiaries, except that such term does not include any such plan or other arrangement which is established or maintained—

(i) under or pursuant to one or more agreements which the Secretary finds to be collective bargaining agreements,

(ii) by a rural electric cooperative, or

(iii) by a rural telephone cooperative association.

* * *

(41) The term "single employer plan" means a plan which is not a multiemployer plan.

(42) the term "plan assets" means plan assets as defined by such regulations as the Secretary may prescribe, except that under such regulations the assets of any entity shall not be treated as plan assets if, immediately after the most recent acquisition of any equity interest in the entity, less than 25 percent of the total value of each class of equity interest in the entity is held by benefit plan investors. For purposes of determinations pursuant to this para-

graph, the value of any equity interest held by a person (other than such a benefit plan investor) who has discretionary authority or control with respect to the assets of the entity or any person who provides investment advice for a fee (direct or indirect) with respect to such assets, or any affiliate of such a person, shall be disregarded for purposes of calculating the 25 percent threshold. An entity shall be considered to hold plan assets only to the extent of the percentage of the equity interest held by benefit plan investors. For purposes of this paragraph, the term "benefit plan investor" means an employee benefit plan subject to part 4, any plan to which section 4975 of Title 26 applies, and any entity whose underlying assets include plan assets by reason of a plan's investment in such entity.

§ 4. Coverage (§ 1003)

(a) Except as provided in subsection (b) or (c) of this section and in sections 1051, 1081, and 1101 of this title, this subchapter shall apply to any employee benefit plan if it is established or maintained—

    (1) by any employer engaged in commerce or in any industry or activity affecting commerce; or

    (2) by any employee organization or organizations representing employees engaged in commerce or in any industry or activity affecting commerce; or

    (3) by both.

(b) The provisions of this subchapter shall not apply to any employee benefit plan if—

    (1) such plan is a governmental plan (as defined in section 1002(32) of this title);

    (2) such plan is a church plan (as defined in section 1002(33) of this title) with respect to which no election has been made under section 410(d) of Title 26;

    (3) such plan is maintained solely for the purpose of complying with applicable workmen's compensation laws or unemployment compensation or disability insurance laws;

    (4) such plan is maintained outside of the United States primarily for the benefit of persons substantially all of whom are nonresident aliens; or

    (5) such plan is an excess benefit plan (as defined in section 1002(36) of this title) and is unfunded.

The provisions of part 7 of subtitle B shall not apply to a health insurance issuer (as defined in section 1191b(b)(2) of this title) solely by reason of health insurance coverage (as defined in section 1191b(b)(1) of this title) provided by such issuer in connection with a group health plan (as defined in section 1191b(a)(1) of this title) if the provisions of this subchapter do not apply to such group health plan.

(c) If a pension plan allows an employee to elect to make voluntary employee contributions to accounts and annuities as provided in section 408(q) of Title 26, such accounts and annuities (and contributions thereto) shall not be treated as part of such plan (or as a separate pension plan) for purposes of any provision of this subchapter other than section 1103(c), 1104, or 1105 of this title (relating to exclusive benefit, and fiduciary and co-fiduciary responsibilities) and part 5 of subtitle B of this subchapter (relating to administration and enforcement). Such provisions shall apply to such accounts and annuities in a manner similar to their application to a simplified employee pension under section 408(k) of Title 26.

Subtitle B—Regulatory Provisions

Part 1—Reporting and Disclosure

§ 101. Duty of disclosure and reporting (§ 1021)

(a) **Summary plan description and information to be furnished to participants and beneficiaries**—The administrator of each employee benefit plan shall cause to be furnished in accordance with section 1024(b) of this title to each participant covered under the plan and to each beneficiary who is receiving benefits under the plan—

(1) a summary plan description described in section 1022(a)(1) of this title; and

(2) the information described in subsection (f) and sections 1024(b)(3) and 1025(a) and (c) of this title.

(b) **Reports to be filed with Secretary of Labor**—The administrator shall, in accordance with section 1024(a) of this title, file with the Secretary—

(1) the annual report containing the information required by section 1023 of this title; and

(2) terminal and supplementary reports as required by subsection (c) of this section.

(c) **Terminal and supplementary reports—**

(1) Each administrator of an employee pension benefit plan which is winding up its affairs (without regard to the number of participants remaining in the plan) shall, in accordance with regulations prescribed by the Secretary, file such terminal reports as the Secretary may consider necessary. A copy of such report shall also be filed with the Pension Benefit Guaranty Corporation.

(2) The Secretary may require terminal reports to be filed with regard to any employee welfare benefit plan which is winding up its affairs in accordance with regulations promulgated by the Secretary.

(3) The Secretary may require that a plan described in paragraph (1) or (2) file a supplementary or terminal report with the annual report in the year such plan is terminated and that a copy of such supplementary or terminal report in the case of a plan described in paragraph (1) be also filed with the Pension Benefit Guaranty Corporation.

* * *

(f) **Defined benefit plan funding notices—**

(1) **In general**—The administrator of a defined benefit plan to which subchapter III of this chapter applies shall for each plan year provide a plan funding notice to the Pension Benefit Guaranty Corporation, to each plan participant and beneficiary, to each labor organization representing such participants or beneficiaries, and, in the case of a multiemployer plan, to each employer that has an obligation to contribute to the plan.

* * *

(i) **Notice of blackout periods to participant or beneficiary under individual account plan—**

(1) **Duties of plan administrator**—In advance of the commencement of any blackout period with respect to an individual account plan, the plan administrator shall notify the plan

participants and beneficiaries who are affected by such action in accordance with this subsection.

(2) Notice requirements—

(A) In general—The notices described in paragraph (1) shall be written in a manner calculated to be understood by the average plan participant and shall include—

(i) the reasons for the blackout period,

(ii) an identification of the investments and other rights affected,

(iii) the expected beginning date and length of the blackout period,

(iv) in the case of investments affected, a statement that the participant or beneficiary should evaluate the appropriateness of their current investment decisions in light of their inability to direct or diversify assets credited to their accounts during the blackout period, and

(v) such other matters as the Secretary may require by regulation.

(B) Notice to participants and beneficiaries—Except as otherwise provided in this subsection, notices described in paragraph (1) shall be furnished to all participants and beneficiaries under the plan to whom the blackout period applies at least 30 days in advance of the blackout period.

(C) Exception to 30-day notice requirement—In any case in which—

(i) a deferral of the blackout period would violate the requirements of subparagraph (A) or (B) of section 1104(a)(1) of this title, and a fiduciary of the plan reasonably so determines in writing, or

(ii) the inability to provide the 30-day advance notice is due to events that were unforeseeable or circumstances beyond the reasonable control of the plan administrator, and a fiduciary of the plan reasonably so determines in writing,

subparagraph (B) shall not apply, and the notice shall be furnished to all participants and beneficiaries under the plan to whom the blackout period applies as soon as reasonably possible under the circumstances unless such a notice in advance of the termination of the blackout period is impracticable.

(D) Written notice—The notice required to be provided under this subsection shall be in writing, except that such notice may be in electronic or other form to the extent that such form is reasonably accessible to the recipient.

(E) Notice to issuers of employer securities subject to blackout period—In the case of any blackout period in connection with an individual account plan, the plan administrator shall provide timely notice of such blackout period to the issuer of any employer securities subject to such blackout period.

(3) Exception for blackout periods with limited applicability—In any case in which the blackout period applies only to 1 or more participants or beneficiaries in connection with a merger, acquisition, divestiture, or similar transaction involving the plan or plan sponsor and occurs solely in connection with becoming or ceasing to be a participant or beneficiary under the plan by reason of such merger, acquisition, divestiture, or transaction, the requirement of this subsection that the notice be provided to all participants and beneficiaries shall be treated as met if the notice required under paragraph (1) is provided to such participants or beneficiaries to whom the blackout period applies as soon as reasonably practicable.

(4) Changes in length of blackout period—If, following the furnishing of the notice pursuant to this subsection, there is a change in the beginning date or length of the blackout period (specified in such notice pursuant to paragraph (2)(A)(iii)), the administrator shall provide affected participants and beneficiaries notice of the change as soon as reasonably practicable. In relation to the extended blackout period, such notice shall meet the requirements of paragraph (2)(D) and shall specify any material change in the matters referred to in clauses (i) through (v) of paragraph (2)(A).

(5) Regulatory exceptions—The Secretary may provide by regulation for additional exceptions to the requirements of this subsection which the Secretary determines are in the interests of participants and beneficiaries.

(6) Guidance and model notices—The Secretary shall issue guidance and model notices which meet the requirements of this subsection.

(7) Blackout period—For purposes of this subsection—

(A) In general—The term 'blackout period' means, in connection with an individual account plan, any period for which any ability of participants or beneficiaries under the plan, which is otherwise available under the terms of such plan, to direct or diversify assets credited to their accounts, to obtain loans from the plan, or to obtain distributions from the plan is temporarily suspended, limited, or restricted, if such suspension, limitation, or restriction is for any period of more than 3 consecutive business days.

(B) Exclusions—The term 'blackout period' does not include a suspension, limitation, or restriction—

(i) which occurs by reason of the application of the securities laws (as defined in section 78c(a)(47) of Title 15),

(ii) which is a change to the plan which provides for a regularly scheduled suspension, limitation, or restriction which is disclosed to participants or beneficiaries through any summary of material modifications, any materials describing specific investment alternatives under the plan, or any changes thereto, or

(iii) which applies only to 1 or more individuals, each of whom is the participant, an alternate payee (as defined in section 1056(d)(3)(K) of this title), or any other beneficiary pursuant to a qualified domestic relations order (as defined in section 1056(d)(3)(B)(i) of this title).

(8) Individual account plan—

(A) In general—For purposes of this subsection, the term 'individual account plan' shall have the meaning provided such term in section 1002(34) of this title, except that such term shall not include a one-participant retirement plan.

(B) One-participant retirement plan—For purposes of subparagraph (A), the term 'one-participant retirement plan' means a retirement plan that on the first day of the plan year —

(i) covered only one individual (or the individual and the individual's spouse) and the individual (or the individual and the individual's spouse) owned 100 percent of the plan sponsor (whether or not incorporated), or

(ii) covered only one or more partners (or partners and their spouses) in the plan sponsor.

(j) **Notice of funding-based limitation on certain forms of distribution**—The plan administrator of a single-employer plan shall provide a written notice to plan participants and beneficiaries within 30 days—

(1) after the plan has become subject to a restriction described in paragraph (1) or (3) of section 1056(g) of this title,

(2) in the case of a plan to which section 1056(g)(4) of this title applies, after the valuation date for the plan year described in section 1056(g)(4)(A) of this title for which the plan's adjusted funding target attainment percentage for the plan year is less than 60 percent (or, if earlier, the date such percentage is deemed to be less than 60 percent under section 1056(g)(7) of this title), and

(3) at such other time as may be determined by the Secretary of the Treasury.

The notice required to be provided under this subsection shall be in writing, except that such notice may be in electronic or other form to the extent that such form is reasonably accessible to the recipient. The Secretary of the Treasury, in consultation with the Secretary, shall have the authority to prescribe rules applicable to the notices required under this subsection.

* * *

(m) **Notice of right to divest**—Not later than 30 days before the first date on which an applicable individual of an applicable individual account plan is eligible to exercise the right under section 1054(j) of this title to direct the proceeds from the divestment of employer securities with respect to any type of contribution, the administrator shall provide to such individual a notice—

(1) setting forth such right under such section, and

(2) describing the importance of diversifying the investment of retirement account assets.

The notice required by this subsection shall be written in a manner calculated to be understood by the average plan participant and may be delivered in written, electronic, or other appropriate form to the extent that such form is reasonably accessible to the recipient.

* * *

§ 102. Summary plan description (§ 1022)

(a) A summary plan description of any employee benefit plan shall be furnished to participants and beneficiaries as provided in section 1024(b) of this title. The summary plan description shall include the information described in subsection (b), shall be written in a manner calculated to be understood by the average plan participant, and shall be sufficiently accurate and comprehensive to reasonably apprise such participants and beneficiaries of their rights and obligations under the plan. A summary of any material modification in the terms of the plan and any change in the information required under subsection (b) of this section shall be written in a manner calculated to be understood by the average plan participant and shall be furnished in accordance with section 1024(b)(1) of this title.

(b) The summary plan description shall contain the following information: The name and type of administration of the plan; in the case of a group health plan (as defined in section 1191b(a)(1) of this title), whether a health insurance issuer (as defined in section 1191b(b)(2) of this title) is responsible for the financing or administration (including payment of claims) of the plan and (if so) the name and address of such issuer; the name and address of the person designated as agent for the service of legal process, if such person is not the administrator; the name and address of the administrator; names, titles, and addresses of any trustee or trustees (if they are persons different from the administrator); a description of the relevant provisions of any applicable collective bargaining agreement; the plan's requirements respecting eligibility for participation and benefits; a description of the provisions providing for nonforfeitable pension benefits; circumstances which may result in disqualification, ineligibility, or denial or loss of benefits; the source of financing of the plan and the identity of any organization through which benefits are provided; the date of the end of the plan year and whether the records of the plan are kept on a calendar, policy, or fiscal year basis; the procedures to be followed in presenting claims for benefits under the plan including the office at the Department of Labor through which participants and beneficiaries may seek assistance or information regarding their rights under this chapter and the Health Insurance Portability and Accountability Act of 1996 with respect to health benefits that are offered through a group health plan (as defined in section 1191b(a)(1) of this title), the remedies available under the plan for the redress of claims which are denied in whole or in part (including procedures required under section 1133 of this title), and if the employer so elects for purposes of complying with section 1181(f)(3)(B)(i) of this title, the model notice applicable to the State in which the participants and beneficiaries reside.

§ 103. Annual reports (§ 1023)

(a) Publication and filing—

(1)(A) An annual report shall be published with respect to every employee benefit plan to which this part applies. Such report shall be filed with the Secretary in accordance with section 1024(a) of this title, and shall be made available and furnished to participants in accordance with section 1024(b) of this title.

(B) The annual report shall include the information described in subsections (b) and (c) of this section and where applicable subsections (d), (e) and (f) of this section and shall also include—

(i) a financial statement and opinion, as required by paragraph (3) of this subsection, and

(ii) an actuarial statement and opinion, as required by paragraph (4) of this subsection.

* * *

(3)(A) Except as provided in subparagraph (C), the administrator of an employee benefit plan shall engage, on behalf of all plan participants, an independent qualified public accountant, who shall conduct such an examination of any financial statements of the plan, and of other books and records of the plan, as the accountant may deem necessary to enable the accountant to form an opinion as to whether the financial statements and schedules required to be included in the annual reports by subsection (b) of this section are presented fairly in conformity with generally accepted accounting principles applied on a basis consistent with that of the preceding year. Such examination shall be conducted in accordance with generally accepted auditing standards, and shall involve such tests of the books and records of the plan as are considered necessary by the independent qualified public accountant. The independent qualified public accountant shall also offer his opinion as to whether the separate schedules specified in subsection (b)(3) of this section and the summary material required under section 1024(b)(3) of this title present fairly, and in all material respects the information contained therein when considered in conjunction with the financial statements taken as a whole. The opinion by the independent qualified public accountant shall be made a part of the annual report. In a case where a plan is not required to file an annual report, the requirements of this paragraph shall not apply. In a case where by reason of section 1024(a)(2) of this title a plan is required only to file a simplified annual report, the Secretary may waive the requirements of this paragraph.

* * *

(4)(A) The administrator of an employee pension benefit plan subject to the reporting requirement of subsection (d) of this section shall engage, on behalf of all plan participants, an enrolled actuary who shall be responsible for the preparation of the materials comprising the actuarial statement required under subsection (d) of this section. In a case where a plan is not required to file an annual report, the requirement of this paragraph shall not apply, and, in a case where by reason of section 1024(a)(2) of this title, a plan is required only to file a simplified report, the Secretary may waive the requirement of this paragraph.

(B) The enrolled actuary shall utilize such assumptions and techniques as are necessary to enable him to form an opinion as to whether the contents of the matters reported under subsection (d) of this section—

(i) are in the aggregate reasonably related to the experience of the plan and to reasonable expectations; and

(ii) represent his best estimate of anticipated experience under the plan.

The opinion of the enrolled actuary shall be made with respect to, and shall be made a part of, each annual report.

* * *

§ 104. Filing with Secretary and furnishing information to participants and certain employers (§ 1024)

(a) Filing of annual report, plan description, summary plan description, and modifications and changes with Secretary—

(1) The administrator of any employee benefit plan subject to this part shall file with the Secretary the annual report for a plan year within 210 days after the close of such year (or within such time as may be required by regulations promulgated by the Secretary in order to reduce duplicative filing). The Secretary shall make copies of such annual reports available for inspection in the public document room of the Department of Labor.

(2)(A) With respect to annual reports required to be filed with the Secretary under this part, he may by regulation prescribe simplified annual reports for any pension plan which covers less than 100 participants.

* * *

(b) Publication of summary plan description and annual report to participants and beneficiaries of plan—Publication of the summary plan descriptions and annual reports shall be made to participants and beneficiaries of the particular plan as follows:

(1) The administrator shall furnish to each participant, and each beneficiary receiving benefits under the plan, a copy of the summary plan description, and all modifications and changes referred to in section 1022(a) of this title—

(A) within 90 days after he becomes a participant, or (in the case of a beneficiary) within 90 days after he first receives benefits, or

(B) if later, within 120 days after the plan becomes subject to this part.

The administrator shall furnish to each participant, and each beneficiary receiving benefits under the plan, every fifth year after the plan becomes subject to this part an updated summary plan description described in section 1022 of this title which integrates all plan amendments made within such five-year period, except that in a case where no amendments have been made to a plan during such five-year period this sentence shall not apply. Notwithstanding the foregoing, the administrator shall furnish to each participant, and to each beneficiary receiving benefits under the plan, the summary plan description described in section 1022 of this title every tenth year after the plan becomes subject to this part. If there is a modification or change described in section 1022(a) of this title (other than a material reduction in covered services or benefits provided in the case of a group health plan (as defined in section 1191b(a)(1) of this title)), a summary description of such modification or change shall be furnished not later than 210 days after the end of the plan year in which the change is adopted to each participant, and to each beneficiary who is receiving benefits under the plan. If there is a modification or change described in section 1022(a) of this title that is a material reduction in covered services or benefits provided under a group health plan (as defined in section 1191b(a)(1) of this title), a summary description of such modification or change shall be furnished to participants and beneficiaries not later than 60 days after the date of the adoption of the modification or change. In the alternative, the plan sponsors may provide such description at regular intervals of not more than 90 days.

* * *

(2) The administrator shall make copies of the latest updated summary plan description and the latest annual report and the bargaining agreement, trust agreement, contract, or other instruments under which the plan was established or is operated available for examination by any plan participant or beneficiary in the principal office of the administrator and in such other places as may be necessary to make available all pertinent information to all participants (including such places as the Secretary may prescribe by regulations).

(3) Within 210 days after the close of the fiscal year of the plan, the administrator (other than an administrator of a defined benefit plan to which the requirements of section 1021(f) of this title appl[y]) shall furnish to each participant, and to each beneficiary receiving benefits under the plan, a copy of the statements and schedules, for such fiscal year, described in subparagraphs (A) and (B) of section 1023(b)(3) of this title and such other material (including the percentage determined under section 1023(d)(11) of this title) as is necessary to fairly summarize the latest annual report.

(4) The administrator shall, upon written request of any participant or beneficiary, furnish a copy of the latest updated summary plan description, and the latest annual report, any terminal report, the bargaining agreement, trust agreement, contract, or other instruments under which the plan is established or operated. The administrator may make a reasonable charge to cover the cost of furnishing such complete copies. The Secretary may by regulation prescribe the maximum amount which will constitute a reasonable charge under the preceding sentence.

(5) Identification and basic plan information and actuarial information included in the annual report for any plan year shall be filed with the Secretary in an electronic format which accommodates display on the Internet, in accordance with regulations which shall be prescribed by the Secretary. The Secretary shall provide for display of such information included in the annual report, within 90 days after the date of the filing of the annual report, on an Internet website maintained by the Secretary and other appropriate media. Such information shall also be displayed on any Intranet website maintained by the plan sponsor (or by the plan administrator on behalf of the plan sponsor) for the purpose of communicating with employees and not the public, in accordance with regulations which shall be prescribed by the Secretary.

* * *

§ 105. Reporting of participant's benefit rights (§ 1025)

(a) Requirements to provide pension benefit statements—

(1) Requirements—

(A) Individual account plan—The administrator of an individual account plan (other than a one-participant retirement plan described in section 1021(i)(8)(B) of this title) shall furnish a pension benefit statement—

(i) at least once each calendar quarter to a participant or beneficiary who has the right to direct the investment of assets in his or her account under the plan,

(ii) at least once each calendar year to a participant or beneficiary who has his or her own account under the plan but does not have the right to direct the investment of assets in that account, and

(iii) upon written request to a plan beneficiary not described in clause (i) or (ii).

(B) Defined benefit plan—The administrator of a defined benefit plan (other than a one-participant retirement plan described in section 1021(i)(8)(B) of this title) shall furnish a pension benefit statement—

(i) at least once every 3 years to each participant with a nonforfeitable accrued benefit and who is employed by the employer maintaining the plan at the time the statement is to be furnished, and

(ii) to a participant or beneficiary of the plan upon written request.

Information furnished under clause (i) to a participant may be based on reasonable estimates determined under regulations prescribed by the Secretary, in consultation with the Pension Benefit Guaranty Corporation.

(2) Statements—

(A) In general—A pension benefit statement under paragraph (1)—

(i) shall indicate, on the basis of the latest available information—

(I) the total benefits accrued, and

(II) the nonforfeitable pension benefits, if any, which have accrued, or the earliest date on which benefits will become nonforfeitable,

(ii) shall include an explanation of any permitted disparity under section 401(l) of Title 26 or any floor-offset arrangement that may be applied in determining any accrued benefits described in clause (i),

(iii) shall be written in a manner calculated to be understood by the average plan participant, and

(iv) may be delivered in written, electronic, or other appropriate form to the extent such form is reasonably accessible to the participant or beneficiary.

(B) Additional information—In the case of an individual account plan, any pension benefit statement under clause (i) or (ii) of paragraph (1)(A) shall include—

(i) the value of each investment to which assets in the individual account have been allocated, determined as of the most recent valuation date under the plan, including the value of any assets held in the form of employer securities, without regard to whether such securities were contributed by the plan sponsor or acquired at the direction of the plan or of the participant or beneficiary, and

(ii) in the case of a pension benefit statement under paragraph (1)(A)(i)—

(I) an explanation of any limitations or restrictions on any right of the participant or beneficiary under the plan to direct an investment,

(II) an explanation, written in a manner calculated to be understood by the average plan participant, of the importance, for the long-term retirement security of participants and beneficiaries, of a well-balanced and diversified investment portfolio, including a statement of the risk that holding more than 20 percent of a portfolio in the security of one entity (such as employer securities) may not be adequately diversified, and

(III) a notice directing the participant or beneficiary to the Internet website of the Department of Labor for sources of information on individual investing and diversification.

(C) Alternative notice—The requirements of subparagraph (A)(i)(II) are met if, at least annually and in accordance with requirements of the Secretary, the plan—

(i) updates the information described in such paragraph which is provided in the pension benefit statement, or

(ii) provides in a separate statement such information as is necessary to enable a participant or beneficiary to determine their nonforfeitable vested benefits.

(3) Defined benefit plans—

(A) Alternative notice—In the case of a defined benefit plan, the requirements of paragraph (1)(B)(i) shall be treated as met with respect to a participant if at least once each year the administrator provides to the participant notice of the availability of the pension benefit statement and the ways in which the participant may obtain such statement. Such notice may be delivered in written, electronic, or other appropriate form to the extent such form is reasonably accessible to the participant.

(B) Years in which no benefits accrue—The Secretary may provide that years in which no employee or former employee benefits (within the meaning of section 410(b) of Title 26) under the plan need not be taken into account in determining the 3-year period under paragraph (1)(B)(i).

* * *

excludes WBP's fwy vesting of partnip rules

Part 2—Participation and Vesting

§ 201. Coverage (§ 1051)

This part shall apply to any employee benefit plan described in section 1003(a) of this title (and not exempted under section 1003(b) of this title) other than—

(1) an employee welfare benefit plan;

(2) a plan which is unfunded and is maintained by an employer primarily for the purpose of providing deferred compensation for a select group of management or highly compensated employees;

(3)(A) a plan established and maintained by a society, order, or association described in section 501(c)(8) or (9) of Title 26, if no part of the contributions to or under such plan are made by employers of participants in such plan, or

(B) a trust described in section 501(c)(18) of Title 26;

(4) a plan which is established and maintained by a labor organization described in section 501(c)(5) of Title 26 and which does not at any time after September 2, 1974, provide for employer contributions;

(5) any agreement providing payments to a retired partner or a deceased partner's successor in interest, as described in section 736 of Title 26;

(6) an individual retirement account or annuity described in section 408 of Title 26, or a retirement bond described in section 409 of Title 26 (as effective for obligations issued before January 1, 1984);

(7) an excess benefit plan; or

(8) any plan, fund or program under which an employer, all of whose stock is directly or indirectly owned by employees, former employees or their beneficiaries, proposes through an unfunded arrangement to compensate retired employees for benefits which were forfeited by such employees under a pension plan maintained by a former employer prior to the date such pension plan became subject to this chapter.

§ 202. Minimum participation standards (§ 1052)

(a)(1)(A) No pension plan may require, as a condition of participation in the plan, that an employee complete a period of service with the employer or employers maintaining the plan extending beyond the later of the following dates—

(i) the date on which the employee attains the age of 21; or

(ii) the date on which he completes 1 year of service.

(B)(i) In the case of any plan which provides that after not more than 2 years of service each participant has a right to 100 percent of his accrued benefit under the plan which is nonforfeitable at the time such benefit accrues, clause (ii) of subparagraph (A) shall be applied by substituting "2 years of service" for "1 year of service".

(ii) In the case of any plan maintained exclusively for employees of an educational organization (as defined in section 170(b)(1)(A)(ii) of Title 26) by an employer which is exempt from tax under section 501(a) of Title 26, which provides that each participant having at least 1 year of service has a right to 100 percent of his accrued benefit under the plan which is nonforfeitable at the time such benefit accrues, clause (i) of subparagraph (A) shall be applied by substituting "26" for "21". This clause shall not apply to any plan to which clause (i) applies.

(2) No pension plan may exclude from participation (on the basis of age) employees who have attained a specified age.

(3)(A) For purposes of this section, the term "year of service" means a 12-month period during which the employee has not less than 1,000 hours of service. For purposes of this paragraph, computation of any 12-month period shall be made with reference to the date on which the employee's employment commenced, except that, in accordance with regulations prescribed by the Secretary, such computation may be made by reference to the first day of a plan year in the case of an employee who does not complete 1,000 hours of service during the 12-month period beginning on the date his employment commenced.

(B) In the case of any seasonal industry where the customary period of employment is less than 1,000 hours during a calendar year, the term "year of service" shall be such period as may be determined under regulations prescribed by the Secretary.

(C) For purposes of this section, the term "hour of service" means a time of service determined under regulations prescribed by the Secretary.

(D) For purposes of this section, in the case of any maritime industry, 125 days of service shall be treated as 1,000 hours of service. The Secretary may prescribe regulations to carry out the purposes of this subparagraph.

(4) A plan shall be treated as not meeting the requirements of paragraph (1) unless it provides that any employee who has satisfied the minimum age and service requirements specified in such paragraph, and who is otherwise entitled to participate in the plan, commences participation in the plan no later than the earlier of—

(A) the first day of the first plan year beginning after the date on which such employee satisfied such requirements, or

(B) the date 6 months after the date on which he satisfied such requirements,

unless such employee was separated from the service before the date referred to in subparagraph (A) or (B), whichever is applicable.

(b)(1) Except as otherwise provided in paragraphs (2), (3), and (4) all years of service with the employer or employers maintaining the plan shall be taken into account in computing the period of service for purposes of subsection (a)(1) of this section.

(2) In the case of any employee who has any 1-year break in service (as defined in section 1053(b)(3)(A) of this title) under a plan to which the service requirements of clause (i) of subsection (a)(1)(B) of this section apply, if such employee has not satisfied such requirements, service before such break shall not be required to be taken into account.

(3) In computing an employee's period of service for purposes of subsection (a)(1) of this section in the case of any participant who has any 1-year break in service (as defined in section 1053(b)(3)(A) of this title), service before such break shall not be required to be taken into account under the plan until he has completed a year of service (as defined in subsection (a)(3) of this section) after his return.

(4)(A) For purposes of paragraph (1), in the case of a nonvested participant, years of service with the employer or employers maintaining the plan before any period of consecutive 1-year breaks in service shall not be required to be taken into account in computing the period of service if the number of consecutive 1-year breaks in service within such period equals or exceeds the greater of—

    (i) 5, or

    (ii) the aggregate number of years of service before such period.

    (B) If any years of service are not required to be taken into account by reason of a period of breaks in service to which subparagraph (A) applies, such years of service shall not be taken into account in applying subparagraph (A) to a subsequent period of breaks in service.

    (C) For purposes of subparagraph (A), the term "nonvested participant" means a participant who does not have any nonforfeitable right under the plan to an accrued benefit derived from employer contributions.

* * *

§ 203. Minimum vesting standards (§ 1053)

    (a) Nonforfeitability requirements—Each pension plan shall provide that an employee's right to his normal retirement benefit is nonforfeitable upon the attainment of normal retirement age and in addition shall satisfy the requirements of paragraphs (1) and (2) of this subsection.

    (1) A plan satisfies the requirements of this paragraph if an employee's rights in his accrued benefit derived from his own contributions are nonforfeitable.

    (2)(A)(i) In the case of a defined benefit plan, a plan satisfies the requirements of this paragraph if it satisfies the requirements of clause (ii) or (iii).

    (ii) A plan satisfies the requirements of this clause if an employee who has completed at least 5 years of service has a nonforfeitable right to 100 percent of the employee's accrued benefit derived from employer contributions.

    (iii) A plan satisfies the requirements of this clause if an employee has a nonforfeitable right to a percentage of the employee's accrued benefit derived from employer contributions determined under the following table:

Years of service:	The nonforfeitable percentage is:
3	20
4	40
5	60
6	80
7 or more	100.

    (B)(i) In the case of an individual account plan, a plan satisfies the requirements of this paragraph if it satisfies the requirements of clause (ii) or (iii).

    (ii) A plan satisfies the requirements of this clause if an employee who has completed at least 3 years of service has a nonforfeitable right to 100 percent of the employee's accrued benefit derived from employer contributions.

    (iii) A plan satisfies the requirements of this clause if an employee has a nonforfeitable right to a percentage of the employee's accrued benefit derived from employer contributions determined under the following table:

Years of service:	*The nonforfeitable percentage is:*
2	20
3	40
4	60
5	80
6 or more	100.

(3)(A) A right to an accrued benefit derived from employer contributions shall not be treated as forfeitable solely because the plan provides that it is not payable if the participant dies (except in the case of a survivor annuity which is payable as provided in section 1055 of this title).

(B) A right to an accrued benefit derived from employer contributions shall not be treated as forfeitable solely because the plan provides that the payment of benefits is suspended for such period as the employee is employed, subsequent to the commencement of payment of such benefits—

    (i) in the case of a plan other than a multiemployer plan, by an employer who maintains the plan under which such benefits were being paid; and

    (ii) in the case of a multiemployer plan, in the same industry, in the same trade or craft, and the same geographic area covered by the plan, as when such benefits commenced.

The Secretary shall prescribe such regulations as may be necessary to carry out the purposes of this subparagraph, including regulations with respect to the meaning of the term "employed".

(C) A right to an accrued benefit derived from employer contributions shall not be treated as forfeitable solely because plan amendments may be given retroactive application as provided in section 1082(d)(2) of this title.

* * *

(b) Computation of period of service—

(1) In computing the period of service under the plan for purposes of determining the nonforfeitable percentage under subsection (a)(2) of this section, all of an employee's years of service with the employer or employers maintaining the plan shall be taken into account, except that the following may be disregarded:

    (A) years of service before age 18[;]

    (B) years of service during a period for which the employee declined to contribute to a plan requiring employee contributions[;]

    (C) years of service with an employer during any period for which the employer did not maintain the plan or a predecessor plan, defined by the Secretary of the Treasury;

    (D) service not required to be taken into account under paragraph (3);

    (E) years of service before January 1, 1971, unless the employee has had at least 3 years of service after December 31, 1970;

(F) years of service before this part first applies to the plan if such service would have been disregarded under the rules of the plan with regard to breaks in service, as in effect on the applicable date; and

(G) in the case of a multiemployer plan, years of service—

(i) with an employer after—

(I) a complete withdrawal of such employer from the plan (within the meaning of section 1383 of this title), or

(II) to the extent permitted by regulations prescribed by the Secretary of the Treasury, a partial withdrawal described in section 1385(b)(2)(A)(i) of this title in connection with the decertification of the collective bargaining representative; and

(ii) with any employer under the plan after the termination date of the plan under section 1348 of this title.

(2)(A) For purposes of this section, except as provided in subparagraph (C), the term "year of service" means a calendar year, plan year, or other 12-consecutive month period designated by the plan (and not prohibited under regulations prescribed by the Secretary) during which the participant has completed 1,000 hours of service.

(B) For purposes of this section, the term "hour of service" has the meaning provided by section 1052(a)(3)(C) of this title.

(C) In the case of any seasonal industry where the customary period of employment is less than 1,000 hours during a calendar year, the term "year of service" shall be such period as determined under regulations of the Secretary.

(D) For purposes of this section, in the case of any maritime industry, 125 days of service shall be treated as 1,000 hours of service. The Secretary may prescribe regulations to carry out the purposes of this subparagraph.

(3)(A) For purposes of this paragraph, the term "1-year break in service" means a calendar year, plan year, or other 12-consecutive-month period designated by the plan (and not prohibited under regulations prescribed by the Secretary) during which the participant has not completed more than 500 hours of service.

(B) For purposes of paragraph (1), in the case of any employee who has any 1-year break in service, years of service before such break shall not be required to be taken into account until he has completed a year of service after his return.

(C) For purposes of paragraph (1), in the case of any participant in an individual account plan or an insured defined benefit plan which satisfies the requirements of subsection 1054(b)(1)(F) of this title who has 5 consecutive 1-year breaks in service, years of service after such 5-year period shall not be required to be taken into account for purposes of determining the nonforfeitable percentage of his accrued benefit derived from employer contributions which accrued before such 5-year period.

(D)(i) For purposes of paragraph (1), in the case of a nonvested participant, years of service with the employer or employers maintaining the plan before any period of consecutive 1-year breaks in service shall not be required to be taken into account if the number of consecutive 1-year breaks in service within such period equals or exceeds the greater of—

(I) 5, or

(II) the aggregate number of years of service before such period.

(ii) If any years of service are not required to be taken into account by reason of a period of breaks in service to which clause (i) applies, such years of service shall not be taken into account in applying clause (i) to a subsequent period of breaks in service.

(iii) For purposes of clause (i), the term "nonvested participant" means a participant who docs not have any nonforfeitable right under the plan to an accrued benefit derived from employer contributions.

* * *

(c) Plan amendments altering vesting schedule—

(1)(A) A plan amendment changing any vesting schedule under the plan shall be treated as not satisfying the requirements of subsection (a)(2) of this section if the nonforfeitable percentage of the accrued benefit derived from employer contributions (determined as of the later of the date such amendment is adopted, or the date such amendment becomes effective) of any employee who is a participant in the plan is less than such nonforfeitable percentage computed under the plan without regard to such amendment.

(B) A plan amendment changing any vesting schedule under the plan shall be treated as not satisfying the requirements of subsection (a)(2) of this section unless each participant having not less than 3 years of service is permitted to elect, within a reasonable period after adoption of such amendment, to have his nonforfeitable percentage computed under the plan without regard to such amendment.

(2) Subsection (a) of this section shall not apply to benefits which may not be provided for designated employees in the event of early termination of the plan under provisions of the plan adopted pursuant to regulations prescribed by the Secretary of the Treasury to preclude the discrimination prohibited by section 401(a)(4) of Title 26.

(d) Nonforfeitable benefits after lesser period and in greater amounts than required— A pension plan may allow for nonforfeitable benefits after a lesser period and in greater amounts than are required by this part.

(e) Consent for distribution; present value; covered distributions—

(1) If the present value of any nonforfeitable benefit with respect to a participant in a plan exceeds $5,000, the plan shall provide that such benefit may not be immediately distributed without the consent of the participant.

(2) For purposes of paragraph (1), the present value shall be calculated in accordance with section 1055(g)(3) of this title.

(3) This subsection shall not apply to any distribution of dividends to which section 404(k) of Title 26 applies.

(4) A plan shall not fail to meet the requirements of this subsection if, under the terms of the plan, the present value of the nonforfeitable accrued benefit is determined without regard to that portion of such benefit which is attributable to rollover contributions (and earnings allocable thereto). For purposes of this subparagraph, the term "rollover contributions" means any rollover contribution under sections 402(c), 403(a)(4), 403(b)(8), 408(d)(3)(A)(ii), and 457(e)(16) of Title 26.

(f) Special rules for plans computing accrued benefits by reference to hypothetical account balance or equivalent amounts—

    (1) In general—An applicable defined benefit plan shall not be treated as failing to meet—

        (A) subject to paragraph (2), the requirements of subsection (a)(2) of this section, or

        (B) the requirements of section 1054(c) or 1055(g) of this title, or the requirements of subsection (e), with respect to accrued benefits derived from employer contributions,

solely because the present value of the accrued benefit (or any portion thereof) of any participant is, under the terms of the plan, equal to the amount expressed as the balance in the hypothetical account described in paragraph (3) or as an accumulated percentage of the participant's final average compensation.

    (2) 3-year vesting—In the case of an applicable defined benefit plan, such plan shall be treated as meeting the requirements of subsection (a)(2) of this section only if an employee who has completed at least 3 years of service has a nonforfeitable right to 100 percent of the employee's accrued benefit derived from employer contributions.

    (3) Applicable defined benefit plan and related rules—For purposes of this subsection—

        (A) In general—The term "applicable defined benefit plan" means a defined benefit plan under which the accrued benefit (or any portion thereof) is calculated as the balance of a hypothetical account maintained for the participant or as an accumulated percentage of the participant's final average compensation.

        (B) Regulations to include similar plans—The Secretary of the Treasury shall issue regulations which include in the definition of an applicable defined benefit plan any defined benefit plan (or any portion of such a plan) which has an effect similar to an applicable defined benefit plan.

§ 204. Benefit accrual requirements (§ 1054)

(a) Satisfaction of requirements by pension plans—Each pension plan shall satisfy the requirements of subsection (b)(3) of this section, and—

    (1) in the case of a defined benefit plan, shall satisfy the requirements of subsection (b)(1) of this section; and

    (2) in the case of a defined contribution plan, shall satisfy the requirements of subsection (b)(2) of this section.

(b) Enumeration of plan requirements—

    (1)(A) A defined benefit plan satisfies the requirements of this paragraph if the accrued benefit to which each participant is entitled upon his separation from the service is not less than—

        (i) 3 percent of the normal retirement benefit to which he would be entitled at the normal retirement age if he commenced participation at the earliest possible entry age under the plan and served continuously until the earlier of age 65 or the normal retirement age specified under the plan, multiplied by (**ii**) the number of years (not in excess of 33 1/3) of his participation in the plan.

In the case of a plan providing retirement benefits based on compensation during any period, the normal retirement benefit to which a participant would be entitled shall be determined as if he continued to earn annually the average rate of compensation which he earned during consecutive years of service, not in excess of 10, for which his compensation was the highest. For purposes of this subparagraph, social security benefits and all other relevant factors used to compute benefits shall be treated as remaining constant as of the current year for all years after such current year.

(**B**) A defined benefit plan satisfies the requirements of this paragraph of a particular plan year if under the plan the accrued benefit payable at the normal retirement age is equal to the normal retirement benefit and the annual rate at which any individual who is or could be a participant can accrue the retirement benefits payable at normal retirement age under the plan for any later plan year is not more than 133 1/3 percent of the annual rate at which he can accrue benefits for any plan year beginning on or after such particular plan year and before such later plan year. For purposes of this subparagraph—

(**i**) any amendment to the plan which is in effect for the current year shall be treated as in effect for all other plan years;

(**ii**) any change in an accrual rate which does not apply to any individual who is or could be a participant in the current year shall be disregarded;

(**iii**) the fact that benefits under the plan may be payable to certain employees before normal retirement age shall be disregarded; and

(**iv**) social security benefits and all other relevant factors used to compute benefits shall be treated as remaining constant as of the current year for all years after the current year.

(**C**) A defined benefit plan satisfies the requirements of this paragraph if the accrued benefit to which any participant is entitled upon his separation from the service is not less than a fraction of the annual benefit commencing at normal retirement age to which he would be entitled under the plan as in effect on the date of his separation if he continued to earn annually until normal retirement age the same rate of compensation upon which his normal retirement benefit would be computed under the plan, determined as if he had attained normal retirement age on the date any such determination is made (but taking into account no more than the 10 years of service immediately preceding his separation from service). Such fraction shall be a fraction, not exceeding 1, the numerator of which is the total number of his years of participation in the plan (as of the date of his separation from the service) and the denominator of which is the total number of years he would have participated in the plan if he separated from the service at the normal retirement age. For purposes of this subparagraph, social security benefits and all other relevant factors used to compute benefits shall be treated as remaining constant as of the current year for all years after such current year.

* * *

(**G**) Notwithstanding the preceding subparagraphs, a defined benefit plan shall be treated as not satisfying the requirements of this paragraph if the participant's accrued benefit is reduced on account of any increase in his age or service. The preceding sentence shall not apply to benefits under the plan commencing before benefits payable under title II of the Social Security Act [42 U.S.C.A. § 401 et seq.] which benefits under the plan—

(i) do not exceed social security benefits, and

(ii) terminate when such social security benefits commence.

(H)(i) Notwithstanding the preceding subparagraphs, a defined benefit plan shall be treated as not satisfying the requirements of this paragraph if, under the plan, an employee's benefit accrual is ceased, or the rate of an employee's benefit accrual is reduced, because of the attainment of any age.

(ii) A plan shall not be treated as failing to meet the requirements of this subparagraph solely because the plan imposes (without regard to age) a limitation on the amount of benefits that the plan provides or a limitation on the number of years of service or years of participation which are taken into account for purposes of determining benefit accrual under the plan.

(iii) In the case of any employee who, as of the end of any plan year under a defined benefit plan, has attained normal retirement age under such plan—

(I) if distribution of benefits under such plan with respect to such employee has commenced as of the end of such plan year, then any requirement of this subparagraph for continued accrual of benefits under such plan with respect to such employee during such plan year shall be treated as satisfied to the extent of the actuarial equivalent of in-service distribution of benefits, and

(II) if distribution of benefits under such plan with respect to such employee has not commenced as of the end of such year in accordance with section 1056(a)(3) of this title, and the payment of benefits under such plan with respect to such employee is not suspended during such plan year pursuant to section 1053(a)(3)(B) of this title, then any requirement of this subparagraph for continued accrual of benefits under such plan with respect to such employee during such plan year shall be treated as satisfied to the extent of any adjustment in the benefit payable under the plan during such plan year attributable to the delay in the distribution of benefits after the attainment of normal retirement age.

The preceding provisions of this clause shall apply in accordance with regulations of the Secretary of the Treasury. Such regulations may provide for the application of the preceding provisions of this clause, in the case of any such employee, with respect to any period of time within a plan year.

(iv) Clause (i) shall not apply with respect to any employee who is a highly compensated employee (within the meaning of section 414(q) of Title 26) to the extent provided in regulations prescribed by the Secretary of the Treasury for purposes of precluding discrimination in favor of highly compensated employees within the meaning of subchapter D of chapter 1 of Title 26.

(v) A plan shall not be treated as failing to meet the requirements of clause (i) solely because the subsidized portion of any early retirement benefit is disregarded in determining benefit accruals.

(vi) Any regulations prescribed by the Secretary of the Treasury pursuant to clause (v) of section 411(b)(1)(H) of Title 26 shall apply with respect to the requirements of this subparagraph in the same manner and to the same extent as such regulations apply with respect to the requirements of such section 411(b)(1)(H).

(2)(A) A defined contribution plan satisfies the requirements of this paragraph if, under the plan, allocations to the employee's account are not ceased, and the rate at which amounts are allocated to the employee's account is not reduced, because of the attainment of any age.

(B) A plan shall not be treated as failing to meet the requirements of subparagraph (A) solely because the subsidized portion of any early retirement benefit is disregarded in determining benefit accruals.

(C) Any regulations prescribed by the Secretary of the Treasury pursuant to subparagraphs (B) and (C) of section 411(b)(2) of Title 26 shall apply with respect to the requirements of this paragraph in the same manner and to the same extent as such regulations apply with respect to the requirements of such section 411(b)(2).

* * *

(5) Special rules relating to age—

(A) Comparison to similarly situated younger individual—

(i) In general—A plan shall not be treated as failing to meet the requirements of paragraph (1)(H)(i) if a participant's accrued benefit, as determined as of any date under the terms of the plan, would be equal to or greater than that of any similarly situated, younger individual who is or could be a participant.

(ii) Similarly situated—For purposes of this subparagraph, a participant is similarly situated to any other individual if such participant is identical to such other individual in every respect (including period of service, compensation, position, date of hire, work history, and any other respect) except for age.

(iii) Disregard of subsidized early retirement benefits—In determining the accrued benefit as of any date for purposes of this subparagraph, the subsidized portion of any early retirement benefit or retirement-type subsidy shall be disregarded.

(iv) Accrued benefit—For purposes of this subparagraph, the accrued benefit may, under the terms of the plan, be expressed as an annuity payable at normal retirement age, the balance of a hypothetical account, or the current value of the accumulated percentage of the employee's final average compensation.

(B) Applicable defined benefit plans—

(i) Interest credits—

(I) In general—An applicable defined benefit plan shall be treated as failing to meet the requirements of paragraph (1)(H) unless the terms of the plan provide that any interest credit (or an equivalent amount) for any plan year shall be at a rate which is not greater than a market rate of return. A plan shall not be treated as failing to meet the requirements of this subclause merely because the plan provides for a reasonable minimum guaranteed rate of return or for a rate of return that is equal to the greater of a fixed or variable rate of return.

(II) Preservation of capital—An applicable defined benefit plan shall be treated as failing to meet the requirements of paragraph (1)(H) unless the plan provides that an interest credit (or equivalent amount) of less than zero shall in no event result in the account balance or similar amount being less than the aggregate amount of contributions credited to the account.

(III) Market rate of return—The Secretary of the Treasury may provide by regulation for rules governing the calculation of a market rate of return for purposes of subclause (I) and for permissible methods of crediting interest to the account (including fixed or variable interest rates) resulting in effective rates of return meeting the requirements of subclause (I).

(ii) Special rule for plan conversions—If, after June 29, 2005, an applicable plan amendment is adopted, the plan shall be treated as failing to meet the requirements of paragraph (1)(H) unless the requirements of clause (iii) are met with respect to each individual who was a participant in the plan immediately before the adoption of the amendment.

(iii) Rate of benefit accrual—Subject to clause (iv), the requirements of this clause are met with respect to any participant if the accrued benefit of the participant under the terms of the plan as in effect after the amendment is not less than the sum of—

(I) the participant's accrued benefit for years of service before the effective date of the amendment, determined under the terms of the plan as in effect before the amendment, plus

(II) the participant's accrued benefit for years of service after the effective date of the amendment, determined under the terms of the plan as in effect after the amendment.

(iv) Special rules for early retirement subsidies—For purposes of clause (iii)(I), the plan shall credit the accumulation account or similar amount with the amount of any early retirement benefit or retirement-type subsidy for the plan year in which the participant retires if, as of such time, the participant has met the age, years of service, and other requirements under the plan for entitlement to such benefit or subsidy.

(v) Applicable plan amendment—For purposes of this subparagraph—

(I) In general—The term "applicable plan amendment" means an amendment to a defined benefit plan which has the effect of converting the plan to an applicable defined benefit plan.

(II) Special rule for coordinated benefits—If the benefits of 2 or more defined benefit plans established or maintained by an employer are coordinated in such a manner as to have the effect of the adoption of an amendment described in subclause (I), the sponsor of the defined benefit plan or plans providing for such coordination shall be treated as having adopted such a plan amendment as of the date such coordination begins.

(III) Multiple amendments—The Secretary of the Treasury shall issue regulations to prevent the avoidance of the purposes of this subparagraph through the use of 2 or more plan amendments rather than a single amendment.

(IV) Applicable defined benefit plan—For purposes of this subparagraph, the term "applicable defined benefit plan" has the meaning given such term by section 1053(f)(3) of this title.

(vi) Termination requirements—An applicable defined benefit plan shall not be treated as meeting the requirements of clause (i) unless the plan provides that, upon the termination of the plan—

(I) if the interest credit rate (or an equivalent amount) under the plan is a variable rate, the rate of interest used to determine accrued benefits under the plan shall be equal to the average of the rates of interest used under the plan during the 5-year period ending on the termination date, and

(II) the interest rate and mortality table used to determine the amount of any benefit under the plan payable in the form of an annuity payable at normal retirement age shall be the rate and table specified under the plan for such purpose as of the termination date, except that if such interest rate is a variable rate, the interest rate shall be determined under the rules of subclause (I).

(C) Certain offsets permitted—A plan shall not be treated as failing to meet the requirements of paragraph (1)(H)(i) solely because the plan provides offsets against benefits under the plan to the extent such offsets are otherwise allowable in applying the requirements of section 401(a) of Title 26.

(D) Permitted disparities in plan contributions or benefits—A plan shall not be treated as failing to meet the requirements of paragraph (1)(H) solely because the plan provides a disparity in contributions or benefits with respect to which the requirements of section 401(l) of Title 26 are met.

(E) Indexing permitted—

(i) In general—A plan shall not be treated as failing to meet the requirements of paragraph (1)(H) solely because the plan provides for indexing of accrued benefits under the plan.

(ii) Protection against loss—Except in the case of any benefit provided in the form of a variable annuity, clause (i) shall not apply with respect to any indexing which results in an accrued benefit less than the accrued benefit determined without regard to such indexing.

(iii) Indexing—For purposes of this subparagraph, the term "indexing" means, in connection with an accrued benefit, the periodic adjustment of the accrued benefit by means of the application of a recognized investment index or methodology.

(F) Early retirement benefit or retirement-type subsidy—For purposes of this paragraph, the terms "early retirement benefit" and "retirement-type subsidy" have the meaning given such terms in subsection (g)(2)(A) of this section.

(G) Benefit accrued to date—For purposes of this paragraph, any reference to the accrued benefit shall be a reference to such benefit accrued to date.

(c) Employee's accrued benefits derived from employer and employee contributions—

(1) For purposes of this section and section 1053 of this title an employee's accrued benefit derived from employer contributions as of any applicable date is the excess (if any) of the accrued benefit for such employee as of such applicable date over the accrued benefit derived from contributions made by such employee as of such date.

* * *

(d) Employee service which may be disregarded in determining employee's accrued benefits under plan—Notwithstanding section 1053(b)(1) of this title, for purposes of determining the employee's accrued benefit under the plan, the plan may disregard service performed by the employee with respect to which he has received—

    (1) a distribution of the present value of his entire nonforfeitable benefit if such distribution was in an amount (not more than the dollar limit under section 1053(e)(1) of this title) permitted under regulations prescribed by the Secretary of the Treasury, or

    (2) a distribution of the present value of his nonforfeitable benefit attributable to such service which he elected to receive.

Paragraph (1) shall apply only if such distribution was made on termination of the employee's participation in the plan. Paragraph (2) shall apply only if such distribution was made on termination of the employee's participation in the plan or under such other circumstances as may be provided under regulations prescribed by the Secretary of the Treasury.

(e) Opportunity to repay full amount of distributions which have been reduced through disregarded employee service—For purposes of determining the employee's accrued benefit, the plan shall not disregard service as provided in subsection (d) of this section unless the plan provides an opportunity for the participant to repay the full amount of a distribution described in subsection (d) of this section with, in the case of a defined benefit plan, interest at the rate determined for purposes of subsection (c)(2)(C) of this section and provides that upon such repayment the employee's accrued benefit shall be recomputed by taking into account service so disregarded. This subsection shall apply only in the case of a participant who—

    (1) received such a distribution in any plan year to which this section applies, which distribution was less than the present value of his accrued benefit,

    (2) resumes employment covered under the plan, and

    (3) repays the full amount of such distribution with, in the case of a defined benefit plan, interest at the rate determined for purposes of subsection (c)(2)(C) of this section.

The plan provision required under this subsection may provide that such repayment must be made (A) in the case of a withdrawal on account of separation from service, before the earlier of 5 years after the first date on which the participant is subsequently re-employed by the employer, or the close of the first period of 5 consecutive 1-year breaks in service commencing after the withdrawal; or (B) in the case of any other withdrawal, 5 years after the date of the withdrawal.

* * *

(g) Decrease of accrued benefits through amendment of plan— _applies to pension p's not welfare plans_

    (1) The accrued benefit of a participant under a plan may not be decreased by an amendment of the plan, other than an amendment described in section 1082(d)(2) or 1441 of this title.

    (2) For purposes of paragraph (1), a plan amendment which has the effect of—

        (A) eliminating or reducing an early retirement benefit or a retirement-type subsidy (as defined in regulations), or

        (B) eliminating an optional form of benefit,

with respect to benefits attributable to service before the amendment shall be treated as reducing accrued benefits. In the case of a retirement-type subsidy, the preceding sentence shall apply only with respect to a participant who satisfies (either before or after the amendment) the preamendment conditions for the subsidy. The Secretary of the Treasury shall by regulations provide that this paragraph shall not apply to any plan amendment which reduces or eliminates benefits or subsidies which create significant burdens or complexities for the plan and plan participants, unless such amendment adversely affects the rights of any participant in a more than de minimis manner. The Secretary of the Treasury may by regulations provide that this subparagraph shall not apply to a plan amendment described in subparagraph (B) (other than a plan amendment having an effect described in subparagraph (A)).

* * *

(4)(A) A defined contribution plan (in this subparagraph referred to as the "transferee plan") shall not be treated as failing to meet the requirements of this subsection merely because the transferee plan does not provide some or all of the forms of distribution previously available under another defined contribution plan (in this subparagraph referred to as the "transferor plan") to the extent that

> **(i)** the forms of distribution previously available under the transferor plan applied to the account of a participant or beneficiary under the transferor plan that was transferred from the transferor plan to the transferee plan pursuant to a direct transfer rather than pursuant to a distribution from the transferor plan;

> **(ii)** the terms of both the transferor plan and the transferee plan authorize the transfer described in clause (i);

> **(iii)** the transfer described in clause (i) was made pursuant to a voluntary election by the participant or beneficiary whose account was transferred to the transferee plan;

> **(iv)** the election described in clause (iii) was made after the participant or beneficiary received a notice describing the consequences of making the election; and

> **(v)** the transferee plan allows the participant or beneficiary described in clause (iii) to receive any distribution to which the participant or beneficiary is entitled under the transferee plan in the form of a single sum distribution.

(B) Subparagraph (A) shall apply to plan mergers and other transactions having the effect of a direct transfer, including consolidations of benefits attributable to different employers within a multiple employer plan.

(5) Except to the extent provided in regulations promulgated by the Secretary of the treasury, a defined contribution plan shall not be treated as failing to meet the requirements of this subsection merely because of the elimination of a form of distribution previously available thereunder. this paragraph shall not apply to the elimination of a form of distribution with respect to any participant unless

> **(A)** a single sum payment is available to such participant at the same time or times as the form of distribution being eliminated; and

> **(B)** such single sum payment is based on the same or greater portion of the participant's account as the form of distribution being eliminated.

(h) Notice of significant reduction in benefit accruals—

(1) An applicable pension plan may not be amended so as to provide for a significant reduction in the rate of future benefit accrual unless the plan administrator provides the notice described in paragraph (2) to each applicable individual (and to each employee organization representing applicable individuals) and to each employer who has an obligation to contribute to the plan.

(2) The notice required by paragraph (1) shall be written in a manner calculated to be understood by the average plan participant and shall provide sufficient information (as determined in accordance with regulations prescribed by the Secretary of the treasury) to allow applicable individuals to understand the effect of the plan amendment. the Secretary of the treasury may provide a simplified form of notice for, or exempt from any notice requirement, a plan

    (A) which has fewer than 100 participants who have accrued a benefit under the plan, or

    (B) which offers participants the option to choose between the new benefit formula and the old benefit formula.

(3) Except as provided in regulations prescribed by the Secretary of the Treasury, the notice required by paragraph (1) shall be provided within a reasonable time before the effective date of the plan amendment.

* * *

(6)(A) In the case of any egregious failure to meet any requirement of this subsection with respect to any plan amendment, the provisions of the applicable pension plan shall be applied as if such plan amendment entitled all applicable individuals to the greater of

    (i) the benefits to which they would have been entitled without regard to such amendment, or

    (ii) the benefits under the plan with regard to such amendment.

    (B) For purposes of subparagraph (A), there is an egregious failure to meet the requirements of this subsection if such failure is within the control of the plan sponsor and is

    (i) an intentional failure (including any failure to promptly provide the required notice or information after the plan administrator discovers an unintentional failure to meet the requirements of this subsection),

    (ii) a failure to provide most of the individuals with most of the information they are entitled to receive under this subsection, or

    (iii) a failure which is determined to be egregious under regulations prescribed by the Secretary of the Treasury.

(7) The Secretary of the Treasury may by regulations allow any notice under this subsection to be provided by using new technologies.

(8) For purposes of this subsection

    (A) The term "applicable individual" means, with respect to any plan amendment—

    (i) each participant in the plan; and

(ii) any beneficiary who is an alternate payee (within the meaning of section 1056(d)(3)(K) of this title) under an applicable qualified domestic relations order (within the meaning of section 1056(d)(3)(B)(i) of this title),

whose rate of future benefit accrual under the plan may reasonably be expected to be significantly reduced by such plan amendment.

(B) The term "applicable pension plan" means—

(i) any defined benefit plan; or

(ii) an individual account plan which is subject to the funding standards of section 412 of Title 26.

(9) For purposes of this subsection, a plan amendment which eliminates or reduces any early retirement benefit or retirement-type subsidy (within the meaning of subsection (g)(2)(A)) shall be treated as having the effect of reducing the rate of future benefit accrual.

(i) Prohibition on benefit increases where plan sponsor is in bankruptcy—

(1) In the case of a plan described in paragraph (3) which is maintained by an employer that is a debtor in a case under Title 11 or similar Federal or State law, no amendment of the plan which increases the liabilities of the plan by reason of—

(A) any increase in benefits,

(B) any change in the accrual of benefits, or

(C) any change in the rate at which benefits become nonforfeitable under the plan,

with respect to employees of the debtor, shall be effective prior to the effective date of such employer's plan of reorganization.

(2) Paragraph (1) shall not apply to any plan amendment that—

(A) the Secretary of the Treasury determines to be reasonable and that provides for only de minimis increases in the liabilities of the plan with respect to employees of the debtor,

(B) only repeals an amendment described in section 1082(d)(2) of this title,

(C) is required as a condition of qualification under part I of subchapter D of chapter 1 of Title 26, or

(D) was adopted prior to, or pursuant to a collective bargaining agreement entered into prior to, the date on which the employer became a debtor in a case under Title 11 or similar Federal or State law.

(3) This subsection shall apply only to plans (other than multiemployer plans or CSEC plans) covered under section 1321 of this title for which the funding target attainment percentage (as defined in section 1083(d)(2) of this title) is less than 100 percent after taking into account the effect of the amendment.

(4) For purposes of this subsection, the term "employer" has the meaning set forth in section 1082(b)(1) of this title, without regard to section 1082(b)(2) of this title.

(j) Diversification requirements for certain individual account plans—

(1) In general—An applicable individual account plan shall meet the diversification requirements of paragraphs (2), (3), and (4).[**]

* * *

§ 205. Requirement of joint and survivor annuity and preretirement survivor annuity (§ 1055)

(a) Required contents for applicable plans—Each pension plan to which this section applies shall provide that—

(1) in the case of a vested participant who does not die before the annuity starting date, the accrued benefit payable to such participant shall be provided in the form of a qualified joint and survivor annuity, and

(2) in the case of a vested participant who dies before the annuity starting date and who has a surviving spouse, a qualified preretirement survivor annuity shall be provided to the surviving spouse of such participant.

(b) Applicable plans—

(1) This section shall apply to—

(A) any defined benefit plan,

(B) any individual account plan which is subject to the funding standards of section 1082 of this title, and

(C) any participant under any other individual account plan unless—

(i) such plan provides that the participant's nonforfeitable accrued benefit (reduced by any security interest held by the plan by reason of a loan outstanding to such participant) is payable in full, on the death of the participant, to the participant's surviving spouse (or, if there is no surviving spouse or the surviving spouse consents in the manner required under subsection (c)(2) of this section, to a designated beneficiary),

(ii) such participant does not elect the payment of benefits in the form of a life annuity, and

(iii) with respect to such participant, such plan is not a direct or indirect transferee (in a transfer after December 31, 1984) of a plan which is described in subparagraph (A) or (B) or to which this clause applied with respect to the participant.

Clause (iii) of subparagraph (C) shall apply only with respect to the transferred assets (and income therefrom) if the plan separately accounts for such assets and any income therefrom.

* * *

(4) A plan shall not be treated as failing to meet the requirements of paragraph (1)(C) or (2) merely because the plan provides that benefits will not be payable to the surviving

---

[**] Paragraphs (2)-(7) of § 204(j) are omitted, but IRC § 401(a)(35) mirrors the requirements of these paragraphs.

spouse of the participant unless the participant and such spouse had been married throughout the 1-year period ending on the earlier of the participant's annuity starting date or the date of the participant's death.

(c) Plans meeting requirements of section—

(1) A plan meets the requirements of this section only if—

(A) under the plan, each participant—

(i) may elect at any time during the applicable election period to waive the qualified joint and survivor annuity form of benefit or the qualified preretirement survivor annuity form of benefit (or both),

(ii) if the participant elects a waiver under clause (i), may elect the qualified optional survivor annuity at any time during the applicable election period, and

(iii) may revoke any such election at any time during the applicable election period, and

(B) the plan meets the requirements of paragraphs (2), (3), and (4).

(2) Each plan shall provide that an election under paragraph (1)(A)(i) shall not take effect unless—

(A)(i) the spouse of the participant consents in writing to such election, (ii) such election designates a beneficiary (or a form of benefits) which may not be changed without spousal consent (or the consent of the spouse expressly permits designations by the participant without any requirement of further consent by the spouse), and (iii) the spouse's consent acknowledges the effect of such election and is witnessed by a plan representative or a notary public, or

(B) it is established to the satisfaction of a plan representative that the consent required under subparagraph (A) may not be obtained because there is no spouse, because the spouse cannot be located, or because of such other circumstances as the Secretary of the Treasury may by regulations prescribe.

Any consent by a spouse (or establishment that the consent of a spouse may not be obtained) under the preceding sentence shall be effective only with respect to such spouse.

(3)(A) Each plan shall provide to each participant, within a reasonable period of time before the annuity starting date (and consistent with such regulations as the Secretary of the Treasury may prescribe) a written explanation of—

(i) the terms and conditions of the qualified joint and survivor annuity and of the qualified optional survivor annuity,

(ii) the participant's right to make, and the effect of, an election under paragraph (1) to waive the joint and survivor annuity form of benefit,

(iii) the rights of the participant's spouse under paragraph (2), and

(iv) the right to make, and the effect of, a revocation of an election under paragraph (1).

(B)(i) Each plan shall provide to each participant, within the applicable period with respect to such participant (and consistent with such regulations as the Secretary may prescribe), a written explanation with respect to the qualified preretirement survivor annuity comparable to that required under subparagraph (A).

* * *

(4) Each plan shall provide that, if this section applies to a participant when part or all of the participant's accrued benefit is to be used as security for a loan, no portion of the participant's accrued benefit may be used as security for such loan unless—

(A) the spouse of the participant (if any) consents in writing to such use during the 90-day period ending on the date on which the loan is to be so secured, and

(B) requirements comparable to the requirements of paragraph (2) are met with respect to such consent.

(5)(A) The requirements of this subsection shall not apply with respect to the qualified joint and survivor annuity form of benefit or the qualified preretirement survivor annuity form of benefit, as the case may be, if such benefit may not be waived (or another beneficiary selected) and if the plan fully subsidizes the costs of such benefit.

(B) For purposes of subparagraph (A), a plan fully subsidizes the costs of a benefit if under the plan the failure to waive such benefit by a participant would not result in a decrease in any plan benefits with respect to such participant and would not result in increased contributions from such participant.

(6) If a plan fiduciary acts in accordance with part 4 of this subtitle in—

(A) relying on a consent or revocation referred to in paragraph (1)(A), or

(B) making a determination under paragraph (2),

then such consent, revocation, or determination shall be treated as valid for purposes of discharging the plan from liability to the extent of payments made pursuant to such Act.

(7) For purposes of this subsection, the term "applicable election period" means—

(A) in the case of an election to waive the qualified joint and survivor annuity form of benefit, the 180-day period ending on the annuity starting date, or

(B) in the case of an election to waive the qualified preretirement survivor annuity, the period which begins on the first day of the plan year in which the participant attains age 35 and ends on the date of the participant's death.

In the case of a participant who is separated from service, the applicable election period under subparagraph (B) with respect to benefits accrued before the date of such separation from service shall not begin later than such date.

* * *

(d)(1) "Qualified joint and survivor annuity" defined—For purposes of this section, the term "qualified joint and survivor annuity" means an annuity—

(A) for the life of the participant with a survivor annuity for the life of the spouse which is not less than 50 percent of (and is not greater than 100 percent of) the amount of the annuity which is payable during the joint lives of the participant and the spouse, and

(B) which is the actuarial equivalent of a single annuity for the life of the participant.

Such term also includes any annuity in a form having the effect of an annuity described in the preceding sentence.

(2)(A) For purposes of this section, the term 'qualified optional survivor annuity' means an annuity—

> **(i)** for the life of the participant with a survivor annuity for the life of the spouse which is equal to the applicable percentage of the amount of the annuity which is payable during the joint lives of the participant and the spouse, and

> **(ii)** which is the actuarial equivalent of a single annuity for the life of the participant.

Such term also includes any annuity in a form having the effect of an annuity described in the preceding sentence.

> **(B)(i)** For purposes of subparagraph (A), if the survivor annuity percentage—

>> **(I)** is less than 75 percent, the applicable percentage is 75 percent, and

>> **(II)** is greater than or equal to 75 percent, the applicable percentage is 50 percent.

> **(ii)** For purposes of clause (i), the term 'survivor annuity percentage' means the percentage which the survivor annuity under the plan's qualified joint and survivor annuity bears to the annuity payable during the joint lives of the participant and the spouse.

(e) **"Qualified preretirement survivor annuity" defined**—For purposes of this section—

(1) Except as provided in paragraph (2), the term "qualified preretirement survivor annuity" means a survivor annuity for the life of the surviving spouse of the participant if—

> **(A)** the payments to the surviving spouse under such annuity are not less than the amounts which would be payable as a survivor annuity under the qualified joint and survivor annuity under the plan (or the actuarial equivalent thereof) if—

>> **(i)** in the case of a participant who dies after the date on which the participant attained the earliest retirement age, such participant had retired with an immediate qualified joint and survivor annuity on the day before the participant's date of death, or

>> **(ii)** in the case of a participant who dies on or before the date on which the participant would have attained the earliest retirement age, such participant had—

>>> **(I)** separated from service on the date of death,

>>> **(II)** survived to the earliest retirement age,

>>> **(III)** retired with an immediate qualified joint and survivor annuity at the earliest retirement age, and

>>> **(IV)** died on the day after the day on which such participant would have attained the earliest retirement age, and

> **(B)** under the plan, the earliest period for which the surviving spouse may receive a payment under such annuity is not later than the month in which the participant would have attained the earliest retirement age under the plan.

In the case of an individual who separated from service before the date of such individual's death, subparagraph (A)(ii)(I) shall not apply.

(2) In the case of any individual account plan or participant described in subparagraph (B) or (C) of subsection (b)(1) of this section, the term "qualified preretirement survivor annuity" means an annuity for the life of the surviving spouse the actuarial equivalent of which is not less than 50 percent of the portion of the account balance of the participant (as of the date of death) to which the participant had a nonforfeitable right (within the meaning of section 1053 of this title).

(3) For purposes of paragraphs (1) and (2), any security interest held by the plan by reason of a loan outstanding to the participant shall be taken into account in determining the amount of the qualified preretirement survivor annuity.

(f) Marriage requirements for plan—

(1) Except as provided in paragraph (2), a plan may provide that a qualified joint and survivor annuity (or a qualified preretirement survivor annuity) will not be provided unless the participant and spouse had been married throughout the 1-year period ending on the earlier of—

    (A) the participant's annuity starting date, or

    (B) the date of the participant's death.

(2) For purposes of paragraph (1), if—

    (A) a participant marries within 1 year before the annuity starting date, and

    (B) the participant and the participant's spouse in such marriage have been married for at least a 1-year period ending on or before the date of the participant's death,

such participant and such spouse shall be treated as having been married throughout the 1-year period ending on the participant's annuity starting date.

(g) Distribution of present value of annuity; written consent; determination of present value—

(1) A plan may provide that the present value of a qualified joint and survivor annuity or a qualified preretirement survivor annuity will be immediately distributed if such value does not exceed the amount that can be distributed without the participant's consent under section 1053(e) of this title. No distribution may be made under the preceding sentence after the annuity starting date unless the participant and the spouse of the participant (or where the participant has died, the surviving spouse) consent in writing to such distribution.

    (2) If—

    (A) the present value of the qualified joint and survivor annuity or the qualified preretirement survivor annuity exceeds the amount that can be distributed without the participant's consent under section 1053(e) of this title, and

    (B) the participant and the spouse of the participant (or where the participant has died, the surviving spouse) consent in writing to the distribution,

the plan may immediately distribute the present value of such annuity.

(3)(A) For purposes of paragraphs (1) and (2), the present value shall not be less than the present value calculated by using the applicable mortality table and the applicable interest rate.

    (B) For purposes of subparagraph (A)—

(i) The term "applicable mortality table" means a mortality table, modified as appropriate by the Secretary of the Treasury, based on the mortality table specified for the plan year under subparagraph (A) of section 1083(h)(3) of this title (without regard to subparagraph (C) or (D) of such section).

(ii) The term "applicable interest rate" means the adjusted first, second, and third segment rates applied under rules similar to the rules of section 1083(h)(2)(C) of this title (determined by not taking into account any adjustment under clause (iv) thereof) for the month before the date of the distribution or such other time as the Secretary of the Treasury may by regulations prescribe.

(iii) For purposes of clause (ii), the adjusted first, second, and third segment rates are the first, second, and third segment rates which would be determined under section 1083(h)(2)(C) of this title) (determined by not taking into account any adjustment under clause (iv) thereof) if section 1083(h)(2)(D) of this title were applied by substituting the average yields for the month described in clause (ii) for the average yields for the 24-month period described in such section.

(h) Definitions—For purposes of this section—

(1) The term "vested participant" means any participant who has a nonforfeitable right (within the meaning of section 1002(19) of this title) to any portion of such participant's accrued benefit.

(2)(A) The term "annuity starting date" means—

(i) the first day of the first period for which an amount is payable as an annuity, or

(ii) in the case of a benefit not payable in the form of an annuity, the first day on which all events have occurred which entitle the participant to such benefit.

(B) For purposes of subparagraph (A), the first day of the first period for which a benefit is to be received by reason of disability shall be treated as the annuity starting date only if such benefit is not an auxiliary benefit.

(3) The term "earliest retirement age" means the earliest date on which, under the plan, the participant could elect to receive retirement benefits.

(i) Increased costs from providing annuity—A plan may take into account in any equitable manner (as determined by the Secretary of the Treasury) any increased costs resulting from providing a qualified joint or survivor annuity or a qualified preretirement survivor annuity.

(j) Use of participant's accrued benefit as security for loan as not preventing distribution—If the use of any participant's accrued benefit (or any portion thereof) as security for a loan meets the requirements of subsection (c)(4) of this section, nothing in this section shall prevent any distribution required by reason of a failure to comply with the terms of such loan.

(k) Spousal consent—No consent of a spouse shall be effective for purposes of subsection (g)(1) or (g)(2) of this section (as the case may be) unless requirements comparable to the requirements for spousal consent to an election under subsection (c)(1)(A) of this section are met.

* * *

§ 206. Form and payment of benefits (§ 1056)

(a) Commencement date for payment of benefits—Each pension plan shall provide that unless the participant otherwise elects, the payment of benefits under the plan to the participant shall begin not later than the 60th day after the latest of the close of the plan year in which—

(1) occurs the date on which the participant attains the earlier of age 65 or the normal retirement age specified under the plan,

(2) occurs the 10th anniversary of the year in which the participant commenced participation in the plan, or

(3) the participant terminates his service with the employer.

In the case of a plan which provides for the payment of an early retirement benefit, such plan shall provide that a participant who satisfied the service requirements for such early retirement benefit, but separated from the service (with any nonforfeitable right to an accrued benefit) before satisfying the age requirement for such early retirement benefit, is entitled upon satisfaction of such age requirement to receive a benefit not less than the benefit to which he would be entitled at the normal retirement age, actuarially reduced under regulations prescribed by the Secretary of the Treasury.

(b) Decrease in plan benefits by reason of increases in benefit levels under Social Security Act or Railroad Retirement Act of 1937—If—

(1) a participant or beneficiary is receiving benefits under a pension plan, or

(2) a participant is separated from the service and has nonforfeitable rights to benefits,

a plan may not decrease benefits of such a participant by reason of any increase in the benefit levels payable under title II of the Social Security Act [42 U.S.C.A. § 401 et seq.] or the Railroad Retirement Act of 1937 [45 U.S.C.A. § 231 et seq.], or any increase in the wage base under such title II, if such increase takes place after September 2, 1974, or (if later) the earlier of the date of first entitlement of such benefits or the date of such separation.

(c) Forfeiture of accrued benefits derived from employer contributions—No pension plan may provide that any part of a participant's accrued benefit derived from employer contributions (whether or not otherwise nonforfeitable) is forfeitable solely because of withdrawal by such participant of any amount attributable to the benefit derived from contributions made by such participant. The preceding sentence shall not apply (1) to the accrued benefit of any participant unless, at the time of such withdrawal, such participant has a nonforfeitable right to at least 50 percent of such accrued benefit, or (2) to the extent that an accrued benefit is permitted to be forfeited in accordance with section 1053(a)(3)(D)(iii) of this title.

(d) Assignment or alienation of plan benefits—

(1) Each pension plan shall provide that benefits provided under the plan may not be assigned or alienated.

(2) For the purposes of paragraph (1) of this subsection, there shall not be taken into account any voluntary and revocable assignment of not to exceed 10 percent of any benefit payment, or of any irrevocable assignment or alienation of benefits executed before September 2, 1974. The preceding sentence shall not apply to any assignment or alienation made for the purposes of defraying plan administration costs. For purposes of this paragraph a loan made to a participant or beneficiary shall not be treated as an assignment or alienation if such loan is secured by the participant's accrued nonforfeitable benefit and is exempt from the tax imposed by section 4975 of Title 26 (relating to tax on prohibited transactions) by reason of section 4975(d)(1) of Title 26.

(3)(A) Paragraph (1) shall apply to the creation, assignment, or recognition of a right to any benefit payable with respect to a participant pursuant to a domestic relations order, except that paragraph (1) shall not apply if the order is determined to be a qualified domestic relations order. Each pension plan shall provide for the payment of benefits in accordance with the applicable requirements of any qualified domestic relations order.

(B) For purposes of this paragraph—

(i) the term "qualified domestic relations order" means a domestic relations order—

(I) which creates or recognizes the existence of an alternate payee's right to, or assigns to an alternate payee the right to, receive all or a portion of the benefits payable with respect to a participant under a plan, and

(II) with respect to which the requirements of subparagraphs (C) and (D) are met, and

(ii) the term "domestic relations order" means any judgment, decree, or order (including approval of a property settlement agreement) which—

(I) relates to the provision of child support, alimony payments, or marital property rights to a spouse, former spouse, child, or other dependent of a participant, and

(II) is made pursuant to a State domestic relations law (including a community property law).

(C) A domestic relations order meets the requirements of this subparagraph only if such order clearly specifies—

(i) the name and the last known mailing address (if any) of the participant and the name and mailing address of each alternate payee covered by the order,

(ii) the amount or percentage of the participant's benefits to be paid by the plan to each such alternate payee, or the manner in which such amount or percentage is to be determined,

(iii) the number of payments or period to which such order applies, and

(iv) each plan to which such order applies.

(D) A domestic relations order meets the requirements of this subparagraph only if such order—

(i) does not require a plan to provide any type or form of benefit, or any option, not otherwise provided under the plan,

(ii) does not require the plan to provide increased benefits (determined on the basis of actuarial value), and

(iii) does not require the payment of benefits to an alternate payee which are required to be paid to another alternate payee under another order previously determined to be a qualified domestic relations order.

(E)(i) A domestic relations order shall not be treated as failing to meet the requirements of clause (i) of subparagraph (D) solely because such order requires that payment of benefits be made to an alternate payee—

(I) in the case of any payment before a participant has separated from service, on or after the date on which the participant attains (or would have attained) the earliest retirement age,

(II) as if the participant had retired on the date on which such payment is to begin under such order (but taking into account only the present value of benefits actually accrued and not taking into account the present value of any employer subsidy for early retirement), and

(III) in any form in which such benefits may be paid under the plan to the participant (other than in the form of a joint and survivor annuity with respect to the alternate payee and his or her subsequent spouse).

For purposes of subclause (II), the interest rate assumption used in determining the present value shall be the interest rate specified in the plan or, if no rate is specified, 5 percent.

(ii) For purposes of this subparagraph, the term "earliest retirement age" means the earlier of—

(I) the date on which the participant is entitled to a distribution under the plan, or

(II) the later of the date of the participant attains age 50 or the earliest date on which the participant could begin receiving benefits under the plan if the participant separated from service.

(F) To the extent provided in any qualified domestic relations order—

(i) the former spouse of a participant shall be treated as a surviving spouse of such participant for purposes of section 1055 of this title (and any spouse of the participant shall not be treated as a spouse of the participant for such purposes), and

(ii) if married for at least 1 year, the surviving former spouse shall be treated as meeting the requirements of section 1055(f) of this title.

(G)(i) In the case of any domestic relations order received by a plan—

(I) the plan administrator shall promptly notify the participant and each alternate payee of the receipt of such order and the plan's procedures for determining the qualified status of domestic relations orders, and

(II) within a reasonable period after receipt of such order, the plan administrator shall determine whether such order is a qualified domestic relations order and notify the participant and each alternate payee of such determination.

(ii) Each plan shall establish reasonable procedures to determine the qualified status of domestic relations orders and to administer distributions under such qualified orders. Such procedures—

(I) shall be in writing,

(II) shall provide for the notification of each person specified in a domestic relations order as entitled to payment of benefits under the plan (at the address included in the domestic relations order) of such procedures promptly upon receipt by the plan of the domestic relations order, and

(III) shall permit an alternate payee to designate a representative for receipt of copies of notices that are sent to the alternate payee with respect to a domestic relations order.

(H)(i) During any period in which the issue of whether a domestic relations order is a qualified domestic relations order is being determined (by the plan administrator, by a court of competent jurisdiction, or otherwise), the plan administrator shall separately account for the amounts (hereinafter in this subparagraph referred to as the "segregated amounts") which would have been payable to the alternate payee during such period if the order had been determined to be a qualified domestic relations order.

(ii) If within the 18-month period described in clause (v) the order (or modification thereof) is determined to be a qualified domestic relations order, the plan administrator shall pay the segregated amounts (including any interest thereon) to the person or persons entitled thereto.

(iii) If within the 18-month period described in clause (v)—

(I) it is determined that the order is not a qualified domestic relations order, or

(II) the issue as to whether such order is a qualified domestic relations order is not resolved,

then the plan administrator shall pay the segregated amounts (including any interest thereon) to the person or persons who would have been entitled to such amounts if there had been no order.

(iv) Any determination that an order is a qualified domestic relations order which is made after the close of the 18-month period described in clause (v) shall be applied prospectively only.

(v) For purposes of this subparagraph, the 18-month period described in this clause is the 18-month period beginning with the date on which the first payment would be required to be made under the domestic relations order.

(I) If a plan fiduciary acts in accordance with part 4 of this subtitle in—

(i) treating a domestic relations order as being (or not being) a qualified domestic relations order, or

(ii) taking action under subparagraph (H),

then the plan's obligation to the participant and each alternate payee shall be discharged to the extent of any payment made pursuant to such Act.

(J) A person who is an alternate payee under a qualified domestic relations order shall be considered for purposes of any provision of this chapter a beneficiary under the plan. Nothing in the preceding sentence shall permit a requirement under section 1301 of this title of the payment of more than 1 premium with respect to a participant for any period.

(K) The term "alternate payee" means any spouse, former spouse, child, or other dependent of a participant who is recognized by a domestic relations order as having a right to receive all, or a portion of, the benefits payable under a plan with respect to such participant.

(L) This paragraph shall not apply to any plan to which paragraph (1) does not apply.

* * *

(4) Paragraph (1) shall not apply to any offset of a participant's benefits provided under an employee pension benefit plan against an amount that the participant is ordered or required to pay to the plan if—

(A) the order or requirement to pay arises—

(i) under a judgment of conviction for a crime involving such plan,

(ii) under a civil judgment (including a consent order or decree) entered by a court in an action brought in connection with a violation (or alleged violation) of part 4 of this subtitle [section 1101 et seq. of this title], or

(iii) pursuant to a settlement agreement between the Secretary and the participant, or a settlement agreement between the Pension Benefit Guaranty Corporation and the participant, in connection with a violation (or alleged violation) of part 4 of this subtitle [section 1101 et seq. of this title] by a fiduciary or any other person,

(B) the judgment, order, decree, or settlement agreement expressly provides for the offset of all or part of the amount ordered or required to be paid to the plan against the participant's benefits provided under the plan, and

(C) in a case in which the survivor annuity requirements of section 1055 of this title apply with respect to distributions from the plan to the participant, if the participant has a spouse at the time at which the offset is to be made—

(i) either—

(I) such spouse has consented in writing to such offset and such consent is witnessed by a notary public or representative of the plan (or it is established to the satisfaction of a plan representative that such consent may not be obtained by reason of circumstances described in section 1055(c)(2)(B) of this title), or

(II) an election to waive the right of the spouse to a qualified joint and survivor annuity or a qualified preretirement survivor annuity is in effect in accordance with the requirements of section 1055(c) of this title,

(ii) such spouse is ordered or required in such judgment, order, decree, or settlement to pay an amount to the plan in connection with a violation of part 4 of this subtitle, or

(iii) in such judgment, order, decree, or settlement, such spouse retains the right to receive the survivor annuity under a qualified joint and survivor annuity provided pursuant to section 1055(a)(1) of this title and under a qualified preretirement survivor annuity provided pursuant to section 1055(a)(2) of this title, determined in accordance with paragraph (5).

A plan shall not be treated as failing to meet the requirements of section 1055 of this title solely by reason of an offset under this paragraph.

* * *

(g) Funding-based limits on benefits and benefit accruals under single-employer plans—

(1) Funding-based limitation on shutdown benefits and other unpredictable contingent event benefits under single-employer plans—

(A) In general—If a participant of a defined benefit plan which is a single-employer plan is entitled to an unpredictable contingent event benefit payable with respect to any event occurring during any plan year, the plan shall provide that such benefit may not be provided if the adjusted funding target attainment percentage for such plan year—

(i) is less than 60 percent, or

(ii) would be less than 60 percent taking into account such occurrence.

(B) Exemption—Subparagraph (A) shall cease to apply with respect to any plan year, effective as of the first day of the plan year, upon payment by the plan sponsor of a contribution (in addition to any minimum required contribution under section 1083 of this title) equal to—

(i) in the case of subparagraph (A)(i), the amount of the increase in the funding target of the plan (under section 1083 of this title) for the plan year attributable to the occurrence referred to in subparagraph (A), and

(ii) in the case of subparagraph (A)(ii), the amount sufficient to result in an adjusted funding target attainment percentage of 60 percent.

(C) Unpredictable contingent event benefit—For purposes of this paragraph, the term "unpredictable contingent event benefit" means any benefit payable solely by reason of—

(i) a plant shutdown (or similar event, as determined by the Secretary of the Treasury), or

(ii) an event other than the attainment of any age, performance of any service, receipt or derivation of any compensation, or occurrence of death or disability.

(2) Limitations on plan amendments increasing liability for benefits—

(A) In general—No amendment to a defined benefit plan which is a single-employer plan which has the effect of increasing liabilities of the plan by reason of increases in benefits, establishment of new benefits, changing the rate of benefit accrual, or changing the rate at which benefits become nonforfeitable may take effect during any plan year if the adjusted funding target attainment percentage for such plan year is—

(i) less than 80 percent, or

(ii) would be less than 80 percent taking into account such amendment.

(B) Exemption—Subparagraph (A) shall cease to apply with respect to any plan year, effective as of the first day of the plan year (or if later, the effective date of the amendment), upon payment by the plan sponsor of a contribution (in addition to any minimum required contribution under section 1083 of this title) equal to—

(i) in the case of subparagraph (A)(i), the amount of the increase in the funding target of the plan (under section 1083 of this title) for the plan year attributable to the amendment, and

(ii) in the case of subparagraph (A)(ii), the amount sufficient to result in an adjusted funding target attainment percentage of 80 percent.

(C) **Exception for certain benefit increases**—Subparagraph (A) shall not apply to any amendment which provides for an increase in benefits under a formula which is not based on a participant's compensation, but only if the rate of such increase is not in excess of the contemporaneous rate of increase in average wages of participants covered by the amendment.

(3) Limitations on accelerated benefit distributions—

(A) **Funding percentage less than 60 percent**—A defined benefit plan which is a single-employer plan shall provide that, in any case in which the plan's adjusted funding target attainment percentage for a plan year is less than 60 percent, the plan may not pay any prohibited payment after the valuation date for the plan year.

(B) **Bankruptcy**—A defined benefit plan which is a single-employer plan shall provide that, during any period in which the plan sponsor is a debtor in a case under title 11, or similar Federal or State law, the plan may not pay any prohibited payment. The preceding sentence shall not apply on or after the date on which the enrolled actuary of the plan certifies that the adjusted funding target attainment percentage of such plan (determined by not taking into account any adjustment of segment rates under section 303(h)(2)(c)(IV)) is not less than 100 percent.

(C) **Limited payment if percentage at least 60 percent but less than 80 percent—**

(i) **In general**—A defined benefit plan which is a single-employer plan shall provide that, in any case in which the plan's adjusted funding target attainment percentage for a plan year is 60 percent or greater but less than 80 percent, the plan may not pay any prohibited payment after the valuation date for the plan year to the extent the amount of the payment exceeds the lesser of—

(I) 50 percent of the amount of the payment which could be made without regard to this subsection, or

(II) the present value (determined under guidance prescribed by the Pension Benefit Guaranty Corporation, using the interest and mortality assumptions under section 1055(g) of this title) of the maximum guarantee with respect to the participant under section 1322 of this title.

(ii) **One-time application—**

(I) **In general**—The plan shall also provide that only 1 prohibited payment meeting the requirements of clause (i) may be made with respect to any participant during any period of consecutive plan years to which the limitations under either subparagraph (A) or (B) or this subparagraph applies.

(II) **Treatment of beneficiaries**—For purposes of this clause, a participant and any beneficiary on his behalf (including an alternate payee, as defined in subsection (d)(3)(K) of this section) shall be treated as 1 participant. If the accrued benefit of a participant is allocated to such an alternate payee and

1 or more other persons, the amount under clause (i) shall be allocated among such persons in the same manner as the accrued benefit is allocated unless the qualified domestic relations order (as defined in subsection (d)(3)(B)(i) of this section) provides otherwise.

(D) Exception—This paragraph shall not apply to any plan for any plan year if the terms of such plan (as in effect for the period beginning on September 1, 2005, and ending with such plan year) provide for no benefit accruals with respect to any participant during such period.

(E) Prohibited payment—For purpose of this paragraph, the term "prohibited payment" means—

(i) any payment, in excess of the monthly amount paid under a single life annuity (plus any social security supplements described in the last sentence of section 1054(b)(1)(G) of this title), to a participant or beneficiary whose annuity starting date (as defined in section 1055(h)(2) of this title) occurs during any period a limitation under subparagraph (A) or (B) is in effect,

(ii) any payment for the purchase of an irrevocable commitment from an insurer to pay benefits, and

(iii) any other payment specified by the Secretary of the Treasury by regulations.

Such term shall not include the payment of a benefit which under section 1053(e) of this title may be immediately distributed without the consent of the participant.

(4) Limitation on benefit accruals for plans with severe funding shortfalls—

(A) In general—A defined benefit plan which is a single-employer plan shall provide that, in any case in which the plan's adjusted funding target attainment percentage for a plan year is less than 60 percent, benefit accruals under the plan shall cease as of the valuation date for the plan year.

(B) Exemption—Subparagraph (A) shall cease to apply with respect to any plan year, effective as of the first day of the plan year, upon payment by the plan sponsor of a contribution (in addition to any minimum required contribution under section 1083 of this title) equal to the amount sufficient to result in an adjusted funding target attainment percentage of 60 percent.

(5) Rules relating to contributions required to avoid benefit limitations—

(A) Security may be provided—

(i) **In general**—For purposes of this subsection, the adjusted funding target attainment percentage shall be determined by treating as an asset of the plan any security provided by a plan sponsor in a form meeting the requirements of clause (ii).

(ii) **Form of security**—The security required under clause (i) shall consist of—

(I) a bond issued by a corporate surety company that is an acceptable surety for purposes of section 1112 of this title,

(II) cash, or United States obligations which mature in 3 years or less, held in escrow by a bank or similar financial institution, or

(III) such other form of security as is satisfactory to the Secretary of the Treasury and the parties involved.

(iii) Enforcement—Any security provided under clause (i) may be perfected and enforced at any time after the earlier of—

(I) the date on which the plan terminates,

(II) if there is a failure to make a payment of the minimum required contribution for any plan year beginning after the security is provided, the due date for the payment under section 1083(j) of this title, or

(III) if the adjusted funding target attainment percentage is less than 60 percent for a consecutive period of 7 years, the valuation date for the last year in the period.

(iv) Release of security—The security shall be released (and any amounts thereunder shall be refunded together with any interest accrued thereon) at such time as the Secretary of the Treasury may prescribe in regulations, including regulations for partial releases of the security by reason of increases in the adjusted funding target attainment percentage.

(B) Prefunding balance or funding standard carryover balance may not be used—No prefunding balance or funding standard carryover balance under section 1083(f) of this title may be used under paragraph (1), (2), or (4) to satisfy any payment an employer may make under any such paragraph to avoid or terminate the application of any limitation under such paragraph.

(C) Deemed reduction of funding balances—

(i) In general—Subject to clause (iii), in any case in which a benefit limitation under paragraph (1), (2), (3), or (4) would (but for this subparagraph and determined without regard to paragraph (1)(B), (2)(B), or (4)(B)) apply to such plan for the plan year, the plan sponsor of such plan shall be treated for purposes of this [chapter] as having made an election under section 1083(f) of this title to reduce the prefunding balance or funding standard carryover balance by such amount as is necessary for such benefit limitation to not apply to the plan for such plan year.

(ii) Exception for insufficient funding balances—Clause (i) shall not apply with respect to a benefit limitation for any plan year if the application of clause (i) would not result in the benefit limitation not applying for such plan year.

(iii) Restrictions of certain rules to collectively bargained plans—With respect to any benefit limitation under paragraph (1), (2), or (4), clause (i) shall only apply in the case of a plan maintained pursuant to 1 or more collective bargaining agreements between employee representatives and 1 or more employers.

(6) New plans—Paragraphs (1), (2), and (4) shall not apply to a plan for the first 5 plan years of the plan. For purposes of this paragraph, the reference in this paragraph to a plan shall include a reference to any predecessor plan.

(7) Presumed underfunding for purposes of benefit limitations—

(A) Presumption of continued underfunding—In any case in which a benefit limitation under paragraph (1), (2), (3), or (4) has been applied to a plan with respect to the plan year preceding the current plan year, the adjusted funding target attainment percentage of the plan for the current plan year shall be presumed to be equal to the adjusted funding target attainment percentage of the plan for the preceding plan year until the enrolled actuary of the plan certifies the actual adjusted funding target attainment percentage of the plan for the current plan year.

(B) Presumption of underfunding after 10th month—In any case in which no certification of the adjusted funding target attainment percentage for the current plan year is made with respect to the plan before the first day of the 10th month of such year, for purposes of paragraphs (1), (2), (3), and (4), such first day shall be deemed, for purposes of such paragraph, to be the valuation date of the plan for the current plan year and the plan's adjusted funding target attainment percentage shall be conclusively presumed to be less than 60 percent as of such first day.

(C) Presumption of underfunding after 4th month for nearly underfunded plans—In any case in which—

(i) a benefit limitation under paragraph (1), (2), (3), or (4) did not apply to a plan with respect to the plan year preceding the current plan year, but the adjusted funding target attainment percentage of the plan for such preceding plan year was not more than 10 percentage points greater than the percentage which would have caused such paragraph to apply to the plan with respect to such preceding plan year, and

(ii) as of the first day of the 4th month of the current plan year, the enrolled actuary of the plan has not certified the actual adjusted funding target attainment percentage of the plan for the current plan year,

until the enrolled actuary so certifies, such first day shall be deemed, for purposes of such paragraph, to be the valuation date of the plan for the current plan year and the adjusted funding target attainment percentage of the plan as of such first day shall, for purposes of such paragraph, be presumed to be equal to 10 percentage points less than the adjusted funding target attainment percentage of the plan for such preceding plan year.

(8) Treatment of plan as of close of prohibited or cessation period—For purposes of applying this part—

(A) Operation of plan after period—Unless the plan provides otherwise, payments and accruals will resume effective as of the day following the close of the period for which any limitation of payment or accrual of benefits under paragraph (3) or (4) applies.

(B) Treatment of affected benefits—Nothing in this paragraph shall be construed as affecting the plan's treatment of benefits which would have been paid or accrued but for this subsection.

(9) Terms relating to funding target attainment percentage—For purposes of this subsection—

(A) In general—The term "funding target attainment percentage" has the same meaning given such term by section 1083(d)(2) of this title.

(B) Adjusted funding target attainment percentage—The term "adjusted funding target attainment percentage" means the funding target attainment percentage which is determined under subparagraph (A) by increasing each of the amounts under subparagraphs (A) and (B) of section 1083(d)(2) of this title by the aggregate amount of purchases of annuities for employees other than highly compensated employees (as defined in section 414(q) of Title 26) which were made by the plan during the preceding 2 plan years.

(C) Application to plans which are fully funded without regard to reductions for funding balances—In the case of a plan for any plan year, if the funding target attainment percentage is 100 percent or more (determined without regard to the reduction in the value of assets under section 1083(f)(4) of this title), the funding target attainment percentage for purposes of subparagraphs (A) and (B) shall be determined without regard to such reduction.

* * *

(12) CSEC plans—This subsection shall not apply to a CSEC plan (as defined in section 1060(f) of this title).

§ 208. Mergers and consolidations of plans or transfers of plan assets (§ 1058)

A pension plan may not merge or consolidate with, or transfer its assets or liabilities to, any other plan after September 2, 1974, unless each participant in the plan would (if the plan then terminated) receive a benefit immediately after the merger, consolidation, or transfer which is equal to or greater than the benefit he would have been entitled to receive immediately before the merger, consolidation, or transfer (if the plan had then terminated). The preceding sentence shall not apply to any transaction to the extent that participants either before or after the transaction are covered under a multiemployer plan to which subchapter III of this chapter applies.

Part 3—Funding

§ 301. Coverage (§ 1081)

(a) Plans excepted from applicability of this part—This part shall apply to any employee pension benefit plan described in section 1003(a) of this title, (and not exempted under section 1003(b) of this title), other than—

(1) an employee welfare benefit plan;

(2) an insurance contract plan described in subsection (b) of this section;

(3) a plan which is unfunded and is maintained by an employer primarily for the purpose of providing deferred compensation for a select group of management or highly compensated employees;

(4)(A) a plan which is established and maintained by a society, order, or association described in section 501(c)(8) or (9) of title 26, if no part of the contributions to or under such plan are made by employers of participants in such plan; or

(B) a trust described in section 501(c)(18) of Title 26;

(5) a plan which has not at any time after September 2, 1974, provided for employer contributions;

(6) an agreement providing payments to a retired partner or deceased partner or a deceased partner's successor in interest as described in section 736 of Title 26;

(7) an individual retirement account or annuity as described in section 408(a) of Title 26, or a retirement bond described in section 409 of Title 26 (as effective for obligations issued before January 1, 1984);

(8) an individual account plan (other than a money purchase plan) and a defined benefit plan to the extent it is treated as an individual account plan (other than a money purchase plan) under section 1002(35)(B) of this title;

(9) an excess benefit plan; or

(10) any plan, fund or program under which an employer, all of whose stock is directly or indirectly owned by employees, former employees or their beneficiaries, proposes through an unfunded arrangement to compensate retired employees for benefits which were forfeited by such employees under a pension plan maintained by a former employer prior to the date such pension plan became subject to this chapter.

* * *

§ 302. Minimum funding standards (§ 1082)

(a) Requirement to meet minimum funding standard—

(1) In general—A plan to which this part applies shall satisfy the minimum funding standard applicable to the plan for any plan year.

(2) Minimum funding standard—For purposes of paragraph (1), a plan shall be treated as satisfying the minimum funding standard for a plan year if—

(A) in the case of a defined benefit plan which is a single-employer plan (other than a CSEC plan), the employer makes contributions to or under the plan for the plan year which, in the aggregate, are not less than the minimum required contribution determined under section 1083 of this title for the plan for the plan year,

(B) in the case of a money purchase plan which is a single-employer plan, the employer makes contributions to or under the plan for the plan year which are required under the terms of the plan,

(C) in the case of a multiemployer plan, the employers make contributions to or under the plan for any plan year which, in the aggregate, are sufficient to ensure that the plan does not have an accumulated funding deficiency under section 1084 of this title as of the end of the plan year, and

(D) in the case of a CSEC plan, the employers make contributions to or under the plan for any plan year which, in the aggregate, are sufficient to ensure that the plan does not have an accumulated funding deficiency under section 1085a of this title as of the end of the plan year.

(b) Liability for contributions—

(1) In general—Except as provided in paragraph (2), the amount of any contribution required by this section (including any required installments under paragraphs (3) and (4) of section 1083(j) of this title or under section 1085a(f) of this title) shall be paid by the employer responsible for making contributions to or under the plan.

(2) Joint and several liability where employer member of controlled group— If the employer referred to in paragraph (1) is a member of a controlled group, each member of such group shall be jointly and severally liable for payment of such contributions.

(3) Multiemployer plans in critical status—Paragraph (1) shall not apply in the case of a multiemployer plan for any plan year in which the plan is in critical status pursuant to section 1085 of this title. This paragraph shall only apply if the plan sponsor adopts a rehabilitation plan in accordance with section 1085(e) of this title and complies with the terms of such rehabilitation plan (and any updates or modifications of the plan).

(c) Variance from minimum funding standards—

    (1) Waiver in case of business hardship—

        (A) In general—If—

            (i) an employer is (or in the case of a multiemployer plan or a CSEC plan, 10 percent or more of the number of employers contributing to or under the plan are) unable to satisfy the minimum funding standard for a plan year without temporary substantial business hardship (substantial business hardship in the case of a multiemployer plan), and

            (ii) application of the standard would be adverse to the interests of plan participants in the aggregate,

the Secretary of the Treasury may, subject to subparagraph (C), waive the requirements of subsection (a) for such year with respect to all or any portion of the minimum funding standard. The Secretary of the Treasury shall not waive the minimum funding standard with respect to a plan for more than 3 of any 15 (5 of any 15 in the case of a multiemployer plan) consecutive plan years.

        (B) Effects of waiver—If a waiver is granted under subparagraph (A) for any plan year—

            (i) in the case of a single-employer plan (other than a CSEC plan), the minimum required contribution under section 1083 of this title for the plan year shall be reduced by the amount of the waived funding deficiency and such amount shall be amortized as required under section 1083(e) of this title,

            (ii) in the case of a multiemployer plan, the funding standard account shall be credited under section 1084(b)(3)(C) of this title with the amount of the waived funding deficiency and such amount shall be amortized as required under section 1084(b)(2)(C) of this title, and

            (iii) in the case of a CSEC plan, the funding standard account shall be credited under section 1085a(b)(3)(C) of this title with the amount of the waived funding deficiency and such amount shall be amortized as required under section 1085a(b)(2)(C) of this title.

        (C) Waiver of amortized portion not allowed—The Secretary of the Treasury may not waive under subparagraph (A) any portion of the minimum funding standard under subsection (a) for a plan year which is attributable to any waived funding deficiency for any preceding plan year.

    (2) Determination of business hardship—For purposes of this subsection, the factors taken into account in determining temporary substantial business hardship (substantial business hardship in the case of a multiemployer plan) shall include (but shall not be limited to) whether or not—

        (A) the employer is operating at an economic loss,

        (B) there is substantial unemployment or underemployment in the trade or business and in the industry concerned,

        (C) the sales and profits of the industry concerned are depressed or declining, and

(D) it is reasonable to expect that the plan will be continued only if the waiver is granted.

(3) Waived funding deficiency—For purposes of this part, the term "waived funding deficiency" means the portion of the minimum funding standard under subsection (a) (determined without regard to the waiver) for a plan year waived by the Secretary of the Treasury and not satisfied by employer contributions.

(4) Security for waivers for single-employer plans, consultations—

(A) Security may be required—

(i) In general—Except as provided in subparagraph (C), the Secretary of the Treasury may require an employer maintaining a defined benefit plan which is a single-employer plan (within the meaning of section 1301(a)(15) of this title) to provide security to such plan as a condition for granting or modifying a waiver under paragraph (1) or for granting an extension under section 1085a(d) of this title.

(ii) Special rules—Any security provided under clause (i) may be perfected and enforced only by the Pension Benefit Guaranty Corporation, or at the direction of the Corporation, by a contributing sponsor (within the meaning of section 1301(a)(13) of this title), or a member of such sponsor's controlled group (within the meaning of section 1301(a)(14) of this title).

(B) Consultation with the pension benefit guaranty corporation—Except as provided in subparagraph (C), the Secretary of the Treasury shall, before granting or modifying a waiver under this subsection or an extension under [section] 1085a(d) of this title with respect to a plan described in subparagraph (A)(i)—

(i) provide the Pension Benefit Guaranty Corporation with—

(I) notice of the completed application for any waiver or modification, and

(II) an opportunity to comment on such application within 30 days after receipt of such notice, and

(ii) consider—

(I) any comments of the Corporation under clause (i)(II), and

(II) any views of any employee organization (within the meaning of section 1002(4) of this title) representing participants in the plan which are submitted in writing to the Secretary of the Treasury in connection with such application.

Information provided to the Corporation under this subparagraph shall be considered tax return information and subject to the safeguarding and reporting requirements of section 6103(p) of Title 26.

(C) Exception for certain waivers or extensions—

(i) In general—The preceding provisions of this paragraph shall not apply to any plan with respect to which the sum of—

(I) the aggregate unpaid minimum required contributions for the plan year and all preceding plan years, or the accumulated funding deficiency under section 1085a of this title, whichever is applicable,

(II) the present value of all waiver amortization installments determined for the plan year and succeeding plan years under section 1083(e)(2) of this title or section 1085a(b)(2)(C) of this title, whichever is applicable, and

(III) the total amounts not paid by reason of an extension in effect under section 1805a(d) of this title,

is less than $1,000,000.

(ii) Treatment of waivers or extensions for which applications are pending—The amount described in clause (i)(I) shall include any increase in such amount which would result if all applications for waivers or extensions with respect to the minimum funding standard under this subsection which are pending with respect to such plan were denied.

(iii) Unpaid minimum required contribution—For purposes of this subparagraph—

(I) In general—The term "unpaid minimum required contribution" means, with respect to any plan year, any minimum required contribution under section 1083 of this title for the plan year which is not paid on or before the due date (as determined under section 1083(j)(1) of this title) for the plan year.

(II) Ordering rule—For purposes of subclause (I), any payment to or under a plan for any plan year shall be allocated first to unpaid minimum required contributions for all preceding plan years on a first-in, first-out basis and then to the minimum required contribution under section 1083 of this title for the plan year.

(5) Special rules for single-employer plans—

(A) Application must be submitted before date 2 1/2 months after close of year—In the case of a single-employer plan, no waiver may be granted under this subsection with respect to any plan for any plan year unless an application therefor is submitted to the Secretary of the Treasury not later than the 15th day of the 3rd month beginning after the close of such plan year.

(B) Special rule if employer is member of controlled group—In the case of a single-employer plan, if an employer is a member of a controlled group, the temporary substantial business hardship requirements of paragraph (1) shall be treated as met only if such requirements are met—

(i) with respect to such employer, and

(ii) with respect to the controlled group of which such employer is a member (determined by treating all members of such group as a single employer).

The Secretary of the Treasury may provide that an analysis of a trade or business or industry of a member need not be conducted if such Secretary determines such analysis is not necessary because the taking into account of such member would not significantly affect the determination under this paragraph.

(6) Advance notice—

(A) In general—The Secretary of the Treasury shall, before granting a waiver under this subsection, require each applicant to provide evidence satisfactory to such Secretary that the applicant has provided notice of the filing of the application for such waiver to each affected party (as defined in section 1301(a)(21) of this title). Such notice shall include a description of the extent to which the plan is funded for benefits which are guaranteed under subchapter III of this chapter and for benefit liabilities.

(B) Consideration of relevant information—The Secretary of the Treasury shall consider any relevant information provided by a person to whom notice was given under subparagraph (A).

(7) Restriction on plan amendments—

(A) In general—No amendment of a plan which increases the liabilities of the plan by reason of any increase in benefits, any change in the accrual of benefits, or any change in the rate at which benefits become nonforfeitable under the plan shall be adopted if a waiver under this subsection or an extension of time under section 1084(d) of this title or section 1085a(d) of this title is in effect with respect to the plan, or if a plan amendment described in subsection (d)(2) which reduces the accrued benefit of any participant has been made at any time in the preceding 12 months (24 months in the case of a multiemployer plan). If a plan is amended in violation of the preceding sentence, any such waiver, or extension of time, shall not apply to any plan year ending on or after the date on which such amendment is adopted.

(B) Exception—Subparagraph (A) shall not apply to any plan amendment which—

(i) the Secretary of the Treasury determines to be reasonable and which provides for only de minimis increases in the liabilities of the plan,

(ii) only repeals an amendment described in subsection (d)(2) of this section, or

(iii) is required as a condition of qualification under part I of subchapter D of chapter 1 of title 26.

(8) Cross reference—For corresponding duties of the Secretary of the Treasury with regard to implementation of Title 26, see section 412(c) of such title.

(d) Miscellaneous rules—

(1) Change in method or year—If the funding method or a plan year for a plan is changed, the change shall take effect only if approved by the Secretary of the Treasury.

(2) Certain retroactive plan amendments—For purposes of this section, any amendment applying to a plan year which—

(A) is adopted after the close of such plan year but no later than 2 1/2 months after the close of the plan year (or, in the case of a multiemployer plan, no later than 2 years after the close of such plan year),

(B) does not reduce the accrued benefit of any participant determined as of the beginning of the first plan year to which the amendment applies, and

(C) does not reduce the accrued benefit of any participant determined as of the time of adoption except to the extent required by the circumstances,

shall, at the election of the plan administrator, be deemed to have been made on the first day of such plan year. No amendment described in this paragraph which reduces the accrued benefits of any participant shall take effect unless the plan administrator files a notice with the Secretary of the Treasury notifying him of such amendment and such Secretary has approved such amendment, or within 90 days after the date on which such notice was filed, failed to disapprove such amendment. No amendment described in this subsection shall be approved by the Secretary of the Treasury unless such Secretary determines that such amendment is necessary because of a temporary substantial business hardship (as determined under subsection (c)(2) of this section) or a substantial business hardship (as so determined) in the case of a multiemployer plan and that a waiver under subsection (c) of this section (or, in the case of a multiemployer plan or a CSEC plan, any extension of the amortization period under section 1084(d) of this title or section 1085a(d) of this title) is unavailable or inadequate.

(3) Controlled group—For purposes of this section, the term "controlled group" means any group treated as a single employer under subsection (b), (c), (m), or (o) of section 414 of Title 26.

§ 303. Minimum funding standards for single-employer defined benefit pension plans (§ 1083)

(a) Minimum required contribution—For purposes of this section and section 1082(a)(2)(A) of this title, except as provided in subsection (f) of this section, the term "minimum required contribution" means, with respect to any plan year of a single-employer plan—

(1) in any case in which the value of plan assets of the plan (as reduced under subsection (f)(4)(B) of this section) is less than the funding target of the plan for the plan year, the sum of—

(A) the target normal cost of the plan for the plan year,

(B) the shortfall amortization charge (if any) for the plan for the plan year determined under subsection (c), and

(C) the waiver amortization charge (if any) for the plan for the plan year as determined under subsection (e); or

(2) in any case in which the value of plan assets of the plan (as reduced under subsection (f)(4)(B) of this section) equals or exceeds the funding target of the plan for the plan year, the target normal cost of the plan for the plan year reduced (but not below zero) by such excess.

(b) Target normal cost—For purposes of this section:

(1) In general—Except as provided in subsection (i)(2) with respect to plans in at-risk status, the term "target normal cost" means, for any plan year, the excess of—

(A) the sum of—

(i) the present value of all benefits which are expected to accrue or to be earned under the plan during the plan year, plus

(ii) the amount of plan-related expenses expected to be paid from plan assets during the plan year, over

(B) the amount of mandatory employee contributions expected to be made during the plan year.

(2) Special rule for increase in compensation—For purposes of this subsection, if any benefit attributable to services performed in a preceding plan year is increased by reason of any increase in compensation during the current plan year, the increase in such benefit shall be treated as having accrued during the current plan year.

(c) Shortfall amortization charge—

(1) In general—For purposes of this section, the shortfall amortization charge for a plan for any plan year is the aggregate total (not less than zero) of the shortfall amortization installments for such plan year with respect to any shortfall amortization base which has not been fully amortized under this subsection.

(2) Shortfall amortization installment—For purposes of paragraph (1)—

(A) Determination—The shortfall amortization installments are the amounts necessary to amortize the shortfall amortization base of the plan for any plan year in level annual installments over the 7-plan-year period beginning with such plan year.

(B) Shortfall installment—The shortfall amortization installment for any plan year in the 7-plan-year period under subparagraph (A) with respect to any shortfall amortization base is the annual installment determined under subparagraph (A) for that year for that base.

(C) Segment rates—In determining any shortfall amortization installment under this paragraph, the plan sponsor shall use the segment rates determined under subparagraph (C) of subsection (h)(2) of this section, applied under rules similar to the rules of subparagraph (B) of subsection (h)(2) of this section.

(D) Special election for eligible plan years—

(i) In general—If a plan sponsor elects to apply this subparagraph with respect to the shortfall amortization base of a plan for any eligible plan year (in this subparagraph and paragraph (7) referred to as an 'election year'), then, notwithstanding subparagraphs (A) and (B)—

(I) the shortfall amortization installments with respect to such base shall be determined under clause (ii) or (iii), whichever is specified in the election, and

(II) the shortfall amortization installment for any plan year in the 9-plan-year period described in clause (ii) or the 15-plan-year period described in clause (iii), respectively, with respect to such shortfall amortization base is the annual installment determined under the applicable clause for that year for that base.

(ii) 2 plus 7 amortization schedule—The shortfall amortization installments determined under this clause are—

(I) in the case of the first 2 plan years in the 9-plan-year period beginning with the election year, interest on the shortfall amortization base of the plan for the election year (determined using the effective interest rate for the plan for the election year), and

(II) in the case of the last 7 plan years in such 9-plan-year period, the amounts necessary to amortize the remaining balance of the shortfall amortization base of the plan for the election year in level annual installments over such last 7 plan years (using the segment rates under subparagraph (C) for the election year).

(iii) 15-year amortization—The shortfall amortization installments determined under this subparagraph are the amounts necessary to amortize the shortfall amortization base of the plan for the election year in level annual installments over the 15-plan-year period beginning with the election year (using the segment rates under subparagraph (C) for the election year).

(iv) Election—

(I) In general—The plan sponsor of a plan may elect to have this subparagraph apply to not more than 2 eligible plan years with respect to the plan, except that in the case of a plan described in section 106 of the Pension Protection Act of 2006, the plan sponsor may only elect to have this subparagraph apply to a plan year beginning in 2011.

(II) Amortization schedule—Such election shall specify whether the amortization schedule under clause (ii) or (iii) shall apply to an election year, except that if a plan sponsor elects to have this subparagraph apply to 2 eligible plan years, the plan sponsor must elect the same schedule for both years.

(III) Other rules—Such election shall be made at such time, and in such form and manner, as shall be prescribed by the Secretary of the Treasury, and may be revoked only with the consent of the Secretary of the Treasury. The Secretary of the Treasury shall, before granting a revocation request, provide the Pension Benefit Guaranty Corporation an opportunity to comment on the conditions applicable to the treatment of any portion of the election year shortfall amortization base that remains unamortized as of the revocation date.

(v) Eligible plan year—For purposes of this subparagraph, the term "eligible plan year" means any plan year beginning in 2008, 2009, 2010, or 2011, except that a plan year shall only be treated as an eligible plan year if the due date under subsection (j)(1) for the payment of the minimum required contribution for such plan year occurs on or after June 25, 2010.

(vi) Reporting—A plan sponsor of a plan who makes an election under clause (i) shall—

(I) give notice of the election to participants and beneficiaries of the plan, and

(II) inform the Pension Benefit Guaranty Corporation of such election in such form and manner as the Director of the Pension Benefit Guaranty Corporation may prescribe.

(vii) Increases in required installments in certain cases—For increases in required contributions in cases of excess compensation or extraordinary dividends or stock redemptions, see paragraph (7).

(3) Shortfall amortization base—For purposes of this section, the shortfall amortization base of a plan for a plan year is—

(A) the funding shortfall of such plan for such plan year, minus

(B) the present value (determined using the segment rates determined under subparagraph (C) of subsection (h)(2) of this section, applied under rules similar to the rules of subparagraph (B) of subsection (h)(2) of this section) of the aggregate total of the shortfall amortization installments and waiver amortization installments which have been determined for such plan year and any succeeding plan year with respect to the shortfall amortization bases and waiver amortization bases of the plan for any plan year preceding such plan year.

(4) Funding shortfall—For purposes of this section, the funding shortfall of a plan for any plan year is the excess (if any) of—

(A) the funding target of the plan for the plan year, over

(B) the value of plan assets of the plan (as reduced under subsection (f)(4)(B) of this section) for the plan year which are held by the plan on the valuation date.

(5) Exemption from new shortfall amortization base—In any case in which the value of plan assets of the plan (as reduced under subsection (f)(4)(A) of this section) is equal to or greater than the funding target of the plan for the plan year, the shortfall amortization base of the plan for such plan year shall be zero.

(6) Early deemed amortization upon attainment of funding target—In any case in which the funding shortfall of a plan for a plan year is zero, for purposes of determining the shortfall amortization charge for such plan year and succeeding plan years, the shortfall amortization bases for all preceding plan years (and all shortfall amortization installments determined with respect to such bases) shall be reduced to zero.

(7) Increases in alternate required installments in cases of excess compensation or extraordinary dividends or stock redemptions—

(A) In general—If there is an installment acceleration amount with respect to a plan for any plan year in the restriction period with respect to an election year under paragraph (2)(D), then the shortfall amortization installment otherwise determined and payable under such paragraph for such plan year shall, subject to the limitation under subparagraph (B), be increased by such amount.

(B) Total installments limited to shortfall base---Subject to rules prescribed by the Secretary of the Treasury, if a shortfall amortization installment with respect to any shortfall amortization base for an election year is required to be increased for any plan year under subparagraph (A)—

(i) such increase shall not result in the amount of such installment exceeding the present value of such installment and all succeeding installments with respect to such base (determined without regard to such increase but after application of clause (ii)), and

(ii) subsequent shortfall amortization installments with respect to such base shall, in reverse order of the otherwise required installments, be reduced to the extent necessary to limit the present value of such subsequent shortfall amortization installments (after application of this paragraph) to the present value of the remaining unamortized shortfall amortization base.

(C) Installment acceleration amount—For purposes of this paragraph—

(i) In general—The term "installment acceleration amount" means, with respect to any plan year in a restriction period with respect to an election year, the sum of—

(I) the aggregate amount of excess employee compensation determined under subparagraph (D) with respect to all employees for the plan year, plus

(II) the aggregate amount of extraordinary dividends and redemptions determined under subparagraph (E) for the plan year.

(ii) Annual limitation—The installment acceleration amount for any plan year shall not exceed the excess (if any) of—

(I) the sum of the shortfall amortization installments for the plan year and all preceding plan years in the amortization period elected under paragraph (2)(D) with respect to the shortfall amortization base with respect to an election year, determined without regard to paragraph (2)(D) and this paragraph, over

(II) the sum of the shortfall amortization installments for such plan year and all such preceding plan years, determined after application of paragraph (2)(D) (and in the case of any preceding plan year, after application of this paragraph).

(iii) Carryover of excess installment acceleration amounts—

(I) In general—If the installment acceleration amount for any plan year (determined without regard to clause (ii)) exceeds the limitation under clause (ii), then, subject to subclause (II), such excess shall be treated as an installment acceleration amount with respect to the succeeding plan year.

(II) Cap to apply—If any amount treated as an installment acceleration amount under subclause (I) or this subclause with respect any succeeding plan year, when added to other installment acceleration amounts (determined without regard to clause (ii)) with respect to the plan year, exceeds the limitation under clause (ii), the portion of such amount representing such excess shall be treated as an installment acceleration amount with respect to the next succeeding plan year.

(III) Limitation on years to which amounts carried for—No amount shall be carried under subclause (I) or (II) to a plan year which begins after the first plan year following the last plan year in the restriction period (or after the second plan year following such last plan year in the case of an election year with respect to which 15-year amortization was elected under paragraph (2)(D)).

(IV) Ordering rules—For purposes of applying subclause (II), installment acceleration amounts for the plan year (determined without regard to any carryover under this clause) shall be applied first against the limitation under clause (ii) and then carryovers to such plan year shall be applied against such limitation on a first-in, first-out basis.

(D) Excess employee compensation—For purposes of this paragraph—

(i) In general—The term "excess employee compensation" means, with respect to any employee for any plan year, the excess (if any) of—

(I) the aggregate amount includible in income under chapter 1 of Title 26 for remuneration during the calendar year in which such plan year begins for services performed by the employee for the plan sponsor (whether or not performed during such calendar year), over

(II) $1,000,000.

(ii) Amounts set aside for nonqualified deferred compensation—If during any calendar year assets are set aside or reserved (directly or indirectly) in a trust (or other arrangement as determined by the Secretary of the Treasury), or transferred to such a trust or other arrangement, by a plan sponsor for purposes of paying deferred compensation of an employee under a nonqualified deferred compensation plan (as defined in section 409A of such title) of the plan sponsor, then, for purposes of clause (i), the amount of such assets shall be treated as remuneration of the employee includible in income for the calendar year unless such amount is otherwise includible in income for such year. An amount to which the preceding sentence applies shall not be taken into account under this paragraph for any subsequent calendar year.

(iii) Only remuneration for certain post-2009 services counted— Remuneration shall be taken into account under clause (i) only to the extent attributable to services performed by the employee for the plan sponsor after February 28, 2010.

(iv) Exception for certain equity payments—

(I) In general—There shall not be taken into account under clause (i)(I) any amount includible in income with respect to the granting after February 28, 2010, of service recipient stock (within the meaning of section 409A of Title 26) that, upon such grant, is subject to a substantial risk of forfeiture (as defined under section 83(c)(1) of such title) for at least 5 years from the date of such grant.

(II) Secretarial authority—The Secretary of the Treasury may by regulation provide for the application of this clause in the case of a person other than a corporation.

(v) Other exceptions—The following amounts includible in income shall not be taken into account under clause (i)(I):

(I) Commissions—Any remuneration payable on a commission basis solely on account of income directly generated by the individual performance of the individual to whom such remuneration is payable.

(II) Certain payments under existing contracts—Any remuneration consisting of nonqualified deferred compensation, restricted stock, stock options, or stock appreciation rights payable or granted under a written binding contract that was in effect on March 1, 2010, and which was not modified in any material respect before such remuneration is paid.

(vi) Self-employed individual treated as employee—The term "employee" includes, with respect to a calendar year, a self-employed individual who is treated as an employee under section 401(c) of such title for the taxable year ending during such calendar year, and the term 'compensation' shall include earned income of such individual with respect to such self-employment.

(vii) Indexing of amount—In the case of any calendar year beginning after 2010, the dollar amount under clause (i)(II) shall be increased by an amount equal to—

(I) such dollar amount, multiplied by

(II) the cost-of-living adjustment determined under section 1(f)(3) of such title for the calendar year, determined by substituting "calendar year 2009" for "calendar year 1992" in subparagraph (B) thereof.

If the amount of any increase under clause (i) is not a multiple of $1,000, such increase shall be rounded to the next lowest multiple of $1,000.

(E) Extraordinary dividends and redemptions—

(i) In general—The amount determined under this subparagraph for any plan year is the excess (if any) of the sum of the dividends declared during the plan year by the plan sponsor plus the aggregate amount paid for the redemption of stock of the plan sponsor redeemed during the plan year over the greater of—

(I) the adjusted net income (within the meaning of section 1343 of this title) of the plan sponsor for the preceding plan year, determined without regard to any reduction by reason of interest, taxes, depreciation, or amortization, or

(II) in the case of a plan sponsor that determined and declared dividends in the same manner for at least 5 consecutive years immediately preceding such plan year, the aggregate amount of dividends determined and declared for such plan year using such manner.

(ii) Only certain post-2009 dividends and redemptions counted—For purposes of clause (i), there shall only be taken into account dividends declared, and redemptions occurring, after February 28, 2010.

(iii) Exception for intra-group dividends—Dividends paid by one member of a controlled group (as defined in section 1082(d)(3) of this title) to another member of such group shall not be taken into account under clause (i).

(iv) Exception for certain redemptions—Redemptions that are made pursuant to a plan maintained with respect to employees, or that are made on account of the death, disability, or termination of employment of an employee or shareholder, shall not be taken into account under clause (i).

(v) Exception for certain preferred stock—

(I) In general—Dividends and redemptions with respect to applicable preferred stock shall not be taken into account under clause (i) to the extent that dividends accrue with respect to such stock at a specified rate in all events and without regard to the plan sponsor's income, and interest accrues on any unpaid dividends with respect to such stock.

(II) Applicable preferred stock—For purposes of subclause (I), the term "applicable preferred stock" means preferred stock which was issued before March 1, 2010 (or which was issued after such date and is held by an employee benefit plan subject to the provisions of this subchapter).

(F) Other definitions and rules—For purposes of this paragraph—

(i) Plan sponsor—The term " plan sponsor" includes any member of the plan sponsor's controlled group (as defined in section 1082(d)(3) of this title).

(ii) Restriction period—The term "restriction period" means, with respect to any election year—

(I) except as provided in subclause (II), the 3-year period beginning with the election year (or, if later, the first plan year beginning after December 31, 2009), and

(II) if the plan sponsor elects 15-year amortization for the shortfall amortization base for the election year, the 5-year period beginning with the election year (or, if later, the first plan year beginning after December 31, 2009).

(iii) Elections for multiple plans—If a plan sponsor makes elections under paragraph (2)(D) with respect to 2 or more plans, the Secretary of the Treasury shall provide rules for the application of this paragraph to such plans, including rules for the ratable allocation of any installment acceleration amount among such plans on the basis of each plan's relative reduction in the plan's shortfall amortization installment for the first plan year in the amortization period described in subparagraph (A) (determined without regard to this paragraph).

(iv) Mergers and acquisitions—The Secretary of the Treasury shall prescribe rules for the application of paragraph (2)(D) and this paragraph in any case where there is a merger or acquisition involving a plan sponsor making the election under paragraph (2)(D).

(d) Rules relating to funding target—For purposes of this section—

(1) Funding target—Except as provided in subsection (i)(1) with respect to plans in at-risk status, the funding target of a plan for a plan year is the present value of all benefits accrued or earned under the plan as of the beginning of the plan year.

(2) Funding target attainment percentage—The "funding target attainment percentage" of a plan for a plan year is the ratio (expressed as a percentage) which—

(A) the value of plan assets for the plan year (as reduced under subsection (f)(4)(B) of this section), bears to

(B) the funding target of the plan for the plan year (determined without regard to subsection (i)(1) of this section).

(e) Waiver amortization charge—

(1) Determination of waiver amortization charge—The waiver amortization charge (if any) for a plan for any plan year is the aggregate total of the waiver amortization installments for such plan year with respect to the waiver amortization bases for each of the 5 preceding plan years.

(2) Waiver amortization installment—For purposes of paragraph (1)—

(A) Determination—The waiver amortization installments are the amounts necessary to amortize the waiver amortization base of the plan for any plan year in level annual installments over a period of 5 plan years beginning with the succeeding plan year.

(B) Waiver installment—The waiver amortization installment for any plan year in the 5-year period under subparagraph (A) with respect to any waiver amortization base is the annual installment determined under subparagraph (A) for that year for that base.

(3) Interest rate—In determining any waiver amortization installment under this subsection, the plan sponsor shall use the segment rates determined under subparagraph (C) of subsection (h)(2) of this section, applied under rules similar to the rules of subparagraph (B) of subsection (h)(2) of this section.

(4) Waiver amortization base—The waiver amortization base of a plan for a plan year is the amount of the waived funding deficiency (if any) for such plan year under section 1082(c) of this title.

(5) Early deemed amortization upon attainment of funding target—In any case in which the funding shortfall of a plan for a plan year is zero, for purposes of determining the waiver amortization charge for such plan year and succeeding plan years, the waiver amortization bases for all preceding plan years (and all waiver amortization installments determined with respect to such bases) shall be reduced to zero.

(f) Reduction of minimum required contribution by prefunding balance and funding standard carryover balance—

(1) Election to maintain balances—

(A) Prefunding balance—The plan sponsor of a single-employer plan may elect to maintain a prefunding balance.

(B) Funding standard carryover balance—

(i) In general—In the case of a single-employer plan described in clause (ii), the plan sponsor may elect to maintain a funding standard carryover balance, until such balance is reduced to zero.

(ii) Plans maintaining funding standard account in 2007—A plan is described in this clause if the plan—

(I) was in effect for a plan year beginning in 2007, and

(II) had a positive balance in the funding standard account under section 1082(b) of this title as in effect for such plan year and determined as of the end of such plan year.

(2) Application of balances—A prefunding balance and a funding standard carryover balance maintained pursuant to this paragraph—

(A) shall be available for crediting against the minimum required contribution, pursuant to an election under paragraph (3),

(B) shall be applied as a reduction in the amount treated as the value of plan assets for purposes of this section, to the extent provided in paragraph (4), and

(C) may be reduced at any time, pursuant to an election under paragraph (5).

(3) Election to apply balances against minimum required contribution—

(A) In general—Except as provided in subparagraphs (B) and (C), in the case of any plan year in which the plan sponsor elects to credit against the minimum required contribution for the current plan year all or a portion of the prefunding balance or the funding standard carryover balance for the current plan year (not in excess of such minimum required contribution), the minimum required contribution for the plan year shall be reduced as of the first day of the plan year by the amount so credited by the plan sponsor. For purposes of the preceding sentence, the minimum required contribution shall be determined after taking into account any waiver under section 1082(c) of this title.

(B) Coordination with funding standard carryover balance—To the extent that any plan has a funding standard carryover balance greater than zero, no amount of the prefunding balance of such plan may be credited under this paragraph in reducing the minimum required contribution.

(C) Limitation for underfunded plans—The preceding provisions of this paragraph shall not apply for any plan year if the ratio (expressed as a percentage) which—

(i) the value of plan assets for the preceding plan year (as reduced under paragraph (4)(C)), bears to

(ii) the funding target of the plan for the preceding plan year (determined without regard to subsection (i)(1)),

is less than 80 percent. In the case of plan years beginning in 2008, the ratio under this subparagraph may be determined using such methods of estimation as the Secretary of the Treasury may prescribe.

(D) Special rule for certain years of plans maintained by charities—

(i) In general—For purposes of applying subparagraph (C) for plan years beginning after August 31, 2009, and before September 1, 2011, the ratio determined under such subparagraph for the preceding plan year shall be the greater of—

(I) such ratio, as determined without regard to this subparagraph, or

(II) the ratio for such plan for the plan year beginning after August 31, 2007, and before September 1, 2008, as determined under rules prescribed by the Secretary of the Treasury.

(ii) Special rule—In the case of a plan for which the valuation date is not the first day of the plan year—

(I) clause (i) shall apply to plan years beginning after December 31, 2008, and before January 1, 2011, and

(II) clause (i)(II) shall apply based on the last plan year beginning before September 1, 2007, as determined under rules prescribed by the Secretary of the Treasury.

(iii) Limitation to charities—This subparagraph shall not apply to any plan unless such plan is maintained exclusively by one or more organizations described in section 501(c)(3) of Title 26.

(4) Effect of balances on amounts treated as value of plan assets—In the case of any plan maintaining a prefunding balance or a funding standard carryover balance pursuant to this subsection, the amount treated as the value of plan assets shall be deemed to be such amount, reduced as provided in the following subparagraphs:

(A) Applicability of shortfall amortization base—For purposes of subsection (c)(5) of this section, the value of plan assets is deemed to be such amount, reduced by the amount of the prefunding balance, but only if an election under paragraph (3) applying any portion of the prefunding balance in reducing the minimum required contribution is in effect for the plan year.

(B) Determination of excess assets, funding shortfall, and funding target attainment percentage—

(i) **In general**—For purposes of subsections (a), (c)(4)(B), and (d)(2)(A) of this section, the value of plan assets is deemed to be such amount, reduced by the amount of the prefunding balance and the funding standard carryover balance.

(ii) **Special rule for certain binding agreements with PBGC**—For purposes of subsection (c)(4)(B) of this section, the value of plan assets shall not be deemed to be reduced for a plan year by the amount of the specified balance if, with respect to such balance, there is in effect for a plan year a binding written agreement with the Pension Benefit Guaranty Corporation which provides that such balance is not available to reduce the minimum required contribution for the plan year. For purposes of the preceding sentence, the term "specified balance" means the prefunding balance or the funding standard carryover balance, as the case may be.

(C) Availability of balances in plan year for crediting against minimum required contribution—For purposes of paragraph (3)(C)(i) of this subsection, the value of plan assets is deemed to be such amount, reduced by the amount of the prefunding balance.

(5) Election to reduce balance prior to determinations of value of plan assets and crediting against minimum required contribution—

(A) In general—The plan sponsor may elect to reduce by any amount the balance of the prefunding balance and the funding standard carryover balance for any plan year (but not below zero). Such reduction shall be effective prior to any determination of the value of plan assets for such plan year under this section and application of the balance in reducing the minimum required contribution for such plan for such plan year pursuant to an election under paragraph (2).

(B) Coordination between prefunding balance and funding standard carryover balance—To the extent that any plan has a funding standard carryover balance greater than zero, no election may be made under subparagraph (A) with respect to the prefunding balance.

(6) Prefunding balance—

(A) In general—A prefunding balance maintained by a plan shall consist of a beginning balance of zero, increased and decreased to the extent provided in subparagraphs (B) and (C), and adjusted further as provided in paragraph (8).

(B) Increases—

(i) **In general**—As of the first day of each plan year beginning after 2008, the prefunding balance of a plan shall be increased by the amount elected by the plan sponsor for the plan year. Such amount shall not exceed the excess (if any) of—

(I) the aggregate total of employer contributions to the plan for the preceding plan year, over—

(II) the minimum required contribution for such preceding plan year.

(ii) **Adjustments for interest**—Any excess contributions under clause (i) shall be properly adjusted for interest accruing for the periods between the first day of the current plan year and the dates on which the excess contributions were made, determined by using the effective interest rate for the preceding plan year and by treating contributions as being first used to satisfy the minimum required contribution.

(iii) Certain contributions necessary to avoid benefit limitations disregarded—The excess described in clause (i) with respect to any preceding plan year shall be reduced (but not below zero) by the amount of contributions an employer would be required to make under paragraph (1), (2), or (4) of section 1056(g) of this title to avoid a benefit limitation which would otherwise be imposed under such paragraph for the preceding plan year. Any contribution which may be taken into account in satisfying the requirements of more than 1 of such paragraphs shall be taken into account only once for purposes of this clause.

(C) Decrease—The prefunding balance of a plan shall be decreased (but not below zero) by—

(i) as of the first day of each plan year after 2008, the amount of such balance credited under paragraph (2) (if any) in reducing the minimum required contribution of the plan for the preceding plan year, and

(ii) as of the time specified in paragraph (5)(A), any reduction in such balance elected under paragraph (5).

(7) Funding standard carryover balance—

(A) In general—A funding standard carryover balance maintained by a plan shall consist of a beginning balance determined under subparagraph (B), decreased to the extent provided in subparagraph (C), and adjusted further as provided in paragraph (8).

(B) Beginning balance—The beginning balance of the funding standard carryover balance shall be the positive balance described in paragraph (1)(B)(ii)(II).

(C) Decreases—The funding standard carryover balance of a plan shall be decreased (but not below zero) by—

(i) as of the first day of each plan year after 2008, the amount of such balance credited under paragraph (2) (if any) in reducing the minimum required contribution of the plan for the preceding plan year, and

(ii) as of the time specified in paragraph (5)(A), any reduction in such balance elected under paragraph (5).

(8) Adjustments for investment experience—In determining the prefunding balance or the funding standard carryover balance of a plan as of the first day of the plan year, the plan sponsor shall, in accordance with regulations prescribed by the Secretary of the Treasury, adjust such balance to reflect the rate of return on plan assets for the preceding plan year. Notwithstanding subsection (g)(3) of this section, such rate of return shall be determined on the basis of fair market value and shall properly take into account, in accordance with such regulations, all contributions, distributions, and other plan payments made during such period.

(9) Elections—Elections under this subsection shall be made at such times, and in such form and manner, as shall be prescribed in regulations of the Secretary of the Treasury.

(g) Valuation of plan assets and liabilities—

(1) Timing of determinations—Except as otherwise provided under this subsection, all determinations under this section for a plan year shall be made as of the valuation date of the plan for such plan year.

(2) Valuation date—For purposes of this section—

(A) In general—Except as provided in subparagraph (B), the valuation date of a plan for any plan year shall be the first day of the plan year.

(B) Exception for small plans—If, on each day during the preceding plan year, a plan had 100 or fewer participants, the plan may designate any day during the plan year as its valuation date for such plan year and succeeding plan years. For purposes of this subparagraph, all defined benefit plans which are single-employer plans and are maintained by the same employer (or any member of such employer's controlled group) shall be treated as 1 plan, but only participants with respect to such employer or member shall be taken into account.

(C) Application of certain rules in determination of plan size—For purposes of this paragraph—

(i) Plans not in existence in preceding year—In the case of the first plan year of any plan, subparagraph (B) shall apply to such plan by taking into account the number of participants that the plan is reasonably expected to have on days during such first plan year.

(ii) Predecessors—Any reference in subparagraph (B) to an employer shall include a reference to any predecessor of such employer.

(3) Determination of value of plan assets—For purposes of this section—

(A) In general—Except as provided in subparagraph (B), the value of plan assets shall be the fair market value of the assets.

(B) Averaging allowed—A plan may determine the value of plan assets on the basis of the averaging of fair market values, but only if such method—

(i) is permitted under regulations prescribed by the Secretary of the Treasury,

(ii) does not provide for averaging of such values over more than the period beginning on the last day of the 25th month preceding the month in which the valuation date occurs and ending on the valuation date (or a similar period in the case of a valuation date which is not the 1st day of a month), and

(iii) does not result in a determination of the value of plan assets which, at any time, is lower than 90 percent or greater than 110 percent of the fair market value of such assets at such time.

Any such averaging shall be adjusted for contributions, distributions, and expected earnings (as determined by the plan's actuary on the basis of an assumed earnings rate specified by the actuary but not in excess of the third segment rate applicable under subsection (h)(2)(C)(iii)), as specified by the Secretary of the Treasury.

(4) Accounting for contribution receipts—For purposes of determining the value of assets under paragraph (3)—

(A) Prior year contributions—If—

(i) an employer makes any contribution to the plan after the valuation date for the plan year in which the contribution is made, and

(ii) the contribution is for a preceding plan year,

the contribution shall be taken into account as an asset of the plan as of the valuation date, except that in the case of any plan year beginning after 2008, only the present value (determined as of the valuation date) of such contribution may be taken into account. For purposes of the preceding sentence, present value shall be determined using the effective interest rate for the preceding plan year to which the contribution is properly allocable.

(B) Special rule for current year contributions made before valuation date—If any contributions for any plan year are made to or under the plan during the plan year but before the valuation date for the plan year, the assets of the plan as of the valuation date shall not include—

(i) such contributions, and

(ii) interest on such contributions for the period between the date of the contributions and the valuation date, determined by using the effective interest rate for the plan year.

(h) Actuarial assumptions and methods—

(1) In general—Subject to this subsection, the determination of any present value or other computation under this section shall be made on the basis of actuarial assumptions and methods—

(A) each of which is reasonable (taking into account the experience of the plan and reasonable expectations), and

(B) which, in combination, offer the actuary's best estimate of anticipated experience under the plan.

(2) Interest rates—

(A) Effective interest rate—For purposes of this section, the term "effective interest rate" means, with respect to any plan for any plan year, the single rate of interest which, if used to determine the present value of the plan's accrued or earned benefits referred to in subsection (d)(1) of this section, would result in an amount equal to the funding target of the plan for such plan year.

(B) Interest rates for determining funding target—For purposes of determining the funding target and normal cost of a plan for any plan year, the interest rate used in determining the present value of the benefits of the plan shall be—

(i) in the case of benefits reasonably determined to be payable during the 5-year period beginning on the valuation date for the plan year, the first segment rate with respect to the applicable month,

(ii) in the case of benefits reasonably determined to be payable during the 15-year period beginning at the end of the period described in clause (i), the second segment rate with respect to the applicable month, and

(iii) in the case of benefits reasonably determined to be payable after the period described in clause (ii), the third segment rate with respect to the applicable month.

(C) Segment rates—For purposes of this paragraph—

(i) First segment rate—The term "first segment rate" means, with respect to any month, the single rate of interest which shall be determined by the Secretary of the Treasury for such month on the basis of the corporate bond yield curve for such month, taking into account only that portion of such yield curve which is based on bonds maturing during the 5-year period commencing with such month.

(ii) Second segment rate—The term "second segment rate" means, with respect to any month, the single rate of interest which shall be determined by the Secretary of the Treasury for such month on the basis of the corporate bond yield curve for such month, taking into account only that portion of such yield curve which is based on bonds maturing during the 15-year period beginning at the end of the period described in clause (i).

(iii) Third segment rate—The term "third segment rate" means, with respect to any month, the single rate of interest which shall be determined by the Secretary of the Treasury for such month on the basis of the corporate bond yield curve for such month, taking into account only that portion of such yield curve which is based on bonds maturing during periods beginning after the period described in clause (ii).

(iv) Segment rate stabilization—

(I) In general—If a segment rate described in clause (i), (ii), or (iii) with respect to any applicable month (determined without regard to this clause) is less than the applicable minimum percentage, or more than the applicable maximum percentage, of the average of the segment rates described in such clause for years in the 25-year period ending with September 30 of the calendar year preceding the calendar year in which the plan year begins, then the segment rate described in such clause with respect to the applicable month shall be equal to the applicable minimum percentage or the applicable maximum percentage of such average, whichever is closest. The Secretary of the Treasury shall determine such average on an annual basis and may prescribe equivalent rates for years in any such 25-year period for which the rates described in any such clause are not available.

(II) Applicable minimum percentage; applicable maximum percentage—For purposes of subclause (I), the applicable minimum percentage and the applicable maximum percentage for a plan year beginning in a calendar year shall be determined in accordance with the following table:

If the calendar year is:	The applicable minimum percentage is:	The applicable maximum percentage is:
2012, 3013, 2014, 2015, 2016, 2017, 2018, 2019, or 2020	90%	110%
2021	85%	115%
2022	80%	120%
2023	75%	125%
After 2023	70%	130%

(D) Corporate bond yield curve—For purposes of this paragraph—

(i) In general—The term "corporate bond yield curve" means, with respect to any month, a yield curve which is prescribed by the Secretary of the Treasury for such month and which reflects the average, for the 24-month period ending with the month preceding such month, of monthly yields on investment grade corporate bonds with varying maturities and that are in the top 3 quality levels available.

(ii) Election to use yield curve—Solely for purposes of determining the minimum required contribution under this section, the plan sponsor may, in lieu of the segment rates determined under subparagraph (C), elect to use interest rates under the corporate bond yield curve. For purposes of the preceding sentence such curve shall be determined without regard to the 24-month averaging described in clause (i). Such election, once made, may be revoked only with the consent of the Secretary of the Treasury.

(E) Applicable month—For purposes of this paragraph, the term "applicable month" means, with respect to any plan for any plan year, the month which includes the valuation date of such plan for such plan year or, at the election of the plan sponsor, any of the 4 months which precede such month. Any election made under this subparagraph shall apply to the plan year for which the election is made and all succeeding plan years, unless the election is revoked with the consent of the Secretary of the Treasury.

(F) Publication requirements—The Secretary of the Treasury shall publish for each month the corporate bond yield curve (and the corporate bond yield curve reflecting the modification described in section 1055(g)(3)(B)(iii)(I) of this title for such month) and each of the rates determined under subparagraph (C) and the averages determined under subparagragh (C)(iv) for such month. The Secretary of the Treasury shall also publish a description of the methodology used to determine such yield curve and such rates which is sufficiently detailed to enable plans to make reasonable projections regarding the yield curve and such rates for future months based on the plan's projection of future interest rates.

* * *

(3) Mortality tables—

(A) In general—Except as provided in subparagraph (C) or (D), the Secretary of the Treasury shall by regulation prescribe mortality tables to be used in determining any present value or making any computation under this section. Such tables shall be based on the actual experience of pension plans and projected trends in such experience. In prescribing such tables, the Secretary of the Treasury shall take into account results of available independent studies of mortality of individuals covered by pension plans.

(B) Periodic revision—The Secretary of the Treasury shall (at least every 10 years) make revisions in any table in effect under subparagraph (A) to reflect the actual experience of pension plans and projected trends in such experience.

(C) Substitute mortality table—

(i) In general—Upon request by the plan sponsor and approval by the Secretary of the Treasury, a mortality table which meets the requirements of clause (iii) shall be used in determining any present value or making any computation under this section during the period of consecutive plan years (not to exceed 10) specified in the request.

(ii) Early termination of period—Notwithstanding clause (i), a mortality table described in clause (i) shall cease to be in effect as of the earliest of—

(I) the date on which there is a significant change in the participants in the plan by reason of a plan spinoff or merger or otherwise, or

(II) the date on which the plan actuary determines that such table does not meet the requirements of clause (iii).

(iii) Requirements—A mortality table meets the requirements of this clause if—

(I) there is a sufficient number of plan participants, and the pension plans have been maintained for a sufficient period of time, to have credible information necessary for purposes of subclause (II), and

(II) such table reflects the actual experience of the pension plans maintained by the sponsor and projected trends in general mortality experience.

(iv) All plans in controlled group must use separate table—Except as provided by the Secretary of the Treasury, a plan sponsor may not use a mortality table under this subparagraph for any plan maintained by the plan sponsor unless—

(I) a separate mortality table is established and used under this subparagraph for each other plan maintained by the plan sponsor and if the plan sponsor is a member of a controlled group, each member of the controlled group, and

(II) the requirements of clause (iii) are met separately with respect to the table so established for each such plan, determined by only taking into account the participants of such plan, the time such plan has been in existence, and the actual experience of such plan.

(v) Deadline for submission and disposition of application—

(I) Submission—The plan sponsor shall submit a mortality table to the Secretary of the Treasury for approval under this subparagraph at least 7 months before the 1st day of the period described in clause (i).

(II) Disposition—Any mortality table submitted to the Secretary of the Treasury for approval under this subparagraph shall be treated as in effect as of the 1st day of the period described in clause (i) unless the Secretary of the Treasury, during the 180-day period beginning on the date of such submission, disapproves of such table and provides the reasons that such table fails to meet the requirements of clause (iii). The 180-day period shall be extended upon mutual agreement of the Secretary of the Treasury and the plan sponsor.

(D) Separate mortality tables for the disabled—Notwithstanding subparagraph (A)—

(i) In general—The Secretary of the Treasury shall establish mortality tables which may be used (in lieu of the tables under subparagraph (A)) under this subsection for individuals who are entitled to benefits under the plan on account of disability. The Secretary of the Treasury shall establish separate tables for individuals whose disabilities occur in plan years beginning before January 1, 1995, and for individuals whose disabilities occur in plan years beginning on or after such date.

(ii) **Special rule for disabilities occurring after 1994**—In the case of disabilities occurring in plan years beginning after December 31, 1994, the tables under clause (i) shall apply only with respect to individuals described in such subclause who are disabled within the meaning of title II of the Social Security Act [42 U.S.C.A. § 401 et seq.] and the regulations thereunder.

(iii) **Periodic revision**—The Secretary of the Treasury shall (at least every 10 years) make revisions in any table in effect under clause (i) to reflect the actual experience of pension plans and projected trends in such experience.

(4) Probability of benefit payments in the form of lump sums or other optional forms—For purposes of determining any present value or making any computation under this section, there shall be taken into account—

(A) the probability that future benefit payments under the plan will be made in the form of optional forms of benefits provided under the plan (including lump sum distributions, determined on the basis of the plan's experience and other related assumptions), and

(B) any difference in the present value of such future benefit payments resulting from the use of actuarial assumptions, in determining benefit payments in any such optional form of benefits, which are different from those specified in this subsection.

(5) Approval of large changes in actuarial assumptions—

(A) In general—No actuarial assumption used to determine the funding target for a plan to which this paragraph applies may be changed without the approval of the Secretary of the Treasury.

(B) Plans to which paragraph applies—This paragraph shall apply to a plan only if—

(i) the plan is a single-employer plan to which title IV applies,

(ii) the aggregate unfunded vested benefits as of the close of the preceding plan year (as determined under section 1306(a)(3)(E)(iii) of this title) of such plan and all other plans maintained by the contributing sponsors (as defined in section 1301(a)(13) of this title) and members of such sponsors' controlled groups (as defined in section 1301(a)(14) of this title) which are covered by subchapter III of this chapter (disregarding plans with no unfunded vested benefits) exceed $50,000,000, and

(iii) the change in assumptions (determined after taking into account any changes in interest rate and mortality table) results in a decrease in the funding shortfall of the plan for the current plan year that exceeds $50,000,000, or that exceeds $5,000,000 and that is 5 percent or more of the funding target of the plan before such change.

(i) Special rules for at-risk plans—

(1) Funding target for plans in at-risk status—

(A) In general—In the case of a plan which is in at-risk status for a plan year, the funding target of the plan for the plan year shall be equal to the sum of—

(i) the present value of all benefits accrued or earned under the plan as of the beginning of the plan year, as determined by using the additional actuarial assumptions described in subparagraph (B), and

(ii) in the case of a plan which also has been in at-risk status for at least 2 of the 4 preceding plan years, a loading factor determined under subparagraph (C).

(B) **Additional actuarial assumptions**—The actuarial assumptions described in this subparagraph are as follows:

(i) All employees who are not otherwise assumed to retire as of the valuation date but who will be eligible to elect benefits during the plan year and the 10 succeeding plan years shall be assumed to retire at the earliest retirement date under the plan but not before the end of the plan year for which the at-risk funding target and at-risk target normal cost are being determined.

(ii) All employees shall be assumed to elect the retirement benefit available under the plan at the assumed retirement age (determined after application of clause (i)) which would result in the highest present value of benefits.

(C) **Loading factor**—The loading factor applied with respect to a plan under this paragraph for any plan year is the sum of—

(i) $700, times the number of participants in the plan, plus

(ii) 4 percent of the funding target (determined without regard to this paragraph) of the plan for the plan year.

(2) **Target normal cost of at-risk plans**—In the case of a plan which is in at-risk status for a plan year, the target normal cost of the plan for such plan year shall be equal to the sum of—

(A) the excess of—

(i) the sum of—

(I) the present value of all benefits which are expected to accrue or to be earned under the plan during the plan year, determined using the additional actuarial assumptions described in paragraph (1)(B), plus

(II) the amount of plan-related expenses expected to be paid from plan assets during the plan year, over

(ii) the amount of mandatory employee contributions expected to be made during the plan year, plus

(B) in the case of a plan which also has been in at-risk status for at least 2 of the 4 preceding plan years, a loading factor equal to 4 percent of the amount determined under subsection (b)(1)(A)(i) with respect to the plan for the plan year.

(3) **Minimum amount**—In no event shall—

(A) the at-risk funding target be less than the funding target, as determined without regard to this subsection, or

(B) the at-risk target normal cost be less than the target normal cost, as determined without regard to this subsection.

(4) **Determination of at-risk status**—For purposes of this subsection—

(A) In general—A plan is in at-risk status for a plan year if—

(i) the funding target attainment percentage for the preceding plan year (determined under this section without regard to this subsection) is less than 80 percent, and

(ii) the funding target attainment percentage for the preceding plan year (determined under this section by using the additional actuarial assumptions described in paragraph (1)(B) in computing the funding target) is less than 70 percent.

* * *

(5) Transition between applicable funding targets and between applicable target normal costs—

(A) In general—In any case in which a plan which is in at-risk status for a plan year has been in such status for a consecutive period of fewer than 5 plan years, the applicable amount of the funding target and of the target normal cost shall be, in lieu of the amount determined without regard to this paragraph, the sum of—

(i) the amount determined under this section without regard to this subsection, plus

(ii) the transition percentage for such plan year of the excess of the amount determined under this subsection (without regard to this paragraph) over the amount determined under this section without regard to this subsection.

(B) Transition percentage—For purposes of subparagraph (A), the transition percentage shall be determined in accordance with the following table:

In the consecutive number of years (including the plan year) the plan is in at-risk status is—	The transition percentage is—
1	20
2	40
3	60
4	80

(C) Years before effective date—For purposes of this paragraph, plan years beginning before 2008 shall not be taken into account.

(6) Small plan exception—If, on each day during the preceding plan year, a plan had 500 or fewer participants, the plan shall not be treated as in at-risk status for the plan year. For purposes of this paragraph, all defined benefit plans (other than multiemployer plans) maintained by the same employer (or any member of such employer's controlled group) shall be treated as 1 plan, but only participants with respect to such employer or member shall be taken into account and the rules of subsection (g)(2)(C) of this section shall apply.

(j) Payment of minimum required contributions—

(1) In general—For purposes of this section, the due date for any payment of any minimum required contribution for any plan year shall be 8 1/2 months after the close of the plan year.

(2) Interest—Any payment required under paragraph (1) for a plan year that is made on a date other than the valuation date for such plan year shall be adjusted for interest accruing for the period between the valuation date and the payment date, at the effective rate of interest for the plan for such plan year.

(3) Accelerated quarterly contribution schedule for underfunded plans—

(A) Failure to timely make required installment—In any case in which the plan has a funding shortfall for the preceding plan year, the employer maintaining the plan shall make the required installments under this paragraph and if the employer fails to pay the full amount of a required installment for the plan year, then the amount of interest charged under paragraph (2) on the underpayment for the period of underpayment shall be determined by using a rate of interest equal to the rate otherwise used under paragraph (2) plus 5 percentage points. In the case of plan years beginning in 2008, the funding shortfall for the preceding plan year may be determined using such methods of estimation as the Secretary of the Treasury may provide.

(B) Amount of underpayment, period of underpayment—For purposes of subparagraph (A)—

(i) Amount—The amount of the underpayment shall be the excess of—

(I) the required installment, over

(II) the amount (if any) of the installment contributed to or under the plan on or before the due date for the installment.

(ii) Period of underpayment—The period for which any interest is charged under this paragraph with respect to any portion of the underpayment shall run from the due date for the installment to the date on which such portion is contributed to or under the plan.

(iii) Order of crediting contributions—For purposes of clause (i)(II), contributions shall be credited against unpaid required installments in the order in which such installments are required to be paid.

(C) Number of required installments; due dates—For purposes of this paragraph—

(i) Payable in 4 installments—There shall be 4 required installments for each plan year.

(ii) Time for payment of installments—The due dates for required installments are set forth in the following table:

In the case of the following required installment—	The due date is—
1st	April 15
2nd	July 15
3rd	October 15
4th	January 15 of the following year.

(D) Amount of required installment—For purposes of this paragraph—

(i) In general—The amount of any required installment shall be 25 percent of the required annual payment.

(ii) Required annual payment—For purposes of clause (i), the term "required annual payment" means the lesser of—

(I) 90 percent of the minimum required contribution (determined without regard to this subsection) to the plan for the plan year under this section, or

(II) 100 percent of the minimum required contribution (determined without regard to this subsection or to any waiver under section 1082(c) of this title) to the plan for the preceding plan year.

Subclause (II) shall not apply if the preceding plan year referred to in such clause was not a year of 12 months.

(E) Fiscal years, short years, and years with alternate valuation date—

(i) Fiscal years—In applying this paragraph to a plan year beginning on any date other than January 1, there shall be substituted for the months specified in this paragraph, the months which correspond thereto.

(ii) Short plan year—This subparagraph shall be applied to plan years of less than 12 months in accordance with regulations prescribed by the Secretary of the Treasury.

(iii) Plan with alternate valuation date—The Secretary of the Treasury shall prescribe regulations for the application of this paragraph in the case of a plan which has a valuation date other than the first day of the plan year.

(F) Quarterly contributions not to include certain increased contributions— Subparagraph (D) shall be applied without regard to any increase under subsection (c)(7).

(4) Liquidity requirement in connection with quarterly contributions—

(A) In general—A plan to which this paragraph applies shall be treated as failing to pay the full amount of any required installment under paragraph (3) to the extent that the value of the liquid assets paid in such installment is less than the liquidity shortfall (whether or not such liquidity shortfall exceeds the amount of such installment required to be paid but for this paragraph).

(B) Plans to which paragraph applies—This paragraph shall apply to a plan (other than a plan described in subsection (g)(2)(B) of this section) which—

(i) is required to pay installments under paragraph (3) for a plan year, and

(ii) has a liquidity shortfall for any quarter during such plan year.

(C) Period of underpayment—For purposes of paragraph (3)(A), any portion of an installment that is treated as not paid under subparagraph (A) shall continue to be treated as unpaid until the close of the quarter in which the due date for such installment occurs.

(D) Limitation on increase—If the amount of any required installment is increased by reason of subparagraph (A), in no event shall such increase exceed the amount which, when added to prior installments for the plan year, is necessary to increase the funding target attainment percentage of the plan for the plan year (taking into account the expected increase in funding target due to benefits accruing or earned during the plan year) to 100 percent.

(E) Definitions—For purposes of this paragraph—

(i) Liquidity shortfall—The term "liquidity shortfall" means, with respect to any required installment, an amount equal to the excess (as of the last day of the quarter for which such installment is made) of—

(I) the base amount with respect to such quarter, over

(II) the value (as of such last day) of the plan's liquid assets.

(ii) Base amount—

(I) In general—The term "base amount" means, with respect to any quarter, an amount equal to 3 times the sum of the adjusted disbursements from the plan for the 12 months ending on the last day of such quarter.

(II) Special rule—If the amount determined under subclause (I) exceeds an amount equal to 2 times the sum of the adjusted disbursements from the plan for the 36 months ending on the last day of the quarter and an enrolled actuary certifies to the satisfaction of the Secretary of the Treasury that such excess is the result of nonrecurring circumstances, the base amount with respect to such quarter shall be determined without regard to amounts related to those nonrecurring circumstances.

(iii) Disbursements from the plan—The term "disbursements from the plan" means all disbursements from the trust, including purchases of annuities, payments of single sums and other benefits, and administrative expenses.

(iv) Adjusted disbursements—The term "adjusted disbursements" means disbursements from the plan reduced by the product of—

(I) the plan's funding target attainment percentage for the plan year, and

(II) the sum of the purchases of annuities, payments of single sums, and such other disbursements as the Secretary of the Treasury shall provide in regulations.

(v) Liquid assets—The term "liquid assets" means cash, marketable securities, and such other assets as specified by the Secretary of the Treasury in regulations.

(vi) Quarter—The term "quarter" means, with respect to any required installment, the 3-month period preceding the month in which the due date for such installment occurs.

(F) Regulations—The Secretary of the Treasury may prescribe such regulations as are necessary to carry out this paragraph.

(k) Imposition of lien where failure to make required contributions—

(1) In general—In the case of a plan to which this subsection applies (as provided under paragraph (2)), if—

(A) any person fails to make a contribution payment required by section 1082 of this title and this section before the due date for such payment, and

(B) the unpaid balance of such payment (including interest), when added to the aggregate unpaid balance of all preceding such payments for which payment was not made before the due date (including interest), exceeds $1,000,000,

then there shall be a lien in favor of the plan in the amount determined under paragraph (3) upon all property and rights to property, whether real or personal, belonging to such person and any other person who is a member of the same controlled group of which such person is a member.

(2) Plans to which subsection applies—This subsection shall apply to a single-employer plan covered under section 1321 of this title for any plan year for which the funding target attainment percentage (as defined in subsection (d)(2)) of such plan is less than 100 percent.

(3) Amount of lien—For purposes of paragraph (1), the amount of the lien shall be equal to the aggregate unpaid balance of contribution payments required under this section and section 1082 of this title for which payment has not been made before the due date.

(4) Notice of failure; lien—

(A) Notice of failure—A person committing a failure described in paragraph (1) shall notify the Pension Benefit Guaranty Corporation of such failure within 10 days of the due date for the required contribution payment.

(B) Period of lien—The lien imposed by paragraph (1) shall arise on the due date for the required contribution payment and shall continue until the last day of the first plan year in which the plan ceases to be described in paragraph (1)(B). Such lien shall continue to run without regard to whether such plan continues to be described in paragraph (2) during the period referred to in the preceding sentence.

(C) Certain rules to apply—Any amount with respect to which a lien is imposed under paragraph (1) shall be treated as taxes due and owing the United States and rules similar to the rules of subsections (c), (d), and (e) of section 1368 of this title shall apply with respect to a lien imposed by subsection (a) and the amount with respect to such lien.

(5) Enforcement—Any lien created under paragraph (1) may be perfected and enforced only by the Pension Benefit Guaranty Corporation, or at the direction of the Pension Benefit Guaranty Corporation, by the contributing sponsor (or any member of the controlled group of the contributing sponsor).

(6) Definitions—For purposes of this subsection—

(A) Contribution payment—The term "contribution payment" means, in connection with a plan, a contribution payment required to be made to the plan, including any required installment under paragraphs (3) and (4) of subsection (j).

(B) Due date; required installment—The terms "due date" and "required installment" have the meanings given such terms by subsection (j).

(C) Controlled group—The term "controlled group" means any group treated as a single employer under subsections (b), (c), (m), and (o) of section 414 of Title 26.

(l) Qualified transfers to health benefit accounts—In the case of a qualified transfer (as defined in section 420 of Title 26), any assets so transferred shall not, for purposes of this section, be treated as assets in the plan.

§ 304. Minimum funding standards for multiemployer plans (§ 1084)

(a) In general—For purposes of section 1082 of this title, the accumulated funding deficiency of a multiemployer plan for any plan year is the amount, determined as of the end of the plan year, equal to the excess (if any) of the total charges to the funding standard account of the plan for all plan years (beginning with the first plan year for which this part applies to the plan) over the total credits to such account for such years.

* * *

§ 305. Additional funding rules for multiemployer plans in endangered status or critical status (§ 1085)

(a) General rule—For purposes of this part, in the case of a multiemployer plan in effect on July 16, 2006—

(1) if the plan is in endangered status—

(A) the plan sponsor shall adopt and implement a funding improvement plan in accordance with the requirements of subsection (c) of this section, and

(B) the requirements of subsection (d) of this section shall apply during the funding plan adoption period and the funding improvement period,

(2) if the plan is in critical status—

(A) the plan sponsor shall adopt and implement a rehabilitation plan in accordance with the requirements of subsection (e) of this section, and

(B) the requirements of subsection (f) of this section shall apply during the rehabilitation plan adoption period and the rehabilitation period, and

(3) If the plan is in critical and declining status—

(A) the requirements of paragraph (2) shall apply to the plan; and

(B) the plan sponsor may, by plan amendment, suspend benefits in accordance with the requirements of subsection (e)(9).

* * *

§ 306. Minimum funding standards (§ 1085a)

(a) General rule—For purposes of section 1082 of this title, the term "accumulated funding deficiency" for a CSEC plan means the excess of the total charges to the funding standard account for all plan years (beginning with the first plan year to which section 1082 of this title applies) over the total credits to such account for such years or, if less, the excess of the total charges to the alternative minimum funding standard account for such plan years over the total credits to such account for such years.

(b) Funding standard account—

(1) Account required—Each plan to which this section applies shall establish and maintain a funding standard account. Such account shall be credited and charged solely as provided in this section.

(2) Charges to account—For a plan year, the funding standard account shall be charged with the sum of—

(A) the normal cost of the plan for the plan year,

(B) the amounts necessary to amortize in equal annual installments (until fully amortized)—

    (i) in the case of a plan in existence on January 1, 1974, the unfunded past service liability under the plan on the first day of the first plan year to which section 1082 of this title applies, over a period of 40 plan years,

    (ii) in the case of a plan which comes into existence after January 1, 1974, but before the first day of the first plan year beginning after December 31, 2013, the unfunded past service liability under the plan on the first day of the first plan year to which section 1082 of this title applies, over a period of 30 plan years,

    (iii) separately, with respect to each plan year, the net increase (if any) in unfunded past service liability under the plan arising from plan amendments adopted in such year, over a period of 15 plan years,

    (iv) separately, with respect to each plan year, the net experience loss (if any) under the plan, over a period of 5 plan years, and

    (v) separately, with respect to each plan year, the net loss (if any) resulting from changes in actuarial assumptions used under the plan, over a period of 10 plan years,

(C) the amount necessary to amortize each waived funding deficiency (within the meaning of section 1082(c)(3) of this title for each prior plan year in equal annual installments (until fully amortized) over a period of 5 plan years,

(D) the amount necessary to amortize in equal annual installments (until fully amortized) over a period of 5 plan years any amount credited to the funding standard account under paragraph (3)(D), and

(E) the amount necessary to amortize in equal annual installments (until fully amortized) over a period of 20 years the contributions which would be required to be made under the plan but for the provisions of section 1082(c)(7)(A)(i)(I) of this title (as in effect on the day before the enactment of the Pension Protection Act of 2006 [enacted Aug. 17, 2006]).

(3) Credits to account—For a plan year, the funding standard account shall be credited with the sum of—

(A) the amount considered contributed by the employer to or under the plan for the plan year,

(B) the amount necessary to amortize in equal annual installments (until fully amortized)—

    (i) separately, with respect to each plan year, the net decrease (if any) in unfunded past service liability under the plan arising from plan amendments adopted in such year, over a period of 15 plan years,

    (ii) separately, with respect to each plan year, the net experience gain (if any) under the plan, over a period of 5 plan years, and

    (iii) separately, with respect to each plan year, the net gain (if any) resulting from changes in actuarial assumptions used under the plan, over a period of 10 plan years,

(C) the amount of the waived funding deficiency (within the meaning of section 1082(c)(3) of this title) for the plan year, and

(D) in the case of a plan year for which the accumulated funding deficiency is determined under the funding standard account if such plan year follows a plan year for which such deficiency was determined under the alternative minimum funding standard, the excess (if any) of any debit balance in the funding standard account (determined without regard to this subparagraph) over any debit balance in the alternative minimum funding standard account.

(4) Combining and offsetting amounts to be amortized—Under regulations prescribed by the Secretary of the Treasury, amounts required to be amortized under paragraph (2) or paragraph (3), as the case may be—

(A) may be combined into one amount under such paragraph to be amortized over a period determined on the basis of the remaining amortization period for all items entering into such combined amount, and

(B) may be offset against amounts required to be amortized under the other such paragraph, with the resulting amount to be amortized over a period determined on the basis of the remaining amortization periods for all items entering into whichever of the two amounts being offset is the greater.

(5) Interest—

(A) In general—Except as provided in subparagraph (B), the funding standard account (and items therein) shall be charged or credited (as determined under regulations prescribed by the Secretary of the Treasury) with interest at the appropriate rate consistent with the rate or rates of interest used under the plan to determine costs.

(B) Exception—The interest rate used for purposes of computing the amortization charge described in subsection (b)(2)(C) or for purposes of any arrangement under subsection (d) for any plan year shall be the greater of—

(i) 150 percent of the Federal mid-term rate (as in effect under section 1274 of Title 26 for the 1st month of such plan year), or

(ii) the rate of interest determined under subparagraph (A).

(6) Amortization schedules in effect—Amortization schedules for amounts described in paragraphs (2) and (3) that are in effect as of the last day of the last plan year beginning before January 1, 2014, by reason of section 104 of the Pension Protection Act of 2006 [26 U.S.C.A. § 401 note] shall remain in effect pursuant to their terms and this section, except that such amounts shall not be amortized again under this section.

* * *

Part 4—Fiduciary Responsibility

§ 401. Coverage (§ 1101)

(a) Scope of coverage—This part shall apply to any employee benefit plan described in section 1003(a) of this title (and not exempted under section 1003(b) of this title), other than—

(1) a plan which is unfunded and is maintained by an employer primarily for the purpose of providing deferred compensation for a select group of management or highly compensated employees; or

(2) any agreement described in section 736 of Title 26, which provides payments to a retired partner or deceased partner or a deceased partner's successor in interest.

(b) Securities or policies deemed to be included in plan assets—For purposes of this part:

(1) In the case of a plan which invests in any security issued by an investment company registered under the Investment Company Act of 1940 [15 U.S.C.A. § 80a-1 et seq.], the assets of such plan shall be deemed to include such security but shall not, solely by reason of such investment, be deemed to include any assets of such investment company.

(2) In the case of a plan to which a guaranteed benefit policy is issued by an insurer, the assets of such plan shall be deemed to include such policy, but shall not, solely by reason of the issuance of such policy, be deemed to include any assets of such insurer. For purposes of this paragraph:

(A) The term "insurer" means an insurance company, insurance service, or insurance organization, qualified to do business in a State.

(B) The term "guaranteed benefit policy" means an insurance policy or contract to the extent that such policy or contract provides for benefits the amount of which is guaranteed by the insurer. Such term includes any surplus in a separate account, but excludes any other portion of a separate account

(c) Clarification of application of ERISA to insurance company general accounts—

(1)(A) Not later than June 30, 1997, the Secretary shall issue proposed regulations to provide guidance for the purpose of determining, in cases where an insurer issues 1 or more policies to or for the benefit of an employee benefit plan (and such policies are supported by assets of such insurer's general account), which assets held by the insurer (other than plan assets held in its separate accounts) constitute assets of the plan for purposes of this part and section 4975 of Title 26 and to provide guidance with respect to the application of this subchapter to the general account assets of insurers.

(B) The proposed regulations under subparagraph (A) shall be subject to public notice and comment until September 30, 1997.

(C) The Secretary shall issue final regulations providing the guidance described in subparagraph (A) not later than December 31, 1997.

(D) Such regulations shall only apply with respect to policies which are issued by an insurer on or before December 31, 1998, to or for the benefit of an employee benefit plan which is supported by assets of such insurer's general account. With respect to policies issued on or before December 31, 1998, such regulations shall take effect at the end of the 18-month period following the date on which such regulations become final.

(2) The Secretary shall ensure that the regulations issued under paragraph (1)—

(A) are administratively feasible, and

(B) protect the interests and rights of the plan and of its participants and beneficiaries (including meeting the requirements of paragraph (3)).

(3) The regulations prescribed by the Secretary pursuant to paragraph (1) shall require, in connection with any policy issued by an insurer to or for the benefit of an employee benefit plan to the extent that the policy is not a guaranteed benefit policy (as defined in subsection (b)(2)(B) of this section)—

(A) that a plan fiduciary totally independent of the insurer authorize the purchase of such policy (unless such purchase is a transaction exempt under section 1108(b)(5) of this title),

(B) that the insurer describe (in such form and manner as shall be prescribed in such regulations), in annual reports and in policies issued to the policyholder after the date on which such regulations are issued in final form pursuant to paragraph (1)(C)—

(i) a description of the method by which any income and expenses of the insurer's general account are allocated to the policy during the term of the policy and upon the termination of the policy, and

(ii) for each report, the actual return to the plan under the policy and such other financial information as the Secretary may deem appropriate for the period covered by each such annual report,

(C) that the insurer disclose to the plan fiduciary the extent to which alternative arrangements supported by assets of separate accounts of the insurer (which generally hold plan assets) are available, whether there is a right under the policy to transfer funds to a separate account and the terms governing any such right, and the extent to which support by assets of the insurer's general account and support by assets of separate accounts of the insurer might pose differing risks to the plan, and

(D) that the insurer manage those assets of the insurer which are assets of such insurer's general account (irrespective of whether any such assets are plan assets) with the care, skill, prudence, and diligence under the circumstances then prevailing that a prudent man acting in a like capacity and familiar with such matters would use in the conduct of an enterprise of a like character and with like aims, taking into account all obligations supported by such enterprise.

(4) Compliance by the insurer with all requirements of the regulations issued by the Secretary pursuant to paragraph (1) shall be deemed compliance by such insurer with sections 1104, 1106, and 1107 of this title with respect to those assets of the insurer's general account which support a policy described in paragraph (3).

(5)(A) Subject to subparagraph (B), any regulations issued under paragraph (1) shall not take effect before the date on which such regulations become final.

(B) No person shall be subject to liability under this part or section 4975 of Title 26 for conduct which occurred before the date which is 18 months following the date described in subparagraph (A) on the basis of a claim that the assets of an insurer (other than plan assets held in a separate account) constitute assets of the plan, except—

(i) as otherwise provided by the Secretary in regulations intended to prevent avoidance of the regulations issued under paragraph (1), or

(ii) as provided in an action brought by the Secretary pursuant to paragraph (2) or (5) of section 1132(a) of this title for a breach of fiduciary responsibilities which would also constitute a violation of Federal or State criminal law.

The Secretary shall bring a cause of action described in clause (ii) if a participant, beneficiary, or fiduciary demonstrates to the satisfaction of the Secretary that a breach described in clause (ii) has occurred.

(6) Nothing in this subsection shall preclude the application of any Federal criminal law.

(7) For purposes of this subsection, the term "policy" includes a contract.

§ 402. Establishment of plan (§ 1102)

(a) Named fiduciaries—

written instrument required

(1) Every employee benefit plan shall be established and maintained pursuant to a written instrument. Such instrument shall provide for one or more named fiduciaries who jointly or severally shall have authority to control and manage the operation and administration of the plan.

(2) For purposes of this subchapter, the term "named fiduciary" means a fiduciary who is named in the plan instrument, or who, pursuant to a procedure specified in the plan, is identified as a fiduciary (A) by a person who is an employer or employee organization with respect to the plan or (B) by such an employer and such an employee organization acting jointly.

(b) Requisite features of plan—Every employee benefit plan shall—

(1) provide a procedure for establishing and carrying out a funding policy and method consistent with the objectives of the plan and the requirements of this subchapter,

(2) describe any procedure under the plan for the allocation of responsibilities for the operation and administration of the plan (including any procedure described in section 1105(c)(1) of this title),

(3) provide a procedure for amending such plan, and for identifying the persons who have authority to amend the plan, and

(4) specify the basis on which payments are made to and from the plan.

(c) Optional features of plan—Any employee benefit plan may provide—

(1) that any person or group of persons may serve in more than one fiduciary capacity with respect to the plan (including service both as trustee and administrator);

(2) that a named fiduciary, or a fiduciary designated by a named fiduciary pursuant to a plan procedure described in section 1105(c)(1) of this title, may employ one or more persons to render advice with regard to any responsibility such fiduciary has under the plan; or

(3) that a person who is a named fiduciary with respect to control or management of the assets of the plan may appoint an investment manager or managers to manage (including the power to acquire and dispose of) any assets of a plan.

§ 403. Establishment of trust (§ 1103)

(a) Benefit plan assets to be held in trust; authority of trustees—Except as provided in subsection (b) of this section, all assets of an employee benefit plan shall be held in trust by one or more trustees. Such trustee or trustees shall be either named in the trust instrument or in the plan instrument described in section 1102(a) of this title or appointed by a person who is a named fiduciary, and upon acceptance of being named or appointed, the trustee or trustees shall have exclusive authority and discretion to manage and control the assets of the plan, except to the extent that—

(1) the plan expressly provides that the trustee or trustees are subject to the direction of a named fiduciary who is not a trustee, in which case the trustees shall be subject to proper directions of such fiduciary which are made in accordance with the terms of the plan and which are not contrary to this chapter, or

(2) authority to manage, acquire, or dispose of assets of the plan is delegated to one or more investment managers pursuant to section 1102(c)(3) of this title.

(b) Exceptions—The requirements of subsection (a) of this section shall not apply—

(1) to any assets of a plan which consist of insurance contracts or policies issued by an insurance company qualified to do business in a State;

(2) to any assets of such an insurance company or any assets of a plan which are held by such an insurance company;

(3) to a plan—

(A) some or all of the participants of which are employees described in section 401(c)(1) of Title 26; or

(B) which consists of one or more individual retirement accounts described in section 408 of Title 26;

to the extent that such plan's assets are held in one or more custodial accounts which qualify under section 401(f) or 408(h) of Title 26, whichever is applicable.

(4) to a plan which the Secretary exempts from the requirement of subsection (a) of this section and which is not subject to any of the following provisions of this chapter—

(A) part 2 of this subtitle,

(B) part 3 of this subtitle, or

(C) subchapter III of this chapter;

(5) to a contract established and maintained under section 403(b) of Title 26 to the extent that the assets of the contract are held in one or more custodial accounts pursuant to section 403(b)(7) of Title 26; or

(6) Any plan, fund or program under which an employer, all of whose stock is directly or indirectly owned by employees, former employees or their beneficiaries, proposes through an unfunded arrangement to compensate retired employees for benefits which were forfeited by such employees under a pension plan maintained by a former employer prior to the date such pension plan became subject to this chapter.

(c) Assets of plan not to inure to benefit of employer; allowable purposes of holding plan assets—

(1) Except as provided in paragraph (2), (3), or (4) or subsection (d) of this section, or under sections 1342 and 1344 of this title (relating to termination of insured plans), or under section 420 of Title 26 (as in effect on July 31, 2015), the assets of a plan shall never inure to the benefit of any employer and shall be held for the exclusive purposes of providing benefits to participants in the plan and their beneficiaries and defraying reasonable expenses of administering the plan.

(2)(A) In the case of a contribution, or a payment of withdrawal liability under part 1 of subtitle E of subchapter III of this chapter—

(i) if such contribution or payment is made by an employer to a plan (other than a multiemployer plan) by a mistake of fact, paragraph (1) shall not prohibit the return of such contribution to the employer within one year after the payment of the contribution, and

(ii) if such contribution or payment is made by an employer to a multiemployer plan by a mistake of fact or law (other than a mistake relating to whether the plan is described in section 401(a) of Title 26 or the trust which is part of such plan is exempt from taxation under section 501(a) of Title 26), paragraph (1) shall not prohibit the return of such contribution or payment to the employer within 6 months after the plan administrator determines that the contribution was made by such a mistake.

(B) If a contribution is conditioned on initial qualification of the plan under section 401 or 403(a) of Title 26, and if the plan receives an adverse determination with respect to its initial qualification, then paragraph (1) shall not prohibit the return of such contribution to the employer within one year after such determination, but only if the application for the determination is made by the time prescribed by law for filing the employer's return for the taxable year in which such plan was adopted, or such later date as the Secretary of the Treasury may prescribe.

(C) If a contribution is conditioned upon the deductibility of the contribution under section 404 of Title 26, then, to the extent the deduction is disallowed, paragraph (1) shall not prohibit the return to the employer of such contribution (to the extent disallowed) within one year after the disallowance of the deduction.

(3) In the case of a withdrawal liability payment which has been determined to be an overpayment, paragraph (1) shall not prohibit the return of such payment to the employer within 6 months after the date of such determination.

(d) Termination of plan—

(1) Upon termination of a pension plan to which section 1321 of this title does not apply at the time of termination and to which this part applies (other than a plan to which no employer contributions have been made) the assets of the plan shall be allocated in accordance with the provisions of section 1344 of this title, except as otherwise provided in regulations of the Secretary.

(2) The assets of a welfare plan which terminates shall be distributed in accordance with the terms of the plan, except as otherwise provided in regulations of the Secretary.

§ 404. Fiduciary duties (§ 1104)

(a) Prudent man standard of care—

(1) Subject to sections 1103(c) and (d), 1342, and 1344 of this title, a fiduciary shall discharge his duties with respect to a plan solely in the interest of the participants and beneficiaries and—

(A) for the exclusive purpose of:

(i) providing benefits to participants and their beneficiaries; and

(ii) defraying reasonable expenses of administering the plan;

(B) with the care, skill, prudence, and diligence under the circumstances then prevailing that a prudent man acting in a like capacity and familiar with such matters would use in the conduct of an enterprise of a like character and with like aims;

(C) by diversifying the investments of the plan so as to minimize the risk of large losses, unless under the circumstances it is clearly prudent not to do so; and

(D) in accordance with the documents and instruments governing the plan insofar as such documents and instruments are consistent with the provisions of this subchapter and subchapter III of this chapter.

(2) In the case of an eligible individual account plan (as defined in section 1107(d)(3) of this title), the diversification requirement of paragraph (1)(C) and the prudence requirement (only to the extent that it requires diversification) of paragraph (1)(B) is not violated by acquisition or holding of qualifying employer real property or qualifying employer securities (as defined in section 1107(d)(4) and (5) of this title).

(b) Indicia of ownership of assets outside jurisdiction of district courts—Except as authorized by the Secretary by regulations, no fiduciary may maintain the indicia of ownership of any assets of a plan outside the jurisdiction of the district courts of the United States.

(c) Control over assets by participant or beneficiary—

(1)(A) In the case of a pension plan which provides for individual accounts and permits a participant or beneficiary to exercise control over the assets in his account, if a participant or beneficiary exercises control over the assets in his account (as determined under regulations of the Secretary)—

> **(i)** such participant or beneficiary shall not be deemed to be a fiduciary by reason of such exercise, and

> **(ii)** no person who is otherwise a fiduciary shall be liable under this part for any loss, or by reason of any breach, which results from such participant's or beneficiary's exercise of control, except that this clause shall not apply in connection with such participant or beneficiary for any blackout period during which the ability of such participant or beneficiary to direct the investment of the assets in his or her account is suspended by a plan sponsor or fiduciary.

> **(B)** If a person referred to in subparagraph (A)(ii) meets the requirements of this subchapter in connection with authorizing and implementing the blackout period, any person who is otherwise a fiduciary shall not be liable under this subchapter for any loss occurring during such period.

> **(C)** For purposes of this paragraph, the term 'blackout period' has the meaning given such term by section 1021(i)(7) of this title.

(2) In the case of a simple retirement account established pursuant to a qualified salary reduction arrangement under section 408(p) of Title 26, a participant or beneficiary shall, for purposes of paragraph (1), be treated as exercising control over the assets in the account upon the earliest of—

> **(A)** an affirmative election among investment options with respect to the initial investment of any contribution,

> **(B)** a rollover to any other simple retirement account or individual retirement plan, or

> **(C)** one year after the simple retirement account is established.

No reports, other than those required under section 1021(g) of this title, shall be required with respect to a simple retirement account established pursuant to such a qualified salary reduction arrangement.

(3) In the case of a pension plan which makes a transfer to an individual retirement account or annuity of a designated trustee or issuer under section 401(a)(31)(B) of [Title 26], the participant or beneficiary shall, for purposes of paragraph (1), be treated as exercising control over the assets in the account or annuity upon—

(A) the earlier of—

(i) a rollover of all or a portion of the amount to another individual retirement account or annuity; or

(ii) one year after the transfer is made; or

(B) a transfer that is made in a manner consistent with guidance provided by the Secretary.

(4)(A) In any case in which a qualified change in investment options occurs in connection with an individual account plan, a participant or beneficiary shall not be treated for purposes of paragraph (1) as not exercising control over the assets in his account in connection with such change if the requirements of subparagraph (C) are met in connection with such change.

(B) For purposes of subparagraph (A), the term "qualified change in investment options" means, in connection with an individual account plan, a change in the investment options offered to the participant or beneficiary under the terms of the plan, under which—

(i) the account of the participant or beneficiary is reallocated among one or more remaining or new investment options which are offered in lieu of one or more investment options offered immediately prior to the effective date of the change, and

(ii) the stated characteristics of the remaining or new investment options provided under clause (i), including characteristics relating to risk and rate of return, are, as of immediately after the change, reasonably similar to those of the existing investment options as of immediately before the change.

(C) The requirements of this subparagraph are met in connection with a qualified change in investment options if—

(i) at least 30 days and no more than 60 days prior to the effective date of the change, the plan administrator furnishes written notice of the change to the participants and beneficiaries, including information comparing the existing and new investment options and an explanation that, in the absence of affirmative investment instructions from the participant or beneficiary to the contrary, the account of the participant or beneficiary will be invested in the manner described in subparagraph (B),

(ii) the participant or beneficiary has not provided to the plan administrator, in advance of the effective date of the change, affirmative investment instructions contrary to the change, and

(iii) the investments under the plan of the participant or beneficiary as in effect immediately prior to the effective date of the change were the product of the exercise by such participant or beneficiary of control over the assets of the account within the meaning of paragraph (1).

(5) Default investment arrangements—

(A) In general—For purposes of paragraph (1), a participant or beneficiary in an individual account plan meeting the notice requirements of subparagraph (B) shall be treated as exercising control over the assets in the account with respect to the amount of contributions and earnings which, in the absence of an investment election by the participant or beneficiary, are invested by the plan in accordance with regulations prescribed by the Secretary. The regulations under this subparagraph shall provide guidance on the appropriateness of designating default investments that include a mix of asset classes consistent with capital preservation or long-term capital appreciation, or a blend of both.

(B) Notice requirements—

(i) In general—The requirements of this subparagraph are met if each participant or beneficiary—

(I) receives, within a reasonable period of time before each plan year, a notice explaining the employee's right under the plan to designate how contributions and earnings will be invested and explaining how, in the absence of any investment election by the participant or beneficiary, such contributions and earnings will be invested, and

(II) has a reasonable period of time after receipt of such notice and before the beginning of the plan year to make such designation.

(ii) Form of notice—The requirements of clauses (i) and (ii) of section 401(k)(12)(D) of Title 26 shall apply with respect to the notices described in this subparagraph.

* * *

§ 405. Liability for breach of co-fiduciary (§ 1105)

(a) Circumstances giving rise to liability—In addition to any liability which he may have under any other provisions of this part, a fiduciary with respect to a plan shall be liable for a breach of fiduciary responsibility of another fiduciary with respect to the same plan in the following circumstances:

(1) if he participates knowingly in, or knowingly undertakes to conceal, an act or omission of such other fiduciary, knowing such act or omission is a breach;

(2) if, by his failure to comply with section 1104(a)(1) of this title in the administration of his specific responsibilities which give rise to his status as a fiduciary, he has enabled such other fiduciary to commit a breach; or

(3) if he has knowledge of a breach by such other fiduciary, unless he makes reasonable efforts under the circumstances to remedy the breach.

(b) Assets held by two or more trustees—

(1) Except as otherwise provided in subsection (d) of this section and in section 1103(a)(1) and (2) of this title, if the assets of a plan are held by two or more trustees—

(A) each shall use reasonable care to prevent a co-trustee from committing a breach; and

(B) they shall jointly manage and control the assets of the plan, except that nothing in this subparagraph (B) shall preclude any agreement, authorized by the trust instrument, allocating specific responsibilities, obligations, or duties among trustees, in which event a trustee to whom certain responsibilities, obligations, or duties have not been allocated shall not be liable by reason of this subparagraph (B) either individually or as a trustee for any loss resulting to the plan arising from the acts or omissions on the part of another trustee to whom such responsibilities, obligations, or duties have been allocated.

(2) Nothing in this subsection shall limit any liability that a fiduciary may have under subsection (a) of this section or any other provision of this part.

(3)(A) In the case of a plan the assets of which are held in more than one trust, a trustee shall not be liable under paragraph (1) except with respect to an act or omission of a trustee of a trust of which he is a trustee.

> **(B)** No trustee shall be liable under this subsection for following instructions referred to in section 1103(a)(1) of this title.

(c) Allocation of fiduciary responsibility; designated person to carry out fiduciary responsibilities—

(1) The instrument under which a plan is maintained may expressly provide for procedures (A) for allocating fiduciary responsibilities (other than trustee responsibilities) among named fiduciaries, and (B) for named fiduciaries to designate persons other than named fiduciaries to carry out fiduciary responsibilities (other than trustee responsibilities) under the plan.

(2) If a plan expressly provides for a procedure described in paragraph (1), and pursuant to such procedure any fiduciary responsibility of a named fiduciary is allocated to any person, or a person is designated to carry out any such responsibility, then such named fiduciary shall not be liable for an act or omission of such person in carrying out such responsibility except to the extent that—

> **(A)** the named fiduciary violated section 1104(a)(1) of this title—
>
>> **(i)** with respect to such allocation or designation,
>>
>> **(ii)** with respect to the establishment or implementation of the procedure under paragraph (1), or
>>
>> **(iii)** in continuing the allocation or designation; or
>
> **(B)** the named fiduciary would otherwise be liable in accordance with subsection (a) of this section.

(3) For purposes of this subsection, the term "trustee responsibility" means any responsibility provided in the plan's trust instrument (if any) to manage or control the assets of the plan, other than a power under the trust instrument of a named fiduciary to appoint an investment manager in accordance with section 1102(c)(3) of this title.

(d) Investment managers—

(1) If an investment manager or managers have been appointed under section 1102(c)(3) of this title, then, notwithstanding subsections (a)(2) and (3) and subsection (b) of this section, no trustee shall be liable for the acts or omissions of such investment manager or managers, or be under an obligation to invest or otherwise manage any asset of the plan which is subject to the management of such investment manager.

(2) Nothing in this subsection shall relieve any trustee of any liability under this part for any act of such trustee.

§ 406. Prohibited transactions (§ 1106)

(a) Transactions between plan and party in interest—Except as provided in section 1108 of this title:

(1) A fiduciary with respect to a plan shall not cause the plan to engage in a transaction, if he knows or should know that such transaction constitutes a direct or indirect—

(A) sale or exchange, or leasing, of any property between the plan and a party in interest;

(B) lending of money or other extension of credit between the plan and a party in interest;

(C) furnishing of goods, services, or facilities between the plan and a party in interest;

(D) transfer to, or use by or for the benefit of, a party in interest, of any assets of the plan; or

(E) acquisition, on behalf of the plan, of any employer security or employer real property in violation of section 1107(a) of this title.

(2) No fiduciary who has authority or discretion to control or manage the assets of a plan shall permit the plan to hold any employer security or employer real property if he knows or should know that holding such security or real property violates section 1107(a) of this title.

(b) Transactions between plan and fiduciary—A fiduciary with respect to a plan shall not—

(1) deal with the assets of the plan in his own interest or for his own account,

(2) in his individual or in any other capacity act in any transaction involving the plan on behalf of a party (or represent a party) whose interests are adverse to the interests of the plan or the interests of its participants or beneficiaries, or

(3) receive any consideration for his own personal account from any party dealing with such plan in connection with a transaction involving the assets of the plan.

(c) Transfer of real or personal property to plan by party in interest—A transfer of real or personal property by a party in interest to a plan shall be treated as a sale or exchange if the property is subject to a mortgage or similar lien which the plan assumes or if it is subject to a mortgage or similar lien which a party-in-interest placed on the property within the 10-year period ending on the date of the transfer.

§ 407. Limitation with respect to acquisition and holding of employer securities and employer real property by certain plans (§ 1107)

(a) Percentage limitation—Except as otherwise provided in this section and section 1114 of this title:

(1) A plan may not acquire or hold—

(A) any employer security which is not a qualifying employer security, or

(B) any employer real property which is not qualifying employer real property.

(2) A plan may not acquire any qualifying employer security or qualifying employer real property, if immediately after such acquisition the aggregate fair market value of employer securities and employer real property held by the plan exceeds 10 percent of the fair market value of the assets of the plan.

* * *

(b) Exception—

(1) Subsection (a) of this section shall not apply to any acquisition or holding of qualifying employer securities or qualifying employer real property by an eligible individual account plan.

(2)(A) If this paragraph applies to an eligible individual account plan, the portion of such plan which consists of applicable elective deferrals (and earnings allocable thereto) shall be treated as a separate plan—

    (i) which is not an eligible individual account plan, and

    (ii) to which the requirements of this section apply.

    (B)(i) This paragraph shall apply to any eligible individual account plan if any portion of the plan's applicable elective deferrals (or earnings allocable thereto) are required to be invested in qualifying employer securities or qualifying employer real property or both—

        (I) pursuant to the terms of the plan, or

        (II) at the direction of a person other than the participant on whose behalf such elective deferrals are made to the plan (or a beneficiary).

    (ii) This paragraph shall not apply to an individual account plan for a plan year if, on the last day of the preceding plan year, the fair market value of the assets of all individual account plans maintained by the employer equals not more than 10 percent of the fair market value of the assets of all pension plans (other than multiemployer plans) maintained by the employer.

    (iii) This paragraph shall not apply to an individual account plan that is an employee stock ownership plan as defined in section 4975(e)(7) of Title 26.

    (iv) This paragraph shall not apply to an individual account plan if, pursuant to the terms of the plan, the portion of any employee's applicable elective deferrals which is required to be invested in qualifying employer securities and qualifying employer real property for any year may not exceed 1 percent of the employee's compensation which is taken into account under the plan in determining the maximum amount of the employee's applicable elective deferrals for such year.

    (C) For purposes of this paragraph, the term "applicable elective deferral" means any elective deferral (as defined in section 402(g)(3)(A) of Title 26) which is made pursuant to a qualified cash or deferred arrangement as defined in section 401(k) of Title 26.

* * *

(d) Definitions—For purposes of this section—

(1) The term "employer security" means a security issued by an employer of employees covered by the plan, or by an affiliate of such employer. A contract to which section 1108(b)(5) of this title applies shall not be treated as a security for purposes of this section.

(2) The term "employer real property" means real property (and related personal property) which is leased to an employer of employees covered by the plan, or to an affiliate of such employer. For purposes of determining the time at which a plan acquires employer real property for purposes of this section, such property shall be deemed to be acquired by the plan on the date on which the plan acquires the property or on the date on which the lease to the employer (or affiliate) is entered into, whichever is later.

(3)(A) The term "eligible individual account plan" means an individual account plan which is (i) a profit-sharing, stock bonus, thrift, or savings plan; (ii) an employee stock ownership plan; or (iii) a money purchase plan which was in existence on September 2, 1974, and which on such date invested primarily in qualifying employer securities. Such term excludes an individual retirement account or annuity described in section 408 of Title 26.

(B) Notwithstanding subparagraph (A), a plan shall be treated as an eligible individual account plan with respect to the acquisition or holding of qualifying employer real property or qualifying employer securities only if such plan explicitly provides for acquisition and holding of qualifying employer securities or qualifying employer real property (as the case may be). In the case of a plan in existence on September 2, 1974, this subparagraph shall not take effect until January 1, 1976.

(C) The term "eligible individual account plan" does not include any individual account plan the benefits of which are taken into account in determining the benefits payable to a participant under any defined benefit plan.

(4) The term "qualifying employer real property" means parcels of employer real property—

(A) if a substantial number of the parcels are dispersed geographically;

(B) if each parcel of real property and the improvements thereon are suitable (or adaptable without excessive cost) for more than one use;

(C) even if all of such real property is leased to one lessee (which may be an employer, or an affiliate of an employer); and

(D) if the acquisition and retention of such property comply with the provisions of this part (other than section 1104(a)(1)(B) of this title to the extent it requires diversification, and sections 1104(a)(1)(C), 1106 of this title, and subsection (a) of this section).

(5) The term "qualifying employer security" means an employer security which is—

(A) stock,

(B) a marketable obligation (as defined in subsection (e)), or

(C) an interest in a publicly traded partnership (as defined in section 7704(b) of Title 26), but only if such partnership is an existing partnership as defined in section 10211(c)(2)(A) of the Revenue Act of 1987 (Public Law 100-203).

After December 17, 1987, in the case of a plan other than an eligible individual account plan, an employer security described in subparagraph (A) or (C) shall be considered a qualifying employer security only if such employer security satisfies the requirements of subsection (f)(1).

(6) The term "employee stock ownership plan" means an individual account plan—

(A) which is a stock bonus plan which is qualified, or a stock bonus plan and money purchase plan both of which are qualified, under section 401 of Title 26, and which is designed to invest primarily in qualifying employer securities, and

(B) which meets such other requirements as the Secretary of the Treasury may prescribe by regulation.

(7) A corporation is an affiliate of an employer if it is a member of any controlled group of corporations (as defined in section 1563(a) of Title 26, except that "applicable percentage" shall be substituted for "80 percent" wherever the latter percentage appears in such section) of which the employer who maintains the plan is a member. For purposes of the preceding sentence, the term "applicable percentage" means 50 percent, or such lower percentage as the Secretary may prescribe by regulation.

* * *

(e) Marketable obligations—For purposes of subsection (d)(5) of this section, the term "marketable obligation" means a bond, debenture, note, or certificate, or other evidence of indebtedness (hereinafter in this subsection referred to as "obligation") if—

(1) such obligation is acquired—

(A) on the market, either (i) at the price of the obligation prevailing on a national securities exchange which is registered with the Securities and Exchange Commission, or (ii) if the obligation is not traded on such a national securities exchange, at a price not less favorable to the plan than the offering price for the obligation as established by current bid and asked prices quoted by persons independent of the issuer;

(B) from an underwriter, at a price (i) not in excess of the public offering price for the obligation as set forth in a prospectus or offering circular filed with the Securities and Exchange Commission, and (ii) at which a substantial portion of the same issue is acquired by persons independent of the issuer; or

(C) directly from the issuer, at a price not less favorable to the plan than the price paid currently for a substantial portion of the same issue by persons independent of the issuer;

(2) immediately following acquisition of such obligation—

(A) not more than 25 percent of the aggregate amount of obligations issued in such issue and outstanding at the time of acquisition is held by the plan, and

(B) at least 50 percent of the aggregate amount referred to in subparagraph (A) is held by persons independent of the issuer; and

(3) immediately following acquisition of the obligation, not more than 25 percent of the assets of the plan is invested in obligations of the employer or an affiliate of the employer.

(f) Maximum percentage of stock held by plan; time of holding or acquisition; necessity of legally binding contract—

(1) Stock satisfies the requirements of this paragraph if, immediately following the acquisition of such stock—

(A) no more than 25 percent of the aggregate amount of stock of the same class issued and outstanding at the time of acquisition is held by the plan, and

(B) at least 50 percent of the aggregate amount referred to in subparagraph (A) is held by persons independent of the issuer.

* * *

§ 408. Exemptions from prohibited transactions (§ 1108)

(a) Grant of exemptions—The Secretary shall establish an exemption procedure for purposes of this subsection. Pursuant to such procedure, he may grant a conditional or unconditional exemption of any fiduciary or transaction, or class of fiduciaries or transactions, from all or part of the restrictions imposed by sections 1106 and 1107(a) of this title. Action under this subsection may be taken only after consultation and coordination with the Secretary of the Treasury. An exemption granted under this section shall not relieve a fiduciary from any other applicable provision of this chapter. The Secretary may not grant an exemption under this subsection unless he finds that such exemption is—

(1) administratively feasible,

(2) in the interests of the plan and of its participants and beneficiaries, and

(3) protective of the rights of participants and beneficiaries of such plan.

Before granting an exemption under this subsection from section 1106(a) or 1107(a) of this title, the Secretary shall publish notice in the Federal Register of the pendency of the exemption, shall require that adequate notice be given to interested persons, and shall afford interested persons opportunity to present views. The Secretary may not grant an exemption under this subsection from section 1106(b) of this title unless he affords an opportunity for a hearing and makes a determination on the record with respect to the findings required by paragraphs (1), (2), and (3) of this subsection.

(b) Enumeration of transactions exempted from section 1106 prohibitions—The prohibitions provided in section 1106 of this title shall not apply to any of the following transactions:

(1) Any loans made by the plan to parties in interest who are participants or beneficiaries of the plan if such loans (A) are available to all such participants and beneficiaries on a reasonably equivalent basis, (B) are not made available to highly compensated employees (within the meaning of section 414(q) of Title 26) in an amount greater than the amount made available to other employees, (C) are made in accordance with specific provisions regarding such loans set forth in the plan, (D) bear a reasonable rate of interest, and (E) are adequately secured. A loan made by a plan shall not fail to meet the requirements of the preceding sentence by reason of a loan repayment suspension described under section 414(u)(4) of Title 26.

(2) Contracting or making reasonable arrangements with a party in interest for office space, or legal, accounting, or other services necessary for the establishment or operation of the plan, if no more than reasonable compensation is paid therefor.

(3) A loan to an employee stock ownership plan (as defined in section 1107(d)(6) of this title), if—

(A) such loan is primarily for the benefit of participants and beneficiaries of the plan, and

(B) such loan is at an interest rate which is not in excess of a reasonable rate.

If the plan gives collateral to a party in interest for such loan, such collateral may consist only of qualifying employer securities (as defined in section 1107(d)(5) of this title).

(4) The investment of all or part of a plan's assets in deposits which bear a reasonable interest rate in a bank or similar financial institution supervised by the United States or a State, if such bank or other institution is a fiduciary of such plan and if—

    (A) the plan covers only employees of such bank or other institution and employees of affiliates of such bank or other institution, or

    (B) such investment is expressly authorized by a provision of the plan or by a fiduciary (other than such bank or institution or affiliate thereof) who is expressly empowered by the plan to so instruct the trustee with respect to such investment.

(5) Any contract for life insurance, health insurance, or annuities with one or more insurers which are qualified to do business in a State, if the plan pays no more than adequate consideration, and if each such insurer or insurers is—

    (A) the employer maintaining the plan, or

    (B) a party in interest which is wholly owned (directly or indirectly) by the employer maintaining the plan, or by any person which is a party in interest with respect to the plan, but only if the total premiums and annuity considerations written by such insurers for life insurance, health insurance, or annuities for all plans (and their employers) with respect to which such insurers are parties in interest (not including premiums or annuity considerations written by the employer maintaining the plan) do not exceed 5 percent of the total premiums and annuity considerations written for all lines of insurance in that year by such insurers (not including premiums or annuity considerations written by the employer maintaining the plan).

(6) The providing of any ancillary service by a bank or similar financial institution supervised by the United States or a State, if such bank or other institution is a fiduciary of such plan, and if—

    (A) such bank or similar financial institution has adopted adequate internal safeguards which assure that the providing of such ancillary service is consistent with sound banking and financial practice, as determined by Federal or State supervisory authority, and

    (B) the extent to which such ancillary service is provided is subject to specific guidelines issued by such bank or similar financial institution (as determined by the Secretary after consultation with Federal and State supervisory authority), and adherence to such guidelines would reasonably preclude such bank or similar financial institution from providing such ancillary service (i) in an excessive or unreasonable manner, and (ii) in a manner that would be inconsistent with the best interests of participants and beneficiaries of employee benefit plans.

Such ancillary services shall not be provided at more than reasonable compensation.

(7) The exercise of a privilege to convert securities, to the extent provided in regulations of the Secretary, but only if the plan receives no less than adequate consideration pursuant to such conversion.

(8) Any transaction between a plan and (i) a common or collective trust fund or pooled investment fund maintained by a party in interest which is a bank or trust company supervised by a State or Federal agency or (ii) a pooled investment fund of an insurance company qualified to do business in a State, if—

(A) the transaction is a sale or purchase of an interest in the fund,

(B) the bank, trust company, or insurance company receives not more than reasonable compensation, and

(C) such transaction is expressly permitted by the instrument under which the plan is maintained, or by a fiduciary (other than the bank, trust company, or insurance company, or an affiliate thereof) who has authority to manage and control the assets of the plan.

(9) The making by a fiduciary of a distribution of the assets of the plan in accordance with the terms of the plan if such assets are distributed in the same manner as provided under section 1344 of this title (relating to allocation of assets).

(10) Any transaction required or permitted under part 1 of subtitle E of subchapter III of this chapter.

(11) A merger of multiemployer plans, or the transfer of assets or liabilities between multiemployer plans, determined by the Pension Benefit Guaranty Corporation to meet the requirements of section 1141 of this title.

(12) The sale by a plan to a party in interest on or after December 18, 1987, of any stock, if—

(A) the requirements of paragraphs (1) and (2) of subsection (e) are met with respect to such stock,

(B) on the later of the date on which the stock was acquired by the plan, or January 1, 1975, such stock constituted a qualifying employer security (as defined in section 1107(d)(5) of this title as then in effect), and

(C) such stock does not constitute a qualifying employer security (as defined in section 1107(d)(5) of this title as in effect at the time of the sale).

(13) Any transfer made before January 1, 2026, of excess pension assets from a defined benefit plan to a retiree health account in a qualified transfer permitted under section 420 of Title 26 (as in effect on July 31, 2015).

(14) Any transaction in connection with the provision of investment advice described in section 1002(21)(A)(ii) of this title to a participant or beneficiary of an individual account plan that permits such participant or beneficiary to direct the investment of assets in their individual account, if—

(A) the transaction is—

(i) the provision of the investment advice to the participant or beneficiary of the plan with respect to a security or other property available as an investment under the plan,

(ii) the acquisition, holding, or sale of a security or other property available as an investment under the plan pursuant to the investment advice, or

(iii) the direct or indirect receipt of fees or other compensation by the fiduciary adviser or an affiliate thereof (or any employee, agent, or registered representative of the fiduciary adviser or affiliate) in connection with the provision of the advice or in connection with an acquisition, holding, or sale of a security or other property available as an investment under the plan pursuant to the investment advice; and

(B) the requirements of subsection (g)* are met.

(15)(A) Any transaction involving the purchase or sale of securities, or other property (as determined by the Secretary), between a plan and a party in interest (other than a fiduciary described in section 1002(21)(A) of this title) with respect to a plan if—

    (i) the transaction involves a block trade,

    (ii) at the time of the transaction, the interest of the plan (together with the interests of any other plans maintained by the same plan sponsor), does not exceed 10 percent of the aggregate size of the block trade,

    (iii) the terms of the transaction, including the price, are at least as favorable to the plan as an arm's[-]length transaction, and

    (iv) the compensation associated with the purchase and sale is not greater than the compensation associated with an arm's length transaction with an unrelated party.

(B) For purposes of this paragraph, the term "block trade" means any trade of at least 10,000 shares or with a market value of at least $200,000 which will be allocated across two or more unrelated client accounts of a fiduciary.

(16) Any transaction involving the purchase or sale of securities, or other property (as determined by the Secretary), between a plan and a party in interest if—

(A) the transaction is executed through an electronic communication network, alternative trading system, or similar execution system or trading venue subject to regulation and oversight by—

    (i) the applicable Federal regulating entity, or

    (ii) such foreign regulatory entity as the Secretary may determine by regulation,

(B) either—

    (i) the transaction is effected pursuant to rules designed to match purchases and sales at the best price available through the execution system in accordance with applicable rules of the Securities and Exchange Commission or other relevant governmental authority, or

    (ii) neither the execution system nor the parties to the transaction take into account the identity of the parties in the execution of trades,

(C) the price and compensation associated with the purchase and sale are not greater than the price and compensation associated with an arm's length transaction with an unrelated party,

---

* Subsection (g) of § 408 is omitted, but its provisions are mirrored by IRC § 4975(f)(8).

(D) if the party in interest has an ownership interest in the system or venue described in subparagraph (A), the system or venue has been authorized by the plan sponsor or other independent fiduciary for transactions described in this paragraph, and

(E) not less than 30 days prior to the initial transaction described in this paragraph executed through any system or venue described in subparagraph (A), a plan fiduciary is provided written or electronic notice of the execution of such transaction through such system or venue.

(17)(A) Transactions described in subparagraphs (A), (B), and (D) of section 1106(a)(1) of this title between a plan and a person that is a party in interest other than a fiduciary (or an affiliate) who has or exercises any discretionary authority or control with respect to the investment of the plan assets involved in the transaction or renders investment advice (within the meaning of section 1002(21)(A)(ii) of this title) with respect to those assets, solely by reason of providing services to the plan or solely by reason of a relationship to such a service provider described in subparagraph (F), (G), (H), or (I) of section 1002(14) of this title, or both, but only if in connection with such transaction the plan receives no less, nor pays no more, than adequate consideration.

(B) For purposes of this paragraph, the term "adequate consideration" means—

(i) in the case of a security for which there is a generally recognized market—

(I) the price of the security prevailing on a national securities exchange which is registered under section 78f of Title 15, taking into account factors such as the size of the transaction and marketability of the security, or

(II) if the security is not traded on such a national securities exchange, a price not less favorable to the plan than the offering price for the security as established by the current bid and asked prices quoted by persons independent of the issuer and of the party in interest, taking into account factors such as the size of the transaction and marketability of the security, and

(ii) in the case of an asset other than a security for which there is a generally recognized market, the fair market value of the asset as determined in good faith by a fiduciary or fiduciaries in accordance with regulations prescribed by the Secretary.

(18) Foreign exchange transactions. Any foreign exchange transactions, between a bank or broker-dealer (or any affiliate of either), and a plan (as defined in section 1002(3) of this title) with respect to which such bank or broker-dealer (or affiliate) is a trustee, custodian, fiduciary, or other party in interest, if—

(A) the transaction is in connection with the purchase, holding, or sale of securities or other investment assets (other than a foreign exchange transaction unrelated to any other investment in securities or other investment assets),

(B) at the time the foreign exchange transaction is entered into, the terms of the transaction are not less favorable to the plan than the terms generally available in comparable arm's length foreign exchange transactions between unrelated parties, or the terms afforded by the bank or broker-dealer (or any affiliate of either) in comparable arm's-length foreign exchange transactions involving unrelated parties,

(C) the exchange rate used by such bank or broker-dealer (or affiliate) for a particular foreign exchange transaction does not deviate by more than 3 percent from the interbank bid and asked rates for transactions of comparable size and maturity at the time of the transaction as displayed on an independent service that reports rates of exchange in the foreign currency market for such currency, and

(D) the bank or broker-dealer (or any affiliate of either) does not have investment discretion, or provide investment advice, with respect to the transaction.

(19) Cross trading. Any transaction described in sections 1006(a)(1)(A) and 1106(b)(2) of this title involving the purchase and sale of a security between a plan and any other account managed by the same investment manager, if—

(A) the transaction is a purchase or sale, for no consideration other than cash payment against prompt delivery of a security for which market quotations are readily available,

(B) the transaction is effected at the independent current market price of the security (within the meaning of section 270.17a-7(b) of title 17, Code of Federal Regulations),

(C) no brokerage commission, fee (except for customary transfer fees, the fact of which is disclosed pursuant to subparagraph (D)), or other remuneration is paid in connection with the transaction,

(D) a fiduciary (other than the investment manager engaging in the cross-trades or any affiliate) for each plan participating in the transaction authorizes in advance of any cross-trades (in a document that is separate from any other written agreement of the parties) the investment manager to engage in cross trades at the investment manager's discretion, after such fiduciary has received disclosure regarding the conditions under which cross trades may take place (but only if such disclosure is separate from any other agreement or disclosure involving the asset management relationship), including the written policies and procedures of the investment manager described in subparagraph (H),

(E) each plan participating in the transaction has assets of at least $100,000,000, except that if the assets of a plan are invested in a master trust containing the assets of plans maintained by employers in the same controlled group (as defined in section 1107(d)(7) of this title), the master trust has assets of at least $100,000,000,

(F) the investment manager provides to the plan fiduciary who authorized cross trading under subparagraph (D) a quarterly report detailing all cross trades executed by the investment manager in which the plan participated during such quarter, including the following information, as applicable: (i) the identity of each security bought or sold; (ii) the number of shares or units traded; (iii) the parties involved in the cross-trade; and (iv) trade price and the method used to establish the trade price,

(G) the investment manager does not base its fee schedule on the plan's consent to cross trading, and no other service (other than the investment opportunities and cost savings available through a cross trade) is conditioned on the plan's consent to cross trading,

(H) the investment manager has adopted, and cross-trades are effected in accordance with, written cross-trading policies and procedures that are fair and equitable to all accounts participating in the cross-trading program, and that include a description of the manager's pricing policies and procedures, and the manager's policies and procedures for allocating cross trades in an objective manner among accounts participating in the cross-trading program, and

(I) the investment manager has designated an individual responsible for periodically reviewing such purchases and sales to ensure compliance with the written policies and procedures described in subparagraph (H), and following such review, the individual shall issue an annual written report no later than 90 days following the period to which it relates signed under penalty of perjury to the plan fiduciary who authorized cross trading under subparagraph (D) describing the steps performed during the course of the review, the level of compliance, and any specific instances of non-compliance.

The written report under subparagraph (I) shall also notify the plan fiduciary of the plan's right to terminate participation in the investment manager's cross-trading program at any time.

(20)(A) Except as provided in subparagraphs (B) and (C), a transaction described in section 1006(a) of this title in connection with the acquisition, holding, or disposition of any security or commodity, if the transaction is corrected before the end of the correction period.

(B) Subparagraph (A) does not apply to any transaction between a plan and a plan sponsor or its affiliates that involves the acquisition or sale of an employer security (as defined in section 1107(d)(1) of this title) or the acquisition, sale, or lease of employer real property (as defined in section 1107(d)(2) of this title).

(C) In the case of any fiduciary or other party in interest (or any other person knowingly participating in such transaction), subparagraph (A) does not apply to any transaction if, at the time the transaction occurs, such fiduciary or party in interest (or other person) knew (or reasonably should have known) that the transaction would (without regard to this paragraph) constitute a violation of section 1106(a) of this title.

(D) For purposes of this paragraph, the term 'correction period' means, in connection with a fiduciary or party in interest (or other person knowingly participating in the transaction), the 14-day period beginning on the date on which such fiduciary or party in interest (or other person) discovers, or reasonably should have discovered, that the transaction would (without regard to this paragraph) constitute a violation of section 1106(a) of this title.

(E) For purposes of this paragraph—

(i) The term "security" has the meaning given such term by section 475(c)(2) of Title 26 (without regard to subparagraph (F)(iii) and the last sentence thereof).

(ii) The term "commodity" has the meaning given such term by section 475(e)(2) of Title 26 (without regard to subparagraph (D)(iii) thereof).

(iii) The term "correct" means, with respect to a transaction—

(I) to undo the transaction to the extent possible and in any case to make good to the plan or affected account any losses resulting from the transaction, and

(II) to restore to the plan or affected account any profits made through the use of assets of the plan.

(c) Fiduciary benefits and compensation not prohibited by section 1106—Nothing in section 1106 of this title shall be construed to prohibit any fiduciary from—

(1) receiving any benefit to which he may be entitled as a participant or beneficiary in the plan, so long as the benefit is computed and paid on a basis which is consistent with the terms of the plan as applied to all other participants and beneficiaries;

(2) receiving any reasonable compensation for services rendered, or for the reimbursement of expenses properly and actually incurred, in the performance of his duties with the plan; except that no person so serving who already receives full-time pay from an employer or an association of employers, whose employees are participants in the plan, or from an employee organization whose members are participants in such plan shall receive compensation from such plan, except for reimbursement of expenses properly and actually incurred; or

(3) serving as a fiduciary in addition to being an officer, employee, agent, or other representative of a party in interest.

(d) Owner-employees; family members; shareholder employees—

(1) Section 1107(b) of this title and subsections (b), (c), and (e) of this section shall not apply to a transaction in which a plan directly or indirectly—

(A) lends any part of the corpus or income of the plan to,

(B) pays any compensation for personal services rendered to the plan to, or

(C) acquires for the plan any property from, or sells any property to,

any person who is with respect to the plan an owner-employee (as defined in section 401(c)(3) of Title 26), a member of the family (as defined in section 267(c)(4) of such title) of any such owner-employee, or any corporation in which any such owner-employee owns, directly or indirectly, 50 percent or more of the total combined voting power of all classes of stock entitled to vote or 50 percent or more of the total value of shares of all classes of stock of the corporation.

(2)(A) For purposes of paragraph (1), the following shall be treated as owner-employees:

(i) A shareholder-employee.

(ii) A participant or beneficiary of an individual retirement plan (as defined in section 7701(a)(37) of Title 26).

(iii) An employer or association of employees which establishes such an individual retirement plan under section 408(c) of such title.

(B) Paragraph (1)(C) shall not apply to a transaction which consists of a sale of employer securities to an employee stock ownership plan (as defined in section 1107(d)(6) of this title) by a shareholder-employee, a member of the family (as defined in section 267(c)(4) of [Title 26]) of any such owner-employee, or a corporation in which such a shareholder-employee owns stock representing a 50 percent or greater interest described in paragraph (1).

(C) For purposes of paragraph (1)(A), the term "owner-employee" shall only include a person described in clause (ii) or (iii) of subparagraph (A).

(3) For purposes of paragraph (2), the term "shareholder-employee" means an employee or officer of an S corporation (as defined in section 1361(a)(1) of Title 26) who owns (or is considered as owning within the meaning of section 318(a)(1) of Title 26) more than 5 percent of the outstanding stock of the corporation on any day during the taxable year of such corporation.

(e) Acquisition or sale by plan of qualifying employer securities; acquisition, sale, or lease by plan of qualifying employer real property—Sections 1106 and 1107 of this title shall not apply to the acquisition or sale by a plan of qualifying employer securities (as defined in section 1107(d)(5) of this title) or acquisition, sale or lease by a plan of qualifying employer real property (as defined in section 1107(d)(4) of this title)—

(1) if such acquisition, sale, or lease is for adequate consideration (or in the case of a marketable obligation, at a price not less favorable to the plan than the price determined under section 1107(e)(1) of this title),

(2) if no commission is charged with respect thereto, and

(3) if—

(A) the plan is an eligible individual account plan (as defined in section 1107(d)(3) of this title), or

(B) in the case of an acquisition or lease of qualifying employer real property by a plan which is not an eligible individual account plan, or of an acquisition of qualifying employer securities by such a plan, the lease or acquisition is not prohibited by section 1107(a) of this title.

* * *

§ 409. Liability for breach of fiduciary duty (§ 1109)

(a) Any person who is a fiduciary with respect to a plan who breaches any of the responsibilities, obligations, or duties imposed upon fiduciaries by this subchapter shall be personally liable to make good to such plan any losses to the plan resulting from each such breach, and to restore to such plan any profits of such fiduciary which have been made through use of assets of the plan by the fiduciary, and shall be subject to such other equitable or remedial relief as the court may deem appropriate, including removal of such fiduciary. A fiduciary may also be removed for a violation of section 1111 of this title.

(b) No fiduciary shall be liable with respect to a breach of fiduciary duty under this subchapter if such breach was committed before he became a fiduciary or after he ceased to be a fiduciary.

§ 410. Exculpatory provisions; insurance (§ 1110)

(a) Except as provided in sections 1105(b)(1) and 1105(d) of this title, any provision in an agreement or instrument which purports to relieve a fiduciary from responsibility or liability for any responsibility, obligation, or duty under this part shall be void as against public policy.

(b) Nothing in this subpart shall preclude—

(1) a plan from purchasing insurance for its fiduciaries or for itself to cover liability or losses occurring by reason of the act or omission of a fiduciary, if such insurance permits recourse by the insurer against the fiduciary in the case of a breach of a fiduciary obligation by such fiduciary;

(2) a fiduciary from purchasing insurance to cover liability under this part from and for his own account; or

(3) an employer or an employee organization from purchasing insurance to cover potential liability of one or more persons who serve in a fiduciary capacity with regard to an employee benefit plan.

§ 411. Persons prohibited from holding certain positions (§ 1111)

(a) **Conviction of imprisonment**—No person who has been convicted of, or has been imprisoned as a result of his conviction of, robbery, bribery, extortion, embezzlement, fraud, grand larceny, burglary, arson, a felony violation of Federal or State law involving substances defined in section 802(6) of Title 21, murder, rape, kidnaping, perjury, assault with intent to kill, any crime described in section 80a-9(a)(1) of Title 15, a violation of any provision of this chapter, a violation of section 186 of this title, a violation of chapter 63 of title 18, a violation of section 874, 1027, 1503, 1505, 1506, 1510, 1951, or 1954 of title 18, a violation of the Labor-Management Reporting and Disclosure Act of 1959 (29 U.S.C. 401), any felony involving abuse or misuse of such person's position or employment in a labor organization or employee benefit plan to seek or obtain an illegal gain at the expense of the members of the labor organization or the beneficiaries of the employee benefit plan, or conspiracy to commit any such crimes or attempt to commit any such crimes, or a crime in which any of the foregoing crimes is an element, shall serve or be permitted to serve—

(1) as an administrator, fiduciary, officer, trustee, custodian, counsel, agent, employee, or representative in any capacity of any employee benefit plan,

(2) as a consultant or adviser to an employee benefit plan, including but not limited to any entity whose activities are in whole or substantial part devoted to providing goods or services to any employee benefit plan, or

(3) in any capacity that involves decisionmaking authority or custody or control of the moneys, funds, assets, or property of any employee benefit plan,

during or for the period of thirteen years after such conviction or after the end of such imprisonment, whichever is later, unless the sentencing court on the motion of the person convicted sets a lesser period of at least three years after such conviction or after the end of such imprisonment, whichever is later, or unless prior to the end of such period, in the case of a person so convicted or imprisoned (A) his citizenship rights, having been revoked as a result of such conviction, have been fully restored, or (B) if the offense is a Federal offense, the sentencing judge or, if the offense is a State or local offense, the United States district court for the district in which the offense was committed, pursuant to sentencing guidelines and policy statements under section 994(a) of title 28, determines that such person's service in any capacity referred to in paragraphs (1) through (3) would not be contrary to the purposes of this subchapter. Prior to making any such determination the court shall hold a hearing and shall give notice to such proceeding by certified mail to the Secretary of Labor and to State, county, and Federal prosecuting officials in the jurisdiction or jurisdictions in which such person was convicted. The court's determination in any such proceeding shall be final. No person shall knowingly hire, retain, employ, or otherwise place any other person to serve in any capacity in violation of this subsection. Notwithstanding the preceding provisions of this subsection, no corporation or partnership will be precluded from acting as an administrator, fiduciary, officer, trustee, custodian, counsel, agent, or employee of any employee benefit plan or as a consultant to any employee benefit plan without a notice, hearing, and determination by such court that such service would be inconsistent with the intention of this section.

(b) **Penalty**—Any person who intentionally violates this section shall be fined not more than $10,000 or imprisoned for not more than five years, or both.

(c) **Definitions**—For the purpose of this section—

(1) A person shall be deemed to have been "convicted" and under the disability of "conviction" from the date of the judgment of the trial court, regardless of whether that judgment remains under appeal.

(2) The term "consultant" means any person who, for compensation, advises, or

represents an employee benefit plan or who provides other assistance to such plan, concerning the establishment or operation of such plan.

(3) A period of parole or supervised release shall not be considered as part of a period of imprisonment.

(d) Salary of person barred from employee benefit plan office during appeal of conviction—Whenever any person—

(1) by operation of this section, has been barred from office or other position in an employee benefit plan as a result of a conviction, and

(2) has filed an appeal of that conviction,

any salary which would be otherwise due such person by virtue of such office or position, shall be placed in escrow by the individual or organization responsible for payment of such salary. Payment of such salary into escrow shall continue for the duration of the appeal or for the period of time during which such salary would be otherwise due, whichever period is shorter. Upon the final reversal of such person's conviction on appeal, the amounts in escrow shall be paid to such person. Upon the final sustaining of that person's conviction on appeal, the amounts in escrow shall be returned to the individual or organization responsible for payments of those amounts. Upon final reversal of such person's conviction, such person shall no longer be barred by this statute from assuming any position from which such person was previously barred.

§ 413. Limitation of actions (§ 1113)

No action may be commenced under this subchapter with respect to a fiduciary's breach of any responsibility, duty, or obligation under this part, or with respect to a violation of this part, after the earlier of—

(1) six years after (A) the date of the last action which constituted a part of the breach or violation, or (B) in the case of an omission, the latest date on which the fiduciary could have cured the breach or violation, or

(2) three years after the earliest date on which the plaintiff had actual knowledge of the breach or violation;

except that in the case of fraud or concealment, such action may be commenced not later than six years after the date of discovery of such breach or violation.

Part 5—Administration and Enforcement

§ 501. Criminal penalties (§ 1131)

(a) Any person who willfully violates any provision of part 1 of this subtitle, or any regulation or order issued under any such provision, shall upon conviction be fined not more than $100,000 or imprisoned not more than 10 years, or both; except that in the case of such violation by a person not an individual, the fine imposed upon such person shall be a fine not exceeding $500,000.

(b) Any person that violates section 519 shall upon conviction be imprisoned not more than 10 years or fined under title 18, United States Code, or both.

§ 502. Civil enforcement (§ 1132)

(a) **Persons empowered to bring a civil action**—A civil action may be brought—

(1) by a participant or beneficiary—

(A) for the relief provided for in subsection (c) of this section, or

(B) to recover benefits due to him under the terms of his plan, to enforce his rights under the terms of the plan, or to clarify his rights to future benefits under the terms of the plan;

(2) by the Secretary, or by a participant, beneficiary or fiduciary for appropriate relief under section 1109 of this title;

(3) by a participant, beneficiary, or fiduciary (A) to enjoin any act or practice which violates any provision of this subchapter or the terms of the plan, or (B) to obtain other appropriate equitable relief (i) to redress such violations or (ii) to enforce any provisions of this subchapter or the terms of the plan;

(4) by the Secretary, or by a participant, or beneficiary for appropriate relief in the case of a violation of 1025(c) of this title;

(5) except as otherwise provided in subsection (b), by the Secretary (A) to enjoin any act or practice which violates any provision of this subchapter, or (B) to obtain other appropriate equitable relief (i) to redress such violation or (ii) to enforce any provision of this subchapter;

(6) by the Secretary to collect any civil penalty under paragraph (2), (4), (5), (6). (7), (8), or (9) of subsection (c) or under subsection (i) or (l);

(7) by a State to enforce compliance with a qualified medical child support order (as defined in section 1169(a)(2)(A) of this title);

(8) by the Secretary, or by an employer or other person referred to in section 1021(f)(1) of this title, (A) to enjoin any act or practice which violates subsection (f) of section 1021 of this title, or (B) to obtain appropriate equitable relief (i) to redress such violation or (ii) to enforce such subsection; or

(9) in the event that the purchase of an insurance contract or insurance annuity in connection with termination of an individual's status as a participant covered under a pension plan with respect to all or any portion of the participant's pension benefit under such plan constitutes a violation of part 4 of this title or the terms of the plan, by the Secretary, by any individual who was a participant or beneficiary at the time of the alleged violation, or by a fiduciary, to obtain appropriate relief, including the posting of security if necessary, to assure receipt by the participant or beneficiary of the amounts provided or to be provided by such insurance contract or annuity, plus reasonable prejudgment interest on such amounts.

(10) in the case of a multiemployer plan that has been certified by the actuary to be in endangered or critical status under section 1085 of this title, if the plan sponsor—

(A) has not adopted a funding improvement or rehabilitation plan under that section by the deadline established in such section, or

(B) fails to update or comply with the terms of the funding improvement or rehabilitation plan in accordance with the requirements of such section,

by an employer that has an obligation to contribute with respect to the multiemployer plan or an employee organization that represents active participants in the multiemployer plan, for an order compelling the plan sponsor to adopt a funding improvement or rehabilitation plan or to update or comply with the terms of the funding improvement or rehabilitation plan in accordance with the requirements of such section and the funding improvement or rehabilitation plan; or

(11) In the case of a multiemployer plan, by an employee representative, or any employer that has an obligation to contribute to the plan, (A) to enjoin any act or practice which violates subsection (k) of section 1021 of this title (or, in the case of an employer, subsection (l) of such section), or (B) to obtain appropriate equitable relief (i) to redress such violation or (ii) to enforce such subsection.

* * *

(c) Administrator's refusal to supply requested information; penalty for failure to provide annual report in complete form—

(1) Any administrator (A) who fails to meet the requirements of paragraph (1) or (4) of section 1166 of this title, section 1021(e)(1) of this title or section 1021(f), or section 1025(a) of this title with respect to a participant or beneficiary, or (B) who fails or refuses to comply with a request for any information which such administrator is required by this subchapter to furnish to a participant or beneficiary (unless such failure or refusal results from matters reasonably beyond the control of the administrator) by mailing the material requested to the last known address of the requesting participant or beneficiary within 30 days after such request may in the court's discretion be personally liable to such participant or beneficiary in the amount of up to $100 a day from the date of such failure or refusal, and the court may in its discretion order such other relief as it deems proper. For purposes of this paragraph, each violation described in subparagraph (A) with respect to any single participant, and each violation described in subparagraph (B) with respect to any single participant or beneficiary, shall be treated as a separate violation.

(2) The Secretary may assess a civil penalty against any plan administrator of up to $1,000 a day from the date of such plan administrator's failure or refusal to file the annual report required to be filed with the Secretary under section 1021(b)(4) of this title. For purposes of this paragraph, an annual report that has been rejected under section 1024(a)(4) of this title for failure to provide material information shall not be treated as having been filed with the Secretary.

(3) Any employer maintaining a plan who fails to meet the notice requirement of section 1021(d) of this title with respect to any participant or beneficiary or who fails to meet the requirements of section 1021(e)(2) of this title with respect to any person or who fails to meet the requirements of section 1082(d)(12)(E) of this title with respect to any person may in the court's discretion be liable to such participant or beneficiary or to such person in the amount of up to $100 a day from the date of such failure, and the court may in its discretion order such other relief as it deems proper.

(4) The Secretary may assess a civil penalty of not more than $1,000 a day for each violation by any person of subsection (j), (k), or (l) of section 1021 of this title or section 1144(e)(3) of this title.

(5) The Secretary may assess a civil penalty against any person of up to $1,000 a day from the date of the person's failure or refusal to file the information required to be filed by such person with the Secretary under regulations prescribed pursuant to section 1021(g) of this title.

(6) If, within 30 days of a request by the Secretary to a plan administrator for documents under section 1024(a)(6) of this title, the plan administrator fails to furnish the material requested to the Secretary, the Secretary may assess a civil penalty against the plan administrator of up to $100 a day from the date of such failure (but in no event in excess of $1,000 per request). No penalty shall be imposed under this paragraph for any failure resulting from matters reasonably beyond the control of the plan administrator.

(7) The Secretary may assess a civil penalty against a plan administrator of up to $100 a day from the date of the plan administrator's failure or refusal to provide notice to participants and beneficiaries in accordance with subsection (i) or (m) of section 1021 of this title. For purposes of this paragraph, each violation with respect to any single participant or beneficiary shall be treated as a separate violation.

(8) The Secretary may assess against any plan sponsor of a multiemployer plan a civil penalty of not more than $1,100 per day—

(A) for each violation by such sponsor of the requirement under section 1085 of this title to adopt by the deadline established in that section a funding improvement plan or rehabilitation plan with respect to a multiemployer which is in endangered or critical status, or

(B) in the case of a plan in endangered status which is not in seriously endangered status, for failure by the plan to meet the applicable benchmarks under section 1085 of this title by the end of the funding improvement period with respect to the plan.

(9)(A) The Secretary may assess a civil penalty against any employer of up to $100 a day from the date of the employer's failure to meet the notice requirement of section 1181(f)(3)(B)(i)(I) of this title. For purposes of this subparagraph, each violation with respect to any single employee shall be treated as a separate violation.

(B) The Secretary may assess a civil penalty against any plan administrator of up to $100 a day from the date of the plan administrator's failure to timely provide to any State the information required to be disclosed under section 1181(f)(3)(B)(ii) of this title. For purposes of this subparagraph, each violation with respect to any single participant or beneficiary shall be treated as a separate violation.

(10) **Secretarial enforcement authority relating to use of genetic information—**

(A) **General rule**—The Secretary may impose a penalty against any plan sponsor of a group health plan, or any health insurance issuer offering health insurance coverage in connection with the plan, for any failure by such sponsor or issuer to meet the requirements of subsection (a)(1)(F), (b)(3), (c), or (d) of section 1182 of this title or section 1181 or 1182(b)(1) of this title with respect to genetic information, in connection with the plan.

* * *

(11) The Secretary and the Secretary of Health and Human Services shall maintain such ongoing consultation as may be necessary and appropriate to coordinate enforcement under this subsection with enforcement under section 1144(c)(8) of the Social Security Act [42 U.S.C.A. § 1320b-14(c)(8)].

(12) The Secretary may assess a civil penalty against any sponsor of a CSEC plan of up to $100 a day from the date of the plan sponsor's failure to comply with the requirements of section 1085a(j)(3) of this title to establish or update a funding restoration plan.

(d) **Status of employee benefit plan as entity—**

(1) An employee benefit plan may sue or be sued under this subchapter as an entity. Service of summons, subpoena, or other legal process of a court upon a trustee or an admin-

istrator of an employee benefit plan in his capacity as such shall constitute service upon the employee benefit plan. In a case where a plan has not designated in the summary plan description of the plan an individual as agent for the service of legal process, service upon the Secretary shall constitute such service. The Secretary, not later than 15 days after receipt of service under the preceding sentence, shall notify the administrator or any trustee of the plan of receipt of such service.

(2) Any money judgment under this subchapter against an employee benefit plan shall be enforceable only against the plan as an entity and shall not be enforceable against any other person unless liability against such person is established in his individual capacity under this subchapter.

(e) Jurisdiction—

(1) Except for actions under subsection (a)(1)(B) of this section, the district courts of the United States shall have exclusive jurisdiction of civil actions under this subchapter brought by the Secretary or by a participant, beneficiary, fiduciary, or any person referred to in section 1021(f)(1) of this title. State courts of competent jurisdiction and district courts of the United States shall have concurrent jurisdiction of actions under paragraphs (1)(B) and (7) of subsection (a) of this section.

(2) Where an action under this subchapter is brought in a district court of the United States, it may be brought in the district where the plan is administered, where the breach took place, or where a defendant resides or may be found, and process may be served in any other district where a defendant resides or may be found.

(f) Amount in controversy; citizenship of parties—The district courts of the United States shall have jurisdiction, without respect to the amount in controversy or the citizenship of the parties, to grant the relief provided for in subsection (a) of this section in any action.

(g) Attorney's fees and costs; awards in actions involving delinquent contributions—

(1) In any action under this subchapter (other than an action described in paragraph (2)) by a participant, beneficiary, or fiduciary, the court in its discretion may allow a reasonable attorney's fee and costs of action to either party.

(2) In any action under this subchapter by a fiduciary for or on behalf of a plan to enforce section 1145 of this title in which a judgment in favor of the plan is awarded, the court shall award the plan—

(A) the unpaid contributions,

(B) interest on the unpaid contributions,

(C) an amount equal to the greater of—

(i) interest on the unpaid contributions, or

(ii) liquidated damages provided for under the plan in an amount not in excess of 20 percent (or such higher percentage as may be permitted under Federal or State law) of the amount determined by the court under subparagraph (A),

(D) reasonable attorney's fees and costs of the action, to be paid by the defendant, and

(E) such other legal or equitable relief as the court deems appropriate.

For purposes of this paragraph, interest on unpaid contributions shall be determined by using the rate provided under the plan, or, if none, the rate prescribed under section 6621 of Title 26.

(h) Service upon Secretary of Labor and Secretary of the Treasury—A copy of the complaint in any action under this subchapter by a participant, beneficiary, or fiduciary (other than an action brought by one or more participants or beneficiaries under subsection (a)(1)(B) of this section which is solely for the purpose of recovering benefits due such participants under the terms of the plan) shall be served upon the Secretary and the Secretary of the Treasury by certified mail. Either Secretary shall have the right in his discretion to intervene in any action, except that the Secretary of the Treasury may not intervene in any action under part 4 of this subtitle. If the Secretary brings an action under subsection (a) of this section on behalf of a participant or beneficiary, he shall notify the Secretary of the Treasury.

(i) Administrative assessment of civil penalty—In the case of a transaction prohibited by section 1106 of this title by a party in interest with respect to a plan to which this part applies, the Secretary may assess a civil penalty against such party in interest. The amount of such penalty may not exceed 5 percent of the amount involved in each such transaction (as defined in section 4975(f)(4) of Title 26) for each year or part thereof during which the prohibited transaction continues, except that, if the transaction is not corrected (in such manner as the Secretary shall prescribe in regulations which shall be consistent with section 4975(f)(5) of Title 26) within 90 days after notice from the Secretary (or such longer period as the Secretary may permit), such penalty may be in an amount not more than 100 percent of the amount involved. This subsection shall not apply to a transaction with respect to a plan described in section 4975(e)(1) of Title 26.

(j) Direction and control of litigation by Attorney General—In all civil actions under this subchapter, attorneys appointed by the Secretary may represent the Secretary (except as provided in section 518(a) of Title 28), but all such litigation shall be subject to the direction and control of the Attorney General.

(k) Jurisdiction of actions against the Secretary of Labor—Suits by an administrator, fiduciary, participant, or beneficiary of an employee benefit plan to review a final order of the Secretary, to restrain the Secretary from taking any action contrary to the provisions of this chapter, or to compel him to take action required under this subchapter, may be brought in the district court of the United States for the district where the plan has its principal office, or in the United States District Court for the District of Columbia.

(l) Civil penalties on violations by fiduciaries—

   (1) In the case of—

      (A) any breach of fiduciary responsibility under (or other violation of) part 4 of this subtitle by a fiduciary, or

      (B) any knowing participation in such a breach or violation by any other person,

the Secretary shall assess a civil penalty against such fiduciary or other person in an amount equal to 20 percent of the applicable recovery amount.

   (2) For purposes of paragraph (1), the term "applicable recovery amount" means any amount which is recovered from a fiduciary or other person with respect to a breach or violation described in paragraph (1)—

      (A) pursuant to any settlement agreement with the Secretary, or

(B) ordered by a court to be paid by such fiduciary or other person to a plan or its participants and beneficiaries in a judicial proceeding instituted by the Secretary under subsection (a)(2) or (a)(5) of this section.

(3) The Secretary may, in the Secretary's sole discretion, waive or reduce the penalty under paragraph (1) if the Secretary determines in writing that—

(A) the fiduciary or other person acted reasonably and in good faith, or

(B) it is reasonable to expect that the fiduciary or other person will not be able to restore all losses to the plan (or to provide the relief ordered pursuant to subsection (a)(9) of this section) without severe financial hardship unless such waiver or reduction is granted.

(4) The penalty imposed on a fiduciary or other person under this subsection with respect to any transaction shall be reduced by the amount of any penalty or tax imposed on such fiduciary or other person with respect to such transaction under subsection (i) of this section and section 4975 of Title 26.

(m) In the case of a distribution to a pension plan participant or beneficiary in violation of section 1056(e) of this title by a plan fiduciary, the Secretary shall assess a penalty against such fiduciary in an amount equal to the value of the distribution. Such penalty shall not exceed $10,000 for each such distribution.

§ 503. Claims procedure (§ 1133)

In accordance with regulations of the Secretary, every employee benefit plan shall—

(1) provide adequate notice in writing to any participant or beneficiary whose claim for benefits under the plan has been denied, setting forth the specific reasons for such denial, written in a manner calculated to be understood by the participant, and

(2) afford a reasonable opportunity to any participant whose claim for benefits has been denied for a full and fair review by the appropriate named fiduciary of the decision denying the claim.

§ 504. Investigative authority (§ 1134)

(a) Investigation and submission of reports, books, etc.—The Secretary shall have the power, in order to determine whether any person has violated or is about to violate any provision of this subchapter or any regulation or order thereunder—

(1) to make an investigation, and in connection therewith to require the submission of reports, books, and records, and the filing of data in support of any information required to be filed with the Secretary under this subchapter, and

(2) to enter such places, inspect such books and records and question such persons as he may deem necessary to enable him to determine the facts relative to such investigation, if he has reasonable cause to believe there may exist a violation of this subchapter or any rule or regulation issued thereunder or if the entry is pursuant to an agreement with the plan.

The Secretary may make available to any person actually affected by any matter which is the subject of an investigation under this section, and to any department or agency of the United States, information concerning any matter which may be the subject of such investigation; except that any information obtained by the Secretary pursuant to section 6103(g) of Title 26 shall be made available only in accordance with regulations prescribed by the Secretary of the Treasury.

(b) Frequency of submission of books and records—The Secretary may not under the authority of this section require any plan to submit to the Secretary any books or records of the plan more than once in any 12 month period, unless the Secretary has reasonable cause to believe there may exist a violation of this subchapter or any regulation or order thereunder.

* * *

§ 510. Interference with protected rights (§ 1140)

It shall be unlawful for any person to discharge, fine, suspend, expel, discipline, or discriminate against a participant or beneficiary for exercising any right to which he is entitled under the provisions of an employee benefit plan, this subchapter, section 1201 of this title, or the Welfare and Pension Plans Disclosure Act [29 U.S.C.A. § 301 et seq.], or for the purpose of interfering with the attainment of any right to which such participant may become entitled under the plan, this subchapter, or the Welfare and Pension Plans Disclosure Act. It shall be unlawful for any person to discharge, fine, suspend, expel, or discriminate against any person because he has given information or has testified or is about to testify in any inquiry or proceeding relating to this chapter or the Welfare and Pension Plans Disclosure Act. In the case of a multiemployer plan, it shall be unlawful for the plan sponsor or any other person to discriminate against any contributing employer for exercising rights under this chapter or for giving information or testifying in any inquiry or proceeding relating to this chapter before Congress. The provisions of section 1132 of this title shall be applicable in the enforcement of this section.

§ 511. Coercive interference (§ 1141)

It shall be unlawful for any person through the use of fraud, force, violence, or threat of the use of force or violence, to restrain, coerce, intimidate, or attempt to restrain, coerce, or intimidate any participant or beneficiary for the purpose of interfering with or preventing the exercise of any right to which he is or may become entitled under the plan, this subchapter, section 1201 of this title, or the Welfare and Pension Plans Disclosure Act [29 U.S.C.A. § 301 et seq.]. Any person who willfully violates this section shall be fined $100,000 or imprisoned for not more than 10 years, or both.

§ 514. Other laws (§ 1144)

(a) Supersedure; effective date—Except as provided in subsection (b) of this section, the provisions of this subchapter and subchapter III of this chapter shall supersede any and all State laws insofar as they may now or hereafter relate to any employee benefit plan described in section 1003(a) of this title and not exempt under section 1003(b) of this title. This section shall take effect on January 1, 1975.

(b) Construction and application—

(1) This section shall not apply with respect to any cause of action which arose, or any act or omission which occurred, before January 1, 1975.

(2)(A) Except as provided in subparagraph (B), nothing in this subchapter shall be construed to exempt or relieve any person from any law of any State which regulates insurance, banking, or securities.

(B) Neither an employee benefit plan described in section 1003(a) of this title, which is not exempt under section 1003(b) of this title (other than a plan established primarily for the purpose of providing death benefits), nor any trust established under such a plan, shall be deemed to be an insurance company or other insurer, bank, trust company, or investment company or to be engaged in the business of insurance or

[handwritten: deemer clause]

[handwritten: When the employer self-insures, the plan is outside the insurance savings clause & state regulation is preempted.]

banking for purposes of any law of any State purporting to regulate insurance companies, insurance contracts, banks, trust companies, or investment companies.

(3) Nothing in this section shall be construed to prohibit use by the Secretary of services or facilities of a State agency as permitted under section 1136 of this title.

(4) Subsection (a) of this section shall not apply to any generally applicable criminal law of a State.

(5)(A) Except as provided in subparagraph (B), subsection (a) of this section shall not apply to the Hawaii Prepaid Health Care Act (Haw.Rev.Stat. §§ 393-1 through 393-51).

(B) Nothing in subparagraph (A) shall be construed to exempt from subsection (a) of this section—

(i) any State tax law relating to employee benefit plans, or

(ii) any amendment of the Hawaii Prepaid Health Care Act enacted after September 2, 1974, to the extent it provides for more than the effective administration of such Act as in effect on such date.

(C) Notwithstanding subparagraph (A), parts 1 and 4 of this subtitle, and the preceding sections of this part to the extent they govern matters which are governed by the provisions of such parts 1 and 4, shall supersede the Hawaii Prepaid Health Care Act (as in effect on or after January 14, 1983), but the Secretary may enter into cooperative arrangements under this paragraph and section 1136 of this title with officials of the State of Hawaii to assist them in effectuating the policies of provisions of such Act which are superseded by such parts 1 and 4 and the preceding sections of this part.

(6)(A) Notwithstanding any other provision of this section—

(i) in the case of an employee welfare benefit plan which is a multiple employer welfare arrangement and is fully insured (or which is a multiple employer welfare arrangement subject to an exemption under subparagraph (B)), any law of any State which regulates insurance may apply to such arrangement to the extent that such law provides—

(I) standards, requiring the maintenance of specified levels of reserves and specified levels of contributions, which any such plan, or any trust established under such a plan, must meet in order to be considered under such law able to pay benefits in full when due, and

(II) provisions to enforce such standards, and

(ii) in the case of any other employee welfare benefit plan which is a multiple employer welfare arrangement, in addition to this subchapter, any law of any State which regulates insurance may apply to the extent not inconsistent with the preceding sections of this subchapter.

(B) The Secretary may, under regulations which may be prescribed by the Secretary, exempt from subparagraph (A)(ii), individually or by class, multiple employer welfare arrangements which are not fully insured. Any such exemption may be granted with respect to any arrangement or class of arrangements only if such arrangement or each arrangement which is a member of such class meets the requirements of section 1002(1) and section 1003 of this title necessary to be considered an employee welfare benefit plan to which this subchapter applies.

(C) Nothing in subparagraph (A) shall affect the manner or extent to which the provisions of this subchapter apply to an employee welfare benefit plan which is not a multiple employer welfare arrangement and which is a plan, fund, or program participating in, subscribing to, or otherwise using a multiple employer welfare arrangement to fund or administer benefits to such plan's participants and beneficiaries.

(D) For purposes of this paragraph, a multiple employer welfare arrangement shall be considered fully insured only if the terms of the arrangement provide for benefits the amount of all of which the Secretary determines are guaranteed under a contract, or policy of insurance, issued by an insurance company, insurance service, or insurance organization, qualified to conduct business in a State.

(7) Subsection (a) of this section shall not apply to qualified domestic relations orders (within the meaning of section 1056(d)(3)(B)(i) of this title), qualified medical child support orders (within the meaning of section 1169(a)(2)(A) of this title), and the provisions of law referred to in section 1169(a)(2)(B)(ii) of this title to the extent they apply to qualified medical child support orders.

(8) Subsection (a) of this section shall not be construed to preclude any State cause of action—

(A) with respect to which the State exercises its acquired rights under section 1169(b)(3) of this title with respect to a group health plan (as defined in section 1167(1) of this title), or

(B) for recoupment of payment with respect to items or services pursuant to a State plan for medical assistance approved under title XIX of the Social Security Act [42 U.S.C.A. § 1396 et seq.] which would not have been payable if such acquired rights had been executed before payment with respect to such items or services by the group health plan.

(9) For additional provisions relating to group health plans, see section 1191 of this title.

(c) Definitions—For purposes of this section:

(1) The term "State law" includes all laws, decisions, rules, regulations, or other State action having the effect of law, of any State. A law of the United States applicable only to the District of Columbia shall be treated as a State law rather than a law of the United States.

(2) The term "State" includes a State, any political subdivisions thereof, or any agency or instrumentality of either, which purports to regulate, directly or indirectly, the terms and conditions of employee benefit plans covered by this subchapter.

(d) Alteration, amendment, modification, invalidation, impairment, or supersedure of any law of the United States prohibited—Nothing in this subchapter shall be construed to alter, amend, modify, invalidate, impair, or supersede any law of the United States (except as provided in sections 1031 and 1137(b) of this title) or any rule or regulation issued under any such law.

(e)(1) Notwithstanding any other provision of this section, this subchapter shall supersede any law of a State which would directly or indirectly prohibit or restrict the inclusion in any plan of an automatic contribution arrangement. The Secretary may prescribe regulations which would establish minimum standards that such an arrangement would be required to satisfy in order for this subsection to apply in the case of such arrangement.

(2) For purposes of this subsection, the term 'automatic contribution arrangement' means an arrangement—

(A) under which a participant may elect to have the plan sponsor make payments as contributions under the plan on behalf of the participant, or to the participant directly in cash,

(B) under which a participant is treated as having elected to have the plan sponsor make such contributions in an amount equal to a uniform percentage of compensation provided under the plan until the participant specifically elects not to have such contributions made (or specifically elects to have such contributions made at a different percentage), and

(C) under which such contributions are invested in accordance with regulations prescribed by the Secretary under section 1104(c)(5) of this title.

(3)(A) The plan administrator of an automatic contribution arrangement shall, within a reasonable period before such plan year, provide to each participant to whom the arrangement applies for such plan year notice of the participant's rights and obligations under the arrangement which—

(i) is sufficiently accurate and comprehensive to apprise the participant of such rights and obligations, and

(ii) is written in a manner calculated to be understood by the average participant to whom the arrangement applies.

(B) A notice shall not be treated as meeting the requirements of subparagraph (A) with respect to a participant unless—

(i) the notice includes an explanation of the participant's right under the arrangement not to have elective contributions made on the participant's behalf (or to elect to have such contributions made at a different percentage),

(ii) the participant has a reasonable period of time, after receipt of the notice described in clause (i) and before the first elective contribution is made, to make such election, and

(iii) the notice explains how contributions made under the arrangement will be invested in the absence of any investment election by the participant.

Part 6—Group Health Plans

§ 601. Plans must provide continuation coverage to certain individuals (§ 1161)

(a) In general—The plan sponsor of each group health plan shall provide, in accordance with this part, that each qualified beneficiary who would lose coverage under the plan as a result of a qualifying event is entitled, under the plan, to elect, within the election period, continuation coverage under the plan.

(b) Exception for certain plans—Subsection (a) of this section shall not apply to any group health plan for any calendar year if all employers maintaining such plan normally employed fewer than 20 employees on a typical business day during the preceding calendar year.

§ 602. Continuation coverage (§ 1162)

For purposes of section 1161 of this title, the term "continuation coverage" means coverage under the plan which meets the following requirements:

(1) Type of benefit coverage—The coverage must consist of coverage which, as of the time the coverage is being provided, is identical to the coverage provided under the plan to similarly situated beneficiaries under the plan with respect to whom a qualifying event has not occurred. If coverage is modified under the plan for any group of similarly situated beneficiaries, such coverage shall also be modified in the same manner for all individuals who are qualified beneficiaries under the plan pursuant to this part in connection with such group.

(2) Period of coverage—The coverage must extend for at least the period beginning on the date of the qualifying event and ending not earlier than the earliest of the following:

(A) Maximum required period—

(i) General rule for terminations and reduced hours—In the case of a qualifying event described in section 1163(2) of this title, except as provided in clause (ii), the date which is 18 months after the date of the qualifying event.

(ii) Special rule for multiple qualifying events—If a qualifying event (other than a qualifying event described in section 1163(6) of this title) occurs during the 18 months after the date of a qualifying event described in section 1163(2) of this title, the date which is 36 months after the date of the qualifying event described in section 1163(2) of this title.

(iii) Special rule for certain bankruptcy proceedings—In the case of a qualifying event described in section 1163(6) of this title (relating to bankruptcy proceedings), the date of the death of the covered employee or qualified beneficiary (described in section 1167(3)(C)(iii) of this title), or in the case of the surviving spouse or dependent children of the covered employee, 36 months after the date of the death of the covered employee.

(iv) General rule for other qualifying events—In the case of a qualifying event not described in section 1163(2) or 1163(6) of this title, the date which is 36 months after the date of the qualifying event.

(v) Special rule for PBGC recipients—In the case of a qualifying event described in section 1163(2) of this title with respect to a covered employee who (as of such qualifying event) has a nonforfeitable right to a benefit any portion of which is to be paid by the Pension Benefit Guaranty Corporation under subchapter III of this chapter, notwithstanding clause (i) or (ii), the date of the death of the covered employee, or in the case of the surviving spouse or dependent children of the covered employee, 24 months after the date of the death of the covered employee. The preceding sentence shall not require any period of coverage to extend beyond January 1, 2014.

(vi) Special rule for TAA-eligible individuals—In the case of a qualifying event described in section 1163(2) of this title with respect to a covered employee who is (as of the date that the period of coverage would, but for this clause or clause (vii), otherwise terminate under clause (i) or (ii)) a TAA-eligible individual (as defined in section 1165(b)(4)(B) of this title), the period of coverage shall not terminate by reason of clause (i) or (ii), as the case may be, before the later of the date specified in such clause or the date on which such individual ceases to be such a TAA-eligible individual. The preceding sentence shall not require any period of coverage to extend beyond January 1, 2014.

(vii) Medicare entitlement followed by qualifying event—In the case of a qualifying event described in section 1163(2) of this title that occurs less than 18 months after the date the covered employee became entitled to benefits under title XVIII of the Social Security Act [42 U.S.C.A. § 1395 et seq.], the period of coverage for qualified beneficiaries other than the covered employee shall not terminate under this subparagraph before the close of the 36-month period beginning on the date the covered employee became so entitled.

(viii) Special rule for disability—In the case of a qualified beneficiary who is determined, under title II or XVI of the Social Security Act [42 U.S.C.A. § 401 et seq. or 1381 et seq.], to have been disabled at any time during the first 60 days of continuation coverage under this part, any reference in clause (i) or (ii) to 18 months is deemed a reference to 29 months (with respect to all qualified beneficiaries), but only if the qualified beneficiary has provided notice of such determination under section 1166(3) of this title before the end of such 18 months.

(B) End of plan—The date on which the employer ceases to provide any group health plan to any employee.

(C) Failure to pay premium—The date on which coverage ceases under the plan by reason of a failure to make timely payment of any premium required under the plan with respect to the qualified beneficiary. The payment of any premium (other than any payment referred to in the last sentence of paragraph (3)) shall be considered to be timely if made within 30 days after the date due or within such longer period as applies to or under the plan.

(D) Group health plan coverage or Medicare entitlement—The date on which the qualified beneficiary first becomes, after the date of the election—

(i) covered under any other group health plan (as an employee or otherwise) which does not contain any exclusion or limitation with respect to any preexisting condition of such beneficiary (other than such an exclusion or limitation which does not apply to (or is satisfied by) such beneficiary by reason of chapter 100 of Title 26, part 7 of this subtitle, or title XXVII of the Public Health Service Act [42 U.S.C.A. § 300gg et seq.]), or

(ii) in the case of a qualified beneficiary other than a qualified beneficiary described in section 1167(3)(C) of this title, entitled to benefits under title XVIII of the Social Security Act [42 U.S.C.A. § 1395 et seq.].

(E) Termination of extended coverage for disability—In the case of a qualified beneficiary who is disabled at any time during the first 60 days of continuation coverage under this part, the month that begins more than 30 days after the date of the final determination under title II or XVI of the Social Security Act [42 U.S.C.A. § 401 et seq. or 1381 et seq.] that the qualified beneficiary is no longer disabled.

(3) Premium requirements—The plan may require payment of a premium for any period of continuation coverage, except that such premium—

(A) shall not exceed 102 percent of the applicable premium for such period, and

(B) may, at the election of the payor, be made in monthly installments.

In no event may the plan require the payment of any premium before the day which is 45 days after the day on which the qualified beneficiary made the initial election for continuation coverage. In the case of an individual described in the last sentence of paragraph (2)(A), any reference in subparagraph (A) of this paragraph to "102 percent" is deemed a reference to "150 percent" for any month after the 18th month of continuation coverage described in clause (i) or (ii) of paragraph (2)(A).

(4) No requirement of insurability—The coverage may not be conditioned upon, or discriminate on the basis of lack of, evidence of insurability.

(5) Conversion option—In the case of a qualified beneficiary whose period of continuation coverage expires under paragraph (2)(A), the plan must, during the 180-day period ending on such expiration date, provide to the qualified beneficiary the option of enrollment under a conversion health plan otherwise generally available under the plan.

§ 603. Qualifying event (§ 1163)

For purposes of this part, the term "qualifying event" means, with respect to any covered employee, any of the following events which, but for the continuation coverage required under this part, would result in the loss of coverage of a qualified beneficiary:

(1) The death of the covered employee.

(2) The termination (other than by reason of such employee's gross misconduct), or reduction of hours, of the covered employee's employment.

(3) The divorce or legal separation of the covered employee from the employee's spouse.

(4) The covered employee becoming entitled to benefits under title XVIII of the Social Security Act [42 U.S.C.A. § 1395 et seq.].

(5) A dependent child ceasing to be a dependent child under the generally applicable requirements of the plan.

(6) A proceeding in a case under title 11, commencing on or after July 1, 1986, with respect to the employer from whose employment the covered employee retired at any time.

In the case of an event described in paragraph (6), a loss of coverage includes a substantial elimination of coverage with respect to a qualified beneficiary described in section 1167(3)(C) of this title within one year before or after the date of commencement of the proceeding.

§ 604. Applicable premium (§ 1164)

For purposes of this part—

(1) In general—The term "applicable premium" means, with respect to any period of continuation coverage of qualified beneficiaries, the cost to the plan for such period of the coverage for similarly situated beneficiaries with respect to whom a qualifying event has not occurred (without regard to whether such cost is paid by the employer or employee).

* * *

§ 605. Election (§ 1165)

(a) In general—For purposes of this part—

(1) Election period—The term "election period" means the period which—

(A) begins not later than the date on which coverage terminates under the plan by reason of a qualifying event,

(B) is of at least 60 days' duration, and

(C) ends not earlier than 60 days after the later of—

(i) the date described in subparagraph (A), or

(ii) in the case of any qualified beneficiary who receives notice under section 1166[(a)](4) of this title, the date of such notice.

* * *

§ 606. Notice requirement (§ 1166)

(a) In general—In accordance with regulations prescribed by the Secretary—

(1) the group health plan shall provide, at the time of commencement of coverage under the plan, written notice to each covered employee and spouse of the employee (if any) of the rights provided under this subsection.

(2) the employer of an employee under a plan must notify the administrator of a qualifying event described in paragraph (1), (2), (4), or (6) of section 1163 of this title within 30 days (or, in the case of a group health plan which is a multiemployer plan, such longer period of time as may be provided in the terms of the plan) of the date of the qualifying event,

(3) each covered employee or qualified beneficiary is responsible for notifying the administrator of the occurrence of any qualifying event described in paragraph (3) or (5) of section 1163 of this title within 60 days after the qualifying event and each qualified beneficiary who is determined, under title II or XVI of the Social Security Act [42 U.S.C.A. § 401 et seq. or 1381 et seq.], to have been disabled at any time during the first 60 days of continuation coverage under this part is responsible for notifying the plan administrator of such determination within 60 days after the date of the determination and for notifying the plan administrator within 30 days after the date of any final determination under such title or titles that the qualified beneficiary is no longer disabled, and

(4) the administrator shall notify—

(A) in the case of a qualifying event described in paragraph (1), (2), (4), or (6) of section 1163 of this title, any qualified beneficiary with respect to such event, and

(B) in the case of a qualifying event described in paragraph (3) or (5) of section 1163 of this title where the covered employee notifies the administrator under paragraph (3), any qualified beneficiary with respect to such event,

of such beneficiary's rights under this subsection.

* * *

§ 607. Definitions and special rules (§ 1167)

For purposes of this part—

(1) Group health plan—The term "group health plan" means an employee welfare benefit plan providing medical care (as defined in section 213(d) of Title 26) to participants or beneficiaries directly or through insurance, reimbursement, or otherwise. Such term shall not include any plan substantially all of the coverage under which is for qualified long-term care services (as defined in section 7702B(c) of Title 26).

(2) Covered employee—The term "covered employee" means an individual who is (or was) provided coverage under a group health plan by virtue of the performance of services by the individual for 1 or more persons maintaining the plan (including as an employee defined in section 401(c)(1) of Title 26).

(3) Qualified beneficiary—

(A) In general—The term "qualified beneficiary" means, with respect to a covered employee under a group health plan, any other individual who, on the day before the qualifying event for that employee, is a beneficiary under the plan—

(i) as the spouse of the covered employee, or

(ii) as the dependent child of the employee.

Such term shall also include a child who is born to or placed for adoption with the covered employee during the period of continuation coverage under this part.

(B) Special rule for terminations and reduced employment—In the case of a qualifying event described in section 1163(2) of this title, the term "qualified beneficiary" includes the covered employee.

(C) Special rule for retirees and widows—In the case of a qualifying event described in section 1163(6) of this title, the term "qualified beneficiary" includes a covered employee who had retired on or before the date of substantial elimination of coverage and any other individual who, on the day before such qualifying event, is a beneficiary under the plan—

(i) as the spouse of the covered employee,

(ii) as the dependent child of the employee, or

(iii) as the surviving spouse of the covered employee.

(4) Employer—Subsection (n) (relating to leased employees) and subsection (t) (relating to application of controlled group rules to certain employee benefits) of section 414 of Title 26 shall apply for purposes of this part in the same manner and to the same extent as such subsections apply for purposes of section 106 of Title 26. Any regulations prescribed by the Secretary pursuant to the preceding sentence shall be consistent and coextensive with any regulations prescribed for similar purposes by the Secretary of the Treasury (or such Secretary's delegate) under such subsections.

(5) Optional extension of required periods—A group health plan shall not be treated as failing to meet the requirements of this part solely because the plan provides both—

(A) that the period of extended coverage referred to in section 1162(2) of this title commences with the date of the loss of coverage, and

(B) that the applicable notice period provided under section 1166(a)(2) of this title commences with the date of the loss of coverage.

§ 609. Additional standards for group health plans (§ 1169)

(a) Group health plan coverage pursuant to medical child support orders—

(1) In general—Each group health plan shall provide benefits in accordance with the applicable requirements of any qualified medical child support order. A qualified medical child support order with respect to any participant or beneficiary shall be deemed to apply to each group health plan which has received such order, from which the participant or beneficiary is eligible to receive benefits, and with respect to which the requirements of paragraph (4) are met.

(2) **Definitions**—For purposes of this subsection—

(A) **Qualified medical child support order**—The term "qualified medical child support order" means a medical child support order—

(i) which creates or recognizes the existence of an alternate recipient's right to, or assigns to an alternate recipient the right to, receive benefits for which a participant or beneficiary is eligible under a group health plan, and

(ii) with respect to which the requirements of paragraphs (3) and (4) are met.

(B) **Medical child support order**—The term "medical child support order" means any judgment, decree, or order (including approval of a settlement agreement) which—

(i) provides for child support with respect to a child of a participant under a group health plan or provides for health benefit coverage to such a child, is made pursuant to a State domestic relations law (including a community property law), and relates to benefits under such plan, or

(ii) is made pursuant to a law relating to medical child support described in section 1908 of the Social Security Act [42 U.S.C.A. § 1396g-1] (as added by section 13822 of the Omnibus Budget Reconciliation Act of 1993) with respect to a group health plan,

if such judgment, decree, or order (I) is issued by a court of competent jurisdiction or (II) is issued through an administrative process established under State law and has the force and effect of law under applicable State law. For purposes of this subparagraph, an administrative notice which is issued pursuant to an administrative process referred to in subclause (II) of the preceding sentence and which has the effect of an order described in clause (i) or (ii) of the preceding sentence shall be treated as such an order.

(C) **Alternate recipient**—The term "alternate recipient" means any child of a participant who is recognized under a medical child support order as having a right to enrollment under a group health plan with respect to such participant.

(D) **Child**—The term "child" includes any child adopted by, or placed for adoption with, a participant of a group health plan.

(3) **Information to be included in qualified order**—A medical child support order meets the requirements of this paragraph only if such order clearly specifies—

(A) the name and the last known mailing address (if any) of the participant and the name and mailing address of each alternate recipient covered by the order, except that, to the extent provided in the order, the name and mailing address of an official of a State or a political subdivision thereof may be substituted for the mailing address of any such alternate recipient,

(B) a reasonable description of the type of coverage to be provided to each such alternate recipient, or the manner in which such type of coverage is to be determined, and

(C) the period to which such order applies.

(4) **Restriction on new types or forms of benefits**—A medical child support order meets the requirements of this paragraph only if such order does not require a plan to provide any type or form of benefit, or any option, not otherwise provided under the plan, except to the extent necessary to meet the requirements of a law relating to medical child sup-

port described in section 1908 of the Social Security Act [42 U.S.C.A. § 1396g-1] (as added by section 13822 of the Omnibus Budget Reconciliation Act of 1993).

(5) Procedural requirements—

(A) Timely notifications and determinations—In the case of any medical child support order received by a group health plan—

(i) the plan administrator shall promptly notify the participant and each alternate recipient of the receipt of such order and the plan's procedures for determining whether medical child support orders are qualified medical child support orders, and

(ii) within a reasonable period after receipt of such order, the plan administrator shall determine whether such order is a qualified medical child support order and notify the participant and each alternate recipient of such determination.

(B) Establishment of procedures for determining qualified status of orders— Each group health plan shall establish reasonable procedures to determine whether medical child support orders are qualified medical child support orders and to administer the provision of benefits under such qualified orders. Such procedures—

(i) shall be in writing,

(ii) shall provide for the notification of each person specified in a medical child support order as eligible to receive benefits under the plan (at the address included in the medical child support order) of such procedures promptly upon receipt by the plan of the medical child support order, and

(iii) shall permit an alternate recipient to designate a representative for receipt of copies of notices that are sent to the alternate recipient with respect to a medical child support order.

(C) National Medical Support Notice deemed to be a qualified medical child support order—

(i) **In general**—If the plan administrator of a group health plan which is maintained by the employer of a noncustodial parent of a child or to which such an employer contributes receives an appropriately completed National Medical Support Notice promulgated pursuant to section 401(b) of the Child Support Performance and Incentive Act of 1998 in the case of such child, and the Notice meets the requirements of paragraphs (3) and (4), the Notice shall be deemed to be a qualified medical child support order in the case of such child.

(ii) **Enrollment of child in plan**—In any case in which an appropriately completed National Medical Support Notice is issued in the case of a child of a participant under a group health plan who is a noncustodial parent of the child, and the Notice is deemed under clause (i) to be a qualified medical child support order, the plan administrator, within 40 business days after the date of the Notice, shall—

(I) notify the State agency issuing the Notice with respect to such child whether coverage of the child is available under the terms of the plan and, if so, whether such child is covered under the plan and either the effective date of the coverage or, if necessary, any steps to be taken by the custodial parent (or by the official of a State or political subdivision thereof substituted for the name of such child pursuant to paragraph (3)(A)) to effectuate the coverage; and

> **(II)** provide to the custodial parent (or such substituted official) a description of the coverage available and any forms or documents necessary to effectuate such coverage.

(iii) Rule of construction—Nothing in this subparagraph shall be construed as requiring a group health plan, upon receipt of a National Medical Support Notice, to provide benefits under the plan (or eligibility for such benefits) in addition to benefits (or eligibility for benefits) provided under the terms of the plan as of immediately before receipt of such Notice.

(6) Actions taken by fiduciaries—If a plan fiduciary acts in accordance with part 4 of this subtitle in treating a medical child support order as being (or not being) a qualified medical child support order, then the plan's obligation to the participant and each alternate recipient shall be discharged to the extent of any payment made pursuant to such act of the fiduciary.

(7) Treatment of alternate recipients—

(A) Treatment as beneficiary generally—A person who is an alternate recipient under a qualified medical child support order shall be considered a beneficiary under the plan for purposes of any provision of this chapter.

(B) Treatment as participant for purposes of reporting and disclosure requirements—A person who is an alternate recipient under any medical child support order shall be considered a participant under the plan for purposes of the reporting and disclosure requirements of part 1 of this subtitle.

(8) Direct provision of benefits provided to alternate recipients—Any payment for benefits made by a group health plan pursuant to a medical child support order in reimbursement for expenses paid by an alternate recipient or an alternate recipient's custodial parent or legal guardian shall be made to the alternate recipient or the alternate recipient's custodial parent or legal guardian.

(9) Payment to State official treated as satisfaction of plan's obligation to make payment to alternate recipient—Payment of benefits by a group health plan to an official of a State or a political subdivision thereof whose name and address have been substituted for the address of an alternate recipient in a qualified medical child support order, pursuant to paragraph (3)(A), shall be treated, for purposes of this subchapter, as payment of benefits to the alternate recipient.

* * *

Part 7—Group Health Plan Requirements

§ 701. Increased portability through limitation on preexisting condition exclusions (§ 1181)

(a) Limitation on preexisting condition exclusion period; crediting for periods of previous coverage—Subject to subsection (d), a group health plan, and a health insurance issuer offering group health insurance coverage, may, with respect to a participant or beneficiary, impose a preexisting condition exclusion only if—

(1) such exclusion relates to a condition (whether physical or mental), regardless of the cause of the condition, for which medical advice, diagnosis, care, or treatment was recommended or received within the 6-month period ending on the enrollment date;

(2) such exclusion extends for a period of not more than 12 months (or 18 months in the case of a late enrollee) after the enrollment date; and

(3) the period of any such preexisting condition exclusion is reduced by the aggregate of the periods of creditable coverage (if any, as defined in subsection (c)(1) of this section) applicable to the participant or beneficiary as of the enrollment date.

(b) Definitions—For purposes of this part—

(1) Preexisting condition exclusion—

(A) In general—The term "preexisting condition exclusion" means, with respect to coverage, a limitation or exclusion of benefits relating to a condition based on the fact that the condition was present before the date of enrollment for such coverage, whether or not any medical advice, diagnosis, care, or treatment was recommended or received before such date.

(B) Treatment of genetic information—Genetic information shall not be treated as a condition described in subsection (a)(1) of this section in the absence of a diagnosis of the condition related to such information.

(2) Enrollment date—The term "enrollment date" means, with respect to an individual covered under a group health plan or health insurance coverage, the date of enrollment of the individual in the plan or coverage or, if earlier, the first day of the waiting period for such enrollment.

(3) Late enrollee—The term "late enrollee" means, with respect to coverage under a group health plan, a participant or beneficiary who enrolls under the plan other than during—

(A) the first period in which the individual is eligible to enroll under the plan, or

(B) a special enrollment period under subsection (f) of this section.

(4) Waiting period—The term "waiting period" means, with respect to a group health plan and an individual who is a potential participant or beneficiary in the plan, the period that must pass with respect to the individual before the individual is eligible to be covered for benefits under the terms of the plan.

(c) Rules relating to crediting previous coverage—

(1) "Creditable coverage" defined—For purposes of this part, the term "creditable coverage" means, with respect to an individual, coverage of the individual under any of the following:

(A) A group health plan.

(B) Health insurance coverage.

(C) Part A or part B of title XVIII of the Social Security Act 42 U.S.C.A. § 1395c et seq. or 1395j et seq.].

(D) Title XIX of the Social Security Act [42 U.S.C.A. § 1396 et seq.], other than coverage consisting solely of benefits under section 1928 [42 U.S.C.A. § 1396s].

(E) Chapter 55 of title 10.

(F) A medical care program of the Indian Health Service or of a tribal organization.

(G) A State health benefits risk pool.

(H) A health plan offered under chapter 89 of title 5.

(I) A public health plan (as defined in regulations).

(J) A health benefit plan under section 2504(e) of Title 22.

Such term does not include coverage consisting solely of coverage of excepted benefits (as defined in section 1191b(c) of this title).

(2) Not counting periods before significant breaks in coverage—

(A) In general—A period of creditable coverage shall not be counted, with respect to enrollment of an individual under a group health plan, if, after such period and before the enrollment date, there was a 63-day period during all of which the individual was not covered under any creditable coverage.

(B) Waiting period not treated as a break in coverage—For purposes of subparagraph (A) and subsection (d)(4) of this section, any period that an individual is in a waiting period for any coverage under a group health plan (or for group health insurance coverage) or is in an affiliation period (as defined in subsection (g)(2) of this section) shall not be taken into account in determining the continuous period under subparagraph (A).

* * *

(3) Method of crediting coverage—

(A) Standard method—Except as otherwise provided under subparagraph (B), for purposes of applying subsection (a)(3) of this section, a group health plan, and a health insurance issuer offering group health insurance coverage, shall count a period of creditable coverage without regard to the specific benefits covered during the period.

(B) Election of alternative method—A group health plan, or a health insurance issuer offering group health insurance coverage, may elect to apply subsection (a)(3) of this section based on coverage of benefits within each of several classes or categories of benefits specified in regulations rather than as provided under subparagraph (A). Such election shall be made on a uniform basis for all participants and beneficiaries. Under such election a group health plan or issuer shall count a period of creditable coverage with respect to any class or category of benefits if any level of benefits is covered within such class or category.

(C) Plan notice—In the case of an election with respect to a group health plan under subparagraph (B) (whether or not health insurance coverage is provided in connection with such plan), the plan shall—

(i) prominently state in any disclosure statements concerning the plan, and state to each enrollee at the time of enrollment under the plan, that the plan has made such election, and

(ii) include in such statements a description of the effect of this election.

(4) Establishment of period—Periods of creditable coverage with respect to an individual shall be established through presentation of certifications described in subsection (e) of this section or in such other manner as may be specified in regulations.

(d) Exceptions—

(1) Exclusion not applicable to certain newborns—Subject to paragraph (4), a group health plan, and a health insurance issuer offering group health insurance coverage, may not impose any preexisting condition exclusion in the case of an individual who, as of the last day of the 30-day period beginning with the date of birth, is covered under creditable coverage.

(2) Exclusion not applicable to certain adopted children—Subject to paragraph (4), a group health plan, and a health insurance issuer offering group health insurance coverage, may not impose any preexisting condition exclusion in the case of a child who is adopted or placed for adoption before attaining 18 years of age and who, as of the last day of the 30-day period beginning on the date of the adoption or placement for adoption, is covered under creditable coverage. The previous sentence shall not apply to coverage before the date of such adoption or placement for adoption.

(3) Exclusion not applicable to pregnancy—A group health plan, and health insurance issuer offering group health insurance coverage, may not impose any preexisting condition exclusion relating to pregnancy as a preexisting condition.

(4) Loss if break in coverage—Paragraphs (1) and (2) shall no longer apply to an individual after the end of the first 63-day period during all of which the individual was not covered under any creditable coverage.

* * *

§ 702. Prohibiting discrimination against individual participants and beneficiaries based on health status (§ 1182)

(a) In eligibility to enroll—

(1) In general—Subject to paragraph (2), a group health plan, and a health insurance issuer offering group health insurance coverage in connection with a group health plan, may not establish rules for eligibility (including continued eligibility) of any individual to enroll under the terms of the plan based on any of the following health status-related factors in relation to the individual or a dependent of the individual:

(A) Health status.

(B) Medical condition (including both physical and mental illnesses).

(C) Claims experience.

(D) Receipt of health care.

(E) Medical history.

(F) Genetic information.

(G) Evidence of insurability (including conditions arising out of acts of domestic violence).

(H) Disability.

(2) No application to benefits or exclusions—To the extent consistent with section 1181 of this title, paragraph (1) shall not be construed—

(A) to require a group health plan, or group health insurance coverage, to provide particular benefits other than those provided under the terms of such plan or coverage, or

(B) to prevent such a plan or coverage from establishing limitations or restrictions on the amount, level, extent, or nature of the benefits or coverage for similarly situated individuals enrolled in the plan or coverage.

(3) Construction—For purposes of paragraph (1), rules for eligibility to enroll under a plan include rules defining any applicable waiting periods for such enrollment.

(b) In premium contributions—

(1) In general—A group health plan, and a health insurance issuer offering health insurance coverage in connection with a group health plan, may not require any individual (as a condition of enrollment or continued enrollment under the plan) to pay a premium or contribution which is greater than such premium or contribution for a similarly situated individual enrolled in the plan on the basis of any health status-related factor in relation to the individual or to an individual enrolled under the plan as a dependent of the individual.

(2) Construction—Nothing in paragraph (1) shall be construed—

(A) to restrict the amount that an employer may be charged for coverage under a group health plan except as provided in paragraph (3); or

(B) to prevent a group health plan, and a health insurance issuer offering group health insurance coverage, from establishing premium discounts or rebates or modifying otherwise applicable copayments or deductibles in return for adherence to programs of health promotion and disease prevention.

(3) No group-based discrimination on basis of genetic information—

(A) In general— For purposes of this section, a group health plan, and a health insurance issuer offering group health insurance coverage in connection with a group health plan, may not adjust premium or contribution amounts for the group covered under such plan on the basis of genetic information.

(B) Rule of construction—Nothing in subparagraph (A) or in paragraphs (1) and (2) of subsection (d) shall be construed to limit the ability of a health insurance issuer offering health insurance coverage in connection with a group health plan to increase the premium for an employer based on the manifestation of a disease or disorder of an individual who is enrolled in the plan. In such case, the manifestation of a disease or disorder in one individual cannot also be used as genetic information about other group members and to further increase the premium for the employer.

(c) Genetic testing—

(1) Limitation on requesting or requiring genetic testing—A group health plan, and a health insurance issuer offering health insurance coverage in connection with a group health plan, shall not request or require an individual or a family member of such individual to undergo a genetic test.

(2) Rule of construction—Paragraph (1) shall not be construed to limit the authority of a health care professional who is providing health care services to an individual to request that such individual undergo a genetic test.

(3) Rule of construction regarding payment—

(A) In general—Nothing in paragraph (1) shall be construed to preclude a group health plan, or a health insurance issuer offering health insurance coverage in connection with a group health plan, from obtaining and using the results of a genetic test in making a determination regarding payment (as such term is defined for the purposes of applying the regulations promulgated by the Secretary of Health and Human Services under part C of title XI of the Social Security Act and section 264 of the Health Insurance Portability and Accountability Act of 1996, as may be revised from time to time) consistent with subsection (a).

(B) Limitation—For purposes of subparagraph (A), a group health plan, or a health insurance issuer offering health insurance coverage in connection with a group health plan, may request only the minimum amount of information necessary to accomplish the intended purpose.

(4) Research exception—Notwithstanding paragraph (1), a group health plan, or a health insurance issuer offering health insurance coverage in connection with a group health plan, may request, but not require, that a participant or beneficiary undergo a genetic test if each of the following conditions is met:

(A) The request is made, in writing, pursuant to research that complies with part 46 of title 45, Code of Federal Regulations, or equivalent Federal regulations, and any applicable State or local law or regulations for the protection of human subjects in research.

(B) The plan or issuer clearly indicates to each participant or beneficiary, or in the case of a minor child, to the legal guardian of such beneficiary, to whom the request is made that—

(i) compliance with the request is voluntary; and

(ii) non-compliance will have no effect on enrollment status or premium or contribution amounts.

(C) No genetic information collected or acquired under this paragraph shall be used for underwriting purposes.

(D) The plan or issuer notifies the Secretary in writing that the plan or issuer is conducting activities pursuant to the exception provided for under this paragraph, including a description of the activities conducted.

(E) The plan or issuer complies with such other conditions as the Secretary may by regulation require for activities conducted under this paragraph.

(d) Prohibition on collection of genetic information—

(1) In general—A group health plan, and a health insurance issuer offering health insurance coverage in connection with a group health plan, shall not request, require, or purchase genetic information for underwriting purposes (as defined in section 1191b of this title).

(2) Prohibition on collection of genetic information prior to enrollment—A group health plan, and a health insurance issuer offering health insurance coverage in connection with a group health plan, shall not request, require, or purchase genetic information with respect to any individual prior to such individual's enrollment under the plan or coverage in connection with such enrollment.

(3) Incidental collection—If a group health plan, or a health insurance issuer offering health insurance coverage in connection with a group health plan, obtains genetic information incidental to the requesting, requiring, or purchasing of other information concerning any individual, such request, requirement, or purchase shall not be considered a violation of paragraph (2) if such request, requirement, or purchase is not in violation of paragraph (1).

(e) Application to all plans—The provisions of subsections (a)(1)(F), (b)(3), (c), and (d), and subsection (b)(1) and section 1181 of this title with respect to genetic information, shall apply to group health plans and health insurance issuers without regard to section 1191a(a) of this title.

(f) Genetic information of a fetus or embryo—Any reference in this part to genetic information concerning an individual or family member of an individual shall—

(1) with respect to such an individual or family member of an individual who is a pregnant woman, include genetic information of any fetus carried by such pregnant woman; and

(2) with respect to an individual or family member utilizing an assisted reproductive technology, include genetic information of any embryo legally held by the individual or family member.

§ 711. Standards relating to benefits for mothers and newborns (§ 1185)

(a) Requirements for minimum hospital stay following birth—

(1) In general—A group health plan, and a health insurance issuer offering group health insurance coverage, may not—

(A) except as provided in paragraph (2)—

(i) restrict benefits for any hospital length of stay in connection with childbirth for the mother or newborn child, following a normal vaginal delivery, to less than 48 hours, or

(ii) restrict benefits for any hospital length of stay in connection with childbirth for the mother or newborn child, following a cesarean section, to less than 96 hours; or

(B) require that a provider obtain authorization from the plan or the issuer for prescribing any length of stay required under subparagraph (A) (without regard to paragraph (2)).

(2) Exception—Paragraph (1)(A) shall not apply in connection with any group health plan or health insurance issuer in any case in which the decision to discharge the mother or her newborn child prior to the expiration of the minimum length of stay otherwise required under paragraph (1)(A) is made by an attending provider in consultation with the mother.

* * *

§ 712. Parity in mental health and substance use disorder benefits (§ 1185a)

(a) In general—

(1) Aggregate lifetime limits—In the case of a group health plan (or health insurance coverage offered in connection with such a plan) that provides both medical and surgical benefits and mental health or substance use disorder benefits—

(A) No lifetime limit—If the plan or coverage does not include an aggregate lifetime limit on substantially all medical and surgical benefits, the plan or coverage may not impose any aggregate lifetime limit on mental health or substance use disorder benefits.

(B) Lifetime limit—If the plan or coverage includes an aggregate lifetime limit on substantially all medical and surgical benefits (in this paragraph referred to as the "applicable lifetime limit"), the plan or coverage shall either—

(i) apply the applicable lifetime limit both to the medical and surgical benefits to which it otherwise would apply and to mental health and substance use disorder benefits and not distinguish in the application of such limit between such medical and surgical benefits and mental health and substance use disorder benefits; or

(ii) not include any aggregate lifetime limit on mental health or substance use disorder benefits that is less than the applicable lifetime limit.

* * *

(2) Annual limits—In the case of a group health plan (or health insurance coverage offered in connection with such a plan) that provides both medical and surgical benefits and mental health benefits—

(A) No annual limit—If the plan or coverage does not include an annual limit on substantially all medical and surgical benefits, the plan or coverage may not impose any annual limit on mental health or substance use disorder benefits.

(B) Annual limit—If the plan or coverage includes an annual limit on substantially all medical and surgical benefits (in this paragraph referred to as the "applicable annual limit"), the plan or coverage shall either—

(i) apply the applicable annual limit both to medical and surgical benefits to which it otherwise would apply and to mental health and substance use disorder benefits and not distinguish in the application of such limit between such medical and surgical benefits and mental health and substance use disorder benefits; or

(ii) not include any annual limit on mental health or substance use disorder benefits that is less than the applicable annual limit.

* * *

(b) Construction—Nothing in this section shall be construed—

(1) as requiring a group health plan (or health insurance coverage offered in connection with such a plan) to provide any mental health or substance use disorder benefits; or

(2) in the case of a group health plan (or health insurance coverage offered in connection with such a plan) that provides mental health or substance use disorder benefits, as affecting the terms and conditions of the plan or coverage relating to such benefits under the plan or coverage, except as provided in subsection (a).

(c) Exemptions—

(1) Small employer exemption—

(A) In general—This section shall not apply to any group health plan (and group health insurance coverage offered in connection with a group health plan) for any plan year of a small employer.

(B) Small employer— For purposes of subparagraph (A), the term "small employer" means, in connection with a group health plan with respect to a calendar year and a plan year, an employer who employed an average of at least 2 (or 1 in the case of an employer residing in a State that permits small groups to include a single individual) but not more than 50 employees on business days during the preceding calendar year.

* * *

(2) Cost exemption—

(A) In general—With respect to a group health plan (or health insurance coverage offered in connection with such a plan), if the application of this section to such plan (or coverage) results in an increase for the plan year involved of the actual total costs of coverage with respect to medical and surgical benefits and mental health and substance use disorder benefits under the plan (as determined and certified under subparagraph (C)) by an amount that exceeds the applicable percentage described in subparagraph (B) of the actual total plan costs, the provisions of this section shall not apply to such plan (or coverage) during the following plan year, and such exemption shall apply to the plan (or coverage) for 1 plan year. An employer may elect to continue to apply mental health and substance use disorder parity pursuant to this section with respect to the group health plan (or coverage) involved regardless of any increase in total costs.

(B) Applicable percentage—With respect to a plan (or coverage), the applicable percentage described in this subparagraph shall be—

(i) 2 percent in the case of the first plan year in which this section is applied; and

(ii) 1 percent in the case of each subsequent plan year.

* * *

(e) Definitions—For purposes of this section—

* * *

(4) Mental health benefits—The term "mental health benefits" means benefits with respect to services for mental health conditions, as defined under the terms of the plan and in accordance with applicable Federal and State law.

(5) Substance use disorder benefits—The term "substance use disorder benefits" means benefits with respect to services for substance use disorders, as defined under the terms of the plan and in accordance with applicable Federal and State law.

* * *

§ 713. Required coverage for reconstructive surgery following mastectomies (§ 1185b)

(a) In general—A group health plan, and a health insurance issuer providing health insurance coverage in connection with a group health plan, that provides medical and surgical benefits with respect to a mastectomy shall provide, in a case of a participant or beneficiary who is receiving benefits in connection with a mastectomy and who elects breast reconstruction in connection with such mastectomy, coverage for—

(1) all stages of reconstruction of the breast on which the mastectomy has been performed;

(2) surgery and reconstruction of the other breast to produce a symmetrical appearance; and

(3) prostheses and physical complications of mastectomy, including lymphedemas;

in a manner determined in consultation with the attending physician and the patient. Such coverage may be subject to annual deductibles and coinsurance provisions as may be deemed appropriate and as are consistent with those established for other benefits under the plan or coverage. Written notice of the availability of such coverage shall be delivered to the participant upon enrollment and annually thereafter.

* * *

§ 715. Additional market reforms (§ 1185d)

(a) General rule. Except as provided in subsection (b)—

(1) the provisions of part A of title XXVII of the Public Health Service Act (as amended by the Patient Protection and Affordable Care Act) shall apply to group health plans, and health insurance issuers providing health insurance coverage in connection with group health plans, as if included in this subpart; and

(2) to the extent that any provision of this part conflicts with a provision of such part A with respect to group health plans, or health insurance issuers providing health insurance coverage in connection with group health plans, the provisions of such part A shall apply.

(b) Exception. Notwithstanding subsection (a), the provisions of sections 2716 and 2718 of title XXVII of the Public Health Service Act (as amended by the Patient Protection and Affordable Care Act) shall not apply with respect to self-insured group health plans, and the provisions of this part shall continue to apply to such plans as if such sections of the Public Health Service Act (as so amended) had not been enacted.

§ 731. Preemption; State flexibility; construction (§ 1191)

(a) Continued applicability of State law with respect to health insurance issuers—

(1) In general—Subject to paragraph (2) and except as provided in subsection (b) of this section, this part shall not be construed to supersede any provision of State law which establishes, implements, or continues in effect any standard or requirement solely relating to health insurance issuers in connection with group health insurance coverage except to the extent that such standard or requirement prevents the application of a requirement of this part.

(2) Continued preemption with respect to group health plans—Nothing in this part shall be construed to affect or modify the provisions of section 1144 of this title with respect to group health plans.

(b) Special rules in case of portability requirements—

(1) In general—Subject to paragraph (2), the provisions of this part relating to health insurance coverage offered by a health insurance issuer supersede any provision of State law which establishes, implements, or continues in effect a standard or requirement applicable to imposition of a preexisting condition exclusion specifically governed by section 1181 of this title which differs from the standards or requirements specified in such section.

(2) Exceptions—Only in relation to health insurance coverage offered by a health insurance issuer, the provisions of this part do not supersede any provision of State law to the extent that such provision—

(A) substitutes for the reference to "6-month period" in section 1181(a)(1) of this title a reference to any shorter period of time;

(B) substitutes for the reference to "12 months" and "18 months" in section 1181(a)(2) of this title a reference to any shorter period of time;

(C) substitutes for the references to "63 days" in sections 1181(c)(2)(A) and (d)(4)(A) of this title a reference to any greater number of days;

(D) substitutes for the reference to "30-day period" in sections 1181(b)(2) and (d)(1) of this title a reference to any greater period;

(E) prohibits the imposition of any preexisting condition exclusion in cases not described in section 1181(d) of this title or expands the exceptions described in such section;

(F) requires special enrollment periods in addition to those required under section 1181(f) of this title; or

(G) reduces the maximum period permitted in an affiliation period under section 1181(g)(1)(B) of this title.

(c) Rules of construction—Except as provided in section 1185 of this title, nothing in this part shall be construed as requiring a group health plan or health insurance coverage to provide specific benefits under the terms of such plan or coverage.

(d) Definitions—For purposes of this section—

(1) State law—The term "State law" includes all laws, decisions, rules, regulations, or other State action having the effect of law, of any State. A law of the United States applicable only to the District of Columbia shall be treated as a State law rather than a law of the United States.

(2) State—The term "State" includes a State, the Northern Mariana Islands, any political subdivisions of a State or such Islands, or any agency or instrumentality of either.

§ 733. Definitions (§ 1191b)

(a) Group health plan—For purposes of this part—

(1) In general—The term "group health plan" means an employee welfare benefit plan to the extent that the plan provides medical care (as defined in paragraph (2) and including items and services paid for as medical care) to employees or their dependents (as defined under the terms of the plan) directly or through insurance, reimbursement, or otherwise.

(2) Medical care—The term "medical care" means amounts paid for—

(A) the diagnosis, cure, mitigation, treatment, or prevention of disease, or amounts paid for the purpose of affecting any structure or function of the body,

(B) amounts paid for transportation primarily for and essential to medical care referred to in subparagraph (A), and

(C) amounts paid for insurance covering medical care referred to in subparagraphs (A) and (B).

(b) Definitions relating to health insurance—For purposes of this part—

(1) Health insurance coverage—The term "health insurance coverage" means benefits consisting of medical care (provided directly, through insurance or reimbursement, or otherwise and including items and services paid for as medical care) under any hospital or medical service policy or certificate, hospital or medical service plan contract, or health maintenance organization contract offered by a health insurance issuer.

(2) Health insurance issuer—The term "health insurance issuer" means an insurance company, insurance service, or insurance organization (including a health maintenance organization, as defined in paragraph (3)) which is licensed to engage in the business of insurance in a State and which is subject to State law which regulates insurance (within the meaning of section 1144(b)(2) of this title). Such term does not include a group health plan.

(3) Health maintenance organization—The term "health maintenance organization" means—

(A) a federally qualified health maintenance organization (as defined in section 1301(a) of the Public Health Service Act (42 U.S.C. 300e(a))),

(B) an organization recognized under State law as a health maintenance organization, or

(C) a similar organization regulated under State law for solvency in the same manner and to the same extent as such a health maintenance organization.

(4) Group health insurance coverage—The term "group health insurance coverage" means, in connection with a group health plan, health insurance coverage offered in connection with such plan.

(c) Excepted benefits—For purposes of this part, the term "excepted benefits" means benefits under one or more (or any combination thereof) of the following:

(1) Benefits not subject to requirements—

(A) Coverage only for accident, or disability income insurance, or any combination thereof.

(B) Coverage issued as a supplement to liability insurance.

(C) Liability insurance, including general liability insurance and automobile liability insurance.

(D) Workers' compensation or similar insurance.

(E) Automobile medical payment insurance.

(F) Credit-only insurance.

(G) Coverage for on-site medical clinics.

(H) Other similar insurance coverage, specified in regulations, under which benefits for medical care are secondary or incidental to other insurance benefits.

(2) Benefits not subject to requirements if offered separately—

(A) Limited scope dental or vision benefits.

(B) Benefits for long-term care, nursing home care, home health care, community-based care, or any combination thereof.

(C) Such other similar, limited benefits as are specified in regulations.

(3) Benefits not subject to requirements if offered as independent, noncoordinated benefits—

(A) Coverage only for a specified disease or illness.

(B) Hospital indemnity or other fixed indemnity insurance.

(4) Benefits not subject to requirements if offered as separate insurance policy— Medicare supplemental health insurance (as defined under section 1395ss(g)(1) of Title 42), coverage supplemental to the coverage provided under chapter 55 of title 10, United States Code, and similar supplemental coverage provided to coverage under a group health plan.

(d) Other definitions—For purposes of this part—

(1) COBRA continuation provision—The term "COBRA continuation provision" means any of the following:

(A) Part 6 of this subtitle.

(B) Section 4980B of Title 26, other than subsection (f)(1) of such section insofar as it relates to pediatric vaccines.

(C) Title XXII of the Public Health Service Act [42 U.S.C.A. § 300bb-1 et seq.].

(2) Health status-related factor—The term "health status-related factor" means any of the factors described in section 1182(a)(1) of this title.

(3) Network plan—The term "network plan" means health insurance coverage offered by a health insurance issuer under which the financing and delivery of medical care (including items and services paid for as medical care) are provided, in whole or in part, through a defined set of providers under contract with the issuer.

(4) Placed for adoption—The term "placement", or being "placed", for adoption, has the meaning given such term in section 1169(c)(3)(B) of this title.

(5) Family member—The term "family member" means, with respect to an individual—

(A) a dependent (as such term is used for purposes of section 1181(f)(2) of this title) of such individual, and

(B) any other individual who is a first-degree, second-degree, third-degree, or fourth-degree relative of such individual or of an individual described in subparagraph (A).

(6) Genetic information—

(A) In general—The term "genetic information" means, with respect to any individual, information about—

(i) such individual's genetic tests,

(ii) the genetic tests of family members of such individual, and

(iii) the manifestation of a disease or disorder in family members of such individual.

(B) Inclusion of genetic services and participation in genetic research—Such term includes, with respect to any individual, any request for, or receipt of, genetic services, or participation in clinical research which includes genetic services, by such individual or any family member of such individual.

(C) Exclusions—The term "genetic information" shall not include information about the sex or age of any individual.

(7) Genetic test—

(A) In general—The term "genetic test" means an analysis of human DNA, RNA, chromosomes, proteins, or metabolites, that detects genotypes, mutations, or chromosomal changes.

(B) Exceptions—The term "genetic test" does not mean—

(i) an analysis of proteins or metabolites that does not detect genotypes, mutations, or chromosomal changes; or

(ii) an analysis of proteins or metabolites that is directly related to a manifested disease, disorder, or pathological condition that could reasonably be detected by a health care professional with appropriate training and expertise in the field of medicine involved.

(8) Genetic services—The term "genetic services" means—

(A) a genetic test;

(B) genetic counseling (including obtaining, interpreting, or assessing genetic information); or

(C) genetic education.

(9) Underwriting purposes—The term "underwriting purposes" means, with respect to any group health plan, or health insurance coverage offered in connection with a group health plan—

(A) rules for, or determination of, eligibility (including enrollment and continued eligibility) for benefits under the plan or coverage;

(B) the computation of premium or contribution amounts under the plan or coverage;

(C) the application of any pre-existing condition exclusion under the plan or coverage; and

(D) other activities related to the creation, renewal, or replacement of a contract of health insurance or health benefits.

Title IV (Subchapter III)—Plan Termination Insurance

Subtitle A—Pension Benefit Guaranty Corporation

§ 4001. Definitions (§ 1301)

(a) For purposes of this subchapter, the term—

(1) "administrator" means the person or persons described in paragraph (16) of section 1002 of this title;

(2) "substantial employer", for any plan year of a single-employer plan, means one or more persons—

(A) who are contributing sponsors of the plan in such plan year,

(B) who, at any time during such plan year, are members of the same controlled group, and

(C) whose required contributions to the plan for each plan year constituting one of—

(i) the two immediately preceding plan years, or

(ii) the first two of the three immediately preceding plan years,

total an amount greater than or equal to 10 percent of all contributions required to be paid to or under the plan for such plan year;

(3) "multiemployer plan" means a plan—

(A) to which more than one employer is required to contribute,

(B) which is maintained pursuant to one or more collective bargaining agreements between one or more employee organizations and more than one employer, and

(C) which satisfies such other requirements as the Secretary of Labor may prescribe by regulation,

except that, in applying this paragraph—

(i) a plan shall be considered a multiemployer plan on and after its termination date if the plan was a multiemployer plan under this paragraph for the plan year preceding such termination, and

(ii) for any plan year which began before September 26, 1980, the term "multiemployer plan" means a plan described in section 414(f) of Title 26 as in effect immediately before such date;

(4) "corporation", except where the context clearly requires otherwise, means the Pension Benefit Guaranty Corporation established under section 1302 of this title;

(5) "fund" means the appropriate fund established under section 1305 of this title;

(6) "basic benefits" means benefits guaranteed under section 1322 of this title (other than under section 1322(c) of this title), or under section 1322a of this title (other than under section 1322a(g) of this title);

(7) "non-basic benefits" means benefits guaranteed under section 1322(c) of this title or 1322a(g) of this title;

(8) "nonforfeitable benefit" means, with respect to a plan, a benefit for which a participant has satisfied the conditions for entitlement under the plan or the requirements of this chapter (other than submission of a formal application, retirement, completion of a required waiting period, or death in the case of a benefit which returns all or a portion of a participant's accumulated mandatory employee contributions upon the participant's death), whether or not the benefit may subsequently be reduced or suspended by a plan amendment, an occurrence of any condition, or operation of this chapter or Title 26;

(9) [Repealed]

(10) "plan sponsor" means, with respect to a multiemployer plan—

(A) the plan's joint board of trustees, or

(B) if the plan has no joint board of trustees, the plan administrator;

(11) "contribution base unit" means a unit with respect to which an employer has an obligation to contribute under a multiemployer plan, as defined in regulations prescribed by the Secretary of the Treasury;

(12) "outstanding claim for withdrawal liability" means a plan's claim for the unpaid balance of the liability determined under part 1 of subtitle E for which demand has been made, valued in accordance with regulations prescribed by the corporation;

(13) "contributing sponsor", of a single-employer plan, means a person described in section 1082(b)(1) of this title (without regard to section 1082(b)(2) of this title) or section 412(b)(1) of Title 26 (without regard to section 412(b)(2) of Title 26).

(14) in the case of a single-employer plan—

(A) "controlled group" means, in connection with any person, a group consisting of such person and all other persons under common control with such person;

(B) the determination of whether two or more persons are under "common control" shall be made under regulations of the corporation which are consistent and coextensive with regulations prescribed for similar purposes by the Secretary of the Treasury under subsections (b) and (c) of section 414 of Title 26; and

* * *

(15) "single-employer plan" means any defined benefit plan (as defined in section 1002(35) of this title) which is not a multiemployer plan;

(16) "benefit liabilities" means the benefits of employees and their beneficiaries under the plan (within the meaning of section 401(a)(2) of Title 26);

(17) "amount of unfunded guaranteed benefits", of a participant or beneficiary as of any date under a single-employer plan, means an amount equal to the excess of—

(A) the actuarial present value (determined as of such date on the basis of assumptions prescribed by the corporation for purposes of section 1344 of this title) of the benefits of the participant or beneficiary under the plan which are guaranteed under section 1322 of this title, over

(B) the current value (as of such date) of the assets of the plan which are required to be allocated to those benefits under section 1344 of this title;

(18) "amount of unfunded benefit liabilities" means, as of any date, the excess (if any) of—

(A) the value of the benefit liabilities under the plan (determined as of such date on the basis of assumptions prescribed by the corporation for purposes of section 1344 of this title), over

(B) the current value (as of such date) of the assets of the plan;

(19) "outstanding amount of benefit liabilities" means, with respect to any plan, the excess (if any) of—

(A) the value of the benefit liabilities under the plan (determined as of the termination date on the basis of assumptions prescribed by the corporation for purposes of section 1344 of this title), over

(B) the value of the benefit liabilities which would be so determined by only taking into account benefits which are guaranteed under section 1322 of this title or to which assets of the plan are allocated under section 1344 of this title;

(20) "person" has the meaning set forth in section 1002(9) of this title;

(21) "affected party" means, with respect to a plan—

(A) each participant in the plan,

(B) each beneficiary under the plan who is a beneficiary of a deceased participant or who is an alternate payee (within the meaning of section 1056(d)(3)(K) of this title) under an applicable qualified domestic relations order (within the meaning of section 1056(d)(3)(B)(i) of this title),

(C) each employee organization representing participants in the plan, and

(D) the corporation,

except that, in connection with any notice required to be provided to the affected party, if an affected party has designated, in writing, a person to receive such notice on behalf of the affected party, any reference to the affected party shall be construed to refer to such person.

(b)(1) An individual who owns the entire interest in an unincorporated trade or business is treated as his own employer, and a partnership is treated as the employer of each partner who is an employee within the meaning of section 401(c)(1) of Title 26. For purposes of this subchapter, under regulations prescribed by the corporation, all employees of trades or businesses (whether or not incorporated) which are under common control shall be treated as employed by a single employer and all such trades and businesses as a single employer. The regulations prescribed under the preceding sentence shall be consistent and coextensive with regulations prescribed for similar purposes by the Secretary of the Treasury under section 414(c) of Title 26.

(2) For purposes of subtitle E of this subchapter—

(A) except as otherwise provided in subtitle E of this subchapter, contributions or other payments shall be considered made under a plan for a plan year if they are made within the period prescribed under section 412(c)(10) of Title 26 (determined, in the case of a terminated plan, as if the plan had continued beyond the termination date), and

(B) the term "Secretary of the Treasury" means the Secretary of the Treasury or such Secretary's delegate.

§ 4002. Pension Benefit Guaranty Corporation (§ 1302)

(a) Establishment within Department of Labor—There is established within the Department of Labor a body corporate to be known as the Pension Benefit Guaranty Corporation. In carrying out its functions under this subchapter, the corporation shall be administered by a Director, who shall be appointed by the President, by and with the advice and consent of the Senate, and who shall act in accordance with the policies established by the board. The purposes of this subchapter, which are to be carried out by the corporation, are—

(1) to encourage the continuation and maintenance of voluntary private pension plans for the benefit of their participants,

(2) to provide for the timely and uninterrupted payment of pension benefits to participants and beneficiaries under plans to which this subchapter applies, and

(3) to maintain premiums established by the corporation under section 1306 of this title at the lowest level consistent with carrying out its obligations under this subchapter.

* * *

§ 4003. Operation of corporation (§ 1303)

(a) Investigatory authority; audit of statistically significant number of terminating plans—The corporation may make such investigations as it deems necessary to enforce any provision of this subchapter or any rule or regulation thereunder, and may require or permit any person to file with it a statement in writing, under oath or otherwise as the corporation shall determine, as to all the facts and circumstances concerning the matter to be investigated. The corporation shall annually audit a statistically significant number of plans terminating under section 1341(b) of this title to determine whether participants and beneficiaries have received their benefit commitments and whether section 1350(a) of this title has been satisfied. Each audit shall include a statistically significant number of participants and beneficiaries.

(b) Discovery powers vested in board members or officers designated by the chairman—For the purpose of any such investigation, or any other proceeding under this subchapter, the Director, any member of the board of directors of the corporation, or any officer designated by the Director or chairman, may administer oaths and affirmations, subpena witnesses, compel their attendance, take evidence, and require the production of any books, papers, correspondence, memoranda, or other records which the corporation deems relevant or material to the inquiry.

(c) Contempt—In case of contumacy by, or refusal to obey a subpena issued to, any person, the corporation may invoke the aid of any court of the United States within the jurisdiction of which such investigation or proceeding is carried on, or where such person resides or carries on business, in requiring the attendance and testimony of witnesses and the production of books, papers, correspondence, memoranda, and other records. The court may issue an order requiring such person to appear before the corporation, or member or officer designated by the corporation, and to produce records or to give testimony related to the matter under investigation or in question. Any failure to obey such order of the court may be punished by the court as a contempt thereof. All process in any such case may be served in the judicial district in which such person is an inhabitant or may be found.

* * *

(e) Civil actions by corporation; jurisdiction; process; expeditious handling of case; costs; limitation on actions—

(1) Civil actions may be brought by the corporation for appropriate relief, legal or equitable or both, to enforce (A) the provisions of this subchapter, and (B) in the case of a plan which is covered under this subchapter (other than a multiemployer plan) and for which the conditions for imposition of a lien described in section 1083(k)(1)(A) and (B) or 1085a(g)(1)(A) and (B) of this title or section 430(k)(1)(A) and (B) or 433(g)(1)(A) and (B) of Title 26 have been met, section 1082 of this title and section 412 of Title 26.

(2) Except as otherwise provided in this subchapter, where such an action is brought in a district court of the United States, it may be brought in the district where the plan is administered, where the violation took place, or where a defendant resides or may be found, and process may be served in any other district where a defendant resides or may be found.

(3) The district courts of the United States shall have jurisdiction of actions brought by the corporation under this subchapter without regard to the amount in controversy in any such action.

(4) [Repealed]

(5) In any action brought under this subchapter, whether to collect premiums, penalties, and interest under section 1307 of this title or for any other purpose, the court may award to the corporation all or a portion of the costs of litigation incurred by the corporation in connection with such action.

(6)(A) Except as provided in subparagraph (C), an action under this subsection may not be brought after the later of—

    (i) 6 years after the date on which the cause of action arose, or

    (ii) 3 years after the applicable date specified in subparagraph (B).

    (B)(i) Except as provided in clause (ii), the applicable date specified in this subparagraph is the earliest date on which the corporation acquired or should have acquired actual knowledge of the existence of such cause of action.

        (ii) If the corporation brings the action as a trustee, the applicable date specified in this subparagraph is the date on which the corporation became a trustee with respect to the plan if such date is later than the date described in clause (i).

    (C) In the case of fraud or concealment, the period described in subparagraph (A)(ii) shall be extended to 6 years after the applicable date specified in subparagraph (B).

(f) Civil actions against corporation; appropriate court; award of costs and expenses; limitation on actions; jurisdiction; removal of actions—

(1) Except with respect to withdrawal liability disputes under part 1 of subtitle E, any person who is a plan sponsor, fiduciary, employer, contributing sponsor, member of a contributing sponsor's controlled group, participant, or beneficiary, and is adversely affected by any action of the corporation with respect to a plan in which such person has an interest, or who is an employee organization representing such a participant or beneficiary so adversely affected for purposes of collective bargaining with respect to such plan, may bring an action against the corporation for appropriate equitable relief in the appropriate court.

(2) For purposes of this subsection, the term "appropriate court" means—

    (A) the United States district court before which proceedings under section 1341 or 1342 of this title are being conducted,

    (B) if no such proceedings are being conducted, the United States district court for the judicial district in which the plan has its principal office, or

    (C) the United States District Court for the District of Columbia.

(3) In any action brought under this subsection, the court may award all or a portion of the costs and expenses incurred in connection with such action to any party who prevails or substantially prevails in such action.

(4) This subsection shall be the exclusive means for bringing actions against the corporation under this subchapter, including actions against the corporation in its capacity as a trustee under section 1342 or 1349 of this title.

(5)(A) Except as provided in subparagraph (C), an action under this subsection may not be brought after the later of—

    (i) 6 years after the date on which the cause of action arose, or

    (ii) 3 years after the applicable date specified in subparagraph (B).

(B)(i) Except as provided in clause (ii), the applicable date specified in this subparagraph is the earliest date on which the plaintiff acquired or should have acquired actual knowledge of the existence of such cause of action.

    (ii) In the case of a plaintiff who is a fiduciary bringing the action in the exercise of fiduciary duties, the applicable date specified in this subparagraph is the date on which the plaintiff became a fiduciary with respect to the plan if such date is later than the date specified in clause (i).

    (C) In the case of fraud or concealment, the period described in subparagraph (A)(ii) shall be extended to 6 years after the applicable date specified in subparagraph (B).

(6) The district courts of the United States have jurisdiction of actions brought under this subsection without regard to the amount in controversy.

(7) In any suit, action, or proceeding in which the corporation is a party, or intervenes under section 1451 of this title, in any State court, the corporation may, without bond or security, remove such suit, action, or proceeding from the State court to the United States district court for the district or division in which such suit, action, or proceeding is pending by following any procedure for removal now or hereafter in effect.

§ 4005. Pension benefit guaranty funds (§ 1305)

(a) Establishment of four revolving funds on books of Treasury of the United States— There are established on the books of the Treasury of the United States four revolving funds to be used by the corporation in carrying out its duties under this subchapter. One of the funds shall be used with respect to basic benefits guaranteed under section 1322 of this title, one of the funds shall be used with respect to basic benefits guaranteed under section 1322a of this title, one of the funds shall be used with respect to nonbasic benefits guaranteed under section 1322 of this title (if any), and the remaining fund shall be used with respect to nonbasic benefits guaranteed under section 1322a of this title (if any), other than subsection (g)(2) thereof (if any). Whenever in this subchapter reference is made to the term "fund" the reference shall be considered to refer to the appropriate fund established under this subsection.

(b) Credits to funds; availability of funds; investment of moneys in excess of current needs—

* * *

(3)(A) Whenever the corporation determines that the moneys of any fund are in excess of current needs, it may request the investment of such amounts as it determines advisable by the Secretary of the Treasury in obligations issued or guaranteed by the United States.

* * *

§ 4006. Premium rates (§ 1306)

(a) **Schedules for premium rates and bases for application; establishment, coverage, etc.—**

(1) The corporation shall prescribe such schedules of premium rates and bases for the application of those rates as may be necessary to provide sufficient revenue to the fund for the corporation to carry out its functions under this subchapter. The premium rates charged by the corporation for any period shall be uniform for all plans, other than multiemployer plans, insured by the corporation with respect to basic benefits guaranteed by it under section 1322 of this title, and shall be uniform for all multiemployer plans with respect to basic benefits guaranteed by it under section 1322a of this title.

* * *

(3)(A) Except as provided in subparagraph (C), the annual premium rate payable to the corporation by all plans for basic benefits guaranteed under this subchapter is—

(i) in the case of a single-employer plan, an amount for each individual who is a participant in such plan during the plan year equal to the sum of the additional premium (if any) determined under subparagraph (E) and—

(I) for plan years beginning after December 31, 2005, and before January 1, 2013, $30;

(II) for plan years beginning after December 31, 2012, and before January 1, 2014, $42;

(III) for plan years beginning after December 31, 2013[,] and before January 1, 2015,[,] $49.[;]

(IV) for plan years beginning after December 31, 2014, and before January 1, 2016, $57;

(V) for plan years beginning after December 31, 2015, and before January 1, 2017, $64;

(VI) for plan years beginning after December 31, 2016, and before January 1, 2018, $69;

(VII) for plan years beginning after December 31, 2017, and before January 1, 2019, $74; and

(VIII) for plan years beginning after December 31, 2018, $80.

* * *

(iv) in the case of a multiemployer plan, for plan years beginning after December 31, 2005, and before January 1, 2013, $8.00 for each individual who is a participant in such plan during the applicable plan year,

(v) in the case of a multiemployer plan, for plan years beginning after December 31, 2012, $12.00 for each individual who is a participant in such plan during the applicable plan year, or

(vi) in the case of a multiemployer plan, for plan years beginning after December 31, 2014, $26 for each individual who is a participant in such plan during the applicable plan year.

* * *

(vii)(E)(i) Except as provided in subparagraph (H), the additional premium determined under this subparagraph with respect to any plan for any plan year—

(I) shall be an amount equal to the amount determined under clause (ii) divided by the number of participants in such plan as of the close of the preceding plan year; and

(II) in the case of plan years beginning in a calendar year after 2012 and before 2016, shall not exceed $400[;] and

(III) in the case of plan years beginning in a calendar year after 2015, shall not exceed $500.

(ii) The amount determined under this clause for any plan year shall be an amount equal to the applicable dollar amount under paragraph (8) for each $1,000 (or fraction thereof) of unfunded vested benefits under the plan as of the close of the preceding plan year.

* * *

(G) For each plan year beginning in a calendar year after 2016, there shall be substituted for the premium rate specified in clause (i) of subparagraph (A) an amount equal to the greater of—

(i) the product derived by multiplying the premium rate specified in clause (i) of subparagraph (A) by the ratio of—

(I) the national average wage index (as defined in section 409(k)(1) of Title 42) for the first of the 2 calendar years preceding the calendar year in which such plan year begins, to

(II) the national average wage index (as so defined) for 2017; and

(ii) the premium rate in effect under clause (i) of subparagraph (A) for plan years beginning in the preceding calendar year.

If the amount determined under this subparagraph is not a multiple of $1, such product shall be rounded to the nearest multiple of $1.

(H) For each plan year beginning in a calendar year after 2006, there shall be substituted for the premium rate specified in clause (iv) of subparagraph (A) an amount equal to the greater of—

(i) the product derived by multiplying the premium rate specified in clause (iv) of subparagraph (A) by the ratio of—

(I) the national average wage index (as defined in section 409(k)(1) of Title 42) for the first of the 2 calendar years preceding the calendar year in which such plan year begins, to

(II) the national average wage index (as so defined) for 2004; and

(ii) the premium rate in effect under clause (iv) of subparagraph (A) for plan years beginning in the preceding calendar year.

If the amount determined under this subparagraph is not a multiple of $1, such product shall be rounded to the nearest multiple of $1.

(I)(i) In the case of an employer who has 25 or fewer employees on the first day of the plan year, the additional premium determined under subparagraph (E) for each participant shall not exceed $5 multiplied by the number of participants in the plan as of the close of the preceding plan year.

(ii) For purposes of clause (i), whether an employer has 25 or fewer employees on the first day of the plan year is determined by taking into consideration all of the employees of all members of the contributing sponsor's controlled group. In the case of a plan maintained by two or more contributing sponsors, the employees of all contributing sponsors and their controlled groups shall be aggregated for purposes of determining whether the 25-or-fewer-employees limitation has been satisfied.

* * *

(7) Premium rate for certain terminated single-employer plans—

(A) In general—If there is a termination of a single-employer plan under clause (ii) or (iii) of section 1341(c)(2)(B) or section 1342 of this title, there shall be payable to the corporation, with respect to each applicable 12-month period, a premium at a rate equal to $1,250 multiplied by the number of individuals who were participants in the plan immediately before the termination date. Such premium shall be in addition to any other premium under this section.

(B) Special rule for plans terminated in bankruptcy reorganization—In the case of a single-employer plan terminated under section 1341(c)(2)(B)(ii) or under section 1342 of this title during pendency of any bankruptcy reorganization proceeding under chapter 11 of Title 11, or under any similar law of a State or a political subdivision of a State (or a case described in section 1341(c)(2)(B)(i) of this title filed by or against such person has been converted, as of such date, to such a case in which reorganization is sought), subparagraph (A) shall not apply to such plan until the date of the discharge or dismissal of such person in such case.

(C) Applicable 12-month period—For purposes of subparagraph (A)—

(i) **In general**—The term "applicable 12-month period" means—

(I) the 12-month period beginning with the first month following the month in which the termination date occurs, and

(II) each of the first two 12-month periods immediately following the period described in subclause (I).

(ii) **Plans terminated in bankruptcy reorganization**— In any case in which the requirements of subparagraph (B) are met in connection with the termination of the plan with respect to 1 or more persons described in such subparagraph, the 12-month period described in clause (i)(I) shall be the 12-month period beginning with the first month following the month which includes the earliest date as of which each such person is discharged or dismissed in the case described in such clause in connection with such person.

* * *

Subtitle B—Coverage

§ 4021. Coverage (§ 1321)

(a) **Plans covered**—Except as provided in subsection (b), this subchapter applies to any plan (including a successor plan) which, for a plan year—

(1) is an employee pension benefit plan (as defined in paragraph (2) of section 1002 of this title) established or maintained—

(A) by an employer engaged in commerce or in any industry or activity affecting commerce, or

(B) by any employee organization, or organization representing employees, engaged in commerce or in any industry or activity affecting commerce, or

(C) by both,

which has, in practice, met the requirements of part I of subchapter D of chapter 1 of Title 26 (as in effect for the preceding 5 plan years of the plan) applicable to the plans described in paragraph (2) for the preceding 5 plan years; or

(2) is, or has been determined by the Secretary of the Treasury to be, a plan described in section 401(a) of Title 26, or which meets, or has been determined by the Secretary of the Treasury to meet, the requirements of section 404(a)(2) of Title 26.

For purposes of this subchapter, a successor plan is considered to be a continuation of a predecessor plan. For this purpose, unless otherwise specifically indicated in this subchapter, a successor plan is a plan which covers a group of employees which includes substantially the same employees as a previously established plan, and provides substantially the same benefits as that plan provided.

(b) Plans not covered—This section does not apply to any plan—

(1) which is an individual account plan, as defined in paragraph (34) of section 1002 of this title[;]

(2) established and maintained for its employees by the Government of the United States, by the government of any State or political subdivision thereof, or by any agency or instrumentality of any of the foregoing, or to which the Railroad Retirement Act of 1935 or 1937 [45 U.S.C.A. § 231 et seq.] applies and which is financed by contributions required under that Act, or which is described in the last sentence of section 1002(32) of this title[;]

(3) which is a church plan as defined in section 414(e) of Title 26, unless that plan has made an election under section 410(d) of Title 26, and has notified the corporation in accordance with procedures prescribed by the corporation, that it wishes to have the provisions of this part apply to it[;]

(4)(A) established and maintained by a society, order, or association described in section 501(c)(8) or (9) of Title 26, if no part of the contributions to or under the plan is made by employers of participants in the plan, or

(B) of which a trust described in section 501(c)(18) of Title 26 is a part;

(5) which has not at any time after September 2, 1974, provided for employer contributions;

(6) which is unfunded and which is maintained by an employer primarily for the purpose of providing deferred compensation for a select group of management or highly compensated employees;

(7) which is established and maintained outside of the United States primarily for the benefit of individuals substantially all of whom are nonresident aliens;

(8) which is maintained by an employer solely for the purpose of providing benefits for certain employees in excess of the limitations on contributions and benefits imposed by section 415 of Title 26 on plans to which that section applies, without regard to whether the plan is funded, and, to the extent that a separable part of a plan (as determined by the corporation) maintained by an employer is maintained for such purpose, that part shall be treated for purposes of this subchapter, as a separate plan which is an excess benefit plan;

(9) which is established and maintained exclusively for substantial owners;

(10) of an international organization which is exempt from taxation under the International Organizations Immunities Act [22 U.S.C.A. § 288 et seq.];

(11) maintained solely for the purpose of complying with applicable workmen's compensation laws or unemployment compensation or disability insurance laws;

(12) which is a defined benefit plan, to the extent that it is treated as an individual account plan under paragraph (35)(B) of section 1002 of this title; or

(13) established and maintained by a professional service employer which does not at any time after September 2, 1974, have more than 25 active participants in the plan.

(c) Definitions—

(1) For purposes of subsection (b)(1) of this section, the term "individual account plan" does not include a plan under which a fixed benefit is promised if the employer or his representative participated in the determination of that benefit.

(2) For purposes of this paragraph and for purposes of subsection (b)(13) of this section—

(A) the term "professional service employer" means any proprietorship, partnership, corporation, or other association or organization (i) owned or controlled by professional individuals or by executors or administrators of professional individuals, (ii) the principal business of which is the performance of professional services, and

(B) the term "professional individuals" includes but is not limited to, physicians, dentists, chiropractors, osteopaths, optometrists, other licensed practitioners of the healing arts, attorneys at law, public accountants, public engineers, architects, draftsmen, actuaries, psychologists, social or physical scientists, and performing artists.

(3) In the case of a plan established and maintained by more than one professional service employer, the plan shall not be treated as a plan described in subsection (b)(13) of this section if, at any time after September 2, 1974, the plan has more than 25 active participants.

(d) For purposes of subsection (b)(9) of this section, the term "substantial owner" means an individual who, at any time during the 60-month period ending on the date the determination is being made—

(1) owns the entire interest in an unincorporated trade or business,

(2) in the case of a partnership, is a partner who owns, directly or indirectly, more than 10 percent of either the capital interest or the profits interest in such partnership, or

(3) in the case of a corporation, owns, directly or indirectly, more than 10 percent in value of either the voting stock of that corporation or all the stock of that corporation.

For purposes of paragraph (3), the constructive ownership rules of section 1563(e) of Title 26 (other than paragraph (3)(C) thereof) shall apply, including the application of such rules under section 414(c) of Title 26.

§ 4022. Single-employer plan benefits guaranteed (§ 1322)

(a) Nonforfeitable benefits—Subject to the limitations contained in subsection (b) of this section, the corporation shall guarantee, in accordance with this section, the payment of all nonforfeitable benefits (other than benefits becoming nonforfeitable solely on account of the termination of a plan) under a single-employer plan which terminates at a time when this subchapter applies to it.

(b) Exceptions—

(1) Except to the extent provided in paragraph (7)—

(A) no benefits provided by a plan which has been in effect for less than 60 months at the time the plan terminates shall be guaranteed under this section, and

(B) any increase in the amount of benefits under a plan resulting from a plan amendment which was made, or became effective, whichever is later, within 60 months before the date on which the plan terminates shall be disregarded.

(2) For purposes of this subsection, the time a successor plan (within the meaning of section 1321(a) of this title) has been in effect includes the time a previously established plan (within the meaning of section 1321(a) of this title) was in effect. For purposes of determining what benefits are guaranteed under this section in the case of a plan to which section 1321 of this title does not apply on September 3, 1974, the 60-month period referred to in paragraph (1) shall be computed beginning on the first date on which such section does apply to the plan.

(3) The amount of monthly benefits described in subsection (a) of this section provided by a plan, which are guaranteed under this section with respect to a participant, shall not have an actuarial value which exceeds the actuarial value of a monthly benefit in the form of a life annuity commencing at age 65 equal to the lesser of—

(A) his average monthly gross income from his employer during the 5 consecutive calendar year period (or, if less, during the number of calendar years in such period in which he actively participates in the plan) during which his gross income from that employer was greater than during any other such period with that employer determined by dividing 1/12 of the sum of all such gross income by the number of such calendar years in which he had such gross income, or

(B) $750 multiplied by a fraction, the numerator of which is the contribution and benefit base (determined under section 230 of the Social Security Act [42 U.S.C.A. § 430]) in effect at the time the plan terminates and the denominator of which is such contribution and benefit base in effect in calendar year 1974.

The provisions of this paragraph do not apply to non-basic benefits. The maximum guaranteed monthly benefit shall not be reduced solely on account of the age of a participant in the case of a benefit payable by reason of disability that occurred on or before the termination date, if the participant demonstrates to the satisfaction of the corporation that the Social Security Administration has determined that the participant satisfies the definition of disability under title II [42 U.S.C.A. § 401 et seq.] or XVI [42 U.S.C.A. § 1381 et seq.] of the Social Security Act, and the regulations thereunder. If a benefit payable by reason of disability is converted to an early or normal retirement benefit for reasons other than a change in the health of the participant, such early or normal retirement benefit shall be treated as a continuation of the benefit payable by reason of disability and this subparagraph shall continue to apply.

* * *

(5)(A) For purposes of this paragraph, the term 'majority owner' means an individual who, at any time during the 60-month period ending on the date the determination is being made—

> **(i)** owns the entire interest in an unincorporated trade or business,

> **(ii)** in the case of a partnership, is a partner who owns, directly or indirectly, 50 percent or more of either the capital interest or the profits interest in such partnership, or

> **(iii)** in the case of a corporation, owns, directly or indirectly, 50 percent or more in value of either the voting stock of that corporation or all the stock of that corporation.

For purposes of clause (iii), the constructive ownership rules of section 1563(e) of Title 26 (other than paragraph (3)(C) thereof) shall apply, including the application of such rules under section 414(c) of Title 26.

> **(B)** In the case of a participant who is a majority owner, the amount of benefits guaranteed under this section shall equal the product of—

> > **(i)** a fraction (not to exceed 1) the numerator of which is the number of years from the later of the effective date or the adoption date of the plan to the termination date, and the denominator of which is 10, and

> > **(ii)** the amount of benefits that would be guaranteed under this section if the participant were not a majority owner.

(6)(A) No benefits accrued under a plan after the date on which the Secretary of the Treasury issues notice that he has determined that any trust which is a part of a plan does not meet the requirements of section 401(a) of Title 26, or that the plan does not meet the requirements of section 404(a)(2) of Title 26, are guaranteed under this section unless such determination is erroneous. This subparagraph does not apply if the Secretary subsequently issues a notice that such trust meets the requirements of section 401(a) of Title 26 or that the plan meets the requirements of section 404(a)(2) of Title 26 and if the Secretary determines that the trust or plan has taken action necessary to meet such requirements during the period between the issuance of the notice referred to in the preceding sentence and the issuance of the notice referred to in this sentence.

> **(B)** No benefits accrued under a plan after the date on which an amendment of the plan is adopted which causes the Secretary of the Treasury to determine that any trust under the plan has ceased to meet the requirements of section 401(a) of Title 26 or that the plan has ceased to meet the requirements of section 404(a)(2) of Title 26, are guaranteed under this section unless such determination is erroneous. This subparagraph shall not apply if the amendment is revoked as of the date it was first effective or amended to comply with such requirements.

(7) Benefits described in paragraph (1) are guaranteed only to the extent of the greater of—

> **(A)** 20 percent of the amount which, but for the fact that the plan or amendment has not been in effect for 60 months or more, would be guaranteed under this section, or

> **(B)** $20 per month,

multiplied by the number of years (but not more than 5) the plan or amendment, as the case may be, has been in effect. In determining how many years a plan or amendment has been in effect for purposes of this paragraph, the first 12 months beginning with the date on which the plan or amendment is made or first becomes effective (whichever is later) constitutes one year, and each consecutive period of 12 months thereafter constitutes an additional year. This paragraph does not apply to benefits payable under a plan unless the corporation finds substantial evidence that the plan was terminated for a reasonable business purpose and not for the purpose of obtaining the payment of benefits by the corporation under this subchapter.

(8) If an unpredictable contingent event benefit (as defined in section 1056(g)(1) of this title) is payable by reason of the occurrence of any event, this section shall be applied as if a plan amendment had been adopted on the date such event occurred.

(c) Payment by corporation to participants and beneficiaries of recovery percentage of outstanding amount of benefit liabilities—

(1) In addition to benefits paid under the preceding provisions of this section with respect to a terminated plan, the corporation shall pay the portion of the amount determined under paragraph (2) which is allocated with respect to each participant under section 1344(a) of this title. Such payment shall be made to such participant or to such participant's beneficiaries (including alternate payees, within the meaning of section 1056(d)(3)(K) of this title).

* * *

(g) Bankruptcy filing substituted for termination date—If a contributing sponsor of a plan has filed or has had filed against such person a petition seeking liquidation or reorganization in a case under title 11 or under any similar Federal law or law of a State or political subdivision, and the case has not been dismissed as of the termination date of the plan, then this section shall be applied by treating the date such petition was filed as the termination date of the plan.

* * *

Subtitle C—Terminations

§ 4041. Termination of single-employer plans (§ 1341)

(a) General rules governing single-employer plan terminations—

(1) Exclusive means of plan termination—Except in the case of a termination for which proceedings are otherwise instituted by the corporation as provided in section 1342 of this title, a single-employer plan may be terminated only in a standard termination under subsection (b) of this section or a distress termination under subsection (c) of this section.

(2) 60-day notice of intent to terminate—Not less than 60 days before the proposed termination date of a standard termination under subsection (b) of this section or a distress termination under subsection (c) of this section, the plan administrator shall provide to each affected party (other than the corporation in the case of a standard termination) a written notice of intent to terminate stating that such termination is intended and the proposed termination date. The written notice shall include any related additional information required in regulations of the corporation.

(3) Adherence to collective bargaining agreements—The corporation shall not proceed with a termination of a plan under this section if the termination would violate the terms and conditions of an existing collective bargaining agreement. Nothing in the preceding sentence shall be construed as limiting the authority of the corporation to institute proceedings to involuntarily terminate a plan under section 1342 of this title.

(b) Standard termination of single-employer plans—

(1) General requirements—A single-employer plan may terminate under a standard termination only if—

(A) the plan administrator provides the 60-day advance notice of intent to terminate to affected parties required under subsection (a)(2) of this section,

(B) the requirements of subparagraphs (A) and (B) of paragraph (2) are met,

(C) the corporation does not issue a notice of noncompliance under subparagraph (C) of paragraph (2), and

(D) when the final distribution of assets occurs, the plan is sufficient for benefit liabilities (determined as of the termination date).

* * *

(3) Methods of final distribution of assets—

(A) In general—In connection with any final distribution of assets pursuant to the standard termination of the plan under this subsection, the plan administrator shall distribute the assets in accordance with section 1344 of this title. In distributing such assets, the plan administrator shall—

(i) purchase irrevocable commitments from an insurer to provide all benefit liabilities under the plan, or

(ii) in accordance with the provisions of the plan and any applicable regulations, otherwise fully provide all benefit liabilities under the plan. A transfer of assets to the corporation in accordance with section 1350 of this title on behalf of a missing participant shall satisfy this subparagraph with respect to such participant.

* * *

(c) Distress termination of single-employer plans—

(1) In general—A single-employer plan may terminate under a distress termination only if—

(A) the plan administrator provides the 60-day advance notice of intent to terminate to affected parties required under subsection (a)(2) of this section,

(B) the requirements of subparagraph (A) of paragraph (2) are met, and

(C) the corporation determines that the requirements of subparagraphs (B) and (D) of paragraph (2) are met.

(2) Termination requirements—

(A) Information submitted to the corporation—As soon as practicable after the date on which the notice of intent to terminate is provided pursuant to subsection (a)(2) of this section, the plan administrator shall provide the corporation, in such form as may be prescribed by the corporation in regulations, the following information:

* * *

(B) Determination by the corporation of necessary distress criteria—Upon receipt of the notice of intent to terminate required under subsection (a)(2) of this section and the information required under subparagraph (A), the corporation shall determine whether the requirements of this subparagraph are met as provided in clause (i), (ii), or (iii). The requirements of this subparagraph are met if each person who is (as of the proposed termination date) a contributing sponsor of such plan or a member of such sponsor's controlled group meets the requirements of any of the following clauses:

(i) Liquidation in bankruptcy or insolvency proceedings—The requirements of this clause are met by a person if—

(I) such person has filed or has had filed against such person, as of the proposed termination date, a petition seeking liquidation in a case under Title 11 or under any similar Federal law or law of a State or political subdivision of a State (or a case described in clause (ii) filed by or against such person has been converted, as of such date, to a case in which liquidation is sought), and

(II) such case has not, as of the proposed termination date, been dismissed.

(ii) Reorganization in bankruptcy or insolvency proceedings—The requirements of this clause are met by a person if—

(I) such person has filed, or has had filed against such person, as of the proposed termination date, a petition seeking reorganization in a case under Title 11 or under any similar law of a State or political subdivision of a State (or a case described in clause (i) filed by or against such person has been converted, as of such date, to such a case in which reorganization is sought),

(II) such case has not, as of the proposed termination date, been dismissed,

(III) such person timely submits to the corporation any request for the approval of the bankruptcy court (or other appropriate court in a case under such similar law of a State or political subdivision) of the plan termination, and

(IV) the bankruptcy court (or such other appropriate court) determines that, unless the plan is terminated, such person will be unable to pay all its debts pursuant to a plan of reorganization and will be unable to continue in business outside the Chapter 11 reorganization process and approves the termination.

(iii) Termination required to enable payment of debts while staying in business or to avoid unreasonably burdensome pension costs caused by declining workforce—The requirements of this clause are met by a person if such person demonstrates to the satisfaction of the corporation that—

(I) unless a distress termination occurs, such person will be unable to pay such person's debts when due and will be unable to continue in business, or

(II) the costs of providing pension coverage have become unreasonably burdensome to such person, solely as a result of a decline of such person's workforce covered as participants under all single-employer plans of which such person is a contributing sponsor.

* * *

(D) Disclosure of termination information—

(i) In general—A plan administrator that has filed a notice of intent to terminate under subsection (a)(2) shall provide to an affected party any information provided to the corporation under subparagraph (A) or the regulations under subsection (a)(2) of this section not later than 15 days after—

(I) receipt of a request from the affected party for the information; or

(II) the provision of new information to the corporation relating to a previous request.

* * *

§ 4042. Institution of termination proceedings by the corporation (§ 1342)

(a) Authority to institute proceedings to terminate a plan—The corporation may institute proceedings under this section to terminate a plan whenever it determines that—

(1) the plan has not met the minimum funding standard required under section 412 of Title 26, or has been notified by the Secretary of the Treasury that a notice of deficiency under section 6212 of Title 26 has been mailed with respect to the tax imposed under section 4971(a) of Title 26,

(2) the plan will be unable to pay benefits when due,

(3) the reportable event described in section 1343(c)(7) of this title has occurred, or

(4) the possible long-run loss of the corporation with respect to the plan may reasonably be expected to increase unreasonably if the plan is not terminated.

The corporation shall as soon as practicable institute proceedings under this section to terminate a single-employer plan whenever the corporation determines that the plan does not have assets available to pay benefits which are currently due under the terms of the plan. The corporation may prescribe a simplified procedure to follow in terminating small plans as long as that procedure includes substantial safeguards for the rights of the participants and beneficiaries under the plans, and for the employers who maintain such plans (including the requirement for a court decree under subsection (c) of the section). Notwithstanding any other provision of this subchapter, the corporation is authorized to pool assets of terminated plans for purposes of administration, investment, payment of liabilities of all such terminated plans, and such other purposes as it determines to be appropriate in the administration of this subchapter.

* * *

§ 4043. Reportable events (§ 1343)

(a) Notification that event has occurred—Within 30 days after the plan administrator or the contributing sponsor knows or has reason to know that a reportable event described in subsection (c) of this section has occurred, he shall notify the corporation that such event has occurred, unless a notice otherwise required under this subsection has already been provided with respect to such event. The corporation is authorized to waive the requirement of the preceding sentence with respect to any or all reportable events with respect to any plan, and to require the notification to be made by including the event in the annual report made by the plan.

(b) Notification that event is about to occur—

(1) The requirements of this subsection shall be applicable to a contributing sponsor if, as of the close of the preceding plan year—

(A) the aggregate unfunded vested benefits (as determined under section 1306(a)(3)(E)(iii) of this title) of plans subject to this subchapter which are maintained by such sponsor and members of such sponsor's controlled groups (disregarding plans with no unfunded vested benefits) exceed $50,000,000, and

(B) the funded vested benefit percentage for such plans is less than 90 percent.

For purposes of subparagraph (B), the funded vested benefit percentage means the percentage which the aggregate value of the assets of such plans bears to the aggregate vested benefits of such plans (determined in accordance with section 1306(a)(3)(E)(iii) of this title).

(2) This subsection shall not apply to an event if the contributing sponsor, or the member of the contributing sponsor's controlled group to which the event relates, is—

(A) a person subject to the reporting requirements of section 13 or 15(d) of the Securities Exchange Act of 1934 [15 U.S.C.A. § 78m or 78o(d)], or

(B) a subsidiary (as defined for purposes of such Act [15 U.S.C.A. § 78a et seq.]) of a person subject to such reporting requirements.

(3) No later than 30 days prior to the effective date of an event described in paragraph (9), (10), (11), (12), or (13) of subsection (c) of this section, a contributing sponsor to which the requirements of this subsection apply shall notify the corporation that the event is about to occur.

(4) The corporation may waive the requirement of this subsection with respect to any or all reportable events with respect to any contributing sponsor.

(c) Enumeration of reportable events—For purposes of this section a reportable event occurs—

(1) when the Secretary of the Treasury issues notice that a plan has ceased to be a plan described in section 1321(a)(2) of this title, or when the Secretary of Labor determines the plan is not in compliance with title I of this chapter;

(2) when an amendment of the plan is adopted if, under the amendment, the benefit payable with respect to any participant may be decreased;

(3) when the number of active participants is less than 80 percent of the number of such participants at the beginning of the plan year, or is less than 75 percent of the number of such participants at the beginning of the previous plan year;

(4) when the Secretary of the Treasury determines that there has been a termination or partial termination of the plan within the meaning of section 411(d)(3) of Title 26, but the occurrence of such a termination or partial termination does not, by itself, constitute or require a termination of a plan under this subchapter;

(5) when the plan fails to meet the minimum funding standards under section 412 of Title 26 (without regard to whether the plan is a plan described in section 1321(a)(2) of this title) or under section 1082 of this title;

(6) when the plan is unable to pay benefits thereunder when due;

(7) when there is a distribution under the plan to a participant who is a substantial owner as defined in section 1321(d) of this title if—

(A) such distribution has a value of $10,000 or more;

(B) such distribution is not made by reason of the death of the participant; and

(C) immediately after the distribution, the plan has nonforfeitable benefits which are not funded;

(8) when a plan merges, consolidates, or transfers its assets under section 1058 of this title, or when an alternative method of compliance is prescribed by the Secretary of Labor under section 1030 of this title;

(9) when, as a result of an event, a person ceases to be a member of the controlled group;

(10) when a contributing sponsor or a member of a contributing sponsor's controlled group liquidates in a case under Title 11, or under any similar Federal law or law of a State or political subdivision of a State;

(11) when a contributing sponsor or a member of a contributing sponsor's controlled group declares an extraordinary dividend (as defined in section 1059(c) of Title 26) or redeems, in any 12-month period, an aggregate of 10 percent or more of the total combined voting power of all classes of stock entitled to vote, or an aggregate of 10 percent or more of the total value of shares of all classes of stock, of a contributing sponsor and all members of its controlled group;

(12) when, in any 12-month period, an aggregate of 3 percent or more of the benefit liabilities of a plan covered by this subchapter and maintained by a contributing sponsor or a member of its controlled group are transferred to a person that is not a member of the controlled group or to a plan or plans maintained by a person or persons that are not such a contributing sponsor or a member of its controlled group; or

(13) when any other event occurs that may be indicative of a need to terminate the plan and that is prescribed by the corporation in regulations.

For purposes of paragraph (7), all distributions to a participant within any 24-month period are treated as a single distribution.

* * *

§ 4044. Allocation of assets (§ 1344)

(a) Order of priority of participants and beneficiaries—In the case of the termination of a single-employer plan, the plan administrator shall allocate the assets of the plan (available to provide benefits) among the participants and beneficiaries of the plan in the following order:

(1) First, to that portion of each individual's accrued benefit which is derived from the participant's contributions to the plan which were not mandatory contributions.

(2) Second, to that portion of each individual's accrued benefit which is derived from the participant's mandatory contributions.

(3) Third, in the case of benefits payable as an annuity—

(A) in the case of the benefit of a participant or beneficiary which was in pay status as of the beginning of the 3-year period ending on the termination date of the plan, to each such benefit, based on the provisions of the plan (as in effect during the 5-year period ending on such date) under which such benefit would be the least,

(B) in the case of a participant's or beneficiary's benefit (other than a benefit described in subparagraph (A)) which would have been in pay status as of the beginning of such 3-year period if the participant had retired prior to the beginning of the 3-year period and if his benefits had commenced (in the normal form of annuity under the plan) as of the beginning of such period, to each such benefit based on the provisions of the plan (as in effect during the 5-year period ending on such date) under which such benefit would be the least.

For purposes of subparagraph (A), the lowest benefit in pay status during a 3-year period shall be considered the benefit in pay status for such period.

(4) Fourth—

(A) to all other benefits (if any) of individuals under the plan guaranteed under this subchapter (determined without regard to section 1322b(a) of this title), and

(B) to the additional benefits (if any) which would be determined under subparagraph (A) if section 1322(b)(5)(B) of this title did not apply.

For purposes of this paragraph, section 1321 of this title shall be applied without regard to subsection (c) thereof.

(5) Fifth, to all other nonforfeitable benefits under the plan.

(6) Sixth, to all other benefits under the plan.

* * *

(d) Distribution of residual assets; restrictions on reversions pursuant to recently amended plans; assets attributable to employee contributions; calculation of remaining assets—

(1) Subject to paragraph (3), any residual assets of a single-employer plan may be distributed to the employer if—

(A) all liabilities of the plan to participants and their beneficiaries have been satisfied,

(B) the distribution does not contravene any provision of law, and

(C) the plan provides for such a distribution in these circumstances.

(2)(A) In determining the extent to which a plan provides for the distribution of plan assets to the employer for purposes of paragraph (1)(C), any such provision, and any amendment increasing the amount which may be distributed to the employer, shall not be treated as effective before the end of the fifth calendar year following the date of the adoption of such provision or amendment.

(B) A distribution to the employer from a plan shall not be treated as failing to satisfy the requirements of this paragraph if the plan has been in effect for fewer than 5 years and the plan has provided for such a distribution since the effective date of the plan.

(C) Except as otherwise provided in regulations of the Secretary of the Treasury, in any case in which a transaction described in section 1058 of this title occurs, subparagraph (A) shall continue to apply separately with respect to the amount of any assets transferred in such transaction.

(D) For purposes of this subsection, the term "employer" includes any member of the controlled group of which the employer is a member. For purposes of the preceding sentence, the term "controlled group" means any group treated as a single employer under subsection (b), (c), (m) or (o) of section 414 of Title 26.

(3)(A) Before any distribution from a plan pursuant to paragraph (1), if any assets of the plan attributable to employee contributions remain after satisfaction of all liabilities described in subsection (a) of this section, such remaining assets shall be equitably distributed to the participants who made such contributions or their beneficiaries (including alternate payees, within the meaning of section 1056(d)(3)(K) of this title).

(B) For purposes of subparagraph (A), the portion of the remaining assets which are attributable to employee contributions shall be an amount equal to the product derived by multiplying—

(i) the market value of the total remaining assets, by

(ii) a fraction—

(I) the numerator of which is the present value of all portions of the accrued benefits with respect to participants which are derived from participants' mandatory contributions (referred to in subsection (a)(2) of this section), and

(II) the denominator of which is the present value of all benefits with respect to which assets are allocated under paragraphs (2) through (6) of subsection (a) of this section.

(C) For purposes of this paragraph, each person who is, as of the termination date—

(i) a participant under the plan, or

(ii) an individual who has received, during the 3-year period ending with the termination date, a distribution from the plan of such individual's entire nonforfeitable benefit in the form of a single sum distribution in accordance with section 1053(e) of this title or in the form of irrevocable commitments purchased by the plan from an insurer to provide such nonforfeitable benefit,

shall be treated as a participant with respect to the termination, if all or part of the nonforfeitable benefit with respect to such person is or was attributable to participants' mandatory contributions (referred to in subsection (a)(2) of this section).

(4) Nothing in this subsection shall be construed to limit the requirements of section 4980(d) of Title 26 (as in effect immediately after the enactment of the Omnibus Budget Reconciliation Act of 1990) or section 1104(d) of this title with respect to any distribution of residual assets of a single-employer plan to the employer.

(e) Bankruptcy filing substituted for termination date—If a contributing sponsor of a plan has filed or has had filed against such person a petition seeking liquidation or reorganization in a case under title 11 or under any similar Federal law or law of a State or political subdivision, and the case has not been dismissed as of the termination date of the plan, then subsection (a)(3) of this section shall be applied by treating the date such petition was filed as the termination date of the plan.

(f) Valuation of section 1362(c) liability for determining amounts payable by corporation to participants and beneficiaries—

(1) In general—In the case of a terminated plan, the value of the recovery of liability under section 1362(c) of this title allocable as a plan asset under this section for purposes of determining the amount of benefits payable by the corporation shall be determined by multiplying—

    (A) the amount of liability under section 1362(c) of this title as of the termination date of the plan, by

    (B) the applicable section 1362(c) recovery ratio.

(2) Section 1362(c) recovery ratio—For purposes of this subsection—

    (A) In general—Except as provided in subparagraph (C), the term "section 1362(c) recovery ratio" means the ratio which—

        (i) the sum of the values of all recoveries under section 1362(c) of this title determined by the corporation in connection with plan terminations described under subparagraph (B), bears to

        (ii) the sum of all the amounts of liability under section 1362(c) of this title with respect to such plans as of the termination date in connection with any such prior termination.

    (B) Prior terminations—A plan termination described in this subparagraph is a termination with respect to which—

        (i) the value of recoveries under section 1362(c) of this title have been determined by the corporation, and

        (ii) notices of intent to terminate were provided (or in the case of a termination by the corporation, a notice of determination under section 1342 of this title was issued) during the 5-Federal fiscal year period ending with the third fiscal year preceding the fiscal year in which occurs the date of the notice of intent to terminate (or the notice of determination under section 1342 of this title) with respect to the plan termination for which the recovery ratio is being determined.

    (C) Exception—In the case of a terminated plan with respect to which the outstanding amount of benefit liabilities exceeds $20,000,000, the term "section 1362(c) recovery ratio" means, with respect to the termination of such plan, the ratio of—

        (i) the value of the recoveries on behalf of the plan under section 1362(c) of this title, to

        (ii) the amount of the liability owed under section 1362(c) of this title as of the date of plan termination to the trustee appointed under section 1342(b) or (c) of this title.

(3) Subsection not to apply—This subsection shall not apply with respect to the determination of—

    (A) whether the amount of outstanding benefit liabilities exceeds $20,000,000, or

    (B) the amount of any liability under section 1362 of this title to the corporation or the trustee appointed under section 1362(b) or (c) of this title.

(4) Determinations—Determinations under this subsection shall be made by the corporation. Such determinations shall be binding unless shown by clear and convincing evidence to be unreasonable.

§ 4045. Recapture of payments (§ 1345)

(a) Authorization to recover benefits—Except as provided in subsection (c) of this section, the trustee is authorized to recover for the benefit of a plan from a participant the recoverable amount (as defined in subsection (b) of this section) of all payments from the plan to him which commenced within the 3-year period immediately preceding the time the plan is terminated.

(b) Recoverable amount—For purposes of subsection (a) of this section the recoverable amount is the excess of the amount determined under paragraph (1) over the amount determined under paragraph (2).

(1) The amount determined under this paragraph is the sum of the amount of the actual payments received by the participant within the 3-year period.

(2) The amount determined under this paragraph is the sum of—

(A) the sum of the amount such participant would have received during each consecutive 12-month period within the 3 years if the participant received the benefit in the form described in paragraph (3),

(B) the sum for each of the consecutive 12-month periods of the lesser of—

(i) the excess, if any, of $10,000 over the benefit in the form described in paragraph (3), or

(ii) the excess of the actual payment, if any, over the benefit in the form described in paragraph (3), and

(C) the present value at the time of termination of the participant's future benefits guaranteed under this subchapter as if the benefits commenced in the form described in paragraph (3).

(3) The form of benefit for purposes of this subsection shall be the monthly benefit the participant would have received during the consecutive 12-month period, if he had elected at the time of the first payment made during the 3-year period, to receive his interest in the plan as a monthly benefit in the form of a life annuity commencing at the time of such first payment.

(c) Payments made on or after death or disability of participant; waiver of recovery in case of hardship—

(1) In the event of a distribution described in section 1343(b)(7) of this title the 3-year period referred to in subsection (b) of this section shall not end sooner than the date on which the corporation is notified of the distribution.

(2) The trustee shall not recover any payment made from a plan after or on account of the death of a participant, or to a participant who is disabled (within the meaning of section 72(m)(7) of Title 26).

(3) The corporation is authorized to waive, in whole or in part, the recovery of any amount which the trustee is authorized to recover for the benefit of a plan under this section in any case in which it determines that substantial economic hardship would result to the participant or his beneficiaries from whom such amount is recoverable.

§ 4047. Restoration of plans (§ 1347)

Whenever the corporation determines that a plan which is to be terminated under section 1341 or 1342 of this title, or which is in the process of being terminated under section 1341 or

1342 of this title, should not be terminated under section 1341 or 1342 of this title as a result of such circumstances as the corporation determines to be relevant, the corporation is authorized to cease any activities undertaken to terminate the plan, and to take whatever action is necessary and within its power to restore the plan to its status prior to the determination that the plan was to be terminated under section 1341 or 1342 of this title. In the case of a plan which has been terminated under section 1341 or 1342 of this title the corporation is authorized in any such case in which the corporation determines such action to be appropriate and consistent with its duties under this subchapter, to take such action as may be necessary to restore the plan to its pretermination status, including, but not limited to, the transfer to the employer or a plan administrator of control of part or all of the remaining assets and liabilities of the plan.

§ 4048. Termination date (§ 1348)

(a) For purposes of this subchapter the termination date of a single-employer plan is—

(1) in the case of a plan terminated in a standard termination in accordance with the provisions of section 1341(b) of this title, the termination date proposed in the notice provided under section 1341(a)(2) of this title,

(2) in the case of a plan terminated in a distress termination in accordance with the provisions of section 1341(c) of this title, the date established by the plan administrator and agreed to by the corporation,

(3) in the case of a plan terminated in accordance with the provisions of section 1342 of this title, the date established by the corporation and agreed to by the plan administrator, or

(4) in the case of a plan terminated under section 1341(c) or 1342 of this title in any case in which no agreement is reached between the plan administrator and the corporation (or the trustee), the date established by the court.

(b) For purposes of this subchapter, the date of termination of a multiemployer plan is—

(1) in the case of a plan terminated in accordance with the provisions of section 1341a of this title, the date determined under subsection (b) of that section; or

(2) in the case of a plan terminated in accordance with the provisions of section 1342 of this title, the date agreed to between the plan administrator and the corporation (or the trustee appointed under section 1342(b)(2) of this title, if any), or, if no agreement is reached, the date established by the court.

Subtitle D—Liability

§ 4062. Liability for termination of single-employer plans under a distress termination or a termination by corporation (§ 1362)

(a) **In general**—In any case in which a single-employer plan is terminated in a distress termination under section 1341(c) of this title or a termination otherwise instituted by the corporation under section 1342 of this title, any person who is, on the termination date, a contributing sponsor of the plan or a member of such a contributing sponsor's controlled group shall incur liability under this section. The liability under this section of all such persons shall be joint and several. The liability under this section consists of—

(1) liability to the corporation, to the extent provided in subsection (b) of this section, and

(2) liability to the trustee appointed under subsection (b) or (c) of section 1342 of this title, to the extent provided in subsection (c) of this section.

(b) Liability to corporation—

(1) Amount of liability—

(A) In general—Except as provided in subparagraph (B), the liability to the corporation of a person described in subsection (a) of this section shall be the total amount of the unfunded benefit liabilities (as of the termination date) to all participants and beneficiaries under the plan, together with interest (at a reasonable rate) calculated from the termination date in accordance with regulations prescribed by the corporation.

* * *

(c) Liability to section 1342 trustee—A person described in subsection (a) of this section shall be subject to liability under this subsection to the trustee appointed under subsection (b) or (c) of section 1342 of this title. The liability of such person under this subsection shall consist of—

(1) the sum of the shortfall amortization charge (within the meaning of section 1083(c)(1) of this title and [section] 430(d)(1) of Title 26) with respect to the plan (if any) for the plan year in which the termination date occurs, plus the aggregate total of shortfall amortization installments (if any) determined for succeeding plan years under section 1083(c)(2) of this title and section 430(d)(2) of Title 26 (which, for purposes of this subparagraph, shall include any increase in such sum which would result if all applications for waivers of the minimum funding standard under section 1082(c) of this title and section 412(c) of Title 26 which are pending with respect to such plan were denied and if no additional contributions (other than those already made by the termination date) were made for the plan year in which the termination date occurs or for any previous plan year), and

(2) the sum of the waiver amortization charge (within the meaning of section 1083(e)(1) of this title and [section] 430(e)(1) of Title 26) with respect to the plan (if any) for the plan year in which the termination date occurs, plus the aggregate total of waiver amortization installments (if any) determined for succeeding plan years under section 1083(e)(2) of this title and section 430(e)(2) of Title 26,

together with interest (at a reasonable rate) calculated from the termination date in accordance with regulations prescribed by the corporation. The liability under this subsection shall be due and payable to such trustee as of the termination date, in cash or securities acceptable to such trustee.

* * *

§ 4068. Lien for liability (§ 1368)

(a) Creation of lien—If any person liable to the corporation under section 1362, 1363, or 1364 of this title neglects or refuses to pay, after demand, the amount of such liability (including interest), there shall be a lien in favor of the corporation in the amount of such liability (including interest) upon all property and rights to property, whether real or personal, belonging to such person, except that such lien may not be in an amount in excess of 30 percent of the collective net worth of all persons described in section 1362(a) of this title.

(b) Term of lien—The lien imposed by subsection (a) arises on the date of termination of a plan, and continues until the liability imposed under section 1362, 1363, or 1364 of this title is satisfied or becomes unenforceable by reason of lapse of time.

(c) Priority—

(1) Except as otherwise provided under this section, the priority of a lien imposed under subsection (a) of this section shall be determined in the same manner as under section 6323 of Title 26 (as in effect on April 7, 1986).

* * *

(2) In a case under Title 11 or in insolvency proceedings, the lien imposed under subsection (a) shall be treated in the same manner as a tax due and owing to the United States for purposes of Title 11 or section 3713 of Title 31.

* * *

§ 4069. Treatment of transactions to evade liability; effect of corporate reorganization (§ 1369)

(a) Treatment of transactions to evade liability—If a principal purpose of any person in entering into any transaction is to evade liability to which such person would be subject under this subtitle and the transaction becomes effective within five years before the termination date of the termination on which such liability would be based, then such person and the members of such person's controlled group (determined as of the termination date) shall be subject to liability under this subtitle in connection with such termination as if such person were a contributing sponsor of the terminated plan as of the termination date. This subsection shall not cause any person to be liable under this subtitle in connection with such plan termination for any increases or improvements in the benefits provided under the plan which are adopted after the date on which the transaction referred to in the preceding sentence becomes effective.

(b) Effect of corporate reorganization—For purposes of this subtitle, the following rules apply in the case of certain corporate reorganizations:

(1) Change of identity, form, etc.—If a person ceases to exist by reason of a reorganization which involves a mere change in identity, form, or place of organization, however effected, a successor corporation resulting from such reorganization shall be treated as the person to whom this subtitle applies.

(2) Liquidation into parent corporation—If a person ceases to exist by reason of liquidation into a parent corporation, the parent corporation shall be treated as the person to whom this subtitle applies.

(3) Merger, consolidation, or division—If a person ceases to exist by reason of a merger, consolidation, or division, the successor corporation or corporations shall be treated as the person to whom this subtitle applies.

AGE DISCRIMINATION IN EMPLOYMENT ACT OF 1967

29 U.S.C. § 621 et seq.

§ 2. Congressional statement of findings and purpose (§ 621)

(a) The Congress hereby finds and declares that—

(1) in the face of rising productivity and affluence, older workers find themselves disadvantaged in their efforts to retain employment, and especially to regain employment when displaced from jobs;

(2) the setting of arbitrary age limits regardless of potential for job performance has become a common practice, and certain otherwise desirable practices may work to the disadvantage of older persons;

(3) the incidence of unemployment, especially long-term unemployment with resultant deterioration of skill, morale, and employer acceptability is, relative to the younger ages, high among older workers; their numbers are great and growing; and their employment problems grave;

(4) the existence in industries affecting commerce, of arbitrary discrimination in employment because of age, burdens commerce and the free flow of goods in commerce.

(b) It is therefore the purpose of this chapter to promote employment of older persons based on their ability rather than age; to prohibit arbitrary age discrimination in employment; to help employers and workers find ways of meeting problems arising from the impact of age on employment.

§ 4. Prohibition of age discrimination (§ 623)

(a) **Employer practices**—It shall be unlawful for an employer—

(1) to fail or refuse to hire or to discharge any individual or otherwise discriminate against any individual with respect to his compensation, terms, conditions, or privileges of employment, because of such individual's age;

(2) to limit, segregate, or classify his employees in any way which would deprive or tend to deprive any individual of employment opportunities or otherwise adversely affect his status as an employee, because of such individual's age; or

(3) to reduce the wage rate of any employee in order to comply with this Act.

* * *

(f) **Lawful practices; age an occupational qualification; other reasonable factors; laws of foreign workplace; seniority system; employee benefit plans; discharge or discipline for good cause**—It shall not be unlawful for an employer, employment agency, or labor organization—

(1) to take any action otherwise prohibited under subsections (a), (b), (c), or (e) of this section where age is a bona fide occupational qualification reasonably necessary to the normal operation of the particular business, or where the differentiation is based on reasonable factors other than age, or where such practices involve an employee in a workplace in a foreign country, and compliance with such subsections would cause such employer, or a corporation controlled by such employer, to violate the laws of the country in which such workplace is located;

535

(2) to take any action otherwise prohibited under subsection (a), (b), (c), or (e) of this section—

    (A) to observe the terms of a bona fide seniority system that is not intended to evade the purposes of this Act, except that no such seniority system shall require or permit the involuntary retirement of any individual specified by section 631(a) of this title because of the age of such individual; or

    (B) to observe the terms of a bona fide employee benefit plan—

        (i) where, for each benefit or benefit package, the actual amount of payment made or cost incurred on behalf of an older worker is no less than that made or incurred on behalf of a younger worker, as permissible under section 1625.10, title 29, Code of Federal Regulations (as in effect on June 22, 1989); or

        (ii) that is a voluntary early retirement incentive plan consistent with the relevant purpose or purposes of this chapter.

Notwithstanding clause (i) or (ii) of subparagraph (B), no such employee benefit plan or voluntary early retirement incentive plan shall excuse the failure to hire any individual, and no such employee benefit plan shall require or permit the involuntary retirement of any individual specified by section 631(a) of this title, because of the age of such individual. An employer, employment agency, or labor organization acting under subparagraph (A), or under clause (i) or (ii) of subparagraph (B), shall have the burden of proving that such actions are lawful in any civil enforcement proceeding brought under this Act; or

* * *

(i) Employee pension benefit plans; cessation or reduction of benefit accrual or of allocation to employee account; distribution of benefits after attainment of normal retirement age; compliance; highly compensated employees—

(1) Except as otherwise provided in this subsection, it shall be unlawful for an employer, an employment agency, a labor organization, or any combination thereof to establish or maintain an employee pension benefit plan which requires or permits—

    (A) in the case of a defined benefit plan, the cessation of an employee's benefit accrual, or the reduction of the rate of an employee's benefit accrual, because of age, or

    (B) in the case of a defined contribution plan, the cessation of allocations to an employee's account, or the reduction of the rate at which amounts are allocated to an employee's account, because of age.

(2) Nothing in this section shall be construed to prohibit an employer, employment agency, or labor organization from observing any provision of an employee pension benefit plan to the extent that such provision imposes (without regard to age) a limitation on the amount of benefits that the plan provides or a limitation on the number of years of service or years of participation which are taken into account for purposes of determining benefit accrual under the plan.

(3) In the case of any employee who, as of the end of any plan year under a defined benefit plan, has attained normal retirement age under such plan—

    (A) if distribution of benefits under such plan with respect to such employee has commenced as of the end of such plan year, then any requirement of this subsection for continued accrual of benefits under such plan with respect to such employee during such plan year shall be treated as satisfied to the extent of the actuarial equivalent of in-service distribution of benefits, and

(B) if distribution of benefits under such plan with respect to such employee has not commenced as of the end of such year in accordance with section 1056(a)(3) of this title and section 401(a)(14)(C) of Title 26, and the payment of benefits under such plan with respect to such employee is not suspended during such plan year pursuant to section 1053(a)(3)(B) of this title or section 411(a)(3)(B) of Title 26, then any requirement of this subsection for continued accrual of benefits under such plan with respect to such employee during such plan year shall be treated as satisfied to the extent of any adjustment in the benefit payable under the plan during such plan year attributable to the delay in the distribution of benefits after the attainment of normal retirement age.

The provisions of this paragraph shall apply in accordance with regulations of the Secretary of the Treasury. Such regulations shall provide for the application of the preceding provisions of this paragraph to all employee pension benefit plans subject to this subsection and may provide for the application of such provisions, in the case of any such employee, with respect to any period of time within a plan year.

(4) Compliance with the requirements of this subsection with respect to an employee pension benefit plan shall constitute compliance with the requirements of this section relating to benefit accrual under such plan.

(5) Paragraph (1) shall not apply with respect to any employee who is a highly compensated employee (within the meaning of section 414(q) of Title 26) to the extent provided in regulations prescribed by the Secretary of the Treasury for purposes of precluding discrimination in favor of highly compensated employees within the meaning of subchapter D of chapter 1 of Title 26.

(6) A plan shall not be treated as failing to meet the requirements of paragraph (1) solely because the subsidized portion of any early retirement benefit is disregarded in determining benefit accruals or it is a plan permitted by subsection (m) of this section.

(7) Any regulations prescribed by the Secretary of the Treasury pursuant to clause (v) of section 411(b)(1)(H) of Title 26 and subparagraphs (C) and (D) of section 411(b)(2) of Title 26 shall apply with respect to the requirements of this subsection in the same manner and to the same extent as such regulations apply with respect to the requirements of such sections 411(b)(1)(H) and 411(b)(2).

(8) A plan shall not be treated as failing to meet the requirements of this section solely because such plan provides a normal retirement age described in section 1002(24)(B) of this title and section 411(a)(8)(B) of Title 26.

(9) For purposes of this subsection—

(A) The terms "employee pension benefit plan", "defined benefit plan", "defined contribution plan", and "normal retirement age" have the meanings provided such terms in section 1002 of this title.

(B) The term "compensation" has the meaning provided by section 414(s) of Title 26.

(10) Special rules relating to age—

(A) Comparison to similarly situated younger individual—

(i) In general—A plan shall not be treated as failing to meet the requirements of paragraph (1) if a participant's accrued benefit, as determined as of any date under the terms of the plan, would be equal to or greater than that of any similarly situated, younger individual who is or could be a participant.

(ii) Similarly situated—For purposes of this subparagraph, a participant is similarly situated to any other individual if such participant is identical to such other individual in every respect (including period of service, compensation, position, date of hire, work history, and any other respect) except for age.

(iii) Disregard of subsidized early retirement benefits—In determining the accrued benefit as of any date for purposes of this clause, the subsidized portion of any early retirement benefit or retirement-type subsidy shall be disregarded.

(iv) Accrued benefit—For purposes of this subparagraph, the accrued benefit may, under the terms of the plan, be expressed as an annuity payable at normal retirement age, the balance of a hypothetical account, or the current value of the accumulated percentage of the employee's final average compensation.

(B) Applicable defined benefit plans—

(i) Interest credits—

(I) In general—An applicable defined benefit plan shall be treated as failing to meet the requirements of paragraph (1) unless the terms of the plan provide that any interest credit (or an equivalent amount) for any plan year shall be at a rate which is not greater than a market rate of return. A plan shall not be treated as failing to meet the requirements of this subclause merely because the plan provides for a reasonable minimum guaranteed rate of return or for a rate of return that is equal to the greater of a fixed or variable rate of return.

(II) Preservation of capital—An interest credit (or an equivalent amount) of less than zero shall in no event result in the account balance or similar amount being less than the aggregate amount of contributions credited to the account.

(III) Market rate of return—The Secretary of the Treasury may provide by regulation for rules governing the calculation of a market rate of return for purposes of subclause (I) and for permissible methods of crediting interest to the account (including fixed or variable interest rates) resulting in effective rates of return meeting the requirements of subclause (I). In the case of a governmental plan (as defined in the first sentence of section 414(d) of Title 26, a rate of return or a method of crediting interest established pursuant to any provision of Federal, State, or local law (including any administrative rule or policy adopted in accordance with any such law) shall be treated as a market rate of return for purposes of subclause (I) and a permissible method of crediting interest for purposes of meeting the requirements of subclause (I), except that this sentence shall only apply to a rate of return or method of crediting interest if such rate or method does not violate any other requirement of this chapter.

(ii) Special rule for plan conversions—If, after June 29, 2005, an applicable plan amendment is adopted, the plan shall be treated as failing to meet the requirements of paragraph (1)(H) unless the requirements of clause (iii) are met with respect to each individual who was a participant in the plan immediately before the adoption of the amendment.

(iii) Rate of benefit accrual—Subject to clause (iv), the requirements of this clause are met with respect to any participant if the accrued benefit of the participant under the terms of the plan as in effect after the amendment is not less than the sum of—

(I) the participant's accrued benefit for years of service before the effective date of the amendment, determined under the terms of the plan as in effect before the amendment, plus

(II) the participant's accrued benefit for years of service after the effective date of the amendment, determined under the terms of the plan as in effect after the amendment.

(iv) Special rules for early retirement subsidies—For purposes of clause (iii)(I), the plan shall credit the accumulation account or similar amount with the amount of any early retirement benefit or retirement-type subsidy for the plan year in which the participant retires if, as of such time, the participant has met the age, years of service, and other requirements under the plan for entitlement to such benefit or subsidy.

(v) Applicable plan amendment—For purposes of this subparagraph—

(I) In general—The term "applicable plan amendment" means an amendment to a defined benefit plan which has the effect of converting the plan to an applicable defined benefit plan.

(II) Special rule for coordinated benefits—If the benefits of 2 or more defined benefit plans established or maintained by an employer are coordinated in such a manner as to have the effect of the adoption of an amendment described in subclause (I), the sponsor of the defined benefit plan or plans providing for such coordination shall be treated as having adopted such a plan amendment as of the date such coordination begins.

(III) Multiple amendments—The Secretary of the Treasury shall issue regulations to prevent the avoidance of the purposes of this subparagraph through the use of 2 or more plan amendments rather than a single amendment.

(IV) Applicable defined benefit plan—For purposes of this subparagraph, the term "applicable defined benefit plan" has the meaning given such term by section 1053(f)(3) of this title.

(vi) Termination requirements—An applicable defined benefit plan shall not be treated as meeting the requirements of clause (i) unless the plan provides that, upon the termination of the plan—

(I) if the interest credit rate (or an equivalent amount) under the plan is a variable rate, the rate of interest used to determine accrued benefits under the plan shall be equal to the average of the rates of interest used under the plan during the 5-year period ending on the termination date, and

(II) the interest rate and mortality table used to determine the amount of any benefit under the plan payable in the form of an annuity payable at normal retirement age shall be the rate and table specified under the plan for such purpose as of the termination date, except that if such interest rate is a variable rate, the interest rate shall be determined under the rules of subclause (I).

(C) Certain offsets permitted—A plan shall not be treated as failing to meet the requirements of paragraph (1) solely because the plan provides offsets against benefits under the plan to the extent such offsets are allowable in applying the requirements of section 401(a) of Title 26.

(D) Permitted disparities in plan contributions or benefits—A plan shall not be treated as failing to meet the requirements of paragraph (1) solely because the plan provides a disparity in contributions or benefits with respect to which the requirements of section 401(l) of Title 26 are met.

(E) Indexing permitted—

(i) In general—A plan shall not be treated as failing to meet the requirements of paragraph (1) solely because the plan provides for indexing of accrued benefits under the plan.

(ii) Protection against loss—Except in the case of any benefit provided in the form of a variable annuity, clause (i) shall not apply with respect to any indexing which results in an accrued benefit less than the accrued benefit determined without regard to such indexing.

(iii) Indexing—For purposes of this subparagraph, the term "indexing" means, in connection with an accrued benefit, the periodic adjustment of the accrued benefit by means of the application of a recognized investment index or methodology.

(F) Early retirement benefit or retirement-type subsidy—For purposes of this paragraph, the terms "early retirement benefit" and "retirement-type subsidy" have the meaning given such terms in section 1054(g)(2)(A) of this title.

(G) Benefit accrued to date—For purposes of this paragraph, any reference to the accrued benefit shall be a reference to such benefit accrued to date.

* * *

(l) Lawful practices; minimum age as condition of eligibility for retirement benefits; deductions from severance pay; reduction of long-term disability benefits—Notwithstanding clause (i) or (ii) of subsection (f)(2)(B) of this section—

(1)(A) It shall not be a violation of subsection (a), (b), (c), or (e) of this section solely because—

(i) an employee pension benefit plan (as defined in section 1002(2) of this title) provides for the attainment of a minimum age as a condition of eligibility for normal or early retirement benefits; or

(ii) a defined benefit plan (as defined in section 1002(35) of this title) provides for—

(I) payments that constitute the subsidized portion of an early retirement benefit; or

(II) social security supplements for plan participants that commence before the age and terminate at the age (specified by the plan) when participants are eligible to receive reduced or unreduced old-age insurance benefits under title II of the Social Security Act (42 U.S.C. 401 et seq.), and that do not exceed such old-age insurance benefits.

(B) A voluntary early retirement incentive plan that—

(i) is maintained by—

(I) a local educational agency (as defined in section 7801 of Title 20), or

(II) an education association which principally represents employees of 1 or more agencies described in subclause (I) and which is described in section 501(c)(5) or (6) of Title 26 and exempt from taxation under section 501(a) of Title 26, and

(ii) makes payments or supplements described in subclauses (I) and (II) of subparagraph (A)(ii) in coordination with a defined benefit plan (as so defined) maintained by an eligible employer described in section 457(e)(1)(A) of Title 26 or by an education association described in clause (i)(II),

shall be treated solely for purposes of subparagraph (A)(ii) as if it were a part of the defined benefit plan with respect to such payments or supplements. Payments or supplements under such a voluntary early retirement incentive plan shall not constitute severance pay for purposes of paragraph (2).

(2)(A) It shall not be a violation of subsection (a), (b), (c), or (e) of this section solely because following a contingent event unrelated to age—

(i) the value of any retiree health benefits received by an individual eligible for an immediate pension;

(ii) the value of any additional pension benefits that are made available solely as a result of the contingent event unrelated to age and following which the individual is eligible for not less than an immediate and unreduced pension; or

(iii) the values described in both clauses (i) and (ii);

are deducted from severance pay made available as a result of the contingent event unrelated to age.

* * *

(3) It shall not be a violation of subsection (a), (b), (c), or (e) of this section solely because an employer provides a bona fide employee benefit plan or plans under which long-term disability benefits received by an individual are reduced by any pension benefits (other than those attributable to employee contributions)—

(A) paid to the individual that the individual voluntarily elects to receive; or

(B) for which an individual who has attained the later of age 62 or normal retirement age is eligible.

(m) Notwithstanding subsection (f)(2)(b) of this section, it shall not be a violation of subsection (a), (b), (c), or (e) of this section solely because a plan of an institution of higher education (as defined in section 1001 of title 20) offers employees who are serving under a contract of unlimited tenure (or similar arrangement providing for unlimited tenure) supplemental benefits upon voluntary retirement that are reduced or eliminated on the basis of age, if—

(1) such institution does not implement with respect to such employees any age-based reduction or cessation of benefits that are not such supplemental benefits, except as permitted by other provisions of this chapter;

(2) such supplemental benefits are in addition to any retirement or severance benefits which have been offered generally to employees serving under a contract of unlimited tenure (or similar arrangement providing for unlimited tenure), independent of any early retirement or exit-incentive plan, within the preceding 365 days; and

(3) any employee who attains the minimum age and satisfies all non-age-based conditions for receiving a benefit under the plan has an opportunity lasting not less than 180 days to elect to retire and to receive the maximum benefit that could then be elected by a younger but otherwise similarly situated employee, and the plan does not require retirement to occur sooner than 180 days after such election.

§ 7. Recordkeeping, investigation, and enforcement (§ 626)

* * *

(f) Waiver—

(1) An individual may not waive any right or claim under this chapter unless the waiver is knowing and voluntary. Except as provided in paragraph (2), a waiver may not be considered knowing and voluntary unless at a minimum—

(A) the waiver is part of an agreement between the individual and the employer that is written in a manner calculated to be understood by such individual, or by the average individual eligible to participate;

(B) the waiver specifically refers to rights or claims arising under this chapter;

(C) the individual does not waive rights or claims that may arise after the date the waiver is executed;

(D) the individual waives rights or claims only in exchange for consideration in addition to anything of value to which the individual already is entitled;

(E) the individual is advised in writing to consult with an attorney prior to executing the agreement;

(F)(i) the individual is given a period of at least 21 days within which to consider the agreement; or

(ii) if a waiver is requested in connection with an exit incentive or other employment termination program offered to a group or class of employees, the individual is given a period of at least 45 days within which to consider the agreement;

(G) the agreement provides that for a period of at least 7 days following the execution of such agreement, the individual may revoke the agreement, and the agreement shall not become effective or enforceable until the revocation period has expired;

(H) if a waiver is requested in connection with an exit incentive or other employment termination program offered to a group or class of employees, the employer (at the commencement of the period specified in subparagraph (F)) informs the individual in writing in a manner calculated to be understood by the average individual eligible to participate, as to—

(i) any class, unit, or group of individuals covered by such program, any eligibility factors for such program, and any time limits applicable to such program; and

(ii) the job titles and ages of all individuals eligible or selected for the program, and the ages of all individuals in the same job classification or organizational unit who are not eligible or selected for the program.

* * *

(3) In any dispute that may arise over whether any of the requirements, conditions, and circumstances set forth in subparagraph (A), (B), (C), (D), (E), (F), (G), or (H) of paragraph (1), or subparagraph (A) or (B) of paragraph (2), have been met, the party asserting the validity of a waiver shall have the burden of proving in a court of competent jurisdiction that a waiver was knowing and voluntary pursuant to paragraph (1) or (2).

(4) No waiver agreement may affect the Commission's rights and responsibilities to enforce this chapter. No waiver may be used to justify interfering with the protected right of an employee to file a charge or participate in an investigation or proceeding conducted by the Commission.

§ 12. Age limits (§ 631)

(a) Individuals at least 40 years of age—The prohibitions in this chapter shall be limited to individuals who are at least 40 years of age.

* * *

(c) Bona fide executives or high policymakers—

(1) Nothing in this chapter shall be construed to prohibit compulsory retirement of any employee who has attained 65 years of age and who, for the 2-year period immediately before retirement, is employed in a bona fide executive or a high policymaking position, if such employee is entitled to an immediate nonforfeitable annual retirement benefit from a pension, profit-sharing, savings, or deferred compensation plan, or any combination of such plans, of the employer of such employee, which equals, in the aggregate, at least $44,000.

(2) In applying the retirement benefit test of paragraph (1) of this subsection, if any such retirement benefit is in a form other than a straight life annuity (with no ancillary benefits), or if employees contribute to any such plan or make rollover contributions, such benefit shall be adjusted in accordance with regulations prescribed by the Equal Employment Opportunity Commission, after consultation with the Secretary of the Treasury, so that the benefit is the equivalent of a straight life annuity (with no ancillary benefits) under a plan to which employees do not contribute and under which no rollover contributions are made.

AMERICANS WITH DISABILITIES ACT OF 1990

42 U.S.C. § 12101 et seq.

§ 3. Definition of disability (§ 12102)

As used in this chapter:

(1) Disability—The term "disability" means, with respect to an individual—

(A) a physical or mental impairment that substantially limits one or more major life activities of such individual;

(B) a record of such an impairment; or

(C) being regarded as having such an impairment (as described in paragraph (3)).

(2) Major life activities—

(A) In general—For purposes of paragraph (1), major life activities include, but are not limited to, caring for oneself, performing manual tasks, seeing, hearing, eating, sleeping, walking, standing, lifting, bending, speaking, breathing, learning, reading, concentrating, thinking, communicating, and working.

(B) Major bodily functions—For purposes of paragraph (1), a major life activity also includes the operation of a major bodily function, including but not limited to, functions of the immune system, normal cell growth, digestive, bowel, bladder, neurological, brain, respiratory, circulatory, endocrine, and reproductive functions.

(3) Regarded as having such an impairment—For purposes of paragraph (1)(C):

(A) An individual meets the requirement of "being regarded as having such an impairment" if the individual establishes that he or she has been subjected to an action prohibited under this chapter because of an actual or perceived physical or mental impairment whether or not the impairment limits or is perceived to limit a major life activity.

(B) Paragraph (1)(C) shall not apply to impairments that are transitory and minor. A transitory impairment is an impairment with an actual or expected duration of 6 months or less.

(4) Rules of construction regarding the definition of disability—The definition of "disability" in paragraph (1) shall be construed in accordance with the following:

(A) The definition of disability in this chapter shall be construed in favor of broad coverage of individuals under this chapter, to the maximum extent permitted by the terms of this chapter.

(B) The term "substantially limits" shall be interpreted consistently with the findings and purposes of the ADA Amendments Act of 2008.

(C) An impairment that substantially limits one major life activity need not limit other major life activities in order to be considered a disability.

(D) An impairment that is episodic or in remission is a disability if it would substantially limit a major life activity when active.

(E)(i) The determination of whether an impairment substantially limits a major life activity shall be made without regard to the ameliorative effects of mitigating measures such as—

(I) medication, medical supplies, equipment, or appliances, low-vision devices (which do not include ordinary eyeglasses or contact lenses), prosthetics including limbs and devices, hearing aids and cochlear implants or other implantable hearing devices, mobility devices, or oxygen therapy equipment and supplies;

(II) use of assistive technology;

(III) reasonable accommodations or auxiliary aids or services; or

(IV) learned behavioral or adaptive neurological modifications.

(ii) The ameliorative effects of the mitigating measures of ordinary eyeglasses or contact lenses shall be considered in determining whether an impairment substantially limits a major life activity.

(iii) As used in this subparagraph—

(I) the term "ordinary eyeglasses or contact lenses" means lenses that are intended to fully correct visual acuity or eliminate refractive error; and

(II) the term "low-vision devices" means devices that magnify, enhance, or otherwise augment a visual image.

§ 101. Definitions (§ 12111)

As used in this subchapter:

* * *

(8) Qualified individual—The term "qualified individual" means an individual who, with or without reasonable accommodation, can perform the essential functions of the employment position that such individual holds or desires. For the purposes of this subchapter, consideration shall be given to the employer's judgment as to what functions of a job are essential, and if an employer has prepared a written description before advertising or interviewing applicants for the job, this description shall be considered evidence of the essential functions of the job.

* * *

§ 102. Discrimination (§ 12112)

(a) General rule—No covered entity shall discriminate against a qualified individual on the basis of disability in regard to job application procedures, the hiring, advancement, or discharge of employees, employee compensation, job training, and other terms, conditions, and privileges of employment.

* * *

§ 501. Construction (§ 12201)

* * *

(c) **Insurance**—Subchapters I through III of this chapter and Title IV of this Act shall not be construed to prohibit or restrict—

(1) an insurer, hospital or medical service company, health maintenance organization, or any agent, or entity that administers benefit plans, or similar organizations from underwriting risks, classifying risks, or administering such risks that are based on or not inconsistent with State law; or

(2) a person or organization covered by this chapter from establishing, sponsoring, observing or administering the terms of a bona fide benefit plan that are based on underwriting risks, classifying risks, or administering such risks that are based on or not inconsistent with State law; or

(3) a person or organization covered by this chapter from establishing, sponsoring, observing or administering the terms of a bona fide benefit plan that is not subject to State laws that regulate insurance.

Paragraphs (1), (2), and (3) shall not be used as a subterfuge to evade the purposes of subchapter[s] I and III.

* * *

ERISA REORGANIZATION PLAN

REORGANIZATION PLAN NO. 4 OF 1978

5 U.S.C.—Appendix 1.

Prepared by the President and transmitted to the Senate and the House of Representatives in Congress assembled, August 10, 1978, pursuant to the provisions of Chapter 9 of Title 5 of the United States Code.

EMPLOYEE RETIREMENT INCOME SECURITY ACT TRANSFERS

§ 101. Transfer to the Secretary of the Treasury

Except as otherwise provided in Sections 104 and 106 of this Plan, all authority of the Secretary of Labor to issue the following described documents pursuant to the statutes hereinafter specified is hereby transferred to the Secretary of the Treasury:

(a) regulations, rulings, opinions, variances and waivers under Parts 2 [section 1051 et seq. of Title 29] and 3 [section 1081 et seq. of Title 29] of Subtitle B of Title I and subsection 1012(c) [set out as a note under section 411 of Title 26] of Title II of the Employee Retirement Income Security Act of 1974 (29 U.S.C. 1001 note) (hereinafter referred to as "ERISA"), *except* for sections and subsections 201, 203(a)(3)(B), 209, and 301(a) of ERISA [sections 1051, 1053(a)(3)(B), 1059, and 1081(a) of Title 29];

(b) such regulations, rulings, and opinions which are granted to the Secretary of Labor under Sections 404, 410, 411, 412, and 413 of the Internal Revenue Code of 1986, as amended [Title 26, (hereinafter referred to as the "Code")[,] *except* for subsection 411(a)(3)(B) of the Code and the definitions of "collectively bargained plan" and "collective bargaining agreement" contained in subsections 404 (a)(1)(B) and (a)(1)(C), 410(b)(2)(A) and (b)(2)(B), and 413(a)(1) of the Code; and

(c) regulations, rulings, and opinions under subsections 3(19), 3(22), 3(23), 3(24), 3(25), 3(27), 3(28), 3(29), 3(30), and 3(31) of Subtitle A of Title I of ERISA [section 1002(19), (22), (23), (24), (25), (27), (28), (29), (30), and (31) of Title 29].

§ 102. Transfers to the Secretary of Labor

Except as otherwise provided in Section 105 of this Plan, all authority of the Secretary of the Treasury to issue the following described documents pursuant to the statutes hereinafter specified is hereby transferred to the Secretary of Labor:

(a) regulations, rulings, opinions, and exemptions under section 4975 of the Code, except for (i) subsections 4975(a), (b), (c)(3), (d)(3), (e)(1), and (e)(7) of the Code; (ii) to the extent necessary for the continued enforcement of subsections 4975(a) and (b) by the Secretary of the Treasury, subsections 4975(f)(1), (f)(2), (f)(4), (f)(5) and (f)(6) of the Code; and (iii) exemptions with respect to transactions that are exempted by subsection 404(c) of ERISA from the provisions of Part 4 of Subtitle B of Title I of ERISA [section 1101 et seq. of Title 29]; and

(b) regulations, rulings, and opinions under subsection 2003(c) of ERISA [set out as a note under section 4975 of Title 26, except for subsection 2003(c)(1)(B).

§ 103. Coordination Concerning Certain Fiduciary Actions

In the case of fiduciary actions which are subject to Part 4 of Subtitle B of Title I of ERISA [section 1101 et seq. of Title 29], the Secretary of the Treasury shall notify the Secretary of Labor prior to the time of commencing any proceeding to determine whether the action violates the exclusive benefit rule of subsection 401(a) of the Code, but not later than prior to issuing a preliminary notice of intent to disqualify under that rule, and the Secretary of the Treasury shall not issue a determination that a plan or trust does not satisfy the requirements of subsection 401(a) by reason of the exclusive benefit rule of subsection 401(a), unless within 90 days after the date on which the Secretary of the Treasury notifies the Secretary of Labor of pending action, the Secretary of Labor certifies that he has no objection to the disqualification or the Secretary of Labor fails to respond to the Secretary of the Treasury. The requirements of this paragraph do not apply in the case of any termination or jeopardy assessment under sections 6851 or 6861 of the Code that has been approved in advance by the Commissioner of Internal Revenue, or, as delegated, the Assistant Commissioner for Employee Plans and Exempt Organizations.

§ 104. Enforcement by the Secretary of Labor

The transfers provided for in Section 101 of this Plan shall not affect the ability of the Secretary of Labor, subject to the provisions of Title III of ERISA [section 1201 et seq. of Title 29] relating to jurisdiction, administration, and enforcement, to engage in enforcement under Section 502 of ERISA [section 1132 of Title 29] or to exercise the authority set forth under Title III of ERISA [section 1201 et seq. of Title 29], including the ability to make interpretations necessary to engage in such enforcement or to exercise such authority. However, in bringing such actions and in exercising such authority with respect to Parts 2 [section 1051 et seq. of Title 29] and 3 [section 1081 et seq. of Title 29] of Subtitle B of Title I of ERISA and any definitions for which the authority of the Secretary of Labor is transferred to the Secretary of the Treasury as provided in Section 101 of this Plan, the Secretary of Labor shall be bound by the regulations, rulings, opinions, variances, and waivers issued by the Secretary of the Treasury.

§ 105. Enforcement by the Secretary of the Treasury

The transfers provided for in Section 102 of this Plan shall not affect the ability of the Secretary of the Treasury, subject to the provisions of Title III of ERISA [section 1201 et seq. of Title 29] relating to jurisdiction, administration, and enforcement, (a) to audit plans and employers and to enforce the excise tax provisions of subsections 4975(a) and 4975(b) of the Code, to exercise the authority set forth in subsections 502(b)(1) and 502(h) of ERISA [section 1132(b)(1) and (h) of Title 29], or to exercise the authority set forth in Title III of ERISA [section 1201 et seq. of Title 29], including the ability to make interpretations necessary to audit, to enforce such taxes, and to exercise such authority; and (b) consistent with the coordination requirements under Section 103 of this Plan, to disqualify, under section 401 of the Code, a plan subject to Part 4 of Subtitle B of Title I of ERISA [section 1101 et seq. of Title 29], including the ability to make the interpretations necessary to make such disqualification. However, in enforcing such excise taxes and, to the extent applicable, in disqualifying such plans the Secretary of the Treasury shall be bound by the regulations, rulings, opinions, and exemptions issued by the Secretary of Labor pursuant to the authority transferred to the Secretary of Labor as provided in Section 102 of this Plan.

§ 106. Coordination for Section 101 Transfers

(a) The Secretary of the Treasury shall not exercise the functions transferred pursuant to Section 101 of this Plan to issue in proposed or final form any of the documents described in subsection (b) of this Section in any case in which such documents would significantly impact on or substantially affect collectively bargained plans unless, within 100 calendar days after the

Secretary of the Treasury notifies the Secretary of Labor of such proposed action, the Secretary of Labor certifies that he has no objection or he fails to respond to the Secretary of the Treasury. The fact of such a notification, except for such notification for documents described in subsection (b)(iv) of this Section, from the Secretary of the Treasury to the Secretary of Labor shall be announced by the Secretary of Labor to the public within ten days following the date of receipt of the notification by the Secretary of Labor.

(b) The documents to which this Section applies are:

(i) amendments to regulations issued pursuant to subsections 202(a)(3), 203(b)(2) and (3)(A), 204(b)(3)(A), (C), and (E), and 210(a)(2) of ERISA [sections 1052(a)(3), 1053(b)(2) and (3)(A), 1054(b)(3)(A), (C), and (E), and 1060(a)(2) of Title 29], and subsections 410(a)(3) and 411(a)(5), (6)(A), and (b)(3)(A), (C), and (E), 413(b)(4) and (c)(3) and 414(f) of the Code;

(ii) regulations issued pursuant to subsections 204(b)(3)(D), 302(d)(2), and 304(d)(1), (d)(2), and (e)(2)(A) of ERISA [29 U.S.C.A. §§ 1054(b)(3)(D), 1082(d)(2), and 1084(d)(1), (d)(2), and (E)(2)(A)], and subsections 411(b)(3)(D), 412(c)(2) and 431(d)(1), (d)(2), and (e)(2)(A)of the Code; and

(iii) revenue rulings (within the meaning of 26 CFR Section 601.201(a)(6)), revenue procedures, and similar publications, if the rulings, procedures and publications are issued under one of the statutory provisions listed in (i) and (ii) of this subsection; and

(iv) rulings (within the meaning of 26 CFR Section 601.201(a)(2)) issued prior to the issuance of a published regulation under one of the statutory provisions listed in (i) and (ii) of this subsection and not issued under a published Revenue Ruling.

(c) For those documents described in subsections (b)(i), (b)(ii) and (b)(iii) of this Section, the Secretary of Labor may request the Secretary of the Treasury to initiate the actions described in this Section 106 of this Plan.

* * *

TREASURY REGULATIONS

§ 1.83-1. Property transferred in connection with the performance of services.

(a) *Inclusion in gross income*—(1) **General rule**. Section 83 provides rules for the taxation of property transferred to an employee or independent contractor (or beneficiary thereof) in connection with the performance of services by such employee or independent contractor. In general, such property is not taxable under section 83(a) until it has been transferred (as defined in § 1.83-3(a)) to such person and become substantially vested (as defined in § 1.83-3(b)) in such person. In that case, the excess of—

(i) The fair market value of such property (determined without regard to any lapse restriction, as defined in § 1.83-3(i)) at the time that the property becomes substantially vested, over

(ii) The amount (if any) paid for such property, shall be included as compensation in the gross income of such employee or independent contractor for the taxable year in which the property becomes substantially vested. Until such property becomes substantially vested, the transferor shall be regarded as the owner of such property, and any income from such property received by the employee or independent contractor (or beneficiary thereof) or the right to the use of such property by the employee or independent contractor constitutes additional compensation and shall be included in the gross income of such employee or independent contractor for the taxable year in which such income is received or such use is made available. This paragraph applies to a transfer of property in connection with the performance of services even though the transferor is not the person for whom such services are performed.

(2) **Life insurance**. The cost of life insurance protection under a life insurance contract, retirement income contract, endowment contract, or other contract providing life insurance protection is taxable generally under section 61 and the regulations thereunder during the period such contract remains substantially nonvested (as defined in § 1.83-3(b)). For the taxation of life insurance protection under a split-dollar life insurance arrangement (as defined in § 1.61-22(b)(1) or (2)), see § 1.61-22.

(3) **Cross references**. For rules concerning the treatment of employers and other transferors of property in connection with the performance of services, see section 83(h) and § 1.83-6. For rules concerning the taxation of beneficiaries of an employees' trust that is not exempt under section 501(a), see section 402(b) and the regulations thereunder.

(b) *Subsequent sale, forfeiture, or other disposition of nonvested property*. (1) If substantially nonvested property (that has been transferred in connection with the performance of services) is subsequently sold or otherwise disposed of to a third party in an arm's length transaction while still substantially nonvested, the person who performed such services shall realize compensation in an amount equal to the excess of—

(i) The amount realized on such sale or other disposition, over

(ii) The amount (if any) paid for such property.

Such amount of compensation is includible in his gross income in accordance with his method of accounting. Two preceding sentences also apply when the person disposing of the property has received it in a non-arm's length transaction described in paragraph (c) of this section. In addition, section 83(a) and paragraph (a) of this section shall thereafter cease to apply with respect to such property.

(2) If substantially nonvested property that has been transferred in connection with

550

the performance of services to the person performing such services is forfeited while still substantially nonvested and held by such person, the difference between the amount paid (if any) and the amount received upon forfeiture (if any) shall be treated as an ordinary gain or loss. This paragraph (b)(2) does not apply to property to which § 1.83-2(a) applies.

(3) This paragraph (b) shall not apply to, and no gain shall be recognized on, any sale, forfeiture, or other disposition described in this paragraph to the extent that any property received in exchange therefor is substantially nonvested. Instead, section 83 and this section shall apply with respect to such property received (as if it were substituted for the property disposed of).

(c) *Dispositions of nonvested property not at arm's length.* If substantially nonvested property (that has been transferred in connection with the performance of services) is disposed of in a transaction which is not at arm's length and the property remains substantially nonvested, the person who performed such services realizes compensation equal in amount to the sum of any money and the fair market value of any substantially vested property received in such disposition. Such amount of compensation is includible in his gross income in accordance with his method of accounting. However, such amount of compensation shall not exceed the fair market value of the property disposed of at the time of disposition (determined without regard to any lapse restriction), reduced by the amount paid for such property. In addition, section 83 and these regulations shall continue to apply with respect to such property, except that any amount previously includible in gross income under this paragraph (c) shall thereafter be treated as an amount paid for such property. For example, if in 1971 an employee pays $50 for a share of stock which has a fair market value of $100 and is substantially nonvested at that time and later in 1971 (at a time when the property still has a fair market value of $100 and is still substantially nonvested) the employee disposes of, in a transaction not at arm's length, the share of stock to his wife for

$10, the employee realizes compensation of $10 in 1971. If in 1972, when the share of stock has a fair market value of $120, it becomes substantially vested, the employee realizes additional compensation in 1972 in the amount of $60 (the $120 fair market value of the stock less both the $50 price paid for the stock and the $10 taxed as compensation in 1971). For purposes of this paragraph, if substantially nonvested property has been transferred to a person other than the person who performed the services, and the transferee dies holding the property while the property is still substantially nonvested and while the person who performed the services is alive, the transfer which results by reason of the death of such transferee is a transfer not at arm's length.

(d) *Certain transfers upon death.* If substantially nonvested property has been transferred in connection with the performance of services and the person who performed such services dies while the property is still substantially nonvested, any income realized on or after such death with respect to such property under this section is income in respect of a decedent to which the rules of section 691 apply. In such a case the income in respect of such property shall be taxable under section 691 (except to the extent not includible under section 101(b)) to the estate or beneficiary of the person who performed the services, in accordance with section 83 and the regulations thereunder. However, if an item of income is realized upon such death before July 21, 1978, because the property became substantially vested upon death, the person responsible for filing decedent's income tax return for decedent's last taxable year may elect to treat such item as includible in gross income for decedent's last taxable year by including such item in gross income on the return or amended return filed for decedent's last taxable year.

(e) *Forfeiture after substantial vesting.* If a person is taxable under section 83(a) when the property transferred becomes substantially vested and thereafter the person's beneficial interest in such property is nevertheless forfeited pursuant to a lapse restriction, any loss incurred by such person (but not by a beneficiary of such person) upon such forfeiture shall be an ordinary loss to the extent the basis in such property has been increased as a result of the recognition of income by such person under section 83(a) with respect to such property.

(f) *Examples.* The provisions of this section may be illustrated by the following examples:

Example (1). On November 1, 1978, X corporation sells to E, an employee, 100 shares of X corporation stock at $10 per share. At the time of such sale the fair market value of the X corporation stock is $100 per share. Under the terms of the sale each share of stock is subject to a substantial risk of forfeiture which will not lapse until November 1, 1988. Evidence of this restriction is stamped on the face of E's stock certificates, which are therefore nontransferable (within the meaning of § 1.83-3(d)). Since in 1978 E's stock is substantially nonvested, E does not include any of such amount in his gross income as compensation in 1978. On November 1, 1988, the fair market value of the X corporation stock is $250 per share. Since the X corporation stock becomes substantially vested in 1988, E must include $24,000 (100 shares of X corporation stock $250 fair market value per share less $10 price paid by E for each share) as compensation for 1988. Dividends paid by X to E on E's stock after it was transferred to E on November 1, 1973, are taxable to E as additional compensation during the period E's stock is substantially nonvested and are deductible as such by X.

Example (2). Assume the facts are the same as in example (1), except that on November 1, 1985, each share of stock of X corporation in E's hands could as a matter of law be transferred to a bona fide purchaser who would not be required to forfeit the stock if the risk of forfeiture materialized. In the event, however, that the risk materializes, E would be liable in damages to X. On November 1, 1985, the fair market value of the X corporation stock is $230 per share. Since E's stock is transferable within the meaning of § 1.83-3(d)

in 1985, the stock is substantially vested and E must include $22,000 (100 shares of X corporation stock X $230 fair market value per share less $10 price paid by E for each share) as compensation for 1985.

Example (3). Assume the facts are the same as in example (1) except that, in 1984 E sells his 100 shares of X corporation stock in an arm's length sale to I, an investment company, for $120 per share. At the time of this sale each share of X corporation's stock has a fair market value of $200. Under paragraph (b) of this section, E must include $11,000 (100 shares of X corporation stock X $120 amount realized per share less $10 price paid by E per share) as compensation for 1984 notwithstanding that the stock remains nontransferable and is still subject to a substantial risk of forfeiture at the time of such sale. Under § 1.83-4(b)(2), I's basis in the X corporation stock is $120 per share.

§ 1.83-2. Election to include in gross income in year of transfer.

(a) *In general.* If property is transferred (within the meaning of § 1.83-3(a)) in connection with the performance of services, the person performing such services may elect to include in gross income under section 83(b) the excess (if any) of the fair market value of the property at the time of transfer (determined without regard to any lapse restriction, as defined in § 1.83-3(i)) over the amount (if any) paid for such property, as compensation for services. The fact that the transferee has paid full value for the property transferred, realizing no bargain element in the transaction, does not preclude the use of the election as provided for in this section. If this election is made, the substantial vesting rules of section 83(a) and the regulations thereunder do not apply with respect to such property, and except as otherwise provided in section 83(d)(2) and the regulations thereunder (relating to the cancellation of a nonlapse restriction), any subsequent appreciation in the value of the property is not taxable as compensation to the person who performed the services. Thus, property with respect to which this election is made shall be includible in gross income as of the time of transfer, even though such property is substantially nonvested (as defined in § 1.83-3(b)) at the time of transfer, and no compensation will be includible in gross income when such property becomes substantially vested (as defined in § 1.83-3(b)). In computing the gain or loss from the subsequent sale or exchange of such property, its basis shall be the amount paid for the property increased by the amount included in gross income under section 83(b). If property for which a section 83(b) election is in effect is forfeited while substantially nonvested, such forfeiture shall be treated as a sale or exchange upon which there is realized a loss equal to the excess (if any) of—

(1) The amount paid (if any) for such property, over,

(2) The amount realized (if any) upon such forfeiture.

If such property is a capital asset in the hands of the taxpayer, such loss shall be a capital loss. A sale or other disposition of the property that is in substance a forfeiture, or is made in contemplation of a forfeiture, shall be treated as a forfeiture under the two immediately preceding sentences.

(b) *Time for making election.* Except as provided in the following sentence, the election referred to in paragraph (a) of this section shall be filed not later than 30 days after the date the property was transferred (or, if later, January 29, 1970) and may be filed prior to the date of transfer. Any statement filed before February 15, 1970, which was amended not later than February 16, 1970, in order to make it conform to the requirements of paragraph (e) of this section, shall be deemed a proper election under section 83(b).

(c) *Manner of making election.* The election referred to in paragraph (a) of this section is made by filing one copy of a written statement with the internal revenue office with whom the person who performed the services files his return.

(d) *Additional copies.* The person who performed the services shall also submit a copy of the statement referred to in paragraph (c) of this section to the person for whom the services are performed. In addition, if the person who performs the services and the transferee of such property are not the same person, the person who performs the services shall submit a copy of such statement to the transferee of the property.

(e) Content of statement. The statement shall be signed by the person making the election and shall indicate that it is being made under section 83(b) of the Code, and shall contain the following information:

(1) The name, address and taxpayer identification number of the taxpayer;

(2) A description of each property with respect to which the election is being made;

(3) The date or dates on which the property is tansferred and the taxable year (for example, "calendar year 1970" or "fiscal year ending May 31, 1970") for which such election was made;

(4) The nature of the restriction or restrictions to which the property is subject;

(5) The fair market value at the time of transfer (determined without regard to any lapse restriction, as defined in § 1.83-3(i)) of each property with respect to which the election is being made;

(6) The amount (if any) paid for such property; and

(7) With respect to elections made after July 21, 1978, a statement to the effect that copies have been furnished to other persons as provided in paragraph (d) of this section.

(f) *Revocability of election.* An election under section 83(b) may not be revoked except with the consent of the Commissioner. Consent will be granted only in the case where the transferee is under a mistake of fact as to the underlying transaction and must be requested within 60 days of the date on which the mistake of fact first became known to the person who made the election. In any event, a mistake as to the value, or decline in the value, of the property with respect to which an election under section 83(b) has been made or a failure to perform an act contemplated at the time of transfer of such property does not constitute a mistake of fact.

(g) Effective/applicability date. Paragraph (c) of this section applies to property transferred on or after January 1, 2016.

§ 1.83-3. Meaning and use of certain terms.

(a) *Transfer*—(1) **In general**. For purposes of section 83 and the regulations thereunder, a transfer of property occurs when a person acquires a beneficial ownership interest in such property (disregarding any lapse restriction, as defined in § 1.83-3(i)). For special rules applying to the transfer of a life insurance contract (or an undivided interest therein) that is part of a split-dollar life insurance arrangement (as defined in § 1.61-22(b)(1) or (2)), see § 1.61-22(g).

(2) **Option**. The grant of an option to purchase certain property does not constitute a transfer of such property. However, see § 1.83-7 for the extent to which the grant of the option itself is subject to section 83. In addition, if the amount paid for the transfer of property is an indebtedness secured by the transferred property, on which there is no personal liability to pay all or a substantial part of such indebtedness, such transaction may be in substance the same as the grant of an option. The determination of the substance of the transaction shall be based upon all the facts and circumstances. The factors to be taken into account include the type of property involved, the extent to which the risk that the property will decline in value has been transferred, and the likelihood that the purchase price will, in fact, be paid. See also § 1.83-4(c) for the treatment of forgiveness of indebtedness that has constituted an amount paid.

(3) **Requirement that property be returned**. Similarly, no transfer may have occurred where property is transferred under conditions that require its return upon the happening of an event that is certain to occur, such as the termination of employment. In such a case, whether there is, in fact, a transfer depends upon all the facts and circumstances. Factors which indicate that no transfer has occurred are described in paragraph (a)(4), (5), and (6) of this section.

(4) **Similarity to option**. An indication that no transfer has occurred is the extent to which the conditions relating to a transfer are similar to an option.

(5) **Relationship to fair market value**. An indication that no transfer has occurred is the extent to which the consideration to be paid the transferee upon surrendering the property does not approach the fair market value of the property at the time of surrender. For purposes of paragraph (a) (5) and (6) of this section, fair market value includes fair market value determined under the rules of § 1.83-5(a)(1), relating to the valuation of property subject to nonlapse restrictions. Therefore, the existence of a nonlapse restriction referred to in § 1.83-5(a)(1) is not a factor indicating no transfer has occurred.

(6) **Risk of loss**. An indication that no transfer has occurred is the extent to which the transferee does not incur the risk of a beneficial owner that the value of the property at the time of transfer will decline substantially. Therefore, for purposes of this (6), risk of decline in property value is not limited to the risk that any amount paid for the property may be lost.

(7) **Examples**. The provisions of this paragraph may be illustrated by the following examples:

Example (1). On January 3, 1971, X corporation sells for $500 to S, a salesman of X, 10 shares of stock in X corporation with a fair market value of $1,000. The stock is nontransferable and subject to return to the corporation (for $500) if S's sales do not reach a certain level by December 31, 1971. Disregarding the restriction concerning S's sales (since the restrictions is a lapse restriction), S's interest in the stock is that of a beneficial owner and therefore a transfer occurs on January 3, 1971.

Example (2). On November 17, 1972, W sells to E 100 shares of stock in W corporation with a fair market value of $10,000 in exchange for a $10,000 note without personal liability. The note requires E to make yearly payments of $2,000 commencing in 1973. E collects the dividends, votes the stock and pays the interest on the note. However, he makes no payments toward the face amount of the note. Because E has no personal liability on the note, and since E is making no payments towards the face amount of the note, the likelihood of E paying the full purchase price is in substantial doubt. As a result E has not incurred the risks of a beneficial owner that the value of the stock will decline. Therefore, no transfer of the stock has occurred on November 17, 1972, but an option to purchase the stock has been granted to E.

Example (3). On January 3, 1971, X corporation purports to transfer to E, an employee, 100 shares of stock in X corporation. The X stock is subject to the sole restriction that E must sell such stock to X on termination of employment for any reason for an amount which is equal to the excess (if any) of the book value of the X stock at termination of employment over book value on January 3, 1971. The stock is not transferable by E and the restrictions on transfer are stamped on the certificate. Under these facts and circumstances, there is no transfer of the X stock within the meeting of section 83.

Example (4). Assume the same facts as in example (3) except that E paid $3,000 for the stock and that the restriction required E upon termination of employment to sell the stock to M for the total amount of dividends that have been declared on the stock since September 2, 1971, or $3,000 whichever is higher. Again, under the facts and circumstances, no transfer of the X stock has occurred.

Example (5). On July 4, 1971, X corporation purports to transfer to G, an employee, 100 shares of X stock. The stock is subject to the sole restriction that upon termination of employment G must sell the stock to X for the greater of its fair market value at such time or $100, the amount G paid for the stock. On July 4, 1971 the X stock has a fair market value of $100. Therefore, G does not incur the risk of a beneficial owner that the value of the stock at the time of transfer ($100) will decline substantially. Under these facts and circumstances, no transfer has occurred.

(b) *Substantially vested and substantially nonvested property.* For purposes of section 83 and the regulations thereunder, property is substantially nonvested when it is subject to a substantial risk of forfeiture, within the meaning of paragraph (c) of this section, and is nontransferable, within the meaning of paragraph (d) of this section. Property is substantially vested for such purposes when it is either transferable or not subject to a substantial risk of forfeiture.

(c) *Substantial risk of forfeiture*—(1) **In general.** For purposes of section 83 and these regulations, whether a risk of forfeiture is substantial or not depends upon the facts and circumstances. Except as set forth in paragraphs (j) and (k) of this section, a substantial risk of forfeiture exists only if rights in property that are transferred are conditioned, directly or indirectly, upon the future performance (or refraining from performance) of substantial services by any person, or upon the occurrence of a condition related to a purpose of the transfer if the possibility of forfeiture is substantial. Property is not transferred subject to a substantial risk of forfeiture if at the time of transfer the facts and circumstances demonstrate that the forfeiture condition is unlikely to be enforced. Further, property is not transferred subject to a substantial risk of forfeiture to the extent that the employer is required to pay the fair market value of a portion of such property to the employee upon the return of such property. The risk that the value of property will decline during a certain period of time does not constitute a substantial risk of forfeiture. A nonlapse restriction, standing by itself, will not result in a substantial risk of forfeiture. A restriction on the transfer of property, whether contractual or byoperation of applicable law, will result in a substantial risk of forfeiture only if and to the extent that the restriction is described in paragraph (j) or

(k) of this section. For this purpose, transfer restrictions that will not result in a substantial risk of forfeiture include, but are not limited to, restrictions that if violated, whether by transfer or attempted transfer of the property, would result in the forfeiture of some or all of the property, or liability by the employee for any damages, penalties, fees, or other amount.

(2) **Illustrations of substantial risks of forfeiture**. The regularity of the performance of services and the time spent in performing such services tend to indicate whether services required by a condition are substantial. The fact that the person performing services has the right to decline to perform such services without forfeiture may tend to establish that services are insubstantial. Where stock is transferred to an underwriter prior to a public offering and the full enjoyment of such stock is expressly or impliedly conditioned upon the successful completion of the underwriting, the stock is subject to a substantial risk of forfeiture. Where an employee receives property from an employer subject to a requirement that it be returned if the total earnings of the employer do not increase, such property is subject to a substantial risk of forfeiture. On the other hand, requirements that the property be returned to the employer if the employee is discharged for cause or for committing a crime will not be considered to result in a substantial risk of forfeiture. An enforceable requirement that the property be returned to the employer if the employee accepts a job with a competing firm will not ordinarily be considered to result in a substantial risk of forfeiture unless the particular facts and circumstances indicate to the contrary. Factors which may be taken into account in determining whether a covenant not to compete constitutes a substantial risk of forfeiture are the age of the employee, the availability of alternative employment opportunities, the likelihood of the employee's obtaining such other employment, the degree of skill possessed by the employee, the employee's health, and the practice (if any) of the employer to enforce such covenants. Similarly, rights in property transferred to a retiring employee subject to the sole requirement that it be returned unless he renders consulting services upon the request of his former employer will not be considered subject to a substantial risk of forfeiture unless he is in fact expected to perform substantial services.

(3) **Enforcement of forfeiture condition**. In determining whether the possibility of forfeiture is substantial in the case of rights in property transferred to an employee of a corporation who owns a significant amount of the total combined voting power or value of all classes of stock of the employer corporation or of its parent corporation, there will be taken into account (i) the employee's relationship to other stockholders and the extent of their control, potential control and possible loss of control of the corporation, (ii) the position of the employee in the corporation and the extent to which he is subordinate to other employees, (iii) the employee's relationship to the officers and directors of the corporation, (iv) the person or persons who must approve the employee's discharge, and (v) past actions of the employer in enforcing the provisions of the restrictions. For example, if an employee would be considered as having received rights in property subject to a substantial risk of forfeiture, but for the fact that the employee owns 20 percent of the single class of stock in the transferor corporation, and if the remaining 80 percent of the class of stock is owned by an unrelated individual (or members of such an individual's family) so that the possibility of the corporation enforcing a restriction on such rights is substantial, then such rights are subject to a substantial risk of forfeiture. On the other hand, if 4 percent of the voting power of all the stock of a corporation is owned by the president of such corporation and the remaining stock is so diversely held by the public that the president, in effect, controls the corporation, then the possibility of the corporation enforcing a restriction on rights in property transferred to the president is not substantial, and such rights are not subject to a substantial risk of forfeiture.

(4) **Examples**. The rules contained in paragraph (c)(1) of this section may be illustrated by the following examples. In each example it is assumed that, if the conditions on

transfer are not satisfied, the forfeiture provision will be enforced.

Example (1). On November 1, 1971, corporation X transfers in connection with the performance of services to E, an employee, 100 shares of corporation X stock for $90 per share. Under the terms of the transfer, E will be subject to a binding commitment to resell the stock to corporation X at $90 per share if he leaves the employment of corporation X for any reason prior to the expiration of a 2-year period from the date of such transfer. Since E must perform substantial services for corporation X and will not be paid more than $90 for the stock, regardless of its value, if he fails to perform such services during such 2-year period, E's rights in the stock are subject to a substantial risk of forfeiture during such period.

Example (2). On November 10, 1971, corporation X transfers in connection with the performance of services to a trust for the benefit of employees, $100x. Under the terms of the trust any child of an employee who is an enrolled full-time student at an accredited educational institution as a candidate for a degree will receive an annual grant of cash for each academic year the student completes as a student in good standing, up to a maximum of four years. E, an employee, has a child who is enrolled as a full-time student at an accredited college as a candidate for a degree. Therefore, E has a beneficial interest in the assets of the trust equalling the value of four cash grants. Since E's child must complete one year of college in order to receive a cash grant, E's interest in the trust assets are subject to a substantial risk of forfeiture to the extent E's child has not become entitled to any grants.

Example (3). On November 25, 1971, corporation X gives to E, an employee, in connection with his performance of services to corporation X, a bonus of 100 shares of corporation X stock. Under the terms of the bonus arrangement E is obligated to return the corporation X stock to corporation X if he terminates his employment for any reason. However, for each year occurring after November 25, 1971, during which E remains employed with

corporation X, E ceases to be obligated to return 10 shares of the corporation X stock. Since in each year occurring after November 25, 1971, for which E remains employed he is not required to return 10 shares of corporation X's stock, E's rights in 10 shares each year for 10 years cease to be subject to a substantial risk of forfeiture for each year he remains so employed.

Example (4). (a) Assume the same facts as in example (3) except that for each year occurring after November 25, 1971, for which E remains employed with corporation X, X agrees to pay, in redemption of the bonus shares given to E if he terminates employment for any reason, 10 percent of the fair market value of each share of stock on the date of such termination of employment. Since corporation X will pay E 10 percent of the value of his bonus stock for each of the 10 years after November 25, 1971, in which he remains employed by X, and the risk of a decline in value is not a substantial risk of forfeiture, E's interest in 10 percent of such bonus stock becomes substantially vested in each of those years.

(b) The following chart illustrates the fair market value of the bonus stock and the fair market value of the portion of bonus stock that becomes substantially vested on November 25, for the following years:

	Fair market value of	
		Portion of
		stock that
Year	All stock	becomes vested
1972	$200	$20
1973	$300	$30
1974	$150	$15
1975	$150	$15
1976	$100	$10

If E terminates his employment on July 1, 1977, when the fair market value of the bonus stock is $100, E must return the bonus stock to X, and X must pay, in redemption of the bonus stock, $50 (50 percent of the value of the bonus stock on the date of termination of employment). E has recognized income under section 83(a) and § 1.83-1(a) with respect to 50 percent of the bonus stock, and E's basis in that portion of the stock equals the amount of income recognized, $90. Under § 1.83-1(e), the $40 loss E incurred upon forfeiture ($90 basis less $50 redemption payment) is an ordinary loss.

Example (5). On January 7, 1971, corporation X, a computer service company, transfers to E, 100 shares of corporation X stock for $50. E is a highly compensated salesman who sold X's products in a three-state area since 1960. At the time of transfer each share of X stock has a fair market value of $100. The stock is transferred to E in connection with his termination of employment with X. Each share of X stock is subject to the sole condition that E can keep such share only if he does not engage in competition with X for a 5-year period in the three-state area where E had previously sold X's products. E, who is 45 years old, has no intention of retiring from the work force. In order to earn a salary comparable to his current compensation, while preventing the risk of forfeiture from arising, E will have to expend a substantial amount of time and effort in another industry or market to establish the necessary business contacts. Thus, under these facts and circumstances E's rights in the stock are subject to a substantial risk of forfeiture.

Example (6). On April 3, 2013, Y corporation grants to Q, an officer of Y, a nonstatutory option to purchase Y common stock. Although the option is immediately exercisable, it has no readily ascertainable fair market value when it is granted. Under the option, Q has the right to purchase 100 shares of Y common stock for $0 per share, which is the fair market value of a Y share on the date of grant of the option. On August 1, 2013, Y sells its common stock in an initial public offering. Pursuant to an underwriting agreement entered into in connection with the initial public offering, Q agrees not to sell, otherwise dispose of, or hedge any Y common stock from August 1 through February 1 of 2014 ("the lock-up period"). Q exercises the option and Y shares are transferred to Q on November 15, 2013, during the lock-up period. The underwriting agreement does not impose a substantial risk

of forfeiture on the Y shares acquired by Q because the provisions of the agreement do not condition Q's rights in the shares upon anyone's future performance (or refraining from performance) of substantial services or on the occurrence of a condition related to the purpose of the transfer of shares to Q. Accordingly, neither section 83(c)(3) nor the imposition of the lock-up period by the underwriting agreement precludes taxation under section 83 when the shares resulting from exercise of the option are transferred to Q.

Example (7). Assume the same facts as in Example 6, except that on August 1, 2013, Y also adopts an insider trading compliance program, under which, as applied to 2013, insiders (such as Q) may trade Y shares only during a limited number of days following each quarterly earnings release ("a trading window"). Under the program, if Q trades Y shares outside a trading window without Y's permission, Y has the right to terminate Q's employment. However, the exercise of the nonstatutory options outside a trading window for Y shares is not prohibited under the insider trading compliance program. Q fully exercises the option, and Y shares are transferred to Q, on November 15, 2013. The exercise of the option occurs outside a trading window, and, on the date of exercise, Q is in possession of material nonpublic information concerning Y that would subject him to liability under Rule 10b-5 under the Securities Exchange Act of 1934 if Q sold the Y shares while in possession of such information. Neither the insider trading compliance program nor the potential liability under Rule 10b-5 impose a substantial risk of forfeiture on the Y shares acquired by Q because the provisions of the program and Rule 10b-5 do not condition Q's rights in the shares upon anyone's future performance (or refraining from performance) of substantial services or on the occurrence of a condition related to the purpose of the transfer of shares to Q. Accordingly, none of section 83(c)(3), the imposition of the trading windows by the insider trading compliance program, and the potential liability under Rule 10b-5 preclude taxation under section 83 when the shares resulting from exercise of the option are transferred to Q.

(d) *Transferability of property.* For purposes of section 83 and the regulations thereunder, the rights of a person in property are transferable if such person can transfer any interest in the property to any person other than the transferor of the property, but only if the rights in such property of such transferee are not subject to a substantial risk of forfeiture. Accordingly, property is transferable if the person performing the services or receiving the property can sell, assign, or pledge (as collateral for a loan, or as security for the performance of an obligation, or for any other purpose) his interest in the property to any person other than the transferor of such property and if the transferee is not required to give up the property or its value in the event the substantial risk of forfeiture materializes. On the other hand, property is not considered to be transferable merely because the person performing the services or receiving the property may designate a beneficiary to receive the property in the event of his death.

(e) *Property.* For purposes of section 83 and the regulations thereunder, the term "property" includes real and personal property other than either money or an unfunded and unsecured promise to pay money or property in the future. The term also includes a beneficial interest in assets (including money) which are transferred or set aside from the claims of creditors of the transferor, for example, in a trust or escrow account. See, however, § 1.83-8(a) with respect to employee trusts and annuity plans subject to section 402(b) and section 403(c). In the case of a transfer of a life insurance contract, retirement income contract, endowment contract, or other contract providing life insurance protection, or any undivided interest therein, the policy cash value and all other rights under such contract (including any supplemental agreements thereto and whether or not guaranteed), other than current life insurance protection, are treated as property for purposes of this section. However, in the case of the transfer of a life insurance contract, retirement income con-

tract, endowment contract, or other contract providing life insurance protection, which was part of a split-dollar arrangement (as defined in § 1.61-22(b)) entered into (as defined in § 1.61-22(j)) on or before September 17, 2003, and which is not materially modified (as defined in § 1.61-22(j)(2)) after September 17, 2003, only the cash surrender value of the contract is considered to be property. Where rights in a contract providing life insurance protection are substantially nonvested, see § 1.83-1(a)(2) for rules relating to taxation of the cost of life insurance protection.

(f) *Property transferred in connection with the performance of services.* Property transferred to an employee or an independent contractor (or beneficiary thereof) in recognition of the performance of, or the refraining from performance of, services is considered transferred in connection with the performance of services within the meaning of section 83. The existence of other persons entitled to buy stock on the same terms and conditions as an employee, whether pursuant to a public or private offering may, however, indicate that in such circumstances a transfer to the employee is not in recognition of the performance of, or the refraining from performance of, services. The transfer of property is subject to section 83 whether such transfer is in respect of past, present, or future services.

(g) *Amount paid.* For purposes of section 83 and the regulations thereunder, the term "amount paid" refers to the value of any money or property paid for the transfer of property to which section 83 applies, and does not refer to any amount paid for the right to use such property or to receive the income therefrom. Such value does not include any stated or unstated interest payments. For rules regarding the calculation of the amount of unstated interest payments, see § 1.483-1(c). When section 83 applies to the transfer of property pursuant to the exercise of an option, the term "amount paid" refers to any amount paid for the grant of the option plus any amount paid as the exercise price of the option. For rules regarding the forgiveness of indebtedness treated as an amount paid, see § 1.83-4(c).

(h) *Nonlapse restriction*. For purposes of section 83 and the regulations thereunder, a restriction which by its terms will never lapse (also referred to as a "nonlapse restriction") is a permanent limitation on the transferability of property—

(1) Which will require the transferee of the property to sell, or offer to sell, such property at a price determined under a formula, and

(2) Which will continue to apply to and be enforced against the transferee or any subsequent holder (other than the transferor).

A limitation subjecting the property to a permanent right of first refusal in a particular person at a price determined under a formula is a permanent nonlapse restriction. Limitations imposed by registration requirements of State or Federal security laws or similar laws imposed with respect to sales or other dispositions of stock or securities are not nonlapse restrictions. An obligation to resell or to offer to sell property transferred in connection with the performance of services to a specific person or persons at its fair market value at the time of such sale is not a nonlapse restriction. See § 1.83-5(c) for examples of nonlapse restrictions.

(i) *Lapse restriction*. For purposes of section 83 and the regulations thereunder, the term "lapse restriction" means a restriction other than a nonlapse restriction as defined in paragraph (h) of this section, and includes (but is not limited to) a restriction that carries a substantial risk of forfeiture.

(j) *Sales which may give rise to suit under section 16(b) of the Securities Exchange Act of 1934*—(1) **In general**. For purposes of section 83 and the regulations thereunder if the sale of property at a profit within six months after the purchase of the property could subject a person to suit under section 16(b) of the Securities Exchange Act of 1934, the person's rights in the property are treated as subject to a substantial risk of forfeiture and as not transferable until the earlier of (i) the expiration of such six-month period, or (ii) the first day on which the sale of such property at a profit will

not subject the person to suit under section 16(b) of the Securities Exchange Act of 1934. However, whether an option is "transferable by the optionee" for purposes of § 1.83-7(b)(2)(i) is determined without regard to section 83(c)(3) and this paragraph (j).

(2) **Examples**. The provisions of this paragraph may be illustrated by the following examples:

Example (1). On January 1, 1983, X corporation sells to P, a beneficial owner of 12% of X corporation stock, in connection with P's performance of services, 100 shares of X corporation stock at $10 per share. At the time of the sale the fair market value of the X corporation stock is $100 per share. P, as a beneficial owner of more 10% of X corporation stock, is liable to suit under section 16(b) of the Securities Exchange Act of 1934 for recovery of any profit from any sale and purchase or purchase and sale of X corporation stock within a six-month period, but no other restrictions apply to the stock. Because the section 16(b) restriction is applicable to P, P's rights in the 100 shares of stock purchased on January 1, 1983, are treated as subject to a substantial risk of forfeiture and as not transferable through June 29, 1983. P chooses not to make an election under section 83 (b) and therefore does not include any amount with respect to the stock purchase in gross income as compensation on the date of purchase. On June 30, 1983, the fair market value of X corporation stock is $250 per share. P must include $24,000 (100 shares of X corporation stock $240 ($250 fair market value per share less $10 price paid by P for each share)) in gross income as compensation on June 30, 1983. If, in this example, restrictions other than section 16(b) applied to the stock, such other restrictions (but not section 16(b) would be taken into account in determining whether the stock is subject to a substantial risk of forfeiture and is nontransferable for periods after June 29, 1983.

Example (2). Assume the same facts as in example (1) except that P is not an insider on or after May 1, 1983, and the section 16(b) restriction does not apply beginning on that date. On May 1, 1983, P must include in gross income as compensation the difference between the fair market value of the stock on that date and the amount paid for the stock.

Example (3). Assume the same facts as in example (1) except that on June 1, 1983, X corporation sells to P an additional 100 shares of X corporation stock at $20 per share. At the time of the sale the fair market value of the X corporation stock is $150 per share. On June 30, 1983, P must include $24,000 in gross income as compensation with respect to the January 1, 1983 purchase. On November 30, 1983, the fair market value of X corporation stock is $200 per share. Accordingly, on that date P must include $18,000 (100 shares of X corporation stock X $180 ($200 fair market value per share less $20 price paid by P for each share)) in gross income as compensation with respect to the June 1, 1983 purchase.

Example (4). (i) On June 3, 2013, Y corporation grants to Q, an officer of Y, a nonstatutory option to purchase Y common stock. Y stock is traded on an established securities market. Although the option is immediately exercisable, it has no readily ascertainable fair market value when it is granted. Under the option, Q has the right to purchase 100 shares of Y common stock for $10 per share, which is the fair market value of a Y share on the date of grant of the option. The grant of the option is not one that satisfies the requirements for a transaction that is exempt from section 16(b) of the Securities Exchange Act of 1934. On December 15, 2013, Y stock is trading at more than $10 per share. On that date, Q fully exercises the option, paying the exercise price in cash, and receives 100 Y shares. Q's rights in the shares received as a result of the exercise are not conditioned upon the future performance of substantial services. Because no exemption from section 16(b) was available for the June 3, 2013 grant of the option, the section 16(b) liability period expires on December 1, 2013. Accordingly, the section 16(b) liability period expires before the date that Q exercises the option and the Y common stock is transferred to Q. Thus, the shares acquired by Q pursuant to the exercise of the option are not subject to a substantial risk of forfeiture under section 83(c)(3) as a result of section 16(b). As a result, section 83(c)(3) does not preclude taxation under section 83 when the shares acquired pursuant to the December 15, 2013 exercise of the option are transferred to Q.

(ii) Assume the same facts as in paragraph (i) of this Example 4 except that Q exercises the nonstatutory option on October 30, 2013 when Y stock is trading at more than $10 per share. The shares acquired are subject to a substantial risk of forfeiture under section 83(c)(3) as a result of section 16(b) through December 1, 2013.

(iii) Assume the same facts as in paragraph (i) of this Example 4 except that on November 5, 2013, Q also purchases 100 shares of Y common stock on the public market. The purchase of the shares is not a transaction exempt from section 16(b) of the Securities Exchange Act of 1934. Because no exemption from section 16(b) was available for the November 5, 2013 purchase of shares, the section 16(b) liability period with respect to such shares will last for a period of six months after the November 5, 2013 purchase of shares. Notwithstanding the non-exempt purchase of Y common stock on November 5, 2013, the shares acquired by Q pursuant to the December 15, 2013 exercise of the option are not subject to a substantial risk of forfeiture under section 83(c)(3) as a result of section 16(b). As a result, section 83(c)(3) does not preclude taxation under section 83 when the shares acquired pursuant to the December 15, 2013 exercise of the option are transferred to Q.

(k) For purposes of section 83 and the regulations thereunder, property is subject to substantial risk of forfeiture and is not transferable so long as the property is subject to a restriction on transfer to comply with the "Pooling-of-Interests Accounting" rules set forth in Accounting Series Release Numbered 130 ((10/5/72) 37 FR 20937; 17 CFR 211.130) and Accounting Series Release Numbered 135 ((1/18/73) 38 FR 1734; 17 CFR 211.135).

(l) **Effective/applicability date**. This section applies to property transferred on or after January 1, 2013. For rules relating to property transferred before that date, see § 1.83-3 as contained in 26 CFR part 1 (as of April 1, 2012).

§ 1.83-4. Special rules.

(a) *Holding period*. Under section 83(f), the holding period of transferred property to which section 83(a) applies shall begin just after such property is substantially vested. However, if the person who has performed the services in connection with which property is transferred has made an election under section 83(b), the holding period of such property shall begin just after the date such property is transferred. If property to which section 83 and the regulations thereunder apply is transferred at arm's length, the holding period of such property in the hands of the transferee shall be determined in accordance with the rules provided in section 1223.

(b) *Basis*. (1) Except as provided in paragraph (b)(2) of this section, if property to which section 83 and the regulations thereunder apply is acquired by any person (including a person who acquires such property in a subsequent transfer which is not at arm's length), while such property is still substantially nonvested, such person's basis for the property shall reflect any amount paid for such property and any amount includible in the gross income of the person who performed the services (including any amount so includible as a result of a disposition by the person who acquired such property.) Such basis shall also reflect any adjustments to basis provided under sections 1015 and 1016.

(2) If property to which § 1.83-1 applies is transferred at arm's length, the basis of the property in the hands of the transferee shall be determined under section 1012 and the regulations thereunder.

(b) *Forgiveness of indebtedness treated as an amount paid*. If an indebtedness that has been treated as an amount paid under § 1.83-1(a)(1)(ii) is subsequently cancelled, forgiven or satisfied for an amount less than the amount of such indebtedness, the amount that is not, in fact, paid shall be includible in the gross income of the service provider in the taxable year in which such cancellation, forgiveness or satisfaction occurs.

§ 1.83-5. Restrictions that will never lapse.

(a) *Valuation*. For purposes of section 83 and the regulations thereunder, in the case of property subject to a nonlapse restriction (as defined in § 1.83-3(h)), the price determined under the formula price will be considered to be the fair market value of the property unless established to the contrary by the Commissioner, and the burden of proof shall be on the commissioner with respect to such value. If stock in a corporation is subject to a nonlapse restriction which requires the transferee to sell such stock only at a formula price based on book value, a reasonable multiple of earnings or a reasonable combination thereof, the price so determined will ordinarily be regarded as determinative of the fair market value of such property for purposes of section 83. However, in certain circumstances the formula price will not be considered to be the fair market value of property subject to such a formula price restriction, even though the formula price restriction is a substantial factor in determining such value. For example, where the formula price is the current book value of stock, the book value of the stock at some time in the future may be a more accurate measure of the value of the stock than the current book value of the stock for purposes of determining the fair market value of the stock at the time the stock becomes substantially vested.

(b) *Cancellation*—(1) **In general.** Under section 83(d)(2), if a nonlapse restriction imposed on property that is subject to section 83 is cancelled, then, unless the taxpayer establishes—

(i) That such cancellation was not compensatory, and

(ii) That the person who would be allowed a deduction, if any, if the cancellation were treated as compensatory, will treat the transaction as not compensatory, as provided in paragraph (c)(2) of this section, the excess of the fair market value of such property (computed without regard to such restriction) at the time of cancellation, over the sum of—

(iii) The fair market value of such property (computed by taking the restriction into account) immediately before the cancellation, and

(iv) The amount, if any, paid for the cancellation, shall be treated as compensation for the taxable year in which such cancellation occurs. Whether there has been a noncompensatory cancellation of a nonlapse restriction under section 83(d)(2) depends upon the particular facts and circumstances. Ordinarily the fact that the employee or independent contractor is required to perform additional services or that the salary or payment of such a person is adjusted to take the cancellation into account indicates that such cancellation has a compensatory purpose. On the other hand, the fact that the original purpose of a restriction no longer exists may indicate that the purpose of such cancellation is non-compensatory. Thus, for example, if a so-called "buy-sell" restriction was imposed on a corporation's stock to limit ownership of such stock and is being cancelled in connection with a public offering of the stock, such cancellation will generally be regarded as noncompensatory. However, the mere fact that the employer is willing to forego a deduction under section 83(h) is insufficient evidence to establish a noncompensatory cancellation of a nonlapse restriction. The refusal by a corporation or shareholder to repurchase stock of the corporation which is subject to a permanent right of first refusal will generally be treated as a cancellation of a nonlapse restriction. The preceding sentence shall not apply where there is no nonlapse restriction, for example, where the price to be paid for the stock subject to the right of first refusal is the fair market value of the stock. Section 83(d)(2) and this (1) do not apply where immediately after the cancellation of a nonlapse restriction the property is still substantially nonvested and no section

83(b) election has been made with respect to such property. In such a case the rules of section 83(a) and § 1.83-1 shall apply to such property.

(2) **Evidence of noncompensatory cancellation.** In addition to the information necessary to establish the factors described in paragraph (b)(1) of this section, the taxpayer shall request the employer to furnish the taxpayer with a written statement indicating that the employer will not treat the cancellation of the nonlapse restriction as a compensatory event, and that no deduction will be taken with respect to such cancellation. The taxpayer shall file such written statement with his income tax return for the taxable year in which or with which such cancellation occurs.

(c) **Examples**. The provisions of this section may be illustrated by the following examples:

Example (1). On November 1, 1971, X corporation whose shares are closely held and not regularly traded, transfers to E, an employee, 100 shares of X corporation stock subject to the condition that, if he desires to dispose of such stock during the period of his employment, he must resell the stock to his employer at its then existing book value. In addition, E or E's estate is obligated to offer to sell the stock at his retirement or death to his employer at its then existing book value. Under these facts and circumstances, the restriction to which the shares of X corporation stock are subject is a nonlapse restriction. Consequently, the fair market value of the X stock is includible in E's gross income as compensation for taxable year 1971. However, in determining the fair market value of the X stock, the book value formula price will ordinarily be regarded as being determinative of such value.

Example (2). Assume the facts are the same as in example (1), except that the X stock is subject to the condition that if E desires to dispose of the stock during the period of his employment he must resell the stock to his employer at a multiple of earnings per share that is in this case a reasonable approximation of value at the time of transfer to E. In addition, E or E's estate is obligated to offer to sell the stock at his retirement or death to his employer at the same multiple of earnings. Under these facts and circumstances, the restriction to which the X corporation stock is subject is a nonlapse restriction. Consequently, the fair market value of the X stock is includible in E's gross income for taxable year 1971. However, in determining the fair market value of the X stock, the multiple-of-earnings formula price will ordinarily be regarded as determinative of such value.

Example (3). On January 4, 1971, X corporation transfers to E, an employee, 100 shares of stock in X corporation. Each such share of stock is subject to an agreement between X and E whereby E agrees that such shares are to be held solely for investment purposes and not for resale (a so-called investment letter restriction). E's rights in such stock are substantially vested upon transfer, causing the fair market value of each share of X corporation stock to be includible in E's gross income as compensation for taxable year 1971. Since such an investment letter restriction does not constitute a nonlapse restriction, in determining the fair market value of each share, the investment letter restriction is disregarded.

Example (4). On September 1, 1971, X corporation transfers to B, an independent contractor, 500 shares of common stock in X corporation in exchange for B's agreement to provide services in the construction of an office building on property owned by X corporation. X corporation has 100 shares of preferred stock outstanding and an additional 500 shares of common stock outstanding. The preferred stock has a liquidation value of $1,000x, which is equal to the value of all assets owned by X. Therefore, the book value of the common stock in X corporation is $0. Under the terms of the transfer, if B wishes to dispose of the stock, B must offer to sell the stock to X for 150 percent of the then existing book value of B's common stock. The stock is also subject to a substantial risk of forfeiture until B performs the agreed-upon services. B makes a

timely election under section 83(b) to include the value of the stock in gross income in 1971. Under these facts and circumstances, the restriction to which the shares of X corporation common stock are subject is a nonlapse restriction. In determining the fair market value of the X common stock at the time of transfer, the book value formula price would ordinarily be regarded as determinative of such value. However, the fair market value of X common stock at the time of transfer, subject to the book value restriction, is greater than $0 since B was willing to agree to provide valuable personal services in exchange for the stock. In determining the fair market value of the stock, the expected book value after construction of the office building would be given great weight. The likelihood of completion of construction would be a factor in determining the expected book value after completion of construction.

§ 1.83-6. Deduction by employer.

(a) *Allowance of deduction*—(1) **General Rule.** In the case of a transfer of property in connection with the performance of services, or a compensatory cancellation of a nonlapse restriction described in section 83(d) and § 1.83-5, a deduction is allowable under section 162 or 212 to the person for whom the services were performed. The amount of the deduction is equal to the amount included as compensation in the gross income of the service provider under section 83 (a), (b), or (d)(2), but only to the extent the amount meets the requirements of section 162 or 212 and the regulations thereunder. The deduction is allowed only for the taxable year of that person in which or with which ends the taxable year of the service provider in which the amount is included as compensation. For purposes of this paragraph, any amount excluded from gross income under section 79 or section 101(b) or subchapter N is considered to have been included in gross income.

(2) **Special Rule.** For purposes of paragraph (a)(1) of this section, the service provider is deemed to have included the amount as compensation in gross income if the person

for whom the services were performed satisfies in a timely manner all requirements of section 6041 or section 6041A , and the regulations thereunder, with respect to that amount of compensation. For purposes of the preceding sentence, whether a person for whom services were performed satisfies all requirements of section 6041 or section 6041A , and the regulations thereunder, is determined without regard to § 1.6041-3(c) (exception for payments to corporations). In the case of a disqualifying disposition of stock described in section 421(b), an employer that otherwise satisfies all requirements of section 6041 and the regulations thereunder will be considered to have done so timely for purposes of this paragraph (a)(2) if Form W-2 or Form W-2c, as appropriate, is furnished to the employee or former employee, and is filed with the federal government, on or before the date on which the employer files the tax return claiming the deduction relating to the disqualifying disposition.

(3) **Exceptions.** Where property is substantially vested upon transfer, the deduction shall be allowed to such person in accordance with his method of accounting (in conformity with sections 446 and 461). In the case of a transfer to an employee benefit plan described in § 1.162-10(a) or a transfer to an employees' trust or annuity plan described in section 404(a)(5) and the regulations thereunder, section 83(h) and this section do not apply.

(4) **Capital expenditure, etc**. No deduction is allowed under section 83(h) to the extent that the transfer of property constitutes a capital expenditure, an item of deferred expense, or an amount properly includible in the value of inventory items. In the case of a capital expenditure, for example, the basis of the property to which such capital expenditure relates shall be increased at the same time and to the same extent as any amount includible in the employee's gross income in respect of such transfer. Thus, for example, no deduction is allowed to a corporation in respect of a transfer of its stock to a promoter upon its organization, notwithstanding that such promoter must include the value of such stock in

his gross income in accordance with the rules under section 83.

(5) **Transfer of life insurance contract (or an undivided interest therein)**—(i) **General rule**. In the case of a transfer of a life insurance contract (or an undivided interest therein) described in § 1.61-22(c)(3) in connection with the performance of services, a deduction is allowable under paragraph (a)(1) of this section to the person for whom the services were performed. The amount of the deduction, if allowable, is equal to the sum of the amount included as compensation in the gross income of the service provider under § 1.61-22(g)(1) and the amount determined under § 1.61-22(g)(1)(ii).

(ii) **Effective date**—(A) General rule— Paragraph (a)(5)(i) of this section applies to any split-dollar life insurance arrangement (as defined in § 1.61-22(b)(1) or (2)) entered into after September 17, 2003. For purposes of this paragraph (a)(5), an arrangement is entered into as determined under § 1.61-22(j)(1)(ii).

(B) Modified arrangements treated as new arrangements. If an arrangement entered into on or before September 17, 2003 is materially modified (within the meaning of § 1.61-22(j)(2)) after September 17, 2003, the arrangement is treated as a new arrangement entered into on the date of the modification.

(6) **Effective date**. Paragraphs (a)(1) and (2) of this section apply to deductions for taxable years beginning on or after January 1, 1995. However, taxpayers may also apply paragraphs (a)(1) and (2) of this section when claiming deductions for taxable years beginning before that date if the claims are not barred by the statute of limitations. Paragraphs (a) (3) and (4) of this section are effective as set forth in § 1.83-8(b).

(b) *Recognition of gain or loss*. Except as provided in section 1032 , at the time of a transfer of property in connection with the performance of services the transferor recognizes gain to the extent that the transferor receives an amount that exceeds the transferor's basis in the property. In addition, at the time a deduction is allowed under section 83(h) and paragraph (a) of this section, gain or loss is recognized to the extent of the difference between (1) the sum of the amount paid plus the amount allowed as a deduction under section 83(h), and (2) the sum of the taxpayer's basis in the property plus any amount recognized pursuant to the previous sentence.

(c) *Forfeitures.* If, under section 83(h) and paragraph (a) of this section, a deduction, an increase in basis, or a reduction of gross income was allowable (disregarding the reasonableness of the amount of compensation) in respect of a transfer of property and such property is subsequently forfeited, the amount of such deduction, increase in basis or reduction of gross income shall be includible in the gross income of the person to whom it was allowable for the taxable year of forfeiture. The basis of such property in the hands of the person to whom it is forfeited shall include any such amount includible in the gross income of such person, as well as any amount such person pays upon forfeiture.

(d) *Special rules for transfers by shareholders*—(1) **Transfers**. If a shareholder of a corporation transfers property to an employee of such corporation or to an independent contractor (or to a beneficiary thereof), in consideration of services performed for the corporation, the transaction shall be considered to be a contribution of such property to the capital of such corporation by the shareholder, and immediately thereafter a transfer of such property by the corporation to the employee or independent contractor under paragraphs (a) and (b) of this section. For purposes of this (1), such a transfer will be considered to be in consideration for services performed for the corporation if either the property transferred is substantially nonvested at the time of transfer or an amount is includible in the gross income of the employee or independent contractor at the time of transfer under § 1.83-1(a)(1) or § 1.83-2(a). In the case of such a transfer, any money or other property paid to the shareholder for such stock shall be considered to be paid to the corporation and transferred immediately thereafter by the corporation to the shareholder as a distribution to which section

302 applies. For special rules that may apply to a corporation's transfer of its own stock to any person in consideration of services performed for another corporation or partnership, see § 1.1032-3. The preceding sentence applies to transfers of stock and amounts paid for such stock occurring on or after May 16, 2000.

(2) **Forfeiture.** If, following a transaction described in paragraph (d)(1) of this section, the transferred property is forfeited to the shareholder, paragraph (c) of this section shall apply both with respect to the shareholder and with respect to the corporation. In addition, the corporation shall in the taxable year of forfeiture be allowed a loss (or realize a gain) to offset any gain (or loss) realized under paragraph (b) of this section. For example, if a shareholder transfers property to an employee of the corporation as compensation, and as a result the shareholder's basis of $200x in such property is allocated to his stock in such corporation and such corporation recognizes a short-term capital gain of $800x, and is allowed a deduction of $1,000x on such transfer, upon a subsequent forfeiture of the property to the shareholder, the shareholder shall take $200x into gross income, and the corporation shall take $1,000x into gross income and be allowed a short-term capital loss of $800x.

(e) *Options.* [Reserved]

(f) *Reporting requirements.* [Reserved]

§ 1.83-7. Taxation of nonqualified stock options.

(a) *In general.* If there is granted to an employee or independent contractor (or beneficiary thereof) in connection with the performance of services, an option to which section 421 (relating generally to certain qualified and other options) does not apply, section 83(a) shall apply to such grant if the option has a readily ascertainable fair market value (determined in accordance with paragraph (b) of this section) at the time the option is granted. The person who performed such services realizes compensation upon such grant at the time and in the amount determined under section 83(a). If section 83(a) does not apply to the grant of such an option because the option does not have a readily ascertainable fair market value at the time of grant, sections 83(a) and 83(b) shall apply at the time the option is exercised or otherwise disposed of, even though the fair market value of such option may have become readily ascertainable before such time. If the option is exercised, sections 83(a) and 83(b) apply to the transfer of property pursuant to such exercise, and the employee or independent contractor realizes compensation upon such transfer at the time and in the amount determined under section 83(a) or 83(b). If the option is sold or otherwise disposed of in an arm's length transaction, sections 83(a) and 83(b) apply to the transfer of money or other property received in the same manner as sections 83(a) and 83(b) would have applied to the transfer of property pursuant to an exercise of the option. The preceding sentence does not apply to a sale or other disposition of the option to a person related to the service provider that occurs on or after July 2, 2003. For this purpose, a person is related to the service provider if—

(1) The person and the service provider bear a relationship to each other that is specified in section 267(b) or 707(b)(1), subject to the modifications that the language "20 percent" is used instead of "50 percent" each place it appears in sections 267(b) and 707(b)(1), and section 267(c)(4) is applied as if the family of an individual includes the spouse of any member of the family; or

(2) The person and the service provider are engaged in trades or businesses under common control (within the meaning of section 52(a) and (b); provided that a person is not related to the service provider if the person is the service recipient with respect to the option or the grantor of the option.

(b) *Readily ascertainable defined*—(1) **Actively traded on an established market**. Options have a value at the time they are granted, but that value is ordinarily not readily ascertainable unless the option is actively traded on an established market. If an option is actively traded on an established market, the fair market value of such option is readily ascertainable for purposes of this section by applying the rules of valuation set forth in §20.2031-2.

(2) **Not actively traded on an established market**. When an option is not actively traded on an established market, it does not have a readily ascertainable fair market value unless its fair market value can otherwise be measured with reasonable accuracy. For purposes of this section, if an option is not actively traded on an established market, the option does not have a readily ascertainable fair market value when granted unless the taxpayer can show that all of the following conditions exist:

(i) The option is transferable by the optionee;

(ii) The option is exerciseable immediately in full by the optionee;

(iii) The option or the property subject to the option is not subject to any restriction or condition (other than a lien or other condition to secure the payment of the purchase price) which has a significant effect upon the fair market value of the option; and

(iv) The fair market value of the option privilege is readily ascertainable in accordance with paragraph (b)(3) of this section.

(3) **Option privilege**. The option privilege in the case of an option to buy is the opportunity to benefit during the option's exercise period from any increase in the value of property subject to the option during such period, without risking any capital. Similarly, the option privilege in the case of an option to sell is the opportunity to benefit during the exercise period from a decrease in the value of property subject to the option. For example, if at some time during the exercise period of an option to buy, the fair market value of the property subject to the option is greater than the option's exercise price, a profit may be realized by exercising the option and immediately selling the property so acquired for its higher fair market value. Irrespective of

whether any such gain may be realized immediately at the time an option is granted, the fair market value of an option to buy includes the value of the right to benefit from any future increase in the value of the property subject to the option (relative to the option exercise price), without risking any capital. Therefore, the fair market value of an option is not merely the difference that may exist at a particular time between the option's exercise price and the value of the property subject to the option, but also includes the value of the option privilege for the remainder of the exercise period. Accordingly, for purposes of this section, in determining whether the fair market value of an option is readily ascertainable, it is necessary to consider whether the value of the entire option privilege can be measured with reasonable accuracy. In determining whether the value of the option privilege is readily ascertainable, and in determining the amount of such value when such value is readily ascertainable, it is necessary to consider—

(i) Whether the value of the property subject to the option can be ascertained;

(ii) The probability of any ascertainable value of such property increasing or decreasing; and

(iii) The length of the period during which the option can be exercised.

(c) *Reporting requirements.* [Reserved]

(d) This section applies on and after July 2, 2003. For transactions prior to that date, see § 1.83-7 as published in 26 CFR part 1 (revised as of April 1, 2003).

§ 1.83-8. Applicability of section and transitional rules.

(a) *Scope of section 83.* Section 83 is not applicable to—

(1) A transaction concerning an option to which section 421 applies;

(2) A transfer to or from a trust described in section 401(a) for the benefit of employees or their beneficiaries, or a transfer under an annuity plan that meets the requirements of section 404(a)(2) for the benefit of employees or their beneficiaries;

(3) The transfer of an option without a readily ascertainable fair market value (as defined in § 1.83-7(b)(1)); or

(4) The transfer of property pursuant to the exercise of an option with a readily ascertainable fair market value at the date of grant. Section 83 applies to a transfer to or from a trust or under an annuity plan for the benefit of employees, independent contractors, or their beneficiaries (except as provided in paragraph (a)(2) of this section), but to the extent a transfer is subject to section 402(b) or 403(c), section 83 applies to such a transfer only as provided for in section 402(b) or 403(c).

(b) *Transitional rules*—(1) **In general.** Except as otherwise provided in this paragraph, section 83 and the regulations thereunder shall apply to property transferred after June 30, 1969.

(2) **Binding written contracts.** Section 83 and the regulations thereunder shall not apply to property transferred pursuant to a binding written contract entered into before April 22, 1969. For purposes of this paragraph, a binding written contract means only a written contract under which the employee or independent contractor has an enforceable right to compel the transfer of property or to obtain damages upon the breach of such contract. A contract which provides that a person's right to such property is contingent upon the happening of an event (including the passage of time) may satisfy the requirements of this paragraph. However, if the event itself, or the determination of whether the event has occurred, rests with the board of directors or any other individual or group acting on behalf of the employer (other than an arbitrator), the contract will not be treated as giving the person an enforceable right for purposes of this paragraph.

The fact that the board of directors has the power (either expressly or impliedly) to terminate employment of an officer pursuant to a contract that contemplates the completion of services over a fixed or ascertainable period does not negate the existence of a binding written contract. Nor will the binding nature of the contract be negated by a provision in such contract which allows the employee or independent contractor to terminate the contract for any year and receive cash instead of property if such election would cause a substantial penalty, such as a forfeiture of part or all of the property received in connection with the performance of services in an earlier year.

(3) **Options granted before April 22, 1969.** Section 83 shall not apply to property received upon the exercise of an option granted before April 22, 1969.

(4) **Certain written plans.** Section 83 shall not apply to property transferred (whether or not by the exercise of an option) before May 1, 1970, pursuant to a written plan adopted and approved before July 1, 1969. A plan is to be considered as having been adopted and approved before July 1, 1969, only if prior to such date the transferor of the property undertook an ascertainable course of conduct which under applicable State law does not require further approval by the board of directors or the stockholders of any corporation. For example, if a corporation transfers property to an employee in connection with the performance of services pursuant to a plan adopted and approved before July 1, 1969, by the board of directors of such corporation, it is not necessary that the stockholders have adopted or approved such plan if State law does not require such approval. However, such approval is necessary if required by the articles of incorporation or the bylaws or if, by its terms, such plan will not become effective without such approval.

(5) **Certain options granted pursuant to a binding written contract.** Section 83 shall not apply to property transferred before January 1, 1973, upon the exercise of an option granted pursuant to a binding written contract (as defined in paragraph (b)(2) of this section) entered into before April 22, 1969, between a corporation and the transferor of such property requiring the transferor to grant options to employees of such corporation (or a subsidi-ary of such corporation) to purchase a determinable number of shares of stock of such corporation, but only if the transferee was an employee of such corporation (or a subsidiary of such corporation) on or before April 22, 1969.

(6) **Certain tax free exchanges.** Section 83 shall not apply to property transferred in exchange for (or pursuant to the exercise of a conversion privilege contained in) property transferred before July 1, 1969, or in exchange for property to which section 83 does not apply (by reason of paragraphs (1), (2), (3), or (4) of section 83(i)), if section 354, 355, 356, or 1036 (or so much of section 1031 as relates to section 1036) applies, or if gain or loss is not otherwise required to be recognized upon the exercise of such conversion privilege, and if the property received in such exchange is subject to restrictions and conditions substantially similar to those to which the property given in such exchange was subject.

§ 1.162-27. Certain employee remuneration in excess of $1,000,000.

(a) *Scope.* This section provides rules for the application of the $1 million deduction limit under section 162(m) of the Internal Revenue Code. Paragraph (b) of this section provides the general rule limiting deductions under section 162(m). Paragraph (c) of this section provides definitions of generally applicable terms. Paragraph (d) of this section provides an exception from the deduction limit for compensation payable on a commission basis. Paragraph (e) of this section provides an exception for qualified performance-based compensation. Paragraphs (f) and (g) of this section provide special rules for corporations that become publicly held corporations and payments that are subject to section 280G, respectively. Paragraph (h) of this section provides transition rules, including the rules for contracts that are grandfathered and not subject to section 162(m). Paragraph (j) of this section contains the effective date provisions. For rules concerning the deductibility of compensation for services that are not covered by section 162(m) and this section, see section

162(a)(1) and § 1.162-7. This section is not determinative as to whether compensation meets the requirements of section 162(a)(1).

(b) *Limitation on deduction.* Section 162(m) precludes a deduction under chapter 1 of the Internal Revenue Code by any publicly held corporation for compensation paid to any covered employee to the extent that the compensation for the taxable year exceeds $1,000,000.

(c) *Definitions*—(1) **Publicly held corporation**—(i) **General rule.** A publicly held corporation means any corporation issuing any class of common equity securities required to be registered under section 12 of the Exchange Act. A corporation is not considered publicly held if the registration of its equity securities is voluntary. For purposes of this section, whether a corporation is publicly held is determined based solely on whether, as of the last day of its taxable year, the corporation is subject to the reporting obligations of section 12 of the Exchange Act.

(ii) **Affiliated groups.** A publicly held corporation includes an affiliated group of corporations, as defined in section 1504 (determined without regard to section 1504(b)). For purposes of this section, however, an affiliated group of corporations does not include any subsidiary that is itself a publicly held corporation. Such a publicly held subsidiary, and its subsidiaries (if any), are separately subject to this section. If a covered employee is paid compensation in a taxable year by more than one member of an affiliated group, compensation paid by each member of the affiliated group is aggregated with compensation paid to the covered employee by all other members of the group. Any amount disallowed as a deduction by this section must be prorated among the payor corporations in proportion to the amount of compensation paid to the covered employee by each such corporation in the taxable year.

(2) **Covered employee**—(i) **General rule**. A covered employee means any individual who, on the last day of the taxable year, is—

(A) The chief executive officer of the corporation or is acting in such capacity; or

(B) Among the four highest compensated officers (other than the chief executive officer).

(ii) **Application of rules of the Securities and Exchange Commission.** Whether an individual is the chief executive officer described in paragraph (c)(2)(i)(A) of this section or an officer described in paragraph (c)(2)(i)(B) of this section is determined pursuant to the executive compensation disclosure rules under the Exchange Act.

(3) **Compensation**—(i) **In general.** For purposes of the deduction limitation described in paragraph (b) of this section, compensation means the aggregate amount allowable as a deduction under chapter 1 of the Internal Revenue Code for the taxable year (determined without regard to section 162(m) for remuneration for services performed by a covered employee, whether or not the services were performed during the taxable year.

(ii) **Exceptions.** Compensation does not include—

(A) Remuneration covered in section 3121(a)(5)(A) through section 3121(a)(5)(D) (concerning remuneration that is not treated as wages for purposes of the Federal Insurance Contributions Act); and

(B) Remuneration consisting of any benefit provided to or on behalf of an employee if, at the time the benefit is provided, it is reasonable to believe that the employee will be able to exclude it from gross income. In addition, compensation does not include salary reduction contributions described in section 3121(v)(1).

(4) **Compensation Committee.** The compensation committee means the committee of directors (including any subcommittee of directors) of the publicly held corporation that has the authority to establish and administer performance goals described in paragraph (e)(2) of this section, and to certify that performance goals are attained, as described in paragraph (e)(5) of this section. A committee

of directors is not treated as failing to have the authority to establish performance goals merely because the goals are ratified by the board of directors of the publicly held corporation or, if applicable, any other committee of the board of directors. See paragraph (e)(3) of this section for rules concerning the composition of the compensation committee.

(5) **Exchange Act.** The Exchange Act means the Securities Exchange Act of 1934.

(6) **Examples.** This paragraph (c) may be illustrated by the following examples:

Example 1. Corporation X is a publicly held corporation with a July 1 to June 30 fiscal year. For Corporation X's taxable year ending on June 30, 1995, Corporation X pays compensation of $2,000,000 to A, an employee. However, A's compensation is not required to be reported to shareholders under the executive compensation disclosure rules of the Exchange Act because A is neither the chief executive officer nor one of the four highest compensated officers employed on the last day of the taxable year. A's compensation is not subject to the deduction limitation of paragraph (b) of this section.

Example 2. C, a covered employee, performs services and receives compensation from Corporations X, Y, and Z, members of an affiliated group of corporations. Corporation X, the parent corporation, is a publicly held corporation. The total compensation paid to C from all affiliated group members is $3,000,000 for the taxable year, of which Corporation X pays $1,500,000; Corporation Y pays $900,000; and Corporation Z pays $600,000. Because the compensation paid by all affiliated group members is aggregated for purposes of section 162(m), $2,000,000 of the aggregate compensation paid is nondeductible. Corporations X, Y, and Z each are treated as paying a ratable portion of the nondeductible compensation. Thus, two thirds of each corporation's payment will be nondeductible. Corporation X has a nondeductible compensation expense of $1,000,000 ($1,500,000x$2,000,000/$3,000,000). Corporation Y has a nondeductible compensation expense of $600,000 ($900,000x$2,000,000/$3,000,000). Corporation Z has a nondeductible compensation expense of $400,000 ($600,000x$2,000,000/$3,000,000).

Example 3. Corporation W, a calendar year taxpayer, has total assets equal to or exceeding $5 million and a class of equity security held of record by 500 or more persons on December 31, 1994. However, under the Exchange Act, Corporation W is not required to file a registration statement with respect to that security until April 30, 1995. Thus, Corporation W is not a publicly held corporation on December 31, 1994, but is a publicly held corporation on December 31, 1995.

Example 4. The facts are the same as in Example 3, except that on December 15, 1996, Corporation W files with the Securities and Exchange Commission to disclose that Corporation W is no longer required to be registered under section 12 of the Exchange Act and to terminate its registration of securities under that provision. Because Corporation W is no longer subject to Exchange Act reporting obligations as of December 31, 1996, Corporation W is not a publicly held corporation for taxable year 1996, even though the registration of Corporation W's securities does not terminate until 90 days after Corporation W files with the Securities and Exchange Commission.

(d) *Exception for compensation paid on a commission basis.* The deduction limit in paragraph (b) of this section shall not apply to any compensation paid on a commission basis. For this purpose, compensation is paid on a commission basis if the facts and circumstances show that it is paid solely on account of income generated directly by the individual performance of the individual to whom the compensation is paid. Compensation does not fail to be attributable directly to the individual merely because support services, such as secretarial or research services, are utilized in generating the income. However, if compensation is paid on account of broader performance standards, such as income produced by a business unit of the corporation, the compensation does not qualify for the exception provided under this paragraph (d).

(e) *Exception for qualified performance-based compensation*—(1) **In general.** The deduction limit in paragraph (b) of this section does not apply to qualified performance-based compensation. Qualified performance-based compensation is compensation that meets all of the requirements of paragraphs (e)(2) through (e)(5) of this section.

(2) **Performance goal requirement**—(i) **Preestablished goal.** Qualified performance-based compensation must be paid solely on account of the attainment of one or more preestablished, objective performance goals. A performance goal is considered preestablished if it is established in writing by the compensation committee not later than 90 days after the commencement of the period of service to which the performance goal relates, provided that the outcome is substantially uncertain at the time the compensation committee actually establishes the goal. However, in no event will a performance goal be considered to be preestablished if it is established after 25 percent of the period of service (as scheduled in good faith at the time the goal is established) has elapsed. A performance goal is objective if a third party having knowledge of the relevant facts could determine whether the goal is met. Performance goals can be based on one or more business criteria that apply to the individual, a business unit, or the corporation as a whole. Such business criteria could include, for example, stock price, market share, sales, earnings per share, return on equity, or costs. A performance goal need not, however, be based upon an increase or positive result under a business criterion and could include, for example, maintaining the status quo or limiting economic losses (measured, in each case, by reference to a specific business criterion). A performance goal does not include the mere continued employment of the covered employee. Thus, a vesting provision based solely on continued employment would not constitute a performance goal. See paragraph (e)(2)(vi) of this section for rules on

compensation that is based on an increase in the price of stock.

(ii) **Objective compensation formula.** A preestablished performance goal must state, in terms of an objective formula or standard, the method for computing the amount of compensation payable to the employee if the goal is attained. A formula or standard is objective if a third party having knowledge of the relevant performance results could calculate the amount to be paid to the employee. In addition, a formula or standard must specify the individual employees or class of employees to which it applies.

(iii) **Discretion.**

(A) The terms of an objective formula or standard must preclude discretion to increase the amount of compensation payable that would otherwise be due upon attainment of the goal. A performance goal is not discretionary for purposes of this paragraph (e)(2)(iii) merely because the compensation committee reduces or eliminates the compensation or other economic benefit that was due upon attainment of the goal. However, the exercise of negative discretion with respect to one employee is not permitted to result in an increase in the amount payable to another employee. Thus, for example, in the case of a bonus pool, if the amount payable to each employee is stated in terms of a percentage of the pool, the sum of these individual percentages of the pool is not permitted to exceed 100 percent. If the terms of an objective formula or standard fail to preclude discretion to increase the amount of compensation merely because the amount of compensation to be paid upon attainment of the performance goal is based, in whole or in part, on a percentage of salary or base pay and the dollar amount of the salary or base pay is not fixed at the time the performance goal is established, then the objective formula or standard will not be considered discretionary for purposes of this paragraph (e)(2)(iii) if the maximum dollar amount to be paid is fixed at that time.

(B) If compensation is payable upon or after the attainment of a performance goal, and a change is made to accelerate the payment of compensation to an earlier date after the attainment of the goal, the change will be treated as an increase in the amount of compensation, unless the amount of compensation paid is discounted to reasonably reflect the time value of money. If compensation is payable upon or after the attainment of a performance goal, and a change is made to defer the payment of compensation to a later date, any amount paid in excess of the amount that was originally owed to the employee will not be treated as an increase in the amount of compensation if the additional amount is based either on a reasonable rate of interest or on one or more predetermined actual investments (whether or not assets associated with the amount originally owed are actually invested therein) such that the amount payable by the employer at the later date will be based on the actual rate of return of a specific investment (including any decrease as well as any increase in the value of an investment). If compensation is payable in the form of property, a change in the timing of the transfer of that property after the attainment of the goal will not be treated as an increase in the amount of compensation for purposes of this paragraph (e)(2)(iii). Thus, for example, if the terms of a stock grant provide for stock to be transferred after the attainment of a performance goal and the transfer of the stock also is subject to a vesting schedule, a change in the vesting schedule that either accelerates or defers the transfer of stock will not be treated as an increase in the amount of compensation payable under the performance goal.

(C) Compensation attributable to a stock option, stock appreciation right, or other stock-based compensation does not fail to satisfy the requirements of this paragraph (e)(2) to the extent that a change in the grant or award is made to reflect a change in corporate capitalization, such as a stock split or dividend, or a corporate transaction, such as any merger of a corporation into another corporation, any consolidation of two or more corporations into another corporation, any separation of a corporation (including a spinoff or other distribution of stock or property by a corporation), any reorganization of a corporation (whether or not such reorganization comes within the definition of such term in section 368), or any partial or complete liquidation by a corporation.

(iv) **Grant-by-grant determination.** The determination of whether compensation satisfies the requirements of this paragraph (e)(2) generally shall be made on a grant-by-grant basis. Thus, for example, whether compensation attributable to a stock option grant satisfies the requirements of this paragraph (e)(2) generally is determined on the basis of the particular grant made and without regard to the terms of any other option grant, or other grant of compensation, to the same or another employee. As a further example, except as provided in paragraph (e)(2)(vi), whether a grant of restricted stock or other stock-based compensation satisfies the requirements of this paragraph (e)(2) is determined without regard to whether dividends, dividend equivalents, or other similar distributions with respect to stock, on such stock-based compensation are payable prior to the attainment of the performance goal. Dividends, dividend equivalents, or other similar distributions with respect to stock that are treated as separate grants under this paragraph (e)(2)(iv) are not performance-based compensation unless they separately satisfy the requirements of this paragraph (e)(2).

(v) **Compensation contingent upon attainment of performance goal.** Compensation does not satisfy the requirements of this paragraph (e)(2) if the facts and circumstances indicate that the employee would receive all or part of the compensation regardless of whether the performance goal is attained. Thus, if the payment of compensation under a grant or award is only nominally or partially contingent on attaining a performance goal, none of the compensation payable under the grant or award will be considered performance-based. For example, if an employee is entitled to a bonus under either of two arrangements, where payment under a nonperformance-based arrangement is contingent upon the failure to attain the performance goals under an otherwise performance-based arrangement, then neither arrangement provides for compensation that satisfies the requirements of this paragraph (e)(2). Compensation does not fail to be qualified performance-based compensation merely because the plan allows the compensation to be payable upon death, disability, or change of ownership or control, although compensation actually paid on account of those events prior to the attainment of the performance goal would not satisfy the requirements of this paragraph (e)(2). As an exception to the general rule set forth in the first sentence of paragraph (e)(2)(iv) of this section, the facts-and-circumstances determination referred to in the first sentence of this paragraph (e)(2)(v) is made taking into account all plans, arrangements, and agreements that provide for compensation to the employee.

(vi) **Application of requirements to stock options and stock appreciation rights**—(A) **In general.** Compensation attributable to a stock option or a stock appreciation right is deemed to satisfy the requirements of this paragraph (e)(2) if the grant or award is made by the compensation committee; the plan under which the option or right is granted states the maximum number of shares with respect to which options or rights may be granted during a specified period to any individual employee; and, under the terms of the option or right, the amount of compensation the employee may receive is based solely on an increase in the value of the stock after the date of the grant or award. A plan may satisfy the requirement to provide a maximum number of shares with respect to which stock options and stock appreciation rights may be granted to any individual employee during a specified period if the plan specifies an aggregate maximum number of shares with respect to which stock options, stock appreciation rights, restricted stock, restricted stock units and other equity-based awards that may be granted to any individual employee during a specified period under a plan approved by shareholders in accordance with § 1.162-27(e)(4). If the amount of compensation the employee may receive under the grant or award is not based solely on an increase in the value of the stock after the date of grant or award (for example, in the case of restricted stock, or an option that is granted with an exercise price that is less than the fair market value of the stock as of the date of grant), none of the compensation attributable to the grant or award is qualified performance-based compensation under this paragraph (e)(2)(vi)(A). Whether a stock option grant is based solely on an increase in the value of the stock after the date of grant is determined without regard to any dividend equivalent that may be payable, provided that payment of the dividend equivalent is not made contingent on the exercise of the option. The rule that the compensation attributable to a stock option or stock appreciation right must be based solely on an increase in the value of the stock after the date of grant or award does not apply if the grant or award is made on account of, or if the vesting or exercisability of the grant or award is contingent on, the attainment of a performance goal that satisfies the requirements of this paragraph (e)(2).

(B) **Cancellation and repricing.** Compensation attributable to a stock option or stock appreciation right does not satisfy the requirements of this paragraph (e)(2) to the extent that the number of options granted exceeds the maximum number of shares for which options may be granted to the employee as specified in the plan. If an option is canceled, the canceled option continues to be counted against the maximum number of shares for which options may be granted to the employee under the plan. If, after grant, the exercise price of an option is reduced, the transaction is treated as a cancellation of the option and a grant of a new option. In such case, both the option that is deemed to be canceled and the option that is deemed to be granted reduce the maximum number of shares for which options may be granted to the employee under the plan. This paragraph (e)(2)(vi)(B) also applies in the case of a stock appreciation right where, after the award is made, the base amount on which stock appreciation is calculated is reduced to reflect a reduction in the fair market value of stock.

(vii) **Examples.** This paragraph (e)(2) may be illustrated by the following examples:

Example 1. No later than 90 days after the start of a fiscal year, but while the outcome is substantially uncertain, Corporation S establishes a bonus plan under which A, the chief executive officer, will receive a cash bonus of $500,000, if year-end corporate sales are increased by at least 5 percent. The compensation committee retains the right, if the performance goal is met, to reduce the bonus payment to A if, in its judgment, other subjective factors warrant a reduction. The bonus will meet the requirements of this paragraph (e)(2).

Example 2. The facts are the same as in Example 1, except that the bonus is based on a percentage of Corporation S's total sales for the fiscal year. Because Corporation S is virtually certain to have some sales for the fiscal year, the outcome of the performance goal is not substantially uncertain, and therefore the bonus does not meet the requirements of this paragraph (e)(2).

Example 3. The facts are the same as in Example 1, except that the bonus is based on a percentage of Corporation S's total profits for the fiscal year. Although some sales are virtually certain for virtually all public companies, it is substantially uncertain whether a company will have profits for a specified future period even if the company has a history of profitability. Therefore, the bonus will meet the requirements of this paragraph (e)(2).

Example 4. B is the general counsel of Corporation R, which is engaged in patent litigation with Corporation S. Representatives of Corporation S have informally indicated to Corporation R a willingness to settle the litigation for $50,000,000. Subsequently, the compensation committee of Corporation R agrees to pay B a bonus if B obtains a formal settlement for at least $50,000,000. The bonus to B does not meet the requirement of this paragraph (e)(2) because the performance goal was not established at a time when the outcome was substantially uncertain.

Example 5. Corporation S, a public utility, adopts a bonus plan for selected salaried employees that will pay a bonus at the end of a 3-year period of $750,000 each if, at the end of the 3 years, the price of S stock has increased by 10 percent. The plan also provides that the 10-percent goal will automatically adjust upward or downward by the percentage change in a published utilities index. Thus, for example, if the published utilities index shows a net increase of 5 percent over a 3-year period, then the salaried employees would receive a bonus only if Corporation S stock has increased by 15 percent. Conversely, if the published utilities index shows a net decrease of 5 percent over a 3-year period, then the salaried employees would receive a bonus if Corporation S stock has increased by 5 percent. Because these automatic adjustments in the performance goal are preestablished, the bonus meets the requirement of this paragraph (e)(2), notwithstanding the potential changes in the performance goal.

Example 6. The facts are the same as in Example 5, except that the bonus plan provides that, at the end of the 3-year period, a bonus of $750,000 will be paid to each salaried employee if either the price of Corporation S stock has increased by 10 percent or the earnings per share on Corporation S stock have increased by 5 percent. If both the earnings-per-share goal and the stock-price goal are preestablished, the compensation committee's discretion to choose to pay a bonus under either of the two goals does not cause any bonus paid under the plan to fail to meet the requirement of this paragraph (e)(2) because each goal independently meets the requirements of this paragraph (e)(2). The choice to pay under either of the two goals is tantamount to the discretion to choose not to pay under one of the goals, as provided in paragraph (e)(2)(iii) of this section.

Example 7. Corporation U establishes a bonus plan under which a specified class of employees will participate in a bonus pool if certain preestablished performance goals are attained. The amount of the bonus pool is determined under an objective formula. Under the terms of the bonus plan, the compensation committee retains the discretion to determine the fraction of the bonus pool that each employee may receive. The bonus plan does not satisfy the requirements of this paragraph (e)(2). Although the aggregate amount of the bonus plan is determined under an objective formula, a third party could not determine the amount that any individual could receive under the plan.

Example 8. The facts are the same as in Example 7, except that the bonus plan provides that a specified share of the bonus pool is payable to each employee, and the total of these shares does not exceed 100% of the pool. The bonus plan satisfies the requirements of this paragraph (e)(2). In addition, the bonus plan will satisfy the requirements of this paragraph (e)(2) even if the compensation committee retains the discretion to reduce the compensation payable to any individual employee, provided that a reduction in the amount of one employee's bonus does not result in an increase in the amount of any other employee's bonus.

Example 9. Corporation V establishes a stock option plan for salaried employees. The terms of the stock option plan specify that no individual salaried employee shall receive options for more than 100,000 shares over any 3–year period. The compensation committee grants options for 50,000 shares to each of several salaried employees. The exercise price of each option is equal to or greater than the fair market value of a share of V stock at the time of each grant. Compensation attributable to the exercise of the options satisfies the requirements of paragraph (e)(2)(vi) of this section. If, however, the terms of the options provide that the exercise price is less than fair market value of a share of V stock at the date of grant, no compensation attributable to the exercise of those options satisfies the requirements of this paragraph (e)(2) unless issuance or exercise of the options was contingent upon the attainment of a preestablished performance goal that satisfies this paragraph (e)(2). If, however, the terms of the plan also provide that Corporation V could grant options to pur-

chase no more than 900,000 shares over any 3–year period, but did not provide a limitation on the number of shares that any individual employee could purchase, then no compensation attributable to the exercise of those options satisfies the requirements of paragraph (e)(2)(vi) of this section.

Example 10. The facts are the same as in Example 9, except that, within the same 3-year grant period, the fair market value of Corporation V stock is significantly less than the exercise price of the options. The compensation committee reprices those options to that lower current fair market value of Corporation V stock. The repricing of the options for 50,000 shares held by each salaried employee is treated as the grant of new options for an additional 50,000 shares to each employee. Thus, each of the salaried employees is treated as having received grants for 100,000 shares. Consequently, if any additional options are granted to those employees during the 3-year period, compensation attributable to the exercise of those additional options would not satisfy the requirements of this paragraph (e)(2). The results would be the same if the compensation committee canceled the outstanding options and issued new options to the same employees that were exercisable at the fair market value of Corporation V stock on the date of reissue.

Example 11. Corporation W maintains a plan under which each participating employee may receive incentive stock options, nonqualified stock options, stock appreciation rights, or grants of restricted Corporation W stock. The plan specifies that each participating employee may receive options, stock appreciation rights, restricted stock, or any combination of each, for no more than 20,000 shares over the life of the plan. The plan provides that stock options may be granted with an exercise price of less than, equal to, or greater than fair market value on the date of grant. Options granted with an exercise price equal to, or greater than, fair market value on the date of grant do not fail to meet the requirements of this paragraph (e)(2) merely because the compensation committee has the discretion to determine the types of awards (i.e., options, rights, or restricted stock) to be granted to each employee or the discretion to issue options or make other compensation awards under the plan that would not meet the requirements of this paragraph (e)(2). Whether an option granted under the plan satisfies the requirements of this paragraph (e)(2) is determined on the basis of the specific terms of the option and without regard to other options or awards under the plan.

Example 12. Corporation X maintains a plan under which stock appreciation rights may be awarded to key employees. The plan permits the compensation committee to make awards under which the amount of compensation payable to the employee is equal to the increase in the stock price plus a percentage "gross up" intended to offset the tax liability of the employee. In addition, the plan permits the compensation committee to make awards under which the amount of compensation payable to the employee is equal to the increase in the stock price, based on the highest price, which is defined as the highest price paid for Corporation X stock (or offered in a tender offer or other arms-length offer) during the 90 days preceding exercise. Compensation attributable to awards under the plan satisfies the requirements of paragraph (e)(2)(vi) of this section, provided that the terms of the plan specify the maximum number of shares for which awards may be made.

Example 13. Corporation W adopts a plan under which a bonus will be paid to the CEO only if there is a 10% increase in earnings per share during the performance period. The plan provides that earnings per share will be calculated without regard to any change in accounting standards that may be required by the Financial Accounting Standards Board after the goal is established. After the goal is established, such a change in accounting standards occurs. Corporation W's reported earnings, for purposes of determining earnings per share under the plan, are adjusted pursuant to this plan provision to factor out this change in standards. This adjustment will not be considered an exercise of impermissible discre-

tion because it is made pursuant to the plan provision.

Example 14. Corporation X adopts a performance-based incentive pay plan with a four-year performance period. Bonuses under the plan are scheduled to be paid in the first year after the end of the performance period (year 5). However, in the second year of the performance period, the compensation committee determines that any bonuses payable in year 5 will instead, for bona fide business reasons, be paid in year 10. The compensation committee also determines that any compensation that would have been payable in year 5 will be adjusted to reflect the delay in payment. The adjustment will be based on the greater of the future rate of return of a specified mutual fund that invests in blue chip stocks or of a specified venture capital investment over the five-year deferral period. Each of these investments, considered by itself, is a predetermined actual investment because it is based on the future rate of return of an actual investment. However, the adjustment in this case is not based on predetermined actual investments within the meaning of paragraph (e)(2)(iii)(B) of this section because the amount payable by Corporation X in year 10 will be based on the greater of the two investment returns and, thus, will not be based on the actual rate of return on either specific investment.

Example 15. The facts are the same as in Example 14, except that the increase will be based on Moody's Average Corporate Bond Yield over the five-year deferral period. Because this index reflects a reasonable rate of interest, the increase in the compensation payable that is based on the index's rate of return is not considered an impermissible increase in the amount of compensation payable under the formula.

Example 16. The facts are the same as in Example 14, except that the increase will be based on the rate of return for the Standard & Poor's 500 Index. This index does not measure interest rates and thus does not represent a reasonable rate of interest. In addition, this index does not represent an actual investment.

Therefore, any additional compensation payable based on the rate of return of this index will result in an impermissible increase in the amount payable under the formula. If, in contrast, the increase were based on the rate of return of an existing mutual fund that is invested in a manner that seeks to approximate the Standard & Poor's 500 Index, the increase would be based on a predetermined actual investment within the meaning of paragraph (e)(2)(iii)(B) of this section and thus would not result in an impermissible increase in the amount payable under the formula.

(3) **Outside directors**—(i) **General rule**. The performance goal under which compensation is paid must be established by a compensation committee comprised solely of two or more outside directors. A director is an outside director if the director—

(A) Is not a current employee of the publicly held corporation;

(B) Is not a former employee of the publicly held corporation who receives compensation for prior services (other than benefits under a tax-qualified retirement plan) during the taxable year;

(C) Has not been an officer of the publicly held corporation; and

(D) Does not receive remuneration from the publicly held corporation, either directly or indirectly, in any capacity other than as a director. For this purpose, remuneration includes any payment in exchange for goods or services.

(ii) **Remuneration received.** For purposes of this paragraph (e)(3), remuneration is received, directly or indirectly, by a director in each of the following circumstances:

(A) If remuneration is paid, directly or indirectly, to the director personally or to an entity in which the director has a beneficial ownership interest of greater than 50 percent. For this purpose, remuneration is considered paid when actually paid (and throughout the remainder of that taxable year of the corporation) and, if earlier, throughout the period

when a contract or agreement to pay remuneration is outstanding.

(B) If remuneration, other than de minimis remuneration, was paid by the publicly held corporation in its preceding taxable year to an entity in which the director has a beneficial ownership interest of at least 5 percent but not more than 50 percent. For this purpose, remuneration is considered paid when actually paid or, if earlier, when the publicly held corporation becomes liable to pay it.

(C) If remuneration, other than de minimis remuneration, was paid by the publicly held corporation in its preceding taxable year to an entity by which the director is employed or self-employed other than as a director. For this purpose, remuneration is considered paid when actually paid or, if earlier, when the publicly held corporation becomes liable to pay it.

(iii) **De minimis remuneration**—(A) **In general.** For purposes of paragraphs (e)(3)(ii)(B) and (C) of this section, remuneration that was paid by the publicly held corporation in its preceding taxable year to an entity is de minimis if payments to the entity did not exceed 5 percent of the gross revenue of the entity for its taxable year ending with or within that preceding taxable year of the publicly held corporation.

(B) **Remuneration for personal services and substantial owners.** Notwithstanding paragraph (e)(3)(iii)(A) of this section, remuneration in excess of $60,000 is not de minimis if the remuneration is paid to an entity described in paragraph (e)(3)(ii)(B) of this section, or is paid for personal services to an entity described in paragraph (e)(3)(ii)(C) of this section.

(iv) **Remuneration for personal services.** For purposes of paragraph (e)(3)(iii)(B) of this section, remuneration from a publicly held corporation is for personal services if—

(A) The remuneration is paid to an entity for personal or professional services, consisting of legal, accounting, investment banking, and management consulting services (and other similar services that may be specified by the Commissioner in revenue rulings, notices, or other guidance published in the Internal Revenue Bulletin), performed for the publicly held corporation, and the remuneration is not for services that are incidental to the purchase of goods or to the purchase of services that are not personal services; and

(B) The director performs significant services (whether or not as an employee) for the corporation, division, or similar organization (within the entity) that actually provides the services described in paragraph (e)(3)(iv)(A) of this section to the publicly held corporation, or more than 50 percent of the entity's gross revenues (for the entity's preceding taxable year) are derived from that corporation, subsidiary, or similar organization.

(v) Entity defined. For purposes of this paragraph (e)(3), entity means an organization that is a sole proprietorship, trust, estate, partnership, or corporation. The term also includes an affiliated group of corporations as defined in section 1504 (determined without regard to section 1504(b)) and a group of organizations that would be an affiliated group but for the fact that one or more of the organizations are not incorporated. However, the aggregation rules referred to in the preceding sentence do not apply for purposes of determining whether a director has a beneficial ownership interest of at least 5 percent or greater than 50 percent.

(vi) **Employees and former officers.** Whether a director is an employee or a former officer is determined on the basis of the facts at the time that the individual is serving as a director on the compensation committee. Thus, a director is not precluded from being an outside director solely because the director is a former officer of a corporation that previously was an affiliated corporation of the publicly held corporation. For example, a director of a parent corporation of an affiliated group is not precluded from being an outside director solely because that director is a former officer of an affiliated subsidiary that was spun off or liquidated. However, an outside director would no longer be an outside director if a corporation in which the director was previ-

ously an officer became an affiliated corporation of the publicly held corporation.

(vii) **Officer.** Solely for purposes of this paragraph (e)(3), officer means an administrative executive who is or was in regular and continued service. The term implies continuity of service and excludes those employed for a special and single transaction. An individual who merely has (or had) the title of officer but not the authority of an officer is not considered an officer. The determination of whether an individual is or was an officer is based on all of the facts and circumstances in the particular case, including without limitation the source of the individual's authority, the term for which the individual is elected or appointed, and the nature and extent of the individual's duties.

(viii) **Members of affiliated groups.** For purposes of this paragraph (e)(3), the outside directors of the publicly held member of an affiliated group are treated as the outside directors of all members of the affiliated group.

(ix) **Examples.** This paragraph (e)(3) may be illustrated by the following examples:

Example 1. Corporations X and Y are members of an affiliated group of corporations as defined in section 1504, until July 1, 1994, when Y is sold to another group. Prior to the sale, A served as an officer of Corporation Y. After July 1, 1994, A is not treated as a former officer of Corporation X by reason of having been an officer of Y.

Example 2. Corporation Z, a calendar-year taxpayer, uses the services of a law firm by which B is employed, but in which B has a less-than-5-percent ownership interest. The law firm reports income on a July 1 to June 30 basis. Corporation Z appoints B to serve on its compensation committee for calendar year 1998 after determining that, in calendar year 1997, it did not become liable to the law firm for remuneration exceeding the lesser of $60,000 or five percent of the law firm's gross revenue (calculated for the year ending June 30, 1997). On October 1, 1998, Corporation Z becomes liable to pay remuneration of $50,000 to the law firm on June 30, 1999. For the year ending June 30, 1998, the law firm's gross revenue was less than $1 million. Thus, in calendar year 1999, B is not an outside director. However, B may satisfy the requirements for an outside director in calendar year 2000, if, in calendar year 1999, Corporation Z does not become liable to the law firm for additional remuneration. This is because the remuneration actually paid on June 30, 1999 was considered paid on October 1, 1998 under paragraph (e)(3)(ii)(C) of this section.

Example 3. Corporation Z, a publicly held corporation, purchases goods from Corporation A. D, an executive and less-than-5-percent owner of Corporation A, sits on the board of directors of Corporation Z and on its compensation committee. For 1997, Corporation Z obtains representations to the effect that D is not eligible for any commission for D's sales to Corporation Z and that, for purposes of determining D's compensation for 1997, Corporation A's sales to Corporation Z are not otherwise treated differently than sales to other customers of Corporation A (including its affiliates, if any) or are irrelevant. In addition, Corporation Z has no reason to believe that these representations are inaccurate or that it is otherwise paying remuneration indirectly to D personally. Thus, in 1997, no remuneration is considered paid by Corporation Z indirectly to D personally under paragraph (e)(3)(ii)(A) of this section.

Example 4. (i) Corporation W, a publicly held corporation, purchases goods from Corporation T. C, an executive and less-than-5-percent owner of Corporation T, sits on the board of directors of Corporation W and on its compensation committee. Corporation T develops a new product and agrees on January 1, 1998 to pay C a bonus of $500,000 if Corporation W contracts to purchase the product. Even if Corporation W purchases the new product, sales to Corporation W will represent less than 5 percent of Corporation T's gross revenues. In 1999, Corporation W contracts to purchase the new product and, in 2000, C receives the $500,000 bonus from Corporation T. In 1998, 1999, and 2000, Corporation W does not obtain any representations relating to

indirect remuneration to C personally (such as the representations described in Example 3).

(ii) Thus, in 1998, 1999, and 2000, remuneration is considered paid by Corporation W indirectly to C personally under paragraph (e)(3)(ii)(A) of this section. Accordingly, in 1998, 1999, and 2000, C is not an outside director of Corporation W. The result would have been the same if Corporation W had obtained appropriate representations but nevertheless had reason to believe that it was paying remuneration indirectly to C personally.

Example 5. Corporation R, a publicly held corporation, purchases utility service from Corporation Q, a public utility. The chief executive officer, and less-than-5-percent owner, of Corporation Q is a director of Corporation R. Corporation R pays Corporation Q more than $60,000 per year for the utility service, but less than 5 percent of Corporation Q's gross revenues. Because utility services are not personal services, the fees paid are not subject to the $60,000 de minimis rule for remuneration for personal services within the meaning of paragraph (e)(3)(iii)(B) of this section. Thus, the chief executive officer qualifies as an outside director of Corporation R, unless disqualified on some other basis.

Example 6. Corporation A, a publicly held corporation, purchases management consulting services from Division S of Conglomerate P. The chief financial officer of Division S is a director of Corporation A. Corporation A pays more than $60,000 per year for the management consulting services, but less than 5 percent of Conglomerate P's gross revenues. Because management consulting services are personal services within the meaning of paragraph (e)(3)(iv)(A) of this section, and the chief financial officer performs significant services for Division S, the fees paid are subject to the $60,000 de minimis rule as remuneration for personal services. Thus, the chief financial officer does not qualify as an outside director of Corporation A.

Example 7. The facts are the same as in Example 6, except that the chief executive officer, and less-than-5-percent owner, of the parent company of Conglomerate P is a director of Corporation A and does not perform significant services for Division S. If the gross revenues of Division S do not constitute more than 50 percent of the gross revenues of Conglomerate P for P's preceding taxable year, the chief executive officer will qualify as an outside director of Corporation A, unless disqualified on some other basis.

(4) **Shareholder approval requirement**—(i) **General rule.** The material terms of the performance goal under which the compensation is to be paid must be disclosed to and subsequently approved by the shareholders of the publicly held corporation before the compensation is paid. The requirements of this paragraph (e)(4) are not satisfied if the compensation would be paid regardless of whether the material terms are approved by shareholders. The material terms include the employees eligible to receive compensation; a description of the business criteria on which the performance goal is based; and either the maximum amount of compensation that could be paid to any employee or the formula used to calculate the amount of compensation to be paid to the employee if the performance goal is attained (except that, in the case of a formula based, in whole or in part, on a percentage of salary or base pay, the maximum dollar amount of compensation that could be paid to the employee must be disclosed).

(ii) **Eligible employees.** Disclosure of the employees eligible to receive compensation need not be so specific as to identify the particular individuals by name. A general description of the class of eligible employees by title or class is sufficient, such as the chief executive officer and vice presidents, or all salaried employees, all executive officers, or all key employees.

(iii) **Description of business criteria**—(A) **In general.** Disclosure of the business criteria on which the performance goal is based need not include the specific targets that must be satisfied under the performance goal. For example, if a bonus plan provides that a bonus will be paid if earnings per share increase by 10 percent, the 10-percent figure is a target that need not be disclosed to shareholders. However, in that case, disclosure must be made that the bonus plan is based on an earnings-per-share business criterion. In the case of a plan under which employees may be granted stock options or stock appreciation rights, no specific description of the business criteria is required if the grants or awards are based on a stock price that is no less than current fair market value.

(B) **Disclosure of confidential information.** The requirements of this paragraph (e)(4) may be satisfied even though information that otherwise would be a material term of a performance goal is not disclosed to shareholders, provided that the compensation committee determines that the information is confidential commercial or business information, the disclosure of which would have an adverse effect on the publicly held corporation. Whether disclosure would adversely affect the corporation is determined on the basis of the facts and circumstances. If the compensation committee makes such a determination, the disclosure to shareholders must state the compensation committee's belief that the information is confidential commercial or business information, the disclosure of which would adversely affect the company. In addition, the ability not to disclose confidential information does not eliminate the requirement that disclosure be made of the maximum amount of compensation that is payable to an individual under a performance goal. Confidential information does not include the identity of an executive or the class of executives to which a performance goal applies or the amount of compensation that is payable if the goal is satisfied.

(iv) **Description of compensation.** Disclosure as to the compensation payable under a performance goal must be specific enough so that shareholders can determine the maximum amount of compensation that could be paid to any indivicual employee during a specified period. If the terms of the performance goal do not provide for a maximum dollar amount, the disclosure must include the formula under which the compensation would be calculated. Thus, if compensation attributable to the exercise of stock options is equal to the difference between the exercise price and the current value of the stock, then disclosure of the maximum number of shares for which grants may be made to any individual employee during a specified period and the exercise price of those options (for example, fair market value on date of grant) would satisfy the requirements of this paragraph (e)(4)(iv). In that case, shareholders could calculate the maximum amount of compensation that would be attributable to the exercise of options on the basis of their assumptions as to the future stock price.

(v) **Disclosure requirements of the Securities and Exchange Commission.** To the extent not otherwise specifically provided in this paragraph (e)(4), whether the material terms of a performance goal are adequately disclosed to shareholders is determined under the same standards as apply under the Exchange Act.

(vi) **Frequency of disclosure.** Once the material terms of a performance goal are disclosed to and approved by shareholders, no additional disclosure or approval is required unless the compensation committee changes the material terms of the performance goal. If, however, the compensation committee has authority to change the targets under a performance goal after shareholder approval of the goal, material terms of the performance goal must be disclosed to and reapproved by shareholders no later than the first shareholder meeting that occurs in the fifth year following the year in which shareholders previously approved the performance goal.

(vii) **Shareholder vote.** For purposes of this paragraph (e)(4), the material terms of a performance goal are approved by shareholders if, in a separate vote, a majority of the votes cast on the issue (including abstentions to the extent abstentions are counted as voting under applicable state law) are cast in favor of approval.

(viii) **Members of affiliated group.** For purposes of this paragraph (e)(4), the share-holders of the publicly held member of the affiliated group are treated as the shareholders of all members of the affiliated group.

(ix) **Examples.** This paragraph (e)(4) may be illustrated by the following examples:

Example 1. Corporation X adopts a plan that will pay a specified class of its executives an annual cash bonus based on the overall increase in corporate sales during the year. Under the terms of the plan, the cash bonus of each executive equals $100,000 multiplied by the number of percentage points by which sales increase in the current year when compared to the prior year. Corporation X discloses to its shareholders prior to the vote both the class of executives eligible to receive awards and the annual formula of $100,000 multiplied by the percentage increase in sales. This disclosure meets the requirements of this paragraph (e)(4). Because the compensation committee does not have the authority to establish a different target under the plan, Corporation X need not redisclose to its shareholders and obtain their reapproval of the material terms of the plan until those material terms are changed.

Example 2. The facts are the same as in Example 1 except that Corporation X discloses only that bonuses will be paid on the basis of the annual increase in sales. This disclosure does not meet the requirements of this paragraph (e)(4) because it does not include the formula for calculating the compensation or a maximum amount of compensation to be paid if the performance goal is satisfied.

Example 3. Corporation Y adopts an incentive compensation plan in 1995 that will pay a specified class of its executives a bonus every 3 years based on the following 3 factors: increases in earnings per share, reduction in costs for specified divisions, and increases in sales by specified divisions. The bonus is payable in cash or in Corporation Y stock, at the option of the executive. Under the terms of the plan, prior to the beginning of each 3-year period, the compensation committee determines the specific targets under each of the three factors (i.e., the amount of the increase in earnings per share, the reduction in costs, and the amount of sales) that must be met in order for the executives to receive a bonus. Under the terms of the plan, the compensation committee retains the discretion to determine whether a bonus will be paid under any one of the goals. The terms of the plan also specify that no executive may receive a bonus in excess of $1,500,000 for any 3-year period. To satisfy the requirements of this paragraph (e)(4), Corporation Y obtains shareholder approval of the plan at its 1995 annual shareholder meeting. In the proxy statement issued to shareholders, Corporation Y need not disclose to shareholders the specific targets that are set by the compensation committee. However, Corporation Y must disclose that bonuses are paid on the basis of earnings per share, reductions in costs, and increases in sales of specified divisions. Corporation Y also must disclose the maximum amount of compensation that any executive may receive under the plan is $1,500,000 per 3-year period. Unless changes in the material terms of the plan are made earlier, Corporation Y need not disclose the material terms of the plan to the shareholders and obtain their reapproval until the first shareholders' meeting held in 2000.

Example 4. The same facts as in Example 3, except that prior to the beginning of the second 3-year period, the compensation committee determines that different targets will be set under the plan for that period with regard to all three of the performance criteria (i.e., earnings per share, reductions in costs, and increases in sales). In addition, the compensation committee raises the maximum dollar amount that can be paid under the plan for a 3-year period to $2,000,000. The increase in the maximum dollar amount of compensation under the plan is a changed material term. Thus, to satisfy the requirements of this paragraph (e)(4), Corporation Y must disclose to and obtain approval by the shareholders of the plan as amended.

Example 5. In 1998, Corporation Z establishes a plan under which a specified group of executives will receive a cash bonus not to exceed $750,000 each if a new product that

has been in development is completed and ready for sale to customers by January 1, 2000. Although the completion of the new product is a material term of the performance goal under this paragraph (e)(4), the compensation committee determines that the disclosure to shareholders of the performance goal would adversely affect Corporation Z because its competitors would be made aware of the existence and timing of its new product. In this case, the requirements of this paragraph (e)(4) are satisfied if all other material terms, including the maximum amount of compensation, are disclosed and the disclosure affirmatively states that the terms of the performance goal are not being disclosed because the compensation committee has determined that those terms include confidential information, the disclosure of which would adversely affect Corporation Z.

(5) **Compensation committee certification.** The compensation committee must certify in writing prior to payment of the compensation that the performance goals and any other material terms were in fact satisfied. For this purpose, approved minutes of the compensation committee meeting in which the certification is made are treated as a written certification. Certification by the compensation committee is not required for compensation that is attributable solely to the increase in the value of the stock of the publicly held corporation.

(f) *Companies that become publicly held, spinoffs, and similar transactions*—(1) **In general.** In the case of a corporation that was not a publicly held corporation and then becomes a publicly held corporation, the deduction limit of paragraph (b) of this section does not apply to any remuneration paid pursuant to a compensation plan or agreement that existed during the period in which the corporation was not publicly held. However, in the case of such a corporation that becomes publicly held in connection with an initial public offering, this relief applies only to the extent that the prospectus accompanying the initial public offering disclosed information concerning those plans or agreements that satisfied all applicable securities laws then in effect. In accordance with paragraph (c)(1)(ii) of this section, a corporation that is a member of an affiliated group that includes a publicly held corporation is considered publicly held and, therefore, cannot rely on this paragraph (f)(1).

(2) **Reliance period.** Paragraph (f)(1) of this section may be relied upon until the earliest of—

(i) The expiration of the plan or agreement;

(ii) The material modification of the plan or agreement, within the meaning of paragraph (h)(1)(iii) of this section;

(iii) The issuance of all employer stock and other compensation that has been allocated under the plan; or

(iv) The first meeting of shareholders at which directors are to be elected that occurs after the close of the third calendar year following the calendar year in which the initial public offering occurs or, in the case of a privately held corporation that becomes publicly held without an initial public offering, the first calendar year following the calendar year in which the corporation becomes publicly held.

(3) **Stock-based compensation.** Paragraph (f)(1) of this section will apply to any compensation received pursuant to the exercise of a stock option or stock appreciation right, or the substantial vesting of restricted property, granted under a plan or agreement described in paragraph (f)(1) of this section if the grant occurs on or before the earliest of the events specified in paragraph (f)(2) of this section. This paragraph does not apply to any form of stock-based compensation other than the forms listed in the immediately preceding sentence. Thus, for example, compensation payable under a restricted stock unit arrangement or a phantom stock arrangement must be paid, rather than merely granted, on or before the occurrence of the earliest of the events specified in paragraph (f)(2) of this section in order for paragraph (f)(1) of this section to apply.

(4) **Subsidiaries that become separate publicly held corporations**—(i) **In general.** If a subsidiary that is a member of the affiliated group described in paragraph (c)(1)(ii) of this section becomes a separate publicly held corporation (whether by spinoff or otherwise), any remuneration paid to covered employees of the new publicly held corporation will satisfy the exception for performance-based compensation described in paragraph (e) of this section if the conditions in either paragraph (f)(4)(ii) or (f)(4)(iii) of this section are satisfied.

(ii) **Prior establishment and approval.** Remuneration satisfies the requirements of this paragraph (f)(4)(ii) if the remuneration satisfies the requirements for performance-based compensation set forth in paragraphs (e)(2), (e)(3), and (e)(4) of this section (by application of paragraphs (e)(3)(viii) and (e)(4)(viii) of this section) before the corporation becomes a separate publicly held corporation, and the certification required by paragraph (e)(5) of this section is made by the compensation committee of the new publicly held corporation (but if the performance goals are attained before the corporation becomes a separate publicly held corporation, the certification may be made by the compensation committee referred to in paragraph (e)(3)(viii) of this section before it becomes a separate publicly held corporation). Thus, this paragraph (f)(4)(ii) requires that the outside directors and shareholders (within the meaning of paragraphs (e)(3)(viii) and (e)(4)(viii) of this section) of the corporation before it becomes a separate publicly held corporation establish and approve, respectively, the performance-based compensation for the covered employees of the new publicly held corporation in accordance with paragraphs (e)(3) and (e)(4) of this section.

(iii) **Transition period.** Remuneration satisfies the requirements of this paragraph (f)(4)(iii) if the remuneration satisfies all of the requirements of paragraphs (e)(2), (e)(3), and (e)(5) of this section. The outside directors (within the meaning of paragraph (e)(3)(viii) of this section) of the corporation before it becomes a separate publicly held corporation, or the outside directors of the new publicly held corporation, may establish and administer the performance goals for the covered employees of the new publicly held corporation for purposes of satisfying the requirements of paragraphs (e)(2) and (e)(3) of this section. The certification required by paragraph (e)(5) of this section must be made by the compensation committee of the new publicly held corporation. However, a taxpayer may rely on this paragraph (f)(4)(iii) to satisfy the requirements of paragraph (e) of this section only for compensation paid, or stock options, stock appreciation rights, or restricted property granted, prior to the first regularly scheduled meeting of the shareholders of the new publicly held corporation that occurs more than 12 months after the date the corporation becomes a separate publicly held corporation. Compensation paid, or stock options, stock appreciation rights, or restricted property granted, on or after the date of that meeting of shareholders must satisfy all requirements of paragraph (e) of this section, including the shareholder approval requirement of paragraph (e)(4) of this section, in order to satisfy the requirements for performance-based compensation.

(5) **Example.** The following example illustrates the application of paragraph (f)(4)(ii) of this section:

Example. Corporation P, which is publicly held, decides to spin off Corporation S, a wholly owned subsidiary of Corporation P. After the spinoff, Corporation S will be a separate publicly held corporation. Before the spinoff, the compensation committee of Corporation P, pursuant to paragraph (e)(3)(viii) of this section, establishes a bonus plan for the executives of Corporation S that provides for bonuses payable after the spinoff and that satisfies the requirements of paragraph (e)(2) of this section. If, pursuant to paragraph (e)(4)(viii) of this section, the shareholders of Corporation P approve the plan prior to the spinoff, that approval will satisfy the requirements of paragraph (e)(4) of this section with respect to compensation paid pursuant to the bonus plan after the spinoff. However, the compensation committee of Corporation S will be required to certify that the goals are satisfied prior to the payment of the bonuses in order for the bonuses to be considered performance-based compensation.

(g) *Coordination with disallowed excess parachute payments.* The $1,000,000 limitation in paragraph (b) of this section is reduced (but not below zero) by the amount (if any) that would have been included in the compensation of the covered employee for the taxable year but for being disallowed by reason of section 280G. For example, assume that during a taxable year a corporation pays $1,500,000 to a covered employee and no portion satisfies the exception in paragraph (d) of this section for commissions or paragraph (e) of this section for qualified performance-based compensation. Of the $1,500,000, $600,000 is an excess parachute payment, as defined in section 280G(b)(1) and is disallowed by reason of that section. Because the excess parachute payment reduces the limitation of paragraph (b) of this section, the corporation can deduct $400,000, and $500,000 of the otherwise deductible amount is nondeductible by reason of section 162(m).

(h) *Transition rules*—(1) **Compensation payable under a written binding contract which was in effect on February 17, 1993**— (i) **General rule.** The deduction limit of paragraph (b) of this section does not apply to any compensation payable under a written binding contract that was in effect on February 17, 1993. The preceding sentence does not apply unless, under applicable state law, the corporation is obligated to pay the compensation if the employee performs services. However, the deduction limit of paragraph (b) of this section does apply to a contract that is renewed after February 17, 1993. A written binding contract that is terminable or cancelable by the corporation after February 17, 1993, without the employee's consent is treated as a new contract as of the date that any such termination or cancellation, if made, would be effective. Thus, for example, if the terms of a contract provide that it will be automatically renewed as of a certain date unless either the corporation or the employee gives notice of termination of the contract at least 30 days before that date, the contract is treated as a new contract as of the date that termination would be effective if that notice were given. Similarly, for example, if the terms of a contract provide that the contract will be terminated or canceled as of a certain date unless either the corporation or the employee elects to renew within 30 days of that date, the contract is treated as renewed by the corporation as of that date. Alternatively, if the corporation will remain legally obligated by the terms of a contract beyond a certain date at the sole discretion of the employee, the contract will not be treated as a new contract as of that date if the employee exercises the discretion to keep the corporation bound to the contract. A contract is not treated as terminable or cancelable if it can be terminated or canceled only by terminating the employment relationship of the employee.

(ii) **Compensation payable under a plan or arrangement.** If a compensation plan or arrangement meets the requirements of paragraph (h)(1)(i) of this section, the compensation paid to an employee pursuant to the plan or arrangement will not be subject to the deduction limit of paragraph (b) of this section even though the employee was not eligible to participate in the plan as of February 17, 1993. However, the preceding sentence does not apply unless the employee was employed on February 17, 1993, by the corporation that maintained the plan or arrangement, or the employee had the right to participate in the plan or arrangement under a written binding contract as of that date.

(iii) **Material modifications.**

(A) Paragraph (h)(1)(i) of this section will not apply to any written binding contract that is materially modified. A material modification occurs when the contract is amended to increase the amount of compensation payable to the employee. If a binding written contract is materially modified, it is treated as a new contract entered into as of the date of the material modification. Thus, amounts received by

an employee under the contract prior to a material modification are not affected, but amounts received subsequent to the material modification are not treated as paid under a binding, written contract described in paragraph (h)(1)(i) of this section.

(B) A modification of the contract that accelerates the payment of compensation will be treated as a material modification unless the amount of compensation paid is discounted to reasonably reflect the time value of money. If the contract is modified to defer the payment of compensation, any compensation paid in excess of the amount that was originally payable to the employee under the contract will not be treated as a material modification if the additional amount is based on either a reasonable rate of interest or one or more predetermined actual investments (whether or not assets associated with the amount originally owed are actually invested therein) such that the amount payable by the employer at the later date will be based on the actual rate of return of the specific investment (including any decrease as well as any increase in the value of the investment).

(C) The adoption of a supplemental contract or agreement that provides for increased compensation, or the payment of additional compensation, is a material modification of a binding, written contract where the facts and circumstances show that the additional compensation is paid on the basis of substantially the same elements or conditions as the compensation that is otherwise paid under the written binding contract. However, a material modification of a written binding contract does not include a supplemental payment that is equal to or less than a reasonable cost-of-living increase over the payment made in the preceding year under that written binding contract. In addition, a supplemental payment of compensation that satisfies the requirements of qualified performance-based compensation in paragraph (e) of this section will not be treated as a material modification.

(iv) **Examples.** The following examples illustrate the exception of this paragraph (h)(1):

Example 1. Corporation X executed a 3-year compensation arrangement with C on February 15, 1993, that constitutes a written binding contract under applicable state law. The terms of the arrangement provide for automatic extension after the 3-year term for additional 1-year periods, unless the corporation exercises its option to terminate the arrangement within 30 days of the end of the 3-year term or, thereafter, within 30 days before each anniversary date. Termination of the compensation arrangement does not require the termination of C's employment relationship with Corporation X. Unless terminated, the arrangement is treated as renewed on February 15, 1996, and the deduction limit of paragraph (b) of this section applies to payments under the arrangement after that date.

Example 2. Corporation Y executed a 5-year employment agreement with B on January 1, 1992, providing for a salary of $900,000 per year. Assume that this agreement constitutes a written binding contract under applicable state law. In 1992 and 1993, B receives the salary of $900,000 per year. In 1994, Corporation Y increases B's salary with a payment of $20,000. The $20,000 supplemental payment does not constitute a material modification of the written binding contract because the $20,000 payment is less than or equal to a reasonable cost-of-living increase from 1993. However, the $20,000 supplemental payment is subject to the limitation in paragraph (b) of this section. On January 1, 1995, Corporation Y increases B's salary to $1,200,000. The $280,000 supplemental payment is a material modification of the written binding contract because the additional compensation is paid on the basis of substantially the same elements or conditions as the compensation that is otherwise paid under the written binding contract and it is greater than a reasonable, annual cost-of-living increase. Because the written binding contract is materially modified as of January 1, 1995, all compensation paid to B in 1995 and thereafter is subject to the deduction limitation of section 162(m).

Example 3. Assume the same facts as in Example 2, except that instead of an increase in salary, B receives a restricted stock grant subject to B's continued employment for the balance of the contract. The restricted stock grant is not a material modification of the binding written contract because any additional compensation paid to B under the grant is not paid on the basis of substantially the same elements and conditions as B's salary because it is based both on the stock price and B's continued service. However, compensation attributable to the restricted stock grant is subject to the deduction limitation of section 162(m).

(2) **Special transition rule for outside directors.** A director who is a disinterested director is treated as satisfying the requirements of an outside director under paragraph (e)(3) of this section until the first meeting of shareholders at which directors are to be elected that occurs on or after January 1, 1996. For purposes of this paragraph (h)(2) and paragraph (h)(3) of this section, a director is a disinterested director if the director is disinterested within the meaning of Rule 16b-3(c)(2)(i), 17 CFR 240.16b-3(c)(2)(i), under the Exchange Act (including the provisions of Rule 16b-3(d)(3), as in effect on April 30, 1991).

(3) **Special transition rule for previously-approved plans**—(i) **In general.** Any compensation paid under a plan or agreement approved by shareholders before December 20, 1993, is treated as satisfying the requirements of paragraphs (e)(3) and (e)(4) of this section, provided that the directors administering the plan or agreement are disinterested directors and the plan was approved by shareholders in a manner consistent with Rule 16b-3(b), 17 CFR 240.16b-3(b), under the Exchange Act or Rule 16b-3(a), 17 CFR 240.16b-3(a) (as contained in 17 CFR part 240 revised April 1, 1990). In addition, for purposes of satisfying the requirements of paragraph (e)(2)(vi) of this section, a plan or agreement is treated as stating a maximum number of shares with respect to which an option or right may be granted to any employee if the plan or agreement that was approved by the shareholders provided for an aggregate limit, consistent with Rule 16b-3(b), 17 CFR

250.16b-3(b), on the shares of employer stock with respect to which awards may be made under the plan or agreement.

(ii) **Reliance period.** The transition rule provided in this paragraph (h)(3) shall continue and may be relied upon until the earliest of—

(A) The expiration or material modification of the plan or agreement;

(B) The issuance of all employer stock and other compensation that has been allocated under the plan; or

(C) The first meeting of shareholders at which directors are to be elected that occurs after December 31, 1996.

(iii) **Stock-based compensation.** This paragraph (h)(3) will apply to any compensation received pursuant to the exercise of a stock option or stock appreciation right, or the substantial vesting of restricted property, granted under a plan or agreement described in paragraph (h)(3)(i) of this section if the grant occurs on or before the earliest of the events specified in paragraph (h)(3)(ii) of this section.

(iv) **Example.** The following example illustrates the application of this paragraph (h)(3):

Example. Corporation Z adopted a stock option plan in 1991. Pursuant to Rule 16b-3 under the Exchange Act, the stock option plan has been administered by disinterested directors and was approved by Corporation Z shareholders. Under the terms of the plan, shareholder approval is not required again until 2001. In addition, the terms of the stock option plan include an aggregate limit on the number of shares available under the plan. Option grants under the Corporation Z plan are made with an exercise price equal to or greater than the fair market value of Corporation Z stock. Compensation attributable to the exercise of options that are granted under the plan before the earliest of the dates specified in paragraph (h)(3)(ii) of this section will be treated as satisfying the requirements of paragraph (e) of this section for qualified perfor-

mance-based compensation, regardless of when the options are exercised.

(i) (*Reserved*)

(j) *Effective date*—(1) **In general.** Section 162(m) and this section apply to compensation that is otherwise deductible by the corporation in a taxable year beginning on or after January 1, 1994.

(2) **Delayed effective date for certain provisions**—(i) **Date on which remuneration is considered paid.** Notwithstanding paragraph (j)(1) of this section, the rules in the second sentence of each of paragraphs (e)(3)(ii)(A), (e)(3)(ii)(B), and (e)(3)(ii)(C) of this section for determining the date or dates on which remuneration is considered paid to a director are effective for taxable years beginning on or after January 1, 1995. Prior to those taxable years, taxpayers must follow the rules in paragraphs (e)(3)(ii)(A), (e)(3)(ii)(B), and (e)(3)(ii)(C) of this section or another reasonable, good faith interpretation of section 162(m) with respect to the date or dates on which remuneration is considered paid to a director.

(ii) **Separate treatment of publicly held subsidiaries.** Notwithstanding paragraph (j)(1) of this section, the rule in paragraph (c)(1)(ii) of this section that treats publicly held subsidiaries as separately subject to section 162(m) is effective as of the first regularly scheduled meeting of the shareholders of the publicly held subsidiary that occurs more than 12 months after December 2, 1994. The rule for stock-based compensation set forth in paragraph (f)(3) of this section will apply for this purpose, except that the grant must occur before the shareholder meeting specified in this paragraph (j)(2)(ii). Taxpayers may choose to rely on the rule referred to in the first sentence of this paragraph (j)(2)(ii) for the period prior to the effective date of the rule.

(iii) **Subsidiaries that become separate publicly held corporations.** Notwithstanding paragraph (j)(1) of this section, if a subsidiary of a publicly held corporation becomes a separate publicly held corporation as described in paragraph (f)(4)(i) of this section, then, for the duration of the reliance period described in paragraph (f)(2) of this section, the rules of paragraph (f)(1) of this section are treated as applying (and the rules of paragraph (f)(4) of this section do not apply) to remuneration paid to covered employees of that new publicly held corporation pursuant to a plan or agreement that existed prior to December 2, 1994, provided that the treatment of that remuneration as performance-based is in accordance with a reasonable, good faith interpretation of section 162(m). However, if remuneration is paid to covered employees of that new publicly held corporation pursuant to a plan or agreement that existed prior to December 2, 1994, but that remuneration is not performance-based under a reasonable, good faith interpretation of section 162(m), the rules of paragraph (f)(1) of this section will be treated as applying only until the first regularly scheduled meeting of shareholders that occurs more than 12 months after December 2, 1994. The rules of paragraph (f)(4) of this section will apply as of that first regularly scheduled meeting. The rule for stock-based compensation set forth in paragraph (f)(3) of this section will apply for purposes of this paragraph (j)(2)(iii), except that the grant must occur before the shareholder meeting specified in the preceding sentence if the remuneration is not performance-based under a reasonable, good faith interpretation of section 162(m). Taxpayers may choose to rely on the rules of paragraph (f)(4) of this section for the period prior to the applicable effective date referred to in the first or second sentence of this paragraph (j)(2)(iii).

(iv) **Bonus pools.** Notwithstanding paragraph (j)(1) of this section, the rules in paragraph (e)(2)(iii)(A) that limit the sum of individual percentages of a bonus pool to 100 percent will not apply to remuneration paid before January 1, 2001, based on performance in any performance period that began prior to December 20, 1995.

(v) **Compensation based on a percentage of salary or base pay.** Notwithstanding paragraph (j)(1) of this section, the require-ment in paragraph (e)(4)(i) of this section that, in the case of certain formulas based on a percentage of salary or base pay, a corporation disclose to shareholders the maximum dollar amount of compensation that could be paid to the employee, will apply only to plans approved by shareholders after April 30, 1995.

(vi) The modifications to paragraphs (e)(2)(vi)(A), (e)(2)(vii) Example 9, and (e)(4)(iv) of this section concerning the maximum number of shares with respect to which a stock option or stock appreciation right that may be granted and the amount of compensation that may be paid to any individual employee apply to compensation attributable to stock options and stock appreciation rights that are granted on or after June 24, 2011. The last two sentences of §1.162-27(f)(3) apply to remuneration that is otherwise deductible resulting from a stock option, stock appreciation right, restricted stock (or other property), restricted stock unit, or any other form of equity-based remuneration that is granted on or after April 1, 2015.

§ 1.280G-1. Golden parachute payments.

The following questions and answers relate to the treatment of golden parachute payments under section 280G of the Internal Revenue Code of 1986, as added by section 67 of the Tax Reform Act of 1984 (Pub. L. No. 98-369; 98 Stat. 585) and amended by section 1804(j) of the Tax Reform Act of 1986 (Pub. L. No. 99-514; 100 Stat. 2807), section 1018(d)(6)-(8) of the Technical and Miscellaneous Revenue Act of 1988 (Pub. L. No. 100-647; 102 Stat. 3581), and section 1421 of the Small Business Job Protection Act of 1996 (Pub. L. No. 104-188; 110 Stat. 1755). The following is a table of subjects covered in this section:

Overview

589

Definition of corporation — Q/A-45

Treatment of affiliated group as one corporation — Q/A-46

Effective Date

General effective date of section 280G — Q/A-47

Effective date of regulations — Q/A-48

Overview

Q-1: *What is the effect of Internal Revenue Code section 280G?*

A-1: (a) Section 280G disallows a deduction for any excess parachute payment paid or accrued. For rules relating to the imposition of a nondeductible 20-percent excise tax on the recipient of any excess parachute payment, see Internal Revenue Code sections 4999, 275(a)(6), and 3121(v)(2)(A).

(b) The disallowance of a deduction under section 280G is not contingent on the imposition of the excise tax under section 4999. The imposition of the excise tax under section 4999 is not contingent on the disallowance of a deduction under section 280G. Thus, for example, because the imposition of the excise tax under section 4999 is not contingent on the disallowance of a deduction under section 280G, a payee may be subject to the 20-percent excise tax under section 4999 even though the disallowance of the deduction for the excess parachute payment may not directly affect the federal taxable income of the payor.

Q-2: *What is a parachute payment for purposes of section 280G?*

A-2: (a) The term parachute payment means any payment (other than an exempt payment described in Q/A-5) that—

(1) Is in the nature of compensation;

(2) Is made or is to be made to (or for the benefit of) a disqualified individual;

(3) Is contingent on a change—

(i) In the ownership of a corporation;

(ii) In the effective control of a corporation; or

(iii) In the ownership of a substantial portion of the assets of a corporation; and

(4) Has (together with other payments described in paragraphs (a)(1), (2), and (3) of this A-2 with respect to the same disqualified individual) an aggregate present value of at least 3 times the individual's base amount.

(b) Hereinafter, a change referred to in paragraph (a)(3) of this A-2 is generally referred to as a change in ownership or control. For a discussion of the application of paragraph (a)(1), see Q/A-11 through Q/A-14; paragraph (a)(2), Q/A-15 through Q/A-21; paragraph (a)(3), Q/A-22 through Q/A-29; and paragraph (a)(4), Q/A-30 through Q/A-36.

(c) The term parachute payment also includes any payment in the nature of compensation to (or for the benefit of) a disqualified individual that is pursuant to an agreement that violates a generally enforced securities law or regulation. This type of parachute payment is referred to in this section as a securities violation parachute payment. See Q/A-37 for the definition and treatment of securities violation parachute payments.

Q-3: *What is an excess parachute payment for purposes of section 280G?*

A-3: The term excess parachute payment means an amount equal to the excess of any parachute payment over the portion of the base amount allocated to such payment. Subject to certain exceptions and limitations, an excess parachute payment is reduced by any portion of the payment which the taxpayer establishes by clear and convincing evidence is reasonable compensation for personal services actually rendered by the disqualified individual before the date of the change in ownership or control. For a discussion of the nonreduction of a securities violation parachute payment by reasonable compensation, see Q/A-37. For a discussion of the computation of excess parachute payments and their reduction by reasonable compensation, see Q/A-38 through Q/A-44.

Q-4: *What is the effective date of section 280G and this section?*

A-4: In general, section 280G applies to payments under agreements entered into or renewed after June 14, 1984. Section 280G also applies to certain payments under agreements entered into on or before June 14, 1984, and amended or supplemented in significant relevant respect after that date. This section applies to any payment that is contingent on a change in ownership or control and the change in ownership or control occurs on or after January 1, 2004. For a discussion of the application of the effective date, see Q/A-47 and Q/A-48.

Exempt Payments

Q-5: *Are some types of payments exempt from the definition of the term parachute payment?*

A-5: (a) Yes, the following five types of payments are exempt from the definition of parachute payment—

(1) Payments with respect to a small business corporation (described in Q/A-6 of this section);

(2) Certain payments with respect to a corporation no stock in which is readily tradeable on an established securities market (or otherwise) (described in Q/A-6 of this section);

(3) Payments to or from a qualified plan (described in Q/A-8 of this section);

(4) Certain payments made by a corporation undergoing a change in ownership or control that is described in any of the following sections of the Internal Revenue Code: section 501(c) (but only if such organization is subject to an express statutory prohibition against inurement of net earnings to the benefit of any private shareholder or individual, or if the organization is described in section 501(c)(1) or section 501(c)(21), section 501(d), or section 529, collectively referred to as tax-exempt organizations (described in Q/A-6 of this section); and

(5) Certain payments of reasonable compensation for services to be rendered on or after the change in ownership or control (described in Q/A-9 of this section).

(b) Deductions for payments exempt from the definition of parachute payment are not disallowed by section 280G, and such exempt payments are not subject to the 20-percent excise tax of section 4999. In addition, such exempt payments are not taken into account in applying the 3-times-base-amount test of Q/A-30 of this section.

Q-6: *Which payments with respect to a corporation referred to in paragraph (a)(1), (a)(2), or (a)(4) of Q/A-5 of this section are exempt from the definition of parachute payment?*

A-6: (a) The term parachute payment does not include—

(1) Any payment to a disqualified individual with respect to a corporation which (immediately before the change in ownership or control) would qualify as a small business corporation (as defined in section 1361(b) but without regard to section 1361(b)(1)(C) thereof), without regard to whether the corporation had an election to be treated as a corporation under section 1361 in effect on the date of the change in ownership or control;

(2) Any payment to a disqualified individual with respect to a corporation (other than a small business corporation described in paragraph (a)(1) of this A-6) if—

(i) Immediately before the change in ownership or control, no stock in such corporation was readily tradeable on an established securities market or otherwise; and

(ii) The shareholder approval requirements described in Q/A-7 of this section are met with respect to such payment; or

(3) Any payment to a disqualified individual made by a corporation which is a tax-exempt organization (as defined in paragraph (a)(4) of Q/A-5 of this section), but only if the corporation meets the definition of a tax-exempt organization both immediately before

and immediately after the change in ownership or control.

(b) For purposes of paragraph (a)(1) of this A-6, the members of an affiliated group are not treated as one corporation.

(c) The requirements of paragraph (a)(2)(i) of this A-6 are not met with respect to a corporation if a substantial portion of the assets of any entity consists (directly or indirectly) of stock in such corporation and any ownership interest in such entity is readily tradeable on an established securities market or otherwise. For this purpose, such stock constitutes a substantial portion of the assets of an entity if the total fair market value of the stock is equal to or exceeds one third of the total gross fair market value of all of the assets of the entity. For this purpose, gross fair market value means the value of the assets of the entity, determined without regard to any liabilities associated with such assets. If a corporation is a member of an affiliated group (which group is treated as one corporation under A-46 of this section), the requirements of paragraph (a)(2)(i) of this A-6 are not met if any stock in any member of such group is readily tradeable on an established securities market or otherwise.

(d) For purposes of paragraph (a)(2)(i) of this A-6, the term stock does not include stock described in section 1504(a)(4) if the payment does not adversely affect the redemption and liquidation rights of any shareholder owning such stock.

(e) For purposes of paragraph (a)(2)(i) of this A-6, stock is treated as readily tradeable if it is regularly quoted by brokers or dealers making a market in such stock.

(f) For purposes of paragraph (a)(2)(i) of this A-6, the term established securities market means an established securities market as defined in § 1.897-1(m).

(g) The following examples illustrate the application of this exemption:

Example 1. A small business corporation (within the meaning of paragraph (a)(1) of this A-6) operates two businesses. The corporation sells the assets of one of its businesses, and these assets represent a substantial portion of the assets of the corporation. Because of the sale, the corporation terminates its employment relationship with persons employed in the business the assets of which are sold. Several of these employees are highly-compensated individuals to whom the owners of the corporation make severance payments in excess of 3 times each employee's base amount. Since the corporation is a small business corporation immediately before the change in ownership or control, the payments are not parachute payments.

Example 2. Assume the same facts as in Example 1, except that the corporation is not a small business corporation within the meaning of paragraph (a)(1) of this A-6. If no stock in the corporation is readily tradeable on an established securities market (or otherwise) immediately before the change in ownership or control and the shareholder approval requirements described in Q/A-7 of this section are met, the payments are not parachute payments.

Example 3. Stock of Corporation S is owned by Corporation P, stock in which is readily tradeable on an established securities market. The Corporation S stock equals or exceeds one third of the total gross fair market value of the assets of Corporation P, and thus, represents a substantial portion of the assets of Corporation P. Corporation S makes severance payments to several of its highly-compensated individuals that are parachute payments under section 280G and Q/A-2 of this section. Because stock in Corporation P is readily tradeable on an established securities market, the payments are not exempt from the definition of parachute payments under this A-6.

Example 4. A is a corporation described in section 501(c)(3), and accordingly, its net earnings are prohibited from inuring to the benefit of any private shareholder or individual. A transfers substantially all of its assets to another corporation resulting in a change in ownership or control. Contingent on the change in ownership or control, A makes a payment that, but for the potential application of the exemption described in A-5(a)(4), would constitute a parachute payment. However, one or more aspects of the transaction that constitutes the change in ownership or control causes A to fail to be described in section 501(c)(3). Accordingly, A fails to meet the definition of a tax-exempt organization both immediately before and immediately after the change in ownership or control, as required by this A-6. As a result, the payment made by A that was contingent on the change in ownership or control is not exempt from the definition of parachute payment under this A-6.

Example 5. B is a corporation described in section 501(c)(15). B does not meet the definition of a tax-exempt organization because section 501(c)(15) does not expressly prohibit inurement of B's net earnings to the benefit of any private shareholder or individual. Accordingly, if B has a change in ownership or control and makes a payment that would otherwise meet the definition of a parachute payment, such payment is not exempt from the definition of the term parachute payment for purposes of this A-6.

Q-7: *How are the shareholder approval requirements referred to in paragraph (a)(2)(ii) of Q/A-6 of this section met?*

A-7: (a) General rule. The shareholder approval requirements referred to in paragraph (a)(2)(ii) of Q/A-6 of this section are met with respect to any payment if—

(1) Such payment is approved by more than 75 percent of the voting power of all outstanding stock of the corporation entitled to vote (as described in this A-7) immediately before the change in ownership or control; and

(2) Before the vote, there was adequate disclosure to all persons entitled to vote (as described in this A-7) of all material facts concerning all material payments which (but for Q/A-6 of this section) would be parachute payments with respect to a disqualified individual.

(b) Voting requirements—(1) General rule. The vote described in paragraph (a)(1) of this A-7 must determine the right of the disqualified individual to receive the payment, or, in the case of a payment made before the vote, the right of the disqualified individual to retain the payment. Except as otherwise provided in this A-7, the normal voting rules of the corporation are applicable. Thus, for example, an optionholder is generally not permitted to vote for purposes of this A-7. For purposes of this A-7, the vote can be on less than the full amount of the payment(s) to be made. Shareholder approval can be a single vote on all payments to any one disqualified individual, or on all payments to more than one disqualified individual. The total payment(s) submitted for shareholder approval, however, must be separately approved by the shareholders. The requirements of this paragraph (b)(1) are not satisfied if approval of the change in ownership or control is contingent, or otherwise conditioned, on the approval of any payment to a disqualified individual that would be a parachute payment but for Q/A-6 of this section.

(2) Special rule. A vote to approve the payment does not fail to be a vote of the outstanding stock of the corporation entitled to vote immediately before the change in ownership or control merely because the determination of the shareholders entitled to vote on the payment is based on the shareholders of record as of any day within the six-month period immediately prior to and ending on date of the change in ownership or control, provided the disclosure requirements described in paragraph (c) of this A-7 are met.

(3) Entity shareholder. (i) Approval of a payment by any shareholder that is not an individual (an entity shareholder) generally must be made by the person authorized by the entity shareholder to approve the payment. See paragraph (b)(4) of this A-7 if the person so authorized by the entity shareholder is a disqualified individual who would receive a parachute payment if the shareholder approval requirements of this A-7 are not met.

(ii) However, if a substantial portion of the assets of an entity shareholder consists (directly or indirectly) of stock in the corporation undergoing the change in ownership or control, approval of the payment by that entity shareholder must be made by a separate vote of the persons who hold, immediately before the change in ownership or control, more than 75 percent of the voting power of the entity shareholder entitled to vote. The preceding sentence does not apply if the value of the stock of the corporation owned, directly or indirectly, by or for the entity shareholder does not exceed 1 percent of the total value of the outstanding stock of the corporation undergoing a change in ownership or control. Where approval of a payment by an entity shareholder must be made by a separate vote of the owners of the entity shareholder, the normal voting rights of the entity shareholder determine which owners shall vote. For purposes of this (b)(3)(ii), stock represents a substantial portion of the assets of an entity shareholder if the total fair market value of the stock held by the entity shareholder in the corporation undergoing the change in ownership or control is equal to or exceeds one third of the total gross fair market value of all of the assets of the entity shareholder. For this purpose, gross fair market value means the value of the assets of the entity, determined without regard to any liabilities associated with such assets.

(4) Disqualified individuals and attribution of stock ownership. In determining the persons entitled to vote referred to in paragraph (a)(1) or (b)(3) of this A-7, stock that would otherwise be entitled to vote is not counted as outstanding stock and is not considered in determining whether the more than 75 percent vote has been obtained under this A-7 if the stock is actually owned or constructively owned under section 318(a) by or for a disqualified individual who receives (or is to receive) payments that would be parachute payments if the shareholder approval requirements described in paragraph (a) of this A-7 are not met. Likewise, stock is not counted as outstanding stock if the owner is considered under section 318(a) to own any part of the stock owned directly or indirectly by or for a disqualified individual described in the preceding sentence. In addition, if the person authorized to vote the stock of an entity shareholder is a disqualified individual who would receive a parachute payment if the shareholder approval requirements described in this A-7 are not met, such person is not permitted to vote such shares, but the entity shareholder is permitted to appoint an equity interest holder in the entity shareholder, or in the case of a trust another person eligible to vote on behalf of the trust, to vote the otherwise eligible shares. However, if all persons who hold voting power in the corporation undergoing the change in ownership or control are disqualified individuals or related persons described in this paragraph (b)(4), then such stock is counted as outstanding stock and votes by such persons are considered in determining whether the more than 75 percent vote has been obtained.

(c) Adequate disclosure. To be adequate disclosure for purposes of paragraph (a)(2) of this A-7, disclosure must be full and truthful disclosure of the material facts and such additional information as is necessary to make the disclosure not materially misleading at the time the disclosure is made. Disclosure of such information must be made to every shareholder of the corporation entitled to vote under this A-7. For each disqualified individual, material facts that must be disclosed include, but are not limited to, the event triggering the payment or payments, the total amount of the payments that would be parachute payments if the shareholder approval requirements described in paragraph (a) of this A-7 are not met, and a brief description of each payment (e.g., accelerated vesting of options, bonus, or salary). An omitted fact is considered a material fact if there is a substantial likelihood that a reasonable shareholder would consider it important.

(d) Corporation without shareholders. If a corporation does not have shareholders, the exemption described in Q/A-6(a)(2) of this section and the shareholder approval requirements described in this A-7 do not apply.

Solely for purposes of this paragraph (d), a shareholder does not include a member in an association, joint stock company, or insurance company.

(e) Examples. The following examples illustrate the application of this A-7:

Example 1. Corporation S has two shareholders—Corporation P, which owns 76 percent of the stock of Corporation S, and A, a disqualified individual who would receive a parachute payment if the shareholder approval requirements of this A-7 are not met. No stock of Corporation P or S is readily tradeable on an established securities market (or otherwise). The value of the stock of Corporation S equals or exceeds one third of the gross fair market value of the assets of Corporation P, and thus, represents a substantial portion of the assets of Corporation P. All of the stock of Corporation S is sold to Corporation M. Contingent on the change in ownership of Corporation S, severance payments are made to certain officers of Corporation S in excess of 3 times each officer's base amount. If the payments are approved by a separate vote of the persons who hold, immediately before the sale, more than 75 percent of the voting power of the outstanding stock entitled to vote of Corporation P and the disclosure rules of paragraph (a)(2) of this A-7 are complied with, the shareholder approval requirements of this A-7 are met, and the payments are exempt from the definition of parachute payment pursuant to A-6 of this section.

Example 2. (i) Stock of Corporation X, none of which is traded on an established market, is acquired by Corporation Y. In the voting ballot concerning the sale, the Corporation X shareholders are asked to vote either "yes" on the sale and "yes" to paying parachute payments to A, a disqualified individual with respect to Corporation A, or "no" on the sale and "no" to paying parachute payments to A.

(ii) Because the approval of the change in ownership or control is conditioned on the approval of the payments to A, the shareholder approval requirements of this A-7 are not

satisfied. If the payments are made to A, the payments are not exempt from the definition of parachute payment pursuant to Q/A-6 of this section.

(iii) Assume the same facts as in paragraph (i) of this Example 2, except that the acquisition agreement between Corporation X and Corporation Y states that the acquisition is approved only if there are no parachute payments made to A. If the shareholder approval and the disclosure requirements described in this A-7 are met, the payments will not be parachute payments. Alternatively, if the shareholders do not approve the payments, the payments cannot be made (or retained). Thus, the transaction is not conditioned on the approval of the parachute payments. If the payments are made and the requirements of this A-7 are met, the payments are exempt from the definition of parachute payment pursuant to Q/A-6 of this section.

Example 3. Corporation M is wholly owned by Partnership P. No interest in either M or P is readily tradeable on an established securities market (or otherwise). The value of the stock of Corporation M equals or exceeds one third of the gross fair market value of the assets of Partnership P, and thus, represents a substantial portion of the assets of Partnership P. Corporation M undergoes a change in ownership or control. Partnership P has one general partner and 200 limited partners. The general partner is not a disqualified individual. None of the limited partners are entitled to vote on issues involving the management of the partnership investments. If the payments that would be parachute payments if the shareholder approval requirements of this A-7 are not met are approved by the general partner and the disclosure rules of paragraph (a)(2) of this A-7 are complied with, the shareholder approval requirements of this A-7 are met, and the payments are exempt from the definition of parachute payment pursuant to A-6 of this section.

Example 4. Corporation A has several shareholders including X and Y, who are disqualified individuals with respect to Corporation A and would receive parachute payments if the shareholder approval requirements of this A-7 are not met. No stock of Corporation A is readily tradeable on an established securities market (or otherwise). Corporation A undergoes a change in ownership or control. Contingent on the change in ownership or control, severance payments are payable to X and Y that are in excess of 3 times each individual's base amount. To determine whether the shareholder approval requirements of paragraph (a)(1) of this A-7 are satisfied regarding the payments to X and Y, the stock of X and Y is not considered outstanding, and X and Y are not entitled to vote.

Example 5. Assume the same facts as in Example 4, except that after adequate disclosure of all material facts (within the meaning of paragraph (a)(2) of this A-7) to all shareholders entitled to vote, 60 percent of the shareholders who are entitled to vote approve the payments to X and Y. Because more than 75 percent of the shareholders holding outstanding stock who were entitled to vote did not approve the payments to X and Y, the payments cannot be made.

Example 6. Assume the same facts as in Example 4 except that disclosure of all the material facts (within the meaning of paragraph (a)(2) of this A-7) regarding the payments to X and Y is made to two of Corporation A's shareholders, who collectively own 80 percent of Corporation A's stock entitled to vote and approve the payment. Both shareholders approve the payments. Assume further that no adequate disclosure of the material facts regarding the payments to X and Y is made to other Corporation A shareholders who are entitled to vote within the meaning of this A-7. Notwithstanding that 80 percent of the shareholders entitled to vote approve the payments, because disclosure regarding the payments to X and Y is not made to all of Corporation A's shareholders who were entitled to vote, the disclosure requirements of paragraph (a)(2) of this A-7 are not met, and the payments are not exempt from the definition of parachute payment pursuant to Q/A-6.

Example 7. Corporation C has three shareholders—Partnership, which owns 20

percent of the stock of Corporation C; A, an individual who owns 60 percent of the stock of Corporation C; and B, an individual who owns 20 percent of Corporation C. Stock of Corporation C does not represent a substantial portion of the assets of Partnership. No interest in either Partnership or Corporation C is readily tradeable on an established securities market (or otherwise). P, a one-third partner in Partnership, is a disqualified individual with respect to Corporation C. Corporation C undergoes a change in ownership or control. Contingent on the change, a severance payment is payable to P in excess of 3 times P's base amount. To determine the persons who are entitled to vote referred to in paragraph (a)(1) of this A-7, one-third of the stock held by Partnership is not considered outstanding stock. If P is the person authorized by Partnership to approve the payment, none of the shares of Partnership are considered outstanding stock. However, Partnership is permitted to appoint an equity interest holder in Partnership (who is not a disqualified individual who would receive a parachute payment if the requirements of this A-7 are not met), to vote the two-thirds of the shares held by Partnership that are otherwise entitled to be voted.

Example 8. X, Y, and Z are all employees and disqualified individuals with respect to Corporation E. No stock in Corporation E is readily tradeable on an established securities market (or otherwise). Each individual has a base amount of $100,000. Corporation E undergoes a change in ownership or control. Contingent on the change, a severance payment of $400,000 is payable to X; $600,000 is payable to Y; and $1,000,000 is payable to Z. Corporation E provides each Corporation E shareholder entitled to vote (as determined under this A-7) with a ballot listing and describing the payments of $400,000 to X; $600,000 to Y; and $1,000,000 to Z and the triggering event that generated the payments. Next to each name and corresponding amount on the ballot, Corporation E requests approval (with a "yes" and "no" box) of each total payment to be made to each individual and states that if the payment is not approved the payment will not be made. Adequate disclosure, within the meaning of this A-7 is made to each shareholder entitled to vote under this A-7. More than 75 percent of the Corporation E shareholders who are entitled to vote under paragraph (a)(1) of this A-7 approve each payment to each individual. The shareholder approval requirements of this A-7 are met, and the payments are exempt from the definition of parachute payment pursuant to A-6 of this section.

Example 9. Assume the same facts as in Example 8 except that the ballot does not request approval of each total payment to each individual separately. Instead, the ballot states that $2,000,000 in payments will be made to X, Y, and Z and requests approval of the $2,000,000 payments. Assuming the triggering event and amount of the payments to X, Y, and Z are separately described to the shareholders entitled to vote under this A-7, the shareholder approval requirements of paragraph (a)(1) of this A-7 are met, and the payments are exempt from the definition of parachute payment pursuant to A-6 of this section.

Example 10. B, an employee of Corporation X, is a disqualified individual with respect to Corporation X. Stock of Corporation X is not readily tradeable on an established securities market (or otherwise). Corporation X undergoes a change in ownership or control. B's base amount is $205,000. Under B's employment agreement with Corporation X, in the event of a change in ownership or control, B's stock options will vest and B will receive severance and bonus payments. Contingent on the change in ownership or control, B's stock options with a fair market value of $500,000 immediately vest, $200,000 of which is contingent on the change, and B will receive a $200,000 bonus payment and a $400,000 severance payment. Corporation X distributes a ballot to every shareholder of Corporation X who immediately before the change is entitled to vote as described in this A-7. The ballot contains adequate disclosure of all material facts and lists the following payments to be made to B: The contingent payment of $200,000 attributable to options, a $200,000 bonus payment, and a $400,000 severance

payment. The ballot requests shareholder approval of the $200,000 bonus payment to B and states that whether or not the $200,000 bonus payment is approved, B will receive $200,000 attributable to options and a $400,000 severance payment. More than 75 percent of the shareholders entitled to vote as described by this A-7 approve the $200,000 bonus payment to B. The shareholder approval requirements of this A-7 are met, and the $200,000 payment is exempt from the definition of parachute payment pursuant to A-6 of this section.

Q-8: *Which payments under a qualified plan are exempt from the definition of parachute payment?*

A-8: The term parachute payment does not include any payment to or from—

(a) A plan described in section 401(a) which includes a trust exempt from tax under section 501(a);

(b) An annuity plan described in section 403(a);

(c) A simplified employee pension (as defined in section 408(k)); or

(d) A simple retirement account (as defined in section 408(p)).

Q-9: *Which payments of reasonable compensation are exempt from the definition of parachute payment?*

A-9: Except in the case of securities violation parachute payment s, the term parachute payment does not include any payment (or portion thereof) which the taxpayer establishes by clear and convincing evidence is reasonable compensation for personal services to be rendered by the disqualified individual on or after the date of the change in ownership or control. See Q/A-37 of this section for the definition and treatment of securities violation parachute payments. See Q/A-40 through Q/A-44 of this section for rules on determining amounts of reasonable compensation.

Payor of Parachute Payments

Q-10: *Who may be the payor of parachute payments?*

A-10: Parachute payments within the meaning of Q/A-2 of this section may be paid, directly or indirectly, by—

(i) The corporation referred to in paragraph (a)(3) of Q/A-2 of this section;

(ii) A person acquiring ownership or effective control of that corporation or ownership of a substantial portion of that corporation's assets; or

(iii) Any person whose relationship to such corporation or other person is such as to require attribution of stock ownership between the parties under section 318(a).

Payments in the Nature of Compensation

Q-11: *What types of payments are in the nature of compensation?*

A-11: (a) General rule. For purposes of this section, all payments—in whatever form—are payments in the nature of compensation if they arise out of an employment relationship or are associated with the performance of services. For this purpose, the performance of services includes holding oneself out as available to perform services and refraining from performing services (such as under a covenant not to compete or similar arrangement). Payments in the nature of compensation include (but are not limited to) wages and salary, bonuses, severance pay, fringe benefits, life insurance, pension benefits, and other deferred compensation (including any amount characterized by the parties as interest thereon). A payment in the nature of compensation also includes cash when paid, the value of the right to receive cash (including the value of accelerated vesting under Q/A-24(c), or a transfer of property. However, payments in the nature of compensation do not include attorney's fees or court costs paid or incurred in connection with the payment of any amount described in paragraphs (a)(1), (2), and (3) of Q/A-2 of this section or a reasonable rate of interest accrued on any amount during the period the parties contest whether a payment will be made.

(b) When payment is considered to be made. Except as otherwise provided in A-11 through Q/A-13 of this section, a payment in the nature of compensation is considered made (and is subject to the excise tax under section 4999) in the taxable year in which it is includible in the disqualified individual's gross income or, in the case of fringe benefits and other benefits excludible from income, in the taxable year the benefits are received.

(c) Prepayment rule. Notwithstanding the general rule described in paragraph (b) of this A-11, a disqualified individual may, in the year of the change in ownership or control, or any later year, prepay the excise tax under section 4999, provided that the payor and disqualified individual treat the payment of the excise tax consistently and the payor satisfies its obligations under section 4999(c) in the year of prepayment. The prepayment of the excise tax for purposes of section 4999 must be based on the present value of the excise tax that would be due in the year the excess parachute payment would actually be paid (calculated using the discount rate equal to 120 percent of the applicable Federal rate (determined under section 1274(d) and regulations thereunder; see Q/A-32)). For purposes of projecting the future value of a payment that provides for interest to be credited at a variable interest rate, it is permissible to make a reasonable assumption regarding this variable rate. A disqualified individual is not required to adjust the excise tax paid under this paragraph (c) merely because the interest rates in the future are not the same as the rate used for purposes of projecting the future value of the payment. However, a disqualified individual may not apply this paragraph (c) of this A-11 to a payment to be made in cash if the present value of the payment would be considered not reasonably ascertainable under section 3121(v) and § 31.3121(v)(2)-1(e)(4) of this Chapter or to a payment related to health benefits or coverage. The Commissioner may provide additional guidance regarding the applicability of this paragraph (c) to certain payments in published guidance of general applicability under § 601.601(d)(2) of this Chapter.

(d) Transfers of property. Transfers of property are treated as payments for purposes of this A-11. See Q/A-12 of this section for rules on determining when such payments are considered made and the amount of such payments. See Q/A-13 of this section for special rules on transfers of stock options.

(e) The following example illustrates the principles of this A-11:

Example. D is a disqualified individual with respect to Corporation X. D has a base amount of $100,000 and is entitled to receive two parachute payments, one of $200,000 and the other of $400,000. A change in ownership or control of Corporation X occurs on May 1, 2005, and the $200,000 payment is made to D at the time of the change in ownership or control. The $400,000 payment is to be made on October 1, 2010. Corporation X and D agree that D will prepay the excise tax and X will satisfy its obligations under section 4999(c) with respect to the $400,000 payment. Using discount rate determined under Q/A-32, Corporation X and D determine that the present value of the $400,000 payment is $300,000 on the date of the change in ownership or control. The portions of the base amount allocated to these payments are $40,000 (($200,000/$500,000) x $100,000) and $60,000 (($300,000/$500,000 x $100,000), respectively. Thus, the amount of the first excess parachute payment is $160,000 ($200,000 − $40,000) and that of the second excess parachute payment is $340,000 ($400,000 − $60,000). The excise tax on the $400,000 payment is $68,000 ($340,000 x 20 percent). Assume the present value (calculated in accordance with paragraph (c) of this A-11) of $68,000 is $50,000. To prepay the excise tax due on the $400,000 payment, Corporation X must satisfy its obligations under section 4999 with respect to the $50,000, in addition to the $32,000 withholding required with respect to the $200,000 payment.

Q-12: *If a property transfer to a disqualified individual is a payment in the nature of compensation, when is the payment considered made (or to be made), and how is the amount of the payment determined?*

A-12: (a) Except as provided in this A-12 and Q/A-13 of this section, a transfer of property is considered a payment made (or to be made) in the taxable year in which the property transferred is includible in the gross income of the disqualified individual under section 83 and the regulations thereunder. Thus, in general, such a payment is considered made (or to be made) when the property is transferred (as defined in § 1.83-3(a)) to the disqualified individual and becomes substantially vested (as defined in § 1.83-3(b) and (j)) in such individual. The amount of the payment is determined under section 83 and the regulations thereunder. Thus, in general, the amount of the payment is equal to the excess of the fair market value of the transferred property (determined without regard to any lapse restriction, as defined in § 1.83-3(i)) at the time that the property becomes substantially vested, over the amount (if any) paid for the property.

(b) An election made by a disqualified individual under section 83(b) with respect to transferred property will not apply for purposes of this A-12. Thus, even if such an election is made with respect to a property transfer that is a payment in the nature of compensation, for purposes of this section, the payment is generally considered made (or to be made) when the property is transferred to and becomes substantially vested in such individual.

(c) See Q/A-13 of this section for rules on applying this A-12 to transfers of stock options.

(d) The following example illustrates the principles of this A-12:

Example. On January 1, 2006, Corporation M gives to A, a disqualified individual, a bonus of 100 shares of Corporation M stock in connection with the performance of services to Corporation M. Under the terms of the bonus arrangement A is obligated to return the Corporation M stock to Corporation M unless the earnings of Corporation M double by January 1, 2009, or there is a change in ownership or control of Corporation M before that date. A's rights in the stock are treated as substantially nonvested (within the meaning of

§ 1.83-3(b)) during that period because A's rights in the stock are subject to a substantial risk of forfeiture (within the meaning of § 1.83-3(c)) and are nontransferable (within the meaning of § 1.83-3(d)). On January 1, 2008, a change in ownership or control of Corporation M occurs. On that day, the fair market value of the Corporation M stock is $250 per share. Because A's rights in the Corporation M stock become substantially vested (within the meaning of § 1.83-3(b)) on that day, the payment is considered made on that day, and the amount of the payment for purposes of this section is equal to $25,000 (100 x $250). See Q/A-38 through 41 for rules relating to the reduction of the excess parachute payment by the portion of the payment which is established to be reasonable compensation for personal services actually rendered before the date of a change in ownership or control.

Q-13: *How are transfers of statutory and nonstatutory stock options treated?*

A-13: (a) For purposes of this section, an option (including an option to which section 421 applies) is treated as property that is transferred when the option becomes vested (regardless of whether the option has a readily ascertainable fair market value as defined in § 1.83-7(b)). For purposes of this A-13, vested means substantially vested within the meaning of § 1.83-3(b) and (j) or the right to the payment is not otherwise subject to a substantial risk of forfeiture within the meaning of section 83(c). Thus, for purposes of this section, the vesting of such an option is treated as a payment in the nature of compensation. The value of an option at the time the option vests is determined under all the facts and circumstances in the particular case. Factors relevant to such a determination include, but are not limited to: The difference between the option's exercise price and the value of the property subject to the option at the time of vesting; the probability of the value of such property increasing or decreasing; and the length of the period during which the option can be exercised. Thus, an option is treated as a payment in the nature of compensation on the date of grant or vesting, as applicable, without regard to whether such option has an ascertainable fair market value. For purposes of this A-13, valuation may be determined by any method prescribed by the Commissioner in published guidance of general applicability under § 601.601(d)(2) of this Chapter.

(b) Any money or other property transferred to the disqualified individual on the exercise, or as consideration on the sale or other disposition, of an option described in paragraph (a) of this Λ-13 after the time such option vests is not treated as a payment in the nature of compensation to the disqualified individual under Q/A-11 of this section. Nonetheless, the amount of the otherwise allowable deduction under section 162 or 212 with respect to such transfer is reduced by the amount of the payment described in paragraph (a) of this A-13 treated as an excess parachute payment.

Q-14: *Are payments in the nature of compensation reduced by consideration paid by the disqualified individual?*

A-14: Yes, to the extent not otherwise taken into account under Q/A-12 and Q/A-13 of this section, the amount of any payment in the nature of compensation is reduced by the amount of any money or the fair market value of any property (owned by the disqualified individual without restriction) that is (or will be) transferred by the disqualified individual in exchange for the payment. For purposes of the preceding sentence, the fair market value of property is determined as of the date the property is transferred by the disqualified individual.

Disqualified Individuals

Q-15: *Who is a disqualified individual?*

A- 5: (a) For purposes of this section, an individual is a disqualified individual with respect to a corporation if, at any time during the disqualified individual determination period (as defined in Q/A-20 of this section), the individual is an employee or independent contractor of the corporation and is, with respect to the corporation—

(1) A shareholder (but see Q/A-17 of this section);

(2) An officer (see Q/A-18 of this section); or

(3) A highly-compensated individual (see Q/A-19 of this section).

(b) For purposes of this A-15, a director is a disqualified individual with respect to a corporation if, at any time during the disqualified individual determination period, the director is, with respect to the corporation, a shareholder (see Q/A-17 of this section), an officer (see Q/A-18 of this section), or a highly-compensated individual (see Q/A-19 of this section).

(c) For purposes of this A-15, an individual who is an employee or independent contractor of a corporation other than the corporation undergoing a change in ownership or control is disregarded for purposes of determining who is a disqualified individual if such individual is employed by the corporation undergoing the change in ownership or control only on the last day of the disqualified individual determination period. Thus, for example, assume that E is an employee of Corporation X, that Y is acquired by Corporation X, and that Y undergoes a change in ownership or control. If E becomes an employee of Y on the date of the acquisition, in determining the disqualified individuals with respect to Y, E is disregarded under this paragraph (c).

Q-16: *Is a personal service corporation treated as an individual?*

A-16: (a) Yes. For purposes of this section, a personal service corporation (as defined in section 269A(b)(1)), or a noncorporate entity that would be a personal service corporation if it were a corporation, is treated as an individual.

(b) The following example illustrates the principles of this A-16:

Example. Corporation N, a personal service corporation (as defined in section 269A(b)(1)), has a single individual as its sole shareholder and employee. Corporation N performs personal services for Corporation M. The compensation paid to Corporation N by Corporation M puts Corporation N within the group of highly-compensated individuals of Corporation M as determined under A-19 of this section. Thus, Corporation N is treated as a highly-compensated individual with respect to Corporation M.

Q-17: *Are all shareholders of a corporation considered shareholders for purposes of paragraphs (a)(1) and (b) of Q/A-15 of this section?*

A-17: (a) No. Only an individual who owns stock of a corporation with a fair market value that exceeds 1 percent of the fair market value of the outstanding shares of all classes of the corporation's stock is treated as a disqualified individual with respect to the corporation by reason of stock ownership. An individual who owns a lesser amount of stock may, however, be a disqualified individual with respect to the corporation if such individual is an officer (see Q/A-18) or highly-compensated individual (see Q/A-19) with respect to the corporation.

(b) For purposes of determining the amount of stock owned by an individual for purposes of paragraph (a) of this A-17, the constructive ownership rules of section 318(a) apply. Stock underlying a vested option is considered owned by an individual who holds the vested option (and the stock underlying an unvested option is not considered owned by an individual who holds the unvested option). For purposes of the preceding sentence, however, if the option is exercisable for stock that is not substantially vested (as defined by §§ 1.83-3(b) and (j)), the stock underlying the option is not treated as owned by the individual who holds the option. Solely for purposes of determining the amount of stock owned by an individual for purposes of this A-17, mutual and cooperative corporations are treated as having stock.

(c) The following examples illustrates the principles of this A-17:

Example 1. E, an employee of Corporation A, received options under Corporation

A's Stock Option Plan. E's stock options vest three years after the date of grant. E is not an officer or highly compensated individual during the disqualified individual determination period. E does not own, and is not considered to own under section 318, any other Corporation A stock. Two years after the options are granted to E, all of Corporation A's stock is acquired by Corporation B. Under Corporation A's Stock Option Plan, E's options are converted to Corporation B options and the vesting schedule remains the same. Under paragraph (b) of this A-17, the stock underlying the unvested options held by E on the date of the change in ownership or control is not considered owned by E. Because E is not considered to own Corporation A stock with a fair market value exceeding 1 percent of the total fair market value of all of the outstanding shares of all classes of Corporation A and E is not an officer or highly-compensated individual during the disqualified individual determination period, E is not a disqualified individual within the meaning of Q&A-15 of this section with respect to Corporation A.

Example 2. Assume the same facts as in Example 1, except that Corporation A's Stock Option Plan provides that all unvested options will vest immediately on a change in ownership or control. Under paragraph (b) of this A-17, the stock underlying the options that vest on the change in ownership or control is considered owned by E. If the stock considered owned by E exceeds 1 percent of the total fair market value of all of the outstanding shares of all classes of Corporation A stock (including for this purpose, all stock owned or constructively owned by all shareholders, provided that no share of stock is counted more than once), E is a disqualified individual within the meaning of Q/A-15 of this section with respect to Corporation A.

Example 3. Assume the same facts as in Example 1 except that E received nonstatutory stock options that are exercisable for stock subject to a substantial risk of forfeiture under section 83. Assume further that under Corporation A's Stock Option Plan, the nonstatutory options will vest on a change in ownership or

control. Under paragraph (b) of this A-17, E is not considered to own the stock underlying the options that vest on the change in ownership or control because the options are exercisable for stock subject to a substantial risk of forfeiture within the meaning of section 83. Because E is not considered to own Corporation A stock with a fair market value exceeding 1 percent of the total fair market value of all of the outstanding shares of all classes of Corporation A stock and E is not an officer or highly compensated individual during the disqualified individual determination period, E is not a disqualified individual within the meaning of Q/A-15 of this section with respect to Corporation A.

Q-18: *Who is an officer?*

A-18: (a) For purposes of this section, whether an individual is an officer with respect to a corporation is determined on the basis of all the facts and circumstances in the particular case (such as the source of the individual's authority, the term for which the individual is elected or appointed, and the nature and extent of the individual's duties). Any individual who has the title of officer is presumed to be an officer unless the facts and circumstances demonstrate that the individual does not have the authority of an officer. However, an individual who does not have the title of officer may nevertheless be considered an officer if the facts and circumstances demonstrate that the individual has the authority of an officer. Generally, the term officer means an administrative executive who is in regular and continued service. The term officer implies continuity of service and excludes those employed for a special and single transaction.

(b) An individual who is an officer with respect to any member of an affiliated group that is treated as one corporation pursuant to Q/A-46 of this section is treated as an officer of such one corporation.

(c) No more than 50 employees (or, if less, the greater of 3 employees, or 10 percent of the employees (rounded up to the nearest integer)) of the corporation (in the case of an affiliated group treated as one corporation, each member of the affiliated group) are treated as disqualified individuals with respect to a corporation by reason of being an officer of the corporation. For purposes of the preceding sentence, the number of employees of the corporation is the greatest number of employees the corporation has during the disqualified individual determination period (as defined in Q/A-20 of this section). If the number of officers of the corporation exceeds the number of employees who may be treated as officers under the first sentence of this paragraph (c), then the employees who are treated as officers for purposes of this section are the highest paid 50 employees (or, if less, the greater of 3 employees, or 10 percent of the employees (rounded up to the nearest integer)) of the corporation when ranked on the basis of compensation (as determined under Q/A-21 of this section) paid during the disqualified individual determination period.

(d) In determining the total number of employees of a corporation for purposes of this A-18, employees are not counted if they normally work less than 17 1/2 hours per week (as defined in section 414(q)(5)(B) and the regulations thereunder) or if they normally work during not more than 6 months during any year (as defined in section 414(q)(5)(C) and the regulations thereunder). However, an employee who is not counted for purposes of the preceding sentence may still be an officer.

Q-19: *Who is a highly-compensated individual?*

A-19: (a) For purposes of this section, a highly-compensated individual with respect to a corporation is any individual who is, or would be if the individual were an employee, a member of the group consisting of the lesser of the highest paid 1 percent of the employees of the corporation (rounded up to the nearest integer), or the highest paid 250 employees of the corporation, when ranked on the basis of compensation (as determined under Q/A-21 of this section) earned during the disqualified individual determination period (as defined in Q/A-20 of this section). For purposes of the preceding sentence, the number of employees

of the corporation is the greatest number of employees the corporation has during the disqualified individual determination period (as defined in Q/A-20 of this section). However, no individual whose annualized compensation during the disqualified individual determination period is less than the amount described in section 414(q)(1)(B)(i) for the year in which the change in ownership or control occurs will be treated as a highly-compensated individual.

(b) An individual who is not an employee of the corporation is not treated as a highly-compensated individual with respect to the corporation on account of compensation received for performing services (such as brokerage, legal, or investment banking services) in connection with a change in ownership or control of the corporation, if the services are performed in the ordinary course of the individual's trade or business and the individual performs similar services for a significant number of clients unrelated to the corporation.

(c) The total number of employees of a corporation for purposes of this A-19 is determined in accordance with Q/A-18(d) of this section. However, an employee who is not counted for purposes of the preceding sentence may still be a highly-compensated individual.

Q-20: *What is the disqualified individual determination period?*

A-20: The disqualified individual determination period is the twelve-month period prior to and ending on the date of the change in ownership or control of the corporation.

Q-21: *How is compensation defined for purposes of determining who is a disqualified individual?*

A-21: (a) For purposes of determining who is a disqualified individual, the term compensation means the compensation which was earned by the individual for services performed for the corporation with respect to which the change in ownership or control occurs (changed corporation), for a predecessor entity, or for a related entity. Such compensation is determined without regard to sections 125, 132(f)(4), 402(e)(3), and 402(h)(1)(B). Thus, for example, compensation includes elective or salary reduction contributions to a cafeteria plan, cash or deferred arrangement or tax-sheltered annuity, and amounts credited under a nonqualified deferred compensation plan.

(b) For purposes of this A-21, a predecessor entity is any entity which, as a result of a merger, consolidation, purchase or acquisition of property or stock, corporate separation, or other similar business transaction transfers some or all of its employees to the changed corporation or to a related entity or to a predecessor entity of the changed corporation. The term related entity includes—

(1) All members of a controlled group of corporations (as defined in section 414(b)) that includes the changed corporation or a predecessor entity;

(2) All trades or businesses (whether or not incorporated) that are under common control (as defined in section 414(c)) if such group includes the changed corporation or a predecessor entity;

(3) All members of an affiliated service group (as defined in section 414(m)) that includes the changed corporation or a predecessor entity; and

(4) Any other entities required to be aggregated with the changed corporation or a predecessor entity pursuant to section 414(o) and the regulations thereunder (except leasing organizations as defined in section 414(n)).

(c) For purposes of Q/A-18 and Q/A-19 of this section, compensation that was contingent on the change in ownership or control and that was payable in the year of the change is not treated as compensation.

Contingent on Change in Ownership or Control

Q-22: *When is a payment contingent on a change in ownership or control?*

A-22: (a) In general, a payment is treated as contingent on a change in ownership or control if the payment would not, in fact, have been made had no change in ownership or control occurred, even if the payment is also conditioned on the occurrence of another event. A payment generally is treated as one which would not, in fact, have been made in the absence of a change in ownership or control unless it is substantially certain, at the time of the change, that the payment would have been made whether or not the change occurred. (But see Q/A-23 of this section regarding payments under agreements entered into after a change in ownership or control.) A payment that becomes vested as a result of a change in ownership or control is not treated as a payment which was substantially certain to have been made whether or not the change occurred. For purposes of this A-22, vested means the payment is substantially vested within the meaning of § 1.83-3(b) and (j) or the right to the payment is not otherwise subject to a substantial risk of forfeiture as defined by section 83(c).

(b)(1) For purposes of paragraph (a), a payment is treated as contingent on a change in ownership or control if—

(i) The payment is contingent on an event that is closely associated with a change in ownership or control;

(ii) A change in ownership or control actually occurs; and

(iii) The event is materially related to the change in ownership or control.

(2) For purposes of paragraph (b)(1)(i) of this A-22, a payment is treated as contingent on an event that is closely associated with a change in ownership or control unless it is substantially certain, at the time of the event, that the payment would have been made whether or not the event occurred. An event is considered closely associated with a change in ownership or control if the event is of a type often preliminary or subsequent to, or otherwise closely associated with, a change in ownership or control. For example, the following events are considered closely associated with a change in the ownership or control of a corporation: The onset of a tender offer

with respect to the corporation; a substantial increase in the market price of the corporation's stock that occurs within a short period (but only if such increase occurs prior to a change in ownership or control); the cessation of the listing of the corporation's stock on an established securities market; the acquisition of more than 5 percent of the corporation's stock by a person (or more than one person acting as a group) not in control of the corporation; the voluntary or involuntary termination of the disqualified individual's employment; a significant reduction in the disqualified individual's job responsibilities; and a change in ownership or control as defined in the disqualified individual's employment agreement (or elsewhere) that does not meet the definition of a change in ownership or control described in Q/A-27, 28, or 29 of this section. Whether other events are treated as closely associated with a change in ownership or control is based on all the facts and circumstances of the particular case.

(3) For purposes of determining whether an event (as described in paragraph (b)(2) of this A-22) is materially related to a change in ownership or control, the event is presumed to be materially related to a change in ownership or control if such event occurs within the period beginning one year before and ending one year after the date of the change in ownership or control. If such event occurs outside of the period beginning one year before and ending one year after the date of change in ownership or control, the event is presumed not materially related to the change in ownership or control. A payment does not fail to be contingent on a change in ownership or control merely because it is also contingent on the occurrence of a second event (without regard to whether the second event is closely associated with or materially related to a change in ownership or control). Similarly, a payment that is treated as contingent on a change in ownership or control because it is contingent on a closely associated event does not fail to be treated as contingent on a change in ownership or control merely because it is also contingent on the occurrence of a second event (without regard to whether the second event is closely associ-

ated with or materially related to a change in ownership or control).

(c) A payment that would in fact have been made had no change in ownership or control occurred is treated as contingent on a change in ownership or control if the change in ownership or control (or the occurrence of an event that is closely associated with and materially related to a change in ownership or control within the meaning of paragraph (b)(1) of this A-22), accelerates the time at which the payment is made. Thus, for example, if a change in ownership or control accelerates the time of payment of deferred compensation that is vested without regard to the change in ownership or control, the payment may be treated as contingent on the change. See Q/A-24 of this section regarding the portion of a payment that is so treated. See also Q/A-8 of this section regarding the exemption for certain payments under qualified plans and Q/A-40 of this section regarding the treatment of a payment as reasonable compensation.

(d) A payment is treated as contingent on a change in ownership or control even if the employment or independent contractor relationship of the disqualified individual is not terminated (voluntarily or involuntarily) as a result of the change.

(e) The following examples illustrate the principles of this A-22:

Example 1. A corporation grants a stock appreciation right to a disqualified individual, A, more than one year before a change in ownership or control. After the stock appreciation right vests and becomes exercisable, a change in ownership or control of the corporation occurs, and A exercises the right. Assuming neither the granting nor the vesting of the stock appreciation right is contingent on a change in ownership or control, the payment made on exercise is not contingent on the change in ownership or control.

Example 2. A contract between a corporation and B, a disqualified individual, provides that a payment will be made to B if the corporation undergoes a change in ownership or control and B's employment with the corporation is terminated at any time over the succeeding 5 years. Eighteen months later, a change in the ownership of the corporation occurs. Two years after the change in ownership, B's employment is terminated and the payment is made to B. Because it was not substantially certain that the corporation would have made the payment to B on B's termination of employment if there had not been a change in ownership, the payment is treated as contingent on the change in ownership under paragraph (a) of this A-22. This is true even though B's termination of employment is presumed not to be, and in fact may not be, materially related to the change in ownership or control.

Example 3. A contract between a corporation and C, a disqualified individual, provides that a payment will be made to C if C's employment is terminated at any time over the succeeding 3 years (without regard to whether or not there is a change in ownership or control). Eighteen months after the contract is entered into, a change in the ownership or control of the corporation occurs. Six months after the change in ownership or control, C's employment is terminated and the payment is made to C. Termination of employment is considered an event closely associated with a change in ownership or control. Because the termination occurred within one year after the date of the change in ownership or control, the termination of C's employment is presumed to be materially related to the change in ownership or control under paragraph (b)(3) of this A-22. If this presumption is not successfully rebutted, the payment will be treated as contingent on the change in ownership or control under paragraph (b) of this A-22.

Example 4. A contract between a corporation and a disqualified individual, D, provides that a payment will be made to D upon the onset of a tender offer for shares of the corporation's stock. A tender offer is made on December 1, 2008, and the payment is made to D. Although the tender offer is unsuccessful, it leads to a negotiated merger with another entity on June 1, 2009, which results in a change in the ownership or control of the cor-

poration. It was not substantially certain, at the time of the onset of the tender offer, that the payment would have been made had no tender offer taken place. The onset of a tender offer is considered closely associated with a change in ownership or control. Because the tender offer occurred within one year before the date of the change in ownership or control of the corporation, the onset of the tender offer is presumed to be materially related to the change in ownership or control. If this presumption is not rebutted, the payment will be treated as contingent on the change in ownership or control. If no change in ownership or control had occurred, the payment would not be treated as contingent on a change in ownership or control; however, the payment still could be a parachute payment under Q/A-37 of this section if the contract violated a generally enforced securities law or regulation.

Example 5. A contract between a corporation and a disqualified individual, E, provides that a payment will be made to E if the corporation's level of product sales or profits reaches a specified level. At the time the contract was entered into, the parties had no reason to believe that such an increase in the corporation's level of product sales or profits would be preliminary or subsequent to, or otherwise closely associated with, a change in ownership or control of the corporation. Eighteen months later, a change in the ownership or control of the corporation occurs and within one year after the date of the change of ownership or control, the corporation's level of product sales or profits reaches the specified level. Under these facts and circumstances (and in the absence of contradictory evidence), the increase in product sales or profits of the corporation is not an event closely associated with the change in ownership or control of the corporation. Accordingly, even if the increase is materially related to the change in ownership or control, the payment will not be treated as contingent on a change in ownership or control.

Q-23: *May a payment be treated as contingent on a change in ownership or control if the payment is made under an agreement entered into after the change?*

A-23: (a) No. Payments are not treated as contingent on a change in ownership or control if they are made (or are to be made) pursuant to an agreement entered into after the change (a post-change agreement). For this purpose, an agreement that is executed after a change in ownership or control pursuant to a legally enforceable agreement that was entered into before the change is considered to have been entered into before the change. (See Q/A-9 of this section regarding the exemption for reasonable compensation for services rendered on or after a change in ownership or control.) If an individual has a right to receive a payment that would be a parachute payment if made under an agreement entered into prior to a change in ownership or control (pre-change agreement) and gives up that right as bargained—for consideration for benefits under a post-change agreement, the agreement is treated as a post-change agreement only to the extent the value of the payments under the agreement exceed the value of the payments under the pre-change agreement. To the extent payments under the agreement have the same value as the payments under the pre-change agreement, such payments retain their character as parachute payments subject to this section.

(b) The following examples illustrate the principles of this A-23:

Example 1. Assume that a disqualified individual is an employee of a corporation. A change in ownership or control of the corporation occurs, and thereafter the individual enters into an employment agreement with the acquiring company. Because the agreement is entered into after the change in ownership or control occurs, payments to be made under the agreement are not treated as contingent on the change.

Example 2. Assume the same facts as in Example 1, except that the agreement between the disqualified individual and the acquiring company is executed after the change in ownership or control, pursuant to a legally enforceable agreement entered into before the change. Payments to be made under the agreement may be treated as contingent on the change in ownership or control pursuant to Q/A-22 of this section. However, see Q/A-9 of this section regarding the exemption from the definition of parachute payment for certain amounts of reasonable compensation.

Example 3. Assume the same facts as in Example 1, except that prior to the change in ownership or control, the individual and corporation enter into an agreement under which the individual will receive parachute payments in the event of a change in ownership or control of the corporation. After the change, the individual agrees to give up the right to payments under the pre-change agreement that would be parachute payments if made, in exchange for compensation under a new agreement with the acquiring corporation. Because the individual gave up the right to parachute payments under the pre-change agreement in exchange for other payments under the post-change agreement, payments in an amount equal to the parachute payments under the pre-change agreement are treated as contingent on the change in ownership or control under this A-23. Because the post-change agreement was entered into after the change, payments in excess of this amount are not treated as parachute payments.

Q-24: *If a payment is treated as contingent on a change in ownership or control, is the full amount of the payment so treated?*

A-24: (a)(1) General rule. Yes. If the payment is a transfer of property, the amount of the payment is determined under Q/A-12 or Q/A-13 of this section. For all other payments, the amount of the payment is determined under Q/A-11 of this section. However, in certain circumstances, described in paragraphs (b) and (c) of this A-24, only a portion of the payment is treated as contingent on the change. Paragraph (b) of this A-24 applies to a payment that is vested, without regard to the change in ownership or control, and is treated as contingent on the change in ownership or control because the change accelerates the time at which the payment is made. Paragraph

(c) of this A-24 applies to a payment that becomes vested as a result of the change in ownership or control if, without regard to the change in ownership or control, the payment was contingent only on the continued performance of services for the corporation for a specified period of time and if the payment is attributable, at least in part, to services performed before the date the payment becomes vested. Paragraph (b) or (c) does not apply to any payment (or portion thereof) if the payment is treated as contingent on the change in ownership or control pursuant to Q/A-25 of this section. For purposes of this A-24, vested has the same meaning as provided in Q/A-22(a).

(2) Reduction by reasonable compensation. The amount of a payment under paragraph (a)(1) of this A-24 is reduced by any portion of such payment that the taxpayer establishes by clear and convincing evidence is reasonable compensation for personal services rendered by the disqualified individual on or after the date of the change of control. See Q/A-9 and Q/A-38 through 44 of this section for rules concerning reasonable compensation. The portion of an amount treated as contingent under paragraph (b) or (c) of this A-24 may not be reduced by reasonable compensation.

(b) Vested payments. This paragraph (b) applies if a payment is vested, without regard to the change in ownership or control, and is treated as contingent on the change in ownership or control because the change accelerates the time at which the payment is made. In such a case, the portion of the payment, if any, that is treated as contingent on the change in ownership or control is the amount by which the amount of the accelerated payment exceeds the present value of the payment absent the acceleration. If the value of such a payment absent the acceleration is not reasonably ascertainable, and the acceleration of the payment does not significantly increase the present value of the payment absent the acceleration, the present value of the payment absent the acceleration is treated as equal to the amount of the accelerated payment. If the value of the payment absent the acceleration is

not reasonably ascertainable, but the acceleration significantly increases the present value of the payment, the future value of such payment is treated as equal to the amount of the accelerated payment. For rules on determining present value, see paragraph (e) of this A-24, Q/A-32, and Q/A-33 of this section.

(c)(1) Nonvested payments. This paragraph (c) applies to a payment that becomes vested as a result of the change in ownership or control to the extent that—

(i) Without regard to the change in ownership or control, the payment was contingent only on the continued performance of services for the corporation for a specified period of time; and

(ii) The payment is attributable, at least in part, to the performance of services before the date the payment is made or becomes certain to be made.

(2) The portion of the payment subject to paragraph (c) of this A-24 that is treated as contingent on the change in ownership or control is the amount described in paragraph (b) of this A-24, plus an amount, as determined in paragraph (c)(4) of this A-24, to reflect the lapse of the obligation to continue to perform services. In no event can the portion of the payment treated as contingent on the change in ownership or control under this paragraph (c) exceed the amount of the accelerated payment, or, if the payment is not accelerated, the present value of the payment.

(3) For purposes of this paragraph (c) of this A-24, the acceleration of the vesting of a stock option or the lapse of a restriction on restricted stock is considered to significantly increase the value of a payment.

(4) The amount reflecting the lapse of the obligation to continue to perform services (described in paragraph (c)(2) of this A-24) is 1 percent of the amount of the accelerated payment multiplied by the number of full months between the date that the individual's right to receive the payment is vested and the date that, absent the acceleration, the payment would have been vested. This paragraph (c)(4)

applies to the accelerated vesting of a payment in the nature of compensation even if the time at which the payment is made is not accelerated. In such a case, the amount reflecting the lapse of the obligation to continue to perform services is 1 percent of the present value of the future payment multiplied by the number of full months between the date that the individual's right to receive the payment is vested and the date that, absent the acceleration, the payment would have been vested.

(d) Application of this A-24 to certain payments.—(1) Benefits under a nonqualified deferred compensation plan. In the case of a payment of benefits under a nonqualified deferred compensation plan, paragraph (b) of this A-24 applies to the extent benefits under the plan are vested without regard to the change in ownership or control. Paragraph (c) of this A-24 applies to the extent benefits under the plan become vested as a result of the change in ownership or control and are attributable, at least in part, to the performance of services prior to vesting. Any other payment of benefits under a nonqualified deferred compensation plan is a payment in the nature of compensation subject to the general rule of paragraph (a) of this A-24 and the rules in Q/A-11 of this section.

(2) Employment agreements. The general rule of paragraph (a) of this A-24 (and not the rules in paragraphs (b) or (c)) applies to the payment of amounts due under an employment agreement on a termination of employment or a change in ownership or control that otherwise would be attributable to the performance of services (or refraining from the performance of services) during any period that begins after the date of termination of employment or change in ownership or control, as applicable. For purposes of this paragraph (d)(2) of this A-24, an employment agreement means an agreement between an employee or independent contractor and employer or service recipient which describes, among other things, the amount of compensation or remuneration payable to the employee or independent contractor. See Q/A-42(b) and 44 of this section for the treatment of the remaining

amounts of salary under an employment agreement.

(3) Vesting due to an event other than services. Neither paragraph (b) nor (c) of this A-24 applies to a payment if (without regard to the change in ownership or control) vesting of the payment depends on an event other than the performance of services, such as the attainment of a performance goal, and the event does not occur prior to the change in ownership or control. In such circumstances, the full amount of the accelerated payment is treated as contingent on the change in ownership or control under paragraph (a) of this A-24. However, see Q/A-39 of this section for rules relating to the reduction of the excess parachute payment by the portion of the payment which is established to be reasonable compensation for personal services actually rendered before the date of a change in ownership or control.

(e) Present value. For purposes of this A-24, the present value of a payment is determined as of the date on which the accelerated payment is made.

(f) Examples. The following examples illustrate the principles of this A-24:

Example 1. (i) Corporation maintains a qualified plan and a nonqualified supplemental retirement plan (SERP) for its executives. Benefits under the SERP are not paid to participants until retirement. E, a disqualified individual with respect to Corporation, has a vested account balance of $500,000 under the SERP. A change in ownership or control of Corporation occurs. The SERP provides that in the event of a change in ownership or control, all vested accounts will be paid to SERP participants.

(ii) Because E was vested in $500,000 of benefits under the SERP prior to the change in ownership or control and the change merely accelerated the time at which the payment was made to E, only a portion of the payment, as determined under paragraph (b) of this A-24, is treated as contingent on the change. Thus, the portion of the payment that is treated as contingent on the change is the amount by which the amount of the accelerated payment ($500,000) exceeds the present value of the payment absent the acceleration.

(iii) Assume the same facts as in paragraph (i) of this Example 1, except that E's account balance of $500,000 is not vested. Instead, assume that E will vest in E's account balance of $500,000 in 2 years if E continues to perform services for the next 2 years. Assume further that the SERP provides that all unvested SERP benefits vest immediately on a change in ownership or control and are paid to the participants. Because the vesting of the SERP payment, without regard to the change, depends only on the performance of services for a specified period of time and the payment is attributable, in part, to the performance of services before the change in ownership or control, only a portion of the $500,000 payment, as determined under paragraph (c) of this A-24, is treated as contingent on the change. The portion of the payment that is treated as contingent on the change is the lesser of the amount of the accelerated payment or the amount by which the accelerated payment exceeds the present value of the payment absent the acceleration, plus an amount to reflect the lapse of the obligation to continue to perform services.

(iv) Assume the same facts as in paragraph (i) of this Example 1, except that in addition to the pay out of the vested account balance of $500,000 on the change in ownership or control, an additional $70,000 will be credited to E's account and included in the payment to E. Because the $500,000 was vested without regard to the change in ownership or control, paragraph (b) of this A-24 applies to the $500,000 payment. Because the $70,000 is not vested, without regard to the change, and is not attributable to the performance of services prior to the change, the entire $70,000 payment is contingent on the change in ownership or control under paragraph (a) of this A-24.

(v) Assume the same facts as in paragraph (i) of this Example 1, except that the benefit under the SERP is calculated using a percentage of final average compensation multiplied by years of service. If, contingent on the change in ownership or control, E is credited with additional years of service, an adjustment to final average compensation, or an increase in the applicable percentage, any increase in the benefit payable under the SERP is not attributable to the performance of services prior to the change, and the entire increase in the benefit is contingent on the change in ownership or control under paragraph (a) of this A-24.

Example 2. As a result of a change in the effective control of a corporation D, a disqualified individual with respect to the corporation, receives accelerated payment of D's vested account balance in a nonqualified deferred compensation account plan. Actual interest and other earnings on the plan assets are credited to each account as earned before distribution. Investment of the plan assets is not restricted in such a manner as would prevent the earning of a market rate of return on the plan assets. The date on which D would have received D's vested account balance absent the change in ownership or control is uncertain, and the rate of earnings on the plan assets is not fixed. Thus, the amount of the payment absent the acceleration is not reasonably ascertainable. Under these facts, acceleration of the payment does not significantly increase the present value of the payment absent the acceleration, and the present value of the payment absent the acceleration is treated as equal to the amount of the accelerated payment. Accordingly, no portion of the payment is treated as contingent on the change.

Example 3. (i) On January 15, 2006, a corporation and a disqualified individual, F, enter into a contract providing for a retention bonus of $500,000 to be paid to F on January 15, 2011. The payment of the bonus will be forfeited by F if F does not remain employed by the corporation for the entire 5-year period. However, the contract provides that the full amount of the payment will be made immediately on a change in ownership or control of the corporation during the 5-year period. On January 15, 2009, a change in ownership or control of the corporation occurs and the full amount of the payment ($500,000) is made on that date to F. Under these facts, the payment of $500,000 was contingent only on F's performance of services for a specified period and is attributable, in part, to the performance of services before the change in ownership or control. Therefore, only a portion of the payment, as determined under paragraph (c) of this A-24 is treated as contingent on the change. The portion of the payment that is treated as contingent on the change is the amount by which the amount of the accelerated payment (i.e., $500,000, the amount paid to the individual because of the change in ownership) exceeds the present value of the payment that was expected to have been made absent the acceleration (i.e., $406,838, the present value on January 15, 2009, of a $500,000 payment on January 15, 2011), plus $115,000 (1 percent x 23 months x $500,000) which is the amount reflecting the lapse of the obligation to continue to perform services. Accordingly, the amount of the payment treated as contingent on the change in ownership or control is $208,162, the sum of $93,162 ($500,000 − $406,838) + $115,000). This result does not change if F actually remains employed until the end of the 5-year period.

(ii) Assume the same facts as in paragraph (i) of this Example 3, except that the retention bonus will vest on the change in ownership or control, but will not be paid until January 15, 2011 (the original date in the contract). Because the payment of $500,000 was contingent only on F's performance of services for a specified period and is attributable, in part, to the performance of services before the change in ownership or control, only a portion of the $500,000 payment is treated as contingent on the change in ownership or control as determined under paragraph (c) of this A-24. Because there is accelerated vesting of the bonus, the portion of the payment treated as contingent on the change is the amount described in paragraph (b) of this A-27, which is $0 under these facts, plus an amount reflecting the lapse of the obligation to continue to perform services which is $93,573 (1 percent x 23 months x $406,838 (the present value of a $500,000 payment).

Example 4. (i) On January 15, 2006, a corporation gives to a disqualified individual, in connection with her performance of services to the corporation, a bonus of 1,000 shares of the corporation's stock. Under the terms of the bonus arrangement, the individual is obligated to return the stock to the corporation if she terminates her employment for any reason prior to January 15, 2011. However, if there is a change in the ownership or effective control of the corporation prior to January 15, 2011, she ceases to be obligated to return the stock. The individual's rights in the stock are treated as substantially nonvested (within the meaning of § 1.83-3(b) and (j)) during that period. On January 15, 2009, a change in the ownership of the corporation occurs. On that day, the fair market value of the stock is $500,000.

(ii) Under these facts, the payment was contingent only on performance of services for a specified period and is attributable, in part, to the performance of services before the change in ownership or control. Thus, only a portion of the payment, as determined under paragraph (c) of this A-24, is treated as contingent on the change in ownership or control. The portion of the payment that is treated as contingent on the change is the amount by which the present value of the accelerated payment on January 15, 2009 ($500,000), exceeds the present value of the payment that was expected to have been made on January 15, 2011, plus an amount reflecting the lapse of the obligation to continue to perform services. At the time of the change, it cannot be reasonably ascertained what the value of the stock would have been on January 15, 2011. The acceleration of the lapse of a restriction on stock is treated as significantly increasing the value of the payment. Therefore, the value of such stock on January 15, 2011, is deemed to be $500,000, the amount of the accelerated payment. The present value on January 15, 2009, of a $500,000 payment to be made on January 15, 2011, is $406,838. Thus, the portion of the payment treated as contingent on the change is $208,162, the sum of $93,162 ($500,000 − $406,838), plus $115,000 (1 percent x 23 months x $500,000), the amount reflecting the lapse of the obligation to continue to perform services.

Example 5. (i) On January 15, 2006, a corporation grants to a disqualified individual nonqualified stock options to purchase 30,000 shares of the corporation's stock. The options will be forfeited by the individual if he fails to perform personal services for the corporation until January 15, 2009. The options will, however, vest in the individual at an earlier date if there is a change in ownership or control of the corporation. On January 16, 2008, a change in the ownership or control of the corporation occurs and the options become vested in the individual. The value of the options on January 16, 2008, determined in accordance with Q/A-13, is $600,000.

(ii) The payment of the options to purchase 30,000 shares was contingent only on performance of services for the corporation until January 15, 2009, and is attributable, in part, to the performance of services before the change in ownership or control. Therefore, only a portion of the payment is treated as contingent on the change. The portion of the payment that is treated as contingent on the change is the amount by which the accelerated payment on January 16, 2008 ($600,000) exceeds the present value on January 16, 2008, of the payment that was expected to have been made on January 15, 2009, absent the acceleration, plus an amount reflecting the lapse of the obligation to continue to perform services. At the time of the change, it cannot be reasonably ascertained what the value of the options would have been on January 15, 2009. The acceleration of vesting in the options is treated as significantly increasing the value of the payment. Therefore, the value of such options on January 15, 2009, is deemed to be $600,000, the amount of the accelerated payment. The present value on January 16, 2008, of a $600,000 payment to be made on January 15, 2009, is $549,964. Thus, the portion of the payment treated as contingent on the change is $116,036, the sum of $50,036 ($600,000 − $549,964), plus an amount reflecting the lapse of the obligation to continue to perform ser-

vices which is $66,000 (1 percent x 11 months x $600,000).

Example 6. (i) Assume the same facts as in Example 5, except that the options become vested periodically (absent a change in ownership or control), with one-third of the options vesting on January 15, 2007, 2008, and 2009, respectively. Thus, options to purchase 20,000 shares vest independently of the January 16, 2008, change in ownership or control and the options to purchase the remaining 10,000 shares vest as a result of the change in ownership or control.

(ii) The payment of the options to purchase 10,000 shares was contingent only on performance of services for the corporation until January 15, 2009, and is attributable, in part, to the performance of services before the change in ownership or control. Therefore, only a portion of the payment as determined under paragraph (c) of this A-24 is treated as contingent on the change in ownership or control. The portion of the payment that is treated as contingent on the change in ownership or control is the amount by which the accelerated payment on January 16, 2008 ($200,000) exceeds the present value on January 16, 2008, of the payment that was expected to have been made on January 15, 2009, absent the acceleration, plus an amount reflecting the lapse of the obligation to perform services. At the time of the change in ownership or control, it cannot be reasonably ascertained what the value of the options would have been on January 15, 2009. The acceleration of vesting in the options is treated as significantly increasing the value of the payment. Therefore, the value of such options on January 15, 2009, is deemed to be $200,000, the amount of the accelerated payment. The present value on January 16, 2008, of a $200,000 payment to be made on January 15, 2009, is $183,328.38. Thus, the portion of the payment treated as contingent on the change is $38,671.62, the sum of $16,671.62 ($200,000 − $183,328.38), plus an amount reflecting the lapse of the obligation to continue to perform services which is $22,000 (1 percent x 11 months x $200,000).

Example 7. Assume the same facts as in Example 5, except that the option agreement provides that the options will vest either on the corporation's level of profits reaching a specified level, or if earlier, on the date on which there is a change in ownership or control of the corporation. The corporation's level of profits do not reach the specified level prior to January 16, 2008. In such case, the full amount of the payment, $600,000, is treated as contingent on the change in ownership or control under paragraph (a) of this A-24. Because the payment was not contingent only on the performance of services for the corporation for a specified period, the rules of paragraph (b) and (c) of this A-24 do not apply. See Q/A-39 of this section for rules relating to the reduction of the excess parachute payment by the portion of the payment which is established to be reasonable compensation for personal services actually rendered before the date of a change in ownership or control.

Example 8. On January 1, 2005, E, a disqualified individual with respect to Corporation X, enters into an employment agreement with Corporation X under which E will be paid wages of $200,000 each year during the 5-year employment agreement. The employment agreement provides that if a change in ownership or control of Corporation X occurs, E will be paid the present value of the remaining salary under the employment agreement. On January 1, 2006, a change in ownership or control of Corporation X occurs, E is terminated, and E receives a payment of the present value of $200,000 for each of the 4 years remaining under the employment agreement. Because the payment represents future salary under an employment agreement (i.e., amounts otherwise attributable to the performance of services for periods that begin after the termination of employment), the general rule of paragraph (a) of this A-24 applies to the payment and not the rules of paragraphs (b) and (c) of this A-24. See Q/A-42(c) and 44 of this section for the treatment of the remaining payments under an employment agreement.

Presumption That Payment Is Contingent on Change

Q-25: *Is there a presumption that certain payments are contingent on a change in ownership or control?*

A-25: Yes, for purposes of this section, any payment is presumed to be contingent on such a change unless the contrary is established by clear and convincing evidence if the payment is made pursuant to—

(a) An agreement entered into within one year before the date of a change in ownership or control; or

(b) An amendment that modifies a previous agreement in any significant respect, if the amendment is made within one year before the date of a change in ownership or control. In the case of an amendment described in paragraph (b) of this A-25, only the portion of any payment that exceeds the amount of such payment that would have been made in the absence of the amendment is presumed, by reason of the amendment, to be contingent on the change in ownership or control.

Q-26: *How may the presumption described in Q/A-25 of this section be rebutted?*

A-26: (a) To rebut the presumption described in Q/A-25 of this section, the taxpayer must establish by clear and convincing evidence that the payment is not contingent on the change in ownership or control. Whether the payment is contingent on such change is determined on the basis of all the facts and circumstances of the particular case. Factors relevant to such a determination include, but are not limited to, the content of the agreement or amendment and the circumstances surrounding the execution of the agreement or amendment, such as whether it was entered into at a time when a takeover attempt had commenced and the degree of likelihood that a change in ownership or control would actually occur. However, even if the presumption is rebutted with respect to an agreement, some or all of the payments under the agreement may still be contingent on the change in ownership or control pursuant to Q/A-22 of this section.

(b) In the case of an agreement described in Q/A-25 of this section, clear and convincing evidence that the agreement is one of the three following types will generally rebut the presumption that payments under the agreement are contingent on the change in ownership or control—

(1) A nondiscriminatory employee plan or program as defined in paragraph (c) of this A-26;

(2) A contract between a corporation and an individual that replaces a prior contract entered into by the same parties more than one year before the change in ownership or control, if the new contract does not provide for increased payments (apart from normal increases attributable to increased responsibilities or cost of living adjustments), accelerate the payment of amounts due at a future time, or modify (to the individual's benefit) the terms or conditions under which payments will be made; or

(3) A contract between a corporation and an individual who did not perform services for the corporation prior to the one year period before the change in ownership or control occurs, if the contract does not provide for payments that are significantly different in amount, timing, terms, or conditions from those provided under contracts entered into by the corporation (other than contracts that themselves were entered into within one year before the change in ownership or control and in contemplation of the change) with individuals performing comparable services.

(c) For purposes of this section, the term nondiscriminatory employee plan or program means: a group term life insurance plan that meets the requirements of section 79(d); a self-insured medical reimbursement plan that meets the requirements of section 105(h); a cafeteria plan (within the meaning of section 125);an educational assistance program (within the meaning of section 127); a dependent care assistance program (within the meaning of section 129); a no-additional-cost service (within the meaning of section 132(b)) or qualified employee discount (within the mean-

ing of section 132(c)); a qualified retirement planning services program under section 132(m); an adoption assistance program (within the meaning of section 137); and such other items as provided by the Commissioner in published guidance of general applicability under § 601.601(d)(2). Payments under certain other plans are exempt from the definition of parachute payment under Q/A-8 of this section.

(d) The following examples illustrate the application of the presumption:

Example 1. A corporation and a disqualified individual who is an employee of the corporation enter into an employment contract. The contract replaces a prior contract entered into by the same parties more than one year before the change in ownership or control and the new contract does not provide for any increased payments other than a cost of living adjustment, does not accelerate the payment of amounts due at a future time, and does not modify (to the individual's benefit) the terms or conditions under which payments will be made. Clear and convincing evidence of these facts rebuts the presumption described in A-25 of this section. However, payments under the contract still may be contingent on the change in ownership or control pursuant to Q/A-22 of this section.

Example 2. Assume the same facts as in Example 1, except that the contract is entered into after a tender offer for the corporation's stock had commenced and it was likely that a change in ownership or control would occur and the contract provides for a substantial bonus payment to the individual upon his signing the contract. The individual has performed services for the corporation for many years, but previous employment contracts between the corporation and the individual did not provide for a similar signing bonus. One month after the contract is entered into, a change in the ownership or control of the corporation occurs. All payments under the contract are presumed to be contingent on the change in ownership or control even though the bonus payment would have been legally required even if no change had occurred.

Clear and convincing evidence of these facts rebuts the presumption described in A-25 of this section with respect to all of the payments under the contract with the exception of the bonus payment (which is treated as contingent on the change). However, payments other than the bonus under the contract still may be contingent on the change in ownership or control pursuant to Q/A-22 of this section.

Example 3. A corporation and a disqualified individual, who is an employee of the corporation, enter into an employment contract within one year of a change in ownership or control of the corporation. Under the contract, in the event of a change in ownership or control and subsequent termination of employment, certain payments will be made to the individual. A change in ownership or control occurs, but the individual is not terminated until 2 years after the change in ownership or control. If clear and convincing evidence does not rebut the presumption described in A-25 of this section, because the payment is made pursuant to an agreement entered into within one year of the date of the change in ownership or control, the payment is presumed contingent on the change under A-25 of this section. This is true even though A's termination of employment is presumed not to be materially related to the change in ownership or control under Q/A-22 of this section.

Change in Ownership or Control

Q-27: *When does a change in the ownership of a corporation occur?*

A-27: (a) For purposes of this section, a change in the ownership of a corporation occurs on the date that any one person, or more than one person acting as a group (as defined in paragraph (b) of this A-27), acquires ownership of stock of the corporation that, together with stock held by such person or group, has more than 50 percent of the total fair market value or total voting power of the stock of such corporation. However, if any one person, or more than one person acting as a group, is considered to own more than 50 percent of the total fair market value or total voting power of the stock of a corporation, the acquisition of

additional stock by the same person or persons is not considered to cause a change in the ownership of the corporation (or to cause a change in the effective control of the corporation (within the meaning of Q/A-28 of this section)). An increase in the percentage of stock owned by any one person, or persons acting as a group, as a result of a transaction in which the corporation acquires its stock in exchange for property will be treated as an acquisition of stock for purposes of this section. This A-27 applies only when there is a transfer of stock of a corporation (or issuance of stock of a corporation) and stock in such corporation remains outstanding after the transaction. (See Q/A-29 for rules regarding the transfer of assets of a corporation).

(b) For purposes of paragraph (a) of this A-27, persons will not be considered to be acting as a group merely because they happen to purchase or own stock of the same corporation at the same time, or as a result of the same public offering. However, persons will be considered to acting as a group if they are owners of a corporation that enters into a merger, consolidation, purchase or acquisition of stock, or similar business transaction with the corporation. If a person, including an entity shareholder, owns stock in both corporations that enter into a merger, consolidation, purchase or acquisition of stock, or similar transaction, such shareholder is considered to be acting as a group with other shareholders in a corporation only with respect to the ownership in that corporation prior to the transaction giving rise to the change and not with respect to the ownership interest in the other corporation.

(c) For purposes of this A-27 (and Q/A-28 and 29), section 318(a) applies to determine stock ownership. Stock underlying a vested option is considered owned by the individual who holds the vested option (and the stock underlying an unvested option is not considered owned by the individual who holds the unvested option). For purposes of the preceding sentence, however, if the option is exercisable for stock that is not substantially vested (as defined by sections 1.83-3(b) and (j)), the stock underlying the option is not treated as owned by the individual who holds the option. In addition, mutual and cooperative corporations are treated as having stock for purposes of this A-27.

(d) The following examples illustrate the principles of this A-27:

Example 1. Corporation M has owned stock with a fair market value equal to 19 percent of the value of the stock of Corporation N (anotherwise unrelated corporation) for many years prior to 2006. Corporation M acquires additional stock with a fair market value equal to 15 percent of the value of the stock of Corporation N on January 1, 2006, and an additional 18 percent on February 21, 2007. As of February 21, 2007, Corporation M has acquired stock with a fair market value greater than 50 percent of the value of the stock of Corporation N. Thus, a change in the ownership of Corporation N is considered to occur on February 21, 2007 (assuming that Corporation M did not have effective control of Corporation N immediately prior to the acquisition on that date).

Example 2. All of the corporation's stock is owned by the founders of the corporation. The board of directors of the corporation decides to offer shares of the corporation to the public. After the public offering, the founders of the corporation own a total of 40 percent of the corporation's stock, and members of the public own 60 percent. If no one person (or more than one person acting as a group) owns more than 50 percent of the corporation's stock (by value or voting power) after the public offering, there is no change in the ownership of the corporation.

Example 3. Corporation P merges into Corporation O (a previously unrelated corporation). In the merger, the shareholders of Corporation P receive Corporation O stock in exchange for their Corporation P stock. Immediately after the merger, the former shareholders of Corporation P own stock with a fair market value equal to 60 percent of the value of the stock of Corporation O, and the former shareholders of Corporation O own stock with

a fair market value equal to 40 percent of the value of the stock of Corporation O. The former shareholders of Corporation P will be treated as acting as a group in their acquisition of Corporation O stock. Thus, a change in the ownership of Corporation O occurs on the date of the merger. See Q/A-29, Example 3, regarding whether there is a change in ownership or control of P.

Example 4. Assume the same facts as in Example 3, except that immediately after the change, the former shareholders of Corporation P own stock with a fair market value of 51 percent of the value of Corporation O stock and the former shareholders of Corporation O own stock with a fair market value equal to 49 percent of the value of Corporation O stock. Assume further that prior to the merger several Corporation O shareholders also owned Corporation P stock (overlapping shareholders). In the merger, those O shareholders received additional O stock by virtue of their ownership of P stock with a fair market value of 5 percent of the value of Corporation O stock. Including the O stock attributable to the P shares, the O shareholders hold 54 percent of O after the transaction. However, those overlapping shareholders that owned both Corporation O stock and Corporation P stock prior to the merger are treated as acting as a group with the Corporation O shareholders only with respect to their ownership interest in Corporation O prior to the transaction. Therefore, because the Corporation O shareholders owned 49 percent of the value of Corporation O stock, a change in the ownership of Corporation O occurs on the date of the merger. See Q/A-29, Example 3, regarding whether there is a change in ownership or control of P.

Example 5. A, an individual, owns stock with a fair market value equal to 20 percent of the value of the stock of Corporation Q. On January 1, 2007, Corporation Q acquires in a redemption for cash all of the stock held by shareholders other than A. Thus, A is left as the sole shareholder of Corporation O. A change in ownership of Corporation O is considered to occur on January 1, 2007 (assuming that A did not have effective control of Corporation Q immediately prior to the redemption).

Example 6. Assume the same facts as in Example 5, except that A owns stock with a fair market value equal to 51 percent of the value of all the stock of Corporation Q immediately prior to the redemption. There is no change in the ownership of Corporation Q as a result of the redemption.

Q-28: *When does a change in the effective control of a corporation occur?*

A-28: (a) Notwithstanding that a corporation has not undergone a change in ownership under Q/A-27, for purposes of this section, a change in the effective control of a corporation is presumed to occur on the date that either—

(1) Any one person, or more than one person acting as a group (as determined under paragraph (e) of this A-28), acquires (or has acquired during the 12-month period ending on the date of the most recent acquisition by such person or persons) ownership of stock of the corporation possessing 20 percent or more of the total voting power of the stock of such corporation; or

(2) A majority of members of the corporation's board of directors is replaced during any 12-month period by directors whose appointment or election is not endorsed by a majority of the members of the corporation's board of directors prior to the date of the appointment or election.

(b) The presumption of paragraph (a) of this A-28 may be rebutted by establishing that such acquisition or acquisitions of the corporation's stock, or such replacement of the majority of the members of the corporation's board of directors, does not transfer the power to control (directly or indirectly) the management and policies of the corporation from any one person (or more than one person acting as a group) to another person (or group). For purposes of this section, in the absence of an event described in paragraph (a)(1) or (2) of this A-28, a change in the effective control of

a corporation is presumed not to have occurred.

(c) In no event does a change in effective control under this A-28 occur in any transaction in which either of the two corporations involved in the transaction has a change in ownership or control under Q/A-27 or 29 of this section. Thus, for example, assume Corporation P transfers more than one-third of the total gross fair market value of its assets to Corporation O in exchange for 20 percent of O's stock. Because P has undergone a change in ownership of a substantial portion of its assets under Q/A-29 of this section, O does not have a change in effective control under Q/A-28.

(d) If any one person, or more than one person acting as a group, is considered to effectively control a corporation (within the meaning of this A-28), the acquisition of additional control of the corporation by the same person or persons is not considered to cause a change in the effective control of the corporation (or to cause a change in the ownership of the corporation within the meaning of Q/A-27 of this section).

(e) For purposes of this A-28, persons will not be considered to be acting as a group merely because they happen to purchase or own stock of the same corporation at the same time, or as a result of the same public offering. However, persons will be considered to be acting as a group if they are owners of a corporation that enters into a merger, consolidation, purchase or acquisition of stock, or similar business transaction with the corporation. If a person, including an entity shareholder, owns stock in both corporations that enter into a merger, consolidation, purchase or acquisition of stock, or similar transaction, such shareholder is considered to be acting as a group with other shareholders in a corporation only with respect to the ownership in that corporation prior to the transaction giving rise to the change and not with respect to the ownership interest in the other corporation.

(f) For purposes of determining stock ownership, see Q/A-27(c).

(g) The following examples illustrate the principles of this A-28:

Example 1. Shareholder A acquired the following percentages of the voting stock of Corporation M (an otherwise unrelated corporation) on the following dates: 16 percent on January 1, 2005; 10 percent on January 10, 2006; 8 percent on February 10, 2006; 11 percent on March 1, 2007; and 8 percent on March 10, 2007. Thus, on March 10, 2007, A owns a total of 53 percent of M's voting stock. Because A did not acquire 20 percent or more of M's voting stock during any 12-month period, there is no presumption of a change in effective control pursuant to paragraph (a)(1) of this A-28. In addition, under these facts there is a presumption that no change in the effective control of Corporation M occurred. If this presumption is not rebutted (and thus no change in effective control of Corporation M is treated as occurring prior to March 10, 2007), a change in the ownership of Corporation M is treated as having occurred on March 10, 2007 (pursuant to Q/A-27 of this section) because A had acquired more than 50 percent of Corporation M's voting stock as of that date.

Example 2. A minority group of shareholders of a corporation opposes the practices and policies of the corporation's current board of directors. A proxy contest ensues. The minority group presents its own slate of candidates for the board at the next annual meeting of the corporation's shareholders, and candidates of the minority group are elected to replace a majority of the current members of the board. A change in the effective control of the corporation is presumed to have occurred on the date the election of the new board of directors becomes effective.

Q-29: *When does a change in the ownership of a substantial portion of a corporation's assets occur?*

A-29: (a) For purposes of this section, a change in the ownership of a substantial portion of a corporation's assets occurs on the date that any one person, or more than one person acting as a group (as determined in paragraph (c) of this A-29), acquires (or has acquired during the 12-month period ending on the date of the most recent acquisition by such person or persons) assets from the corporation that have a total gross fair market value equal to or more than one-third of the total gross fair market value of all of the assets of the corporation immediately prior to such acquisition or acquisitions. For this purpose, gross fair market value means the value of the assets of the corporation, or the value of the assets being disposed of, determined without regard to any liabilities associated with such assets. This A-29 applies in any situation other than one involving the transfer of stock (or issuance of stock) in a parent corporation and stock in such corporation remains outstanding after the transaction. Thus, this A-29 applies to the sale of stock in a subsidiary (when that subsidiary is treated as a single corporation with the parent pursuant to Q/A-46) and to mergers involving the creation of a new corporation orwith respect to the corporation that is not surviving entity.

(b) (1) There is no change in ownership or control under this A-29 when there is a transfer to an entity that is controlled by the shareholders of the transferring corporation immediately after the transfer, as provided in this paragraph (b). A transfer of assets by a corporation is not treated as a change in the ownership of such assets if the assets are transferred to—

(i) A shareholder of the corporation (immediately before the asset transfer) in exchange for or with respect to its stock;

(ii) An entity, 50 percent or more of the total value or voting power of which is owned, directly or indirectly, by the corporation;

(iii) A person, or more than one person acting as a group, that owns, directly or indirectly, 50 percent or more of the total value or voting power of all the outstanding stock of the corporation; or

(iv) An entity, at least 50 percent of the total value or voting power is owned, directly or indirectly, by a person described in paragraph (b)(1)(iii) of this A-29.

(2) For purposes of paragraph (b) and except as otherwise provided, a person's status is determined immediately after the transfer of the assets. For example, a transfer to a corporation in which the transferor corporation has no ownership interest in before the transaction, but which is a majority-owned subsidiary of the transferor corporation after the transaction is not treated as a change in the ownership of the assets of the transferor corporation.

(c) For purposes of this A-29, persons will not be considered to be acting as a group merely because they happen to purchase assets of the same corporation at the same time, or as a result of the same public offering. However, persons will be considered to be acting as a group if they are owners of a corporation that enters into a merger, consolidation, purchase or acquisition of assets, or similar business transaction with the corporation. If a person, including an entity shareholder, owns stock in both corporations that enter into a merger, consolidation, purchase or acquisition of stock, or similar transaction, such shareholder is considered to be acting as a group with other shareholders in a corporation only to the extent of the ownership in that corporation prior to the transaction giving rise to the change and not with respect to the ownership interest in the other corporation.

(d) For purposes of determining stock ownership, see Q/A-27(c).

(e) The following examples illustrate the principles of this A-29:

Example 1. Corporation M acquires assets having a gross fair market value of $500,000 from Corporation N (an unrelated corporation) on January 1, 2006. The total gross fair market value of Corporation N's assets immediately prior to the acquisition was $3 million. Since the value of the assets acquired by Corporation M is less than one-third of the total gross fair market value of Corporation N's total assets immediately prior to the acquisition, the acquisition does not represent a change in the ownership of a substantial portion of Corporation N's assets.

Example 2. Assume the same facts as in Example 1. Also assume that on November 1, 2006, Corporation M acquires from Corporation N additional assets having a fair market value of $700,000. Thus, Corporation M has acquired from Corporation N assets worth a total of $1.2 million during the 12-month period ending on November 1, 2006. Since $1.2 million is more than one-third of the total gross fair market value of all of Corporation N's assets immediately prior to the earlier of these acquisitions ($3 million), a change in the ownership of a substantial portion of Corporation N's assets is considered to have occurred on November 1, 2006.

Example 3. (i) All of the assets of Corporation P are transferred to Corporation O (an unrelated corporation). In exchange, the shareholders of Corporation P receive Corporation O stock. Immediately after the transfer, the former shareholders of Corporation P own 60 percent of the fair market value of the outstanding stock of Corporation O and the former shareholders of Corporation O own 40 percent of the fair market value of the outstanding stock of Corporation O. Because Corporation O is an entity more than 50 percent of the fair market value of the outstanding stock of which is owned by the former shareholders of Corporation P (based on ownership of Corporation P prior the change), the transfer of assets is not treated as a change in ownership of a substantial portion of the assets of Corporation P. However, a change in the ownership (within the meaning of Q/A-27) of Corporation O occurs.

(ii) The result in paragraph (i) would be the same if immediately after the change, the former shareholders of Corporation P own stock with a fair market value of 51 percent of the value of Corporation O stock because Corporation O is an entity more than 50 percent of the fair market value of the outstanding stock of which is owned by the former shareholders of Corporation P. See Q/A-27, Example 4, regarding whether there is a change in ownership or control of O.

Example 4. Corporation P sells all of the stock of its wholly-owned subsidiary, S, to

Corporation Y. The fair market value of the affiliated group, determined without regard to its liabilities, is $210 million. The fair market value of S, determined without regard to its liabilities, is $80 million. Because there is a change in more than one-third of the gross fair market value of the total assets of the affiliated group, there is a change in the ownership of a substantial portion of the assets of the affiliated group.

Three-Times-Base-Amount Test for Parachute Payments

Q-30: *Are all payments that are in the nature of compensation, are made to a disqualified individual, and are contingent on a change in ownership or control, parachute payments?*

A-30: (a) No. To determine whether such payments are parachute payments, they must be tested against the individual's base amount (as defined in Q/A-34 of this section). To do this, the aggregate present value of all payments in the nature of compensation that are made or to be made to (or for the benefit of) the same disqualified individual and are contingent on the change in ownership or control must be determined. If this aggregate present value equals or exceeds the amount equal to 3 times the individual's base amount, the payments are parachute payments. If this aggregate present value is less than the amount equal to 3 times the individual's base amount, no portion of the payment is a parachute payment. See Q/A-31, Q/A-32, and Q/A-33 of this section for rules on determining present value. Parachute payments that are securities violation parachute payments are not included in the foregoing computation if they are not contingent on a change in ownership or control. See Q/A-37 of this section for the definition and treatment of securities violation parachute payments.

(b) The following examples illustrate the principles of this A-30:

Example 1. A is a disqualified individual with respect to Corporation M. A's base amount is $100,000. Payments in the nature of compensation that are contingent on a change in the ownership or control of Corporation M totaling $400,000 are made to A on the date of the change in ownership or control. The payments are parachute payments because they have an aggregate present value at least equal to 3 times A's base amount of $100,000 (3 x $100,000 = $300,000).

Example 2. Assume the same facts as in Example 1, except that the payments contingent on the change in the ownership or control of Corporation M total $290,000. Because the payments do not have an aggregate present value at least equal to 3 times A's base amount, no portion of the payments is a parachute payment.

Q-31: *As of what date is the present value of a payment determined?*

A-31: (a) Except as provided in this section, the present value of a payment is determined as of the date on which the change in ownership or control occurs, or, if a payment is made prior to such date, the date on which the payment is made.

(b)(1) For purposes of determining whether a payment is a parachute payment, if a payment in the nature of compensation is the right to receive payments in a year (or years) subsequent to the year of the change in ownership or control, the value of the payment is the present value of such payment (or payments) calculated in accordance with Q/A-32 of this section and based on reasonable actuarial assumptions.

(2) If the payment in the nature of compensation is an obligation to provide health care, then for purposes of this A-31 and for applying the 3-times-base-amount test under Q/A-30 of this section, the present value of such obligation should be calculated in accordance with generally accepted accounting principles. For purposes of Q/A-30 and this A-31, the obligation to provide health care is permitted to be measured by projecting the cost of premiums for purchased health care insurance, even if no health care insurance is actually purchased. If the obligation to provide health care is made in coordination with a health care plan that the corporation makes

available to a group, then the premiums used for this purpose may be group premiums.

Q-32: *What discount rate is to be used to determine present value?*

A-32: For purposes of this section, present value generally is determined by using a discount rate equal to 120 percent of the applicable Federal rate (determined under section 1274(d) and the regulations thereunder) compounded semiannually. The applicable Federal rate to be used for this purpose is the Federal rate that is in effect on the date as of which the present value is determined, using the period until the payment would have been made without regard to the change in ownership or control as the term of the debt instrument under section 1274(d). See Q/A-24 and 31 of this section. However, for any payment, the corporation and the disqualified individual may elect to use the applicable Federal rate that is in effect on the date that the contract which provides for the payment is entered into, if such election is made in the contract.

Q-33: *If the present value of a payment to be made in the future is contingent on an uncertain future event or condition, how is the present value of the payment determined?*

A-33: (a) In certain cases, it may be necessary to apply the 3-times-base-amount test of Q/A-30 of this section, or to allocate a portion of the base amount to a payment described in paragraphs (a)(1), (2), and (3) of Q/A-2 of this section, at a time when the aggregate present value of all such payments cannot be determined with certainty because the time, amount, or right to receive one or more such payments is contingent on the occurrence of an uncertain future event or condition. For example, a disqualified individual's right to receive a payment may be contingent on the involuntary termination of such individual's employment with the corporation. In such a case, it must be reasonably estimated whether the payment will be made. If it is reasonably estimated that there is a 50-percent or greater probability that the payment will be made, the full amount of the payment is considered for purposes of the 3-times-base-

amount test and the allocation of the base amount. Conversely, if it is reasonably estimated that there is a less than 50-percent probability that the payment will be made, the payment is not considered for either purpose.

(b) If the estimate made under paragraph (a) of this A-33 is later determined to be incorrect, the 3-times-base-amount test described in Q/A-30 of this section must be reapplied (and the portion of the base amount allocated to previous payments must be reallocated (if necessary) to such payments) to reflect the actual time and amount of the payment. Whenever the 3-times-base-amount test is applied (or whenever the base amount is allocated), the aggregate present value of the payments received or to be received by the disqualified individual is redetermined as of the date described in A-31 of this section, using the discount rate described in A-32 of this section. This redetermination may affect the amount of any excess parachute payment for a prior taxable year. Alternatively, if, based on the application of the 3-times-base-amount test without regard to the payment described in paragraph (a) of this A-33, a disqualified individual is determined to have an excess parachute payment or payments, then the 3-times-base-amount test does not have to be reapplied when a payment described in paragraph (a) of this A-33 is made (or becomes certain to be made) if no base amount is allocated to such payment.

(c) To the extent provided in published guidance of general applicability under § 601.601(d)(2) of this Chapter, an initial estimate of the value of an option subject to Q/A-13 of this section is permitted to be made, with the valuation subsequently redetermined, and the 3-times-base-amount test reapplied.

(d) The following examples illustrate the principles of this A-33:

Example 1. A, a disqualified individual with respect to Corporation M, has a base amount of $100,000. Under A's employment agreement with Corporation M, A is entitled to receive a payment in the nature of compensation in the amount of $250,000 contingent on a change in ownership or control of Corporation M. In addition, the agreement provides that if A's employment is terminated within 1 year after the change in ownership or control, A will receive an additional payment in the nature of compensation in the amount of $150,000, payable 1 year after the date of the change in ownership or control. A change in ownership or control of Corporation M occurs and A receives the first payment of $250,000. Corporation M reasonably estimates that there is a 50-percent probability that, as a result of the change, A's employment will be terminated within 1 year of the date of the change. For purposes of applying the 3-times-base-amount test (and if the first payment is determined to be a parachute payment, for purposes of allocating a portion of A's base amount to that payment), because M reasonably estimates that there is a 50-percent or greater probability that, as a result of the change, A's employment will be terminated within 1 year of the date of the change, Corporation M must assume that the $150,000 payment will be made to A as a result of the change in ownership or control. The present value of the additional payment is determined under Q/A-31 and Q/A-32 of this section.

Example 2. Assume the same facts as in Example 1, except that Corporation M reasonably estimates that there is a less than 50-percent probability that, as a result of the change, A's employment will be terminated within 1 year of the date of the change. For purposes of applying the 3-times-base-amount test, because Corporation M reasonably estimates that there is a less than 50-percent probability that, as a result of the change, A's employment will be terminated within 1 year of the date of the change, Corporation M must assume that the $150,000 payment will not be made to A as a result of the change in ownership or control.

Example 3. B, a disqualified individual with respect to Corporation P, has a base amount of $200,000. Under B's employment agreement with Corporation P, if there is a change in ownership or control of Corporation

P, B will receive a severance payment of $600,000 and a bonus payment of $400,000. In addition, the agreement provides that if B's employment is terminated within 1 year after the change, B will receive an additional payment in the nature of compensation of $500,000. A change in ownership or control of Corporation P occurs, and B receives the $600,000 and $400,000 payments. At the time of the change in ownership or control, Corporation P reasonably estimates that there is a less than 50-percent probability that B's employment will be terminated within 1 year of the change. For purposes of applying the 3-times-base-amount test, because Corporation P reasonably estimates that there is a less than 50-percent probability that B's employment will be terminated within 1 year of the date of the change, Corporation P assumes that the $500,000 payment will not be made to B. Eleven months after the change in ownership or control, B's employment is terminated, and the $500,000 payment is made to B. Because B was determined to have excess parachute payments without regard to the $500,000 payment, the 3-times-base-amount test is not reapplied and the base amount is not reallocated to include the $500,000 payment. The entire $500,000 payment is treated as an excess parachute payment.

Q-34: *What is the base amount?*

A-34: (a) The base amount of a disqualified individual is the average annual compensation for services performed for the corporation with respect to which the change in ownership or control occurs (or for a predecessor entity or a related entity as defined in Q/A-21 of this section) which was includible in the gross income of such individual for taxable years in the base period (including amounts that were excluded under section 911), or which would have been includible in such gross income if such person had been a United States citizen or resident. See Q/A-35 of this section for the definition of base period and for examples of base amount computations.

(b) If the base period of a disqualified individual includes a short taxable year or less than all of a taxable year, compensation for such short or incomplete taxable year must be annualized before determining the average annual compensation for the base period. In annualizing compensation, the frequency with which payments are expected to be made over an annual period must be taken into account. Thus, any amount of compensation for such a short or incomplete taxable year that represents a payment that will not be made more often than once per year is not annualized.

(c) Because the base amount includes only compensation that is includible in gross income, the base amount does not include certain items that constitute parachute payments. For example, payments in the form of excludible fringe benefits are not included in the base amount but may be treated as parachute payments.

(d) The base amount includes the amount of compensation included in income under section 83(b) during the base period. See Q/A-35 for the definition of base period.

(e) The following example illustrates the principles of this A-34:

Example. A disqualified individual, D, receives an annual salary of $500,000 per year during the 5-year base period. D defers $100,000 of D's salary each year under the corporation's nonqualified deferred compensation plan. D's base amount is $400,000 ($400,000 x (5/5)).

Q-35: What is the base period?

A-35: (a) The base period of a disqualified individual is the most recent 5 taxable years of the individual ending before the date of the change in ownership or control. For this purpose, the date of the change in ownership or control is the date the corporation experiences one of the events described in Q/A-27, Q/A-28, or Q/A-29 of this section. However, if the disqualified individual was not an employee or independent contractor of the corporation with respect to which the change in ownership or control occurs (or a predecessor entity or a related entity as defined in Q/A-21 of this section) for this entire 5-year period, the individual's base period is the portion of

such 5-year period during which the individual performed personal services for the corporation or predecessor entity or related entity.

(b) The following examples illustrate the principles of Q/A-34 of this section and this Q/A-35:

Example 1. A disqualified individual, D, was employed by a corporation for 2 years and 4 months preceding the taxable year in which a change in ownership or control of the corporation occurs. D's includible compensation income from the corporation was $30,000 for the 4-month period, $120,000 for the first full year, and $150,000 for the second full year. D's base amount is $120,000, ((3 x $30,000) + $120,000 + $150,000)/3.

Example 2. Assume the same facts as in Example 1, except that D also received a $60,000 signing bonus when D's employment with the corporation commenced at the beginning of the 4-month period. D's base amount is $140,000, (($60,000 + (3 x $30,000)) + $120,000 + $150,000) / 3. Since the bonus will not be paid more often than once per year, the amount of the bonus is not increased in annualizing D's compensation for the 4-month period.

Example 3. E is a disqualified individual with respect to Corporation X who was not an employee or independent contractor for the full 5-year base period. In 2004 and 2005, E is a director of X and receives $30,000 per year for E's services. In 2006, E becomes an officer of X. E's includible compensation from Corporation X is $250,000 for 2006 and 2007, and $300,000 for 2008. In 2008, X undergoes a change in ownership or control. E's base amount is $140,000 ((2 x $250,000) + (2 x $30,000)/4).

Q-36: *How is the base amount determined in the case of a disqualified individual who did not perform services for the corporation (or a predecessor entity or a related entity as defined in Q/A-21 of this section), prior to the individual's taxable year in which the change in ownership or control occurs?*

A-36: (a) In such a case, the individual's base amount is the annualized compensation for services performed for the corporation (or a predecessor entity or related entity) which—

(1) Was includible in the individual's gross income for that portion, prior to such change, of the individual's taxable year in which the change occurred (including amounts that were excluded under section 911), or would have been includible in such gross income if such person had been a United States citizen or resident;

(2) Was not contingent on the change in ownership or control; and

(3) Was not a securities violation parachute payment.

(b) The following examples illustrate the principles of this A-36:

Example 1. On January 1, 2006, A, an individual whose taxable year is the calendar year, enters into a 4-year employment contract with Corporation M as an officer of the corporation. A has not previously performed services for Corporation M (or any predecessor entity or related entity as defined in Q/A-21 of this section). Under the employment contract, A is to receive an annual salary of $120,000 for each of the 4 years that he remains employed by Corporation M with any remaining unpaid balance to be paid immediately in the event that A's employment is terminated without cause. On July 1, 2006, after A has received compensation of $60,000, a change in the ownership or control of Corporation M occurs. Because of the change, A's employment is terminated without cause, and he receives a payment of $420,000. It is established by clear and convincing evidence that the $60,000 in compensation is not contingent on the change in ownership or control, but the presumption that the $420,000 payment is contingent on the change is not rebutted. Thus, the payment of $420,000 is treated as contingent on the change in ownership or control of Corporation M. In this case, A's base amount is $120,000 (2 x $60,000). Since the present value of the payment which is contingent on the change in ownership of Corporation M

($420,000) is more than 3 times A's base amount of $120,000 (3 x $120,000 = $360,000), the payment is a parachute payment.

Example 2. Assume the same facts as in Example 1, except that A also receives a signing bonus of $50,000 from Corporation M on January 1, 2006. It is established by clear and convincing evidence that the bonus is not contingent on the change in ownership or control. When the change in ownership or control occurs on July 1, 2006, A has received compensation of $110,000 (the $50,000 bonus plus $60,000 in salary). In this case, A's base amount is $170,000 ($50,000 + (2 x $60,000)). Because the $50,000 bonus will not be paid more than once per year, the amount of the bonus is not increased in annualizing A's compensation. The present value of the potential parachute payment ($420,000) is less than 3 times A's base amount of $170,000 (3 x $170,000 = $510,000), and therefore no portion of the payment is a parachute payment.

Securities Violation Parachute Payments

Q-37: *Must a payment be contingent on a change in ownership or control in order to be a parachute payment?*

A-37: (a) No, the term parachute payment also includes any payment (other than a payment exempted under Q/A-6 or Q/A-8 of this section) that is in the nature of compensation and is to (or for the benefit of) a disqualified individual, if such payment is a securities violation payment. A securities violation payment is a payment made or to be made—

(1) Pursuant to an agreement that violates any generally enforced Federal or state securities laws or regulations; and

(2) In connection with a potential or actual change in ownership or control.

(b) A violation is not taken into account under paragraph (a)(1) of this A-37 if it is merely technical in character or is not materially prejudicial to shareholders or potential shareholders. Moreover, a violation will be presumed not to exist unless the existence of the violation has been determined or admitted in a civil or criminal action (or an administrative action by a regulatory body charged with enforcing the particular securities law or regulation) which has been resolved by adjudication or consent. Parachute payments described in this A-37 are referred to in this section as securities violation payments.

(c) Securities violation parachute payments that are not contingent on a change in ownership or control within the meaning of Q/A-22 of this section are not taken into account in applying the 3-times-base-amount test of Q/A-30 of this section. Such payments are considered parachute payments regardless of whether such test is met with respect to the disqualified individual (and are included in allocating base amount under Q/A-38 of this section). Moreover, the amount of a securities violation parachute payment treated as an excess parachute payment shall not be reduced by the portion of such payment that is reasonable compensation for personal services actually rendered before the date of a change in ownership or control if such payment is not contingent on such change. Likewise, the amount of a securities violation parachute payment includes the portion of such payment that is reasonable compensation for personal services to be rendered on or after the date of a change in ownership or control if such payment is not contingent on such change.

(d) The rules in paragraph (b) of this A-37 also apply to securities violation parachute payments that are contingent on a change in ownership or control if the application of these rules results in greater total excess parachute payments with respect to the disqualified individual than would result if the payments were treated simply as payments contingent on a change in ownership or control (and hence were taken into account in applying the 3-times-base-amount test and were reduced by, or did not include, any applicable amount of reasonable compensation).

(e) The following examples illustrate the principles of this A-37:

Example 1. A, a disqualified individual with respect to Corporation M, receives two payments in the nature of compensation that are contingent on a change in the ownership or control of Corporation M. The present value of the first payment is equal to A's base amount and is not a securities violation parachute payment. The present value of the second payment is equal to 1.5 times A's base amount and is a securities violation parachute payment. Neither payment includes any reasonable compensation. If the second payment is treated simply as a payment contingent on a change in ownership or control, the amount of A's total excess parachute payments is zero because the aggregate present value of the payments does not equal or exceed 3 times A's base amount. If the second payment is treated as a securities violation parachute payment subject to the rules of paragraph (b) of this A-37, the amount of A's total excess parachute payments is 0.5 times A's base amount. Thus, the second payment is treated as a securities violation parachute payment.

Example 2. Assume the same facts as in Example 1, except that the present value of the first payment is equal to 2 times A's base amount. If the second payment is treated simply as a payment contingent on a change in ownership or control, the total present value of the payments is 3.5 times A's base amount, and the amount of A's total excess parachute payments is 2.5 times A's base amount. If the second payment is treated as a securities violation parachute payment, the amount of A's total excess parachute payments is 0.5 times A's base amount. Thus, the second payment is treated simply as a payment contingent on a change in ownership or control.

Example 3. B, a disqualified individual with respect to Corporation N, receives two payments in the nature of compensation that are contingent on a change in the control of Corporation N. The present value of the first payment is equal to 4 times B's base amount and is a securities violation parachute payment. The present value of the second payment is equal to 2 times B's base amount and is not a securities violation parachute payment. B establishes by clear and convincing evidence that the entire amount of the first payment is reasonable compensation for personal services to be rendered after the change in ownership or control. If the first payment is treated simply as a payment contingent on a change in ownership or control, it is exempt from the definition of parachute payment pursuant to Q/A-9 of this section. Thus, the amount of B's total excess parachute payment is zero because the present value of the second payment does not equal or exceed 3 times B's basc amount. However, if the first payment is treated as a securities violation parachute payment, the amount of B's total excess parachute payments is 3 times B's base amount. Thus, the first payment is treated as a securities violation parachute payment.

Example 4. Assume the same facts as in Example 3, except that B does not receive the second payment and B establishes by clear and convincing evidence that the first payment is reasonable compensation for services actually rendered before the change in the control of Corporation N. If the payment is treated simply as a payment contingent on a change in ownership or control, the amount of B's excess parachute payment is zero because the amount treated as an excess parachute payment is reduced by the amount that B establishes as reasonable compensation. However, if the payment is treated as a securities violation parachute payment, the amount of B's excess parachute payment is 3 times B's base amount. Thus, the payment is treated as a securities violation parachute payment.

Computation and Reduction of Excess Parachute Payments

Q-38: *How is the amount of an excess parachute payment computed?*

A-38: (a) The amount of an excess parachute payment is the excess of the amount of any parachute payment over the portion of the disqualified individual's base amount that is allocated to such payment. For this purpose, the portion of the base amount allocated to any parachute payment is the amount that bears the same ratio to the base amount as the present value of such parachute payment bears to the aggregate present value of all parachute payments made or to be made to (or for the benefit of) the same disqualified individual. Thus, the portion of the base amount allocated to any parachute payment is determined by multiplying the base amount by a fraction, the numerator of which is the present value of such parachute payment and the denominator of which is the aggregate present value of all such payments. See Q/A-31, Q/A-32, and Q/A-33 of this section for rules on determining present value and Q/A-34 of this section for the definition of base amount.

(b) The following example illustrates the principles of this A-38:

Example. An individual with a base amount of $100,000 is entitled to receive two parachute payments, one of $200,000 and the other of $400,000. The $200,000 payment is made at the time of the change in ownership or control, and the $400,000 payment is to be made at a future date. The present value of the $400,000 payment is $300,000 on the date of the change in ownership or control. The portions of the base amount allocated to these payments are $40,000 (($200,000/$500,000) x $100,000) and $60,000 (($300,000/$500,000) x $100,000), respectively. Thus, the amount of the first excess parachute payment is $160,000 ($200,000-$40,000) and that of the second is $340,000 ($400,000-$60,000).

Q-39: *May the amount of an excess parachute payment be reduced by reasonable compensation for personal services actually rendered before the change in ownership or control?*

A-39: (a) Generally, yes. Except in the case of payments treated as securities violation parachute payments or when the portion of a payment that is treated as contingent on the change in ownership or control is determined under paragraph (b) or (c) of Q/A-24 of this section, the amount of an excess parachute payment is reduced by any portion of the payment that the taxpayer establishes by clear and convincing evidence is reasonable compensation for personal services actually rendered by the disqualified individual before the date of the change in ownership or control.

Services reasonably compensated for by payments that are not parachute payments (for example, because the payments are not contingent on a change in ownership or control and are not securities violation parachute payments, or because the payments are exempt from the definition of parachute payment under Q/A-6 through Q/A-9 of this section) are not taken into account for this purpose. The portion of any parachute payment that is established as reasonable compensation is first reduced by the portion of the disqualified individual's base amount that is allocated to such parachute payment; any remaining portion of the parachute payment established as reasonable compensation then reduces the excess parachute payment.

(b) The following examples illustrate the principles of this A-39:

Example 1. Assume that a parachute payment of $600,000 is made to a disqualified individual, and the portion of the individual's base amount that is allocated to the parachute payment is $100,000. Also assume that $300,000 of the $600,000 parachute payment is established as reasonable compensation for personal services actually rendered by the disqualified individual before the date of the change in ownership or control. Before the reasonable compensation is taken into account, the amount of the excess parachute payment is $500,000 ($600,000-$100,000). In reducing the excess parachute payment by reasonable compensation, the portion of the parachute payment that is established as reasonable compensation ($300,000) is first reduced by the portion of the disqualified individual's base amount that is allocated to the parachute payment ($100,000), and the remainder ($200,000) then reduces the excess parachute payment. Thus, in this case, the excess parachute payment of $500,000 is reduced by $200,000 of reasonable compensation.

Example 2. Assume the same facts as in Example 1, except that the full amount of the $600,000 parachute payment is established as reasonable compensation. In this case, the excess parachute payment of $500,000 is re-

duced to zero by $500,000 of reasonable compensation. As a result, no portion of any deduction for the payment is disallowed by section 280G [26 USCS § 280G], and no portion of the payment is subject to the 20-percent excise tax of section 4999 [26 USCS § 4999].

Determination of Reasonable Compensation

Q-40: *How is it determined whether payments are reasonable compensation?*

A-40: (a) In general, whether payments are reasonable compensation for personal services actually rendered, or to be rendered, by the disqualified individual is determined on the basis of all the facts and circumstances of the particular case. Factors relevant to such a determination include, but are not limited to, the following—

(1) The nature of the services rendered or to be rendered;

(2) The individual's historic compensation for performing such services; and

(3) The compensation of individuals performing comparable services in situations where the compensation is not contingent on a change in ownership or control.

(b) For purposes of section 280G, reasonable compensation for personal services includes reasonable compensation for holding oneself out as available to perform services and refraining from performing services (such as under a covenant not to compete).

Q-41: *Is any particular type of evidence generally considered clear and convincing evidence of reasonable compensation for personal services?*

A-41: Yes. A showing that payments are made under a nondiscriminatory employee plan or program (as defined in Q/A-26 of this section) generally is considered to be clear and convincing evidence that the payments are reasonable compensation. This is true whether the personal services for which the payments are made are actually rendered before, or are to be rendered on or after, the date of change in ownership or control. Q/A-46 of this section (relating to the treatment of an affiliated group as one corporation) does not apply for purposes of this A-41. No determination of reasonable compensation is needed for payments under qualified plans to be exempt from the definition of parachute payment under Q/A-8 of this section.

Q-42: *Is any particular type of evidence generally considered clear and convincing evidence of reasonable compensation for personal services to be rendered on or after the date of a change in ownership or control?*

A-42: (a) Yes, if payments are made or to be made to (or on behalf of) a disqualified individual for personal services to be rendered on or after the date of a change in ownership or control, a showing of the following generally is considered to be clear and convincing evidence that the payments are reasonable compensation for services to be rendered on or after the date of the change in ownership or control—

(1) The payments were made or are to be made only for the period the individual actually performs such personal services; and

(2) If the individual's duties and responsibilities are substantially the same after the change in ownership or control, the individual's annual compensation for such services is not significantly greater than such individual's annual compensation prior to the change in ownership or control, apart from normal increases attributable to increased responsibilities or cost of living adjustments. If the scope of the individual's duties and responsibilities are not substantially the same, the annual compensation after the change is not significantly greater than the annual compensation customarily paid by the employer or by comparable employers to persons performing comparable services. However, except as provided in paragraph (b) and (c) of this A-42, such clear and convincing evidence will not exist if the individual does not, in fact, perform the services contemplated in exchange for the compensation.

(b) Generally, an agreement under which the disqualified individual must refrain from performing services (e.g., a covenant not to compete) is an agreement for the performance of personal services for purposes of this A-42 to the extent that it is demonstrated by clear and convincing evidence that the agreement substantially constrains the individual's ability to perform services and there is a reasonable likelihood that the agreement will be enforced against the individual. In the absence of clear and convincing evidence, payments under the agreement are treated as severance payments under Q/A-44 of this section.

(c) If the employment of a disqualified individual is involuntarily terminated before the end of a contract term and the individual is paid damages for breach of contract, a showing of the following factors generally is considered clear and convincing evidence that the payment is reasonable compensation for personal services to be rendered on or after the date of change in ownership or control—

(1) The contract was not entered into, amended, or renewed in contemplation of the change in ownership or control;

(2) The compensation the individual would have received under the contract would have qualified as reasonable compensation under section 162;

(3) The damages do not exceed the present value (determined as of the date of receipt) of the compensation the individual would have received under the contract if the individual had continued to perform services for the employer until the end of the contract term;

(4) The damages are received because an offer to provide personal services was made by the disqualified individual but was rejected by the employer (including involuntary termination or constructive discharge); and

(5) The damages are reduced by mitigation. Mitigation will be treated as occurring when such damages are reduced (or any payment of such damages is returned) to the extent of the disqualified individual's earned income (within the meaning of section 911(d)(2)(A)) during the remainder of the

period in which the contract would have been in effect. See Q/A-44 of this section for rules regarding damages for a failure to make severance payments.

(d) The following examples illustrate the principles of this A-42:

Example 1. A, a disqualified individual, has a three-year employment contract with Corporation M, a publicly traded corporation. Under this contract, A is to receive a salary for $100,000 for the first year of the contract and, for each succeeding year, an annual salary that is 10 percent higher than the prior year's salary. During the third year of the contract, Corporation N acquires all the stock of Corporation M. Prior to the change in ownership, Corporation N arranges to retain A's services by entering into an employment contract with A that is essentially the same as A's contract with Corporation M. Under the new contract, Corporation N is to fulfill Corporation M's obligations for the third year of the old contract, and, for each of the succeeding years, pay A an annual salary that is 10 percent higher than A's prior year's salary. Amounts are payable under the new contract only for the portion of the contract term during which A remains employed by Corporation N. A showing of the facts described above (and in the absence of contradictory evidence) is regarded as clear and convincing evidence that all payments under the new contract are reasonable compensation for personal services to be rendered on or after the date of the change in ownership. Therefore, the payments under this agreement are exempt from the definition of parachute payment pursuant to Q/A-9 of this section.

Example 2. Assume the same facts as in Example 1, except that A does not perform the services described in the new contract, but receives payment under the new contract. Because services were not rendered after the change, the payments under this contract are not exempt from the definition of parachute payment pursuant to Q/A-9 of this section.

Example 3. Assume the same facts as in Example 1, except that under the new contract

A agrees to perform consulting services to Corporation N, when and if Corporation N requires A's services. Assume further that when Corporation N does not require A's services, the contract provides that A must not perform services for any other competing company. Corporation N previously enforced similar contracts against former employees of Corporation N. Because A is substantially constrained under this contract and Corporation N is reasonably likely to enforce the contract against A, the agreement is an agreement for the performance of services under paragraph (b) of this A-42. Assuming the requirements of paragraph (a) of this A-42 are met and there is clear and convincing evidence that all payments under the new contract are reasonable compensation for personal services to be rendered on or after the date of the change in ownership, the payments under this contract are exempt from the definition of parachute payment pursuant to Q/A-9 of this section.

Example 4. Assume the same facts as in Example 1, except that instead of agreeing not to compete with Corporation N, under the new agreement A agrees not to disparage either Corporation M or Corporation N. Because the nondisparagement agreement does not substantially constrain A's ability to perform services, no amount of the payments under this contract are reasonable compensation for the nondisparagement agreement.

Example 5. Assume the same facts as in Example 1, except that the employment contract with Corporation N does not provide that amounts are payable under the contract only for the portion of the term for which A remains employed by Corporation N. Shortly after the change in ownership, and despite A's request to remain employed by Corporation N, A's employment with Corporation N is involuntarily terminated. Shortly thereafter, A obtains employment with Corporation O. A commences a civil action against Corporation N, alleging breach of the employment contract. In settlement of the litigation, A receives an amount equal to the present value of the compensation A would have received under the contract with Corporation N, reduced by the amount of compensation A otherwise receives from Corporation O during the period that the contract would have been in effect. A showing of the facts described above (and in the absence of contradictory evidence) is regarded as clear and convincing evidence that the amount A receives as damages is reasonable compensation for personal services to be rendered on or after the date of the change in ownership. Therefore, the amount received by A is exempt from the definition of parachute payment pursuant to Q/A-9 of this section.

Q-43: *Is any particular type of payment generally considered reasonable compensation for personal services actually rendered before the date of a change in ownership or control?*

A-43: Yes, payments of compensation earned before the date of a change in ownership or control generally are considered reasonable compensation for personal services actually rendered before the date of a change in ownership or control if they qualify as reasonable compensation under section 162.

Q-44: *May severance payments be treated as reasonable compensation?*

A-44: (a) No, severance payments are not treated as reasonable compensation for personal services actually rendered before, or to be rendered on or after, the date of a change in ownership or control. Moreover, any damages paid for a failure to make severance payments are not treated as reasonable compensation for personal services actually rendered before, or to be rendered on or after, the date of such change. For purposes of this section, the term severance payment means any payment that is made to (or for the benefit of) a disqualified individual on account of the termination of such individual's employment prior to the end of a contract term, but does not include any payment that otherwise would be made to (or for the benefit of) such individual on the termination of such individual's employment, whenever occurring.

(b) The following example illustrates the principles of this A-44:

Example. A, a disqualified individual, has a three-year employment contract with Corporation X. Under the contract, A will receive a salary of $200,000 for the first year of the contract, and for each succeeding year, an annual salary that is $100,000 higher than the previous year. In the event of A's termination of employment following a change in ownership or control, the contract provides that A will receive the remaining salary due under the employment contract. At the beginning of the second year of the contract, Corporation Y acquires all of the stock of Corporation X, A's employment is terminated, and A receives $700,000 ($300,000 for the second year of the contract plus $400,000 for the third year of the contract) representing the remaining salary due under the employment contract. Because the $700,000 payment is treated as a severance payment, it is not reasonable compensation for personal services on or after the date of the change in ownership or control. Thus, the full amount of the $700,000 is a parachute payment.

Miscellaneous Rules

Q-45: *How is the term corporation defined?*

A-45: For purposes of this section, the term corporation has the meaning prescribed by section 7701(a)(3) and § 301.7701-2(b) of this Chapter. For example, a corporation, for purposes of this section, includes a publicly traded partnership treated as a corporation under section 7704(a); an entity described in § 301.7701-3(c)(1)(v)(A) of this Chapter; a real estate investment trust under section 856(a); a corporation that has mutual or cooperative (rather than stock) ownership, such as a mutual insurance company, a mutual savings bank, or a cooperative bank (as defined in section 7701(a)(32)), and a foreign corporation as defined under section 7701(a)(5).

Q-46: *How is an affiliated group treated?*

A-46: For purposes of this section, and except as otherwise provided in this section, all members of the same affiliated group (as defined in section 1504, determined without regard to section 1504(b)) are treated as one corporation. Rules affected by this treatment of an affiliated group include (but are not limited to) rules relating to exempt payments of certain corporations (Q/A-6, Q/A-7 of this section (except as provided therein)), payor of parachute payments (Q/A-10 of this section), disqualified individuals (Q/A-15 through Q/A-21 of this section (except as provided therein)), rebuttal of the presumption that payments are contingent on a change (Q/A-26 of this section (except as provide therein)), change in ownership or control (Q/A-27, 28, and 29 of this section), and reasonable compensation (Q/A-42, 43, and 44 of this section).

Effective Date

Q-47: *What is the general effective date of section 280G?*

A-47: (a) Generally, section 280G applies to payments under agreements entered into or renewed after June 14, 1984. Any agreement that is entered into before June 15, 1984, and is renewed after June 14, 1984, is treated as a new contract entered into on the day the renewal takes effect.

(b) For purposes of paragraph (a) of this A-47, a contract that is terminable or cancellable unconditionally at will by either party to the contract without the consent of the other, or by both parties to the contract, is treated as a new contract entered into on the date any such termination or cancellation, if made, would be effective. However, a contract is not treated as so terminable or cancellable if it can be terminated or cancelled only by terminating the employment relationship or independent contractor relationship of the disqualified individual.

(c) Section 280G applies to payments under a contract entered into on or before June 14, 1984, if the contract is amended or supplemented after June 14, 1984, in significant relevant respect. For this purpose, a supplement to a contract is defined as a new contract entered into after June 14, 1984, that affects the trigger, amount, or time of receipt of a payment under an existing contract.

(d)(1) Except as otherwise provided in paragraph (e) of this A-47, a contract is considered to be amended or supplemented in significant relevant respect if provisions for payments contingent on a change in ownership or control (parachute provisions), or provisions in the nature of parachute provisions, are added to the contract, or are amended or supplemented to provide significant additional benefits to the disqualified individual. Thus, for example, a contract generally is treated as amended or supplemented in significant relevant respect if it is amended or supplemented—

(i) To add or modify, to the disqualified individual's benefit, a change in ownership or control trigger;

(ii) To increase amounts payable that are contingent on a change in ownership or control (or, where payment is to be made under a formula, to modify the formula to the disqualified individual's advantage); or

(iii) To accelerate, in the event of a change in ownership or control, the payment of amounts otherwise payable at a later date.

(2) For purposes of paragraph (a) of this A-47, a payment is not treated as being accelerated in the event of a change in ownership or control if the acceleration does not increase the present value of the payment.

(e) A contract entered into on or before June 14, 1984, is not treated as amended or supplemented in significant relevant respect merely by reason of normal adjustments in the terms of employment relationship or independent contractor relationship of the disqualified individual. Whether an adjustment in the terms of such a relationship is considered normal for this purpose depends on all of the facts and circumstances of the particular case. Relevant factors include, but are not limited to, the following—

(1) The length of time between the adjustment and the change in ownership or control;

(2) The extent to which the corporation, at the time of the adjustment, viewed itself as a likely takeover candidate;

(3) A comparison of the adjustment with historical practices of the corporation;

(4) The extent of overlap between the group receiving the benefits of the adjustment and those members of that group who are the beneficiaries of pre-June 15, 1984, parachute contracts; and

(5) The size of the adjustment, both in absolute terms and in comparison with the benefits provided to other members of the group receiving the benefits of the adjustment.

Q-48: *What is the effective date of this section?*

A-48: This section applies to any payments that are contingent on a change in ownership or control if the change in ownership or control occurs on or after January 1, 2004. Taxpayers may rely on these regulations after August 4, 2003, for the treatment of any parachute payment.

§ 1.401-1. Qualified pension, profit-sharing, and stock bonus plans.

(a) *Introduction.*

* * *

(2) A qualified pension, profit-sharing, or stock bonus plan is a definite written program and arrangement which is communicated to the employees and which is established and maintained by an employer—

(i) In the case of a pension plan, to provide for the livelihood of the employees or their beneficiaries after the retirement of such employees through the payment of benefits determined without regard to profits (see paragraph (b)(1)(i) of this section);

(ii) In the case of a profit-sharing plan, to enable employees or their beneficiaries to participate in the profits of the employer's trade or business, or in the profits of an affiliated employer who is entitled to deduct his contributions to the plan under section 404(a)(3)(B), pursuant to a definite formula for allocating

the contributions and for distributing the funds accumulated under the plan (see paragraph (b)(1)(ii) of this section); and

(iii) In the case of a stock bonus plan, to provide employees or their beneficiaries benefits similar to those of profit-sharing plans, except that such benefits are distributable in stock of the employer, and that the contributions by the employer are not necessarily dependent upon profits. If the employer's contributions are dependent upon profits, the plan may enable employees or their beneficiaries to participate not only in the profits of the employer, but also in the profits of an affiliated employer who is entitled to deduct his contributions to the plan under section 404(a)(3)(B) (see paragraph (b)(1)(iii) of this section).

* * *

(b) *General rules.* (1)(i) A pension plan within the meaning of section 401(a) is a plan established and maintained by an employer primarily to provide systematically for the payment of definitely determinable benefits to his employees over a period of years, usually for life, after retirement. Retirement benefits generally are measured by, and based on, such factors as years of service and compensation received by the employees. The determination of the amount of retirement benefits and the contributions to provide such benefits are not dependent upon profits. Benefits are not definitely determinable if funds arising from forfeitures on termination of service, or other reason, may be used to provide increased benefits for the remaining participants (see § 1.401-7, relating to the treatment of forfeitures under a qualified pension plan). A plan designed to provide benefits for employees or their beneficiaries to be paid upon retirement or over a period of years after retirement will, for the purposes of section 401(a), be considered a pension plan if the employer contributions under the plan can be determined actuarially on the basis of definitely determinable benefits, or, as in the case of money purchase pension plans, such contributions are fixed without being geared to profits. A pension plan may provide for the payment of a pension due to disability and may also provide for the payment of incidental death benefits through insurance or otherwise. However, a plan is not a pension plan if it provides for the payment of benefits not customarily included in a pension plan such as layoff benefits or benefits for sickness, accident, hospitalization, or medical expenses (except medical benefits described in section 401(h) as defined in paragraph (a) of § 1.401-14).

(ii) A profit-sharing plan is a plan established and maintained by an employer to provide for the participation in his profits by his employees or their beneficiaries. The plan must provide a definite predetermined formula for allocating the contributions made to the plan among the participants and for distributing the funds accumulated under the plan after a fixed number of years, the attainment of a stated age, or upon the prior occurrence of some event such as layoff, illness, disability, retirement, death, or severance of employment. A formula for allocating the contributions among the participants is definite if, for example, it provides for an allocation in proportion to the basic compensation of each participant. A plan (whether or not it contains a definite predetermined formula for determining the profits to be shared with the employees) does not qualify under section 401(a) [26 USCS § 401(a)] if the contributions to the plan are made at such times or in such amounts that the plan in operation discriminates in favor of officers, shareholders, persons whose principal duties consist in supervising the work of other employees, or highly compensated employees. For the rules with respect to discrimination, see §§ 1.401-3 and 1.401-4. A profit-sharing plan within the meaning of section 401 [26 USCS § 401] is primarily a plan of deferred compensation, but the amounts allocated to the account of a participant may be used to provide for him or his family incidental life or accident or health insurance. See §§ 1.72-15, 1.72-16, and 1.402(a)-1(e) for rules regarding the tax treatment of incidental life or accident or health insurance

(iii) A stock bonus plan is a plan established and maintained by an employer to provide benefits similar to those of a profit-sharing plan, except that the contributions by the employer are not necessarily dependent upon profits and the benefits are distributable in stock of the employer company. For the purpose of allocating and distributing the stock of the employer which is to be shared among his employees or their beneficiaries, such a plan is subject to the same requirements as a profit-sharing plan. See §§ 1.72-15, 1.72-16, and 1.402(a)-1(e) for rules regarding the tax treatment of incidental life or accident or health insurance.

* * *

(2) The term "plan" implies a permanent as distinguished from a temporary program. Thus, although the employer may reserve the right to change or terminate the plan, and to discontinue contributions thereunder, the abandonment of the plan for any reason other than business necessity within a few years after it has taken effect will be evidence that the plan from its inception was not a bona fide program for the exclusive benefit of employees in general. Especially will this be true if, for example, a pension plan is abandoned soon after pensions have been fully funded for persons in favor of whom discrimination is prohibited under section 401(a). The permanency of the plan will be indicated by all of the surrounding facts and circumstances, including the likelihood of the employer's ability to continue contributions as provided under the plan. In the case of a profit-sharing plan, other than a profit-sharing plan which covers employees and owner-employees (see section 401(d)(2)(B)), it is not necessary that the employer contribute every year or that he contribute the same amount or contribute in accordance with the same ratio every year. However, merely making a single or occasional contribution out of profits for employees does not establish a plan of profit-sharing. To be a profit-sharing plan, there must be recurring and substantial contributions out of profits for the employees. In the event a plan is abandoned, the employer should promptly notify the district director, stating the circum-

stances which led to the discontinuance of the plan.

* * *

§ 1.401-2. Impossibility of diversion under the trust instrument.

(a) *In general.* (1) Under section 401(a)(2) a trust is not qualified unless under the trust instrument it is impossible (in the taxable year and at any time thereafter before the satisfaction of all liabilities to employees or their beneficiaries covered by the trust) for any part of the trust corpus or income to be used for, or diverted to, purposes other than for the exclusive benefit of such employees or their beneficiaries.

* * *

(b) *Meaning of "liabilities".* (1) The intent and purpose in section 401(a)(2) of the phrase "prior to the satisfaction of all liabilities with respect to employees and their beneficiaries under the trust" is to permit the employer to reserve the right to recover at the termination of the trust, and only at such termination, any balance remaining in the trust which is due to erroneous actuarial computations during the previous life of the trust. A balance due to an "erroneous actuarial computation" is the surplus arising because actual requirements differ from the expected requirements even though the latter were based upon previous actuarial valuations of liabilities or determinations of costs of providing pension benefits under the plan and were made by a person competent to make such determinations in accordance with reasonable assumptions as to mortality, interest, etc., and correct procedures relating to the method of funding. For example, a trust has accumulated assets of $1,000,000 at the time of liquidation, determined by acceptable actuarial procedures using reasonable assumptions as to interest, mortality, etc., as being necessary to provide the benefits in accordance with the provisions of the plan. Upon such liquidation it is found that $950,000 will satisfy all of the liabilities under the plan. The surplus of $50,000 arises, therefore, because of the difference between the amounts actuarially determined and the amounts actually required to satisfy the liabilities. This $50,000, therefore, is the amount which may be returned to the employer as the result of an erroneous actuarial computation. If, however, the surplus of $50,000 had been accumulated as a result of a change in the benefit provisions or in the eligibility requirements of the plan, the $50,000 could not revert to the employer because such surplus would not be the result of an erroneous actuarial computation.

(2) The term "liabilities" as used in section 401(a)(2) includes both fixed and contingent obligations to employees. For example, if 1,000 employees are covered by a trust forming part of a pension plan, 300 of whom have satisfied all the requirements for a monthly pension, while the remaining 700 employees have not yet completed the required period of service, contingent obligations to such 700 employees have nevertheless arisen which constitute "liabilities" within the meaning of that term.

(b)* * *

§ 1.401(a)-1. Post-ERISA qualified plans and qualified trusts; In general.

(a) *Introduction*—(1) *In general.* This section and the following regulation sections under section 401 reflect the provisions of section 401 after amendment by the Employee Retirement Income Security Act of 1974 (Pub.L. 93-406) ("ERISA").

(2) [Reserved]

(b) *Requirements for pension plans*—(1) *Definitely determinable benefits.* (i) In order for a pension plan to be a qualified plan under section 401(a), the plan must be established and maintained by an employer primarily to provide systematically for the payment of definitely determinable benefits to its employees over a period of years, usually for life, after retirement or attainment of normal retirement age (subject to paragraph (b)(2) of this section). A plan does not fail to satisfy this paragraph (b)(1)(i) merely because the plan provides, in accordance with section 401(a)(36), that a distribution may be made from the plan to an employee who has attained age 62 and who is not separated from employment at the time of such distribution.

(ii) Section 1.401-1(b)(1)(i), a pre-ERISA regulation, provides rules applicable to this requirement, and that regulation is applicable except as otherwise provided.

(iii) The use of the type of plan provision described in § 1.415(a)-1(d)(1) which automatically freezes or reduces the rate of benefit accrual or the annual addition to insure that the limitations of section 415 will not be exceeded, will not be considered to violate the requirements of this subparagraph provided that the operation of such provision precludes discretion by the employer.

(2) *Normal retirement age*—(i) *General rule.* The normal retirement age under a plan must be an age that is not earlier than the earliest age that is reasonably representative of the typical retirement age for the industry in which the covered workforce is employed.

(ii) *Age 62 safe harbor.* A normal retirement age under a plan that is age 62 or later is deemed to be not earlier than the earliest age that is reasonably representative of the typical retirement age for the industry in which the covered workforce is employed.

(iii) *Age 55 to age 62.* In the case of a normal retirement age that is not earlier than age 55 and is earlier than age 62, whether the age is not earlier than the earliest age that is reasonably representative of the typical retirement age for the industry in which the covered workforce is employed is based on all of the relevant facts and circumstances.

(iv) *Under age 55.* A normal retirement age that is lower than age 55 is presumed to be earlier than the earliest age that is reasonably representative of the typical retirement age for the industry in which the covered workforce is employed, unless the Commissioner determines that under the facts and circumstances the normal retirement age is not earlier than the earliest age that is reasonably representative of the typical retirement age for the industry in which the covered workforce is employed.

(v) *Age 50 safe harbor for qualified public safety employees.* A normal retirement age under a plan that is age 50 or later is deemed to be not earlier than the earliest age that is reasonably representative of the typical retirement age for the industry in which the covered workforce is employed if substantially all of the participants in the plan are qualified public safety employees (within the meaning of section 72(t)(10)(B)).

(3) Benefit distribution prior to retirement. For purposes of paragraph (b)(1)(i) of this section, retirement does not include a mere reduction in the number of hours that an employee works. Accordingly, benefits may not be distributed prior to normal retirement age solely due to a reduction in the number of hours that an employee works.

* * *

§ 1.401(a)-13. Assignment or alienation of benefits.

* * *

(b) *No assignment or alienation*—(1) *General rule.* Under section 401(a)(13), a trust will not be qualified unless the plan of which the trust is a part provides that benefits provided under the plan may not be anticipated, assigned (either at law or in equity), alienated or subject to attachment, garnishment, levy, execution or other legal or equitable process.

(2) Federal tax levies and judgments. A plan provision satisfying the requirements of subparagraph (1) of this paragraph shall not preclude the following:

(i) The enforcement of a Federal tax levy made pursuant to section 6331.

(ii) The collection by the United States on a judgment resulting from an unpaid tax assessment.

(c) *Definition of assignment and alienation*—(1) *In general.* For purposes of this section, the terms "assignment" and "alienation" include—

(i) Any arrangement providing for the payment to the employer of plan benefits which otherwise would be due the participant under the plan, and

(ii) Any direct or indirect arrangement (whether revocable or irrevocable) whereby a party acquires from a participant or beneficiary a right or interest enforceable against the plan in, or to, all or any part of a plan benefit payment which is, or may become, payable to the participant or beneficiary.

(2) *Specific arrangements not considered an assignment or alienation.* The terms "assignment" and "alienation" do not include, and paragraph (e) of this section does not apply to, the following arrangements:

(i) Any arrangement for the recovery of amounts described in section 4045(b) of the Employee Retirement Income Security Act of 1974, 88 Stat. 1027 (relating to the recapture of certain payments),

(ii) Any arrangement for the withholding of Federal, State or local tax from plan benefit payments,

(iii) Any arrangement for the recovery by the plan of overpayments of benefits previously made to a participant,

(iv) Any arrangement for the transfer of benefit rights from the plan to another plan, or

(v) Any arrangement for the direct deposit of benefit payments to an account in a bank, savings and loan association or credit union, provided such arrangement is not part of an arrangement constituting an assignment or alienation. Thus, for example, such an arrangement could provide for the direct deposit of a participant's benefit payments to a bank account held by the participant and the participant's spouse as joint tenants.

(d) *Exceptions to general rule prohibiting assignments or alienations*—(1) *Certain voluntary and revocable assignments or alienations.* Notwithstanding paragraph (b)(1) of this section, a plan may provide that once a participant or beneficiary begins receiving benefits under the plan, the participant or beneficiary may assign or alienate the right to future bene-

fit payments provided that the provision is limited to assignments or alienations which—

(i) Are voluntary and revocable;

(ii) Do not in the aggregate exceed 10 percent of any benefit payment; and

(iii) Are neither for the purpose, nor have the effect, of defraying plan administration costs.

For purposes of this subparagraph, an attachment, garnishment, levy, execution, or other legal or equitable process is not considered a voluntary assignment or alienation.

(2) *Benefits assigned or alienated as security for loans.* (i) Notwithstanding paragraph (b)(1) of this section, a plan may provide for loans from the plan to a participant or a beneficiary to be secured (by whatever means) by the participant's accrued nonforfeitable benefit provided that the following conditions are met.

(ii) The plan provision providing for the loans must be limited to loans from the plan. A plan may not provide for the use of benefits accrued or to be accrued under the plan as security for a loan from a party other than the plan, regardless of whether these benefits are nonforfeitable within the meaning of section 411 and the regulations thereunder.

(iii) The loan, if made to a participant or beneficiary who is a disqualified person (within the meaning of section 4975(e)(2)), must be exempt from the tax imposed by section 4975 (relating to the tax imposed on prohibited transactions) by reason of section 4975(d)(1). If the loan is made to a participant or beneficiary who is not a disqualified person, the loan must be one which would be exempt from the tax imposed by section 4975 by reason of section 4975(d)(1) if the loan were made to a disqualified person.

* * *

§ 1.401(a)-20. **Requirements of qualified joint and survivor annuity and qualified preretirement survivor annuity.**

* * *

Q-28: Does consent contained in an antenuptial agreement or similar contract entered into prior to marriage satisfy the consent requirements of sections 401(a)(11) and 417?

A-28: No. An agreement entered into prior to marriage does not satisfy the applicable consent requirements, even if the agreement is executed within the applicable election period.

* * *

§ 1.401(a)(4)-1. Nondiscrimination requirements of section 401(a)(4).

(a) *In general.* Section 401(a)(4) provides that a plan is a qualified plan only if the contributions or the benefits provided under the plan do not discriminate in favor of HCEs. Whether a plan satisfies this requirement depends on the form of the plan and on its effect in operation. In making this determination, intent is irrelevant. This section sets forth the exclusive rules for determining whether a plan satisfies section 401(a)(4). A plan that complies in form and operation with the rules in this section therefore satisfies section 401(a)(4).

(b) *Requirements a plan must satisfy*—(1) *In general.* In order to satisfy section 401(a)(4), a plan must satisfy each of the requirements of this paragraph (b).

(2) *Nondiscriminatory amount of contributions or benefits*—(i) *General rule.* Either the contributions or the benefits provided under the plan must be nondiscriminatory in amount. It need not be shown that both the contributions and the benefits provided are nondiscriminatory in amount, but only that either the contributions alone or the benefits alone are nondiscriminatory in amount.

(ii) *Defined contribution plans*—(A) *General rule.* A defined contribution plan satisfies this paragraph (b)(2) if the contributions allocated under the plan (including forfeitures) are nondiscriminatory in amount under § 1.401(a)(4)-2. Alternatively, a defined contribution plan (other than an ESOP) satisfies this paragraph (b)(2) if the equivalent benefits provided under the plan are nondiscriminatory in amount under § 1.401(a)(4)-

8(b). Section 1.401(a)(4)-8(b) includes a safe-harbor testing method for contributions provided under a target benefit plan.

(B) *Section 401(k) plans and section 401(m) plans.* A section 401(k) plan is deemed to satisfy this paragraph (b)(2) because § 1.410(b)-9 defines a section 401(k) plan as a plan consisting of elective contributions under a qualified cash or deferred arrangement (i.e., one that satisfies section 401(k)(3), the nondiscriminatory amount requirement applicable to qualified cash or deferred arrangements). A section 401(m) plan satisfies this paragraph (b)(2) only if the plan satisfies §§ 1.401(m)-1(b) and 1.401(m)-2. Contributions under a nonqualified cash or deferred arrangement, elective contributions described in § 1.401(k)-1(b)(4)(iv) that fail to satisfy the allocation and compensation requirements of § 1.401(k)-1(b)(4)(i), matching contributions that fail to satisfy § 1.401(m)-1(b)(4)(ii)(A), and qualified nonelective contributions treated as elective or matching contributions for certain purposes under §§ 1.401(k)-1(b)(5) and 1.401(m)-1(b)(5), respectively, are not subject to the special rule in this paragraph (b)(2)(ii)(B), because they are not treated as part of a section 401(k) plan or section 401(m) plan as those terms are defined in § 1.410(b)-9. The contributions described in the preceding sentence must satisfy paragraph (b)(2)(ii)(A) of this section.

(iii) *Defined benefit plans.* A defined benefit plan satisfies this paragraph (b)(2) if the benefits provided under the plan are nondiscriminatory in amount under § 1.401(a)(4)-3. Alternatively, a defined benefit plan satisfies this paragraph (b)(2) if the equivalent allocations provided under the plan are nondiscriminatory in amount under § 1.401(a)(4)-8(c). Section 1.401(a)(4)-8(c) includes a safe-harbor testing method for benefits provided under a cash balance plan. In addition, § 1.401(a)(4)-8(d) provides a safe-harbor testing method for benefits provided under a defined benefit plan that is part of a floor-offset arrangement.

(3) *Nondiscriminatory availability of benefits, rights, and features.* All benefits, rights,

and features provided under the plan must be made available in the plan in a nondiscriminatory manner. Rules for determining whether this requirement is satisfied are set forth in § 1.401(a)(4)-4.

(4) *Nondiscriminatory effect of plan amendments and terminations.* The timing of plan amendments must not have the effect of discriminating significantly in favor of HCEs. Rules for determining whether this requirement is satisfied are set forth in § 1.401(a)(4)-5(a). Section 1.401(a)(4)-5(b) provides additional requirements regarding plan terminations.

(c) *Application of requirements*—(1) *In general.* The requirements of paragraph (b) of this section must be applied in accordance with the rules set forth in this paragraph (c).

(2) *Interpretation.* The provisions of §§ 1.401(a)(4)-1 through 1.401(a)(4)-13 must be interpreted in a reasonable manner consistent with the purpose of preventing discrimination in favor of HCEs.

(3) *Plan-year basis of testing.* The requirements of paragraph (b) of this section are generally applied on the basis of the plan year and on the basis of the terms of the plan in effect during the plan year. Thus, unless otherwise provided, the compensation, contributions, benefit accruals, and other items used to apply these requirements must be determined with respect to the plan year being tested. However, § 1.401(a)(4)-11(g) provides rules allowing for corrective amendments made after the close of the plan year to be taken into account in satisfying certain requirements under paragraph (b) of this section.

(4) *Application of section 410(b) rules*— (i) *Relationship between sections 401(a)(4) and 410(b).* To be a qualified plan, a plan must satisfy both sections 410(b) and 401(a)(4). Section 410(b) requires that a plan benefit a nondiscriminatory group of employees, and section 401(a)(4) requires that the contributions or benefits provided to employees benefiting under the plan not discriminate in favor of HCEs. Consistent with this requirement, the definition of a plan subject to

testing under section 401(a)(4) is the same as the definition of a plan subject to testing under section 410(b), i.e., the plan determined after applying the mandatory disaggregation rules of § 1.410(b)-7(c) and the permissive aggregation rules of § 1.410(b)-7(d). In addition, whichever testing option is used for the plan year under § 1.410(b)-8(a) (e.g., quarterly testing) must also be used for purposes of determining whether the plan satisfies section 401(a)(4) for the plan year.

(ii) *Special rules for certain aggregated plans.* Special rules are set forth in § 1.401(a)(4)-9(b) for applying the nondiscriminatory amount and availability requirements of paragraphs (b)(2) and (b)(3) of this section to a plan that includes one or more defined benefit plans and one or more defined contribution plans that have been permissively aggregated under § 1.410(b)-7(d).

(iii) *Restructuring.* In certain circumstances, a plan may be restructured on the basis of employee groups and treated as comprising two or more plans, each of which is treated as a separate plan that must independently satisfy sections 401(a)(4) and 410(b). Rules relating to restructuring plans for purposes of applying the requirements of paragraph (b) of this section are set forth in § 1.401(a)(4)-9(c).

(iv) *References to section 410(b).* Except as otherwise specifically provided, references to satisfying section 410(b) in §§ 1.401(a)(4)-1 through 1.401(a)(4)-13 mean satisfying § 1.410(b)-2 (taking into account any special rules available in satisfying that section, other than the permissive aggregation rules of § 1.410(b)-7(d)). In the case of a plan described in section 410(c)(1) that has not made the election described in section 410(d) and is not subject to section 403(b)(12)(A)(i), references in §§ 1.401(a)(4)-1 through 1.401(a)(4)-13 to satisfying section 410(b) mean satisfying section 410(c)(2).

(5) *Collectively-bargained plans.* The requirements of paragraph (b) of this section are treated as satisfied by a collectively-bargained

plan that automatically satisfies section 410(b) under § 1.410(b)-2(b)(7).

(6) *Former employees.* In applying the nondiscriminatory amount and availability requirements of paragraphs (b)(2) and (b)(3) of this section, former employees are tested separately from active employees, unless otherwise provided. Rules for applying paragraphs (b)(2) and (b)(3) of this section to former employees are set forth in § 1.401(a)(4)-10.

(7) *Employee-provided contributions and benefits.* In applying the nondiscriminatory amount requirement of paragraph (b)(2) of this section, employee-provided contributions and benefits are tested separately from employer-provided contributions and benefits, unless otherwise provided. Rules for determining the amount of employer-provided benefits under a defined benefit plan that include employee contributions not allocated to separate accounts are set forth in § 1.401(a)(4)-6(b), and rules for applying paragraph (b)(2) of this section to employee contributions under such a plan are set forth in § 1.401(a)(4)-6(c). See paragraph (b)(2)(ii)(B) of this section for rules applicable to employee contributions allocated to separate accounts.

(8) *Allocation of earnings.* Notwithstanding any other provision in §§ 1.401(a)(4)-1 through 1.401(a)(4)-13, a defined contribution plan does not satisfy paragraph (b)(2) of this section if the manner in which income, expenses, gains, or losses are allocated to accounts under the plan discriminates in favor of HCEs or former HCEs.

(9) *Rollovers, transfers, and buybacks.* In applying the requirements of paragraph (b) of this section, rollover (including direct rollover) contributions described in section 402(c), 402(e)(6), 403(a)(4), 403(a)(5), or 408(d)(3), elective transfers described in § 1.411(d)-4, Q&A-3(b), transfers of assets and liabilities described in section 414(l), and employee buybacks are treated in accordance with the rules set forth in § 1.401(a)(4)-11(b).

(10) *Vesting.* A plan does not satisfy the nondiscriminatory amount requirement of paragraph (b)(2) of this section unless it satisfies § 1.401(a)(4)-11(c) with respect to the manner in which employees vest in their accrued benefits.

(11) *Crediting service.* A plan does not satisfy paragraphs (b)(2) and (b)(3) of this section unless it satisfies § 1.401(a)(4)-11(d) with respect to the manner in which employees' service is credited under the plan. Service other than actual service with the employer may not be taken into account in determining whether the plan satisfies paragraphs (b)(2) and (b)(3) of this section except as provided in § 1.401(a)(4)-11(d).

* * *

§ 1.401(a)(4)-2. Nondiscrimination in amount of employer contributions under a defined contribution plan.

(a) *Introduction*—(1) *Overview.* This section provides rules for determining whether the employer contributions allocated under a defined contribution plan are nondiscriminatory in amount as required by § 1.401(a)(4)-1(b)(2)(ii)(A). Certain defined contribution plans that provide uniform allocations are permitted to satisfy this requirement by meeting one of the safe harbors in paragraph (b) of this section. Plans that do not provide uniform allocations may satisfy this requirement by satisfying the general test in paragraph (c) of this section. See § 1.401(a)(4)-1(b)(2)(ii)(B) for the exclusive tests applicable to section 401(k) plans and section 401(m) plans.

(2) *Alternative methods of satisfying nondiscriminatory amount requirement.* A defined contribution plan is permitted to satisfy paragraph (b)(2) or (c) of this section on a restructured basis pursuant to § 1.401(a)(4)-9(c). Alternatively, a defined contribution plan (other than an ESOP) is permitted to satisfy the nondiscriminatory amount requirement of § 1.401(a)(4)-1(b)(2)(ii)(A) on the basis of equivalent benefits pursuant to § 1.401(a)(4)-8(b).

(b) *Safe harbors*—(1) *In general.* The employer contributions allocated under a defined contribution plan are nondiscriminatory in amount for a plan year if the plan satisfies either of the safe harbors in paragraph (b)(2) or (b)(3) of this section. Paragraph (b)(4) of this section provides exceptions for certain plan provisions that do not cause a plan to fail to satisfy this paragraph (b).

(2) *Safe harbor for plans with uniform allocation formula*—(i) *General rule*. A defined contribution plan satisfies the safe harbor in this paragraph (b)(2) for a plan year if the plan allocates all amounts taken into account under paragraph (c)(2)(ii) of this section for the plan year under an allocation formula that allocates to each employee the same percentage of plan year compensation, the same dollar amount, or the same dollar amount for each uniform unit of service (not to exceed one week) performed by the employee during the plan year.

(ii) *Permitted disparity*. If a plan satisfies section 401(l) in form, differences in employees' allocations under the plan attributable to uniform disparities permitted under § 1.401(l)-2 (including differences in disparities that are deemed uniform under § 1.401(l)-2(c)(2)) do not cause the plan to fail to satisfy this paragraph (b)(2).

(3) *Safe harbor for plans with uniform points allocation formula*—(i) *General rule*. A defined contribution plan (other than an ESOP) satisfies the safe harbor in this paragraph (b)(3) for a plan year if it satisfies both of the following requirements:

(A) The plan must allocate amounts under a uniform points allocation formula. A uniform points allocation formula defines each employee's allocation for the plan year as the product of the total of all amounts taken into account under paragraph (c)(2)(ii) of this section and a fraction, the numerator of which is the employee's points for the plan year and the denominator of which is the sum of the points of all employees in the plan for the plan year. For this purpose, an employee's points for a plan year equal the sum of the employee's points for age, service, and units of plan year compensation for the plan year. Under a uniform points allocation formula, each employee must receive the same number of points for

each year of age, the same number of points for each year of service, and the same number of points for each unit of plan year compensation. (See § 1.401(a)(4)-11(d)(3) regarding service that may be taken into account as years of service.) A uniform points allocation formula need not grant points for both age and service, but it must grant points for at least one of them. If the allocation formula grants points for years of service, the plan is permitted to limit the number of years of service taken into account to a single maximum number of years of service. A uniform points allocation formula need not grant points for units of plan year compensation, but if it does, the unit used must be a single dollar amount for all employees that does not exceed $200.

(B) For the plan year, the average of the allocation rates for the HCEs in the plan must not exceed the average of the allocation rates for the NHCEs in the plan. For this purpose, allocation rates are determined in accordance with paragraph (c)(2) of this section, without imputing permitted disparity and without grouping allocation rates under paragraphs (c)(2)(iv) and (v) of this section, respectively.

* * *

(c) *General test for nondiscrimination in amount of contributions*—(1) *General rule*. The employer contributions allocated under a defined contribution plan are nondiscriminatory in amount for a plan year if each rate group under the plan satisfies section 410(b). For purposes of this paragraph (c), a rate group exists under a plan for each HCE and consists of the HCE and all other employees in the plan (both HCEs and NHCEs) who have an allocation rate greater than or equal to the HCE's allocation rate. Thus, an employee is in the rate group for each HCE who has an allocation rate less than or equal to the employee's allocation rate.

(2) *Determination of allocation rates*—(i) *General rule*. The allocation rate for an employee for a plan year equals the sum of the allocations to the employee's account for the plan year, expressed either as a percentage of plan year compensation or as a dollar amount.

(ii) *Allocations taken into account.* The amounts taken into account in determining allocation rates for a plan year include all employer contributions and forfeitures that are allocated or treated as allocated to the account of an employee under the plan for the plan year, other than amounts described in paragraph (c)(2)(iii) of this section. For this purpose, employer contributions include annual additions described in § 1.415(c)-1(b)(4) (regarding amounts arising from certain transactions between the plan and the employer). In the case of a defined contribution plan subject to section 412, an employer contribution is taken into account in the plan year for which it is required to be contributed and allocated to employees' accounts under the plan, even if all or part of the required contribution is not actually made.

(iii) *Allocations not taken into account.* Allocations of income, expenses, gains, and losses attributable to the balance in an employee's account are not taken into account in determining allocation rates.

(iv) *Imputation of permitted disparity.* The disparity permitted under section 401(l) may be imputed in accordance with the rules of § 1.401(a)(4)-7.

(v) *Grouping of allocation rates*—(A) *General rule.* An employer may treat all employees who have allocation rates within a specified range above and below a midpoint rate chosen by the employer as having an allocation rate equal to the midpoint rate within that range. Allocation rates within a given range may not be grouped under this paragraph (c)(2)(v) if the allocation rates of HCEs within the range generally are significantly higher than the allocation rates of NHCEs in the range. The specified ranges within which all employees are treated as having the same allocation rate may not overlap and may be no larger than provided in paragraph (c)(2)(v)(B) of this section. Allocation rates of employees that are not within any of these specified ranges are determined without regard to this paragraph (c)(2)(v).

(B) *Size of specified ranges.* The lowest and highest allocation rates in the range must be within five percent (not five percentage points) of the midpoint rate. If allocation rates are determined as a percentage of plan year compensation, the lowest and highest allocation rates need not be within five percent of the midpoint rate, if they are no more than one quarter of a percentage point above or below the midpoint rate.

(vi) *Consistency requirement.* Allocation rates must be determined in a consistent manner for all employees for the plan year.

(3) *Satisfaction of section 410(b) by a rate group*—(i) *General rule.* For purposes of determining whether a rate group satisfies section 410(b), the rate group is treated as if it were a separate plan that benefits only the employees included in the rate group for the plan year. Thus, for example, under § 1.401(a)(4)-1(c)(4)(iv), the ratio percentage of the rate group is determined taking into account all nonexcludable employees regardless of whether they benefit under the plan. Paragraph (c)(3) (ii) and (iii) of this section provide additional special rules for determining whether a rate group satisfies section 410(b).

(ii) *Application of nondiscriminatory classification test.* A rate group satisfies the nondiscriminatory classification test of § 1.410(b)-4 (including the reasonable classification requirement of § 1.410(b)-4(b)) if and only if the ratio percentage of the rate group is greater than or equal to the lesser of—

(A) The midpoint between the safe and the unsafe harbor percentages applicable to the plan; and

(B) The ratio percentage of the plan.

(iii) *Application of average benefit percentage test.* A rate group satisfies the average benefit percentage test of § 1.410(b)-5 if the plan of which it is a part satisfies § 1.410(b)-5 (without regard to § 1.410(b)-5(f)). In the case of a plan that relies on § 1.410(b)-5(f) to satisfy the average benefit percentage test, each rate group under the plan satisfies the average benefit percentage test (if applicable) only if the rate group separately satisfies § 1.410(b)-5(f).

(4) *Examples*. The following examples illustrate the general test in this paragraph (c):

Example 1. Employer X maintains two defined contribution plans, Plan A and Plan B, that are aggregated and treated as a single plan for purposes of sections 410(b) and 401(a)(4) pursuant to § 1.410(b)-7(d). For the 1994 plan year, Employee M has plan year compensation of $10,000 and receives an allocation of $200 under Plan A and an allocation of $800 under Plan B. Employee M's allocation rate under the aggregated plan for the 1994 plan year is 10 percent (i.e., $1,000 divided by $10,000).

* * *

Example 3. (a) Employer Y has only six nonexcludable employees, all of whom benefit under Plan D. The HCEs are H1 and H2, and the NHCEs are N1 through N4. For the 1994 plan year, H1 and N1 through N4 have an allocation rate of 5.0 percent of plan year compensation. For the same plan year, H2 has an allocation rate of 7.5 percent of plan year compensation.

(b) There are two rate groups under Plan D. Rate group 1 consists of H1 and all those employees who have an allocation rate greater than or equal to H1's allocation rate (5.0 percent). Thus, rate group 1 consists of H1, H2, and N1 through N4. Rate group 2 consists only of H2 because no other employee has an allocation rate greater than or equal to H2's allocation rate (7.5 percent).

(c) The ratio percentage for rate group 2 is zero percent—i.e., zero percent (the percentage of all nonhighly compensated nonexcludable employees who are in the rate group) divided by 50 percent (the percentage of all highly compensated nonexcludable employees who are in the rate group). Therefore rate group 2 does not satisfy the ratio percentage test under § 1.410(b)-2(b)(2). Rate group 2 also does not satisfy the nondiscriminatory classification test of § 1.410(b)-4 (as modified by paragraph (c)(3) of this section). Rate

group 2 therefore does not satisfy section 410(b) and, as a result, Plan D does not satisfy the general test in paragraph (c)(1) of this section. This is true regardless of whether rate group 1 satisfies § 1.410(b)-2(b)(2).

Example 4. (a) The facts are the same as in Example 3, except that N4 has an allocation rate of 8.0 percent.

(b) There are two rate groups in Plan D. Rate group 1 consists of H1 and all those employees who have an allocation rate greater than or equal to H1's allocation rate (5.0 percent). Thus, rate group 1 consists of H1, H2 and N1 through N4. Rate group 2 consists of H2, and all those employees who have an allocation rate greater than or equal to H2's allocation rate (7.5 percent). Thus, rate group 2 consists of H2 and N4.

(c) Rate group 1 satisfies the ratio percentage test under § 1.410(b)-2(b)(2) because the ratio percentage of the rate group is 100 percent—i.e., 100 percent (the percentage of all nonhighly compensated nonexcludable employees who are in the rate group) divided by 100 percent (the percentage of all highly compensated nonexcludable employees who are in the rate group).

(d) Rate group 2 does not satisfy the ratio percentage test of § 1.410(b)-2(b)(2) because the ratio percentage of the rate group is 50 percent—i.e., 25 percent (the percentage of all nonhighly compensated nonexcludable employees who are in the rate group) divided by 50 percent (the percentage of all highly compensated nonexcludable employees who are in the rate group).

(e) However, rate group 2 does satisfy the nondiscriminatory classification test of § 1.410(b)-4 because the ratio percentage of the rate group (50 percent) is greater than the safe harbor percentage applicable to the plan under § 1.410(b)-4(c)(4) (45.5 percent).

(f) Under paragraph (c)(3)(iii) of this section, rate group 2 satisfies the average benefit percentage test, if Plan D satisfies the average benefit percentage test. (The requirement that Plan D satisfy the average benefit percentage test applies even though Plan D satisfies the ratio percentage test and would ordinarily not need to run the average benefit percentage test.) If Plan D satisfies the average benefit percentage test, then rate group 2 satisfies section 410(b) and thus, Plan D satisfies the general test in paragraph (c)(1) of this section, because each rate group under the plan satisfies section 410(b).

* * *

§ 1.401(a)(4)-3. Nondiscrimination in amount of employer-provided benefits under a defined benefit plan.

(a) *Introduction*—(1) *Overview.* This section provides rules for determining whether the employer-provided benefits under a defined benefit plan are nondiscriminatory in amount as required by § 1.401(a)(4)-1(b)(2)(iii). Certain defined benefit plans that provide uniform benefits are permitted to satisfy this requirement by meeting one of the safe harbors in paragraph (b) of this section. Plans that do not provide uniform benefits may satisfy this requirement by satisfying the general test in paragraph (c) of this section. Paragraph (d) of this section provides rules for determining the individual benefit accrual rates needed for the general test. Paragraph (e) of this section provides rules for determining compensation for purposes of applying the requirements of this section. Paragraph (f) of this section provides additional rules that apply generally for purposes of both the safe harbors in paragraph (b) of this section and the general test in paragraph (c) of this section. See § 1.401(a)(4)-6 for rules for determining the amount of employer-provided benefits under a contributory DB plan, and for determining whether the employee-provided benefits under such a plan are nondiscriminatory in amount.

(2) *Alternative methods of satisfying non-discriminatory amount requirement.* A defined benefit plan is permitted to satisfy paragraph (b) or (c) of this section on a restructured basis pursuant to § 1.401(a)(4)-9(c). Alternatively, a defined benefit plan is permitted to satisfy the nondiscriminatory amount requirement of

§ 1.401(a)(4)-1(b)(2)(iii) on the basis of equivalent allocations pursuant to § 1.401(a)(4)-8(c). In addition, a defined benefit plan that is part of a floor-offset arrangement is permitted to satisfy this section pursuant to § 1.401(a)(4)-8(d).

(b) *Safe harbors*—(1) *In general.* The employer-provided benefits under a defined benefit plan are nondiscriminatory in amount for a plan year if the plan satisfies each of the uniformity requirements of paragraph (b)(2) of this section and any one of the safe harbors in paragraphs (b)(3) (unit credit plans), (b)(4) (fractional accrual plans), and (b)(5) (insurance contract plans) of this section. Paragraph (b)(6) of this section provides exceptions for certain plan provisions that do not cause a plan to fail to satisfy this paragraph (b). Paragraph (f) of this section provides additional rules that apply in determining whether a plan satisfies this paragraph (b).

(2) *Uniformity requirements*—(i) *Uniform normal retirement benefit.* The same benefit formula must apply to all employees. The benefit formula must provide all employees with an annual benefit payable in the same form commencing at the same uniform normal retirement age. The annual benefit must be the same percentage of average annual compensation or the same dollar amount for all employees who will have the same number of years of service at normal retirement age. (See § 1.401(a)(4)-11(d)(3) regarding service that may be taken into account as years of service.) The annual benefit must equal the employee's accrued benefit at normal retirement age (within the meaning of section 411(a)(7)(A)(i)) and must be the normal retirement benefit under the plan (within the meaning of section 411(a)(9)).

(ii) *Uniform post-normal retirement benefit.* With respect to an employee with a given number of years of service at any age after normal retirement age, the annual benefit commencing at that employee's age must be the same percentage of average annual compensation or the same dollar amount that would be payable commencing at normal retirement age to an employee who had that same number of years of service at normal retirement age.

(iii) *Uniform subsidies.* Each subsidized optional form of benefit available under the plan must be currently available (within the meaning of § 1.401(a)(4)-4(b)(2)) to substantially all employees. Whether an optional form of benefit is considered subsidized for this purpose may be determined using any reasonable actuarial assumptions.

(iv) *No employee contributions.* The plan must not be a contributory DB plan.

(v) *Period of accrual.* Each employee's benefit must be accrued over the same years of service that are taken into account in applying the benefit formula under the plan to that employee. For this purpose, any year in which the employee benefits under the plan (within the meaning of § 1.410(b)-3(a)) is included as a year of service in which a benefit accrues. Thus, for example, a plan does not satisfy the safe harbor in paragraph (b)(4) of this section unless the plan uses the same years of service to determine both the normal retirement benefit under the plan's benefit formula and the fraction by which an employee's fractional rule benefit is multiplied to derive the employee's accrued benefit as of any plan year.

(vi) *Examples.* The following examples illustrate the rules in this paragraph (b)(2):

Example 1. Plan A provides a normal retirement benefit equal to two percent of average annual compensation times each year of service commencing at age 65 for all employees. Plan A provides that employees of Division S receive their benefit in the form of a straight life annuity and that employees of Division T receive their benefit in the form of a life annuity with an automatic cost-of-living increase. Plan A does not provide a uniform normal retirement benefit within the meaning of paragraph (b)(2)(i) of this section because the annual benefit is not payable in the same form to all employees.

Example 2. Plan B provides a normal retirement benefit equal to 1.5 percent of average annual compensation times each year of

service at normal retirement age for all employees. The normal retirement age under the plan is the earlier of age 65 or the age at which the employee completes 10 years of service, but in no event earlier than age 62. Plan B does not provide a uniform normal retirement benefit within the meaning of paragraph (b)(2)(i) of this section because the same uniform normal retirement age does not apply to all employees.

＊ ＊ ＊

(3) *Safe harbor for unit credit plans*—(i) *General rule.* A plan satisfies the safe harbor in this paragraph (b)(3) for a plan year if it satisfies both of the following requirements:

(A) The plan must satisfy the 133 1/3 percent accrual rule of section 411(b)(1)(B).

(B) Each employee's accrued benefit under the plan as of any plan year must be determined by applying the plan's benefit formula to the employee's years of service and (if applicable) average annual compensation, both determined as of that plan year.

(ii) *Example.* The following example illustrates the rules in this paragraph (b)(3):

Example. Plan A provides that the accrued benefit of each employee as of any plan year equals the employee's average annual compensation times a percentage that depends on the employee's years of service determined as of that plan year. The percentage is 2 percent for each of the first 10 years of service, plus 1.5 percent for each of the next 10 years of service, plus 2 percent for all additional years of service. Plan A satisfies this paragraph (b)(3).

(4) *Safe harbor for plans using fractional accrual rule*—(i) *General rule.* A plan satisfies the safe harbor in this paragraph (b)(4) for a plan year if it satisfies each of the following requirements:

(A) The plan must satisfy the fractional accrual rule of section 411(b)(1)(C).

(B) Each employee's accrued benefit under the plan as of any plan year before the employee reaches normal retirement age must be determined by multiplying the employee's fractional rule benefit (within the meaning of § 1.411(b)-1(b)(3)(ii)(A)) by a fraction, the numerator of which is the employee's years of service determined as of the plan year, and the denominator of which is the employee's projected years of service as of normal retirement age.

(C) The plan must satisfy one of the following requirements:

(1) Under the plan, it must be impossible for any employee to accrue in a plan year a portion of the normal retirement benefit described in paragraph (b)(2)(i) of this section that is more than one-third larger than the portion of the same benefit accrued in that or any other plan year by any other employee, when each portion of the benefit is expressed as a percentage of each employee's average annual compensation or as a dollar amount. In making this determination, actual and potential employees in the plan with any amount of service at normal retirement must be taken into account (other than employees with more than 33 years of service at normal retirement age). In addition, in the case of a plan that satisfies section 401(l) in form, an employee is treated as accruing benefits at a rate equal to the excess benefit percentage in the case of a defined benefit excess plan or at a rate equal to the gross benefit percentage in the case of an offset plan.

(2) The normal retirement benefit under the plan must be a flat benefit that requires a minimum of 25 years of service at normal retirement age for an employee to receive the unreduced flat benefit, determined without regard to section 415. For this purpose, a flat benefit is a benefit that is the same percentage of average annual compensation or the same dollar amount for all employees who have a minimum number of years of service at normal retirement age (e.g., 50 percent of average annual compensation), with a pro rata reduction in the flat benefit for employees who have less than the minimum number of years of service at normal retirement age. An employee is permitted to accrue the maximum benefit permitted under section 415 over a period of

less than 25 years, provided that the flat benefit under the plan, determined without regard to section 415, can accrue over no less than 25 years.

(3) The plan must satisfy the requirements of paragraph (b)(4)(i)(C)(2) of this section (other than the requirement that the minimum number of years of service for receiving the unreduced flat benefit is at least 25 years), and, for the plan year, the average of the normal accrual rates for all nonhighly compensated nonexcludable employees must be at least 70 percent of the average of the normal accrual rates for all highly compensated nonexcludable employees. The averages in the preceding sentence are determined taking into account all nonexcludable employees (regardless of whether they benefit under the plan). In addition, contributions and benefits under other plans of the employer are disregarded. For purposes of this paragraph (b)(4)(i)(C)(3), normal accrual rates are determined under paragraph (d) of this section.

(ii) *Examples.* The following examples illustrate the rules in this paragraph (b)(4). In each example, it is assumed that the plan has never permitted employee contributions.

Example 1. Plan A provides a normal retirement benefit equal to 1.6 percent of average annual compensation times each year of service up to 25. Plan A further provides that an employee's accrued benefit as of any plan year equals the employee's fractional rule benefit multiplied by a fraction, the numerator of which is the employee's years of service as of the plan year, and the denominator of which is the employee's projected years of service as of normal retirement age. The greatest benefit that an employee could accrue in any plan year is 1.6 percent of average annual compensation (this is the case for an employee with 25 or fewer years of projected service at normal retirement age). Among potential employees with 33 or fewer years of projected service at normal retirement age, the lowest benefit that an employee could accrue in any plan year is 1.212 percent of average annual compensation (this is the case for an employee with 33 years of projected service at normal retirement age). Plan A satisfies paragraph (b)(4)(i)(C)(1) of this section because 1.6 percent is not more than one third larger than 1.212 percent.

* * *

(6) *Use of safe harbors not precluded by certain plan provisions*—(i) *In general.* A plan does not fail to satisfy this paragraph (b) merely because the plan contains one or more of the provisions described in this paragraph (b)(6). Unless otherwise provided, any such provision must apply uniformly to all employees.

(ii) *Section 401(l) permitted disparity.* The plan takes permitted disparity into account in a manner that satisfies section 401(l) in form. Thus, differences in employees' benefits under the plan attributable to uniform disparities permitted under § 1.401(l)-3 (including differences in disparities that are deemed uniform under § 1.401(l)-3(c)(2)) do not cause a plan to fail to satisfy this paragraph (b).

(iii) *Different entry dates.* The plan provides one or more entry dates during the plan year as permitted by section 410(a)(4).

(iv) *Certain conditions on accruals.* The plan provides that an employee's accrual for the plan year is less than a full accrual (including a zero accrual) because of a plan provision permitted by the year-of-participation rules of section 411(b)(4).

(v) *Certain limits on accruals.* The plan limits benefits otherwise provided under the benefit formula or accrual method to a maximum dollar amount or to a maximum percentage of average annual compensation (e.g., by limiting service taken into account in the benefit formula) or in accordance with section 401(a)(5)(D), applies the limits of section 415, or limits the dollar amount of compensation taken into account in determining benefits.

(vi) *Dollar accrual per uniform unit of service.* The plan determines accruals based on the same dollar amount for each uniform unit of service (not to exceed one week) performed by each employee with the same number of years of service under the plan during

the plan year. The preceding sentence applies solely for purposes of the unit credit safe harbor in paragraph (b)(3) of this section.

(vii) *Prior benefits accrued under a different formula.* The plan determines benefits for years of service after a fresh-start date for all employees under a benefit formula and accrual method that differ from the benefit formula and accrual method previously used to determine benefit accruals for employees in a fresh-start group for years of service before the fresh-start date. This paragraph (b)(6)(vii) applies solely to plans that satisfy § 1.401(a)(4)-13(c) with respect to the fresh start.

(viii) *Employee contributions.* The plan is a contributory DB plan that would satisfy the requirements of paragraph (b) of this section if the plan's benefit formula provided benefits at employees' employer-provided benefit rates determined under § 1.401(a)(4)-6(b). This paragraph (b)(6)(viii) does not apply to a plan tested under paragraph (b)(4) or (b)(5) of this section unless the plan satisfies one of the methods in § 1.401(a)(4)-6(b)(4) through (b)(6). A minimum benefit added to the plan solely to satisfy § 1.401(a)(4)-6(b)(3) is not taken into account in determining whether this paragraph (b)(6)(viii) is satisfied.

(ix) *Certain subsidized optional forms.* The plan provides a subsidized optional form of benefit that is available to fewer than substantially all employees because the optional form of benefit has been eliminated prospectively as provided in § 1.401(a)(4)-4(b)(3).

(x) *Lower benefits for HCEs*—(A) *General rule.* The benefits (including any subsidized optional form of benefit) provided to one or more HCEs under the plan are inherently less valuable to those HCEs (determined by applying the principles of § 1.401(a)(4)-4(d)(4)) than the benefits that would otherwise be provided to those HCEs if the plan satisfied this paragraph (b) (determined without regard to this paragraph (b)(6)(x)). These inherently less valuable benefits are deemed to satisfy this paragraph (b).

* * *

(c) *General test for nondiscrimination in amount of benefits*—(1) *General rule.* The employer-provided benefits under a defined benefit plan are nondiscriminatory in amount for a plan year if each rate group under the plan satisfies section 410(b). For purposes of this paragraph (c)(1), a rate group exists under a plan for each HCE and consists of the HCE and all other employees (both HCEs and NHCEs) who have a normal accrual rate greater than or equal to the HCE's normal accrual rate, and who also have a most valuable accrual rate greater than or equal to the HCE's most valuable accrual rate. Thus, an employee is in the rate group for each HCE who has a normal accrual rate less than or equal to the employee's normal accrual rate, and who also has a most valuable accrual rate less than or equal to the employee's most valuable accrual rate.

(2) *Satisfaction of section 410(b) by a rate group.* For purposes of determining whether a rate group satisfies section 410(b), the same rules apply as in § 1.401(a)(4)-2(c)(3). See paragraph (c)(4) of this section and § 1.401(a)(4)-2(c)(4), Example 3 through Example 5, for examples of this rule.

* * *

(d) *Determination of accrual rates*—(1) *Definitions*—(i) *Normal accrual rate.* The normal accrual rate for an employee for a plan year is the increase in the employee's accrued benefit (within the meaning of section 411(a)(7)(A)(i)) during the measurement period, divided by the employee's testing service during the measurement period, and expressed either as a dollar amount or as a percentage of the employee's average annual compensation.

(ii) *Most valuable accrual rate.* The most valuable accrual rate for an employee for a plan year is the increase in the employee's most valuable optional form of payment of the accrued benefit during the measurement period, divided by the employee's testing service during the measurement period, and expressed either as a dollar amount or as a percentage of the employee's average annual compensation. The employee's most valuable optional form

of payment of the accrued benefit is determined by calculating for the employee the normalized QJSA associated with the accrued benefit that is potentially payable in the current or any future plan year at any age under the plan and selecting the largest (per year of testing service). If the plan provides a QSUPP, the most valuable accrual rate also takes into account the QSUPP payable in conjunction with the QJSA at each age under the plan. Thus, the most valuable accrual rate reflects the value of all benefits accrued or treated as accrued under section 411(d)(6) that are payable in any form and at any time under the plan, including early retirement benefits, retirement-type subsidies, early retirement window benefits, and QSUPPs. In addition, the most valuable accrual rate must take into account any such benefits that are available during a plan year, even if the benefits cease to be available before the end of the current or any future plan year.

(iii) *Measurement period.* The measurement period can be—

(A) The current plan year;

(B) The current plan year and all prior years; or

(C) The current plan year and all prior and future years.

(iv) *Testing service*—(A) *General rule.* Testing service means an employee's years of service as defined in the plan for purposes of applying the benefit formula under the plan, subject to the requirements of paragraph (d)(1)(iv)(B) of this section. Alternatively, testing service means service determined for all employees in a reasonable manner that satisfies the requirements of paragraph (d)(1)(iv)(B) of this section. For example, the number of plan years that an employee has benefited under the plan within the meaning of § 1.410(b)-3(a) is an acceptable definition of testing service because it determines service in a reasonable manner and satisfies paragraph (d)(1)(iv)(B) of this section. See also § 1.401(a)(4)-11(d)(3) (additional limits on service that may be taken into account as testing service).

(B) *Requirements for testing service*—(1) Employees not credited with years of service under the benefit formula. An employee must be credited with testing service for any year in which the employee benefits under the plan (within the meaning of § 1.410(b)-3(a)), unless that year is part of a period of service that may not be taken into account under § 1.401(a)(4)-11(d)(3). This rule applies even if the employee does not receive service credit under the benefit formula for that year (e.g., because of a service cap in the benefit formula or because of a transfer out of the group of employees covered by the plan).

(2) *Current year testing service.* In the case of a measurement period that is the current plan year, testing service for the plan year equals one (1).

* * *

§ 1.401(a)(4)-4. Nondiscriminatory availability of benefits, rights, and features.

(a) *Introduction.* This section provides rules for determining whether the benefits, rights, and features provided under a plan (i.e., all optional forms of benefit, ancillary benefits, and other rights and features available to any employee under the plan) are made available in a nondiscriminatory manner. Benefits, rights, and features provided under a plan are made available to employees in a nondiscriminatory manner only if each benefit, right, or feature satisfies the current availability requirement of paragraph (b) of this section and the effective availability requirement of paragraph (c) of this section. Paragraph (d) of this section provides special rules for applying these requirements. Paragraph (e) of this section defines optional form of benefit, ancillary benefit, and other right or feature.

(b) *Current availability*—(1) *General rule.* The current availability requirement of this paragraph (b) is satisfied if the group of employees to whom a benefit, right, or feature is currently available during the plan year satisfies section 410(b) (without regard to the average benefit percentage test of § 1.410(b)-5). In determining whether the group of employees satisfies section 410(b), an employee is treated as benefiting only if the benefit, right, or feature is currently available to the employee.

(2) *Determination of current availability*—(i) *General rule.* Whether a benefit, right, or feature that is subject to specified eligibility conditions is currently available to an employee generally is determined based on the current facts and circumstances with respect to the employee (e.g., current compensation, accrued benefit, position, or net worth).

(ii) *Certain conditions disregarded*—(A) *Certain age and service conditions*—(1) *General rule.* Notwithstanding paragraph (b)(2)(i) of this section, any specified age or service condition with respect to an optional form of benefit or a social security supplement is disregarded in determining whether the optional form of benefit or the social security supplement is currently available to an employee. Thus, for example, an optional form of benefit that is available to all employees who terminate employment on or after age 55 with at least 10 years of service is treated as currently available to an employee, without regard to the employee's current age or years of service, and without regard to whether the employee could potentially meet the age and service conditions prior to attaining the plan's normal retirement age.

(2) *Time-limited age or service conditions not disregarded.* Notwithstanding paragraph (b)(2)(ii)(A)(1) of this section, an age or service condition is not disregarded in determining the current availability of an optional form of benefit or social security supplement if the condition must be satisfied within a limited period of time. However, in determining the current availability of an optional form of benefit or a social security supplement subject to such an age or service condition, the age and service of employees may be projected to the last date by which the age condition or service condition must be satisfied in order to be eligible for the optional form of benefit or social security supplement under the plan. Thus, for example, an optional form of benefit that is available only to employees who terminate employment between July 1, 1995, and

December 31, 1995, after attainment of age 55 with at least 10 years of service is treated as currently available to an employee only if the employee could satisfy those age and service conditions by December 31, 1995.

(B) *Certain other conditions*. Specified conditions on the availability of a benefit, right, or feature requiring a specified percentage of the employee's accrued benefit to be nonforfeitable, termination of employment, death, satisfaction of a specified health condition (or failure to meet such condition), disability, hardship, family status, default on a plan loan secured by a participant's account balance, execution of a covenant not to compete, application for benefits or similar ministerial or mechanical acts, election of a benefit form, execution of a waiver of rights under the Age Discrimination in Employment Act or other federal or state law, or absence from service, are disregarded in determining the employees to whom the benefit, right, or feature is currently available. In addition, if a multiemployer plan includes a reasonable condition that limits eligibility for an ancillary benefit, or other right or feature, to those employees who have recent service under the plan (e.g., a condition on a death benefit that requires an employee to have a minimum number of hours credited during the last two years) and the condition applies to all employees in the multiemployer plan (including the collectively bargained employees) to whom the ancillary benefit, or other right or feature, is otherwise currently available, then the condition is disregarded in determining the employees to whom the ancillary benefit, or other right or feature, is currently available.

(C) *Certain conditions relating to mandatory cash-outs*. In the case of a plan that provides for mandatory cash-outs of all terminated employees who have a vested accrued benefit with an actuarial present value less than or equal to a specified dollar amount (not to exceed the cash-out limit in effect under § 1.411(a)-11(c)(3)(ii)) as permitted by sections 411(a)(11) and 417(e), the implicit condition on any benefit, right, or feature (other than the mandatory cash-out) that requires the employee to have a vested accrued benefit with an actuarial present value in excess of the specified dollar amount is disregarded in determining the employees to whom the benefit, right, or feature is currently available.

(D) *Other dollar limits*. A condition that the amount of an employee's vested accrued benefit or the actuarial present value of that benefit be less than or equal to a specified dollar amount is disregarded in determining the employees to whom the benefit, right, or feature is currently available.

(E) *Certain conditions on plan loans*. In the case of an employee's right to a loan from the plan, the condition that an employee must have an account balance sufficient to be eligible to receive a minimum loan amount specified in the plan (not to exceed $1,000) is disregarded in determining the employees to whom the right is currently available.

(3) *Benefits, rights, and features that are eliminated prospectively*—(i) *Special testing rule*. Notwithstanding paragraph (b)(1) of this section, a benefit, right, or feature that is eliminated with respect to benefits accrued after the later of the eliminating amendment's adoption or effective date (the elimination date), but is retained with respect to benefits accrued as of the elimination date, and that satisfies this paragraph (b) as of the elimination date, is treated as satisfying this paragraph (b) for all subsequent periods. This rule does not apply if the terms of the benefit, right, or feature (including the employees to whom it is available) are changed after the elimination date.

(ii) *Elimination of a benefit, right, or feature*—(A) *General rule*. For purposes of this paragraph (b)(3), a benefit, right, or feature provided to an employee is eliminated with respect to benefits accrued after the elimination date if the amount or value of the benefit, right, or feature depends solely on the amount of the employee's accrued benefit (within the meaning of section 411(a)(7)) as of the elimination date, including subsequent income, expenses, gains, and losses with respect to that benefit in the case of a defined contribution plan.

(B) *Special rule for benefits, rights, and features that are not section 411(d)(6)-protected benefits*. Notwithstanding paragraph (b)(3)(ii)(A) of this section, in the case of a benefit, right, or feature under a defined contribution plan that is not a section 411(d)(6)-protected benefit (within the meaning of § 1.411(d)-4, Q&A-1), e.g., the availability of plan loans, for purposes of this paragraph (b)(3)(ii) each employee's accrued benefit as of the elimination date may be treated, on a uniform basis, as consisting exclusively of the dollar amount of the employee's account balance as of the elimination date.

(C) *Special rule for benefits, rights, and features that depend on adjusted accrued benefits*. For purposes of this paragraph (b)(3), a benefit, right, or feature provided to an employee under a plan that has made a fresh start does not fail to be eliminated as of an elimination date that is the fresh-start date merely because it depends solely on the amount of the employee's adjusted accrued benefit (within the meaning of § 1.401(a)(4)-13(d)(8)).

(c) *Effective availability*—(1) *General rule*. Based on all of the relevant facts and circumstances, the group of employees to whom a benefit, right, or feature is effectively available must not substantially favor HCEs.

(2) *Examples*. The following examples illustrate the rules of this paragraph (c):

Example 1. Employer X maintains Plan A, a defined benefit plan that covers both of its highly compensated nonexcludable employees and nine of its 12 nonhighly compensated nonexcludable employees. Plan A provides for a normal retirement benefit payable as an annuity and based on a normal retirement age of 65, and an early retirement benefit payable upon termination in the form of an annuity to employees who terminate from service with the employer on or after age 55 with 30 or more years of service. Both HCEs of Employer X currently meet the age and service requirement, or will have 30 years of service by the time they reach age 55. All but two of the nine NHCEs of Employer X who are covered by Plan A were hired on or after

age 35 and, thus, cannot qualify for the early retirement benefit. Even though the group of employees to whom the early retirement benefit is currently available satisfies the ratio percentage test of § 1.410(b)-2(b)(2) when age and service are disregarded pursuant to paragraph (b)(2)(ii)(A) of this section, absent other facts, the group of employees to whom the early retirement benefit is effectively available substantially favors HCEs.

Example 2. Employer Y maintains Plan B, a defined benefit plan that provides for a normal retirement benefit payable as an annuity and based on a normal retirement age of 65. By a plan amendment first adopted and effective December 1, 1998, Employer Y amends Plan B to provide an early retirement benefit that is available only to employees who terminate employment by December 15, 1998, and who are at least age 55 with 30 or more years of service. Assume that all employees were hired prior to attaining age 25 and that the group of employees who have, or will have, attained age 55 with 30 years of service by December 15, 1998, satisfies the ratio percentage test of § 1.410(b)-2(b)(2). Assume, further, that the employer takes no steps to inform all eligible employees of the early retirement option on a timely basis and that the only employees who terminate from employment with the employer during the two-week period in which the early retirement benefit is available are HCEs. Under these facts, the group of employees to whom this early retirement window benefit is effectively available substantially favors HCEs.

* * *

§ 1.401(a)(4)-5. Plan amendments and plan terminations.

(a) *Introduction*—(1) *Overview*. This paragraph (a) provides rules for determining whether the timing of a plan amendment or series of amendments has the effect of discriminating significantly in favor of HCEs or former HCEs. For purposes of this section, a plan amendment includes, for example, the establishment or termination of the plan, and any change in the benefits, rights, or features, benefit formulas, or allocation formulas under the plan. Paragraph (b) of this section sets forth additional requirements that must be satisfied in the case of a plan termination.

(2) *Facts-and-circumstances determination.* Whether the timing of a plan amendment or series of plan amendments has the effect of discriminating significantly in favor of HCEs or former HCEs is determined at the time the plan amendment first becomes effective for purposes of section 401(a), based on all of the relevant facts and circumstances. These include, for example, the relative numbers of current and former HCEs and NHCEs affected by the plan amendment, the relative length of service of current and former HCEs and NHCEs, the length of time the plan or plan provision being amended has been in effect, and the turnover of employees prior to the plan amendment. In addition, the relevant facts and circumstances include the relative accrued benefits of current and former HCEs and NHCEs before and after the plan amendment and any additional benefits provided to current and former HCEs and NHCEs under other plans (including plans of other employers, if relevant). In the case of a plan amendment that provides additional benefits based on an employee's service prior to the amendment, the relevant facts and circumstances also include the benefits that employees and former employees who do not benefit under the amendment would have received had the plan, as amended, been in effect throughout the period on which the additional benefits are based.

(3) *Safe harbor for certain grants of benefits for past periods.* The timing of a plan amendment that credits (or increases benefits attributable to) years of service for a period in the past is deemed not to have the effect of discriminating significantly in favor of HCEs or former HCEs if the period for which the service credit (or benefit increase) is granted does not exceed the five years immediately preceding the year in which the amendment first becomes effective, the service credit (or benefit increase) is granted on a reasonably uniform basis to all employees, benefits at-tributable to the period are determined by applying the current plan formula, and the service credited is service (including pre-participation or imputed service) with the employer or a previous employer that may be taken into account under § 1.401(a)(4)-11(d)(3) (without regard to § 1.401(a)(4)-11(d)(3)(i)(B)). However, this safe harbor is not available if the plan amendment granting the service credit (or increasing benefits) is part of a pattern of amendments that has the effect of discriminating significantly in favor of HCEs or former HCEs.

(4) *Examples.* The following examples illustrate the rules in this paragraph (a):

Example 1. Plan A is a defined benefit plan that covered both HCEs and NHCEs for most of its existence. The employer decides to wind up its business. In the process of ceasing operations, but at a time when the plan covers only HCEs, Plan A is amended to increase benefits and thereafter is terminated. The timing of this plan amendment has the effect of discriminating significantly in favor of HCEs.

* * *

Example 4. Plan D provides for a benefit of one percent of average annual compensation per year of service. Ten years after Plan D is adopted, it is amended to provide a benefit of two percent of average annual compensation per year of service, including years of service prior to the amendment. The amendment is effective only for employees currently employed at the time of the amendment. The ratio of HCEs to former HCEs is significantly higher than the ratio of NHCEs to former NHCEs. In the absence of any additional factors, the timing of this plan amendment has the effect of discriminating significantly in favor of HCEs.

Example 5. The facts are the same as in *Example 4*, except that, in addition, the years of prior service are equivalent between HCEs and NHCEs who are current employees, and the group of current employees with prior service would satisfy the nondiscriminatory classification test of § 1.410(b)-4 in the current and all prior plan years for which past service credit is granted. The timing of this plan amendment does not have the effect of discriminating significantly in favor of HCEs or former HCEs.

* * *

Example 7. Employer W currently has six nonexcludable employees, two of whom, H1 and H2, are HCEs, and the remaining four of whom, N1 through N4, are NHCEs. The ratio of HCEs to former HCEs is significantly higher than the ratio of NHCEs to former NHCEs. Employer W establishes Plan F, a defined benefit plan providing a benefit of one percent of average annual compensation per year of service, including years of service prior to the establishment of the plan. H1 and H2 each have 15 years of prior service, N1 has nine years of past service, N2 has five years, N3 has three years, and N4 has one year. The timing of this plan establishment has the effect of discriminating significantly in favor of HCEs.

Example 8. Assume the same facts as in *Example 7,* except that N1 through N4 were hired in the current year, and Employer W never employed any NHCEs prior to the current year. Thus, no NHCEs would have received additional benefits had Plan F been in existence during the preceding 15 years. The timing of this plan establishment does not have the effect of discriminating significantly in favor of HCEs or former HCEs.

Example 9. The facts are the same as in *Example 7,* except that Plan F limits the grant of past service credit to five years, and the grant of past service otherwise satisfies the safe harbor in paragraph (a)(3) of this section. The timing of this plan establishment is deemed not to have the effect of discriminating significantly in favor of HCEs or former HCEs.

Example 10. The facts are the same as in *Example 9,* except that, five years after the establishment of Plan F, Employer W amends the plan to provide a benefit equal to two percent of average annual compensation per year of service, taking into account all years of service since the establishment of the plan. The ratio of HCEs to former HCEs who ter-

minated employment during the five-year period since the establishment of the plan is significantly higher than the ratio of NHCEs to former NHCEs who terminated employment during the five-year period since the establishment of the plan. Although the amendment described in this example might separately satisfy the safe harbor in paragraph (a)(3) of this section, the safe harbor is not available with respect to the amendment because, under these facts, the amendment is part of a pattern of amendments that has the effect of discriminating significantly in favor of HCEs.

* * *

(b) *Pre-termination restrictions*—(1) *Required provisions in defined benefit plans.* A defined benefit plan has the effect of discriminating significantly in favor of HCEs or former HCEs unless it incorporates provisions restricting benefits and distributions as described in paragraph (b)(2) and (3) of this section at the time the plan is established or, if later, as of the first plan year to which §§ 1.401(a)(4)-1 through 1.401(a)(4)-13 apply to the plan under § 1.401(a)(4)-13(a) or (b). This paragraph (b) does not apply if the Commissioner determines that such provisions are not necessary to prevent the prohibited discrimination that may occur in the event of an early termination of the plan. The restrictions in this paragraph (b) apply to a plan within the meaning of § 1.410(b)-7(b) (i.e., a section 414(l) plan). Any plan containing a provision described in this paragraph (b) satisfies section 411(d)(2) and does not fail to satisfy section 411(a) or (d)(3) merely because of the provision.

(2) *Restriction of benefits upon plan termination.* A plan must provide that, in the event of plan termination, the benefit of any HCE (and any former HCE) is limited to a benefit that is nondiscriminatory under section 401(a)(4).

(3) *Restrictions on distributions*—(i) *General rule.* A plan must provide that, in any year, the payment of benefits to or on behalf of a restricted employee shall not exceed an amount equal to the payments that would be

made to or on behalf of the restricted employee in that year under—

(A) A straight life annuity that is the actuarial equivalent of the accrued benefit and other benefits to which the restricted employee is entitled under the plan (other than a social security supplement); and

(B) A social security supplement, if any, that the restricted employee is entitled to receive.

(ii) *Restricted employee defined.* For purposes of this paragraph (b), the term restricted employee generally means any HCE or former HCE. However, an HCE or former HCE need not be treated as a restricted employee in the current year if the HCE or former HCE is not one of the 25 (or a larger number chosen by the employer) nonexcludable employees and former employees of the employer with the largest amount of compensation in the current or any prior year. Plan provisions defining or altering this group can be amended at any time without violating section 411(d)(6).

(iii) *Benefit defined.* For purposes of this paragraph (b), the term benefit includes, among other benefits, loans in excess of the amounts set forth in section 72(p)(2)(A), any periodic income, any withdrawal values payable to a living employee or former employee, and any death benefits not provided for by insurance on the employee's or former employee's life.

(iv) *Nonapplicability in certain cases.* The restrictions in this paragraph (b)(3) do not apply, however, if any one of the following requirements is satisfied:

(A) After taking into account payment to or on behalf of the restricted employee of all benefits payable to or on behalf of that restricted employee under the plan, the value of plan assets must equal or exceed 110 percent of the value of current liabilities, as defined in section 412(l)(7).

(B) The value of the benefits payable to or on behalf of the restricted employee must be less than one percent of the value of current liabilities before distribution.

(C) The value of the benefits payable to or on behalf of the restricted employee must not exceed the amount described in section 411(a)(11)(A) (restrictions on certain mandatory distributions).

* * *

§ 1.401(a)(4)-7. Imputation of permitted disparity.

(a) *Introduction.* In determining whether a plan satisfies section 401(a)(4) with respect to the amount of contributions or benefits, section 401(a)(5)(C) allows the disparities permitted under section 401(l) to be taken into account. For purposes of satisfying the safe harbors of §§ 1.401(a)(4)-2(b)(2) and 1.401(a)(4)-3(b), permitted disparity may be taken into account only by satisfying section 401(l) in form in accordance with § 1.401(l)-2 or 1.401(l)-3, respectively. For purposes of the general tests of §§ 1.401(a)(4)-2(c) and 1.401(a)(4)-3(c), permitted disparity may be taken into account only in accordance with the rules of this section. In general, this section allows permitted disparity to be arithmetically imputed with respect to employer-provided contributions or benefits by determining an adjusted allocation or accrual rate that appropriately accounts for the permitted disparity with respect to each employee. Paragraph (b) of this section provides rules for imputing permitted disparity with respect to employer-provided contributions by adjusting each employee's unadjusted allocation rate. Paragraph (c) of this section provides rules for imputing permitted disparity with respect to employer-provided benefits by adjusting each employee's unadjusted accrual rate. Paragraph (d) of this section provides rules of general application.

(b) *Adjusting allocation rates*—(1) *In general.* The rules in this paragraph (b) produce an adjusted allocation rate for each employee by determining the excess contribution percentage under the hypothetical formula that would yield the allocation actually received by the employee, if the plan took into account the full disparity permitted under section 401(l)(2) and used the taxable wage base as the integration level. This adjusted allocation rate is used to determine whether the amount of contributions under the plan satisfies the general test of § 1.401(a)(4)-2(c) and to apply the average benefit percentage test on the basis of contributions under § 1.410(b)-5(d). Paragraphs (b)(2) and (b)(3) of this section apply to employees whose plan year compensation does not exceed and does exceed, respectively, the taxable wage base, and paragraph (b)(4) of this section provides definitions.

(2) *Employees whose plan year compensation does not exceed taxable wage base.* If an employee's plan year compensation does not exceed the taxable wage base, the employee's adjusted allocation rate is the lesser of the A rate and the B rate determined under the formulas below, where the permitted disparity rate and the unadjusted allocation rate are determined under paragraph (b)(4)(ii) and (iv) of this section, respectively.

A Rate = 2 x unadjusted allocation rate

B Rate = unadjusted allocation rate + permitted disparity rate

(3) *Employees whose plan year compensation exceeds taxable wage base.* If an employee's plan year compensation exceeds the taxable wage base, the employee's adjusted allocation rate is the lesser of the C rate and the D rate determined under the formulas below, where allocations and the permitted disparity rate are determined under paragraph (b)(4)(i) and (ii) of this section, respectively.

C Rate =

$$\frac{\text{allocations}}{\text{plan year compensation - 1/2 taxable wage base}}$$

D Rate =

$$\frac{\text{allocations + (permitted disparity rate x taxable wage base)}}{\text{plan year compensation}}$$

(4) *Definitions.* In applying this paragraph (b), the following definitions govern—

(i) *Allocations.* Allocations means the amount determined by multiplying the employee's plan year compensation by the employee's unadjusted allocation rate.

(ii) *Permitted disparity rate*—(A) General rule. Permitted disparity rate means the rate in effect as of the beginning of the plan year under section 401(l)(2)(A)(ii) (e.g., 5.7 percent for plan years beginning in 1990).

* * *

(iii) *Taxable wage base.* Taxable wage base means the taxable wage base, as defined in § 1.401(l)-1(c)(32), in effect as of the beginning of the plan year.

(iv) *Unadjusted allocation rate.* Unadjusted allocation rate means the employee's allocation rate determined under § 1.401(a)(4)-2(c)(2)(i) for the plan year (expressed as a percentage of plan year compensation), without imputing permitted disparity under this section.

(5) *Example.* The following example illustrates the rules in this paragraph (b):

Example. (a) Employees M and N participate in a defined contribution plan maintained by Employer X. Employee M has plan year compensation of $30,000 in the 1990 plan year and has an unadjusted allocation rate of five percent. Employee N has plan year compensation of $100,000 in the 1990 plan year and has an unadjusted allocation rate of eight percent. The taxable wage base in 1990 is $51,300.

(b) Because Employee M's plan year compensation does not exceed the taxable wage base, Employee M's A rate is 10 percent (2 x 5 percent), and Employee M's B rate is 10.7 percent (5 percent + 5.7 percent). Thus, Employee M's adjusted allocation rate is 10 percent, the lesser of the A rate and the B rate.

(c) Employee N's allocations are $8,000 (8 percent x $100,000). Because Employee N's plan year compensation exceeds the taxable wage base, Employee N's C rate is 10.76 percent ($8,000 divided by ($100,000 - (½ x $51,300))), and Employee N's D rate is 10.92 percent (($8,000 + (5.7 percent x $51,300)) divided by $100,000). Thus, Employee N's adjusted allocation rate is 10.76 percent, the lesser of the C rate and the D rate.

(c) *Adjusting accrual rates*—(1) *In general*. The rules in this paragraph (c) produce an adjusted accrual rate for each employee by determining the excess benefit percentage under the hypothetical plan formula that would yield the employer-provided accrual actually received by the employee, if the plan took into account the full permitted disparity under section 401(l)(3)(A) in each of the first 35 years of an employee's testing service under the plan and used the employee's covered compensation as the integration level. This adjusted accrual rate is used to determine whether the amount of employer-provided benefits under the plan satisfies the alternative safe harbor for flat benefit plans under § 1.401(a)(4)-3(b)(4)(i)(C)(3) or the general test of § 1.401(a)(4)-3(c), and to apply the average benefit percentage test on the basis of benefits under § 1.410(b)-5. Paragraphs (c)(2) and (c)(3) of this section apply to employees whose average annual compensation does not exceed and does exceed, respectively, covered compensation, and paragraph (c)(4) of this section provides definitions. Paragraph (c)(5) of this section provides a special rule for employees with negative unadjusted accrual rates.

* * *

§ 1.401(a)(4)-8. Cross-testing.

(a) *Introduction*. This section provides rules for testing defined benefit plans on the basis of equivalent employer-provided contributions and defined contribution plans on the basis of equivalent employer-provided benefits under § 1.401(a)(4)-1(b)(2). Paragraphs (b)(1) and (c)(1) of this section provide general tests for nondiscrimination based on individual equivalent accrual or allocation rates determined under paragraphs (b)(2) and (c)(2) of this section, respectively. Paragraphs (b)(3), (c)(3), and (d) of this section provide additional safe-harbor testing methods for target benefit plans, cash balance plans, and defined benefit plans that are part of floor-offset arrangements, respectively, that generally may be satisfied on a design basis.

(b) *Nondiscrimination in amount of benefits provided under a defined contribution plan*—(1) *General rule and gateway*—(i) *General rule*. Equivalent benefits under a defined contribution plan (other than an ESOP) are nondiscriminatory in amount for a plan year if—

(A) The plan would satisfy § 1.401(a)(4)-2(c)(1) for the plan year if an equivalent accrual rate, as determined under paragraph (b)(2) of this section, were substituted for each employee's allocation rate in the determination of rate groups; and

(B) For plan years beginning on or after January 1, 2002, the plan satisfies one of the following conditions—

(1) The plan has broadly available allocation rates (within the meaning of paragraph (b)(1)(iii) of this section) for the plan year;

(2) The plan has age-based allocation rates that are based on either a gradual age or service schedule (within the meaning of paragraph (b)(1)(iv) of this section) or a uniform target benefit allocation (within the meaning of paragraph (b)(1)(v) of this section) for the plan year; or

(3) The plan satisfies the minimum allocation gateway of paragraph (b)(1)(vi) of this section for the plan year.

(ii) *Allocations after testing age*. A plan does not fail to satisfy paragraph (b)(1)(i)(A) of this section merely because allocations are made at the same rate for employees who are older than their testing age (determined without regard to the current-age rule in paragraph (4) of the definition of testing age in § 1.401(a)(4)-12) as they are made for employees who are at that age.

(iii) *Broadly available allocation rates*—(A) *In general*. A plan has broadly available allocation rates for the plan year if each allocation rate under the plan is currently available during the plan year (within the meaning of § 1.401(a)(4)-4(b)(2)), to a group of employees that satisfies section 410(b) (without regard to the average benefit percentage test of § 1.410(b)-5). For this purpose, if two allocation rates could be permissively aggregated under § 1.401(a)(4)-4(d)(4), assuming the allocation rates were treated as benefits, rights or features, they may be aggregated and treated as a single allocation rate. In addition, the disregard of age and service conditions described in § 1.401(a)(4)-4(b)(2)(ii)(A) does not apply for purposes of this paragraph (b)(1)(iii)(A).

* * *

(iv) *Gradual age or service schedule—* (A) *In general.* A plan has a gradual age or service schedule for the plan year if the allocation formula for all employees under the plan provides for a single schedule of allocation rates under which—

(1) The schedule defines a series of bands based solely on age, years of service, or the number of points representing the sum of age and years of service (age and service points), under which the same allocation rate applies to all employees whose age, years of service, or age and service points are within each band; and

(2) The allocation rates under the schedule increase smoothly at regular intervals, within the meaning of paragraphs (b)(1)(iv)(B) and (C) of this section.

(B) *Smoothly increasing schedule of allocation rates.* A schedule of allocation rates increases smoothly if the allocation rate for each band within the schedule is greater than the allocation rate for the immediately preceding band (i.e., the band with the next lower number of years of age, years of service, or age and service points)' but by no more than 5 percentage points. However, a schedule of allocation rates will not be treated as increasing smoothly if the ratio of the allocation rate for any band to the rate for the immediately preceding band is more than 2.0 or if it exceeds the ratio of allocation rates between the two immediately preceding bands.

(C) *Regular intervals.* A schedule of allocation rates has regular intervals of age, years of service or age and service points, if each band, other than the band associated with the highest age, years of service, or age and service points, is the same length. For this purpose, if the schedule is based on age, the first band is deemed to be of the same length as the other bands if it ends at or before age 25. If the first age band ends after age 25, then, in determining whether the length of the first band is the same as the length of other bands, the starting age for the first age band is permitted to be treated as age 25 or any age earlier than 25. For a schedule of allocation rates based on age and service points, the rules of the preceding two sentences are applied by substituting 25 age and service points for age 25. For a schedule of allocation rates based on service, the starting service for the first service band is permitted to be treated as one year of service or any lesser amount of service.

(D) *Minimum allocation rates permitted.* A schedule of allocation rates under a plan does not fail to increase smoothly at regular intervals, within the meaning of paragraphs (b)(1)(iv)(B) and (C) of this section, merely because a minimum uniform allocation rate is provided for all employees or the minimum benefit described in section 416(c)(2) is provided for all non-key employees (either because the plan is top heavy or without regard to whether the plan is top heavy) if the schedule satisfies one of the following conditions—

(1) The allocation rates under the plan that are greater than the minimum allocation rate can be included in a hypothetical schedule of allocation rates that increases smoothly at regular intervals, within the meaning of paragraphs (b)(1)(iv)(B) and (C) of this section, where the hypothetical schedule has a lowest allocation rate no lower than 1% of plan year compensation; or

(2) For a plan using a schedule of allocation rates based on age, for each age band in the schedule that provides an allocation rate greater than the minimum allocation rate, there could be an employee in that age band with an equivalent accrual rate that is less than or equal to the equivalent accrual rate that would apply to an employee whose age is the highest age for which the allocation rate equals the minimum allocation rate.

(v) *Uniform target benefit allocations.* A plan has allocation rates that are based on a uniform target benefit allocation for the plan year if the plan fails to satisfy the requirements for the safe harbor testing method in paragraph (b)(3) of this section merely because the determination of the allocations under the plan differs from the allocations determined under that safe harbor testing method for any of the following reasons—

(A) The interest rate used for determining the actuarial present value of the stated plan benefit and the theoretical reserve is lower than a standard interest rate;

(B) The stated benefit is calculated assuming compensation increases at a specified rate; or

(C) The plan computes the current year contribution using the actual account balance instead of the theoretical reserve.

(vi) *Minimum allocation gateway*—(A) *General rule.* A plan satisfies the minimum allocation gateway of this paragraph (b)(1)(vi) if each NHCE has an allocation rate that is at least one third of the allocation rate of the HCE with the highest allocation rate.

(B) *Deemed satisfaction.* A plan is deemed to satisfy the minimum allocation gateway of this paragraph (b)(1)(vi) if each NHCE receives an allocation of at least 5% of the NHCE's compensation within the meaning of section 415(c)(3), measured over a period of time permitted under the definition of plan year compensation.

(vii) *Determination of allocation rate.* For purposes of paragraph (b)(1)(i)(B) of this section, allocations and allocation rates are determined under § 1.401(a)(4)-2(c)(2), but without taking into account the imputation of permitted disparity under § 1.401(a)(4)-7. However, in determining whether the plan has broadly available allocation rates as provided in paragraph (b)(1)(iii) of this section, differences in allocation rates attributable solely to the use of permitted disparity described in § 1.401(l)-2 are disregarded.

* * *

(2) *Determination of equivalent accrual rates*—(i) *Basic definition.* An employee's equivalent accrual rate for a plan year is the annual benefit that is the result of normalizing the increase in the employee's account balance during the measurement period, divided by the number of years in which the employee benefited under the plan during the measurement period, and expressed either as a dollar amount or as a percentage of the employee's average annual compensation. A measurement period that includes future years may not be used for this purpose.

* * *

(c) *Nondiscrimination in amount of contributions under a defined benefit plan*—(1) *General rule.* Equivalent allocations under a defined benefit plan are nondiscriminatory in amount for a plan year if the plan would satisfy § 1.401(a)(4)-3(c)(1) (taking into account § 1.401(a)(4)-3(c)(3)) for the plan year if an equivalent normal and most valuable allocation rate, as determined under paragraph (c)(2) of this section, were substituted for each employee's normal and most valuable accrual rate, respectively, in the determination of rate groups.

(2) *Determination of equivalent allocation rates*—(i) *Basic definitions.* An employee's equivalent normal and most valuable allocation rates for a plan year are, respectively, the actuarial present value of the increase over the plan year in the benefit that would be taken into account in determining the employee's normal and most valuable accrual rates for the plan year, expressed either as a dollar amount or as a percentage of the employee's plan year compensation. In the case of a contributory DB plan, the rules in § 1.401(a)(4)-6(b)(1), (b)(5), or (b)(6) must be used to determine the amount of each employee's employer-provided benefit that would be taken into account for this purpose.

* * *

§ 1.401(a)(4)-9. Plan aggregation and restructuring.

(a) *Introduction.* Two or more plans that are permissively aggregated and treated as a single plan under §§ 1.410(b)-7(d) must also be treated as a single plan for purposes of section 401(a)(4). See § 1.401(a)(4)-12 (definition of plan). An aggregated plan is generally tested under the same rules applicable to single plans. Paragraph (b) of this section, however, provides special rules for determining whether a plan that consists of one or more defined contribution plans and one or more defined benefit plans (a DB/DC plan) satisfies section 401(a)(4) with respect to the amount of employer-provided benefits and the availability of benefits, rights, and features. Paragraph (c) of this section provides rules allowing a plan to be treated as consisting of separate component plans and allowing the component plans to be tested separately under section 401(a)(4).

(b) *Application of nondiscrimination requirements to DB/DC plans*—(1) *General rule.* Except as provided in paragraph (b)(2) of this section, whether a DB/DC plan satisfies section 401(a)(4) is determined using the same rules applicable to a single plan. In addition, paragraph (b)(3) of this section provides an optional rule for demonstrating nondiscrimination in availability of benefits, rights, and features provided under a DB/DC plan.

* * *

(c) *Plan restructuring*—(1) *General rule.* A plan may be treated, in accordance with this paragraph (c), as consisting of two or more component plans for purposes of determining whether the plan satisfies section 401(a)(4). If each of the component plans of a plan satisfies all of the requirements of sections 401(a)(4) and 410(b) as if it were a separate plan, then the plan is treated as satisfying section 401(a)(4).

(2) *Identification of component plans.* A plan may be restructured into component plans, each consisting of all the allocations, accruals, and other benefits, rights, and features provided to a selected group of employees. The employer may select the group of employees used for this purpose in any man-

ner, and the composition of the groups may be changed from plan year to plan year. Every employee must be included in one and only one component plan under the same plan for a plan year.

(3) *Satisfaction of section 401(a)(4) by a component plan*—(i) *General rule.* The rules applicable in determining whether a component plan satisfies section 401(a)(4) are the same as those applicable to a plan. Thus, for this purpose, any reference to a plan in section 401(a)(4) and the regulations thereunder (other than this paragraph (c)) is interpreted as a reference to a component plan. As is true for a plan, whether a component plan satisfies the uniformity and other requirements applicable to safe harbor plans under §§ 1.401(a)(4)-2(b) and 1.401(a)(4)-3(b) is determined on a design basis. Thus, for example, plan provisions are not disregarded merely because they do not currently apply to employees in the component plan if they will apply to those employees as a result of the mere passage of time.

(ii) *Restructuring not available for certain testing purposes.* The safe harbor in § 1.401(a)(4)-2(b)(3) for plans with uniform points allocation formulas is not available in testing (and thus cannot be satisfied by) contributions under a component plan. Similarly, component plans cannot be used for purposes of determining whether a plan provides broadly available allocation rates (as defined in § 1.401(a)(4)-8(b)(1)(iii)), determining whether a plan has a gradual age or service schedule (as defined in § 1.401(a)(4)-8(b)(1)(iv)), determining whether a plan has allocation rates that are based on a uniform target benefit allocation (as defined in § 1.401(a)(4)-8(b)(1)(v)), or determining whether a plan is primarily defined benefit in character or consists of broadly available separate plans (as defined in paragraphs (b)(2)(v)(B) and (C) of this section). In addition, the minimum allocation gateway of § 1.401(a)(4)-8(b)(1)(vi) and the minimum aggregate allocation gateway of paragraph (b)(2)(v)(D) of this section cannot be satisfied on the basis of component plans. See §§ 1.401(k)-1(b)(4)(iv)(B) and 1.401(m)-1(b)(4)(iv)(B) for rules regarding the inapplicability of restructuring to section 401(k) plans and section 401(m) plans.

(4) *Satisfaction of section 410(b) by a component plan*—(i) *General rule.* The rules applicable in determining whether a component plan satisfies section 410(b) are generally the same as those applicable to a plan. However, a component plan is deemed to satisfy the average benefit percentage test of § 1.410(b)-5 if the plan of which it is a part satisfies § 1.410(b)-5 (without regard to § 1.410(b)-5(f)). In the case of a component plan that is part of a plan that relies on § 1.410(b)-5(f) to satisfy the average benefit percentage test, the component plan is deemed to satisfy the average benefit percentage test only if the component plan separately satisfies § 1.410(b)-5(f). In addition, all component plans of a plan are deemed to satisfy the average benefit percentage test if the plan makes an early retirement window benefit (within the meaning of § 1.401(a)(4)-3(f)(4)(iii)) currently available (within the meaning of § 1.401(a)(4)-3(f)(4)(ii)(A)) to a group of employees that satisfies section 410(b) (without regard to the average benefit percentage test), and if it would not be necessary for the plan or any rate group or component plan of the plan to satisfy that test in order for the plan to satisfy sections 401(a)(4) and 410(b) in the absence of the early retirement window benefit.

(ii) *Relationship to satisfaction of section 410(b) by the plan.* Satisfaction of section 410(b) by a component plan is relevant solely for purposes of determining whether the plan of which it is a part satisfies section 401(a)(4), and not for purposes of determining whether the plan satisfies section 410(b) itself. The plan must still independently satisfy section 410(b) in order to be a qualified plan. Similarly, satisfaction of section 410(b) by a plan is relevant solely for purposes of determining whether the plan, and not the component plan, satisfies section 410(b). Thus, for example, a component plan that does not satisfy the ratio percentage test of § 1.410(b)-2(b)(2) must still satisfy the average benefit test of § 1.410(b)-2(b)(3), even though the plan of which it is a part satisfies the ratio percentage test.

(5) *Effect of restructuring under other sections.* The restructuring rules provided in this paragraph (c) apply solely for purposes of sections 401(a)(4) and 401(l), and those portions of sections 410(b), 414(s), and any other provisions that are specifically applicable in determining whether the requirements of section 401(a)(4) are satisfied. Thus, for example, a component plan is not treated as a separate plan under section 401(a)(26).

(6) *Examples.* The following examples illustrate the rules in this paragraph (c):

Example 1. Employer X maintains a defined benefit plan. The plan provides a normal retirement benefit equal to 1.0 percent of average annual compensation times years of service to employees at Plant S, and 1.5 percent of average annual compensation times years of service to employees at Plant T. Under paragraph (c)(2) of this section, the plan may be treated as consisting of two component defined benefit plans, one providing retirement benefits equal to 1.0 percent of average annual compensation times years of service to the employees at Plant S, and another providing benefits equal to 1.5 percent of average annual compensation times years of service to employees at Plant T. If each component plan satisfies sections 401(a)(4) and 410(b) as if it were a separate plan under the rules of this paragraph (c), then the entire plan satisfies section 401(a)(4).

Example 2. (a) Employer Y maintains Plan A, a defined benefit plan, for its Employees M, N, O, P, Q, and R. Plan A provides benefits under a uniform formula that satisfies the requirements of § 1.401(a)(4)-3(b)(2) and (b)(3) before it is amended on February 14, 1994. The amendment provides an early retirement window benefit that is a subsidized optional form of benefit under § 1.401(a)(4)-3(b)(2)(iii) and that is available on the same terms to all employees who satisfy the eligibility requirements for the window. The early retirement window benefit is available only to employees who retire between June 1, 1994, and November 30, 1994.

(b) Assume that Employees M, N, and O will be eligible to receive the window benefit by the end of the window period and Employees P, Q, and R will not. Because substantially all employees will not satisfy the eligibility requirements for the early retirement window benefit by the close of the early retirement window benefit period, Plan A fails to satisfy the uniform subsidies requirement of §1.401(a)(4)-3(b)(2)(iii). See §1.401(a)(4)-3(b)(2)(vi), Example 6.

(c) Under paragraph (c)(2) of this section, Employees M, N, O, P, Q, and R may be grouped into two component plans, one consisting of Employees M, N, and O, and all their accruals and other benefits, rights, and features under the plan (including the early retirement window benefit), and another consisting of Employees P, Q, and R, and all their accruals and other benefits, rights, and features under the plan. Each of the component plans identified in this manner satisfies the uniform subsidies requirement of §1.401(a)(4)-3(b)(2)(iii), and thus satisfies §1.401(a)(4)-3(b). The entire plan satisfies section 401(a)(4) under the rules of this paragraph (c), if each of these component plans also satisfies section 410(b) as if it were a separate plan (including, if applicable, the reasonable classification requirement of §1.410(b)-4(b), and taking into account the special rule of paragraph (c)(4)(i) of this section that forgives the average benefit percentage test in certain situations in which the average benefit percentage test would be required solely as a result of the early retirement window benefit).

* * *

§1.401(a)(4)-13. Effective dates and fresh-start rules.

* * *

(c) *Fresh-start rules for defined benefit plans*—(1) *Introduction.* This paragraph (c) provides rules that must be satisfied in order to use the fresh-start testing options for defined benefit plans in §1.401(a)(4)-3(b)(6)(vii) and (d)(3)(iii), relating to the safe harbors and the general test, respectively.

Those fresh-start options are designed to allow a plan to be tested without regard to benefits accrued before a selected fresh-start date. To the extent provided in paragraph (d) of this section, those options also may be used to disregard certain increases in benefits attributable to compensation increases after a fresh-start date. Although this paragraph (c) generally requires a plan to be amended to freeze employees' accrued benefits as of a fresh-start date and to provide any additional accrued benefits after the fresh-start date solely in accordance with certain specified formulas, certain of these requirements do not apply to a plan that is tested under the general test of §1.401(a)(4)-3(c). See §1.401(a)(4)-3(b)(6)(vii) and (d)(3)(iii).

(2) *General rule.* A defined benefit plan satisfies this paragraph (c) if—

(i) Accrued benefits of employees in the fresh-start group are frozen as of the fresh-start date in accordance with paragraph (c)(3) of this section;

(ii) Accrued benefits after the fresh-start date for employees in the fresh-start group are determined under one of the fresh-start formulas in paragraph (c)(4) of this section; and

(iii) Paragraph (c)(5) of this section is satisfied.

(3) *Definition of frozen*—(i) *General rule.* An employee's accrued benefit under a plan is frozen as of the fresh-start date if it is determined as if the employee terminated employment with the employer as of the fresh-start date (or the date the employee actually terminated employment with the employer, if earlier), and without regard to any amendment to the plan adopted after that date, other than amendments recognized as effective as of or before that date under section 401(b) or §1.401(a)(4)-11(g). The assumption that an employee has terminated employment applies solely for purposes of this paragraph (c)(3). Thus, for example, the fresh start has no effect on the service taken into account for purposes of determining vesting and eligibility for benefits, rights, and features under the plan.

* * *

(4) *Fresh-start formulas*—(i) *Formula without wear-away*. An employee's accrued benefit under the plan is equal to the sum of—

(A) The employee's frozen accrued benefit; and

(B) The employee's accrued benefit determined under the formula applicable to benefit accruals in the current plan year (current formula) as applied to the employee's years of service after the fresh-start date.

(ii) *Formula with wear-away*. An employee's accrued benefit under the plan is equal to the greater of—

(A) The employee's frozen accrued benefit; or

(B) The employee's accrued benefit determined under the current formula as applied to the employee's total years of service (before and after the fresh-start date) taken into account under the current formula.

(iii) *Formula with extended wear-away*. An employee's accrued benefit under the plan is equal to the greater of—

(A) The amount determined under paragraph (c)(4)(i) of this section; or

(B) The amount determined under paragraph (c)(4)(ii)(B) of this section.

* * *

§ 1.401(a)(9)-2. Distributions commencing during an employee's lifetime.

Q-1. In the case of distributions commencing during an employee's lifetime, how must the employee's entire interest be distributed in order to satisfy section 401(a)(9)(A)?

A-1. (a) In order to satisfy section 401(a)(9)(A), the entire interest of each employee must be distributed to such employee not later than the required beginning date, or must be distributed, beginning not later than the required beginning date, over the life of the employee or joint lives of the employee and a designated beneficiary or over a period not extending beyond the life expectancy of the employee or the joint life and last survivor expectancy of the employee and the designated beneficiary.

(b) Section 401(a)(9)(G) provides that lifetime distributions must satisfy the incidental death benefit requirements.

(c) The amount required to be distributed for each calendar year in order to satisfy section 401(a)(9)(A) and (G) generally depends on whether a distribution is in the form of distributions under a defined contribution plan or annuity payments under a defined benefit plan or under an annuity contract. For the method of determining the required minimum distribution in accordance with section 401(a)(9)(A) and (G) from an individual account under a defined contribution plan, see § 1.401(a)(9)-5. For the method of determining the required minimum distribution in accordance with section 401(a)(9)(A) and (G) in the case of annuity payments from a defined benefit plan or an annuity contract, see § 1.401(a)(9)-6.

Q-2. For purposes of section 401(a)(9)(C), what does the term required beginning date mean?

A-2. (a) Except as provided in paragraph (b) of this A-2 with respect to a 5-percent owner, as defined in paragraph (c) of this A-2, the term required beginning date means April 1 of the calendar year following the later of the calendar year in which the employee attains age 70½ or the calendar year in which the employee retires from employment with the employer maintaining the plan.

(b) In the case of an employee who is a 5-percent owner, the term required beginning date means April 1 of the calendar year following the calendar year in which the employee attains age 70½.

(c) For purposes of section 401(a)(9), a 5-percent owner is an employee who is a 5-percent owner (as defined in section 416) with respect to the plan year ending in the calendar year in which the employee attains age 70½.

(d) Paragraph (b) of this A-2 does not apply in the case of a governmental plan (within the meaning of section 414(d)) or a church plan. For purposes of this paragraph, the term church plan means a plan maintained by a church for church employees, and the term church means any church (as defined in section 3121(w)(3)(A)) or qualified church-controlled organization (as defined in section 3121(w)(3)(B)).

(e) A plan is permitted to provide that the required beginning date for purposes of section 401(a)(9) for all employees is April 1 of the calendar year following the calendar year in which an employee attains age 70½ regardless of whether the employee is a 5-percent owner.

Q-3. When does an employee attain age 70½?

A-3. An employee attains age 70½ as of the date six calendar months after the 70th anniversary of the employee's birth. For example, if an employee's date of birth was June 30, 1933, the 70th anniversary of such employee's birth is June 30, 2003. Such employee attains age 70½ on December 30, 2003. Consequently, if the employee is a 5-percent owner or retired, such employee's required beginning date is April 1, 2004. However, if the employee's date of birth was July 1, 1933, the 70th anniversary of such employee's birth would be July 1, 2003. Such employee would then attain age 70½ on January 1, 2004 and such employee's required beginning date would be April 1, 2005.

Q-4. Must distributions made before the employee's required beginning date satisfy section 401(a)(9)?

A-4. Lifetime distributions made before the employee's required beginning date for calendar years before the employee's first distribution calendar year, as defined in A-1(b) of § 1.401(a)(9)-5, need not be made in accordance with section 401(a)(9). However, if distributions commence before the employee's required beginning date under a particular distribution option, such as in the form of an annuity, the distribution option fails to satisfy section 401(a)(9) at the time distributions commence if, under terms of the particular

distribution option, distributions to be made for the employee's first distribution calendar year or any subsequent distribution calendar year will fail to satisfy section 401(a)(9).

Q-5. If distributions have begun to an employee during the employee's lifetime (in accordance with section 401(a)(9)(A)(ii)), how must distributions be made after an employee's death?

A-5. Section 401(a)(9)(B)(i) provides that if the distribution of the employee's interest has begun in accordance with section 401(a)(9)(A)(ii) and the employee dies before his entire interest has been distributed to him, the remaining portion of such interest must be distributed at least as rapidly as under the distribution method being used under section 401(a)(9)(A)(ii) as of the date of his death. The amount required to be distributed for each distribution calendar year following the calendar year of death generally depends on whether a distribution is in the form of distributions from an individual account under a defined contribution plan or annuity payments under a defined benefit plan. For the method of determining the required minimum distribution in accordance with section 401(a)(9)(B)(i) from an individual account, see § 1.401(a)(9)-5. In the case of annuity payments from a defined benefit plan or an annuity contract, see § 1.401(a)(9)-6.

Q-6. For purposes of section 401(a)(9)(B), when are distributions considered to have begun to the employee in accordance with section 401(a)(9)(A)(ii)?

A-6. (a) General rule. Except as otherwise provided in A-10 of § 1.401(a)(9)-6, distributions are not treated as having begun to the employee in accordance with section 401(a)(9)(A)(ii) until the employee's required beginning date, without regard to whether payments have been made before that date. Thus, section 401(a)(9)(B)(i) only applies if an employee dies on or after the employee's required beginning date. For example, if employee A retires in 2003, the calendar year A attains age 65½, and begins receiving installment distributions from a profit-sharing plan over a period not exceeding the joint life and last survivor expectancy of A and A's spouse, benefits are not treated as having begun in accordance with section 401(a)(9)(A)(ii) until April 1, 2009 (the April 1 following the calendar year in which A attains age 70½). Consequently, if A dies before April 1, 2009 (A's required beginning date), distributions after A's death must be made in accordance with section 401(a)(9)(B)(ii) or (iii) and (iv) and § 1.401(a)(9)-3, and not section 401(a)(9)(B)(i). This is the case without regard to whether the plan has distributed the minimum distribution for the first distribution calendar year (as defined in A-1(b) of § 1.401(a)(9)-5) before A's death.

(b) If a plan provides, in accordance with A-2(e) of this section, that the required beginning date for purposes of section 401(a)(9) for all employees is April 1 of the calendar year following the calendar year in which an employee attains age 70½, an employee who dies on or after the required beginning date determined under the plan terms is treated as dying after the employee's distributions have begun for purposes of this A-6 even though the employee dies before the April 1 following the calendar year in which the employee retires.

§ 1.401(a)(9)-3. Death before required beginning date.

Q-1. If an employee dies before the employee's required beginning date, how must the employee's entire interest be distributed in order to satisfy section 401(a)(9)?

A-1. (a) Except as otherwise provided in A-10 of § 1.401(a)(9)-6, if an employee dies before the employee's required beginning date (and, thus, before distributions are treated as having begun in accordance with section 401(a)(9)(A)(ii)), distribution of the employee's entire interest must be made in accordance with one of the methods described in section 401(a)(9)(B)(ii) or (iii) and (iv). One method (the 5-year rule in section 401(a)(9)(B)(ii)) requires that the entire interest of the employee be distributed within 5 years of the employee's death regardless of who or what entity receives the distribution. Another method

(the life expectancy rule in section 401(a)(9)(B)(iii) and (iv)) requires that any portion of an employee's interest payable to (or for the benefit of) a designated beneficiary be distributed, commencing within one year of the employee's death, over the life of such beneficiary (or over a period not extending beyond the life expectancy of such beneficiary). Section 401(a)(9)(B)(iv) provides special rules where the designated beneficiary is the surviving spouse of the employee, including a special commencement date for distributions under section 401(a)(9)(B)(iii) to the surviving spouse.

(b) See A-4 of this section for the rules for determining which of the methods described in paragraph (a) of this A-1 applies. See A-3 of this section to determine when distributions under the exception to the 5-year rule in section 401(a)(9)(B)(iii) and (iv) must commence. See A-2 of this section to determine when the 5-year period in section 401(a)(9)(B)(ii) ends. For distributions using the life expectancy rule in section 401(a)(9)(B)(iii) and (iv), see §1.401(a)(9)-4 in order to determine the designated beneficiary under section 401(a)(9)(B)(iii) and (iv), see § 1.401(a)(9)-5 for the rules for determining the required minimum distribution under a defined contribution plan, and see § 1.401(a)(9)-6 for required minimum distributions under defined benefit plans.

Q-2. By when must the employee's entire interest be distributed in order to satisfy the 5-year rule in section 401(a)(9)(B)(ii)?

A-2. In order to satisfy the 5-year rule in section 401(a)(9)(B)(ii), the employee's entire interest must be distributed by the end of the calendar year which contains the fifth anniversary of the date of the employee's death. For example, if an employee dies on January 1, 2003, the entire interest must be distributed by the end of 2008, in order to satisfy the 5-year rule in section 401(a)(9)(B)(ii).

Q-3. When are distributions required to commence in order to satisfy the life expectancy rule in section 401(a)(9)(B)(iii) and (iv)?

A-3. (a) *Nonspouse beneficiary*. In order to satisfy the life expectancy rule in section 401(a)(9)(B)(iii), if the designated beneficiary is not the employee's surviving spouse, distributions must commence on or before the end of the calendar year immediately following the calendar year in which the employee died. This rule also applies to the distribution of the entire remaining benefit if another individual is a designated beneficiary in addition to the employee's surviving spouse. See A-2 and A-3 of §1.401(a)(9)-8, however, if the employee's benefit is divided into separate accounts.

(b) *Spousal beneficiary*. In order to satisfy the rule in section 401(a)(9)(B)(iii) and (iv), if the sole designated beneficiary is the employee's surviving spouse, distributions must commence on or before the later of—

(1) The end of the calendar year immediately following the calendar year in which the employee died; and

(2) The end of the calendar year in which the employee would have attained age 70½.

Q-4. How is it determined whether the 5-year rule in section 401(a)(9)(B)(ii) or the life expectancy rule in section 401(a)(9)(B)(iii) and (iv) applies to a distribution?

A-4. (a) *No plan provision*. If a plan does not adopt an optional provision described in paragraph (b) or (c) of this A-4 specifying the method of distribution after the death of an employee, distribution must be made as follows:

(1) If the employee has a designated beneficiary, as determined under §1.401(a)(9)-4, distributions are to be made in accordance with the life expectancy rule in section 401(a)(9)(B)(iii) and (iv).

(2) If the employee has no designated beneficiary, distributions are to be made in accordance with the 5-year rule in section 401(a)(9)(B)(ii).

(b) *Optional plan provisions*. A plan may adopt a provision specifying either that the 5-year rule in section 401(a)(9)(B)(ii) will apply to certain distributions after the death of an employee even if the employee has a designated beneficiary or that distribution in every case will be made in accordance with the 5-year rule in section 401(a)(9)(B)(ii). Further, a plan need not have the same method of distribution for the benefits of all employees in order to satisfy section 401(a)(9).

(c) *Elections*. A plan may adopt a provision that permits employees (or beneficiaries) to elect on an individual basis whether the 5-year rule in section 401(a)(9)(B)(ii) or the life expectancy rule in section 401(a)(9)(B)(iii) and (iv) applies to distributions after the death of an employee who has a designated beneficiary. Such an election must be made no later than the earlier of the end of the calendar year in which distribution would be required to commence in order to satisfy the requirements for the life expectancy rule in section 401(a)(9)(B)(iii) and (iv) (see A-3 of this section for the determination of such calendar year) or the end of the calendar year which contains the fifth anniversary of the date of death of the employee. As of the last date the election may be made, the election must be irrevocable with respect to the beneficiary (and all subsequent beneficiaries) and must apply to all subsequent calendar years. If a plan provides for the election, the plan may also specify the method of distribution that applies if neither the employee nor the beneficiary makes the election. If neither the employee nor the beneficiary elects a method and the plan does not specify which method applies, distribution must be made in accordance with paragraph (a) of this A-4.

Q-5. If the employee's surviving spouse is the employee's sole designated beneficiary and such spouse dies after the employee, but before distributions have begun to the surviving spouse under section 401(a)(9)(B)(iii) and (iv), how is the employee's interest to be distributed?

A-5. Pursuant to section 401(a)(9)(B)(iv)(II), if the surviving spouse is the employee's sole designated beneficiary and dies after the employee, but before distributions to such spouse have begun under section 401(a)(9)(B)(iii) and (iv), the 5-year rule in section 401(a)(9)(B)(ii) and the life expectancy rule in section 401(a)(9)(B)(iii) are to be applied as if the surviving spouse were the employee. In applying this rule, the date of death of the surviving spouse shall be substituted for the date of death of the employee. However, in such case, the rules in section 401(a)(9)(B)(iv) are not available to the surviving spouse of the deceased employee's surviving spouse.

Q-6. For purposes of section 401(a)(9)(B)(iv)(II), when are distributions considered to have begun to the surviving spouse?

A-6. Distributions are considered to have begun to the surviving spouse of an employee, for purposes of section 401(a)(9)(B)(iv)(II), on the date, determined in accordance with A-3 of this section, on which distributions are required to commence to the surviving spouse, even though payments have actually been made before that date. See A-11 of §1.401(a)(9)-6 for a special rule for annuities.

§ 1.401(a)(9)-4. Determination of the designated beneficiary.

Q-1. Who is a designated beneficiary under section 401(a)(9)(E)?

A-1. A designated beneficiary is an individual who is designated as a beneficiary under the plan. An individual may be designated as a beneficiary under the plan either by the terms of the plan or, if the plan so provides, by an affirmative election by the employee (or the employee's surviving spouse) specifying the beneficiary. A beneficiary designated as such under the plan is an individual who is entitled to a portion of an employee's benefit, contingent on the employee's death or another specified event. For example, if a distribution is in the form of a joint and survivor annuity over the life of the employee and another individual, the plan does not satisfy section 401(a)(9) unless such other individual is a designated beneficiary under the plan. A designated beneficiary need not be specified by name in the plan or by the employee to the plan in order to be a designated beneficiary so long as the individual who is to be the benefi-

ciary is identifiable under the plan. The members of a class of beneficiaries capable of expansion or contraction will be treated as being identifiable if it is possible, to identify the class member with the shortest life expectancy. The fact that an employee's interest under the plan passes to a certain individual under a will or otherwise under applicable state law does not make that individual a designated beneficiary unless the individual is designated as a beneficiary under the plan. See A-6 of § 1.401(a)(9)-8 for rules which apply to qualified domestic relation orders.

Q-2. Must an employee (or the employee's spouse) make an affirmative election specifying a beneficiary for a person to be a designated beneficiary under section 401(a)(9)(E)?

A-2. No, a designated beneficiary is an individual who is designated as a beneficiary under the plan whether or not the designation under the plan was made by the employee. The choice of beneficiary is subject to the requirements of sections 401(a)(11), 414(p), and 417.

Q-3. May a person other than an individual be considered to be a designated beneficiary for purposes of section 401(a)(9)?

A-3. No, only individuals may be designated beneficiaries for purposes of section 401(a)(9). A person that is not an individual, such as the employee's estate, may not be a designated beneficiary. If a person other than an individual is designated as a beneficiary of an employee's benefit, the employee will be treated as having no designated beneficiary for purposes of section 401(a)(9), even if there are also individuals designated as beneficiaries. However, see A-5 of this section for special rules that apply to trusts and A-2 and A-3 of § 1.401(a)(9)-8 for rules that apply to separate accounts.

Q-4. When is the designated beneficiary determined?

A-4. (a) General rule. In order to be a designated beneficiary, an individual must be a beneficiary as of the date of death. Except as provided in paragraph (b) and §1.401(a)(9)-6, the employee's designated beneficiary will be determined based on the beneficiaries designated as of the date of death who remain beneficiaries as of September 30 of the calendar year following the calendar year of the employee's death. Consequently, except as provided in § 1.401(a)(9)-6, any person who was a beneficiary as of the date of the employee's death, but is not a beneficiary as of that September 30 (e.g., because the person receives the entire benefit to which the person is entitled before that September 30), is not taken into account in determining the employee's designated beneficiary for purposes of determining the distribution period for required minimum distributions after the employee's death. Accordingly, if a person disclaims entitlement to the employee's benefit, pursuant to a disclaimer that satisfies section 2518 by that September 30 thereby allowing other beneficiaries to receive the benefit in lieu of that person, the disclaiming person is not taken into account in determining the employee's designated beneficiary.

(b) *Surviving spouse.* As provided in A-5 of § 1.401(a)(9)-3, if the employee's spouse is the sole designated beneficiary as of September 30 of the calendar year following the calendar year of the employee's death, and the surviving spouse dies after the employee and before the date on which distributions have begun to the surviving spouse under section 401(a)(9)(B)(iii) and (iv), the rule in section 401(a)(9)(B)(iv)(II) will apply. Thus, for example, the relevant designated beneficiary for determining the distribution period after the death of the surviving spouse is the designated beneficiary of the surviving spouse. Similarly, such designated beneficiary will be determined based on the beneficiaries designated as of the date of the surviving spouse's death and who remain beneficiaries as of September 30 of the calendar year following the calendar year of the surviving spouse's death. Further, if, as of that September 30, there is no designated beneficiary under the plan with respect to that surviving spouse, distribution must be made in accordance with the 5-year rule in

section 401(a)(9)(B)(ii) and A-2 of § 1.401(a)(9)-3.

(c) *Deceased beneficiary.* For purposes of this A-4, an individual who is a beneficiary as of the date of the employee's death and dies prior to September 30 of the calendar year following the calendar year of the employee's death without disclaiming continues to be treated as a beneficiary as of the September 30 of the calendar year following the calendar year of the employee's death in determining the employee's designated beneficiary for purposes of determining the distribution period for required minimum distributions after the employee's death, without regard to the identity of the successor beneficiary who is entitled to distributions as the beneficiary of the deceased beneficiary. The same rule applies in the case of distributions to which A-5 of § 1.401(a)(9)-3 applies so that, if an individual is designated as a beneficiary of an employee's surviving spouse as of the spouse's date of death and dies prior to September 30 of the year following the year of the surviving spouse's death, that individual will continue to be treated as a designated beneficiary.

Q-5. If a trust is named as a beneficiary of an employee, will the beneficiaries of the trust with respect to the trust's interest in the employee's benefit be treated as having been designated as beneficiaries of the employee under the plan for purposes of determining the distribution period under section 401(a)(9)?

A-5. (a) If the requirements of paragraph (b) of this A-5 are met with respect to a trust that is named as the beneficiary of an employee under the plan, the beneficiaries of the trust (and not the trust itself) will be treated as having been designated as beneficiaries of the employee under the plan for purposes of determining the distribution period under section 401(a)(9).

(b) The requirements of this paragraph (b) are met if, during any period during which required minimum distributions are being determined by treating the beneficiaries of the trust as designated beneficiaries of the employee, the following requirements are met—

(1) The trust is a valid trust under state law, or would be but for the fact that there is no corpus.

(2) The trust is irrevocable or will, by its terms, become irrevocable upon the death of the employee.

(3) The beneficiaries of the trust who are beneficiaries with respect to the trust's interest in the employee's benefit are identifiable within the meaning of A-1 of this section from the trust instrument.

(4) The documentation described in A-6 of this section has been provided to the plan administrator.

(c) In the case of payments to a trust having more than one beneficiary, see A-7 of § 1.401(a)(9)-5 for the rules for determining the designated beneficiary whose life expectancy will be used to determine the distribution period and A-3 of this section for the rules that apply if a person other than an individual is designated as a beneficiary of an employee's benefit. However, the separate account rules under A-2 of § 1.401(a)(9)-8 are not available to beneficiaries of a trust with respect to the trust's interest in the employee's benefit.

(d) If the beneficiary of the trust named as beneficiary of the employee's interest is another trust, the beneficiaries of the other trust will be treated as being designated as beneficiaries of the first trust, and thus, having been designated by the employee under the plan for purposes of determining the distribution period under section 401(a)(9)(A)(ii), provided that the requirements of paragraph (b) of this A-5 are satisfied with respect to such other trust in addition to the trust named as beneficiary.

Q-6. If a trust is named as a beneficiary of an employee, what documentation must be provided to the plan administrator?

A-6. (a) *Required minimum distributions before death*. If an employee designates a trust as the beneficiary of his or her entire benefit and the employee's spouse is the sole beneficiary of the trust, in order to satisfy the docu-

mentation requirements of this A-6 so that the spouse can be treated as the sole designated beneficiary of the employee's benefits (if the other requirements of paragraph (b) of A-5 of this section are satisfied), the employee must either—

(1) Provide to the plan administrator a copy of the trust instrument and agree that if the trust instrument is amended at any time in the future, the employee will, within a reasonable time, provide to the plan administrator a copy of each such amendment; or

(2) Provide to the plan administrator a list of all of the beneficiaries of the trust (including contingent and remaindermen beneficiaries with a description of the conditions on their entitlement sufficient to establish that the spouse is the sole beneficiary) for purposes of section 401(a)(9); certify that, to the best of the employee's knowledge, this list is correct and complete and that the requirements of paragraph (b)(1), (2), and (3) of A-5 of this section are satisfied; agree that, if the trust instrument is amended at any time in the future, the employee will, within a reasonable time, provide to the plan administrator corrected certifications to the extent that the amendment changes any information previously certified; and agree to provide a copy of the trust instrument to the plan administrator upon demand.

(b) *Required minimum distributions after death*. In order to satisfy the documentation requirement of this A-6 for required minimum distributions after the death of the employee (or spouse in a case to which A-5 of § 1.401(a)(9)-3 applies), by October 31 of the calendar year immediately following the calendar year in which the employee died, the trustee of the trust must either—

(1) Provide the plan administrator with a final list of all beneficiaries of the trust (including contingent and remaindermen beneficiaries with a description of the conditions on their entitlement) as of September 30 of the calendar year following the calendar year of the employee's death; certify that, to the best of the trustee's knowledge, this list is correct

and complete and that the requirements of paragraph (b)(1), (2), and (3) of A-5 of this section are satisfied; and agree to provide a copy of the trust instrument to the plan administrator upon demand; or

(2) Provide the plan administrator with a copy of the actual trust document for the trust that is named as a beneficiary of the employee under the plan as of the employee's date of death.

* * *

§ 1.401(a)(9)-5. Required minimum distributions from defined contribution plans.

Q-1. If an employee's benefit is in the form of an individual account under a defined contribution plan, what is the amount required to be distributed for each calendar year?

A-1. (a) *General rule.* If an employee's accrued benefit is in the form of an individual account under a defined contribution plan, the minimum amount required to be distributed for each distribution calendar year, as defined in paragraph (b) of this A-1, is equal to the quotient obtained by dividing the account (determined under A-3 of this section) by the applicable distribution period (determined under A-4 or A-5 of this section, whichever is applicable). However, the required minimum distribution amount will never exceed the entire account balance on the date of the distribution. See A-8 of this section for rules that apply if a portion of the employee's account is not vested. Further, the minimum distribution required to be distributed on or before an employee's required beginning date is always determined under section 401(a)(9)(A)(ii) and this A-1 and not section 401(a)(9)(A)(i).

(b) *Distribution calendar year.* A calendar year for which a minimum distribution is required is a distribution calendar year. If an employee's required beginning date is April 1 of the calendar year following the calendar year in which the employee attains age 70½, the employee's first distribution calendar year is the year the employee attains age 70½. If an employee's required beginning date is April 1

of the calendar year following the calendar year in which the employee retires, the employee's first distribution calendar year is the calendar year in which the employee retires. In the case of distributions to be made in accordance with the life expectancy rule in § 1.401(a)(9)-3 and in section 401(a)(9)(B)(iii) and (iv), the first distribution calendar year is the calendar year containing the date described in A-3(a) or A-3(b) of § 1.401(a)(9)-3, whichever is applicable.

(c) *Time for distributions.* The distribution required to be made on or before the employee's required beginning date shall be treated as the distribution required for the employee's first distribution calendar year (as defined in paragraph (b) of this A-1). The required minimum distribution for other distribution calendar years, including the required minimum distribution for the distribution calendar year in which the employee's required beginning date occurs, must be made on or before the end of that distribution calendar year.

(d) *Minimum distribution incidental benefit requirement.* If distributions of an employee's account balance under a defined contribution plan are made in accordance with this section, the minimum distribution incidental benefit requirement of section 401(a)(9)(G) is satisfied. Further, with respect to the retirement benefits provided by that account balance, to the extent the incidental benefit requirement of § 1.401-1(b)(1)(i) requires a distribution, that requirement is deemed to be satisfied if distributions satisfy the minimum distribution incidental benefit requirement of section 401(a)(9)(G) and this section.

(e) *Annuity contracts.* Instead of satisfying this A-1, the minimum distribution requirement may be satisfied by the purchase of an annuity contract from an insurance company in accordance with A-4 of § 1.401(a)(9)-6 with the employee's entire individual account. If such an annuity is purchased after distributions are required to commence (the required beginning date, in the case of distributions commencing before death, or the date determined under A-3 of § 1.401(a)(9)-3, in the case of distributions commencing after death), payments under the annuity contract purchased will satisfy section 401(a)(9) for distribution calendar years after the calendar year of the purchase if payments under the annuity contract are made in accordance with § 1.401(a)(9)-6. In such a case, payments under the annuity contract will be treated as distributions from the individual account for purposes of determining if the individual account satisfies section 401(a)(9) for the calendar year of the purchase. An employee may also purchase an annuity contract with a portion of the employee's account under the rules of A-2(a)(3) of § 1.401(a)(9)-8.

Q-2. If an employee's benefit is in the form of an individual account and, in any calendar year, the amount distributed exceeds the minimum required, will credit be given in subsequent calendar years for such excess distribution?

A-2. If, for any distribution calendar year, the amount distributed exceeds the minimum required, no credit will be given in subsequent calendar years for such excess distribution.

Q-3. What is the amount of the account of an employee used for determining the employee's required minimum distribution in the case of an individual account?

A-3. (a) In the case of an individual account, the benefit used in determining the required minimum distribution for a distribution calendar year is the account balance as of the last valuation date in the calendar year immediately preceding that distribution calendar year (valuation calendar year) adjusted in accordance with paragraphs (b), (c) and (d) of this A-3.

(b) The account balance is increased by the amount of any contributions or forfeitures allocated to the account balance as of dates in the valuation calendar year after the valuation date. For this purpose, contributions that are allocated to the account balance as of dates in the valuation calendar year after the valuation date, but that are not actually made during the valuation calendar year, are permitted to be excluded.

(c) The account balance is decreased by distributions made in the valuation calendar year after the valuation date.

(d) The account balance does not include the value of any qualifying longevity annuity contract (QLAC), defined in A-17 of § 1.401(a)(9)-6, that is held under the plan. This paragraph (d) applies only to contracts purchased on or after July 2, 2014.

(e) If an amount is distributed from a plan and rolled over to another plan (receiving plan), A-2 of § 1.401(a)(9)-7 provides additional rules for determining the benefit and required minimum distribution under the receiving plan. If an amount is transferred from one plan (transferor plan) to another plan (transferee plan), in a transfer to which § 414(l) applies, A-3 and A-4 of § 1.401(a)(9)-7 provide additional rules for determining the amount of the required minimum distribution and the benefit under both the transferor and transferee plans.

Q-4. For required minimum distributions during an employee's lifetime, what is the applicable distribution period?

A-4. (a) *General rule.* Except as provided in paragraph (b) of this A-4, the applicable distribution period for required minimum distributions for distribution calendar years up to and including the distribution calendar year that includes the employee's date of death is determined using the Uniform Lifetime Table in A-2 of § 1.401(a)(9)-9 for the employee's age as of the employee's birthday in the relevant distribution calendar year. If an employee dies on or after the required beginning date, the distribution period applicable for calculating the amount that must be distributed during the distribution calendar year that includes the employee's death is determined as if the employee had lived throughout that year. Thus, a minimum required distribution, determined as if the employee had lived throughout that year, is required for the year of the employee's death and that amount must be distributed to a beneficiary to the extent it has not already been distributed to the employee.

(b) *Spouse is sole beneficiary*—(1) *General rule.* Except as otherwise provided in paragraph (b)(2) of this A-4, if the sole designated beneficiary of an employee is the employee's surviving spouse, for required minimum distributions during the employee's lifetime, the applicable distribution period is the longer of the distribution period determined in accordance with paragraph (a) of this A-4 or the joint life expectancy of the employee and spouse using the employee's and spouse's attained ages as of the employee's and the spouse's birthdays in the distribution calendar year. The spouse is sole designated beneficiary for purposes of determining the applicable distribution period for a distribution calendar year during the employee's lifetime only if the spouse is the sole beneficiary of the employee's entire interest at all times during the distribution calendar year.

(2) *Change in marital status.* If the employee and the employee's spouse are married on January 1 of a distribution calendar year, but do not remain married throughout that year (i.e., the employee or the employee's spouse die or they become divorced during that year), the employee will not fail to have a spouse as the employee's sole beneficiary for that year merely because they are not married throughout that year. If an employee's spouse predeceases the employee, the spouse will not fail to be the employee's sole beneficiary for the distribution calendar year that includes the date of the spouse's death solely because, for the period remaining in that year after the spouse's death, someone other than the spouse is named as beneficiary. However, the change in beneficiary due to the death or divorce of the spouse will be effective for purposes of determining the applicable distribution period under section 401(a)(9) in the distribution calendar year following the distribution calendar year that includes the date of the spouse's death or divorce.

Q-5. For required minimum distributions after an employee's death, what is the applicable distribution period?

A-5. (a) *Death on or after the employee's required beginning date.* If an employee dies after distribution has begun as determined under A-6 of § 1.401(a)(9)-2 (generally on or after the employee's required beginning date), in order to satisfy section 401(a)(9)(B)(i), the applicable distribution period for distribution calendar years after the distribution calendar year containing the employee's date of death is either—

(1) If the employee has a designated beneficiary as of the date determined under A-4 of § 1.401(a)(9)-4, the longer of—

(i) The remaining life expectancy of the employee's designated beneficiary determined in accordance with paragraph (c)(1) or (2) of this A-5; and

(ii) The remaining life expectancy of the employee determined in accordance with paragraph (c)(3) of this A-5; or

(2) If the employee does not have a designated beneficiary as of the date determined under A-4 of § 1.401(a)(9)-4, the remaining life expectancy of the employee determined in accordance with paragraph (c)(3) of this A-5.

(b) *Death before an employee's required beginning date.* If an employee dies before distribution has begun, as determined under A-5 of § 1.401(a)(9)-2 (generally before the employee's required beginning date), in order to satisfy section 401(a)(9)(B)(iii) or (iv) and the life expectancy rule described in A-1 of § 1.401(a)(9)-3, the applicable distribution period for distribution calendar years after the distribution calendar year containing the employee's date of death is determined in accordance with paragraph (c) of this A-5. See A-4 of § 1.401(a)(9)-3 to determine when the 5-year rule of in section 401(a)(9)(B)(ii) applies (e.g., there is no designated beneficiary or the 5-year rule is elected or specified by plan provision).

(c) *Life expectancy*—(1) *Nonspouse designated beneficiary.* Except as otherwise provided in paragraph (c)(2), the applicable distribution period measured by the beneficiary's remaining life expectancy is determined using the beneficiary's age as of the beneficiary's birthday in the calendar year immediately following the calendar year of the employee's death. In subsequent calendar years, the applicable distribution period is reduced by one for each calendar year that has elapsed after the calendar year immediately following the calendar year of the employee's death.

(2) *Spouse designated beneficiary*. If the surviving spouse of the employee is the employee's sole beneficiary, the applicable distribution period is measured by the surviving spouse's life expectancy using the surviving spouse's birthday for each distribution calendar year after the calendar year of the employee's death up through the calendar year of the spouse's death. For calendar years after the calendar year of the spouse's death, the applicable distribution period is the life expectancy of the spouse using the age of the spouse as of the spouse's birthday in the calendar year of the spouse's death, reduced by one for each calendar year that has elapsed after the calendar year of the spouse's death.

(3) *No designated beneficiary*. If the employee does not have a designated beneficiary, the applicable distribution period measured by the employee's remaining life expectancy is the life expectancy of the employee using the age of the employee as of the employee's birthday in the calendar year of the employee's death. In subsequent calendar years the applicable distribution period is reduced by one for each calendar year that has elapsed after the calendar year of the employee's death.

Q-6. What life expectancies must be used for purposes of determining required minimum distributions under section 401(a)(9)?

A-6. Life expectancies for purposes of determining required minimum distributions under section 401(a)(9) must be computed using the Single Life Table in A-1 of § 1.401(a)(9)-9 and the Joint and Last Survivor Table in A-3 of § 1.401(a)(9)-9.

Q-7. If an employee has more than one designated beneficiary, which designated beneficiary's life expectancy will be used to determine the applicable distribution period?

A-7. (a) *General rule*—(1) Except as otherwise provided in paragraph (c) of this A-7, if more than one individual is designated as a beneficiary with respect to an employee as of the applicable date for determining the designated beneficiary under A-4 of § 1.401(a)(9)-4, the designated beneficiary with the shortest life expectancy will be the designated beneficiary for purposes of determining the applicable distribution period.

(2) See A-3 of § 1.401(a)(9)-4 for rules that apply if a person other than an individual is designated as a beneficiary and see A-2 and A-3 of § 1.401(a)(9)-8 for special rules that apply if an employee's benefit under a plan is divided into separate accounts and the beneficiaries with respect to a separate account differ from the beneficiaries of another separate account.

(b) *Contingent beneficiary*. Except as provided in paragraph (c)(1) of this A-7, if a beneficiary's entitlement to an employee's benefit after the employee's death is a contingent right, such contingent beneficiary is nevertheless considered to be a beneficiary for purposes of determining whether a person other than an individual is designated as a beneficiary (resulting in the employee being treated as having no designated beneficiary under the rules of A-3 of § 1.401(a)(9)-4) and which designated beneficiary has the shortest life expectancy under paragraph (a) of this A-7.

(c) *Successor beneficiary*—(1) A person will not be considered a beneficiary for purposes of determining who is the beneficiary with the shortest life expectancy under paragraph (a) of this A-7, or whether a person who is not an individual is a beneficiary, merely because the person could become the successor to the interest of one of the employee's beneficiaries after that beneficiary's death. However, the preceding sentence does not apply to a person who has any right (including a contingent right) to an employee's benefit beyond being a mere potential successor to the interest of one of the employee's beneficiaries upon that beneficiary's death. Thus, for example, if the first beneficiary has a right to all income with respect to an employee's individual account during that beneficiary's life and a second beneficiary has a right to the principal but only after the death of the first income beneficiary (any portion of the principal distributed during the life of the first income beneficiary to be held in trust until that first beneficiary's death), both beneficiaries must be taken into account in determining the beneficiary with the shortest life expectancy and whether only individuals are beneficiaries.

(2) If the individual beneficiary whose life expectancy is being used to calculate the distribution period dies after September 30 of the calendar year following the calendar year of the employee's death, such beneficiary's remaining life expectancy will be used to determine the distribution period without regard to the life expectancy of the subsequent beneficiary.

(3) This paragraph (c) is illustrated by the following examples:

Example 1. (i) Employer M maintains a defined contribution plan, Plan X. Employee A, an employee of M, died in 2005 at the age of 55, survived by spouse, B, who was 50 years old. Prior to A's death, M had established an account balance for A in Plan X. A's account balance is invested only in productive assets. A named a testamentary trust (Trust P) established under A's will as the beneficiary of all amounts payable from A's account in Plan X after A's death. A copy of the Trust P and a list of the trust beneficiaries were provided to the plan administrator of Plan X by October 31 of the calendar year following the calendar year of A's death. As of the date of A's death, the Trust P was irrevocable and was a valid trust under the laws of the state of A's domicile. A's account balance in Plan X was includible in A's gross estate under § 2039.

(ii) Under the terms of Trust P, all trust income is payable annually to B, and no one has the power to appoint Trust P principal to any person other than B. A's children, who are all younger than B, are the sole remainder beneficiaries of the Trust P. No other person has a beneficial interest in Trust P. Under the terms of the Trust P, B has the power, exercisable annually, to compel the trustee to withdraw from A's account balance in Plan X an amount equal to the income earned on the assets held in A's account in Plan X during the calendar year and to distribute that amount through Trust P to B. Plan X contains no prohibition on withdrawal from A's account of amounts in excess of the annual required minimum distributions under section 401(a)(9). In accordance with the terms of Plan X, the trustee of Trust P elects, in order to satisfy section 401(a)(9), to receive annual required minimum distributions using the life expectancy rule in section 401(a)(9)(B)(iii) for distributions over a distribution period equal to B's life expectancy. If B exercises the withdrawal power, the trustee must withdraw from A's account under Plan X the greater of the amount of income earned in the account during the calendar year or the required minimum distribution. However, under the terms of Trust P, and applicable state law, only the portion of the Plan X distribution received by the trustee equal to the income earned by A's account in Plan X is required to be distributed to B (along with any other trust income.)

(iii) Because some amounts distributed from A's account in Plan X to Trust P may be accumulated in Trust P during B's lifetime for the benefit of A's children, as remaindermen beneficiaries of Trust P, even though access to those amounts are delayed until after B's death, A's children are beneficiaries of A's account in Plan X in addition to B and B is not the sole designated beneficiary of A's account. Thus the designated beneficiary used to determine the distribution period from A's account in Plan X is the beneficiary with the shortest life expectancy. B's life expectancy is the shortest of all the potential beneficiaries of the testamentary trust's interest in A's account in Plan X (including remainder beneficiaries). Thus, the distribution period for purposes of section 401(a)(9)(B)(iii) is B's life expectancy. Because B is not the sole designated beneficiary of the testamentary trust's interest in A's account in Plan X, the special rule in 401(a)(9)(B)(iv) is not available and the annual required minimum distributions from the account to Trust M must begin no later than the end of the calendar year immediately following the calendar year of A's death.

Example 2. (i) The facts are the same as Example 1 except that the testamentary trust instrument provides that all amounts distributed from A's account in Plan X to the trustee while B is alive will be paid directly to B upon receipt by the trustee of Trust P.

(ii) In this case, B is the sole designated beneficiary of A's account in Plan X for purposes of determining the designated beneficiary under section 401(a)(9)(B)(iii) and (iv). No amounts distributed from A's account in Plan X to Trust P are accumulated in Trust P during B's lifetime for the benefit of any other beneficiary. Therefore, the residuary beneficiaries of Trust P are mere potential successors to B's interest in Plan X. Because B is the sole beneficiary of the testamentary trust's interest in A's account in Plan X, the annual required minimum distributions from A's account to Trust P must begin no later than the end of the calendar year in which A would have attained age 70½, rather than the calendar year immediately following the calendar year of A's death.

Q-8. If a portion of an employee's individual account is not vested as of the employee's required beginning date, how is the determination of the required minimum distribution affected?

A-8. If the employee's benefit is in the form of an individual account, the benefit used to determine the required minimum distribution for any distribution calendar year will be determined in accordance with A-1 of this section without regard to whether or not all of the employee's benefit is vested. If any portion of the employee's benefit is not vested, distributions will be treated as being paid from the vested portion of the benefit first. If, as of the end of a distribution calendar year (or as of the employee's required beginning date, in the case of the employee's first distribution calendar year), the total amount of the employee's vested benefit is less than the required minimum distribution for the calendar year, only

the vested portion, if any, of the employee's benefit is required to be distributed by the end of the calendar year (or, if applicable, by the employee's required beginning date). However, the required minimum distribution for the subsequent distribution calendar year must be increased by the sum of amounts not distributed in prior calendar years because the employee's vested benefit was less than the required minimum distribution.

Q-9. Which amounts distributed from an individual account are taken into account in determining whether section 401(a)(9) is satisfied and which amounts are not taken into account in determining whether section 401(a)(9) is satisfied?

A-9. (a) *General rule.* Except as provided in paragraph (b), all amounts distributed from an individual account are distributions that are taken into account in determining whether section 401(a)(9) is satisfied, regardless of whether the amount is includible in income. Thus, for example, amounts that are excluded from income as recovery of investment in the contract under section 72 are taken into account for purposes of determining whether section 401(a)(9) is satisfied for a distribution calendar year. Similarly, amounts excluded from income as net unrealized appreciation on employer securities also are amounts distributed for purposes of determining if section 401(a)(9) is satisfied.

(b) *Exceptions.* The following amounts are not taken into account in determining whether the required minimum amount has been distributed for a calendar year:

(1) Elective deferrals and employee contributions that, pursuant to § 1.415-6(b)(6)(iv), are returned (together with the income allocable to these corrective distributions) as a result of the application of the section 415 limitations.

(2) Corrective distributions of excess deferrals as described in § 1.402(g)-1(e)(3), together with the income allocable to these distributions.

(3) Corrective distributions of excess contributions under a qualified cash or deferred arrangement under section 401(k)(8) and excess aggregate contributions under section 401(m)(6), together with the income allocable to these distributions.

(4) Loans that are treated as deemed distributions pursuant to section 72(p).

(5) Dividends described in section 404(k) that are paid on employer securities. (Amounts paid to the plan that, pursuant to section 404(k)(2)(A)(iii)(II), are included in the account balance and subsequently distributed from the account lose their character as dividends.)

(6) The costs of life insurance coverage (P.S. 58 costs).

(7) Similar items designated by the Commissioner in revenue rulings, notices, and other guidance published in the Internal Revenue Bulletin. See § 601.601(d)(2)(ii)(b) of this chapter.

§ 1.401(a)(9)-6. Required minimum distributions for defined benefit plans and annuity contracts.

Q-1. How must distributions under a defined benefit plan be paid in order to satisfy section 401(a)(9)?

A-1. (a) *General rules.* In order to satisfy section 401(a)(9), except as otherwise provided in this section, distributions of the employee's entire interest under a defined benefit plan must be paid in the form of periodic annuity payments for the employee's life (or the joint lives of the employee and beneficiary) or over a period certain that does not exceed the maximum length of the period certain determined in accordance with A-3 of this section. The interval between payments for the annuity must be uniform over the entire distribution period and must not exceed one year. Once payments have commenced over a period, the period may only be changed in accordance with A-13 of this section. Life (or joint and survivor) annuity payments must satisfy the minimum distribution incidental benefit requirements of A-2 of this section. Except as

otherwise provided in this section (such as permitted increases described in A-14 of this section), all payments (whether paid over an employee's life, joint lives, or a period certain) also must be nonincreasing.

(b) *Life annuity with period certain.* The annuity may be a life annuity (or joint and survivor annuity) with a period certain if the life (or lives, if applicable) and period certain each meet the requirements of paragraph (a) of this A-1. For purposes of this section, if distributions are permitted to be made over the lives of the employee and the designated beneficiary, references to a life annuity include a joint and survivor annuity.

(c) *Annuity commencement.* (1) Annuity payments must commence on or before the employee's required beginning date (within the meaning of A-2 of § 1.401(a)(9)-2). The first payment, which must be made on or before the employee's required beginning date, must be the payment which is required for one payment interval. The second payment need not be made until the end of the next payment interval even if that payment interval ends in the next calendar year. Similarly, in the case of distributions commencing after death in accordance with section 401(a)(9)(B)(iii) and (iv), the first payment, which must be made on or before the date determined under A-3(a) or (b) (whichever is applicable) of § 1.401(a)(9)-3, must be the payment which is required for one payment interval. Payment intervals are the periods for which payments are received, e.g., bimonthly, monthly, semi-annually, or annually. All benefit accruals as of the last day of the first distribution calendar year must be included in the calculation of the amount of annuity payments for payment intervals ending on or after the employee's required beginning date.

(2) This paragraph (c) is illustrated by the following example:

Example. A defined benefit plan (Plan X) provides monthly annuity payments of $500 for the life of unmarried participants with a 10-year period certain. An unmarried, retired participant (A) in Plan X attains age 70½ in

2005. In order to meet the requirements of this paragraph, the first monthly payment of $500 must be made on behalf of A on or before April 1, 2006, and the payments must continue to be made in monthly payments of $500 thereafter for the life and 10-year period certain.

(d) *Single sum distributions.* In the case of a single sum distribution of an employee's entire accrued benefit during a distribution calendar year, the amount that is the required minimum distribution for the distribution calendar year (and thus not eligible for rollover under section 402(c)) is determined using either the rule in paragraph (d)(1) or the rule in paragraph (d)(2) of this A-1.

(1) The portion of the single sum distribution that is a required minimum distribution is determined by treating the single sum distribution as a distribution from an individual account plan and treating the amount of the single sum distribution as the employee's account balance as of the end of the relevant valuation calendar year. If the single sum distribution is being made in the calendar year containing the required beginning date and the required minimum distribution for the employee's first distribution calendar year has not been distributed, the portion of the single sum distribution that represents the required minimum distribution for the employee's first and second distribution calendar years is not eligible for rollover.

(2) The portion of the single sum distribution that is a required minimum distribution is permitted to be determined by expressing the employee's benefit as an annuity that would satisfy this section with an annuity starting date as of the first day of the distribution calendar year for which the required minimum distribution is being determined, and treating one year of annuity payments as the required minimum distribution for that year, and not eligible for rollover. If the single sum distribution is being made in the calendar year containing the required beginning date and the required minimum distribution for the employee's first distribution calendar year has not been made, the benefit must be expressed as

an annuity with an annuity starting date as of the first day of the first distribution calendar year and the payments for the first two distribution calendar years would be treated as required minimum distributions, and not eligible for rollover.

(e) *Death benefits.* The rule in paragraph (a) of this A-1, prohibiting increasing payments under an annuity applies to payments made upon the death of an employee. However, for purposes of this section, an ancillary death benefit described in this paragraph (e) may be disregarded in applying that rule. Such an ancillary death benefit is excluded in determining an employee's entire interest and the rules prohibiting increasing payments do not apply to such an ancillary death benefit. A death benefit with respect to an employee's benefit is an ancillary death benefit for purposes of this A-1 if—

(1) It is not paid as part of the employee's accrued benefit or under any optional form of the employee's benefit; and

(2) The death benefit, together with any other potential payments with respect to the employee's benefit that may be provided to a survivor, satisfy the incidental benefit requirement of § 1.401-1(b)(1)(i).

(f) *Additional guidance.* Additional guidance regarding how distributions under a defined benefit plan must be paid in order to satisfy section 401(a)(9) may be issued by the Commissioner in revenue rulings, notices, or other guidance published in the Internal Revenue Bulletin. See § 601.601(d)(2)(ii)(b) of this chapter.

Q-2. How must distributions in the form of a life (or joint and survivor) annuity be made in order to satisfy the minimum distribution incidental benefit (MDIB) requirement of section 401(a)(9)(G) and the distribution component of the incidental benefit requirement of § 1.401-1(b)(1)(i)?

A-2. (a) *Life annuity for employee.* If the employee's benefit is payable in the form of a life annuity for the life of the employee satisfying section 401(a)(9) without regard to the

MDIB requirement, the MDIB requirement of section 401(a)(9)(G) will be satisfied.

(b) *Joint and survivor annuity, spouse beneficiary.* If the employee's sole beneficiary, as of the annuity starting date for annuity payments, is the employee's spouse and the distributions satisfy section 401(a)(9) without regard to the MDIB requirement, the distributions to the employee will be deemed to satisfy the MDIB requirement of section 401(a)(9)(G). For example, if an employee's benefit is being distributed in the form of a joint and survivor annuity for the lives of the employee and the employee's spouse and the spouse is the sole beneficiary of the employee, the amount of the periodic payment payable to the spouse would not violate the MDIB requirement if it was 100 percent of the annuity payment payable to the employee, regardless of the difference in the ages between the employee and the employee's spouse.

(c) *Joint and survivor annuity, nonspouse beneficiary*—(1) *Explanation of rule.* If distributions commence under a distribution option that is in the form of a joint and survivor annuity for the joint lives of the employee and a beneficiary other than the employee's spouse, the minimum distribution incidental benefit requirement will not be satisfied as of the date distributions commence unless under the distribution option, the annuity payments to be made on and after the employee's required beginning date will satisfy the conditions of this paragraph (c). The periodic annuity payment payable to the survivor must not at any time on and after the employee's required beginning date exceed the applicable percentage of the annuity payment payable to the employee using the table in paragraph (c)(2) of this A-2. The applicable percentage is based on the adjusted employee/beneficiary age difference. The adjusted employee/beneficiary age difference is determined by first calculating the excess of the age of the employee over the age of the beneficiary based on their ages on their birthdays in a calendar year. Then, if the employee is younger than age 70, the age difference determined in the previous sentence is reduced by the number of years that the employee is younger than age 70 on the employee's birthday in the calendar year that contains the annuity starting date. In the case of an annuity that provides for increasing payments, the requirement of this paragraph (c) will not be violated merely because benefit payments to the beneficiary increase, provided the increase is determined in the same manner for the employee and the beneficiary.

(2) *Table.*

Excess of age of employee over age of beneficiary	Applicable percentage
10 years or less	100%
11	96%
12	93%
13	90%
14	87%
15	84%
16	82%
17	79%
18	77%
19	75%
20	73%
21	72%
22	70%
23	68%
24	67%
25	66%
26	64%
27	63%
28	62%
29	61%
30	60%
31	59%
32	59%
33	58%
34	57%
35	56%
36	56%
37	55%
38	55%
39	54%
40	54%
41	53%
42	53%
43	53%
44 and greater	52%

(3) *Example.* This paragraph (c) is illustrated by the following example:

Example. Distributions commence on January 1, 2003 to an employee (Z), born March 1, 1937, after retirement at age 65. Z's daughter (Y), born February 5, 1967, is Z's beneficiary. The distributions are in the form of a joint and survivor annuity for the lives of Z and Y with payments of $500 a month to Z and upon Z's death of $500 a month to Y, i.e., the projected monthly payment to Y is 100 percent of the monthly amount payable to Z. Accordingly, under A-10 of this section, compliance with the rules of this section is determined as of the annuity starting date. The adjusted employee/beneficiary age difference is calculated by taking the excess of the employee's age over the beneficiary's age and subtracting the number of years the employee is younger than age 70. In this case, Z is 30 years older than Y and is commencing benefit 4 years before attaining age 70 so the adjusted employee/beneficiary age difference is 26 years. Under the table in paragraph (c)(2) of this A-2, the applicable percentage for a 26-year adjusted employee/beneficiary age difference is 64 percent. As of January 1, 2003 (the annuity starting date) the plan does not satisfy the MDIB requirement because, as of such date, the distribution option provides that, as of Z's required beginning date, the monthly payment to Y upon Z's death will exceed 66 percent of Z's monthly payment.

(d) *Period certain and annuity features.* If a distribution form includes a period certain, the amount of the annuity payments payable to the beneficiary need not be reduced during the period certain, but in the case of a joint and survivor annuity with a period certain, the amount of the annuity payments payable to the beneficiary must satisfy paragraph (c) of this A-2 after the expiration of the period certain.

(e) *Deemed satisfaction of incidental benefit rule.* Except in the case of distributions with respect to an employee's benefit that include an ancillary death benefit described in paragraph A-1(e) of this section, to the extent

the incidental benefit requirement of § 1.401-1(b)(1)(i) requires a distribution, that requirement is deemed to be satisfied if distributions satisfy the minimum distribution incidental benefit requirement of this A-2. If the employee's benefits include an ancillary death benefit described in paragraph A-1(e) of this section, the benefits (including the ancillary death benefit) must be distributed in accordance with the incidental benefit requirement described in § 1.401-1(b)(1)(i) and the benefits (excluding the ancillary death benefit) must also satisfy the minimum distribution incidental benefit requirement of this A-2.

* * *

Q-14. Are annuity payments permitted to increase?

A-14. (a) *General rules.* Except as otherwise provided in this section, all annuity payments (whether paid over an employee's life, joint lives, or a period certain) must be nonincreasing or increase only in accordance with one or more of the following—

(1) With an annual percentage increase that does not exceed the percentage increase in an eligible cost-of-living index as defined in paragraph (b) of this A-14 for a 12-month period ending in the year during which the increase occurs or the prior year;

(2) With a percentage increase that occurs at specified times (e.g., at specified ages) and does not exceed the cumulative total of annual percentage increases in an eligible cost-of-living index as defined in paragraph (b) of this A-14 since the annuity starting date, or if later, the date of the most recent percentage increase. However, in cases providing such a cumulative increase, an actuarial increase may not be provided to reflect the fact that increases were not provided in the interim years;

(3) To the extent of the reduction in the amount of the employee's payments to provide for a survivor benefit, but only if there is no longer a survivor benefit because the beneficiary whose life was being used to determine the period described in section 401(a)(9)(A)(ii) over which payments were

being made dies or is no longer the employee's beneficiary pursuant to a qualified domestic relations order within the meaning of section 414(p);

(4) To pay increased benefits that result from a plan amendment;

(5) To allow a beneficiary to convert the survivor portion of a joint and survivor annuity into a single sum distribution upon the employee's death; or

(6) To the extent increases are permitted in accordance with paragraph (c) or (d) of this A-14.

(b)(1) For purposes of this A-14, an eligible cost-of-living index means an index described in paragraphs (b)(2), (b)(3), or (b)(4) of this A-14.

(2) A consumer price index that is based on prices of all items (or all items excluding food and energy) and issued by the Bureau of Labor Statistics, including an index for a specific population (such as urban consumers or urban wage earners and clerical workers) and an index for a geographic area or areas (such as a given metropolitan area or state).

(3) A percentage adjustment based on a cost-of-living index described in paragraph (b)(2) of this A-14, or a fixed percentage if less. In any year when the cost-of-living index is lower than the fixed percentage, the fixed percentage may be treated as an increase in an eligible cost-of-living index, provided it does not exceed the sum of:

(i) The cost-of-living index for that year, and

(ii) The accumulated excess of the annual cost-of-living index from each prior year over the fixed annual percentage used in that year (reduced by any amount previously utilized under this paragraph (b)(3)(ii)).

(4) A percentage adjustment based on the increase in compensation for the position held by the employee at the time of retirement, and provided under either the terms of a governmental plan within the meaning of section

414(d) or under the terms of a nongovernmental plan as in effect on April 17, 2002.

(c) *Additional permitted increases for annuity payments under annuity contracts purchased from insurance companies.* In the case of annuity payments paid from an annuity contract purchased from an insurance company, if the total future expected payments (determined in accordance with paragraph (e)(3) of this A-14) exceed the total value being annuitized (within the meaning of paragraph (e)(1) of this A-14), the payments under the annuity will not fail to satisfy the nonincreasing payment requirement in A-1(a) of this section merely because the payments are increased in accordance with one or more of the following—

(1) By a constant percentage, applied not less frequently than annually;

(2) To provide a final payment upon the death of the employee that does not exceed the excess of the total value being annuitized (within the meaning of paragraph (e)(1) of this A-14) over the total of payments before the death of the employee;

(3) As a result of dividend payments or other payments that result from actuarial gains (within the meaning of paragraph (e)(2) of this A-14), but only if actuarial gain is measured no less frequently than annually and the resulting dividend payments or other payments are either paid no later than the year following the year for which the actuarial experience is measured or paid in the same form as the payment of the annuity over the remaining period of the annuity (beginning no later than the year following the year for which the actuarial experience is measured); and

(4) An acceleration of payments under the annuity (within the meaning of paragraph (e)(4) of this A-14).

(d) *Additional permitted increases for annuity payments from a qualified trust.* In the case of annuity payments paid under a defined benefit plan qualified under section 401(a) (other than annuity payments under an annuity contract purchased from an insurance company that satisfy paragraph (c) of this section), the payments under the annuity will not fail to satisfy the nonincreasing payment requirement in A-1(a) of this section merely because the payments are increased in accordance with one of the following—

(1) By a constant percentage, applied not less frequently than annually, at a rate that is less than 5 percent per year;

(2) To provide a final payment upon the death of the employee that does not exceed the excess of the actuarial present value of the employee's accrued benefit (within the meaning of section 411(a)(7)) calculated as the annuity starting date using the applicable interest rate and the applicable mortality table under section 417(e) (or, if greater, the total amount of employee contributions) over the total of payments before the death of the employee; or

(3) As a result of dividend payments or other payments that result from actuarial gains (within the meaning of paragraph (e)(2) of this A-14), but only if—

(i) Actuarial gain is measured no less frequently than annually;

(ii) The resulting dividend payments or other payments are either paid no later than the year following the year for which the actuarial experience is measured or paid in the same form as the payment of the annuity over the remaining period of the annuity (beginning no later than the year following the year for which the actuarial experience is measured);

(iii) The actuarial gain taken into account is limited to actuarial gain from investment experience;

(iv) The assumed interest used to calculate such actuarial gains is not less than 3 percent; and

(v) The payments are not increasing by a constant percentage as described in paragraph (d)(1) of this A-14.

* * *

Q-17. What is a qualifying longevity annuity contract?

A-17. (a) Definition of qualifying longevity annuity contract. A qualifying longevity annuity contract (QLAC) is an annuity contract that is purchased from an insurance company for an employee and that, in accordance with the rules of application of paragraph (d) of this A-17, satisfies each of the following requirements—

(1) Premiums for the contract satisfy the requirements of paragraph (b) of this A-17;

(2) The contract provides that distributions under the contract must commence not later than a specified annuity starting date that is no later than the first day of the month next following the 85th anniversary of the employee's birth;

(3) The contract provides that, after distributions under the contract commence, those distributions must satisfy the requirements of this section (other than the requirement in A-1(c) of this section that annuity payments commence on or before the required beginning date);

(4) The contract does not make available any commutation benefit, cash surrender right, or other similar feature;

(5) No benefits are provided under the contract after the death of the employee other than the benefits described in paragraph (c) of this A-17;

(6) When the contract is issued, the contract (or a rider or endorsement with respect to that contract) states that the contract is intended to be a QLAC; and

(7) The contract is not a variable contract under section 817, an indexed contract, or a similar contract, except to the extent provided by the Commissioner in revenue rulings, notices, or other guidance published in the Internal Revenue Bulletin and made available by the Superintendent of Documents, U.S. Government Printing Office, Washington, DC 20402 and on the IRS Web site at http://www.irs.gov.

* * *

§ 1.401(a)(9)-7. Rollovers and Transfers.

Q-1. If an amount is distributed by one plan (distributing plan) and is rolled over to another plan, is the required minimum distribution under the distributing plan affected by the rollover?

A-1. No, if an amount is distributed by one plan and is rolled over to another plan, the amount distributed is still treated as a distribution by the distributing plan for purposes of section 401(a)(9), notwithstanding the rollover. See A-1 of § 1.402(c)-2 for the definition of a rollover and A-7 of § 1.402(c)-2 for rules for determining the portion of any distribution that is not eligible for rollover because it is a required minimum distribution.

Q-2. If an amount is distributed by one plan (distributing plan) and is rolled over to another plan (receiving plan), how are the benefit and the required minimum distribution under the receiving plan affected?

A-2. If an amount is distributed by one plan (distributing plan) and is rolled over to another plan (receiving plan), the benefit of the employee under the receiving plan is increased by the amount rolled over for purposes of determining the required minimum distribution for the calendar year immediately following the calendar year in which the amount rolled over is distributed. If the amount rolled over is received after the last valuation date in the calendar year under the receiving plan, the benefit of the employee as of such valuation date, adjusted in accordance with A-3 of § 1.401(a)(9)-5, will be increased by the rollover amount valued as of the date of receipt. In addition, if the amount rolled over is received in a different calendar year from the calendar year in which it is distributed, the amount rolled over is deemed to have been received by the receiving plan in the calendar year in which it was distributed.

Q-3. In the case of a transfer of an amount of an employee's benefit from one plan (transferor plan) to another plan (transferee plan), are there any special rules for satisfying section 401(a)(9) or determining the employee's benefit under the transferor plan?

A-3. (a) In the case of a transfer of an amount of an employee's benefit from one plan (transferor plan) to another (transferee plan), the transfer is not treated as a distribution by the transferor plan for purposes of section 401(a)(9). Instead, the benefit of the employee under the transferor plan is decreased by the amount transferred. However, if any portion of an employee's benefit is transferred in a distribution calendar year with respect to that employee, in order to satisfy section 401(a)(9), the transferor plan must determine the amount of the required minimum distribution with respect to that employee for the calendar year of the transfer using the employee's benefit under the transferor plan before the transfer. Additionally, if any portion of an employee's benefit is transferred in the employee's second distribution calendar year but on or before the employee's required beginning date, in order to satisfy section 401(a)(9), the transferor plan must determine the amount of the minimum distribution requirement for the employee's first distribution calendar year based on the employee's benefit under the transferor plan before the transfer. The transferor plan may satisfy the minimum distribution requirement for the calendar year of the transfer (and the prior year if applicable) by segregating the amount which must be distributed from the employee's benefit and not transferring that amount. Such amount may be retained by the transferor plan and must be distributed on or before the date required under section 401(a)(9).

(b) For purposes of determining any required minimum distribution for the calendar year immediately following the calendar year in which the transfer occurs, in the case of a transfer after the last valuation date for the calendar year of the transfer under the transferor plan, the benefit of the employee as of such valuation date, adjusted in accordance with A-3 of § 1.401(a)(9)-5, will be decreased by the amount transferred, valued as of the date of the transfer.

Q-4. If an amount of an employee's benefit is transferred from one plan (transferor plan) to another plan (transferee plan), how are the benefit and the required minimum distribution under the transferee plan affected?

A-4. In the case of a transfer from one plan (transferor plan) to another (transferee plan), the benefit of the employee under the transferee plan is increased by the amount transferred in the same manner as if it were a plan receiving a rollover contribution under A-2 of this section.

Q-5. How is a spinoff, merger or consolidation (as defined in § 1.414(l)-1) treated for purposes of determining an employee's benefit and required minimum distribution under section 401(a)(9)?

A-5. For purposes of determining an employee's benefit and required minimum distribution under section 401(a)(9), a spinoff, a merger, or a consolidation (as defined in § 1.414(l)-1) will be treated as a transfer of the benefits of the employees involved. Consequently, the benefit and required minimum distribution of each employee involved under the transferor and transferee plans will be determined in accordance with A-3 and A-4 of this section.

§ 1.401(a)(9)-9. Life expectancy and distribution period tables.

Q-1. What is the life expectancy for an individual for purposes of determining required minimum distributions under section 401(a)(9)?

A-1. The following table, referred to as the Single Life Table, is used for determining the life expectancy of an individual:

Single Life Table

Age	Life Expectancy	Age	Life Expectancy	Age	Life Expectancy	Age	Life Expectancy
0	82.4	29	54.3	58	27.0	87	6.7
1	81.6	30	53.3	59	26.1	88	6.3
2	80.6	31	52.4	60	25.2	89	5.9
3	79.7	32	51.4	61	24.4	90	5.5
4	78.7	33	50.4	62	23.5	91	5.2
5	77.7	34	49.4	63	22.7	92	4.9
6	76.7	35	48.5	64	21.8	93	4.6
7	75.8	36	47.5	65	21.0	94	4.3
8	74.8	37	46.5	66	20.2	95	4.1
9	73.8	38	45.6	67	19.4	96	3.8
10	72.8	39	44.6	68	18.6	97	3.6
11	71.8	40	43.6	69	17.8	98	3.4
12	70.8	41	42.7	70	17.0	99	3.1
13	69.9	42	41.7	71	16.3	100	2.9
14	68.9	43	40.7	72	15.5	101	2.7
15	67.9	44	39.8	73	14.8	102	2.5
16	66.9	45	38.8	74	14.1	103	2.3
17	66.0	46	37.9	75	13.4	104	2.1
18	65.0	47	37.0	76	12.7	105	1.9
19	64.0	48	36.0	77	12.1	106	1.7
20	63.0	49	35.1	78	11.4	107	1.5
21	62.1	50	34.2	79	10.8	108	1.4
22	61.1	51	33.3	80	10.2	109	1.2
23	60.1	52	32.3	81	9.7	110	1.1
24	59.1	53	31.4	82	9.1	111+	1.0
25	58.2	54	30.5	83	8.6		
26	57.2	55	29.6	84	8.1		
27	56.2	56	28.7	85	7.6		
28	55.3	57	27.9	86	7.1		

Q-2. What is the applicable distribution period for an individual account for purposes of determining required minimum distributions during an employee's lifetime under section 401(a)(9)?

A-2. Table for determining distribution period. The following table, referred to as the Uniform Lifetime Table, is used for determining the distribution period for lifetime distributions to an employee in situations in which the employee's spouse is either not the sole designated beneficiary or is the sole designated beneficiary but is not more than 10 years younger than the employee.

Uniform Lifetime Table

Age of the employee	Distribution period
70	27.4
71	26.5
72	25.6
73	24.7
74	23.8
75	22.9
76	22.0
77	21.2
78	20.3
79	19.5
80	18.7
81	17.9
82	17.1
83	16.3
84	15.5
85	14.8
86	14.1
87	13.4
88	12.7
89	12.0
90	11.4
91	10.8
92	10.2
93	9.6
94	9.1
95	8.6
96	8.1
97	7.6
98	7.1
99	6.7
100	6.3
101	5.9
102	5.5
103	5.2
104	4.9
105	4.5
106	4.2
107	3.9
108	3.7
109	3.4
110	3.1
111	2.9
112	2.6
113	2.4
114	2.1
115 and older	1.9

Q-3. What is the joint life and last survivor expectancy of an individual and beneficiary for purposes of determining required minimum distributions under section 401(a)(9)?

A-3. The following table, referred to as the Joint and Last Survivor Table, is used for determining the joint and last survivor life expectancy of two individuals:

Joint and Last Survivor Table

* * *

§ 1.401(a)(17)-1. Limitation on annual compensation.

* * *

(c) *Limit on compensation for nondiscrimination rules*—(1) *General rule.* The annual compensation limit applies for purposes of applying the nondiscrimination rules under sections 401(a)(4), 401(a)(5), 401(l), 401(k)(3), 401(m)(2), 403(b)(12), 404(a)(2) and 410(b)(2). The annual compensation limit also applies in determining whether an alternative method of determining compensation impermissibly discriminates under section 414(s)(3). Thus, for example, the annual compensation limit applies when determining a self-employed individual's total earned income that is used to determine the equivalent alternative compensation amount under § 1.414(s)-1(g)(1). This paragraph (c) provides rules for applying the annual compensation limit for these purposes. For purposes of this paragraph (c), compensation means the compensation used in applying the applicable nondiscrimination rule.

* * *

§ 1.401(a)(26)-1. Minimum participation requirements.

* * *

(b) *Exceptions to section 401(a)(26)*—(1) Plans that do not benefit any highly compensated employees. A plan, other than a frozen defined benefit plan as defined in § 1.401(a)(26)-2(b), satisfies section 401(a)(26) for a plan year if the plan is not a top-heavy plan under section 416 and the plan meets the following requirements:

(i) The plan benefits no highly compensated employee or highly compensated former employee of the employer; and

(ii) The plan is not aggregated with any other plan of the employer to enable the other plan to satisfy section 401(a)(4) or 410(b). The plan may, however, be aggregated with the employer's other plans for purposes of the average benefit percentage test in section 410(b)(2)(A)(ii).

* * *

§ 1.401(a)(31)-1. Requirement to offer direct rollover of eligible rollover distributions; questions and answers.

* * *

Q-3: What is a direct rollover that satisfies section 401(a)(31), and how is it accomplished?

A-3: A direct rollover that satisfies section 401(a)(31) is an eligible rollover distribution that is paid directly to an eligible retirement plan for the benefit of the distributee. A direct rollover may be accomplished by any reasonable means of direct payment to an eligible retirement plan. Reasonable means of direct payment include, for example, a wire transfer or the mailing of a check to the eligible retirement plan. If payment is made by check, the check must be negotiable only by the trustee of the eligible retirement plan. If the payment is made by wire transfer, the wire

transfer must be directed only to the trustee of the eligible retirement plan. In the case of an eligible retirement plan that does not have a trustee (such as a custodial individual retirement account or an individual retirement annuity), the custodian of the plan or issuer of the contract under the plan, as appropriate, should be substituted for the trustee for purposes of this Q&A-3, and Q&A-4 of this section.

Q-4: Is providing a distributee with a check for delivery to an eligible retirement plan a reasonable means of accomplishing a direct rollover?

A-4: Providing the distributee with a check and instructing the distributee to deliver the check to the eligible retirement plan is a reasonable means of direct payment, provided that the check is made payable as follows: [Name of the trustee] as trustee of [name of the eligible retirement plan]. For example, if the name of the eligible retirement plan is "Individual Retirement Account of John Q. Smith," and the name of the trustee is "ABC Bank," the payee line of a check would read "ABC Bank as trustee of Individual Retirement Account of John Q. Smith." Unless the name of the distributee is included in the name of the eligible retirement plan, the check also must indicate that it is for the benefit of the distributee. If the eligible retirement plan is not an individual retirement account or an individual retirement annuity, the payee line of the check need not identify the trustee by name. For example, the payee line of a check for the benefit of distributee Jane Doe might read, "Trustee of XYZ Corporation Savings Plan FBO Jane Doe."

* * *

§ 1.401(b)-1. Certain retroactive changes in plan.

(a) *General rule.* Under section 401(b) a stock bonus, pension, profit-sharing, annuity, or bond purchase plan which does not satisfy the requirements of section 401(a) on any day solely as a result of a disqualifying provision (as defined in paragraph (b) of this section) shall be considered to have satisfied such requirements on such date if, on or before the last day of the remedial amendment period (as determined under paragraphs (d), (e) and (f) of this section) with respect to such disqualifying provision, all provisions of the plan which are necessary to satisfy all requirements of sections 401(a), 403(a), or 405(a) are in effect and have been made effective for all purposes for the whole of such period. Under some facts and circumstances, it may not be possible to amend a plan retroactively so that all provisions of the plan which are necessary to satisfy the requirements of section 401(a) are in fact made effective for the whole remedial amendment period. If it is not possible, the requirements of this section will not be satisfied even if the employer adopts a retroactive plan amendment which, in form, appears to satisfy such requirements. Section 401(b) does not permit a plan to be made retroactively effective, for qualification purposes, for a taxable year prior to the taxable year of the employer in which the plan was adopted by such employer.

(b) *Disqualifying provisions*. For purposes of this section, with respect to a plan described in paragraph (a) of this section, the term "disqualifying provision" means:

(1) A provision of a new plan, the absence of a provision from a new plan, or an amendment to an existing plan, which causes such plan to fail to satisfy the requirements of the Code applicable to qualification of such plan as of the date such plan or amendment is first made effective

* * *

(3) A plan provision designated by the Commissioner, at the Commissioner's discretion, as a disqualifying provision that either—

(i) Results in the failure of the plan to satisfy the qualification requirements of the Internal Revenue Code by reason of a change in those requirements; or

(ii) Is integral to a qualification requirement of the Internal Revenue Code that has been changed.

(c) *Special rules applicable to disqualifying provisions*—(1) *Absence of plan provision*. For purposes of paragraphs (b)(2) and (3) of this section, a disqualifying provision includes the absence from a plan of a provision required by, or, if applicable, integral to the applicable change to the qualification requirements of the Internal Revenue Code, if the plan was in effect on the date the change became effective with respect to the plan.

(2) *Method of designating disqualifying provisions*. The Commissioner may designate a plan provision as a disqualifying provision pursuant to paragraph (b)(3) of this section only in revenue rulings, notices, and other guidance published in the Internal Revenue Bulletin. See § 601.601(d)(2) of this chapter.

(3) *Authority to impose limitations*. In the case of a provision that has been designated as a disqualifying provision by the Commissioner pursuant to paragraph (b)(3) of this section, the Commissioner may impose limits and provide additional rules regarding the amendments that may be made with respect to that disqualifying provision during the remedial amendment period. The Commissioner may provide guidance in revenue rulings, notices, and other guidance published in the Internal Revenue Bulletin. See § 601.601(d)(2) of this chapter.

(d) *Remedial amendment period*. (1) The remedial amendment period with respect to a disqualifying provision begins:

(i) In the case of a provision of, or absence of a provision from, a new plan, described in paragraph (b)(1) of this section, the date the plan is put into effect,

(ii) In the case of an amendment to an existing plan, described in paragraph (b)(1) of this section, the date the plan amendment is adopted or put into effect (whichever is earlier),

* * *

(iv) In the case of a disqualifying provision described in paragraph (b)(3)(i) of this section, the date on which the change effected by an amendment to the Internal Revenue

Code became effective with respect to the plan; or

(v) In the case of a disqualifying provision described in paragraph (b)(3)(ii) of this section, the first day on which the plan was operated in accordance with such provision, as amended, unless another time is specified by the Commissioner in revenue rulings, notices, and other guidance published in the Internal Revenue Bulletin. See § 601.601(d)(2) of this chapter.

(2) Unless further extended as provided by paragraph (e) of this section, the remedial amendment period ends with the latest of:

(i) In the case of a plan maintained by one employer, the time prescribed by law, including extensions, for filing the income tax return (or partnership return of income) of the employer for the employer's taxable year in which falls the latest of:

(A) The date on which the remedial amendment period begins.

(B) The date on which a plan amendment described in paragraph (b)(1) of this section is adopted, or

(C) The date on which a plan amendment described in paragraph (b)(1) of this section is made effective,

(ii) In the case of a plan maintained by one employer, the last day of the plan year within which falls the latest of:

(A) The date on which the remedial amendment period begins,

(B) The date on which a plan amendment described in paragraph (b)(1) of this section is adopted, or

(C) The date on which a plan amendment described in paragraph (b)(1) of this section is made effective,

* * *

(f) *Discretionary extensions.* At his discretion, the Commissioner may extend the remedial amendment period or may allow a particular plan to be amended after the expira-

tion of its remedial amendment period and any applicable extension of such period. In determining whether such an extension will be granted, the Commissioner shall consider, among other factors, whether substantial hardship to the employer would result if such an extension were not granted, whether such an extension is in the best interest of plan participants, and whether the granting of the extension is adverse to the interests of the Government.

* * *

§ 1.401(k)-1. Certain cash or deferred arrangements.

(a) *General rules*—(1) *Certain plans permitted to include cash or deferred arrangements.* A plan, other than a profit-sharing, stock bonus, pre-ERISA money purchase pension, or rural cooperative plan, does not satisfy the requirements of section 401(a) if the plan includes a cash or deferred arrangement. A profit-sharing, stock bonus, pre-ERISA money purchase pension, or rural cooperative plan does not fail to satisfy the requirements of section 401(a) merely because the plan includes a cash or deferred arrangement. A cash or deferred arrangement is part of a plan for purposes of this section if any contributions to the plan, or accruals or other benefits under the plan, are made or provided pursuant to the cash or deferred arrangement.

(2) *Rules applicable to cash or deferred arrangements generally*—(i) *Definition of cash or deferred arrangement.* Except as provided in paragraphs (a)(2)(ii) and (iii) of this section, a cash or deferred arrangement is an arrangement under which an eligible employee may make a cash or deferred election with respect to contributions to, or accruals or other benefits under, a plan that is intended to satisfy the requirements of section 401(a) (including a contract that is intended to satisfy the requirements of section 403(a)).

(ii) *Treatment of after-tax employee contributions.* A cash or deferred arrangement does not include an arrangement under which amounts contributed under a plan at an employee's election are designated or treated at the time of contribution as after-tax employee contributions (e.g., by treating the contributions as taxable income subject to applicable withholding requirements). See also section 414(h)(1). A designated Roth contribution, however, is not treated as an after-tax contribution for purposes of this section, § 1.401(k)-2 through § 1.401(k)-6 and § 1.401(m)-1 through § 1.401(m)-5. A contribution can be an after-tax employee contribution under the rule of this paragraph (a)(2)(ii) even if the employee's election to make after-tax employee contributions is made before the amounts subject to the election are currently available to the employee.

(iii) *Treatment of ESOP dividend election.* A cash or deferred arrangement does not include an arrangement under an ESOP under which dividends are either distributed or invested pursuant to an election made by participants or their beneficiaries in accordance with section 404(k)(2)(A)(iii).

(iv) *Treatment of elective contributions as plan assets.* The extent to which elective contributions constitute plan assets for purposes of the prohibited transaction provisions of section 4975 and Title I of the Employee Retirement Income Security Act of 1974 is determined in accordance with regulations and rulings issued by the Department of Labor. See 29 CFR 2510.3-102.

(3) *Rules applicable to cash or deferred elections generally*—(i) *Definition of cash or deferred election.* A cash or deferred election is any direct or indirect election (or modification of an earlier election) by an employee to have the employer either—

(A) Provide an amount to the employee in the form of cash (or some other taxable benefit) that is not currently available; or

(B) Contribute an amount to a trust, or provide an accrual or other benefit, under a plan deferring the receipt of compensation.

(ii) *Automatic enrollment.* For purposes of determining whether an election is a cash or deferred election, it is irrelevant whether the default that applies in the absence of an affirmative election is described in paragraph (a)(3)(i)(A) of this section (i.e., the employee receives an amount in cash or some other taxable benefit) or in paragraph (a)(3)(i)(B) of this section (i.e., the employer contributes an amount to a trust or provides an accrual or other benefit under a plan deferring the receipt of compensation).

(iii) *Rules related to timing*—(A) *Requirement that amounts not be currently available.* A cash or deferred election can only be made with respect to an amount that is not currently available to the employee on the date of the election. Further, a cash or deferred election can only be made with respect to amounts that would (but for the cash or deferred election) become currently available after the later of the date on which the employer adopts the cash or deferred arrangement or the date on which the arrangement first becomes effective.

(B) *Contribution may not precede election.* A contribution is made pursuant to a cash or deferred election only if the contribution is made after the election is made.

(C) *Contribution may not precede services*—(1) *General rule.* Contributions are made pursuant to a cash or deferred election only if the contributions are made after the employee's performance of service with respect to which the contributions are made (or when the cash or other taxable benefit would be currently available, if earlier).

(2) *Exception for bona fide administrative considerations.* The timing of contributions will not be treated as failing to satisfy the requirements of this paragraph (a)(3)(iii)(C) merely because contributions for a pay period are occasionally made before the services with respect to that pay period are performed, provided the contributions are made early in order to accommodate bona fide administrative considerations (for example, the temporary absence of the bookkeeper with responsibility to transmit contributions to the plan) and are not paid early with a principal purpose of accelerating deductions.

(iv) *Current availability defined.* Cash or another taxable benefit is currently available to the employee if it has been paid to the employee or if the employee is able currently to receive the cash or other taxable benefit at the employee's discretion. An amount is not currently available to an employee if there is a significant limitation or restriction on the employee's right to receive the amount currently. Similarly, an amount is not currently available as of a date if the employee may under no circumstances receive the amount before a particular time in the future. The determination of whether an amount is currently available to an employee does not depend on whether it has been constructively received by the employee for purposes of section 451.

(v) *Certain one-time elections not treated as cash or deferred elections.* A cash or deferred election does not include a one-time irrevocable election made no later than the employee's first becoming eligible under the plan or any other plan or arrangement of the employer that is described in section 219(g)(5)(A) (whether or not such other plan or arrangement has terminated), to have contributions equal to a specified amount or percentage of the employee's compensation (including no amount of compensation) made by the employer on the employee's behalf to the plan and a specified amount or percentage of the employee's compensation (including no amount of compensation) divided among all other plans or arrangements of the employer (including plans or arrangements not yet established) for the duration of the employee's employment with the employer, or in the case of a defined benefit plan to receive accruals or other benefits (including no benefits) under such plans. Thus, for example, employer contributions made pursuant to a one-time irrevocable election described in this paragraph are not treated as having been made pursuant to a cash or deferred election and are not includible in an employee's gross income by reason of § 1.402(a)-1(d).

* * *

(vi) *Tax treatment of employees.* An amount generally is includible in an employ-

ee's gross income for the taxable year in which the employee actually or constructively receives the amount. But for section 402(e)(3), an employee is treated as having received an amount that is contributed to an exempt trust or plan described in section 401(a) or 403(a) pursuant to the employee's cash or deferred election. This is the case even if the election to defer is made before the year in which the amount is earned, or before the amount is currently available. See § 1.402(a)-1(d).

(vii) *Examples.* The following examples illustrate the application of this paragraph (a)(3):

Example 1. (i) An employer maintains a profit-sharing plan under which each eligible employee has an election to defer an annual bonus payable on January 30 each year. The bonus equals 10% of compensation during the previous calendar year. Deferred amounts are not treated as after-tax employee contributions. The bonus is currently available on January 30.

(ii) An election made prior to January 30 to defer all or part of the bonus is a cash or deferred election, and the bonus deferral arrangement is a cash or deferred arrangement.

Example 2. (i) An employer maintains a profit-sharing plan which provides for discretionary profit sharing contributions and under which each eligible employee may elect to reduce his compensation by up to 10% and to have the employer contribute such amount to the plan. The employer pays each employee every two weeks for services during the immediately preceding two weeks. The employee's election to defer compensation for a payroll period must be made prior to the date the amount would otherwise be paid. The employer contributes to the plan the amount of compensation that each employee elected to defer, at the time it would otherwise be paid to the employee, and does not treat the contribution as an after-tax employee contribution.

(ii) The election is a cash or deferred election and the contributions are elective contributions.

Example 3. (i) The facts are the same as in Example 2, except that the employer makes a $10,000 contribution on January 31 of the plan year that is in addition to the contributions that satisfy the employer's obligation to make contributions with respect to cash or deferred elections for prior payroll periods. Employee A makes an election on February 15 to defer $2,000 from compensation that is not currently available and the employer reduces the employee's compensation to reflect the election.

(ii) None of the additional $10,000 contributed January 31 is a contribution made pursuant to Employee A's cash or deferred election, because the contribution was made before the election was made. Accordingly, the employer must make an additional contribution of $2,000 in order to satisfy its obligation to contribute an amount to the plan pursuant to Employee A's election. The $10,000 contribution may be allocated under the plan terms providing for discretionary profit sharing contributions.

Example 4. (i) The facts are the same as in Example 3, except that Employee A had an outstanding election to defer $500 from each payroll period's compensation. The $10,000 additional payment that is contributed early is not made early in order to accommodate bona fide administrative considerations.

(ii) None of the additional $10,000 contributed January 31 is a contribution made pursuant to Employee A's cash or deferred election for future payroll periods, because the contribution was made before the earlier of Employee A's performance of services to which the contribution is attributable or when the compensation would be currently available. Furthermore, the exception for early contributions in paragraph (a)(3)(iii)(C)(2) of this section does not apply. Accordingly, the employer must make an additional contribution of $500 per payroll period in order to satisfy its obligation to contribute an amount to the plan pursuant to Employee A's election. The $10,000 contribution may be allocated under the plan terms providing for discretionary profit sharing contributions.

Example 5. (i) Employer B establishes a money purchase pension plan in 1986. This is the first qualified plan established by Employer B. All salaried employees are eligible to participate under the plan. Hourly-paid employees are not eligible to participate under the plan. In 2000, Employer B establishes a profit-sharing plan under which all employees (both salaried and hourly) are eligible. Employer B permits all employees on the effective date of the profit-sharing plan to make a one-time irrevocable election to have Employer B contribute 5% of compensation on their behalf to the plan and make no other contribution to any other plan of Employer B (including plans not yet established) for the duration of the employee's employment with Employer B, and have their salaries reduced by 5%.

(ii) The election provided under the profit-sharing plan is not a one-time irrevocable election within the meaning of paragraph (a)(3)(v) of this section with respect to the salaried employees of Employer B who, before becoming eligible to participate under the profit-sharing plan, became eligible to participate under the money purchase pension plan. The election under the profit-sharing plan is a one-time irrevocable election within the meaning of paragraph (a)(3)(v) of this section with respect to the hourly employees, because they were not previously eligible to participate under another plan of the employer.

(4) *Rules applicable to qualified cash or deferred arrangements*—(i) *Definition of qualified cash or deferred arrangement.* A qualified cash or deferred arrangement is a cash or deferred arrangement that satisfies the requirements of paragraphs (b), (c), (d), and (e) of this section.

(ii) *Treatment of elective contributions as employer contributions.* Except as otherwise provided in § 1.401(k)-2(b)(3), elective contributions under a qualified cash or deferred arrangement (including designated Roth contributions) are treated as employer contributions. Thus, for example, elective contributions under such an arrangement are treated as employer contributions for purposes of sections 401(a), 401(k), 402, 404, 409, 411, 412, 415, 416, and 417.

(iii) *Tax treatment of employees.* Except as provided in section 402(g), 402A (effective for taxable years beginning after December 31, 2005), or § 1.401(k)-2(b)(3), elective contributions under a qualified cash or deferred arrangement are neither includible in an employee's gross income at the time the cash would have been includible in the employee's gross income (but for the cash or deferred election), nor at the time the elective contributions are contributed to the plan. See § 1.402(a)-1(d)(2)(i).

(iv) *Application of nondiscrimination requirements to plan that includes a qualified cash or deferred arrangement*—(A) *Exclusive means of amounts testing.* Elective contributions (including elective contributions that are designated Roth contributions) under a qualified cash or deferred arrangement satisfy the requirements of section 401(a)(4) with respect to amounts if and only if the amount of elective contributions satisfies the nondiscrimination test of section 401(k) under paragraph (b)(1) of this section. See § 1.401(a)(4)-1(b)(2)(ii)(B).

(B) *Testing benefits, rights and features.* A plan that includes a qualified cash or deferred arrangement must satisfy the requirements of section 401(a)(4) with respect to benefits, rights and features in addition to the requirements regarding amounts described in paragraph (a)(4)(iv)(A) of this section. For example, the right to make each level of elective contributions under a cash or deferred arrangement and the right to make designated Roth contributions are rights or features subject to the requirements of section 401(a)(4). See § 1.401(a)(4)-4(e)(3)(i) and (iii)(D). Thus, for example, if all employees are eligible to make a stated level of elective contributions under a cash or deferred arrangement, but that level of contributions can only be made from compensation in excess of a stated amount, such as the Social Security taxable wage base, the arrangement will generally favor HCEs with respect to the availability of elective con-

tributions and thus will generally not satisfy the requirements of section 401(a)(4).

(C) *Minimum coverage requirement.* A qualified cash or deferred arrangement is treated as a separate plan that must satisfy the requirements of section 410(b). See § 1.410(b)-7(c)(1) for special rules. The determination of whether a cash or deferred arrangement satisfies the requirements of section 410(b) must be made without regard to the modifications to the disaggregation rules set forth in paragraph (b)(4)(v) of this section. See also § 1.401(a)(4)-11(g)(3)(vii)(A), relating to corrective amendments that may be made to satisfy the minimum coverage requirements of section 410(b).

(5) *Rules applicable to nonqualified cash or deferred arrangements*—(i) *Definition of nonqualified cash or deferred arrangement.* A nonqualified cash or deferred arrangement is a cash or deferred arrangement that fails to satisfy one or more of the requirements in paragraph (b), (c), (d) or (e) of this section.

(ii) *Treatment of elective contributions as nonelective contributions.* Except as specifically provided otherwise, elective contributions under a nonqualified cash or deferred arrangement are treated as nonelective employer contributions. Thus, for example, the elective contributions under such an arrangement are treated as nonelective employer contributions for purposes of sections 401(a) (including section 401(a)(4)) and 401(k), 404, 409, 411, 412, 415, 416, and 417 and are not subject to the requirements of section 401(m).

(iii) *Tax treatment of employees.* Elective contributions under a nonqualified cash or deferred arrangement are includible in an employee's gross income at the time the cash or other taxable amount that the employee would have received (but for the cash or deferred election) would have been includible in the employee's gross income. See § 1.402(a)-1(d)(1).

(iv) *Qualification of plan that includes a nonqualified cash or deferred arrangement*—(A) *In general.* A profit-sharing, stock bonus, pre-ERISA money purchase pension, or rural cooperative plan does not fail to satisfy the requirements of section 401(a) merely because the plan includes a nonqualified cash or deferred arrangement. In determining whether the plan satisfies the requirements of section 401(a)(4), the nondiscrimination tests of sections 401(k), paragraph (b)(1) of this section, section 401(m)(2) and § 1.401(m)-1(b) may not be used. See §§ 1.401(a)(4)-1(b)(2)(ii)(B) and 1.410(b)-9 (definition of section 401(k) plan).

(B) *Application of section 401(a)(4) to certain plans.* The amount of employer contributions under a nonqualified cash or deferred arrangement is treated as satisfying section 401(a)(4) if the arrangement is part of a collectively bargained plan that automatically satisfies the requirements of section 410(b). See §§ 1.401(a)(4)-(c)(5) and 1.410(b)-2(b)(7). Additionally, the requirements of sections 401(a)(4) and 410(b) do not apply to a governmental plan (within the meaning of section 414(d)) maintained by a State or local government or political subdivision thereof (or agency or instrumentality thereof). See sections 401(a)(5) and 410(c)(1)(A).

(v) *Example.* The following example illustrates the application of this paragraph (a)(5):

Example. (i) For the 2006 plan year, Employer A maintains a collectively bargained plan that includes a cash or deferred arrangement. Employer contributions under the cash or deferred arrangement do not satisfy the nondiscrimination test of section 401(k) and paragraph (b) of this section.

(ii) The arrangement is a nonqualified cash or deferred arrangement. The employer contributions under the cash or deferred arrangement are considered to be nondiscriminatory under section 401(a)(4), and the elective contributions are generally treated as employer contributions under paragraph (a)(5)(ii) of this section. Under paragraph (a)(5)(iii) of this section and under § 1.402(a)-1(d)(1), however, the elective contributions are includible in each employee's gross income.

(6) *Rules applicable to cash or deferred arrangements of self-employed individuals—* (i) *Application of general rules.* Generally, a partnership or sole proprietorship is permitted to maintain a cash or deferred arrangement, and individual partners or owners are permitted to make cash or deferred elections with respect to compensation attributable to services rendered to the entity, under the same rules that apply to other cash or deferred arrangements. For example, any contributions made on behalf of an individual partner or owner pursuant to a cash or deferred arrangement of a partnership or sole proprietorship are elective contributions unless they are designated or treated as after-tax employee contributions. In the case of a partnership, a cash or deferred arrangement includes any arrangement that directly or indirectly permits individual partners to vary the amount of contributions made on their behalf. Consistent with § 1.402(a)-1(d), the elective contributions under such an arrangement are includible in income and are not deductible under section 404(a) unless the arrangement is a qualified cash or deferred arrangement (i.e., the requirements of section 401(k) and this section are satisfied). Also, even if the arrangement is a qualified cash or deferred arrangement, the elective contributions are includible in gross income and are not deductible under section 404(a) to the extent they exceed the applicable limit under section 402(g). See also § 1.401(a)-30.

(ii) *Treatment of matching contributions made on behalf of self-employed individuals.* Under section 402(g)(8), matching contributions made on behalf of a self-employed individual are not treated as elective contributions made pursuant to a cash or deferred election, without regard to whether such matching contributions indirectly permit individual partners to vary the amount of contributions made on their behalf.

(iii) *Timing of self-employed individual's cash or deferred election.* For purposes of paragraph (a)(3)(iv) of this section, a partner's compensation is deemed currently available on the last day of the partnership taxable year and a sole proprietor's compensation is deemed currently available on the last day of the individual's taxable year. Accordingly, a self-employed individual may not make a cash or deferred election with respect to compensation for a partnership or sole proprietorship taxable year after the last day of that year. See § 1.401(k)-2(a)(4)(ii) for the rules regarding when these contributions are treated as allocated.

(iv) *Special rule for certain payments to self-employed individuals.* For purposes of sections 401(k) and 401(m), the earned income of a self-employed individual for a taxable year constitutes payment for services during that year. Thus, for example, if a partnership provides for cash advance payments during the taxable year to be made to a partner based on the value of the partner's services prior to the date of payment (and which do not exceed a reasonable estimate of the partner's earned income for the taxable year), a contribution of a portion of these payments to a profit sharing plan in accordance with an election to defer the portion of the advance payments does not fail to be made pursuant to a cash or deferred election within the meaning of paragraph (a)(3)(iii) of this section merely because the contribution is made before the amount of the partner's earned income is finally determined and reported. However, see § 1.401(k)-2(a)(4)(ii) for rules on when earned income is treated as received.

* * *

(d) *Distribution limitation*—(1) *General rule.* A cash or deferred arrangement satisfies this paragraph (d) only if amounts attributable to elective contributions may not be distributed before one of the following events, and any distributions so permitted also satisfy the additional requirements of paragraphs (d)(2) through (5) of this section (to the extent applicable)—

(i) The employee's death, disability, or severance from employment;

(ii) In the case of a profit-sharing, stock bonus or rural cooperative plan, the employ-

ee's attainment of age 59 1/2, or the employee's hardship; or

(iii) The termination of the plan.

(2) *Rules applicable to distributions upon severance from employment.* An employee has a severance from employment when the employee ceases to be an employee of the employer maintaining the plan. An employee does not have a severance from employment if, in connection with a change of employment, the employee's new employer maintains such plan with respect to the employee. For example, a new employer maintains a plan with respect to an employee by continuing or assuming sponsorship of the plan or by accepting a transfer of plan assets and liabilities (within the meaning of section 414(l)) with respect to the employee.

(3) *Rules applicable to hardship distributions*—(i) *Distribution must be on account of hardship.* A distribution is treated as made after an employee's hardship for purposes of paragraph (d)(1)(ii) of this section if and only if it is made on account of the hardship. For purposes of this rule, a distribution is made on account of hardship only if the distribution both is made on account of an immediate and heavy financial need of the employee and is necessary to satisfy the financial need. The determination of the existence of an immediate and heavy financial need and of the amount necessary to meet the need must be made in accordance with nondiscriminatory and objective standards set forth in the plan.

(ii) *Limit on maximum distributable amount*—(A) *General rule.* A distribution on account of hardship must be limited to the maximum distributable amount. The maximum distributable amount is equal to the employee's total elective contributions as of the date of distribution, reduced by the amount of previous distributions of elective contributions. Thus, the maximum distributable amount does not include earnings, QNECs or QMACs, unless grandfathered under paragraph (d)(3)(ii)(B) of this section.

* * *

(iii) *Immediate and heavy financial need*—(A) *In general.* Whether an employee has an immediate and heavy financial need is to be determined based on all the relevant facts and circumstances. Generally, for example, the need to pay the funeral expenses of a family member would constitute an immediate and heavy financial need. A distribution made to an employee for the purchase of a boat or television would generally not constitute a distribution made on account of an immediate and heavy financial need. A financial need may be immediate and heavy even if it was reasonably foreseeable or voluntarily incurred by the employee.

(B) *Deemed immediate and heavy financial need.* A distribution is deemed to be on account of an immediate and heavy financial need of the employee if the distribution is for—

(1) Expenses for (or necessary to obtain) medical care that would be deductible under section 213(d) (determined without regard to whether the expenses exceed 7.5% of adjusted gross income);

(2) Costs directly related to the purchase of a principal residence for the employee (excluding mortgage payments);

(3) Payment of tuition, related educational fees, and room and board expenses, for up to the next 12 months of post-secondary education for the employee, or the employee's spouse, children, or dependents (as defined in section 152, and, for taxable years beginning on or after January 1, 2005, without regard to section 152(b)(1), (b)(2) and (d)(1)(B));

(4) Payments necessary to prevent the eviction of the employee from the employee's principal residence or foreclosure on the mortgage on that residence;

(5) Payments for burial or funeral expenses for the employee's deceased parent, spouse, children or dependents (as defined in section 152, and, for taxable years beginning on or after January 1, 2005, without regard to section 152(d)(1)(B)); or

(6) Expenses for the repair of damage to the employee's principal residence that would qualify for the casualty deduction under section 165 (determined without regard to whether the loss exceeds 10% of adjusted gross income).

(iv) *Distribution necessary to satisfy financial need*—(A) *Distribution may not exceed amount of need.* A distribution is treated as necessary to satisfy an immediate and heavy financial need of an employee only to the extent the amount of the distribution is not in excess of the amount required to satisfy the financial need. For this purpose, the amount required to satisfy the financial need may include any amounts necessary to pay any federal, state, or local income taxes or penalties reasonably anticipated to result from the distribution.

(B) *No alternative means available.* A distribution is not treated as necessary to satisfy an immediate and heavy financial need of an employee to the extent the need may be relieved from other resources that are reasonably available to the employee. This determination generally is to be made on the basis of all the relevant facts and circumstances. For purposes of this paragraph (d)(3)(iv), the employee's resources are deemed to include those assets of the employee's spouse and minor children that are reasonably available to the employee. Thus, for example, a vacation home owned by the employee and the employee's spouse, whether as community property, joint tenants, tenants by the entirety, or tenants in common, generally will be deemed a resource of the employee. However, property held for the employee's child under an irrevocable trust or under the Uniform Gifts to Minors Act (or comparable State law) is not treated as a resource of the employee.

(C) *Employer reliance on employee representation.* For purposes of paragraph (d)(3)(iv)(B) of this section, an immediate and heavy financial need generally may be treated as not capable of being relieved from other resources that are reasonably available to the employee, if the employer relies upon the employee's representation (made in writing or such other form as may be prescribed by the Commissioner), unless the employer has actual knowledge to the contrary, that the need cannot reasonably be relieved— (1) Through reimbursement or compensation by insurance or otherwise;

(2) By liquidation of the employee's assets;

(3) By cessation of elective contributions or employee contributions under the plan;

(4) By other currently available distributions (including distribution of ESOP dividends under section 404(k)) and nontaxable (at the time of the loan) loans, under plans maintained by the employer or by any other employer; or

(5) By borrowing from commercial sources on reasonable commercial terms in an amount sufficient to satisfy the need.

(D) *Employee need not take counterproductive actions.* For purposes of this paragraph (d)(3)(iv), a need cannot reasonably be relieved by one of the actions described in paragraph (d)(3)(iv)(C) of this section if the effect would be to increase the amount of the need. For example, the need for funds to purchase a principal residence cannot reasonably be relieved by a plan loan if the loan would disqualify the employee from obtaining other necessary financing.

(E) *Distribution deemed necessary to satisfy immediate and heavy financial need.* A distribution is deemed necessary to satisfy an immediate and heavy financial need of an employee if each of the following requirements are satisfied—

(1) The employee has obtained all other currently available distributions (including distribution of ESOP dividends under section 404(k), but not hardship distributions) and nontaxable (at the time of the loan) loans, under the plan and all other plans maintained by the employer; and

(2) The employee is prohibited, under the terms of the plan or an otherwise legally enforceable agreement, from making elective

contributions and employee contributions to the plan and all other plans maintained by the employer for at least 6 months after receipt of the hardship distribution.

(F) *Definition of other plans.* For purposes of paragraph (d)(3)(iv)(C)(4) and (E)(1) of this section, the phrase plans maintained by the employer means all qualified and nonqualified plans of deferred compensation maintained by the employer, including a cash or deferred arrangement that is part of a cafeteria plan within the meaning of section 125. However, it does not include the mandatory employee contribution portion of a defined benefit plan or a health or welfare benefit plan (including one that is part of a cafeteria plan). In addition, for purposes of paragraph (d)(3)(iv)(E)(2) of this section, the phrase plans maintained by the employer also includes a stock option, stock purchase, or similar plan maintained by the employer. See § 1.401(k)-6 for the continued treatment of suspended employees as eligible employees.

(v) *Commissioner may expand standards.* The Commissioner may prescribe additional guidance of general applicability, published in the Internal Revenue Bulletin (see § 601.601(d)(2) of this chapter), expanding the list of deemed immediate and heavy financial needs and prescribing additional methods for distributions to be deemed necessary to satisfy an immediate and heavy financial need.

* * *

(e) *Additional requirements for qualified cash or deferred arrangements*—(1) *Qualified plan requirement.* A cash or deferred arrangement satisfies this paragraph (e) only if the plan of which it is a part is a profit-sharing, stock bonus, pre-ERISA money purchase or rural cooperative plan that otherwise satisfies the requirements of section 401(a) (taking into account the cash or deferred arrangement). A plan that includes a cash or deferred arrangement may provide for other contributions, including employer contributions (other than elective contributions), employee contributions, or both. However, except as expressly permitted under section

401(m), 410(b)(2)(A)(ii) or 416(c)(2)(A), elective contributions and matching contributions taken into account under § 1.401(k)-2(a) may not be taken into account for purposes of determining whether any other contributions under any plan (including the plan to which the contributions are made) satisfy the requirements of section 401(a).

(2) *Election requirements*—(i) *Cash must be available.* A cash or deferred arrangement satisfies this paragraph (e) only if the arrangement provides that the amount that each eligible employee may defer as an elective contribution is available to the employee in cash. Thus, for example, if an eligible employee is provided the option to receive a taxable benefit (other than cash) or to have the employer contribute on the employee's behalf to a profit-sharing plan an amount equal to the value of the taxable benefit, the arrangement is not a qualified cash or deferred arrangement. Similarly, if an employee has the option to receive a specified amount in cash or to have the employer contribute an amount in excess of the specified cash amount to a profit-sharing plan on the employee's behalf, any contribution made by the employer on the employee's behalf in excess of the specified cash amount is not treated as made pursuant to a qualified cash or deferred arrangement, but would be treated as a matching contribution. This cash availability requirement applies even if the cash or deferred arrangement is part of a cafeteria plan within the meaning of section 125.

(ii) *Frequency of elections.* A cash or deferred arrangement satisfies this paragraph (e) only if the arrangement provides an employee with an effective opportunity to make (or change) a cash or deferred election at least once during each plan year. Whether an employee has an effective opportunity is determined based on all the relevant facts and circumstances, including the adequacy of notice of the availability of the election, the period of time during which an election may be made, and any other conditions on elections.

(3) *Separate accounting requirement*—(i) *General rule.* A cash or deferred arrangement

satisfies this paragraph (e) only if the portion of an employee's benefit subject to the requirements of paragraphs (c) and (d) of this section is determined by an acceptable separate accounting between that portion and any other benefits. Separate accounting is not acceptable unless contributions and withdrawals are attributed to the separate accounts and gains, losses, and other credits or charges are separately allocated on a reasonable and consistent basis to the accounts subject to the requirements of paragraphs (c) and (d) of this section and to other accounts. Subject to section 401(a)(4), forfeitures are not required to be allocated to the accounts in which benefits are subject to paragraphs (c) and (d) of this section. The separate accounting requirement of this paragraph (e)(3)(i) applies at the time the elective contribution is contributed to the plan and continues to apply until the contribution is distributed under the plan.

(ii) *Satisfaction of separate accounting requirement.* The requirements of paragraph (e)(3)(i) of this section are treated as satisfied if all amounts held under a plan that includes a qualified cash or deferred arrangement (and, if applicable, under another plan to which QNECs and QMACs are made) are subject to the requirements of paragraphs (c) and (d) of this section.

* * *

(6) *Other benefits not contingent upon elective contributions*—(i) *General rule.* A cash or deferred arrangement satisfies this paragraph (e) only if no other benefit is conditioned (directly or indirectly) upon the employee's electing to make or not to make elective contributions under the arrangement. The preceding sentence does not apply to—

(A) Any matching contribution (as defined in § 1.401(m)-1(a)(2)) made by reason of such an election;

(B) Any benefit, right or feature (such as a plan loan) that requires, or results in, an amount to be withheld from an employee's pay (e.g. to pay for the benefit or to repay the loan), to the extent the cash or deferred arrangement restricts elective contributions to amounts available after such withholding from the employee's pay (after deduction of all applicable income and employment taxes);

(C) Any reduction in the employer's top-heavy contributions under section 416(c)(2) because of matching contributions that resulted from the elective contributions; or

(D) Any benefit that is provided at the employee's election under a plan described in section 125(d) in lieu of an elective contribution under a qualified cash or deferred arrangement.

(ii) *Definition of other benefits.* For purposes of this paragraph (e)(6), other benefits include, but are not limited to, benefits under a defined benefit plan; nonelective contributions under a defined contribution plan; the availability, cost, or amount of health benefits; vacations or vacation pay; life insurance; dental plans; legal services plans; loans (including plan loans); financial planning services; subsidized retirement benefits; stock options; property subject to section 83; and dependent care assistance. Also, increases in salary, bonuses or other cash remuneration (other than the amount that would be contributed under the cash or deferred election) are benefits for purposes of this paragraph (e)(6). The ability to make after-tax employee contributions is a benefit, but that benefit is not contingent upon an employee's electing to make or not make elective contributions under the arrangement merely because the amount of elective contributions reduces dollar-for-dollar the amount of after-tax employee contributions that may be made. Additionally, benefits under any other plan or arrangement (whether or not qualified) are not contingent upon an employee's electing to make or not to make elective contributions under a cash or deferred arrangement merely because the elective contributions are or are not taken into account as compensation under the other plan or arrangement for purposes of determining benefits.

(iii) *Effect of certain statutory limits.* Any benefit under an excess benefit plan described in section 3(36) of the Employee Retirement Income Security Act of 1974 that is dependent on the employee's electing to make or not to make elective contributions is not treated as contingent. Deferred compensation under a nonqualified plan of deferred compensation that is dependent on an employee's having made the maximum elective deferrals under section 402(g) or the maximum elective contributions permitted under the terms of the plan also is not treated as contingent.

(iv) *Nonqualified deferred compensation.* Except as otherwise provided in paragraph (e)(6)(iii) of this section, participation in a nonqualified deferred compensation plan is treated as contingent for purposes of this paragraph (e)(6) to the extent that an employee may receive additional deferred compensation under the nonqualified plan to the extent the employee makes or does not make elective contributions.

(v) *Plan loans and distributions.* A loan or distribution of elective contributions is not a benefit conditioned on an employee's electing to make or not make elective contributions under the arrangement merely because the amount of the loan or distribution is based on the amount of the employee's account balance.

* * *

(7) *Plan provision requirement.* A plan that includes a cash or deferred arrangement satisfies this paragraph (e) only if it provides that the nondiscrimination requirements of section 401(k) will be met. Thus, the plan must provide for satisfaction of one of the specific alternatives described in paragraph (b)(1)(ii) of this section and, if with respect to that alternative there are optional choices, which of the optional choices will apply. For example, a plan that uses the ADP test of section 401(k)(3), as described in paragraph (b)(1)(ii)(A) of this section, must specify whether it is using the current year testing method or prior year testing method. Additionally, a plan that uses the prior year testing method must specify whether the ADP for eligible NHCEs for the first plan year is 3% or the ADP for the eligible NHCEs for the first plan year. Similarly, a plan that uses the safe

harbor method of section 401(k)(12), as described in paragraph (b)(1)(ii)(B) of this section, must specify whether the safe harbor contribution will be the nonelective safe harbor contribution or the matching safe harbor contribution and is not permitted to provide that ADP testing will be used if the requirements for the safe harbor are not satisfied. In addition, a plan that uses the safe harbor method of section 401(k)(13), as described in paragraph (b)(1)(ii)(C) of this section, must specify the default percentages that apply for the plan year and whether the safe harbor contribution will be the nonelective safe harbor contribution or the matching safe harbor contribution, and is not permitted to provide that ADP testing will be used if the requirements for the safe harbor are not satisfied. For purposes of this paragraph (e)(7), a plan may incorporate by reference the provisions of section 401(k)(3) and § 1.401(k)-2 if that is the nondiscrimination test being applied. The Commissioner may, in guidance of general applicability, published in the Internal Revenue Bulletin (see § 601.601(d)(2) of this chapter), specify the options that will apply under the plan if the nondiscrimination test is incorporated by reference in accordance with the preceding sentence.

(8) *Section 415 compensation required.* With respect to compensation that is paid (or would have been paid but for a cash or deferred election) in plan years beginning on or after July 1, 2007, a cash or deferred arrangement satisfies this paragraph (e) only if cash or deferred elections can only be made with respect to amounts that are compensation within the meaning of section 415(c)(3) and § 1.415(c)-2. Thus, for example, the arrangement is not a qualified cash or deferred arrangement if an eligible employee who is not in qualified military service (as that term is defined in section 414(u)) and who is not permanently and totally disabled (as defined in section 22(e)(3)) can make a cash or deferred election with respect to an amount paid after severance from employment, unless the amount is paid by the later of 2 1/2 months after severance from employment or the end of the year that includes the date of severance

from employment and is described in § 1.415(c)-2(e)(3)(ii) or (iii).

(f) *Special rules for designated Roth contributions*—(1) *In general.* The term designated Roth contribution means an elective contribution under a qualified cash or deferred arrangement that, to the extent permitted under the plan, is—

(i) Designated irrevocably by the employee at the time of the cash or deferred election as a designated Roth contribution that is being made in lieu of all or a portion of the pre-tax elective contributions the employee is otherwise eligible to make under the plan;

(ii) Treated by the employer as not excludible from the employee's gross income (in accordance with paragraph (f)(2) of this section);

(iii) Maintained by the plan in a separate account (in accordance with paragraph (f)(3) of this section).

(2) *Inclusion treatment.* An elective contribution is generally treated as not excludible from gross income if it is treated as includible in gross income by the employer (e.g., by treating the contribution as wages subject to applicable income tax withholding). However, in the case of a self-employed individual, an elective contribution is treated as not excludible from gross income only if the individual does not claim a deduction for such amount. If an elective contribution would not have been includible in gross income if the amount had been paid directly to the employee (rather than being subject to a cash or deferral election), the elective contribution is nevertheless permitted to be a designated Roth contribution, provided the employee is entitled to treat the amount as an investment in the contract pursuant to section 72(f)(2).

(3) *Separate accounting required.* Under the separate accounting requirement of this paragraph (f)(3), contributions and withdrawals of designated Roth contributions must be credited and debited to a designated Roth account maintained for the employee and the plan must maintain a record of the employee's

investment in the contract (that is, designated Roth contributions that have not been distributed) with respect to the employee's designated Roth account. In addition, gains, losses, and other credits or charges must be separately allocated on a reasonable and consistent basis to the designated Roth account and other accounts under the plan. However, forfeitures may not be allocated to the designated Roth account and no contributions other than designated Roth contributions and rollover contributions described in section 402A(c)(3)(B) may be allocated to such account. The separate accounting requirement applies at the time the designated Roth contribution is contributed to the plan and must continue to apply until the designated Roth account is completely distributed. See A-13 of § 1.402A-1 for additional requirements for separate accounting.

(4) *Designated Roth contributions must satisfy rules applicable to elective contributions*—(i) *In general.* A designated Roth contribution must satisfy the requirements applicable to elective contributions made under a qualified cash or deferred arrangement. Thus, for example, a designated Roth contribution must satisfy the requirements of paragraphs (c) and (d) of this section and is treated as an employer contribution for purposes of sections 401(a), 401(k), 402, 404, 409, 411, 412, 415, 416 and 417. In addition, the designated Roth contributions are treated as elective contributions for purposes of the ADP test. Similarly, the designated Roth account under the plan is subject to the rules of section 401(a)(9)(A) and (B) in the same manner as an account that contains pre-tax elective contributions.

(ii) *Special rules for direct rollovers.* A direct rollover from a designated Roth account under a qualified cash or deferred arrangement may only be made to another designated Roth account under an applicable retirement plan described in section 402A(e)(1) or to a Roth IRA described in section 408A, and only to the extent the rollover is permitted under the rules of section 402(c). Moreover, a participant's designated Roth account and the participant's other accounts under a plan are treated

as accounts held under two separate plans (within the meaning of section 414(l)) for purposes of applying the automatic rollover rules for mandatory distributions under section 401(a)(31)(B)(i)(I) and the special rules in A-9 through A-11 of § 1.401(a)(31)-1.

(5) *Rules regarding designated Roth contribution elections*—(i) *Frequency of elections.* The rules under paragraph (e)(2)(ii) of this section regarding frequency of elections apply in the same manner to both pre-tax elective contributions and designated Roth contributions. Thus, an employee must have an effective opportunity to make (or change) an election to make designated Roth contributions at least once during each plan year.

(ii) *Default elections*—(A) In the case of a plan that provides for both pre-tax elective contributions and designated Roth contributions and in which, under paragraph (a)(3)(ii) of this section, the default in the absence of an affirmative election is to make a contribution under the cash or deferred arrangement, the plan terms must provide the extent to which the default contributions are pre-tax elective contributions and the extent to which the default contributions are designated Roth contributions.

(B) If the default contributions under the plan are designated Roth contributions, then an employee who has not made an affirmative election is deemed to have irrevocably designated the contributions (in accordance with section 402A(c)(1)(B)) as designated Roth contributions.

* * *

§ 1.401(k)-2. ADP test.

(a) *Actual deferral percentage (ADP) test*—(1) *In general*—(i) *ADP test formula.* A cash or deferred arrangement satisfies the ADP test for a plan year only if—

(A) The ADP for the eligible HCEs for the plan year is not more than the ADP for the eligible NHCEs for the applicable year multiplied by 1.25; or

(B) The excess of the ADP for the eligible HCEs for the plan year over the ADP for the eligible NHCEs for the applicable year is not more than 2 percentage points, and the ADP for the eligible HCEs for the plan year is not more than the ADP for the eligible NHCEs for the applicable year multiplied by 2.

(ii) *HCEs as sole eligible employees.* If, for the applicable year for determining the ADP of the NHCEs for a plan year, there are no eligible NHCEs (i.e., all of the eligible employees under the cash or deferred arrangement for the applicable year are HCEs), the arrangement is deemed to satisfy the ADP test for the plan year.

* * *

(2) *Determination of ADP*—(i) *General rule.* The ADP for a group of eligible employees (either eligible HCEs or eligible NHCEs) for a plan year or applicable year is the average of the ADRs of the eligible employees in that group for that year. The ADP for a group of eligible employees is calculated to the nearest hundredth of a percentage point.

(ii) *Determination of applicable year under current year and prior year testing method.* The ADP test is applied using the prior year testing method or the current year testing method. Under the prior year testing method, the applicable year for determining the ADP for the eligible NHCEs is the plan year immediately preceding the plan year for which the ADP test is being performed. Under the prior year testing method, the ADP for the eligible NHCEs is determined using the ADRs for the eligible employees who were NHCEs in that preceding plan year, regardless of whether those NHCEs are eligible employees or NHCEs in the plan year for which the ADP test is being calculated. Under the current year testing method, the applicable year for determining the ADP for the eligible NHCEs is the same plan year as the plan year for which the ADP test is being performed. Under either method, the ADP for eligible HCEs is the average of the ADRs of the eligible HCEs for the plan year for which the ADP test is being performed. See paragraph (c) of this section

for additional rules for the prior year testing method.

(3) *Determination of ADR*—(i) *General rule.* The ADR of an eligible employee for a plan year or applicable year is the sum of the employee's elective contributions taken into account with respect to such employee for the year, determined under the rules of paragraphs (a)(4) and (5) of this section, and the qualified nonelective contributions and qualified matching contributions taken into account with respect to such employee under paragraph (a)(6) of this section for the year, divided by the employee's compensation taken into account for the year. The ADR is calculated to the nearest hundredth of a percentage point. If no elective contributions, qualified nonelective contributions, or qualified matching contributions are taken into account under this section with respect to an eligible employee for the year, the ADR of the employee is zero.

* * *

(4) *Elective contributions taken into account under the ADP test*—(i) *General rule.* An elective contribution is taken into account in determining the ADR for an eligible employee for a plan year or applicable year only if each of the following requirements is satisfied—

(A) The elective contribution is allocated to the eligible employee's account under the plan as of a date within that year. For purposes of this rule, an elective contribution is considered allocated as of a date within a year only if—

(1) The allocation is not contingent on the employee's participation in the plan or performance of services on any date subsequent to that date; and

(2) The elective contribution is actually paid to the trust no later than the end of the 12-month period immediately following the year to which the contribution relates.

(B) The elective contribution relates to compensation that either—

(1) Would have been received by the employee in the year but for the employee's election to defer under the arrangement; or

(2) Is attributable to services performed by the employee in the year and, but for the employee's election to defer, would have been received by the employee within 2 1/2 months after the close of the year, but only if the plan provides for elective contributions that relate to compensation that would have been received after the close of a year to be allocated to such prior year rather than the year in which the compensation would have been received.

(ii) *Elective contributions for partners and self-employed individuals.* For purposes of this paragraph (a)(4), a partner's distributive share of partnership income is treated as received on the last day of the partnership taxable year and a sole proprietor's compensation is treated as received on the last day of the individual's taxable year. Thus, an elective contribution made on behalf of a partner or sole proprietor is treated as allocated to the partner's account for the plan year that includes the last day of the partnership taxable year, provided the requirements of paragraph (a)(4)(i) of this section are met.

(iii) *Elective contributions for HCEs.* Elective contributions of an HCE must include any excess deferrals, as described in § 1.402(g)-1(a), even if those excess deferrals are distributed, pursuant to § 1.402(g)-1(e).

(5) *Elective contributions not taken into account under the ADP test*—(i) *General rule.* Elective contributions that do not satisfy the requirements of paragraph (a)(4)(i) of this section may not be taken into account in determining the ADR of an eligible employee for the plan year or applicable year with respect to which the contributions were made, or for any other plan year. Instead, the amount of the elective contributions must satisfy the requirements of section 401(a)(4) (without regard to the ADP test) for the plan year for which they are allocated under the plan as if they were nonelective contributions and were the only nonelective contributions for that

year. See §§ 1.401(a)(4)-1(b)(2)(ii)(B) and 1.410(b)-7(c)(1).

(ii) *Elective contributions for NHCEs.* Elective contributions of an NHCE shall not include any excess deferrals, as described in § 1.402(g)-1(a), to the extent the excess deferrals are prohibited under section 401(a)(30). However, to the extent that the excess deferrals are not prohibited under section 401(a)(30), they are included in elective contributions even if distributed pursuant to § 1.402(g)-1(e).

(iii) *Elective contributions treated as catch-up contributions.* Elective contributions that are treated as catch-up contributions under section 414(v) because they exceed a statutory limit or employer-provided limit (within the meaning of § 1.414(v)-1(b)(1)) are not taken into account under paragraph (a)(4) of this section for the plan year for which the contributions were made, or for any other plan year.

(iv) *Elective contributions used to satisfy the ACP test.* Except to the extent necessary to demonstrate satisfaction of the requirement of § 1.401(m)-2(a)(6)(ii), elective contributions taken into account for the ACP test under § 1.401(m)-2(a)(6) are not taken into account under paragraph (a)(4) of this section.

(v) *Additional elective contributions pursuant to section 414(u).* Additional elective contributions made pursuant to section 414(u) by reason of an eligible employee's qualified military service are not taken into account under paragraph (a)(4) of this section for the plan year for which the contributions are made, or for any other plan year.

(vi) *Default elective contributions pursuant to section 414(w).* Default elective contributions made under an eligible automatic contribution arrangement (within the meaning of § 1.414(w)-1(b)) that are distributed pursuant to § 1.414(w)-1(c) for plan years beginning on or after January 1, 2008, are not taken into account under paragraph (a)(4) of this section for the plan year for which the contributions are made, or for any other plan year.

(6) *Qualified nonelective contributions and qualified matching contributions that may be taken into account under the ADP test.* Qualified nonelective contributions and qualified matching contributions may be taken into account in determining the ADR for an eligible employee for a plan year or applicable year but only to the extent the contributions satisfy the following requirements—

(i) *Timing of allocation.* The qualified nonelective contribution or qualified matching contribution is allocated to the employee's account as of a date within that year within the meaning of paragraph (a)(4)(i)(A) of this section. Consequently, under the prior year testing method, in order to be taken into account in calculating the ADP for the eligible NHCEs for the applicable year, a qualified nonelective contribution or qualified matching contribution must be contributed no later than the end of the 12-month period immediately following the applicable year even though the applicable year is different than the plan year being tested.

* * *

(iv) *Disproportionate contributions not taken into account—(A) General rule.* Qualified nonelective contributions cannot be taken into account for a plan year for an NHCE to the extent such contributions exceed the product of that NHCE's compensation and the greater of 5% or two times the plan's representative contribution rate. Any qualified nonelective contribution taken into account under an ACP test under § 1.401(m)-2(a)(6) (including the determination of the representative contribution rate for purposes of § 1.401(m)-2(a)(6)(v)(B)), is not permitted to be taken into account for purposes of this paragraph (a)(6) (including the determination of the representative contribution rate under paragraph (a)(6)(iv)(B) of this section).

(B) *Definition of representative contribution rate.* For purposes of this paragraph (a)(6)(iv), the plan's representative contribution rate is the lowest applicable contribution rate of any eligible NHCE among a group of eligible NHCEs that consists of half of all

eligible NHCEs for the plan year (or, if greater, the lowest applicable contribution rate of any eligible NHCE in the group of all eligible NHCEs for the plan year and who is employed by the employer on the last day of the plan year).

(C) *Definition of applicable contribution rate.* For purposes of this paragraph (a)(6)(iv), the applicable contribution rate for an eligible NHCE is the sum of the qualified matching contributions taken into account under this paragraph (a)(6) for the eligible NHCE for the plan year and the qualified nonelective contributions made for the eligible NHCE for the plan year, divided by the eligible NHCE's compensation for the same period.

* * *

(b) *Correction of excess contributions—(1) Permissible correction methods—(i) In general.* A cash or deferred arrangement does not fail to satisfy the requirements of section 401(k)(3) and paragraph (a)(1) of this section if the employer, in accordance with the terms of the plan that includes the cash or deferred arrangement, uses any of the following correction methods—

(A) *Qualified nonelective contributions or qualified matching contributions.* The employer makes qualified nonelective contributions or qualified matching contributions that are taken into account under this section and, in combination with other amounts taken into account under paragraph (a) of this section, allow the cash or deferred arrangement to satisfy the requirements of paragraph (a)(1) of this section.

(B) *Excess contributions distributed.* Excess contributions are distributed in accordance with paragraph (b)(2) of this section.

(C) *Excess contributions recharacterized.* Excess contributions are recharacterized in accordance with paragraph (b)(3) of this section.

(ii) *Combination of correction methods.* A plan may provide for the use of any of the correction methods described in paragraph (b)(1)(i) of this section, may limit elective contributions in a manner designed to prevent excess contributions from being made, or may use a combination of these methods, to avoid or correct excess contributions. A plan may permit an HCE to elect whether any excess contributions are to be recharacterized or distributed. Similarly, a plan may permit an HCE with elective contributions for a year that includes both pre-tax elective contributions and designated Roth contributions to elect whether the excess contributions are to be attributed to pre-tax elective contributions or designated Roth contributions. If the plan uses a combination of correction methods, any contribution made under paragraph (b)(1)(i)(A) of this section must be taken into account before application of the correction methods in paragraph (b)(1)(i)(B) or (C) of this section.

(iii) *Exclusive means of correction.* A failure to satisfy the requirements of paragraph (a)(1) of this section may not be corrected using any method other than the ones described in paragraphs (b)(1)(i) and (ii) of this section. Thus, excess contributions for a plan year may not remain unallocated or be allocated to a suspense account for allocation to one or more employees in any future year. In addition, excess contributions may not be corrected using the retroactive correction rules of § 1.401(a)(4)-11(g). See § 1.401(a)(4)-11(g)(3)(vii) and (5).

(2) *Corrections through distribution*—(i) *General rule.* This paragraph (b)(2) contains the rules for correction of excess contributions through a distribution from the plan. Correction through a distribution generally involves a 4-step process. First, the plan must determine, in accordance with paragraph (b)(2)(ii) of this section, the total amount of excess contributions that must be distributed under the plan. Second, the plan must apportion the total amount of excess contributions among HCEs in accordance with paragraph (b)(2)(iii) of this section. Third, the plan must determine the income allocable to excess contributions in accordance with paragraph (b)(2)(iv) of this section. Finally, the plan must distribute the apportioned excess contributions and allocable income in accordance with paragraph (b)(2)(v)

of this section. Paragraph (b)(2)(vi) of this section provides rules relating to the tax treatment of these distributions. Paragraph (b)(2)(vii) provides other rules relating to these distributions.

(ii) *Calculation of total amount to be distributed.* The following procedures must be used to determine the total amount of the excess contributions to be distributed—

(A) *Calculate the dollar amount of excess contributions for each HCE.* The amount of excess contributions attributable to a given HCE for a plan year is the amount (if any) by which the HCE's contributions taken into account under this section must be reduced for the HCE's ADR to equal the highest permitted ADR under the plan. To calculate the highest permitted ADR under a plan, the ADR of the HCE with the highest ADR is reduced by the amount required to cause that HCE's ADR to equal the ADR of the HCE with the next highest ADR. If a lesser reduction would enable the arrangement to satisfy the requirements of paragraph (b)(2)(ii)(C) of this section, only this lesser reduction is used in determining the highest permitted ADR.

(B) *Determination of the total amount of excess contributions.* The process described in paragraph (b)(2)(ii)(A) of this section must be repeated until the arrangement would satisfy the requirements of paragraph (b)(2)(ii)(C) of this section. The sum of all reductions for all HCEs determined under paragraph (b)(2)(ii)(A) of this section is the total amount of excess contributions for the plan year.

(C) *Satisfaction of ADP.* A cash or deferred arrangement satisfies this paragraph (b)(2)(ii)(C) if the arrangement would satisfy the requirements of paragraph (a)(1)(ii) of this section if the ADR for each HCE were determined after the reductions described in paragraph (b)(2)(ii)(A) of this section.

(iii) *Apportionment of total amount of excess contributions among the HCEs.* The following procedures must be used in apportioning the total amount of excess contributions determined under paragraph (b)(2)(ii) of this section among the HCEs:

(A) *Calculate the dollar amount of excess contributions for each HCE.* The contributions of the HCE with the highest dollar amount of contributions taken into account under this section are reduced by the amount required to cause that HCE's contributions to equal the dollar amount of the contributions taken into account under this section for the HCE with the next highest dollar amount of contributions taken into account under this section. If a lesser apportionment to the HCE would enable the plan to apportion the total amount of excess contributions, only the lesser apportionment would apply.

(B) *Limit on amount apportioned to any individual.* For purposes of this paragraph (b)(2)(iii), the amount of contributions taken into account under this section with respect to an HCE who is an eligible employee in more than one plan of an employer is determined by taking into account all contributions otherwise taken into account with respect to such HCE under any plan of the employer during the plan year of the plan being tested as being made under the plan being tested. However, the amount of excess contributions apportioned for a plan year with respect to any HCE must not exceed the amount of contributions actually contributed to the plan for the HCE for the plan year. Thus, in the case of an HCE who is an eligible employee in more than one plan of the same employer to which elective contributions are made and whose ADR is calculated in accordance with paragraph (a)(3)(ii) of this section, the amount required to be distributed under this paragraph (b)(2)(iii) shall not exceed the contributions actually contributed to the plan and taken into account under this section for the plan year.

(C) *Apportionment to additional HCEs.* The procedure in paragraph (b)(2)(iii)(A) of this section must be repeated until the total amount of excess contributions determined under paragraph (b)(2)(ii) of this section has been apportioned.

(iv) *Income allocable to excess contributions*—(A) *General rule.* For plan years beginning on or after January 1, 2008, the income allocable to excess contributions is

equal to the allocable gain or loss through the end of the plan year. See paragraph (b)(2)(iv)(D) of this section for rules that apply to plan years beginning before January 1, 2008.

(B) *Method of allocating income.* A plan may use any reasonable method for computing the income allocable to excess contributions, provided that the method does not violate section 401(a)(4), is used consistently for all participants and for all corrective distributions under the plan for the plan year, and is used by the plan for allocating income to participant's accounts. See § 1.401(a)(4)-1(c)(8). A plan will not fail to use a reasonable method for computing the income allocable to excess contributions merely because the income allocable to excess contributions is determined on a date that is no more than 7 days before the distribution.

(C) *Alternative method of allocating plan year income.* A plan may allocate income to excess contributions for the plan year by multiplying the income for the plan year allocable to the elective contributions and other amounts taken into account under this section (including contributions made for the plan year), by a fraction, the numerator of which is the excess contributions for the employee for the plan year, and the denominator of which is the sum of the—

(1) Account balance attributable to elective contributions and other contributions taken into account under this section as of the beginning of the plan year, and

(2) Any additional amount of such contributions made for the plan year.

* * *

(v) *Distribution.* Within 12 months after the close of the plan year in which the excess contribution arose, the plan must distribute to each HCE the excess contributions apportioned to such HCE under paragraph (b)(2)(iii) of this section and the allocable income. Except as otherwise provided in this paragraph (b)(2)(v) and paragraph (b)(4)(i) of this section, a distribution of excess contributions must be in addition to any other distributions made during the year and must be designated as a corrective distribution by the employer. In the event of a complete termination of the plan during the plan year in which an excess contribution arose, the corrective distribution must be made as soon as administratively feasible after the date of termination of the plan, but in no event later than 12 months after the date of termination. If the entire account balance of an HCE is distributed prior to when the plan makes a distribution of excess contributions in accordance with this paragraph (b)(2), the distribution is deemed to have been a corrective distribution of excess contributions (and income) to the extent that a corrective distribution would otherwise have been required.

(vi) *Tax treatment of corrective distributions*—(A) *Corrective distributions for plan years beginning on or after January 1, 2008.* Except as provided in this paragraph (b)(2)(vi), for plan years beginning on or after January 1, 2008, a corrective distribution of excess contributions (and allocable income) is includible in the employee's gross income for the employee's taxable year in which distributed. In addition, the corrective distribution is not subject to the early distribution tax of section 72(t). See paragraph (b)(5) of this section for additional rules relating to the employer excise tax on amounts distributed more than 2 1/2 months (6 months in the case of certain plans that include an eligible automatic contribution arrangement within the meaning of section 414(w)) after the end of the plan year. See also § 1.402(c)-2, A-4 for restrictions on rolling over distributions that are excess contributions.

* * *

(C) *Corrective distributions attributable to designated Roth contributions.* Notwithstanding paragraphs (b)(2)(vi)(A) and (B) of this section, a distribution of excess contributions is not includible in gross income to the extent it represents a distribution of designated Roth contributions. However, the income allocable to a corrective distribution of excess contributions that are designated Roth contri-

butions is included in gross income in accordance with paragraph (b)(2)(vi)(A) or (B) of this section (i.e., in the same manner as income allocable to a corrective distribution of excess contributions that are pre-tax elective contributions).

(vii) *Other rules*—(A) *No employee or spousal consent required.* A corrective distribution of excess contributions (and income) may be made under the terms of the plan without regard to any notice or consent otherwise required under sections 411(a)(11) and 417.

(B) *Treatment of corrective distributions as elective contributions.* Excess contributions are treated as employer contributions for purposes of sections 404 and 415 even if distributed from the plan.

(C) *No reduction of required minimum distribution.* A distribution of excess contributions (and income) is not treated as a distribution for purposes of determining whether the plan satisfies the minimum distribution requirements of section 401(a)(9). See § 1.401(a)(9)-5, A-9(b).

(D) *Partial distributions.* Any distribution of less than the entire amount of excess contributions (and allocable income) with respect to any HCE is treated as a pro rata distribution of excess contributions and allocable income.

* * *

(3) *Recharacterization of excess contributions*—(i) *General rule.* Excess contributions are recharacterized in accordance with this paragraph (b)(3) only if the excess contributions that would have to be distributed under (b)(2) of this section if the plan was correcting through distribution of excess contributions are recharacterized as described in paragraph (b)(3)(ii) of this section, and all of the conditions set forth in paragraph (b)(3)(iii) of this section are satisfied.

(ii) *Treatment of recharacterized excess contributions.* Recharacterized excess contributions are includible in the employee's gross income as if such amounts were distributed under paragraph (b)(2) of this section. The recharacterized excess contributions are treated as employee contributions for purposes of section 72, sections 401(a)(4), 401(m), § 1.401(k)-1(d) and § 1.401(k)-2. This requirement is not treated as satisfied unless the payor or plan administrator reports the recharacterized excess contributions as employee contributions to the Internal Revenue Service and the employee by timely providing such Federal tax forms and accompanying instructions and timely taking such other action as is prescribed by the Commissioner in revenue rulings, notices and other guidance published in the Internal Revenue Bulletin (see § 601.601(d)(2) of this chapter) as well as the applicable Federal tax forms and accompanying instructions.

(iii) *Additional rules*—(A) *Time of recharacterization.* Excess contributions may not be recharacterized under this paragraph (b)(3) after 2 1/2 months after the close of the plan year to which the recharacterization relates. Recharacterization is deemed to have occurred on the date on which the last of those HCEs with excess contributions to be recharacterized is notified in accordance with paragraph (b)(3)(ii) of this section.

(B) *Employee contributions must be permitted under plan.* The amount of recharacterized excess contributions, in combination with the employee contributions actually made by the HCE, may not exceed the maximum amount of employee contributions (determined without regard to the ACP test of section 401(m)(2)) permitted under the provisions of the plan as in effect on the first day of the plan year.

(C) *Treatment of recharacterized excess contributions.* Recharacterized excess contributions continue to be treated as employer contributions for all purposes under the Internal Revenue Code (other than those specified in paragraph (b)(3)(ii) of this section), including section 401(a) and sections 404, 409, 411, 412, 415, 416, and 417. Thus, for example, recharacterized excess contributions remain subject to the requirements of § 1.401(k)-1(c); must be deducted under section 404; and are

treated as employer contributions described in section 415(c)(2)(A).

(4) *Rules applicable to all corrections*—(i) *Coordination with distribution of excess deferrals*—(A) *Treatment of excess deferrals that reduce excess contributions.* The amount of excess contributions (and allocable income) to be distributed under paragraph (b)(2) of this section or the amount of excess contributions recharacterized under paragraph (b)(3) of this section with respect to an employee for a plan year, is reduced by any amounts previously distributed to the employee from the plan to correct excess deferrals for the employee's taxable year ending with or within the plan year in accordance with section 402(g)(2).

(B) *Treatment of excess contributions that reduce excess deferrals.* Under § 1.402(g)-1(e), the amount required to be distributed to correct an excess deferral to an employee for a taxable year is reduced by any excess contributions (and allocable income) previously distributed or excess contributions recharacterized with respect to the employee for the plan year beginning with or within the taxable year. The amount of excess contributions includible in the gross income of the employee, and the amount of excess contributions reported by the payer or plan administrator as includible in the gross income of the employee, does not include the amount of any reduction under § 1.402(g)-1(e)(6).

(ii) *Forfeiture of match on distributed excess contributions.* A matching contribution is taken into account under section 401(a)(4) even if the match is with respect to an elective contribution that is distributed or recharacterized under this paragraph (b). This requires that, after correction of excess contributions, each level of matching contributions be currently and effectively available to a group of employees that satisfies section 410(b). See § 1.401(a)(4)-4(e)(3)(iii)(G). Thus, a plan that provides the same rate of matching contributions to all employees will not meet the requirements of section 401(a)(4) if elective contributions are distributed under this paragraph (b) to HCEs to the extent needed to meet the requirements of section 401(k)(3), while matching contributions attributable to those elective contributions remain allocated to the HCEs' accounts. Under section 411(a)(3)(G) and § 1.411(a)-4(b)(7), a plan may forfeit matching contributions attributable to excess contributions, excess aggregate contributions or excess deferrals to avoid a violation of section 401(a)(4). See also § 1.401(a)(4)-11(g)(3)(vii)(B) regarding the use of additional allocations to the accounts of NHCEs for the purpose of correcting a discriminatory rate of matching contributions.

(iii) *Permitted forfeiture of QMAC.* Pursuant to section 401(k)(8)(E), a qualified matching contribution is not treated as forfeitable under § 1.401(k)-1(c) merely because under the plan it is forfeited in accordance with paragraph (b)(4)(ii) of this section or § 1.414(w)-1(d)(2).

(iv) *No requirement for recalculation.* If excess contributions are distributed or recharacterized in accordance with paragraphs (b)(2) and (3) of this section, the cash or deferred arrangement is treated as meeting the nondiscrimination test of section 401(k)(3) regardless of whether the ADP for the HCEs, if recalculated after the distributions or recharacterizations, would satisfy section 401(k)(3).

(v) *Treatment of excess contributions that are catch-up contributions.* A cash or deferred arrangement does not fail to meet the requirements of section 401(k)(3) and paragraph (a)(1) of this section merely because excess contributions that are catch-up contributions because they exceed the ADP limit, as described in § 1.414(v)-1(b)(1)(iii), are not corrected in accordance with this paragraph (b).

(5) *Failure to timely correct*—(i) *Failure to correct within 2 1/2 months after end of plan year.* If a plan does not correct excess contributions within 2 1/2 months after the close of the plan year for which the excess contributions are made, the employer will be liable for a 10% excise tax on the amount of the excess contributions. See section 4979 and § 54.4979-1 of this chapter. Qualified nonelective contributions and qualified matching contributions properly taken into account under paragraph (a)(6) of this section for a plan year may enable a plan to avoid having excess contributions, even if the contributions are made after the close of the 2 1/2 month period.

(ii) *Failure to correct within 12 months after end of plan year.* If excess contributions are not corrected within 12 months after the close of the plan year for which they were made, the cash or deferred arrangement will fail to satisfy the requirements of section 401(k)(3) for the plan year for which the excess contributions are made and all subsequent plan years during which the excess contributions remain in the trust.

(iii) Special rule for eligible automatic contribution arrangements. In the case of excess contributions under a plan that includes an eligible automatic contribution arrangement within the meaning of section 414(w), 6 months is substituted for 2 1/2 months in paragraph (b)(5)(i) of this section. The additional time described in this paragraph (b)(5)(iii) applies to a distribution of excess contributions for a plan year beginning on or after January 1, 2010 only where all the eligible NHCEs and eligible HCEs are covered employees under the eligible automatic contribution arrangement (within the meaning of § 1.414(w)-1(e)(3)) for the entire plan year (or for the portion of the plan year that the eligible NHCEs and eligible HCEs are eligible employees).

* * *

§ **1.402(a)-1. Taxability of beneficiary under a trust which meets the requirements of section 401(a).**

* * *

(d) *Salary reduction, cash or deferred arrangements*—(1) *Inclusion in income.* Whether a contribution to an exempt trust or plan described in section 401(a) or 403(a) is made by the employer or the employee is determined on the basis of the particular facts and circumstances of each case. Nevertheless, an amount contributed to a plan or trust will, except as otherwise provided under paragraph (d)(2) of this section, be treated as contributed by the employee if it was contributed at the employee's election, even though the election was made before the year in which the amount was earned by the employee or before the year in which the amount became currently available to the employee. Any amount treated as contributed by the employee is includible in the gross income of the employee for the year in which the amount would have been received by the employee but for the election. Thus, for example, amounts contributed to an exempt trust or plan by reason of a salary reduction agreement under a cash or deferred arrangement are treated as received by the employee when they would have been received by the employee but for the election to defer. Accordingly, they are includible in the gross income of the employee for that year (except as provided under paragraph (d)(2) of this section). See § 1.401(k)-1(a)(3)(iii) and (2)(i) for the meaning of currently available and cash or deferred arrangement, respectively.

(2) *Amounts not included in income—(i) Qualified cash or deferred arrangement.* Elective contributions as defined in § 1.401(k)-1(g)(3) for a plan year made by an employer on behalf of an employee pursuant to a cash or deferred election under a qualified cash or deferred arrangement, as defined in § 1.401(k)-1(a)(4)(i), are not treated as received by or distributed to the employee or as employee contributions. For plan years beginning after December 31, 1992, whether a cash or deferred election is made under a qualified cash or deferred arrangement is determined without regard to the special rules for certain collectively bargained plans contained in § 1.401(k)-1(a)(7). As a result, elective contributions under these plans are treated as employee contributions for purposes of this section if the cash or deferred arrangement does not satisfy the actual deferral percentage test of section 401(k)(3) or otherwise fails to be a qualified cash or deferred arrangement.

(ii) *Matching contributions.* Matching contributions described in § 1.401(m)-1(f)(12) and section 401(m)(4) are not treated as contributed by an employee merely because they are made by the employer as a result of an employee's election.

(iii) *Effect of certain one-time elections.* Amounts contributed to an exempt plan or trust described in section 401(a) or 403(a) pursuant to the one-time irrevocable employee election to participate in a plan described in § 1.401(k)-1(a)(3)(iv) are not treated as contributed by an employee. Similarly, amounts contributed to an exempt plan or trust described in section 401(a) or 403(a) in which self-employed individuals may participate pursuant to the one-time irrevocable election described in § 1.401(k)-1(a)(6)(ii)(C) are not treated as contributed by an employee.

* * *

§ 1.402(c)-2. Eligible rollover distributions; questions and answers.

* * *

Q-4: Are there other amounts that are not eligible rollover distributions?

A-4: Yes. The following amounts are not eligible rollover distributions:

(a) Elective deferrals, as defined in section 402(g)(3), and employee contributions that, pursuant to rules prescribed by the Commissioner in revenue rulings, notices, or other guidance published in the Internal Revenue Bulletin (see § 601.601(d)(2) of this chapter), are returned to the employee (together with the income allocable thereto) in order to comply with the section 415 limitations.

(b) Corrective distributions of excess deferrals as described in § 1.402(g)-1(e)(3), together with the income allocable to these corrective distributions.

(c) Corrective distributions of excess contributions under a qualified cash or deferred arrangement described in § 1.401(k)-2(b)(2) and excess aggregate contributions described in § 1.401(m)-2(b)(2), together with the income allocable to these distributions.

(d) Loans that are treated as deemed distributions pursuant to section 72(p).

(e) Dividends paid on employer securities as described in section 404(k).

(f) The costs of life insurance coverage (P.S. 58 costs).

(g) Prohibited allocations that are treated as deemed distributions pursuant to section 409(p).

(h) A distribution that is a permissible withdrawal from an eligible automatic contribution arrangement within the meaning of section 414(w).

(i) [Reserved]

(j) Distributions of premiums for accident or health insurance under § 1.402(a)-1(e)(1)(i). This paragraph A-4(j) applies for taxable years beginning on or after January 1, 2015.

(k) Similar items designated by the Commissioner in revenue rulings, notices, and other guidance published in the Internal Revenue Bulletin. See § 601.601(d)(2)(ii)(b) of this chapter.

* * *

Q-7: When is a distribution from a plan a required minimum distribution under section 401(a)(9)?

A-7: (a) *General rule.* Except as provided in paragraphs (b) and (c) of this Q&A, if a minimum distribution is required for a calendar year, the amounts distributed during that calendar year are treated as required minimum distributions under section 401(a)(9), to the extent that the total required minimum distribution under section 401(a)(9) for the calendar year has not been satisfied. Accordingly, these amounts are not eligible rollover distributions. For example, if an employee is required under section 401(a)(9) to receive a required minimum distribution for a calendar year of $5,000 and the employee receives a total of $7,200 in that year, the first $5,000 distributed will be treated as the required minimum distribution and will not be an eligible rollover distribution and the remaining $2,200 will be an eligible rollover distribution if it otherwise qualifies. If the total section 401(a)(9) required minimum

distribution for a calendar year is not distributed in that calendar year (e.g., when the distribution for the calendar year in which the employee reaches age 70 1/2 is made on the following April 1), the amount that was required but not distributed is added to the amount required to be distributed for the next calendar year in determining the portion of any distribution in the next calendar year that is a required minimum distribution.

(b) *Distribution before age 70 1/2.* Any amount that is paid before January 1 of the year in which the employee attains (or would have attained) age 70 1/2 will not be treated as required under section 401(a)(9) and, thus, is an eligible rollover distribution if it otherwise qualifies.

(c) *Special rule for annuities.* In the case of annuity payments from a defined benefit plan, or under an annuity contract purchased from an insurance company (including a qualified plan distributed annuity contract (as defined in Q&A-10 of this section)), the entire amount of any such annuity payment made on or after January 1 of the year in which an employee attains (or would have attained) age 70 1/2 will be treated as an amount required under section 401(a)(9) and, thus, will not be an eligible rollover distribution.

Q-8: How are amounts that are not includible in gross income allocated for purposes of determining the required minimum distribution?

A-8: If section 401(a)(9) has not yet been satisfied by the plan for the year with respect to an employee, a distribution is made to the employee that exceeds the amount required to satisfy section 401(a)(9) for the year for the employee, and a portion of that distribution is excludible from gross income, the following rule applies for purposes of determining the amount of the distribution that is an eligible rollover distribution. The portion of the distribution that is excludible from gross income is first allocated toward satisfaction of section 401(a)(9) and then the remaining portion of the required minimum distribution, if any, is satisfied from the portion of the distribution that is includible in gross income. For example, assume an employee is required under section 401(a)(9) to receive a minimum distribution for a calendar year of $4,000 and the employee receives a $4,800 distribution, of which $1,000 is excludible from income as a return of basis. First, the $1,000 return of basis is allocated toward satisfying the required minimum distribution. Then, the remaining $3,000 of the required minimum distribution is satisfied from the $3,800 of the distribution that is includible in gross income, so that the remaining balance of the distribution, $800, is an eligible rollover distribution if it otherwise qualifies.

Q-9: What is a distribution of a plan loan offset amount, and is it an eligible rollover distribution?

A-9: (a) *General rule.* A distribution of a plan loan offset amount, as defined in paragraph (b) of this Q&A, is an eligible rollover distribution if it satisfies Q&A-3 of this section. Thus, an amount equal to the plan loan offset amount can be rolled over by the employee (or spousal distributee) to an eligible retirement plan within the 60-day period under section 402(c)(3), unless the plan loan offset amount fails to be an eligible rollover distribution for another reason. See § 1.401(a)(31)-1, Q&A-16 for guidance concerning the offering of a direct rollover of a plan loan offset amount. See § 31.3405(c)-1, Q&A-11 of this chapter for guidance concerning special withholding rules with respect to plan loan offset amounts.

(b) *Definition of plan loan offset amount.* For purposes of section 402(c), a distribution of a plan loan offset amount is a distribution that occurs when, under the plan terms governing a plan loan, the participant's accrued benefit is reduced (offset) in order to repay the loan (including the enforcement of the plan's security interest in a participant's accrued benefit). A distribution of a plan loan offset amount can occur in a variety of circumstances, e.g., where the terms governing a plan loan require that, in the event of the employee's termination of employment or request for a distribution, the loan be repaid immediately or

treated as in default. A distribution of a plan loan offset amount also occurs when, under the terms governing the plan loan, the loan is cancelled, accelerated, or treated as if it were in default (e.g., where the plan treats a loan as in default upon an employee's termination of employment or within a specified period thereafter). A distribution of a plan loan offset amount is an actual distribution, not a deemed distribution under section 72(p).

(c) *Examples.* The rules with respect to a plan loan offset amount in this Q&A-9, § 1.401(a)(31)-1, Q&A-16 and § 31.3405(c)-1, Q&A-11 of this chapter are illustrated by the following examples:

Example 1. (a) In 1996, Employee A has an account balance of $10,000 in Plan Y, of which $3,000 is invested in a plan loan to Employee A that is secured by Employee A's account balance in Plan Y. Employee A has made no after-tax employee contributions to Plan Y. Plan Y does not provide any direct rollover option with respect to plan loans. Upon termination of employment in 1996, Employee A, who is under age 70½, elects a distribution of Employee A's entire account balance in Plan Y, and Employee A's outstanding loan is offset against the account balance on distribution. Employee A elects a direct rollover of the distribution.

(b) In order to satisfy section 401(a)(31), Plan Y must pay $7,000 directly to the eligible retirement plan chosen by Employee A in a direct rollover. When Employee A's account balance was offset by the amount of the $3,000 unpaid loan balance, Employee A received a plan loan offset amount (equivalent to $3,000) that is an eligible rollover distribution. However, under § 1.401(a)(31)-1, Q&A-16 Plan Y satisfies section 401(a)(31), even though a direct rollover option was not provided with respect to the $3,000 plan loan offset amount.

(c) No withholding is required under section 3405(c) on account of the distribution of the $3,000 plan loan offset amount because no cash or other property (other than the plan loan offset amount) is received by Employee

A from which to satisfy the withholding. Employee A may roll over $3,000 to an eligible retirement plan within the 60 day period provided in section 402(c)(3).

Example 2. (a) The facts are the same as in Example 1, except that the terms governing the plan loan to Employee A provide that, upon termination of employment, Employee A's account balance is automatically offset by the amount of any unpaid loan balance to repay the loan. Employee A terminates employment but does not request a distribution from Plan Y. Nevertheless, pursuant to the terms governing the plan loan, Employee A's account balance is automatically offset by the amount of the $3,000 unpaid loan balance.

(b) The $3,000 plan loan offset amount attributable to the plan loan in this example is treated in the same manner as the $3,000 plan loan offset amount in Example 1.

Example 3. (a) The facts are the same as in Example 2, except that, instead of providing for an automatic offset upon termination of employment to repay the plan loan, the terms governing the plan loan require full repayment of the loan by Employee A within 30 days of termination of employment. Employee A terminates employment, does not elect a distribution from Plan Y, and also fails to repay the plan loan within 30 days. The plan administrator of Plan Y declares the plan loan to Employee A in default and executes on the loan by offsetting Employee A's account balance by the amount of the $3,000 unpaid loan balance.

(b) The $3,000 plan loan offset amount attributable to the plan loan in this example is treated in the same manner as the $3,000 plan loan offset amount in Example 1 and in Example 2. The result in this Example 3 is the same even though the plan administrator treats the loan as in default before offsetting Employee A's accrued benefit by the amount of the unpaid loan.

Example 4. (a) The facts are the same as in Example 1, except that Employee A elects to receive the distribution of the account balance that remains after the $3,000 offset to

repay the plan loan, instead of electing a direct rollover of the remaining account balance.

(b) In this case, the amount of the distribution received by Employee A is $10,000, not $3,000. Because the amount of the $3,000 offset attributable to the loan is included in determining the amount that equals 20 percent of the eligible rollover distribution received by Employee A, withholding in the amount of $2,000 (20 percent of $10,000) is required under section 3405(c). The $2,000 is required to be withheld from the $7,000 to be distributed to Employee A in cash, so that Employee A actually receives a check for $5,000.

Example 5. The facts are the same as in Example 4, except that the $7,000 distribution to Employee A after the offset to repay the loan consists solely of employer securities within the meaning of section 402(e)(4)(E). In this case, no withholding is required under section 3405(c) because the distribution consists solely of the $3,000 plan loan offset amount and the $7,000 distribution of employer securities. This is the result because the total amount required to be withheld does not exceed the sum of the cash and the fair market value of other property distributed, excluding plan loan offset amounts and employer securities. Employee A may roll over the employer securities and $3,000 to an eligible retirement plan within the 60-day period provided in section 402(c)(3).

Example 6. Employee B, who is age 40, has an account balance in Plan Z, a profit sharing plan qualified under section 401(a) that includes a qualified cash or deferred arrangement described in section 401(k). Plan Z provides for no after-tax employee contributions. In 1990, Employee B receives a loan from Plan Z, the terms of which satisfy section 72(p)(2), and which is secured by elective contributions subject to the distribution restrictions in section 401(k)(2)(B). In 1996, the loan fails to satisfy section 72(p)(2) because Employee B stops repayment. In that year, pursuant to section 72(p), Employee B is taxed on a deemed distribution equal to the amount of the unpaid loan balance. Under Q&A-4 of this section, the deemed distribution is not an eligible rollover distribution. Because Employee B has not separated from service or experienced any other event that permits the distribution under section 401(k)(2)(B) of the elective contributions that secure the loan, Plan Z is prohibited from executing on the loan. Accordingly, Employee B's account balance is not offset by the amount of the unpaid loan balance at the time Employee B stops repayment on the loan. Thus, there is no distribution of an offset amount that is an eligible rollover distribution in 1996.

* * *

Q-12: How does section 402(c) apply to a distributee who is not the employee?

A-12: (a) *Spousal distributee.* If any distribution attributable to an employee is paid to the employee's surviving spouse, section 402(c) applies to the distribution in the same manner as if the spouse were the employee. The same rule applies if any distribution attributable to an employee is paid in accordance with a qualified domestic relations order (as defined in section 414(p)) to the employee's spouse or former spouse who is an alternate payee. Therefore, a distribution to the surviving spouse of an employee (or to a spouse or former spouse who is an alternate payee under a qualified domestic relations order), including a distribution of ancillary death benefits attributable to the employee, is an eligible rollover distribution if it meets the requirements of section 402(c)(2) and (4) and Q&A-3 through Q&A-10 and Q&A-14 of this section. However, a qualified plan (as defined in Q&A-2 of this section) is not treated as an eligible retirement plan with respect to a surviving spouse. Only an individual retirement plan is treated as an eligible retirement plan with respect to an eligible rollover distribution to a surviving spouse.

(b) *Non-spousal distributee.* A distributee other than the employee or the employee's surviving spouse (or a spouse or former spouse who is an alternate payee under a qualified domestic relations order) is not permitted to roll over distributions from a qualified plan. Therefore, those distributions do not constitute

eligible rollover distributions under section 402(c)(4) and are not subject to the 20-percent income tax withholding under section 3405(c).

* * *

§ 1.404(a)-12. Contributions of an employer under a plan that does not meet the requirements of section 401(a); application of section 404(a)(5).

(a) *In general.* Section 404(a)(5) covers all cases for which deductions are allowable under section 404(a) (for contributions paid by an employer under a stock bonus, pension, profit sharing, or annuity plan or for any compensation paid on account of any employee under a plan deferring the receipt of such compensation) but not allowable under paragraph (1), (2), (3), (4), or (7) of such section. For the rules with respect to the taxability of an employee when rights under a nonexempt trust become substantially vested, see section 402(b) and the regulations thereunder.

(b) *Contributions made after August 1, 1969*—(1) *In general.* A deduction is allowable for a contribution paid after August 1, 1969, under section 404(a)(5) only in the taxable year of the employer in which or with which ends the taxable year of an employee in which an amount attributable to such contribution is includible in his gross income as compensation, and then only to the extent allowable under section 404(a). See § 1.404(a)-1. For example, if an employer A contributes $1,000 to the account of its employee E for its taxable (calendar) year 1977, but the amount in the account attributable to that contribution is not includible in E's gross income until his taxable (calendar) year 1980 (at which time the includible amount is $1,150), A's deduction for that contribution is $1,000 in 1980 (if allowable under section 404(a)). For purposes of this (1), a contribution is considered to be so includible where the employee or his beneficiary excludes it from his gross income under section 101(b) or subchapter N. To the extent that property of the employer is transferred in connection with such a contribution, such transfer will constitute a disposition of such property by the employer upon which gain or loss is recognized, except as provided in section 1032 and the regulations thereunder. The amount of gain or loss recognized from such disposition shall be the difference between the value of such property used to measure the deduction allowable under this section and the employer's adjusted basis in such property.

(2) *Special rule for unfunded pensions and certain death benefits.* If unfunded pensions are paid directly to former employees, such payments are includible in their gross income when paid, and accordingly, such amounts are deductible under section 404(a)(5) when paid. Similarly, if amounts are paid as a death benefit to the beneficiaries of an employee (for example, by continuing his salary for a reasonable period), and if such amounts meet the requirements of section 162 or 212, such amounts are deductible under section 404(a)(5) in any case when they are not includible under the other paragraphs of section 404(a).

(3) *Separate accounts for funded plans with more than one employee.* In the case of a funded plan under which more than one employee participates, no deduction is allowable under section 404(a)(5) for any contribution unless separate accounts are maintained for each employee. The requirement of separate accounts does not require that a separate trust be maintained for each employee. However, a separate account must be maintained for each employee to which employer contributions under the plan are allocated, along with any income earned thereon. In addition, such accounts must be sufficiently separate and independent to qualify as separate shares under section 663(c). Nothing shall preclude a trust which loses its exemption under section 501(a) from setting up such accounts and meeting the separate account requirement of section 404(a)(5) with respect to the taxable years in which such accounts are set up and maintained.

* * *

§ 1.408-4. Treatment of distributions from individual retirement arrangements.

(a) *General rule*—(1) *Inclusion in income.* Except as otherwise provided in this section, any amount actually paid or distributed or deemed paid or distributed from an individual retirement account or individual retirement annuity shall be included in the gross income of the payee or distributee for the taxable year in which the payment or distribution is received.

(2) *Zero basis.* Notwithstanding section 1015(d) or any other provision of the Code, the basis (or investment in the contract) of any person in such an account or annuity is zero. For purposes of this section, an assignment of an individual's rights under an individual retirement account or an individual retirement annuity shall, except as provided in § 1.408-4(g) (relating to transfer incident to divorce), be deemed a distribution to such individual from such account or annuity of the amount assigned.

* * *

(g) *Transfer incident to divorce*—(1) *General rule.* The transfer of an individual's interest, in whole or in part, in an individual retirement account, individual retirement annuity, or a retirement bond, to his former spouse under a valid divorce decree or a written instrument incident to such divorce shall not be considered to be a distribution from such an account or annuity to such individual or his former spouse; nor shall it be considered a taxable transfer by such individual to his former spouse notwithstanding any other provision of Subtitle A of the Code.

(2) *Spousal account.* The interest described in this paragraph (g) which is transferred to the former spouse shall be treated as an individual retirement account of such spouse if the interest is an individual retirement account; an individual retirement annuity of such spouse if such interest is an individual retirement annuity; and a retirement bond of such spouse if such interest is a retirement bond.

§ 1.408-8. Distribution requirements for individual retirement plans.

The following questions and answers relate to the distribution rules for IRAs provided in sections 408(a)(6) and 408(b)(3).

Q-1. Is an IRA subject to the distribution rules provided in section 401(a)(9) for qualified plans?

A-1. (a) Yes, an IRA is subject to the required minimum distribution rules provided in section 401(a)(9). In order to satisfy section 401(a)(9) for purposes of determining required minimum distributions for calendar years beginning on or after January 1, 2003, the rules of §§ 1.401(a)(9)-1 through 1.401(a)(9)-9 and 1.401(a)(9)-6T for defined contribution plans must be applied, except as otherwise provided in this section. For example, whether the 5-year rule or the life expectancy rule applies to distributions after death occurring before the IRA owner's required beginning date is determined in accordance with § 1.401(a)(9)-3 and the rules of § 1.401(a)(9)-4 apply for purposes of determining an IRA owner's designated beneficiary. Similarly, the amount of the minimum distribution required for each calendar year from an individual account is determined in accordance with § 1.401(a)(9)-5. For purposes of this section, the term IRA means an individual retirement account or annuity described in section 408(a) or (b). The IRA owner is the individual for whom an IRA is originally established by contributions for the benefit of that individual and that individual's beneficiaries.

(b) For purposes of applying the required minimum distribution rules in §§ 1.401(a)(9)-1 through 1.401(a)(9)-9 and 1.401(a)(9)-6 for qualified plans, the IRA trustee, custodian, or issuer is treated as the plan administrator, and the IRA owner is substituted for the employee.

(c) See A-14 and A-15 of § 1.408A-6 for rules under section 401(a)(9) that apply to a Roth IRA.

Q-2. Are IRAs that receive employer contributions under a simplified employee pension (defined in section 408(k)) or a SIMPLE IRA (defined in section 408(p)) treated as IRAs for purposes of section 401(a)(9)?

A-2. Yes, IRAs that receive employer contributions under a simplified employee pension (defined in section 408(k)) or a SIMPLE plan (defined in section 408(p)) are treated as IRAs, rather than employer plans, for purposes of section 401(a)(9) and are, therefore, subject to the distribution rules in this section.

Q-3. In the case of distributions from an IRA, what does the term required beginning date mean?

A-3. In the case of distributions from an IRA, the term required beginning date means April 1 of the calendar year following the calendar year in which the individual attains age 70½.

Q-4. What portion of a distribution from an IRA is not eligible for rollover because the amount is a required minimum distribution?

A-4. The portion of a distribution that is a required minimum distribution from an IRA and thus not eligible for rollover is determined in the same manner as provided in A-7 of § 1.402(c)-2 for distributions from qualified plans. For example, if a minimum distribution is required under section 401(a)(9) for a calendar year, an amount distributed during a calendar year from an IRA is treated as a required minimum distribution under section 401(a)(9) to the extent that the total required minimum distribution for the year under section 401(a)(9) for that IRA has not been satisfied. This requirement may be satisfied by a distribution from the IRA or, as permitted under A-9 of this section, from another IRA.

Q-5. May an individual's surviving spouse elect to treat such spouse's entire interest as a beneficiary in an individual's IRA upon the death of the individual (or the remaining part of such interest if distribution to the spouse has commenced) as the spouse's own account?

A-5. (a) The surviving spouse of an individual may elect, in the manner described in paragraph (b) of this A-5, to treat the spouse's entire interest as a beneficiary in an individual's IRA (or the remaining part of such interest if distribution thereof has commenced to the spouse) as the spouse's own IRA. This election is permitted to be made at any time after the individual's date of death. In order to make this election, the spouse must be the sole beneficiary of the IRA and have an unlimited right to withdraw amounts from the IRA. If a trust is named as beneficiary of the IRA, this requirement is not satisfied even if the spouse is the sole beneficiary of the trust. If the surviving spouse makes the election, the required minimum distribution for the calendar year of the election and each subsequent calendar year is determined under section 401(a)(9)(A) with the spouse as IRA owner and not section 401(a)(9)(B) with the surviving spouse as the deceased IRA owner's beneficiary. However, if the election is made in the calendar year containing the IRA owner's death, the spouse is not required to take a required minimum distribution as the IRA owner for that calendar year. Instead, the spouse is required to take a required minimum distribution for that year, determined with respect to the deceased IRA owner under the rules of A-4(a) of § 1.401(a)(9)-5, to the extent such a distribution was not made to the IRA owner before death.

(b) The election described in paragraph (a) of this A-5 is made by the surviving spouse redesignating the account as an account in the name of the surviving spouse as IRA owner rather than as beneficiary. Alternatively, a surviving spouse eligible to make the election is deemed to have made the election if, at any time, either of the following occurs—

(1) Any amount in the IRA that would be required to be distributed to the surviving spouse as beneficiary under section 401(a)(9)(B) is not distributed within the time period required under section 401(a)(9)(B); or

(2) Any additional amount is contributed to the IRA which is subject, or deemed to be subject, to the lifetime distribution requirements of section 401(a)(9)(A).

(c) The result of an election described in paragraph (b) of this A-5 is that the surviving spouse shall then be considered the IRA owner for whose benefit the trust is maintained for all purposes under the Internal Revenue Code (e.g., section 72(t)).

Q-6. How is the benefit determined for purposes of calculating the required minimum distribution from an IRA?

A-6. For purposes of determining the minimum distribution required to be made from an IRA in any calendar year, the account balance of the IRA as of December 31 of the calendar year immediately preceding the calendar year for which distributions are required to be made is substituted in A-3 of § 1.401(a)(9)-5 for the account balance of the employee. Except as provided in A-7 and A-8 of this section, no adjustments are made for contributions or distributions after that date.

Q-7. What rules apply in the case of a rollover to an IRA of an amount distributed by a qualified plan or another IRA?

A-7. If the surviving spouse of an employee rolls over a distribution from a qualified plan, such surviving spouse may elect to treat the IRA as the spouse's own IRA in accordance with the provisions in A-5 of this section. In the event of any other rollover to an IRA of an amount distributed by a qualified plan or another IRA, the rules in § 1.401(a)(9)-7 will apply for purposes of determining the account balance for the receiving IRA and the required minimum distribution from the receiving IRA. However, because the value of the account balance is determined as of December 31 of the year preceding the year for which the required minimum distribution is being determined and not as of a valuation date in the preceding year, the account balance of the receiving IRA is only adjusted if the amount is not received in the calendar year in which the amount rolled over is distributed. In that case, for purposes of determining the required minimum distribution for the calendar year in which such amount is actually received, the account balance of the receiving IRA as of December 31 of the preceding year must be adjusted by the amount received in accordance with A-2 of § 1.401(a)(9)-7.

Q-8. What rules apply in the case of a transfer (including a recharacterization) from one IRA to another?

A-8. (a) *General rule*. In the case of a trustee-to-trustee transfer from one IRA to another IRA that is not a distribution and rollover, the transfer is not treated as a distribution by the transferor IRA for purposes of section 401(a)(9). Accordingly, the minimum distribution requirement with respect to the transferor IRA must still be satisfied. Except as provided in paragraph (b) of this A-8 for recharacterizations, after the transfer the employee's account balance and the required minimum distribution under the transferee IRA are determined in the same manner as an account balance and required minimum distribution are determined under an IRA receiving a rollover contribution under A-7 of this section.

(b) *Recharacterizations*. If an amount is contributed to a Roth IRA that is a conversion contribution or failed conversion contribution and that amount (plus net income allocable to that amount) is transferred to another IRA (transferee IRA) in a subsequent year as a recharacterized contribution, the recharacterized contribution (plus allocable net income) must be added to the December 31 account balance of the transferee IRA for the year in which the conversion or failed conversion occurred.

Q-9. Is the required minimum distribution from one IRA of an owner permitted to be distributed from another IRA in order to satisfy section 401(a)(9)?

A-9. Yes, the required minimum distribution must be calculated separately for each IRA. The separately calculated amounts may then be totaled and the total distribution taken from any one or more of the individual's IRAs under the rules set forth in this A-9. Generally, only amounts in IRAs that an individual holds as the IRA owner may be aggregated. However, amounts in IRAs that an individual holds as a beneficiary of the same decedent and which are being distributed under the life expectancy rule in section 401(a)(9)(B)(iii) or

(iv) may be aggregated, but such amounts may not be aggregated with amounts held in IRAs that the individual holds as the IRA owner or as the beneficiary of another decedent. Distributions from section 403(b) contracts or accounts will not satisfy the distribution requirements from IRAs, nor will distributions from IRAs satisfy the distribution requirements from section 403(b) contracts or accounts. Distributions from Roth IRAs (defined in section 408A) will not satisfy the distribution requirements applicable to IRAs or section 403(b) accounts or contracts and distributions from IRAs or section 403(b) contracts or accounts will not satisfy the distribution requirements from Roth IRAs.

Q-10. Is any reporting required by the trustee, custodian, or issuer of an IRA with respect to the minimum amount that is required to be distributed from that IRA?

A-10. Yes, the trustee, custodian, or issuer of an IRA is required to report information with respect to the minimum amount required to be distributed from the IRA for each calendar year to individuals or entities, at the time, and in the manner, prescribed by the Commissioner in revenue rulings, notices, and other guidance published in the Internal Revenue Bulletin (see § 601.601(d)(2)(ii)(b) of this chapter) as well as the applicable Federal tax forms and accompanying instructions.

Q-11. Which amounts distributed from an IRA are taken into account in determining whether section 401(a)(9) is satisfied?

A-11. (a) *General rule*. Except as provided in paragraph (b) of this A-11, all amounts distributed from an IRA are taken into account in determining whether section 401(a)(9) is satisfied, regardless of whether the amount is includible in income.

(b) *Amounts not taken into account*. The following amounts are not taken into account in determining whether the required minimum amount with respect to an IRA for a calendar year has been distributed—

(1) Contributions returned pursuant to section 408(d)(4), together with the income allocable to these contributions;

(2) Contributions returned pursuant to section 408(d)(5);

(3) Corrective distributions of excess simplified employee pension contributions under section 408(k)(6)(C), together with the income allocable to these distributions; and

(4) Similar items designated by the Commissioner in revenue rulings, notices, and other guidance published in the Internal Revenue Bulletin. See § 601.601(d)(2)(ii)(b) of this chapter.

Q-12. How does the special rule in A-3(d) of § 1.401(a)(9)-5 for a qualifying longevity annuity contract (QLAC) apply to an IRA?

A-12. (a) General rule. The special rule in A-3(d) of § 1.401(a)(9)-5 for a QLAC, defined in A-17 of § 1.401(a)(9)-6, applies to an IRA, subject to the exceptions set forth in this A-12. See A-14(d) of § 1.408A-6 for special rules relating to Roth IRAs.

(b) Limitations on premiums—(1) In general. In lieu of the limitations described in A-17(b) of § 1.401(a)(9)-6, the premiums paid with respect to the contract on a date are not permitted to exceed the lesser of the dollar limitation in paragraph (b)(2) of this A-12 or the percentage limitation in paragraph (b)(3) of this A-12.

(2) Dollar limitation. The dollar limitation is an amount equal to the excess of—

(i) $125,000 (as adjusted under A-17(d)(2) of § 1.401(a)(9)-6), over

(ii) The sum of—

(A) The premiums paid before that date with respect to the contract, and

(B) The premiums paid on or before that date with respect to any other contract that is intended to be a QLAC and that is purchased for the IRA owner under the IRA, or any other plan, annuity, or account described in section 401(a), 403(a), 403(b), or 408 or eligible governmental plan under section 457(b).

(3) Percentage limitation. The percentage limitation is an amount equal to the excess of—

(i) 25 percent of the total account balances of the IRAs (other than Roth IRAs) that an individual holds as the IRA owner (including the value of any QLAC held under those IRAs) as of December 31 of the calendar year immediately preceding the calendar year in which a premium is paid, over

(ii) The sum of—

(A) The premiums paid before that date with respect to the contract, and

(B) The premiums paid on or before that date with respect to any other contract that is intended to be a QLAC and that is held or was purchased for the individual under those IRAs.

(c) Reliance on representations. For purposes of the limitations described in paragraphs (b)(2) and (3) of this A-12, unless the trustee, custodian, or issuer of an IRA has actual knowledge to the contrary, the trustee, custodian, or issuer may rely on the IRA owner's representation (made in writing or such other form as may be prescribed by the Commissioner) of—

(1) The amount of the premiums described in paragraphs (b)(2)(ii)(B) and (b)(3)(ii)(B) of this A-12 that are not paid under the IRA, and

(2) The amount of the account balances described in paragraph (b)(3)(i) of this A-12 (other than the account balance under the IRA).

(d) Permitted delay in setting beneficiary designation. In case of a contract that is rolled over from a plan to an IRA before the required beginning date under the plan, the contract will not violate the rule in A-17(c)(2)(v) of § 1.401(a)(9)-6 that a non-spouse beneficiary must be irrevocably selected on or before the later of the date of purchase or the required beginning date under the IRA, provided that the contract requires a beneficiary to be irrevocably selected by the end of the year following the year of the rollover.

(e) Roth IRAs. A contract that is purchased under a Roth IRA is not treated as a contract that is intended to be a QLAC for purposes of applying the dollar and percentage limitation rules in paragraphs (b)(2)(ii)(B) and (b)(3)(ii)(B) of this A-12. See A-14(d) of § 1.408A-6. If a QLAC is purchased or held under a plan, annuity, account, or traditional IRA, and that contract is later rolled over or converted to a Roth IRA, the contract is not treated as a contract that is intended to be a QLAC after the date of the rollover or conversion. Thus, premiums paid with respect to the contract will not be taken into account under paragraph (b)(2)(ii)(B) or paragraph (b)(3)(ii)(B) of this A-12 after the date of the rollover or conversion.

(f) Effective/applicability date. This A-12 applies to contracts purchased on or after July 2, 2014.

§ 1.409A-1. Definitions and covered plans.

(a) *Nonqualified deferred compensation plan*—(1) **In general.** Except as otherwise provided in this paragraph (a), the term nonqualified deferred compensation plan means any plan (within the meaning of paragraph (c) of this section) that provides for the deferral of compensation (within the meaning of paragraph (b) of this section). Whether a plan provides for the deferral of compensation generally is determined at the time the service provider obtains a legally binding right to the compensation under the plan, and is not affected by any retroactive change to the plan to characterize the right as one that does not provide for the deferral of compensation. For example, amounts deferred under a nonqualified deferred compensation plan do not become an excluded death benefit if the plan is amended so that the amounts are payable only upon the death of the service provider. If a principal purpose of a plan is to achieve a result with respect to a deferral of compensation that is inconsistent with the purposes of section 409A, the Commissioner may treat the plan as a nonqualified deferred compensation

plan for purposes of section 409A and the regulations thereunder.

(2) **Qualified employer plans.** The term nonqualified deferred compensation plan does not include a qualified employer plan. The term qualified employer plan means any of the following plans:

(i) Any plan described in section 401(a) and a trust exempt from tax under section 501(a) or that is described in section 402(d).

(ii) Any annuity plan described in section 403(a).

(iii) Any annuity contract described in section 403(b).

(iv) Any simplified employee pension (within the meaning of section 408(k)).

(v) Any simple retirement account (within the meaning of section 408(p)).

(vi) Any plan under which an active participant makes deductible contributions to a trust described in section 501(c)(18).

(vii) Any eligible deferred compensation plan (within the meaning of section 457(b).

(viii) Any plan described in section 415(m).

(ix) Any plan described in § 1022(i)(2) of the Employee Retirement Income Security Act of 1974, Public Law 93-406 (88 Stat. 829, 942) (Sept. 2, 1974) (ERISA).

(3) **Certain foreign plans**—(i) **Participation addressed by treaty.** With respect to an individual for a taxable year, the term nonqualified deferred compensation plan does not include any scheme, trust, arrangement, or plan maintained with respect to such individual, to the extent contributions made by or on behalf of such individual to such scheme, trust, arrangement, or plan, or credited allocations, accrued benefits, earnings, or other amounts constituting income, of such individual under such scheme, trust, arrangement, or plan, are excludable by such individual for Federal income tax purposes pursuant to any bilateral income tax convention, or other bilat-

eral or multilateral agreement, to which the United States is a party.

(ii) **Participation by nonresident aliens, certain resident aliens, and bona fide residents of possessions.** With respect to an alien individual for a taxable year during which such individual is a nonresident alien, a resident alien classified as a resident alien solely under section 7701(b)(1)(A)(ii) (and not section 7701(b)(1)(A)(i)), or a bona fide resident of a possession (within the meaning of section 937(a)), the term nonqualified deferred compensation plan does not include any broad-based foreign retirement plan (within the meaning of paragraph (a)(3)(v) of this section).

(iii) **Participation by U.S. citizens and lawful permanent residents.** With respect to an individual for a given taxable year during which such individual is a U.S. citizen or a resident alien classified as a resident alien under section 7701(b)(1)(A)(i), other than an individual who is also a bona fide resident of a possession (within the meaning of section 937(a)), the term nonqualified deferred compensation plan does not include a broad-based foreign retirement plan (within the meaning of paragraph (a)(3)(v) of this section), but only with respect to a plan, or a portion of a plan where such portion may be distinguished, providing for nonelective deferrals of modified foreign earned income, and earnings with respect to such nonelective deferrals, and only to the extent that the amounts deferred under all such plans of the service recipient, or all portions of such plans, in which the service provider participates in such taxable year, do not exceed the applicable limits under section 415(b) (applied to nonaccount balance plans as defined in paragraph (c)(2)(i)(C) of this section) and section 415(c) (applied to account balance plans as defined in paragraph (c)(2)(i)(A) of this section) that would be applicable if such plans were plans subject to section 415 and the modified foreign earned income of such individual were treated as compensation for purposes of applying section 415(b) and (c). For purposes of this paragraph (a)(3)(iii), the term modified foreign earned income means foreign earned income as defined in section 911(b)(1) without regard to section 911(b)(1)(B)(iv) and without regard to the requirement that the income be attributable to services performed during the period described in section 911(d)(1)(A) or (B). The provisions of this paragraph (a)(3)(iii) do not apply to any individual with respect to any taxable year in which the individual is simultaneously eligible to participate in a broad-based foreign retirement plan and a qualified employer plan described in paragraph (a)(2) of this section. For purposes of this paragraph (a)(3)(iii), an individual is eligible to participate in a qualified employer plan if under the terms of the plan and without further amendment or action by the plan sponsor, the individual is eligible to make or receive contributions or accrue benefits under the plan (regardless of whether the individual has elected to participate in the plan).

(iv) **Plans subject to a totalization agreement and similar plans.** The term nonqualified deferred compensation plan does not include any social security system of a jurisdiction to the extent that benefits provided under or contributions made to the system are subject to an agreement entered into pursuant to section 233 of the Social Security Act (42 U.S.C. 433) with any foreign jurisdiction. In addition, the term nonqualified deferred compensation plan does not include a social security system of a foreign jurisdiction to the extent that benefits are provided under or contributions are made to a government-mandated plan as part of that foreign jurisdiction's social security system.

(v) **Broad-based foreign retirement plan.** The term broad-based foreign retirement plan means a scheme, trust, arrangement, or plan (regardless of whether sponsored by a U.S. person) that is written and that, in the case of an employer-maintained plan, satisfies the following conditions:

(A) The plan is nondiscriminatory insofar as the employees who, under the terms of the plan (alone or in combination with other comparable plans) and without further amendment or action by the employer, are eligible to make or receive contributions or accrue benefits under the plan other than earnings (regardless of whether the employee has elected to participate in the plan), are a wide range of employees, substantially all of whom are nonresident aliens, resident aliens classified as resident aliens solely under section 7701(b)(1)(A)(ii) (and not section 7701(b)(1)(A)(i)), or bona fide residents of a possession (within the meaning of section 937(a)), including rank and file employees.

(B) The plan (alone or in combination with other comparable plans) actually provides significant benefits for a substantial majority of such covered employees.

(C) The benefits actually provided under the plan to such covered employees are nondiscriminatory.

(D) The plan contains provisions or is the subject of tax law provisions or other legal restrictions that generally discourage employees from using plan benefits for purposes other than retirement or restrict access to plan benefits before separation from service, including (but not limited to), restricting in-service distributions except in events similar to an unforeseeable emergency (as defined in § 1.409A-3(i)(3)(i)) or hardship (as defined for purposes of section 401(k)(2)(B)(i)(IV)), or for educational purposes or the purchase of a primary residence.

(4) **Section 457 plans.** A nonqualified deferred compensation plan under section 457(f) may constitute a nonqualified deferred compensation plan for purposes of this paragraph (a). The rules of section 409A apply to nonqualified deferred compensation plans separately and in addition to any requirements applicable to such plans under section 457(f). In addition, nonelective deferred compensation of non-employees described in section 457(e)(12) and a grandfathered plan or arrangement described in § 1.457-2(k)(4) may constitute a nonqualified deferred compensation plan for purposes of this paragraph (a). The term nonqualified deferred compensation plan does not include a length of service award to a bona fide volunteer under section

457(e)(11)(A)(ii). For purposes of the application of section 409A to a plan to which section 457 applies, a payment under the plan generally means the provision of cash or property to the service provider, provided that for purposes of the application of the short-term deferral rule set forth in paragraph (b)(4) of this section, the inclusion in income of an amount under section 457(f) is treated as a payment of the amount.

(5) **Certain welfare benefits.** The term nonqualified deferred compensation plan does not include a plan, or a portion of a plan, to the extent that the plan provides bona fide vacation leave, sick leave, compensatory time, disability pay, or death benefits. For these purposes, the terms "disability pay" and "death benefits" have the same meanings as provided in § 31.3121(v)(2)-1(b)(4)(iv)(C) of this chapter, provided that for purposes of this paragraph, such disability pay and death benefits may be provided through insurance and the lifetime benefits payable under the plan are not treated as including the value of any taxable term life insurance coverage or taxable disability insurance coverage provided under the plan. The term nonqualified deferred compensation plan also does not include any Archer Medical Savings Account as described in section 220, any Health Savings Account as described in section 223, or any other medical reimbursement arrangement, including a health reimbursement arrangement, that satisfies the requirements of section 105 and section 106 such that the benefits or reimbursements provided under such arrangement are not includible in income.

(b) *Deferral of compensation*—(1) **In general.** Except as otherwise provided in paragraphs (b)(3) through (b)(12) of this section, a plan provides for the deferral of compensation if, under the terms of the plan and the relevant facts and circumstances, the service provider has a legally binding right during a taxable year to compensation that, pursuant to the terms of the plan, is or may be payable to (or on behalf of) the service provider in a later taxable year. Such compensation is deferred compensation for purposes of section 409A, this section and §§ 1.409A-2 through 1.409A-6. A legally binding right to an amount that will be excluded from income when and if received does not constitute a deferral of compensation, unless the service provider has received the right in exchange for, or has the right to exchange the right for, an amount that will be includible in income (other than due to participation in a cafeteria plan described in section 125). A service provider does not have a legally binding right to compensation to the extent that compensation may be reduced unilaterally or eliminated by the service recipient or other person after the services creating the right to the compensation have been performed. However, if the facts and circumstances indicate that the discretion to reduce or eliminate the compensation is available or exercisable only upon a condition, or the discretion to reduce or eliminate the compensation lacks substantive significance, a service provider will be considered to have a legally binding right to the compensation. Whether the discretion to reduce or eliminate the compensation lacks substantive significance depends on all the relevant facts and circumstances. However, where the service provider to whom the compensation may be paid has effective control of the person retaining the discretion to reduce or eliminate the compensation, or has effective control over any portion of the compensation of the person retaining the discretion to reduce or eliminate the compensation, or is a member of the family (as defined in section 267(c)(4) applied as if the family of an individual includes the spouse of any member of the family) of the person retaining the discretion to reduce or eliminate the compensation, the discretion to reduce or eliminate the compensation will not be treated as having substantive significance. For this purpose, compensation is not considered subject to unilateral reduction or elimination merely because it may be reduced or eliminated by operation of the objective terms of the plan, such as the application of a nondiscretionary, objective provision creating a substantial risk of forfeiture. Similarly, a service provider does not fail to have a legally binding right to compensation merely because the amount of compensation is determined under a formula that provides for benefits to be offset by benefits provided under another plan (including a plan that is qualified under section 401(a)), or because benefits are reduced due to actual or notional investment losses, or, in a final average pay plan, subsequent decreases in compensation.

(2) **Earnings.** References to the deferral of compensation or deferred compensation include references to earnings. When the right to earnings is specified under the terms of the plan, the legally binding right to earnings arises at the time of the deferral of the compensation to which the earnings relate. A plan may provide that the time and form of payment of earnings is treated separately from the time and form of payment of the underlying compensation, so that, provided that the rules of section 409A are otherwise met, a plan may provide that earnings will be paid at a separate time or in a separate form from the payment of the underlying compensation. For the application of the deferral election rules to current payments of earnings and dividend equivalents, see § 1.409A-3(e).

(3) **Compensation payable pursuant to the service recipient's customary payment timing arrangement.** A deferral of compensation does not occur solely because compensation is paid after the last day of the service provider's taxable year pursuant to the timing arrangement under which the service recipient normally compensates service providers for services performed during a payroll period described in section 3401(b), or with respect to a non-employee service provider, a period not longer than the payroll period described in section 3401(b) or if no such payroll period exists, a period not longer than the earlier of the normal timing arrangement under which the service provider normally compensates non-employee service providers or 30 days after the end of the service provider's taxable year.

(4) **Short-term deferral**—(i) **In general.** A deferral of compensation does not occur under a plan with respect to any payment (as defined in § 1.409A-2(b)(2)) that is not a de-

ferred payment, provided that the service provider actually or constructively receives such payment on or before the last day of the applicable 2 1/2 month period. The following rules apply for purposes of this paragraph (b)(4)(i):

(A) The applicable 2 1/2 month period is the period ending on the later of the 15th day of the third month following the end of the service provider's first taxable year in which the right to the payment is no longer subject to a substantial risk of forfeiture or the 15th day of the third month following the end of the service recipient's first taxable year in which the right to the payment is no longer subject to a substantial risk of forfeiture.

(B) A payment is treated as actually or constructively received if the payment is includible in income, including if the payment is includible in income under section 83, the economic benefit doctrine, section 402(b), or section 457(f).

(C) A right to a payment that is never subject to a substantial risk of forfeiture is considered to be no longer subject to a substantial risk of forfeiture on the first date the service provider has a legally binding right to the payment.

(D) A payment is a deferred payment if it is made pursuant to a provision of a plan that provides for the payment to be made or completed on or after any date, or upon or after the occurrence of any event, that will or may occur later than the end of the applicable 2 1/2 month period, such as a separation from service, death, disability, change in control event, specified time or schedule of payment, or unforeseeable emergency, regardless of whether an amount is actually paid as a result of the occurrence of such a payment date or event during the applicable 2 1/2 month period. If a plan provides that the service provider or service recipient may make an election under the plan (including an election under § 1.409A-2(a)(4)) of a different payment date, schedule, or event, such right is disregarded for this purpose. In such cases, whether a plan provides for a deferred payment is determined based on the payment date, schedule, or event that

would apply if no such election were made, except that if the plan would not provide for a deferred payment absent such an election, and the service provider or service recipient makes such an election, whether the plan provides for a deferred payment is determined based upon the payment date, schedule, or event that the service provider or service recipient in fact elected.

(E) A stock right provides for a deferred payment if such right includes any provision pursuant to which the holder of the stock right will or may have the right to exercise the stock right after the applicable 2 1/2 month period.

(F) This paragraph (b)(4)(i) is applied separately to each payment (as defined in § 1.409A-2(b)(2)) required to be made under a plan.

(G) If a plan provides for a deferred payment with respect to part of a payment (for example a life annuity or a series of installment amounts treated as a single payment), the plan provides for a deferred payment with respect to the entire payment.

(ii) **Certain delayed payments.** A payment that otherwise qualifies as a short-term deferral under paragraph (b)(4)(i) of this section but is made after the applicable 2 1/2 month period may continue to qualify as a short-term deferral if the taxpayer establishes that it was administratively impracticable to make the payment by the end of the applicable 2 1/2 month period and, as of the date upon which the legally binding right to the compensation arose, such impracticability was unforeseeable, or the taxpayer establishes that making the payment by the end of the applicable 2 1/2 month period would have jeopardized the ability of the service recipient to continue as a going concern, and provided further that the payment is made as soon as administratively practicable or as soon as the payment would no longer have such effect. For purposes of this paragraph (b)(4)(ii), an action or failure to act of the service provider or a person under the service provider's control, such as a failure to provide necessary information or documentation, is not an unforeseeable event. In addition, a payment that otherwise qualifies as a short-term deferral under paragraph (b)(4)(i) of this section but is made after the applicable 21/2 month period may continue to qualify as a short-term deferral if the taxpayer establishes that the service recipient reasonably anticipated that the service recipient's deduction with respect to such payment otherwise would not be permitted by application of section 162(m), and, as of the date the legally binding right to the payment arose, a reasonable person would not have anticipated the application of section 162(m) at the time of the payment, and provided further that the payment is made as soon as reasonably practicable following the first date on which the service recipient anticipates or reasonably should anticipate that, if the payment were made on such date, the service recipient's deduction with respect to such payment would no longer be restricted due to the application of section 162(m). For additional rules applicable to certain transaction-based compensation, see § 1.409A-3(i)(5)(iv)(A).

(iii) **Examples.** The following examples illustrate the provisions of this paragraph (b)(4). In these examples, except as otherwise noted, each employee and each employer has a calendar year taxable year and each employee is an individual who is employed by the specified employer.

Example 1. On November 1, 2008, Employer Z awards a bonus to Employee A such that Employee A has a legally binding right to the payment as of November 1, 2008, that is not subject to a substantial risk of forfeiture. The bonus plan does not provide for a payment date or a deferred payment. The bonus plan will not be considered to have provided for a deferral of compensation if the bonus is paid or made available to Employee A on or before March 15, 2009.

Example 2. Employer Y has a taxable year ending August 31. On November 1, 2008, Employer Y awards a bonus to Employee B so that Employee B has a legally binding right to the payment as of November 1, 2008, that is not subject to a substantial risk of forfeiture. The bonus plan does not provide for a

payment date or a deferred payment. The bonus plan will not be considered to have provided for a deferral of compensation if the bonus is paid or made available to Employee B on or before November 15, 2009.

Example 3. On November 1, 2008, Employer X awards a bonus to Employee C such that Employee C has a legally binding right to the payment as of November 1, 2008. Under the bonus plan, Employee C will forfeit the bonus unless Employee C continues performing services through December 31, 2010. The right to the payment is subject to a substantial risk of forfeiture through December 31, 2010. Employee C has the right to make a written election not later than December 31, 2009, to receive the bonus on or after December 31, 2015, but Employee C does not make such election. The bonus plan does not provide for a default payment date or a deferred payment in the absence of an election by Employee C. The bonus plan will not be considered to have provided for a deferral of compensation if the bonus is paid or made available to Employee C on or before March 15, 2011.

Example 4. On November 1, 2008, Employer W awards a bonus to Employee D such that Employee D has a legally binding right to the payment as of November 1, 2008. Under the bonus plan, the bonus will be determined based on services performed during the period from January 1, 2009 through December 31, 2010. The bonus is scheduled to be paid as a lump sum payment on February 15, 2011. Under the bonus plan, Employee D will forfeit the bonus unless Employee D continues performing services through the scheduled payment date (February 15, 2011). Provided that at all times before the scheduled payment date Employee D is required to continue to perform services to retain the right to the bonus, and the bonus is paid on or before March 15, 2012, the bonus plan will not be considered to have provided for a deferral of compensation.

Example 5. On November 1, 2008, Employer V awards a bonus to Employee E such that Employee E has a legally binding right to the payment as of November 1, 2008. Under the bonus plan, Employee E will forfeit the bonus unless Employee E continues performing services through December 31, 2010. Under the bonus plan, the bonus is scheduled to be paid as a lump sum payment on July 1, 2011. By specifying a payment date after the applicable 21/2 month period, the bonus plan provides for a deferred payment. The bonus plan provides for a deferral of compensation, and will not qualify as a short-term deferral regardless of whether the bonus is paid or made available on or before March 15, 2011 (and generally any payment before June 1, 2011 would constitute an impermissible acceleration of a payment).

Example 6. On November 1, 2008, Employer U awards a bonus to Employee F such that Employee F has a legally binding right to the payment as of November 1, 2008, that is not subject to a substantial risk of forfeiture. The bonus plan provides for a lump sum payment upon Employee F's separation from service. Because the separation from service is an event that may occur after the applicable 21/2 month period, the bonus plan provides for a deferred payment and therefore provides for a deferral of compensation. Accordingly, the bonus plan will not qualify as a short-term deferral regardless of whether Employee F separates from service and the bonus is paid or made available on or before March 15, 2009.

Example 7. On November 1, 2008, Employer T grants Employee G a legally binding right to the payment of a life annuity with the first annuity payment on November 1, 2013, provided that Employee G continues performing services for Employer T continuously through November 1, 2013. Because the life annuity is treated as a single payment, and because all payments of the life annuity may not occur during the applicable 21/2 month period, the plan provides for a deferred payment and none of the amounts payable under the annuity will qualify as a short-term deferral, so that section 409A applies to all amounts that are payable under the plan.

Example 8. On November 1, 2008, Employer S grants Employee H a stock right providing for an exercise price less than the fair market value of the underlying stock on November 1, 2008. The stock right is subject to a substantial risk of forfeiture requiring services through November 1, 2010. The stock right becomes exercisable when the substantial risk of forfeiture lapses and expires on November 1, 2013. Employee H continues providing services through November 1, 2010, at which time the substantial risk of forfeiture lapses. The stock right provides for a deferred payment and will not qualify as a short-term deferral regardless of whether Employee H exercises the stock right on or before March 15, 2011.

(5) **Stock options, stock appreciation rights, and other equity-based compensation**—(i) **Stock rights**—(A) **Nonstatutory stock options not providing for the deferral of compensation.** An option to purchase service recipient stock does not provide for a deferral of compensation if—

(1) The exercise price may never be less than the fair market value of the underlying stock (disregarding lapse restrictions as defined in § 1.83-3(i)) on the date the option is granted and the number of shares subject to the option is fixed on the original date of grant of the option;

(2) The transfer or exercise of the option is subject to taxation under section 83 [26 USCS § 83] and § 1.83-7; and

(3) The option does not include any feature for the deferral of compensation other than the deferral of recognition of income until the later of the following:

(i) The exercise or disposition of the option under § 1.83-7.

(ii) The time the stock acquired pursuant to the exercise of the option first becomes substantially vested (as defined in § 1.83-3(b)).

(B) **Stock appreciation rights not providing for the deferral of compensation.** A right to compensation based on the appreciation in value of a specified number of shares of service recipient stock occurring between the date of grant and the date of exercise of such right (a stock appreciation right) does not provide for a deferral of compensation if—

(1) Compensation payable under the stock appreciation right cannot be greater than the excess of the fair market value of the stock (disregarding lapse restrictions as defined in § 1.83-3(i)) on the date the stock appreciation right is exercised over an amount specified on the date of grant of the stock appreciation right (the stock appreciation right exercise price), with respect to a number of shares fixed on or before the date of grant of the right;

(2) The stock appreciation right exercise price may never be less than the fair market value of the underlying stock (disregarding lapse restrictions as defined in § 1.83-3(i)) on the date the right is granted; and

(3) The stock appreciation right does not include any feature for the deferral of compensation other than the deferral of recognition of income until the exercise of the stock appreciation right.

(C) **Stock rights that may provide for the deferral of compensation.** An option to purchase stock other than service recipient stock, or a stock appreciation right with respect to stock other than service recipient stock, generally will provide for the deferral of compensation within the meaning of this paragraph (b). If under the terms of an option to purchase service recipient stock (other than an incentive stock option described in section 422 [26 USCS § 422] or a stock option granted under an employee stock purchase plan described in section 423 [26 USCS § 423]), the exercise price is or could become less than the fair market value of the stock (disregarding lapse restrictions as defined in § 1.83-3(i)) on the date of grant, the grant of the option generally will provide for the deferral of compensation within the meaning of this paragraph (b). If under the terms of a stock appreciation right with respect to service recipient stock, the compensation payable under the stock appreciation right is or could be any amount greater than, with respect to a predetermined number of shares, the excess of the

fair market value of the stock (disregarding lapse restrictions as defined in § 1.83-3(i)) on the date the stock appreciation right is exercised over the fair market value of the stock (disregarding lapse restrictions as defined in § 1.83-3(i)) on the date of grant of the stock appreciation right, the grant of the stock appreciation right generally will provide for a deferral of compensation within the meaning of this paragraph (b).

(D) **Feature for the deferral of compensation.** To the extent a stock right provides a right other than the right to receive cash or stock on the date of exercise and such additional right would otherwise allow compensation to be deferred beyond the date of exercise, the entire arrangement (including the underlying stock right) provides for the deferral of compensation. For purposes of this paragraph (b)(5)(i), neither the right to receive substantially nonvested stock (as defined in § 1.83-3(b)) upon the exercise of a stock right, nor the right to pay the exercise price with previously acquired shares, constitutes a feature for the deferral of compensation.

(E) **Rights to dividends.** For purposes of this paragraph (b)(5)(i), the right, directly or indirectly contingent upon the exercise of a stock right, to receive an amount equal to all or part of the dividends or other distributions (other than stock dividends described in paragraph (b)(5)(v)(H) of this section) declared and paid on the number of shares underlying the stock right between the date of grant and the date of exercise of the stock right constitutes an offset to the exercise price of the stock option or an increase in the amount payable under the stock appreciation right (generally causing such stock right to be subject to section 409A [26 USCS § 409A]). A plan providing a right to dividends or other distributions declared and paid on the number of shares underlying a stock right, the payment of which is not contingent upon, or otherwise payable on, the exercise of the stock right, may provide for a deferral of compensation, but the existence of the right to receive such an amount will not be treated as a reduction to the exercise price of (or an increase to the compensation payable under) the stock right. Thus, a right to such dividends or distributions that is not contingent, directly or indirectly, upon the exercise of a stock right will not cause the related stock right to fail to satisfy the requirements of the exclusion from the definition of a deferral of compensation provided in paragraphs (b)(5)(i)(A) and (B) of this section.

(ii) **Statutory stock options.** The grant of an incentive stock option as described in section 422 [26 USCS § 422], or the grant of an option under an employee stock purchase plan described in section 423 [26 USCS § 423] (including the grant of an option with an exercise price discounted in accordance with section 423(b)(6) [26 USCS § 423(b)(6)] and the accompanying regulations), does not constitute a deferral of compensation. However, the exclusion for statutory stock options under this paragraph (b)(5)(ii) does not apply to a modification, extension, or renewal of a statutory option that is treated as the grant of a new option that is not a statutory option. See § 1.424-1(e). In such event, the option is treated for purposes of this paragraph (b) as if it had been a nonstatutory stock option from the date of the original grant. Accordingly, if such modification, extension, or renewal of the stock option would have been treated as the grant of a new option or as causing the option to have had a deferral feature from the date of grant under paragraph (b)(5)(v) of this section, the modification, extension, or renewal of the stock option is treated as the grant of a new option or as causing the option to have had a deferral feature from the date of grant for purposes of this paragraph (b)(5).

(iii) **Service recipient stock**—(A) **In general.** Except as otherwise provided in paragraphs (b)(5)(iii)(B), (C), and (D) of this section, the term service recipient stock means a class of stock that, as of the date of grant, is common stock for purposes of section 305 [26 USCS § 305] and the regulations thereunder of a corporation that is an eligible issuer of service recipient stock (as defined in paragraph (b)(5)(iii)(E) of this section). Notwithstanding the foregoing, the term service recip-

ient stock does not include a class of stock that has any preference as to distributions other than distributions of service recipient stock and distributions in liquidation of the issuer. The term service recipient stock also does not include any stock that is subject to a mandatory repurchase obligation (other than a right of first refusal), or a put or call right that is not a lapse restriction as defined in § 1.83-3(i), if the stock price under such right or obligation is based on a measure other than the fair market value (disregarding lapse restrictions as defined in § 1.83-3(i)) of the equity interest in the corporation represented by the stock.

(B) **American depositary receipts.** An American depositary receipt or American depositary share may constitute service recipient stock, to the extent that the stock traded on a foreign securities market to which the American depositary receipt or American depositary share relates qualifies as service recipient stock.

(C) **Mutual company units.** Mutual company units may constitute service recipient stock. For this purpose, the term mutual company unit means a fixed percentage of the overall value of a non-stock mutual company or association. For purposes of determining the value of the mutual company unit, the unit may be valued in accordance with the rules set forth in paragraph (b)(5)(iv)(B) of this section governing valuation of service recipient stock the shares of which are not traded on an established securities market, applied as if the mutual company were a stock corporation with one class of common stock and the number of shares of such stock determined according to such fixed percentage. For example, an appreciation right based on the appreciation of 10 mutual company units, where each unit is defined as one percent of the overall value of the mutual company, would be valued as if the appreciation right were based upon 10 shares of a corporation, with 100 shares of common stock (and no other class of stock), the shares of which are not readily tradable on an established securities market.

(D) **Other entities.** An interest in an entity other than a corporation or non-stock mutual company or association may constitute service recipient stock to the extent designated by the Commissioner in revenue procedures, notices, or other guidance published in the Internal Revenue Bulletin (see § 601.601(d)(2) of this chapter).

(E) **Eligible issuer of service recipient stock**—(1) **In general.** The term eligible issuer of service recipient stock means only the corporation for which the service provider provides direct services on the date of grant of the stock right (if the entity receiving such services is a corporation), and any corporation in a chain of corporations or other entities in which each corporation or other entity has a controlling interest in another corporation or other entity in the chain, ending with the corporation or other entity that has a controlling interest in the corporation or other entity for which the service provider provides direct services on the date of grant of the stock right. For this purpose, the term controlling interest has the same meaning as provided in § 1.414(c)-2(b)(2)(i), provided that the language "at least 50 percent" is used instead of "at least 80 percent" each place it appears in § 1.414(c)-2(b)(2)(i). In addition, where the use of such stock with respect to the grant of a stock right to such service provider is based upon legitimate business criteria, the term controlling interest has the same meaning as provided in § 1.414(c)-(b)(2)(i), provided that the language "at least 20 percent" is used instead of "at least 80 percent" each place it appears in § 1.414(c)-2(b)(2)(i). For purposes of determining ownership of an interest in an organization, the rules of §§ 1.414(c)-3 and 1.414(c)-4 apply. The determination of whether a grant is based on legitimate business criteria is based on the facts and circumstances, focusing primarily on whether there is a sufficient nexus between the service provider and the issuer of the stock right so that the grant serves a legitimate non-tax business purpose other than simply providing compensation to the service provider that is excluded from the requirements of section 409A [26 USCS § 409A]. For example, stock of a corporation that owns an interest in a joint venture involving an operating business, used with respect to

stock rights granted to service providers of the joint venture who are former service providers of such corporation, generally will constitute use of service recipient stock based upon legitimate business criteria, and therefore could constitute service recipient stock with respect to such service providers if the corporation owns at least 20 percent of the joint venture and the other requirements of this paragraph (b)(5)(iii) are met. Similarly, the legitimate business criteria requirement generally would be met if the corporate venturer issued such a right to an employee of the joint venture who it reasonably expected would in the future become an employee of the corporate venturer. However, where a service provider has no real nexus with a corporate venturer, such as generally happens when the corporate venturer is a passive investor in the service recipient joint venture, a stock right issued to that employee on the investor corporation's stock generally would not be based upon legitimate business criteria. Similarly, where a corporation holds only a minority interest in an entity that in turn holds a minority interest in the entity for which the service provider performs services, such that the corporation holds only an insubstantial indirect interest in the entity receiving the services, legitimate business criteria generally would not exist for issuing a stock right on the corporation's stock to the service provider.

(2) **Investment vehicles.** Notwithstanding the provisions of paragraph (b)(5)(iii)(E)(1) of this section, except as to a service provider providing services directly to such corporation, for purposes of this paragraph (b)(5), an eligible issuer of service recipient stock does not include any corporation whose primary purpose is to serve as an investment vehicle with respect to the corporation's minority ownership interests in entities other than the service recipient.

(3) **Corporate structures established or transactions undertaken for purposes of avoiding coverage under section 409A** [26 USCS § 409A]. Notwithstanding the provisions of paragraph (b)(5)(iii)(E)(1) of this section, an eligible issuer of service recipient

stock does not include any corporation within a group of entities treated as a single service recipient if a purpose of the establishment of the structure of the ownership, or a purpose of a significant transaction between or among two or more entities comprising a single service recipient, is to provide deferred compensation not subject to the application of section 409A [26 USCS § 409A]. If an entity becomes a member of a group of corporations or other entities treated as a single service recipient, and the primary source of income or value of such entity arises from the provision of management services to other members of the service recipient group, it is presumed that such structure was established for purposes of avoiding the application of section 409A [26 USCS § 409A] if any stock rights are issued with respect to such entity.

(4) **Substitutions and assumptions by reason of a corporate transaction.** If the requirements of paragraph (b)(5)(v)(D) of this section are met such that the substitution of a new stock right pursuant to a corporate transaction for an outstanding stock right, or the assumption of an outstanding stock right pursuant to a corporate transaction, would not be treated as the grant of a new stock right or a change in the form of payment for purposes of this section and §§ 1.409A-2 through 1.409A-6, the stock underlying the stock right that replaced the stock right that is substituted or assumed will be treated as service recipient stock for purposes of applying this paragraph (b)(5) to the replacement stock rights if such underlying stock otherwise satisfies the requirements of paragraph (b)(5)(iii)(A) of this section. For example, if by reason of a spinoff transaction (under which the stock of a subsidiary corporation is distributed to the stockholders of a distributing corporation), a stock option to purchase distributing corporation stock is replaced with a stock option to purchase distributing corporation stock and a stock option to purchase the spun off subsidiary corporation's stock (each otherwise satisfying the requirements of paragraph (b)(5)(iii)(A) of this section), and where such substitution is not treated as a modification of the original stock option pursuant to paragraph

(b)(5)(v)(D) of this section, both the distributing corporation stock and the subsidiary corporation stock are treated as service recipient stock for purposes of applying this paragraph (b)(5) to the replacement stock options.

(iv) **Determination of the fair market value of service recipient stock**—(A) **Stock readily tradable on an established securities market.** For purposes of paragraph (b)(5)(i) of this section, in the case of service recipient stock that is readily tradable on an established securities market, the fair market value of the stock may be determined based upon the last sale before or the first sale after the grant, the closing price on the trading day before or the trading day of the grant, the arithmetic mean of the high and low prices on the trading day before or the trading day of the grant, or any other reasonable method using actual transactions in such stock as reported by such market. The determination of fair market value also may be determined using an average selling price during a specified period that is within 30 days before or 30 days after the applicable valuation date, provided that the program under which the stock right is granted, including a program with a single participant, must irrevocably specify the commitment to grant the stock right with an exercise price set using such an average selling price before the beginning of the specified period. For this purpose, the term average selling price refers to the arithmetic mean of such selling prices on all trading days during the specified period, or the average of such prices over the specified period weighted based on the volume of trading of such stock on each trading day during such specified period. To satisfy this requirement, the service recipient must designate the recipient of the stock right, the number and class of shares of stock that are subject to the stock right, and the method for determining the exercise price including the period over which the averaging will occur, before the beginning of the specified averaging period. Notwithstanding the forgoing provisions of this paragraph (b)(5)(iv)(A), where applicable foreign law requires that a compensatory stock right be priced based upon a specific price averaging method and period, a stock right granted in accordance with such applicable foreign law will be treated as meeting the requirements of this paragraph (b)(5)(iv)(A), provided that the averaging period does not exceed 30 days.

(B) **Stock not readily tradable on an established securities market**—(1) **In general.** For purposes of paragraph (b)(5)(i) of this section, in the case of service recipient stock that is not readily tradable on an established securities market, the fair market value of the stock as of a valuation date means a value determined by the reasonable application of a reasonable valuation method. The determination whether a valuation method is reasonable, or whether an application of a valuation method is reasonable, is made based on the facts and circumstances as of the valuation date. Factors to be considered under a reasonable valuation method include, as applicable, the value of tangible and intangible assets of the corporation, the present value of anticipated future cash-flows of the corporation, the market value of stock or equity interests in similar corporations and other entities engaged in trades or businesses substantially similar to those engaged in by the corporation the stock of which is to be valued, the value of which can be readily determined through nondiscretionary, objective means (such as through trading prices on an established securities market or an amount paid in an arm's length private transaction), recent arm's length transactions involving the sale or transfer of such stock or equity interests, and other relevant factors such as control premiums or discounts for lack of marketability and whether the valuation method is used for other purposes that have a material economic effect on the service recipient, its stockholders, or its creditors. The use of a valuation method is not reasonable if such valuation method does not take into consideration in applying its methodology all available information material to the value of the corporation. Similarly, the use of a value previously calculated under a valuation method is not reasonable as of a later date if such calculation fails to reflect information available after the date of the calculation that may materially affect the value of the corporation

(for example, the resolution of material litigation or the issuance of a patent) or the value was calculated with respect to a date that is more than 12 months earlier than the date for which the valuation is being used. The service recipient's consistent use of a valuation method to determine the value of its stock or assets for other purposes, including for purposes unrelated to compensation of service providers, is also a factor supporting the reasonableness of such valuation method.

(2) **Presumption of reasonableness.** For purposes of this paragraph (b)(5)(iv)(B), the use of any of the following methods of valuation is presumed to result in a reasonable valuation, provided that the Commissioner may rebut such a presumption upon a showing that either the valuation method or the application of such method was grossly unreasonable:

(i) A valuation of a class of stock determined by an independent appraisal that meets the requirements of section 401(a)(28)(C) [26 USCS § 401(a)(28)(C)] and the regulations as of a date that is no more than 12 months before the relevant transaction to which the valuation is applied (for example, the date of grant of a stock option).

(ii) A valuation based upon a formula that, if used as part of a nonlapse restriction (as defined in § 1.83-3(h)) with respect to the stock, would be considered to be the fair market value of the stock pursuant to § 1.83-5, provided that such stock is valued in the same manner for purposes of any transfer of any shares of such class of stock (or any substantially similar class of stock) to the issuer or any person that owns stock possessing more than 10 percent of the total combined voting power of all classes of stock of the issuer (applying the stock attribution rules of § 1.424-1(d)), other than an arm's length transaction involving the sale of all or substantially all of the outstanding stock of the issuer, and such valuation method is used consistently for all such purposes, and provided further that this paragraph (b)(5)(iv)(B)(2)(ii) does not apply with respect to stock subject to a stock right payable in stock, where the stock acquired pursuant to the exercise of the stock right is transferable other than through the operation of a nonlapse restriction.

(iii) A valuation, made reasonably and in good faith and evidenced by a written report that takes into account the relevant factors described in paragraph (b)(5)(iv)(B)(1) of this section, of illiquid stock of a start-up corporation. For this purpose, illiquid stock of a start-up corporation means service recipient stock of a corporation that has no material trade or business that it or any predecessor to it has conducted for a period of 10 years or more and has no class of equity securities that are traded on an established securities market (as defined in paragraph (k) of this section), where such stock is not subject to any put, call, or other right or obligation of the service recipient or other person to purchase such stock (other than a right of first refusal upon an offer to purchase by a third party that is unrelated to the service recipient or service provider and other than a right or obligation that constitutes a lapse restriction as defined in § 1.83-3(i)), and provided that this paragraph (b)(5)(iv)(B)(2)(iii) does not apply to the valuation of any stock if the service recipient or service provider may reasonably anticipate, as of the time the valuation is applied, that the service recipient will undergo a change in control event as described in § 1.409A-3(i)(5)(v) or § 1.409A-3(i)(5)(vii) within the 90 days following the action to which the valuation is applied, or make a public offering of securities within the 180 days following the action to which the valuation is applied. For purposes of this paragraph (b)(5)(iv)(B)(2)(iii), a valuation will not be treated as made reasonably and in good faith unless the valuation is performed by a person or persons that the corporation reasonably determines is qualified to perform such a valuation based on the person's or persons" significant knowledge, experience, education, or training. Generally, a person will be qualified to perform such a valuation if a reasonable individual, upon being apprised of such knowledge, experience, education, and training, would reasonably rely on the advice of such person with respect to valuation in deciding whether to accept an offer to purchase or sell the stock being valued. For this purpose, significant experience generally means at least five years of relevant experience in business valuation or appraisal, financial accounting, investment banking, private equity, secured lending, or other comparable experience in the line of business or industry in which the service recipient operates.

(3) **Use of alternative methods.** For purposes of this paragraph (b)(5), a different valuation method may be used for each separate action for which a valuation is relevant, provided that a single valuation method is used for each separate action and, once used, may not retroactively be altered. For example, one valuation method may be used to establish the exercise price of a stock option, and a different valuation method may be used to determine the value at the date of the repurchase of stock pursuant to a put or call right. However, once an exercise price or amount to be paid has been established, the exercise price or amount to be paid may not be changed through the retroactive use of another valuation method. In addition, notwithstanding the foregoing, where after the date of grant, but before the date of exercise or transfer, of the stock right, the service recipient stock to which the stock right relates becomes readily tradable on an established securities market, the service recipient must use the valuation method set forth in paragraph (b)(5)(iv)(A) of this section for purposes of determining the payment at the date of exercise or the purchase of the stock, as applicable.

(v) **Modifications, extensions, substitutions, and assumptions of stock rights—(A) Treatment of modified and extended stock rights.** A modification of the terms of a stock right within the meaning of paragraph (b)(5)(v)(B) of this section is considered to be the grant of a new stock right. The new stock right may or may not constitute a deferral of compensation under paragraph (b)(5)(i) of this section, determined at the date of grant of the new stock right. If there is an extension of a stock right (within the meaning of paragraph (b)(5)(v)(C) of this section), the stock right is treated as having had an additional deferral feature from the original date of grant of the stock right, and therefore will be treated as a plan providing for the deferral of compensation from the original grant date for purposes of this paragraph (b).

(B) **Modification in general.** Except as otherwise provided in paragraph (b)(5)(v) of this section, the term modification means any change in the terms of the stock right (or change in the terms of the plan pursuant to which the stock right was granted or in the terms of any other agreement governing the stock right) that may provide the holder of the stock right with a direct or indirect reduction in the exercise price of the stock right regardless of whether the holder in fact benefits from the change in terms. A change in the terms of the stock right shortening the period during which the stock right is exercisable is not a modification. It is not a modification to add a feature providing the ability to tender previously acquired stock for the stock purchasable under the stock right, or to withhold or have withheld shares of stock to facilitate the payment of the exercise price or the employment taxes or required withholding taxes resulting from the exercise of the stock right. In addition, it is not a modification for the grantor to exercise discretion specifically reserved under a stock right with respect to the transferability of the stock right.

(C) **Extensions**—(1) **In general.** An extension of a stock right refers to the provision to the holder of an additional period of time within which to exercise the stock right beyond the time originally prescribed under the terms of the stock right, the conversion or exchange of a stock right for a legally binding right to compensation in a future taxable year, or the addition of any feature for the deferral of compensation not permitted in paragraph (b)(5)(i)(A)(3) of this section (in the case of a stock option) or not permitted in paragraph (b)(5)(i)(B)(3) of this section (in the case of a stock appreciation right) to the terms of the stock right, other than at a time when the exercise price of the stock right equals or exceeds the fair market value of the service recipient stock that could be purchased (in the case of an option) or the fair market value of the service recipient stock used to determine the payment to the service provider (in the case of a stock appreciation right), and includes a renewal of such right that has such effect. It is not an extension if the exercise period of a stock right is extended to a date no later than the earlier of the latest date upon which the stock right could have expired by its original terms under any circumstances or the 10th anniversary of the original date of grant of the stock right. If the exercise period of a stock right is extended at a time when the exercise price of the stock right equals or exceeds the fair market value of the service recipient stock that could be purchased (in the case of an option) or the fair market value of the service recipient stock used to determine the payment to the service provider (in the case of a stock appreciation right), it is not an extension of the original stock right. Instead, in such a case, the original stock right is treated as modified rather than extended and a new stock right is treated as having been granted for purposes of this section. In addition, it is not an extension of a stock right if the expiration of the stock right is tolled while the holder cannot exercise the stock right because such an exercise would violate an applicable Federal, state, local, or foreign law, or would jeopardize the ability of the service recipient to continue as a going concern, provided that the period during which the stock right may be exercised is not extended more than 30 days after the exercise of the stock right first would no longer violate an applicable Federal, state, local, and foreign laws or would first no longer jeopardize the ability of the service recipient to continue as a going concern. For this purpose, a provision of foreign law shall be considered applicable only to foreign earned income (as defined under section 911(b)(1) [26 USCS § 911(b)(1)] without regard to section 911(b)(1)(B)(iv) [26 USCS § 911(b)(1)(B)(iv)] and without regard to the requirement that the income be attributable to services performed during the period described in section 911(d)(1)(A) or (B) [26 USCS § 911(d)(1)(A) or (B)]) from sources within the foreign country that promulgated such law.

(2) **Certain extensions before April 10, 2007.** An extension of a stock right before April 10, 2007 solely in order to provide the holder of such stock right an additional period of time beyond the time originally prescribed under the terms of such stock right within which to exercise the stock right is disregarded for purposes of applying the rules contained in paragraph (b)(5)(v)(C)(1) of this section. For purposes of applying the rules contained in paragraph (b)(5)(v)(C)(1) of this section on and after April 10, 2007, such a stock right is treated as having specified at the date of grant the time within which to exercise such stock right that was prescribed under the terms of such stock right in effect on April 10, 2007. Nothing in this paragraph (b)(5)(v)(C)(2) affects any other action treated as the extension of a stock right, including the addition of a deferral feature.

(3) **Examples.** The following examples illustrate the provisions of this paragraph (b)(5)(v)(C). In the examples, each employee is an individual employed by the specified employer, and each employee and each employer has a calendar year taxable year.

Example 1. On July 1, 2009, Employer Z grants Employee A a nonstatutory stock option that does not provide for the deferral of compensation in accordance with paragraph (b)(5)(i)(A) of this section. The terms of the nonstatutory stock option provide that the exercise period of the stock option expires on the earlier of July 1, 2019, or 3 months after Employee A's separation from service. On July 1, 2011, Employee A separates from service. On the same day, Employee A and Employer Z change the exercise period of the option so that it expires on July 1, 2013. Because the exercise period of the stock right is not extended beyond July 1, 2019, the change is not an extension for purposes of this paragraph (b)(5)(v)(C).

Example 2. The facts are the same as in Example 1 except that Employee A separates from service on July 1, 2018, and on the same day, Employee A and Employer Z change the exercise period of the option so that it expires on July 1, 2020. As of July 1, 2018, the fair market value of the underlying stock exceeds the exercise price. Because the exercise period of the stock right is extended beyond July 1, 2019, the change is an extension for purposes of this paragraph (b)(5)(v)(C).

Example 3. The facts are the same as in Example 2 except that as of July 1, 2018, the fair market value of the underlying stock is less than the exercise price of the option. Because the exercise period of the stock right is extended at a time when the fair market value of the underlying stock is less than the exercise price, the change is not an extension for purposes of this paragraph (b)(5)(v)(C) and the change is treated as a modification of the option, resulting in the extension of the exercise period being treated as the grant of a new option on July 1, 2018.

Example 4. On July 1, 2009, Employer Y grants to Employee B a stock appreciation right with respect to 200 shares of Employer Y common stock that does not provide for the deferral of compensation in accordance with paragraph (b)(5)(i)(B) of this section. Upon exercise of the stock appreciation right, Employee B is entitled to receive the excess of the fair market value of a share of Employer Y common stock on the date of exercise over $100 (the fair market value of a share of Employer Y common stock on July 1, 2009), multiplied by the number of shares with respect to which Employee B is exercising the right. The exercise period of the right expires on the earlier of July 1, 2019, or 3 months after Employee B separates from service. Employee B cannot exercise the stock appreciation right with respect to more than 100 shares unless Employee B continues to be employed by Employer Y through June 30, 2014. On July 1, 2011, when the fair market value of a share of Employer Y common stock is $200, Employee B and Employer Y amend the stock appreciation right to provide that the right will be exercisable only during calendar year 2018, except that before January 1, 2017, Employee B may elect to designate calendar year 2023 or any subsequent calendar year before 2033 as the year in which the right will be exercisable. The amendment constitutes an extension of the stock appreciation right under paragraph (b)(5)(v)(C)(1) of this section. Under paragraph (b)(5)(v)(A) of this section, the stock appreciation right is treated as having had an additional deferral feature from the original date of grant (July 1, 2009) of the right, and therefore is treated as a plan providing for the deferral of compensation from that date. During the period from July 1, 2009, through June 30, 2011, the provisions of the stock appreciation right relating to the time and form of payment did not satisfy the requirements of § 1.409A-3(a). Therefore, the stock appreciation right provides for a deferral of compensation that does not comply with section 409A [26 USCS § 409A].

(D) **Substitutions and assumptions of stock rights by reason of a corporate transaction.** If the requirements of § 1.424-1 (without regard to the requirement described in § 1.424-1(a)(2) that an eligible corporation be the employer of the optionee) would be met if the stock right were a statutory option, the substitution of a new stock right pursuant to a corporate transaction (as defined in § 1.424-1(a)(3)) for an outstanding stock right or the assumption of an outstanding stock right pursuant to a corporate transaction will not be treated as the grant of a new stock right or a change in the form of payment for purposes of this section and §§ 1.409A-2 through 1.409A-6. For purposes of the preceding sentence, the requirement of § 1.424-1(a)(5)(iii) will be deemed to be satisfied if the ratio of the exercise price to the fair market value of the shares subject to the stock right immediately after the substitution or assumption is not greater than the ratio of the exercise price to the fair market value of the shares subject to the stock right immediately before the substitution or assumption. In the case of a transaction described in section 355 [26 USCS § 355] in which the stock of the distributing corporation and the stock distributed in the transaction are both readily tradable on an established securities market immediately after the transaction, for purposes of this paragraph (b)(5)(v), the

requirements of § 1.424-1(a)(5) related to the fair market value of the stock may be satisfied by—

(1) Using the last sale before or the first sale after the specified date as of which such valuation is being made, the closing price on the last trading day before or the trading day of a specified date, the arithmetic mean of the high and low prices on the last trading day before or the trading day of such specified date, or any other reasonable method using actual transactions in such stock as reported by such market on a specified date, for the stock of the distributing corporation and the stock distributed in the transaction, provided the specified date is designated before such specified date, and such specified date is not more than 60 days after the transaction;

(2) Using the arithmetic mean of such market prices on trading days during a specified period designated before the beginning of such specified period, where such specified period is not longer than 30 days and ends no later than 60 days after the transaction; or

(3) Using an average of such prices during such prespecified period weighted based on the volume of trading of such stock on each trading day during such prespecified period.

(E) **Acceleration of date when exercisable.** Although with respect to a stock right not immediately exercisable in full, a change in the terms of the right solely to accelerate or delay, within the original term of the stock right, the time at which the stock right (or any portion of such stock right) may be exercised is not a modification for purposes of this section, with respect to a stock right subject to section 409A [26 USCS § 409A], such an acceleration may constitute an impermissible acceleration of a payment date under § 1.409A-3(j) or a subsequent deferral under § 1.409A-2(b).

(F) **Discretionary added benefits.** If a change to a stock right provides, either by its terms or in substance, that the holder may receive an additional benefit under the stock right at the future discretion of the grantor, and the addition of such benefit would constitute a modification or extension, then the addition of such discretion is a modification or extension at the time that the stock right is changed to provide such discretion.

(G) **Change in underlying stock increasing value.** A change in the terms of the stock subject to a stock right that increases the value of the stock is a modification of such stock right, except to the extent that a new stock right is substituted for such stock right by reason of the change in the terms of the stock in accordance with paragraph (b)(5)(v)(D) of this section.

(H) **Change in the number of shares purchasable.** If a stock right is amended solely to increase the number of shares subject to the stock right, the increase is not considered a modification of the stock right but is treated as the grant of a new additional stock right to which the additional shares are subject. Notwithstanding the previous sentence, if the exercise price and number of shares subject to a stock right are proportionally adjusted to reflect a stock split (including a reverse stock split) or stock dividend, and the only effect of the stock split or stock dividend is to increase (or decrease) on a pro rata basis the number of shares owned by each shareholder of the class of stock subject to the stock right, then there is no modification of the stock right if it is proportionally adjusted to reflect the stock split or stock dividend and the aggregate exercise price of the stock right is not less than the aggregate exercise price before the stock split or stock dividend.

(I) **Rescission of changes.** A change to the terms of a stock right (or change in the terms of the plan pursuant to which the stock right was granted or in the terms of any other agreement governing the right) is not considered a modification or extension of the stock right to the extent the change in the terms of the stock right is rescinded by the earlier of the date the stock right is exercised or the last day of the service provider's taxable year during which such change occurred. Thus, for example, if the terms of a stock right granted to an individual employee with a calendar year taxable year are changed on March 1 in a

manner that would result in an extension of the stock right, and the change is rescinded on November 1 of the same year, and the stock right is not exercised before the change is rescinded, the stock right is not considered extended under this paragraph (b)(5)(v).

(J) **Successive modifications and extensions.** The rules of this paragraph (b)(5)(v) apply as well to successive modifications and extensions.

(K) **Modifications and extensions in effect on October 23, 2004.** For purposes of the application of section 409A [26 USCS § 409A] and these regulations to a stock right, if a legally binding right to a modification or extension of such stock right existed on October 23, 2004, such modification or extension is disregarded, and the stock right is treated as if granted with the terms and conditions in effect on October 23, 2004.

(vi) **Meaning and use of certain terms**—(A) **Option.** The term option means the right or privilege of an individual to purchase stock from a corporation by virtue of an offer of the corporation continuing for a stated period of time, whether or not irrevocable, to sell such stock at a price determined under paragraph (b)(5)(vi)(D) of this section, such individual being under no obligation to purchase. While no particular form of words is necessary, the option must express an offer to sell at the option price, the maximum number of shares purchasable under the option, and the period of time during which the offer remains open. The term option includes a warrant that meets the requirements of this paragraph (b)(5)(vi)(A). An option may be granted as part of or in conjunction with an employee stock purchase plan or subscription contract. An option must be in writing (in paper or electronic form) provided that such writing is adequate to establish an option right or privilege that is enforceable under applicable law.

(B) **Date of grant of option.** (1) The language the date of grant of the option, and similar phrases, refer to the date when the granting corporation completes the corporate action necessary to create the legally binding right constituting the option. A corporate action creating the legally binding right constituting the option is not considered complete until the date on which the maximum number of shares that can be purchased under the option and the minimum exercise price are fixed or determinable, and the class of underlying stock and the identity of the service provider is designated. Ordinarily, if the corporate action provides for an immediate offer of stock for sale to a service provider, or provides for a particular date on which such offer is to be made, the date of the granting of the option is the date of such corporate action if the offer is to be made immediately, or the date provided as the date of the offer, as the case may be. However, an unreasonable delay in the giving of notice of such offer to the service provider will be taken into account as indicating that the corporation provided that the offer was to be made at the subsequent date on which such notice is given.

(2) If the corporation imposes a condition on the granting of an option (as distinguished from a condition governing the exercise of the option), such condition generally will be given effect in accordance with the intent of the corporation. However, if the grant of an option is subject to approval by stockholders, the date of grant of the option will be determined as if the option had not been subject to such approval. A condition that does not require corporate action, such as the approval of, or registration with, some regulatory or government agency, for example, a stock exchange or the Securities and Exchange Commission, is ordinarily considered a condition upon the exercise of the option unless the corporate action clearly indicates that the option is not to be granted until such condition has been satisfied.

(3) In general, a condition imposed upon the exercise of an option will not operate to make ineffective the granting of the option. For example, on June 1, 2008, Corporation A grants to X, an employee, an option to purchase 5,000 shares of the corporation's common stock, exercisable by X on or after June 1, 2009, provided X is employed by the corporation on June 1, 2009, and provided that A's

profits during the fiscal year preceding the year of exercise exceed $200,000. Such an option is granted to X on June 1, 2008, and will be treated as outstanding as of such date.

(C) **Stock.** The term stock means capital stock of any class, including voting or nonvoting common or preferred stock. Except as otherwise provided, the term stock includes both treasury stock and stock of original issue. Special classes of stock authorized to be issued to and held by employees are within the scope of the term stock for this purpose, provided such stock otherwise possesses the rights and characteristics of capital stock.

(D) **Exercise price.** The term exercise price means the consideration in cash or property that, pursuant to the terms of the option, is the price at which the stock subject to the option is purchased. The term exercise price does not include any amounts paid as interest under a deferred payment plan or treated as interest.

(E) **Exercise.** The term exercise, when used in reference to an option, means the act of acceptance by the holder of the option of the offer to sell contained in the option. In general, the time of exercise is the time when there is a sale or a contract to sell between the corporation and the individual. A promise to pay the exercise price does not constitute an exercise of the option unless the holder of the option is subject to personal liability on such promise. An agreement or undertaking by the service provider to make payments under a stock purchase plan does not constitute the exercise of an option to the extent the payments made remain subject to withdrawal by or refund to the service provider.

(F) **Transfer.** The term transfer, when used in reference to the transfer to an individual of a share of stock pursuant to the exercise of an option, means the transfer of ownership of such share, or the transfer of substantially all the rights of ownership. Such transfer must, within a reasonable time, be evidenced on the books of the corporation. A transfer may occur even if a share of stock is subject to a substantial risk of forfeiture or is not otherwise transferable immediately after the date of exercise. A transfer does not fail to occur merely because, under the terms of the arrangement, the individual may not dispose of the share for a specified period of time, or the share is subject to a right of first refusal or a right to acquire the share at the share's fair market value at the time of the sale.

(G) **Readily tradable.** For purposes of this section and §§ 1.409A-2 through 1.409A-6, stock is treated as readily tradable if it is regularly quoted by brokers or dealers making a market in such stock.

(H) **Application to stock appreciation rights.** For purposes of this section and §§ 1.409A-2 through 1.409A-6, the definitions provided in paragraphs (b)(5)(vi)(A) through (G) of this section may be applied by analogy to the issuance of, exercise of, or payment upon the exercise of, a stock appreciation right.

(6) **Restricted property, section 402(b) [26 USCS § 402(b)] trusts, and section 403(c) [26 USCS § 403(c)] annuities—(i) In general.** If a service provider receives property from, or pursuant to, a plan maintained by a service recipient, there is no deferral of compensation merely because the value of the property is not includible in income by reason of the property being substantially nonvested (as defined in § 1.83-3(b)), or is includible in income solely due to a valid election under section 83(b) [26 USCS § 83(b)]. For purposes of this paragraph (b)(6)(i), a transfer of property includes the transfer of a beneficial interest in a trust or annuity plan, or a transfer to or from a trust or under an annuity plan, to the extent such a transfer is subject to section 83 [26 USCS § 83], section 402(b) [26 USCS § 402(b)] or section 403(c) [26 USCS § 403(c)]. In addition, for purposes of this paragraph (b), a right to compensation income that will be required to be included in income under section (b)(4)(A) is not a deferral of compensation.

(ii) **Promises to transfer property.** A plan under which a service provider obtains a legally binding right to receive property in a

future taxable year where the property will be substantially vested (as defined in § 1.83-3(b)) at the time of transfer of the property may provide for the deferral of compensation and, accordingly, may constitute a nonqualified deferred compensation plan. A legally binding right to receive property in a future taxable year where the property will be substantially nonvested (as defined in § 1.83-3(b)) at the time of transfer of the property will not provide for the deferral of compensation and, accordingly, will not constitute a nonqualified deferred compensation plan unless offered in conjunction with another legally binding right that constitutes a deferral of compensation.

(7) **Arrangements between partnerships and partners.** [Reserved.]

(8) **Certain foreign plans—(i) Plans with respect to compensation covered by treaty or other international agreement.** A plan in which a service provider participates does not provide for a deferral of compensation for purposes of this paragraph (b) to the extent that the compensation under the plan would have been excluded from gross income for Federal income tax purposes under the provisions of any bilateral income tax convention or other bilateral or multilateral agreement to which the United States is a party if the compensation had been paid to the service provider at the time that the legally binding right to the compensation first arose or, if later, the time that the legally binding right was no longer subject to a substantial risk of forfeiture.

(ii) **Plans with respect to certain other compensation.** A plan in which a service provider participates does not provide for a deferral of compensation for purposes of this paragraph (b) to the extent that compensation under the plan would not have been includible in gross income for Federal tax purposes if it had been paid to the service provider at the time that the legally binding right to the compensation first arose or, if later, the time that the legally binding right was no longer subject to a substantial risk of forfeiture, due to one of the following:

(A) The service provider was a nonresident alien at such time and the compensation would not have been includible in gross income under section 872 [26 USCS § 872].

(B) The service provider was a qualified individual (as defined in section 911(d)(1) [26 USCS § 911(d)(1)]) at such time, the compensation would have been foreign earned income within the meaning of section 911(b)(1) [26 USCS § 911(b)(1)] (without regard to section 911(b)(1)(B)(iv) [26 USCS § 911(b)(1)(B)(iv)]) if paid at such time, and the amount of such compensation was equal to or less than the excess (if any) of the maximum exclusion amount under section 911(b)(2)(D) [26 USCS § 911(b)(2)(D)] for such taxable year over the amount of foreign earned income actually excluded from gross income by such qualified individual for such taxable year under section 911(a)(1) [26 USCS § 911(a)(1)].

(C) The compensation would have been excludible from gross income under section 893 [26 USCS § 893].

(D) The compensation would have been excludible from gross income under section 931 [26 USCS § 931] or section 933 [26 USCS § 933].

(iii) **Tax equalization agreements.** A tax equalization agreement does not provide for a deferral of compensation if payments made under such tax equalization agreement are made no later than the end of the second taxable year of the service provider beginning after the taxable year of the service provider in which the service provider's U.S. Federal income tax return is required to be filed (including any extensions) for the year to which the compensation subject to the tax equalization payment relates, or, if later, the second taxable year of the service provider beginning after the latest such taxable year in which the service provider's foreign tax return or payment is required to be filed or made for the year to which the compensation subject to the tax equalization payment relates. Where such payments arise due to an audit, litigation or similar proceeding, the right to the payments

will not be treated as resulting in a deferral of compensation if the payments are scheduled and made in accordance with the provisions of § 1.409A-3(i)(1)(v) (timing of tax gross-up payments). For purposes of this paragraph (b)(8)(iii), the term tax equalization agreement refers to an agreement, method, program, or other arrangement that provides payments intended to compensate the service provider for some or all of the excess of the taxes actually imposed by a foreign jurisdiction on the compensation paid by the service recipient to the service provider over the taxes that would be imposed if the compensation were subject solely to United States Federal, state, and local income tax, or some or all of the excess of the United States Federal, state, and local income tax actually imposed on the compensation paid by the service to the service provider over the taxes that would be imposed if the compensation were subject solely to taxes in the foreign jurisdiction, provided that the payment made under such agreement, method, program, or other arrangement may not exceed such excess and the amount necessary to compensate for the additional taxes on the amount paid under the agreement, method, program, or other arrangement.

(iv) **Certain limited deferrals of a nonresident alien.** With respect to a nonresident alien, a foreign plan does not provide for a deferral of compensation if the amounts deferred under the foreign plan based upon services performed by the nonresident alien in the United States (including amounts deferred based upon service credits or compensation received due to services performed in the United States) do not exceed the applicable dollar amount under section 402(g)(1)(B) [26 USCS § 402(g)(1)(B)] for the taxable year. If the amounts deferred under the foreign plan based upon the services performed by the nonresident alien in the United States exceed the applicable dollar amount, an amount of such deferrals equal to such amount is treated as not deferred under a nonqualified deferred compensation plan. For purposes of this paragraph (b)(8)(iv), the term foreign plan means a plan that, together with all substantially similar plans, is maintained by a service recipient for a substantial number of participants, substantially all of whom are nonresident aliens or resident aliens classified as resident aliens solely under section 7701(b)(1)(A)(ii) [26 USCS § 7701(b)(1)(A)(ii)] (and not section 7701(b)(1)(A)(i) [26 USCS § 7701(b)(1)(A)(i)]).

(v) **Additional foreign plans.** A plan in which a service provider participates does not provide for a deferral of compensation for purposes of this paragraph (b) to the extent designated by the Commissioner in revenue procedures, notices, or other guidance published in the Internal Revenue Bulletin (see § 601.601(d)(2) of this chapter).

(vi) **Earnings.** Earnings on compensation excluded from the definition of deferral of compensation pursuant to this paragraph (b)(8) are also not treated as a deferral of compensation.

(9) **Separation pay plans**—(i) **In general.** A plan that otherwise provides for a deferral of compensation under this paragraph (b) does not fail to provide a deferral of compensation merely because the right to payment of the compensation is conditioned upon a separation from service. However, paragraphs (b)(9)(ii), (iii), (iv), and (v) of this section provide rules concerning the extent to which certain separation pay plans do not provide for the deferral of compensation. The exceptions contained in paragraphs (b)(9)(ii), (iii), (iv), and (v) of this section may be used in combination, such that compensation under a plan that would be excepted under one of those paragraphs may be treated as excepted under another of those paragraphs, so that other compensation under a plan may be treated as excepted under the first of such paragraphs. Notwithstanding any other provision of this paragraph (b)(9), any payment or benefit, or entitlement to a payment or benefit, that acts as a substitute for, or replacement of, amounts deferred by the service recipient under a separate nonqualified deferred compensation plan constitutes a payment or a deferral of compensation under the separate nonqualified deferred compensation plan, and does not constitute a payment or deferral of compensation

under a separation pay plan. If a service provider receives a payment at separation from service and also has a legally binding right to an amount of deferred compensation that would be forfeited upon the separation from service, whether the payment acts as an acceleration of vesting and substitute payment for the amount of deferred compensation forfeited, or whether the deferred compensation is treated as forfeited and the amount paid is treated as a separate payment of current compensation, is determined based on the facts and circumstances, provided that, where the separation from service is voluntary, it is presumed that the payment results from an acceleration of vesting followed by a payment of the deferred compensation that is subject to section 409A [26 USCS § 409A]. Accordingly, any change in the payment schedule to accelerate or defer the payments would be subject to the rules of section 409A [26 USCS § 409A]. The presumption that a right to a payment is not a new right, but is instead a right substituted for a pre-existing forfeited right, may be rebutted by demonstrating that the service provider would have obtained the right to the payment regardless of the forfeiture of the nonvested right. A factor indicating that the service provider would have obtained a right to a payment regardless of the forfeiture of the nonvested right is that the amount to which the service provider obtains a right is materially less than an amount equal to the present value of the forfeited amount multiplied by a fraction, the numerator of which is the period of service the service provider actually completed, and the denominator of which is the full period of service the service provider would have been required to complete to receive the full amount of the payment. For example, where a service provider is entitled to a future payment only if the service provider completes three years of service and at the time of termination the service provider has completed one year of service, the presumption could be rebutted if the payment to the service provider is materially less than the present value of one-third of the nonvested amount. Another such factor is that the payment to the service provider is of a type customarily made to service providers who separate from service with the service recipient and do not forfeit nonvested rights to deferred compensation (for example, a payment of accrued but unused leave or a payment for a release of actual or potential claims).

(ii) **Collectively bargained separation pay plans.** A separation pay plan does not provide for a deferral of compensation to the extent the plan is a collectively bargained separation pay plan that provides for separation pay only upon an involuntary separation from service or pursuant to a window program. Only the portion of the separation pay plan attributable to employees covered by a bona fide collective bargaining agreement is considered to be provided under a collectively bargained separation pay plan. A collectively bargained separation pay plan is a separation pay plan that meets the following conditions:

(A) The separation pay plan is contained within an agreement that the Secretary of Labor determines to be a collective bargaining agreement.

(B) The separation pay provided by the collective bargaining agreement was the subject of arm's length negotiations between employee representatives and one or more employers, and the agreement between employee representatives and one or more employers satisfies section 7701(a)(46) [26 USCS § 7701(a)(46)].

(C) The circumstances surrounding the agreement evidence good faith bargaining between adverse parties over the separation pay to be provided under the agreement.

(iii) **Separation pay due to involuntary separation from service or participation in a window program.** A separation pay plan that is not described in paragraph (b)(9)(ii) of this section and that provides for separation pay only upon an involuntary separation from service (as defined in paragraph (n) of this section) or pursuant to a window program does not provide for a deferral of compensation to the extent that the separation pay, or portion of the separation pay, provided under the plan meets the following requirements:

(A) The separation pay (other than amounts described in paragraphs (b)(9)(iv) and (v) of this section) does not exceed two times the lesser of—

(1) The sum of the service provider's annualized compensation based upon the annual rate of pay for services provided to the service recipient for the taxable year of the service provider preceding the taxable year of the service provider in which the service provider has a separation from service with such service recipient (adjusted for any increase during that year that was expected to continue indefinitely if the service provider had not separated from service); or

(2) The maximum amount that may be taken into account under a qualified plan pursuant to section 401(a)(17) [26 USCS § 401(a)(17)] for the year in which the service provider has a separation from service.

(B) The plan provides that the separation pay described in paragraph (b)(9)(iii)(A) of this section must be paid no later than the last day of the second taxable year of the service provider following the taxable year of the service provider in which occurs the separation from service.

(iv) **Foreign separation pay plans.** A separation pay plan (including a plan providing payments upon a voluntary separation from service) does not provide for deferred compensation to the extent the plan provides for amounts of separation pay required to be provided under the applicable law of a foreign jurisdiction. For this purpose, a provision of foreign law shall be considered applicable only to foreign earned income (as defined under section 911(b)(1) [26 USCS § 911(b)(1)] without regard to section 911(b)(1)(B)(iv) [26 USCS § 911(b)(1)(B)(iv)] and without regard to the requirement that the income be attributable to services performed during the period described in section 911(d)(1)(A) or (B) [26 USCS § 911(d)(1)(A) or (B)]) from sources within the foreign country that promulgated such law.

(v) **Reimbursements and certain other separation payments**—(A) **In general.** To the extent a separation pay plan (including a plan providing payments upon a voluntary separation from service) entitles a service provider to payment by the service recipient of reimbursements that are not otherwise excludible from gross income for expenses that the service provider could otherwise deduct under section 162 [26 USCS § 162] or section 167 [26 USCS § 167] as business expenses incurred in connection with the performance of services (ignoring any applicable limitation based on adjusted gross income), or of reasonable outplacement expenses and reasonable moving expenses actually incurred by the service provider and directly related to the termination of services for the service recipient, such plan does not provide for a deferral of compensation to the extent such rights apply during a limited period of time (regardless of whether such rights extend beyond the limited period of time). For purposes of this paragraph (b)(9)(v)(A), the reimbursement of reasonable moving expenses includes the reimbursement of all or part of any loss the service provider actually incurs due to the sale of a primary residence in connection with a separation from service.

(B) **Medical benefits.** To the extent a separation pay plan (including a plan providing payments due to a voluntary separation from service) entitles a service provider to reimbursement by the service recipient of payments of medical expenses incurred and paid by the service provider but not reimbursed by a person other than the service recipient and allowable as a deduction under section 213 [26 USCS § 213](disregarding the requirement of section 213(a) [26 USCS § 213(a)] that the deduction is available only to the extent that such expenses exceed 7.5 percent of adjusted gross income), such plan does not provide for a deferral of compensation to the extent such rights apply during the period of time during which the service provider would be entitled (or would, but for such plan, be entitled) to continuation coverage under a group health plan of the service recipient under section 4980B [26 USCS § 4980B]

(COBRA) if the service provider elected such coverage and paid the applicable premiums.

(C) **In-kind benefits and direct service recipient payments.** A service provider's entitlement to in-kind benefits from the service recipient, or a payment by the service recipient directly to the person providing the goods or services to the service provider, is treated as not providing for a deferral of compensation for purposes of this paragraph (b), if a right to reimbursement by the service recipient for a payment for such benefits, goods, or services by the service provider would not be treated as providing for a deferral of compensation under this paragraph (b)(9)(v).

(D) **Limited payments.** If not otherwise excluded, a taxpayer may treat a right or rights under a separation pay plan to a payment or payments as not providing for a deferral of compensation to the extent such payments in the aggregate do not exceed the applicable dollar amount under section 402(g)(1)(B) [26 USCS § 402(g)(1)(B)] for the year of the separation from service.

(E) **Limited period of time.** For purposes of paragraphs (b)(9)(v)(A) and (C) of this section, a limited period of time in which expenses may be incurred, or in which in-kind benefits may be provided by the service recipient or a third party that the service recipient will pay, does not include periods beyond the last day of the second taxable year of the service provider following the taxable year of the service provider in which the separation from service occurred, provided that the period during which the reimbursements for such expenses must be paid may not extend beyond the third taxable year of the service provider following the taxable year of the service provider in which the separation from service occurred.

(vi) **Window programs—definition**. The term window program refers to a program established by a service recipient in connection with an impending separation from service to provide separation pay, where such program is made available by the service recipient for a limited period of time (no longer than 12 months) to service providers who separate from service during that period or to service providers who separate from service during that period under specified circumstances. A program will not be considered a window program if a service recipient establishes a pattern of repeatedly providing for similar separation pay in similar situations for substantially consecutive, limited periods of time. Whether the recurrence of these programs constitutes a pattern is determined based on the facts and circumstances. Although no one factor is determinative, relevant factors include whether the benefits are on account of a specific business event or condition, the degree to which the separation pay relates to the event or condition, and whether the event or condition is temporary or discrete or is a permanent aspect of the employer's business.

(10) **Certain indemnification and liability insurance plans.** A plan in which a service provider participates does not provide for a deferral of compensation for purposes of this paragraph (b) to the extent that the plan provides (to the extent permissible under applicable law), for the indemnification of, or the purchase of an insurance policy providing for payments of, all or part of the expenses incurred or damages paid or payable by a service provider with respect to a bona fide claim against the service provider or service recipient, including amounts paid or payable by the service provider upon the settlement of a bona fide claim against the service provider or service recipient, where such claim is based on actions or failures to act by the service provider in his or her capacity as a service provider of the service recipient.

(11) **Legal settlements.** An agreement to which a service provider is a party does not provide for a deferral of compensation for purposes of this paragraph (b) to the extent that the agreement provides for amounts paid as settlements or awards resolving bona fide legal claims based on wrongful termination, employment discrimination, the Fair Labor Standards Act, or worker's compensation statutes, including claims under applicable Federal, state, local, or foreign laws, or for reimbursements or payments of reasonable attorneys fees or other reasonable expenses incurred by the service provider related to such bona fide legal claims, regardless of whether such settlements, awards, or reimbursement or payment of expenses pursuant to such claims are treated as compensation or wages for Federal tax purposes. Whether the execution of a waiver of any or all of such types of claims indicates that the amounts are paid as an award or settlement of an actual bona fide claim for damages under applicable law is determined based on the facts and circumstances. This paragraph (b)(11) does not apply to any deferred amounts that did not arise as a result of an actual bona fide claim for damages under applicable law, such as amounts that would have been deferred or paid regardless of the existence of such claim, even if such amounts are paid or modified as part of a settlement or award resolving an actual bona fide claim. For this purpose, a provision of foreign law shall be considered applicable only to foreign earned income (as defined under section 911(b)(1) [26 USCS § 911(b)(1)] without regard to section 911(b)(1)(B)(iv) [26 USCS § 911(b)(1)(B)(iv)] and without regard to the requirement that the income be attributable to services performed during the period described in section 911(d)(1)(A) or (B) [26 USCS § 911(d)(1)(A) or (B)]) from sources within the foreign country that promulgated such law.

(12) **Certain educational benefits.** A plan in which a service provider participates does not provide for a deferral of compensation to the extent the plan provides for taxable educational benefits. For purposes of this paragraph (b)(12), the term educational benefits refers solely to benefits provided to a service provider, consisting solely of educational assistance for the education of the service provider, as defined in section 127(c) [26 USCS § 127(c)] and the accompanying regulations, and does not refer to any benefits provided for the education of any other person, including any spouse, child, or other family member of the service provider.

(c) *Plan*—(1) **In general.** The term plan includes any agreement, method, program, or other arrangement, including an agreement, method, program, or other arrangement that applies to one person or individual. A plan may be adopted unilaterally by the service recipient or may be negotiated or agreed to by the service recipient and one or more service providers or service provider representatives. An agreement, method, program, or other arrangement may constitute a plan regardless of whether it is an employee benefit plan under section 3(3) of ERISA, as amended (29 U.S.C. 1002(3)). The requirements of section 409A [26 USCS § 409A] are applied as if a separate plan or plans is maintained for each service provider. For purposes of determining the terms of a plan, general provisions of the plan that purport to nullify noncompliant plan terms, or to supply any specific plan terms required by this section, § 1.409A-2 or § 1.409A-3, are disregarded.

(2) **Plan aggregation rules**—(i) **In general.** Except as otherwise provided, the following rules apply with respect to the application of this section and §§ 1.409A-2 through 1.409A-6 to deferrals of compensation with respect to a service provider:

(A) All deferrals of compensation at the election of that service provider under all plans of the service recipient that are account balance plans, except to the extent that the plan is described in paragraph (c)(2)(i)(D), (E), (F), (G), or (H) of this section, are treated as deferred under a single plan. For purposes of this paragraph, the term account balance plan means—

(1) An agreement, method, program, or other arrangement that is an account balance plan as defined in § 31.3121(v)(2)-1(c)(1)(ii)(A) of this chapter, including mandatorily bifurcating the agreement, method, program, or other arrangement in accordance with the rules provided in § 31.3121(v)-1(c)(1)(iii)(B) of this chapter; or

(2) An agreement, method, program, or other arrangement that would be described in paragraph (c)(2)(i)(A)(1) of this section if the service provider were an employee.

(B) All deferrals of compensation other than at the election of that service provider, including deferrals reflecting matching by the service recipient with respect to amounts a service provider elects to defer, under all plans of the service recipient that are account balance plans, except to the extent the plan is described in paragraph (c)(2)(i)(D), (E), (F), (G), or (H) of this section, are treated as deferred under a single plan. For purposes of this paragraph (c)(2)(i)(B), the term "account balance plan" has the same meaning as provided in paragraph (c)(2)(i)(A) of this section.

(C) All deferrals of compensation with respect to that service provider under all plans of the service recipient that are nonaccount balance plans, except to the extent such plan is described in paragraph (c)(2)(i)(D), (E), (F), (G), or (H) of this section, are treated as deferred under a single plan. For purposes of this paragraph (c)(2)(i)(C), the term nonaccount balance plan means—

(1) An agreement, method, program, or other arrangement that is a nonaccount balance plan as defined in § 31.3121(v)(2)-1(c)(2)(i) of this chapter, including mandatorily bifurcating the agreement, method, program, or other arrangement in accordance with the rules provided in § 31.3121(v)-1(c)(1)(iii)(B) of this chapter; or

(2) An agreement, method, program, or other arrangement that would be described in paragraph (c)(2)(i)(C)(1) of this section if the service provider were an employee.

(D) All deferrals of compensation with respect to that service provider under all separation pay plans (as defined in paragraph (m) of this section) of the service recipient to the extent an amount deferred under the plans is not described in paragraph (c)(2)(i)(E) of this section and is payable solely upon an involuntary separation from service within the meaning of paragraph (n) of this section or as a result of participation in a window program, are treated as deferred under a single plan.

(E) All deferrals of compensation with respect to that service provider under all plans of the service recipient to the extent such amounts deferred consist of rights to in-kind benefits or reimbursements of expenses, such as membership fees, or expenses related to aircraft or vehicle usage, to the extent that the right to the in-kind benefit or reimbursement, separately or in the aggregate, does not constitute a substantial portion of either the overall compensation earned by the service provider for performing services for the service recipient or the overall compensation received due to a separation from service, are treated as deferred under a single plan.

(F) All deferrals of compensation with respect to that service provider under all plans of the service recipient to the extent that the taxation of such compensation is governed by § 1.61-22 or § 1.7872-15 (split-dollar life insurance arrangements), or the taxation of such compensation would be governed by § 1.61-22 or § 1.7872-15 but for the operation of § 1.61-22(j) (effective date provisions), are treated as deferred under a single plan.

(G) All deferrals of compensation with respect to that service provider under all agreements, methods, programs, or other arrangements of the service recipient to the extent the deferrals under the agreements, methods, programs, or other arrangements are deferrals of amounts that would be treated as modified foreign earned income (meaning foreign earned income as defined under section 911(b)(1) [26 USCS § 911(b)(1)] without regard to section 911(b)(1)(B)(iv) [26 USCS § 911(b)(1)(B)(iv)] and without regard to the requirement that the income be attributable to services performed during the period described in section 911(d)(1)(A) or (B) [26 USCS § 911(d)(1)(A) or (B)]) if paid to the service provider at the time the amount is first deferred, and provided further that substantially all the participants in such agreements, methods, programs, or other arrangements and any substantially similar agreements, methods, programs, or other arrangements are nonresident aliens and that the service provider does not participate in a substantially identical agreement, method, program, or other arrangement that does not meet the requirements of this paragraph (c)(2)(i)(G) (a domestic arrangement), are treated as deferred under a single plan.

(H) All deferrals of compensation with respect to that service provider under all plans of the service recipient to the extent such plans are stock rights (as defined in paragraph (l) of this section) subject to section 409A, are treated as deferred under a single plan.

(I) All deferrals of compensation with respect to that service provider under all plans of the service recipient to the extent such plans are not described in paragraph (c)(2)(i)(A), (B), (C), (D), (E), (F), (G), or (H) of this section are treated as deferred under a single plan.

(ii) **Dual status.** Agreements, methods, programs, and other arrangements in which a service provider participates are not aggregated with other agreements, methods, programs, and other arrangements to the extent the service provider participates in one set of agreements, methods, programs, and other arrangements due to status as an employee of the service recipient (employee arrangements) and another set of agreements, methods, programs, and other arrangements due to status as an independent contractor of the service recipient (independent contractor arrangements). For example, where a service provider deferred amounts under an independent contractor arrangement while providing services as an independent contractor, and then becomes eligible for and defers amounts under a separate employee arrangement after being hired as an employee, the two arrangements will not be aggregated for purposes of this paragraph (c)(2). Where an employee also is a member of the board of directors of the service recipient (or a similar position with respect to a noncorporate service recipient), the arrangements under which the employee participates as a director (director arrangements) are not aggregated with employee arrangements, provided that the director arrangements are substantially similar to arrangements provided to service providers providing services only as directors (or similar positions with respect to non-corporate service recipients). For example, an employee director who participates in an employee arrangement and a director arrangement generally may treat the two arrangements as separate plans, provided that the director arrangement is substantially similar to arrangements providing benefits to non-employee directors. To the extent a plan in which an employee director participates is not substantially similar to arrangements in which non-employee directors participate, such plan is treated as an employee plan for purposes of this paragraph (c)(2). Director plans and independent contractor plans are aggregated for purposes of this paragraph (c)(2).

(3) **Establishment of plan**—(i) **In general.** A plan does not satisfy the requirements of section 409A [26 USCS § 409A] and this section and §§ 1.409A-2 through 1.409A-3 and §§ 1.409A-5 through 1.409A-6, unless the plan is established and maintained by a service recipient in accordance with the requirements of this section, §§ 1.409A-2 through 1.409A-3 and §§ 1.409A-5 through 1.409A-6. For purposes of this paragraph (c)(3), a plan is established on the latest of the date on which it is adopted, the date on which it is effective, and the date on which the material terms of the plan are set forth in writing. The material terms of the plan may be set forth in writing in one or more documents. For purposes of this paragraph (c)(3)(i), a plan will be deemed to be set forth in writing if it is set forth in any other form that is approved by the Commissioner. The material terms of the plan include the amount (or the method or formula for determining the amount) of deferred compensation to be provided under the plan and the time and form of payment. Notwithstanding the foregoing, a plan will be deemed to be established as of the date the participant obtains a legally binding right to a deferral of compensation, provided that the plan is otherwise established under the rules of this paragraph (c)(3)(i) by the end of the taxable year of the service provider in which the legally binding right arises, or with respect to an amount not payable in the year immediately following the taxable year of the service provider in which

the legally binding right arises (the subsequent year), the 15th day of the third month of the subsequent year.

(ii) **Initial deferral election provisions.** If a plan provides a service provider or a service recipient with an initial deferral election, the plan satisfies the requirements of this paragraph (c)(3) if the plan sets forth in writing, on or before the date the applicable election is required to be irrevocable to satisfy the requirements of § 1.409A-2(a), the conditions under which such election may be made.

(iii) **Subsequent deferral election provisions.** If a plan permits a subsequent deferral election described in § 1.409A-2(b), the plan satisfies the requirements of this paragraph (c)(3) if the plan sets forth in writing, on or before the date the election is required to be irrevocable to meet the requirements of § 1.409A-2(b), the conditions under which such election may be made.

(iv) **Payment accelerations.** Except as explicitly provided in § 1.409A-3, a plan is not required to set forth in writing the conditions under which a payment may be accelerated if such acceleration is permitted under § 1.409A-3(j)(4).

(v) **Six-month delay for specified employees.** A plan must provide that distributions to a specified employee may not be made before the date that is six months after the date of separation from service or, if earlier, the date of death (the six-month delay rule). The six-month delay rule, required for payments due to the separation from service of a specified employee, must be written in the plan. A plan does not fail to be established and maintained merely because it does not contain the six-month delay rule when the service provider who has a right to compensation deferred under such plan is not a specified employee. However, such provision must be set forth in writing on or before the date such service provider first becomes a specified employee. In general, this means the provision must be set forth in writing on or before the specified employee effective date (as defined in paragraph (i)(3) of this section) for the first list of specified employees that includes such service provider.

(vi) **Plan amendments.** In the case of an amendment that increases the amount deferred under a nonqualified deferred compensation plan, the plan is not considered established with respect to the additional amount deferred until the plan, as amended, is established in accordance with paragraph (c)(3)(i) of this section.

(vii) **Transition rule for written plan requirement.** For purposes of this paragraph (c)(3), a legally enforceable unwritten plan that was adopted and effective before December 31, 2007, is treated as established under this section as of the later of the date on which it was adopted or became effective, provided that the material terms of the plan are set forth in writing on or before December 31, 2007.

(viii) **Plan aggregation rules.** The plan aggregation rules of paragraph (c)(2)(i) of this section do not apply to the written plan requirements of this paragraph (c)(3). Accordingly, deferrals of compensation under an agreement, method, program, or other arrangement that fails to meet the requirements of section 409A [26 USCS § 409A] solely due to a failure to meet the written plan requirements of this paragraph (c)(3) are not aggregated with deferrals of compensation under other agreements, methods, programs, or other arrangements that meet such requirements.

(d) *Substantial risk of forfeiture*—(1) **In general.** Compensation is subject to a substantial risk of forfeiture if entitlement to the amount is conditioned on the performance of substantial future services by any person or the occurrence of a condition related to a purpose of the compensation, and the possibility of forfeiture is substantial. For purposes of this paragraph (d), a condition related to a purpose of the compensation must relate to the service provider's performance for the service recipient or the service recipient's business activities or organizational goals (for example, the attainment of a prescribed level of earnings or equity value or completion of an initial public offering). For purposes of this para-

graph (d), if a service provider's entitlement to the amount is conditioned on the occurrence of the service provider's involuntary separation from service without cause, the right is subject to a substantial risk of forfeiture if the possibility of forfeiture is substantial. An amount is not subject to a substantial risk of forfeiture merely because the right to the amount is conditioned, directly or indirectly, upon the refraining from the performance of services. Except as provided with respect to certain transaction-based compensation under § 1.409A-3(i)(5)(iv), the addition of any risk of forfeiture after the legally binding right to the compensation arises, or any extension of a period during which compensation is subject to a risk of forfeiture, is disregarded for purposes of determining whether such compensation is subject to a substantial risk of forfeiture. An amount will not be considered subject to a substantial risk of forfeiture beyond the date or time at which the recipient otherwise could have elected to receive the amount of compensation, unless the present value of the amount subject to a substantial risk of forfeiture (disregarding, in determining the present value, the risk of forfeiture) is materially greater than the present value of the amount the recipient otherwise could have elected to receive absent such risk of forfeiture. For this purpose, compensation that the service provider would receive for continuing to perform services regardless of whether the service provider elected to receive the amount that is subject to a substantial risk of forfeiture is not taken into account in determining whether the present value of the right to the amount subject to a substantial risk of forfeiture is materially greater than the amount the recipient otherwise could have elected to receive absent such risk of forfeiture. For example, a salary deferral generally may not be made subject to a substantial risk of forfeiture. But, for example, where a bonus plan provides an election between a cash payment or restricted stock units with a present value that is materially greater (disregarding the risk of forfeiture) than the present value of such cash payment and that will be forfeited absent continued services for a period of years, the right to the restricted stock units generally will be treated as subject to a substantial risk of forfeiture.

(2) **Stock rights.** A stock right is not subject to a substantial risk of forfeiture at the earlier of the first date the holder may exercise the stock right and receive cash or property that is substantially vested (as defined in § 1.83-3(b)) or the first date that the stock right is not subject to a forfeiture condition that would constitute a substantial risk of forfeiture. Accordingly, a stock option that the service provider may exercise immediately and receive substantially vested stock is not subject to a substantial risk of forfeiture, even if the stock option automatically terminates upon the service provider's separation from service.

(3) **Enforcement of forfeiture condition**—(i) **In general.** In determining whether the possibility of forfeiture is substantial in the case of rights to compensation granted by a service recipient to a service provider that owns a significant amount of the total combined voting power or value of all classes of equity of the service recipient (where the service provider's ownership is determined with application of the attribution rules under section 318 [26 USCS § 318] if the service recipient is a corporation, or if the service recipient is an entity that is not a corporation, with application by analogy of the attribution rules under section 318 [26 USCS § 318]), all relevant facts and circumstances will be taken into account in determining whether the probability of the service recipient enforcing such condition is substantial, including—

(A) The service provider's relationship to other equity holders and the extent of their control, potential control and possible loss of control of the service recipient;

(B) The position of the service provider in the service recipient and the extent to which the service provider is subordinate to other service providers;

(C) The service provider's relationship to the officers and directors of the service recipient (or similar positions with respect to a noncorporate service recipient);

(D) The person or persons who must approve the service provider's discharge; and

(E) Past actions of the service recipient in enforcing the restrictions.

(ii) **Examples.** The following examples illustrate the rules of paragraph (d)(3)(i) of this section:

Example 1. A service provider would be considered as having deferred compensation subject to a substantial risk of forfeiture, but for the fact that the service provider owns 20 percent of the single class of stock in the transferor corporation. If the remaining 80 percent of the class of stock is owned by an unrelated individual (or members of such an individual's family) so that the possibility of the corporation enforcing a restriction on such rights is substantial, then such rights are subject to a substantial risk of forfeiture.

Example 2. A service provider would be considered as having deferred compensation subject to a substantial risk of forfeiture, but for the fact that the service provider, who is president of the corporation, also owns 4 percent of the voting power of all the stock of a corporation. If the remaining stock is so diversely held by the public that the president, in effect, controls the corporation, then the possibility of the corporation enforcing a restriction on the right to deferred compensation of the president is not substantial, and such rights are not subject to a substantial risk of forfeiture.

(e) *Performance-based compensation*— (1) **In general.** The term performance-based compensation means compensation the amount of which, or the entitlement to which, is contingent on the satisfaction of preestablished organizational or individual performance criteria relating to a performance period of at least 12 consecutive months. Organizational or individual performance criteria are considered preestablished if established in writing by not later than 90 days after the commencement of the period of service to which the criteria relates, provided that the outcome is substantially uncertain at the time the criteria are established. Performance-based compensation may include payments based on performance criteria that are not approved by a compensation committee of the board of directors (or similar entity in the case of a non-corporate service recipient) or by the stockholders or members of the service recipient. Performance-based compensation does not include any amount or portion of any amount that will be paid either regardless of performance, or based upon a level of performance that is substantially certain to be met at the time the criteria is established. In addition, except as provided in paragraph (e)(3) of this section, compensation is not performance-based compensation merely because the amount of such compensation is determined by reference to the value of the service recipient or the stock of the service recipient. Where a portion of an amount of compensation would qualify as performance-based compensation if the portion were the sole amount available under the plan, that portion of the award will not fail to qualify as performance-based compensation if that portion is designated separately or otherwise separately identifiable under the terms of the plan, and the amount of each portion is determined independently of the other. Compensation may be performance-based compensation where the amount will be paid regardless of satisfaction of the performance criteria due to the service provider's death, disability, or a change in control event (as defined in § 1.409A-3(i)(5)(i)), provided that a payment made under such circumstances without regard to the satisfaction of the performance criteria will not constitute performance-based compensation. For purposes of this paragraph (e)(1), a disability refers to any medically determinable physical or mental impairment resulting in the service provider's inability to perform the duties of his or her position or any substantially similar position, where such impairment can be expected to result in death or can be expected to last for a continuous period of not less than six months.

(2) **Payments based upon subjective performance criteria.** The term performance-based compensation includes payments based upon subjective performance criteria, provided that—

(i) The subjective performance criteria are bona fide and relate to the performance of the participant service provider, a group of service providers that includes the participant service provider, or a business unit for which the participant service provider provides services (which may include the entire organization); and

(ii) The determination that any subjective performance criteria have been met is not made by the participant service provider or a family member of the participant service provider (as defined in section 267(c)(4) [26 USCS § 267(c)(4)] applied as if the family of an individual includes the spouse of any member of the family), or a person under the effective control of the participant service provider or such a family member, and no amount of the compensation of the person making such determination is effectively controlled in whole or in part by the service provider or such a family member.

(3) **Equity-based compensation.** Compensation is performance-based compensation if it is based solely on an increase in the value of the service recipient, or a share of stock in the service recipient, after the date of a grant or award. However, compensation payable for a service period that is equal to the value of a predetermined number of shares of stock, and is variable only to the extent that the value of such shares appreciates or depreciates, generally will not be performance-based compensation. Notwithstanding the foregoing, the attainment of a prescribed value for the service recipient (or a portion thereof), or a share of stock in the service recipient, may be used as a preestablished organizational criterion for purposes of providing performance-based compensation, provided that the other requirements of paragraph (e)(1) of this section are satisfied. In addition, an award of equity-based compensation may constitute performance-based compensation if entitlement to the compensation is subject to a condition that would cause the award to otherwise qualify as performance-based compensation, such as a performance-based vesting condition. A provision that allows a service provider to defer

compensation that would be realized upon the exercise of a stock right generally constitutes an additional deferral feature for purposes of the definition of a deferral of compensation under paragraph (b)(5) of this section.

(f) *Service provider*—(1) **In general.** The term service provider includes an individual, corporation, subchapter S corporation, partnership, personal service corporation (as defined in section 269A(b)(1) [26 USCS § 269A(b)(1)]), noncorporate entity that would be a personal service corporation if it were a corporation, qualified personal service corporation (as defined in section 448(d)(2) [26 USCS § 448(d)(2)]), and noncorporate entity that would be a qualified personal service corporation if it were a corporation, for any taxable year in which such individual, corporation, subchapter S corporation, partnership, or other entity accounts for gross income from the performance of services under the cash receipts and disbursements method of accounting. The term service provider generally includes a person who has separated from service (a former service provider).

(2) **Independent contractors**—(i) **In general.** Except as otherwise provided in paragraph (f)(2)(iv) of this section, section 409A [26 USCS § 409A] does not apply to an amount deferred under a plan between a service provider and service recipient with respect to a particular trade or business in which the service provider participates, including earnings credited to such deferred amount, if during the service provider's taxable year in which the service provider obtains a legally binding right to the payment of the amount deferred each of the following applies:

(A) The service provider is actively engaged in the trade or business of providing services, other than as an employee or as a member of the board of directors of a corporation (or similar position with respect to an entity that is not a corporation).

(B) The service provider provides significant services to two or more service recipients to which the service provider is not related

and that are not related to one another (as defined in paragraph (f)(2)(ii) of this section).

(C) The service provider is not related to the service recipient, applying the definition of related person contained in paragraph (f)(2)(ii) of this section subject to the modification that the language "20 percent" is not used instead of "50 percent" each place "50 percent" appears in sections 267(b) and 707(b)(1) [26 USCS §§ 267(b) and 707(b)(1)].

(ii) **Related person.** For purposes of this paragraph (f)(2), a person is related to another person if the persons bear a relationship to each other that is specified in section 267(b) or 707(b)(1) [26 USCS § 267(b) or 707(b)(1)], subject to the modifications that the language "20 percent" is used instead of "50 percent" each place it appears in sections 267(b) and 707(b)(1) [26 USCS §§ 267(b) and 707(b)(1)], and section 267(c)(4) [26 USCS § 267(c)(4)] is applied as if the family of an individual includes the spouse of any member of the family; or the persons are engaged in trades or businesses under common control (within the meaning of section 52(a) and (b) [26 USCS § 52(a) and (b)]). In addition, an individual is related to an entity if the individual is an officer of an entity that is a corporation, or holds a position substantially similar to an officer of a corporation with an entity that is not a corporation.

(iii) **Significant services.** Whether a service provider is providing significant services depends on the facts and circumstances of each case. However, for purposes of paragraph (f)(2)(i) of this section, a service provider who provides services to two or more service recipients to which the service provider is not related and that are not related to one another is deemed to be providing significant services to two or more of such service recipients for a given taxable year, if the revenues generated from the services provided to any service recipient or group of related service recipients during such taxable year do not exceed 70 percent of the total revenue generated by the service provider from the trade or business of providing such services. In addition, in the case of a service provider who has been providing services in a trade or business for a period of not less than three consecutive years, for purposes of paragraph (f)(2)(i) of this section, a service provider who provides services to two or more service recipients to which the service provider is not related and that are not related to one another is deemed to be providing significant services to two or more of such service recipients for a given taxable year if in each of the prior three taxable years the revenues generated from the services provided to any service recipient or group of related service recipients during such prior taxable years did not exceed 70 percent of the total revenue generated by the service provider from the trade or business of providing such services and, at the time an amount is deferred, the service provider does not know or have reason to anticipate that the revenues generated from the services provided to any service recipient or group of related service recipients during the current year will exceed 70 percent of the total revenue generated by the service provider from the trade or business of providing such services.

(iv) **Management services.** This paragraph (f)(2) does not apply to a service provider to the extent the service provider provides management services to a service recipient. For purposes of this paragraph (f)(2)(iv), the term management services means services that involve the actual or de facto direction or control of the financial or operational aspects of a trade or business of the service recipient, or investment management or advisory services provided to a service recipient whose primary trade or business includes the investment of financial assets (including investments in real estate), such as a hedge fund or a real estate investment trust.

(v) **Services provided to related persons.** Section 409A [26 USCS § 409A] does not apply to an amount deferred under a plan that is a bona fide agreement, method, program, or other arrangement between a service provider and a related service recipient arising in the ordinary course of a particular trade or business in which the service provider is engaged to the extent that—

(A) The service provider provides services to the service recipient as an independent contractor;

(B) During the service provider's taxable year in which the amount is deferred, the service provider qualifies for the safe harbor provided in paragraph (f)(2)(iii) of this section with respect to such trade or business; and

(C) Such agreement, method, program, or other arrangement and the practices thereunder (including billing and collection practices), are substantially similar to the agreements, methods, programs, or other arrangements and practices applicable to one or more unrelated service recipients to whom the service provider provides substantial services and that produce a majority of the total revenue that the service provider earns from the trade or business of providing such services during the taxable year.

(g) *Service recipient.* Except as otherwise specifically provided in these regulations, the term service recipient means the person for whom the services are performed and with respect to whom the legally binding right to compensation arises, and all persons with whom such person would be considered a single employer under section 414(b) [26 USCS § 414(b)] (employees of controlled group of corporations), and all persons with whom such person would be considered a single employer under section 414(c) [26 USCS § 414(c)] (employees of partnerships, proprietorships, etc., under common control). For example, if the service provider is an employee, the service recipient generally is the employer (including all persons treated as a single employer under section 414(b) or (c) [26 USCS § 414(b) or (c)]). Notwithstanding the foregoing, section 409A [26 USCS § 409A] applies to a plan that provides for the deferral of compensation, even if the payment of the compensation is not made by the person for whom services are performed.

(h) *Separation from service*—(1) **Employees**—(i) **In general.** An employee separates from service with the employer if the employee dies, retires, or otherwise has a termination of employment with the employer. However, for purposes of this paragraph (h)(1), the employment relationship is treated as continuing intact while the individual is on military leave, sick leave, or other bona fide leave of absence if the period of such leave does not exceed six months, or if longer, so long as the individual retains a right to reemployment with the service recipient under an applicable statute or by contract. For purposes of this paragraph (h)(1), a leave of absence constitutes a bona fide leave of absence only if there is a reasonable expectation that the employee will return to perform services for the employer. If the period of leave exceeds six months and the individual does not retain a right to reemployment under an applicable statute or by contract, the employment relationship is deemed to terminate on the first date immediately following such six-month period. Notwithstanding the foregoing, where a leave of absence is due to any medically determinable physical or mental impairment that can be expected to result in death or can be expected to last for a continuous period of not less than six months, where such impairment causes the employee to be unable to perform the duties of his or her position of employment or any substantially similar position of employment, a 29-month period of absence may be substituted for such six-month period.

(ii) **Termination of employment.** Whether a termination of employment has occurred is determined based on whether the facts and circumstances indicate that the employer and employee reasonably anticipated that no further services would be performed after a certain date or that the level of bona fide services the employee would perform after such date (whether as an employee or as an independent contractor) would permanently decrease to no more than 20 percent of the average level of bona fide services performed (whether as an employee or an independent contractor) over the immediately preceding 36-month period (or the full period of services to the employer if the employee has been providing services to the employer less than 36 months). Facts and circumstances to be considered in making this determination include, but are not limited to, whether the employee continues to be treated as an employee for other purposes (such as continuation of salary and participation in employee benefit programs), whether similarly situated service providers have been treated consistently, and whether the employee is permitted, and realistically available, to perform services for other service recipients in the same line of business. An employee is presumed to have separated from service where the level of bona fide services performed decreases to a level equal to 20 percent or less of the average level of services performed by the employee during the immediately preceding 36-month period. An employee will be presumed not to have separated from service where the level of bona fide services performed continues at a level that is 50 percent or more of the average level of service performed by the employee during the immediately preceding 36-month period. No presumption applies to a decrease in the level of bona fide services performed to a level that is more than 20 percent and less than 50 percent of the average level of bona fide services performed during the immediately preceding 36-month period. The presumption is rebuttable by demonstrating that the employer and the employee reasonably anticipated that as of a certain date the level of bona fide services would be reduced permanently to a level less than or equal to 20 percent of the average level of bona fide services provided during the immediately preceding 36-month period or full period of services provided to the employer if the employee has been providing services to the service recipient for a period of less than 36 months (or that the level of bona fide services would not be so reduced). For example, an employee may demonstrate that the employer and employee reasonably anticipated that the employee would cease providing services, but that, after the original cessation of services, business circumstances such as termination of the employee's replacement caused the employee to return to employment. Although the employee's return to employment may cause the employee to be presumed to have continued in employment because the employee is providing services at a rate equal to the rate at which the employee was providing services before the termination of employment, the facts and circumstances in this case would demonstrate that at the time the employee originally ceased to provide services, the employee and the service recipient reasonably anticipated that the employee would not provide services in the future. Notwithstanding the foregoing provisions of this paragraph (h)(1)(ii), a plan may treat another level of reasonably anticipated permanent reduction in the level of bona fide services as a separation from service, provided that the level of reduction required must be designated in writing as a specific percentage, and the reasonably anticipated reduced level of bona fide services must be greater than 20 percent but less that 50 percent of the average level of bona fide services provided in the immediately preceding 36 months. The plan must specify the definition of separation from service on or before the date on which a separation from service is designated as a time of payment of the applicable amount deferred, and once designated, any change to the definition of separation from service with respect to such amount deferred will be subject to the rules regarding subsequent deferrals and the acceleration of payments. For purposes of this paragraph (h)(1)(ii), for periods during which an employee is on a paid bona fide leave of absence (as defined in paragraph (h)(1)(i) of this section) and has not otherwise terminated employment pursuant to paragraph (h)(1)(i) of this section, the employee is treated as providing bona fide services at a level equal to the level of services that the employee would have been required to perform to receive the compensation paid with respect to such leave of absence. Periods during which an employee is on an unpaid bona fide leave of absence (as defined in paragraph (h)(1)(i) of this section) and has not otherwise terminated employment pursuant to paragraph (h)(1)(i) of this section, are disregarded for purposes of this paragraph (h)(1)(ii) (including for purposes of determining the applicable 36-month (or shorter) period).

(2) **Independent contractors**—(i) **In general.** An independent contractor is consid-

ered to have a separation from service with the service recipient upon the expiration of the contract (or in the case of more than one contract, all contracts) under which services are performed for the service recipient if the expiration constitutes a good-faith and complete termination of the contractual relationship. An expiration does not constitute a good faith and complete termination of the contractual relationship if the service recipient anticipates a renewal of a contractual relationship or the independent contractor becoming an employee. For this purpose, a service recipient is considered to anticipate the renewal of the contractual relationship with an independent contractor if it intends to contract again for the services provided under the expired contract, and neither the service recipient nor the independent contractor has eliminated the independent contractor as a possible provider of services under any such new contract. Further, a service recipient is considered to intend to contract again for the services provided under an expired contract if the service recipient's doing so is conditioned only upon incurring a need for the services, the availability of funds, or both.

(ii) **Special rule.** Notwithstanding paragraph (h)(2)(i) of this section, a plan is considered to satisfy the requirement described in § 1.409A-3(a)(1) with respect to an amount payable upon a separation from service if, with respect to amounts payable to a service provider who is an independent contractor, the plan provides that—

(A) No amount will be paid to the service provider before a date at least 12 months after the day on which the contract expires under which the service provider performs services for the service recipient (or, in the case of more than one contract, all such contracts expire); and

(B) No amount payable to the service provider on that date will be paid to the service provider if, after the expiration of the contract (or contracts) and before that date, the service provider performs services for the service recipient as an independent contractor or an employee.

(3) **Definition of service recipient and employer.** For purposes of this paragraph (h), the term service recipient or employer means the service recipient as defined in paragraph (g) of this section, provided that in applying section 1563(a)(1), (2), and (3) [26 USCS § 1563(a)(1), (2), and (3)] for purposes of determining a controlled group of corporations under section 414(b) [26 USCS § 414(b)], the language "at least 50 percent" is used instead of "at least 80 percent" each place it appears in section 1563(a)(1), (2), and (3) [26 USCS § 1563(a)(1), (2), and (3)], and in applying § 1.414(c)-2 for purposes of determining trades or businesses (whether or not incorporated) that are under common control for purposes of section 414(c) [26 USCS § 414(c)], "at least 50 percent" is used instead of "at least 80 percent" each place it appears in § 1.414(c)-2. A plan may provide with respect to a deferral of compensation under the plan that in applying sections 1563(a)(1), (2), and (3) [26 USCS §§ 1563(a)(1), (2), and (3)] for purposes of determining a controlled group of corporations under section 414(b) [26 USCS § 414(b)], another defined percentage greater than 50 percent, but not greater than 80 percent, is used instead of "at least 80 percent" at each place it appears in sections 1563(a)(1), (2), and (3) [26 USCS §§ 1563(a)(1), (2), and (3)], and in applying § 1.414(c)-2 for purposes of determining trades or businesses (whether or not incorporated) that are under common control for purposes of section 414(c) [26 USCS § 414(c)], another defined percentage greater than 50 percent, but not greater than 80 percent, is used instead of "at least 80 percent" at each place it appears in § 1.414(c)-2. In addition, where the use of such definition of service recipient for purposes of determining a separation from service is based upon legitimate business criteria, the plan may provide that for purposes of a deferral of compensation under the plan that in applying sections 1563(a)(1), (2), and (3) [26 USCS §§ 1563(a)(1), (2), and (3)] for purposes of determining a controlled group of corporations under section 414(b) [26 USCS § 414(b)], the language "at least 20 percent" or another defined percentage not less than 20 percent but

not greater than 50 percent is used instead of "at least 80 percent" at each place it appears in sections 1563(a)(1), (2), and (3) [26 USCS §§ 1563(a)(1), (2), and (3)], and in applying § 1.414(c)-2 for purposes of determining trades or businesses (whether or not incorporated) that are under common control for purposes of section 414(c) [26 USCS § 414(c)], the language "at least 20 percent" or another defined percentage not less than 20 percent but not greater than 50 percent is used instead of "at least 80 percent" at each place it appears in § 1.414(c)-2. Where a definition of service recipient or employer other than the definition provided in the first sentence of this paragraph (h)(3) (the 50 percent standard) is used, the plan must designate in writing the alternate definition no later than the last date at which the time and form of payment of the applicable amount deferred must be elected in accordance with § 1.409A-2(a), and any change in the definition for such amounts deferred will constitute a change in the time and form of payment subject to the rules governing subsequent deferral elections under § 1.409A-2(b) and the acceleration of payments under § 1.409A-3(j).

(4) **Asset purchase transactions.** Where as part of a sale or other disposition of assets by one service recipient (seller) to an unrelated service recipient (buyer), a service provider of the seller would otherwise experience a separation from service with the seller, the seller and the buyer may retain the discretion to specify, and may specify, whether a service provider providing services to the seller immediately before the asset purchase transaction and providing services to the buyer after and in connection with the asset purchase transaction has experienced a separation from service for purposes of this paragraph (h), provided that the asset purchase transaction results from bona fide, arm's length negotiations, all service providers providing services to the seller immediately before the asset purchase transaction and providing services to the buyer after and in connection with the asset purchase transaction are treated consistently (regardless of position at the seller) for purposes of applying the provisions of any non-

qualified deferred compensation plan, and such treatment is specified in writing no later than the closing date of the asset purchase transaction. For purposes of this paragraph (h)(4), references to a sale or other disposition of assets, or an asset purchase transaction, refer only to a transfer of substantial assets, such as a plant or division or substantially all the assets of a trade or business. For purposes of this paragraph (h)(4), whether a service recipient is related to another service recipient is determined under the rules provided in paragraph (f)(2)(ii) of this section.

(5) **Dual status.** If a service provider provides services both as an employee of a service recipient and as an independent contractor of a service recipient, the service provider must separate from service both as an employee and as an independent contractor to be treated as having separated from service. If a service provider ceases providing services as an independent contractor and begins providing services as an employee, or ceases providing services as an employee and begins providing services as an independent contractor, the service provider will not be considered to have a separation from service until the service provider has ceased providing services in both capacities. Notwithstanding the foregoing, if a service provider provides services both as an employee of a service recipient and a member of the board of directors of a corporate service recipient (or an analogous position with respect to a non-corporate service recipient), the services provided as a director are not taken into account in determining whether the service provider has a separation from service as an employee for purposes of a nonqualified deferred compensation plan in which the service provider participates as an employee that is not aggregated with any plan in which the service provider participates as a director under paragraph (c)(2)(ii) of this section. In addition, if a service provider provides services both as an employee of a service recipient and a member of the board of directors of a corporate service recipient (or an analogous position with respect to a non-corporate service recipient), the services provided as an employee are not taken into account in determining whether

the service provider has a separation from service as a director for purposes of a non-qualified deferred compensation plan in which the service provider participates as a director that is not aggregated with any plan in which the service provider participates as an employee under paragraph (c)(2)(ii) of this section.

(6) **Collectively bargained plans covering multiple employers.** Notwithstanding the foregoing provisions of this paragraph (h), to the extent a plan is established pursuant to a bona fide collective bargaining agreement covering services performed by employees for multiple employers, such plan may define a separation from service in a reasonable manner that treats the employee as not having separated from service during periods in which the employee is not providing services but is available to perform services covered by the collective bargaining agreement for one or more employers, provided that the definition also provides that the employee must be deemed to have separated from service at a specified date not later than the end of any period of at least 12 consecutive months during which the employee has not provided any services covered by the collective bargaining agreement to any participating employer. This paragraph (h)(6) applies only if the definition of separation from service provided by the collective bargaining agreement was the subject of arm's length negotiations between employee representatives and two or more employers, the agreement between employee representatives and such employers satisfies section 7701(a)(46) [26 USCS § 7701(a)(46)], and the circumstances surrounding the agreement evidence good faith bargaining between adverse parties over such definition.

(i) *Specified employee*—(1) **In general.** The term specified employee means a service provider who, as of the date of the service provider's separation from service, is a key employee of a service recipient any stock of which is publicly traded on an established securities market or otherwise. For purposes of this paragraph (i)(1), a service provider is a key employee if the service provider meets the requirements of section 416(i)(1)(A)(i), (ii), or (iii) [26 USCS § 416(i)(1)(A)(i), (ii), or (iii)] (applied in accordance with the regulations thereunder and disregarding section 416(i)(5) [26 USCS § 416(i)(5)]) at any time during the 12-month period ending on a specified employee identification date. If a service provider is a key employee as of a specified employee identification date, the service provider is treated as a key employee for purposes of this paragraph (i) for the entire 12-month period beginning on the specified employee effective date.

(2) **Definition of compensation.** For purposes of identifying a specified employee by applying the requirements of section 416(i)(1)(A)(i), (ii), and (iii) [26 USCS § 416(i)(1)(A)(i), (ii), and (iii)], the definition of compensation under § 1.415(c)-2(a) is used, applied as if the service recipient were not using any safe harbor provided in § 1.415(c)-2(d), were not using any of the elective special timing rules provided in § 1.415(c)-2(e), and were not using any of the elective special rules provided in § 1.415(c)-2(g). Notwithstanding the foregoing, a service recipient may elect to use any available definition of compensation under section 415 [26 USCS § 415] and the regulations thereunder in accordance with the election requirements set forth in paragraph (i)(8) of this section, including any available safe harbor and any available election under the timing rules or special rules, provided that the definition is applied consistently to all employees of the service recipient for purposes of identifying specified employees. A service recipient may elect to use such an alternative definition regardless of whether another definition of compensation is being used for purposes of a qualified plan sponsored by the service recipient. However, once a list of specified employees has become effective, the service recipient cannot change the definition of compensation for purposes of identifying specified employees for the period with respect to which such list is effective.

(3) **Specified employee identification date.** Unless another date is designated in accordance with the requirements of this para-graph (i)(3) and paragraph (i)(8) of this section, the specified employee identification date is December 31. A service recipient may designate in accordance with the requirements of paragraph (i)(8) of this section any other date as the specified employee identification date, provided that a service recipient must use the same specified employee identification date with respect to all nonqualified deferred compensation plans, and any change to the specified employee identification date may not be effective for a period of at least 12 months. The service recipient may designate a specified employee identification date in each plan or in a separate document applicable to all plans, provided that the service recipient will not be treated as having designated a specified employee identification date before the designation is legally binding on the service recipient and all affected service providers. Any designation of a specified employee identification date made on or before December 31, 2007, may be applied to any separation from service occurring on or after January 1, 2005, unless and until subsequently changed pursuant to this paragraph (i)(3).

(4) **Specified employee effective date.** Unless another date is designated in accordance with the requirements of this paragraph (i)(4) and paragraph (i)(8) of this section, the specified employee effective date is the first day of the fourth month following the specified employee identification date. A service recipient may designate in accordance with the requirements of paragraph (i)(8) of this section any date following the specified employee identification date as the specified employee effective date, provided that such date may not be later than the first day of the fourth month following the specified employee identification date, and provided further that a service recipient must use the same specified employee effective date with respect to all nonqualified deferred compensation plans, and any change to the specified employee effective date may not be effective for a period of at least 12 months. The service recipient may designate a specified employee effective date through inclusion in each plan document or through a separate document applicable to all

plans, provided that the service recipient will not be treated as having designated a specified employee effective date on any date before the designation is legally binding on the service recipient and all affected service providers. Any designation of a specified employee effective date made on or before December 31, 2007, may be applied to any separation from service occurring on or after January 1, 2005, unless and until subsequently changed pursuant to this paragraph (i)(4).

(5) **Alternative methods of satisfying the six-month delay rule.** A plan may provide, in accordance with the requirements of paragraph (i)(8) of this section, for an alternative method to identify service providers who will be subject to the six-month delay rule provided in section 409A(a)(2)(B)(i) [26 USCS § 409A(a)(2)(B)(i)], provided that the alternative method is reasonably designed to include all specified employees (determined without respect to any available service recipient elections), the alternative method is an objectively determinable standard providing no direct or indirect election to any service provider regarding its application, and the alternative method results in either all service providers or no more than 200 service providers being identified in the class as of any date. Use of such an alternative method will not be treated as a change in the time and form of payment for purposes of § 1.409A-2(b) (the subsequent deferral rules), even if the service provider is not a specified employee when the payment is delayed.

(6) **Corporate transactions**—(i) **Mergers and acquisitions of public service recipients.** If as a result of a corporate transaction, two or more separate service recipients, more than one of which has stock outstanding that is publicly traded on an established securities market or otherwise immediately before the transaction, become one service recipient, any stock of which is publicly traded on an established securities market or otherwise immediately after the transaction (resulting public service recipient), the resulting public service recipient's next specified employee identification date and specified employee

effective date following the corporate transaction are the specified employee identification date and specified employee effective date that the acquiring service recipient would have been required to use absent such transaction. For this purpose, in the case of a corporate merger, the acquiring service recipient is the service recipient that included the surviving corporation in such merger, in the case of an acquisition by a corporation of the stock of another corporation, the acquiring service recipient is the service recipient that included the corporation that acquired such stock, and in all other cases, the surviving service recipient is determined on the basis of all of the facts and circumstances. For the period between the transaction and the next specified employee effective date, the list of specified employees of the resulting public service recipient is determined by combining the lists of specified employees of all service recipients participating in the transaction that were in effect at the date of the corporate transaction, ranking such specified employees in order of the amount of compensation used to determine each specified employee's status as a specified employee, and treating the top 50 of such specified employees, plus any employees described in section 416(i)(1)(ii) [26 USCS § 416(i)(1)(ii)] or section 416(i)(1)(iii) [26 USCS § 416(i)(1)(iii)] and the regulations thereunder (relating to 1-percent and 5-percent owners) who are not included in such top 50 specified employees, as specified employees for the period between the corporate transaction and the next specified employee effective date. Alternatively, the resulting service recipient may elect in accordance with the requirements of paragraph (i)(8) of this section to use any reasonable method to determine the specified employees of the resulting service recipient, including the use of an alternative method of compliance described in paragraph (i)(5) of this section, provided that such method is adopted no later than 90 days after the corporate transaction and applied prospectively from the date the method is adopted.

(ii) **Mergers and acquisitions of non-public service recipients.** If as part of a corporate transaction a service recipient that does not have outstanding stock that is publicly traded on an established securities market or otherwise immediately before the transaction (initial private service recipient), and a service recipient with stock outstanding that is publicly traded on an established securities market or otherwise immediately before the transaction (initial public service recipient), become a single service recipient having stock that is publicly traded on an established securities market or otherwise immediately after the transaction (resulting public service recipient), the resulting public service recipient's next specified employee identification date and specified employee effective date following the corporate transaction are the specified employee identification date and specified employee effective date that the initial public service recipient would have been required to use absent such transaction. For the period after the date of the corporate transaction and before the next specified employee effective date, the specified employees of the initial public service recipient immediately before the transaction continue to be the specified employees of the resulting public service recipient, and no service providers of the initial private service recipient are required to be treated as specified employees.

(iii) **Spinoffs.** If as part of a corporate transaction, a service recipient with stock outstanding that is publicly traded on an established securities market or otherwise immediately before the transaction (initial public service recipient), becomes two or more separate service recipients, each with stock outstanding that is publicly traded on an established securities market or otherwise immediately after the transaction (post-transaction public service recipients), the next specified employee identification date of each of the post-transaction public service recipients is the specified employee identification date that the initial public service recipient would have been required to use absent such transaction. For the period after the date of the corporate transaction and before the next specified employee effective date, the specified employees of the initial public service recipient immediately before the transaction continue to be the specified

employees of the post-transaction public service recipients.

(iv) **Public offerings and other corporate transactions.** If as part of an initial public offering or corporate transaction not described in paragraph (i)(6)(ii) or (iii) of this section, a service recipient with no outstanding stock that is publicly traded on an established securities market or otherwise immediately before such offering or other transaction (initial private service recipient), becomes one or more service recipients with stock outstanding that is publicly traded on an established securities market or otherwise immediately after such offering or other transaction (post-transaction public service recipient), each post-transaction public service recipient has a specified employee identification date of December 31 and a specified employee effective date of April 1, effective retroactively to the December 31 and April 1 next preceding the offering or other transaction for purposes of identifying the specified employees between the corporation transaction and the next December 31. Alternatively, a post-transaction public service recipient may elect in accordance with the requirements of paragraph (i)(8) of this section, a specified employee identification date and specified employee effective date on or before the date of the offering or other transaction. If a public service recipient makes such an election, for the period after the offering or other transaction and before the next specified employee effective date, the specified employees of the post-transaction public service recipient consist of the service providers that at the time of the offering or other transaction would have been classified as specified employees of the initial private service recipient, had the initial private service recipient elected the same specified employee identification date and specified employee effective date as selected by the post-transaction public service recipient, and had such initial private service recipient had stock publicly traded on an established securities market or otherwise as of the specified employee identification date preceding the transaction.

(v) **Alternative methods of compliance.** For purposes of this paragraph (i)(6), references to specified employees as of a corporate transaction or offering include any specified employees identified through the use of an alternative method described in paragraph (i)(5) of this section, where the use of such alternative method was established and effective at the time of the corporate transaction or offering.

(7) **Nonresident alien employees.** For purposes of determining whether an employee meets the requirements of section 416(i)(1)(A)(i), (ii), or (iii) [26 USCS § 416(i)(1)(A)(i), (ii), or (iii)] (applied in accordance with the regulations thereunder and disregarding section 416(i)(5) [26 USCS § 416(i)(5)]), and therefore is a key employee, the incorporation of the rules of § 1.415(c)-2(g)(5) regarding the definition of compensation applies. Accordingly, the rule of § 1.415(c)-2(g)(5)(i), generally requiring the treatment as compensation of certain compensation excludible from an employee's gross income due to the location of the services or the identity of the employer, applies. In addition, a service recipient may elect in accordance with paragraph (i)(8) of this section to apply the rule of § 1.415(c)-2(g)(5)(ii) to not treat as compensation certain compensation excludible from an employee's gross income on account of the location of the services or the identity of the employer that is not effectively connected with the conduct of a trade or business within the United States. A service recipient may elect to apply the rule of § 1.415-2(g)(5)(ii) regardless of whether the service recipient has elected to apply the rule to a qualified plan sponsored by the service recipient; however, once a list of specified employees has become effective, any election of the rule for that period may not be changed. Notwithstanding the foregoing, any election of the rule made before January 1, 2008, may be effective with respect to any specified employee identification date on or before December 31, 2007.

(8) **Elections affecting the identification of specified employees.** The elections described in paragraphs (i)(2) through (7) of this section are effective only as of the date that all necessary corporate action has been taken to make such elections binding for purposes of all affected nonqualified deferred compensation plans in which the service providers of the service recipient that would become a specified employee due to the application of such election participate. Where a taxpayer attempts to make an election under paragraph (i)(2), (3), (4), (5), (6), or (7) of this section but such election is not binding on all the affected nonqualified deferred compensation plans and applied consistently to all such service providers, the election is not effective and the rule under paragraph (i)(2), (3), (4), (5), (6), or (7) of this section, as applicable, that would apply absent an election is applicable for identifying specified employees.

(j) *Nonresident alien.* (1) Except as provided in paragraph (j)(2) of this section, the term nonresident alien means an individual who is—

(i) A nonresident alien within the meaning of section 7701(b)(1)(B) [26 USCS § 7701(b)(1)(B)]; or

(ii) A dual resident taxpayer within the meaning of § 301.7701(b)-7(a)(1) of this chapter with respect to any taxable year in which such individual is treated as a nonresident alien for purposes of computing the individual's U.S. income tax liability.

(2) The term nonresident alien does not include—

(i) A nonresident alien with respect to whom an election is in effect for the taxable year under section 6013(g) [26 USCS § 6013(g)] to be treated as a resident of the United States;

(ii) A former citizen or long-term resident (within the meaning of section 877(e)(2) [26 USCS § 877(e)(2)]) who expatriated after June 3, 2004, and has not complied with the requirements of section 7701(n) [26 USCS § 7701(n)]; or

(iii) An individual who is treated as a citizen or resident of the United States for the taxable year under section 877(g) [26 USCS § 877(g)].

(k) *Established securities market.* The term established securities market means an established securities market within the meaning of § 1.897-1(m).

(l) *Stock right.* The term stock right means a stock option (other than an incentive stock option described in section 422 [26 USCS § 422] or an option granted pursuant to an employee stock purchase plan described in section 423 [26 USCS § 423]) or a stock appreciation right.

(m) *Separation pay plan.* The term separation pay plan means any plan that provides separation pay or, where a plan provides both amounts that are separation pay and that are not separation pay, that portion of the plan that provides separation pay. The term separation pay means any deferral of compensation (before the application of the exclusions from the definition of a deferral of compensation set forth in paragraph (b)(9) of this section) that will not be paid under any circumstances unless the service provider has had a separation from service, whether voluntary or involuntary, including payments in the form of reimbursements of expenses incurred, and the provision of in-kind benefits. A deferral of compensation that the service provider may receive without a separation from service does not become separation pay merely because the service provider elects to receive or receives the payment after or upon a separation from service. A deferral of compensation does not fail to be separation pay merely because the payment is conditioned upon the execution of a release of claims, noncompetition or nondisclosure provisions, or other similar requirements. Notwithstanding the foregoing, any amount, or entitlement to any amount, that acts as a substitute for, or replacement of, amounts deferred by the service recipient under a nonqualified deferred compensation plan constitutes a payment of compensation or deferral of compensation under such nonqualified deferred compensation plan.

(n) *Involuntary separation from service*—
(1) **In general.** An involuntary separation from service means a separation from service due to the independent exercise of the unilateral authority of the service recipient to terminate the service provider's services, other than due to the service provider's implicit or explicit request, where the service provider was willing and able to continue performing services. An involuntary separation from service may include the service recipient's failure to renew a contract at the time such contract expires, provided that the service provider was willing and able to execute a new contract providing terms and conditions substantially similar to those in the expiring contract and to continue providing such services. The determination of whether a separation from service is involuntary is based on all the facts and circumstances. Any characterization of the separation from service as voluntary or involuntary by the service provider and the service recipient in the documentation of the separation from service is presumed to properly characterize the nature of the separation from service. However, the presumption may be rebutted where the facts and circumstances indicate otherwise. For example, if a separation from service is designated as a voluntary separation from service or resignation, but the facts and circumstances indicate that absent such voluntary separation from service the service recipient would have terminated the service provider's services, and that the service provider had knowledge that the service provider would be so terminated, the separation from service is involuntary.

(2) **Separations from service for good reason**—(i) **In general.** Notwithstanding paragraph (n)(1) of this section, a service provider's voluntary separation from service will be treated for purposes of this section and §§ 1.409A-2 through 1.409A-6 as an involuntary separation from service if the separation from service occurs under certain limited bona fide conditions, where the avoidance of the requirements of section 409A [26 USCS § 409A] is not a purpose of the inclusion of these conditions in the plan or of the actions by the service recipient in connection with the

satisfaction of these conditions, and a voluntary separation from service under such conditions effectively constitutes an involuntary separation from service. Generally such conditions will be prespecified under an agreement to provide compensation upon a separation from service for good reason. Such a good reason (or a similar condition) must be defined to require actions taken by the service recipient resulting in a material negative change to the service provider in the service relationship, such as the duties to be performed, the conditions under which such duties are to be performed, or the compensation to be received for performing such services. Other factors taken into account in determining whether a separation from service for good reason effectively constitutes an involuntary separation from service include the extent to which the payments upon a separation from service for good reason are in the same amount and are to be made at the same time and in the same form as payments available upon an actual involuntary separation from service, and whether the service provider is required to give the service recipient notice of the existence of the condition that would result in treatment as a separation from service for good reason and a reasonable opportunity to remedy the condition.

(ii) **Safe harbor.** For purposes of this section and §§ 1.409A-2 through 1.409A-6, if a plan provides that a voluntary separation from service will be treated as an involuntary separation from service if the separation from service occurs under certain express conditions, a separation from service satisfying the conditions set forth in the plan will be treated as an involuntary separation from the service if the necessary conditions (or set of conditions) require the following:

(A) The separation from service must occur during a pre-determined limited period of time not to exceed two years following the initial existence of one or more of the following conditions arising without the consent of the service provider:

(1) A material diminution in the service provider's base compensation.

(2) A material diminution in the service provider's authority, duties, or responsibilities.

(3) A material diminution in the authority, duties, or responsibilities of the supervisor to whom the service provider is required to report, including a requirement that a service provider report to a corporate officer or employee instead of reporting directly to the board of directors of a corporation (or similar governing body with respect to an entity other than a corporation).

(4) A material diminution in the budget over which the service provider retains authority.

(5) A material change in the geographic location at which the service provider must perform the services.

(6) Any other action or inaction that constitutes a material breach by the service recipient of the agreement under which the service provider provides services.

(B) The amount, time, and form of payment upon the separation from service must be substantially identical to the amount, time and form of payment payable due to an actual involuntary separation from service, to the extent such a right exists.

(C) The service provider must be required to provide notice to the service recipient of the existence of the condition described in paragraph (n)(2)(ii)(A) of this section within a period not to exceed 90 days of the initial existence of the condition, upon the notice of which the service recipient must be provided a period of at least 30 days during which it may remedy the condition and not be required to pay the amount.

(3) **Special rule for certain collectively bargained plans.** Notwithstanding the foregoing, for purposes of this paragraph (n), to the extent a plan is subject to a bona fide collective bargaining agreement covering services performed for multiple employers under which an employee must separate from service with all such employers in order to receive a payment, such plan may use any reasonable definition of involuntary separation

from service, provided that such definition is consistent with any definition of a separation from service adopted under paragraph (h)(6) of this section, and provided further that the definition of an involuntary separation from service provided by the collective bargaining agreement was the subject of arm's length negotiations between employee representatives and two or more employers, the agreement between employee representatives and such employers satisfies section 7701(a)(46) [26 USCS § 7701(a)(46)], and the circumstances surrounding the agreement evidence good faith bargaining between adverse parties over such definition.

(o) *Earnings.* Whether a deferred amount constitutes earnings on an amount deferred, or actual or notional income attributable to an amount deferred, is determined under the principles defining income attributable to the amount taken into account under § 31.3121(v)(2)-1(d)(2) of this chapter. Accordingly, with respect to an account balance plan, earnings on an amount deferred generally include an amount credited on behalf of a service provider under the terms of the plan that reflects a rate of return that does not exceed either the rate of return on a predetermined actual investment or, if the income does not reflect the rate of return on a predetermined actual investment, a reasonable rate of interest. With respect to nonaccount balance plans, earnings on an amount deferred generally include an increase, due solely to the passage of time, in the present value of the future payments to which the service provider has obtained a legally binding right, the present value of which constituted the amount deferred (determined as of the date such amount was deferred), but only if the amount deferred was determined using reasonable actuarial assumptions and methods. A right to earnings on an amount deferred generally is treated as a right to a deferral of compensation for purposes of this section and §§ 1.409A-2 through 1.409A-6. However, for purposes of any provision of this section and §§ 1.409A-2 through 1.409A-6 referring to earnings on deferred compensation (or similar terms), the use of an unreasonable rate of return, or unreasonable

actuarial assumptions and methods, generally will result in the treatment of some or all of such a right to deferred compensation as a right only to deferred compensation, and not a right to earnings on deferred compensation, so that the provision will not be applicable. With respect to plans that are neither account balance plans nor nonaccount balance plans, these rules apply by analogy.

(p) *In-kind benefits.* The term in-kind benefits refers to services provided to or on behalf of a service provider, such as financial planning services, or tangible personal or real property made available for use by or on behalf of the service provider, such as the use of an aircraft or vehicle, and does not refer to a transfer of property within the meaning of section 83 [26 USCS § 83] and the regulations thereunder, or a promise to transfer, or an option to purchase or receive, property in the future.

(q) *Application of definitions and rules.* The definitions and rules set forth in paragraphs (a) through (p) of this section apply for purposes of section 409A [26 USCS § 409A], this section, and §§ 1.409A-2 through 1.409A-6.

§ 1.409A-2. Deferral elections.

(a) *Initial elections as to the time and form of payment*—(1) **In general.** A plan that is, or constitutes part of, a nonqualified deferred compensation plan meets the requirements of section 409A(a)(4)(B) [26 USCS § 409A(a)(4)(B)] only if under the terms of the plan, compensation for services performed during a service provider's taxable year (the service year) may be deferred at the service provider's election only if the election to defer such compensation is made and becomes irrevocable not later than the latest date permitted in this paragraph (a). An election will not be considered to be revocable merely because the service provider or service recipient may make an election to change the time and form of payment pursuant to paragraph (b) of this section, or the service recipient may accelerate the time of payment pursuant to § 1.409A-3(j)(4) (exceptions to prohibition on accelerated payments). Whether a plan provides a service provider an opportunity to elect the time or form of payment of compensation is determined based upon all the facts and circumstances surrounding the determination of the time and form of payment of the compensation. For purposes of this section, an election to defer includes an election as to the time of the payment, an election as to the form of the payment or an election as to both the time and the form of the payment, but does not include an election as to the medium of payment (for example, an election between a payment of cash or a payment of property). Except as otherwise expressly provided in this section, an election will not be considered made until such election becomes irrevocable under the terms of the applicable plan. Accordingly, a plan may provide that an election to defer may be changed at any time before the last permissible date for making such an election. Where a plan provides the service provider a right to make an initial deferral election, and further provides that the election remains in effect until terminated or modified by the service provider, the election will be treated as made as of the date such election becomes irrevocable as to compensation for services performed during the relevant service year. For example, where a plan provides that a service provider's election to defer a set percentage will remain in effect until changed or revoked, but that as of each December 31 the election becomes irrevocable with respect to salary payable in connection with servicesperformed in the immediately following year, the initial deferral election with respect to salary payable with respect to services performed in the immediately following year will be deemed to have been made as of the December 31 upon which the election became irrevocable. For purposes of this paragraph (a), the reference to a service period or a performance period refers to the period of service for which the right to the compensation arises, and may include periods before the grant of a legally binding right to the compensation. For example, where a service recipient grants a bonus based upon services performed in the calendar year 2010, but retains the discretion to rescind the bonus until

2011 such that the promise of the bonus is not a legally binding right, the period of service or performance period to which the compensation relates is the calendar year 2010.

(2) **Service recipient elections.** A plan that provides for a deferral of compensation for services performed during a service provider's taxable year that does not provide the service provider with an opportunity to elect the time or form of payment of such compensation must designate the time and form of payment by no later than the later of the time the service provider first has a legally binding right to the compensation or, if later, the time the service provider would be required under this section to make such an election if the service provider were provided such an election. Such designation is treated as an initial deferral election for purposes of this section. Where a plan permits a service recipient to exercise discretion to disregard a service provider election as to the time or form of a payment, any service provider election that is subject to such discretion will be treated as revocable so long as such discretion may be exercised.

(3) **General rule.** A plan that is, or constitutes part of, a nonqualified deferred compensation plan meets the requirements of section 409A(a)(4)(B) [26 USCS § 409A(a)(4)(B)] if under the terms of the plan, compensation for services performed during a service provider's taxable year (the service year) may be deferred at the service provider's election only if the election to defer such compensation is made not later than the close of the service provider's taxable year next preceding the service year.

(4) **Initial deferral election with respect to short-term deferrals.** If a service provider has a legally binding right to a payment of compensation in a subsequent taxable year that, absent a deferral election, would be treated as a short-term deferral within the meaning of § 1.409A-1(b)(4), an election to defer such compensation may be made in accordance with the requirements of paragraph (b) of this section, applied as if the amount were a deferral of compensation and the scheduled pay-

ment date for the amount were the date the substantial risk of forfeiture lapses. Notwithstanding the requirements of paragraph (b) of this section, such a deferral election may provide that the deferred amounts will be payable upon a change in control event (as defined in § 1.409A-3(i)(5)) without regard to the five-year additional deferral requirement in paragraph (b) of this section.

(5) **Initial deferral election with respect to certain forfeitable rights.** If a service provider has a legally binding right to a payment in a subsequent year that is subject to a condition requiring the service provider to continue to provide services for a period of at least 12 months from the date the service provider obtains the legally binding right to avoid forfeiture of the payment, an election to defer such compensation may be made on or before the 30th day after the service provider obtains the legally binding right to the compensation, provided that the election is made at least 12 months in advance of the earliest date at which the forfeiture condition could lapse. For purposes of this paragraph (a)(5), a condition will not be treated as failing to require the service provider to continue to provide services for a period of at least 12 months from the date the service provider obtains the legally binding right merely because the condition immediately lapses upon the death or disability (as defined in § 1.409A-3(i)(4)) of the service provider, or upon a change in control event (as defined in § 1.409A-3(i)(5)), provided that if death, disability, or a change in control event occurs and the condition lapses before the end of such 12-month period, a deferral election may be given effect only if the deferral election is permitted under this section without regard to this paragraph (a)(5).

(6) **Initial deferral election with respect to fiscal year compensation.** In the case of a service recipient with a taxable year that is not the same as the taxable year of the service provider, a plan may provide that fiscal year compensation may be deferred at the service provider's election if the election to defer such compensation is made not later than the close of the service recipient's taxable year immedi-

ately preceding the first taxable year of the service recipient in which any services are performed for which such compensation is payable. For purposes of this paragraph (a)(6), the term fiscal year compensation means compensation relating to a period of service coextensive with one or more consecutive taxable years of the service recipient, of which no amount is paid or payable during the service recipient's taxable year or years constituting the period of service. For example, fiscal year compensation generally would include a bonus to an individual employee with a calendar year taxable year that is based on a service period consisting of the service recipient's two consecutive taxable years ending September 30, 2011, where the amount will be paid after the end of the second of such taxable years, but would not include either a bonus based on a service period consisting of one or more calendar years or salary that would otherwise be paid during such taxable years of the service recipient.

(7) **First year of eligibility**—(i) **In general.** In the case of the first year in which a service provider becomes eligible to participate in a plan, the service provider may make an initial deferral election within 30 days after the date the service provider becomes eligible to participate in such plan, with respect to compensation paid for services to be performed after the election. In the case of a plan that does not provide for service provider elections with respect to the time or form of a payment, the time and form of the payment must be specified on or before the date that is 30 days after the date the service provider first becomes eligible to participate in such plan. For compensation that is earned based upon a specified performance period (for example, an annual bonus), where a deferral election is made in the first year of eligibility but after the beginning of the performance period, the election must apply only to the compensation paid for services performed after the election. For this purpose, an election will be deemed to apply to compensation paid for services performed after the election if the election applies to no more than an amount equal to the total amount of the compensation for the perfor-

mance period multiplied by the ratio of the number of days remaining in the performance period after the election over the total number of days in the performance period.

(ii) **Eligibility to participate.** For purposes of this paragraph (a)(7), a service provider is eligible to participate in a plan at any time during which, under the plan's terms and without further amendment or action by the service recipient, the service provider is eligible to accrue an amount of deferred compensation under the plan other than earnings on amounts previously deferred, even if the service provider has elected not to accrue (or has not elected to accrue) an amount of deferred compensation. Where a service provider has been paid all amounts deferred under a plan, and on and before the date of the last payment was not eligible to continue (or to elect to continue) to participate in the plan for periods after the last payment (other than through an election of a different time and form of payment with respect to the amounts paid), the service provider may be treated as initially eligible to participate in a plan as of the first date following such payment that the service provider becomes eligible to accrue an additional amount of deferred compensation. Where a service provider has ceased being eligible to participate in a plan (other than the accrual of earnings), regardless of whether all amounts deferred under the plan have been paid, and subsequently becomes eligible to participate in the plan again, the service provider may be treated as being initially eligible to participate in the plan if the service provider had not been eligible to participate in the plan (other than the accrual of earnings) at any time during the 24-month period ending on the date the service provider again becomes eligible to participate in the plan.

(iii) **Application to excess benefit plans.** For purposes of this paragraph (a)(7), a service provider is treated as initially eligible to participate in an excess benefit plan as of the first day of the service provider's taxable year immediately following the first year the service provider accrues a benefit under the excess benefit plan; and any election made with-

in 30 days following such date is treated as applying to benefits accrued under such plan for services performed before the election. For purposes of this paragraph (a)(7), the term excess benefit plan means all nonqualified deferred compensation plans in which a service provider participates, to the extent such plans do not provide for an election between current compensation (including a short-term deferral) and deferred compensation and solely provide deferred compensation equal to the excess of the benefits the service provider would have accrued under a qualified employer plan (as defined in § 1.409A-1(a)(2)) in which the service provider also participates, in the absence of one or more of the limits incorporated into the plan to reflect one or more of the limits on contributions or benefits applicable to the qualified employer plan under the Internal Revenue Code, over the benefits the service provider actually accrues under the qualified employer plan. For purposes of this paragraph (a)(7), once a service provider has accrued a benefit or deferred compensation under a plan in any year, the service provider will not become eligible for an initial deferral election based upon an accrual or deferral under an excess benefit plan in a subsequent year, even if the benefit or deferred compensation accrued in a previous year is forfeited or eliminated.

(8) **Initial deferral election with respect to performance-based compensation.** In the case of any performance-based compensation (as defined in § 1.409A-1(e)), an initial deferral election may be made with respect to such performance-based compensation on or before the date that is six months before the end of the performance period, provided that the service provider performs services continuously from the later of the beginning of the performance period or the date the performance criteria are established through the date an election is made under this paragraph (a)(8), and provided further that in no event may an election to defer performance-based compensation be made after such compensation has become readily ascertainable. For purposes of this paragraph (a)(8), if the performance-based compensation is a specified or calculable

amount, the compensation is readily ascertainable if and when the amount is first substantially certain to be paid. If the performance-based compensation is not a specified or calculable amount because, for example, the amount may vary based upon the level of performance, the compensation, or any portion of the compensation, is readily ascertainable when the amount is first both calculable and substantially certain to be paid. For this purpose, the performance-based compensation is bifurcated between the portion that is readily ascertainable and the amount that is not readily ascertainable. Accordingly, in general any minimum amount that is both calculable and substantially certain to be paid will be treated as readily ascertainable.

(9) **Nonqualified deferred compensation plans linked to qualified employer plans or certain other arrangements.** If a nonqualified deferred compensation plan provides that the amount deferred under the plan is determined under the formula for determining benefits under a qualified employer plan (as defined in § 1.409A-1(a)(2)) or a broad-based foreign retirement plan (as defined in § 1.409A-1(a)(3)(v)) maintained by the service recipient but applied without regard to one or more limitations applicable to the qualified employer plan under the Internal Revenue Code or to the broad-based foreign retirement plan under other applicable law, or that the amount deferred under the nonqualified deferred compensation plan is determined as an amount offset by some or all of the benefits provided under the qualified employer plan or the broad-based foreign retirement plan or the broad-based foreign retirement plan, an increase in amounts deferred under the nonqualified deferred compensation plan that results directly from the operation of the qualified employer plan or broad-based foreign retirement plan (other than service provider actions described in paragraphs (a)(9)(iii) and (iv) of this section) including changes in benefit limitations applicable to the qualified employer plan or the broad-based foreign retirement plan under the Internal Revenue Code or other applicable law does not constitute a deferral election under the nonqualified deferred compensation plan, pro-

vided that such operation does not otherwise result in a change in the time or form of a payment under the nonqualified deferred compensation plan, and provided further that such change in the amounts deferred under the nonqualified deferred compensation plan does not exceed that change in the amounts deferred under the qualified employer plan or the broad-based foreign retirement plan, as applicable. In addition, with respect to such a nonqualified deferred compensation plan, the following actions or failures to act will not constitute a deferral election under the nonqualified deferred compensation plan even if in accordance with the terms of the nonqualified deferred compensation plan, the actions or inactions result in an increase in the amounts deferred under the plan, provided that such actions or inactions do not otherwise affect the time or form of payment under the nonqualified deferred compensation plan and provided further that with respect to actions or inactions described in paragraphs (a)(9)(i) or (ii), the change in the amount deferred under the nonqualified deferred compensation plan does not exceed the change in the amounts deferred under the qualified employer plan or the broad-based foreign retirement plan, as applicable:

(i) A service provider's action or inaction under the qualified employer plan or broad-based foreign retirement plan with respect to whether to elect to receive a subsidized benefit or an ancillary benefit under the qualified employer plan or broad-based foreign retirement plan.

(ii) The amendment of a qualified employer plan or broad-based foreign retirement plan to add or remove a subsidized benefit or an ancillary benefit, or to freeze or limit future accruals of benefits under the qualified plan or freeze or limit future accruals of benefits or reduce existing benefits under the broad-based foreign retirement plan.

(iii) A service provider's action or inaction under a qualified employer plan with respect to elective deferrals and other employee pre-tax contributions subject to the contribution restrictions under section 401(a)(30) [26

USCS § 401(a)(30)] or section 402(g) [26 USCS § 402(g)], including an adjustment to a deferral election under such qualified employer plan, provided that for any given taxable year, the service provider's action or inaction does not result in an increase in the amounts deferred under all nonqualified deferred compensation plans in which the service provider participates (other than amounts described in paragraph (a)(9)(iv) of this section) in excess of the limit with respect to elective deferrals under section 402(g)(1)(A), (B), and (C) [26 USCS § 402(g)(1)(A), (B), and (C)] in effect for the taxable year in which such action or inaction occurs.

(iv) A service provider's action or inaction under a qualified employer plan with respect to elective deferrals and other employee pre-tax contributions subject to the contribution restrictions under section 401(a)(30) [26 USCS § 401(a)(30)] or section 402(g) [26 USCS § 402(g)], and after-tax contributions by the service provider to a qualified employer plan that provides for such contributions, that affects the amounts that are credited under one or more nonqualified deferred compensation plans as matching amounts or other similar amounts contingent on such elective deferrals, employee pre-tax contributions, or after-tax contributions, provided that the total of such matching or contingent amounts, as applicable, never exceeds 100 percent of the matching or contingent amounts that would be provided under the qualified employer plan absent any plan-based restrictions that reflect limits on qualified plan contributions under the Internal Revenue Code.

(10) **Changes in elections under a cafeteria plan.** A change in an election under a cafeteria plan does not constitute a deferral election with respect to an amount deferred under a nonqualified deferred compensation plan to the extent that the change in the amount deferred under the nonqualified deferred compensation plan results solely from the application of the change in amount eligible to be treated as compensation under the terms of the nonqualified deferred compensation plan resulting from the election change

under the cafeteria plan, to a benefit formula under the nonqualified deferred compensation plan based upon the service provider's eligible compensation, and only to the extent that such change applies in the same manner as any other increase or decrease in compensation would apply to such benefit formula.

(11) **Initial deferral election with respect to certain separation pay.** In the case of separation pay (as defined in § 1.409A-1(m)), where such separation pay is the subject of bona fide, arm's length negotiations at the time of the separation from service, an initial deferral election may be made at any time up to the time the service provider obtains a legally binding right to the payment. This paragraph (a)(11) does not apply to any separation pay to which the service provider obtained a legally binding right before the negotiations at the time of the separation from service, including a right to a payment subject to a condition such as that the service provider separate from service other than for cause. In the case of separation pay due to participation in a window program (as defined in § 1.409A-1(b)(9)(vi)), an initial deferral election may be made at any time before the time the election to participate in the window program becomes irrevocable.

(12) **Initial deferral election with respect to certain commissions—(i) Sales commission compensation.** For purposes of this paragraph (a), a service provider earning sales commission compensation is treated as providing the services to which such compensation relates only in the service provider's taxable year in which the customer remits payment to the service recipient or, if applied consistently to all similarly situated service providers, the service provider's taxable year in which the sale occurs. For purposes of this paragraph (a)(12), the term sales commission compensation means compensation or portions of compensation earned by a service provider if a substantial portion of the services provided by such service provider to a service recipient consist of the direct sale of a product or service to an unrelated customer, the compensation paid by the service recipient to the

service provider consists of either a portion of the purchase price for the product or service or an amount substantially all of which is calculated by reference to the volume of sales, and payment of the compensation is either contingent upon the service recipient receiving payment from an unrelated customer for the product or services or, if applied consistently to all similarly situated service providers, is contingent upon the closing of the sales transaction and such other requirements as may be specified by the service recipient before the closing of the sales transaction. For this purpose, a customer is treated as an unrelated customer only if the customer is not related to either the service provider or the service recipient. A person is treated as related to another person if the person would be treated as related to the other person under § 1.409A-1(f)(2)(ii) or the person would be treated as providing management services to the other person under § 1.409A-1(f)(2)(iv).

(ii) **Investment commission compensation.** For purposes of this paragraph (a), a service provider earning investment commission compensation is treated as providing the services to which such compensation relates over the 12 months preceding the date as of which the overall value of the assets or asset accounts is determined for purposes of the calculation of the investment commission compensation. For purposes of this paragraph (a)(12), the term investment commission compensation means the compensation or the portion of compensation earned by a service provider if a substantial portion of the services provided by such service provider to a service recipient to which such compensation relates consists of sales of financial products or other direct customer services to an unrelated customer with respect to customer assets or customer asset accounts, the customer retains the right to terminate the customer relationship and may move or liquidate the assets or asset accounts without undue delay (which may be subject to a reasonable notice period), such compensation consists of a portion of the value of the overall assets or asset account balance, an amount substantially all of which is calculated by reference to the increase in the value of the

overall assets or account balance during a specified period, or both, and the value of the overall assets or account balance and investment commission compensation is determined at least annually. For this purpose, a customer is treated as an unrelated customer only if the customer is not related to either the service provider or the service recipient. A person is treated as related to another person if the person would be treated as related to the other person under § 1.409A-1(f)(2)(ii) or the person would be treated as providing management services to the other person under § 1.409A-1(f)(2)(iv).

(iii) **Commission compensation and related persons.** The rules of paragraphs (a)(12)(i) and (ii) of this section apply to sales commission compensation and investment commission compensation involving a related customer, provided that substantial sales from which commission compensation arises are made, or substantial services from which commission compensation arises are provided, to unrelated customers by the service recipient, the sales and service arrangement and the commission arrangement with respect to the related customer are bona fide, arise from the service recipient's ordinary course of business, and are substantially the same, both in terms and in practice, as the terms and practices applicable to unrelated customers (as defined in such paragraphs) to which individually or in the aggregate substantial sales are made or substantial services provided by the service recipient.

(13) **Initial deferral election with respect to compensation paid for final payroll period**—(i) **In general.** Unless a plan provides otherwise, compensation payable after the last day of the service provider's taxable year solely for services performed during the final payroll period described in section 3401(b) [26 USCS § 3401(b)] containing the last day of the service provider's taxable year or, with respect to a non-employee service provider, a period not longer than the payroll period described in section 3401(b) [26 USCS § 3401(b)], where such amount is payable pursuant to the timing arrangement under

which the service recipient normally compensates service providers for services performed during a payroll period described in section 3401(b) [26 USCS § 3401(b)], or with respect to a non-employee service provider, a period not longer than the payroll period described in section 3401(b) [26 USCS § 3401(b)], is treated as compensation for services performed in the subsequent taxable year in which the payment is made. The preceding sentence does not apply to any compensation paid during such period for services performed during any period other than such final payroll period, such as a payment of an annual bonus. Any amendment of a plan after December 31, 2007, to add a provision providing for a differing treatment of such compensation may not be effective for 12 months from the date the amendment is executed and enacted.

(ii) **Transition rule.** For purposes of this paragraph (a)(13), a plan that was adopted and effective before December 31, 2007, whether written or unwritten, will be treated as designating such compensation for services performed in the taxable year in which the payroll period ends, unless otherwise set forth in writing before December 31, 2007.

(14) **Elections to annualize recurring part-year compensation.** In the case of a service provider receiving recurring part-year compensation, an election to defer all or a portion of the recurring part-year compensation to be earned during a particular service period is considered to meet the requirements of this paragraph (a) if the election is made before the services for which the recurring part-year compensation is paid begin, and the election does not defer payment of any of the recurring part-year compensation to a date beyond the last day of the 13th month following the first date of the service period. For purposes of this paragraph (a)(14), the term recurring part-year compensation means compensation paid for services rendered in a position that the service recipient and service provider reasonably anticipate will continue on similar terms and conditions in subsequent years, and will require services to be provided during successive service periods each of

which comprises less than 12 months (for example, a teacher providing services during a school year comprised of 10 consecutive months), and each of which periods begins in one taxable year of the service provider and ends in the next such taxable year. The rules of this paragraph (a)(14) apply to a particular amount of compensation only once, so that an amount deferred under this rule may not again be treated as recurring part-year compensation for purposes of this paragraph and subject to a second deferral election under this paragraph (a)(14).

(15) **USERRA rights.** The requirements of this paragraph (a) are deemed satisfied to the extent an initial deferral election is provided to satisfy the requirements of the Uniformed Service Employment and Reemployment Rights Act of 1994, as amended, 38 U.S.C. 4301-4334.

(b) *Subsequent changes in time and form of payment*—(1) **In general.** A plan that permits under a subsequent election a delay in a payment or a change in the form of payment (a subsequent deferral election), including a subsequent deferral election made by a service provider or a service recipient, satisfies the requirements of section 409A(a)(4)(C) [26 USCS § 409A(a)(4)(C)] only if the conditions of this paragraph (b) are met. For purposes of this paragraph (b), except as otherwise expressly provided in this section, a subsequent deferral election is not considered made until such election becomes irrevocable under the terms of the plan. Accordingly, a plan may provide that a subsequent deferral election may be changed at any time before the last permissible date for making such a subsequent deferral election. Where a plan permits a subsequent deferral election, the requirements of this paragraph are satisfied only if the following conditions are met:

(i) The plan requires that such election not take effect until at least 12 months after the date on which the election is made.

(ii) In the case of an election related to a payment not described in § 1.409A-3(a)(2) (payment on account of disability), § 1.409A-

3(a)(3) (payment on account of death), or § 1.409A-3(a)(6) (payment on account of the occurrence of an unforeseeable emergency), the plan requires that the payment with respect to which such election is made be deferred for a period of not less than five years from the date such payment would otherwise have been paid (or in the case of a life annuity or installment payments treated as a single payment, five years from the date the first amount was scheduled to be paid).

(iii) The plan requires that any election related to a payment described in § 1.409A-3(a)(4) (payment at a specified time or pursuant to a fixed schedule) be made not less than 12 months before the date the payment is scheduled to be paid (or in the case of a life annuity or installment payments treated as a single payment, 12 months before the date the first amount was scheduled to be paid).

(2) **Definition of payments for purposes of subsequent changes in the time or form of payment**—(i) **In general.** Except as provided in paragraphs (b)(2)(ii) and (iii) of this section, the term payment refers to each separately identified amount to which a service provider is entitled to payment under a plan on a determinable date, and includes amounts applied for the benefit of the service provider. An amount is separately identified only if the amount may be objectively determined under a nondiscretionary formula. For example, an amount identified as 10 percent of the account balance as of a specified payment date would be a separately identified amount. A payment includes the provision of any taxable benefit, including payment in cash or in kind. In addition, a payment includes, but is not limited to, the transfer, cancellation, or reduction of an amount of deferred compensation in exchange for benefits under a welfare benefit plan, a fringe benefit excludible under section 119 [26 USCS § 119] or section 132 [26 USCS § 132], or any other benefit that is excludible from gross income. For additional rules relating to the application of this paragraph (b) to amounts payable at a fixed time or pursuant to a fixed schedule, see § 1.409A-3(i)(1).

(ii) **Life annuities**—(A) **In general.** The entitlement to a life annuity is treated as the entitlement to a single payment. Accordingly, an election to delay payment of a life annuity, or to change the form of payment of a life annuity, must be made at least 12 months before the scheduled commencement of the life annuity, and must defer the payment for a period of not less than five years from the originally scheduled commencement of the life annuity. For purposes of § 1.409A-1, this section, and §§ 1.409A-3 through 1.409A-6, the term life annuity means a series of substantially equal periodic payments, payable not less frequently than annually, for the life (or life expectancy) of the service provider, or a series of substantially equal periodic payments, payable not less frequently than annually, for the life (or life expectancy) of the service provider, followed upon the death or end of the life expectancy of the service provider by a series of substantially equal periodic payments, payable not less frequently than annually, for the life (or life expectancy) of the service provider's designated beneficiary (if any). Notwithstanding the foregoing, a schedule of payments does not fail to be an annuity solely because such plan provides for an immediate payment of the actuarial present value of all remaining annuity payments if the actuarial present value of the remaining annuity payments falls below a predetermined amount, and the immediate payment of such amount does not constitute an accelerated payment for purposes of § 1.409A-3(j), provided that such feature, including the predetermined amount, is established by no later than the time and form of payment is otherwise required to be established, and provided further that any change in such feature, including the predetermined amount, is a change in the time and form of payment. A change in designated beneficiary before any annuity payment has been made under the plan is not a change in the time or form of payment. A change in the form of a payment before any annuity payment has been made under the plan, from one type of life annuity to another type of life annuity with the same scheduled date for the first annuity payment, is not considered a change in the time and form of a payment, provided that the annuities are actuarially equivalent applying reasonable actuarial methods and assumptions. For purposes of this paragraph (b)(2)(ii), a requirement that a service provider obtain the consent of a spouse or other potential recipient of a survivor annuity to change a beneficiary or form of payment is disregarded, so that any annuity form that the service recipient could elect to receive with such consent is considered currently available.

(B) **Certain features disregarded.** Notwithstanding the foregoing provisions of this paragraph (b)(2)(ii), the following features are disregarded for purposes of determining whether a payment form is a life annuity within the meaning of this paragraph (b)(2)(ii), but are not disregarded for purposes of determining whether a life annuity is the actuarial equivalent of another life annuity except as otherwise provided in this paragraph (b)(2)(ii):

(1) Term certain features under which annuity payments continue for the longer of the life of the annuitant or a fixed period of time.

(2) Pop-up features under which payments increase upon the death of the beneficiary or another event that eliminates the right to a survivor annuity.

(3) Cash refund features under which payment is provided upon the death of the last annuitant in an amount that is not greater than the excess of the present value of the annuity at the annuity starting date over the total of payments before the death of the last annuitant.

(4) Features under which an annuity form of payment provides higher periodic payments before the expected commencement of benefits under the Social Security Act (42 U.S.C. ch. 7) or the Railroad Retirement Act (45 U.S.C. 231 et seq.) and lower periodic payments after such expected commencement date, so that the combined periodic payments under the arrangement and the Social Security Act or the Railroad Retirement Act, as applicable, are approximately level before and after such expected commencement date (Social

Security or Railroad Retirement leveling features).

(5) Features providing for an increase in the annuity payment in a manner described in §1.401(a)(9)-6, Q&A-14(a)(1) or (2) (eligible cost-of-living adjustments).

(C) **Subsidized joint and survivor annuities.** For purposes of this paragraph (b)(2)(ii), a joint and survivor annuity will not fail to be treated as actuarially equivalent to a single life annuity due solely to the value of a subsidized survivor annuity benefit, provided that the annual lifetime annuity benefit available to the service provider under the joint and survivor annuity is not greater than the annual lifetime annuity benefit available to the service provider under the single life annuity alternative, and provided that the annual survivor annuity benefit is not greater than the annual lifetime annuity benefit available to the service provider under the joint and survivor annuity.

(D) **Actuarial assumptions and methods.** For purposes of this paragraph (b)(2)(ii), at any given time the same actuarial assumptions and methods must be used in valuing each annuity payment option, in determining whether the payments are actuarially equivalent and such assumptions must be reasonable. This requirement applies over the entire term of the service provider's participation in the plan, such that the annuity payment must be actuarially equivalent at all times for the annuity payment options to be treated as one time and form of payment. There is no requirement that the same actuarial methods and assumptions be used over the term of a service provider's participation in a plan. Accordingly, a plan may change the actuarial assumptions and methods used to determine the life annuity payments provided that all of the actuarial assumptions and methods are reasonable.

(iii) **Installment payments.** The entitlement to a series of installment payments that is not a life annuity is treated as the entitlement to a single payment, unless the plan provides at all times with respect to the amount deferred that the right to the series of installment payments is to be treated as a right to a series of separate payments. For purposes of § 1.409A-1, this section, and §§ 1.409A-3 through 1.409A-6, a series of installment payments refers to an entitlement to the payment of a series of substantially equal periodic amounts to be paid over a predetermined period of years, except to the extent any increase (or decrease) in the amount reflects reasonable earnings (or losses) through the date the amount is paid. For this purpose, a series of installment payments over a predetermined period and a series of installment payments over a shorter or longer period, or a series of installment payments over the same predetermined period but with a different commencement date, are different times and forms of payment. Accordingly, a change in the predetermined period or the commencement date is a change in the time and form of payment. Notwithstanding the foregoing, a schedule of payments does not fail to be an installment payment solely because such plan provides for an immediate payment of all remaining installments if the present value of the deferred amount to be paid in the remaining installment payments falls below a predetermined amount, and the immediate payment of such amount does not constitute an accelerated payment for purposes of § 1.409A-3(j), provided that such feature including the predetermined amount is established by no later than the time and form of payment is otherwise required to be established, and provided further that any change in such feature including the predetermined amount is a change in the time and form of payment.

(iv) **Transition rule.** For purposes of this section, a plan that was adopted and effective before December 31, 2007, whether written or unwritten, that fails to make a designation as to whether the entitlement to a series of payments is to be treated as an entitlement to a series of separate payments under paragraph (b)(2)(iii) of this section, may make such designation on or before December 31, 2007, provided such designation is set forth in writing on or before December 31, 2007.

(3) **Beneficiaries.** The rules of this paragraph (b) governing changes in the time and form of payment apply to elections by beneficiaries with respect to the time and form of payment, as well as elections by service providers or service recipients with respect to the time and form of payment to beneficiaries. An election to change the identity of a beneficiary does not constitute a change in the time and form of payment merely because the election changes the identity of the recipient of the payment, if the time and form of the payment is not otherwise changed. In addition, an election to change the identity of a beneficiary before the initial payment of a life annuity does not constitute a change in the time and form of payment if the change in the time of payments stems solely from the different life expectancy of the new beneficiary, such as in the case of a joint and survivor annuity.

(4) **Domestic relations orders.** The rules of this paragraph (b) governing changes in the time and form of payment do not apply to elections by individuals other than a service provider, with respect to payments to a person other than the service provider, to the extent such elections are reflected in, or made in accordance with, the terms of a domestic relations order (as defined in section 414(p)(1)(B) [26 USCS § 414(p)(1)(B)]).

(5) **Coordination with prohibition against acceleration of payments.** For purposes of applying the prohibition against the acceleration of payments in § 1.409A-3(j), the definition of payment is the same as the definition in paragraph (b)(2) of this section. Accordingly, a change in the form of a payment that results in a more rapid schedule for payments generally will not constitute an acceleration of a payment, if the change in the form of payment is made in compliance with the subsequent deferral rules. For example, a change in form from a 10-year installment payment treated as a single payment to a lump-sum payment would not constitute an acceleration if the change in the form of the payment is made in compliance with the requirements of paragraph (b)(1) of this section, generally meaning that the election to change to a lump-sum payment must be made at least 12 months before the installment payments

were scheduled to commence and the lump-sum payment could not be made until at least five years after the date the installment payments were scheduled to commence. See §1.409A-3(j)(4)(i) with respect to situations in which the failure to accelerate a payment or the modification of a plan term relating to certain accelerated payments will not be subject to the rules of this paragraph (b).

(6) **Application to multiple payment events.** In the case of a plan that permits a payment upon each of a number of potential permissible payment events, such as the earlier of a fixed date or separation from service, the requirements of paragraph (b)(1) of this section are applied separately to each payment (as defined in paragraph (b)(2) of this section) due upon each payment event. Notwithstanding the foregoing, the addition or deletion of a permissible payment event to a plan under which amounts were previously deferred is subject to the rules of this paragraph (b) where the addition or deletion of the permissible payment event may result in a change in the time or form of payment of the amount deferred. For application of the rules governing accelerations of payments to the addition of a permissible payment event to amounts deferred, see §1.409A-3(j).

(7) **Delay of payments under certain circumstances.** A payment may be delayed to a date after the designated payment date under any of the circumstances described in this paragraph (b)(7), and the provision will not fail to meet the requirements of establishing a permissible payment event and the delay in the payment will not constitute a subsequent deferral election, so long as the service recipient treats all payments to similarly situated service providers on a reasonably consistent basis.

(i) **Payments subject to section 162(m)** [26 USCS § 162(m)]. A payment may be delayed to the extent that the service recipient reasonably anticipates that if the payment were made as scheduled, the service recipient's deduction with respect to such payment would not be permitted due to the application of section 162(m) [26 USCS § 162(m)], pro-

vided that the payment is made either during the service provider's first taxable year in which the service recipient reasonably anticipates, or should reasonably anticipate, that if the payment is made during such year, the deduction of such payment will not be barred by application of section 162(m) [26 USCS § 162(m)] or during the period beginning with the date of the service provider's separation from service and ending on the later of the last day of the taxable year of the service recipient in which the service provider separates from service or the 15th day of the third month following the service provider's separation from service, and provided further that where any scheduled payment to a specific service provider in a service recipient's taxable year is delayed in accordance with this paragraph, the delay in payment will be treated as a subsequent deferral election unless all scheduled payments to that service provider that could be delayed in accordance with this paragraph are also delayed. Where the payment is delayed to a date on or after the service provider's separation from service, the payment will be considered a payment upon a separation from service for purposes of the rules under §1.409A-3(i)(2) (payments to specified employees upon a separation from service) and, in the case of a specified employee, the date that is six months after a service provider's separation from service is substituted for any reference to a service provider's separation from service in the first sentence of this paragraph. No election may be provided to the service provider with respect to the timing of the payment under this paragraph (b)(7)(i).

(ii) **Payments that would violate Federal securities laws or other applicable law.** A payment may be delayed where the service recipient reasonably anticipates that the making of the payment will violate Federal securities laws or other applicable law; provided that the payment is made at the earliest date at which the service recipient reasonably anticipates that the making of the payment will not cause such violation. The making of a payment that would cause inclusion in gross income or the application of any penalty provision or other provision of the Internal Revenue

Code is not treated as a violation of applicable law.

(iii) **Other events and conditions.** A service recipient may delay a payment upon such other events and conditions as the Commissioner may prescribe in generally applicable guidance published in the Internal Revenue Bulletin (see § 601.601(d)(2) of this chapter). For additional rules applicable to certain delayed payments pursuant to a change in control event, see § 1.409A-3(i)(5)(iv). For additional rules applicable to amounts payable because of an unforeseeable emergency, see § 1.409A-3(i)(3).

(8) **USERRA rights.** The requirements of this paragraph (b) are deemed met to the extent an election to change the time or form of a payment of deferred compensation is provided to satisfy the requirements of the Uniformed Services Employment and Reemployment Rights Act of 1994, as amended, 38 U.S.C. 4301-4344.

(9) **Examples.** The following examples illustrate the application of the provisions of this section. For purposes of these examples, each employee is an individual with a calendar year taxable year, and is employed by the specified employer:

Example 1. Initial election to defer salary.

Employer ZZ sponsors a plan under which Employee A may elect to defer a percentage of Employee A's salary. Employee A has participated in the plan in prior years. To satisfy the requirements of this section with respect to salary earned in calendar year 2008, if Employee A elects to defer any amount of such salary, the deferral election (including an election as to the time and form of payment) must be made no later than December 31, 2007.

Example 2. Designation of time and form of payment where an initial deferral election is not provided.

Employer YY has a taxable year ending September 30. On July 1, 2008, Employer YY enters into a legally binding obligation to pay Employee B a $10,000 bonus. The amount is not subject to a substantial risk of forfeiture and does not qualify as performance-based compensation as described in § 1.409A-1(e). Employer YY does not provide Employee B an election as to the time and form of payment. Unless the amount is to be paid in accordance with the short-term deferral rule of § 1.409A-1(b)(4), Employer YY must specify the time and form of payment on or before July 1, 2008, to satisfy the requirements of this section.

Example 3. Initial election to defer bonus payable based on services during calendar year.

Employer XX has a taxable year ending September 30. Employee C participates in a bonus plan under which Employee C is entitled to a bonus for services performed during the calendar year that, absent an election by Employee C, will be paid on March 15 of the following year. The amount is not subject to a substantial risk of forfeiture and does not qualify as performance-based compensation as described in § 1.409A-1(e). If Employee C elects to defer the payment of the bonus with respect to services rendered during calendar year 2008, Employee C must elect the time and form of payment not later than December 31, 2007, to satisfy the requirements of this section.

Example 4. Initial election to defer bonus payable based on services during fiscal year other than calendar year.

Employer WW has a taxable year ending September 30. Employee D participates in a bonus plan under which Employee D is entitled to a bonus for services performed during Employer WW's fiscal year that, absent an election by Employee D, will be paid on December 15 of the calendar year in which the fiscal year ends. The amount is not subject to a substantial risk of forfeiture and does not qualify as performance-based compensation as described in § 1.409A-1(e). The amount qualifies as fiscal year compensation. If Employee D elects to defer the payment of the amount related to the fiscal year ending September 30,

2009, to satisfy the requirements of this section Employee D must elect the time and form of payment not later than September 30, 2008.

Example 5. Initial election to defer bonus payable only if service provider completes at least 12 months of services after the election.

Employer VV has a calendar year taxable year. On March 1, 2008, Employer VV grants Employee E a $10,000 bonus, payable on March 1, 2010 (with reasonable interest), provided that Employee E continues performing services as an employee of Employer VV through March 1, 2010. The amount does not qualify as performance-based compensation as described in § 1.409A-1(e), and Employee E already participates in another account balance nonqualified deferred compensation plan. Employee E may make an initial deferral election on or before March 31, 2008 (within 30 days after obtaining a legally binding right), because at least 12 months of additional services are required after the date of election for the risk of forfeiture to lapse.

Example 6. Initial election to defer bonus that would otherwise constitute a short-term deferral.

The same facts as Example 5, except that Employee E does not make an initial deferral election on or before March 31, 2008. Because the right to the compensation would not be treated as a deferral of compensation pursuant to § 1.409A-1(b)(4) absent a deferral election (because the arrangement would be treated as a short-term deferral), Employee E may make an initial deferral election provided that the election may not become effective for 12 months and must defer the payment at least 5 years from March 1, 2010 (the first date the payment could become substantially vested). Accordingly, Employee E may make an election before March 1, 2009, provided that the election defers the payment to a date on or after March 1, 2015 (other than a payment due to death, disability, unforeseeable emergency, or a change in control event).

Example 7. Initial election to defer sales commissions.

Employer UU has a calendar year taxable year. As part of Employee F's services for Employer UU, Employee F sells refrigerators to customers unrelated to Employee F or Employer UU. Under the employment arrangement, Employee F is entitled to 10% of the sales price of any refrigerator Employee F sells, payable only upon the receipt of payment from the customer who purchased the refrigerator. For purposes of the initial deferral rule, Employee F is treated as performing the services related to each refrigerator sale in the calendar year in which each customer pays for the refrigerator.

Example 8. Initial election to defer renewal sales commissions.

The same facts as Example 7, except that Employee F also sells warranties related to the refrigerators sold. Under the warranty arrangement, refrigerator warranty customers are entitled in a future year to extend the warranty for an additional cost to be paid at the time of the extension. Under Employee F's arrangement with Employer UU, Employee F is entitled to 10% of the amount paid for an extension of any warranty, payable upon the receipt of payment from the customer extending the warranty. For purposes of the initial deferral election rule, Employee F is treated as performing the services related to the amount paid for the extension of the warranty in the taxable year in which the customer pays for the warranty extension.

Example 9. Initial election to defer investment commissions. Employer TT is in the trade or business of managing financial assets for customer accounts. Customers who deposit funds in an account with Employer TT are entitled to remove the account balance of such account upon 60-days notice to Employer TT. Employee G sells financial products and provides continuing customer service to certain unrelated customers involving the deposit and maintenance of funds in customer accounts managed by Employer TT. Under the employment arrangement, Employee G is entitled to a set percentage of the aggregate value of the assets held in the accounts of customers to whom Employee G sold financial products and provides customer service. Under the arrangement, the aggregate value of the assets held in the accounts is determined as of June 30 of each year, and unless Employee G elects to defer the payment, the amount is payable to Employee G in a lump sum on December 31 of the year in which the valuation is made. Employee G has no control over the valuation of the assets held in the accounts, or the calculation of the amount due Employee G. For purposes of the initial deferral rule, Employee G is treated as providing the services to which a payment relates during the July 1 through June 30 period ending on the June 30 date as of which the assets held in the account are valued.

Example 10. Initial election to defer part-year compensation. Employee H provides services as a teacher to Employer SS, a school system. The period of services routinely begins on the second Monday of August of one year and ends on the first Friday of June of the subsequent year. Employer SS provides an election to Employee H to receive the compensation for the period of services ratably over the period beginning on the second Monday of August of one year and ending on the last day of August of the subsequent year. Because the compensation constitutes recurring part-year compensation, as defined in paragraph (a)(14) of this section, and because the schedule will provide that all of the recurring part-year compensation is paid no later than September 30 of the subsequent year, Employee H will be deemed to have made a timely deferral election with respect to such recurring part-year compensation if Employee H elects before the first day of the service period to have the recurring part-year compensation paid under such schedule.

Example 11. Initial election to defer negotiated separation pay. Employer RR decides to terminate Employee J's employment involuntarily. As part of the process of terminating Employee J, Employer RR enters into bona fide, arm's length negotiations with respect to the terms of Employee J's termination of employment. As part of the process, Employer RR offers Employee J an amount that is in

addition to any amounts to which Employee J is otherwise entitled, payable either as a lump sum payment at the end of 3 years or in 3 annual payments starting at the date of termination of employment. The election of the time and form of payment by Employee J may be made at any time before Employee J accepts the offer and obtains a legally binding right to the additional amount. The election may not apply to any amount to which Employee J already had a legally binding right.

Example 12. Election of time and form of payments under a window program. Employer QQ establishes a window program, as defined in § 1.409A-1(b)(9)(vi). Individuals who elect to terminate employment under the window program are entitled to receive an amount equal to 2-weeks pay multiplied by every year of service with Employer QQ. The individuals participating in the window program may elect to receive the payment as either a lump sum payment payable on the first day of the month after making the election to participate in the window program, or as a payment of 3 equal annual installments on each January 1 of the first 3 years following the election to participate in the window program. Employee K is eligible to participate in the window program. Employee K will be treated as making a timely deferral election if the election as to the time and form of payment is made on or before the date Employee K's election to participate in the window program becomes irrevocable.

Example 13. Initial election to defer salary earned during final payroll period beginning in one calendar year and ending in the subsequent calendar year. Employer PP pays the salary of its employees, including Employee L, on a bi-weekly basis. One bi-weekly payroll period runs from December 24, 2008, through January 6, 2009, with a scheduled payment date of January 13, 2009. Employer PP sponsors, and Employee L participates in, a nonqualified deferred compensation plan under which Employee L may defer a specified percentage of his annual salary. The plan does not specify that any salary compensation paid for the payroll period in which falls January 1 is to be treated as compensation for services performed during the year preceding the year in which falls that January 1. For purposes of applying the initial deferral election rules, Employee L is deemed to have performed the services for the payroll period December 24, 2008, through January 6, 2009, during the calendar year 2009.

Example 14. Application of deferral election rules and anti-acceleration rules to a nonqualified deferred compensation plan linked to a qualified plan. Employee M participates in a qualified retirement plan that is a defined benefit plan that offers a subsidized early retirement benefit to employees who have attained age 55 and completed 30 years of service. Employee M, who has attained age 55 and completed 30 years of service, also participates in a nonqualified deferred compensation plan, under which the benefit payable is calculated under a formula, with that benefit then reduced by any benefit that Employee M has accrued under the qualified retirement plan. In 2008, Employee M fails to elect the subsidized early retirement benefit under the qualified retirement plan, with the effect that the amounts payable under the nonqualified deferred compensation plan are increased by an amount equal to the reduction in the benefit payable under the qualified plan. In 2009, Employer NN amends the qualified retirement plan to increase benefits under the plan, resulting in a decrease in the amounts payable under the nonqualified deferred compensation plan equal to the increase in the benefit payable under the qualified plan. Neither of these actions constitutes a deferral election or an acceleration of a payment under the nonqualified deferred compensation plan.

Example 15. Subsequent deferral election. Employee N participates in a nonqualified deferred compensation plan. Employee N elects to be paid in a lump sum payment at the earlier of age 65 or separation from service. Employee N anticipates that he will work after age 65, and wishes to defer payment to a later date. Provided that Employee N continues in employment and makes the election by his 64th birthday, Employee N may elect to re-

ceive a lump sum payment at the earlier of age 70 or separation from service.

Example 16. Subsequent deferral election rule—change in form of payment from lump sum payment to life annuity. Employee P participates in a nonqualified deferred compensation plan. Employee P elects to be paid in a lump sum payment at age 65. Employee P wishes to change the payment form to a life annuity. Provided that Employee P makes the election on or before his 64th birthday, Employee P may elect to receive a life annuity commencing at age 70.

Example 17. Subsequent deferral election rule—change in form of payment from life annuity to lump sum payment. Employee Q participates in a nonqualified deferred compensation plan. Employee Q elects to be paid in a life annuity at age 65. Employee Q wishes to change the payment form to a lump sum payment. Provided that Employee Q makes the election on or before his 64th birthday, Employee Q may elect to receive a lump sum payment at age 70.

Example 18. Subsequent deferral election rule—installment payments designated as separate payments. Employee R, whose taxable year is the calendar year, participates in a nonqualified deferred compensation plan that provides for payment in a series of 5 equal annual amounts, each designated as a separate payment. The first payment is scheduled to be made on January 1, 2010. Provided that Employee R makes the election on or before January 1, 2009, Employee R may elect for the first payment scheduled to be made on January 1, 2010, to be made on January 1, 2015. If Employee R makes that election, but does not elect to defer the remaining payments, the remaining payments continue to be due upon January 1 of the 4 consecutive calendar years commencing on January 1, 2011.

Example 19. Subsequent deferral election rule—change in form of payment from installment payments not designated as separate payments to lump sum payment.

Employee S participates in a nonqualified deferred compensation plan that provides for payment in a series of 5 equal annual amounts that are not designated as a series of 5 separate payments. The first amount is scheduled to be paid on January 1, 2010. Employee S wishes to receive the entire amount equal to the sum of all 5 of the amounts to be paid as a lump sum payment. Provided that Employee S makes the election on or before January 1, 2009, Employee S may elect to receive a lump sum payment on or after January 1, 2015.

Example 20. Subsequent deferral election rule—change in form of payment from installment payments designated as separate payments to lump sum payment.

Employee T participates in a nonqualified deferred compensation plan that provides for payment in a series of 5 equal annual amounts each of which is designated as a separate payment. The first amount is scheduled to be paid on January 1, 2010. Employee T wishes to receive the entire amount equal to the sum of all 5 of the amounts in a single lump sum payment. Provided that Employee T makes the election on or before January 1, 2009, Employee T may elect to receive a lump sum payment on or after January 1, 2019.

Example 21. Subsequent deferral election rule—change in form of payment from one life annuity form to another life annuity form.

Employee U participates in a nonqualified deferred compensation plan that permits Employee U to elect before Employee U's separation from service whether to be paid in the form of a single life annuity beginning on the first day of the month following Employee U's separation from service, or an annuity beginning on the first day of the month following Employee U's separation from service under which annuity payments continue for Employee U's lifetime but not less than 10 years. The two types of annuities are actuarially equivalent at all times applying reasonable actuarial methods and assumptions. For purposes of this section, the two types of annuities are treated as a single form of payment. Accordingly, the election provided under the plan is not treated as providing a subsequent deferral election or accelerated payment, and an election by Em-

ployee U under the plan between the two annuity options made before the first scheduled payment date for an annuity payment is not treated as a subsequent deferral election or an acceleration of a payment.

Example 22. Subsequent deferral election rule—change in time of payment from payment at specified age to payment at later of specified age or separation from service.

Employee V participates in a nonqualified deferred compensation plan that provides for a lump sum payment at age 65. Employee V wishes to modify the plan so that the deferred amount will be payable upon the later of Employee V's attainment of a specified age or separation from service. Provided that Employee V makes such election on or before his 64th birthday, Employee V may modify the plan so Employee V will receive a lump sum payment upon the later of age 70 or separation from service.

Example 23. Subsequent deferral election rule—change in time of payment from payment at separation from service to payment at later of separation from service or specified age.

Employee W participates in a nonqualified deferred compensation plan that provides for a lump sum payment at separation from service. Employee W wishes to make the payment payable upon the later of separation from service or a predetermined age. Provided that Employee W makes such election on or before the date 1 year before a separation from service, Employee W may elect to receive a lump sum payment upon the later of the date 5 years following a separation from service or at a specified age.

Example 24. Subsequent deferral election rule—change in time of payment from payment at separation from service to payment at a change in control event.

Employee X participates in a nonqualified deferred compensation plan that provides for a lump sum payment at separation from service. Employee X wishes to change the payment provision such that the payment is payable upon a change in control event. A change in the distribution provision to provide for a payment only upon a change in control event will violate the rules governing payment provisions, because the change could result in an acceleration if the change in control event occurs before Employee X separates from service, or a subsequent deferral if the change in control does not occur until after Employee X separates from service. However, provided that Employee X makes such election on or before the date 1 year before a separation from service, Employee X may elect to receive a payment upon the later of a change in control event or 5 years following a separation from service.

(c) *Special rules for certain resident aliens.* For the first taxable year of an individual in which such individual is a resident alien, a nonqualified deferred compensation plan is deemed to meet the requirements of paragraph (a) of this section if, with respect to compensation payable for services performed during that first taxable year or with respect to compensation the right to which is subject to a substantial risk of forfeiture as of the first day of that first taxable year, an initial deferral election is made by the end of such first taxable year, provided that the initial deferral election may not apply to amounts that have already been paid or made available to the service provider before the election is made. For any year after the first taxable year in which an individual is classified as a resident alien, this paragraph (c) does not apply, provided that a taxable year may again be treated as the first taxable year in which an individual is classified as a resident alien if such individual is classified as a resident alien in that taxable year and has not been classified as a resident alien for the three consecutive taxable years immediately preceding that taxable year.

§ 1.409A-3. Permissible payments.

(a) *In general.* The requirements of section 409A(a)(2)(A) [26 USCS § 409A(a)(2)(A)] are met only if the plan provides that an amount of deferred compensation under the plan may be paid only upon an

event or at a time set forth in this paragraph (a):

(1) The service provider's separation from service (as defined in § 1.409A-1(h) and in accordance with paragraph (i)(2) of this section).

(2) The service provider becoming disabled (in accordance with paragraph (i)(4) of this section).

(3) The service provider's death.

(4) A time or a fixed schedule specified under the plan (in accordance with paragraph (i)(1) of this section).

(5) A change in the ownership or effective control of the corporation, or in the ownership of a substantial portion of the assets of the corporation (in accordance with paragraph (i)(5) of this section).

(6) The occurrence of an unforeseeable emergency (in accordance with paragraph (i)(3) of this section).

(b) *Designation of payment upon a permissible payment event.* Except as otherwise specified in this section, a plan provides for the payment upon an event described in paragraph (a)(1), (2), (3), (5), or (6) of this section if the plan provides the date of the event is the payment date, or specifies another payment date that is objectively determinable and nondiscretionary at the time the event occurs. A plan may also provide that a payment upon an event described in paragraph (a)(1), (2), (3), (5), or (6) of this section is to be made in accordance with a schedule that is objectively determinable and nondiscretionary based on the date the event occurs and that would qualify as a fixed schedule under paragraph (i)(1) of this section if the payment event were instead a fixed date, provided that the schedule must be fixed at the time the permissible payment event is designated. In addition, a plan may provide that a payment, including a payment that is part of a schedule, is to be made during a designated taxable year of the service provider that is objectively determinable and nondiscretionary at the time the payment event occurs such as, for example, a schedule of three substantially equal payments payable during the first three taxable years following the taxable year in which a separation from service occurs. A plan may also provide that a payment, including a payment that is part of a schedule, is to be made during a designated period objectively determinable and nondiscretionary at the time the payment event occurs, but only if the designated period both begins and ends within one taxable year of the service provider or the designated period is not more than 90 days and the service provider does not have a right to designate the taxable year of the payment (other than an election that complies with the subsequent deferral election rules of § 1.409A-2(b)). Where a plan provides for a period of more than one day following a payment event during which a payment may be made, such as within 90 days following the date of the event, the payment date for purposes of the subsequent deferral rules under § 1.409A-2(b) is treated as the first possible date upon which a payment could be made under the terms of the plan. A plan may provide for payment upon the earliest or latest of more than one event or time, provided that each event or time is described in paragraphs (a)(1) through (6) of this section. For examples illustrating the provisions of this paragraph, see paragraph (i)(1)(vi) of this section.

(c) *Designation of alternative specified dates or payment schedules based upon date of permissible event.* Except as otherwise provided in this paragraph (c), for an amount of deferred compensation under a plan, the plan may designate only one time and form of payment upon the occurrence of each event described in paragraph (a)(1), (2), (3), (5), or (6) of this section. For example, a plan does not satisfy the requirements of this paragraph (c) if it provides for one payment date or schedule of payments if a specified event occurs on a Monday, but another payment date or schedule of payments if the event occurs on any other day of the week. However, a plan that provides for a payment upon an event described in paragraph (a)(2), (3), (5), or (6) of this section may allow for an alternative payment schedule if the event occurs on or before one (but not more than one) specified

date, provided that the addition or deletion of such a different time and form of payment applicable to an existing deferral is subject to § 1.409A-2(b) (subsequent deferral elections) and paragraph (j) of this section (accelerated payments). For example, a plan may provide that a service provider will receive a lump sum payment of the service provider's entire benefit under the plan on the first day of the month following a change in control event that occurs before the service provider attains age 55, but will receive 5 substantially equal annual payments commencing on the first day of the month following a change in control event that occurs on or after the service provider attains age 55. In the case of a plan that provides that a payment upon an event described in paragraph (a)(1) of this section (a payment upon a separation from service), a different time and form of payment may be designated with respect to a separation from service under each of the following conditions, provided that the addition or deletion of such a different time and form of payment applicable to an existing deferral is subject to § 1.409A-2(b) and paragraph (j) of this section:

(1) A separation from service during a limited period of time not to exceed two years following a change in control event (as defined in paragraph (i)(5) of this section).

(2) A separation from service before or after a specified date (for example, the attainment of a specified age), or a separation from service before or after a combination of a specified date, such as attaining a specified age, and a specified period of service determined under a predetermined, nondiscretionary, objective formula or pursuant to the method for crediting service under a qualified plan sponsored by the service recipient.

(3) A separation from service not described in paragraphs (c)(1) or (c)(2) of this section.

(d) *When a payment is treated as made upon the designated payment date.* Except as otherwise specified in this section, a payment is treated as made upon the date specified under the plan (including a date specified under paragraph (a)(4) of this section) if the payment is made at such date or a later date within the same taxable year of the service provider or, if later, by the 15th day of the third calendar month following the date specified under the plan and the service provider is not permitted, directly or indirectly, to designate the taxable year of the payment. In addition, a payment is treated as made upon the date specified under the plan (including a date specified under paragraph (a)(4) of this section) and is not treated as an accelerated payment if the payment is made no earlier than 30 days before the designated payment date and the service provider is not permitted, directly or indirectly to designate the taxable year of the payment. For purposes of this paragraph, if the date specified is only a designated taxable year of the service provider, or a period of time during such a taxable year, the date specified under the plan is treated as the first day of such taxable year or the first day of the period of time during such taxable year, as applicable. The payment with respect to a stock right generally occurs upon the exercise of the stock right, so that where a stock right designates a fixed exercise date, the stock right will be deemed to have been paid at such date if the exercise and payment occur on such date or a later date within the same taxable year of the service provider or, if later, by the 15th day of the third calendar month following the exercise date specified under the plan. If calculation of the amount of the payment is not administratively practicable due to events beyond the control of the service provider (or service provider's beneficiary), the payment will be treated as made upon the date specified under the plan if the payment is made during the first taxable year of the service provider in which the calculation of the amount of the payment is administratively practicable. For purposes of this paragraph, the inability of a service recipient to calculate the amount or timing of a payment due to a failure of a service provider (or service provider's beneficiary) to provide reasonably available information necessary to make such calculation does not constitute an event beyond the control of the service provider. Similarly, if the making of the pay-

ment at the date specified under the plan would jeopardize the ability of the service recipient to continue as a going concern, the payment will be treated as made upon the date specified under the plan if the payment is made during the first taxable year of the service provider in which the making of the payment would not have such effect.

(e) *Designation of time and form of payment with respect to earnings.* A nonqualified deferred compensation plan that provides for actual or notional earnings to be credited on amounts of deferred compensation may specify, in accordance with the requirements of § 1.409A-2(a) (initial deferral elections), that such earnings are treated separately from the right to the other amounts deferred under the plan for purposes of designating the time and form of payments under such plan, provided that to satisfy the requirements of this paragraph (e), actual or notional earnings must be credited at least annually. For these purposes, a right to dividend equivalents may be treated analogously to a right to actual or notional earnings on an amount of deferred compensation. For purposes of this paragraph (e), the term dividend equivalents means the right to an amount equal to all or a specified portion of dividends declared and paid, if any, on a specified number of shares of stock.

(f) *Substitutions.* Except as otherwise provided under these regulations, the payment of an amount as a substitute for a payment of deferred compensation will be treated as a payment of the deferred compensation. A forfeiture or voluntary relinquishment of an amount of deferred compensation will not be treated as a payment of the compensation, but there is no forfeiture or voluntary relinquishment for this purpose if an amount is paid, or a legally binding right to a payment is created, that acts as a substitute for the forfeited or voluntarily relinquished amount. Whether a payment or a right to a payment acts as a substitute for a payment of deferred compensation is determined based on all the facts and circumstances. However, where the payment of an amount results in an actual or potential reduction of, or current or future offset to, an amount of deferred compensation, or if the service provider receives a loan the repayment of which is secured by or may be accomplished through an offset of or a reduction in an amount deferred under a nonqualified deferred compensation plan, the payment or loan is a substitute for the deferred compensation. In addition, where a service provider's right to deferred compensation is made subject to anticipation, alienation, sale, transfer, assignment, pledge, encumbrance, attachment, or garnishment by creditors of the service provider or the service provider's beneficiary, the deferred compensation is treated as having been paid. For the treatment of certain offsets, see paragraph (j)(4)(xiii) of this section. Even where there is no explicit reduction or offset, the payment of an amount or creation of a new right to a payment proximate to the purported forfeiture or voluntary relinquishment of a right to deferred compensation is presumed to be a substitute for the deferred compensation. The presumption is rebuttable by a showing that the compensation paid would have been received regardless of the forfeiture or voluntary relinquishment of the right to deferred compensation. Factors indicating that a payment would have been received regardless of such forfeiture or voluntarily relinquishment include that the amount paid is materially less than the forfeited or relinquished amount, or consists of a type of payment customarily made in the ordinary course of business of the service recipient to service providers who do not forfeit or relinquish deferred compensation (for example, a payment of accrued but unused leave or a payment for a release of actual or potential claims). See § 1.409A-1(b)(9)(i) with respect to certain separation pay plans.

(g) *Disputed payments and refusals to pay.* If a service recipient fails to make a payment in whole or in part as of the date specified under a plan, either intentionally or unintentionally, other than with the express or implied consent of the service provider, the payment will be treated as made upon the date specified under the plan if the service provider accepts the portion (if any) of the payment that the service recipient is willing to make (unless such acceptance will result in a relinquishment of the claim to all or part of the remaining amount), makes prompt and reasonable, good faith efforts to collect the remaining portion of the payment, and any further payment (including payment of a lesser amount that satisfies the obligation to make the payment) is made no later than the end of the first taxable year of the service provider in which the service recipient and the service provider enter into a legally binding settlement of such dispute, the service recipient concedes that the amount is payable, or the service recipient is required to make such payment pursuant to a final and nonappealable judgment or other binding decision. For purposes of this paragraph (g), efforts to collect the payment will be presumed not to be prompt, reasonable, good faith efforts, unless the service provider provides notice to the service recipient within 90 days of the latest date upon which the payment could have been timely made in accordance with the terms of the plan and these regulations, and unless, if not paid, the service provider takes further enforcement measures within 180 days after such latest date. For purposes of this paragraph (g), a service recipient is not treated as having failed to make a payment where pursuant to the terms of the plan the service provider is required to request payment, or otherwise provide information or take any other action, and the service provider has failed to take such action. In addition, for purposes of this paragraph (g), the service provider is deemed to have requested that a payment not be made, rather than the service recipient having failed to make such payment, where the service recipient's decision to refuse to make the payment is made by the service provider or a member of the service provider's family (as defined in section 267(c)(4) [26 USCS § 267(c)(4)] applied as if the family of an individual includes the spouse of any member of the family), or any person or group of persons over whom the service provider or service provider's family member has effective control, or any person any portion of whose compensation is controlled the service provider or service provider's family member.

(h) *Special rule for certain resident aliens.* An agreement, method, program, or other arrangement that is, or constitutes part of, a nonqualified deferred compensation plan is deemed to meet the requirements of this section with respect to any amount payable in the first taxable year of the service provider in which a service provider is a resident alien, and with respect to any amount payable in a subsequent taxable year if no later than the last day of the first taxable year of the service provider in which the service provider is a resident alien, the plan is amended as necessary so that the times and forms of payment of amounts payable in a subsequent year comply with the provisions of this section. For any year after the first taxable year of an individual in which the individual is a resident alien, this paragraph (h) does not apply, provided that a taxable year may again be treated as the first taxable year in which an individual is a resident alien if such individual has not been a resident alien for at least three consecutive taxable years immediately preceding the taxable year in which the service provider is again a resident alien.

(i) *Definitions and special rules*—(1) **Specified time or fixed schedule**—(i) **In general.** Amounts are payable at a specified time or pursuant to a fixed schedule if objectively determinable amounts are payable at a date or dates that are nondiscretionary and objectively determinable at the time the amount is deferred. An amount is objectively determinable for this purpose if the amount is specifically identified or if the amount may be determined at the time payment is due pursuant to an objective, nondiscretionary formula specified at the time the amount is deferred (for example, 50 percent of a specified account balance). Except as otherwise provided in paragraph (i)(1) of this section, an amount is not objectively determinable if the amount of the payment is based all or in part upon the occurrence of an event, including the consummation of a transaction by, or a payment of an amount to, a service recipient. If an amount is payable in a service provider's taxable year (or pursuant to a fixed schedule of taxable years of the service provider) that is

designated at the time the amount is deferred and that is objectively determinable, the amount is treated as payable at a specified time (or pursuant to a fixed schedule), provided that for purposes of the application of the subsequent deferral rules contained in § 1.409A-2(b), the specified time or fixed schedule of payments is deemed to refer to the first day of the relevant taxable year or years. A specified time or fixed schedule also includes the designation at the time the amount is deferred of a defined period or periods within the service provider's taxable year or taxable years that are objectively determinable, provided that no such defined period may begin within one taxable year and end within another taxable year, and provided further that for purposes of the application of the subsequent deferral rules contained in § 1.409A-2(b), the specified time or fixed schedule of payments is deemed to refer to the first day of the relevant period in which the payment will be made. A plan may provide that a payment upon the lapse of a substantial risk of forfeiture is to be made in accordance with a fixed schedule that is objectively determinable based on the date the substantial risk of forfeiture lapses (disregarding any discretionary acceleration of the lapse of the substantial risk of forfeiture), provided that the schedule must be fixed on the date the time and form of payment are designated, and any change in the fixed schedule will constitute a change in the time and form of payment. For example, a plan that provides for a bonus payment subject to the condition that the service provider complete three years of service, and subject to the further condition that such requirement of continued services will lapse upon the occurrence of an initial public offering, which condition if applied alone would constitute a substantial risk of forfeiture, may provide that a service provider is entitled to substantially equal payments on each of the first three anniversaries of the date the substantial risk of forfeiture lapses (the earlier of three years of service or the date of an initial public offering).

(ii) **Payment schedules with formula and fixed limitations**—(A) **Individual limi-**

tations. A schedule of payments does not fail to be a fixed schedule of payments where the amount of a payment or payments that may be paid at a specified time or during a specified period is limited by an objective nondiscretionary formula or a specified amount that is not under the effective control of the service provider and is not subject to the exercise of discretion by the service recipient, where such limitation is established on or before the date the time and form of payment is otherwise required to be set under these regulations, and the plan specifies the time and form of any payment that will be made or completed after its original payment date due to the application of the limitation. A change in the limitation or a change in the time and form of any payment that exceeds the limitation is subject to the requirements of § 1.409A-2(b) (subsequent deferral elections) and paragraph (j) of this section (accelerated payments). For purposes of this paragraph, a plan provision that reduces a schedule of periodic payments on a dollar-for-dollar basis by the amount of Social Security payments received or receivable may be treated as a nondiscretionary, objective formula limitation, if such reduction does not otherwise affect the time of payment of the deferred compensation (other than a forfeiture due to the reduction), including changes based on the service provider's eligibility or elections related to Social Security benefits. Similarly, a plan provision that reduces a schedule of periodic payments on a dollar-for-dollar basis by the amount of bona fide disability pay (within the meaning of § 1.409A-1(a)(5)) received or receivable may be treated as a nondiscretionary, objective formula limitation, if the disability payments are made pursuant to a plan sponsored by the service recipient that covers a substantial number of service providers and was established before the service provider became disabled, and if such reduction does not otherwise affect the time of payment of the deferred compensation (other than a forfeiture due to the reduction). Whether an amendment to, or other change in the benefit payable under, such bona fide disability plan results in an acceleration of a payment for purposes of paragraph (j) of this section or

a subsequent election to delay the time or change the form of payment for purposes of § 1.409A-2(b) is determined based on all of the relevant facts and circumstances.

(B) **Limitations on aggregate payments to all participants in substantially identical plans.** A schedule of payments does not fail to be a fixed schedule of payments where the amount of the aggregate payments that will be made during a specified period of time to all participants in substantially identical plans is limited by an objective nondiscretionary formula or specified amount that is not under the effective control of the service provider and is not subject to the exercise of discretion by the service recipient, where the limit is established on or before the date the time and form of payment of the amount deferred is otherwise required to be set under these regulations, the method of allocating payments among the participants where there is an overall limitation on the aggregate amount that may be paid to a group of service providers during a specified period is an objective nondiscretionary allocation method that is not under the effective control of the service provider and is not subject to the exercise of discretion by the service recipient, the method is established on or before the date the time and form of payment of the amount deferred is otherwise required to be set, and the plan specifies the time and form of any payment of any amount that will be paid after its original payment date due to the application of the limitation. A change in the limitation or a change in the time and form of payment of any payment that is not otherwise made at the scheduled payment date due to application of the formula limitation is subject to the requirements of § 1.409A-2(b) (subsequent deferral elections) and paragraph (j) of this section (accelerated payments).

(iii) **Payment schedules determined by timing of payments received by the service recipient.** A payment schedule determined by reference to the timing of payments received by the service recipient (not including payments from one entity to another entity where both entities are treated as part of a single service recipient), meets the requirements of a specified date or fixed schedule of payments if the following conditions are met:

(A) The payments due to the service recipient arise from bona fide and routine transactions in the ordinary course of business of the service recipient.

(B) The service provider does not have effective control of the service recipient, the person from whom such amounts are due, or the collection of any of the amounts due to the service recipient.

(C) The payment schedule provides an objective, nondiscretionary method of identification of the payments to the service recipient from which the amount of the payment from the service recipient to the service provider is determined.

(D) The payment schedule provides an objective, nondiscretionary schedule under which the payments will be made to the service provider.

(E) The payments to the service recipient from which the amount of the payments from service recipient to the service provider are determined result from sales of a type that the service recipient is in the trade or business of making and makes frequently, and either all such sales by the service recipient are taken into account for purposes of determining the payment to the service provider, or there is a legitimate, non-tax business reason for identifying the specific sales taken into account.

(iv) **Reimbursement or in-kind benefit plans**—(A) **General rule.** A plan that provides for reimbursements of expenses incurred by a service provider, or in-kind benefits, meets the requirements of a specified date or fixed schedule of payments with respect to such reimbursements or benefits if the following conditions are met:

(1) The plan provides an objectively determinable nondiscretionary definition of the expenses eligible for reimbursement or of the in-kind benefits to be provided.

(2) The plan provides for the reimbursement of expenses incurred or for the provision of the in-kind benefits during an objectively and specifically prescribed period (including the lifetime of the service provider).

(3) The plan provides that the amount of expenses eligible for reimbursement, or in-kind benefits provided, during a service provider's taxable year may not affect the expenses eligible for reimbursement, or in-kind benefits to be provided, in any other taxable year.

(4) The reimbursement of an eligible expense is made on or before the last day of the service provider's taxable year following the taxable year in which the expense was incurred.

(5) The right to reimbursement or in-kind benefits is not subject to liquidation or exchange for another benefit.

(B) **Medical reimbursement arrangements.** Notwithstanding the foregoing, an arrangement providing for the reimbursement of expenses referred to in section 105(b) [26 USCS § 105(b)] will not be deemed to fail to meet the requirements of paragraph (i)(1)(iv)(A)(3) of this section solely because the arrangement provides for a limit on the amount of expenses that may be reimbursed under such arrangement over some or all of the period in which the reimbursement arrangement remains in effect.

(v) **Tax gross-up payments.** A plan providing a right to a tax gross-up payment will be treated as providing for payment at a specified time or on a fixed schedule of payments if the plan provides that payment will be made, and the payment is made, by the end of the service provider's taxable year next following the service provider's taxable year in which the service provider remits the related taxes. For purposes of this paragraph (i)(1)(v), the term tax gross-up payment refers to a payment to reimburse the service provider in an amount equal to all or a designated portion of the Federal, state, local, or foreign taxes imposed upon the service provider as a result of compensation paid or made available to the service provider by the service recipient, including the amount of additional taxes imposed upon the service provider due to the service recipient's payment of the initial taxes on such compensation. In addition, a right to the reimbursement of expenses incurred due to a tax audit or litigation addressing the existence or amount of a tax liability, whether Federal, state, local, or foreign, satisfies the requirement of a fixed time and form of payment if the right to the reimbursement provides that payment will be made, and the payment is made, by the end of the service provider's taxable year following the service provider's taxable year in which the taxes that are the subject of the audit or litigation are remitted to the taxing authority, or where as a result of such audit or litigation no taxes are remitted, the end of the service provider's taxable year following the service provider's taxable year in which the audit is completed or there is a final and nonappealable settlement or other resolution of the litigation. Nothing in this paragraph (i)(1)(v) otherwise alters the application of section 409A [26 USCS § 409A] to the underlying compensation arrangement or other arrangement that results in the taxes subject to the right to the tax gross-up payment.

(vi) **Examples.** The following examples (in which each employee is an individual whose taxable year is the calendar year) illustrate the principles of paragraphs (a), (b), (c), (d), and (i)(1) of this section:

Example 1. Employee A provides services as an employee of Employer Z, but is not a specified employee. Employee A participates in a nonqualified deferred compensation plan providing for a lump sum payment payable on or before December 31 of the calendar year in which Employee A separates from service. The plan provides for a payment upon a separation from service in compliance with this section.

Example 2. Employee B provides services as an employee of Employer Y, but is not a specified employee. Employee B participates in a nonqualified deferred compensation plan providing for a lump sum payment payable on or before the 90th day immediately

following the date upon which Employee B separates from service. Employer Y retains the sole discretion to determine when during the 90-day period the payment will be made. Although the plan does not specify a period during one calendar year in which the payment will be made, the plan provides for a payment upon a separation from service in compliance with this section because the period over which the payment may be made is not longer than 90 days.

Example 3. Employee C provides services as an employee of Employer X, but is not a specified employee. Employee C participates in a nonqualified deferred compensation plan providing for a lump sum payment payable on or before the 180th day following the date upon which Employee C separates from service. Employer X retains the sole discretion to determine when during the 180-day period the payment will be made. Because the plan does not specify a period during one calendar year in which the payment will be made, and because the period over which the payment may be made is longer than 90 days, the plan does not provide for a payment upon a separation from service that complies with this section.

Example 4. Employee D provides services as an employee of Employer W, but is not a specified employee. Employee D participates in a nonqualified deferred compensation plan providing for 10 installment payments payable on the first 10 anniversaries of the date Employee D separates from service, provided that no installment payment in any year may be more than 1% of Employer W's net income for the previous calendar year, and provided further that the excess over such limit that would otherwise be payable but is not paid due to application of the limit will become payable as of the first installment payment date at which time such amount, in combination with any installment payment otherwise due Employee D, does not exceed 1% of Employer W's net income for the previous calendar year. Provided that Employee D does not retain effective control of the calculation of Employer W's net income or the amount that Employee D will not be paid due to application of the limit, the plan provides for a schedule of payments upon a separation from service that complies with this section.

Example 5. Employee E and Employee F provide services as employees of Employer V, but neither is a specified employee. Employee E and Employee F both participate in substantially identical nonqualified deferred compensation plans providing for 10 installment payments payable on the first 10 anniversaries of the date the respective employee separates from service, provided that the total amount of installment payments in any year may not be more than 1% of Employer V's net income for the previous year, that where any payments are not made due to application of the limit the determination of the amount not paid to a particular employee will be made by applying the overall limit proportionately based upon the installment payment due the employee that year, and that the excess over such limit that would otherwise be payable but is not paid due to application of the limit will become payable as of the first installment payment date at which time such amount, in combination with any installment payments otherwise due the participants, does not exceed 1% of Employer V's net income for the previous calendar year. Provided that neither Employee E nor Employee F retains effective control of the calculation of Employer V's net income or the amount that the respective employee will not be paid due to application of the limit, the plan provides for a schedule of payments upon a separation from service that complies with this section.

Example 6. Employee G provides services as an employee of Employer U, but is not a specified employee. As a bona fide part of this employment relationship, Employee G provides professional services to clients of Employer U as part of the bona fide, ordinary course of Employer U's trade or business. Under an arrangement between Employee G and Employer U, Employer U agrees to pay Employee G upon Employee G's separation from service an amount equal to 5% of any amount collected from Company T, a client of Em-

ployer U for which Employee G performed services during his employment with Employer U, during the 36 months following Employee G's separation from service. Under the arrangement, the amounts due to Employee G based upon payments received by Employer U during any calendar year are payable to Employee G on April 1 of the subsequent calendar year. Provided that Employee G does not have effective control of Employer U, Company T, or the collection of any amounts due Employer Y from Company T, the arrangement provides for a schedule of payments upon a separation from service that complies with this section.

Example 7. Employee H provides services as an employee of Employer S, but is not a specified employee. Under a plan sponsored by Employer S, Employee H has a legally binding right upon a separation from service to the reimbursement of country club dues paid in the calendar year of the separation from service and each of the next 3 calendar years following the separation from service in an amount not to exceed $30,000 in any calendar year, provided that the amount of dues paid in any calendar year that are eligible for reimbursement equals only the amount actually expended during such calendar year, and the maximum amount available for reimbursement in any calendar year will not be increased or decreased to reflect the amount expended or reimbursed in a prior or subsequent calendar year. The plan further provides that any reimbursement must be paid to Employee H by December 31 of the calendar year following the year in which Employee H pays the country club dues. The reimbursement plan provides for a schedule of payments upon a separation from service that complies with this section.

Example 8. Employee J provides services as an employee of Employer Q, but is not a specified employee. Under a plan sponsored by Employer Q, Employee J has a legally binding right upon a separation from service to the reimbursement of country club dues paid during the calendar year in which the separation from service occurs and the next 3 calendar years in a total amount not to exceed $90,000. The plan further provides that any reimbursement must be paid to Employee J by December 31 of the calendar year following the year in which Employee J pays the country club dues. Because the reimbursement of a payment of country club dues in one calendar year may affect the amount of country club dues available for reimbursement in another calendar year, the plan does not provide for a schedule of payments upon a separation from service that complies with this section.

(2) **Separation from service—required delay in payment to a specified employee pursuant to a separation from service**—(i) **In general.** In the case of any service provider who is a specified employee (as defined in § 1.409A-1(i)) as of the date of a separation from service, the requirements of paragraph (a)(1) of this section permitting a payment upon a separation from service are satisfied only if payments may not be made before the date that is six months after the date of separation from service (or, if earlier than the end of the six-month period, the date of death of the specified employee). For this purpose, a service provider who is not a specified employee as of the date of a separation from service will not be treated as subject to this requirement even if the service provider would have become a specified employee if the service provider had continued to provide services through the next specified employee effective date. Similarly, a service provider who is treated as a specified employee as of the date of a separation from service will be subject to this requirement even if the service provider would not have been treated as a specified employee after the next specified employee effective date had the specified employee continued providing services through the next specified employee effective date. Notwithstanding the foregoing, this paragraph (i)(2)(i) does not apply to a payment made under the circumstances described in paragraph (j)(4)(ii) (domestic relations order), (j)(4)(iii) (conflicts of interest), or (j)(4)(vi) (payment of employment taxes) of this section.

(ii) **Application of payment rules to delayed payments.** The required delay in payment is met if payments to which a specified employee would otherwise be entitled during the first six months following the date of separation from service are accumulated and paid on the first day of the seventh month following the date of separation from service, or if each payment to which a specified employee is otherwise entitled upon a separation from service is delayed by six months. A service recipient may retain discretion to choose which method will be implemented, provided that no direct or indirect election as to the method may be provided to the service provider. For an affected specified employee, a date upon which the plan or the service recipient designates that the payment will be made after the six-month delay is treated as a fixed payment date for purposes of paragraph (d) of this section once the separation from service has occurred.

(3) **Unforeseeable emergency**—(i) **Definition.** For purposes of §§ 1.409A-1 and 1.409A-2, this section, and §§ 1.409A-4 through 1.409A-6, an unforeseeable emergency is a severe financial hardship to the service provider resulting from an illness or accident of the service provider, the service provider's spouse, the service provider's beneficiary, or the service provider's dependent (as defined in section 152 [26 USCS § 152], without regard to section 152(b)(1), (b)(2), and (d)(1)(B) [26 USCS § 152(b)(1), (b)(2), and (d)(1)(B)]); loss of the service provider's property due to casualty (including the need to rebuild a home following damage to a home not otherwise covered by insurance, for example, not as a result of a natural disaster); or other similar extraordinary and unforeseeable circumstances arising as a result of events beyond the control of the service provider. For example, the imminent foreclosure of or eviction from the service provider's primary residence may constitute an unforeseeable emergency. In addition, the need to pay for medical expenses, including non-refundable deductibles, as well as for the costs of prescription drug medication, may constitute an unforeseeable emergency. Finally, the need to pay for the funeral

expenses of a spouse, a beneficiary, or a dependent (as defined in section 152 [26 USCS § 152], without regard to section 152(b)(1), (b)(2), and (d)(1)(B) [26 USCS § 152(b)(1), (b)(2), and (d)(1)(B)]) may also constitute an unforeseeable emergency. Except as otherwise provided in this paragraph (i)(3)(i), the purchase of a home and the payment of college tuition are not unforeseeable emergencies. Whether a service provider is faced with an unforeseeable emergency permitting a distribution under this paragraph (i)(3)(i) is to be determined based on the relevant facts and circumstances of each case, but, in any case, a distribution on account of unforeseeable emergency may not be made to the extent that such emergency is or may be relieved through reimbursement or compensation from insurance or otherwise, by liquidation of the service provider's assets, to the extent the liquidation of such assets would not cause severe financial hardship, or by cessation of deferrals under the plan. A plan may provide for a payment upon a specific type or types of unforeseeable emergency, without providing for payment upon all unforeseeable emergencies, provided that any event upon which a payment may be made qualifies as an unforeseeable emergency.

(ii) **Amount of payment permitted upon an unforeseeable emergency.** Distributions because of an unforeseeable emergency must be limited to the amount reasonably necessary to satisfy the emergency need (which may include amounts necessary to pay any Federal, state, local, or foreign income taxes or penalties reasonably anticipated to result from the distribution). Determinations of amounts reasonably necessary to satisfy the emergency need must take into account any additional compensation that is available if the plan provides for cancellation of a deferral election upon a payment due to an unforeseeable emergency. See paragraph (j)(4)(viii) of this section. However, the determination of amounts reasonably necessary to satisfy the emergency need is not required to take into account any additional compensation that is available from a qualified employer plan as defined in §1.409A-1(a)(2) (including any

amount available by obtaining a loan under the plan), or that due to the unforeseeable emergency is available under another nonqualified deferred compensation plan (including a plan that would provide for deferred compensation except due to the application of the effective date provisions under §1.409A-6). The payment may be made from any plan in which the service provider participates that provides for payment upon an unforeseeable emergency, provided that the plan under which the payment was made must be designated at the time of payment.

(iii) **Payments due to an unforeseeable emergency.** A service provider may retain discretion with respect to whether to apply for a payment upon an unforeseeable emergency, and a service recipient may retain discretion with respect to whether to make a payment available under the plan due to an unforeseeable emergency. A service provider who has experienced an unforeseeable emergency will not be treated as making a subsequent deferral election under §1.409A-2(b) (subsequent deferral election rules) if the service provider does not apply for or elect to receive a payment available under the plan. A service recipient will not be treated as making a subsequent deferral election under §1.409A-2(b) (subsequent deferral election rules) if the service recipient exercises its discretion not to make a payment otherwise available due to an unforeseeable emergency.

(4) **Disability**—(i) **In general.** For purposes of §§1.409A-1 and 1.409A-2, this section, and §§1.409A-4 through 1.409A-6, except as otherwise specifically provided, a service provider is considered disabled if the service provider meets one of the following requirements:

(A) The service provider is unable to engage in any substantial gainful activity by reason of any medically determinable physical or mental impairment that can be expected to result in death or can be expected to last for a continuous period of not less than 12 months.

(B) The service provider is, by reason of any medically determinable physical or mental impairment that can be expected to result in death or can be expected to last for a continuous period of not less than 12 months, receiving income replacement benefits for a period of not less than three months under an accident and health plan covering employees of the service provider's employer.

(ii) **Limited plan definition of disability.** A plan may provide for a payment upon any disability, and need not provide for a payment upon all disabilities, provided that any disability upon which a payment may be made under the plan complies with the provisions of this paragraph (i)(4).

(iii) **Determination of disability.** A plan may provide that a service provider will be deemed disabled if determined to be totally disabled by the Social Security Administration or Railroad Retirement Board. A plan may also provide that a service provider will be deemed disabled if determined to be disabled in accordance with a disability insurance program, provided that the definition of disability applied under such disability insurance program complies with the requirements of this paragraph (i)(4).

(5) **Change in the ownership or effective control of a corporation, or a change in the ownership of a substantial portion of the assets of a corporation**—(i) **In general.** Pursuant to section 409A(a)(2)(A)(v) [26 USCS § 409A(a)(2)(A)(v)], a plan may permit a payment upon the occurrence of a change in the ownership of the corporation (as defined in paragraph (i)(5)(v) of this section), a change in effective control of the corporation (as defined in paragraph (i)(5)(vi) of this section), or a change in the ownership of a substantial portion of the assets of the corporation (as defined in paragraph (i)(5)(vii) of this section) (collectively referred to as a change in control event). To qualify as a change in control event, the occurrence of the event must be objectively determinable and any requirement that any other person or group, such as a plan administrator or compensation committee, certify the occurrence of a change in control event must be strictly ministerial and not involve any discretionary authority. The plan

may provide for a payment on a particular type or types of change in control events, and need not provide for a payment on all such events, provided that each event upon which a payment is provided qualifies as a change in control event. For rules regarding the ability of the service recipient to terminate the plan and pay amounts of deferred compensation upon a change in control event, see paragraph (j)(4)(ix)(B) of this section.

(ii) **Identification of relevant corporation**—(A) **In general.** To constitute a change in control event with respect to the service provider, the change in control event must relate to—

(1) The corporation for whom the service provider is performing services at the time of the change in control event;

(2) The corporation that is liable for the payment of the deferred compensation (or all corporations liable for the payment if more than one corporation is liable) but only if either the deferred compensation is attributable to the performance of service by the service provider for such corporation (or corporations) or there is a bona fide business purpose for such corporation or corporations to be liable for such payment and, in either case, no significant purpose of making such corporation or corporations liable for such payment is the avoidance of Federal income tax; or

(3) A corporation that is a majority shareholder of a corporation identified in paragraph (i)(5)(ii)(A)(1) or (2) of this section, or any corporation in a chain of corporations in which each corporation is a majority shareholder of another corporation in the chain, ending in a corporation identified in paragraph (i)(5)(ii)(A)(1) or (2) of this section.

(B) **Majority shareholder.** For purposes of this paragraph (i)(5)(ii), a majority shareholder is a shareholder owning more than 50 percent of the total fair market value and total voting power of such corporation.

(C) **Example.** The following example illustrates the rules of this paragraph (i)(5)(ii):

Example. Corporation A is a majority shareholder of Corporation B, which is a majority shareholder of Corporation C. A change in ownership of Corporation B constitutes a change in control event to service providers performing services for Corporation B or Corporation C, and to service providers for which Corporation B or Corporation C is solely liable for payments under the plan (for example, former employees), but is not a change in control event as to Corporation A or any other corporation of which Corporation A is a majority shareholder unless the sale constitutes a change in the ownership of a substantial portion of Corporation A's assets (see paragraph (i)(5)(vii) of this section).

(iii) **Attribution of stock ownership.** For purposes of paragraph (i)(5) of this section, section 318(a) [26 USCS § 318(a)] applies to determine stock ownership. Stock underlying a vested option is considered owned by the individual who holds the vested option (and the stock underlying an unvested option is not considered owned by the individual who holds the unvested option). For purposes of the preceding sentence, however, if a vested option is exercisable for stock that is not substantially vested (as defined by § 1.83-3(b) and (j)), the stock underlying the option is not treated as owned by the individual who holds the option.

(iv) **Special rules for certain delayed payments pursuant to a change in control event**—(A) **Certain transaction-based compensation.** Payments of compensation related to a change in control event described in paragraph (i)(5)(v) of this section (change in the ownership of a corporation) or paragraph (i)(5)(vii) of this section (change in the ownership of a substantial portion of a corporation's assets), that occur because a service recipient purchases its stock held by the service provider or because the service recipient or a third party purchases a stock right held by a service provider, or that are calculated by reference to the value of stock of the service recipient (collectively, transaction-based compensation), may be treated as paid at a designated date or pursuant to a payment schedule that complies with the requirements of section 409A [26

USCS § 409A] if the transaction-based compensation is paid on the same schedule and under the same terms and conditions as apply to payments to shareholders generally with respect to stock of the service recipient pursuant to a change in control event described in paragraph (i)(5)(v) of this section (change in the ownership of a corporation) or as apply to payments to the service recipient pursuant to a change in control event described in paragraph (i)(5)(vii) of this section (change in the ownership of a substantial portion of a corporation's assets), and to the extent that the transaction-based compensation is paid not later than five years after the change in control event, the payment of such compensation will not violate the initial or subsequent deferral election rules set out in § 1.409A-2(a) and (b) solely as a result of such transaction-based compensation being paid pursuant to such schedule and terms and conditions. If before and in connection with a change in control event described in paragraph (i)(5)(v) or (i)(5)(vii) of this section, transaction-based compensation that would otherwise be payable as a result of such event is made subject to a condition on payment that constitutes a substantial risk of forfeiture (as defined in § 1.409A-1(d), without regard to the provisions of that section under which additions or extensions of forfeiture conditions are disregarded) and the transaction-based compensation is payable under the same terms and conditions as apply to payments made to shareholders generally with respect to stock of the service recipient pursuant to a change in control event described in paragraph (i)(5)(v) of this section or to payments to the service recipient pursuant to a change in control event described in paragraph (i)(5)(vii) of this section, for purposes of determining whether such transaction-based compensation is a short-term deferral the requirements of § 1.409A-1(b)(4) are applied as if the legally binding right to such transaction-based compensation arose on the date that it became subject to such substantial risk of forfeiture.

(B) **Certain nonvested compensation.** Notwithstanding the provisions of § 1.409A-1(d) (definition of a substantial risk of forfeiture) that disregard the extension or modification of a condition for purposes of determining whether a condition on payment constitutes a substantial risk of forfeiture, a condition that is a substantial risk of forfeiture that otherwise would lapse as a result of a change in control event described in paragraph (i)(5)(v) or (i)(5)(vii) of this section may be extended or modified before and in connection with such event to provide for a condition on payment that will not lapse as a result of such change in control event, and such extended or modified condition will be treated as continuing to subject the amount to a substantial risk of forfeiture, provided that the transaction constituting the change in control event is a bona fide arm's length transaction between the service recipient or its shareholders and one or more parties who are unrelated to the service recipient and service provider (applying the rules of § 1.409A-1(f)(2)(ii)) and the modified or extended condition to which the payment is subject would otherwise be treated as a substantial risk of forfeiture under § 1.409A-1(d) (without regard to the provisions disregarding additions or extensions of forfeiture conditions). In such a case, the continued application of a fixed schedule of payments based upon the lapse of the substantial risk of forfeiture, so that payments commence upon the lapse of the modified or extended condition on payment, will not be treated as a change in the fixed schedule of payments for purposes of § 1.409A-2(b) (subsequent deferral elections) or paragraph (j) of this section (prohibition on the acceleration of payments).

(v) **Change in the ownership of a corporation**—(A) **In general.** Except as provided in paragraph (i)(5)(vi)(C) of this section, a change in the ownership of a corporation occurs on the date that any one person, or more than one person acting as a group (as defined in paragraph (i)(5)(v)(B) of this section), acquires ownership of stock of the corporation that, together with stock held by such person or group, constitutes more than 50 percent of the total fair market value or total voting power of the stock of such corporation. A nonqualified deferred compensation plan may provide that amounts payable upon a change in the ownership of a corporation will be paid only if the conditions in the preceding sentence are satisfied but substituting a percentage specified in the plan that is higher than 50 percent for the words "50 percent" in the preceding sentence, but only if the provision is set forth in the plan no later than the date by which the time and form of payment must be established under § 1.409A-2. However, if any one person, or more than one person acting as a group, is considered to own more than 50 percent of the total fair market value or total voting power of the stock of a corporation (or such higher percentage specified in accordance with the preceding sentence), the acquisition of additional stock by the same person or persons is not considered to cause a change in the ownership of the corporation (or to cause a change in the effective control of the corporation (within the meaning of paragraph (i)(5)(vi) of this section)). An increase in the percentage of stock owned by any one person, or persons acting as a group, as a result of a transaction in which the corporation acquires its stock in exchange for property will be treated as an acquisition of stock for purposes of this section. This section applies only when there is a transfer of stock of a corporation (or issuance of stock of a corporation) and stock in such corporation remains outstanding after the transaction (see paragraph (i)(5)(vii) of this section for rules regarding the transfer of assets of a corporation). See § 1.280G-1, Q&A-27(d), Example 1, Example 2, Example 5, and Example 6.

(B) **Persons acting as a group.** For purposes of paragraph (i)(5)(v)(A) of this section, persons will not be considered to be acting as a group solely because they purchase or own stock of the same corporation at the same time, or as a result of the same public offering. However, persons will be considered to be acting as a group if they are owners of a corporation that enters into a merger, consolidation, purchase or acquisition of stock, or similar business transaction with the corporation. If a person, including an entity, owns stock in both corporations that enter into a merger, consolidation, purchase or acquisition of stock, or similar transaction, such shareholder is considered to be acting as a group with other shareholders only with respect to the ownership in that corporation before the transaction giving rise to the change and not with respect to the ownership interest in the other corporation. See § 1.280G-1, Q&A-27(d), Example 3 and Example 4.

(vi) **Change in the effective control of a corporation**—(A) **In general.** Notwithstanding that a corporation has not undergone a change in ownership under paragraph (i)(5)(v) of this section, a change in the effective control of the corporation occurs only on either of the following dates:

(1) The date any one person, or more than one person acting as a group (as determined under paragraph (i)(5)(v)(B) of this section), acquires (or has acquired during the 12-month period ending on the date of the most recent acquisition by such person or persons) ownership of stock of the corporation possessing 30 percent or more of the total voting power of the stock of such corporation. A nonqualified deferred compensation plan may provide that amounts payable upon an effective change in control of a corporation will be paid only if the conditions in the preceding sentence are satisfied but substituting a percentage specified in the plan that is higher than 30 percent for the word "30 percent" in the preceding sentence, but only if the percentage is set forth in the plan no later than the date by which the time and form of payment must be established under § 1.409A-2).

(2) The date a majority of members of the corporation's board of directors is replaced during any 12-month period by directors whose appointment or election is not endorsed by a majority of the members of the corporation's board of directors before the date of the appointment or election, provided that for purposes of this paragraph (i)(5)(vi)(A) the term corporation refers solely to the relevant corporation identified in paragraph (i)(5)(ii) of this section for which no other corporation is a majority shareholder for purposes of that paragraph. For example, if Corporation A is a publicly held corporation with no majority shareholder, and Corporation A is the majority

shareholder of Corporation B, which is the majority shareholder of Corporation C, the term corporation for purposes of this paragraph (i)(5)(vi)(A)(2) would refer solely to Corporation A. A nonqualified deferred compensation plan may provide that amounts payable upon a change in the effective control of a corporation will be paid only if the conditions in the first sentence of this paragraph are satisfied substituting a portion of the members of the corporation's board of directors that is higher than the words "a majority of the members of the corporation's board of directors" in the first sentence of this paragraph, but only if the higher portion is set forth in the plan no later than the date by which the time and form of payment must be established under § 1.409A-2(a)).

(B) **Multiple change in control events.** A change in effective control may occur in a transaction in which one of the two corporations involved in the transaction has a change in control event under paragraph (i)(5)(v) or (i)(5)(vii) of this section. Thus, for example, assume Corporation P transfers more than 40 percent of the total gross fair market value of its assets to Corporation O in exchange for 35 percent of O's stock. P has undergone a change in ownership of a substantial portion of its assets under paragraph (i)(5)(vii) of this section and O has a change in effective control under this paragraph (i)(5)(vi).

(C) **Acquisition of additional control.** If any one person, or more than one person acting as a group, is considered to effectively control a corporation (within the meaning of this paragraph (i)(5)(vi)), the acquisition of additional control of the corporation by the same person or persons is not considered to cause a change in the effective control of the corporation (or to cause a change in the ownership of the corporation within the meaning of paragraph (i)(5)(v) of this section).

(D) **Persons acting as a group.** Persons will not be considered to be acting as a group solely because they purchase or own stock of the same corporation at the same time, or as a result of the same public offering. However, persons will be considered to be acting as a group if they are owners of a corporation that enters into a merger, consolidation, purchase or acquisition of stock, or similar business transaction with the corporation. If a person, including an entity, owns stock in both corporations that enter into a merger, consolidation, purchase or acquisition of stock, or similar transaction, such shareholder is considered to be acting as a group with other shareholders in a corporation only with respect to the ownership in that corporation before the transaction giving rise to the change and not with respect to the ownership interest in the other corporation. See § 1.280G-1, Q&A-27(d), Example 4.

(vii) **Change in the ownership of a substantial portion of a corporation's assets—** (A) **In general.** A change in the ownership of a substantial portion of a corporation's assets occurs on the date that any one person, or more than one person acting as a group (as determined in paragraph (i)(5)(v)(B) of this section), acquires (or has acquired during the 12-month period ending on the date of the most recent acquisition by such person or persons) assets from the corporation that have a total gross fair market value equal to or more than 40 percent of the total gross fair market value of all of the assets of the corporation immediately before such acquisition or acquisitions (or such higher amount specified by the plan no later than the date by which the time and form of payment must be established under § 1.409A-2). For this purpose, gross fair market value means the value of the assets of the corporation, or the value of the assets being disposed of, determined without regard to any liabilities associated with such assets.

(B) **Transfers to a related person—**(1) There is no change in control event under this paragraph (i)(5)(vii) when there is a transfer to an entity that is controlled by the shareholders of the transferring corporation immediately after the transfer, as provided in this paragraph (i)(5)(vii)(B). A transfer of assets by a corporation is not treated as a change in the ownership of such assets if the assets are transferred to—

(i) A shareholder of the corporation (immediately before the asset transfer) in exchange for or with respect to its stock;

(ii) An entity, 50 percent or more of the total value or voting power of which is owned, directly or indirectly, by the corporation;

(iii) A person, or more than one person acting as a group, that owns, directly or indirectly, 50 percent or more of the total value or voting power of all the outstanding stock of the corporation; or

(iv) An entity, at least 50 percent of the total value or voting power of which is owned, directly or indirectly, by a person described in paragraph (i)(5)(vii)(B)(1)(iii) of this section.

(2) For purposes of this paragraph (i)(5)(vii)(B) and except as otherwise provided in this paragraph (i), a person's status is determined immediately after the transfer of the assets. For example, a transfer to a corporation in which the transferor corporation has no ownership interest before the transaction, but that is a majority-owned subsidiary of the transferor corporation after the transaction is not treated as a change in the ownership of the assets of the transferor corporation.

(C) **Persons acting as a group.** Persons will not be considered to be acting as a group solely because they purchase assets of the same corporation at the same time. However, persons will be considered to be acting as a group if they are owners of a corporation that enters into a merger, consolidation, purchase or acquisition of assets, or similar business transaction with the corporation. If a person, including an entity shareholder, owns stock in both corporations that enter into a merger, consolidation, purchase or acquisition of assets, or similar transaction, such shareholder is considered to be acting as a group with other shareholders in a corporation only to the extent of the ownership in that corporation before the transaction giving rise to the change and not with respect to the ownership interest in the other corporation. See § 1.280G-1, Q&A-27(d), Example 4.

(6) **Certain back-to-back arrangements**—(i) **In general.** This paragraph (i)(6) applies where a service provider is providing services to a service recipient (the intermediate service recipient), who in turn is providing services to another service recipient (the ultimate service recipient), the services provided by the service provider to the intermediate service recipient are closely related to the services provided by the intermediate service recipient to the ultimate service recipient, there is a nonqualified deferred compensation plan providing for payments by the ultimate service recipient to the intermediate service recipient (the ultimate service recipient plan), there is a nonqualified deferred compensation plan or other agreement, method, program, or other arrangement providing for payments of compensation by the intermediate service recipient to the service provider (the intermediate service recipient plan), and the intermediate service recipient plan provides for a payment upon the occurrence of an event described in paragraph (a)(1), (2), (3), (5), or (6) of this section. In such a case, notwithstanding the generally applicable limits on payments in paragraph (a) of this section, the ultimate service recipient plan may provide for a payment to the intermediate service recipient upon the occurrence of a payment event under the intermediate service recipient plan described in paragraph (a)(1), (2), (3), (5), or (6) of this section if the time and form of payment is defined as the same time and form of payment provided under the intermediate service recipient plan, the amount of the payment under the ultimate service recipient plan does not exceed the amount of the payment under the intermediate service recipient plan, and the ultimate service recipient plan and the intermediate service recipient plan otherwise satisfy the requirements of section 409A [26 USCS § 409A] (regardless of whether such plan is subject to section 409A [26 USCS § 409A]).

(ii) **Example.** The provisions of paragraph (i)(6)(i) of this section are illustrated by the following example:

Example. Company B (intermediate service recipient) provides services to Company C (ultimate service recipient). Employee A (service provider) provides services to Company B that are closely related to the services Company B provides to Company C. Pursuant to a nonqualified deferred compensation plan meeting the requirements of section 409A [26 USCS § 409A], Employee A is entitled to a payment of deferred compensation upon a separation from service with Company B (the intermediate service recipient plan). Under an arrangement between Company B and Company C (the ultimate service recipient plan), Company C agrees to pay an amount of deferred compensation to Company B upon Employee A's separation from service with Company B, in accordance with the time, form and amount of payment provided in the intermediate service recipient plan. Provided that the intermediate service recipient plan and the ultimate service recipient plan otherwise comply with the requirements of section 409A [26 USCS § 409A] (regardless of whether such arrangements are subject to section 409A [26 USCS § 409A]), Company C's payment to Company B of the amount due under the ultimate service recipient plan upon the separation from service of Employee A from Company B may constitute a permissible payment event for purposes of paragraph (a) of this section.

(j) *Prohibition on acceleration of payments*—(1) **In general.** Except as provided in paragraph (j)(4) of this section, a nonqualified deferred compensation plan may not permit the acceleration of the time or schedule of any payment or amount scheduled to be paid pursuant to the terms of the plan, and no such accelerated payment may be made whether or not provided for under the terms of such plan. For purposes of determining whether a payment of deferred compensation has been made, the rules of paragraph (f) of this section (substituted payments) apply. For purposes of this paragraph (j), an impermissible acceleration does not occur if payment is made in accordance with plan provisions or an election as to the time and form of payment in effect at the time of initial deferral (or added in accordance with the rules applicable to subsequent deferral elections under § 1.409A-2(b)) pursuant to which payment is required to be made on an accelerated schedule as a result of an intervening event that is an event described in paragraph (a)(1), (2), (3), (5), or (6) of this section. For example, a plan may provide that a participant will receive six installment payments commencing at separation from service, and also provide that if the participant dies after such payments commence but before all payments have been made, all remaining amounts will be paid in a lump sum payment. Additionally, it is not an acceleration of the time or schedule of payment of a deferral of compensation if a service recipient waives or accelerates the satisfaction of a condition constituting a substantial risk of forfeiture applicable to such deferral of compensation, provided that the requirements of section 409A [26 USCS § 409A] (including the requirement that the payment be made upon a permissible payment event) are otherwise satisfied with respect to such deferral of compensation. For example, if a nonqualified deferred compensation plan provides for a lump sum payment of the vested benefit upon separation from service, and the benefit vests under the plan only after 10 years of service, it is not a violation of the requirements of section 409A [26 USCS § 409A] if the service recipient reduces the vesting requirement to five years of service, even if a service provider becomes vested as a result and receives a payment in connection with a separation from service before the service provider would have completed 10 years of service. However, if the plan in this example had provided for a payment at a fixed date, rather than at separation from service, the date of payment could not be accelerated due to the accelerated vesting. For the definition of a payment for purposes of this paragraph (j), see § 1.409A-2(b)(5) (coordination of the subsequent deferral election rules with the prohibition on acceleration of payments). For other permissible payments, see § 1.409A-2(b)(2)(iii) (certain immediate payments of remaining installments) and paragraph (d) of this section (certain payments made no more than 30 days before the designated payment date).

(2) **Application to multiple payment events.** Generally, the addition of a permissible payment event, the deletion of a permissible payment event, or the substitution of one permissible payment event for another permissible payment event, results in an acceleration of a payment if the addition, deletion, or substitution could result in the payment being made at an earlier date than such payment would have been made absent such addition, deletion, or substitution. Notwithstanding the previous sentence, the addition of death, disability (as defined in paragraph (i)(4) of this section), or an unforeseeable emergency (as defined in paragraph (i)(3) of this section), as a potentially earlier alternative payment event to an amount previously deferred will not be treated as resulting in an acceleration of a payment, even if such addition results in the payment being paid at an earlier time than such payment would have been made absent the addition of the payment event. However, the addition of such a payment event as a potentially later alternative payment event generally is subject to the rules governing changes in the time and form of payment (see § 1.409A-2(b)).

(3) **Beneficiaries.** The rules of this paragraph (j) apply to elections by beneficiaries with respect to the time and form of payment, as well as elections by service providers or service recipients with respect to the time and form of payment to beneficiaries. An election to change the identity of a beneficiary does not constitute an acceleration of a payment merely because the election changes the identity of the recipient of the payment, if the time and form of the payment is not otherwise changed. In addition, an election before the commencement of a life annuity to change the identity of a beneficiary does not constitute an acceleration of a payment if the change in the time of payments stems solely from the different life expectancy of the new beneficiary, such as in the case of a joint and survivor annuity, and does not change the commencement date of the life annuity.

(4) **Exceptions**—(i) **In general.** Except as otherwise expressly provided, a plan may

provide for the acceleration of a payment in accordance with paragraphs (j)(4)(ii) through (xiv) of this section, or may provide a service recipient discretion to accelerate payments in accordance with the provisions of paragraphs (j)(4)(ii) through (xiv) of this section. A plan may not provide a service provider discretion with respect to whether a payment will be accelerated, and a service recipient may not provide a service provider a direct or indirect election as to whether the service recipient's discretion to accelerate a payment will be exercised, even if such acceleration would be permitted under paragraphs (j)(4)(ii) through (xiv) of this section. Whether a service recipient has provided a service provider an election as to whether the service recipient's discretion to accelerate a payment will be exercised is determined based on all the facts and circumstances, including whether similarly situated service providers have been treated differently. Except as otherwise provided in paragraphs (j)(4)(ii) through (xiv) of this section, the plan need not set forth the exception in writing, and provided all other requirements of this section are met, the making of such a payment or the addition of a plan term permitting the making of such a payment will not constitute the acceleration of a payment, and the failure to make such a payment or the deletion or modification of a plan term permitting the making of such a payment will not be subject to the rules regarding a change in the time and form of payment under § 1.409A-2(b).

(ii) **Domestic relations order.** A plan may provide for acceleration of the time or schedule of a payment under the plan to an individual other than the service provider, or a payment under such plan may be made to an individual other than the service provider, to the extent necessary to fulfill a domestic relations order (as defined in section 414(p)(1)(B) [26 USCS § 414(p)(1)(B)]).

(iii) **Conflicts of interest—(A) Compliance with ethics agreements with the Federal government.** A plan may provide for acceleration of the time or schedule of a payment under the plan, or a payment may be made under a plan, to the extent necessary for any Federal officer or employee in the executive branch to comply with an ethics agreement with the Federal government.

(B) **Compliance with ethics laws or conflicts of interest laws.** A plan may provide for acceleration of the time or schedule of a payment under the plan, or a payment may be made under a plan, to the extent reasonably necessary to avoid the violation of an applicable Federal, state, local, or foreign ethics law or conflicts of interest law (including where such payment is reasonably necessary to permit the service provider to participate in activities in the normal course of his or her position in which the service provider would otherwise not be able to participate under an applicable rule). A payment is reasonably necessary to avoid the violation of a Federal, state, local, or foreign ethics law or conflicts of interest law if the payment is a necessary part of a course of action that results in compliance with a Federal, state, local, or foreign ethics law or conflicts of interest law that would be violated absent such course of action, regardless of whether other actions would also result in compliance with the Federal, state, local, or foreign ethics law or conflicts of interest law. For this purpose, a provision of foreign law is considered applicable only to foreign earned income (as defined under section 911(b)(1) [26 USCS § 911(b)(1)] without regard to section 911(b)(1)(B)(iv) [26 USCS § 911(b)(1)(B)(iv)] and without regard to the requirement that the income be attributable to services performed during the period described in section 911(d)(1)(A) or (B) [26 USCS § 911(d)(1)(A) or (B)]) from sources within the foreign country that promulgated such law.

(iv) **Section 457 plans** [26 USCS § 457]. A plan subject to section 457(f) [26 USCS § 457(f)] may provide for an acceleration of the time or schedule of a payment to a service provider, or a payment may be made under such a plan, to pay Federal, state, local, and foreign income taxes due upon a vesting event, provided that the amount of such payment is not more than an amount equal to the Federal, state, local, and foreign income tax withholding that would have been remitted by the employer if there had been a payment of wages equal to the income includible by the service provider under section 457(f) [26 USCS § 457(f)] at the time of the vesting.

(v) **Limited cashouts.** A plan may require or provide a service recipient discretion to require (or be amended to require or to provide a service recipient discretion to require), a mandatory lump sum payment of amounts deferred under the plan that do not exceed a specified amount, provided that such plan term or amendment is executed and effective, and any required exercise of service recipient discretion is evidenced in writing, no later than the date of such payment, and provided that—

(A) The payment results in the termination and liquidation of the entirety of the service provider's interest under the plan, including all agreements, methods, programs, or other arrangements with respect to which deferrals of compensation are treated as having been deferred under a single nonqualified deferred compensation plan under § 1.409A-1(c)(2); and

(B) The payment is not greater than the applicable dollar amount under section 402(g)(1)(B) [26 USCS § 402(g)(1)(B)].

(vi) **Payment of employment taxes.** A plan may provide for the acceleration of the time or schedule of a payment, or a payment may be made under the plan, to pay the Federal Insurance Contributions Act (FICA) tax imposed under section 3101 [26 USCS § 3101], section 3121(a) [26 USCS § 3121(a)], and section 3121(v)(2) [26 USCS § 3121(v)(2)], or the Railroad Retirement Act tax imposed under section 3201 [26 USCS § 3201], section 3211 [26 USCS § 3211], section 3231(e)(1) [26 USCS § 3231(e)(1)], and section 3231(e)(8) [26 USCS § 3231(e)(8)], where applicable, on compensation deferred under the plan (the FICA or RRTA amount). Additionally, a plan may provide for the acceleration of the time or schedule of a payment, or a payment may be made under the plan, to pay the income tax at source on wages

imposed under section 3401 [26 USCS § 3401] or the corresponding withholding provisions of applicable state, local, or foreign tax laws as a result of the payment of the FICA or RRTA amount, and to pay the additional income tax at source on wages attributable to the pyramiding section 3401 [26 USCS § 3401] wages and taxes. However, the total payment under this acceleration provision must not exceed the aggregate of the FICA or RRTA amount, and the income tax withholding related to such FICA or RRTA amount.

(vii) **Payment upon income inclusion under section 409A** [26 USCS § 409A]. A plan may provide for the acceleration of the time or schedule of a payment, or a payment under such plan may be made, at any time the plan fails to meet the requirements of section 409A [26 USCS § 409A] and these regulations. Such payment may not exceed the amount required to be included in income as a result of the failure to comply with the requirements of section 409A [26 USCS § 409A] and these regulations.

(viii) **Cancellation of deferrals following an unforeseeable emergency or hardship distribution.** A plan may provide for a cancellation of a service provider's deferral election, or such a cancellation may be made, due to an unforeseeable emergency or a hardship distribution pursuant to § 1.401(k)-1(d)(3). The deferral election must be cancelled, not merely postponed or otherwise delayed. Accordingly, any later deferral election will be subject to the provisions governing initial deferral elections. See § 1.409A-2(a).

(ix) **Plan terminations and liquidations.** A plan may provide for the acceleration of the time and form of a payment, or a payment under such plan may be made, where the acceleration of the payment is made pursuant to a termination and liquidation of the plan in accordance with one of the following:

(A) The service recipient's termination and liquidation of the plan within 12 months of a corporate dissolution taxed under section 331 [26 USCS § 331], or with the approval of a bankruptcy court pursuant to 11 U.S.C. § 503(b)(1)(A), provided that the amounts deferred under the plan are included in the participants' gross incomes in the latest of the following years (or, if earlier, the taxable year in which the amount is actually or constructively received).

(1) The calendar year in which the plan termination and liquidation occurs.

(2) The first calendar year in which the amount is no longer subject to a substantial risk of forfeiture.

(3) The first calendar year in which the payment is administratively practicable.

(B) The service recipient's termination and liquidation of the plan pursuant to irrevocable action taken by the service recipient within the 30 days preceding or the 12 months following a change in control event (as defined in paragraph (i)(5) of this section), provided that this paragraph will only apply to a payment under a plan if all agreements, methods, programs, and other arrangements sponsored by the service recipient immediately after the time of the change in control event with respect to which deferrals of compensation are treated as having been deferred under a single plan under § 1.409A-1(c)(2) are terminated and liquidated with respect to each participant that experienced the change in control event, so that under the terms of the termination and liquidation all such participants are required to receive all amounts of compensation deferred under the terminated agreements, methods, programs, and other arrangements within 12 months of the date the service recipient irrevocably takes all necessary action to terminate and liquidate the agreements, methods, programs, and other arrangements. Solely for purposes of this paragraph (j)(4)(ix)(B), the applicable service recipient with the discretion to liquidate and terminate the agreements, methods, programs, and other arrangements is the service recipient that is primarily liable immediately after the transaction for the payment of the deferred compensation.

(C) The service recipient's termination and liquidation of the plan, provided that—

(1) The termination and liquidation does not occur proximate to a downturn in the financial health of the service recipient;

(2) The service recipient terminates and liquidates all agreements, methods, programs, and other arrangements sponsored by the service recipient that would be aggregated with any terminated and liquidated agreements, methods, programs, and other arrangements under § 1.409A-1(c) if the same service provider had deferrals of compensation under all of the agreements, methods, programs, and other arrangements that are terminated and liquidated;

(3) No payments in liquidation of the plan are made within 12 months of the date the service recipient takes all necessary action to irrevocably terminate and liquidate the plan other than payments that would be payable under the terms of the plan if the action to terminate and liquidate the plan had not occurred;

(4) All payments are made within 24 months of the date the service recipient takes all necessary action to irrevocably terminate and liquidate the plan; and

(5) The service recipient does not adopt a new plan that would be aggregated with any terminated and liquidated plan under § 1.409A-1(c) if the same service provider participated in both plans, at any time within three years following the date the service recipient takes all necessary action to irrevocably terminate and liquidate the plan.

(D) Such other events and conditions as the Commissioner may prescribe in generally applicable guidance published in the Internal Revenue Bulletin (see § 601.601(d)(2) of this chapter).

(x) **Certain distributions to avoid a nonallocation year under section 409(p)** [26 USCS § 409(p)]. A plan may provide for an acceleration of the time and form of a payment, or a payment may be made under such plan, to prevent the occurrence of a nonallocation year (within the meaning of section 409(p)(3) [26 USCS § 409(p)(3)]) in the plan year of an employee stock ownership plan next following the plan year in which such payment is made, provided that the amount distributed may not exceed 125 percent of the minimum amount of distribution necessary to avoid the occurrence of a nonallocation year. Solely for purposes of determining permissible distributions under this paragraph (j)(4)(x), synthetic equity (within the meaning of section 409(p)(6)(C) [26 USCS § 409(p)(6)(C)] and § 1.409(p)-1(f)) granted during the plan year of the employee stock ownership plan in which such payment is made is disregarded for purposes of determining whether the subsequent plan year would result in a nonallocation year.

(xi) **Payment of state, local, or foreign taxes.** A plan may provide for an acceleration of the time and form of a payment, or a payment may be made under such plan, to reflect payment of state, local, or foreign tax obligations arising from participation in the plan that apply to an amount deferred under the plan before the amount is paid or made available to the participant (the state, local, or foreign tax amount). Such payment may not exceed the amount of such taxes due as a result of participation in the plan. Such payment may be made by distributions to the participant in the form of withholding pursuant to provisions of applicable state, local, or foreign law or by distribution directly to the participant. Additionally, an arrangement may provide for the acceleration of the time or schedule of payment, or a payment may be made under such arrangement, to pay the income tax at source on wages imposed under section 3401 [26 USCS § 3401] as a result of such payment and to pay the additional income tax at source on wages imposed under section 3401 [26 USCS § 3401] attributable to such additional section 3401 [26 USCS § 3401] wages and taxes. However, the total payment under this acceleration provision must not exceed the aggregate of the state, local, and foreign tax amount, and the income tax withholding related to such state, local, and foreign tax amount.

(xii) **Cancellation of deferral elections due to disability.** A plan may provide for a cancellation of a service provider's deferral election, or a cancellation of such election may be made, where such cancellation occurs by the later of the end of the taxable year of the service provider or the 15th day of the third month following the date the service provider incurs a disability. For purposes of this paragraph, a disability refers to any medically determinable physical or mental impairment resulting in the service provider's inability to perform the duties of his or her position or any substantially similar position, where such impairment can be expected to result in death or can be expected to last for a continuous period of not less than six months.

(xiii) **Certain offsets.** A plan may provide for the acceleration of the time or schedule of a payment, or a payment may be made under such plan, as satisfaction of a debt of the service provider to the service recipient, where such debt is incurred in the ordinary course of the service relationship between the service recipient and the service provider, the entire amount of reduction in any of the service recipient's taxable years does not exceed $5,000, and the reduction is made at the same time and in the same amount as the debt otherwise would have been due and collected from the service provider.

(xiv) **Bona fide disputes as to a right to a payment.** A plan may provide for the acceleration of the time or schedule of one or more payments, or a payment may be made under such plan, where such payments occur as part of a settlement between the service provider and the service recipient of an arm's length, bona fide dispute as to the service provider's right to the deferred amount. Discretion to accelerate payments, other than due to an arm's length settlement of a bona fide dispute as to the service provider's right to the deferred amount, is not permitted under this paragraph (j)(4)(xiv). Whether a payment qualifies for the exception under this paragraph is based on all relevant facts and circumstances. A payment will be presumed not to meet this exception unless the payment is subject to a substantial reduction in the value of the payment made in relation to the amount that would have been payable had there been no dispute as to the service provider's right to the payment. For this purpose, a reduction that is less than 25 percent of the present value of the deferred amount in dispute generally is not a substantial reduction. In addition, a payment will be presumed not to meet this exception if the payment is made proximate to a downturn in the financial health of the service recipient.

(5) **Nonqualified deferred compensation plans linked to qualified employer plans or certain other arrangements.** If a nonqualified deferred compensation plan provides that the amount deferred under the plan is the amount determined under the formula determining benefits under a qualified employer plan (as defined in § 1.409A-1(a)(2)), or a broad-based foreign retirement plan (as defined in § 1.409A-1(a)(3)(v)) maintained by the service recipient but applied without regard to one or more limitations applicable to the qualified employer plan under the Internal Revenue Code or to the broad-based foreign retirement plan under other applicable law, or that the amount deferred under the nonqualified deferred compensation plan is determined as an amount offset by some or all of the benefits provided under the qualified employer plan or broad-based foreign retirement plan, a decrease in amounts deferred under the nonqualified deferred compensation plan that results directly from the operation of the qualified employer plan or broad-based foreign retirement plan (other than service provider actions described in paragraphs (j)(5)(iii) and (iv) of this section) including changes in benefit limitations applicable to the qualified employer plan or the broad-based foreign retirement plan under the Internal Revenue Code or other applicable law does not constitute an acceleration of a payment under the nonqualified deferred compensation plan, provided that such operation does not otherwise result in a change in the time or form of a payment under the nonqualified deferred compensation plan, and provided further that the change in the amounts deferred under the nonqualified deferred compensation plan does not exceed

such change in the amounts deferred under the qualified employer plan or the broad-based foreign retirement plan, as applicable. In addition, with respect to such a nonqualified deferred compensation plan, the following actions or failures to act will not constitute an acceleration of a payment under the nonqualified deferred compensation plan even if in accordance with the terms of the nonqualified deferred compensation plan, the actions or inactions result in a decrease in the amounts deferred under the plan, provided that such actions or inactions do not otherwise affect the time or form of payment under the nonqualified deferred compensation plan, and provided further that with respect to actions or inactions described in paragraphs (j)(5)(i) and (ii) of this section, the change in the amount deferred under the nonqualified deferred compensation plan does not exceed the change in the amounts deferred under the qualified employer plan or the broad-based foreign retirement plan, as applicable:

(i) A service provider's action or inaction under the qualified employer plan or broad-based foreign retirement plan with respect to whether to elect to receive a subsidized benefit or an ancillary benefit under the qualified employer plan or broad-based foreign retirement plan.

(ii) The amendment of a qualified employer plan or broad-based foreign retirement plan to increase benefits provided under such plan, or to add or remove a subsidized benefit or an ancillary benefit.

(iii) A service provider's action or inaction under a qualified employer plan with respect to elective deferrals and other employee pre-tax contributions subject to the contribution restrictions under section 401(a)(30) [26 USCS § 401(a)(30)] or section 402(g) [26 USCS § 402(g)], including an adjustment to a deferral election under such qualified employer plan, provided that for any given taxable year, the service provider's action or inaction does not result in a decrease in the amounts deferred under all nonqualified deferred compensation plans in which the service provider participates (other than amounts described in paragraph (j)(5)(iv) of this section) in excess of the limit with respect to elective deferrals under section 402(g)(1)(A), (B), and (C) [26 USCS § 402(g)(1)(A), (B), and (C)] in effect for the taxable year in which such action or inaction occurs.

(iv) A service provider's action or inaction under a qualified employer plan with respect to elective deferrals and other employee pre-tax contributions subject to the contributions restrictions under section 401(a)(30) [26 USCS § 401(a)(30)] or section 402(g) [26 USCS § 402(g)], and after-tax contributions by the service provider to a qualified employer plan that provides for such contributions, that affects the amounts that are credited under one or more nonqualified deferred compensation plans as matching amounts or other similar amounts contingent on such elective deferrals, pre-tax contributions, or after-tax contributions, provided that the total of such matching or contingent amounts, as applicable, never exceeds 100 percent of the matching or contingent amounts that would be provided under the qualified employer plan absent any plan-based restrictions that reflect limits on qualified plan contributions under the Internal Revenue Code.

(6) **Changes in elections under a cafeteria plan.** A change in an election under a cafeteria plan (as defined in section 125(d) [26 USCS § 125(d)]) does not result in an accelerated payment of an amount deferred under a nonqualified deferred compensation plan to the extent that the change in the amount deferred under the nonqualified deferred compensation plan results solely from the application of the change in amount eligible to be treated as compensation under the terms of the nonqualified deferred compensation plan resulting from the election change under the cafeteria plan, to a benefit formula under the nonqualified deferred compensation plan based upon the service provider's eligible compensation, and only to the extent that such change applies in the same manner as any other increase or decrease in compensation would apply to such benefit formula.

§ 1.409A-4. Calculation of income inclusion [Reserved]

§ 1.409A-5. Funding [Reserved]

§ 1.409A-6. Application of section 409A [26 USCS § 409A] and effective dates.

(a) *Statutory application and effective dates*—(1) **Application to amounts deferred**—(i) **In general.** Except as otherwise provided in this section, section 409A [26 USCS § 409A] applies with respect to amounts deferred in taxable years beginning after December 31, 2004, and with respect to amounts deferred in taxable years beginning before January 1, 2005, if the plan under which the deferral is made is materially modified after October 3, 2004. For amounts deferred in taxable years beginning before January 1, 2005, under a plan that is materially modified after October 3, 2004, whether the plan complies with the requirements of section 409A [26 USCS § 409A] and these regulations is determined by reference to the terms of the plan in effect as of, and any actions taken under the plan on or after, the date of the material modification. Section 409A [26 USCS § 409A] is applicable with respect to earnings on amounts deferred only to the extent that section 409A [26 USCS § 409A] is applicable with respect to the amounts deferred. Accordingly, section 409A [26 USCS § 409A] does not apply with respect to earnings on amounts deferred before January 1, 2005, unless section 409A [26 USCS § 409A] applies with respect to the amounts deferred. For this purpose, a right to earnings that is subject to a substantial risk of forfeiture (as defined in § 1.83-3(c)) or a requirement to perform further services, on an amount deferred that is not subject to a substantial risk of forfeiture (as defined in § 1.83-3(c)) or a requirement to perform further services, is not treated as earnings on the amount deferred, but a separate right to compensation. Except as otherwise provided in applicable guidance (see § 601.601(d)(2) of this chapter), the provisions of §§ 1.409A-1 through 1.409A-5 and this section provide the exclusive means of identifying agreements, methods, programs, or other arrangements subject to section 409A [26 USCS § 409A], and the exclusive means of satisfying the requirements of section 409A [26 USCS § 409A] with respect to such agreements, methods, programs, or other arrangements.

(ii) **Collectively bargained plans.** Section 409A [26 USCS § 409A] does not apply with respect to amounts deferred under a plan maintained pursuant to one or more bona fide collective bargaining agreements in effect on October 3, 2004, for the period ending on the earlier of the date on which the last of such collective bargaining agreements terminates (determined without regard to any extension thereof after October 3, 2004) or December 31, 2009.

(2) **Identification of date of deferral for statutory effective date purposes.** For purposes of determining whether section 409A [26 USCS § 409A] is applicable with respect to an amount, the amount is considered deferred before January 1, 2005, if before January 1, 2005, the service provider had a legally binding right to be paid the amount, and the right to the amount was earned and vested. For purposes of this paragraph (a)(2), a right to an amount was earned and vested only if the amount was not subject to a substantial risk of forfeiture (as defined in § 1.83-3(c)) or a requirement to perform further services. Amounts to which the service provider did not have a legally binding right before January 1, 2005 (for example, because the service recipient retained discretion to reduce the amount), will not be considered deferred before January 1, 2005. In addition, amounts to which the service provider had a legally binding right before January 1, 2005, but the right to which was subject to a substantial risk of forfeiture or a requirement to perform further services after December 31, 2004, are not considered deferred before January 1, 2005, for purposes of the effective date. Notwithstanding the foregoing, an amount to which the service provider had a legally binding right before January 1, 2005, but for which the service

provider was required to continue performing services to retain the right only through the completion of the payroll period (as defined in § 1.409A-1(b)(3)) that includes December 31, 2004, is not treated as subject to a requirement to perform further services (or a substantial risk of forfeiture) for purposes of the effective date. For purposes of this paragraph (a)(2), a stock option, stock appreciation right, or similar compensation that on or before December 31, 2004, was immediately exercisable for cash or substantially vested property (as defined in § 1.83-3(b)) is treated as earned and vested, regardless of whether the right would terminate if the service provider ceased providing services for the service recipient.

(3) **Calculation of amount of compensation deferred for statutory effective date purposes**—(i) **Nonaccount balance plans.** The amount of compensation deferred before January 1, 2005, under a nonqualified deferred compensation plan that is a nonaccount balance plan (as defined in § 1.409A-1(c)(2)(i)(C)), equals the present value of the amount to which the service provider would have been entitled under the plan if the service provider voluntarily terminated services without cause on December 31, 2004, and received a payment of the benefits available from the plan on the earliest possible date allowed under the plan to receive a payment of benefits following the termination of services, and received the benefits in the form with the maximum value.

Notwithstanding the foregoing, for any subsequent taxable year of the service provider, the grandfathered amount may increase to equal the present value of the benefit the service provider actually becomes entitled to, in the form and at the time actually paid, determined under the terms of the plan (including applicable limits under the Internal Revenue Code), as in effect on October 3, 2004, without regard to any further services rendered by the service provider after December 31, 2004, or any other events affecting the amount of or the entitlement to benefits (other than a participant election with respect to the time or form of an available benefit). For purposes of calculating the present value of a benefit under this paragraph (a)(3)(i), reasonable actuarial assumptions and methods must be used. Whether assumptions and methods are reasonable for this purpose is determined as of each date the benefit is valued for purposes of determining the grandfathered benefit, provided that any reasonable actuarial assumptions and methods that were used by the service recipient with respect to such benefit as of December 31, 2004, will continue to be treated as reasonable assumptions and methods for purposes of calculating the grandfathered benefit.

Actuarial assumptions and methods will be presumed reasonable if they are the same as those used to value benefits under a qualified plan sponsored by the service recipient the benefits under which are part of the benefit formula under, or otherwise impact the amount of benefits under, the nonaccount balance nonqualified deferred compensation plan.

(ii) **Account balance plans.** The amount of compensation deferred before January 1, 2005, under a nonqualified deferred compensation plan that is an account balance plan (as defined in § 1.409A-1(c)(2)(i)(A)), equals the portion of the service provider's account balance as of December 31, 2004, the right to which was earned and vested (as defined in paragraph (a)(2) of this section) as of December 31, 2004, plus any future contributions to the account, the right to which was earned and vested (as defined in paragraph (a)(2) of this section) as of December 31, 2004, to the extent such contributions are actually made.

(iii) **Equity-based compensation plans.** For purposes of determining the amounts deferred before January 1, 2005, under an equity-based compensation plan, the rules of paragraph (a)(3)(ii) of this section governing account balance plans are applied except that the account balance is deemed to be the amount of the payment available to the service provider on December 31, 2004 (or that would be available to the service provider if the right were immediately exercisable) the right to which is earned and vested (as defined in paragraph (a)(2) of this section) as of December 31, 2004. For this purpose, the payment avail-

able to the service provider excludes any exercise price or other amount that must be paid by the service provider.

(iv) **Earnings.** Earnings on amounts deferred under a plan before January 1, 2005, include only income (whether actual or notional) attributable to the amounts deferred under a plan as of December 31, 2004, or to such income. For example, notional interest earned under the plan on amounts deferred in an account balance plan as of December 31, 2004, generally will be treated as earnings on amounts deferred under the plan before January 1, 2005. Similarly, an increase in the amount of payment available pursuant to a stock option, stock appreciation right, or other equity-based compensation above the amount of payment available as of December 31, 2004, due to appreciation in the underlying stock after December 31, 2004, or accrual of other earnings such as dividends, is treated as earnings on the amount deferred. In the case of a nonaccount balance plan, earnings include the increase, due solely to the passage of time, in the present value of the future payments to which the service provider has obtained a legally binding right, the present value of which constituted the amounts deferred under the plan before January 1, 2005. Thus, for each year, there will be an increase (determined using the same interest rate used to determine the amounts deferred under the plan before January 1, 2005) resulting from the shortening of the discount period before the future payments are made, plus, if applicable, an increase in the present value resulting from the service provider's survivorship during the year. However, an increase in the potential benefits under a nonaccount balance plan due to, for example, an application of an increase in compensation after December 31, 2004, to a final average pay plan or subsequent eligibility for an early retirement subsidy, does not constitute earnings on the amounts deferred under the plan before January 1, 2005.

(v) **Definition of plan.** For purposes of paragraphs (a)(1), (2), and (3) of this section, the term "plan" has the meaning provided in § 1.409A-1(c), except that the plan aggregation rules do not apply for purposes of the actuarial assumptions and methods used in paragraph (a)(3)(i) of this section. Accordingly, different reasonable actuarial assumptions and methods may be used to calculate the amounts deferred by a service provider in two different agreements, methods, programs, or other arrangements each of which constitutes a nonaccount balance plan.

(4) **Material modifications**—(i) **In general.** Except as otherwise provided, a modification of a plan is a material modification if a benefit or right existing as of October 3, 2004, is materially enhanced or a new material benefit or right is added, and such material enhancement or addition affects amounts earned and vested before January 1, 2005. Such material benefit enhancement or addition is a material modification whether it occurs pursuant to an amendment or to the service recipient's exercise of discretion under the terms of the plan. For example, an amendment to a plan to add a provision that payments of deferred amounts earned and vested before January 1, 2005, may be allowed upon request if service providers are required to forfeit 20 percent of the amount of the payment (a haircut) would be a material modification to the plan. Similarly, a material modification would occur if a service recipient exercised discretion to accelerate vesting of a benefit under the plan to a date on or before December 31, 2004. However, it is not a material modification for a service recipient to exercise discretion over the time and manner of payment of a benefit to the extent such discretion is provided under the terms of the plan as of October 3, 2004. It is not a material modification for a service provider to exercise a right permitted under the plan as in effect on October 3, 2004. The amendment of a plan to bring the plan into compliance with the provisions of section 409A [26 USCS § 409A] will not be treated as a material modification. However, a plan amendment or the exercise of discretion under the terms of the plan that materially enhances an existing benefit or right or adds a new material benefit or right will be considered a material modification even if the enhanced or added benefit would be permitted under sec-

tion 409A [26 USCS § 409A]. For example, the addition of a right to a payment upon an unforeseeable emergency of an amount earned and vested before January 1, 2005, would be considered a material modification. The reduction of an existing benefit is not a material modification. For example, the removal of a haircut provision generally would not constitute a material modification. The following modifications also are not material modifications for purposes of this paragraph (a)(4)(i):

(A) The establishment of or contributions to a trust or other arrangement from which benefits under the plan are to be paid is not a material modification of the plan, provided that the contribution to the trust or other arrangement would not otherwise cause an amount to be includible in the service provider's gross income.

(B) The modification of a provision requiring the immediate cancellation of a current deferral election, to require the cancellation of deferrals for the same length of time beginning with the first date at which the application of such cancellation would not violate section 409A [26 USCS § 409A] (for example, the first date of the service provider's first taxable year following the cancellation).

(C) Compliance with a domestic relations order (as defined in § 1.409A-3(j)(4)(ii)) with respect to payments to an individual other than the service provider, or an amendment to a plan to require compliance with a domestic relations order with respect to payments to an individual other than the service provider.

(D) The modification of a plan providing a life annuity form of payment to permit an election between the existing life annuity form of payment and other forms of annuity payments that would be treated as a single form of payment with the existing life annuity form of payment under § 1.409A-2(b)(2)(ii).

(E) The modification of a grandfathered plan to add a limited cashout feature consistent with § 1.409A-3(j)(4)(v) (exception to prohibition on accelerated payments).

(ii) **Adoptions of new plans.** It is presumed that the adoption of a new plan or the grant of an additional benefit under an existing plan after October 3, 2004, and before January 1, 2005, constitutes a material modification of a plan. However, the presumption may be rebutted by demonstrating that the adoption of the plan or grant of the additional benefit was consistent with the service recipient's historical compensation practices. For example, the presumption that the grant of a discounted stock option on November 1, 2004, is a material modification of a plan may be rebutted by demonstrating that the grant was consistent with the historic practice of granting substantially similar discounted stock options (both as to terms and amounts) each November for a significant number of years. Notwithstanding paragraph (a)(4)(i) of this section and this paragraph (a)(4)(ii), the grant of an additional benefit under an existing plan that consists of a deferral of additional compensation not otherwise provided under the plan as of October 3, 2004, will be treated as a material modification of the plan only as to the additional deferral of compensation, if the plan explicitly identifies the additional deferral of compensation and provides that the additional deferral of compensation is subject to section 409A [26 USCS § 409A]. Accordingly, amendments to conform a plan to the requirements of section 409A [26 USCS § 409A] with respect to deferrals under a plan occurring after December 31, 2004, will not constitute a material modification of the plan with respect to amounts deferred that are earned and vested on or before December 31, 2004, provided that there is no concurrent material modification with respect to the amount of, or rights to, amounts deferred that were earned and vested on or before December 31, 2004. Similarly, a grant of an additional benefit under a new plan adopted after October 3, 2004, and before January 1, 2005, will not be treated as a material modification of an existing plan to the extent that the new plan explicitly identifies additional deferrals of compensation and provides that the additional deferrals of compensation are subject to section 409A [26 USCS § 409A].

(iii) **Suspension or termination of a plan.** A cessation of deferrals under, or termination of, a plan, pursuant to the provisions of such plan, is not a material modification. Amending a plan to provide participants an election whether to terminate participation in a plan generally constitutes a material modification of the plan.

(iv) **Changes to investment measures— account balance plans.** With respect to an account balance plan (as defined in § 1.409A-1(c)(2)(i)(A)), it is not a material modification to change a notional investment measure to, or to add to an existing investment measure, an investment measure that qualifies as a predetermined actual investment within the meaning of § 31.3121(v)(2)-1(d)(2) of this chapter or, for any given taxable year, reflects a reasonable rate of interest (determined in accordance with § 31.3121(v)(2)-1(d)(2)(i)(C) of this chapter).

(v) **Stock rights.** The modification, extension, or renewal of a stock right will not constitute a material modification of the stock right, if the modification, extension, or renewal would not be treated as the grant of a new stock right under § 1.409A-1(b)(5)(v)(A), and would not result in the stock right being treated as having had a deferral feature from the date of grant pursuant to § 1.409A-1(b)(5)(v)(C).

(vi) **Rescission of modifications.** Any modification to the terms of a plan that would inadvertently result in treatment as a material modification under this section is not considered a material modification of the plan to the extent the modification in the terms of the plan is rescinded by the earlier of a date before the right is exercised (if the change grants a discretionary right) or the last day of the taxable year of the service provider during which such change occurred. Thus, for example, if a service recipient modifies the terms of a plan on March 1 to allow an individual employee to elect a new change in the time or form of payment without realizing that such a change constituted a material modification that would subject the plan to the requirements of section 409A [26 USCS § 409A], and the modification is rescinded on November 1, then if no change in the time or form of payment has been made pursuant to the modification before November 1, the plan is not considered materially modified under this section.

(vii) **Definition of plan.** For purposes of this paragraph (a)(4), the term "plan" has the same meaning provided in § 1.409A-1(c), except that the plan aggregation rules of § 1.409A-1(c)(2) do not apply.

(b) *Regulatory applicability date.* § 1.409A-1, § 1.409A-2, § 1.409A-3 and this section are applicable for taxable years beginning on or after January 1, 2008.

§ 1.410(a)-3. Minimum age and service conditions.

* * *

(d) *Other conditions.* Section 410(a), § 1.410(a)-4, and this section relate solely to age and service conditions and do not preclude a plan from establishing conditions, other than conditions relating to age or service, which must be satisfied by plan participants. For example, such provisions would not preclude a qualified plan from requiring, as a condition of participation, that an employee be employed within a specified job classification. See section 410(b) and the regulations thereunder for rules with respect to coverage of employees under qualified plans.

(e) *Age and service requirements*—(1) *General rule.* For purposes of applying the rules of this section, plan provisions may be treated as imposing age or service requirements even though the provisions do not specifically refer to age or service. Plan provisions which have the effect of requiring an age or service requirement with the employer or employers maintaining the plan will be treated as if they imposed an age or service requirement. In general, a plan under which an employee cannot participate unless he retires will impose an age and service requirement. However, a plan may provide benefits which supplement benefits provided for employees covered under a pension plan, as defined in section 3(2) of the Employee Retirement Income

Security Act of 1974, satisfying the requirements of section 410(a)(1) without violating the age and service rules.

(2) *Examples.* The rules of this paragraph are illustrated by the following examples:

Example (1). Corporation A is divided into two divisions. In order to work in division 2 an employee must first have been employed in division 1 for 5 years. A plan provision which required division 2 employment for participation will be treated as a service requirement because such a provision has the effect of requiring 5 years of service.

Example (2). Plan B requires as a condition of participation that each employee have had a driver's license for 15 years or more. This provision will be treated as an age requirement because such a provision has the effect of requiring an employee to attain a specified age.

* * *

§ 1.410(b)-2. Minimum coverage requirements (after 1993).

(a) *In general.* A plan is a qualified plan for a plan year only if the plan satisfies section 410(b) for the plan year. A plan satisfies section 410(b) for a plan year if and only if it satisfies paragraph (b) of this section with respect to employees for the plan year and paragraph (c) of this section with respect to former employees for the plan year. The rules in paragraphs (a), (b), and (c) of this section apply to all plans as a condition of qualification, including plans under which no employee is able to accrue any additional benefits (for example, frozen plans).

* * *

(b) *Requirements with respect to employees*—(1) *In general.* A plan satisfies this paragraph (b) for a plan year if and only if it satisfies at least one of the tests in paragraphs (b)(2) through (b)(7) of this section for the plan year.

(2) *Ratio percentage test*—(i) *In general.* A plan satisfies this paragraph (b)(2) for a plan year if and only if the plan's ratio per-

centage for the plan year is at least 70 percent. This test incorporates both the percentage test of section 410(b)(1)(A) and the ratio test of section 410(b)(1)(B). See § 1.410(b)-9 for the definition of ratio percentage.

(ii) *Examples.* The following examples illustrate the ratio percentage test of this paragraph (b)(2).

Example 1. For a plan year, Plan A benefits 70 percent of an employer's nonhighly compensated employees and 100 percent of the employer's highly compensated employees. The plan's ratio percentage for the year is 70 percent (70 percent/100 percent), and thus the plan satisfies the ratio percentage test.

Example 2. For a plan year, Plan B benefits 40 percent of the employer's nonhighly compensated employees and 60 percent of the employer's highly compensated employees. Plan B fails to satisfy the ratio percentage test because the plan's ratio percentage is only 66.67 percent (40 percent/60 percent).

(3) *Average benefit test.* A plan satisfies this paragraph (b)(3) for a plan year if and only if the plan satisfies both the nondiscriminatory classification test of § 1.410(b)-4 and the average benefit percentage test of § 1.410(b)-5 for the plan year.

* * *

(5) *Employers with no nonhighly compensated employees.* A plan satisfies this paragraph (b)(5) for a plan year if and only if the plan is maintained by an employer that has no nonhighly compensated employees at any time during the plan year.

(6) *Plans benefiting no highly compensated employees.* A plan satisfies this paragraph (b)(6) for a plan year if and only if the plan benefits no highly compensated employees for the plan year.

(7) *Plans benefiting collectively bargained employees.* A plan that benefits solely collectively bargained employees for a plan year satisfies this paragraph (b)(7) for the plan year. If a plan (within the meaning of § 1.410(b)-7(b)) benefits both collectively

bargained employees and noncollectively bargained employees for a plan year, § 1.410(b)-7(c)(4) provides that the portion of the plan that benefits collectively bargained employees is treated as a separate plan from the portion of the plan that benefits noncollectively bargained employees. Thus, the mandatorily disaggregated portion of the plan that benefits the collectively bargained employees automatically satisfies this paragraph (b)(7) for the plan year and hence section 410(b). See § 1.410(b)-9 for the definitions of collectively bargained employee and noncollectively bargained employee.

* * *

§ 1.410(b)-4.   Nondiscriminatory classification test.

(a) *In general.* A plan satisfies the nondiscriminatory classification test of this section for a plan year if and only if, for the plan year, the plan benefits the employees who qualify under a classification established by the employer in accordance with paragraph (b) of this section, and the classification of employees is nondiscriminatory under paragraph (c) of this section.

(b) *Reasonable classification* established by the employer. A classification is established by the employer in accordance with this paragraph (b) if and only if, based on all the facts and circumstances, the classification is reasonable and is established under objective business criteria that identify the category of employees who benefit under the plan. Reasonable classifications generally include specified job categories, nature of compensation (i.e., salaried or hourly), geographic location, and similar bona fide business criteria. An enumeration of employees by name or other specific criteria having substantially the same effect as an enumeration by name is not considered a reasonable classification.

(c) *Nondiscriminatory classification*—(1) *General rule.* A classification is nondiscriminatory under this paragraph (c) for a plan year if and only if the group of employees included in the classification benefiting under the plan satisfies the requirements of either paragraph (c)(2) or (c)(3) of this section for the plan year.

(2) *Safe harbor.* A plan satisfies the requirement of this paragraph (c)(2) for a plan year if and only if the plan's ratio percentage is greater than or equal to the employer's safe harbor percentage, as defined in paragraph (c)(4)(i) of this section. See § 1.410(b)-9 for the definition of a plan's ratio percentage.

(3) *Facts and circumstances*—(i) *General rule.* A plan satisfies the requirements of this paragraph (c)(3) if and only if—

(A) The plan's ratio percentage is greater than or equal to the unsafe harbor percentage, as defined in paragraph (c)(4)(ii) of this section, and

(B) The classification satisfies the factual determination of paragraph (c)(3)(ii) of this section.

(ii) *Factual determination.* A classification satisfies this paragraph (c)(3)(ii) if and only if, based on all the relevant facts and circumstances, the Commissioner finds that the classification is nondiscriminatory. No one particular fact is determinative. Included among the facts and circumstances relevant in determining whether a classification is nondiscriminatory are the following—

(A) The underlying business reason for the classification. The greater the business reason for the classification, the more likely the classification is to be nondiscriminatory. Reducing the employer's cost of providing retirement benefits is not a relevant business reason.

(B) The percentage of the employer's employees benefiting under the plan. The higher the percentage, the more likely the classification is to be nondiscriminatory.

(C) Whether the number of employees benefiting under the plan in each salary range is representative of the number of employees in each salary range of the employer's workforce. In general, the more representative the percentages of employees benefiting under the plan in each salary range, the more likely the classification is to be nondiscriminatory.

(D) The difference between the plan's ratio percentage and the employer's safe harbor percentage. The smaller the difference, the more likely the classification is to be nondiscriminatory.

(E) The extent to which the plan's average benefit percentage (determined under § 1.410(b)-5) exceeds 70 percent.

(4) *Definitions*—(i) *Safe harbor percentage.* The safe harbor percentage of an employer is 50 percent, reduced by 3/4 of a percentage point for each whole percentage point by which the nonhighly compensated employee concentration percentage exceeds 60 percent. See paragraph (c)(4)(iv) for a table that illustrates the safe harbor percentage and unsafe harbor percentage.

(ii) *Unsafe harbor percentage.* The unsafe harbor percentage of an employer is 40 percent, reduced by 3/4 of a percentage point for each whole percentage point by which the nonhighly compensated employee concentration percentage exceeds 60 percent. However, in no case is the unsafe harbor percentage less than 20 percent.

(iii) *Nonhighly compensated employee concentration percentage.* The nonhighly compensated employee concentration percentage of an employer is the percentage of all the employees of the employer who are nonhighly compensated employees. Employees who are excludable employees for purposes of the average benefit test are not taken into account.

(iv) *Table.* The following table sets forth the safe harbor and unsafe harbor percentages at each nonhighly compensated employee concentration percentage:

Nonhighly compensated employee concentration percentage	Safe harbor percentage	Unsafe harbor percentage
0-60	50.00	40.00
61	49.25	39.25
62	48.50	38.50
63	47.75	37.75
64	47.00	37.00
65	46.25	36.25
66	45.50	35.50
67	44.75	34.75
68	44.00	34.00
69	43.25	33.25
70	42.50	32.50
71	41.75	31.75
72	41.00	31.00
73	40.25	30.25
74	39.50	29.50
75	38.75	28.75
76	38.00	28.00
77	37.25	27.25
78	36.50	26.50
79	35.75	25.75
80	35.00	25.00
81	34.25	24.25
82	33.50	23.50
83	32.75	22.75
84	32.00	22.00
85	31.25	21.25
86	30.50	20.50
87	29.75	20.00
88	29.00	20.00
89	28.25	20.00
90	27.50	20.00
91	26.75	20.00
92	26.00	20.00
93	25.25	20.00
94	24.50	20.00
95	23.75	20.00
96	23.00	20.00
97	22.25	20.00
98	21.50	20.00
99	20.75	20.00

(5) *Examples.* The following examples illustrate the rules in this paragraph (c).

Example 1. Employer A has 200 nonexcludable employees, of whom 120 are nonhighly compensated employees and 80 are highly compensated employees. Employer A maintains a plan that benefits 60 nonhighly compensated employees and 72 highly compensated employees. Thus, the plan's ratio percentage is 55.56 percent ([60/120]/[72/80]=50%/90%=0.5556), which is below the percentage necessary to satisfy the ratio percentage test of § 1.410(b)-2(b)(2). The employer's nonhighly compensated employee concentration percentage is 60 percent (120/200); thus, Employer A's safe harbor percentage is 50 percent and its unsafe harbor percentage is 40 percent. Because the plan's ratio percentage is greater than the safe harbor percentage, the plan's classification satisfies the safe harbor of paragraph (c)(2) of this section.

Example 2. The facts are the same as in *Example 1*, except that the plan benefits only 40 nonhighly compensated employees. The plan's ratio percentage is thus 37.03 percent ([40/120]/[72/80]=33.33%/90%=0.3703). Under these facts, the plan's classification is below the unsafe harbor percentage and is thus considered discriminatory.

Example 3. The facts are the same as in *Example 1*, except that the plan benefits 45 nonhighly compensated employees. The plan's ratio percentage is thus 41.67 percent ([45/120]/[72/80]=37.50%/90%=0.4167), above the unsafe harbor percentage (40 percent) and below the safe harbor percentage (50 percent). The Commissioner may determine that the classification is nondiscriminatory after considering all the relevant facts and circumstances.

* * *

§ 1.411(a)-4. Forfeitures, suspensions, etc.

(a) *Nonforfeitability.* Certain rights in an accrued benefit must be nonforfeitable to satisfy the requirements of section 411(a). This section defines the term "nonforfeitable" for purposes of these requirements. For purposes of section 411 and the regulations thereunder, a right to an accrued benefit is considered to be nonforfeitable at a particular time if, at that time and thereafter, it is an unconditional right. Except as provided by paragraph (b) of this section, a right which, at a particular time, is conditioned under the plan upon a subsequent event, subsequent performance, or subsequent forbearance which will cause the loss of such right is a forfeitable right at that time. Certain adjustments to plan benefits such as

adjustments in excess of reasonable actuarial reductions, can result in rights being forfeitable. Rights which are conditioned upon a sufficiency of plan assets in the event of a termination or partial termination are considered to be forfeitable because of such condition. However, a plan does not violate the nonforfeitability requirements merely because in the event of a termination an employee does not have any recourse toward satisfaction of his nonforfeitable benefits from other than the plan assets or the Pension Benefit Guaranty Corporation. Furthermore, nonforfeitable rights are not considered to be forfeitable by reason of the fact that they may be reduced to take into account benefits which are provided under the Social Security Act or under any other Federal or State law and which are taken into account in determining plan benefits. To the extent that rights are not required to be nonforfeitable to satisfy the minimum vesting standards, or the nondiscrimination requirements of section 401(a)(4), they may be forfeited without regard to the limitations on forfeitability required by this section.

* * *

§ 1.411(a)-11. Restriction and valuation of distributions.

(a) *Scope—*(1) *In general.* Section 411(a)(11) restricts the ability of a plan to distribute any portion of a participant's accrued benefit without the participant's consent. Section 411(a)(11) also restricts the ability of defined benefit plans to distribute any portion of a participant's accrued benefit in optional forms of benefit without complying with specified valuation rules for determining the amount of the distribution. If the consent requirements or the valuation rules of this section are not satisfied, the plan fails to satisfy the requirements of section 411(a).

(2) *Accrued benefit.* For purposes of this section, an accrued benefit is valued taking into consideration the particular optional form in which the benefit is to be distributed. The value of an accrued benefit is the present value of the benefit in the distribution form determined under the plan. For example, a plan

that provides a subsidized early retirement annuity benefit may specify that the optional single sum distribution form of benefit available at early retirement age is the present value of the subsidized early retirement annuity benefit. In this case, the subsidized early retirement annuity benefit must be used to apply the valuation requirements of this section and the resulting amount of the single sum distribution. However, if a plan that provides a subsidized early retirement annuity benefit specifies that the single sum distribution benefit available at early retirement age is the present value of the normal retirement annuity benefit, then the normal retirement annuity benefit is used to apply the valuation requirements of this section and the resulting amount of the single sum distribution available at early retirement age.

* * *

(d) *Distribution valuation requirements.* In determining the present value of any distribution of any accrued benefit from a defined benefit plan, the plan must take into account specified valuation rules. For this purpose, the valuation rules are the same valuation rules for valuing distributions as set forth in section 417(e); see § 1.417(e)-1(d). This paragraph (d) applies both before and after the participant's death regardless of whether the accrued benefit is immediately distributable. This paragraph also applies whether or not the participant's consent is required under paragraphs (b) and (c) of this section.

* * *

§ 1.411(d)-2. Termination or partial termination; discontinuance of contributions.

* * *

(b) *Partial termination*—(1) *General rule.* Whether or not a partial termination of a qualified plan occurs (and the time of such event) shall be determined by the Commissioner with regard to all the facts and circumstances in a particular case. Such facts and circumstances include: the exclusion, by reason of a plan amendment or severance by the

employer, of a group of employees who have previously been covered by the plan; and plan amendments which adversely affect the rights of employees to vest in benefits under the plan.

(2) *Special rule.* If a defined benefit plan ceases or decreases future benefit accruals under the plan, a partial termination shall be deemed to occur if, as a result of such cessation or decrease, a potential reversion to the employer, or employers, maintaining the plan (determined as of the date such cessation or decrease is adopted) is created or increased. If no such reversion is created or increased, a partial termination shall be deemed not to occur by reason of such cessation or decrease. However, the Commissioner may determine that a partial termination of such a plan occurs pursuant to subparagraph (1) of this paragraph for reasons other than such cessation or decrease.

(3) *Effect of partial termination.* If a termination of a qualified plan occurs, the provisions of section 411(d)(3) apply only to the part of the plan that is terminated.

* * *

§ 1.411(d)-3. Section 411(d)(6) protected benefits.

(a) *Protection of accrued benefits*—(1) *General rule.* Under section 411(d)(6)(A), a plan is not a qualified plan (and a trust forming a part of such plan is not a qualified trust) if a plan amendment decreases the accrued benefit of any plan participant, except as provided in section 412(d)(2) (section 412(c)(8) for plan years beginning before January 1, 2008), section 4281 of the Employee Retirement Income Security Act of 1974 as amended (ERISA), or other applicable law (see, for example, sections 418D and 418E of the Internal Revenue Code, and section 1107 of the Pension Protection Act of 2006, Public Law 109-280 (120 Stat. 780, 1063)). However, such an amendment does not violate section 411(d)(6) to the extent it applies with respect to benefits that accrue after the applicable amendment date. The protection of section 411(d)(6) applies to a participant's entire accrued benefit under the plan as of the applicable amendment date, without regard to whether the entire accrued benefit was accrued before a participant's severance from employment or whether any portion was the result of an increase in the accrued benefit of the participant pursuant to a plan amendment adopted after the participant's severance from employment.

(2) *Plan provisions taken into account—*(i) *Direct or indirect reduction in accrued benefit.* For purposes of determining whether a participant's accrued benefit is decreased, all of the amendments to the provisions of a plan affecting, directly or indirectly, the computation of accrued benefits are taken into account. Plan provisions indirectly affecting the computation of accrued benefits include, for example, provisions relating to years of service and compensation.

(ii) *Amendments effective with the same applicable amendment date.* In determining whether a reduction in a participant's accrued benefit has occurred, all plan amendments with the same applicable amendment date are treated as one amendment. Thus, if two amendments have the same applicable amendment date and one amendment, standing alone, increases participants' accrued benefits and the other amendment, standing alone, decreases participants' accrued benefits, the amendments are treated as one amendment and will only violate section 411(d)(6) if, for any participant, the net effect is to decrease participants' accrued benefit as of that applicable amendment date.

(iii) *Multiple amendments—*(A) *General rule.* A plan amendment violates the requirements of section 411(d)(6) if it is one of a series of plan amendments that, when taken together, have the effect of reducing or eliminating a section 411(d)(6) protected benefit in a manner that would be prohibited by section 411(d)(6) if accomplished through a single amendment.

(B) *Determination of the time period for combining plan amendments.* For purposes of applying the rule in paragraph (a)(2)(iii)(A) of this section, generally only plan amendments adopted within a 3-year period are taken into account.

* * *

(g) *Definitions and use of terms.* The definitions in this paragraph (g) apply for purposes of this section.

* * *

(6) *Definitions of types of section 411(d)(6)(B) protected benefits—*(i) *Early retirement benefit.* The term early retirement benefit means the right, under the terms of a plan, to commence distribution of a retirement-type benefit at a particular date after severance from employment with the employer and before normal retirement age. Different early retirement benefits result from differences in terms relating to timing.

(ii) *Optional form of benefit—*(A) *In general.* The term optional form of benefit means a distribution alternative (including the normal form of benefit) that is available under the plan with respect to an accrued benefit or a distribution alternative with respect to a retirement-type benefit. Different optional forms of benefit exist if a distribution alternative is not payable on substantially the same terms as another distribution alternative. The relevant terms include all terms affecting the value of the optional form, such as the method of benefit calculation and the actuarial factors or assumptions used to determine the amount distributed. Thus, for example, different optional forms of benefit may result from differences in terms relating to the payment schedule, timing, commencement, medium of distribution (e.g., in cash or in kind), election rights, differences in eligibility requirements, or the portion of the benefit to which the distribution alternative applies. Likewise, differences in the normal retirement ages of employees or in the form in which the accrued benefit of employees is payable at normal retirement age under a plan are taken into account in determining whether a distribution alternative constitutes one or more optional forms of benefit.

(B) *Death benefits.* If a death benefit is payable after the annuity starting date for a specific optional form of benefit and the same death benefit would not be provided if another optional form of benefit were elected by a participant, then that death benefit is part of the specific optional form of benefit and is thus protected under section 411(d)(6). A death benefit is not treated as part of a specific optional form of benefit merely because the same benefit is not provided to a participant who has received his or her entire accrued benefit prior to death. For example, a $5,000 death benefit that is payable to all participants except any participant who has received his or her accrued benefit in a single-sum distribution is not part of a specific optional form of benefit.

(iii) *Retirement-type benefit.* The term retirement-type benefit means—

(A) The payment of a distribution alternative with respect to an accrued benefit; or

(B) The payment of any other benefit under a defined benefit plan (including a QSUPP as defined in § 1.401(a)(4)-12) that is permitted to be in a qualified pension plan, continues after retirement, and is not an ancillary benefit.

(iv) *Retirement-type subsidy.* The term retirement-type subsidy means the excess, if any, of the actuarial present value of a retirement-type benefit over the actuarial present value of the accrued benefit commencing at normal retirement age or at actual commencement date, if later, with both such actuarial present values determined as of the date the retirement-type benefit commences. Examples of retirement-type subsidies include a subsidized early retirement benefit and a subsidized qualified joint and survivor annuity.

(v) *Subsidized early retirement benefit or early retirement subsidy.* The terms subsidized early retirement benefit or early retirement subsidy mean the right, under the terms of a plan, to commence distribution of a retirement-type benefit at a particular date after severance from employment with the employer and before normal retirement age where the actuarial present value of the optional forms of benefit available to the participant under the plan at that annuity starting date exceeds the actuarial present value of the accrued benefit commencing at normal retirement age (with such actuarial present values determined as of the annuity starting date). Thus, an early retirement subsidy is an early retirement benefit that provides a retirement-type subsidy.

* * *

§ 1.411(d)-4. Section 411(d)(6) protected benefits.

Q-1: What are "section 411(d)(6) protected benefits"?

A-1: (a) *In general.* The term "section 411(d)(6) protected benefit" includes any benefit that is described in one or more of the following categories—

(1) Benefits described in section 411(d)(6)(A),

(2) Early retirement benefits (as defined in § 1.411(d)-3(g)(6)(i)) and retirement-type subsidies (as defined in § 1.411(d)-3(g)(6)(iv)), and

(3) Optional forms of benefit described in section 411(d)(6)(B)(ii).

Such benefits, to the extent they have accrued, are subject to the protection of section 411(d)(6) and, where applicable, the definitely determinable requirement of section 401(a) (including section 401(a)(25)) and cannot, therefore, be reduced, eliminated, or made subject to employer discretion except to the extent permitted by regulations.

(b) *Optional forms of benefit—* (1) *In general.* The term optional form of benefit has the same meaning as in § 1.411(d)-3(g)(6)(ii). Under this definition, different optional forms of benefit exist if a distribution alternative is not payable on substantially the same terms as another distribution alternative. Thus, for example, different optional forms of benefit may result from differences in terms relating to the payment schedule, timing, commencement, medium of distribution (e.g., in cash or in kind), election rights, differences in eligibility requirements, or the portion of the benefit to which the distribution alternative applies.

* * *

(c) *Plan terms*—(1) *General rule.* Generally, benefits described in section 411(d)(6)(A), early retirement benefits, retirement-type subsidies, and optional forms of benefit are section 411(d)(6) protected benefits only if they are provided under the terms of a plan. However, if an employer establishes a pattern of repeated plan amendments providing for similar benefits in similar situations for substantially consecutive, limited periods of time, such benefits will be treated as provided under the terms of the plan, without regard to the limited periods of time, to the extent necessary to carry out the purposes of section 411(d)(6) and, where applicable, the definitely determinable requirement of section 401(a), including section 401(a)(25). A pattern of repeated plan amendments providing that a particular optional form of benefit is available to certain named employees for a limited period of time is within the scope of this rule and may result in such optional form of benefit being treated as provided under the terms of the plan to all employees covered under the plan without regard to the limited period of time and the limited group of named employees.

* * *

(d) *Benefits that are not section 411(d)(6) protected benefits.* The following benefits are examples of items that are not section 411(d)(6) protected benefits:

(1) Ancillary life insurance protection;

(2) Accident or health insurance benefits;

(3) Social security supplements described in section 411(a)(9), except qualified social security supplements as defined in § 1.401(a)(4)-12;

(4) The availability of loans (other than the distribution of an employee's accrued benefit upon default under a loan);

(5) The right to make after-tax employee contributions or elective deferrals described in section 402(g)(3);

(6) The right to direct investments;

(7) The right to a particular form of investment (e.g., investment in employer stock or securities or investment in certain types of securities, commercial paper, or other investment media);

(8) The allocation dates for contributions, forfeitures, and earnings, the time for making contributions (but not the conditions for receiving an allocation of contributions or forfeitures for a plan year after such conditions have been satisfied), and the valuation dates for account balances;

(9) Administrative procedures for distributing benefits, such as provisions relating to the particular dates on which notices are given and by which elections must be made; and

(10) Rights that derive from administrative and operational provisions, such as mechanical procedures for allocating investment experience among accounts in defined contribution plans.

Q-2: To what extent may section 411(d)(6) protected benefits under a plan be reduced or eliminated?

A-2: (a) *Reduction or elimination of section 411(d)(6) protected benefits*—(1) *In general.* A plan is not permitted to be amended to eliminate or reduce a section 411(d)(6) protected benefit that has already accrued, except as provided in § 1.411(d)-3 or this section. This is generally the case even if such elimination or reduction is contingent upon the employee's consent. However, a plan may be amended to eliminate or reduce section 411(d)(6) protected benefits with respect to benefits not yet accrued as of the later of the amendment's adoption date or effective date without violating section 411(d)(6).

(2) *Selection of optional forms of benefit*—(i) *General rule.* A plan may treat a participant as receiving his entire nonforfeitable accrued benefit under the plan if the partici-

pant receives his benefit in an optional form of benefit in an amount determined under the plan that is at least the actuarial equivalent of the employee's nonforfeitable accrued benefit payable at normal retirement age under the plan. This is true even though the participant could have elected to receive an optional form of benefit with a greater actuarial value than the value of the optional form received, such as an optional form including retirement-type subsidies, and without regard to whether such other, more valuable optional form could have commenced immediately or could have become available only upon the employee's future satisfaction of specified eligibility conditions.

* * *

(e) *Permitted plan amendments affecting alternative forms of payment under defined contribution plans*—(1) *General rule.* A defined contribution plan does not violate the requirements of section 411(d)(6) merely because the plan is amended to eliminate or restrict the ability of a participant to receive payment of accrued benefits under a particular optional form of benefit for distributions with annuity starting dates after the date the amendment is adopted if, after the plan amendment is effective with respect to the participant, the alternative forms of payment available to the participant include payment in a single-sum distribution form that is otherwise identical to the optional form of benefit that is being eliminated or restricted.

(2) *Otherwise identical single-sum distribution.* For purposes of this paragraph (e), a single-sum distribution form is otherwise identical to an optional form of benefit that is eliminated or restricted pursuant to paragraph (e)(1) of this Q&A-2 only if the single-sum distribution form is identical in all respects to the eliminated or restricted optional form of benefit (or would be identical except that it provides greater rights to the participant) except with respect to the timing of payments after commencement. For example, a single-sum distribution form is not otherwise identical to a specified installment form of benefit if the single-sum distribution form is not availa-

ble for distribution on the date on which the installment form would have been available for commencement, is not available in the same medium of distribution as the installment form, or imposes any condition of eligibility that did not apply to the installment form. However, an otherwise identical distribution form need not retain rights or features of the optional form of benefit that is eliminated or restricted to the extent that those rights or features would not be protected from elimination or restriction under section 411(d)(6) or this section.

(3) *Example.* The following example illustrates the application of this paragraph (e):

Example. (i) P is a participant in Plan M, a qualified profit-sharing plan with a calendar plan year that is invested in mutual funds. The distribution forms available to P under Plan M include a distribution of P's vested account balance under Plan M in the form of distribution of various annuity contract forms (including a single life annuity and a joint and survivor annuity). The annuity payments under the annuity contract forms begin as of the first day of the month following P's severance from employment (or as of the first day of any subsequent month, subject to the requirements of section 401(a)(9)). P has not previously elected payment of benefits in the form of a life annuity, and Plan M is not a direct or indirect transferee of any plan that is a defined benefit plan or a defined contribution plan that is subject to section 412. Distributions on the death of a participant are made in accordance with plan provisions that comply with section 401(a)(11)(B)(iii)(I). On September 2, 2005, Plan M is amended so that, effective for payments that begin on or after November 1, 2005, P is no longer entitled to any distribution in the form of the distribution of an annuity contract. However, after the amendment is effective, P is entitled to receive a single-sum cash distribution of P's vested account balance under Plan M payable as of the first day of the month following P's severance from employment (or as of the first day of any subsequent month, subject to the requirements of section 401(a)(9)).

(ii) Plan M does not violate the requirements of section 411(d)(6) (or section 401(a)(11)) merely because, as of November 1, 2005, the plan amendment has eliminated P's option to receive a distribution in any of the various annuity contract forms previously available.

* * *

Q-4: May a plan provide that the employer may, through the exercise of discretion, deny a participant a section 411(d)(6) protected benefit for which the participant is otherwise eligible?

A-4: (a) *In general*. Except as provided in paragraph (d) of Q&A-2 of this section with respect to certain employee stock ownership plans, a plan that permits the employer, either directly or indirectly, through the exercise of discretion, to deny a participant a section 411(d)(6) protected benefit provided under the plan for which the participant is otherwise eligible (but for the employer's exercise of discretion) violates the requirements of section 411(d)(6). A plan provision that makes a section 411(d)(6) protected benefit available only to those employees as the employer may designate is within the scope of this prohibition. Thus, for example, a plan provision under which only employees who are designated by the employer are eligible to receive a subsidized early retirement benefit constitutes an impermissible provision under section 411(d)(6). In addition, a pension plan that permits employer discretion to deny the availability of a section 411(d)(6) protected benefit violates the definitely determinable requirement of section 401(a), including section 401(a)(25). See § 1.401-1(b)(1)(i). This is the result even if the plan specifically limits the employer's discretion to choosing among section 411(d)(6) protected benefits, including optional forms of benefit, that are actuarially equivalent. In addition, the provisions of sections 411(a)(11) and 417(e) that allow a plan to make involuntary distributions of certain amounts are not excepted from this limitation on employer discretion. Thus, for example, a plan may not permit employer discretion with respect to whether benefits will be distributed

involuntarily in the event that the present value of the employee's benefit is not more than the cash-out limit in effect under § 1.411(a)-11(c)(3)(ii) within the meaning of sections 411(a)(11) and 417(e). (An exception is provided for such provisions with respect to the nondiscrimination requirements of section 401(a)(4). See § 1.401(a)(4)-4(b)(2)(ii)(C).)

(b) *Exception for administrative discretion*. A plan may permit limited discretion with respect to the ministerial or mechanical administration of the plan, including the application of objective plan criteria specifically set forth in the plan. Such plan provisions do not violate the requirements of section 411(d)(6) or the definitely determinable requirement of section 401(a), including section 401(a)(25). For example, these requirements are not violated by the following provisions that permit limited administrative discretion:

(1) Commencement of benefit payments as soon as administratively feasible after a stated date or event;

(2) Employer authority to determine whether objective criteria specified in the plan (e.g., objective criteria designed to identify those employees with a heavy and immediate financial need or objective criteria designed to determine whether an employee has a permanent and total disability) have been satisfied; and

(3) Employer authority to determine, pursuant to specific guidelines set forth in the plan, whether the participant or spouse is dead or cannot be located.

* * *

Q-6: May a plan condition the availability of a section 411(d)(6) protected benefit on the satisfaction of objective conditions that are specifically set forth in the plan?

A-6: (a) *Certain objective conditions permissible*—(1) *In general*. The availability of a section 411(d)(6) protected benefit may be limited to employees who satisfy certain objective conditions provided the conditions are ascertainable, clearly set forth in the plan and not subject to the employer's discretion except to the extent reasonably necessary to determine whether the objective conditions have been met. Also, the availability of the section 411(d)(6) protected benefit must meet the nondiscrimination requirements of section 401(a)(4). See § 1.401(a)-4.

(2) *Examples of permissible conditions.* The following examples illustrate of permissible objective conditions: a plan may deny a single sum distribution form to employees for whom life insurance is not available at standard rates as defined under the terms of the plan at the time the single sum distribution would otherwise be payable; a plan may provide that a single sum distribution is available only if the employee is in extreme financial need as defined under the terms of the plan at the time the single sum distribution would otherwise be payable; a plan may condition the availability of a single sum distribution on the execution of a covenant not to compete, provided that objective conditions with respect to the terms of such covenant and the employees and circumstances requiring execution of such covenant are set forth in the plan.

(b) *Conditions based on factors within employer's discretion generally impermissible.* A plan may not limit the availability of section 411(d)(6) protected benefits permitted under the plan on objective conditions that are within the employer's discretion. For example, the availability of section 411(d)(6) protected benefits in a plan may not be conditioned on a determination with respect to the level of the plan's funded status, because the amount of plan funding is within the employer's discretion. However, for example, although conditions based on the plan's funded status are impermissible, a plan may limit the availability of a section 411(d)(6) protected benefit (e.g., a single sum distribution) in an objective manner, such as the following:

(1) Single sum distributions of $25,000 and less are available without limit; and

(2) Single sum distributions in excess of $25,000 are available for a year only to the extent that the total amount of such single sum

distributions for the year is not greater than $5,000,000; and

(3) An objective and nondiscriminatory method for determining which particular single sum distributions will not be available during a year in order for the $5,000,000 limit to be satisfied is set forth in the plan.

* * *

§ 1.414(c)-2. Two or more trades or businesses under common control.

(a) *In general.* For purposes of this section, the term "two or more trades or businesses under common control" means any group of trades or businesses which is either a "parent-subsidiary group of trades or businesses under common control" as defined in paragraph (b) of this section, a "brother-sister group of trades or businesses under common control" as defined in paragraph (c) of this section, or a "combined group of trades or businesses under common control" as defined in paragraph (d) of this section. For purposes of this section and §§ 1.414(c)-3 and 1.414(c)-4, the term "organization" means a sole proprietorship, a partnership (as defined in section 7701(a)(2)), a trust, an estate, or a corporation.

(b) *Parent-subsidiary group of trades or businesses under common control*—(1) *In general.* The term "parent-subsidiary group of trades or businesses under common control" means one or more chains of organizations conducting trades or businesses connected through ownership of a controlling interest with a common parent organization if—

(i) A controlling interest in each of the organizations, except the common parent organization, is owned (directly and with the application of § 1.414(c)-4(b)(1), relating to options) by one or more of the other organizations; and

(ii) The common parent organization owns (directly and with the application of § 1.414(c)-4(b)(1), relating to options) a controlling interest in at least one of the other organizations, excluding, in computing such controlling interest, any direct ownership interest by such other organizations.

(2) *Controlling interest defined*—(i) *Controlling interest*. For purposes of paragraphs (b) and (c) of this section, the phrase "controlling interest" means:

(A) In the case of an organization which is a corporation, ownership of stock possessing at least 80 percent of total combined voting power of all classes of stock entitled to vote of such corporation or at least 80 percent of the total value of shares of all classes of stock of such corporation;

(B) In the case of an organization which is a trust or estate, ownership of an actuarial interest of at least 80 percent of such trust or estate;

(C) In the case of an organization which is a partnership, ownership of at least 80 percent of the profits interest or capital interest of such partnership; and

(D) In the case of an organization which is a sole proprietorship, ownership of such sole proprietorship.

(ii) *Actuarial interest*. For purposes of this section, the actuarial interest of each beneficiary of trust or estate shall be determined by assuming the maximum exercise of discretion by the fiduciary in favor of such beneficiary. The factors and methods prescribed in § 20.2031-7 or, for certain prior periods, § 20.2031-7A (Estate Tax Regulations), for use in ascertaining the value of an interest in property for estate tax purposes shall be used for purposes of this subdivision in determining a beneficiary's actuarial interest.

(c) *Brother-sister group of trades or businesses under common control*—(1) *In general*. The term "brother-sister group of trades or businesses under common control" means two or more organizations conducting trades or businesses if (i) the same five or fewer persons who are individuals, estates, or trusts own (directly and with the application of § 1.414(c)-4) a controlling interest in each organization, and (ii) taking into account the ownership of each such person only to the

extent such ownership is identical with respect to each such organization, such persons are in effective control of each organization. The five or fewer persons whose ownership is considered for purposes of the controlling interest requirement for each organization must be the same persons whose ownership is considered for purposes of the effective control requirement.

(2) Effective control defined. For purposes of this paragraph, persons are in "effective control" of an organization if—

(i) In the case of an organization which is a corporation, such persons own stock possessing more than 50 percent of the total combined voting power of all classes of stock entitled to vote or more than 50 percent of the total value of shares of all classes of stock of such corporation;

(ii) In the case of an organization which is a trust or estate, such persons own an aggregate actuarial interest of more than 50 percent of such trust or estate;

(iii) In the case of an organization which is a partnership, such persons own an aggregate of more than 50 percent of the profits interest or capital interest of such partnership; and

(iv) In the case of an organization which is a sole proprietorship, one of such persons owns such sole proprietorship.

(d) *Combined group of trades or businesses under common control*. The term "combined group of trades or businesses under common control" means any group of three or more organizations, if (1) each such organization is a member of either a parent-subsidiary group of trades or businesses under common control or a brother-sister group of trades or businesses under common control, and (2) at least one such organization is the common parent organization of a parent-subsidiary group of trades or businesses under common control and is also a member of a brother-sister group of trades or businesses under common control.

(e) *Examples.* The definitions of parent-subsidiary group of trades or businesses under common control, brother-sister group of trades or businesses under common control, and combined group of trades or businesses under common control may be illustrated by the following examples.

Example (1). (a) The ABC partnership owns stock possessing 80 percent of the total combined voting power of all classes of stock entitled to voting of S corporation. ABC part nership is the common parent of a parent-subsidiary group of trades or businesses under common control consisting of the ABC partnership and S Corporation.

(b) Assume the same facts as in (a) and assume further that S owns 80 percent of the profits interest in the DEF Partnership. The ABC Partnership is the common parent of a parent-subsidiary group of trades or businesses under common control consisting of the ABC Partnership, S Corporation, and the DEF Partnership. The result would be the same if the ABC Partnership, rather than S, owned 80 percent of the profits interest in the DEF Partnership.

Example (2). L Corporation owns 80 percent of the only class of stock of T Corporation, and T, in turn, owns 40 percent of the capital interest in the GHI Partnership. L also owns 80 percent of the only class of stock of N Corporation and N, in turn, owns 40 percent of the capital interest in the GHI Partnership. L is the common parent of a parent-subsidiary group of trades or businesses under common control consisting of L Corporation, T Corporation, N Corporation, and the GHI Partnership.

Example (3). ABC Partnership owns 75 percent of the only class of stock of X and Y Corporations; X owns all the remaining stock of Y, and Y owns all the remaining stock of X. Since interorganization ownership is excluded (that is, treated as not outstanding) for purposes of determining whether ABC owns a controlling interest of at least one of the other organizations, ABC is treated as the owner of stock possessing 100 percent of the voting power and value of all classes of stock of X and of Y for purposes of paragraph (b)(1)(ii) of this section. Therefore, ABC is the common parent of a parent-subsidiary group of trades or businesses under common control consisting of the ABC Partnership, X Corporation, and Y Corporation.

Example (4). Unrelated individuals A, B, C, D, E, and F own an interest in sole proprietorship A, a capital interest in the GHI Partnership, and stock of corporations M, W, X, Y, and Z (each of which has only one class of stock outstanding) in the following proportions:

ORGANIZATIONS

Individuals	A	GHI	M	W	X	Y	Z
A	100%	50%	100%	60%	40%	20%	60%
B	—	40%	—	15%	40%	50%	30%
C	—	—	—	—	10%	10%	10%
D	—	—	—	25%	—	20%	—
E	—	10%	—	—	10%	—	—
	100%	100%	100%	100%	100%	100%	100%

Under these facts the following four brother-sister groups of trades or businesses under common control exist: GHI, X and Z; X, Y and Z; W and Y; A and M. In the case of GHI, X, and Z, for example, A and B together have effective control of each organization because their combined identical ownership of GHI, X and Z is greater than 50%. (A's identical ownership of GHI, X and Z is 40% because A owns at least a 40% interest in each organization. B's identical ownership of GHI, X and Z is 30% because B owns at least a 30% interest in each organization.) A and B (the persons whose ownership is considered for purposes of the effective control requirement) together own a controlling interest in each organization because they own at least 80% of the capital interest of partnership GHI and at least 80% of the total combined voting power of corporations X and Z. Therefore, GHI, X and Z comprise a brother-sister group of trades or businesses under common control. Y is not a member of this group because neither the effective control requirement nor the 80% controlling interest requirement are met. (The effective control requirement is not met because A's and B's combined identical ownership in GHI, X, Y and Z (20% for A and 30% for B) does not exceed 50%. The 80% controlling interest test is not met because A and B together only own 70% of the total combined voting power of the stock of Y.) A and M are not members of this group because B owns no interest in either organization and A's ownership of GHI, X and Z, considered alone, is less than 80%.

* * *

§ 1.414(c)-4. Rules for determining ownership.

(a) *In general*. In determining the ownership of an interest in an organization for purposes of § 1.414(c)-2 and § 1.414(c)-3, the constructive ownership rules of paragraph (b) of this section shall apply, subject to the operating rules contained in paragraph (c). For purposes of this section the term "interest" means: in the case of a corporation, stock; in the case of a trust or estate, an actuarial interest; in the case of a partnership, an interest in the profits or capital; and in the case of a sole proprietorship, the proprietorship.

(b) *Constructive ownership*—(1) *Options*. If a person has an option to acquire any outstanding interest in an organization, such interest shall be considered as owned by such person. For this purpose, an option to acquire an option, and each one of a series of such options shall be considered as an option to acquire such interest.

(2) *Attribution from partnerships*—(i) General. An interest owned, directly or indirectly, by or for a partnership shall be considered as owned by any partner having an interest of 5 percent or more in either the profits or capital of the partnership in proportion to such partner's interest in the profits or capital, whichever such proportion is greater.

* * *

(3) *Attribution from estates and trusts*—(i) *In general*. An interest in an organization (hereinafter called an "organization interest") owned, directly or indirectly, by or for an estate or trust shall be considered as owned by any beneficiary of such estate or trust who has an actuarial interest of 5 percent or more in such organization interest, to the extent of such actuarial interest. For purposes of this subparagraph, the actuarial interest of each beneficiary shall be determined by assuming the maximum exercise of discretion by the fiduciary in favor of such beneficiary and the maximum use of the organization interest to satisfy the beneficiary's rights. A beneficiary of an estate or trust who cannot under any circumstances receive any part of an organization interest held by the estate or trust, including the proceeds from the disposition thereof, or the income therefrom, does not have an actuarial interest in such organization interest. Thus, where stock owned by a decedent's estate has been specifically bequeathed to certain beneficiaries and the remainder of the estate has been specifically bequeathed to other beneficiaries, the stock is attributable only to the beneficiaries to whom it is specifically bequeathed. Similarly a remainderman of a trust who cannot under any circumstances receive any interest in the stock of a corporation which is a part of the corpus of the trust (including any accumulated income therefrom or the proceeds from a disposition thereof) does not have an actuarial interest in such stock. However, an income beneficiary of a trust does have an actuarial interest in stock if he has any right to the income from such stock even though under the terms of the trust in-

strument such stock can never be distributed to him. The factors and methods prescribed in § 20.2031-7 or, for certain prior periods, § 20.2031-7A (Estate Tax Regulations) for use in ascertaining the value of an interest in property for estate tax purposes shall be used for purposes of this subdivision in determining a beneficiary's actuarial interest in an organization interest owned directly or indirectly by or for an estate or trust.

(ii) *Special rules for estates.* (A) For purposes of this paragraph (b)(3) with respect to an estate, property of a decedent shall be considered as owned by his or her estate if such property is subject to administration by the executor or administrator for the purposes of paying claims against the estate and expenses of administration notwithstanding that, under local law, legal title to such property vests in the decedent's heirs, legatees or devisees immediately upon death.

(B) For purposes of this paragraph (b)(3) with respect to an estate, the term "beneficiary" includes any person entitled to receive property of a decedent pursuant to a will or pursuant to laws of descent and distribution.

(C) For purposes of this paragraph (b)(3) with respect to an estate, a person shall no longer be considered a beneficiary of an estate when all the property to which he or she is entitled has been received by him or her, when he or she no longer has a claim against the estate arising out of having been a beneficiary, and when there is only a remote possibility that it will be necessary for the estate to seek the return of property from him or her or to seek payment from him or her by contribution or otherwise to satisfy claims against the estate or expenses of administration.

(iii) *Grantor trusts, etc.* An interest owned, directly or indirectly, by or for any portion of a trust of which a person is considered the owner under subpart E, part I, subchapter J of the Code (relating to grantors and others treated as substantial owners) is considered as owned by such person.

(4) *Attribution from corporations—*(i) *General.* An interest owned, directly or indi-

rectly, by or for a corporation shall be considered as owned by any person who owns (directly and, in the case of a parent-subsidiary group of trades or businesses under common control, with the application of paragraph (b)(1) of this section, or in the case of a brother-sister group of trades or business under common control, with the application of this section), 5 percent or more in value of the stock in that proportion which the value of the stock which such person so owns bears to the total value of all the stock in such corporation.

(ii) *Example.* The provisions of paragraph (b)(4)(i) of this section may be illustrated by the following example:

Example. B, an individual, owns 60 of the 100 shares of the only class of outstanding stock of corporation P. C, an individual, owns 4 shares of the P stock, and corporation X owns 36 shares of the P stock. Corporation P owns, directly and indirectly, 50 shares of the stock of corporation S. Under this subparagraph, B is considered to own 30 shares of the S stock (60/100 x 50), and X is considered to own 18 shares of S stock (36/100 x 50). Since C does not own 5 percent or more in the value of P stock, he is not considered as owning any of the S stock owned by P. If in this example, C's wife had owned directly 1 share of the P stock, C and his wife would each be considered as owning 5 shares of the P stock, and therefore C and his wife would be considered as owning 2.5 shares of the S stock (5/100 x 50).

(5) *Spouse—*(i) *General rule.* Except as provided in paragraph (b)(5)(ii) of this section, an individual shall be considered to own an interest owned, directly or indirectly, by or for his or her spouse, other than a spouse who is legally separated from the individual under a decree of divorce, whether interlocutory or final, or a decree of separate maintenance.

(ii) *Exception.* An individual shall not be considered to own an interest in an organization owned, directly or indirectly, by or for his or her spouse on any day of a taxable year of such organization, provided that each of the following conditions are satisfied with respect to such taxable year:

(A) Such individual does not, at any time during such taxable year, own directly any interest in such organization;

(B) Such individual is not a member of the board of directors, a fiduciary, or an employee of such organization and does not participate in the management of such organization at any time during such taxable year;

(C) Not more than 50 percent of such organization's gross income for such taxable year was derived from royalties, rents, dividends, interest, and annuities; and

(D) Such interest in such organization is not, at any time during such taxable year, subject to conditions which substantially restrict or limit the spouse's right to dispose of such interest and which run in favor of the individual or the individual's children who have not attained the age of 21 years. The principles of § 1.414(c)-3(d)(6)(i) shall apply in determining whether a condition is a condition described in the preceding sentence.

(iii) *Definitions.* For purposes of paragraph (b)(5)(ii)(C) of this section, the gross income of an organization shall be determined under section 61 and the regulations thereunder. The terms "interest", "royalties", "rents", "dividends", and "annuities" shall have the same meaning such terms are given for purposes of section 1244(c) and § 1.1244(c)-1(e)(1).

(6) *Children, grandchildren, parents, and grandparents*—(i) *Children and parents.* An individual shall be considered to own an interest owned, directly or indirectly, by or for the individual's children who have not attained the age of 21 years, and if the individual has not attained the age of 21 years, an interest owned, directly or indirectly, by or for the individual's parents.

(ii) *Children, grandchildren, parents, and grandparents.* If an individual is in effective control (within the meaning of § 1.414(c)-2(c)(2)), directly and with the application of the rules of this paragraph without regard to

this subdivision, of an organization, then such individual shall be considered to own an interest in such organization owned, directly or indirectly, by or for the individual's parents, grandparents, grandchildren, and children who have attained the age of 21 years.

(iii) *Adopted children.* For purposes of this section, a legally adopted child of an individual shall be treated as a child of such individual.

(iv) *Example.* The provisions of this subparagraph (6) may be illustrated by the following example:

Example—(A) *Facts.* Individual F owns directly 40 percent of the profits interest of the DEF Partnership. His son, M, 20 years of age, owns directly 30 percent of the profits interest of DEF, and his son, A, 30 years of age, owns directly 20 percent of the profits interest of DEF. The 10 percent remaining of the profits interest and 100 percent of the capital interest of DEF is owned by an unrelated person.

(B) *F's ownership.* F owns 40 percent of the profits interest in DEF directly and is considered to own the 30 percent profits interest owned directly by M. Since, for purposes of the effective control test contained in paragraph (b)(6)(ii) of this section, F is treated as owning 70 percent of the profits interest of DEF, F is also considered as owning the 20 percent profits interest of DEF owned by his adult son, A. Accordingly, F is considered as owning a total of 90 percent of the profits interest in DEF.

(C) *M's ownership.* Minor son, M. owns 30 percent of the profits interest in DEF directly, and is considered to own the 40 percent profits interest owned directly by his father, F. However, M is not considered to own the 20 percent profits interest of DEF owned directly by his brother, A, and constructively by F, because an interest constructively owned by F by reason of family attribution is not considered as owned by him for purposes of making another member of his family the constructive owner of such interest. (See paragraph (c)(2) of this section.) Accordingly, M is considered as owning a total of 70 percent of the profits interest of the DEF Partnership.

(D) *A's ownership.* Adult son, A, owns 20 percent of the profits interest in DEF directly. Since, for purposes of determining whether A effectively controls DEF under paragraph (b)(6)(ii) of this section, A is treated as owning only the percentage of profits interest he owns directly, he does not satisfy the condition precedent for the attribution of the DEF profits interest from his father. Accordingly, A is considered as owning only the 20 percent profits interest in DEF which he owns directly.

(c) *Operating rules*—(1) *In general.* Except as provided in paragraph (c)(2) of this section, an interest constructively owned by a person by reason of the application of paragraph (b) (1), (2), (3), (4), (5), or (6) of this section shall, for the purposes of applying such paragraph, be treated as actually owned by such person.

(2) *Members of family.* An interest constructively owned by an individual by reason of the application of paragraph (b) (5) or (6) of this section shall not be treated as owned by such individual for purposes of again applying such subparagraphs in order to make another the constructive owner of such interest.

(3) *Precedence of option attribution.* For purposes of this section, if an interest may be considered as owned under paragraph (b)(1) of this section (relating to option attribution) and under any other subparagraph of paragraph (b) of this section, such interest shall be considered as owned by such person under paragraph (b)(1) of this section.

(4) *Examples.* The provisions of this paragraph may be illustrated by the following examples:

Example (1). A, 30 years of age, has a 90 percent interest in the capital and profits of DEF Partnership. DEF owns all the outstanding stock of corporation X and X owns 60 shares of the 100 outstanding shares of corporation Y. Under paragraph (c)(1) of this section, the 60 shares of Y constructively owned by DEF by reason of paragraph (b)(4) of this section are treated as actually owned by DEF for purposes of applying paragraph (b)(2) of this section. Therefore, A is considered as owning 54 shares of the Y stock (90 percent of 60 shares).

Example (2). Assume the same facts as in example (1). Assume further that B, who is 20 years of age and the brother of A, directly owns 40 shares of Y stock. Although the stock of Y owned by B is considered as owned by C (the father of A and B) under paragraph (b)(6)(i) of this section, under paragraph (c)(2) of this section such stock may not be treated as owned by C for purposes of applying paragraph (b)(6)(ii) of this section in order to make A the constructive owner of such stock.

Example (3). Assume the same facts as in example (2), and further assume that C has an option to acquire the 40 shares of Y stock owned by his son, B. The rule contained in paragraph (c)(2) of this section does not prevent the reattribution of such 40 shares to A because, under paragraph (c)(3) of this section, C is considered as owning the 40 shares by reason of option attribution and not by reason of family attribution. Therefore, since A is in effective control of Y under paragraph (b)(6)(ii) of this section, the 40 shares of Y stock constructively owned by C are reattributed to A. A is considered as owning a total of 94 shares of Y stock.

§ 1.414(s)-1. Definition of compensation.

(a) *Introduction*—(1) *In general.* Section 414(s) and this section provide rules for defining compensation for purposes of applying any provision that specifically refers to section 414(s) or this section. For example, section 414(s) is referred to in many of the nondiscrimination provisions applicable to pension, profit-sharing, and stock bonus plans qualified under section 401(a). In accordance with section 414(s)(1), this section defines compensation as compensation within the meaning of section 415(c)(3). It also implements the election provided in section 414(s)(2) to treat certain deferrals as compensation and exercises the authority granted to the Secretary in section 414(s)(3) to prescribe alternative nondiscriminatory definitions of compensation.

(2) *Limitations on scope of section 414(s).* Section 414(s) and this section do not apply unless a provision specifically refers to section 414(s) or this section. For example, even though a definition of compensation permitted under section 414(s) must be used in determining whether the contributions or benefits under a pension, profit-sharing, or stock bonus plan satisfy a certain applicable provision (such as section 401(a)(4)), except as otherwise specified, the plan is not required to use a definition of compensation that satisfies section 414(s) in calculating the amount of contributions or benefits actually provided under the plan.

(3) *Overview.* Paragraph (b) of this section provides rules of general application that govern a definition of compensation that satisfies section 414(s). Paragraph (c) of this section contains specific definitions of compensation that satisfy section 414(s) without satisfying any additional nondiscrimination requirement under section 414(s). Paragraph (d) of this section provides rules permitting the use of alternative definitions of compensation that satisfy section 414(s) as long as the nondiscrimination requirement and other requirements described in paragraph (d) of this section are satisfied. Paragraphs (e) and (f) of this section provide special rules permitting the use of rate of compensation, or prior-employer compensation or imputed compensation, rather than actual compensation, under a definition of compensation that satisfies section 414(s). Paragraph (g) of this section provides other special rules, including a special rule for determining the compensation of a self-employed individual under an alternate definition of compensation. Paragraph (h) of this section provides definitions for certain terms used in this section.

(b) *Rules of general application—(1) Use of a definition.* Any definition of compensation that satisfies section 414(s) may be used when a provision explicitly refers to section 414(s) unless the reference or this section specifically indicates otherwise.

(2) *Consistency rule—(i) General rule.* A definition of compensation selected by an employer for use in satisfying an applicable provision must be used consistently to define the compensation of all employees taken into account in satisfying the requirements of the applicable provision for the determination period. For example, although any definition of compensation that satisfies section 414(s) may be used for section 401(a)(4) purposes, the same definition of compensation generally must be used consistently to define the compensation of all employees taken into account in determining whether a plan satisfies section 401(a)(4). Furthermore, a different definition of compensation that satisfies section 414(s) is permitted to be used to determine whether another plan maintained by the same employer separately satisfies the requirements of section 401(a)(4). Although a definition of compensation must be used consistently, an employer may change its definition of compensation for a subsequent determination period with respect to the applicable provision. Rules provided under any applicable provision may modify the consistency requirements of this paragraph (b)(2).

* * *

(c) *Specific definitions of compensation that satisfy section 414(s)—(1) General rules.* The definitions of compensation provided in paragraphs (c)(2) and (c)(3) of this section satisfy section 414(s) and need not satisfy any additional requirements under section 414(s). Paragraph (c)(2) of this section describes definitions of compensation within the meaning of section 415(c)(3). Paragraph (c)(3) of this section provides a safe harbor alternative definition that excludes certain additional items of compensation. Paragraph (c)(4) of this section permits any definition provided in paragraph (c)(2) or (c)(3) of this section to include certain types of elective contributions and deferred compensation. Paragraph (c)(5) of this section permits certain modifications to a definition otherwise provided under this paragraph (c).

(2) *Compensation within the meaning of section 415(c)(3).* A definition of compensa-

tion that includes all compensation within the meaning of section 415(c)(3) and excludes all other compensation satisfies section 414(s). Sections 1.415(c)-2(b) and (c) provide rules for determining items of compensation included in and excluded from compensation within the meaning of section 415(c)(3). In addition, section 414(s) is satisfied by the safe harbor definitions provided in § 1.415(c)-2(d)(2), (d)(3) and (d)(4) and any additional definitions of compensation prescribed by the Commissioner under the authority provided in § 1.415(c)-2(d)(1) that are treated as satisfying section 415(c)(3).

(3) *Safe harbor alternative definition.* Under the safe harbor alternative definition in this paragraph (c)(3), compensation is compensation as defined in paragraph (c)(2) of this section, reduced by all of the following items (even if includible in gross income): reimbursements or other expense allowances, fringe benefits (cash and noncash), moving expenses, deferred compensation, and welfare benefits.

(4) *Inclusion of certain deferrals in compensation.* Any definition of compensation provided in paragraph (c)(2) or (c)(3) of this section satisfies section 414(s) even though it is modified to include all of the following types of elective contributions and all of the following types of deferred compensation—

(i) Elective contributions that are made by the employer on behalf of its employees that are not includible in gross income under section 125, section 402(e)(3), section 402(h), and section 403(b);

(ii) Compensation deferred under an eligible deferred compensation plan within the meaning of section 457(b) (deferred compensation plans of state and local governments and tax-exempt organizations); and

(iii) Employee contributions (under governmental plans) described in section 414(h)(2) that are picked up by the employing unit and thus are treated as employer contributions.

(5) *Exclusions applicable solely to highly compensated employees.* Any definition of compensation that satisfies paragraph (c)(2) or (c)(3) of this section, with or without the modification permitted by paragraph (c)(4) of this section, may be modified to exclude any portion of the compensation of some or all of the employer's highly compensated employees (including, for example, any one or more of the types of elective contributions or deferred compensation described in paragraph (c)(4) of this section).

(d) *Alternative definitions of compensation that satisfy section 414(s)*—(1) *General rule.* In addition to the definitions provided in paragraph (c) of this section, any definition of compensation satisfies section 414(s) with respect to employees (other than self-employed individuals treated as employees under section 401(c)(1)) if the definition of compensation does not by design favor highly compensated employees, is reasonable within the meaning of paragraph (d)(2) of this section, and satisfies the nondiscrimination requirement in paragraph (d)(3) of this section.

(2) *Reasonable definition of compensation*—(i) *General rule.* An alternative definition of compensation under this paragraph (d) is reasonable under section 414(s) if it is a definition of compensation provided in paragraph (c) of this section, modified to exclude all or any portion of one or more of the types of compensation described in paragraph (d)(2)(ii) of this section. See paragraph (e) of this section, however, for special rules that permit definitions of compensation based on employees' rates of compensation and paragraph (f) of this section for special rules that permit definitions of compensation that include prior-employer compensation or imputed compensation.

(ii) *Items that may be excluded.* A reasonable definition of compensation is permitted to exclude, on a consistent basis, all or any portion of irregular or additional compensation, including (but not limited to) one or more of the following: Any type of additional compensation for employees working outside their regularly scheduled tour of duty (such as overtime pay, premiums for shift differential, and call-in premiums), bonuses, or any one or more of the types of compensation excluded under the safe harbor alternative definition in paragraph (c)(3) of this section. Whether a type of compensation is irregular or additional is determined based on all the relevant facts and circumstances. A reasonable definition is also permitted to include, on a consistent basis, all or any portion of the types of elective contributions or deferred compensation described in paragraph (c)(4) of this section and, thus, need not include all those types of elective contributions or deferred compensation as otherwise required under paragraph (c)(4) of this section.

(iii) *Limits on the amount excluded from compensation.* A definition of compensation is not reasonable if it provides that each employee's compensation is a specified portion of the employee's compensation measured for the otherwise applicable determination period under another definition. For example, a definition of compensation that specifically limits each employee's compensation for a determination period to 95 percent of the employee's compensation using a definition provided in paragraph (c) of this section is not reasonable. Similarly, a definition of compensation that limits each employee's compensation used to satisfy an applicable provision with a 12-month determination period to compensation under a definition provided in paragraph (c) of this section for one month is not a reasonable definition of compensation. However, a definition of compensation is not unreasonable merely because it excludes all compensation in excess of a specified dollar amount.

(3) *Nondiscrimination requirement*—(i) *In general.* An alternative definition of compensation under this paragraph (d) is nondiscriminatory under section 414(s) for a determination period if the average percentage of total compensation included under the alternative definition of compensation for an employer's highly compensated employees, as a group for the determination period does not exceed by more than a de minimis amount the average percentage of total compensation included under the alternative definition for the employer's nonhighly compensated employees as a group.

(ii) *Total compensation*—(A) *General rule.* For purposes of this paragraph (d)(3), total compensation must be determined using a definition of compensation provided in paragraph (c)(2) of this section, either with or without the modification permitted by paragraph (c)(4) of this section. Thus, total compensation does not include prior-employer compensation or imputed compensation described in paragraph (f)(1) of this section (including imputed compensation for a period during which an employee performs services for another employer). Total compensation taken into account for each employee (including, if added, the elective contributions and deferred compensation described in paragraph (c)(4) of this section) may not exceed the annual compensation limit of section 401(a)(17).

(B) *Alternative definitions with exclusions applicable solely to highly compensated employees.* If an alternative definition of compensation contains a provision that excludes amounts from compensation and, as described in paragraph (c)(5) of this section, the provision only applies in defining the compensation of some highly compensated employees, then, for purposes of this paragraph (d)(3), the total compensation of any highly compensated employee subject to the provision must be reduced by any amount excluded from the employee's compensation as a result of the provision. However, if the provision applies consistently in defining the compensation of all highly compensated employees, this adjustment to total compensation is not required.

* * *

§ 1.415(c)-2. Compensation.

(a) *General definition.* Except as otherwise provided in this section, compensation from the employer within the meaning of section 415(c)(3), which is used for purposes of section 415 and regulations promulgated under section 415, means all items of remuneration described in paragraph (b) of this section, but excludes the items of remuneration described in paragraph (c) of this section. Paragraph (d) of this section provides safe harbor definitions of compensation that are permitted to be provided in a plan in lieu of the generally applicable definition of compensation. Paragraph (e) of this section provides timing rules relating to compensation. Paragraph (f) of this section provides rules regarding the application of the rules of section 401(a)(17) to the definition of compensation for purposes of section 415. Paragraph (g) of this section provides special rules relating to the determination of compensation, including rules for determining compensation for a section 403(b) annuity contract, rules for determining the compensation of employees of controlled groups or affiliated service groups, rules for disabled employees, rules relating to foreign compensation, rules regarding deemed section 125 compensation, rules for employees in qualified military service, and rules relating to back pay.

(b) *Items includible as compensation.* For purposes of applying the limitations of section 415, except as otherwise provided in this section, the term compensation means remuneration for services of the following types—

(1) The employee's wages, salaries, fees for professional services, and other amounts received (without regard to whether or not an amount is paid in cash) for personal services actually rendered in the course of employment with the employer maintaining the plan, to the extent that the amounts are includible in gross income (or to the extent amounts would have been received and includible in gross income but for an election under section 125(a), 132(f)(4), 402(e)(3), 402(h)(1)(B), 402(k), or 457(b)). These amounts include, but are not limited to, commissions paid to salespersons, compensation for services on the basis of a percentage of profits, commissions on insurance premiums, tips, bonuses, fringe benefits, and reimbursements or other expense allowances under a nonaccountable plan as described in § 1.62-2(c).

(2) In the case of an employee who is an employee within the meaning of section 401(c)(1) and regulations promulgated under section 401(c)(1), the employee's earned income (as described in section 401(c)(2) and regulations promulgated under section 401(c)(2)), plus amounts deferred at the election of the employee that would be includible in gross income but for the rules of section 402(e)(3), 402(h)(1)(B), 402(k), or 457(b).

(3) Amounts described in section 104(a)(3), 105(a), or 105(h), but only to the extent that these amounts are includible in the gross income of the employee.

(4) Amounts paid or reimbursed by the employer for moving expenses incurred by an employee, but only to the extent that at the time of the payment it is reasonable to believe that these amounts are not deductible by the employee under section 217.

(5) The value of a nonstatutory option (which is an option other than a statutory option as defined in § 1.421-1(b)) granted to an employee by the employer, but only to the extent that the value of the option is includible in the gross income of the employee for the taxable year in which granted.

(6) The amount includible in the gross income of an employee upon making the election described in section 83(b).

(7) Amounts that are includible in the gross income of an employee under the rules of section 409A or section 457(f)(1)(A) or because the amounts are constructively received by the employee.

(c) *Items not includible as compensation.* The term compensation does not include—

(1) Contributions (other than elective contributions described in section 402(e)(3), section 408(k)(6), section 408(p)(2)(A)(i), or section 457(b)) made by the employer to a plan of deferred compensation (including a simplified employee pension described in section 408(k) or a simple retirement account described in section 408(p), and whether or not qualified) to the extent that the contributions are not includible in the gross income of the employee for the taxable year in which contributed. In addition, any distributions from a plan of deferred compensation (wheth-

er or not qualified) are not considered as compensation for section 415 purposes, regardless of whether such amounts are includible in the gross income of the employee when distributed. However, if the plan so provides, any amounts received by an employee pursuant to a nonqualified unfunded deferred compensation plan are permitted to be considered as compensation for section 415 purposes in the year the amounts are actually received, but only to the extent such amounts are includible in the employee's gross income.

(2) Amounts realized from the exercise of a nonstatutory option (which is an option other than a statutory option as defined in § 1.421-1(b)), or when restricted stock or other property held by an employee either becomes freely transferable or is no longer subject to a substantial risk of forfeiture (see section 83 and regulations promulgated under section 83).

(3) Amounts realized from the sale, exchange, or other disposition of stock acquired under a statutory stock option (as defined in § 1.421-1(b)).

(4) Other amounts that receive special tax benefits, such as premiums for group-term life insurance (but only to the extent that the premiums are not includible in the gross income of the employee and are not salary reduction amounts that are described in section 125).

(5) Other items of remuneration that are similar to any of the items listed in paragraphs (c)(1) through (c)(4) of this section.

(d) *Safe harbor rules with respect to plan's definition of compensation*—(1) *In general.* Paragraphs (d)(2) through (4) of this section contain safe harbor definitions of compensation that are automatically considered to satisfy section 415(c)(3) if specified in the plan. The Commissioner may, in revenue rulings, notices, and other guidance of general applicability published in the Internal Revenue Bulletin (see § 601.601(d)(2) of this chapter), provide additional definitions of compensation that are treated as satisfying section 415(c)(3).

(2) *Simplified compensation.* The safe harbor definition of compensation under this paragraph (d)(2) includes only those items specified in paragraph (b)(1) or (2) of this section and excludes all those items listed in paragraph (c) of this section.

(3) *Section 3401(a) wages.* The safe harbor definition of compensation under this paragraph (d)(3) includes wages within the meaning of section 3401(a) (for purposes of income tax withholding at the source), plus amounts that would be included in wages but for an election under section 125(a), 132(f)(4), 402(e)(3), 402(h)(1)(B), 402(k), or 457(b). However, any rules that limit the remuneration included in wages based on the nature or location of the employment or the services performed (such as the exception for agricultural labor in section 3401(a)(2)) are disregarded for this purpose.

(4) *Information required to be reported under sections 6041, 6051 and 6052.* The safe harbor definition of compensation under this paragraph (d)(4) includes amounts that are compensation under the safe harbor definition of paragraph (d)(3) of this section, plus all other payments of compensation to an employee by his employer (in the course of the employer's trade or business) for which the employer is required to furnish the employee a written statement under sections 6041(d), 6051(a)(3), and 6052. See §§ 1.6041-1(a), 1.6041-2(a)(1), 1.6052-1, and 1.6052-2, and also see § 31.6051-1(a)(1)(i)(C) of this chapter. This safe harbor definition of compensation may be modified to exclude amounts paid or reimbursed by the employer for moving expenses incurred by an employee, but only to the extent that, at the time of the payment, it is reasonable to believe that these amounts are deductible by the employee under section 217.

(e) *Timing rules*—(1) *In general*—(i) *Payment during the limitation year.* Except as otherwise provided in this paragraph (e), in order to be taken into account for a limitation year, compensation within the meaning of section 415(c)(3) must be actually paid or made available to an employee (or, if earlier, includible in the gross income of the employee) within the limitation year. For this purpose, compensation is treated as paid on a date if it is actually paid on that date or it would have been paid on that date but for an election under section 125, 132(f)(4), 401(k), 403(b), 408(k), 408(p)(2)(A)(i), or 457(b).

(ii) *Payment prior to severance from employment.* Except as otherwise provided in this paragraph (e), in order to be taken into account for a limitation year, compensation within the meaning of section 415(c)(3) must be paid or treated as paid to the employee (in accordance with the rules of paragraph (e)(1)(i) of this section) prior to the employee's severance from employment with the employer maintaining the plan. See § 1.415(a)-1(f)(5) for the definition of severance from employment.

(2) *Certain minor timing differences.* Notwithstanding the provisions of paragraph (e)(1)(i) of this section, a plan may provide that compensation for a limitation year includes amounts earned during that limitation year but not paid during that limitation year solely because of the timing of pay periods and pay dates if—

(i) These amounts are paid during the first few weeks of the next limitation year;

(ii) The amounts are included on a uniform and consistent basis with respect to all similarly situated employees; and

(iii) No compensation is included in more than one limitation year.

(3) *Compensation paid after severance from employment*—(i) *In general.* Any compensation described in paragraph (e)(3)(ii) of this section does not fail to be compensation (within the meaning of section 415(c)(3)) pursuant to the rule of paragraph (e)(1)(ii) of this section merely because it is paid after the employee's severance from employment with the employer maintaining the plan, provided the compensation is paid by the later of 2 1/2 months after severance from employment with the employer maintaining the plan or the end of the limitation year that includes the date of severance from employment with the employer maintaining the plan. In addition, the plan may provide that amounts described in para-

graph (e)(3)(iii) of this section are included in compensation (within the meaning of section 415(c)(3)) if—

(A) Those amounts are paid by the later of 2 1/2 months after severance from employment with the employer maintaining the plan or the end of the limitation year that includes the date of severance from employment with the employer maintaining the plan; and

(B) Those amounts would have been included in the definition of compensation if they were paid prior to the employee's severance from employment with the employer maintaining the plan.

(ii) *Regular pay after severance from employment.* An amount is described in this paragraph (e)(3)(ii) if—

(A) The payment is regular compensation for services during the employee's regular working hours, or compensation for services outside the employee's regular working hours (such as overtime or shift differential), commissions, bonuses, or other similar payments; and

(B) The payment would have been paid to the employee prior to a severance from employment if the employee had continued in employment with the employer.

(iii) *Leave cashouts and deferred compensation.* An amount is described in this paragraph (e)(3)(iii) if the amount is either—

(A) Payment for unused accrued bona fide sick, vacation, or other leave, but only if the employee would have been able to use the leave if employment had continued; or

(B) Received by an employee pursuant to a nonqualified unfunded deferred compensation plan, but only if the payment would have been paid to the employee at the same time if the employee had continued in employment with the employer and only to the extent that the payment is includible in the employee's gross income.

(iv) *Other post-severance payments.* Any payment that is not described in paragraph (e)(3)(ii) or (iii) of this section is not considered compensation under paragraph (e)(3)(i) of this section if paid after severance from employment with the employer maintaining the plan, even if it is paid within the time period described in paragraph (e)(3)(i) of this section. Thus, compensation does not include severance pay, or parachute payments within the meaning of section 280G(b)(2), if they are paid after severance from employment with the employer maintaining the plan, and does not include post-severance payments under a nonqualified unfunded deferred compensation plan unless the payments would have been paid at that time without regard to the severance from employment.

(4) *Salary continuation payments for military service and disabled participants.* The rule of paragraph (e)(1)(ii) of this section does not apply to payments to an individual who does not currently perform services for the employer by reason of qualified military service (as that term is used in section 414(u)(1)) to the extent those payments do not exceed the amounts the individual would have received if the individual had continued to perform services for the employer rather than entering qualified military service, but only if the plan so provides. In addition, the rule of paragraph (e)(1)(ii) of this section does not apply to compensation paid to a participant who is permanently and totally disabled (as defined in section 22(e)(3)) if the conditions set forth in paragraph (g)(4)(ii)(A) of this section are satisfied (applied by substituting a continuation of compensation for the continuation of contributions), but only if the plan so provides.

(5) *Special rule for governmental plans.* For purposes of applying the rules of paragraph (e)(3) of this section, a governmental plan (as defined in section 414(d)) may provide for the substitution of the calendar year in which the severance from employment with the employer maintaining the plan occurs for the limitation year in which the severance from employment with the employer maintaining the plan occurs.

(6) *Examples.* The provisions of this paragraph (e) are illustrated by the following examples:

Example 1. (i) *Facts.* Participant A was a common law employee of Employer X, performing services as a script writer for Employer X from January 1, 2005 to December 31, 2005. Pursuant to a collective bargaining agreement, Employer X, Employer Y and Employer Z maintain and contribute to Plan T, a multiemployer plan (as defined in section 414(f)) in which Participant A participates. Under the collective bargaining agreement, Participant A is entitled to residual payments whenever television shows that Participant A wrote are re-used commercially (These residual payments constitute compensation described in paragraph (b) of this section and do not constitute compensation described in paragraph (c) of this section.). In the year 2008, Participant A receives residual payments from Employer X for television programs using the scripts that Participant A wrote in the year 2005 that were rebroadcast in the year 2008. In the years 2006, 2007, and 2008, Participant A was a common law employee of Employer Y, and did not perform any services for Employer X.

(ii) *Conclusion.* The residual payments received from Employer X by Participant A in the year 2008 are compensation for purposes of section 415(c)(3). The payments are not treated as made after severance from employment because Plan T is a multiemployer plan (as defined in section 414(f)) and Participant A continues to be employed by an employer maintaining Plan T.

Example 2. (i) *Facts.* The facts are the same as in Example 1, except that Participant A: ceased employment with Employer Y in the year 2006; subsequently moved away from the area in which A formerly worked; performs no services as an employee for any employer; and commenced receiving distributions under Plan T in March, 2006.

(ii) *Conclusion.* Based on the facts and circumstances, A has ceased employment with any employer maintaining Plan T. Pursuant to paragraph (e)(1)(ii) of this section, compensation must be paid prior to an employee's severance from employment with the employer maintaining the plan. Accordingly, the residual payments received by Participant A in the year 2008 are not compensation for purposes of section 415(c)(3).

(f) *Interaction with section 401(a)(17).* Because a plan may not base allocations (in the case of a defined contribution plan) or benefits (in the case of a defined benefit plan) on compensation in excess of the limitation under section 401(a)(17), a plan's definition of compensation for a year that is used for purposes of applying the limitations of section 415 is not permitted to reflect compensation for a year that is in excess of the limitation under section 401(a)(17) that applies to that year. See §§ 1.401(a)(17)-1(a)(3)(i) and 1.401(a)(17)-1(b)(3)(ii) for rules regarding the effective date of increases in the section 401(a)(17) compensation limitation for a plan year and for a 12-month period other than the plan year.

(g) Special rules—(1) Compensation for section 403(b) annuity contract. In the case of an annuity contract described in section 403(b), the term participant's compensation means the participant's includible compensation determined under section 403(b)(3). Accordingly, the rules for determining a participant's compensation pursuant to section 415(c)(3) (other than section 415(c)(3)(E)) and this section do not apply to a section 403(b) annuity contract.

(2) *Employees of controlled groups of corporations, etc.* In the case of an employee of two or more corporations which are members of a controlled group of corporations (as defined in section 414(b) as modified by section 415(h)), the term compensation for such employee includes compensation from all employers that are members of the group, regardless of whether the employee's particular employer has a qualified plan. This special rule is also applicable to an employee of two or more trades or businesses (whether or not incorporated) that are under common control (as defined in section 414(c) as modified by section 415(h)), to an employee of two or more members of an affiliated service group as defined in section 414(m), and to an employee of two or more members of any group of employers who must be aggregated and treated as one employer pursuant to section 414(o).

(3) *Aggregation of section 403(b) annuity with qualified plan of controlled employer.* If a section 403(b) annuity contract is aggregated with a qualified plan of a controlled employer in accordance with § 1.415(f)-1(f)(2), then, in applying the limitations of section 415(c) in connection with the aggregation of the section 403(b) annuity with a qualified plan, the total compensation from both employers is permitted to be taken into account.

(4) *Permanent and total disability of defined contribution plan participant—(i) In general.* Pursuant to section 415(c)(3)(C), if the conditions set forth in paragraph (g)(4)(ii) of this section are satisfied, then, in the case of a participant in any defined contribution plan who is permanently and totally disabled (as defined in section 22(e)(3)), the participant's compensation means the compensation the participant would have received for the year if the participant was paid at the rate of compensation paid immediately before becoming permanently and totally disabled, if such compensation is greater than the participant's compensation determined without regard to this paragraph (g)(4).

(ii) *Conditions for deemed disability compensation.* The rule of paragraph (g)(4)(i) of this section applies only if the following conditions are satisfied—

(A) Either the participant is not a highly compensated employee (as defined in section 414(q)) immediately before becoming disabled, or the plan provides for the continuation of contributions on behalf of all participants who are permanently and totally disabled for a fixed or determinable period;

(B) The plan provides that the rule of this paragraph (g)(4) (treating certain amounts as compensation for a disabled participant) applies with respect to the participant; and

(C) Contributions made with respect to amounts treated as compensation under this paragraph (g)(4) are nonforfeitable when made.

* * *

(8) *Back pay.* Payments awarded by an administrative agency or court or pursuant to a bona fide agreement by an employer to compensate an employee for lost wages are compensation within the meaning of section 415(c)(3) for the limitation year to which the back pay relates, but only to the extent such payments represent wages and compensation that would otherwise be included in compensation under this section.

§ 1.415(d)-1. Cost-of-living adjustments.

(a) *Defined benefit plans*—(1) *Dollar limitation*—(i) *Determination of adjusted limit.* Under section 415(d)(1)(A), the dollar limitation described in section 415(b)(1)(A) applicable to defined benefit plans is adjusted annually to take into account increases in the cost of living. The adjustment of the dollar limitation is made by multiplying the adjustment factor for the year, as described in paragraph (a)(1)(ii)(A) of this section, by $160,000, and rounding the result in accordance with paragraph (a)(1)(iii) of this section. The adjusted dollar limitation is prescribed by the Commissioner and published in the Internal Revenue Bulletin. See § 601.601(d)(2) of this chapter.

(ii) *Determination of adjustment factor*— (A) *Adjustment factor.* The adjustment factor for a calendar year is equal to a fraction, the numerator of which is the value of the applicable index for the calendar quarter ending September 30 of the preceding calendar year, and the denominator of which is the value of such index for the base period. The applicable index is determined consistent with the procedures used to adjust benefit amounts under section 215(i)(2)(A) of the Social Security Act, Public Law 92-336 (86 Stat. 406), as amended. If, however, the value of that fraction is less than one for a calendar year, then the adjustment factor for the calendar year is equal to one.

(B) *Base period.* For the purpose of adjusting the dollar limitation pursuant to paragraph (a)(1)(ii)(A) of this section, the base period is the calendar quarter beginning July 1, 2001.

(iii) *Rounding.* Any increase in the $160,000 amount specified in section 415(b)(1)(A) which is not a multiple of $5,000 is rounded to the next lowest multiple of $5,000.

(2) *Average compensation for high-3 years of service limitation*—(i) *Determination of adjusted limit.* Under section 415(d)(1)(B), with regard to participants who have had a severance from employment with the employer maintaining the plan, the compensation limitation described in section 415(b)(1)(B) is permitted to be adjusted annually to take into account increases in the cost of living. For any limitation year beginning after the severance occurs, the adjustment of the compensation limitation is made by multiplying the annual adjustment factor (as defined in paragraph (a)(2)(ii) of this section) by the compensation limitation applicable to the participant in the prior limitation year. The annual adjustment factor is prescribed by the Commissioner and published in the Internal Revenue Bulletin. See § 601.601(d)(2) of this chapter.

(ii) *Annual adjustment factor.* The annual adjustment factor for a calendar year is equal to a fraction, the numerator of which is the value of the applicable index for the calendar quarter ending September 30 of the preceding calendar year, and the denominator of which is the value of such index for the calendar quarter ending September 30 of the calendar year prior to that preceding calendar year. The applicable index is determined consistent with the procedures used to adjust benefit amounts under section 215(i)(2)(A) of the Social Security Act. If the value of the fraction described in the first sentence of this paragraph (a)(2)(ii) is less than one for a calendar year, then the adjustment factor for the calendar year is equal to one. In such a case, the annual adjustment factor for future calendar years will be determined in accordance with revenue rulings, notices, or other published guidance prescribed by the Commissioner and published in the Internal Revenue Bulletin. See § 601.601(d)(2) of this chapter.

(iii) *Special rule for rehired employees.* If, after having a severance from employment with the employer maintaining the plan, an employee is rehired by the employer maintaining the plan, the employee's compensation limit under section 415(b)(1)(B) is the greater of—

(A) 100 percent of the participant's average compensation for the period of the participant's high-3 years of service, as determined prior to the employee's severance from employment with the employer maintaining the plan, as adjusted pursuant to paragraph (a)(2)(i) of this section (if the plan so provides); or

(B) 100 percent of the participant's average compensation for the period of the participant's high-3 years of service, with the period of the participant's high-3 years of service determined pursuant to § 1.415(b)-1(a)(5)(iii).

(3) *Effective date of adjustment.* The adjusted dollar limitation applicable to defined benefit plans and the adjusted compensation limit applicable to a participant are effective as of January 1 of each calendar year and apply with respect to limitation years ending with or within that calendar year. However, benefit payments (and, in the case of plans that are subject to the requirements of section 411, accrued benefits for a limitation year) cannot exceed the currently applicable dollar limitation or compensation limitation (as in effect before the January 1 adjustment) prior to January 1. Thus, where there is an increase in the limitation under section 415(b)(1), any increase in a participant's benefits associated with the limitation increase is permitted to occur as of a date no earlier than January 1 of the calendar year for which the increase in the limitation is effective, and can only be applied for payments due on or after January 1 of such calendar year. For example, assume that a participant in a defined benefit plan is currently receiving a benefit in the form of a straight life annuity, payable monthly, in an amount

equal to the section 415(b)(1)(A) dollar limit, and the defined benefit plan has a limitation year that runs from July 1 to June 30. If the plan is amended to reflect the section 415(d) increase to the section 415(b)(1)(A) dollar limit that is effective as of January 1, 2009, the associated increase in the participant's monthly benefit payments is only effective for payments due on or after January 1, 2009, and the participant's benefit cannot be increased to reflect the section 415(d) increase that is effective January 1, 2009, with respect to any monthly payment due prior to January 1, 2009.

(4) *Application of adjusted figure—(i) In general.* If the dollar limitation of section 415(b)(1)(A) or the compensation limitation of section 415(b)(1)(B) is adjusted pursuant to section 415(d) for a limitation year, the adjustment is applied as provided in this paragraph (a)(4).

(ii) *Application of adjusted limitations to benefits that have not commenced.* An adjustment to the dollar limitation of section 415(b)(1)(A) is permitted to be applied to a participant who has not commenced benefits before the date on which the adjustment is effective. Annual adjustments to the compensation limit of section 415(b)(1)(B) as described in paragraph (a)(2) of this section are permitted to be made for all limitation years that begin after the participant's severance from employment, and apply to distributions that commence after the effective dates of such adjustments. However, no adjustment to the compensation limit of section 415(b)(1)(B) is made for any limitation year that begins on or before the date of the participant's severance from employment with the employer maintaining the plan.

(iii) *Application of adjusted dollar limitation to remaining payments under benefits that have commenced.* With respect to a distribution of accrued benefits that commenced before the date on which an adjustment to the section 415(b)(1)(A) dollar limitation is effective, a plan is permitted to apply the adjusted limitations to that distribution, but only to the extent that benefits have not been paid. Thus, for example, a plan cannot provide that the adjusted dollar limitation applies to a participant who has previously received the entire plan benefit in a single-sum distribution. However, a plan can provide for an increase in benefits to a participant who accrues additional benefits under the plan that could have been accrued without regard to the adjustment of the dollar limitation (including benefits that accrue as a result of a plan amendment) on or after the effective date of the adjusted limitation.

(iv) *Manner of adjustment for benefits that have commenced.* If a plan is amended to increase benefits payable under the plan in accordance with paragraphs (a)(5) or (a)(6) of this section (or the plan is treated as applying paragraph (a)(5) of this section because the plan incorporates the section 415(d) cost-of-living adjustments automatically by reference pursuant to § 1.415(a)-1(d)(3)(v)), or if benefits payable under the plan are increased pursuant to a form of benefit that is described in § 1.415(b)-1(c)(5), then the distribution as increased will be treated as continuing to satisfy the requirements of section 415(b). If benefits payable under a plan are increased in a manner other than as described in the preceding sentence, the plan must satisfy the requirements of § 1.415(b)-1(b)(1)(iii), treating the commencement of the additional benefit as the commencement of a new distribution that gives rise to a new annuity starting date.

(5) *Safe harbor for annual adjustments to distributions.* An amendment to a plan to incorporate adjustments to the section 415(b) limits that increases a distribution that has previously commenced is described in this paragraph (a)(5) if—

(i) The employee has received one or more distributions that satisfy the requirements of section 415(b) before the date the adjustment to the applicable limits is effective (as determined under paragraph (a)(3) of this section);

(ii) The increased distribution is solely as a result of the amendment of the plan to reflect

the adjustment to the applicable limits pursuant to section 415(d); and

(iii) The amounts payable to the employee on and after the effective date of the adjustment (as determined under paragraph (a)(3) of this section) are not greater than the amounts that would otherwise be payable without regard to the adjustment, multiplied by a fraction determined for the limitation year, the numerator of which is the limitation under section 415(b) (which is the lesser of the applicable dollar limitation under section 415(b)(1)(A), as adjusted for age at commencement, and the applicable compensation-based limitation under section 415(b)(1)(B)) in effect with respect to the distribution taking into account the section 415(d) adjustment, and the denominator of which is the limitation under section 415(b) in effect for the distribution immediately before the adjustment.

(6) *Safe harbor for periodic adjustments to distributions—(i) General rule.* An amendment to a plan that increases a distribution that has previously commenced is made using the safe harbor methodology of this paragraph (a)(6) if—

(A) The employee has received one or more distributions that satisfy the requirements of section 415(b) before the date on which the increase is effective; and

(B) The amounts payable to the employee on and after the effective date of the increase are not greater than the amounts that would otherwise be payable without regard to the increase, multiplied by the cumulative adjustment fraction.

(ii) *Cumulative adjustment fraction.* The cumulative adjustment fraction for purposes of this paragraph (a)(6) is equal to the product of all of the fractions described in paragraph (a)(5)(iii) of this section that would have applied after benefits commence if the plan had been amended each year to incorporate the section 415(d) adjustments to the applicable section 415(b) limits and had otherwise satisfied the safe harbor methodology described in paragraph (a)(5) of this section. For purposes of the preceding sentence, if for the limitation year for which the increase to the section 415(b)(1)(A) dollar limitation pursuant to section 611(a)(1)(A) of the Economic Growth and Tax Relief Reconciliation Act of 2001 (115 Stat. 38), Public Law 107-16 (EGTR-RA), is first effective (generally, the first limitation year beginning after December 31, 2001), the section 415(b)(1)(A) dollar limit applicable to a participant is less than the section 415(b)(1)(B) compensation limit for the participant, then the fraction described in paragraph (a)(5)(iii) of this section for that limitation year is 1.0.

(7) *Examples.* The following examples illustrate the application of this paragraph (a):

Example 1. (i) X is a participant in a qualified defined benefit plan maintained by X's employer. The plan has a calendar year limitation year. Under the terms of the plan, X is entitled to a benefit consisting of a straight life annuity equal to 100 percent of X's average compensation for the period of X's high-3 years of service. X's average compensation for the period of X's high-3 years of service is $50,000. X incurs a severance from employment with the employer maintaining the plan on October 3, 2007, at age 65 with a nonforfeitable right to the accrued benefit after more than 10 years of participation in the plan. X begins to receive annual benefit payments (payable monthly) of $50,000, commencing on November 1, 2007. The dollar limitation for the 2007 limitation year (as adjusted pursuant to section 415(d)) is $180,000. Assume that the dollar limitation for the 2008 limitation year (as adjusted pursuant to section 415(d)) is $185,000 and the annual adjustment factor for adjusting the compensation limitation of section 415(b)(1)(B) for the 2008 limitation year is 1.0334. Effective January 1, 2008, the plan is amended to incorporate these adjustments to the dollar and compensation limitations, and accordingly, X's annual benefit payment is increased, effective for payments due on or after January 1, 2008. Prior to the plan amendment incorporating the application of the adjusted dollar and compensation limitations, X has received one or more distributions that satisfy the requirements of section

415(b). In addition, the adjustment to X's annual benefit payments is solely on account of the plan amendment incorporating the adjusted limitations.

(ii) For the limitation year beginning January 1, 2008, the dollar limit applicable to X under section 415(b)(1)(A) is $185,000, and the compensation limit applicable to X under section 415(b)(1)(B) is $51,670 ($50,000 multiplied by the annual adjustment factor of 1.0334). Accordingly, the adjustment to X's benefit satisfies the safe harbor for cost-of-living adjustments under paragraph (a)(5) of this section if, after the adjustment, X's benefit payable in the 2008 limitation year is no greater than $50,000 multiplied by $51,670 (X's section 415(b) limitation for 2008)/$50,000 (X's section 415(b) limitation for 2007).

Example 2. (i) The facts are the same as in Example 1, except that X's average compensation for the period of X's high-3 consecutive years of service is $200,000. Consequently, X's annual benefit payments commencing on November 1, 2007, are limited to $180,000.

(ii) For the limitation year beginning January 1, 2008, the dollar limit applicable to X under section 415(b)(1)(A) is $185,000, and the compensation limit applicable to X under section 415(b)(1)(B) is $206,680 ($200,000 multiplied by the annual adjustment factor of 1.0334). Accordingly, the adjustment to X's benefit satisfies the safe harbor for cost-of-living adjustments under paragraph (a)(5) of this section if, after the adjustment, X's benefit payable in 2008 is no greater than $180,000 multiplied by $185,000 (X's section 415(b) limitation for 2008)/$180,000 (X's section 415(b) limitation for 2007).

Example 3. (i) X is a participant in Plan T, a qualified defined benefit plan maintained by X's employer. In the year 2008, X receives a single-sum distribution of X's entire accrued benefit under the plan. At the time that X receives the single-sum distribution, X's accrued benefit under Plan T is limited by the section 415(b)(1)(A) age-adjusted dollar limit. X accrues no further benefits under Plan T after X receives the single-sum distribution. In the 2009 limitation year, pursuant to section 415(d) and § 1.415(d)-1, the section 415(b)(1)(A) dollar limit is increased.

(ii) In the 2009 limitation year, Plan T may not provide additional benefits to X on account of the increase in the section 415(b)(1)(A) dollar limit pursuant to section 415(d) and § 1.415(d)-1.

Example 4. (i) X is a participant in Plan T, a qualified defined benefit plan maintained by X's employer, Employer S. Plan T has a calendar limitation year. In 2008, X incurs a severance from employment with Employer S and X commences receiving distributions from Plan T in the form of a single life annuity in an annual amount of $30,000. At the time that X commences receiving distributions from Plan T, X's accrued benefit under Plan T is limited by the section 415(b)(1)(B) compensation limit. In 2009, the annual adjustment factor described in paragraph (a)(2) of this section (which is the factor for adjusting the compensation limit described in section 415(b)(1)(B)) is 1.03. Employer S amends Plan T, effective as of January 1, 2009, to increase the annual benefit of all participants who, prior to January 1, 2009, incurred a severance from employment with Employer S and who have commenced receiving benefits from Plan T by a factor of 1.015. Assume that for limitation years prior to 2009, X's distributions from Plan T satisfy the requirements of section 415(b).

(ii) The increase in X's annual benefit pursuant to the amendment effective January 1, 2009, is within the safe harbor described in paragraph (a)(6) of this section. This is because the amount payable to X under Plan T for the 2009 limitation year and limitation years thereafter (as increased by the amendment effective January 1, 2009) is not greater than the product of the amount payable to X under Plan T for such limitation years (as determined without regard to the amendment increasing X's benefit effective January 1, 2009) and the cumulative adjustment fraction (which, in X's case, is 1.03). Thus, X's annual

benefit, as increased by the amendment, is not determined pursuant to the rules of § 1.415(b)-1(b)(1)(iii).

Example 5. (i) Participant P participated in Plan A, maintained by Employer M, for more than 10 years. Plan A uses a calendar year limitation year and Plan A automatically adjusts a participant's section 415(b)(1)(B) compensation limit for limitation years after the limitation year in which the participant incurs a severance from employment as described in § 1.415(a)-1(d)(3)(v). Prior to separating from employment with M in 2010, P's average compensation for P's period of high-3 years while a participant in Plan A is $50,000, based on P's compensation for 2007, 2008, and 2009, which was $50,000 for each year. P's compensation for year 2010 was $45,000. In year 2012, P is rehired by M and resumes participation in Plan A. P's compensation in year 2012 is $45,000, and is $70,000 in year 2013. Assume that the annual adjustment factor described in § 1.415(d)-1(a)(2)(ii) for the limitation years 2011 through 2013 is 1.03 for each year. Thus, disregarding P's rehire by M, P's average compensation for P's period of high-3 years while a participant in Plan A for the 2013 limitation year would be equal to $54,636 (or 1.03 * 1.03 * 1.03 * $50,000). See § 1.415(b)-1(a)(5)(iii).

(ii) Under § 1.415(d)-1(a)(2)(iii), P's average compensation for P's period of high-3 years while a participant in Plan A for the 2013 limitation year is $54,636.

* * *

§ 54.4980F-1. Notice requirements for certain pension plan amendments significantly reducing the rate of future benefit accrual.

* * *

Q-1. What are the notice requirements of section 4980F(e) of the Internal Revenue Code and section 204(h) of ERISA?

A-1. (a) *Requirements of Internal Revenue Code section 4980F(e) and ERISA section 204(h).* Section 4980F of the Internal Revenue Code (section 4980F) and section 204(h) of the Employee Retirement Income Security Act of 1974, as amended (ERISA), 29 U.S.C. 1054(h) (section 204(h)) each generally requires notice of an amendment to an applicable pension plan that either provides for a significant reduction in the rate of future benefit accrual or that eliminates or significantly reduces an early retirement benefit or retirement-type subsidy. The notice is required to be provided to plan participants and alternate payees who are applicable individuals (as defined in Q&A-10 of this section), to certain employee organizations, and to contributing employers under a multiemployer plan (as described in Q&A-10(a) of this section). The plan administrator must generally provide the notice before the effective date of the plan amendment. Q&A-9 of this section sets forth the time frames for providing notice, Q&A-11 of this section sets forth the content requirements for the notice, and Q&A-12 of this section contains special rules for cases in which participants can choose between the old and new benefit formulas.

(b) *Other notice requirements.* Other provisions of law may require that certain parties be notified of a plan amendment. See, for example, sections 102 and 104 of ERISA, and the regulations thereunder, for requirements relating to summary plan descriptions and summaries of material modifications.

Q-2. What are the differences between section 4980F and section 204(h)?

A-2. The notice requirements of section 4980F generally are parallel to the notice requirements of section 204(h), as amended by the Economic Growth and Tax Relief Reconciliation Act of 2001, Public Law 107-16 (115 Stat. 38) (2001) (EGTRRA). However, the consequences of the failure to satisfy the requirements of the two provisions differ: Section 4980F imposes an excise tax on a failure to satisfy the notice requirements, while section 204(h)(6), as amended by EGTRRA, contains a special rule with respect to an egregious failure to satisfy the notice requirements. See Q&A-14 and Q&A-15 of this section. Except to the extent specifically indicated, these regulations apply both to section 4980F and to section 204(h).

* * *

Q-9. When must section 204(h) notice be provided?

A-9. (a) 45-day general rule. Except as otherwise provided in this Q&A-9, section 204(h) notice must be provided at least 45 days before the effective date of any section 204(h) amendment. See paragraph (e) of this Q&A-9 for special rules for amendments permitting participant choice.

(b) 15-day rule for small plans. Except for amendments described in paragraphs (d)(2) and (g) of this Q&A-9, section 204(h) notice must be provided at least 15 days before the effective date of any section 204(h) amendment in the case of a small plan. For purposes of this section, a small plan is a plan that the plan administrator reasonably expects to have, on the effective date of the section 204(h) amendment, fewer than 100 participants who have an accrued benefit under the plan.

(c) 15-day rule for multiemployer plans. Except for amendments described in paragraphs (d)(2) and (g) of this Q&A-9, section 204(h) notice must be provided at least 15 days before the effective date of any section 204(h) amendment in the case of a multiemployer plan. For purposes of this section, a multiemployer plan means a multiemployer plan as defined in section 414(f) of the Internal Revenue Code.

(d) Special timing rule for business transactions—(1) 15-day rule for section 204(h) amendment in connection with an acquisition or disposition. Except for amendments described in paragraphs (d)(2) and (g) of this Q&A-9, if a section 204(h) amendment is adopted in connection with an acquisition or disposition, section 204(h) notice must be provided at least 15 days before the effective date of the section 204(h) amendment.

(2) Later notice permitted for a section 204(h) amendment significantly reducing early retirement benefit or retirement-type subsidies in connection with certain plan transfers,

mergers, or consolidations. If a section 204(h) amendment is adopted with respect to liabilities that are transferred to another plan in connection with a transfer, merger, or consolidation of assets or liabilities as described in section 414(l) of the Internal Revenue Code and § 1.414(l)-1 of this chapter, the amendment is adopted in connection with an acquisition or disposition, and the amendment significantly reduces an early retirement benefit or retirement-type subsidy, but does not significantly reduce the rate of future benefit accrual, then section 204(h) notice must be provided no later than 30 days after the effective date of the section 204(h) amendment.

(3) *Definition of acquisition or disposition.* For purposes of this paragraph (d), see § 1.410(b)-2(f) of this chapter for the definition of acquisition or disposition.

(e) *Timing rule for amendments permitting participant choice.* In general, section 204(h) notice of a section 204(h) amendment that provides applicable individuals with a choice between the old and the new benefit formulas (as described in Q&A-12 of this section) must be provided in accordance with the time period applicable under paragraphs (a) through (d) of this Q&A-9. See Q&A-12 of this section for additional guidance regarding section 204(h) notice in connection with participant choice.

(f) *Special timing rule for certain plans maintained by commercial airlines. See* section 402 of PPA '06 for a special rule that applies to certain plans maintained by an employer that is a commercial passenger airline or the principal business of which is providing catering services to a commercial passenger airline. Under this special rule, section 204(h) notice must be provided at least 15 days before the effective date of the amendment.

(g) Special timing rules relating to certain section 204(h) amendments that reduce section 411(d)(6) protected benefits—(1) Plan amendments permitted to reduce prior accruals. This paragraph (g) generally provides special rules with respect to a plan amendment that would not violate section 411(d)(6) even

if the amendment were to reduce section 411(d)(6) protected benefits, which are limited to accrued benefits that are attributable to service before the applicable amendment date. For example, this paragraph (g) applies to amendments that are permitted to be effective retroactively under section 412(d)(2) of the Code (section 412(c)(8) for plan years beginning before January 1, 2008), section 418D of the Code, section 418E of the Code, section 4281 of ERISA, or section 1107 of PPA '06. See, generally, § 1.411(d)-3(a)(1).

(2) *General timing rule for amendments to which this paragraph (g) applies.* For an amendment to which this paragraph (g) applies, the amendment is effective on the first date on which the plan is operated as if the amendment were in effect. Thus, except as otherwise provided in this paragraph (g), a section 204(h) notice for an amendment to which paragraph (a) of this section applies that is adopted after the effective date of the amendment must be provided, with respect to any applicable individual, at least 45 days before (or such other date as may apply under paragraph (b), (c), (d), or (f) of this Q&A-9) the date the amendment is put into operational effect.

(3) *Special rules for section 204(h) notices provided in connection with other disclosure requirements*—(i) *In general.* Notwithstanding the requirements in this Q&A-9 and Q&A-11 of this section, if a plan provides one of the notices in paragraph (g)(3)(ii) of this Q&A-9, in accordance with the applicable timing and content rules for such notice, the plan is treated as timely providing a section 204(h) notice with respect to a section 204(h) amendment.

(ii) *Notice requirements.* The notices in this paragraph (g)(3)(ii) are—

(A) A notice required under any revenue ruling, notice, or other guidance published under the authority of the Commissioner in the Internal Revenue Bulletin to affected parties in connection with a retroactive plan amendment described in section 412(d)(2) (section

412(c)(8) for plan years beginning before January 1, 2008);

(B) A notice required under section 101(j) of ERISA if an amendment is adopted to comply with the benefit limitation requirements of section 206(g) of ERISA (section 436 of the Code);

(C) A notice required under section 432(b)(3)(D) of the Code for an amendment adopted to comply with the benefit restrictions under section 432(f)(2);

(D) A notice required under section 418D, or section 4244A(b) of ERISA, for an amendment that reduces or eliminates accrued benefits attributable to employer contributions with respect to a multiemployer plan in reorganization;

(E) A notice required under section 418E, or section 4245(e) of ERISA, relating to the effects of the insolvency status for a multiemployer plan; and

(F) A notice required under section 4281 of ERISA for an amendment of a multiemployer plan reducing benefits pursuant to section 4281(c) of ERISA.

(4) *Delegation of authority to Commissioner.* The Commissioner may provide special rules under section 4980F, in revenue rulings, notices, or other guidance published in the Internal Revenue Bulletin (*See* § 601.601(d)(2)(ii)(*b*) of this chapter), that the Commissioner determines to be necessary or appropriate with respect to a section 204(h) amendment—

(A) That applies to benefits accrued before the applicable amendment date but that does not violate section 411(d)(6); or

(B) For which there is a required notice relating to a reduction in benefits and such notice has timing and content requirements similar to a section 204(h) notice with respect to a significant reduction in the rate of future benefit accruals.

* * *

Q-14. What are the consequences if a plan administrator fails to provide section 204(h) notice?

A-14. (a) Egregious failures—(1) Effect of egregious failure to provide section 204(h) notice. Section 204(h)(6)(A) of ERISA provides that, in the case of any egregious failure to meet the notice requirements with respect to any plan amendment, the plan provisions are applied so that all applicable individuals are entitled to the greater of the benefit to which they would have been entitled without regard to the amendment, or the benefit under the plan with regard to the amendment. For a special rule applicable in the case of a plan termination, see Q&A-17(b) of this section.

(2) Definition of egregious failure. For purposes of section 204(h) of ERISA and this Q&A-14, there is an egregious failure to meet the notice requirements if a failure to provide required notice is within the control of the plan sponsor and is either an intentional failure or a failure, whether or not intentional, to provide most of the individuals with most of the information they are entitled to receive. For this purpose, an intentional failure includes any failure to promptly provide the required notice or information after the plan administrator discovers an unintentional failure to meet the requirements. A failure to give section 204(h) notice is deemed not to be egregious if the plan administrator reasonably determines, taking into account section 4980F, section 204(h), these regulations, other administrative pronouncements, and relevant facts and circumstances, that the reduction in the rate of future benefit accrual resulting from an amendment is not significant (as described in Q&A-8 of this section), or that an amendment does not significantly reduce an early retirement benefit or retirement-type subsidy.

(3) Example. The following example illustrates the provisions of this paragraph (a):

Example. (i) Facts. Plan A is amended to reduce significantly the rate of future benefit accrual effective January 1, 2003. Section 204(h) notice is required to be provided 45 days before January 1, 2003. Timely section

204(h) notice is provided to all applicable individuals (and to each employee organization representing participants who are applicable individuals), except that the employer intentionally fails to provide section 204(h) notice to certain participants until May 16, 2003.

(ii) Conclusion. The failure to provide section 204(h) notice is egregious. Accordingly, for the period from January 1, 2003 through June 30, 2003 (which is the date that is 45 days after May 16, 2003), all participants and alternate payees are entitled to the greater of the benefit to which they would have been entitled under Plan A as in effect before the amendment or the benefit under the plan as amended.

(b) Effect of non-egregious failure to provide section 204(h) notice. If an egregious failure has not occurred, the amendment with respect to which section 204(h) notice is required may become effective with respect to all applicable individuals. However, see section 502 of ERISA for civil enforcement remedies. Thus, where there is a failure, whether or not egregious, to provide section 204(h) notice in accordance with this section, individuals may have recourse under section 502 of ERISA.

(c) Excise taxes. See section 4980F and Q&A-15 of this section for excise taxes that may apply to a failure to notify applicable individuals of a pension plan amendment that provides for a significant reduction in the rate of future benefit accrual or eliminates or significantly reduces an early retirement benefit or retirement-type subsidy, regardless of whether or not the failure is egregious.

Q-15. What are some of the rules that apply with respect to the excise tax under section 4980F?

A-15. (a) Person responsible for excise tax. In the case of a plan other than a multiemployer plan, the employer is responsible for reporting and paying the excise tax. In the case of a multiemployer plan, the plan is responsible for reporting and paying the excise tax.

(b) Excise tax inapplicable in certain cases. Under section 4980F(c)(1) of the Internal Revenue Code, no excise tax is imposed on a failure for any period during which it is established to the satisfaction of the Commissioner that the employer (or other person responsible for the tax) exercised reasonable diligence, but did not know that the failure existed. Under section 4980F(c)(2) of the Internal Revenue Code, no excise tax applies to a failure to provide section 204(h) notice if the employer (or other person responsible for the tax) exercised reasonable diligence and corrects the failure within 30 days after the employer (or other person responsible for the tax) first knew, or exercising reasonable diligence would have known, that such failure existed. For purposes of section 4980F(c)(1) of the Internal Revenue Code, a person has exercised reasonable diligence, but did not know that the failure existed if and only if—

(1) The person exercised reasonable diligence in attempting to deliver section 204(h) notice to applicable individuals by the latest date permitted under this section; and

(2) At the latest date permitted for delivery of section 204(h) notice, the person reasonably believes that section 204(h) notice was actually delivered to each applicable individual by that date.

(c) Example. The following example illustrates the provisions of paragraph (b) of this Q&A-15:

Example. (i) Facts. Plan A is amended to reduce significantly the rate of future benefit accrual. The employer sends out a section 204(h) notice to all affected participants and other applicable individuals and to any employee organization representing applicable individuals, including actual delivery by hand to employees at worksites and by first-class mail for any other applicable individual and to any employee organization representing applicable individuals. However, although the employer exercises reasonable diligence in seeking to deliver the notice, the notice is not delivered to any participants at one worksite due to a failure of an overnight delivery service to provide the notice to appropriate personnel at that site for them to timely hand deliver the notice to affected employees. The error is discovered when the employer subsequently calls to confirm delivery. Appropriate section 204(h) notice is then promptly delivered to all affected participants at the worksite.

(ii) Conclusion. Because the employer exercised reasonable diligence, but did not know that a failure existed, no excise tax applies, assuming that participants at the worksite receive section 204(h) notice within 30 days after the employer first knew, or exercising reasonable diligence would have known, that the failure occurred.

* * *

AGE DISCRIMINATION REGULATIONS

Code of Federal Regulations, Title 29

§ 1625.6. Bona fide occupational qualifications.

(a) Whether occupational qualifications will be deemed to be "bona fide" to a specific job and "reasonably necessary to the normal operation of the particular business," will be determined on the basis of all the pertinent facts surrounding each particular situation. It is anticipated that this concept of a bona fide occupational qualification will have limited scope and application. Further, as this is an exception to the Act it must be narrowly construed.

(b) An employer asserting a BFOQ defense has the burden of proving that (1) the age limit is reasonably necessary to the essence of the business, and either (2) that all or substantially all individuals excluded from the job involved are in fact disqualified, or (3) that some of the individuals so excluded possess a disqualifying trait that cannot be ascertained except by reference to age. If the employer's objective in asserting a BFOQ is the goal of public safety, the employer must prove that the challenged practice does indeed effectuate that goal and that there is no acceptable alternative which would better advance it or equally advance it with less discriminatory impact.

(c) Many State and local governments have enacted laws or administrative regulations which limit employment opportunities based on age. Unless these laws meet the standards for the establishment of a valid bona fide occupational qualification under section 4(f)(1) of the Act, they will be considered in conflict with and effectively superseded by the ADEA.

§ 1625.7. Differentiations based on reasonable factors other than age.

(a) Section 4(f) (1) of the Act provides that * * * it shall not be unlawful for an employer, employment agency, or labor organization * * * to take any action otherwise prohibited under paragraphs (a), (b), (c), or (e) of this section * * * where the differentiation is based on reasonable factors other than age * * *.

(b) When an employment practice uses age as a limiting criterion, the defense that the practice is justified by a reasonable factor other than age is unavailable.

(c) Any employment practice that adversely affects individuals within the protected age group on the basis of older age is discriminatory unless the practice is justified by a "reasonable factor other than age." An individual challenging the allegedly unlawful practice is responsible for isolating and identifying the specific employment practice that allegedly causes any observed statistical disparities.

(d) Whenever the "reasonable factors other than age" defense is raised, the employer bears the burdens of production and persuasion to demonstrate the defense. The "reasonable factors other than age" provision is not available as a defense to a claim of disparate treatment.

(e)(1) A reasonable factor other than age is a non-age factor that is objectively reasonable when viewed from the position of a prudent employer mindful of its responsibilities under the ADEA under like circumstances. Whether a differentiation is based on reasonable factors other than age must be decided on the basis of all the particular facts and circumstances surrounding each individual situation. To establish the RFOA defense, an employer must show that the employment practice was both reasonably designed to further or achieve a legitimate business purpose and administered in a way that reasonably achieves that purpose in light of the particular facts and circumstances that were known, or should have been known, to the employer.

(2) Considerations that are relevant to whether a practice is based on a reasonable

factor other than age include, but are not limited to:

(i) The extent to which the factor is related to the employer's stated business purpose;

(ii) The extent to which the employer defined the factor accurately and applied the factor fairly and accurately, including the extent to which managers and supervisors were given guidance or training about how to apply the factor and avoid discrimination;

(iii) The extent to which the employer limited supervisors' discretion to assess employees subjectively, particularly where the criteria that the supervisors were asked to evaluate are known to be subject to negative age-based stereotypes;

(iv) The extent to which the employer assessed the adverse impact of its employment practice on older workers; and

(v) The degree of the harm to individuals within the protected age group, in terms of both the extent of injury and the numbers of persons adversely affected, and the extent to which the employer took steps to reduce the harm, in light of the burden of undertaking such steps.

(3) No specific consideration or combination of considerations need be present for a differentiation to be based on reasonable factors other than age. Nor does the presence of one of these considerations automatically establish the defense.

(f) A differentiation based on the average cost of employing older employees as a group is unlawful except with respect to employee benefit plans which qualify for the section 4(f)(2) exception to the Act.

§ 1625.10. Costs and benefits under employee benefit plans.

(a)(1) *General.* Section 4(f)(2) of the Act provides that it is not unlawful for an employer, employment agency, or labor organization to observe the terms of any bona fide employee benefit plan such as a retirement, pension, or insurance plan, which is not a subterfuge to evade the purposes of this Act, except that no

such employee benefit plan shall excuse the failure to hire any individual, and no such * * * employee benefit plan shall require or permit the involuntary retirement of any individual specified by section 12(a) of this Act because of the age of such individuals.

The legislative history of this provision indicates that its purpose is to permit age-based reductions in employee benefit plans where such reductions are justified by significant cost considerations. Accordingly, section 4(f)(2) does not apply, for example, to paid vacations and uninsured paid sick leave, since reductions in these benefits would not be justified by significant cost considerations. Where employee benefit plans do meet the criteria in section 4(f)(2), benefit levels for older workers may be reduced to the extent necessary to achieve approximate equivalency in cost for older and younger workers. A benefit plan will be considered in compliance with the statute where the actual amount of payment made, or cost incurred, in behalf of an older worker is equal to that made or incurred in behalf of a younger worker, even though the older worker may thereby receive a lesser amount of benefits or insurance coverage. Since section 4(f)(2) is an exception from the general non-discrimination provisions of the Act, the burden is on the one seeking to invoke the exception to show that every element has been clearly and unmistakably met. The exception must be narrowly construed. The following sections explain three key elements of the exception:

(i) What a "bona fide employee benefit plan" is;

(ii) what it means to "observe the terms" of such a plan; and

(iii) what kind of plan, or plan provision, would be considered "a subterfuge to evade the purposes of [the] Act."

There is also a discussion of the application of the general rules governing all plans with respect to specific kinds of employee benefit plans.

(2) *Relation of section 4(f)(2) to sections 4(a), 4(b) and 4(c)*. Sections 4(a), 4(b) and 4(c) prohibit specified acts of discrimination on the basis of age. Section 4(a) in particular makes it unlawful for an employer to "discriminate against any individual with respect to his compensation, terms, conditions, or privileges of employment, because of such individual's age * * *." Section 4(f)(2) is an exception to this general prohibition. Where an employer under an employee benefit plan provides the same level of benefits to older workers as to younger workers, there is no violation of section 4(a), and accordingly the practice does not have to be justified under section 4(f)(2).

(b) *"Bona fide employee benefit plan."* Section 4(f)(2) applies only to bona fide employee benefit plans. A plan is considered "bona fide" if its terms (including cessation of contributions or accruals in the case of retirement income plans) have been accurately described in writing to all employees and if it actually provides the benefits in accordance with the terms of the plan. Notifying employees promptly of provisions and changes in an employee benefit plan is essential if they are to know how the plan affects them. For these purposes, it would be sufficient under the ADEA for employers to follow the disclosure requirements of ERISA and the regulations thereunder. The plan must actually provide the benefits its provisions describe, since otherwise the notification of the provisions to employees is misleading and inaccurate. An "employee benefit plan" is a plan, such as a retirement, pension, or insurance plan, which provides employees with what are frequently referred to as "fringe benefits." The term does not refer to wages or salary in cash; neither section 4(f)(2) nor any other section of the Act excuses the payment of lower wages or salary to older employees on account of age. Whether or not any particular employee benefit plan may lawfully provide lower benefits to older employees on account of age depends on whether all of the elements of the exception have been met. An "employee-pay-all" employee benefit plan is one of the "terms, conditions, or privileges of employment" with

respect to which discrimination on the basis of age is forbidden under section 4(a)(1). In such a plan, benefits for older workers may be reduced only to the extent and according to the same principles as apply to other plans under section 4(f)(2).

(c) *"To observe the terms"* of a plan. In order for a bona fide employee benefit plan which provides lower benefits to older employees on account of age to be within the section 4(f)(2) exception, the lower benefits must be provided in "observ[ance of] the terms of" the plan. As this statutory text makes clear, the section 4(f)(2) exception is limited to otherwise discriminatory actions which are actually prescribed by the terms of a bona fide employee benefit plan. Where the employer, employment agency, or labor organization is not required by the express provisions of the plan to provide lesser benefits to older workers, section 4(f)(2) does not apply. Important purposes are served by this requirement. Where a discriminatory policy is an express term of a benefit plan, employees presumably have some opportunity to know of the policy and to plan (or protest) accordingly. Moreover, the requirement that the discrimination actually be prescribed by a plan assures that the particular plan provision will be actually applied to all employees of the same age. Where a discriminatory provision is an optional term of the plan, it permits individual, discretionary acts of discrimination, which do not fall within the section 4(f)(2) exception.

(d) *"Subterfuge."* In order for a bona fide employee benefit plan which prescribes lower benefits for older employees on account of age to be within the section 4(f)(2) exception, it must not be "a subterfuge to evade the purposes of [the] Act." In general, a plan or plan provision which prescribes lower benefits for older employees on account of age is not a "subterfuge" within the meaning of section 4(f)(2), provided that the lower level of benefits is justified by age-related cost considerations. (The only exception to this general rule is with respect to certain retirement plans. See paragraph (f)(4) of this section.) There are certain other requirements that must be met in order for a plan not to be a subterfuge. These requirements are set forth below.

(1) *Cost data—General.* Cost data used in justification of a benefit plan which provides lower benefits to older employees on account of age must be valid and reasonable. This standard is met where an employer has cost data which show the actual cost to it of providing the particular benefit (or benefits) in question over a representative period of years. An employer may rely in cost data for its own employees over such a period, or on cost data for a larger group of similarly situated employees. Sometimes, as a result of experience rating or other causes, an employer incurs costs that differ significantly from costs for a group of similarly situated employees. Such an employer may not rely on cost data for the similarly situated employees where such reliance would result in significantly lower benefits for its own older employees. Where reliable cost information is not available, reasonable projections made from existing cost data meeting the standards set forth above will be considered acceptable.

(2) *Cost data—Individual benefit basis and "benefit package" basis.* Cost comparisons and adjustments under section 4(f)(2) must be made on a benefit-by-benefit basis or on a "benefit package" basis, as described below.

(i) *Benefit-by-benefit basis.* Adjustments made on a benefit-by-benefit basis must be made in the amount or level of a specific form of benefit for a specific event or contingency. For example, higher group term life insurance costs for older workers would justify a corresponding reduction in the amount of group term life insurance coverage for older workers, on the basis of age. However, a benefit-by-benefit approach would not justify the substitution of one form of benefit for another, even though both forms of benefit are designed for the same contingency, such as death. See paragraph (f)(1) of this section.

(ii) *"Benefit package" basis.* As an alternative to the benefit-by-benefit basis, cost comparisons and adjustments under section 4(f)(2) may be made on a limited "benefit package" basis. Under this approach, subject to the limitations described below, cost comparisons and adjustments can be made with respect to section 4(f)(2) plans in the aggregate. This alternative basis provides greater flexibility than a benefit-by-benefit basis in order to carry out the declared statutory purpose "to help employers and workers find ways of meeting problems arising from the impact of age on employment." A "benefit package" approach is an alternative approach consistent with this purpose and with the general purpose of section 4(f)(2) only if it is not used to reduce the cost to the employer or the favorability to the employees of overall employee benefits for older employees. A "benefit package" approach used for either of these purposes would be a subterfuge to evade the purposes of the Act. In order to assure that such a "benefit package" approach is not abused and is consistent with the legislative intent, it is subject to the limitations described in paragraph (f) of this section, which also includes a general example.

(3) *Cost data—Five year maximum basis.* Cost comparisons and adjustments under section 4(f)(2) may be made on the basis of age brackets of up to 5 years. Thus a particular benefit may be reduced for employees of any age within the protected age group by an amount no greater than that which could be justified by the additional cost to provide them with the same level of the benefit as younger employees within a specified five-year age group immediately preceding theirs. For example, where an employer chooses to provide unreduced group term life insurance benefits until age 60, benefits for employees who are between 60 and 65 years of age may be reduced only to the extent necessary to achieve approximate equivalency in costs with employees who are 55 to 60 years old. Similarly, any reductions in benefit levels for 65 to 70 year old employees cannot exceed an amount which is proportional to the additional costs for their coverage over 60 to 65 year old employees.

(4) *Employee contributions in support of employee benefit plans—*

(i) *As a condition of employment.* An older employee within the protected age group may not be required as a condition of employment to make greater contributions than a younger employee in support of an employee benefit plan. Such a requirement would be in effect a mandatory reduction in take-home pay, which is never authorized by section 4(f)(2), and would impose an impediment to employment in violation of the specific restrictions in section 4(f)(2).

(ii) *As a condition of participation in a voluntary employee benefit plan.* An older employee within the protected age group may be required as a condition of participation in a voluntary employee benefit plan to make a greater contribution that a younger employee only if the older employee is not thereby required to bear a greater proportion of the total premium cost (employer-paid and employee-paid) than the younger employee. Otherwise the requirement would discriminate against the older employee by making compensation in the form of an employer contribution available on less favorable terms than for the younger employee and denying that compensation altogether to an older employee unwilling or unable to meet the less favorable terms. Such discrimination is not authorized by section 4(f)(2). This principle applies to three different contribution arrangements as follows:

(A) *Employee-pay-all plans.* Older employees, like younger employees, may be required to contribute as a condition of participation up to the full premium cost for their age.

(B) *Non-contributory ("employer-pay-all") plans.* Where younger employees are not required to contribute any portion of the total premium cost, older employees may not be required to contribute any portion.

(C) *Contributory plans.* In these plans employers and participating employees share the premium cost. The required contributions of participants may increase with age so long as the proportion of the total premium required to be paid by the participants does not increase with age.

(iii) *As an option in order to receive an unreduced benefit.* An older employee may be given the option, as an individual, to make the additional contribution necessary to receive the same level of benefits as a younger employee (provided that the contemplated reduction in benefits is otherwise justified by section 4(f)(2).

(5) *Forfeiture clauses.* Clauses in employee benefit plans which state that litigation or participation in any manner in a formal proceeding by an employee will result in the forfeiture of his rights are unlawful insofar as they may be applied to those who seek redress under the Act. This is by reason of section 4(d) which provides that it is unlawful for an employer, employment agency, or labor organization to discriminate against any individual because such individual "has made a charge, testified, assisted, or participated in an investigation, proceeding, or litigation under this Act."

(6) *Refusal to hire clauses.* Any provision of an employee benefit plan which requires or permits the refusal to hire an individual specified in section 12(a) of the Act on the basis of age is a subterfuge to evade the purposes of the Act and cannot be excused under section 4(f)(2).

(7) *Involuntary retirement clauses.* Any provision of an employee benefit plan which requires or permits the involuntary retirement of any individual specified in section 12(a) of the Act on the basis of age is a subterfuge to evade the purpose of the Act and cannot be excused under section 4(f)(2).

(e) *Benefits provided by the Government.* An employer does not violate the Act by permitting certain benefits to be provided by the Government, even though the availability of such benefits may be based on age. For example, it is not necessary for an employer to provide health benefits which are otherwise provided to certain employees by Medicare. However, the availability of benefits from the

Government will not justify a reduction in employer-provided benefits if the result is that, taking the employer-provided and Government-provided benefits together, an older employee is entitled to a lesser benefit of any type (including coverage for family and/or dependents) than a similarly situated younger employee. For example, the availability of certain benefits to an older employee under Medicare will not justify denying an older employee a benefit which is provided to younger employees and is not provided to the older employee by Medicare.

(f) *Application of section 4(f)(2) to various employees benefit plans.* (1) *Benefit-by-benefit approach.* This portion of the interpretation discusses how a benefit-by-benefit approach would apply to four of the most common types of employee benefit plans.

(i) *Life insurance.* It is not uncommon for life insurance coverage to remain constant until a specified age, frequently 65, and then be reduced. This practice will not violate the Act (even if reductions start before age 65), provided that the reduction for an employee of a particular age is no greater than is justified by the increased cost of coverage for that employee's specific age bracket encompassing no more than five years. It should be noted that a total denial of life insurance, on the basis of age, would not be justified under a benefit-by-benefit analysis. However, it is not unlawful for life insurance coverage to cease upon separation from service.

(ii) *Long-term disability.* Under a benefit-by-benefit approach, where employees who are disabled at younger ages are entitled to long-term disability benefits, there is no cost—based justification for denying such benefits altogether, on the basis of age, to employees who are disabled at older ages. It is not unlawful to cut off long-term disability benefits and coverage on the basis of some non-age factor, such as recovery from disability. Reductions on the basis of age in the level or duration of benefits available for disability are justifiable only on the basis of age-related cost considerations as set forth elsewhere in this section. An employer which provides long-term disability coverage to all employees may avoid any increases in the cost to it that such coverage for older employees would entail by reducing the level of benefits available to older employees. An employer may also avoid such cost increases by reducing the duration of benefits available to employees who become disabled at older ages, without reducing the level of benefits. In this connection, the Department would not assert a violation where the level of benefits is not reduced and the duration of benefits is reduced in the following manner:

(A) With respect to disabilities which occur at age 60 or less, benefits cease at age 65.

(B) With respect to disabilities which occur after age 60, benefits cease 5 years after disablement. Cost data may be produced to support other patterns of reduction as well.

(iii) *Retirement plans.* (A) *Participation.* No employee hired prior to normal retirement age may be excluded from a defined contribution plan. With respect to defined benefit plans not subject to the Employee Retirement Income Security Act (ERISA), Pub.L. 93-406, 29 U.S.C. 1001, 1003(a) and (b), an employee hired at an age more than 5 years prior to normal retirement age may not be excluded from such a plan unless the exclusion is justifiable on the basis of cost considerations as set forth elsewhere in this section. With respect to defined benefit plans subject to ERISA, such an exclusion would be unlawful in any case. An employee hired less than 5 years prior to normal retirement age may be excluded from a defined benefit plan, regardless of whether or not the plan is covered by ERISA. Similarly, any employee hired after normal retirement age may be excluded from a defined benefit plan.

(2) *"Benefit Package" Approach.* A "benefit package" approach to compliance under section 4(f)(2) offers greater flexibility than a benefit-by-benefit approach by permitting deviations from a benefit-by-benefit approach so long as the overall result is no lesser cost to the employer and no less favorable benefits for employees. As previously noted, in order

to assure that such an approach is used for the benefit of older workers and not to their detriment, and is otherwise consistent with the legislative intent, it is subject to limitations as set forth below:

(i) A benefit package approach shall apply only to employee benefit plans which fall within section 4(f)(2).

(ii) A benefit package approach shall not apply to a retirement or pension plan. The 1978 legislative history sets forth specific and comprehensive rules governing such plans, which have been adopted above. These rules are not tied to actuarially significant cost considerations but are intended to deal with the special funding arrangements of retirement or pension plans. Variations from these special rules are therefore not justified by variations from the cost-based benefit-by-benefit approach in other benefit plans, nor may variations from the special rules governing pension and retirement plans justify variations from the benefit-by-benefit approach in other benefit plans.

(iii) A benefit package approach shall not be used to justify reductions in health benefits greater than would be justified under a benefit-by-benefit approach. Such benefits appear to be of particular importance to older workers in meeting "problems arising from the impact of age" and were of particular concern to Congress. Therefore, the "benefit package" approach may not be used to reduce health insurance benefits by more than is warranted by the increase in the cost to the employer of those benefits alone. Any greater reduction would be a subterfuge to evade the purpose of the Act.

(iv) A benefit reduction greater than would be justified under a benefit-by-benefit approach must be offset by another benefit available to the same employees. No employees may be deprived because of age of one benefit without an offsetting benefit being made available to them.

(v) Employers who wish to justify benefit reductions under a benefit package approach must be prepared to produce data to show that those reductions are fully justified. Thus employers must be able to show that deviations from a benefit-by-benefit approach do not result in lesser cost to them or less favorable benefits to their employees. A general example consistent with these limitations may be given. Assume two employee benefit plans, providing Benefit "A" and Benefit "B." Both plans fall within section 4(f)(2), and neither is a retirement or pension plan subject to special rules. Both benefits are available to all employees. Age-based cost increases would justify a 10% decrease in both benefits on a benefit-by-benefit basis. The affected employees would, however, find it more favorable—that is, more consistent with meeting their needs—for no reduction to be made in Benefit "A" and a greater reduction to be made in Benefit "B." This "trade-off" would not result in a reduction in health benefits. The "trade-off" may therefore be made. The details of the "trade-off" depend on data on the relative cost to the employer of the two benefits. If the data show that Benefit "A" and Benefit "B" cost the same, Benefit "B" may be reduced up to 20% if Benefit "A" is unreduced. If the data show that Benefit "A" costs only half as much as Benefit "B", however, Benefit "B" may be reduced up to only 15% if Benefit "A" is unreduced, since a greater reduction in Benefit "B" would result in an impermissible reduction in total benefit costs.

(g) *Relation of ADEA to State laws.* The ADEA does not preempt State age discrimination in employment laws. However, the failure of the ADEA to preempt such laws does not affect the issue of whether section 514 of the Employee Retirement Income Security Act (ERISA) preempts State laws which related to employee benefit plans.

ERISA REGULATIONS

Code of Federal Regulations, Title 29

§ 2509.08-1. Supplemental guidance relating to fiduciary responsibility in considering economically targeted investments. [removed and replaced by § 2509.2015-01, below]

§ 2509.08-2. Interpretive bulletin relating to the exercise of shareholder rights and written statements of investment policy, including proxy voting policies or guidelines.

This interpretive bulletin sets forth the Department of Labor's (the Department) interpretation of sections 402, 403 and 404 of the Employee Retirement Income Security Act of 1974 (ERISA) as those sections apply to voting of proxies on securities held in employee benefit plan investment portfolios and the maintenance of and compliance with statements of investment policy, including proxy voting policy. In addition, this interpretive bulletin provides guidance on the appropriateness under ERISA of active monitoring of corporate management by plan fiduciaries. The guidance set forth in this interpretive bulletin modifies and supersedes the guidance set forth in interpretive bulletin 94-2 (29 CFR 2509.94-2).

(1) Proxy Voting

The fiduciary act of managing plan assets that are shares of corporate stock includes the management of voting rights appurtenant to those shares of stock. As a result, the responsibility for voting or deciding not to vote proxies lies exclusively with the plan trustee except to the extent that either (1) the trustee is subject to the direction of a named fiduciary pursuant to ERISA Sec. 403(a)(1); or (2) the power to manage, acquire or dispose of the relevant assets has been delegated by a named fiduciary to one or more investment managers pursuant to ERISA Sec. 403(a)(2). Where the authority to manage plan assets has been delegated to an investment manager pursuant to Sec. 403(a)(2), no person other than the investment manager has authority to make voting decisions for proxies appurtenant to such plan assets except to the extent that the named fiduciary has reserved to itself (or to another named fiduciary so authorized by the plan document) the right to direct a plan trustee regarding the voting of proxies. In this regard, a named fiduciary, in delegating investment management authority to an investment manager, could reserve to itself the right to direct a trustee with respect to the voting of all proxies or reserve to itself the right to direct a trustee as to the voting of only those proxies relating to specified assets or issues.

If the plan document or investment management agreement provides that the investment manager is not required to vote proxies, but does not expressly preclude the investment manager from voting proxies, the investment manager would have exclusive responsibility for proxy voting decisions. Moreover, an investment manager would not be relieved of its own fiduciary responsibilities by following directions of some other person regarding the voting of proxies, or by delegating such responsibility to another person. If, however, the plan document or the investment management contract expressly precludes the investment manager from voting proxies, the responsibility for voting proxies would lie exclusively with the trustee. The trustee, however, consistent with the requirements of ERISA Sec. 403(a)(1), may be subject to the directions of a named fiduciary if the plan so provides.

The fiduciary duties described at ERISA Sec. 404(a)(1)(A) and (B), require that, in voting proxies, regardless of whether the vote is made pursuant to a statement of investment policy, the responsible fiduciary shall consider only those factors that relate to the economic value of the plan's investment and shall not subordinate the interests of the participants and beneficiaries in their retirement income to unrelated objectives. Votes shall only be cast in accordance with a plan's economic interests. If the responsible fiduciary reasonably determines that the cost of voting (including the cost of research, if necessary, to determine how to vote) is likely to exceed the expected economic benefits of voting, or if the exercise of voting results in the imposition of unwarranted trading or other restrictions, the fiduciary has an obligation to refrain from voting. In making this determination, objectives, considerations, and economic effects unrelated to the plan's economic interests cannot be considered. The fiduciary's duties under ERISA Sec. 404(a)(1)(A) and (B) also require that the named fiduciary appointing an investment manager periodically monitor the activities of the investment manager with respect to the management of plan assets, including decisions made and actions taken by the investment manager with regard to proxy voting decisions. The named fiduciary must carry out this responsibility solely in the participants' and beneficiaries' interest in the economic value of the plan assets and without regard to the fiduciary's relationship to the plan sponsor.

It is the view of the Department that compliance with the duty to monitor necessitates proper documentation of the activities that are subject to monitoring. Thus, the investment manager or other responsible fiduciary would be required to maintain accurate records as to proxy voting decisions, including, where appropriate, cost-benefit analyses. Moreover, if the named fiduciary is to be able to carry out its responsibilities under ERISA Sec. 404(a) in determining whether the investment manager is fulfilling its fiduciary obligations in investing plans assets in a manner that justifies the continuation of the management appointment, the proxy voting records must enable the named fiduciary to review not only the investment manager's voting procedure with respect to plan-owned stock, but also to review the actions taken in individual proxy voting situations.

The fiduciary obligations of prudence and loyalty to plan participants and beneficiaries require the responsible fiduciary to vote proxies on issues that may affect the economic value of the plan's investment. However, fiduciaries also need to take into account costs when deciding whether and how to exercise their shareholder rights, including the voting of shares. Such costs include, but are not limited to, expenditures related to developing proxy resolutions, proxy voting services and the analysis of the likely net effect of a particular issue on the economic value of the plan's investment. Fiduciaries must take all of these factors into account in determining whether the exercise of such rights (e.g., the voting of a proxy), independently or in conjunction with other shareholders, is expected to have an effect on the economic value of the plan's investment that will outweigh the cost of exercising such rights. With respect to proxies appurtenant to shares of foreign corporations, a fiduciary, in deciding whether to purchase shares of a foreign corporation, should consider whether any additional difficulty and expense in voting such shares is reflected in their market price.

(2) Statements of Investment Policy

The maintenance by an employee benefit plan of a statement of investment policy designed to further the purposes of the plan and its funding policy is consistent with the fiduciary obligations set forth in ERISA section 404(a)(1)(A) and (B). Because the fiduciary act of managing plan assets that are shares of corporate stock includes the voting, where appropriate, of proxies appurtenant to those shares of stock, a statement of proxy voting policy would be an important part of any comprehensive statement of investment policy. For purposes of this document, the term "statement of investment policy" means a written statement that provides the fiduciaries who are responsible for plan investments with guidelines or general instructions concerning various types or categories of investment management decisions, which may include proxy voting decisions. A statement of investment policy is distinguished from directions as to the purchase or sale of a specific investment at a specific time or as to voting specific plan proxies.

In plans where investment management responsibility is delegated to one or more investment managers appointed by the named fiduciary pursuant to ERISA Sec. 402(c)(3), inherent in the authority to appoint an investment manager, the named fiduciary responsible for appointment of investment managers has the authority to condition the appointment on acceptance of a statement of investment policy. Thus, such a named fiduciary may expressly require, as a condition of the investment management agreement, that an investment manager comply with the terms of a statement of investment policy that sets forth guidelines concerning investments and investment courses of action that the investment manager is authorized or is not authorized to make. Such investment policy may include a policy or guidelines on the voting of proxies on shares of stock for which the investment manager is responsible. Such guidelines must be consistent with the fiduciary obligations set forth in ERISA Sec. 404(a)(1)(A) and (B) and this Interpretive Bulletin, and may not subordinate the economic interests of the plan participants to unrelated objectives. In the absence of such an express requirement to comply with an investment policy, the authority to manage the plan assets placed under the control of the investment manager would lie exclusively with the investment manager. Although a trustee may be subject to the direction of a named fiduciary pursuant to ERISA Sec. 403(a)(1), an investment manager who has authority to make investment decisions, including proxy voting decisions, would never be relieved of its fiduciary responsibility if it followed the direction as to specific investment decisions from the named fiduciary or any other person.

Statements of investment policy issued by a named fiduciary authorized to appoint investment managers would be part of the "documents and instruments governing the plan" within the meaning of ERISA Sec. 404(a)(1)(D). An investment manager to whom such investment policy applies would be required to comply with such policy, pursuant to ERISA Sec. 404(a)(1)(D) insofar as the policy directives or guidelines are consistent with titles I and IV of ERISA. Therefore, if, for example, compliance with the guidelines in a given instance would be imprudent, then the investment manager's failure to follow the guidelines would not violate ERISA Sec. 404(a)(1)(D). Moreover, ERISA Sec. 404(a)(1)(D) does not shield the investment manager from liability for imprudent actions taken in compliance with a statement of investment policy.

The plan document or trust agreement may expressly provide a statement of investment policy to guide the trustee or may authorize a named fiduciary to issue a statement of investment policy applicable to a trustee. Where a plan trustee is subject to an investment policy, the trustee's duty to comply with such investment policy would also be analyzed under ERISA Sec. 404(a)(1)(D). Thus, the trustee would be required to comply with the statement of investment policy unless, for example, it would be imprudent to do so in a given instance.

Maintenance of a statement of investment policy by a named fiduciary does not relieve the named fiduciary of its obligations under ERISA Sec. 404(a) with respect to the appointment and monitoring of an investment manager or trustee. In this regard, the named fiduciary appointing an investment manager must periodically monitor the investment manager's activities with respect to management of the plan assets. Moreover, compliance with ERISA Sec. 404(a)(1)(B) would require maintenance of proper documentation of the activities of the investment manager and of the named fiduciary of the plan in monitoring the activities of the investment manager. In addition, in the view of the Department, a named fiduciary's determination of the terms of a statement of investment policy is an exercise of fiduciary responsibility and, as such, statements may need to take into account factors such as the plan's funding policy and its liquidity needs as well as issues of prudence, diversification and other fiduciary requirements of ERISA.

An investment manager of a pooled investment vehicle that holds assets of more than one employee benefit plan may be subject to a proxy voting policy of one plan that conflicts with the proxy voting policy of another plan. If the investment manager determines that compliance with one of the conflicting voting policies would violate ERISA Sec. 404(a)(1), for example, by being imprudent or not solely in the economic interest of plan participants, the investment manager would be required to ignore the policy and vote in accordance with ERISA's obligations. If, however, the investment manager reasonably concludes that application of each plan's voting policy is consistent with ERISA's obligations, such as when the policies reflect different but reasonable judgments or when the plans have different economic interests, ERISA Sec. 404(a)(1)(D) would generally require the manager, to the extent permitted by applicable law, to vote the proxies in proportion to each plan's interest in the pooled investment vehicle. An investment manager may also require participating investors to accept the investment manager's own investment policy statement, including any statement of proxy voting policy, before they are allowed to invest, which may help to avoid such potential conflicts. As with investment policies originating from named fiduciaries, a policy initiated by an investment manager and adopted by the participating plans would be regarded as an instrument governing the participating plans, and the investment manager's compliance with such a policy would be governed by ERISA Sec. 404(a)(1)(D).

(3) Shareholder Activism

An investment policy that contemplates activities intended to monitor or influence the management of corporations in which the plan owns stock is consistent with a fiduciary's obligations under ERISA where the responsible fiduciary concludes that there is a reasonable expectation that such monitoring or communication with management, by the plan alone or together with other shareholders, will enhance the economic value of the plan's investment in the corporation, after taking into

account the costs involved. Such a reasonable expectation may exist in various circumstances, for example, where plan investments in corporate stock are held as long-term investments or where a plan may not be able to easily dispose such an investment. Active monitoring and communication activities would generally concern such issues as the independence and expertise of candidates for the corporation's board of directors and assuring that the board has sufficient information to carry out its responsibility to monitor management. Other issues may include such matters as consideration of the appropriateness of executive compensation, the corporation's policy regarding mergers and acquisitions, the extent of debt financing and capitalization, the nature of long-term business plans, the corporation's investment in training to develop its work force, other workplace practices and financial and non-financial measures of corporate performance that are reasonably likely to affect the economic value of the plan. Active monitoring and communication may be carried out through a variety of methods including by means of correspondence and meetings with corporate management as well as by exercising the legal rights of a shareholder. In creating an investment policy, a fiduciary shall consider only factors that relate to the economic interest of participants and their beneficiaries in plan assets, and shall not use an investment policy to promote myriad public policy preferences.

(4) Socially-Directed Proxy Voting, Investment Policies and Shareholder Activism.

Plan fiduciaries risk violating the exclusive purpose rule when they exercise their fiduciary authority in an attempt to further legislative, regulatory or public policy issues through the proxy process. In such cases, the Department would expect fiduciaries to be able to demonstrate in enforcement actions their compliance with the requirements of section 404(a)(1)(A) and (B). The mere fact that plans are shareholders in the corporations in which they invest does not itself provide a rationale for a fiduciary to spend plan assets to pursue, support, or oppose such proxy proposals. Because of the heightened potential for abuse in such cases, the fiduciaries must be prepared to articulate a clear basis for concluding that the proxy vote, the investment policy, or the activity intended to monitor or influence the management of the corporation is more likely than not to enhance the economic value of the plan's investment before expending plan assets.

The use of pension plan assets by plan fiduciaries to further policy or political issues through proxy resolutions that have no connection to enhancing the economic value of the plan's investment in a corporation would, in the view of the Department, violate the prudence and exclusive purpose requirements of section 404(a)(1)(A) and (B). For example, the likelihood that the adoption of a proxy resolution or proposal requiring corporate directors and officers to disclose their personal political contributions would enhance the economic value of a plan's investment in the corporation appears sufficiently remote that the expenditure of plan assets to further such a resolution or proposal clearly raises compliance issues under section 404(a)(1)(A) and (B).

§ 2509.75-5. Questions and answers relating to fiduciary responsibility.

* * *

D-1 Q: Is an attorney, accountant, actuary or consultant who renders legal, accounting, actuarial or consulting services to an employee benefit plan (other than an investment adviser to the plan) a fiduciary to the plan solely by virtue of the rendering of such services, absent a showing that such consultant (a) exercises discretionary authority or discretionary control respecting the management of the plan, (b) exercises authority or control respecting management or disposition of the plan's assets, (c) renders investment advice for a fee, direct or indirect, with respect to the assets of the plan, or has any authority or responsibility to do so, or (d) has any discretionary authority or discretionary responsibility in the administration of the plan?

A: No. However, while attorneys, accountants, actuaries and consultants performing their usual professional functions will ordinarily not be considered fiduciaries, if the factual situation in a particular case falls within one of the categories described in clauses (a) through (d) of this question, such persons would be considered to be fiduciaries within the meaning of section 3(21) of the Act. The Internal Revenue Service notes that such persons would also be considered to be fiduciaries within the meaning of section 4975(e)(3) of the Internal Revenue Code of 1954.

* * *

§ 2509.75-8. Questions and answers relating to fiduciary responsibility under the Employee Retirement Income Security Act of 1974.

* * *

D-2 Q: Are persons who have no power to make any decisions as to plan policy, interpretations, practices or procedures, but who perform the following administrative functions for an employee benefit plan, within a framework of policies, interpretations, rules, practices and procedures made by other persons, fiduciaries with respect to the plan:

(1) Application of rules determining eligibility for participation or benefits;

(2) Calculation of services and compensation credits for benefits;

(3) Preparation of employee communications material;

(4) Maintenance of participants' service and employment records;

(5) Preparation of reports required by government agencies;

(6) Calculation of benefits;

(7) Orientation of new participants and advising participants of their rights and options under the plan;

(8) Collection of contributions and application of contributions as provided in the plan;

(9) Preparation of reports concerning participants' benefits;

(10) Processing of claims; and

(11) Making recommendations to others for decisions with respect to plan administration?

A: No. Only persons who perform one or more of the functions described in section 3(21)(A) of the Act with respect to an employee benefit plan are fiduciaries. Therefore, a person who performs purely ministerial functions such as the types described above for an employee benefit plan within a framework of policies, interpretations, rules, practices and procedures made by other persons is not a fiduciary because such person does not have discretionary authority or discretionary control respecting management of the plan, does not exercise any authority or control respecting management or disposition of the assets of the plan, and does not render investment advice with respect to any money or other property of the plan and has no authority or responsibility to do so.

However, although such a person may not be a plan fiduciary, he may be subject to the bonding requirements contained in section 412 of the Act if he handles funds or other property of the plan within the meaning of applicable regulations.

The Internal Revenue Service notes that such persons would not be considered plan fiduciaries within the meaning of section 4975(e)(3) of the Internal Revenue Code of 1954.

* * *

D-4 Q: In the case of a plan established and maintained by an employer, are members of the board of directors of the employer fiduciaries with respect to the plan?

A: Members of the board of directors of an employer which maintains an employee benefit plan will be fiduciaries only to the extent that they have responsibility for the functions described in section 3(21)(A) of the Act. For example, the board of directors may

be responsible for the selection and retention of plan fiduciaries. In such a case, members of the board of directors exercise "discretionary authority or discretionary control respecting management of such plan" and are, therefore, fiduciaries with respect to the plan. However, their responsibility, and, consequently, their liability, is limited to the selection and retention of fiduciaries (apart from co-fiduciary liability arising under circumstances described in section 405(a) of the Act). In addition, if the directors are made named fiduciaries of the plan, their liability may be limited pursuant to a procedure provided for in the plan instrument for the allocation of fiduciary responsibilities among named fiduciaries or for the designation of persons other than named fiduciaries to carry out fiduciary responsibilities, as provided in section 405(c)(2).

* * *

FR-11 Q: In discharging fiduciary responsibilities, may a fiduciary with respect to a plan rely on information, data, statistics or analyses provided by other persons who perform purely ministerial functions for such plan, such as those persons described in D-2 above?

A: A plan fiduciary may rely on information, data, statistics or analyses furnished by persons performing ministerial functions for the plan, provided that he has exercised prudence in the selection and retention of such persons. The plan fiduciary will be deemed to have acted prudently in such selection and retention if, in the exercise of ordinary care in such situation, he has no reason to doubt the competence, integrity or responsibility of such persons.

* * *

FR-17 Q: What are the ongoing responsibilities of a fiduciary who has appointed trustees or other fiduciaries with respect to these appointments?

A: At reasonable intervals the performance of trustees and other fiduciaries should be reviewed by the appointing fiduciary in such manner as may be reasonably expected to ensure that their performance has been in compliance with the terms of the plan and statutory standards, and satisfies the needs of the plan. No single procedure will be appropriate in all cases; the procedure adopted may vary in accordance with the nature of the plan and other facts and circumstances relevant to the choice of the procedure.

§ 2509.2015-01 Interpretive bulletin relating to the fiduciary standard under ERISA in considering economically targeted investments.

This Interpretive Bulletin sets forth the Department of Labor's interpretation of sections 403 and 404 of the Employee Retirement Income Security Act of 1974 (ERISA), as applied to employee benefit plan investments in "economically targeted investments" (ETIs), that is, investments selected for the economic benefits they create apart from their investment return to the employee benefit plan. Sections 403 and 404, in part, require that a fiduciary of a plan act prudently, and to diversify plan investments so as to minimize the risk of large losses, unless under the circumstances it is clearly prudent not to do so. In addition, these sections require that a fiduciary act solely in the interest of the plan's participants and beneficiaries and for the exclusive purpose of providing benefits to their participants and beneficiaries. The Department has construed the requirements that a fiduciary act solely in the interest of, and for the exclusive purpose of providing benefits to, participants and beneficiaries as prohibiting a fiduciary from subordinating the interests of participants and beneficiaries in their retirement income to unrelated objectives.

With regard to investing plan assets, the Department has issued a regulation, at 29 CFR 2550.404a-1, interpreting the prudence requirements of ERISA as they apply to the investment duties of fiduciaries of employee benefit plans. The regulation provides that the prudence requirements of section 404(a)(1)(B) are satisfied if (1) the fiduciary making an investment or engaging in an investment course of action has given appropriate consideration to those facts and circumstances that, given the scope of the fiduciary's investment duties, the fiduciary knows or should know are relevant, and (2) the fiduciary acts accordingly. This includes giving appropriate consideration to the role that the investment or investment course of action plays (in terms of such factors as diversification, liquidity, and risk/return characteristics) with respect to that portion of the plan's investment portfolio within the scope of the fiduciary's responsibility.

Other facts and circumstances relevant to an investment or investment course of action would, in the view of the Department, include consideration of the expected return on alternative investments with similar risks available to the plan. It follows that, because every investment necessarily causes a plan to forgo other investment opportunities, an investment will not be prudent if it would be expected to provide a plan with a lower rate of return than available alternative investments with commensurate degrees of risk or is riskier than alternative available investments with commensurate rates of return.

The fiduciary standards applicable to ETIs are no different than the standards applicable to plan investments generally. Therefore, if the above requirements are met, the selection of an ETI, or the engaging in an investment course of action intended to result in the selection of ETIs, will not violate section 404(a)(1)(A) and (B) and the exclusive purpose requirements of section 403.

§ 2510.3-1. Employee welfare benefit plan.

(a) *General.* (1) The purpose of this section is to clarify the definition of the terms "employee welfare benefit plan" and "welfare plan" for purposes of Title I of the Act and this chapter by identifying certain practices which do not constitute employee welfare benefit plans for those purposes. In addition, the practices listed in this section do not constitute employee pension benefit plans within the meaning of section 3(2) of the Act, and, therefore, do not constitute employee benefit plans within the meaning of section 3(3). Since under section 4(a) of the Act, only employee benefit plans within the meaning of section 3(3) are subject to Title I of the Act, the practices listed in this section are not subject to Title I.

(2) The terms "employee welfare benefit plan" and "welfare plan" are defined in section 3(1) of the Act to include plans providing "(i) medical, surgical, or hospital care or benefits, or benefits in the event of sickness, accident, disability, death or unemployment, or vacation benefits, apprenticeship or other training programs, or day care centers, scholarship funds, or prepaid legal services, or (ii) any benefit described in section 302(c) of the Labor Management Relations Act, 1947 (other than pensions on retirement or death, and insurance to provide such pensions)." Under this definition, only plans which provide benefits described in section 3(1)(A) of the Act or in section 302(c) of the Labor-Management Relations Act, 1947 (hereinafter "the LMRA")(other than pensions on retirement or death) constitute welfare plans. For example, a system of payroll deductions by an employer for deposit in savings accounts owned by its employees is not an employee welfare benefit plan within the meaning of section 3(1) of the Act because it does not provide benefits described in section 3(1)(A) of the Act or section 302(c) of the LMRA. (In addition, if each employee has the right to withdraw the balance in his or her account at any time, such a payroll savings plan does not meet the requirements for a pension plan set forth in section 3(2) of the Act and, therefore, is not an employee benefit plan within the meaning of section 3(3) of the Act).

(3) Section 302(c) of the LMRA lists exceptions to the restrictions contained in subsections (a) and (b) of that section on payments and loans made by an employer to individuals and groups representing employees of the employer. Of these exceptions, only those contained in paragraphs (5), (6), (7) and (8) describe benefits provided through employee benefit plans. Moreover, only paragraph (6) describes benefits not described in section 3(1)(A) of the Act. The benefits described in section 302(c)(6) of the LMRA but not in section 3(1)(A) of the Act are " * * * holiday, severance or similar benefits". Thus, the effect of section 3(1)(B) of the Act is to include within the definition of "welfare plan" those plans which provide holiday and severance benefits, and benefits which are similar (for example, benefits which are in substance severance benefits, although not so characterized).

(4) Some of the practices listed in this section as excluded from the definition of "welfare plan" or mentioned as examples of general categories of excluded practices are inserted in response to questions received by the Department of Labor and, in the Department's judgment, do not represent borderline cases under the definition in section 3(1) of the Act. Therefore, this section should not be read as implicitly indicating the Department's views on the possible scope of section 3(1).

(b) *Payroll practices.* For purposes of Title I of the Act and this chapter, the terms "employee welfare benefit plan" and "welfare plan" shall not include—

(1) Payment by an employer of compensation on account of work performed by an employee, including compensation at a rate in excess of the normal rate of compensation on account of performance of duties under other than ordinary circumstances, such as—

(i) Overtime pay,

(ii) Shift premiums,

(iii) Holiday premiums,

(iv) Weekend premiums;

(2) Payment of an employee's normal compensation, out of the employer's general assets, on account of periods of time during which the employee is physically or mentally

unable to perform his or her duties, or is otherwise absent for medical reasons (such as pregnancy, a physical examination or psychiatric treatment); and

(3) Payment of compensation, out of the employer's general assets, on account of periods of time during which the employee, although physically and mentally able to perform his or her duties and not absent for medical reasons (such as pregnancy, a physical examination or psychiatric treatment) performs no duties; for example—

(i) Payment of compensation while an employee is on vacation or absent on a holiday, including payment of premiums to induce employees to take vacations at a time favorable to the employer for business reasons,

(ii) Payment of compensation to an employee who is absent while on active military duty,

(iii) Payment of compensation while an employee is absent for the purpose of serving as a juror or testifying in official proceedings,

(iv) Payment of compensation on account of periods of time during which an employee performs little or no productive work while engaged in training (whether or not subsidized in whole or in part by Federal, State or local government funds), and

(v) Payment of compensation to an employee who is relieved of duties while on sabbatical leave or while pursuing further education.

(c) *On-premises facilities.* For purposes of Title I of the Act and this chapter, the terms "employee welfare benefit plan" and "welfare plan" shall not include—

(1) The maintenance on the premises of an employer or of an employee organization of recreation, dining or other facilities (other than day care centers) for use by employees or members; and

(2) The maintenance on the premises of an employer of facilities for the treatment of minor injuries or illness or rendering first aid

in case of accidents occurring during working hours.

(d) *Holiday gifts.* For purposes of Title I of the Act and this chapter the terms "employee welfare benefit plan" and "welfare plan" shall not include the distribution of gifts such as turkeys or hams by an employer to employees at Christmas and other holiday seasons.

(e) *Sales to employees.* For purposes of Title I of the Act and this chapter, the terms "employee welfare benefit plan" and "welfare plan" shall not include the sale by an employer to employees of an employer, whether or not at prevailing market prices, of articles or commodities of the kind which the employer offers for sale in the regular course of business.

(f) *Hiring halls.* For purposes of Title I of the Act and this chapter, the terms "employee welfare benefit plan" and "welfare plan" shall not include the maintenance by one or more employers, employee organizations, or both, of a hiring hall facility.

(g) *Remembrance funds.* For purposes of Title I of the Act and this chapter, the terms "employee welfare benefit plan" and "welfare plan" shall not include a program under which contributions are made to provide remembrances such as flowers, an obituary notice in a newspaper or a small gift on occasions such as the sickness, hospitalization, death or termination of employment of employees, or members of an employee organization, or members of their families.

(h) *Strike funds.* For purposes of Title I of the Act and this chapter, the terms "employee welfare benefit plan" and "welfare plan" shall not include a fund maintained by an employee organization to provide payments to its members during strikes and for related purposes.

(i) *Industry advancement programs.* For purposes of Title I of the Act and this chapter, the terms "employee welfare benefit plan" and "welfare plan" shall not include a program maintained by an employer or group or association of employers, which has no employee participants and does not provide benefits to employees or their dependents, regardless of whether the program serves as a conduit through which funds or other assets are channeled to employee benefit plans covered under Title I of the Act.

(j) *Certain group or group-type insurance programs.* For purposes of Title I of the Act and this chapter, the terms "employee welfare benefit plan" and "welfare plan" shall not include a group or group-type insurance program offered by an insurer to employees or members of an employee organization, under which

(1) No contributions are made by an employer or employee organization;

(2) Participation the program is completely voluntary for employees or members;

(3) The sole functions of the employer or employee organization with respect to the program are, without endorsing the program, to permit the insurer to publicize the program to employees or members, to collect premiums through payroll deductions or dues checkoffs and to remit them to the insurer; and

(4) The employer or employee organization receives no consideration in the form of cash or otherwise in connection with the program, other than reasonable compensation, excluding any profit, for administrative services actually rendered in connection with payroll deductions or dues checkoffs.

(k) *Unfunded scholarship programs.* For purposes of Title I of the Act and this chapter, the terms "employee welfare benefit plan" and "welfare plan" shall not include a scholarship program, including a tuition and education expense refund program, under which payments are made solely from the general assets of an employer or employee organization.

§ 2510.3-2. Employee pension benefit plan.

(a) *General.* This section clarifies the terms "employee pension benefit plan" and "pension plan" for purposes of title I of the Act and this chapter by setting forth safe harbors under which certain specific plans, funds and programs would not constitute employee

pension benefit plans when the conditions of this section are satisfied. The safe harbors in this section should not be read as implicitly indicating the Department's views on the possible scope of section 3(2). To the extent that these plans, funds and programs constitute employee welfare benefit plans within the meaning of section 3(1) of the Act and § 2510.3-1 of this part, they will be covered under title I; however, they will not be subject to parts 2 and 3 of title I of the Act.

(b) *Severance pay plans.* (1) For purposes of Title I of the Act and this chapter, an arrangement shall not be deemed to constitute an employee pension benefit plan or pension plan solely by reason of the payment of severance benefits on account of the termination of an employee's service, provided that:

(i) Such payments are not contingent, directly or indirectly, upon the employee's retiring;

(ii) The total amount of such payments does not exceed the equivalent of twice the employee's annual compensation during the year immediately preceding the termination of his service; and

(iii) All such payments to any employee are completed,

(A) In the case of an employee whose service is terminated in connection with a limited program of terminations, within the later of 24 months after the termination of the employee's service, or 24 months after the employee reaches normal retirement age; and

(B) In the case of all other employees, within 24 months after the termination of the employee's service.

(2) For purposes of this paragraph (b),

(i) "Annual compensation" means the total of all compensation, including wages, salary, and any other benefit of monetary value, whether paid in the form of cash or otherwise, which was paid as consideration for the employee's service during the year, or which would have been so paid at the employee's usual rate of compensation if the employee had worked a full year.

(ii) "Limited program of terminations" means a program of terminations:

(A) Which, when begun, was scheduled to be completed upon a date certain or upon the occurrence of one or more specified events;

(B) Under which the number, percentage or class or classes of employees whose services are to be terminated is specified in advance; and

(C) Which is described in a written document which is available to the Secretary upon request, and which contains information sufficient to demonstrate that the conditions set forth in paragraphs (b)(2)(ii)(A) and (B) of this section have been met.

(c) *Bonus program.* For purposes of Title I of the Act and this chapter, the terms "employee pension benefit plan" and "pension plan" shall not include payments made by an employer to some or all of its employees as bonuses for work performed, unless such payments are systematically deferred to the termination of covered employment or beyond, or so as to provide retirement income to employees.

(d) *Individual Retirement Accounts.* (1) For purposes of Title I of the Act and this chapter, the terms "employee pension benefit plan" and "pension plan" shall not include an individual retirement account described in section 408(a) of the Code, an individual retirement annuity described in section 408(b) of the Internal Revenue Code of 1954 (hereinafter "the Code") and an individual retirement bond described in section 409 of the Code, provided that—

(i) No contributions are made by the employer or employee association;

(ii) Participation is completely voluntary for employees or members;

(iii) The sole involvement of the employer or employee organization is without en-

dorsement to permit the sponsor to publicize the program to employees or members, to collect contributions through payroll deductions or dues checkoffs and to remit them to the sponsor; and

(iv) The employer or employee organization receives no consideration in the form of cash or otherwise, other than reasonable compensation for services actually rendered in connection with payroll deductions or dues checkoffs.

* * *

(h) Certain State savings programs. (1) For purposes of title I of the Act and this chapter, the terms "employee pension benefit plan" and "pension plan" shall not include an individual retirement plan (as defined in 26 U.S.C. 7701(a)(37)) established and maintained pursuant to a State payroll deduction savings program, provided that:

(i) The program is specifically established pursuant to State law;

(ii) The program is implemented and administered by the State establishing the program (or by a governmental agency or instrumentality of the State), which is responsible for investing the employee savings or for selecting investment alternatives for employees to choose;

(iii) The State (or governmental agency or instrumentality of the State) assumes responsibility for the security of payroll deductions and employee savings;

(iv) The State (or governmental agency or instrumentality of the State) adopts measures to ensure that employees are notified of their rights under the program, and creates a mechanism for enforcement of those rights;

(v) Participation in the program is voluntary for employees;

(vi) All rights of the employee, former employee, or beneficiary under the program are enforceable only by the employee, former employee, or beneficiary, an authorized representative of such a person, or by the State (or governmental agency or instrumentality of the State);

(vii) The involvement of the employer is limited to the following:

(A) Collecting employee contributions through payroll deductions and remitting them to the program;

(B) Providing notice to the employees and maintaining records regarding the employer's collection and remittance of payments under the program;

(C) Providing information to the State (or governmental agency or instrumentality of the State) necessary to facilitate the operation of the program; and

(D) Distributing program information to employees from the State (or governmental agency or instrumentality of the State) and permitting the State (or governmental agency or instrumentality of the State) to publicize the program to employees;

(viii) The employer contributes no funds to the program and provides no bonus or other monetary incentive to employees to participate in the program; [*59477]

(ix) The employer's participation in the program is required by State law;

(x) The employer has no discretionary authority, control, or responsibility under the program; and

(xi) The employer receives no direct or indirect consideration in the form of cash or otherwise, other than consideration (including tax incentives and credits) received directly from the State (or governmental agency or instrumentality of the State) that does not exceed an amount that reasonably approximates the employer's (or a typical employer's) costs under the program.

(2) A State savings program will not fail to satisfy the provisions of paragraph (h)(1) of this section merely because the program--

(i) Is directed toward those employers that do not offer some other workplace savings arrangement;

(ii) Utilizes one or more service or investment providers to operate and administer the program, provided that the State (or governmental agency or instrumentality of the State) retains full responsibility for the operation and administration of the program; or

(iii) Treats employees as having automatically elected payroll deductions in an amount or percentage of compensation, including any automatic increases in such amount or percentage, unless the employee specifically elects not to have such deductions made (or specifically elects to have the deductions made in a different amount or percentage of compensation allowed by the program), provided that the employee is given adequate advance notice of the right to make such elections and provided, further, that a program may also satisfy this paragraph (h) without requiring or otherwise providing for automatic elections such as those described in this paragraph (h)(2)(iii).

(3) For purposes of this section, the term State shall have the same meaning as defined in section 3(10) of the Act.

§ 2510.3-3. Employee benefit plan.

(a) *General.* This section clarifies the definition in section 3(3) of the term "employee benefit plan" for purposes of Title I of the Act and this chapter. It states a general principle which can be applied to a large class of plans to determine whether they constitute employee benefit plans within the meaning of section 3(3) of the Act. Under section 4(a) of the Act, only employee benefit plans within the meaning of section 3(3) are subject to Title I.

(b) *Plans without employees.* For purposes of Title I of the Act and this chapter, the term "employee benefit plan" shall not include any plan, fund or program, other than an apprenticeship or other training program, under which no employees are participants covered under the plan, as defined in paragraph (d) of this section. For example, a so-called "Keogh" or "H.R. 10" plan under which only partners or only a sole proprietor are participants covered under the plan will not be covered under Title I. However, a Keogh plan under which one or more common law employees, in addition to the self-employed individuals, are participants covered under the plan, will be covered under Title I. Similarly, partnership buy-out agreements described in section 736 of the Internal Revenue Code of 1954 will not be subject to Title I.

(c) *Employees.* For purposes of this section:

(1) An individual and his or her spouse shall not be deemed to be employees with respect to a trade or business, whether incorporated or unincorporated, which is wholly owned by the individual or by the individual and his or her spouse, and

(2) A partner in a partnership and his or her spouse shall not be deemed to be employees with respect to the partnership.

* * *

§ 2510.3-21. Definition of "Fiduciary."

(a) *Investment advice.* For purposes of section 3(21)(A)(ii) of the Employee Retirement Income Security Act of 1974 (Act) and section 4975(e)(3)(B) of the Internal Revenue Code (Code), except as provided in paragraph (c) of this section, a person shall be deemed to be rendering investment advice with respect to moneys or other property of a plan or IRA described in paragraph (g)(6) of this section if-

(1) Such person provides to a plan, plan fiduciary, plan participant or beneficiary, IRA,

or IRA owner the following types of advice for a fee or other compensation, direct or indirect:

(i) A recommendation as to the advisability of acquiring, holding, disposing of, or exchanging, securities or other investment property, or a recommendation as to how securities or other investment property should be invested after the securities or other investment property are rolled over, transferred, or distributed from the plan or IRA;

(ii) A recommendation as to the management of securities or other investment property, including, among other things, recommendations on investment policies or strategies, portfolio composition, selection of other persons to provide investment advice or investment management services, selection of investment account arrangements (e.g., brokerage versus advisory); or recommendations with respect to rollovers, transfers, or distributions from a plan or IRA, including whether, in what amount, in what form, and to what destination such a rollover, transfer, or distribution should be made; and

(2) With respect to the investment advice described in paragraph (a)(1) of this section, the recommendation is made either directly or indirectly (e.g., through or together with any affiliate) by a person who:

(i) Represents or acknowledges that it is acting as a fiduciary within the meaning of the Act or the Code;

(ii) Renders the advice pursuant to a written or verbal agreement, arrangement, or understanding that the advice is based on the particular investment needs of the advice recipient; or

(iii) Directs the advice to a specific advice recipient or recipients regarding the advisability of a particular investment or management decision with respect to securities or other investment property of the plan or IRA.

(b)(1) For purposes of this section, "recommendation" means a communication that, based on its content, context, and presentation, would reasonably be viewed as a suggestion that the advice recipient engage in or refrain from taking a particular course of action. The determination of whether a "recommendation" has been made is an objective rather than subjective inquiry. In addition, the more individually tailored the communication is to a specific advice recipient or recipients about, for example, a security, investment property, or investment strategy, the more likely the communication will be viewed as a recommendation. Providing a selective list of securities to a particular advice recipient as appropriate for that investor would be a recommendation as to the advisability of acquiring securities even if no recommendation is made with respect to any one security. Furthermore, a series of actions, directly or indirectly (e.g., through or together with any affiliate), that may not constitute a recommendation when viewed individually may amount to a recommendation when considered in the aggregate. It also makes no difference whether the communication was initiated by a person or a computer software program.

(2) The provision of services or the furnishing or making available of information and materials in conformance with paragraphs (b)(2)(i) through (iv) of this section is not a "recommendation" for purposes of this section. Determinations as to whether any activity not described in this paragraph (b)(2) constitutes a recommendation must be made by reference to the criteria set forth in paragraph (b)(1) of this section.

(i) *Platform providers.* Marketing or making available to a plan fiduciary of a plan, without regard to the individualized needs of the plan, its participants, or beneficiaries a platform or similar mechanism from which a plan fiduciary may select or monitor investment alternatives, including qualified default investment alternatives, into which plan participants or beneficiaries may direct the investment of assets held in, or contributed to, their individual accounts, provided the plan fiduciary is independent of the person who markets or makes available the platform or similar mechanism, and the person discloses in writing to the plan fiduciary that the person is not undertaking to provide impartial investment advice or to give advice in a fiduciary capacity. A plan participant or beneficiary

or relative of either shall not be considered a plan fiduciary for purposes of this paragraph.

(ii) *Selection and monitoring assistance.* In connection with the activities described in paragraph (b)(2)(i) of this section with respect to a plan,

(A) Identifying investment alternatives that meet objective criteria specified by the plan fiduciary (e.g., stated parameters concerning expense ratios, size of fund, type of asset, or credit quality), provided that the person identifying the investment alternatives discloses in writing whether the person has a financial interest in any of the identified investment alternatives, and if so the precise nature of such interest;

(B) In response to a request for information, request for proposal, or similar solicitation by or on behalf of the plan, identifying a limited or sample set of investment alternatives based on only the size of the employer or plan, the current investment alternatives designated under the plan, or both, provided that the response is in writing and discloses whether the person identifying the limited or sample set of investment alternatives has a financial interest in any of the alternatives, and if so the precise nature of such interest; or

(C) Providing objective financial data and comparisons with independent benchmarks to the plan fiduciary.

(iii) *General Communications.* Furnishing or making available to a plan, plan fiduciary, plan participant or beneficiary, IRA, or IRA owner general communications that a reasonable person would not view as an investment recommendation, including general circulation newsletters, commentary in publicly broadcast talk shows, remarks and presentations in widely attended speeches and conferences, research or news reports prepared for general distribution, general marketing materials, general market data, including data on market performance, market indices, or trading volumes, price quotes, performance reports, or prospectuses.

(iv) *Investment Education.* Furnishing or making available any of the following categories of investment-related information and materials described in paragraphs (b)(2)(iv)(A) through (D) of this section to a plan, plan fiduciary, plan participant or beneficiary, IRA, or IRA owner irrespective of who provides or makes available the information and materials (e.g., plan sponsor, fiduciary or service provider), the frequency with which the information and materials are provided, the form in which the information and materials are provided (e.g., on an individual or group basis, in writing or orally, or via call center, video or computer software), or whether an identified category of information and materials is furnished or made available alone or in combination with other categories of information and materials, provided that the information and materials do not include (standing alone or in combination with other materials) recommendations with respect to specific investment products or specific plan or IRA alternatives, or recommendations with respect to investment or management of a particular security or securities or other investment property, except as noted in paragraphs (b)(2)(iv)(C)(4) and (b)(2)(iv)(D)(6) of this section.

(A) *Plan information.* Information and materials that, without reference to the appropriateness of any individual investment alternative or any individual benefit distribution option for the plan or IRA, or a particular plan participant or beneficiary or IRA owner, describe the terms or operation of the plan or IRA, inform a plan fiduciary, plan participant, beneficiary, or IRA owner about the benefits of plan or IRA participation, the benefits of increasing plan or IRA contributions, the impact of preretirement withdrawals on retirement income, retirement income needs, varying forms of distributions, including rollovers, annuitization and other forms of lifetime income payment options (e.g., immediate annuity, deferred annuity, or incremental purchase of deferred annuity), advantages, disadvantages and risks of different forms of distributions, or describe product features, investor rights and obligations, fee and expense information, applicable trading restrictions, investment objectives and philosophies, risk and return characteristics, historical return infor-

mation, or related prospectuses of investment alternatives available under the plan or IRA.

(B) *General financial, investment, and retirement information.* Information and materials on financial, investment, and retirement matters that do not address specific investment products, specific plan or IRA investment alternatives or distribution options available to the plan or IRA or to plan participants, beneficiaries, and IRA owners, or specific investment alternatives or services offered outside the plan or IRA, and inform the plan fiduciary, plan participant or beneficiary, or IRA owner about:

(1) General financial and investment concepts, such as risk and return, diversification, dollar cost averaging, compounded return, and tax deferred investment;

(2) Historic differences in rates of return between different asset classes (e.g., equities, bonds, or cash) based on standard market indices;

(3) Effects of fees and expenses on rates of return;

(4) Effects of inflation;

(5) Estimating future retirement income needs;

(6) Determining investment time horizons;

(7) Assessing risk tolerance;

(8) Retirement-related risks (e.g., longevity risks, market/interest rates, inflation, health care and other expenses); and

(9) General methods and strategies for managing assets in retirement (e.g., systematic withdrawal payments, annuitization, guaranteed minimum withdrawal benefits), including those offered outside the plan or IRA.

(C) *Asset allocation models.* Information and materials (e.g., pie charts, graphs, or case studies) that provide a plan fiduciary, plan participant or beneficiary, or IRA owner with models of asset allocation portfolios of hypothetical individuals with different time horizons (which may extend beyond an individual's retirement date) and risk profiles, where--

(1) Such models are based on generally accepted investment theories that take into account the historic returns of different asset

classes (e.g., equities, bonds, or cash) over defined periods of time;

(2) All material facts and assumptions on which such models are based (e.g., retirement ages, life expectancies, income levels, financial resources, replacement income ratios, inflation rates, and rates of return) accompany the models;

(3) The asset allocation models are accompanied by a statement indicating that, in applying particular asset allocation models to their individual situations, plan participants, beneficiaries, or IRA owners should consider their other assets, income, and investments (e.g., equity in a home, Social Security benefits, individual retirement plan investments, savings accounts, and interests in other qualified and non-qualified plans) in addition to their interests in the plan or IRA, to the extent those items are not taken into account in the model or estimate; and

(4) The models do not include or identify any specific investment product or investment alternative available under the plan or IRA, except that solely with respect to a plan, asset allocation models may identify a specific investment alternative available under the plan if it is a designated investment alternative within the meaning of 29 CFR 2550.404a-5(h)(4) under the plan subject to oversight by a plan fiduciary independent from the person who developed or markets the investment alternative and the model:

(i) Identifies all the other designated investment alternatives available under the plan that have similar risk and return characteristics, if any; and

(ii) is accompanied by a statement indicating that those other designated investment alternatives have similar risk and return characteristics and identifying where information on those investment alternatives may be obtained, including information described in paragraph (b)(2)(iv)(A) of this section and, if applicable, paragraph (d) of 29 CFR 2550.404a-5.

(D) *Interactive investment materials.* Questionnaires, worksheets, software, and similar materials that provide a plan fiduciary, plan participant or beneficiary, or IRA owner

the means to: Estimate future retirement income needs and assess the impact of different asset allocations on retirement income; evaluate distribution options, products, or vehicles by providing information under paragraphs (b)(2)(iv)(A) and (B) of this section; or estimate a retirement income stream that could be generated by an actual or hypothetical account balance, where--

(1) Such materials are based on generally accepted investment theories that take into account the historic returns of different asset classes (e.g., equities, bonds, or cash) over defined periods of time;

(2) There is an objective correlation between the asset allocations generated by the materials and the information and data supplied by the plan participant, beneficiary or IRA owner;

(3) There is an objective correlation between the income stream generated by the materials and the information and data supplied by the plan participant, beneficiary, or IRA owner;

(4) All material facts and assumptions (e.g., retirement ages, life expectancies, income levels, financial resources, replacement income ratios, inflation rates, rates of return and other features, and rates specific to income annuities or systematic withdrawal plans) that may affect a plan participant's, beneficiary's, or IRA owner's assessment of the different asset allocations or different income streams accompany the materials or are specified by the plan participant, beneficiary, or IRA owner;

(5) The materials either take into account other assets, income and investments (e.g., equity in a home, Social Security benefits, individual retirement plan investments, savings accounts, and interests in other qualified and non-qualified plans) or are accompanied by a statement indicating that, in applying particular asset allocations to their individual situations, or in assessing the adequacy of an estimated income stream, plan participants, beneficiaries, or IRA owners should consider their other assets, income, and investments in addition to their interests in the plan or IRA; and

(6) The materials do not include or identify any specific investment alternative or distribution option available under the plan or IRA, unless such alternative or option is specified by the plan participant, beneficiary, or IRA owner, or it is a designated investment alternative within the meaning of 29 CFR 2550.404a-5(h)(4) under a plan subject to oversight by a plan fiduciary independent from the person who developed or markets the investment alternative and the materials:

(i) Identify all the other designated investment alternatives available under the plan that have similar risk and return characteristics, if any; and

(ii) Are accompanied by a statement indicating that those other designated investment alternatives have similar risk and return characteristics and identifying where information on those investment alternatives may be obtained; including information described in paragraph (b)(2)(iv)(A) of this section and, if applicable, paragraph (d) of 29 CFR 2550.404a-5;

(c) Except for persons who represent or acknowledge that they are acting as a fiduciary within the meaning of the Act or the Code, a person shall not be deemed to be a fiduciary within the meaning of section 3(21)(A)(ii) of the Act or section 4975(e)(3)(B) of the Code solely because of the activities set forth in paragraphs (c)(1), (2), and (3) of this section.

(1) *Transactions with independent fiduciaries with financial expertise* --The provision of any advice by a person (including the provision of asset allocation models or other financial analysis tools) to a fiduciary of the plan or IRA (including a fiduciary to an investment contract, product, or entity that holds plan assets as determined pursuant to sections 3(42) and 401 of the Act and 29 CFR 2510.3-101) who is independent of the person providing the advice with respect to an arm's length sale, purchase, loan, exchange, or other transaction related to the investment of securities or other investment property, if, prior to entering into the transaction the person providing the advice satisfies the requirements of this paragraph (c)(1).

(i) The person knows or reasonably believes that the independent fiduciary of the plan or IRA is:

(A) A bank as defined in section 202 of the Investment Advisers Act of 1940 or similar institution that is regulated and supervised and subject to periodic examination by a State or Federal agency;

(B) An insurance carrier which is qualified under the laws of more than one state to perform the services of managing, acquiring or disposing of assets of a plan;

(C) An investment adviser registered under the Investment Advisers Act of 1940 or, if not registered an as investment adviser under the Investment Advisers Act by reason of paragraph (1) of section 203A of such Act, is registered as an investment adviser under the laws of the State (referred to in such paragraph (1)) in which it maintains its principal office and place of business;

(D) A broker-dealer registered under the Securities Exchange Act of 1934; or

(E) Any independent fiduciary that holds, or has under management or control, total assets of at least $ 50 million (the person may rely on written representations from the plan or independent fiduciary to satisfy this paragraph (c)(1)(i));

(ii) The person knows or reasonably believes that the independent fiduciary of the plan or IRA is capable of evaluating investment risks independently, both in general and with regard to particular transactions and investment strategies (the person may rely on written representations from the plan or independent fiduciary to satisfy this paragraph (c)(1)(ii));

(iii) The person fairly informs the independent fiduciary that the person is not undertaking to provide impartial investment advice, or to give advice in a fiduciary capacity, in connection with the transaction and fairly informs the independent fiduciary of the existence and nature of the person's financial interests in the transaction;

(iv) The person knows or reasonably believes that the independent fiduciary of the plan or IRA is a fiduciary under ERISA or the Code, or both, with respect to the transaction and is responsible for exercising independent judgment in evaluating the transaction (the person may rely on written representations from the plan or independent fiduciary to satisfy this paragraph (c)(1)(iv)); and

(v) The person does not receive a fee or other compensation directly from the plan, plan fiduciary, plan participant or beneficiary, IRA, or IRA owner for the provision of investment advice (as opposed to other services) in connection with the transaction.

(2) *Swap and security-based swap transactions.* The provision of any advice to an employee benefit plan (as described in section 3(3) of the Act) by a person who is a swap dealer, security-based swap dealer, major swap participant, major security-based swap participant, or a swap clearing firm in connection with a swap or security-based swap, as defined in section 1a of the Commodity Exchange Act (7 U.S.C. 1a) and section 3(a) of the Securities Exchange Act of 1934 (15 U.S.C. 78c(a)) if--

(i) The employee benefit plan is represented by a fiduciary under ERISA independent of the person;

(ii) In the case of a swap dealer or security-based swap dealer, the person is not acting as an advisor to the employee benefit plan (within the meaning of section 4s(h) of the Commodity Exchange Act or section 15F(h) of the Securities Exchange Act of 1934) in connection with the transaction;

(iii) The person does not receive a fee or other compensation directly from the plan or plan fiduciary for the provision of investment advice (as opposed to other services) in connection with the transaction; and

(iv) In advance of providing any recommendations with respect to the transaction, or series of transactions, the person obtains a written representation from the independent fiduciary that the independent fiduciary understands that the person is not undertaking to provide impartial investment advice, or to give advice in a fiduciary capacity, in connection with the transaction and that the independent fiduciary is exercising independent judgment in evaluating the recommendation.

(3) *Employees.* (i) In his or her capacity as an employee of the plan sponsor of a plan, as an employee of an affiliate of such plan sponsor, as an employee of an employee benefit plan, as an employee of an employee organization, or as an employee of a plan fiduciary, the person provides advice to a plan fiduciary, or to an employee (other than in his or her capacity as a participant or beneficiary of an employee benefit plan) or independent contractor of such plan sponsor, affiliate, or employee benefit plan, provided the person receives no fee or other compensation, direct or indirect, in connection with the advice beyond the employee's normal compensation for work performed for the employer; or

(ii) In his or her capacity as an employee of the plan sponsor of a plan, or as an employee of an affiliate of such plan sponsor, the person provides advice to another employee of the plan sponsor in his or her capacity as a participant or beneficiary of the plan, provided the person's job responsibilities do not involve the provision of investment advice or investment recommendations, the person is not registered or licensed under federal or state securities or insurance law, the advice he or she provides does not require the person to be registered or licensed under federal or state securities or insurance laws, and the person receives no fee or other compensation, direct or indirect, in connection with the advice beyond the employee's normal compensation for work performed for the employer.

(d) *Scope of fiduciary duty--investment advice.* A person who is a fiduciary with respect to an plan or IRA by reason of rendering investment advice (as defined in paragraph (a) of this section) for a fee or other compensation, direct or indirect, with respect to any securities or other investment property of such plan or IRA, or having any authority or responsibility to do so, shall not be deemed to be a fiduciary regarding any assets of the plan or IRA with respect to which such person does not have any discretionary authority, discretionary control or discretionary responsibility, does not exercise any authority or control, does not render investment advice (as described in paragraph (a)(1) of this section) for a fee or other compensation, and does not have any authority or responsibility to render such investment advice, provided that nothing in this paragraph shall be deemed to:

(1) Exempt such person from the provisions of section 405(a) of the Act concerning liability for fiduciary breaches by other fiduciaries with respect to any assets of the plan; or

(2) Exclude such person from the definition of the term "party in interest" (as set forth in section 3(14)(B) of the Act) or "disqualified person" (as set forth in section 4975(e)(2) of the Code) with respect to any assets of the employee benefit plan or IRA.

(e) *Execution of securities transactions.*
(1) A person who is a broker or dealer registered under the Securities Exchange Act of 1934, a reporting dealer who makes primary markets in securities of the United States Government or of an agency of the United States Government and reports daily to the Federal Reserve Bank of New York its positions with respect to such securities and borrowings thereon, or a bank supervised by the United States or a State, shall not be deemed to be a fiduciary, within the meaning of section 3(21)(A) of the Act or section 4975(e)(3)(B) of the Code, with respect to a plan or IRA solely because such person executes transactions for the purchase or sale of securities on behalf of such plan in the ordinary course of its business as a broker, dealer, or bank, pursuant to instructions of a fiduciary with respect to such plan or IRA, if:

(i) Neither the fiduciary nor any affiliate of such fiduciary is such broker, dealer, or bank; and

(ii) The instructions specify:

(A) The security to be purchased or sold;

(B) A price range within which such security is to be purchased or sold, or, if such security is issued by an open-end investment company registered under the Investment Company Act of 1940 (15 U.S.C. 80a-1, et seq.), a price which is determined in accordance with Rule 22c1 under the Investment Company Act of 1940 (17 CFR 270.22c1);

(C) A time span during which such security may be purchased or sold (not to exceed five business days); and

(D) The minimum or maximum quantity of such security which may be purchased or sold within such price range, or, in the case of a security issued by an open-end investment company registered under the Investment Company Act of 1940, the minimum or maximum quantity of such security which may be purchased or sold, or the value of such security in dollar amount which may be purchased or sold, at the price referred to in paragraph (e)(1)(ii)(B) of this section.

(2) A person who is a broker-dealer, reporting dealer, or bank which is a fiduciary with respect to a plan or IRA solely by reason of the possession or exercise of discretionary authority or discretionary control in the management of the plan or IRA, or the management or disposition of plan or IRA assets in connection with the execution of a transaction or transactions for the purchase or sale of securities on behalf of such plan or IRA which fails to comply with the provisions of paragraph (e)(1) of this section, shall not be deemed to be a fiduciary regarding any assets of the plan or IRA with respect to which such broker-dealer, reporting dealer or bank does not have any discretionary authority, discretionary control or discretionary responsibility, does not exercise any authority or control, does not render investment advice (as defined in paragraph (a) of this section) for a fee or other compensation, and does not have any authority or responsibility to render such investment advice, provided that nothing in this paragraph shall be deemed to:

(i) Exempt such broker-dealer, reporting dealer, or bank from the provisions of section 405(a) of the Act concerning liability for fiduciary breaches by other fiduciaries with respect to any assets of the plan; or

(ii) Exclude such broker-dealer, reporting dealer, or bank from the definition of the term "party in interest" (as set forth in section 3(14)(B) of the Act) or "disqualified person" (as set forth in section 4975(e)(2) of the Code) with respect to any assets of the plan or IRA.

(f) *Internal Revenue Code.* Section 4975(e)(3) of the Code contains provisions parallel to section 3(21)(A) of the Act which define the term "fiduciary" for purposes of the prohibited transaction provisions in Code section 4975. Effective December 31, 1978, section 102 of the Reorganization Plan No. 4 of 1978, 5 U.S.C. App. 237 transferred the authority of the Secretary of the Treasury to promulgate regulations of the type published herein to the Secretary of Labor. All references herein to section 3(21)(A) of the Act should be read to include reference to the parallel provisions of section 4975(e)(3) of the Code. Furthermore, the provisions of this section shall apply for purposes of the application of Code section 4975 with respect to any plan, including any IRA, described in Code section 4975(e)(1).

(g) *Definitions.* For purposes of this section--

(1) The term "affiliate" means any person directly or indirectly, through one or more intermediaries, controlling, controlled by, or under common control with such person; any officer, director, partner, employee, or relative (as defined in paragraph (g)(8) of this section) of such person; and any corporation or partnership of which such person is an officer, director, or partner.

(2) The term "control," for purposes of paragraph (g)(1) of this section, means the power to exercise a controlling influence over the management or policies of a person other than an individual.

(3) The term "fee or other compensation, direct or indirect" means, for purposes of this section and section 3(21)(A)(ii) of the Act, any explicit fee or compensation for the advice received by the person (or by an affiliate) from any source, and any other fee or compensation received from any source in connection with or as a result of the purchase or sale of a security or the provision of investment advice services, including, though not limited to, commissions, loads, finder's fees, revenue sharing payments, shareholder servicing fees, marketing or distribution fees, underwriting compensation, payments to brokerage firms in return for shelf space, recruitment compensation paid in connection with transfers of accounts to a registered representative's new broker-dealer firm, gifts and gratuities, and expense reimbursements. A fee or compensation is paid "in connection with or as a result of" such transaction or service if the fee or compensation would not have been paid but for the transaction or service or if eligibility for or the amount of the fee or compensation is based in whole or in part on the transaction or service.

(4) The term "investment property" does not include health insurance policies, disability insurance policies, term life insurance policies, and other property to the extent the policies or property do not contain an investment component.

(5) The term "IRA owner" means, with respect to an IRA, either the person who is the owner of the IRA or the person for whose benefit the IRA was established.

(6)(i) The term "plan" means any employee benefit plan described in section 3(3) of the Act and any plan described in section 4975(e)(1)(A) of the Code, and

(ii) The term "IRA" means any account or annuity described in Code section 4975(e)(1)(B) through (F), including, for example, an individual retirement account described in section 408(a) of the Code and a health savings account described in section 223(d) of the Code.

(7) The term "plan fiduciary" means a person described in section (3)(21)(A) of the Act and 4975(e)(3) of the Code. For purposes of this section, a participant or beneficiary of the plan or a relative of either is not a "plan fiduciary" with respect to the plan, and the IRA owner or a relative is not a "plan fiduciary" with respect to the IRA.

(8) The term "relative" means a person described in section 3(15) of the Act and section 4975(e)(6) of the Code or a brother, a sister, or a spouse of a brother or sister.

(9) The term "plan participant" or "participant" means, for a plan described in section 3(3) of the Act, a person described in section 3(7) of the Act.

(h) *Effective and applicability dates --(1) Effective date.* This section is effective on June 7, 2016.

(2) *Applicability date.* Paragraphs (a), (b), (c), (d), (f), and (g) of this section apply April 10, 2017.

(3) Until the applicability date under this paragraph (h), the prior regulation under the Act and the Code (as it appeared in the July 1, 2015 edition of 29 CFR part 2510 and the April 1, 2015 edition of 26 CFR part 54) applies.

(i) *Continued applicability of State law regulating insurance, banking, or securities.* Nothing in this part shall be construed to affect or modify the provisions of section 514 of Title I of the Act, including the savings clause in section 514(b)(2)(A) for state laws that regulate insurance, banking, or securities.

(j) [Effective June 7, 2016 through Apr. 10, 2017.] *Temporarily applicable provisions.* (1) During the period between June 7, 2016 and April 10, 2017, this paragraph (j) shall apply.

(i) [Effective June 7, 2016 through Apr. 10, 2017.] A person shall be deemed to be rendering "investment advice" to an employee benefit plan, within the meaning of section 3(21)(A)(ii) of the Act, section 4975(e)(3)(B) of the Code and this paragraph (j), only if:

(A) [Effective June 7, 2016 through Apr. 10, 2017.] Such person renders advice to the plan as to the value of securities or other property, or makes recommendation as to the advisability of investing in, purchasing, or selling securities or other property; and

(B) [Effective June 7, 2016 through Apr. 10, 2017.] Such person either directly or indirectly (e.g., through or together with any affiliate)--

(1) [Effective June 7, 2016 through Apr. 10, 2017.] Has discretionary authority or control, whether or not pursuant to agreement, arrangement or understanding, with respect to purchasing or selling securities or other property for the plan; or

(2) [Effective June 7, 2016 through Apr. 10, 2017.] Renders any advice described in paragraph (j)(1)(i) of this section on a regular basis to the plan pursuant to a mutual agreement, arrangement or understanding, written or otherwise, between such person and the plan or a fiduciary with respect to the plan, that such services will serve as a primary basis for investment decisions with respect to plan assets, and that such person will render individualized investment advice to the plan based on the particular needs of the plan regarding such matters as, among other things, investment policies or strategy, overall portfolio composition, or diversification of plan investments.

(2) [Effective June 7, 2016 through Apr. 10, 2017.] Affiliate and control. (i) For purposes of paragraph (j) of this section, an "affiliate" of a person shall include:

(A) [Effective June 7, 2016 through Apr. 10, 2017.] Any person directly or indirectly, through one or more intermediaries, controlling, controlled by, or under common control with such person;

(B) [Effective June 7, 2016 through Apr. 10, 2017.] Any officer, director, partner, employee or relative (as defined in section 3(15) of the Act) of such person; and

(C) [Effective June 7, 2016 through Apr. 10, 2017.] Any corporation or partnership of which such person is an officer, director or partner.

(ii) [Effective June 7, 2016 through Apr. 10, 2017.] For purposes of this paragraph (j), the term "control" means the power to exercise a controlling influence over the management or policies of a person other than an individual.

(3) [Effective June 7, 2016 through Apr. 10, 2017.] Expiration date. This paragraph (j) expires on April 10, 2017.

§ 2510.3-101. Definition of "plan assets"—plan investments.

(a) *In general.* (1) This section describes what constitute assets of a plan with respect to a plan's investment in another entity for purposes of subtitle A, and parts 1 and 4 of subtitle B, of title I of the Act and section 4975 of the Internal Revenue Code. Paragraph (a)(2) of this section contains a general rule relating to plan investments. Paragraphs (b) through (f) of this section define certain terms that are used in the application of the general rule. Paragraph (g) of this section describes how the rules in this section are to be applied when a plan owns property jointly with others or where it acquires an equity interest whose value relates solely to identified assets of an issuer. Paragraph (h) of this section contains special rules relating to particular kinds of plan investments. Paragraph (i) describes the assets that a plan acquires when it purchases certain guaranteed mortgage certificates. Paragraph (j) of this section contains examples illustrating the operation of this section. The effective date of this section is set forth in paragraph (k) of this section.

(2) Generally, when a plan invests in another entity, the plan's assets include its investment, but do not, solely by reason of such investment, include any of the underlying assets of the entity. However, in the case of a plan's investment in an equity interest of an entity that is neither a publicly-offered security nor a security issued by an investment company registered under the Investment Company Act of 1940 its assets include both the equity interest and an undivided interest in each of the underlying assets of the entity, unless it is established that—

(i) The entity is an operating company, or

(ii) Equity participation in the entity by benefit plan investors is not significant.

Therefore, any person who exercises authority or control respecting the management or disposition of such underlying assets, and any person who provides investment advice with respect to such assets for a fee (direct or indirect), is a fiduciary of the investing plan.

(b) *Equity interests and publicly-offered securities.* (1) The term equity interest means any interest in an entity other than an instrument that is treated as indebtedness under applicable local law and which has no substantial equity features. A profits interest in a partnership, an undivided ownership interest in property and a beneficial interest in a trust are equity interests.

(2) A publicly-offered security is a security that is freely transferable, part of a class of securities that is widely held and either—

(i) Part of a class of securities registered under section 12(b) or 12(g) of the Securities Exchange Act of 1934, or

(ii) Sold to the plan as part of an offering of securities to the public pursuant to an effective registration statement under the Securities Act of 1933 and the class of securities of which such security is a part is registered under the Securities Exchange Act of 1934 within 120 days (or such later time as may be allowed by the Securities and Exchange Commission) after the end of the fiscal year of the issuer during which the offering of such securities to the public occurred.

(3) For purposes of paragraph (b)(2) of this section, a class of securities is "widely-held" only if it is a class of securities that is owned by 100 or more investors independent of the issuer and of one another. A class of securities will not fail to be widely-held solely because subsequent to the initial offering the number of independent investors falls below 100 as a result of events beyond the control of the issuer.

(4) For purposes of paragraph (b)(2) of this section, whether a security is "freely transferable" is a factual question to be determined on the basis of all relevant facts and circumstances. If a security is part of an offering in which the minimum investment is $10,000 or less, however, the following factors ordinarily will not, alone or in combination, affect a finding that such securities are freely transferable:

(i) Any requirement that not less than a minimum number of shares or units of such security be transferred or assigned by any investor, provided that such requirement does not prevent transfer of all of the then remaining shares or units held by an investor;

(ii) Any prohibition against transfer or assignment of such security or rights in respect thereof to an ineligible or unsuitable investor;

(iii) Any restriction on, or prohibition against, any transfer or assignment which would either result in a termination or reclassification of the entity for Federal or state tax purposes or which would violate any state or Federal statute, regulation, court order, judicial decree, or rule of law;

(iv) Any requirement that reasonable transfer or administrative fees be paid in connection with a transfer or assignment;

(v) Any requirement that advance notice of a transfer or assignment be given to the entity and any requirement regarding execution of documentation evidencing such transfer or assignment (including documentation setting forth representations from either or both of the transferor or transferee as to compliance with any restriction or requirement described in this paragraph (b)(4) of this section or requiring compliance with the entity's governing instruments);

(vi) Any restriction on substitution of an assignee as a limited partner of a partnership, including a general partner consent requirement, provided that the economic benefits of ownership of the assignor may be transferred or assigned without regard to such restriction or consent (other than compliance with any other restriction described in this paragraph (b)(4)) of this section;

(vii) Any administrative procedure which establishes an effective date, or an event, such as the completion of the offering, prior to which a transfer or assignment will not be effective; and

(viii) Any limitation or restriction on transfer or assignment which is not created or imposed by the issuer or any person acting for or on behalf of such issuer.

(c) *Operating company.* (1) An "operating company" is an entity that is primarily engaged, directly or through a majority owned subsidiary or subsidiaries, in the production or sale of a product or service other than the investment of capital. The term "operating company" includes an entity which is not described in the preceding sentence, but which is a "venture capital operating company" described in paragraph (d) or a "real estate operating company" described in paragraph (e).

(d) *Venture capital operating company.* (1) An entity is a "venture capital operating company" for the period beginning on an initial valuation date described in paragraph (d)(5)(i) and ending on the last day of the first "annual valuation period" described in paragraph (d)(5)(ii) (in the case of an entity that is not a venture capital operating company immediately before the determination) or for the 12 month period following the expiration of an "annual valuation period" described in paragraph (d)(5)(ii) (in the case of an entity that is a venture capital operating company immediately before the determination) if—

(i) On such initial valuation date, or at any time within such annual valuation period, at least 50 percent of its assets (other than short-term investments pending long-term commitment or distribution to investors), valued at cost, are invested in venture capital investments described in paragraph (d)(3)(i) or derivative investments described in paragraph (d)(4); and

(ii) During such 12 month period (or during the period beginning on the initial valuation date and ending on the last day of the first annual valuation period), the entity, in the ordinary course of its business, actually exercises management rights of the kind described in paragraph (d)(3)(ii) with respect to one or more of the operating companies in which it invests.

(2)(i) A venture capital operating company described in paragraph (d)(1) shall continue to be treated as a venture capital operating company during the "distribution period" described in paragraph (d)(2)(ii). An entity shall not be treated as a venture capital operating company at any time after the end of the distribution period.

(ii) The "distribution period" referred to in paragraph (d)(2)(i) begins on a date established by a venture capital operating company that occurs after the first date on which the venture capital operating company has distributed to investors the proceeds of at least 50 percent of the highest amount of its investments (other than short-term investments made pending long-term commitment or distribution to investors) outstanding at any time from the date it commenced business (determined on the basis of the cost of such investments) and ends on the earlier of—

(A) The date on which the company makes a "new portfolio investment", or

(B) The expiration of 10 years from the beginning of the distribution period.

(iii) For purposes of paragraph (d)(2)(ii)(A), a "new portfolio investment" is an investment other than—

(A) An investment in an entity in which the venture capital operating company had an outstanding venture capital investment at the beginning of the distribution period which has continued to be outstanding at all times during the distribution period, or

(B) A short-term investment pending long-term commitment or distribution to investors.

(3)(i) For purposes of this paragraph (d) a "venture capital investment" is an investment in an operating company (other than a venture capital operating company) as to which the investor has or obtains management rights.

(ii) The term "management rights" means contractual rights directly between the investor and an operating company to substantially participate in, or substantially influence the conduct of, the management of the operating company.

(4)(i) An investment is a "derivative investment" for purposes of this paragraph (d) if it is—

(A) A venture capital investment as to which the investor's management rights have ceased in connection with a public offering of securities of the operating company to which the investment relates, or

(B) An investment that is acquired by a venture capital operating company in the ordinary course of its business in exchange for an existing venture capital investment in connection with:

(1) A public offering of securities of the operating company to which the existing venture capital investment relates, or

(2) A merger or reorganization of the operating company to which the existing venture capital investment relates, provided that such merger or reorganization is made for independent business reasons unrelated to extinguishing management rights.

(ii) An investment ceases to be a derivative investment on the later of:

(A) 10 years from the date of the acquisition of the original venture capital investment to which the derivative investment relates, or

(B) 30 months from the date on which the investment becomes a derivative investment.

(5) For purposes of this paragraph (d) and paragraph (e)—

(i) An "initial valuation date" is the later of—

(A) Any date designated by the company within the 12 month period ending with the effective date of this section, or

(B) The first date on which an entity makes an investment that is not a short-term investment of funds pending long-term commitment.

(ii) An "annual valuation period" is a preestablished annual period, not exceeding 90 days in duration, which begins no later than the anniversary of an entity's initial valuation date. An annual valuation period, once established may not be changed except for good cause unrelated to a determination under this paragraph (d) or paragraph (e).

(e) *Real estate operating company.* An entity is a "real estate operating company" for the period beginning on an initial valuation date described in paragraph (d)(5)(i) and ending on the last day of the first "annual valuation period" described in paragraph (d)(5)(ii) (in the case of an entity that is not a real estate operating company immediately before the determination) or for the 12 month period following the expiration of an annual valuation period described in paragraph (d)(5)(ii) (in the case of an entity that is a real estate operating company immediately before the determination) if:

(1) On such initial valuation date, or on any date within such annual valuation period, at least 50 percent of its assets, valued at cost (other than short-term investments pending long-term commitment or distribution to investors), are invested in real estate which is managed or developed and with respect to which such entity has the right to substantially participate directly in the management or development activities; and

(2) During such 12 month period (or during the period beginning on the initial valuation date and ending on the last day of the first annual valuation period) such entity in the ordinary course of its business is engaged directly in real estate management or development activities.

(f) *Participation by benefit plan investors.* (1) Equity participation in an entity by benefit plan investors is "significant" on any date if, immediately after the most recent acquisition of any equity interest in the entity, 25 percent or more of the value of any class of equity interests in the entity is held by benefit plan investors (as defined in paragraph (f)(2)). For purposes of determinations pursuant to this paragraph (f), the value of any equity interests held by a person (other than a benefit plan investor) who has discretionary authority or control with respect to the assets of the entity or any person who provides investment advice for a fee (direct or indirect) with respect to such assets, or any affiliate of such a person, shall be disregarded.

(2) A "benefit plan investor" is any of the following—

(i) Any employee benefit plan (as defined in section 3(3) of the Act), whether or not it is subject to the provisions of title I of the Act,

(ii) Any plan described in section 4975(e)(1) of the Internal Revenue Code,

(iii) Any entity whose underlying assets include plan assets by reason of a plan's investment in the entity.

(3) An "affiliate" of a person includes any person, directly or indirectly, through one or more intermediaries, controlling, controlled by, or under common control with the person. For purposes of this paragraph (f)(3), "control", with respect to a person other than an individual, means the power to exercise a controlling influence over the management or policies of such person.

(g) *Joint ownership.* For purposes of this section, where a plan jointly owns property with others, or where the value of a plan's equity interest in an entity relates solely to identified property of the entity, such property shall be treated as the sole property of a separate entity.

(h) *Specific rules relating to plan investments.* Notwithstanding any other provision of this section—

(1) Except where the entity is an investment company registered under the Investment Company Act of 1940, when a plan acquires or holds an interest in any of the following entities its assets include its investment and an undivided interest in each of the underlying assets of the entity:

(i) A group trust which is exempt from taxation under section 501(a) of the Internal Revenue Code pursuant to the principles of Rev. Rul. 81-100, 1981-1 C.B. 326,

(ii) A common or collective trust fund of a bank,

(iii) A separate account of an insurance company, other than a separate account that is maintained solely in connection with fixed contractual obligations of the insurance company under which the amounts payable, or credited, to the plan and to any participant or beneficiary of the plan (including an annuitant) are not affected in any manner by the investment performance of the separate account.

(2) When a plan acquires or holds an interest in any entity (other than an insurance company licensed to do business in a State) which is established or maintained for the purpose of offering or providing any benefit described in section 3(1) or section 3(2) of the Act to participants or beneficiaries of the investing plan, its assets will include its investment and an undivided interest in the underlying assets of that entity.

(3) When a plan or a related group of plans owns all of the outstanding equity interests (other than director's qualifying shares) in an entity, its assets include those equity interests and all of the underlying assets of the entity. This paragraph (h)(3) does not apply, however, where all of the outstanding equity interests in an entity are qualifying employer securities described in section 407(d)(5) of the Act, owned by one or more eligible individual account plan(s) (as defined in section 407(d)(3) of the Act) maintained by the same employer, provided that substantially all of the participants in the plan(s) are, or have been, employed by the issuer of such securities or by members of a group of affiliated corporations (as determined under section 407(d)(7) of the Act) of which the issuer is a member.

(4) For purposes of paragraph (h)(3), a "related group" of employee benefit plans consists of every group of two or more employee benefit plans—

(i) Each of which receives 10 percent or more of its aggregate contributions from the same employer or from members of the same controlled group of corporations (as determined under section 1563(a) of the Internal Revenue Code, without regard to section 1563(a)(4) thereof); or

(ii) Each of which is either maintained by, or maintained pursuant to a collective bargaining agreement negotiated by, the same employee organization or affiliated employee organizations. For purposes of this paragraph, an "affiliate" of an employee organization means any person controlling, controlled by, or under common control with such organization, and includes any organization chartered by the same parent body, or governed by the same constitution and bylaws, or having the relation of parent and subordinate.

(i) *Governmental mortgage pools.* (1) Where a plan acquires a guaranteed governmental mortgage pool certificate, as defined in paragraph (i)(2), the plan's assets include the certificate and all of its rights with respect to such certificate under applicable law, but do not, solely by reason of the plan's holding of such certificate, include any of the mortgages underlying such certificate.

(2) A "guaranteed governmental mortgage pool certificate" is a certificate backed by, or evidencing an interest in, specified mortgages or participation interests therein and with respect to which interest and principal payable pursuant to the certificate is guaranteed by the United States or an agency or instrumentality thereof. The term "guaranteed governmental mortgage pool certificate" includes a mortgage pool certificate with respect to which interest and principal payable pursuant to the certificate is guaranteed by:

(i) The Government National Mortgage Association;

(ii) The Federal Home Loan Mortgage Corporation; or

(iii) The Federal National Mortgage Association.

(j) *Examples.* The principles of this section are illustrated by the following examples:

(1) A plan, P, acquires debentures issued by a corporation, T, pursuant to a private offering. T is engaged primarily in investing and reinvesting in precious metals on behalf of its shareholders, all of which are benefit plan investors. By its terms, the debenture is convertible to common stock of T at P's option. At the time of P's acquisition of the debentures, the conversion feature is incidental to T's obligation to pay interest and principal.

Although T is not an operating company, P's assets do not include an interest in the underlying assets of T because P has not acquired an equity interest in T. However, if P exercises its option to convert the debentures to common stock, it will have acquired an equity interest in T at that time and (assuming that the common stock is not a publicly-offered security and that there has been no change in the composition of the other equity investors in T) P's assets would then include an undivided interest in the underlying assets of T.

(2) A plan, P, acquires a limited partnership interest in a limited partnership, U, which is established and maintained by A, a general partner in U. U has only one class of limited partnership interests. U is engaged in the business of investing and reinvesting in securities. Limited partnership interests in U are offered privately pursuant to an exemption from the registration requirements of the Securities Act of 1933. P acquires 15 percent of the value of all the outstanding limited partnership interests in U, and, at the time of P's investment, a governmental plan owns 15 percent of the value of those interests. U is not an operating company because it is engaged primarily in the investment of capital. In addition, equity participation by benefit plan investors is significant because immediately after P's investment such investors hold more than 25 percent of the limited partnership interests in U. Accordingly, P's assets include an undivided interest in the underlying assets of U, and A is a fiduciary of P with respect to such assets by reason of its discretionary authority and control over U's assets. Although the governmental plan's investment is taken into account for purposes of determining whether equity participation by benefit plan investors is significant, nothing in this section imposes fiduciary obligations on A with respect to that plan.

(3) Assume the same facts as in paragraph (j)(2), except that P acquires only 5 percent of the value of all the outstanding limited partnership interests in U, and that benefit plan investors in the aggregate hold only 10 percent of the value of the limited partnership interests in U. Under these facts, there is no significant equity participation by benefit plan investors in U, and, accordingly, P's assets include its limited partnership interest in U, but do not include any of the underlying assets of U. Thus, A would not be a fiduciary of P by reason of P's investment.

(4) Assume the same facts as in paragraph (j)(3) and that the aggregate value of the outstanding limited partnership interests in U is $10,000 (and that the value of the interests held by benefit plan investors is thus $1000). Also assume that an affiliate of A owns limited partnership interests in U having a value of $6500. The value of the limited partnership interests held by A's affiliate are disregarded for purposes of determining whether there is significant equity participation in U by benefit plan investors. Thus, the percentage of the aggregate value of the limited partnership interests held by benefit plan investors in U for purposes of such a determination is approximately 28.6% ($1000/$3500). Therefore there is significant benefit plan investment in T.

(5) A plan, P, invests in a limited partnership, V, pursuant to a private offering. There is significant equity participation by benefit plan investors in V. V acquires equity positions in the companies in which it invests, and, in connection with these investments, V negotiates terms that give it the right to participate in or influence the management of those companies. Some of these investments are in publicly-offered securities and some are in securities acquired in private offerings. During its most recent valuation period, more than 50 percent of V's assets, valued at cost, consisted of investments with respect to which V obtained management rights of the kind described above. V's managers routinely consult informally with, and advise, the management of only one portfolio company with respect to which it has management rights, although it devotes substantial resources to its consultations with that company. With respect to the other portfolio companies, V relies on the managers of other entities to consult with and advise the companies' management. V is a venture capital operating company and therefore P has acquired its limited partnership

investment, but has not acquired an interest in any of the underlying assets of V. Thus, none of the managers of V would be fiduciaries with respect to P solely by reason of its investment. In this situation, the mere fact that V does not participate in or influence the management of all its portfolio companies does not affect its characterization as a venture capital operating company.

(6) Assume the same facts as in paragraph (j)(5) and the following additional facts: V invests in debt securities as well as equity securities of its portfolio companies. In some cases V makes debt investments in companies in which it also has an equity investment; in other cases V only invests in debt instruments of the portfolio company. V's debt investments are acquired pursuant to private offerings and V negotiates covenants that give it the right to substantially participate in or to substantially influence the conduct of the management of the companies issuing the obligations. These covenants give V more significant rights with respect to the portfolio companies' management than the covenants ordinarily found in debt instruments of established, creditworthy companies that are purchased privately by institutional investors. V routinely consults with and advises the management of its portfolio companies. The mere fact that V's investments in portfolio companies are debt, rather than equity, will not cause V to fail to be a venture capital operating company, provided it actually obtains the right to substantially participate in or influence the conduct of the management of its portfolio companies and provided that in the ordinary course of its business it actually exercises those rights.

(7) A plan, P, invests (pursuant to a private offering) in a limited partnership, W, that is engaged primarily in investing and reinvesting assets in equity positions in real property. The properties acquired by W are subject to long-term leases under which substantially all management and maintenance activities with respect to the property are the responsibility of the lessee. W is not engaged in the management or development of real estate merely because it assumes the risks of ownership of income-producing real property, and W is not a real estate operating company. If there is significant equity participation in W by benefit plan investors, P will be considered to have acquired an undivided interest in each of the underlying assets of W.

(8) Assume the same facts as in paragraph (j)(7) except that W owns several shopping centers in which individual stores are leased for relatively short periods to various merchants (rather than owning properties subject to long-term leases under which substantially all management and maintenance activities are the responsibility of the lessee). W retains independent contractors to manage the shopping center properties. These independent contractors negotiate individual leases, maintain the common areas and conduct maintenance activities with respect to the properties. W has the responsibility to supervise and the authority to terminate the independent contractors. During its most recent valuation period more than 50 percent of W's assets, valued at cost, are invested in such properties. W is a real estate operating company. The fact that W does not have its own employees who engage in day-to-day management and development activities is only one factor in determining whether it is actively managing or developing real estate. Thus, P's assets include its interest in W, but do not include any of the underlying assets of W.

(9) A plan, P, acquires a limited partnership interest in X pursuant to a private offering. There is significant equity participation in X by benefit plan investors. X is engaged in the business of making "convertible loans" which are structured as follows: X lends a specified percentage of the cost of acquiring real property to a borrower who provides the remaining capital needed to make the acquisition. This loan is secured by a mortgage on the property. Under the terms of the loan, X is entitled to receive a fixed rate of interest payable out of the initial cash flow from the property and is also entitled to that portion of any additional cash flow which is equal to the percentage of the acquisition cost that is financed

by its loan. Simultaneously with the making of the loan, the borrower also gives X an option to purchase an interest in the property for the original principal amount of the loan at the expiration of its initial term. X's percentage interest in the property, if it exercises this option, would be equal to the percentage of the acquisition cost of the property which is financed by its loan. The parties to the transaction contemplate that the option ordinarily will be exercised at the expiration of the loan term if the property has appreciated in value. X and the borrower also agree that, if the option is exercised, they will form a limited partnership to hold the property. X negotiates loan terms which give it rights to substantially influence, or to substantially participate in, the management of the property which is acquired with the proceeds of the loan. These loan terms give X significantly greater rights to participate in the management of the property than it would obtain under a conventional mortgage loan. In addition, under the terms of the loan, X and the borrower ratably share any capital expenditures relating to the property. During its most recent valuation period, more than 50 percent of the value of X's assets valued at cost consisted of real estate investments of the kind described above. X, in the ordinary course of its business, routinely exercises its management rights and frequently consults with and advises the borrower and the property manager. Under these facts, X is a real estate operating company. Thus, P's assets include its interest in X, but do not include any of the underlying assets of X.

(10) In a private transaction, a plan, P, acquires a 30 percent participation in a debt instrument that is held by a bank. Since the value of the participation certificate relates solely to the debt instrument, that debt instrument is, under paragraph (g), treated as the sole asset of a separate entity. Equity participation in that entity by benefit plan investors is significant since the value of the plan's participation exceeds 25 percent of the value of the instrument. In addition, the hypothetical entity is not an operating company because it is primarily engaged in the investment of capital (i.e., holding the debt instrument). Thus, P's assets include the participation and an undivided interest in the debt instrument, and the bank is a fiduciary of P to the extent it has discretionary authority or control over the debt instrument.

(11) In a private transaction, a plan, P, acquires 30% of the value of a class of equity securities issued by an operating company, Y. These securities provide that dividends shall be paid solely out of earnings attributable to certain tracts of undeveloped land that are held by Y for investment. Under paragraph (g), the property is treated as the sole asset of a separate entity. Thus, even though Y is an operating company, the hypothetical entity whose sole assets are the undeveloped tracts of land is not an operating company. Accordingly, P is considered to have acquired an undivided interest in the tracts of land held by Y. Thus, Y would be a fiduciary of P to the extent it exercises discretionary authority or control over such property.

(12) A medical benefit plan, P, acquires a beneficial interest in a trust, Z, that is not an insurance company licensed to do business in a State. Under this arrangement, Z will provide the benefits to the participants and beneficiaries of P that are promised under the terms of the plan. Under paragraph (h)(2), P's assets include its beneficial interest in Z and an undivided interest in each of its underlying assets. Thus, persons with discretionary authority or control over the assets of Z would be fiduciaries of P.

(k) *Effective date and transitional rules.* (1) In general, this section is effective for purposes of identifying the assets of a plan on or after March 13, 1987. Except as a defense, this section shall not apply to investments in an entity in existence on March 13, 1987, if no plan subject to title I of the Act or plan described in section 4975(e)(1) of the Code (other than a plan described in section 4975(g) (2) or (3)) acquires an interest in the entity from an issuer or underwriter at any time on or after March 13, 1987 except pursuant to a contract binding on the plan in effect on March 13,

1987 with an issuer or underwriter to acquire an interest in the entity.

(2) Notwithstanding paragraph (k)(1), this section shall not, except as a defense, apply to a real estate entity described in section 11018(a) of Pub. L. 99-272.

§ 2530.206. Time and order of issuance of domestic relations orders.

(a) *Scope.* This section implements section 1001 of the Pension Protection Act of 2006 by clarifying certain timing issues with respect to domestic relations orders and qualified domestic relations orders under the Employee Retirement Income Security Act of 1974, as amended (ERISA), 29 U.S.C. 1001 et seq. The examples herein illustrate the application of this section in certain circumstances. This section also applies in circumstances not described in the examples.

(b) *Subsequent domestic relations orders.*

(1) Subject to paragraph (d)(1) of this section, a domestic relations order shall not fail to be treated as a qualified domestic relations order solely because the order is issued after, or revises, another domestic relations order or qualified domestic relations order.

(2) The rule described in paragraph (b)(1) of this section is illustrated by the following examples:

Example (1). Subsequent domestic relations order between the same parties. Participant and Spouse divorce, and the administrator of Participant's 401(k) plan receives a domestic relations order. The administrator determines that the order is a QDRO. The QDRO allocates a portion of Participant's benefits to Spouse as the alternate payee. Subsequently, before benefit payments have commenced, Participant and Spouse seek and receive a second domestic relations order. The second order reduces the portion of Participant's benefits that Spouse was to receive under the QDRO. The second order does not fail to be treated as a QDRO solely because the second order is issued after, and reduces the prior assignment contained in, the first order.

Example (2). Subsequent domestic relations order between different parties. Participant and Spouse divorce, and the administrator of Participant's 401(k) plan receives a domestic relations order. The administrator determines that the order is a QDRO. The QDRO allocates a portion of Participant's benefits to Spouse as the alternate payee. Participant marries Spouse 2, and then they divorce. Participant's 401(k) plan administrator subsequently receives a domestic relations order pertaining to Spouse 2. The order assigns to Spouse 2 a portion of Participant's 401(k) benefits not already allocated to Spouse 1. The second order does not fail to be a QDRO solely because the second order is issued after the plan administrator has determined that an earlier order pertaining to Spouse 1 is a QDRO.

(c) *Timing.*

(1) Subject to paragraph (d)(1) of this section, a domestic relations order shall not fail to be treated as a qualified domestic relations order solely because of the time at which it is issued.

(2) The rule described in paragraph (c)(1) of this section is illustrated by the following examples:

Example (1). Orders issued after death. Participant and Spouse divorce, and the administrator of Participant's plan receives a domestic relations order, but the administrator finds the order deficient and determines that it is not a QDRO. Shortly thereafter, Participant dies while actively employed. A second domestic relations order correcting the defects in the first order is subsequently submitted to the plan. The second order does not fail to be treated as a QDRO solely because it is issued after the death of the Participant. The result would be the same even if no order had been issued before the Participant's death, in other words, the order issued after death were the only order.

Example (2). Orders issued after divorce. Participant and Spouse divorce. As a result, Spouse no longer meets the definition of "surviving spouse" under the terms of the plan.

Subsequently, the plan administrator receives a domestic relations order requiring that Spouse be treated as the Participant's surviving spouse for purposes of receiving a death benefit payable under the terms of the plan only to a participant's surviving spouse. The order does not fail to be treated as a QDRO solely because, at the time it is issued, Spouse no longer meets the definition of a "surviving spouse" under the terms of the plan.

Example (3). Orders issued after annuity starting date. Participant retires and begins receipt of benefits in the form of a straight life annuity, equal to $1,000 per month, and with respect to which Spouse has consented to the waiver of the surviving spousal rights provided under the plan and section 205 of ERISA. Subsequent to the commencement of benefits (in other words, subsequent to the annuity starting date as defined in section 205(h)(2) of ERISA and as further explained in 26 CFR 1.401(a)-20, Q&A-10(b)), Participant and Spouse divorce and present the plan with a domestic relations order requiring 50 percent ($500) of Participant's future monthly annuity payments under the plan to be paid instead to Spouse, as an alternate payee (so that monthly payments of $500 are to be made to Spouse during Participant's lifetime). Pursuant to paragraph (c)(1) of this section, the order does not fail to be a QDRO solely because it is issued after the annuity starting date. If the order instead had required payments to Spouse for the lifetime of Spouse, this would constitute a reannuitization with a new annuity starting date, rather than merely allocating to Spouse a part of the determined annuity payments due to Participant, so that the order, while not failing to be a QDRO because of the timing of the order, would fail to meet the requirements of section 206(d)(3)(D)(i) of ERISA (unless the plan otherwise permits such a change after the participant's annuity starting date). See 29 CFR 2530.206(d)(2), Example (4).

(d) *Requirements and protections*.

(1) Any domestic relations order described in this section shall be subject to the same requirements and protections that apply to qualified domestic relations orders under section 206(d)(3) of ERISA.

(2) The rule described in paragraph (d)(1) of this section is illustrated by the following examples:

Example (1). Type or form of benefit. Participant and Spouse divorce, and their divorce decree provides that the parties will prepare a domestic relations order assigning 50 percent of Participant's benefits under a 401(k) plan to Spouse to be paid in monthly installments over a ten-year period. Shortly thereafter, Participant dies while actively employed. A domestic relations order consistent with the decree is subsequently submitted to the 401(k) plan; however, the plan does not provide for ten-year installment payments of the type described in the order. Pursuant to paragraph (c)(1) of this section, the order does not fail to be treated as a QDRO solely because it is issued after the death of Participant, but the order would fail to be a QDRO under section 206(d)(3)(D)(i) and paragraph (d)(1) of this section because the order requires the plan to provide a type or form of benefit, or any option, not otherwise provided under the plan.

Example (2). Segregation of payable benefits. Participant and Spouse divorce, and the administrator of Participant's plan receives a domestic relations order under which Spouse would begin to receive benefits immediately if the order is determined to be a QDRO. The plan administrator separately accounts for the amounts covered by the domestic relations order as is required under section 206(d)(3)(H)(v) of ERISA. The plan administrator finds the order deficient and determines that it is not a QDRO. Subsequently, after the expiration of the segregation period pertaining to that order, the plan administrator receives a second domestic relations order relating to the same parties under which Spouse would begin to receive benefits immediately if the second order is determined to be a QDRO. Notwithstanding the expiration of the first segregation period, the amounts covered by the second order must be separately accounted for by the plan administrator for an 18-month period, in accordance with section 206(d)(3)(H) of ERISA and paragraph (d)(1) of this section.

Example (3). Previously assigned benefits. Participant and Spouse divorce, and the administrator of Participant's 401(k) plan receives a domestic relations order. The administrator determines that the order is a QDRO. The QDRO assigns a portion of Participant's benefits to Spouse as the alternate payee. Participant marries Spouse 2, and then they divorce. Participant's 401(k) plan administrator subsequently receives a domestic relations order pertaining to Spouse 2. The order assigns to Spouse 2 a portion of Participant's 401(k) benefits already assigned to Spouse 1. The second order does not fail to be treated as a QDRO solely because the second order is issued after the plan administrator has determined that an earlier order pertaining to Spouse 1 is a QDRO. The second order, however, would fail to be a QDRO under section 206(d)(3)(D)(iii) and paragraph (d)(1) of this section because it assigns all or a portion of Participant's benefits that are already assigned to Spouse 1 by the prior QDRO.

Example (4). Type or form of benefit.

Participant retires and commences benefit payments in the form of a straight life annuity based on the life of Participant, with [*32852] respect to which Spouse consents to the waiver of the surviving spousal rights provided under the plan and section 205 of ERISA. Participant and Spouse divorce after the annuity starting date and present the plan with a domestic relations order that eliminates the straight life annuity based on Participant's life and provides for Spouse, as alternate payee, to receive all future benefits in the form of a straight life annuity based on the life of Spouse. The plan does not allow reannuitization with a new annuity starting date, as defined in section 205(h)(2) of ERISA (and as further explained in 26 CFR 1.401(a)-20, Q&A-10(b)). Pursuant to paragraph (c)(1) of this section, the order does not fail to be a QDRO solely because it is issued after the annuity starting date, but the order would fail

to be a QDRO under section 206(d)(3)(D)(i) and paragraph (d)(1) of this section because the order requires the plan to provide a type or form of benefit, or any option, not otherwise provided under the plan. However, the order would not fail to be a QDRO under section 206(d)(3)(D)(i) and paragraph (d)(1) of this section if instead it were to require all of Participant's future payments under the plan to be paid instead to Spouse, as an alternate payee (so that payments that would otherwise be paid to the Participant during the Participant's lifetime are instead to be made to the Spouse during the Participant's lifetime).

§ 2550.404a-1. Investment duties.

(a) *In general.* Section 404(a)(1)(B) of the Employee Retirement Income Security Act of 1974 (the Act) provides, in part, that a fiduciary shall discharge his duties with respect to a plan with the care, skill, prudence, and diligence under the circumstances then prevailing that a prudent man acting in a like capacity and familiar with such matters would use in the conduct of an enterprise of a like character and with like aims.

(b) *Investment duties.* (1) With regard to an investment or investment course of action taken by a fiduciary of an employee benefit plan pursuant to his investment duties, the requirements of section 404(a)(1)(B) of the Act set forth in subsection (a) of this section are satisfied if the fiduciary:

(i) Has given appropriate consideration to those facts and circumstances that, given the scope of such fiduciary's investment duties, the fiduciary knows or should know are relevant to the particular investment or investment course of action involved, including the role the investment or investment course of action plays in that portion of the plan's investment portfolio with respect to which the fiduciary has investment duties; and

(ii) Has acted accordingly.

(2) For purposes of paragraph (b)(1) of this section, "appropriate consideration" shall include, but is not necessarily limited to,

(i) A determination by the fiduciary that the particular investment or investment course of action is reasonably designed, as part of the portfolio (or, where applicable, that portion of the plan portfolio with respect to which the fiduciary has investment duties), to further the purposes of the plan, taking into consideration the risk of loss and the opportunity for gain (or other return) associated with the investment or investment course of action, and

(ii) Consideration of the following factors as they relate to such portion of the portfolio:

(A) The composition of the portfolio with regard to diversification;

(B) The liquidity and current return of the portfolio relative to the anticipated cash flow requirements of the plan; and

(C) The projected return of the portfolio relative to the funding objectives of the plan.

(3) An investment manager appointed, pursuant to the provisions of section 402(c)(3) of the Act, to manage all or part of the assets of a plan, may, for purposes of compliance with the provisions of paragraphs (b)(1) and (2) of this section, rely on, and act upon the basis of, information pertaining to the plan provided by or at the direction of the appointing fiduciary, if—

(i) Such information is provided for the stated purpose of assisting the manager in the performance of his investment duties, and

(ii) The manager does not know and has no reason to know that the information is incorrect.

(c) *Definitions.* For purposes of this section:

(1) The term "investment duties" means any duties imposed upon, or assumed or undertaken by, a person in connection with the investment of plan assets which make or will make such person a fiduciary of an employee benefit plan or which are performed by such person as a fiduciary of an employee benefit plan as defined in section 3(21)(A)(i) or (ii) of the Act.

(2) The term "investment course of action" means any series or program of investments or actions related to a fiduciary's performance of his investment duties.

(3) The term "plan" means an employee benefit plan to which title I of the Act applies.

§ 2550.404a-2. Safe harbor for automatic rollovers to individual retirement plans.

(a) *In general.* (1) Pursuant to section 657(c) of the Economic Growth and Tax Relief Reconciliation Act of 2001, Public Law 107-16, June 7, 2001, 115 Stat. 38, this section provides a safe harbor under which a fiduciary of an employee pension benefit plan subject to Title I of the Employee Retirement Income Security Act of 1974, as amended (the Act), 29 U.S.C. 1001 et seq., will be deemed to have satisfied his or her fiduciary duties under section 404(a) of the Act in connection with an automatic rollover of a mandatory distribution described in section 401(a)(31)(B) of the Internal Revenue Code of 1986, as amended (the Code). This section also provides a safe harbor for certain other mandatory distributions not described in section 401(a)(31)(B) of the Code.

(2) The standards set forth in this section apply solely for purposes of determining whether a fiduciary meets the requirements of this safe harbor. Such standards are not intended to be the exclusive means by which a fiduciary might satisfy his or her responsibilities under the Act with respect to rollovers of mandatory distributions described in paragraphs (c) and (d) of this section.

(b) *Safe harbor.* A fiduciary that meets the conditions of paragraph (c) or paragraph (d) of this section is deemed to have satisfied his or her duties under section 404(a) of the Act with respect to both the selection of an individual retirement plan provider and the investment of funds in connection with the rollover of mandatory distributions described in those paragraphs to an individual retirement plan, within the meaning of section 7701(a)(37) of the Code.

(c) *Conditions.* With respect to an automatic rollover of a mandatory distribution described in section 401(a)(31)(B) of the Code, a fiduciary shall qualify for the safe harbor described in paragraph (b) of this section if:

(1) The present value of the nonforfeitable accrued benefit, as determined under section 411(a)(11) of the Code, does not exceed the maximum amount under section 401(a)(31)(B) of the Code;

(2) The mandatory distribution is to an individual retirement plan within the meaning of section 7701(a)(37) of the Code;

(3) In connection with the distribution of rolled-over funds to an individual retirement plan, the fiduciary enters into a written agreement with an individual retirement plan provider that provides:

(i) The rolled-over funds shall be invested in an investment product designed to preserve principal and provide a reasonable rate of return, whether or not such return is guaranteed, consistent with liquidity;

(ii) For purposes of paragraph (c)(3)(i) of this section, the investment product selected for the rolled-over funds shall seek to maintain, over the term of the investment, the dollar value that is equal to the amount invested in the product by the individual retirement plan;

(iii) The investment product selected for the rolled-over funds shall be offered by a state or federally regulated financial institution, which shall be: A bank or savings association, the deposits of which are insured by the Federal Deposit Insurance Corporation; a credit union, the member accounts of which are insured within the meaning of section 101(7) of the Federal Credit Union Act; an insurance company, the products of which are protected by State guaranty associations; or an investment company registered under the Investment Company Act of 1940;

(iv) All fees and expenses attendant to an individual retirement plan, including investments of such plan, (e.g., establishment charg-es, maintenance fees, investment expenses, termination costs and surrender charges) shall not exceed the fees and expenses charged by the individual retirement plan provider for comparable individual retirement plans established for reasons other than the receipt of a rollover distribution subject to the provisions of section 401(a)(31)(B) of the Code; and

(v) The participant on whose behalf the fiduciary makes an automatic rollover shall have the right to enforce the terms of the contractual agreement establishing the individual retirement plan, with regard to his or her rolled-over funds, against the individual retirement plan provider.

(4) Participants have been furnished a summary plan description, or a summary of material modifications, that describes the plan's automatic rollover provisions effectuating the requirements of section 401(a)(31)(B) of the Code, including an explanation that the mandatory distribution will be invested in an investment product designed to preserve principal and provide a reasonable rate of return and liquidity, a statement indicating how fees and expenses attendant to the individual retirement plan will be allocated (i.e., the extent to which expenses will be borne by the account holder alone or shared with the distributing plan or plan sponsor), and the name, address and phone number of a plan contact (to the extent not otherwise provided in the summary plan description or summary of material modifications) for further information concerning the plan's automatic rollover provisions, the individual retirement plan provider and the fees and expenses attendant to the individual retirement plan; and

(5) Both the fiduciary's selection of an individual retirement plan and the investment of funds would not result in a prohibited transaction under section 406 of the Act, unless such actions are exempted from the prohibited transaction provisions by a prohibited transaction exemption issued pursuant to section 408(a) of the Act.

(d) *Mandatory distributions of $1,000 or less.* A fiduciary shall qualify for the protection afforded by the safe harbor described in paragraph (b) of this section with respect to a mandatory distribution of one thousand dollars ($1,000) or less described in section 411(a)(11) of the Code, provided there is no affirmative distribution election by the participant and the fiduciary makes a rollover distribution of such amount into an individual retirement plan on behalf of such participant in accordance with the conditions described in paragraph (c) of this section, without regard to the fact that such rollover is not described in section 401(a)(31)(B) of the Code.

(e) *Effective date.* This section shall be effective and shall apply to any rollover of a mandatory distribution made on or after March 28, 2005.

§ 2550.404c-1. ERISA section 404(c) plans.

(a) *In general.* (1) Section 404(c) of the Employee Retirement Income Security Act of 1974 (ERISA or the Act) provides that if a pension plan that provides for individual accounts permits a participant or beneficiary to exercise control over assets in his account and that participant or beneficiary in fact exercises control over assets in his account, then the participant or beneficiary shall not be deemed to be a fiduciary by reason of his exercise of control and no person who is otherwise a fiduciary shall be liable for any loss, or by reason of any breach, which results from such exercise of control. This section describes the kinds of plans that are "ERISA section 404(c) plans," the circumstances in which a participant or beneficiary is considered to have exercised independent control over the assets in his account as contemplated by section 404(c), and the consequences of a participant's or beneficiary's exercise of control.

(2) The standards set forth in this section are applicable solely for the purpose of determining whether a plan is an ERISA section 404(c) plan and whether a particular transaction engaged in by a participant or beneficiary of such plan is afforded relief by section 404(c). Such standards, therefore, are not intended to be applied in determining whether, or to what extent, a plan which does not meet

the requirements for an ERISA section 404(c) plan or a fiduciary with respect to such a plan satisfies the fiduciary responsibility or other provisions of Title I of the Act.

(b) *ERISA section 404(c) plans.* (1) *In general.* An "ERISA section 404(c) Plan" is an individual account plan described in section 3(34) of the Act that:

(i) Provides an opportunity for a participant or beneficiary to exercise control over assets in his individual account (see paragraph (b)(2) of this section); and

(ii) Provides a participant or beneficiary an opportunity to choose, from a broad range of investment alternatives, the manner in which some or all of the assets in his account are invested (see paragraph (b)(3) of this section).

(2) Opportunity to exercise control. (i) a plan provides a participant or beneficiary an opportunity to exercise control over assets in his account only if:

(A) Under the terms of the plan, the participant or beneficiary has a reasonable opportunity to give investment instructions (in writing or otherwise, with opportunity to obtain written confirmation of such instructions) to an identified plan fiduciary who is obligated to comply with such instructions except as otherwise provided in paragraph (b)(2)(ii)(B) and (d)(2)(ii) of this section; and

(B) The participant or beneficiary is provided or has the opportunity to obtain sufficient information to make informed investment decisions with regard to investment alternatives available under the plan, and incidents of ownership appurtenant to such investments. For purposes of this paragraph, a participant or beneficiary will be considered to have sufficient information if the participant or beneficiary is provided by an identified plan fiduciary (or a person or persons designated by the plan fiduciary to act on his behalf):

(1) An explanation that the plan is intended to constitute a plan described in section

404(c) of the Employee Retirement Income Security Act, and 29 CFR 2550.404c-1, and that the fiduciaries of the plan may be relieved of liability for any losses which are the direct and necessary result of investment instructions given by such participant or beneficiary;

(2) The information required pursuant to 29 CFR 2550.404a-5; and

(3) In the case of plans which offer an investment alternative which is designed to permit a participant or beneficiary to directly or indirectly acquire or sell any employer security (employer security alternative), a description of the procedures established to provide for the confidentiality of information relating to the purchase, holding and sale of employer securities, and the exercise of voting, tender and similar rights, by participants and beneficiaries, and the name, address and phone number of the plan fiduciary responsible for monitoring compliance with the procedures (See paragraphs (d)(2)(ii)(E)(4)(vii), (viii) and (ix) of this section).

(ii) A plan does not fail to provide an opportunity for a participant or beneficiary to exercise control over his individual account merely because it—

(A) Imposes charges for reasonable expenses. A plan may charge participants' and beneficiaries' accounts for the reasonable expenses of carrying out investment instructions, provided that procedures are established under the plan to periodically inform such participants and beneficiaries of actual expenses incurred with respect to their respective individual accounts;

(B) Permits a fiduciary to decline to implement investment instructions by participants and beneficiaries. A fiduciary may decline to implement participant and beneficiary instructions which are described at paragraph (d)(2)(ii) of this section, as well as instructions specified in the plan, including instructions—

(1) Which would result in a prohibited transaction described in ERISA section 406 or section 4975 of the Internal Revenue Code, and

(2) Which would generate income that would be taxable to the plan;

(C) Imposes reasonable restrictions on frequency of investment instructions. A plan may impose reasonable restrictions on the frequency with which participants and beneficiaries may give investment instructions. In no event, however, is such a restriction reasonable unless, with respect to each investment alternative made available by the plan, it permits participants and beneficiaries to give investment instructions with a frequency which is appropriate in light of the market volatility to which the investment alternative may reasonably be expected to be subject, provided that—

(1) At least three of the investment alternatives made available pursuant to the requirements of paragraph (b)(3)(i)(B) of this section, which constitute a broad range of investment alternatives, Permit participants and beneficiaries to give investment instructions no less frequently than once within any three month period; and

(2)(i) At least one of the investment alternatives meeting the requirements of paragraph (b)(2)(ii)(C)(1) of this section permits participants and beneficiaries to give investment instructions with regard to transfers into the investment alternative as frequently as participants and beneficiaries are permitted to give investment instructions with respect to any investment alternative made available by the plan which permits participants and beneficiaries to give investment instructions more frequently than once within any three month period; or

(ii) With respect to each investment alternative which permits participants and beneficiaries to give investment instructions more frequently than once within any three month period, participants and beneficiaries are permitted to direct their investments from such alternative into an income producing, low risk, liquid fund, subfund, or account as frequently as they are permitted to give investment instructions with respect to each such alternative and, with respect to such fund, subfund or account, participants and beneficiaries are permitted to direct investments from the fund, subfund or account to an investment alternative meeting the requirements of paragraph (b)(2)(ii)(C)(1) as frequently as they are permitted to give investment instructions with respect to that investment alternative; and

(3) With respect to transfers from an investment alternative which is designed to permit a participant or beneficiary to directly or indirectly acquire or sell any employer security (employer security alternative) either:

(i) All of the investment alternatives meeting the requirements of paragraph (b)(2)(ii)(C)(1) of this section must permit participants and beneficiaries to give investment instructions with regard to transfers into each of the investment alternatives as frequently as participants and beneficiaries are permitted to give investment instructions with respect to the employer security alternative; or

(ii) Participants and beneficiaries are permitted to direct their investments from each employer security alternative into an income producing, low risk, liquid fund, subfund, or account as frequently as they are permitted to give investment instructions with respect to such employer security alternative and, with respect to such fund, subfund, or account, participants and beneficiaries are permitted to direct investments from the fund, subfund or account to each investment alternative meeting the requirements of paragraph (b)(2)(ii)(C)(1) as frequently as they are permitted to give investment instructions with respect to each such investment alternative.

(iii) Paragraph (c) of this section describes the circumstances under which a participant or beneficiary will be considered to have exercised independent control with respect to a particular transaction.

(3) Broad range of investment alternatives. (i) A plan offers a broad range of investment alternatives only if the available investment alternatives are sufficient to provide the participant or beneficiary with a reasonable opportunity to:

(A) Materially affect the potential return on amounts in his individual account with respect to which he is permitted to exercise control and the degree of risk to which such amounts are subject;

(B) Choose from at least three investment alternatives:

(1) Each of which is diversified;

(2) Each of which has materially different risk and return characteristics;

(3) Which in the aggregate enable the participant or beneficiary by choosing among them to achieve a portfolio with aggregate risk and return characteristics at any point within the range normally appropriate for the participant or beneficiary; and

(4) Each of which when combined with investments in the other alternatives tends to minimize through diversification the overall risk of a participant's or beneficiary's portfolio;

(C) Diversify the investment of that portion of his individual account with respect to which he is permitted to exercise control so as to minimize the risk of large losses, taking into account the nature of the plan and the size of participants' or beneficiaries' accounts. In determining whether a plan provides the participant or beneficiary with a reasonable opportunity to diversify his investments, the nature of the investment alternatives offered by the plan and the size of the portion of the individual's account over which he is permitted to exercise control must be considered. Where such portion of the account of any participant or beneficiary is so limited in size that the opportunity to invest in look-through investment vehicles is the only prudent means to assure an opportunity to achieve appropriate diversification, a plan may satisfy the requirements of this paragraph only by offering look-through investment vehicles.

(ii) Diversification and look-through investment vehicles. Where look-through investment vehicles are available as investment alternatives to participants and beneficiaries, the underlying investments of the look-through investment vehicles shall be considered in determining whether the plan satisfies the requirements of subparagraphs (b)(3)(i)(B) and (b)(3)(i)(C).

(c) *Exercise of control.* (1) *In general.* (i) Sections 404(c)(1) and 404(c)(2) of the Act and paragraphs (a) and (d) of this section apply only with respect to a transaction where a participant or beneficiary has exercised independent control in fact with respect to the investment of assets in his individual account under an ERISA section 404(c) plan.

(ii) For purposes of sections 404(c)(1) and 404(c)(2) of the Act and paragraphs (a) and (d) of this section, a participant or beneficiary will be deemed to have exercised control with respect to voting, tender or similar rights appurtenant to the participant's or beneficiary's ownership interest in an investment alternative, provided that the participant's or beneficiary's investment in the investment alternative was itself the result of an exercise of control; the participant or beneficiary was provided a reasonable opportunity to give instruction with respect to such incidents of ownership, including the provision of the information described in 29 CFR 2550.404a-5(d)(3); and the participant or beneficiary has not failed to exercise control by reason of the circumstances described in paragraph (c)(2) with respect to such incidents of ownership.

(2) Independent control. Whether a participant or beneficiary has exercised independent control in fact with respect to a transaction depends on the facts and circumstances of the particular case. However, a participant's or beneficiary's exercise of control is not independent in fact if:

(i) The participant or beneficiary is subjected to improper influence by a plan fiduciary or the plan sponsor with respect to the transaction;

(ii) A plan fiduciary has concealed material non-public facts regarding the investment from the participant or beneficiary, unless the disclosure of such information by the plan fiduciary to the participant or beneficiary

would violate any provision of federal law or any provision of state law which is not preempted by the Act; or

(iii) The participant or beneficiary is legally incompetent and the responsible plan fiduciary accepts the instructions of the participant or beneficiary knowing him to be legally incompetent.

(3) Transactions involving a fiduciary. In the case of a sale, exchange or leasing of property (other than a transaction described in paragraph (d)(2)(ii)(E) of this section) between an ERISA section 404(c) plan and a plan fiduciary or an affiliate of such a fiduciary, or a loan to a plan fiduciary or an affiliate of such a fiduciary, the participant or beneficiary will not be deemed to have exercised independent control unless the transaction is fair and reasonable to him. For purposes of this paragraph (c)(3), a transaction will be deemed to be fair and reasonable to a participant or beneficiary if he pays no more than, or receives no less than, adequate consideration (as defined in section 3(18) of the Act) in connection with the transaction.

(4) No obligation to advise. A fiduciary has no obligation under part 4 of Title I of the Act to provide investment advice to a participant or beneficiary under an ERISA section 404(c) plan.

(d) *Effect of independent exercise of control—*

(1) *Participant or beneficiary not a fiduciary.* If a participant or beneficiary of an ERISA section 404(c) plan exercises independent control over assets in his individual account in the manner described in paragraph (c), then such participant or beneficiary is not a fiduciary of the plan by reason of such exercise of control.

(2) *Limitation on liability of plan fiduciaries.* (i) If a participant or beneficiary of an ERISA section 404(c) plan exercises independent control over assets in his individual account in the manner described in paragraph (c), then no other person who is a fiduciary with respect to such plan shall be liable for

any loss, or with respect to any breach of part 4 of Title I of the Act, that is the direct and necessary result of that participant's or beneficiary's exercise of control.

(ii) Paragraph (d)(2)(i) does not apply with respect to any instruction, which if implemented—

(A) Would not be in accordance with the documents and instruments governing the plan insofar as such documents and instruments are consistent with the provisions of Title I of ERISA;

(B) Would cause a fiduciary to maintain the indicia of ownership of any assets of the plan outside the jurisdiction of the district courts of the United States other than as permitted by section 404(b) of the Act and 29 CFR 2550.404b-1;

(C) Would jeopardize the plan's tax qualified status under the Internal Revenue Code;

(D) Could result in a loss in excess of a participant's or beneficiary's account balance; or

(E) Would result in a direct or indirect:

(1) Sale, exchange, or lease of property between a plan sponsor or any affiliate of the sponsor and the plan except for the acquisition or disposition of any interest in a fund, subfund or portfolio managed by a plan sponsor or an affiliate of the sponsor, or the purchase or sale of any qualifying employer security (as defined in section 407(d)(5) of the Act) which meets the conditions of section 408(e) of ERISA and section (d)(2)(ii)(E)(4) below;

(2) Loan to a plan sponsor or any affiliate of the sponsor;

(3) Acquisition or sale of any employer real property (as defined in section 407(d)(2) of the Act); or

(4) Acquisition or sale of any employer security except to the extent that:

(i) Such securities are qualifying employer securities (as defined in section 407(d)(5) of the Act);

(ii) Such securities are stock or an equity interest in a publicly traded partnership (as defined in section 7704(b) of the Internal Revenue Code of 1986), but only if such partnership is an existing partnership as defined in section 10211(c)(2)(A) of the Revenue Act of 1987 (Public Law 100-203);

(iii) Such securities are publicly traded on a national exchange or other generally recognized market;

(iv) Paragraph (d)(2)(i) does not serve to relieve a fiduciary from its duty to prudently select and monitor any service provider or designated investment alternative offered under the plan.

(v) Information provided to shareholders of such securities is provided to participants and beneficiaries with accounts holding such securities;

(vi) Voting, tender and similar rights with respect to such securities are passed through to participants and beneficiaries with accounts holding such securities;

(vii) Information relating to the purchase, holding, and sale of securities, and the exercise of voting, tender and similar rights with respect to such securities by participants and beneficiaries, is maintained in accordance with procedures which are designed to safeguard the confidentiality of such information, except to the extent necessary to comply with Federal laws or state laws not preempted by the Act;

(viii) The plan designates a fiduciary who is responsible for ensuring that: The procedures required under subparagraph (d)(2)(ii)(E)(4) (vii) are sufficient to safeguard the confidentiality of the information described in that subparagraph, such procedures are being followed, and the independent fiduciary required by subparagraph (d)(2)(ii)(E)(4)(ix) is appointed; and

(ix) An independent fiduciary is appointed to carry out activities relating to any situations which the fiduciary designated by the plan for purposes of subparagraph (d)(2)(ii)(E)(4)(viii) determines involve a potential for undue employer influence upon participants and beneficiaries with regard to the direct or indirect exercise of shareholder rights. For purposes of this subparagraph, a fiduciary is not independent if the fiduciary is affiliated with any sponsor of the plan.

(iii) The individual investment decisions of an investment manager who is designated directly by a participant or beneficiary or who manages a look-through investment vehicle in which a participant or beneficiary has invested are not direct and necessary results of the designation of the investment manager or of investment in the look-through investment vehicle. However, this paragraph (d)(2)(iii) shall not be construed to result in liability under section 405 of ERISA with respect to a fiduciary (other than the investment manager) who would otherwise be relieved of liability by reason of section 404(c)(2) of the Act and paragraph (d) of this section.

(3) *Prohibited Transactions.* The relief provided by section 404(c) of the Act and this section applies only to the provisions of part 4 of title I of the Act. Therefore, nothing in this section relieves a disqualified person from the taxes imposed by sections 4975 (a) and (b) of the Internal Revenue Code with respect to the transactions prohibited by section 4975(c)(1) of the Code.

(e) *Definitions.* For purposes of this section:

(1) Look-through investment vehicle means:

(i) An investment company described in section 3(a) of the Investment Company Act of 1940, or a series investment company described in section 18(f) of the 1940 Act or any of the segregated portfolios of such company;

(ii) A common or collective trust fund or a pooled investment fund maintained by a bank or similar institution, a deposit in a bank or similar institution, or a fixed rate investment contract of a bank or similar institution;

(iii) A pooled separate account or a fixed rate investment contract of an insurance company qualified to do business in a State; or

(iv) Any entity whose assets include plan assets by reason of a plan's investment in the entity;

(2) Adequate consideration has the meaning given it in section 3(18) of the Act and in any regulations under this title;

(3) An affiliate of a person includes the following:

(i) Any person directly or indirectly controlling, controlled by, or under common control with the person;

(ii) Any officer, director, partner, employee, an employee of an affiliated employer, relative (as defined in section 3(15) of ERISA), brother, sister, or spouse of a brother or sister, of the person; and

(iii) Any corporation or partnership of which the person is an officer director or partner.

For purposes of this paragraph (e)(3), the term "control" means, with respect to a person other than an individual, the power to exercise a controlling influence over the management or policies of such person.

(4) A designated investment alternative is a specific investment identified by a plan fiduciary as an available investment alternative under the plan.

(f) *Examples.* The provisions of this section are illustrated by the following examples. Examples (5) through (11) assume that the participant has exercised independent control with respect to his individual account under an ERISA section 404(c) plan described in paragraph (b) and has not directed a transaction described in paragraph (d)(2)(ii).

(1) Plan A is an individual account plan described in section 3(34) of the Act. The plan states that a plan participant or beneficiary may direct the plan administrator to invest any portion of his individual account in a particular diversified equity fund managed by an

entity which is not affiliated with the plan sponsor, or any other asset administratively feasible for the plan to hold. However, the plan provides that the plan administrator will not implement certain listed instructions for which plan fiduciaries would not be relieved of liability under section 404(c) (See paragraph (d)(2)(ii) of this section). Plan participants and beneficiaries are permitted to give investment instructions during the first week of each month with respect to the equity fund and at any time with respect to other investments. The plan administrator of Plan A provides each participant and beneficiary with the information described in paragraph (b)(2)(i)(B) of this section, including the information that must be provided on or before the date on which a participant or beneficiary can first direct his or her investments and at least annually thereafter pursuant to 29 CFR 2550.404a-5, and provides updated information in the event of any change in the information provided. Subsequent to any investment by a participant or beneficiary, the plan administrator forwards to the investing participant or beneficiary any materials provided to the plan relating to the exercise of voting, tender or similar rights attendant to ownership of an interest in such investment (See paragraph (b)(2)(i)(B)(3) of this section and 29 CFR 2550.404a-5(d)(3)). Upon request, the plan administrator provides each participant or beneficiary with copies of any prospectuses (or similar documents relating to designated investment alternatives that are provided by entities that are not registered under the Securities Act of 1933 or the Investment Company Act of 1940), financial statements and reports, and any other materials relating to the designated investment alternatives available under the plan in accordance with 29 CFR 2550.404a-5(d)(4)(i) through (iv). Also upon request, the plan administrator provides each participant and beneficiary with other information required by 29 CFR 2550.404a-5(d)(4) with respect to the equity fund, which is a designated investment alternative, including a statement of the value of a share or unit of the participant's or beneficiary's interest in the equity fund and the date

of the valuation. Plan A meets the requirements of paragraph (b)(2)(i)(B) of this section regarding the provision of investment information.

NOTE: The regulation imposes no additional obligation on the administrator to furnish or make available materials relating to the companies in which the equity fund invests (e.g., prospectuses, proxies, etc.).

(2) Plan C is an individual account plan described in section 3(34) of the Act under which participants and beneficiaries may choose among three investment alternatives which otherwise meet the requirements of paragraph (b) of this section. The plan permits investment instruction with respect to each investment alternative only on the first 10 days of each calendar quarter, i.e. January 1-10, April 1-10, July 1-10 and October 1-10. Plan C satisfies the condition of paragraph (b)(2)(ii)(C)(*1*) that instruction be permitted not less frequently than once within any three month period, since there is not any three month period during which control could not be exercised.

(3) Assume the same facts as in paragraph (f)(2), except that investment instruction may only be given on January 1, April 4, July 1 and October 1. Plan C is not an ERISA section 404(c) plan because it does not satisfy the condition of paragraph (b)(2)(ii)(C)(*1*) that instruction be permitted not less frequently than once within any three month period. Under these facts, there is a three month period, e.g., January 2 through April 1, during which control could not be exercised by participants and beneficiaries.

(4) Plan D is an individual account plan described in section 3(34) of the Act under which participants and beneficiaries may choose among three diversified investment alternatives which constitute a broad range of investment alternatives. The plan also permits investment instruction with respect to an employer securities alternative but provides that a participant or beneficiary can invest no more than 25% of his account balance in this alternative. This restriction does not affect the

availability of relief under section 404(c) inasmuch as it does not relate to the three diversified investment alternatives and, therefore, does not cause the plan to fail to provide an opportunity to choose from a broad range of investment alternatives.

(5) A participant, P, independently exercises control over assets in his individual account plan by directing a plan fiduciary, F, to invest 100% of his account balance in a single stock. P is not a fiduciary with respect to the plan by reason of his exercise of control and F will not be liable for any losses that necessarily result form P's investment instruction.

(6) Assume the same facts as in paragraph (f)(5), except that P directs F to purchase the stock from B, who is a party in interest with respect to the plan. Neither P nor F has engaged in a transaction prohibited under section 406 of the Act: P because he is not a fiduciary with respect to the plan by reason of his exercise of control and F because he is not liable for any breach of part 4 of Title I that is the direct and necessary consequence of P's exercise of control. However, a prohibited transaction under section 4975(c) of the Internal Revenue Code may have occurred, and, in the absence of an exemption, tax liability may be imposed pursuant to sections 495 (a) and (b) of the Code.

(7) Assume the same facts as in paragraph (f)(5), except that P does not specify that the stock be purchased from B, and F chooses to purchase the stock from B. In the absence of an exemption, F has engaged in a prohibited transaction described in 406(a) of ERISA because the decision to purchase the stock from B is not a direct or necessary result of P's exercise of control.

(8) Pursuant to the terms of the plan, plan fiduciary F designates three reputable investment managers whom participants may appoint to manage assets in their individual accounts. Participant P selects M, one of the designated managers, to manage the assets in his account. M prudently manages P's account for 6 months after which he incurs losses in managing the account through his impru-

dence. M has engaged in a breach of fiduciary duty because M's imprudent management of P's account is not a direct or necessary result of P's exercise of control (the choice of M as manager). F has no fiduciary liability for M's imprudence because he has no affirmative duty to advise P (see paragraph (c)(4)) and because F is relieved of co-fiduciary liability by reason of section 404(c)(2) (see paragraph (d)(2)(iii)). F does have a duty to monitor M's performance to determine the suitability of continuing M as an investment manager, however, and M's imprudence would be a factor which F must consider in periodically reevaluating its decision to designate M.

(9) Participant P instructs plan fiduciary F to appoint G as his investment manager pursuant to the terms of the plan which provide P total discretion in choosing an investment manager. Through G's imprudence, G incurs losses in managing P's account. G has engaged in a breach of fiduciary duty because G's imprudent management of P's account is not a direct or necessary result of P's exercise of control (the choice of G as manager). Plan fiduciary F has no fiduciary liability for G's imprudence because F has no obligation to advise P (see paragraph (c)(4)) and because F is relieved of co-fiduciary liability for G's actions by reason of section 404(c)(2) (see paragraph (d)(2)(iii)). In addition, F also has no duty to determine the suitability of G as an investment manager because the plan does not designate G as an investment manager.

(10) Participant P directs a plan fiduciary, F, a bank, to invest all of the assets in his individual account in a collective trust fund managed by F that is designed to be invested solely in a diversified portfolio of common stocks. Due to economic conditions, the value of the common stocks in the bank collective trust fund declines while the value of publicly-offered fixed income obligations remains relatively stable. F is not liable for any losses incurred by P solely because his individual account was not diversified to include fixed income obligations. Such losses are the direct result of P's exercise of control; moreover, under paragraph (c)(4) of this section F has no

obligation to advise P regarding his investment decisions.

(11) Assume the same facts as in paragraph (f)(10) except that F, in managing the collective trust fund, invests the assets of the fund solely in a few highly speculative stocks. F is liable for losses resulting from its imprudent investment in the speculative stocks and for its failure to diversify the assets of the account. This conduct involves a separate breach of F's fiduciary duty that is not a direct or necessary result of P's exercise of control (see paragraph (d)(2)(iii)).

* * *

§ 2550.404c-5. Fiduciary relief for investments in qualified default investment alternatives.

(a) *In general.* (1) This section implements the fiduciary relief provided under section 404(c)(5) of the Employee Retirement Income Security Act of 1974, as amended (ERISA or the Act), 29 U.S.C. 1001 et seq., under which a participant or beneficiary in an individual account plan will be treated as exercising control over the assets in his or her account for purposes of ERISA section 404(c)(1) with respect to the amount of contributions and earnings that, in the absence of an investment election by the participant, are invested by the plan in accordance with this regulation. If a participant or beneficiary is treated as exercising control over the assets in his or her account in accordance with ERISA section 404(c)(1) no person who is otherwise a fiduciary shall be liable under part 4 of title I of ERISA for any loss or by reason of any breach which results from such participant's or beneficiary's exercise of control. Except as specifically provided in paragraph (c)(6) of this section, a plan need not meet the requirements for an ERISA section 404(c) plan under 29 CFR 2550.404c-1 in order for a plan fiduciary to obtain the relief under this section.

(2) The standards set forth in this section apply solely for purposes of determining whether a fiduciary meets the requirements of this regulation. Such standards are not intended to be the exclusive means by which a fiduciary might satisfy his or her responsibilities under the Act with respect to the investment of assets in the individual account of a participant or beneficiary.

(b) *Fiduciary relief.* (1) Except as provided in paragraphs (b)(2), (3), and (4) of this section, a fiduciary of an individual account plan that permits participants or beneficiaries to direct the investment of assets in their accounts and that meets the conditions of paragraph (c) of this section shall not be liable for any loss, or by reason of any breach under part 4 of title I of ERISA, that is the direct and necessary result of (i) investing all or part of a participant's or beneficiary's account in any qualified default investment alternative within the meaning of paragraph (e) of this section, or (ii) investment decisions made by the entity described in paragraph (e)(3) of this section in connection with the management of a qualified default investment alternative.

(2) Nothing in this section shall relieve a fiduciary from his or her duties under part 4 of title I of ERISA to prudently select and monitor any qualified default investment alternative under the plan or from any liability that results from a failure to satisfy these duties, including liability for any resulting losses.

(3) Nothing in this section shall relieve any fiduciary described in paragraph (e)(3)(i) of this section from its fiduciary duties under part 4 of title I of ERISA or from any liability that results from a failure to satisfy these duties, including liability for any resulting losses.

(4) Nothing in this section shall provide relief from the prohibited transaction provisions of section 406 of ERISA, or from any liability that results from a violation of those provisions, including liability for any resulting losses.

(c) *Conditions.* With respect to the investment of assets in the individual account of a participant or beneficiary, a fiduciary shall qualify for the relief described in paragraph (b)(1) of this section if:

(1) Assets are invested in a qualified default investment alternative within the meaning of paragraph (e) of this section;

(2) The participant or beneficiary on whose behalf the investment is made had the opportunity to direct the investment of the assets in his or her account but did not direct the investment of the assets;

(3) The participant or beneficiary on whose behalf an investment in a qualified default investment alternative may be made is furnished a notice that meets the requirements of paragraph (d) of this section:

(i)(A) At least 30 days in advance of the date of plan eligibility, or at least 30 days in advance of the date of any first investment in a qualified default investment alternative on behalf of a participant or beneficiary described in paragraph (c)(2) of this section; or

(B) On or before the date of plan eligibility provided the participant has the opportunity to make a permissible withdrawal (as determined under section 414(w) of the Internal Revenue Code of 1986, as amended (Code)); and

(ii) Within a reasonable period of time of at least 30 days in advance of each subsequent plan year;

(4) A fiduciary provides to a participant or beneficiary the material set forth in 29 CFR 2550.404c-1(b)(2)(i)(B)(1)(viii) and (ix) and 29 CFR 404c-1(b)(2)(i)(B)(2) relating to a participant's or beneficiary's investment in a qualified default investment alternative;

(5)(i) Any participant or beneficiary on whose behalf assets are invested in a qualified default investment alternative may transfer, in whole or in part, such assets to any other investment alternative available under the plan with a frequency consistent with that afforded to a participant or beneficiary who elected to invest in the qualified default investment alternative, but not less frequently than once within any three month period;

(ii)(A) Except as provided in paragraph (c)(5)(ii)(B) of this section, any transfer de-scribed in paragraph (c)(5)(i), or any permissible withdrawal as determined under section 414(w)(2) of the Code, by a participant or beneficiary of assets invested in a qualified default investment alternative, in whole or in part, resulting from the participant's or beneficiary's election to make such a transfer or withdrawal during the 90-day period beginning on the date of the participant's first elective contribution as determined under section 414(w)(2)(B) of the Code, or other first investment in a qualified default investment alternative on behalf of a participant or beneficiary described in paragraph (c)(2) of this section, shall not be subject to any restrictions, fees or expenses (including surrender charges, liquidation or exchange fees, redemption fees and similar expenses charged in connection with the liquidation of, or transfer from, the investment);

(B) Paragraph (c)(5)(ii)(A) of this section shall not apply to fees and expenses that are charged on an ongoing basis for the operation of the investment itself (such as investment management fees, distribution and/or service fees, "12b-1" fees, or legal, accounting, transfer agent and similar administrative expenses), and are not imposed, or do not vary, based on a participant's or beneficiary's decision to withdraw, sell or transfer assets out of the qualified default investment alternative; and

(iii) Following the end of the 90-day period described in paragraph (c)(5)(ii)(A) of this section, any transfer or permissible withdrawal described in this paragraph (c)(5) of this section shall not be subject to any restrictions, fees or expenses not otherwise applicable to a participant or beneficiary who elected to invest in that qualified default investment alternative; and

(6) The plan offers a "broad range of investment alternatives" within the meaning of 29 CFR 2550.404c-1(b)(3).

(d) *Notice.* The notice required by paragraph (c)(3) of this section shall be written in a manner calculated to be understood by the average plan participant and shall contain the following:

(1) A description of the circumstances under which assets in the individual account of a participant or beneficiary may be invested on behalf of the participant or beneficiary in a qualified default investment alternative; and, if applicable, an explanation of the circumstances under which elective contributions will be made on behalf of a participant, the percentage of such contributions, and the right of the participant to elect not to have such contributions made on the participant's behalf (or to elect to have such contributions made at a different percentage);

(2) An explanation of the right of participants and beneficiaries to direct the investment of assets in their individual accounts;

(3) A description of the qualified default investment alternative, including a description of the investment objectives, risk and return characteristics (if applicable), and fees and expenses attendant to the investment alternative;

(4) A description of the right of the participants and beneficiaries on whose behalf assets are invested in a qualified default investment alternative to direct the investment of those assets to any other investment alternative under the plan, including a description of any applicable restrictions, fees or expenses in connection with such transfer; and

(5) An explanation of where the participants and beneficiaries can obtain investment information concerning the other investment alternatives available under the plan.

(e) *Qualified default investment alternative.* For purposes of this section, a qualified default investment alternative means an investment alternative available to participants and beneficiaries that:

(1)(i) Does not hold or permit the acquisition of employer securities, except as provided in paragraph (ii).

(ii) Paragraph (e)(1)(i) of this section shall not apply to: (A) Employer securities held or acquired by an investment company registered under the Investment Company Act

of 1940 or a similar pooled investment vehicle regulated and subject to periodic examination by a State or Federal agency and with respect to which investment in such securities is made in accordance with the stated investment objectives of the investment vehicle and independent of the plan sponsor or an affiliate thereof; or (B) with respect to a qualified default investment alternative described in paragraph (e)(4)(iii) of this section, employer securities acquired as a matching contribution from the employer/plan sponsor, or employer securities acquired prior to management by the investment management service to the extent the investment management service has discretionary authority over the disposition of such employer securities;

(2) Satisfies the requirements of paragraph (c)(5) of this section regarding the ability of a participant or beneficiary to transfer, in whole or in part, his or her investment from the qualified default investment alternative to any other investment alternative available under the plan;

(3) Is:

(i) Managed by: (A) an investment manager, within the meaning of section 3(38) of the Act; (B) a trustee of the plan that meets the requirements of section 3(38)(A), (B) and (C) of the Act; or (C) the plan sponsor, or a committee comprised primarily of employees of the plan sponsor, which is a named fiduciary within the meaning of section 402(a)(2) of the Act;

(ii) An investment company registered under the Investment Company Act of 1940; or

(iii) An investment product or fund described in paragraph (e)(4)(iv) or (v) of this section; and

(4) Constitutes one of the following:

(i) An investment fund product or model portfolio that applies generally accepted investment theories, is diversified so as to minimize the risk of large losses and that is designed to provide varying degrees of long-term appreciation and capital preservation through a mix of equity and fixed income exposures based on the participant's age, target retirement date (such as normal retirement age under the plan) or life expectancy. Such products and portfolios change their asset allocations and associated risk levels over time with the objective of becoming more conservative (i.e., decreasing risk of losses) with increasing age. For purposes of this paragraph (e)(4)(i), asset allocation decisions for such products and portfolios are not required to take into account risk tolerances, investments or other preferences of an individual participant. An example of such a fund or portfolio may be a "life-cycle" or "targeted-retirement-date" fund or account.

(ii) An investment fund product or model portfolio that applies generally accepted investment theories, is diversified so as to minimize the risk of large losses and that is designed to provide long-term appreciation and capital preservation through a mix of equity and fixed income exposures consistent with a target level of risk appropriate for participants of the plan as a whole. For purposes of this paragraph (e)(4)(ii), asset allocation decisions for such products and portfolios are not required to take into account the age, risk tolerances, investments or other preferences of an individual participant. An example of such a fund or portfolio may be a "balanced" fund.

(iii) An investment management service with respect to which a fiduciary, within the meaning of paragraph (e)(3)(i) of this section, applying generally accepted investment theories, allocates the assets of a participant's individual account to achieve varying degrees of long-term appreciation and capital preservation through a mix of equity and fixed income exposures, offered through investment alternatives available under the plan, based on the participant's age, target retirement date (such as normal retirement age under the plan) or life expectancy. Such portfolios are diversified so as to minimize the risk of large losses and change their asset allocations and associated risk levels for an individual account over time with the objective of becoming more con-

servative (i.e., decreasing risk of losses) with increasing age. For purposes of this paragraph (e)(4)(iii), asset allocation decisions are not required to take into account risk tolerances, investments or other preferences of an individual participant. An example of such a service may be a "managed account."

(iv)(A) Subject to paragraph (e)(4)(iv)(B) of this section, an investment product or fund designed to preserve principal and provide a reasonable rate of return, whether or not such return is guaranteed, consistent with liquidity. Such investment product shall for purposes of this paragraph (e)(4)(iv):

(1) Seek to maintain, over the term of the investment, the dollar value that is equal to the amount invested in the product; and

(2) Be offered by a State or federally regulated financial institution.

(B) An investment product described in this paragraph (e)(4)(iv) shall constitute a qualified default investment alternative for purposes of paragraph (e) of this section for not more than 120 days after the date of the participant's first elective contribution (as determined under section 414(w)(2)(B) of the Code).

(v)(A) Subject to paragraph (e)(4)(v)(B) of this section, an investment product or fund designed to preserve principal; provide a rate of return generally consistent with that earned on intermediate investment grade bonds; and provide liquidity for withdrawals by participants and beneficiaries, including transfers to other investment alternatives. Such investment product or fund shall, for purposes of this paragraph (e)(4)(v), meet the following requirements:

(1) There are no fees or surrender charges imposed in connection with withdrawals initiated by a participant or beneficiary; and

(2) Such investment product or fund invests primarily in investment products that are backed by State or federally regulated financial institutions.

(B) An investment product or fund described in this paragraph (e)(4)(v) shall constitute a qualified default investment alternative for purposes of paragraph (e) of this section solely for purposes of assets invested in such product or fund before December 24, 2007.

(vi) An investment fund product or model portfolio that otherwise meets the requirements of this section shall not fail to constitute a product or portfolio for purposes of paragraph (e)(4)(i) or (ii) of this section solely because the product or portfolio is offered through variable annuity or similar contracts or through common or collective trust funds or pooled investment funds and without regard to whether such contracts or funds provide annuity purchase rights, investment guarantees, death benefit guarantees or other features ancillary to the investment fund product or model portfolio.

(f) *Preemption of State laws.*

(1) Section 514(e)(1) of the Act provides that title I of the Act supersedes any State law that would directly or indirectly prohibit or restrict the inclusion in any plan of an automatic contribution arrangement. For purposes of section 514(e) of the Act and this paragraph (f), an automatic contribution arrangement is an arrangement (or the provisions of a plan) under which:

(i) A participant may elect to have the plan sponsor make payments as contributions under the plan on his or her behalf or receive such payments directly in cash;

(ii) A participant is treated as having elected to have the plan sponsor make such contributions in an amount equal to a uniform percentage of compensation provided under the plan until the participant specifically elects not to have such contributions made (or specifically elects to have such contributions made at a different percentage); and

(iii) Contributions are invested in accordance with paragraphs (a) through (e) of this section.

(2) A State law that would directly or indirectly prohibit or restrict the inclusion in any pension plan of an automatic contribution arrangement is superseded as to any pension plan, regardless of whether such plan includes an automatic contribution arrangement as defined in paragraph (f)(1) of this section.

(3) The administrator of an automatic contribution arrangement within the meaning of paragraph (f)(1) of this section shall be considered to have satisfied the notice requirements of section 514(e)(3) of the Act if notices are furnished in accordance with paragraphs (c)(3) and (d) of this section.

(4) Nothing in this paragraph (f) precludes a pension plan from including an automatic contribution arrangement that does not meet the conditions of paragraphs (a) through (e) of this section.

§ 2550.408b-1. General statutory exemption for loans to plan participants and beneficiaries who are parties in interest with respect to the plan.

* * *

(f) *Adequate Security.* (1) A loan will be considered to be adequately secured if the security posted for such loan is something in addition to and supporting a promise to pay, which is so pledged to the plan that it may be sold, foreclosed upon, or otherwise disposed of upon default of repayment of the loan, the value and liquidity of which security is such that it may reasonably be anticipated that loss of principal or interest will not result from the loan. The adequacy of such security will be determined in light of the type and amount of security which would be required in the case of an otherwise identical transaction in a normal commercial setting between unrelated parties on arm's-length terms. A participant's vested accrued benefit under a plan may be used as security for a participant loan to the extent of the plan's ability to satisfy the participant's outstanding obligation in the event of default.

(2) For purposes of this paragraph, (i) no more than 50% of the present value of a par-

ticipant's vested accrued benefit may be considered by a plan as security for the outstanding balance of all plan loans made to that participant; (ii) a plan will be in compliance with paragraph (f)(2)(i) of this section if, with respect to any participant, it meets the provisions of paragraph (f)(2)(i) of this section immediately after the origination of each participant loan secured in whole or in part by that participant's vested accrued benefit; and (iii) any loan secured in whole or in part by a portion of a participant's vested accrued benefit must also meet the requirements of paragraph (f)(1) of this section.